Oxford
Idioms
Dictionary
for learners of English

OXFORD
UNIVERSITY PRESS

Great Clarendon Street, Oxford OX2 6DP

Oxford University Press is a department of the University of Oxford.
It furthers the University's objective of excellence in research, scholarship,
and education by publishing worldwide in

Oxford New York

Auckland Bangkok Buenos Aires Cape Town Chennai Dar es Salaam Delhi
Hong Kong Istanbul Karachi Kolkata Kuala Lumpur Madrid Melbourne
Mexico City Mumbai Nairobi São Paulo Shanghai Taipei Tokyo Toronto

OXFORD and OXFORD ENGLISH are registered trade marks of
Oxford University Press in the UK and in certain other countries

Photocopying

ISBN-13: 978 0 19 431723 8
ISBN-10: 0 19 431723 4

Text capture and typesetting by Oxford University Press
Printed in China

ACKNOWLEDGEMENTS

Advisory Board: Dr Keith Brown; Prof. Guy Cook; Dr Alan Cruse; Ruth Gairns;
Moira Runcie; Prof. Gabriele Stein; Dr Norman Whitney; Prof. Henry Widdowson
Phonetics editor: Michael Ashby
Senior editor: Dilys Parkinson
Editor: Ben Francis
Illustrations: Lorna Barnard; Sophie Grillet; Karen Hiscock; Martin Shovel;
John Taylor; Technical Graphics Department, OUP; Harry Venning

Contents

Guide to Using the Dictionary

Key to Dictionary Entries

Idioms are listed under a keyword:

keyword

idiom

opposite

blue triangle shows a related word

stress marks show pronunciation
of idiom

note on the origin of the idiom

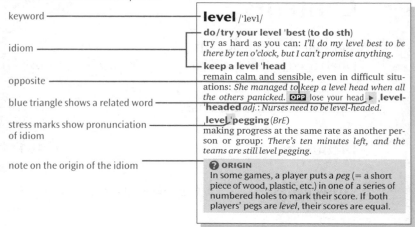

level /'levl/

do/try your level 'best (to do sth)
try as hard as you can: *I'll do my level best to be there by ten o'clock, but I can't promise anything.*

keep a level 'head
remain calm and sensible, even in difficult situations: *She managed to keep a level head when all the others panicked.* **OPP** lose your head ▶ ,level-'headed *adj.*: *Nurses need to be level-headed.*

,level 'pegging (*BrE*)
making progress at the same rate as another person or group: *There's ten minutes left, and the teams are still level pegging.*

> **❓ ORIGIN**
> In some games, a player puts a *peg* (= a short piece of wood, plastic, etc.) in one of a series of numbered holes to mark their score. If both players' pegs are *level*, their scores are equal.

How to find an idiom
Which word to look for?

Idioms are defined at the first important or 'full' word. 'Full' words are nouns, verbs, adverbs and adjectives.

Grammatical words such as articles and prepositions are ignored.

double /'dʌbl/

in a ,double 'bind
in a situation in which it is difficult to choose what to do because whatever you choose will have negative results: *Students are caught in a double bind between a lack of jobs if they leave school and a huge bill for higher education if they stay.*

If you look for an idiom in the wrong place, a link shows you where the idiom can be found.

bind /baɪnd/

• double → in a double bind

Finding a keyword

Keywords are arranged alphabetically. Plural nouns (e.g. *horses*), inflected forms of verbs (e.g. *happens*) and comparative/superlative adjectives (e.g. *longest*) can all be keywords.

In this idiom only the –**ing** form is used.

spoiling /'spɔɪlɪŋ/

be ,spoiling for a 'fight, argument, etc.
want to fight, argue, etc. with sb very much: *Are you spoiling for a fight?* ◇ *The teachers' union is spoiling for a fight with the Government.*

Common words

Some common verbs and adjectives, for example *get* and *bad*, have so many idioms that it is not possible to show them all under these keywords.

> a note tells you to look at the next noun, adjective, etc.

cut /kʌt/

> Most idioms containing **cut** are at the entries for the nouns or adjectives in the idioms, for example **cut corners** is at **corners**.

Idioms that only contain grammar words, or grammar words and very common verbs, are given at the first fixed word in the idiom.

above /ə'bʌv/

above 'all ('else)
especially; most important of all: *Don't spend too much money, don't forget to write, but above all, have a good time!* ◇ *He misses his family above all else.*

Homonyms

If two words are **homonyms** (= spelled the same but pronounced differently) they are divided into two forms and marked with a number.

lead¹ /liːd/

lead² /led/

Variations within idioms

Sometimes one word in an idiom can be replaced with another. In this case the idiom is defined at the first word that is **fixed**.

> different forms are shown separated by slashes

tricks /trɪks/

a bag/box of 'tricks (*informal*)
a set of methods or equipment that sb can use: *Hotel managers are using a whole new bag of tricks to attract their guests.*

When there are a large number of possible words that could be used, common examples are shown followed by 'etc.'

> the idiom is defined at the first fixed word

packet /'pækɪt/

make, lose, spend, etc. a 'packet (*informal*)
make, etc. a large amount of money: *He went to the USA and made a packet in office property.*

Variant idioms

If the structure of an idiom can take more than one form, the different forms are shown separated by ♦ :

quiet /'kwaɪət/

keep quiet about ♦ keep sth quiet
say nothing about sth; keep sth secret: *I've decided to resign but I'd rather you kept quiet about it.*

Sometimes an idiom has a variant which is very different or which belongs to a particular variety of English such as American English. In this case, the variant is shown in brackets:

> an American variant

,eat humble 'pie (*BrE*) (*AmE* **eat 'crow**)
say and show that you are sorry for a mistake that you made: *I had to eat humble pie when Harry, who I said would never have any success, won first prize.*

Ordering of idioms within the same keyword group

Idioms that appear under the same keyword are arranged in alphabetical order, ignoring the following words:

possessive pronouns unless this is fixed (e.g. **my** word)

pronouns unless this is fixed (e.g. **I** dare say)

articles (a, an, the)

bag /bæg/

(not) your 'bag (*informal*)
(not) sth that you are interested in or good at: *Poetry isn't really my bag.*

,bag and 'baggage
with all your belongings: *If you don't pay the rent, you'll be thrown out, bag and baggage.*

a 'bag lady (*informal*)
a woman who has no home and who walks around carrying her possessions with her

Links

Links are arranged alphabetically by keyword:

keyword where idiom can be found

idiom

variant

idiom where the variant can be found

fingers /'fɪŋɡəz; *AmE* 'fɪŋɡərz/

- **green** → green fingers
- **slip** → slip through sb's fingers
- **snap** → snap your fingers
- **sticky** → have sticky fingers
- **thumbs** → be all fingers and thumbs **SEE** all thumbs

Further Information and Practice

There is a 36-page section of study pages in the middle of the dictionary. These pages will help you to focus on certain idiomatic phrases and give you practice using them.

You can find the answers to the exercises in the 'Key to Study Pages' section at the back of the dictionary.

A a

A /eɪ/

from A to 'B
from one place to another: *I don't care what kind of car it is as long as it gets me from A to B.*

from A to 'Z
very thoroughly and in detail: *We need an expert who knows the subject from A to Z.*

● **easy** → (as) easy as ABC/pie/falling off a log
● **straight** → (earn/get) straight A's

aah /ɑː/

● **um** → um and aah (about sth)

aback /əˈbæk/

be taken a'back (by sb/sth)
be shocked or surprised by sb/sth: *She was completely taken aback by his anger.*

abandon /əˈbændən/

● **gay** → with gay abandon

ABC /ˌeɪ biː ˈsiː/

● **easy** → (as) easy as ABC/pie/falling off a log

about /əˈbaʊt/

be about to do sth
be going to do sth immediately: *I was about to phone him when he walked into the room.*

how/what about…?
1 used when asking for information about sb/sth: *How about Ruth? Have you heard from her?* ◇ *I'm having fish. What about you?*
2 used to make a suggestion or offer: *How about going for a walk?* ◇ *You look cold. How about a nice hot drink?*
3 used for introducing sb/sth into a conversation or reminding sb of sb/sth: *I know she's very happy now, but what about him?* ◇ *'I've never been to Spain before.' 'What about the conference you went to in Madrid?'*

how/what about 'that (, then)! (*informal*)
used for expressing surprise, praise, great respect, etc: *'Have you heard Jane's been offered a film part in Hollywood?' 'Well, how about that, then!'*

not be about to do sth
not be willing to do sth; not intend to do sth: *I've never done any cooking and I'm not about to start now.*

that's about 'all/'it
used to say that you have finished telling sb about sth and there is nothing to add: *'Anything else?' 'No, that's about it for now.'*

above /əˈbʌv/

above 'all ('else)
especially; most important of all: *Don't spend too much, don't forget to write, but above all, have a good time!* ◇ *He misses his family above all else.*

a,bove and be'yond sth (*formal*)
more than (your duty, etc.): *They showed commitment to the job above and beyond what was expected of them.*

be/get a'bove yourself (*disapproving*)
behave as if you are better or more important than you really are: *She's getting a bit above herself. She's only been working for me for two weeks and already she's telling me what to do!*

abreast /əˈbrest/

keep a'breast of sth
make sure that you know all the most recent facts about a subject: *It is almost impossible to keep abreast of all the latest developments in computing.*

absence /ˈæbsəns/

,absence makes the heart grow 'fonder (*saying*)
used to say that when you are away from sb that you love, you love them even more **OPP** out of sight, out of mind

leave of 'absence (*formal*)
permission to be away from work for a particular period of time: *Several of my colleagues have had leave of absence to go on training courses.*

● **conspicuous** → conspicuous by your absence

accident /ˈæksɪdənt/

by 'accident
in a way that is not planned or organized: *We met by accident at the airport.* ◇ *Helen got into acting purely by accident.*

(whether) by ,accident or de'sign
if you say that sth happens **by accident or design**, you mean that you do not know if it has been planned or not: *Mary was wearing the same T-shirt as me — whether by accident or design, I never knew.*

● **waiting** → an accident/a disaster waiting to happen

accidentally /ˌæksɪˈdentəli/

acci,dentally on 'purpose (*informal, ironic*)
intending to do sth, but wanting to appear to have done it by accident: *'We'd just finished our meal when John realized he'd accidentally left his chequebook at home.' 'Accidentally on purpose, you mean!'*

accidents /ˈæksɪdənts/

,accidents will 'happen (*saying*)
said when a small accident has happened, for example when sth has been broken, to show that you do not consider it to be serious, or to excuse yourself for causing it: *'I'm so sorry, I've just broken a plate.' 'Oh, never mind, accidents will happen.'*

● **chapter** → a chapter of accidents

accompli /əˈkɒmpliː; AmE əˈkɑːm-/

• fait → a fait accompli

accomplished /əˈkʌmplɪʃt/

• mission → mission accomplished

accord /əˈkɔːd; AmE əˈkɔːrd/

of your own ac'cord
without being asked or forced: *I didn't need to tell her to apologize; she did it of her own accord.*

account /əˈkaʊnt/

of little/no ac'count (*formal*)
not considered important: *His past achievements were of no account when it came to competing with the younger men.*

on account of sb/sth ♦ on sb's account
because of sb/sth: *Flights were delayed on account of the bad weather.* ◊ *I can't go, but don't stay in on my account.*

on 'no account ♦ not on 'any account
not for any reason: *On no account (should you) try to fix the heater yourself. All repairs should be done by a trained engineer.*

on your own ac'count
1 for yourself: *In 1992 Smith set up in business on his own account.*
2 because you want to and you have decided, not sb else: *No one sent me, I am here on my own account.*

put/turn sth to good ac'count (*formal*)
make good use of money, an ability, etc: *He put his experience as a teacher to good account as a writer of children's books.*

take sth into ac'count ♦ take account of sth
consider sth when making a calculation or decision: *It's clear he didn't take his family's wishes into account when deciding to change jobs.* ◊ *We mustn't forget to take account of price increases when we do the budget for next year.*

• call → call sb to account (for/over sth)
• settle → settle a score/an account (with sb)
• square → square your/an account (with sb)

accounted /əˈkaʊntɪd/

• present → all present and accounted for SEE all present and correct

accounting /əˈkaʊntɪŋ/

there's no accounting for 'taste(s) (*saying*)
used to express surprise at another person's likes and dislikes which are different from your own: *'She's just painted her whole room purple.' 'Well, there's no accounting for taste!'*

accounts /əˈkaʊnts/

by/from 'all accounts
used when the speaker does not have direct experience of the thing mentioned but is reporting the ideas, etc. of others: *I've never seen any of her movies, but she's a brilliant director, by all accounts.* ◊ *It was, from all accounts, a very interesting discussion.*

• square → square accounts (with sb)

ace /eɪs/

play your 'ace
use your best argument, etc. in order to get an advantage in a situation: *I think it's time we played our ace, which is the fact that without us they wouldn't be able to run this place.*

> **NOTE**
> This expression refers to card-playing. The *ace* usually has the highest value, and is associated with success.

within an ace of sth/of doing sth (*BrE*)
very close to sth: *We came within an ace of victory.*

• sleeve → have an ace in the hole SEE have an ace/a trick up your sleeve

aces /ˈeɪsɪz/

have/hold (all) the 'aces (also **hold all the 'cards**)
be in a controlling position because you have certain advantages over another person: *The Labour Party candidate holds all the aces — he's local and well liked.*

Achilles /əˈkɪliːz/

an/sb's Achilles' 'heel
a hidden weakness or fault in sb which may be used to harm them: *His pride proved to be his Achilles' heel.*

> **❶ ORIGIN**
> This expression is named after the Greek hero *Achilles*. When he was a small child, his mother dipped him into the river Styx, which meant that he could not be injured. She held him by his heel, which therefore was not touched by the water. Achilles died after being wounded by an arrow in the heel.

acid /ˈæsɪd/

the ˌacid 'test (of sth) (also **the 'litmus test** especially in *AmE*)
a situation which finally proves whether sth is good or bad, true or false, etc: *They've always been good friends, but the acid test will come when they have to share a flat.*

> **❶ ORIGIN**
> Both these expressions originally referred to chemical tests. The *acid test* uses nitric acid to test if something is made of gold. The *litmus test* uses litmus paper to test for acids and alkalis.

acorns /ˈeɪkɔːnz; AmE -kɔːrnz/

• oaks → great/tall oaks from little acorns grow

acquaintance /əˈkweɪntəns/

make sb's acquaintance ◆ make the acquaintance of sb (*formal*)
meet sb for the first time: *I am delighted to make your acquaintance, Mrs Baker.* ◇ *I made the acquaintance of several musicians at that time.*

● **nodding** → have a nodding acquaintance with sb/sth
● **scrape** → scrape (up) an acquaintance with sb

acquired /əˈkwaɪəd; *AmE* əˈkwaɪərd/

an acquired 'taste
a thing which you find unpleasant or do not appreciate at first but which you gradually learn to like: *Whisky is an acquired taste.*

Act /ækt/

● **read¹** → read (sb) the Riot Act

act /ækt/

an ,act of 'God (*law*)
an event caused by natural forces which people cannot control or prevent, for example a hurricane (= a very strong wind), an earthquake, etc: *The insurance covers your house against all types of damage, excluding those caused by acts of God.*

a 'balancing/'juggling act
a process in which sb tries to please two or more people or groups who want different things: *The UN must perform a delicate balancing act between the different sides involved in the conflict.*

Managing her home life and work was proving to be something of a juggling act.

be/get in on the 'act (*informal*)
be/become involved in a particular activity only after it has become successful: *Sales of 'green' products have increased dramatically and now a lot of manufacturers are trying to get in on the act.*

do/perform/stage a disap'pearing/'vanishing act (*informal*)
go away or be impossible to find when people need or want you: *Ian always does a disappearing act when it's time to wash the dishes.*

> **❷ ORIGIN**
> This refers to a magic trick done by a magician in which they make themselves or another person disappear.

get your 'act together ◆ get sth/it to'gether (*informal*) (also **get/have your 'shit together** ⚠, *slang*)
manage to organize or control sth better than you have done before: *If Sally got her act together she'd be a great musician.* ◇ *He's been trying to get his life together.* ◇ *He seems to be getting it together at last.*

a hard/tough act to 'follow
a person or a group that is so good or successful at sth that it will be difficult for anyone else who comes after them to be as good or successful: *The last head teacher achieved a lot — she'll be a hard act to follow.*

> **NOTE**
> An *act* is one of several short pieces of entertainment in a show.

● **age** → act/be your age
● **catch** → catch sb in the act (of doing sth)
● **clean** → clean up your act
● **fool** → act/play the fool
● **goat** → act/play the goat
● **think** → behave/act as if you own the place **SEE** think you own the place

action /ˈækʃn/

'action stations (*spoken, especially BrE*)
used as an order to get ready for action: *Action stations! There's a bus full of tourists arriving in five minutes.*

in 'action
working, operating, etc.; doing a particular activity: *John's a great cook — you should see him in action.*

out of 'action
not working or operating as normal because of illness, injury, damage, etc: *Jane's broken leg will put her out of action for a while.* ◇ *He can't give you a lift today — his car's out of action.*

a piece/slice of the 'action (*informal*)
a share or role in an interesting or exciting activity, especially in order to make money: *Foreign firms will all want a piece of the action if the new airport goes ahead.*

where the 'action is
where the most exciting or important events are happening: *I'd hate to live out in the country — I like to be where the action is.*

● **course** → a course of action
● **spring** → spring to/into life/action
● **swing** → swing into action

actions /'ækʃnz/

,actions speak ,louder than 'words (*saying*)
what you do is more important than what you say: *You said you'd help me, but you know what they say: actions speak louder than words!*

ad /æd/

,ad 'hoc (*from Latin*)
arranged or happening when necessary and not planned in advance: *The meetings will be held on an ad hoc basis.*

,ad infi'nitum (*from Latin*)
without ever coming to an end; again and again: *You cannot stay here ad infinitum without paying any rent.* ◇ *The problem would be repeated ad infinitum.*

> **NOTE**
> The meaning of the Latin phrase is 'to infinity'.

,ad 'nauseam (*from Latin*)
if a person says or does sth again and again so that it becomes boring or annoying: *Television sports commentators repeat the same phrases ad nauseam.*

> **NOTE**
> The meaning of the Latin phrase is 'to sickness'.

Adam /'ædəm/

● know → not know sb from Adam

Adams / ,ædəmz/

● sweet Fanny Adams SEE sweet FA

add /æd/

add ,fuel to the 'fire/'flames
do or say sth which makes a difficult situation worse, or makes sb even more angry, etc: *She was already furious and his apologies and excuses only added fuel to the flames.* **OPP** pour oil on troubled water(s)

add ,insult to 'injury
make a bad relationship with sb worse by offending them even more: *She forgot to send me an invitation to her party and then added insult to injury by asking to borrow my jacket!*

ado /ə'duː/

without further/more a'do (*old-fashioned*)
without delaying; immediately: *So without further ado, let's get on with tonight's show.*

advance /əd'vɑːns; AmE -'væns/

in ad'vance (of sth)
before the time that is expected; before sth happens: *a week/month/year in advance* ◇ *It's cheaper if you book the tickets in advance.* ◇ *People were evacuated from the coastal regions in advance of the hurricane.* **OPP** in the wake of sb/sth

● time → be ahead of/before/in advance of your time

advantage /əd'vɑːntɪdʒ; AmE -'væn-/

take ad'vantage of sth/sb
1 make good use of sth; to make use of an opportunity: *We made sure that we took full advantage of the hotel facilities.* ◇ *Take advantage of our special offer and get two books for the price of one!*
2 make use of sb/sth in a way that is unfair or dishonest: *He took advantage of my generosity* (= for example, by taking more than I had intended to give).

to sb's ad'vantage
so that sb benefits: *The rise in the value of the pound will work to the advantage of those planning a trip abroad this summer.*

to (good, better, etc.) ad'vantage
in a way that produces a good result: *You would be spending your time to better advantage if you did what I suggested.* ◇ *That's a lovely picture but it's not seen to its best advantage on that wall.*

turn sth to your (own) ad'vantage
use or change a bad situation so that it helps you: *She had three empty rooms in the house after her children left home, so she decided to turn this to her advantage and rent them out to students.*

● press → press home your advantage

advocate /'ædvəkət/

● devil → a/the devil's advocate

affairs /ə'feəz; AmE ə'ferz/

● state → a state of affairs

afield /ə'fiːld/

far/farther/further a'field
far away from home; to or in places that are not near: *You can hire a car if you want to explore further afield.* ◇ *Journalists came from as far afield as China and Brazil.*

aforethought /ə'fɔːθɔːt; AmE ə'fɔːrθ-/

● malice → with malice aforethought

afraid /ə'freɪd/

I'm afraid (that)... (*spoken*)
used as a polite way of telling sb sth that is unpleasant or disappointing, or sth that you are sorry about: *I'm afraid I can't come to your party.* ◇ *'Have you got change for ten pounds?' 'I'm afraid not.'* ◇ *I've got some bad news, I'm afraid.* ◇ *'Is this the best you can do?' 'I'm afraid so.'*

after /'ɑːftə(r); AmE 'æf-/

after 'all
1 used to show that sth is the opposite of what you first intend to do or expect to happen: *I think I will have something to eat after all.* ◇ *We could have left our coats at home — it didn't rain after all.*
2 used when you are explaining sth or giving a reason: *Can't I stay up late tonight? After all, there's no school tomorrow!* ◇ *You got a fair price for your car. It's six years old, after all.*

again /əˈgen; əˈgeɪn/

aˌgain and aˈgain
many times; repeatedly: *I've told him again and again to shut the door but he always leaves it open.*

then/there aˈgain (*informal*)
used for introducing an extra piece of information which explains sth or gives another explanation for sth: *I thought he liked me, but then again maybe he didn't.*

age /eɪdʒ/

ˌact/ˌbe your ˈage (*informal*)
(often used as a command) stop behaving like a child: *You're behaving like a couple of kids. Act your age!*

ˌcome of ˈage
1 reach the age when you are considered by the law to be an adult: *He will inherit his father's money when he comes of age.*
2 (of an organization, etc.) become established and accepted: *With more and more people now aware of environmental issues, 'green' politics has really come of age.*

ˌlook your ˈage
seem as old as you really are and not younger or older: *I was surprised when I last saw her — she's really starting to look her age now.*

ˌunder ˈage
not yet an adult according to the law: *We don't serve alcohol to teenagers who are under age/to under-age teenagers.*

* awkward → the awkward age
* certain → of a certain age
* day → in this day and age
* feel → feel your age
* golden → the golden age (of sth)
* grand → a/the grand old age
* ripe → at/to a ripe old age
* tender → at a tender age

aggregate /ˈægrɪgət/

on ˈaggregate (*BrE, sport*)
when the scores of a number of games are added together: *They won 4-2 on aggregate.*

agony /ˈægəni/

* pile → pile on the agony/gloom
* prolong → prolong the agony

agree /əˈgriː/

aˌgree to ˈdiffer
(of two or more people) allow each other to have different opinions about sth, especially in order to avoid more argument: *Our views on this matter are so different that we'll just have to agree to differ.*

I ˌcouldn't agree (with you) ˈmore
I completely agree (with you): *I couldn't agree with you more about the need to hire extra staff.*

agreement /əˈgriːmənt/

* gentleman → a gentlemen's agreement **SEE** a gentleman's agreement

aid /eɪd/

in aid of sb/sth (*BrE*)
in order to help sb/sth: *The children spent the day collecting money in aid of charity.*

what's (all) ˈthis, etc. in aid of? (*BrE, spoken*)
what is the purpose or cause of sth?: *What's all this crying in aid of?*

aim /eɪm/

take ˈaim at sb/sth (*AmE*)
direct your criticism at or your attention to sb/sth: *The unions are taking aim at the government.* ◇ *Several retail giants have now decided to take aim at the youth market.*

air /eə(r)/

float/walk on ˈair (*informal*)
be very happy about sth: *When I passed my driving test, I was walking on air for days.*

in the ˈair
(of an idea, a feeling, a piece of information, etc.) felt by a number of people to exist or to be happening: *Spring is in the air.* ◇ *There was a strong feeling of excitement in the air.*

(up) in the ˈair
(of plans, etc.) uncertain; not yet decided: *Our plans for the summer are still very much up in the air.* ◇ *At the end of the meeting, the matter was left in the air.*

ˌon/ˌoff the ˈair
(being) broadcast/not (being) broadcast on radio or television: *'Going Live' will go off the air for the summer, returning for a new series in the autumn.*

* breath → a breath of fresh air
* castles → (build) castles in the air
* clear → clear the air
* free → (as) free as (the) air/as a bird
* hot → hot air
* light → (as) light as air/a feather
* nose → with your nose in the air
* open → in the open air
* pluck → pluck sth out of the air
* thin → appear, etc. out of thin air
* thin → disappear, etc. into thin air

airs /eəz; *AmE* erz/

ˌairs and ˈgraces (*BrE, disapproving*)
behaviour which is elegant but unnatural and intended to impress others: *Her airs and graces didn't impress her fellow students at all.*

ˌgive yourself/ˌput on ˈairs
behave in a way which shows that you feel you are important: *The nice thing about her is that, in spite of being so rich, she doesn't put on any airs.*

aisle /aɪl/

go/walk down the 'aisle (*informal*)
get married: *I never thought you'd be the first one to walk down the aisle — you used to say you'd never marry!*

> **NOTE**
> The *aisle* is the passage down the middle of a church between the two blocks of seats.

aisles /aɪlz/

• **rolling** → rolling in the aisles

aitches /'eɪtʃɪz/

• **drop** → drop your aitches

Aladdin /ə'lædɪn/

an Aladdin's 'cave
a place full of valuable or interesting objects: *He kept for his private pleasure an Aladdin's cave of stolen masterpieces.*

> **❷ ORIGIN**
> This expression comes from a story in *The Arabian Nights*. Aladdin was trapped in a cave full of gold and jewels by a magician.

alarm /ə'lɑːm; AmE ə'lɑːrm/

• **false** → a false alarm

alec /'ælɪk/

• **smart** → a smart alec/aleck

alert /ə'lɜːt; AmE ə'lɜːrt/

• **red** → on red alert

alike /ə'laɪk/

• **share** → share and share alike

alive /ə'laɪv/

a,live and 'kicking (*informal*)
still existing and strong or active: *The old prejudices were still very much alive and kicking.*

bring sth a'live
make sth interesting: *Maps and pictures bring the book alive.*

come a'live
1 (of a subject or an event) become interesting and exciting: *The game came alive in the second half.*
2 (of a place) become busy and full of activity: *The city starts to come alive after dark.*
3 (of a person) show interest in sth and become excited about it: *She came alive as she talked about her job.*

• **eat** → eat sb alive
• **skin** → skin sb alive

all /ɔːl/

your 'all
everything you have: *The team gave their all in the game on Saturday.*

all a'long
from the beginning: *I've said all along that this would happen.* ◇ *He knew who they were all along but he pretended he didn't.*

'all but
1 almost: *The snow all but covered the path, making it difficult to walk.* ◇ *The patient was all but dead when the doctor arrived.*
2 all (the people or things mentioned) except…: *'Have you done your homework?' 'Yes, all but the last two questions.'*

,all 'in
1 (of a price) with nothing extra to pay; inclusive: *The trip cost $550 all in.* ◇ *These are all-in prices — room, breakfast, service and tax.*
2 (*old-fashioned, informal*) very tired: *At the end of the race he felt all in.*

all in 'all
when everything is considered: *All in all the conference was a great success, despite the problems at the beginning.*

all of sth
(of size, weight, distance, etc.) at least: *'How old is she?' 'Oh, she must be all of fifty.'* ◇ (*ironic*) *He never visits his mother and she lives all of three miles away.*

all or 'nothing
a situation which will end either in complete success or complete failure

all 'over
1 everywhere: *We looked all over for the ring.* ◇ *The news was all over the office within minutes.*
2 what you would expect of the person mentioned: *That sounds like my sister all over.*

all 'round (*BrE*) (*AmE* **all a'round**)
1 in every way; in all respects: *a good performance all round*
2 for each person: *She bought drinks all round.*

,all 'there (*informal*)
having a healthy mind; thinking clearly: *He behaves very oddly at times — I don't think he's quite all there.*

and 'all
1 also; included: *They're coming to stay for the weekend, dog and all.*
2 (*spoken*) too; as well: *And he stole money from me, and all.*
3 (*informal*) and other (connected) things: *She doesn't go out much in the evenings now, what with her work and all.*

and all 'that (rubbish, stuff, etc.) (*informal*)
and other similar things: *He was an intellectual — read Beckett and Barthes and all that.* ◇ *They're always kissing and all that romantic stuff.*

(not) at 'all
(used with a negative, in a question or in an *if* - clause) in any way; to any degree: *This isn't at all what I expected.* ◇ *Are you hungry at all?* ◇ *If you're at all unhappy about taking the job, then don't.*

be all about sb/sth (*informal*)
used to describe the subject or purpose of sth: *This book is all about Greece.* ◇ *Now then, what's this all about* (= what is the problem)*?* ◇ *It's all about money these days.*

be all sb can/could 'do (not) to do sth
(*informal*)
be very difficult (not) to do sth: *His face looked so funny that it was all she could do not to laugh.*

(not) be/take all 'day, 'morning, etc. (to do sth) ◆ **not have all 'day, etc.** (*informal*)
(used as a request to hurry up) (not) take a long time (to do sth): *'Are you going to take all day shaving?' she shouted to him through the bathroom door.* ◇ *Come on! We haven't got all day!*

be all for sth/for doing sth
believe strongly that sth should be done: *They're all for saving money where they can.* **OPP** be (dead) set against sth/against doing sth

be all 'go (*BrE, informal*)
be (a situation where people are) very active or busy: *It was all go in the office today.*

be all 'over sb (*informal*)
show a lot of affection for or enthusiasm about sb: *He was all over her at the party.*

be all the same to sb (also **be all 'one to sb** *old-fashioned*)
not be important to sb: *If it's all the same to you, I'd prefer to go shopping on my own.*

be all 'that (*AmE, informal*)
be very attractive or impressive: *He thinks he's all that.*

in 'all
as a total quantity or number: *We've got six litres of milk in all.* ◇ *That's €24 in all, please.*

it's/they're ,all 'yours
used when passing the responsibility for sb/sth or the use of sth to another person: *'There you are, Mr Brown,' she said, taking him into the classroom full of children, 'they're all yours.'*

not all that 'good, 'well, etc.
not particularly good, well, etc: *He doesn't sing all that well.*

not as bad(ly), tall, etc. as all 'that
not as much as has been suggested: *They're not as rich as all that.*

,not at 'all
used to politely accept thanks or to agree to sth: *'Thanks a lot.' 'Not at all.'* ◇ *'Will it bother you if I smoke?' 'Not at all.'*

of ,all the 'cheek, 'nerve, stupid things to 'do, etc.! (*informal*)
used to express annoyance, impatience, etc. at what another person has done or said: *Of all the idiots, leaving his car unlocked in the middle of town!*

NOTE
This expression is often used without a noun, especially to show that somebody is annoyed: *She said I was fat? Well, of all the …!*

all-clear /ˌɔːl ˈklɪə(r); AmE ˈklɪr/

give sb/get the all-'clear
give sb/get a sign that a particular situation is no longer dangerous: *She got the all-clear from the doctor and was sent home from the hospital.*

❷ ORIGIN
This idiom refers to the signal that is sounded in wartime when a bombing raid is over.

alley /ˈæli/

● blind → a blind alley
● street → be (right) up your alley **SEE** be (right) up your street

allow /əˈlaʊ/

allow 'me (*spoken*)
used to offer help politely: *'I'll just take these bags upstairs.' 'Allow me.'*

● rein → give/allow sb/sth free/full rein

allowances /əˈlaʊənsɪz/

make al'lowances for sb
not judge sb too strictly because of certain problems or difficulties: *The court was asked to make allowances for the age of the accused.*

almighty /ɔːlˈmaɪti/

● God → God almighty

alone /əˈləʊn; AmE əˈloʊn/

go it a'lone (*informal*)
do sth, especially sth difficult, without the help or support of others: *Andrew decided to go it alone and start his own business.*

leave/let sb a'lone ◆ **leave/let sb 'be**
stop annoying sb or trying to get their attention: *She's asked to be left alone but the press photographers follow her everywhere.* ◇ *Leave him be — he obviously doesn't want to talk about it.*

leave/let sth a'lone ◆ **leave/let sth 'be**
stop touching, changing or moving sth: *I've told you before — leave my things alone!*

let a'lone
used after a statement to emphasize that because the first thing is not true or possible, the next thing cannot be true or possible either: *I wouldn't speak to him, let alone trust him or lend him money.* ◇ *She didn't even apologize, let alone offer to pay for the damage.*

● well → let well enough alone **SEE** leave/let well alone

along /əˈlɒŋ; AmE əˈlɔːŋ/

along with sth
in addition to sth: *Tobacco is taxed in most countries, along with alcohol.*

aloud /əˈlaʊd/

● think → think aloud

always /ˈɔːlweɪz/

as ˈalways
as usually happens or is expected: *As always, Polly was late for school.*

amends /əˈmendz/

make aˈmends (to sb) (for sth/for doing sth)
do sth for sb in order to show that you are sorry for sth wrong or unfair that you have done: *I'm sorry I upset you — how can I make amends?* ◇ *He finished third in the 200 metres, but hopes to make amends in the 100 metres.*

American /əˈmerɪkən/

as Aˌmerican as apple ˈpie
used to say that sth is typical of America: *For me, baseball is as American as apple pie.*

amiss /əˈmɪs/

not come/go aˈmiss (*BrE*)
be useful or pleasant in a particular situation: *A little luck wouldn't go amiss right now!*

take sth aˈmiss (*BrE*)
feel offended by sth, perhaps because you have understood it in the wrong way: *Would she take it amiss if I offered to help?* **OPP** take sth in good part

amok /əˈmɒk; *AmE* əˈmɑːk/

run aˈmok
behave in a wild or uncontrolled way: *The crowd ran amok through the city streets when they heard their leaders had been killed.*

> **❷ ORIGIN**
> *Amok* comes from the Malay word for 'attack fiercely'.

amount /əˈmaʊnt/

any aˈmount/ˈnumber of sth
a large quantity of sth: *There was any amount of food and drink at the party.* ◇ *You won't have any difficulty selling your car — there are any number of people who would buy it.*

no aˈmount of sth
used for saying that sth will have no effect: *No amount of encouragement would make him jump into the pool.*

● thing → amount/come to the same thing

amused /əˈmjuːzd/

keep sb aˈmused
give sb interesting things to do, or entertain them so that they do not become bored: *Playing with water can keep children amused for hours.*

analysis /əˈnæləsɪs/

in the ˌlast/ˌfinal aˈnalysis
used to say what is most important after everything has been discussed or considered: *In the final analysis, humour is a matter of individual interpretation.*

anchor /ˈæŋkə(r)/

● weigh → weigh anchor

angels /ˈeɪndʒlz/

● side → be on the side of the angels

anger /ˈæŋɡə(r)/

● sorrow → do sth more in sorrow than in anger

answer /ˈɑːnsə(r); *AmE* ˈæn-/

the ˌanswer to sb's ˈprayers
a thing or a person that sb has waited for or wanted for a long time: *If you've been looking for a good quality fleece at a reasonable price, this one could be the answer to your prayers.*

not take ˌno for an ˈanswer
refuse to accept that sb does not want sth, will not do sth, etc: *You're coming and I won't take no for an answer!*

● dusty → a dusty answer

answers /ˈɑːnsəz; *AmE* ˈænsərz/

have/know all the ˈanswers
be or seem to be more intelligent or know more than others: *He's an economist who thinks he knows all the answers.*

ante /ˈænti/

raise/up the ˈante
increase the level of sth, especially demands or sums of money: *His ex-wife has upped the ante in her alimony suit against him.*

> **NOTE**
> The *ante* is the amount of money that players bet in a card game such as poker.

ants /ænts/

have ants in your pants (*informal*)
be unable to stay still because you are anxious or excited about sth: *Relax and enjoy yourself — you've really got ants in your pants about something tonight!*

anything /ˈeniθɪŋ/

anything ˈbut
certainly not; just the opposite of sth: *Ecologists are anything but optimistic about a change in the Government's attitude towards 'green' issues.* ◇ *'I suppose the weather in Scotland was terrible.' 'Oh no, anything but.'*

anything 'goes
there are no rules about how sb should behave; anything is acceptable: *John always has to wear a suit and tie to the office, but where I work anything goes.*

anything 'like
(*used with a negative, in a question or in an if - clause*) in any way similar to; nearly: *If the meal's anything like the one we had there, you'll really enjoy it.* ◇ *Our car isn't anything like as fast as yours.*

(as) easy, clear, quick, etc. as anything
(*informal*)
very easy, clear, quick, etc: *It was only a small gift but Phil was as pleased as anything with it.*

like 'anything (BrE, informal)
very much: *My head hurt like anything.*

not for 'anything (informal)
definitely not: *I wouldn't give it up for anything.*

or anything (spoken)
or another thing of a similar type: *If you want to call a meeting or anything, just let me know.*

apart /ə'pɑːt; AmE ə'pɑːrt/

be 'poles/'worlds apart
be widely separated; have no interests that you share: *Politically, the two leaders are poles apart.* ◇ *What you learn in the classroom and what happens on the job are often worlds apart.*

come/fall apart at the 'seams (informal)
begin to fail or collapse: *The Government's economic policy is falling apart at the seams.* ◇ *After only six months, their marriage has come apart at the seams.*

> **NOTE**
> If a piece of clothing *comes apart at the seams*, it begins to separate along the lines where the pieces of cloth are sewn together.

● joking → joking apart/aside
● miles → be miles apart
● rip → rip sb/sth apart/to shreds, bits, etc.

ape /eɪp/

go 'ape (*also* **go 'apeshit** ⚠) (*slang, especially AmE*)
become extremely angry or excited: *The manager went ape when the team lost yet another game.*

apology /ə'pɒlədʒi; AmE ə'pɑːl-/

an apology for sth
a very poor example of sth: *I'm sorry this is a bit of an apology for lunch — we'll have a proper meal tonight.*

make no a'pology/a'pologies for sth
if you say that you **make no apology/apologies** for sth, you mean that you do not feel that you have said or done sth wrong: *Having grown up in the north of the country, I make no apologies for saying that people there are more friendly than people in the south.*

appearances /ə'pɪərənsɪz; AmE ə'pɪr-/

keep up ap'pearances
hide the true situation and pretend that everything is still going well: *She's lost all her money, but she's determined to keep up appearances.*

to all ap'pearances
if sth/sb is judged only by what you can see: *The house was, to all appearances, empty.*

appetite /'æpɪtaɪt/

● whet → whet sb's appetite

apple /'æpl/

the apple doesn't fall/never falls far from the 'tree (saying, especially AmE)
a child usually behaves in a similar way to his or her parent(s): *'You have an adorable daughter.' 'Ah, well, you know what they say. The apple doesn't fall too far from the tree.'*

the ˌapple of sb's 'eye
a person, usually a child, who sb loves very much; a favourite child: *The second child, John, was the apple of his mother's eye.*

> **❓ ORIGIN**
> In the past, the *pupil* (= the small round black area at the centre of the eye) was called the 'apple' of the eye, the part that had to be protected most carefully.

a bad/rotten 'apple
one bad person who has a bad effect on others in a group: *In response to the allegations of mass corruption within the team, a former player said today, 'There may be the odd rotten apple in the pack, but the majority are clean and honest.'*

● American → as American as apple pie
● upset → upset the/sb's apple cart

apple-pie /'æpl paɪ/

in apple-pie 'order
neat and very well organized: *She keeps the accounts in apple-pie order.*

apples /'æplz/

ˌapples and 'oranges (AmE)
used to describe a situation in which two people or things are completely different from each other: *He was no competition for me: it was like apples and oranges.*

how do you like 'them apples? ◆ how about 'them apples? (AmE, informal, usually spoken)
used after telling sb an unpleasant fact or truth, to say that they should accept it: *Either you deliver the dresses for the price we agreed on, or I'm going to go someplace else. How do you like them apples?*

she's 'apples (AustralE, New Zealand, informal)
used to say that sth or everything is all right: *I reckon I'll sell the car when the suspension gets tired, but for now, she's apples.*

> **❓ ORIGIN**
> This comes from rhyming slang; *apples and rice* or *apples and spice*, meaning *nice*.

approach /əˈprəʊtʃ; AmE əˈprəʊtʃ/

• softly-softly → a/the softly-softly approach

approval /əˈpruːvl/

on apˈproval
(of goods) not paid for and to be returned, usually within a few days, if the customer decides not to buy them: *I've got it on seven days approval, so if you don't like it I can take it back.*

• seal → a seal of approval

apron /ˈeɪprən/

(tied to) your mother's, wife's, etc. ˈapron strings
(too much under) the influence and control of sb, especially your mother, wife, etc: *The British prime minister is too apt to cling to Washington's apron strings.*

area /ˈeəriə; AmE ˈeriə/

• disaster → a disaster area
• grey → a grey area
• no-go → a no-go area

argue /ˈɑːɡjuː; AmE ˈɑːrɡ-/

ˌargue the ˈtoss (*BrE, informal*)
continue to disagree about a decision, especially when it is too late to change it or it is not very important: *Look, just do it your way. I've got better things to do than stand here all day arguing the toss with you.*

argument /ˈɑːɡjumənt; AmE ˈɑːrɡ-/

• sake → for the sake of argument

ark /ɑːk; AmE ɑːrk/

be out of the ˈark ♦ went out with the ˈark (*BrE, spoken*)
(of an object or a custom) extremely old or old-fashioned: *She was using a dictionary that was straight out of the ark.*

> ❷ ORIGIN
> This idiom refers to a story in the Bible. The *ark* was a large boat which Noah built to save his family and two of every type of animal from the flood.

arm /ɑːm; AmE ɑːrm/

cost/pay an ˌarm and a ˈleg (*informal*)
cost/pay a lot of money: *We want to redecorate the living room, but I'm afraid it's going to cost us an arm and a leg.*

keep sb at arm's ˈlength
avoid becoming too friendly with sb: *He's the kind of man who's best kept at arm's length.*

put the ˈarm/ˈbite on sb (*AmE, informal*)
ask sb for sth, especially money: *To pay for the tax reductions, the government will put the bite on smokers and motorists.*

• chance → chance your arm
• long → as long as your arm
• long → the long arm of the law
• right → would give your right arm for sth/to do sth
• shot → a shot in the arm
• twist → twist sb's arm

armchair /ˈɑːmtʃeə(r); ɑːmˈtʃeə(r); AmE ˈɑːrmtʃer; ɑːrmˈtʃer/

an armchair critic, traveller, etc.
a person who knows about a subject only from what they have heard or read and not from personal experience: *He's what you might call an 'armchair traveller', having never actually been outside Europe.*

armed /ɑːmd; AmE ɑːrmd/

ˌarmed to the ˈteeth (with sth) (*informal*)
carrying a lot of weapons or a lot of things needed for a particular purpose: *The tourists got out of the coach, armed to the teeth with cameras, binoculars, and guidebooks.*

armour (*BrE*) (*AmE* **armor**) /ˈɑːmə(r); AmE ˈɑːrm-/

• chink → a chink in sb's armour
• knight → a knight in shining armour

arms /ɑːmz; AmE ɑːrmz/

up in ˈarms (about/over sth) (*informal*)
very angry and protesting very strongly (about sth): *Local residents are up in arms over plans to build a new motorway.*

• babe → a babe in arms
• fold → fold sb in your arms
• hands → throw up your hands/arms in despair, horror, etc.
• lay → lay down your arms
• open → with open arms

arrive /əˈraɪv/

• scene → arrive/come on the scene

arrow /ˈærəʊ; AmE ˈæroʊ/

• straight → (as) straight as an arrow

arrows /ˈærəʊz; AmE ˈæroʊz/

• slings → the slings and arrows (of sth)

arse /ɑːs; AmE ɑːrs/

My arse! (*BrE, △, slang*)
used by some people to show they do not believe what sb has said: *An appointment at the dentist my arse! She's gone shopping!*

work your 'arse off (*BrE*) (*AmE* **work your 'ass off**) (⚠, *slang*)
work very hard

● **kiss** → kiss (sb's) arse
● **know** → not know your arse from your elbow
● **lick** → lick sb's arse SEE lick sb's boots
● **pain** → a pain in the arse/bum/backside SEE a pain in the neck
● **think** → think the sun shines out of sb's arse/backside

arsed /ɑːst; *AmE* ɑːrst/

can't be 'arsed (to do sth) (*BrE*, ⚠, *slang*)
not want to do sth because it is too much trouble: *I was supposed to do some work this weekend but I couldn't be arsed.*

NOTE
A more polite way to express this is 'can't be bothered (to do something)'.

art /ɑːt; *AmE* ɑːrt/

● **fine** → have sth down to a fine art
● **state** → state of the art

artistic /ɑːˈtɪstɪk; *AmE* ɑːrˈt-/

● **licence** → artistic/poetic licence

as /əz; æz/

as against sth
in contrast with sth: *They got 27% of the vote as against 32% at the last election.*

,as and 'when
whenever; at the moment when: *We'll deal with individual problems as and when they arise.*

as for sb/sth
turning to the subject of sb/sth: *I like Sue very much, but as for her boyfriend — I wouldn't care if I never saw him again!*

'as from (also **'as of** *especially AmE*)
used to indicate the time or date from which something starts: *As from next Monday she'll have a new secretary.* ◇ *We shall be at our new address as of mid-June.*

as 'if (*spoken*)
used to express anger at or disapproval of a suggestion, an explanation, etc., or to deny a possibility: *As if I really cared!* ◇ *'Don't tell Tom I said that, will you?' 'Oh, as if (I would)!'*

as if/as though
in a way that suggests sth: *He behaved as if nothing had happened.* ◇ *It sounds as though you had a good time.*

,as it 'is
as the situation is at the moment (often in contrast to what was expected): *I wanted to have this report ready for tomorrow but as it is, it may not be done until Thursday.* ◇ *We won't be able to buy a new car this year — we can only just afford a holiday as it is.*

as to sth
used when you are referring to sth: *As to tax, that will be deducted from your salary.*

as you 'do (*BrE*)
used as a comment on sth that you have just said to say that it is normal behaviour: *He smiled and I smiled back, as you do.* ◇ (*ironic*) *She's just gone off to Bermuda for three weeks on holiday. As you do!*

it isn't as if/though ✦ **it's not as if/as though**
used to show that a particular explanation for sth is not the correct one: *It isn't as if he didn't recognize me! He just walked straight past me as I stood there.*

ashes /ˈæʃɪz/

● **rake** → rake over the ashes/the past
● **rise** → rise from the ashes
● **sackcloth** → put on, wear, etc. sackcloth and ashes

aside /əˈsaɪd/

● **joking** → joking apart/aside

ask /ɑːsk; *AmE* æsk/

'ask for trouble/it (*informal*)
(usually used in the progressive tenses) behave in a way that is likely to result in problems: *They're asking for trouble, leaving young children alone in the house like that.* ◇ *She's really asking for it, the way she comes in late every day.*

,don't 'ask (*spoken*, *informal*)
if you say **don't ask** to sb, you mean that you do not want to reply to their question, because it would be awkward, embarrassing, etc: *'How was your trip?' 'Don't ask! It was a disaster!'*

,don't ask 'me (*spoken*, *informal*)
if you say **don't ask me**, you mean that you do not know the answer to a question and are annoyed that you have been asked: *Don't ask me — nobody tells me anything around here.*

I 'ask you! (*spoken*, *informal*)
used to show strong surprise, disbelief, shock, etc: *So they just arrived without telling you they were coming? Well, I ask you!*

if you ask 'me (*spoken*, *informal*)
in my personal opinion: *If you ask me, Mark shouldn't have bought that car — it just wasn't worth the money.*

● **hand** → ask for/win sb's hand
● **moon** → cry/ask for the moon

asking /ˈɑːskɪŋ; *AmE* ˈæskɪŋ/

be sb's for the 'asking
be obtained simply by asking for it; be very easily obtained: *If you want any of the furniture, it's yours for the asking.* ◇ *Fame and money were hers for the asking in those days.*

asleep /əˈsliːp/

asleep at the 'wheel (*especially BrE*) (*AmE* usually **asleep at the 'switch**) (*informal*)
not paying attention to possible problems: *The agency has been asleep at the wheel and has failed to enforce regulations.*

> NOTE
> This refers to someone falling asleep while driving a car or while operating a control on a train track.

- **sound** → sound asleep

ass /æs/

get your 'ass in gear (also **move your 'ass**) (△, *slang, especially AmE*)
a rude way of telling sb to hurry

get your ass over/in 'here, etc. (△, *slang, especially AmE*)
a rude way of telling sb to come here, etc.

- **arse** → work your ass off SEE work your arse off
- **bust** → bust sb's ass/balls/butt/hump
- **bust** → bust your ass/balls/butt/hump
- **cover** → cover your ass SEE cover your back
- **haul** → haul ass
- **kick** → kick (some/sb's) ass/butt
- **kiss** → kiss (sb's) ass
- **know** → not know your ass from your elbow SEE not know your arse from your elbow
- **lick** → lick sb's ass SEE lick sb's boots
- **pain** → a pain in the ass/butt SEE a pain in the neck
- **think** → think the sun shines out of sb's ass SEE think the sun shines out of sb's arse/backside

assured /əˈʃʊəd; əˈʃɔːd; AmE əˈʃʊrd/

- **rest** → rest assured (that…)

astray /əˈstreɪ/

go a'stray
1 become lost; be stolen: *Several letters went astray or were not delivered.* ◇ *We locked up our valuables so they wouldn't go astray.*
2 go in the wrong direction or have the wrong result: *Fortunately the gunman's shots went astray.*

- **lead¹** → lead sb astray

atmosphere /ˈætməsfɪə(r); AmE -fɪr/

you could ,cut the atmosphere with a 'knife (*informal*)
used to say that the emotional tension, embarrassment, etc. shared by a group of people is very great: *When John came in with his new girlfriend, you could have cut the atmosphere with a knife.*

- **heavy** → a heavy silence/atmosphere

attached /əˈtætʃt/

- **strings** → (with) no strings attached

attempt /əˈtempt/

- **last-ditch** → a last-ditch stand/attempt/effort

attendance /əˈtendəns/

be in at'tendance (*formal*)
be present at a special event: *Several heads of state were in attendance at the funeral.*

take at'tendance (*AmE*)
check who is present and who is not present at a place and mark this information on a list of names: *The teacher took attendance at the beginning of every class.*

- **dance** → dance attendance on sb

attention /əˈtenʃn/

- **undivided** → get/have sb's undivided attention

attitude /ˈætɪtjuːd; AmE ˈætɪtuːd/

- **strike** → strike a pose/an attitude

attract /əˈtrækt/

- **opposites** → opposites attract

authority /ɔːˈθɒrəti; AmE əˈθɔːr-; əˈθɑːr-/

have sth on good au'thority
be able to believe sth because you trust the person who gave you the information: *I have it on good authority that the chairman is going to resign.*

automatic /ˌɔːtəˈmætɪk/

be on ,automatic 'pilot
do sth without thinking because you have done the same thing many times before: *I got up and dressed on automatic pilot.*

> NOTE
> The *automatic pilot* is the device in an aircraft that keeps it on a fixed course without the need for a person to control it. It is often shortened to 'autopilot': *I did the journey on autopilot.*

avail /əˈveɪl/

of little/no a'vail (*formal*)
of little or no use: *Your ability to argue is of little avail if you get your facts wrong.*

to little/no a'vail (*formal*)
with little or no success: *The doctors tried everything to keep him alive but to no avail.*

averages /ˈævərɪdʒɪz/

- **law** → the law of averages

avoid /əˈvɔɪd/

avoid sb/sth like the 'plague (*informal*)
avoid sb/sth completely: *It was the sort of restaurant that I would normally have avoided like the plague.*

> NOTE
> A *plague* is an infectious disease that kills a lot of people.

- **trap** → fall into/avoid the trap of doing sth

bad. ◇ *No, it's my bad. I'm the one that got caught taking stuff.*

not (so/too) 'bad (*spoken*)
quite good: *'How are you feeling today?' 'Not too bad, thanks.'* ◇ *Some of his recent books are really not bad.*

take the ˌbad with the 'good
accept the bad aspects of sth as well as the good ones: *You must learn to take the bad with the good in this job. Things don't always go as well as you think they should.*

(it's) too 'bad (*spoken*)
1 used to show sympathy or disappointment: *It's too bad you can't come to the party.*
2 used to show that you are not sympathetic: *I know you don't want me to go. Well, too bad, I'm going!*

badly /'bædli/

be badly 'off
1 not having much money; poor
2 not in a good situation: *I've got quite a big room so I'm not too badly off.* **OPP** be well off

be badly 'off for sth
not have enough of sth: *My father also studied history at college, so I'm not badly off for books* (= I've got quite a lot).

bag /bæg/

(not) your 'bag (*informal*)
(not) sth that you are interested in or good at: *Poetry isn't really my bag.*

ˌbag and 'baggage
with all your belongings: *If you don't pay the rent, you'll be thrown out, bag and baggage.*

a 'bag lady (*informal*)
a woman who has no home and who walks around carrying her possessions with her

a ˌbag of 'bones (*informal*)
a very thin person or animal: *She refused to eat until eventually she was a bag of bones.*

in the 'bag (*informal*)
(of a successful result) almost certain to be achieved: *With a three-goal lead and only ten minutes left to play, victory seemed in the bag.*

- **cat** → let the cat out of the bag
- **holding** → leave sb holding the bag **SEE** leave sb holding the baby
- **mixed** → be a mixed bag/bunch
- **nerves** → a bag/bundle of nerves
- **old** → an old bag
- **punch** → he, she, etc. couldn't punch his, her, etc. way out of a paper bag
- **tricks** → a bag/box of tricks

baggage /'bægɪdʒ/

- **bag** → bag and baggage

bags /bægz/

bags (I)… (*BrE*) (*AmE* **'dibs on…**) (*informal*)
used especially by children for claiming the right to have or do sth before anyone else: *Bags I sit in the front seat!*

- **pack** → pack your bags
- **three** → (yes sir, no sir) three bags full (sir)

bait /beɪt/

- **fish** → fish or cut bait
- **rise** → rise to the bait
- **swallow** → swallow the bait

baker /'beɪkə(r)/

a baker's 'dozen (*old-fashioned*)
thirteen

> **❷ ORIGIN**
> This phrase comes from bakers' old custom of adding one extra loaf to an order of a dozen (= twelve).

balance /'bæləns/

(be/hang) in the 'balance
(be) at a point where sth could either develop well or badly; be uncertain: *With the election results due to be announced this afternoon, the future of the country still hangs very much in the balance.*

> **NOTE**
> A *balance* is an instrument for weighing things. It has a bar that is supported in the middle and dishes hanging from each end.

(catch/throw sb) off 'balance
1 make sb/sth unsteady and in danger of falling: *I was thrown off balance by the sudden gust of wind.*
2 make sb surprised and no longer calm: *The senator was clearly caught off balance by the unexpected question.*

on 'balance
when advantages and disadvantages, successes and failures, etc. have been compared: *It has been decided that, on balance, she is the best person for the job despite her lack of experience.*

- **redress** → redress the balance
- **strike** → strike a balance (between A and B)
- **tip** → swing the balance **SEE** tip the balance/scales

balances /'bælənsɪz/

- **checks** → checks and balances

balancing /'bælənsɪŋ/

- **act** → a balancing/juggling act

bald /bɔːld/

(as) bald as a 'coot
having no hair on your head at all: *Why did you buy him a hairbrush? He's as bald as a coot!*

> **NOTE**
> A *coot* is a black bird with a white patch on its forehead that lives on or near water.

ball /bɔːl/

a ,ball and 'chain (*BrE*)
1 a problem that prevents you from doing what you would like to do: *The business never made any money and was regarded more as a ball and chain than anything else.*
2 (*humorous*) sb's husband or wife: *I must get home to the ball and chain!*

> ❷ ORIGIN
>
> In the past, prisoners had to wear a heavy metal ball on a chain around one leg so that they couldn't escape.

the ball is in your/sb's 'court
it is sb's turn to speak, act, etc. next: *I've given them a list of the changes that I think are necessary, so the ball's in their court now.*

be on the 'ball
be aware of what is happening and be able to react or deal with it quickly: *For the assistant manager's job we need someone who's really on the ball.*

a (whole) different/new 'ball game (*informal*)
a completely different kind of situation: *They used to go out every night, but now they've got a baby it's a whole new ball game.*

get/keep/set/start the 'ball rolling
begin/continue an activity, discussion, etc: *I will start the ball rolling by introducing the first speaker.*

have (yourself) a 'ball (*informal, especially AmE*)
enjoy yourself very much: *When these exams are finally over, we're going to have a ball.*

have something/a lot on the 'ball
(*AmE, informal*)
be capable of doing a job very well; be intelligent: *I think she has a lot on the ball and would make an excellent senator.*

play 'ball (with sb) (*informal*)
be willing to work with other people in a helpful way, especially so that sb can get what they want: *We need their help, but will they play ball? ◇ So he won't play ball, eh? He'll soon realize he can't manage without us.*

the whole ball of 'wax (*AmE, informal*)
the whole thing; everything: *I panicked, I cried — the whole ball of wax.*

• **carry** → carry the ball
• **drop** → drop the ball
• **eight** → behind the eight ball
• **eye** → keep your eye on the ball
• **spike** → spike the ball

ballistic /bəˈlɪstɪk/

go bal'listic (*informal*)
become very angry: *He went ballistic when I told him about the accident.*

> ❷ ORIGIN
>
> A *ballistic missile* is a weapon that is sent through the air and that explodes when it hits the thing that it is aimed at. When it goes *ballistic* it starts to fall towards its target and so becomes very dangerous.

balloon /bəˈluːn/

when the bal'loon goes up (*informal*)
when the trouble or important event begins: *I don't want to be there when the balloon goes up.*

• **lead²** → go down like a lead balloon

ballpark /ˈbɔːlpɑːk; AmE -pɑːrk/

a 'ballpark figure
a number which is approximately correct: *I know we haven't really discussed costs yet, but can you give me a ballpark figure?*

be in the same/right 'ballpark (*especially AmE*)
be within the same/the right area or range of figures, etc: *The offers for the contract were all in the same ballpark.*

balls /bɔːlz/

break sb's 'balls (*AmE, △, slang*)
criticize sb in an angry or annoying way: *His wife's breaking his balls about the bills not being paid.* ► **'ball-breaker** *noun*: *That nephew of yours, he's a real ball-breaker.*

break your 'balls (*AmE, △, slang*)
make a very great effort

• **bust** → bust sb's ass/balls/butt/hump
• **bust** → bust your ass/balls/butt/hump

banana /bəˈnɑːnə; AmE bəˈnænə/

• **slip** → slip on a banana skin

bananas /bəˈnɑːnəz; AmE bəˈnænəz/

go ba'nanas (*slang*)
become angry, crazy or silly: *If I'm late again my Dad'll go bananas. ◇ The clock's going bananas* (= isn't working correctly).

bandwagon /ˈbændwægən/

climb/jump on the 'bandwagon (*informal, disapproving*)
do sth that others are already doing because it is successful or fashionable: *As soon as their policies became popular, all the other parties started to climb on the bandwagon.*

> ❷ ORIGIN
>
> At political celebrations in the USA, there was often a band on a large decorated vehicle (= a bandwagon). If somebody joined a particular 'bandwagon', they publicly supported that politician in order to benefit from their success.

bane /beɪn/

the bane of sb's 'life/e'xistence
a person or thing that makes sb's life unpleasant
or unhappy: *That car is always breaking down! It's
the bane of my life.* **OPP** a ray of sunshine

bang /bæŋ/

,**bang for your 'buck** (*AmE, slang*)
if you get more, better, etc. **bang for your buck,**
you get better value for the money you spend or
the effort you put in to sth: *Buyers get more bang
for their buck with our cars.*

> **NOTE**
> *Buck* is an informal word for a dollar.

bang goes sth (*informal*)
sth is suddenly gone, finished, lost, etc: *I twisted
my ankle and bang went my chances of playing in
the match.*

bang/spot 'on (*informal*)
(of an estimate, a description, etc.) exactly right:
*She was bang on when she called him an idiot: that's
just what he is! ◇ Your sales estimate was spot on.
Well done!*

bang to 'rights (*BrE*) (*AmE* **dead to 'rights**)
(*informal*)
in the act of committing a crime, so that you cannot claim to be innocent: *We've got you bang to
rights handling stolen property.*

go 'bang (*informal*)
burst or explode with a loud noise; make a sudden
loud noise: *A balloon suddenly went bang.*

go (off) with a 'bang (*informal*)
(of an event, etc.) be very successful: *Last night's
party really went off with a bang.*

● **drum** → bang/beat the drum (for sb/sth)
● **heads** → bang/knock your/their heads together
● **time** → bang on time **SEE** (right) on time

bank /bæŋk/

not ,break the 'bank (*informal*)
not cost a lot of money, or more than you can
afford: *Just lend me $20. That won't break the
bank, will it?*

> **NOTE**
> If you *break the bank* in a game or competition,
> you win more money than the bank holds.

● **laugh** → laugh all the way to the bank

baptism /'bæptɪzəm/

a ,baptism of 'fire
an unpleasant or a frightening first experience of
sth: *Her first day in the job was a real baptism of
fire because she had to deal with a very difficult case
immediately.*

bar /bɑː(r)/

bar 'none
without exception: *This is the best apple pie I've
ever tasted, bar none.*

be all over ,bar the 'shouting
(of a performance, contest, etc.) be finished or
decided, with only the audience's reaction or the
official announcement to follow: *Now that the first
few election results have been declared, it's really all
over bar the shouting.*

> **NOTE**
> *Bar* in these two expressions is a preposition
> meaning 'apart from'.

not have a 'bar of sth (*AustralE, New Zealand*)
have nothing to do with sth: *That's a ridiculous
proposal and we won't have a bar of it. ◇ He tried
to persuade her to come but she wouldn't have a bar
of it.*

● **kitchen** → everything but/bar the kitchen sink
● **prop** → prop up the bar

bare /beə(r); *AmE* ber/

the bare 'bones (of sth)
the main or basic facts of a matter: *I had so little
time that I could only tell him the bare bones of the
story and had to supply the details later.*

bare your 'soul
tell sb your deepest feelings: *Finally she bared her
soul to him, saying she had always loved him.*

> **NOTE**
> If you *bare* something, you remove the cover-
> ing from it, especially from part of the body.

bare your 'teeth
show your teeth in a fierce and threatening way:
The dog bared its teeth and growled.

with your bare 'hands
with your hands only, without any tools or
weapons: *He said he'd killed a crocodile with his
bare hands!*

● **cupboard** → the cupboard is bare
● **lay** → lay sth bare

bargain /'bɑːgən; *AmE* 'bɑːrgən/

into the 'bargain (*AmE* **in the 'bargain**)
as well; in addition: *She gave us tea and some useful information into the bargain.*

● **drive** → drive a hard bargain
● **strike** → strike a bargain/deal (with sb)

bargaining /'bɑːgənɪŋ; *AmE* 'bɑːrgənɪŋ/

a 'bargaining counter (*BrE*) (also **a 'bargaining
chip** *AmE, BrE*)
a special advantage in negotiations, disputes, etc.
which can be offered in exchange for sth: *The proposed troop reductions were a useful bargaining
counter in the disarmament talks.*

bargepole /ˈbɑːdʒpəʊl; AmE ˈbɑːrdʒpoʊl/

● touch → not touch sb/sth with a bargepole

bark /bɑːk; AmE bɑːrk/

his, her, etc. bark is worse than his, her, etc. bite (*informal*)
sb is not really as angry or unkind as they seem: *Don't worry about my father being angry — his bark is worse than his bite.*

> **NOTE**
> A *bark* is the short loud sound made by dogs, especially when they are angry.

● dog → why keep a dog and bark yourself?

barking /ˈbɑːkɪŋ; AmE ˈbɑːrkɪŋ/

be barking 'mad ♦ be 'barking (*BrE, informal*)
completely crazy: *You're playing tennis in this weather? You're barking mad!*

be barking up the wrong 'tree
be mistaken about sth: *The police are barking up the wrong tree if they think I had anything to do with the crime. I wasn't even in the country when it happened!*

barn /bɑːn; AmE bɑːrn/

● stable → shut, etc. the barn door after the horse has escaped **SEE** shut/lock/close the stable door after the horse has bolted

barred /bɑːd; AmE bɑːrd/

● holds → (with) no holds barred

barrel /ˈbærəl/

(get/have sb) over a 'barrel (*informal*)
(put/have sb) in a position where they are forced to do what you want: *She has us over a barrel — if we don't pay her, we'll lose everything.*

> **❷ ORIGIN**
> This may refer to a person who has been saved from drowning and is held over a *barrel* (= a large round container) in order to empty their lungs of water.

● candy → be like shooting fish in a barrel **SEE** be like taking candy from a baby
● laughs → a barrel/bundle of laughs
● lock → lock, stock and barrel
● scrape → scrape (the bottom of) the barrel

barrelhead /ˈbærəlˌhed/

● cash → cash on the barrelhead

bars /bɑːz; AmE bɑːrz/

behind 'bars (*informal*)
in prison: *Criminals like him ought to be put behind bars for life.*

base /beɪs/

off 'base (*AmE, informal*)
1 completely wrong about sth: *You're way off base with that guess.*
2 unprepared: *The question caught her off base.*

> **NOTE**
> In baseball, a *base* is one of the four positions that a player must reach in order to score points.

● first → get to first base (with sb/sth)
● first → reach/make first base (with sb/sth) **SEE** get to first base (with sb/sth)
● touch → touch base (with sb)

bases /ˈbeɪsɪz/

● cover → cover all the/your bases

bash /bæʃ/

have a bash at (doing) sth (*BrE, spoken*)
make an attempt at sth: *I'm going to have a bash at fixing the car myself.*

basics /ˈbeɪsɪks/

get/go back to 'basics
think about the simple or most important ideas within a subject or an activity instead of new ideas or complicated details: *It's time for us all to get back to basics and concentrate on what really matters.*

bask /bɑːsk; AmE bæsk/

● reflected → bathe/bask in reflected glory

basket /ˈbɑːskɪt; AmE ˈbæs-/

a 'basket case (*informal*)
1 a country or an organization whose economic situation is very bad: *A few years ago, the country was an economic basket case, but now things are different.*
2 a person who is slightly crazy and who has problems dealing with situations: *'How did the interview go?' 'Terrible! I'm sure they thought I was a complete basket case.'*

● eggs → put all your eggs into one basket

bat /bæt/

ˌbat your 'eyelashes/'eyes
open and close your eyes quickly, in a way that is supposed to be attractive: *There's no use batting your eyelashes at me, young lady!*

bat a 'thousand (*AmE, informal*)
be very successful: *He's made another sale? He's really batting a thousand!*

go to 'bat for sb (*AmE, informal*)
give sb help and support: *Nursing students are going to go to bat for the homeless.*

like a ˌbat out of 'hell (*informal*)
very fast: *If there were a fire, I wouldn't try to save any possessions. I'd be off like a bat out of hell!*

not bat an 'eyelid (*BrE*) (*AmE* **not bat an 'eye**) (*informal*)
not seem surprised, worried, afraid, etc: *She didn't bat an eyelid when they told her she'd lost her job. She just calmly walked out.*

(right) off the 'bat (*informal, especially AmE*)
immediately; without delay: *They liked each other very much, right off the bat.*

off your own 'bat (*BrE, informal*)
independently, without the encouragement or help of others: *Nobody had even tried to persuade Tim to give up smoking; he did it off his own bat.*

● blind → (as) blind as a bat
● old → an old bat
● straight → play a straight bat SEE play it straight

bated /ˈbeɪtɪd/

with ˌbated 'breath
hardly able to breathe because you are very anxious about sth: *We watched with bated breath as the lion moved slowly towards him.*

bath /bɑːθ; *AmE* bæθ/

take a 'bath (*AmE, informal, business*)
lose a lot of money, for example on a business agreement or an investment: *Big investors sold their shares before the price crashed, but small investors took a bath.* **OPP** make, etc. a mint (of money)

bathe /beɪð/

● reflected → bathe/bask in reflected glory

bathroom /ˈbɑːθruːm; -rʊm; *AmE* ˈbæθ-/

go to the bathroom (*AmE*)
(used about people or animals) to pass liquid or solid waste material from your body: *Oh, no! The dog went to the bathroom on the carpet!*

bathwater /ˈbɑːθwɔːtə(r); *AmE* ˈbæθwɔːtər; -wɑːt-/

● baby → throw the baby out with the bathwater

bats /bæts/

have ˌbats in the 'belfry (*old-fashioned, informal*)
be crazy or eccentric

batten /ˈbætn/

ˌbatten down the 'hatches
prepare yourself for a period of difficulty or trouble: *Hollywood is battening down the hatches in expectation of a strike by actors and writers this summer.*

❓ ORIGIN
A *batten* is a long piece of wood which was used to hold down strong material in order to cover a ship's *hatches* (= openings in the deck of a boat leading to the lower level) in a storm.

batteries /ˈbætriz; -təriz/

● recharge → recharge your batteries

battle /ˈbætl/

the battle lines are 'drawn
used to say that people or groups have shown which side they intend to support in a dispute or contest that is going to begin: *The battle lines are being drawn in the fight for control of the company.*

a battle of 'wills
a competition, an argument or a struggle where each side is very determined to win: *Annie and Phil were engaged in a silent battle of wills, each refusing to leave.*

a battle of 'wits
a competition, an argument or a struggle where each side uses their ability to think quickly to try to win: *It's a battle of wits between the hero and the villain.*

do/join 'battle (with sb)
fight, compete or argue (with sb): *A group of local parents have decided to join battle with the council about their decision to close two of the town's schools.*

● fight → fight a losing battle
● half → half the battle
● pitched → a pitched battle
● running → a running battle
● uphill → an uphill struggle/battle/task

battles /ˈbætlz/

● fight → fight your own battles

bay /beɪ/

at 'bay
when an animal that is being hunted is **at bay**, it must turn and face the dogs and hunters because it is impossible to escape from them

hold/keep sb/sth at 'bay
prevent sb/sth from coming too close or attacking: *Vitamin C helps to keep colds and flu at bay.*

be /biː; bi/

Most idioms containing the verb **be** are at the entries for the nouns and adjectives in the idioms, for example **be the death of sb** is at **death**.

be 'at it (*informal*)
1 be talking or arguing too much: *It's time you two stopped arguing — you've been at it all morning!*
2 be having sex with sb

be your'self
act naturally: *Don't try to act sophisticated — just be yourself.*

so 'be it (*formal*)
used to show that you accept a situation but do not like it: *He never wants to speak to me again? So be it.*

beach /biːtʃ/

● pebble → not the only pebble on the beach

beady /ˈbiːdi/

keep a beady 'eye on sb/sth ✦ have your beady 'eye on sb/sth
watch sb/sth very carefully because you do not really trust them/it: *He always kept a beady eye on his employees.*

be-all /ˈbi ɔːl/

the ˌbe-all and 'end-all (of sth) (*informal*)
the most important thing/person; the only thing/person that matters: *His girlfriend is the be-all and end-all of his existence.* ◇ *I'll never be rich, but money isn't the be-all and end-all, you know.*

beam /biːm/

off 'beam (*informal*)
wrong; incorrect: *No, you're way off beam there.*

> **❷ ORIGIN**
> A radio wave, or *beam*, can be used to guide aircraft. If the aircraft is *off beam* it is not following the correct course as set by the beam.

● broad → broad in the beam
● ear → beam/grin/smile from ear to ear

bean /biːn/

not (have) a 'bean (*BrE, informal*)
(have) no money at all: *'How much have you saved?' 'Not a bean.'*

beans /biːnz/

● full → full of beans
● hill → a hill of beans
● know → not know beans about sth
● spill → spill the beans

bear /beə(r); AmE ber/

bear the 'brunt of sth
suffer most as the result of an attack, a loss, bad luck, etc: *We all lost money when the business collapsed, but I bore the brunt of it because I had invested the most.*

bear 'fruit
have the desired result; be successful: *The tireless efforts of campaigners have finally borne fruit and the prisoners are due to be released tomorrow.*

like a ˌbear with a sore 'head (*informal*)
very bad-tempered: *She's like a bear with a sore head in the mornings.*

● cross → bear/carry your cross
● cross → have a (heavy) cross to bear
● grin → grin and bear it
● loaded → loaded for bear
● mind → bear/keep in mind that...
● mind → bear/keep sb/sth in mind

● pressure → bring pressure to bear (on sb) (to do sth)
● witness → bear/give witness (to sth)

bearings /ˈbeərɪŋz; AmE ˈber-/

find/get your 'bearings
find out exactly where you are, or the details of the situation you are in, especially when this is new and unfamiliar: *We got off the bus right in the centre of town and it took us a moment or two to get our bearings.* ◇ *I've only been in the job for a week so I'm still finding my bearings.*

lose your 'bearings
become lost or suddenly confused: *The old man seemed to have lost his bearings for a moment.*

beast /biːst/

● man → be no good/use to man or beast

beat /biːt/

ˌbeat about the 'bush (*BrE*) (*AmE ˌbeat around the 'bush*)
take too long before saying what you want to say; avoid saying sth directly: *Don't beat about the bush. Tell me exactly what you think is wrong with my work.* **OPP** call a spade a spade

beat sb at their own 'game
be more successful than sb in their special activity, sport, etc.; defeat sb using their own methods: *If you thought someone was trying to cheat you, would you challenge him or try to beat him at his own game?*

beat your 'brains out (*informal, especially AmE*)
think very hard about sth for a long time: *I was beating my brains out all weekend trying to write the script.*

beat the 'bushes (*especially AmE*)
try very hard to find, obtain or achieve sth: *Telephone companies are beating the bushes for new customers.*

beat the 'clock
finish a task, race, etc. before a particular time

beat sb/sth 'hollow
beat sb easily in a contest, etc.; be much better than sb/sth: *As a cook he beats the professionals hollow.*

'beat it (*informal*)
(usually used as a command) go away: *You're not wanted here, so beat it.*

beat a path to sb's 'door
if a lot of people **beat a path to sb's door**, they are all interested in sth that person has to sell, or can do or tell them: *Top theatrical agents are beating a path to the teenager's door.*

beat the 'rap (*AmE, slang*)
escape without being punished: *This time he didn't beat the rap, and got three years in jail for robbery.*

beat a (hasty) re'treat
go away quickly from sb/sth: *I had a terrible headache from all the noise and smoke at the party, so my wife and I beat a hasty retreat.*

beside /bɪ'saɪd/

be'side yourself (with sth)
unable to control yourself because of the strength
of emotion you are feeling: *He was beside himself
with rage when he found out what she'd done.*

best /best/

all the 'best
used when you are saying goodbye or ending a
letter to give sb your best wishes: *All the best, then,
Maria, and we'll see you in two weeks.* ◇ *Here's
wishing you all the best for the coming year.*

as ,best you 'can
not perfectly but as well as you are able: *We'll
manage as best we can.*

at 'best/'worst
taking the most/least hopeful or positive view:
*Smoking is at best unpleasant and expensive, and
at worst lethal.*

at the 'best of times
even when conditions are good: *This car does not
go very fast at the best of times, and with four
people in it, it will go a lot slower.*

be (all) for the 'best
have a good result, though it does not seem good
at first: *I was very disappointed when I didn't get the
job but now I think it was for the best. I don't think I
would have liked it.*

the/your best 'bet (*informal*)
the best thing for you to do in a particular situation: *Your best bet is to leave the car here and get
a bus into town.*

your best bib and 'tucker (*humorous*)
your best clothes that you only wear on special
occasions: *Bill put on his best bib and tucker and
booked a table at a top restaurant for a romantic
dinner.*

> **NOTE**
> *Bib* and *tucker* are both items of clothing worn
> in the past.

the best 'medicine
the best way of improving a situation, especially
of making you feel happier: *Laughter is the best
medicine.*

the best of a bad 'bunch/'lot (*BrE*)
a person or a thing that is a little better than the
rest in a group, although none are very good

the best of 'both/'all (possible) worlds
the advantages of two/many very different situations: *We have the best of both worlds here — it's
a peaceful village but we're only twenty minutes
from the town centre.* **OPP** the worst of both/all (possible) worlds

the best of 'luck (to sb) (*old-fashioned, informal,
often ironic*)
used to wish sb luck in an activity, especially one
in which they are unlikely to be successful: *The
four of you are going to live in that tiny apartment?
The best of luck to you!*

the best of 'three, 'five, etc.
(especially in games and sports) up to three, five,
etc. games played to decide who wins, the winner
being the person or team that wins most of them

the best thing since sliced 'bread (*informal,
spoken*)
if you say that sth is **the best thing since sliced
bread**, you think it is extremely good, interesting,
etc: *My father doesn't like him very much, but my
mother thinks he's the best thing since sliced bread!*

bring out the 'best in sb
make sb show their best qualities: *Sometimes
it takes a crisis to bring out the best in people.*
OPP bring out the worst in sb

do, mean, etc. sth for the 'best
do or say sth in order to achieve a good result or to
help sb: *I just don't know what to do for the best.*
◇ *I'm sorry if my advice offended you — I meant it
for the best.*

**for a/some reason/reasons best known to
him'self, her'self, etc.** (*humorous*)
for a reason or reasons which other people find
hard to understand: *For reasons best known to
himself, he wears two pairs of socks.*

get/have the 'best of sth
gain more advantage from sth than sb else:
I thought you had the best of that discussion.

give it your best 'shot
try as hard as you can to do or achieve sth: *I
probably won't win the game, but I'll give it my best
shot.*

look your/its 'best
look as attractive, neat, etc. as possible: *The garden looks its best when all the flowers are out.*

make the best of sth/things/a bad job
do as well as you can in a difficult situation: *It
wasn't a very large room, but he made the best of it
by using space carefully.* ◇ *I know the lighting isn't
perfect but we'll have to make the best of a bad job
and get the best photos we can.*

put your best foot 'forward
go, work, etc. as fast as you can: *If we put our best
foot forward, we should be there by noon.*

to the best of your be'lief/'knowledge
as far as you know: *He never made a will, to the
best of my knowledge.*

with the 'best of them
as well as anybody: *She may be seventy, but she can
get up and dance with the best of them!*

with the ,best will in the 'world
even though you have tried very hard to be fair,
generous, etc: *He's quite competent, but with the
best will in the world, I can't imagine him as head
of a large company.*

- **better** → had better/best do sth
- **hope** → hope for the best
- **know** → know best
- **level** → do/try your level best (to do sth)
- **man** → man's best friend
- **next** → the next best thing
- **part** → the better/best part of sth

- **past** → be past your/its best
- **second** → second best
- **Sunday** → your Sunday best

bet /bet/

bet the 'farm/'ranch (*AmE*)
risk everything that you have on sth: *It might succeed but don't bet the farm on it.* ◇ *It's a bet-the-farm situation.*

(you can) bet your bottom 'dollar/your 'life (on sth/that…) (*informal*)
(you can) be certain of sth: *You can bet your bottom dollar that he'll forget our anniversary.*

I/I'll 'bet (that…) (*informal*)
1 I am certain (that…): *I bet he'll be late for the meeting — he always is.*
2 used to show that you agree with sb or are not surprised to hear sth: *'I'm furious about what she said to me.' 'I bet (you are)!'*

I wouldn't 'bet on it ◆ **don't 'bet on it** (*spoken*)
used to say that you do not think that sth is very likely: *'She'll soon get used to the idea.' 'I wouldn't bet on it.'*

,you 'bet (*informal*)
certainly: *'Would you like an ice cream?' 'You bet!'* ◇ *'Are you hungry?' 'You bet I am!'*

- **best** → the/your best bet
- **safe** → a safe bet

bête /bet/

your, his, etc. bête 'noire (*from French*)
a person or thing that particularly annoys you and that you do not like: *Edward was furious when he discovered that he would be working with his old bête noire, Richard Watkins.*

> **NOTE**
> The meaning of the French phrase is 'black beast'.

betide /bɪ'taɪd/

- **woe** → woe betide sb

bets /bets/

all bets are 'off
used to say that if a particular event happens then your current prediction, agreement, deal, etc. will no longer apply: *We expect shares to rise unless the economy slows down, in which case all bets are off.*

- **hedge** → hedge your bets

better /'betə(r)/

against your better 'judgement (*especially BrE*) (*AmE* usually **against your better 'judgment**)
although you know that your action, decision, etc. is not sensible: *She was persuaded against her better judgement to lend him the money, and now she's regretting it.*

be better 'off
have more money: *Families will be better off under the new law.* ◇ *Under the new tax regulations I will be a few dollars a month better off.* **OPP** be worse off

be better off (doing sth)
used to say that sb is/would be happier or more satisfied if they were in a particular position or did a particular thing: *She's better off without him.* ◇ *You'd be better off staying at home with that cold.*

,better the ,devil you 'know (than the devil you don't) (*saying*)
it is better to deal with sb/sth bad, difficult, etc. that is familiar than to make a change and perhaps have to deal with sb/sth worse

(all) the better for sth
made better by sth or by doing sth; benefiting from sth: *You'll be all the better for a weekend by the sea.*

,better ,late than 'never (*saying*)
it is better to arrive, do sth, etc. late than not to arrive, do sth, etc. at all: *You were supposed to be here an hour ago, still better late than never, I suppose!*

,better luck 'next time (*spoken*)
used to encourage sb who has not been successful at sth

,better (to be) ,safe than 'sorry (*saying*)
it is better to be too careful than to do sth careless that you may later regret: *We'd better fill the car up with petrol now. It's better to be safe than sorry.*

the ,bigger, ,faster, etc. the 'better
used to say that sth should be as big, fast, etc. as possible: *As far as the hard disk is concerned, the bigger the better.*

do better to do sth
used to say that it would be more sensible to do sth: *You'd do better to buy a good-quality radio, even if it is more expensive.*

for ,better or (for) 'worse
whether the result is good or bad: *I've decided, for better or for worse, to leave my job.*

get the 'better of sb/sth
defeat sb/sth: *She always manages to get the better of me at tennis.* ◇ *Eventually, his curiosity got the better of him and he had to take a look in the box.*

go one 'better (than sb/sth)
do sth better than sb else; improve on sth: *I bought a new tennis racket but my sister had to go one better by buying the most expensive one in the shop.*

had better/best do sth
used to tell sb what you think they should do: *You'd better lock the door before you leave: there are lots of thieves about.* ◇ *Hadn't you better check to see if the baby is all right?* ◇ *'Shall I phone her now?' 'You'd best not. She might be asleep.'*

have seen/known better 'days
be in a worse condition than in the past: *That jacket of yours has seen better days — isn't it time you bought a new one?*

little/no 'better than
almost or just the same as; almost or just as bad as: *The path was no better than a sheep track.*

so much the 'better/'worse (for sb/sth)
it is better/worse for that reason: *'I seem to have made my curry hotter than usual.' 'So much the better. I love hot curries.'*

take a ,turn for the 'better/'worse
become better/worse: *The weather is taking a turn for the worse, I'm afraid.*

that's (much) 'better
1 used to give support to sb who has been upset and is trying to become calmer: *Dry your eyes now. That's better.*
2 used to praise sb who has made an effort to improve: *That's much better — you played the right notes this time.*

you/you'd better be'lieve it! (*spoken*)
used to tell sb that sth is definitely true: *'He's not a bad player, is he?' 'You'd better believe it!'*

- **discretion** → discretion is the better part of valour
- **half** → half a loaf is better than none/no bread
- **half** → your better/other half
- **kiss** → kiss sth better
- **know** → know better (than that/than to do sth)
- **know** → not know any better
- **part** → the better/best part of sth
- **prevention** → an ounce of prevention is better than a pound of cure **SEE** prevention is better than cure
- **said** → the less/least said, the better
- **sooner** → the sooner the better
- **think** → think (the) better of sb
- **think** → think better of it/of doing sth
- **two** → two heads are better than one

betters /'betəz; *AmE* 'betərz/
- **elders** → your elders and betters

betting /'betɪŋ/

what's the 'betting…? ♦ the betting 'is that…
(*informal*)
it seems likely that…: *What's the betting that he arrives late?* ◊ *The betting is that she'll get her own way.*

between /bɪ'twiːn/

between our'selves ♦ between you and 'me
as a secret or private matter that nobody else should know about: *Just between you and me, I've heard that the business made a big loss last year.*

in be'tween
neither one thing nor another, but having some qualities of both; between two states, kinds, sizes, etc: *'Would you call this dress green or blue?' 'I'd say it was in between.'*

betwixt /bɪ'twɪkst/

be,twixt and be'tween (*old-fashioned*)
in a middle position; neither one thing nor the other: *He found himself placed betwixt and between in the debate, agreeing with parts of each side's arguments.*

beyond /bɪ'jɒnd; *AmE* bɪ'jɑːnd/

be be'yond sb (*informal*)
be impossible for sb to imagine, understand or do: *Why she decided to marry such a boring man is beyond me.* ◊ *Some of the questions in that exam were beyond me, I'm afraid.*

bib /bɪb/
- **best** → your best bib and tucker

bide /baɪd/

bide your 'time
wait for a suitable opportunity to do sth: *She's just biding her time until the right job comes along.*

Big /bɪg/

,Big 'Brother (is watching you)
a leader, a person in authority or a government that tries to control every aspect of people's lives: *We live in a society where all kinds of information about the individual may be stored on computer. Big Brother, if not actually watching you, can quickly check on you if he wants to.*

> ❓ **ORIGIN**
> This comes from the novel *Nineteen Eighty-Four* by George Orwell, in which the leader of the government, Big Brother, had total control over people. The slogan 'Big Brother is watch-ing you' reminded people that he knew every-thing they did.

- **Mr** → Mr Big

big /bɪg/

a ,big 'cheese/'wheel (*informal*)
an important person with a lot of influence in an organization, etc: *His father's a big wheel in the tex-tile industry.*

> ❓ **ORIGIN**
> In this sense, 'cheese' comes from the Urdu word *chiz*, meaning 'thing'.

big 'deal (*informal, ironic*)
used for suggesting that sth is not as important or impressive as sb else thinks it is: *'I've got tickets for next Saturday's football match.' 'Big deal! Who's interested in football anyway?'*

the big enchi'lada (*AmE, informal, humorous*)
the most important person or thing: *New Hamp-shire is the big enchilada in American politics.*

> **NOTE**
> An *enchilada* is a Mexican dish with meat and a spicy sauce.

a big 'fish (in a little/small pond)
an important person but only in a small commu-nity, group, etc: *I would rather stay here in the vil-lage and be a big fish in a little pond than go to the city where no one knows me.*

He thought he was important, but Harry was just a big fish in a very small pond.

a ˌbig girl's 'blouse (*informal, humorous*)
used to say that you think the way a boy or a man is behaving is more typical of a woman than a man, especially when they appear weak or not brave: *Don't be a big girl's blouse and start crying!*

a big 'name/'noise ♦ a 'big shot (*informal*)
an important person: *'What does Ian's dad do?' 'Oh, he's a big shot in the City.'* **OPP** small fry

the big 'picture (*informal, especially AmE*)
the situation as a whole: *Right now forget the details and take a look at the big picture.*

'big time (*informal*)
1 (**the big time**) great success in a profession, especially the entertainment business: *a bit-part actor who finally made/hit the big time*
2 on a large scale; to a great extent: *This time they've messed up big time!*

give sb a big 'hand (*informal*)
clap your hands loudly and enthusiastically: *Let's have a big hand, ladies and gentlemen, for our next performer...*

make it 'big
be very successful: *He's hoping to make it big on television.*

me and my big 'mouth (*spoken*)
used when you realize that you have said sth that you should not have said

no big 'deal (*spoken*)
used to say that sth is not important or not a problem: *If I don't win it's no big deal.*

one ˌbig ˌhappy 'family (*informal*)
a group of people who live or work together happily and without disagreements: *We were always together. We were like one big happy family.* ◊ (*ironic*) *'Is your office a happy place to work in?' 'Oh sure, we're just one big happy family. Everybody hates everybody else.'*

too ˌbig for your 'boots (*informal*)
thinking that you are more important than you really are: *His political rivals had decided that he was getting too big for his boots.*

- bite → bite the big one
- dirty → dirty great/big
- hit → hit (it) big

- talk → talk big
- think → think big
- way → do sth in a big/small way

bigger /'bɪɡə(r)/

- eyes → your eyes are bigger than your stomach
- fish → have other/bigger fish to fry

bike /baɪk/

on your bike! (*BrE, informal*)
a rude or humorous way of telling sb to go away: *'Can I borrow some money, Dave?' 'On your bike!'*

Bill /bɪl/

- Old → the Old Bill

bill /bɪl/

head/top the 'bill
be the most important item or performer in a show, play, etc: *Topping the bill tonight will be Robbie Williams.*

- clean → a clean bill of health
- fit → fit the bill
- foot → foot the bill (for sth)

billy-o /'bɪliəʊ; AmE -oʊ/

like 'billy-o (*BrE, informal*)
very much or very enthusiastically: *They worked like billy-o to get it finished on time.*

bind /baɪnd/

in a 'bind (*AmE*)
in a difficult situation that you do not know how to get out of: *I'd be in a bind without a car. I drive everywhere these days.*

- double → in a double bind
- hand → bind/tie sb hand and foot

bird /bɜːd; AmE bɜːrd/

the bird has 'flown
the person who was being chased or looked for has escaped or gone away: *The police raided the house at dawn, but the bird had flown.*

a bird in the ˌhand is worth two in the 'bush (*saying*)
it is better to be satisfied with what you have got than to lose it trying to get sth more or better

a ˌbird of 'passage
a person who does not stay in a place for very long

flip/give/shoot sb the 'bird (*AmE, slang*)
make a rude sign at sb with your middle finger

- dicky → not say/hear a dicky bird
- early → the early bird catches the worm
- eat → eat like a bird
- free → (as) free as (the) air/as a bird
- home → a home bird
- little → a little bird told me (that...)
- rare → a rare bird

birds /bɜːdz; AmE bɜːrdz/

the birds and the 'bees (*old-fashioned* or *humorous*)
the basic facts about sex and reproduction, the 'facts of life', as told to children: *Now that Jamie is eleven, isn't it time you told him about the birds and the bees?*

birds of a 'feather (flock to'gether) (*saying*)
similar people (spend time together): *She spent most of her time abroad with other English speakers, which I suppose is only natural. Birds of a feather flock together, after all.*

(strictly) for the 'birds (*informal*)
not important or interesting: *Fishing? That's strictly for the birds, if you ask me.*

● **kill** → kill two birds with one stone

bird's-eye /'bɜːdz aɪ; AmE 'bɜːrdz/

a ˌbird's-eye 'view (of sth)
a good view of sth from high above: *From the church tower you get a bird's-eye view of the town.*

birth /bɜːθ; AmE bɜːrθ/

give 'birth (to sb/sth)
produce a baby or young animal: *She died shortly after giving birth.* ◇ *Mary gave birth to a healthy baby girl.* ◇ (*figurative*) *It was the study of history that gave birth to the social sciences.*

birthday /'bɜːθdeɪ; AmE 'bɜːrθ-/

in/wearing your 'birthday suit (*informal, humorous*)
wearing no clothes; naked: *The towel fell off, and there he was in his birthday suit!*

biscuit /'bɪskɪt/

take the 'biscuit (*BrE*) (also **take the 'cake** *AmE, BrE*) (*informal*)
be especially surprising, annoying, etc: *Well, that really takes the biscuit! She asks if she can borrow the car, then keeps it for a month!*

bit /bɪt/

be ˌchamping/ˌchomping at the 'bit (also **be ˌchafing at the bit** *more formal*)
be impatient to do or to start doing sth: *The players were champing at the bit as the start of the match was delayed.* ◇ *I know you're chafing at the bit, so we'll start as soon as we can.*

> **NOTE**
> *Champ* and *chomp* mean to bite or eat something noisily. The *bit* is the piece of metal which goes in a horse's mouth and is used to control the horse.

the (whole)... bit (*informal, disapproving*)
behaviour or ideas that are typical of a particular group, type of person or activity: *She couldn't accept the whole drug-culture bit.*

bit by 'bit (also **little by 'little**)
a small amount at a time; gradually: *We managed to save the money bit by bit over a period of ten years.* ◇ *Little by little, she began to feel better after her illness.*

a bit 'much (*informal*)
too much to be acceptable; unreasonable: *Claiming £50 a day for expenses is a bit much, I think.* ◇ *Don't you think it's a bit much of him to give me most of the work and then take the afternoon off?*

a bit of a... (*informal, especially BrE*)
used when talking about unpleasant or negative things or ideas, to mean 'rather a...': *We may have a bit of a problem on our hands.* ◇ *The rail strike is a bit of a pain.*

a bit of all 'right (*BrE, slang*)
a very attractive person: *He's a bit of all right, don't you think, Madge?*

a bit of 'rough (*BrE, slang*)
a person of a low social class who has a sexual relationship with sb of a higher class

a ˌbit on the 'side (*slang*)
a sexual relationship with sb who is not your regular partner: *He's always looking for a bit on the side.*

a bit 'thick/'strong (*old-fashioned, BrE, informal*)
not fair or acceptable: *It's a bit thick of him to expect me to pay every time we go out together.* ◇ *She said it was the worst book she'd ever read, which I think was a bit strong.*

do your 'bit (*informal*)
do your share of a task, help a cause, etc: *Everyone is expected to do their bit to make the business successful.* ◇ *In reusing this old paper I'm doing my bit for conservation of the rainforests.*

every bit as good, bad, etc. (as sb/sth)
just as good, bad, etc.; equally good, bad, etc: *Rome is every bit as beautiful as Paris.*

get/take the bit between your 'teeth (*informal*)
start doing sth in a determined and enthusiastic way: *Once he gets the bit between his teeth in an argument, no one can stop him.*

> **NOTE**
> If the horse learns to hold the *bit* (see previous note) between its teeth, it can no longer be controlled by the rider.

not a 'bit ● not one (little) 'bit
not at all: *'Are you cold?' 'Not a bit.'* ◇ *I don't like that idea one bit.*

not a 'bit of it! (*BrE, informal*)
used for saying that sth that you had expected to happen did not happen: *You'd think he'd be tired after the journey but not a bit of it!* ◇ *I thought she would be glad to see him but not a bit of it — she made some excuse and left as soon as he got here.*

● **biter** → the biter bit
● **blind** → not a blind bit of notice, difference, etc.
● **far** → go a bit far **SEE** go too far
● **steep** → be a bit/rather steep

bitch /bɪtʃ/

● **son** → a/the son of a bitch

bite /baɪt/

a bite at/of the 'cherry (also **a second/another bite at/of the 'cherry**) (*BrE*)
an opportunity to do sth, or a second attempt at doing sth, especially sth you have failed to do earlier: *They all wanted a bite of the cherry.* ◇ *We've lost that contract with the German firm and we probably won't get another bite at the cherry.*

bite the 'big one (*AmE, slang*)
1 be very bad or fail: *This place really bites the big one!*
2 die: *It's a surprise to see him bite the big one at the end of the movie.*

bite the 'bullet (*informal*)
realize that you cannot avoid sth unpleasant, and so accept it: *Getting your car repaired is often an expensive business, but all you can do is bite the bullet and pay up.*

> ❷ ORIGIN
> This expression comes from the old custom of giving soldiers a bullet to bite on during medical operations, which had to be done without any drugs to stop the pain.

bite the 'dust (*informal*)
1 fail, or be defeated or destroyed: *Thousands of small businesses bite the dust every year.*
2 (*humorous*) die

bite the hand that 'feeds you
be unkind or disloyal to sb who has been kind or helpful to you, or who pays your wages: *When you say such nasty things about the organization, you're biting the hand that feeds you.*

bite your 'lip
force yourself not to express the negative emotions that you are feeling: *You could tell she thought the criticism was unfair but she bit her lip and said nothing.* **OPP** let rip (at sb) (with sth)

bite your 'nails/'fingernails
feel very excited, nervous, or afraid ▸ **'nail-biting** *adj.* very exciting or tense: *What an exciting movie that was — real nail-biting stuff!*

bite off ˌmore than you can 'chew (*informal*)
attempt to do sth that is too difficult for you or that you do not have enough time to do: *He's promised to get all this work finished by the weekend but I've got a feeling he's bitten off more than he can chew.*

bite your 'tongue
stop yourself from saying sth that might upset sb or cause an argument, although you want to speak: *I didn't believe her explanation but I bit my tongue.* **OPP** give sb a piece of your mind

I, etc. won't 'bite (you) (*humorous*)
used to tell sb that they do not need to be afraid of sb: *You should tell your teacher that you don't understand — she won't bite you!*

• arm → put the arm/bite on sb
• bark → his, her, etc. bark is worse than his, her, etc. bite
• head → bite/snap sb's head off

biter /'baɪtə(r)/

the biter 'bit
the person who wanted to do harm, cheat sb, etc., has harm done to them, is cheated, etc: *It was a case of the biter bit — she'd tried to make him look foolish and ended up being ridiculed herself.*

bits /bɪts/

ˌbits and 'pieces (also **ˌbits and 'bobs** *BrE*) (*informal*)
small things of various kinds; belongings: *She let me store a few bits and pieces in her apartment while I was abroad.* ◇ *The box contained needles and thread and various bits and bobs for sewing.*

pick, pull, etc. sb/sth to 'bits/'pieces
criticize sb/sth severely and find as many faults with them/it as you can: *The committee pulled his proposal to bits. They didn't have anything positive at all to say about it.* ◇ *As soon as she left the room, everyone started pulling her to pieces.*

to bits
1 into small pieces: *The book fell to bits in my hands.* ◇ *She took the engine to bits, then carefully put it together again.*
2 (*spoken, informal*) very much: *I love my kids to bits.* ◇ *She was thrilled to bits when I said I'd come.*

bitten /'bɪtn/

• bug → be bitten by/have the bug
• once → once bitten, twice shy

bitter /'bɪtə(r)/

a bitter 'pill (for sb) (to swallow)
a thing that is very difficult or unpleasant to accept: *He was a proud man, so having to ask for money must have been a bitter pill to swallow.*

to the bitter 'end
right to the end, no matter how long it takes; until everything possible has been done: *Now that we have begun this project, we must see it through to the bitter end.* ◇ *We are determined to fight to the bitter end.*

black /blæk/

black and 'blue
covered with bruises (= blue, brown or purple marks on the body): *She was black and blue all over after falling down stairs.*

(in) black and 'white
(as) absolutely right or wrong, good or bad, with no grades between them: *My grandmother has very rigid ideas of character and behaviour; she sees everything in black and white.* ◇ *It's not a black-and-white issue.*

a black 'day (for sb)
a day when sth sad, unpleasant or disastrous happens (to sb): *It was a black day for this area when the local steel factory closed down.*

a black 'eye
an area of dark skin (= a bruise) around the eye caused by an accident, sb hitting you, etc: *How did you get that black eye?*

a black 'look
an angry or a disapproving expression on sb's face: *She gave me a black look when I suggested she should clean her room.*

a black 'mark (against sb) (*BrE*)
sth that sb has done which makes other people dislike or disapprove of them: *It was another black mark against her that she had not gone to the last meeting.* **OPP** brownie points

the black 'market
an illegal form of trade in which foreign money, or goods that are difficult to obtain, are bought and sold: *Tickets for the game are being sold on the black market for $200 each.* **OPP** the open market

a/the black 'sheep (of the family)
a person who is different from the rest of their family or another group, and who is considered bad or embarrassing: *Debbie is the black sheep of the family, having left home at seventeen to live with her boyfriend.*

❷ ORIGIN
Shepherds used to dislike black sheep because their wool was not as valuable as white wool.

a 'black spot
a place where accidents often happen, especially on a road: *This junction is a well-known accident black spot.*

in the 'black (*business*)
have money, for example in your bank account; make a profit: *The company is back in the black after a year of heavy losses.* **OPP** in the red

in black and 'white
in print or writing: *I want to see his statement down in black and white.*

he, it, etc. is not as black as he, it, etc. is 'painted
he, it, etc. is not as bad as people say: *The boss is not as black as she's painted; in fact, I find her quite helpful and friendly.*

look 'black
show no signs of hope or improvement: *I know things look black at the moment but I'm sure you'll get a job soon.*

● pot → the pot calling the kettle black

blame /bleɪm/

be to 'blame (for sth)
be responsible for sth bad: *If anyone's to blame, it's me.* ◇ *Which driver was to blame for the accident?*

don't blame 'me (*spoken*)
used to advise sb not to do sth, when you think they will do it despite your advice: *Call her if you like, but don't blame me if she's angry.*

I don't 'blame you/her, etc. (for doing sth) (*spoken*)
used to say that you think what sb did was reasonable and the right thing to do: *'I just put the phone down when he said that.' 'I don't blame you!'*

blanche /blɑːnʃ/

● carte → carte blanche (to do sth)

blank /blæŋk/

a blank 'cheque (*BrE*) (*AmE* **a blank 'check**)
permission to act as you like (especially to spend money) in a particular task or situation: *Just because I asked you to speak on my behalf, that didn't mean you had a blank cheque to promise anything you liked.* ◇ *She was given a blank cheque and told to hire the best singers she could.*

● draw → draw a blank
● point → ask, tell, etc. sb point blank

blanket /ˈblæŋkɪt/

● wet → a wet blanket

blast /blɑːst; AmE blæst/

a ˌblast from the 'past (*informal*)
a person or thing from your past that you see, hear, meet, etc. again in the present: *This song is real blast from the past.*

● full → (at) full blast

blaze /bleɪz/

blaze a/the 'trail
be the first to do sth important or interesting: *As the first female Member of Parliament, she blazed a trail for others to follow.* ▶ **'trailblazer** *noun* a person who is the first to do or discover sth and so makes it possible for others to follow: *a trailblazer in the field of genetic engineering* **'trailblazing** *adj.*: *trailblazing scientific research*

❷ ORIGIN
The original meaning of this expression was to cut marks (=*blazes*) into trees so that others could follow the path you had taken through a forest, etc.

blazes /ˈbleɪzɪz/

like 'blazes (*old-fashioned, spoken*)
very hard; very fast: *By the time they reached the hotel it was raining like blazes.*

what/where/who the 'blazes...?
(*old-fashioned, spoken*)
used to emphasize that you are annoyed and surprised, to avoid using the word 'hell': *What the blazes have you done?*

❷ ORIGIN
This expression refers to the flames associated with hell.

bleed /bliːd/

bleed sb 'dry/'white (*disapproving*)
take away all sb's money: *He used to be quite wealthy, but his children have bled him dry.*

bleeds /bliːdz/

● heart → your heart bleeds for sb

blend

blend /blend/

• woodwork → blend/fade into the woodwork

bless /bles/

bless (*BrE, spoken, approving*)
used to express affection for sb when you hear about sth they have said or done: *'And then he offered to cook supper for us.' 'Oh, bless!'*

,bless his, her, etc. (little) cotton 'socks (*BrE, humorous*)
used to express your affection for sb because of sth they have said or done: *And the kids brought me breakfast in bed — bless their little cotton socks!*

'bless you
1 (*spoken*) said to sb after they have sneezed (= made a loud noise through the nose)
2 (*old-fashioned*) used for expressing thanks or affection: *Bless you, my dear. It's most kind of you to help.*

'bless you, him, etc. (also **,bless your, his, etc. 'heart** *less frequent*) (*spoken*)
used to express affection for sb who has just been mentioned: *Sarah, bless her, had made a cup of tea.* ◇ *Your mother, bless her heart, is the only friend I have.*

• God → God bless

blessing /'blesɪŋ/

a blessing in dis'guise
a thing that seems bad, unpleasant, etc. at first but that has advantages in the end: *Not getting that job was a blessing in disguise, as the firm went out of business only a few months later.*

• mixed → a mixed blessing

blessings /'blesɪŋz/

• count → count your blessings

blind /blaɪnd/

a ,blind 'alley
a course of action which has no useful result in the end: *Our first experiment was a blind alley, but the second one gave us very promising results.*

> **NOTE**
> A *blind alley* is a narrow passage that is closed at one end.

(as) blind as a 'bat (*humorous*)
not able to see well: *I'm as blind as a bat without my glasses.*

a ,blind 'date
a social meeting between two people who have never met before, often arranged by friends, in the hope that it may lead to a love affair: *A friend of mine set up a blind date for me with his girlfriend's sister.*

blind 'drunk (*informal*)
extremely drunk: *I'm not surprised he can't remember what happened — he was blind drunk!*
OPP stone-cold sober

the ,blind leading the 'blind (*saying*)
a situation in which people with almost no experience or knowledge give advice or help to others who also have no experience or knowledge: *I don't know why she asked me to show her how the computer works when I've hardly used it myself. It would be a case of the blind leading the blind!*

a/sb's 'blind spot
a small part of a subject that sb does not understand or know anything about: *I'm a real music lover but I have to say that modern jazz is a bit of a blind spot with me.*

,blind sb with 'science
deliberately confuse sb with your special knowledge, especially by using difficult or technical words which they do not understand: *Every time I ask her a simple question, she tries to blind me with science.*

not a ,blind bit of 'notice, 'difference, etc.
✦ not the ,blindest bit of 'notice, 'difference, etc. (*BrE, spoken*)
no notice, difference, etc. at all: *She didn't take a blind bit of notice when I asked her to stop. She walked straight past me.*

turn a blind 'eye (to sth)
pretend not to see sth or know about sth: *There's so much suffering in the world, you can't just turn a blind eye to it.* ◇ *The police here seem to turn a blind eye to petty crime.* **OPP** watch sb/sth like a hawk

• love → love is blind
• rob → rob sb blind
• swear → swear blind (that)...

blindest /'blaɪndəst/

• blind → not the blindest bit of notice, difference, etc.

blinding /'blaɪndɪŋ/

• effing → effing and blinding

blink /blɪŋk/

in the blink of an 'eye
very quickly; in a short time: *He was gone in the blink of an eye.*

on the 'blink (*informal*)
(of a machine) not working properly: *Can I watch the film at your house? Our TV's on the blink again.*

bliss /blɪs/

• ignorance → ignorance is bliss

block /blɒk; AmE blɑːk/

have been around the 'block (a few times) (*informal*)
have a lot of experience: *She's been around the block a few times and can't be fooled that easily.*

put/lay your head/neck on the block
risk defeat, failure, etc.; put yourself in a situation where you might be blamed, criticized, etc: *The government laid its head on the block and said that if it loses this vote in Parliament tonight it will call an election.* ◇ *I'm prepared to put my neck on the*

block and promise that the new building will be ready by the end of the year.

❷ ORIGIN
In the past when people were *executed* (= killed as a punishment), they had to lay their head on a block so that it could be chopped off.

- chip → a chip off the old block
- knock → I'll knock your block/head off!
- new → a/the new kid on the block

Bloggs /blɒgz; *AmE* blɔːgz; blɑːgz/

- Joe → Joe Bloggs

blood /blʌd/

bad 'blood (between A and B) (*old-fashioned*)
feelings of hatred or strong dislike between two or more people or groups: *There has always been bad blood between the two families.*

be after/out for sb's 'blood (*informal, often humorous*)
want to hurt or harm sb, especially as revenge: *They have been after my blood ever since I accidentally damaged their car.*

blood and 'guts (*informal*)
used to refer to extreme violence when it is shown in films/movies or on television: *Audiences seem to prefer movies with romance and humour rather than the blood and guts stuff.*

blood and 'thunder (*informal*)
sensational and very dramatic incidents in plays, films/movies, stories, contests, etc: *I don't like blood-and-thunder novels.*

blood is thicker than 'water (*saying*)
your family is more important than other people: *Tony was angry with his brother for a while, but blood is thicker than water, and in the end he forgave him.*

your/sb's ˌblood is 'up (*BrE*)
sb feels angry and aggressive: *Normally, he's a quiet man, but when his blood is up he can be very violent.*

ˌblood, sweat and 'tears
very hard work; a lot of effort: *The only way to succeed is through old-fashioned blood, sweat and tears.*

fresh/new/young 'blood
new members of a group or organization who have fresh ideas, skills, etc. and so make the group more efficient: *What this committee really needs is some new blood.*

have (sb's) 'blood on your hands
be responsible for sb's death: *He's a tyrant with the blood of millions of innocent people on his hands.*

in the/sb's 'blood/'genes
part of sb's nature and shared by other members of their family: *Both his father and his mother were writers, so literature runs in his blood.*

like getting ˌblood out of/from a 'stone
extremely difficult to obtain: *Getting an apology from him was like getting blood out of a stone.*

make sb's 'blood boil
make sb very angry: *Seeing him beating that little dog made my blood boil.*

make sb's 'blood run cold ◆ make sb's 'blood freeze
make sb feel horror or extreme fear: *A terrifying scream in the blackness of the night made my blood run cold.*

- burst → burst a blood vessel
- cold → in cold blood
- flesh → flesh and blood
- flesh → more than flesh and blood can stand, endure, etc.
- flesh → your (own) flesh and blood
- rush → have a rush of blood to the head
- spill → spill (sb's) blood
- spit → spit blood/venom/feathers
- stir → stir sb's/the blood
- sweat → sweat blood

bloody /'blʌdi/

- scream → scream bloody murder **SEE** scream blue murder

bloom /bluːm/

in (full) bloom
(of trees, plants, gardens, etc.) with the flowers fully open: *Their garden was in full bloom.*

blot /blɒt; *AmE* blɑːt/

blot your 'copybook (*old-fashioned, informal*)
spoil a previously good record: *He paid back the money he had stolen, but he had blotted his copybook and couldn't hope for promotion.*

❷ ORIGIN
A *copybook* was an exercise book with printed examples of good writing for children to copy. If you *blotted* it, you accidentally spoiled it by making a mark with ink on it.

a blot on the 'landscape
a thing, especially an ugly building, that spoils the appearance of a place: *That power station is rather a blot on the landscape.*

blouse /blaʊz; *AmE* blaʊs/

- big → a big girl's blouse

Blow /bləʊ; *AmE* bloʊ/

- Joe → Joe Blow **SEE** Joe Bloggs

blow /bləʊ; *AmE* bloʊ/

at a (single) 'blow ◆ at one 'blow
with a single action or effort; all at once: *By stopping all payments to her sons, she made all three of them poor at one blow.*

blow away the 'cobwebs (*informal*)
make you feel lively and refreshed, especially after you have been indoors for too long: *After sitting around for hours, we went out and had a long walk along the beach to blow the cobwebs away.*

> NOTE
> A *cobweb* is a fine net of threads made by a spider, often found in rooms or buildings that have not been used for a long time.

blow your/sb's 'brains out (*informal*)
kill yourself/sb by shooting in the head: *He was so depressed about his debts that he wanted to blow his brains out.*

blow 'chunks (*AmE, slang*)
vomit (= bring food from the stomach back out through the mouth): *Harry is green — looks like he's going to blow chunks.*

blow sb's 'cover (*informal*)
discover or reveal the real identity of sb, especially of a spy, etc: *She had been posing as a diplomat, but her cover was blown when she was found sending coded messages to agents.*

blow a 'fuse (*informal*)
get very angry: *It was only a suggestion, Rob. There's no need to blow a fuse.*

> NOTE
> This refers to the fact that if the flow of electricity in a piece of electrical equipment is too strong, the fuse (= a small wire or device inside it) will break (*blow*), often with a loud noise, and stop the current.

blow the 'gaff (on sb/sth) (*BrE, informal*)
reveal a secret: *She didn't want anyone to know where she had been, but her husband blew the gaff.*
OPP keep mum

blow hot and 'cold (*informal*)
keep changing your opinions about sb/sth: *She keeps blowing hot and cold about the job: one day she says it's marvellous, the next she hates it.*

'blow it ♦ blow your 'chances
waste an opportunity: *You had your chance and you blew it.* ◊ *She blew her chances by arriving late for the interview.*

blow 'me! (*old-fashioned, BrE, informal*)
used for expressing great surprise: *'Isn't that Alice over there?' 'Well, blow me! I thought she was in Japan!'*

blow your/sb's 'mind (*informal*)
make you/sb feel extreme pleasure, excitement, etc: *This new game will blow your mind!* ► **'mind-blowing** *adj.*: *We were stunned by the mind-blowing beauty of the landscape.*

blow sb/sth out of the 'water (*informal*)
1 destroy sb/sth completely
2 show that sb/sth is not good at all: *A DVD music system plays discs that look like CDs, but blows them out of the water.*

blow your own 'trumpet (*especially BrE*) (*AmE* usually **blow/toot your own 'horn**) (*informal*)
talk proudly about your own achievements, abilities, etc.; praise yourself: *I don't like to blow my own trumpet, but the office was much better run when I was in charge.*

> ❷ ORIGIN
> This phrase refers to the custom of announcing important guests by blowing a loud musical instrument.

blow sb/sth ,sky-'high (*informal*)
destroy sb/sth completely in an explosion: *The explosives factory was blown sky-high when one of the workers lit a match.*

blow 'smoke (up sb's ass △) (*AmE, slang*)
try to trick sb or lie to sb, particularly by saying that sth is better than it really is: *I won't blow smoke up your ass. Your product is OK but I've seen better.*

blow your 'top (*BrE*) (*AmE* **blow your 'stack**) (*informal*)
suddenly become very angry: *My mum blew her top when she found out that I'd damaged her car.*

blow up in sb's 'face
(of a situation, plan, project, etc.) end or fail suddenly, with bad results: *Starting up the business was difficult, and it all nearly blew up in his face when his partner fell sick at the last minute.*

blow the 'whistle (on sb/sth) (*informal*)
stop sb doing sth illegal or wrong by telling a person in authority about it: *One of the police officers blew the whistle on his colleagues when he found out they were taking bribes.* ► **'whistle-blower** *noun* a person who informs people in authority or the public that the company they work for is doing sth wrong or illegal: *The company has denied a whistle-blower's allegations of poor security.*

> NOTE
> This idiom probably comes from football, where a referee blows a whistle to stop the game when a player breaks the rules.

cushion/soften the 'blow
make sth unpleasant seem less unpleasant and easier to accept: *When he lost his job he was offered a cash payment to soften the blow.*

- **deal** → deal a blow to sb/sth SEE deal sb/sth a blow
- **deal** → deal sb/sth a blow
- **game** → blow/sod this/that for a game of soldiers
- **lark** → blow/sod that for a lark
- **puff** → puff and pant/blow
- **socks** → blow/knock sb's socks off
- **strike** → strike a blow for/against/at sth

blow-by-blow /ˌbləʊ baɪ 'bləʊ; *AmE* ˌbloʊ baɪ 'bloʊ/

a ,blow-by-,blow ac'count, de'scription, etc.
an account, a description, etc. in which all the details of an event are told in the order in which they happened: *He gave us a blow-by-blow account of everything he had done that day.*

blowed /bləʊd; *AmE* bloʊd/

- **damned** → I'm/I'll be blowed if ... SEE I'm/I'll be damned if...

blows /bləʊz; AmE bloʊz/

come to 'blows (over sth)
begin to hit each other: *They were shouting at each other so much that I thought they would come to blows.*

● way → see which way the wind blows

blue /bluː/

out of the 'blue
suddenly and unexpectedly: *She had no idea that anything was wrong until he announced out of the blue that he wanted a divorce.*

(do sth) till you're ,blue in the 'face (*informal*)
(do sth) with a lot of effort and for a very long time without success: *You can argue with John till you're blue in the face, he'll never agree with you.*

● black → black and blue
● bolt → a bolt from the blue
● boys → the boys in blue
● devil → between the devil and the deep blue sea
● fit → have a pink/blue fit
● once → once in a blue moon
● scream → scream blue murder

blue-eyed /,bluː 'aɪd/

your, sb's, etc. ,blue-eyed 'boy (*informal, usually disapproving*)
the favourite, especially of a person in authority; a person that sb thinks is perfect: *Bob is certain to be promoted: he's the manager's blue-eyed boy.*

bluff /blʌf/

● call → call sb's bluff

blushes /'blʌʃɪz/

save/spare sb's 'blushes (*informal*)
not do sth which will make sb feel embarrassed: *Don't tell everybody about his excellent exam results. Spare his blushes.*

> **NOTE**
> A *blush* is the red colour that spreads over your face when you are embarrassed or ashamed.

board /bɔːd; AmE bɔːrd/

above 'board
honest and open; not secret: *All my dealings with the company have been completely above board.*

> **NOTE**
> If card players keep their hands above the table (the *board*), other players can see what they are doing.

a,cross the 'board
affecting everything or everyone in a society, an organization, etc., equally: *The government claims that standards in education have fallen right across the board.* ◇ *The union demanded an across-the-board salary increase.*

,board and 'lodging
accommodation and food: *I pay £70 a week for board and lodging.*

,go by the 'board
(of a plan, an idea, etc.) be abandoned or rejected: *Our research will certainly go by the board if the government doesn't agree to continue financing it.*

on 'board
on or in a ship, an aircraft or a train: *Have the passengers gone on board yet?* ◇ (*figurative*) *It's good to have you on board* (= working with us) *for this project.*

take sth on 'board (*informal*)
accept (an idea, a suggestion, etc.); recognize (a problem, etc.): *I hope the committee takes our comments on board when making a decision.*

● drawing → (it's) back to the drawing board
● drawing → on the drawing board
● stiff → (as) stiff as a board
● sweep → sweep the board

boards /bɔːdz; AmE bɔːrdz/

● tread → tread the boards

boat /bəʊt; AmE boʊt/

be in the ,same 'boat
be in the same difficult position or situation as sb else: *None of us could do the maths exam, so we're all in the same boat.*

● float → float sb's boat
● miss → miss the boat
● push → push the boat out
● rock → rock the boat
● ship → when your ship/boat comes in

boats /bəʊts; AmE boʊts/

● burn → burn your boats SEE burn your bridges
● rising → a rising tide lifts all boats

Bob /bɒb; AmE bɑːb/

(and) Bob's your 'uncle (*BrE, informal*)
often used after explaining how to do sth, solve a problem, etc. to emphasize how easy it is: *To make the alarm go off at the right time, you just press this button, set the clock, and Bob's your uncle!*

> **❷ ORIGIN**
> *Bob* is a short form of the name 'Robert'. This phrase might refer to the prime minister Robert Cecil. In 1887 he unexpectedly decided to give an important government position to his nephew, who was not considered a very important politician.

bobs /bɒbz; AmE bɑːbz/

● bits → bits and bobs SEE bits and pieces

bode /bəʊd; AmE boʊd/

bode 'well/'ill (for sb/sth) (*formal*)
be a good/bad sign for sb/sth: *These figures do not bode well for the company's future.*

body /ˈbɒdi; AmE ˈbɑːdi/

body and ˈsoul
physically and mentally; completely: *She devoted herself body and soul to this political cause.* ◇ *The company doesn't own me body and soul just because it pays my salary.*

keep body and ˈsoul together (*often humorous*)
manage to stay alive: *I hardly earn enough to keep body and soul together.*

● **bone** → not have a...bone in your body
● **dead** → over my dead body

bog /bɒg; AmE bɔːg/

bog ˈstandard (*BrE, informal*)
ordinary; with no special features: *All you need is a bog standard machine — nothing fancy.*

boggles /ˈbɒglz; AmE ˈbɔːglz/

● **mind** → it boggles the mind **SEE** the mind boggles (at sth)

boil /bɔɪl/

off the ˈboil (*BrE*)
past the time of greatest activity, excitement, etc: *The team were playing brilliantly at the start of the season but seem to have gone off the boil now.*

on the ˈboil
in a lively or an active condition: *Fresh discoveries kept their enthusiasm on the boil.*

● **blood** → make sb's blood boil

boils /bɔɪlz/

● **watched** → a watched pot never boils

bold /bəʊld; AmE boʊld/

be/make so ˈbold (as to do sth) (*formal*)
used especially when politely asking a question or making a suggestion which you hope will not offend anyone: *May I make so bold, sir, as to suggest that you try the grilled fish?*

(as) bold as ˈbrass (*BrE, informal*)
without seeming ashamed or embarrassed; very cheeky: *He came up to me, bold as brass, and asked me for five pounds.*

bollocks /ˈbɒləks; AmE ˈbɑːl-/

● **dog** → the dog's bollocks

bolt /bəʊlt; AmE boʊlt/

a ˌbolt from the ˈblue
an event or a piece of news which is sudden and unexpected; a complete surprise: *She had given us no warning she was going to leave; it came as a complete bolt from the blue.*

> **NOTE**
> This refers to a flash of lightning (= a *bolt*) coming from a clear blue sky.

bolt ˈupright
with your back very straight in an upright position: *The noise woke her suddenly and she sat bolt upright in bed.*

make a ˈbolt/ˈdash for it/sth (*informal*)
try to escape or get somewhere quickly: *The prisoners made a bolt for it through an open window.* ◇ *We smelt smoke and made a dash for the door.*

● **shoot** → shoot your bolt

bolted /ˈbəʊltɪd; AmE ˈboʊltɪd/

● **stable** → shut/lock/close the stable door after the horse has bolted

bolts /bəʊlts; AmE boʊlts/

● **nuts** → the nuts and bolts (of sth)

bomb /bɒm; AmE bɑːm/

be the ˈbomb (*AmE*)
be very good; be the best: *Check out the new website. It's the bomb!* **OPP** be the pits

go down a ˈbomb ◆ go (like) a ˈbomb (*BrE*)
be very successful: *Our performance went down a bomb.* ◇ *The party was really going (like) a bomb.* **OPP** go down like a lead balloon

go like a ˈbomb (*BrE*)
(of a vehicle) go very fast: *Her new car goes like a bomb!*

bombshell /ˈbɒmʃel; AmE ˈbɑːm-/

● **drop** → drop a bombshell

bond /bɒnd; AmE bɑːnd/

● **word** → your, his, etc. word is (as good as) your, his, etc. bond

bone /bəʊn; AmE boʊn/

ˌbone ˈidle (*BrE, informal*)
(of a person) very lazy: *The family consists of Vera, her intensely irritating husband and her two bone idle sons.*

a bone of conˈtention
a matter about which there is a lot of disagreement: *The interpretation of this painting has long been a bone of contention among art historians.*

close to/near the ˈbone (*informal*)
likely to offend or upset sb because, for example, a remark contains elements of truth: *Some of the things she said to him about his failure to find work were a bit close to the bone.*

cut, pare, cut etc. sth to the ˈbone
reduce sth to the point where no further reduction is possible: *We have cut the costs of the business to the bone, but they are still too high for us to make any profit.*

have a ˈbone to pick with sb (*informal*)
have sth that you want to complain to sb about: *Here, I've got a bone to pick with you: why did you tell David I wasn't at home when he phoned?*

not have a...bone in your body
have none of the quality mentioned: *She was honest and hard-working, and didn't have an unkind bone in her body.*

throw sb a 'bone
give sb a small part of what they want as a way of showing that you want to help or because you feel sympathy for them: *The government threw a bone to environmentalists by acknowledging the need for cleaner energy.* ◇ (*AmE, informal*) *Throw me a bone here!* (= give me a little help)

- chill → chill sb to the bone/marrow
- dry → (as) dry as a bone
- fingers → work your fingers to the bone
- skin → be (all/just/nothing but) skin and bone(s)

bones /bəʊnz; *AmE* boʊnz/

make no 'bones about sth/about doing sth
not hesitate to do sth; be honest and open about sth: *She made no bones about telling him she wanted a pay rise.* ◇ *He makes no bones about the fact that he's been in prison.*

- bag → a bag of bones
- bare → the bare bones (of sth)
- feel → feel (it) in your bones

bonkers /ˈbɒŋkəz; *AmE* ˈbɑːŋkərz/

- raving → (stark) raving mad/bonkers

bonnet /ˈbɒnɪt; *AmE* ˈbɑːnət/

- bee → have a bee in your bonnet

boo /buː/

- say → he, she, etc. wouldn't say boo to a goose

book /bʊk/

bring sb to 'book (for sth) (*formal, especially BrE*)
make sb explain their actions, or punish them: *This is just another of the many crimes for which nobody was ever brought to book.*

by the 'book
strictly following the rules or the official way of doing sth: *He insists on doing everything by the book.*

in sb's book (*spoken*)
in sb's opinion; according to sb's judgement: *They took the car away without asking me, and in my book that's theft.*

throw the 'book at sb (*informal*)
punish or criticize sb for as many things as possible: *The police stopped me for speeding and threw the book at me for everything — faulty lights, dangerous tyres, no insurance...*

- close[1] → close the book on sth
- closed → a closed book (to sb)
- judge → don't judge a book by its cover
- leaf → take a leaf out of sb's book
- open → an open book
- read[1] → read sb like a book
- suit → suit your/sb's book
- trick → try, use, etc. every trick in the book
- turn-up → a turn-up for the book(s)

books /bʊks/

be in/get into sb's 'good/'bad books (*informal*)
have/not have sb's favour or approval: *I'm in his bad books at the moment because I accidentally broke the window.* ◇ *'Why are you cleaning her shoes?' 'I'm trying to get into her good books!'*

on/off the/sb's 'books (*business*)
included/not included in the official financial records of a company: *The company falsified its accounts and kept billions of dollars in debt off the books.*

one for the 'books (*especially AmE*)
used to say that sth is unusual or unexpected: *Well here's one for the books — a microwave that plays music.*

- cook → cook the books
- history → the history books
- hit → hit the books

boomer /ˈbuːmə(r)/

- baby → a boomer **SEE** a baby boomer

boot /buːt/

the boot is on the other 'foot (*BrE*) (*AmE* **the shoe is on the other 'foot**) (*informal*)
a situation is now the opposite of what it was: *She used to be the one who had to obey orders, but the boot is on the other foot now she's been promoted.*

give sb/get the 'boot (*informal*)
dismiss sb/be dismissed from a job: *He got the boot for stealing money from the firm.*

put/stick the 'boot in (*BrE, informal*)
1 kick sb very hard, especially when they are on the ground.
2 say or do sth cruel or unfair to sb, especially when they have already been harmed in some other way: *She was upset about losing her job and then her sister started putting the boot in, telling her she was lazy.*

to 'boot (*old-fashioned* or *humorous*)
in addition; as well: *She has a big house, an expensive car, and a holiday villa in Italy to boot.*

boots /buːts/

- big → too big for your boots
- fill → fill sb's boots/shoes
- hang → hang up your boots
- lick → lick sb's boots
- quaking → (be) quaking/shaking in your boots/shoes
- tough → (as) tough as old boots

bootstraps /ˈbuːtstræps/

drag/pull yourself up by your (own) 'bootstraps (*informal*)
improve your situation yourself, without help from other people: *Nobody helped her get where she is today — she pulled herself up by her own bootstraps.*

bore /bɔː(r)/

bore sb to 'tears ◆ bore sb 'stiff ◆ bore sb out of their 'mind (*informal*)
(often used in the passive) bore sb very much: *He bored me to tears with stories about his childhood.* ◇ *After listening to the speech for three hours I was bored stiff.*

bored /bɔːd; AmE bɔːrd/

● witless → be scared/bored witless

born /bɔːn; AmE bɔːrn/

be born with a silver 'spoon in your mouth (*saying*)
be born into a very rich family: *They had both been born with silver spoons in their mouths, and never had to worry about money.*

‚born and 'bred
born and brought up (in a place): *He's Liverpool born and bred.* ◇ *Both my parents were born and bred in London.*

I wasn't born 'yesterday (*spoken*)
used to say that you are not stupid enough to believe what sb is telling you: *You don't expect me to believe that, do you? I wasn't born yesterday, you know.*

in all my born 'days (*old-fashioned, informal*)
never in my life (especially used when referring to sth unpleasant): *How dare you say that! I've never been spoken to like that in all my born days!*

there's one born every 'minute (*saying*)
used to say that sb is very stupid: *You really believed he would pay you that money back? There's one born every minute!*

● know → not know you're born
● manner → (as if) to the manner born
● way → be/be born/be made that way

borrow /'bɒrəʊ; AmE 'bɑːroʊ; 'bɔːr-/

● beg → beg, borrow or steal
● beg → beg, steal or borrow SEE beg, borrow or steal

borrowed /'bɒrəʊd; AmE 'bɑːroʊd; 'bɔːr-/

be/live on borrowed 'time
1 (of a person who is seriously ill) live longer than the doctors expected: *The doctors say he's living on borrowed time.*
2 be doing sth that other people are likely to soon stop you from doing: *The government is on borrowed time* (= they are not likely to be in power for long).

bosom /'bʊzəm/

in the bosom of sth
surrounded or protected by sth: *He longed to be back safe in the bosom of his family.*

boss /bɒs; AmE bɔːs/

● show → show sb who's boss

bothered /'bɒðəd; AmE 'bɒðərd; 'bɑː-/

can't be bothered (to do sth) (*BrE, informal*)
not willing to make the effort (to do sth): *I got home so late last night that I couldn't be bothered to cook dinner.* ◇ *He didn't have an excuse for not coming to the party — he just couldn't be bothered.*

I'm not 'bothered (*informal, especially BrE*)
I don't mind: *'What shall we have for supper tonight?' 'I'm not bothered.'*

● hot → (all) hot and bothered

bottle /'bɒtl; AmE 'bɑːtl/

'bottle it (*BrE, informal*)
not do sth, or not finish sth, because you are frightened: *Why should we take a risk when everybody else is bottling it?*

have, show, etc. (a lot of) bottle (*BrE, informal*)
have, show, etc. (a lot of) courage or confidence: *Carol went in and told the boss he wasn't doing his job properly. She's certainly got a lot of bottle!* ◇ *The match was very tough and United just didn't have the bottle for it.*

on the 'bottle (*informal*)
drinking a lot of alcoholic drinks regularly: *I see he's back on the bottle again.*

● catch → catch lightning in a bottle
● genie → the genie is out of the bottle
● genie → let the genie out of the bottle
● hit → hit the bottle

bottom /'bɒtəm; AmE 'bɑːtəm/

at 'bottom
basically; in reality: *She seems rather unfriendly, but at bottom I think she's quite kind.*

at the bottom/top of the 'pile/'heap (*informal*)
in a low/high position in society: *You've no idea what life at the bottom of the pile is like, have you? When do you ever talk to ordinary people?*

be/lie at the 'bottom of sth
be the basic cause of sth: *Racist feelings almost certainly lie at the bottom of these recent attacks.*

the ‚bottom drops/falls out of the 'market
people no longer want to buy a particular product and so it has to be sold very cheaply: *She invested in coffee, but then the bottom dropped out of the market, and she lost a lot of money.*

the ‚bottom drops/falls out of sb's 'world
a person suddenly loses all their happiness, self-confidence, etc: *When his wife left him, the bottom dropped out of his world.*

the ‚bottom 'line (*informal*)
the important conclusion, judgement, or result: *We've had some success this year, but the bottom line is that the business is still losing money.*

the bottom of the 'hour (*especially AmE*)
(on a TV/radio programme, etc.) 30 minutes past the hour on a clock: *The radio station provides hourly newscasts at both the top and bottom of the hour.* **OPP** the top of the hour

from the ˌbottom of your ˈheart
with deep feeling; very sincerely: *I thank you from the bottom of my heart for all your help.*

get to the ˈbottom of sth
find the true cause of sth or the solution to sth: *We're determined to get to the bottom of this mystery.* **OPP** scratch the surface (of sth)

- **bet** → (you can) bet your bottom dollar/your life (on sth/that...)
- **race** → a/the race to the bottom
- **rock** → be at rock bottom
- **rock** → hit/reach rock bottom
- **smooth** → (as) smooth as a baby's bottom **SEE** (as) smooth as silk
- **top** → from top to bottom
- **touch** → touch bottom

bottomless /ˈbɒtəmləs; *AmE* ˈbɑːt-/

a bottomless ˈpit (of sth)
a thing or situation which seems to have no limits or seems never to end: *There isn't a bottomless pit of money for public spending.* ◇ *the bottomless pit of his sorrow*

bottoms /ˈbɒtəmz; *AmE* ˈbɑːtəmz/

bottoms ˈup! (*old-fashioned, spoken*)
used for telling people to finish their drinks, or to express good wishes when drinking alcohol: *Come on everybody, it's time to go home. Bottoms up!*

bouncing /ˈbaʊnsɪŋ/

be ˌbouncing off the ˈwalls (*informal*)
be so full of energy or so excited that you cannot keep still: *He was bouncing off the walls so I told him to go out for a walk.*

bound /baʊnd/

be/feel duty/honour ˈbound to do sth (*BrE*)
(*AmE* **be/feel duty/honor ˈbound to do sth**)
(*formal*)
feel that you must do sth because of your sense of moral duty: *She felt honour bound to attend as she had promised to.* ◇ *Most people think that children are duty bound to look after their parents when they are old.*

bound and deˈtermined (*AmE*)
very determined to do sth: *I came here bound and determined to put the last 12 months behind me.*

bounds /baʊndz/

out of ˈbounds
1 (in some sports) outside the area of play which is allowed: *His shot went out of bounds.*
2 (*AmE*) not reasonable or acceptable: *His demands were out of bounds.*

out of ˈbounds (to/for sb) (*especially BrE*)
(*AmE* usually **ˌoff ˈlimits**)
outside the area sb is allowed to go: *The village is out of bounds to the soldiers in the camp.*

within ˈbounds
within acceptable limits; under control: *Borrowing money from friends is all right as long as it's kept within bounds.*

- **know** → know no bounds
- **leaps** → by/in leaps and bounds

bow¹ /baʊ/

ˌbow and ˈscrape (*disapproving*)
be too polite to sb important in order to gain their approval: *I will not bow and scrape to him just to get a salary increase.*

bow² /bəʊ; *AmE* boʊ/

have another string/more strings to your bow (*BrE*)
something else that you can use or do if the thing you are using or doing fails: *If I don't succeed as an actor, I've got another string to my bow because I'm a trained music teacher.*

bows /baʊz/

- **shot** → (fire) a (warning) shot across sb's bows

box /bɒks; *AmE* bɑːks/

box ˈclever (*BrE, informal*)
act in a clever way to get what you want, sometimes tricking and deceiving sb: *Suzie realized that she had to box clever. She had to let Adam think she trusted him.*

box sb's ˈears ◆ give sb a box on the ˈears (*old-fashioned*)
hit sb with your hand on the side of their head as a punishment: *If you do that one more time I'll box your ears, boy!*

in the ˈbox seat (*AustralE, New Zealand, informal*)
in a position in which you have an advantage: *Australia is in the box seat to reclaim the trophy following its record win over Ireland.*

- **Pandora** → Pandora's box
- **sharpest** → not the sharpest tool in the box **SEE** not the sharpest knife in the drawer
- **think** → think out of/outside the box
- **tree** → be out of your box **SEE** be out of your tree
- **tricks** → a bag/box of tricks

boy /bɔɪ/

a ˈmummy's/ˈmother's boy (*BrE*) (*AmE* **a ˈmama's boy**) (*disapproving*)
a boy or man who is thought to be too weak because he is influenced and controlled by his mother: *He's a bit of a mummy's boy really. He ought to leave home and become a bit more independent.* ◇ *She always makes sure he wears a scarf — he's a real mother's boy.*

- **blue-eyed** → your, sb's, etc. blue-eyed boy
- **golden** → a golden boy
- **man** → man and boy
- **old** → old boy/girl
- **old** → the old boy network
- **poster** → poster child/boy/girl

- whipping → a whipping boy
- wide → a wide boy

boys /bɔɪz/

the boys in 'blue (*old-fashioned, informal* or *humorous*)
police officers: *If you're not careful, you'll get a visit from the boys in blue!*

,boys will be 'boys (*saying*)
you must not criticize boys or men too much for behaving badly, being noisy, etc. as this is a natural way for them to behave: *The children came home covered in mud from head to foot, but I suppose boys will be boys!*

- back-room → the back-room boys
- jobs → jobs for the boys
- lads → be one of the lads/boys/girls
- men → sort out/separate the men from the boys

brain /breɪn/

the 'brain drain
the loss of qualified scientists, doctors, engineers, etc. to another country, especially one where they are paid more for their work

have sb/sth on the 'brain (*informal*)
think and/or talk a lot or too much about sb/sth: *You do nothing but talk about your job; you've got work on the brain!*

brains /breɪnz/

brains and/versus brawn
intelligence and/compared with physical strength: *In this job you need both brains and brawn.*

the 'brains behind sth
the person who thinks of new ideas and makes plans for sb/sth: *Everyone knew that she was the real brains behind the operation.*

- beat → beat your brains out
- blow → blow your/sb's brains out
- pick → pick sb's brains
- rack → wrack your brains **SEE** rack your brains

brake /breɪk/

- jam → jam the brake(s) on **SEE** jam on the brake(s)

branch /brɑːntʃ; AmE bræntʃ/

- olive → hold out/offer an olive branch (to sb)
- root → root and branch

brass /brɑːs; AmE bræs/

,brass 'monkeys ♦ ,brass 'monkey weather (*BrE, slang*)
if you say that it is **brass monkeys** or **brass monkey weather**, you mean that it is very cold weather: *Wear a hat — it's brass monkeys out there!*

> **❷ ORIGIN**
> The full expression is 'cold enough to freeze the balls off a brass monkey', although this is not often used. It may refer to a brass rack called a *monkey* which was used to store cannonballs. When it was very cold, the brass contracted (= got smaller) and the balls fell off.

,brass 'neck/'nerve (*BrE, informal*)
a combination of confidence and lack of respect: *I didn't think she would have the brass neck to do that.*

the brass 'ring (*AmE, informal*)
the opportunity to be successful; success that you have worked hard to get: *The girls' outdoor track team has grabbed the brass ring seven times.*

> **❷ ORIGIN**
> This comes from the custom of giving a free ride to anyone who managed to grab a large ring that was hung above the people riding on a merry-go-round at a fairground.

get down to brass 'tacks (*informal*)
begin to discuss and deal with the really important practical details: *Let's get down to brass tacks — how much will it all cost?*

- bold → (as) bold as brass
- muck → where there's muck there's brass
- top → (the) top brass

brassed /brɑːst; AmE bræst/

- browned → brassed off (with sb/sth) **SEE** browned off (with sb/sth)

brave /breɪv/

a ,brave new 'world (*often ironic*)
a situation or society that changes in a way that is meant to improve people's lives but is often a source of extra problems: *She promises us a brave new world of high salaries and good working conditions after the reforms.*

> **❷ ORIGIN**
> This phrase comes from Shakespeare's play *The Tempest*. It was later used by Aldous Huxley as the title of his most famous book, which described a vision of the future.

put a brave 'face on sth ♦ put on a brave 'face
try to appear brave or cheerful or to be managing well in a difficult situation, when in fact you are frightened or unhappy: *'How's Mrs O'Brien?' 'She's trying to put a very brave face on things, but you can see that she's very unhappy.'*

brawn /brɔːn/

- brains → brains and/versus brawn

breach /briːtʃ/

- step → step into the breach

bread /bred/

your ,bread and 'butter
the work that sb does which provides them with enough money to live: *He's written one or two novels but journalism is his bread and butter.*

- **best** → the best thing since sliced bread
- **daily** → your daily bread
- **half** → half a loaf is better than none/no bread
- **know** → know which side your bread is buttered

breadline /'bredlaɪn/

on the 'breadline
very poor: *Most of the unemployed in this area are on the breadline.*

> **❷ ORIGIN**
> In North America, a *breadline* was a queue of poor people waiting to receive free food from the government.

breadth /bredθ/

- **hair** → a hair's breadth
- **length** → the length and breadth of sth

break /breɪk/

> Most idioms containing the verb **break** are at the entries for the nouns or adjectives in the idioms, for example **break the ice** is at **ice**.

break your 'back doing sth/to do sth
work very hard to achieve sth: *I've been breaking my back to sell as many books as I can.* ► **'back-breaking** adj. (of physical work) very hard and tiring

break the 'back of sth
finish the largest or most difficult part of a task: *I won't finish this report tonight but I'd like to break the back of it before I go to bed.*

breakfast /'brekfəst/

- **dog** → a dog's breakfast/dinner
- **eat** → have/eat sb for breakfast **SEE** eat sb alive

breaking /'breɪkɪŋ/

breaking and 'entering
the act of getting into a building illegally by breaking a window, etc: *Although they hadn't stolen anything, they were still found guilty of breaking and entering.*

without breaking 'stride (*especially AmE*)
without stopping what you are doing: *The police officers looked at him as they passed, but walked on without breaking stride.*

- **omelette** → you can't make an omelette without breaking eggs

breaks /breɪks/

- **hell** → all hell breaks/is let loose
- **straw** → be the straw that breaks the camel's back **SEE** the last/final straw

breast /brest/

- **clean** → make a clean breast of sth

breath /breθ/

a breath of fresh 'air
a person or thing that is new and different and therefore interesting and exciting: *Having these young people living with us is like a breath of fresh air after years on our own.*

get your 'breath back
be able to breathe again properly after running, etc: *She stopped at the top of the stairs to get her breath back.*

hold your 'breath
1 stop breathing for a short time, for example because you are afraid of sth or very anxious about sth: *I held my breath as the car skidded towards me.*
2 be anxious while you are waiting for sth that you are worried about: *'When will you hear about your job application?' 'Not till next week. I'm holding my breath until then.'*
3 (*informal*) **don't hold your breath** used for telling sb that it's not worth waiting for sth: *We'll let you know if there's any work for you, but don't hold your breath.*

out of 'breath
not be able to breathe easily after physical effort: *I'm out of breath now after running for the bus.*

,say, etc. sth in the same 'breath
say sth which appears to be the opposite of what you have just said: *He told me that my work had improved and then in the same breath said that I was lazy.*

take sb's 'breath away
surprise or amaze sb: *It quite took my breath away when they told me how much money I had won.*
► **'breathtaking** adj. very exciting; spectacular: *a breathtaking view*

under your 'breath
in a whisper (= in a low voice), so that others cannot hear: *He muttered something under his breath.*
OPP out loud

- **bated** → with bated breath
- **catch** → catch your breath
- **draw** → draw (a) breath
- **mention** → mention sb/sth in the same breath
- **save** → save your breath
- **waste** → waste your breath (on sb/sth)

breathe /briːð/

breathe (easily/freely) again
no longer need to be afraid, worried, etc: *I was able to breathe easily again once I knew the children were safe.*

breathe down sb's 'neck (*informal*)
watch sb too closely, and so make them feel uncomfortable: *I can't work with people breathing down my neck the whole time.*

breathe your 'last (*formal*)
die: *Later that night, the King breathed his last.*
OPP come into the world

breathe (new) 'life into sth
improve sth by introducing new ideas and making people more interested in it: *She has breathed new life into a product that was tired and out-of-date.*

(not) breathe a 'word (about/of sth) (to sb)
(not) tell sb sth, especially sth secret: *Please don't breathe a word of this to anyone.*

● **live¹** → live and breathe sth

breathing /ˈbriːðɪŋ/

a 'breathing space
a time for resting between two periods of effort; pause: *This holiday will give me a bit of breathing space before I start my new job.*

bred /bred/

● **born** → born and bred

breeds /briːdz/

● **familiarity** → familiarity breeds contempt

breeze /briːz/

● **shoot** → shoot the breeze

brewing /ˈbruːɪŋ/

● **trouble** → there's trouble brewing

brick /brɪk/

be/come up against a brick 'wall (also **hit a brick 'wall**)
be unable to make any progress because there is a difficulty that stops you: *Since he had no more money to spend on the project, he was up against a brick wall.* ◇ *Plans to build a new road around the town hit a brick wall when local residents protested.*

● **built** → be built like a brick shithouse **SEE** be built like a tank
● **drop** → drop a brick/clanger
● **head** → be banging, etc. your head against a brick wall
● **talk** → talk to a brick wall

bricks /brɪks/

bricks and 'mortar
a building, especially when you are thinking of it in connection with how much it cost to build or how much it is worth: *A home isn't just bricks and mortar.* ◇ *We now need funding to turn the plans into bricks and mortar.*

> **NOTE**
> The modern way of doing business through the Internet as well as from buildings and shops can be referred to as *clicks and mortar*, where 'clicks' refers to the use of the mouse and the Internet.

a few, two, etc. ˌbricks short of a 'load (also **a few, two, etc. ˌsandwiches short of a 'picnic**) (*informal*)
(of a person) not very intelligent; slightly crazy: *If you ask me, I think he must be one or two sandwiches short of a picnic!* **OPP** all there

> **NOTE**
> The structure *a few, two, etc....short of a(n)...* is often used to make new idioms, for example *a few cards short of a deck*, *a few letters short of an alphabet*.

make ˌbricks without 'straw (*BrE*)
try to do a piece of work without the necessary materials, equipment or information: *I don't know how you expect me to cook dinner when there's hardly any food in the house. You can't make bricks without straw, you know.*

> **❷ ORIGIN**
> This is based on a story in the Bible. At that time, straw was an essential material for making bricks.

● **cat** → like a cat on hot bricks
● **ton** → be/come down on sb like a ton of bricks

bridge /brɪdʒ/

bridge the 'gap (between A and B) (also **bridge the 'gulf (between A and B)** *less frequent*)
make it easier to move from one thing to another or for two groups to communicate with each other: *The hostel helps to bridge the gap between prison and life on the outside.*

● **cross** → cross a bridge when you come to it
● **painting** → be painting the Forth Bridge
● **water** → be (all) water under the bridge

bridges /ˈbrɪdʒɪz/

● **build** → build bridges (between A and B/with sb)
● **burn** → burn your bridges
● **cross** → cross your bridges when you come to them

brief /briːf/

hold no 'brief for sb/sth (*formal*)
not be in favour of or not support sb/sth, for example a cause, an idea, etc: *I hold no brief for long prison sentences but this terrible crime really deserves one.*

> **NOTE**
> *Brief* in this expression is the summary of facts and legal points in a case that is given to a lawyer to argue in a court. If a lawyer 'holds no brief for' a person, company, etc. this is not one of their clients/cases.

in 'brief
in a few words: *I won't give a you a long history of the dispute; in brief, it led to the business closing.* ◇ *And now, the news in brief.*

brigade /brɪˈɡeɪd/

● **heavy** → the heavy mob/brigade

bright /braɪt/

bright and 'early
early in the morning: *You're up bright and early this morning!*

(as) bright as a 'button (*BrE*)
clever and lively: *That child's as bright as a button!* **OPP** (as) thick as two short planks

the bright 'lights (*informal*)
the big city seen as a centre of entertainment, enjoyment, etc: *Many people from other places are still tempted by the bright lights of London.*

(a) bright 'spark (*BrE, informal, often ironic*)
a lively and intelligent person: *What bright spark* (= stupid person) *left the front door open all night?*

a/the 'bright spot
a good or pleasant part of sth that is unpleasant or bad in all other ways: *The win last week was the only bright spot in their last ten games.*

look on the 'bright side
be cheerful or hopeful about a bad situation, for example by thinking only of the advantages and not the disadvantages: *I know it's inconvenient to be without a car, but look on the bright side — at least you'll save money on petrol.*

bright-eyed /ˌbraɪt 'aɪd/

ˌbright-eyed and ˌbushy-'tailed (*informal*)
lively and cheerful; pleased and proud: *She came in to see me, all bright-eyed and bushy-tailed, and announced she was leaving the next day.*

bring /brɪŋ/

Idioms containing the verb **bring** are at the entries for the nouns and adjectives in the idioms, for example **bring the house down** is at **house**.

brink /brɪŋk/

● teeter → teeter on the brink/edge of sth

broad /brɔːd/

a broad 'church (*BrE*)
an organization that accepts a wide range of opinions

broad in the 'beam (*informal*)
having wide hips: *Her waist is quite small, but she's rather broad in the beam.*

in broad 'daylight
in the clear light of day, when it is easy to see: *He was attacked right in the centre of town in broad daylight.* **OPP** (in) the dead of (the) night

it's as ˌbroad as it's 'long (*old-fashioned, BrE, spoken*)
there is no real difference between two possible alternatives: *'Shall we go today or tomorrow?' 'It's as broad as it's long, isn't it? You choose.'*

● paint → paint sth with a broad brush

broke /brəʊk; AmE broʊk/

go for 'broke (*informal*)
risk everything in one determined effort to do sth: *I decided to go for broke and start my own business.*

if it ain't 'broke, don't 'fix it
used to say that if sth is satisfactory and works well, it should not be changed: *Why do they keep suggesting 'improvements' when everything's working perfectly? If it ain't broke, don't fix it.*

● flat → be stony broke SEE be flat broke

broom /bruːm/

● new → a new broom (sweeps clean)

broth /brɒθ; AmE brɔːθ/

● cooks → too many cooks spoil the broth

Brother /'brʌðə(r)/

● Big → Big Brother (is watching you)

brothers /'brʌðəz; AmE 'brʌðərz/

● skin → be (all) brothers/sisters under the skin

brought /brɔːt/

● cat → (look) like sth the cat brought/dragged in

brow /braʊ/

● sweat → by the sweat of your brow

browned /braʊnd/

ˌbrowned 'off (with sb/sth) (also **ˌbrassed 'off (with sb/sth)**) (*BrE, informal*)
bored, unhappy and/or annoyed: *By now the passengers were getting browned off with the delay.*

brownie /'braʊni/

'brownie points
if sb does sth to earn **brownie points**, they do it to make sb in authority have a good opinion of them: *She's only working late to win brownie points with the boss.* **OPP** a black mark (against sb)

NOTE
The *Brownies* is a club for young girls which trains them in practical skills and does a lot of activities such as camping. The girls are awarded points for good behaviour and achievements.

brows /braʊz/

● knit → knit your brows

brunt /brʌnt/

● bear → bear the brunt of sth

brush /brʌʃ/

● carpet → sweep/brush sth under the carpet
● daft → (as) daft as a brush
● paint → paint sth with a broad brush
● tar → tar sb/sth with the same brush

bubble /'bʌbl/

the bubble 'bursts
there is a sudden end to a good or lucky situation: *When the bubble finally burst, hundreds of people lost their jobs.*

● burst → burst sb's bubble

buck /bʌk/

the buck stops 'here
used for telling sb that you are prepared to accept responsibility for sth: *We don't try to escape our responsibilities. The buck stops here.*

> **❷ ORIGIN**
> This phrase was used by the US President Harry S. Truman to mean that he did not *pass the buck*.

buck up your i'deas ♦ buck your i'deas up (*informal*)
start to work harder or more efficiently; become more willing to do things: *He's been late every day for two weeks. He'll have to buck up his ideas if he wants to keep his job.*

make a fast/quick buck (*informal, often disapproving*)
earn money quickly and easily: *He didn't really care about the business — he just wanted to make a fast buck.*

● bang → bang for your buck
● pass → pass the buck
● stark → buck naked SEE stark naked

bucket /'bʌkɪt/

● drop → a drop in the bucket SEE a drop in the ocean
● kick → kick the bucket

buckets /'bʌkɪts/

● rain → rain buckets

Buckley's /'bʌkliz/

have 'Buckley's (chance) (*AustralE, New Zealand, informal*)
used to suggest that sb has little or no hope of achieving a particular aim: *She has Buckley's of getting any more than $5 000 for her car.*

bucks /bʌks/

● million → look/feel like a million dollars/bucks

bud /bʌd/

● nip → nip sth in the bud

budge /bʌdʒ/

● inch → not budge/give/move an inch

buff /bʌf/

in the 'buff (*informal*)
wearing no clothes: *I'm sure I saw him swimming in the buff!*

buffers /'bʌfəz; AmE 'bʌfərz/

● hit → hit the buffers

bug /bʌg/

be bitten by/have the 'bug (*informal*)
have a sudden strong interest in or enthusiasm for sth: *My mum was never really interested in going abroad until she went to America last year. Now she's been bitten by the travel bug and hates staying at home!*

bug 'off! (*AmE, spoken*)
a rude way of telling sb to go away

● snug → (as) snug as a bug (in a rug)

buggers /'bʌgəz; AmE 'bʌgərz/

● silly → play silly buggers (with sth)

build /bɪld/

build 'bridges (between A and B/with sb)
if you **build bridges** between people who disagree on sth or who do not like each other, you try to find ways to improve the relationship between them: *The police are trying to build bridges with the local community.* ▶ **'bridge-building** *noun*: *The company has a lot of bridge-building to do with angry investors.*

● hopes → build up/raise sb's hopes

built /bɪlt/

be built like a 'tank (also **be built like a ˌbrick 'shithouse** ⚠, *slang*)
(of a person) be very big and strong: *He's a wrestler? Well, that doesn't surprise me — he's built like a tank!*

● Rome → Rome wasn't built in a day

bulging /'bʌldʒɪŋ/

● seams → be bursting/bulging at the seams (with sth)

bull /bʊl/

like a ˌbull in a 'china shop
very careless or clumsy, especially in a situation where you need to be careful: *He was like a bull in a china shop, treading on everyone's feet and apologizing constantly.* ◇ *The Prime Minister went into the negotiations like a bull in a china shop and only made the relations between the two countries worse.*

take the ˌbull by the 'horns (*informal*)
deal with a difficult or dangerous situation in a direct and brave way: *I decided to take the bull by the horns and ask the bank for a loan.*

● cock → a cock and bull story
● red → (like) a red rag to a bull
● red → like waving a red flag in front of/at a bull SEE (like) a red rag to a bull
● shoot → shoot the bull/shit SEE shoot the breeze

bullet /'bʊlɪt/

● bite → bite the bullet

bully /'bʊli/

bully for sb! (*spoken*)
used to show that you do not think that what sb has said or done is very impressive: *'Janet's just won a free holiday in Spain.' 'Oh, bully for her! She's so rich anyway, she can afford to go away whenever she wants to.'*

bum /bʌm/

a bum 'steer (*AmE*, *informal*)
wrong or unhelpful information or advice: *Whoever recommended this software gave you a bum steer, I'm afraid.*

give sb/get the ,bum's 'rush (*slang, especially AmE*)
1 order or use force to make sb leave a place; be made to leave in this way: *The reporter was given the bum's rush out of the club.*
2 dismiss or get rid of sb that you do not want; be dismissed or got rid of: *I got the bum's rush from Smith & Co.*

● **pain** → a pain in the arse/bum/backside **SEE** a pain in the neck

bump /bʌmp/

● **things** → things that go bump in the night

bumper /'bʌmpə(r)/

,bumper to 'bumper
if vehicles are **bumper to bumper**, there is so much traffic that they are very close together and can hardly move: *Being a Friday evening, it was bumper to bumper on the main road leading out of town.*

> **NOTE**
> A *bumper* is the bar fixed to the front and back of a vehicle to reduce the effect if it hits anything.

bumpkin /'bʌmpkɪn/

● **country** → a country bumpkin/cousin

bumpy /'bʌmpi/

give sb/have a bumpy 'ride
make a situation difficult for sb; have a difficult time: *The business has had a bumpy ride over the last twelve months, but profits are growing again now.*

bums /bʌmz/

bums on 'seats (*BrE*, *informal*)
used to refer to the number of people who attend a show, talk, etc., especially when emphasizing the need or desire to attract a large number: *They're not bothered about attracting the right audience — they just want bums on seats.*

bun /bʌn/

have a 'bun in the oven (*informal, humorous*)
be pregnant

bunch /bʌntʃ/

a bunch of 'fives (*old-fashioned* or *humorous*)
a punch (= a hard hit made with a closed hand)

● **best** → the best of a bad bunch/lot
● **mixed** → be a mixed bag/bunch
● **pick** → the pick of the bunch

bundle /'bʌndl/

a bundle of 'joy (*informal*)
a baby

not go a 'bundle on sb/sth (*BrE*, *informal*)
not like sb/sth: *I don't go a bundle on that shirt he's wearing.*

● **laughs** → a barrel/bundle of laughs
● **nerves** → a bag/bundle of nerves

bunk /bʌŋk/

do a 'bunk (*BrE*, *informal*)
leave a place quickly without telling anyone: *I heard Jimmy did a bunk with all their money!*

bunny /'bʌni/

● **happy** → (not) a happy bunny

buried /'berid/

● **dead** → dead and buried/gone

burn /bɜːn; *AmE* bɜːrn/

burn your 'bridges (*BrE* also **burn your 'boats**)
do sth that makes it impossible for you to return to a previous situation: *Once you sign this document, you'll have burned your boats, and will have to go ahead with the sale.* **OPP** keep/leave (all) your options open

burn the candle at both 'ends
make yourself very tired by doing too much, especially by going to bed late and getting up early: *You look exhausted. Been burning the candle at both ends, have you?*

burn the midnight 'oil
work or study until very late at night: *Before my exams, I was burning the midnight oil every night.*

burn sth to a 'cinder/'crisp
cook sth for too long or with too much heat, so that it becomes badly burnt: *Alan left the potatoes for so long that they were burnt to a crisp.*

● **crash** → crash and burn
● **fingers** → burn your fingers **SEE** get your fingers burnt
● **money** → have money to burn
● **slow** → do a slow burn

burner /'bɜːnə(r); *AmE* 'bɜːrn-/

on the back 'burner (*informal*)
(of an idea, a plan, etc.) left for the present time, to be done or considered later: *The job was put on the back burner when more important assignments arrived.*

> **NOTE**
> A *burner* is one of the parts of a cooker/stove that produces a flame.

● **front** → on the front burner

burning /ˈbɜːnɪŋ; AmE ˈbɜːrn-/

• **ears →** his, her, etc. ears are burning

burns /bɜːnz; AmE bɜːrnz/

• **fiddle →** fiddle while Rome burns
• **money →** money burns a hole in your pocket

burnt /bɜːnt; AmE bɜːrnt/

• **fingers →** get your fingers burnt

burst /bɜːst; AmE bɜːrst/

,burst a 'blood vessel (*informal*)
get very angry and excited: *When I told Dad I'd damaged the car, he nearly burst a blood vessel.*

,burst sb's 'bubble
bring an end to sb's hopes, happiness, etc: *Things are going really well for him. I just hope nothing happens to burst his bubble.*

,burst 'open ♦ ,burst (sth) 'open
open suddenly or violently; make sth open in this way: *The door burst open.* ◇ *Firefighters burst the door open and rescued them.*

bursting /ˈbɜːstɪŋ; AmE ˈbɜːrstɪŋ/

be bursting to do sth (*informal*)
want to do sth so much that you can hardly stop yourself: *She was just bursting to tell us the news.*

NOTE

I'm bursting when it is used on its own usually means 'I really need to go to the toilet'.

• **seams →** be full to bursting (with sth) **SEE** be bursting/bulging at the seams (with sth)

bursts /bɜːsts; AmE bɜːrsts/

• **bubble →** the bubble bursts

bury /ˈberi/

,bury the 'hatchet ♦ ,bury your 'differences
(of two people or groups) agree to forget past disagreements and be friends again: *I've said I'm prepared to bury the hatchet, but John says he won't forgive me for what happened.*

❷ ORIGIN
When Native Americans agreed to end fighting and begin a period of peace they held a ceremony in which they buried a *hatchet* or *tomahawk* (= a small axe).

• **head →** bury/hide your head in the sand

bush /bʊʃ/

,bush 'telegraph
the spreading of news quickly from one person to another: *Everyone knew about it before it was officially announced: the bush telegraph had been at work again.*

❷ ORIGIN
Bush in this phrase refers to the areas of wild land in Australia. *Bush telegraph* originally meant the people who informed *bushrangers* (= criminals who lived in the bush) about the movements of the police.

• **beat →** beat about/around the bush
• **bird →** a bird in the hand is worth two in the bush

bushel /ˈbʊʃl/

• **hide →** hide your light under a bushel

bushes /ˈbʊʃɪz/

• **beat →** beat the bushes

bushy-tailed /ˌbʊʃi ˈteɪld/

• **bright-eyed →** bright-eyed and bushy-tailed

business /ˈbɪznəs/

be (back) in 'business
be working or operating (again) as normal: *Once the switch has been fixed, we will be back in business and we can use the machine again.* ◇ *It looks as though we're in business: she's agreed to lend us the money.*

be none of sb's 'business ♦ be no business of sb's (*informal*)
a person has no right to know sth: *'How much do you earn?' 'That's none of your business.'* ◇ *It's no business of yours who I go out with.*

the 'business end (of sth) (*informal*)
the part of a tool, weapon, etc. that performs its particular function: *Never pick up a knife by the business end.*

,business is 'business
a way of saying that financial and commercial matters are the important things to consider and you should not be influenced by friendship, etc: *He's a nice guy but business is business. He owes me money and he'll have to pay it back.*

get down to 'business
start discussing or doing sth seriously, especially after a time of social talk: *Well, it's getting late — perhaps we'd better get down to business.*

go about your 'business
be busy with the things that you do every day: *He looked out onto the street and watched the people going about their daily business.*

have no business doing sth/to do sth
have no right to do sth: *You have no business being here.*

it's business as 'usual
things continue normally, despite difficulties or disturbances: *It was business as usual at the theatre yesterday, in spite of all the building work going on.*

like 'nobody's business (*informal*)
very fast, very much, very hard, etc: *He's been spending money like nobody's business recently.*

not be in the business of doing sth
not intending to do sth (which it would be surprising for you to do): *I'm not in the business of getting other people to do my work for me.*

out of 'business
having stopped operating as a business because there is no more money or work available: *The new regulations will* **put** *many small firms* **out of business.** ◇ *Some travel companies will probably* **go out of business** *this summer.*

● funny → funny business
● mean → mean business
● mind → mind your own business
● monkey → monkey business
● ply → ply for hire/trade/business

busman /ˈbʌsmən/

a busman's 'holiday (*informal*)
a holiday spent doing the same kind of thing that you do at work: *The fire crew's annual outing turned into a busman's holiday when their bus caught fire. Fortunately, no one was hurt in the blaze.*

> ❷ ORIGIN
> This phrase may refer to the drivers of horse-drawn vehicles in the 19th century. When they were not working, they often rode as passengers on their own buses to make sure that the replacement driver was treating their horses well.

bust /bʌst/

bust sb's 'ass/'balls/'butt/'hump (*AmE*, △, *slang*) (also **bust sb's 'chops** *AmE rather old-fashioned*)
criticize sb in an angry or annoying way: *Why are you always busting my balls?* ◇ *This guy keeps busting my chops about my smelly tennis sneakers.*
▶ **'ball-buster** *noun*

bust your 'ass/'balls/'butt/'hump (*AmE*, △, *slang*)
make a very great effort: *I bust my ass to get that job.* ◇ *I've been busting my hump for the last week trying to get the project finished.*

bust a 'gut (*informal*)
1 make a very great effort: *I'm not going to bust a gut trying to be on time when I know she'll probably be late.*
2 (*AmE*) laugh a lot: *That show is hilarious, I bust a gut every time I watch it.*

go 'bust (*informal*)
(of a business) fail financially; become bankrupt: *The firm went bust and fifty workers lost their jobs.*

... or 'bust (*informal*)
used to say that you will try very hard to get somewhere or achieve sth: *For him it's the Olympics or bust.*

● balls → break sb's balls

bustle /ˈbʌsl/

● hustle → hustle and bustle

busy /ˈbɪzi/

(as) busy as a 'bee
very busy

a ,busy 'bee (*informal*)
a cheerful and busy person

keep yourself 'busy
find enough things to do: *Since she retired she's kept herself very busy.*

but /bət/

but for sb/sth
except for sb/sth; without sb/sth: *But for a brief period after leaving college, he had never been unemployed.* ◇ *But for you, we would not have been able to start up the business.*

butcher /ˈbʊtʃə(r)/

have/take a 'butcher's (*BrE, slang*)
have a look at sth: *Come over here and have a butcher's at this!*

> ❷ ORIGIN
> This phrase comes from rhyming slang, in which *butcher's hook* stands for 'look'.

buts /bʌts/

● ifs → ifs and/or buts

butt /bʌt/

be the butt of sth
be the person or thing that other people often joke about or criticize: *She was the butt of some very unkind jokes.*

> NOTE
> *Butt* in this phrase means *target* and was used in the sport of archery (= shooting arrows).

● bust → bust sb's ass/balls/butt/hump
● bust → bust your ass/balls/butt/hump
● kick → kick (some/sb's) ass/butt
● pain → a pain in the ass/butt SEE a pain in the neck

butter /ˈbʌtə(r)/

,butter wouldn't 'melt (in sb's 'mouth) (*spoken*)
a person looks very innocent, but probably is not: *She looks as if butter wouldn't melt in her mouth, but don't be fooled by first impressions!*

● bread → your bread and butter
● knife → like a knife through butter

buttered /ˈbʌtəd; AmE ˈbʌtərd/

● know → know which side your bread is buttered

butterflies /ˈbʌtəflaɪz; AmE -tərf-/

get/have 'butterflies (in your stomach) (*informal*)
get/have a nervous feeling in your stomach before doing sth: *I always get butterflies (in my stomach) before an interview.*

button /ˈbʌtn/

'button it! (*BrE, spoken*)
used to tell sb rudely to be quiet

on the 'button (*informal, especially AmE*)
1 at exactly the right time or at the exact time mentioned: *We arrived at 4 o'clock on the button.*
2 exactly right: *You're on the button there!*

● bright → (as) bright as a button
● cute → (as) cute as a button
● panic → press/push the panic button

buttons /ˈbʌtnz/

● push → press sb's buttons SEE push sb's buttons
● push → push sb's buttons

buy /baɪ/

buy the 'farm (*informal, humorous, especially AmE*)
die: *I'd like to visit India one day, before I buy the farm.*

> **❷ ORIGIN**
> This comes from the military, perhaps referring to the dream of many soldiers and pilots of buying a farm when the war was over.

buy 'time
delay sth that seems about to happen: *This treatment can buy time for the patient, but I'm afraid it will not cure him.*

● pup → sell sb/buy a pup
● song → (buy sth, go, etc.) for a song

buyer /ˈbaɪə(r)/

a ˌbuyer's 'market
a situation in which there is a lot of a particular item for sale, so that prices are low and people buying have a choice: *We got a very good deal on our new car — it really is a buyer's market at the moment.* **OPP** a seller's market

buzz /bʌz/

give sb a 'buzz (*informal*)
1 telephone sb: *I'll give you a buzz before I leave.*
2 (also **get a buzz from sth/from doing sth**) if sth **gives** you **a buzz** or you **get a buzz from** it, it provides interest and enjoyment for you: *If the work gives you a buzz, then you do the job better.*

buzzer /ˈbʌzə(r)/

at the 'buzzer (*AmE*)
at the end of a game or period of play: *He missed a three-point attempt at the buzzer.* ◊ *The Eagles won at the buzzer 66-64.*

> **NOTE**
> A *buzzer* is an electrical device that makes a sound as a signal, for example to show that no time is left in a game.

by /baɪ/

by and 'by (*old-fashioned*)
after a little time; soon: *Things will be better by and by.*

(all) by your'self, him'self, etc.
1 alone; without anyone else: *How long were you by yourself in the house?*
2 without help: *Are you sure he did this exercise all by himself?*

bye /baɪ/

● way → by the by/bye SEE by the way

bygones /ˈbaɪɡɒnz; AmE -ɡɔːnz; -ɡɑːnz/

let ˌbygones be 'bygones
decide to forget about disagreements that happened in the past: *This is a ridiculous situation, avoiding each other like this. Why can't we let bygones be bygones?*

byways /ˈbaɪweɪz/

● highways → highways and byways

Cc

caboodle /kəˈbuːdl/

the ˌwhole ca'boodle ◆ the ˌwhole kit and ca'boodle
everything: *I had new clothes, a new hairstyle — the whole caboodle.*

> **❷ ORIGIN**
> This idiom originally came from the Dutch word *boedel*, meaning 'possessions'.

cackle /ˈkækl/

cut the 'cackle (*informal*)
stop talking and start working, etc. properly; start talking about the important matters: *Let's cut the cackle and get down to business.*

> **NOTE**
> *Cackle* refers to the loud noise made by chickens.

cage /keɪdʒ/

● rattle → rattle sb's cage

cahoots /kəˈhuːts/

be in ca'hoots (with sb) (*informal*)
be planning or doing sth dishonest with sb else: *Some people believe that the company directors are in cahoots with the government.*

Cain /keɪn/

● raise → raise Cain/hell

another: *The recent robberies in Leeds are a carbon copy of those that have occurred in Halifax over the last few months.*

> NOTE
>
> A *carbon copy* is a copy of a document, letter, etc. made by placing *carbon paper* (= thin paper with a dark substance on one side) between two sheets of paper.

card /kɑːd; AmE kɑːrd/

● trump → a/your trump card

cards /kɑːdz; AmE kɑːrdz/

keep/hold/play your cards ˌclose to your ˈchest
not tell others what you are intending to do: *He keeps his cards pretty close to his chest. I don't know whether he plans to buy the house or not.* **OPP** show/ reveal your hand

on the ˈcards (*BrE*) (*AmE* **in the ˈcards**) (*informal*)
likely to happen: *With a rail strike on the cards for next week, airline bookings have been high.*

put/lay your ˈcards on the table (*informal*)
talk honestly and openly about your thoughts and intentions, especially when these have been secret until now: *It's time I put my cards on the table; I can't afford the price you're asking.*

play your ˈcards right (*informal*)
deal successfully with a particular situation so that you achieve some advantage or sth that you want: *If you play your cards right you could get promotion in a year or two.*

● aces → hold all the cards **SEE** have/hold (all) the aces
● house → a house of cards
● stacked → the cards/odds are stacked against sb/sth
● stacked → the cards/odds are stacked in favour of sb/sth

care /keə(r); AmE ker/

ˈcare of sb (*AmE* also **in ˈcare of sb**)
used when writing to sb at another person's address: *Write to me care of my sister, because I'll be touring Africa for six months.*

> NOTE
>
> This expression is usually written as 'c/o' on envelopes.

couldn't care ˈless (*informal*)
used to say, often rudely, that you are not at all interested in or concerned about sth: *I couldn't care less if I fail my exams — I don't want to go to college anyway.*

for all I, you, etc. ˈcare (*spoken*)
used to say that a person is not worried about or interested in what happens to sb/sth: *I could be dead for all he cares!*

in ˈcare (*BrE*)
(of children) living and looked after in an institution owned by the State: *She has been in care ever since her parents died.* ◇ *The social worker said that their baby would have to* **be taken into care.**

not have a ˌcare in the ˈworld ◆ **without a ˌcare in the ˈworld**
not have any worry or anxiety at all: *Sam looked as if he didn't have a care in the world.* ◇ *She skipped along the road, without a care in the world.*

take ˈcare (that …/to do sth)
be careful: *Take care that you don't fall and hurt yourself.* ◇ *He took great care not to let his personal problems interfere with his work.*

take ˈcare of yourself/sb/sth
1 make sure that you are/sb is safe, well, healthy, etc.; look after yourself/sb: *I don't need your help! I can take care of myself quite well, thank you!* ◇ *Don't worry about the children while you're away. They'll be* **taken good care of.**

> NOTE
>
> 'Take care' is often used alone when saying 'goodbye' to somebody: *Bye then! Take care!*

2 be responsible for sb/sth; deal with sb/sth: *Can you take care of the shopping if I do the cooking?* ◇ *There's no need for you to pay the bill. It's all* **taken care of** (= it is already done).

would you care for… ◆ **would you care to…** (*formal*)
used to ask sb politely if they would like sth or would like to do sth, or if they would be willing to do sth: *Would you care for another drink?* ◇ *If you'd care to follow me, I'll show you where his office is.*

● damn → not care/give a damn (about/for sb/sth)
● hoot → not care/give two hoots (about sb/sth) **SEE** not care/give a hoot (about sb/sth)
● tuppence → not care/give tuppence for/about sb/sth

careful /ˈkeəfl; AmE ˈkerfl/

you can't be too ˈcareful
used to warn sb that they should be careful to avoid danger or problems: *Don't stay out in the sun for too long — you can't be too careful.*

cares /keəz; AmE kerz/

who ˈcares? ◆ **what do I, you, etc. care?** (*informal*)
nobody cares; I, you, etc. do not care: *'Who do you think will win the next election?' 'Who cares?'*

caring /ˈkeərɪŋ; AmE ˈker-/

be beyond/past ˈcaring (about sth)
have reached a stage where you no longer care about or are no longer affected by sth: *She can't hurt him now because he's beyond caring about what she says.*

carpet /ˈkɑːpɪt; AmE ˈkɑːrpɪt/

be on the ˈcarpet (*informal, especially AmE*)
be criticized, especially by an employer or sb in authority, because you have done sth wrong: *She's on the carpet for spending too much of the company's money on entertaining guests.*

sweep/brush sth under the 'carpet (*AmE* also **sweep sth under the 'rug**) (*informal*)
hide sth which might cause trouble, or which you do not want other people to know: *No matter how unwelcome the results of the enquiry may be, they must not be swept under the carpet.*

● **pull** → pull the carpet/rug out from under sb's feet
● **red** → the red carpet

carried /ˈkærɪd/

be/get carried a'way
be/get very excited or lose control of your feelings: *I got carried away and started shouting at the television.*

carrot /ˈkærət/

the carrot and/or (the) stick
rewards offered to sb to persuade them to do sth or try harder, and/or punishment threatened if they do not: *She favoured a carrot-and-stick approach to teaching.*

carry /ˈkæri/

carry all be'fore you
be completely successful in a battle, competition, etc: *In three tournaments since June, this young tennis player has carried all before him, winning easy victories each time.*

carry the 'ball (*AmE*, *informal*)
take responsibility for getting sth done: *My co-worker was sick, so I had to carry the ball.* ◇ *We need a couple of Senators who will carry the ball for us in Congress.*

carry the 'can (for sb/sth) (*BrE*, *informal*)
accept the responsibility or blame for sth: *The teachers who were criticized said that they would not carry the can for the faults in the school system.*
OPP pass the buck

> ❷ ORIGIN
> This may come from military slang. The person who *carried the can* was responsible for collecting the can containing beer for the whole group and bringing it back without spilling any.

carry a 'torch for sb
be in love with sb, especially sb who does not love you in return: *She's been carrying a torch for him for years.*

carry 'weight
be important or able to influence sb: *His opinions carry very little weight with his manager.*

● **cross** → bear/carry your cross
● **day** → carry/win the day
● **extremes** → carry/take sth to extremes
● **far** → carry/take sth too, etc. far
● **fast** → as fast as your legs can carry you
● **fetch** → fetch and carry (for sb)

cart /kɑːt; *AmE* kɑːrt/

put the ˌcart before the 'horse
put or do things in the wrong order: *Don't plan the menu before deciding how many people to invite — it's like putting the cart before the horse.*

● **upset** → upset the/sb's apple cart

carte /kɑːt; *AmE* kɑːrt/

ˌcarte 'blanche (to do sth) (*from French*)
complete freedom or authority to do anything you like: *The detective was **given carte blanche** to read any files he liked in his search for the murderer.*

> ❷ ORIGIN
> The French expression means 'blank paper' on which somebody could write their own conditions for an agreement.

carved /kɑːvd; *AmE* kɑːrvd/

● **stone** → be carved/set in stone

case /keɪs/

as the ˌcase may 'be
used to say that one of two or more possibilities is true, but which one is true depends on the circumstances: *There may be an announcement about this tomorrow — or not, as the case may be.*

be on sb's 'case (*informal*)
criticize sb all the time: *She's always on my case about cleaning my room.*

be on the 'case
be dealing with a particular matter, especially a criminal investigation: *We have two of our best agents on the case.*

a case in 'point
a clear example of the problem, situation, etc. that is being discussed: *Many of the students are from Latin America. Carlos is a case in point — he's from Colombia.*

case the 'joint (*informal*)
look carefully around a building so that you can plan how to steal things from it at a later time: *I saw two men here earlier. Do you think they were casing the joint?*

get off sb's 'case (*informal*)
used to tell sb to stop criticizing you or another person: *I'm doing my best, so get off my case, will you?*

in 'any case
whatever may happen or has happened; anyway: *I don't know yet who'll bring it or what time, but in any case you'll get your car back tomorrow.* ◇ *My mother came to stay so I couldn't go to the party, but I didn't really want to go in any case.*

(just) in case
so as to be prepared for what may or may not happen: *Somebody should stay at home in case John phones.* ◇ *'Did Clara say she'd phone?' 'No, but somebody should stay here just in case.'*

in case of sth (*formal*)
if sth happens: *In case of fire, leave the building by the nearest exit.*

in 'that case
if that happens or has happened; if that is the situation: *'I've made up my mind.' 'In that case, there's no point discussing it.'*

make out a case (for sth)
argue in favour of sth: *In her report, she makes out a case for giving more funds to the health service.*

● basket → a basket case
● open-and-shut → an open-and-shut case
● rest → I rest my case

cash /kæʃ/

cash 'down (*BrE*) (also ,cash up 'front *AmE, BrE*)
with immediate payment of cash: *He paid for the car cash down.*

cash in your 'chips (*especially AmE*)
1 finish a gambling game
2 (*slang*) stop what you are doing and leave: *The companies cashed in their chips and moved out of the valley.*
3 (*slang*) die

,**cash in 'hand** (*BrE, informal*)
if you pay for goods and services **cash in hand**, you pay in cash, especially so that the person being paid can avoid paying tax on the amount: *Most of his customers pay him cash in hand.*

,**cash on the 'barrelhead** (*AmE*)
if you pay for sth **cash on the barrelhead**, you pay in full at the time when you buy it: *If I give you cash on the barrelhead, can I get a discount?*

,**cash on de'livery** (*abbr.* **COD**)
a system of paying for goods when they are delivered: *Do I need to pay now or will you take cash on delivery?*

● hard → hard cash
● strapped → be strapped for cash

cast /kɑːst; *AmE* kæst/

cast/run an 'eye/your 'eyes over sth
look at or examine sth quickly: *'This looks great,' he said, casting an eye around the room.* ◇ *Could you just run your eyes over this report for me?*

cast your 'mind back to sth
think about sth in the past: *Cast your mind back to when you were a child.*

cast ,pearls before 'swine (*saying*)
give or offer valuable things to people who do not understand their value: *She decided not to buy the most expensive wine for dinner, thinking that would be casting pearls before swine.*

❷ ORIGIN
This expression comes from the Bible. *Swine* are pigs.

● die → the die is cast
● light → cast/shed/throw (new) light on sth

● lots → cast/draw lots (for sth/to do sth)
● net → cast/spread your net wide
● veil → cast/draw/throw a veil over sth

casting /'kɑːstɪŋ; *AmE* 'kæstɪŋ/

the 'casting couch (*informal, humorous*)
used to refer to a situation in which sb, especially a woman, agrees to have sex with sb else in order to get work in a film/movie, TV programme, etc: *the Hollywood casting couch for starlets*

castle /'kɑːsl; *AmE* 'kæsl/

● Englishman → a man's home is his castle **SEE** an Englishman's home is his castle

castles /'kɑːslz; *AmE* 'kæslz/

(build) ,castles in the 'air
(have) plans, hopes, etc. which are unlikely to become reality: *They talked about moving to Australia, but they knew they were really only building castles in the air.*

cat /kæt/

(play) cat and 'mouse (with sb) (*informal*)
(keep sb) in a state of uncertainty, being sometimes kind, sometimes cruel: *The police were playing cat and mouse with him; letting him feel safe in the hope that he would make a mistake and then they could arrest him.* ◇ *The authorities have been playing a **cat-and-mouse game** with the protestors.*

NOTE
This expression refers to the way a cat plays with a mouse before killing it.

(has the) cat got your tongue? (*informal*)
why don't you say anything?: *What's the matter — cat got your tongue?*

the cat's 'whiskers/py'jamas (*informal, often ironic*)
the best person, idea, thing, etc: *She thinks she's the cat's whiskers.*

let the 'cat out of the bag (*informal*)
make known a secret, usually without realizing what you are doing: *'Who let the cat out of the bag?' 'I'm afraid I did. I thought everybody already knew.'* ◇ *Nobody knew she had been offered the job until her husband let the cat out of the bag.*
OPP keep sth under your hat

(look) like sth the 'cat brought/dragged in (*informal*)
(look) dirty and untidy: *Where have you been? You look like something the cat dragged in!*

like a ,cat on hot 'bricks (*BrE*) (*AmE less frequent* **like a ,cat on a hot tin 'roof**) (*informal*)
very nervous: *He'll be like a cat on hot bricks till he gets his exam results.*

like the ,cat that got, stole, etc. the 'cream
very pleased or satisfied with yourself: *Ever since she won that prize, she's been like the cat that got the cream.*

not have a cat in 'hell's chance (also **not have a 'dog's chance**) (*informal*)
have no chance at all: *You haven't got a cat in hell's chance of buying a decent car for that amount.*
OPP a sporting chance

put/set the cat among the 'pigeons (*BrE, informal*)
do sth that is likely to cause trouble: *She told all the staff they would have to cancel their holidays, and that really set the cat among the pigeons.*

when the cat's a'way the mice will 'play (*saying*)
people enjoy themselves more and behave with greater freedom when the person in charge of them is not there

- curiosity → curiosity killed the cat
- fat → a fat cat
- fight → fight like cat and dog
- grin → grin like a Cheshire cat
- room → no room to swing a cat
- way → there's more than one way to skin a cat

catbird /ˈkætbɜːd; AmE -bɜːrd/

be in the 'catbird seat (*AmE*)
have an advantage over other people or be in control of a situation: *After his recent success, the president is sitting in the catbird seat.* ◇ *With prices falling dramatically, buyers seem to be in the catbird seat.*

catch /kætʃ/

catch your 'breath
stop breathing for a moment (because of surprise, fear, shock, etc.): *The magnificent view made us catch our breath.*

catch your 'death (of cold) (*old-fashioned, informal*)
(usually said to emphasize how cold it is) get a very bad cold: *Don't go out without your coat — you'll catch your death.*

catch sb's 'eye
attract sb's attention: *I liked all the paintings, but the one that really caught my eye was a Matisse.* ◇ *Can you try to catch the waiter's eye?* ▶ **'eye-catching** *adj.*: *an eye-catching advertisement*

catch sb in the 'act (of doing sth)
find sb while they are doing sth they should not be doing: *She turned round to catch him in the act of trying to run upstairs.*

NOTE
This expression is often used in the passive: *He was caught in the act of stealing a car.*

'catch it (*BrE*) (*AmE* **catch 'hell, 'get it**) (*spoken*)
be punished or spoken to angrily about sth: *If your dad finds out you'll really catch it!*

catch sb 'napping (*informal*)
find sb not prepared or not paying attention, and perhaps gain an advantage over them as a result: *Chelsea's defence was caught napping in the final moments of the game when Jones scored his second goal for Liverpool.*

NOTE
Nap means 'sleep', usually for a short time and especially during the day.

catch sb off (their) 'guard
happen when sb is not prepared: *The question caught him off his guard and he couldn't answer.* ◇ *Businesses were caught off guard by the sudden rise in interest rates.*

catch sb on the 'hop (*BrE, informal*)
find sb in a situation where they are unprepared: *The early start of winter that year caught many farmers on the hop.*

catch sb red-'handed
find sb while they are doing sth wrong, committing a crime, etc: *The thief was caught red-handed as she was emptying the till.*

❷ ORIGIN
This originally referred to catching a person with blood still on their hands after killing somebody.

catch some 'rays (*especially AmE, slang*)
sunbathe (= sit or lie in the sun, especially in order to become brown): *Let's go to the beach and catch some rays before the sun goes down.*

catch the 'sun
become red or brown because of spending time in the sun: *Look at the colour of you! You really caught the sun, didn't you?*

catch sb with their 'pants down (*BrE* also **catch sb with their 'trousers down**) (*informal*)
find or trap sb when they are unprepared or not paying attention: *After the devastating attack on its military bases, the country was determined not to be caught with its pants down a second time.*

- drift → catch/get sb's/the drift
- fancy → catch/take/tickle sb's fancy
- hold → catch/get/grab/take (a) hold of sb/sth
- raw → catch/touch sb on the raw
- sprat → (be) a sprat to catch a mackerel
- unawares → catch/take sb unawares
- Z → catch/get some Z's

catch-22 /ˌkætʃ twenti ˈtuː/

(a) **catch-22** ♦ **a catch-22 situation** (*informal*)
a difficult situation from which there is no escape because you need to do one thing before doing a second, and you cannot do the second thing before doing the first: *I can't get a job because I haven't got any experience, but I can't get experience until I get a job — it's a catch-22 situation.*

❷ ORIGIN
Catch 22 is the title of a novel by Joseph Heller, in which the main character pretends to be crazy in order to avoid dangerous situations in war. The authorities say that he cannot be crazy if he is concerned about his own safety.

catch-as-catch-can /ˌkætʃ əz kætʃ 'kæn/

,catch-as-catch-'can (AmE)
using whatever is available: The company took a catch-as-catch-can approach to IT training. ◇ The visit was arranged catch-as-catch-can.

❷ ORIGIN
Catch-as-catch-can was a type of wrestling (= fighting in which people hold each other and try to throw the other to the ground) in which most things were allowed.

catches /'kætʃɪz/

• early → the early bird catches the worm
• sneezes → if A catches a cold, B gets pneumonia SEE when A sneezes, B catches a cold

catch-up /'kætʃ ʌp/

play 'catch-up
try to equal sb that you are competing against in a sport, competition, business, etc: The oil company has spent the last couple of years playing catch-up. ◇ We were forced to play catch-up after a bad start to the season.

cats /kæts/

• rain → rain cats and dogs

caught /kɔːt/

be caught in the 'crossfire
become involved in a situation where two people or groups of people are arguing, and suffer as a result: When two industrial giants clash, small companies can get caught in the crossfire.

NOTE
Crossfire is the firing of guns from two or more directions at the same time.

• dead → sb wouldn't be seen/caught dead…
• short → be caught/taken short

cause /kɔːz/

be (all) for/in a good 'cause
worth doing, because it is helping other people: Most motorists seem to accept that the speed cameras are all in a good cause (= they help to keep people safe on the roads by stopping people driving too fast).

• lost → a lost cause
• root → the root cause (of sth)
• show → show good cause (for sth/for doing sth)
• stir → cause/create a stir

caution /'kɔːʃn/

throw caution to the 'wind(s) (often humorous)
stop caring about how dangerous sth might be; start taking risks: I decided to throw caution to the winds and buy myself a really expensive pair of shoes. ◇ He threw caution to the wind and dived in after the child. **OPP** tread carefully, warily, etc.

cave /keɪv/

• Aladdin → an Aladdin's cave

cease /siːs/

• wonders → wonders will never cease

ceiling /'siːlɪŋ/

• hit → hit the roof/ceiling

cent /sent/

• hundred → a/one hundred per cent
• red → not have a red cent

centre (BrE) (AmE center) /'sentə(r)/

• front → front and center
• left → right, left and centre SEE left, right and centre

cents /sents/

• two → put in your two cents' worth SEE put in your two pennyworth/penn'orth

century /'sentʃəri/

the ,turn of the 'century/'year
the time when a new century/year starts: He was born around the turn of the century.

ceremony /'serəməni; AmE -moʊni/

stand on 'ceremony (BrE)
behave in a very formal way: Come on — don't stand on ceremony! Start eating or the food will get cold!

without 'ceremony
in a very rough or informal way: He found himself pushed without ceremony out of the house and into the street.

cert /sɜːt; AmE sɜːrt/

• dead → a dead cert

certain /'sɜːtn; AmE 'sɜːrtn/

for 'certain
without doubt: No one can say for certain how the world's climate is likely to change.

make 'certain (that…)
find out whether sth is definitely true: I think there's a bus at 8 o'clock but you'd better call to make certain.

make certain of sth/of doing sth
do sth in order to be sure that sth else will happen: You'll have to leave soon to make certain of getting there on time.

of a certain 'age
if you talk about a person being of a certain age, you mean that they are no longer young but not yet old: The show is designed to appeal to an audience of a certain age.

• point → up to a (certain) point

chaff /tʃɑːf; AmE tʃæf/

• wheat → sort out/separate the wheat from the chaff

chafing /'tʃeɪfɪŋ/

• bit → be chafing at the bit SEE be champing/chomping at the bit

chain /tʃeɪn/

• ball → a ball and chain
• link → a link in the chain
• yank → yank sb's chain

chair /tʃeə(r); AmE tʃer/

• edge → on the edge of your seat/chair

chalice /'tʃælɪs/

• poisoned → a poisoned chalice

chalk /tʃɔːk/

(like) ,chalk and 'cheese (also **as different as ,chalk and 'cheese**) (BrE, informal)
very different: It's hard to imagine that Mark and John are brothers — they're like chalk and cheese.

• experience → chalk it up to experience SEE put sth down to experience
• long → not by a long chalk

challenge /'tʃæləndʒ/

• rise → rise to the occasion/challenge

champing /'tʃæmpɪŋ/

• bit → be champing/chomping at the bit

chance /tʃɑːns; AmE tʃæns/

as ,chance/,luck would 'have it (also **as ,chance 'has it**)
happening in a way that was lucky, although it was not planned: He asked whether we had a room to let and, as luck would have it, we did. ◇ I'm going to London myself tomorrow, as chance has it, so perhaps we can travel together.

by 'any chance
used especially in questions, to ask whether sth is true, possible, etc: Are you in love with him, by any chance?

,chance your 'arm (BrE, informal)
take a risk (especially when you are unlikely to succeed): He knew he wasn't likely to win the contest, but decided to chance his arm anyway.

a ,chance in a 'million (informal)
a very unlikely possibility: If you lost your ring on the beach, it's a chance in a million that you'd find it again.

'chance would be a fine thing (BrE, spoken)
used to say that you would like to do sth but will probably not have the opportunity: 'Are you going on holiday this year?' 'Chance would be a fine thing — I can't even afford a day trip to London!'

'no chance (spoken)
there is no possibility of that: 'Will he do it, do you think?' 'No chance!'

on the 'off chance (informal)
hoping that sth will happen, even if it is unlikely: I called at their house on the off chance that they'd let me stay, but they weren't at home.

(not) stand a chance (of doing sth)
(not) have a chance (of doing sth): You stand a very good chance of winning the prize. ◇ He doesn't stand a chance with her (= she won't want to have a relationship with him).

take a 'chance (on sth)
do sth without being sure of success: We took a chance on being able to get tickets on the day of the match, but they were sold out.

• cat → not have a dog's chance SEE not have a cat in hell's chance
• even → have an even chance (of doing sth)
• eye → have an eye to/for the main chance
• fat → (a) fat chance (of sth/doing sth)
• fighting → a fighting chance
• half → give sb half a chance (to do sth)
• ghost → not have a ghost of a chance (of doing sth)
• snowball → not have a snowball's chance in hell (of doing sth)
• sporting → a sporting chance

chances /'tʃɑːnsɪz; AmE 'tʃænsɪz/

(the) chances 'are (that) (informal)
it is likely (that): The chances are that he'll come if he can finish work on time.

take 'chances
do risky things: Take no chances: don't lend money to people you don't know.

take your 'chances (informal)
make as much use as you can of your opportunities: When the offer of a job in Singapore came, I accepted it. After all, you have to take your chances in life.

• blow → blow your chances
• fancy → fancy your/sb's chances

change /tʃeɪndʒ/

change 'hands
pass to a different owner: The house has changed hands several times.

change your 'mind
change your decision or opinion: He was intending to go to the party but now he's changed his mind and decided to stay in.

a ,change of 'heart
a change in your attitude and feelings, especially becoming kinder, more friendly, etc: The Government has had a change of heart over the proposed tax reforms and is now prepared to listen to public opinion.

change the 'subject
start to talk about something different, especially because what was being discussed was embar-

rassing or difficult to talk about: *I don't like talking about the war. Can't we change the subject?*

change your 'tune (*informal*)
change your opinion about or your attitude to sb/sth: *Tom used to say that parents worry too much about their children, but he soon changed his tune when he became a parent himself!*

change your 'ways
start to live or behave in a different way from before: *I've learned my lesson and I'm going to try to change my ways.* ◇ *It's unlikely your boss will change his ways.*

for a 'change
for variety; as an improvement on what usually happens: *We usually go to Cyprus on holiday but this year we've decided to stay at home for a change.* ◇ *Oh good! She's on time for a change.*

get no change out of sb ♦ **not get much/any change out of sb** (*BrE, spoken*)
get no/little help or information from sb: *If you need any help, ask Manuel. You'll get more change out of him than the others.*

a wind/the winds of 'change
an event or a series of events that has started to happen and will cause important changes or results: *There's a wind of change in the attitude of voters.* ◇ *Winds of change were sweeping over the country.*

❷ ORIGIN
The British Prime Minister Harold Macmillan used this phrase in a speech he made in 1960.

● chop → chop and change
● horses → change/swap horses in midstream
● leopard → a leopard cannot change its spots
● places → change/swap places (with sb)
● plus² → plus ça change (, plus c'est la même chose)

changes /ˈtʃeɪndʒɪz/

● ring → ring the changes (on sth)

chapter /ˈtʃæptə(r)/

,chapter and 'verse
the exact details of sth, especially the exact place where particular information may be found: *I can't give you chapter and verse, but I can tell you that the lines she quoted come from a Brecht play.*

❷ ORIGIN
This originally referred to books of the Bible, which are divided into chapters with numbered divisions called verses.

a ,chapter of 'accidents
a series of unlucky events or mistakes in a short period of time: *The reorganization of the company has been a chapter of accidents!*

character /ˈkærəktə(r)/

,in/,out of 'character
(of sb's behaviour, etc.) of the kind you would/would not expect from them; characteristic/uncharacteristic: *That unpleasant remark she made was quite out of character.* ◇ *'I'm sure it was Bill I saw from the bus. He was arguing with a police officer.' 'Well, that's in character, anyway!'*

charge /tʃɑːdʒ; AmE tʃɑːrdʒ/

get a 'charge out of sth (*AmE*)
get a strong feeling of excitement or pleasure from sth: *If you like horror movies then you'll get a charge out of this one.*

in charge (of sb/sth)
having control or command (of sth): *The teacher in charge of the children has to accompany them on the coach.* ◇ *Who's in charge around here?*

take 'charge (of sth)
begin to have control or command: *The Chief Inspector took charge of the investigations into the murder.*

● earth → cost/pay/charge the earth

charity /ˈtʃærəti/

,charity begins at 'home (*saying*)
people should look after their own family before they think about others

charm /tʃɑːm; AmE tʃɑːrm/

,work like a 'charm (*informal*)
quickly have the effect you want; work like magic: *I don't know what she said to him, but it worked like a charm — he's much more cooperative now.*

NOTE
A *charm* is a small object that is believed to bring good luck, or words believed to have magic power.

● third → third time is the charm SEE third time lucky

charmed /tʃɑːmd; AmE tʃɑːrmd/

lead/have a ,charmed 'life
have a lot of good luck, avoiding accidents or harm: *Carol appeared to lead a charmed life, with her successful career in television, money and a happy home life.*

Charming /ˈtʃɑːmɪŋ; AmE ˈtʃɑːrmɪŋ/

● Prince → Prince Charming

charts /tʃɑːts; AmE tʃɑːrts/

off the 'charts
(about a score, number, price, etc.) far higher or better than normal: *Gas prices are off the charts, making this an expensive winter for home heating.* ◇ *The response has been off the charts. Everybody loved it.*

chase /tʃeɪs/

chase your (own) 'tail
be very busy but in fact achieve very little: *In my first month at college I was continually chasing my own tail and being late for everything.* ▸ **'tail-chasing** *noun*

> NOTE
> If a dog or cat *chases its tail*, it runs round in circles trying to bite its own tail.

cut to the 'chase (*informal, especially AmE*)
stop wasting time and do or say the important things that need to be done or said: *Let's cut to the chase. How much is it going to cost me?*

> NOTE
> A film/movie often *cuts* (= changes) from a slow scene to a more exciting one, such as a car chase, to keep the audience interested.

give 'chase
begin to run after sb/sth in order to catch them: *We gave chase along the footpath.*

● wild → a wild goose chase

cheap /tʃiːp/

be going 'cheap (*informal*)
be sold at a low price: *These shirts were going cheap, so I bought two.*

cheap and 'cheerful (*informal*)
something that is **cheap and cheerful** does not cost a lot but is attractive and pleasant: *cheap and cheerful clothes/meals/rugs*

cheap and 'nasty (*informal*)
something that is **cheap and nasty** does not cost a lot and is of poor quality and not very attractive or pleasant: *The furniture was cheap and nasty.*

cheap at the 'price (*BrE*) (*AmE* **cheap at 'twice the price**)
worth more than the price paid, even though it is expensive: *I know £6 000 is a lot of money, but a great car like this is cheap at the price.*

not come 'cheap
be expensive: *Violins like this don't come cheap.* ◇ *Babies certainly don't come cheap* (= it is expensive to buy everything they need).

on the 'cheap (*informal*)
for less than the normal cost (and therefore of poor quality): *He got it on the cheap so I wasn't surprised when it broke after a couple of months.*

● life → life is cheap

check /tʃek/

keep/hold sb/sth in 'check
control sb/sth: *The disease is kept in check with drugs.* ◇ *It was difficult to hold their enthusiasm in check.*

● blank → a blank check **SEE** a blank cheque
● rain → take a rain check (on sth)

checks /tʃeks/

ˌchecks and 'balances
rules that are designed to control the amount of power, especially political power, that one person or group has: *These are the proposals for introducing a new system of checks and balances into the boardrooms of UK companies.*

cheek /tʃiːk/

ˌcheek by 'jowl (with sb/sth)
side by side (with sb/sth); very near: *If he'd known that he was to find himself seated cheek by jowl with his old enemy he wouldn't have attended the dinner.*

> NOTE
> The *jowl* is the lower part of the cheek and so the cheek and the jowl are next to each other.

turn the other 'cheek
make a deliberate decision to remain calm and not to act in an aggressive way when sb has hurt you or made you angry: *It's hard to just turn the other cheek when people are criticizing you unfairly.*

> ❷ ORIGIN
> This is a phrase used by Jesus in the Bible.

● tongue → with your tongue in your cheek **SEE** (with) tongue in cheek

cheeks /tʃiːks/

● roses → put the roses back in your cheeks

cheerful /'tʃɪəfl; AmE 'tʃɪrfl/

● cheap → cheap and cheerful

cheers /tʃɪəz; AmE tʃɪrz/

● three → (give) three cheers (for sb/sth)

cheese /tʃiːz/

● big → a big cheese/wheel
● chalk → as different as chalk and cheese **SEE** (like) chalk and cheese
● hard → hard cheese
● say → say cheese!

cheque (*BrE*) (*AmE* **check**) /tʃek/

● blank → a blank cheque

cherry /'tʃeri/

● bite → a second/another bite at/of the cherry **SEE** a bite at/of the cherry

Cheshire /'tʃeʃə(r); -ʃɪə(r); AmE -ʃɪr/

● grin → grin like a Cheshire cat

chest /tʃest/

ˌget sth off your 'chest (*informal*)
say sth that you have wanted to say for a long time and feel better because you have done this: *If something is worrying you, get it off your chest.*

chord /kɔːd; AmE kɔːrd/

strike/touch a 'chord (with sb)
say or do sth which speaks directly to sb's emotions or memories: *His war poetry struck a chord with people who remembered that period.*

Christmas /'krɪsməs/

● white → a white Christmas

chucking /'tʃʌkɪŋ/

it's 'chucking it down (*BrE, spoken*)
it is raining heavily: *They had to cancel the barbecue, as it started chucking it down.*

chunks /tʃʌŋks/

● blow → blow chunks

church /tʃɜːtʃ; AmE tʃɜːrtʃ/

● broad → a broad church
● poor → (as) poor as a church mouse

cigar /sɪ'gɑː(r)/

● close² → close but no cigar

cinder /'sɪndə(r)/

● burn → burn sth to a cinder/crisp

circle /'sɜːkl; AmE 'sɜːrkl/

‚circle the 'drain (*AmE*)
(usually used in the progressive tenses) if sth **circles the drain** it continues to become worse so that it may not be able to survive much longer: *It appears the governor's political career is circling the drain.*

● full → come/go full circle
● square → square the circle
● vicious → a vicious circle
● wheel → the wheel has come/turned full circle

circles /'sɜːklz; AmE 'sɜːrklz/

go round in 'circles
keep making the same points without making progress in a discussion, an argument, etc: *This discussion is going round and round in circles. Let's make a decision.*

run around in 'circles (*BrE also* **run round in 'circles**) (*informal*)
be busy doing sth without achieving anything important or making progress: *He has a tendency to run around in circles getting more and more worked up.*

circumstance /'sɜːkəmstəns; -stɑːns; -stæns; AmE 'sɜːrkəmstæns/

● force → force of circumstance
● pomp → pomp and circumstance

circumstances /'sɜːkəmstənsɪz; -stɑːnsɪz; -stænsɪz; AmE 'sɜːrkəmstænsɪz/

in/under the 'circumstances
used before or after a statement to show that you have thought about the conditions that affect a situation before making a decision or a statement: *Under the circumstances, it seemed better not to tell him about the accident.* ◇ *She did the job very well in the circumstances.*

in/under no circumstances
used to emphasize that sth should never happen or be allowed: *Under no circumstances should you lend Paul any money.* ◇ *Don't open the door to strangers in any circumstances.*

● reduced → reduced circumstances

claim /kleɪm/

‚claim to 'fame (*often humorous*)
one thing that makes a person or place important or interesting: *His main claim to fame is that he went to school with the President.*

● lay → lay claim to sth
● stake → stake (out) a/your claim to sb/sth

clam /klæm/

● happy → (as) happy as the day is long/as a clam/as Larry

clanger /'klæŋə(r)/

● drop → drop a brick/clanger

clap /klæp/

● eyes → clap/lay/set eyes on sb/sth

Clapham /'klæpəm/

● man → the man (and/or woman) on the Clapham omnibus **SEE** the man (and/or woman) in the street

clappers /'klæpəz; AmE 'klæpərz/

like the 'clappers (*BrE, informal*)
very fast: *We had to drive like the clappers to get there on time.*

class /klɑːs; AmE klæs/

be in a class of your, its, etc. own (also **be in a class by yourself, itself, etc.**)
be much better than any others of the same kind: *The winning competitor was in a class by herself.* ◇ *For originality, Leo's designs are truly in a class of their own.*

● league → not be in the same league/class/street
● touch → have, etc. a touch of class

claw /klɔː/

claw your way back, into sth, out of sth, etc.
gradually achieve sth or move somewhere by using a lot of determination and effort: *She clawed*

her way to the top of her profession. ◇ *Slowly, he clawed his way out from under the collapsed building.*

● red → red in tooth and claw

claws /klɔːz/

get your 'claws into sb
1 (*disapproving*) if a woman **gets her claws** into a man, she tries hard to make him marry her or to have a relationship with her: *He was perfectly happy before she got her claws into him!*
2 criticize sb severely: *Wait until the media gets its claws into her.*

> NOTE
> *Claws* are the sharp curved nails on the end of an animal's or a bird's foot.

clay /kleɪ/

● feet → feet of clay

clean /kliːn/

(as) clean as a 'whistle (*informal*)
1 (also **(as) clean as a new 'pin**) very clean: *She scrubbed the kitchen floor until it was clean as a whistle.*
2 if sb is **as clean as a whistle**, they are not involved in anything illegal: *I don't know why the police want to talk to me. I'm as clean as a whistle!*

a clean bill of 'health
a statement that sb is well or sth is in a satisfactory condition: *The doctor's given her a clean bill of health.*

> ❷ ORIGIN
> A *bill of health* was an official document given to the captain of a ship when leaving a particular port that said that nobody on the ship carried any disease or infection.

a clean 'break
a complete separation from a person, an organization, a way of life, etc: *She wanted to make a clean break with the past and start again.*

clean 'house (*AmE*)
remove people or things that are not necessary or wanted: *The new manager said he wanted to clean house.*

a clean 'sheet/'slate
a record of your work or actions that does not show any mistakes or bad things that you have done: *At the new school, you will start with a clean slate.* ◇ *They kept a clean sheet in the match* (= no goals were scored against them).

clean up your 'act (*informal*)
start behaving in a moral and responsible way: *He cleaned up his act and gave up the cigarettes and alcohol.*

come 'clean (with sb) (about sth) (*informal*)
tell the truth about sth, especially after lying or keeping it secret: *I'll come clean with you — I've been reading your mail.* ◇ *He finally came clean and confessed.*

have clean 'hands ◆ **your hands are 'clean**
not be responsible for crime, dishonesty, etc: *After years of corrupt government, we want politicians with clean hands.*

make a clean 'breast of sth
admit fully sth that you have done wrong: *He decided to make a clean breast of it and tell the police.*

make a clean 'sweep (of sth) (*informal*)
1 remove unwanted things or people: *The Prime Minister is expected to make a clean sweep of his advisers who don't support the new policy.*
2 win all the prizes, etc. that are available: *Kenyan athletes made a clean sweep (of the medals) in yesterday's competition.*

● nose → keep your nose clean
● show → show (sb) a clean pair of heels
● wipe → wipe the slate clean

cleaners /'kliːnəz; AmE 'kliːnərz/

take sb to the 'cleaners (*informal*)
1 make sb lose a lot of money, often by cheating them: *He's heavily in debt — his ex-wife took him to the cleaners at the time of their divorce.*
2 defeat sb completely: *Our team got taken to the cleaners.*

clear /klɪə(r); AmE klɪr/

clear the 'air
remove the causes of disagreement, fear, doubts, etc. by talking about them honestly and openly: *Mary had been bad-tempered with me for days, so in an attempt to clear the air, I asked her what the matter was.*

(as) clear as a 'bell
easily and clearly heard: *'Can you hear me all right?' 'Clear as a bell!'*

(as) clear as 'day
easy to see or understand; obvious: *Although it's written on the door as clear as day, people still don't realize that this room is private.*

(as) clear as 'mud (*spoken*)
not clear at all; very difficult to understand: *The instructions in the manual are as clear as mud.*
OPP crystal clear

clear the 'deck(s)
get ready for some activity by first dealing with anything not essential to it: *We had been doing some painting in the dining room, so we had to spend some time clearing the decks before our visitors came round in the evening.*

clear sb's 'name
prove that sb is innocent: *Throughout his years in prison, his family fought to clear his name.*

clear your 'throat
cough slightly, especially before speaking or to attract sb's attention: *The lawyer stood up, cleared his throat and began to address the jury.*

clear the 'way (for sth/for sth to happen)
remove things that are stopping the progress or movement of sth: *The ruling could clear the way for extradition proceedings.*

have/keep a clear 'head
be able to think clearly, especially because you have not had any alcohol, drugs, etc: *Don't give me any wine, I must keep a clear head for the meeting this afternoon.* **OPP** a thick head

in the 'clear (*informal*)
no longer in danger or likely to be blamed, punished, etc: *She told the police that Jim was with her when the burglary happened, so that put him in the clear.*

steer/stay/keep clear (of sb/sth)
avoid sb/sth: *I'm trying to lose weight so I have to steer clear of fattening foods.* ◇ *It's best to stay clear of the bank at lunchtimes as it gets very busy.*

- coast → the coast is clear
- crystal → crystal clear
- field → leave the field clear for sb
- loud → loud and clear
- plain → be clear sailing SEE be (all) plain sailing

cleft /kleft/

be (caught) in a cleft 'stick (*informal*)
be in a difficult situation when any action you take will have bad results: *I was in a cleft stick — my job was boring but I couldn't move to another firm without losing my company pension.*

clever /'klevə(r)/

'clever Dick (also **'clever clogs**) (*BrE, informal, disapproving*)
a person who thinks that they are always right or that they know everything: *Come on then, clever clogs, tell us the answer!* ◇ (*ironic*) *Some clever Dick has parked his car so close to mine I can't get out!*

- box → box clever

climb /klaɪm/

- bandwagon → climb/jump on the bandwagon

climbing /'klaɪmɪŋ/

be climbing the 'walls (*informal*)
be extremely bored, worried, etc: *It's too cold and wet to play outside, and the kids are climbing the walls with frustration.*

clip /klɪp/

at a fast, good, steady, etc. 'clip (*especially AmE*)
quickly: *Land prices will rise at a healthy clip.*

clip sb's 'wings
limit sb's freedom or power: *The new law was seen as an attempt to clip the wings of the trade unions.*

> **NOTE**
> This refers to cutting some of the feathers from a bird's wings so that it can no longer fly.

clock /klɒk; AmE klɑːk/

around/round the 'clock
for twenty-four hours without stopping: *The police watched the house round the clock but no one went in or came out.* ◇ *Her mother needs round-the-clock care and attention.*

put/turn the 'clock back
return to the past; return to old-fashioned ideas, customs, etc: *Sometimes I wish I could turn the clock back to my days as a student.* ◇ *These new restrictions on medical research will undoubtedly put the clock back (by) 20 years.*

run out the 'clock (*AmE*)
if a sports team tries to **run out the clock** at the end of a game, it stops trying to score and just tries to keep hold of the ball to stop the other team from scoring

- beat → beat the clock
- race → a race against time/the clock
- time → against the clock SEE against time
- watch → watch the clock

clockwork /'klɒkwɜːk; AmE 'klɑːkwɜːrk/

go/run like 'clockwork
(of arrangements, etc.) happen according to plan, without any difficulty or trouble: *The sports day went like clockwork, with every race starting and finishing on time.*

- regular → (as) regular as clockwork

clogs /klɒgz; AmE klɑːgz/

- clever → clever clogs SEE clever Dick
- pop → pop your clogs

close¹ /kləʊz; AmE kloʊz/

close the 'book on sth
stop doing sth because you no longer believe you will be successful or will find a solution: *The police have closed the book on the case* (= they have stopped trying to solve it).

close your 'mind (to sth)
be unwilling or unable to consider new ideas, proposals, etc: *His mind is closed to the possibility of reform.* ▶ **closed-'minded** *adj.* (*disapproving*): *She was accused of being closed-minded and intolerant of other people's opinions.*

close 'ranks
(of the members of a profession, group, etc.) co-operate closely to protect and defend each other: *Although the family quarrelled a good deal among themselves, they quickly closed ranks against any outsider who criticized one of them.*

- door → shut/close the door on sth
- ears → shut/close your ears to sb/sth
- eyes → shut/close your eyes to sth
- stable → shut/lock/close the stable door after the horse has bolted

close² /kləʊs; AmE kloʊs/

at ˌclose 'quarters
from/within a very short distance: *You have to examine the paint at close quarters in order to see the tiny scratches on it.*

close but no ci'gar (*AmE, informal*)
used to say that the answer, result, etc. is not quite
good enough

❓ **ORIGIN**
This expression comes from the old US custom
of giving a cigar as a prize in fairground games
of skill, such as shooting games.

close 'by (sb/sth)
at a short distance (from sb/sth): *Our friends live
close by.* ◇ *The route passes close by the town.*

close on ✦ close to
almost; nearly: *It's close on midnight.* ◇ *They made
a profit close to €20 000.*

a ,close 'shave/'call (*informal*)
a situation where a disaster, an accident, etc.
almost happens: *We didn't actually hit the other
car, but it was a close shave.* ◇ *Phew! That was a
close call — she nearly saw us!*

close 'to ✦ close 'up
in a position very near to sth: *The picture looks
very different when you see it close to.*

close to 'home
if a remark or topic of discussion is **close to home**,
it is accurate or connected with you in a way that
makes you uncomfortable or embarrassed: *Her
remarks about me were embarrassingly close to
home.*

come 'close (to sth/to doing sth)
almost reach or do sth: *He'd come close to death.*
◇ *We didn't win but we came close.*

keep a close 'eye/'watch on sb/sth
watch sb/sth carefully: *Over the next few months
we will keep a close eye on sales.*

run sb/sth 'close (*BrE*)
be nearly as good, fast, successful, etc. as sb/sth
else: *Germany ran Argentina very close in the final.*

too close for 'comfort
so near that you become afraid or anxious: *The
exams are getting a bit too close for comfort.*

- **bone** → close to/near the bone
- **cards** → keep/hold/play your cards close to your chest
- **heart** → be close/dear/near to sb's heart
- **mark** → be close to/near the mark
- **sail** → sail close to the wind
- **thing** → a close/near thing

closed /kləʊzd; *AmE* kloʊzd/

be,hind closed 'doors
in private; without the public being allowed to
attend: *Journalists protested that the trial was
being held behind closed doors.*

a closed 'book (to sb)
a person or a subject that you know nothing
about: *I'm afraid geophysics is rather a closed book
to me.* ◇ *Please let's not talk about her former life,
that's all a closed book now.*

a closed 'shop
a factory, etc. where only people belonging to a
certain union may work

- **eyes** → (be able to do sth) with your eyes shut/closed

close-run /ˌkləʊs 'rʌn; *AmE* ˌkloʊs-/

- **thing** → a close-run thing **SEE** a close/near thing

closet /'klɒzɪt; *AmE* 'klɑːzət/

come out of the 'closet
admit sth openly that you kept secret before, especially because of shame or embarrassment: *Homo-
sexuals in public life are now coming out of the
closet.*

- **skeleton** → a skeleton in the cupboard/closet

cloth /klɒθ; *AmE* klɔːθ/

be ,cut from the same 'cloth
be very similar in character, quality, experience,
etc: *Don't assume all the women in our family are
cut from the same cloth.*

- **coat** → cut your coat according to your cloth
- **man** → a man of God/the cloth

clothes /kləʊðz; kləʊz; *AmE* kloʊðz; kloʊz/

- **emperor** → the emperor's new clothes
- **emperor** → the emperor has no clothes

clothing /'kləʊðɪŋ; *AmE* 'kloʊðɪŋ/

- **wolf** → a wolf in sheep's clothing

cloud /klaʊd/

a cloud hangs over sb/sth
if a **cloud hangs over sb/sth**, sth bad has happened that will affect them/it for a long time: *He
still has a cloud of suspicion hanging over him.*

a (small) cloud on the ho'rizon
a sign of trouble or difficulty to come: *Although we
are making good profits there is one cloud on the
horizon — the government may increase taxes.*

every ,cloud has a silver 'lining (*saying*)
there is always something hopeful about even the
most difficult or unhappy situation

on cloud 'nine (*old-fashioned, informal*)
extremely happy: *She's been on cloud nine ever
since she heard the news.* **OPP** down in the dumps

under a 'cloud
suspected of having done sth wrong; in disgrace:
*He'd been stealing, so he was asked to resign, and he
left under a cloud.*

clouds /klaʊdz/

- **head** → have your head in the clouds

clover /'kləʊvə(r); *AmE* 'kloʊ-/

in 'clover (*informal*)
in comfort or luxury: *Since winning the lottery,
they've been living in clover.*

club /klʌb/

be in the 'club (*BrE, informal*)
be pregnant

- **join** → join the club

colours (BrE) (AmE colors) /'kʌləz; AmE 'kʌlərz/

- flying → with flying colours
- glowing → in glowing terms/colours
- nail → nail your colours to the mast
- true → your, his, etc. true colours

comb /kəʊm; AmE koʊm/

- fine-tooth → go over/through sth with a fine-tooth comb

combine /kəm'baɪn/

- forces → join/combine forces (with sb)

come /kʌm/

> Most idioms containing the verb **come** are at the entries for the nouns or adjectives in the idioms, for example **come a cropper** is at **cropper**.

as ˌclever, ˌstupid, etc. as they ˈcome
very clever, stupid, etc: *He's just about as mean as they come. He wouldn't even lend me a couple of dollars!*

ˌcome aˈgain? (*informal*)
used for asking sb to repeat sth because you have not heard or understood: *'This is Peter — he's a dermatologist.' 'Come again?' 'A dermatologist — you know, a specialist in skin diseases.'*

ˌcome and ˈgo
exist or be there for a short time and then stop or leave: *Newspapers come and go, and unfortunately the time has now come for this one to close.* ◇ *Feel free to come and go as you please.*

ˌcome, ˈcome ◆ ˈcome, now
used for asking sb to act or speak in a sensible or reasonable way: *Come, come! We all know that you were in Manchester the day the crime was committed, so you may as well tell the whole story.*

come ˈeasily, ˈnaturally, etc. to sb
(of an activity, a skill, etc.) be easy, natural, etc. for sb to do: *Acting comes naturally to her.*

ˈcome it (with sb) (*informal*)
try to impress, persuade or deceive sb in the hope of getting their attention, respect, sympathy, etc: *Your leg hurts? Don't come it (with me) — get out there and play with the rest of the team!*

come ˈoff it (*spoken*)
used to show that you do not believe sb/sth or that you disagree with sb: *'I can't afford a holiday this year.' 'Come off it, you've got plenty of money.'*

come to ˈnothing ◆ not ˈcome to anything/ much
not have a successful result: *The latest attempt to end the dispute came to nothing.* ◇ *They had a scheme for making a lot of money quickly, but it never came to anything.*

come to ˈthat ◆ if it comes to ˈthat
used when you are going to add sth to what has just been said: *It's been raining all day today. Come to that, it's been raining non-stop since Friday.*

ˌcome what ˈmay
whatever may happen: *My mother taught us to always tell the truth, come what may.*

to ˈcome
(used after a noun) in the future: *They may well regret the decision in years to come.* ◇ *This will be a problem for some time to come* (= for a period of time in the future).

comes /kʌmz/

when it comes to sth/to doing sth
when it is a question of sth: *When it comes to getting things done, he's useless.*

- goes → what goes around comes around

comeuppance /kʌm'ʌpəns/

get your comeˈuppance (*informal*)
receive a punishment for sth bad that you have done and that other people feel you really deserve: *I was glad to see that the bad guy got his comeuppance at the end of the movie.*

comfort /'kʌmfət; AmE -fərt/

- close² → too close for comfort
- cold → cold comfort

comfortably /'kʌmftəbli; -fət-; AmE -fərt-/

ˌcomfortably ˈoff
having enough money to buy what you want without worrying about the cost: *My brother is very comfortably off. He has a career in finance.*

- sit → sit comfortably/easily/well (with sth)

comforter /'kʌmfətə(r); AmE -fərt-/

- Job → a Job's comforter

coming /'kʌmɪŋ/

have it/that ˈcoming (to you) (*informal*)
be about to experience sth unpleasant, especially if you deserve it: *He's got a shock coming to him when he takes the exams and sees how difficult they are.* ◇ *He thinks he can break all the rules; but, believe me, he's got it coming to him one day.*

see sb ˈcoming (*informal*)
know that sb is innocent or stupid and decide to lie to them or cheat them: *'I paid €500 for it, and it doesn't work!' 'They must have seen you coming.'*

see sth ˈcoming
realize that there is going to be a problem before it happens: *We should have seen it coming. There was no way he could keep going under all that pressure.*
OPP not know what hit you

where sb is ˈcoming from (*informal, spoken*)
somebody's ideas, beliefs, personality, etc. that makes them say what they have said: *I see where you're coming from* (= I understand what you mean).

comings /'kʌmɪŋz/

,comings and 'goings
arrivals and departures; movement of people:
There were a lot of comings and goings at our neigh-bour's house all day.

command /kə'mɑːnd; AmE kə'mænd/

at your com'mand
if you have a skill or an amount of sth **at your command**, you are able to use it well and completely: *With four European languages at her command, she's thinking of working for the EU.*

be at sb's com'mand (*formal*)
be ready to obey sb: *I'm at your command — what would you like me to do?*

• wish → your wish is my command

commando /kə'mɑːndəʊ; AmE kə-'mændoʊ/

go com'mando (*informal, humorous*)
not wear underwear under your clothes

commas /'kɒməz; AmE 'kɑːməz/

• inverted → in inverted commas

comment /'kɒment; AmE 'kɑːm-/

,no 'comment
(said in reply to a question, usually from a journalist) I have nothing to say about that: *'Will you resign, sir?' 'No comment!'*

commission /kə'mɪʃn/

in/out of com'mission
available/not available to be used: *Several of the airline's planes are temporarily out of commission and undergoing safety checks.*

common /'kɒmən; AmE 'kɑːmən/

,common or 'garden (*BrE*) (*AmE* '**garden-variety**) (*informal*)
ordinary; not unusual: *...a pet shop full of snakes and spiders, and not a common or garden rabbit or hamster in sight!*

the common/general 'run (of sth)
the average or usual type (of sth): *This programme is better than the general run of television comedies.*

the ,common 'touch
the ability of a powerful or famous person to talk to and understand ordinary people: *Despite being one of the richest and most famous women in the world, she never lost the common touch.*

have sth in 'common (with sb/sth)
have the same interests, characteristics or experience as sb: *Come and meet my sister. I'm sure you two have got a lot in common.* ◇ *I have nothing in common with Mark, so I find it quite difficult to talk to him.*

in common with sb/sth
together with sb/sth; similar to sb/sth: *The hospital buildings, in common with many others in this country, are sadly out of date.*

• knowledge → be common/public knowledge

company /'kʌmpəni/

the 'company sb keeps
the people with whom sb spends time: *People disapprove of the company he keeps.*

get into/keep bad 'company
be friends with people that others disapprove of: *I'm worried about Joe — I think he's getting into bad company.*

in company with sb/sth (*formal*)
together with or at the same time as sb/sth: *She arrived in company with the ship's captain.* ◇ *The US dollar went through a difficult time, in company with the oil market.*

in good 'company
if you say that sb is **in good company**, you mean that they should not worry about a mistake, etc. because sb else, especially sb more important, has done the same thing: *If you worry about your relationship with your teenage son or daughter, you're in good company. Many parents share the same worries.*

keep sb 'company
spend time with sb so that they are not alone: *I've promised to keep my sister company while her husband is away.*

• part → part company (with/from sb/sth)
• present → excepting present company **SEE** present company excepted
• two → two's company (, three's a crowd)

compare /kəm'peə(r); AmE -'per/

beyond/without com'pare (*literary*)
too good, beautiful, etc. to be compared with anyone or anything else: *The loveliness of the scene was beyond compare.*

compare 'notes (with sb)
exchange ideas or opinions with sb, especially about shared experiences: *We met after the exam to compare notes on how well we had done.*

comparison /kəm'pærɪsn/

by com'parison (*written*)
used especially at the beginning of a sentence when the next thing that is mentioned is compared with sth in the previous sentence: *By comparison, expenditure on education increased last year.*

by/in comparison (with sb/sth)
when compared with sb/sth: *The second half of the game was dull by comparison with the first.* ◇ *The tallest buildings in London are small in comparison with New York's skyscrapers.*

there's no com'parison
used when comparing two people or things to emphasize that one is much better, etc: *'Who is*

the better player, Tom or Anna?' 'Anna is — there's no comparison.'

● pale → pale in/by comparison (with/to sth)

complexion /kəm'plekʃn/

put a new/different com'plexion on sth
change the way that a situation appears: *What the police officer had just told me put quite a different complexion on the mystery.*

compliment /'kɒmplɪmənt; AmE 'kɑːm-/

● backhanded → a left-handed compliment **SEE** a backhanded compliment
● return → return the compliment

compliments /'kɒmplɪmənts; AmE 'kɑːm-/

● fish → fish for compliments

compos /ˌkɒmpəs; AmE ˌkɑːm-/

be ˌcompos 'mentis (*from Latin, formal or humorous*)
having full control of your mind: *Are you sure she was fully compos mentis when she said that?*

concentrate /'kɒnsntreɪt; AmE 'kɑːn-/

ˌconcentrate the 'mind
make you think very clearly and seriously about sth: *Being informed that you are likely to lose your job unless you work harder concentrates the mind wonderfully.*

concern /kən'sɜːn; AmE -'sɜːrn/

a ˌgoing con'cern
a business or an activity that is making a profit and is expected to continue to do well: *He sold the cafe as a going concern.*

conclusion /kən'kluːʒn/

● foregone → a foregone conclusion

conclusions /kən'kluːʒnz/

jump/leap to con'clusions
make a decision about sb/sth too quickly, before you know or have thought about all the facts: *There you go again — jumping to conclusions. Wait till you hear my side of the story!*

condition /kən'dɪʃn/

● mint → in mint condition

confidence /'kɒnfɪdəns; AmE 'kɑːn-/

be in sb's 'confidence
be trusted with sb's secrets: *He is said to be very much in the President's confidence.*

take sb into your 'confidence
tell sb your secret plans, problems, etc: *She's the only person I've taken into my confidence about it.*

conflict /'kɒnflɪkt; AmE 'kɑːn-/

conflict of 'interest(s)
a situation in which there are two jobs, aims, roles, etc. and it is not possible for both of them to be treated equally and fairly at the same time: *There was a conflict of interest between his business dealings and his political activities.*

conjunction /kən'dʒʌŋkʃn/

in con'junction with (*formal*)
together with: *The police are working in conjunction with tax officers on the investigation.* ◇ *The system is designed to be used in conjunction with a word processing program.*

conjure /'kʌndʒə(r)/

● name → a name to conjure with

connect /kə'nekt/

connect the 'dots (*BrE also* **join (up) the 'dots**)
find or show the relationships between different things: *It's not hard to connect the dots between crime and poverty.* ▶ **connect-the-'dots** *adj.*: *a connect-the-dots article*

cons /kɒnz; AmE kɑːnz/

● mod → (with) all mod cons
● pros → the pros and cons (of sth)

conscience /'kɒnʃəns; AmE 'kɑːn-/

in all/good 'conscience
while being honest or just: *You cannot in all conscience think that is fair pay.*

on your 'conscience
making you feel guilty for doing or failing to do sth: *I'll write and apologize. I've had it on my conscience for weeks.*

● prick → your conscience pricks you **SEE** prick your conscience
● search → search your heart/soul/conscience

consequence /'kɒnsɪkwəns; AmE 'kɑːnsəkwens/

in 'consequence (of sth) (*formal*)
as a result of sth: *The child was born deformed in consequence of an injury to its mother.*

consideration /kənˌsɪdə'reɪʃn/

in conside'ration of sth (*formal*)
as payment for sth: *a small sum in consideration of your services*

take sth into conside'ration
think about and include a particular thing or fact when you are forming an opinion or making a decision: *The candidates' experience and qualifications will be taken into consideration when the decision is made.* ◇ *Taking everything into consideration, the event was a great success.*

● mature → on mature reflection/consideration

considered /kən'sɪdə(r)d/

your con,sidered o'pinion
your opinion that is the result of careful thought:
*In my considered opinion, 'Trainspotting' is one of
the best British movies ever made.*

• things → all things considered

conspicuous /kən'spɪkjuəs/

con,spicuous by your 'absence
not present in a situation or place, when it is obvious that you should be there: *When it came to
cleaning up afterwards, Anne was conspicuous by
her absence.*

conspiracy /kən'spɪrəsi/

a con,spiracy of 'silence
an agreement not to talk publicly about sth which
should not remain secret: *While no one was ever
convicted of the murders, it is widely believed that
there may have been a conspiracy of silence maintained by the victims' friends and families.*

contact /'kɒntækt; AmE 'kɑːn-/

• point → point of contact
• touch → lose touch/contact (with sb/sth)

contempt /kən'tempt/

beneath con'tempt
very shameful or disgusting: *Stealing the money
was bad enough. Trying to get someone else blamed
for it was beneath contempt.*

• familiarity → familiarity breeds contempt

content /kən'tent/

• heart → to your heart's content

contention /kən'tenʃn/

in/out of con'tention (for sth)
with/without a chance of winning sth: *Only three
teams are now in contention for the title.* ◇ *With
that defeat, Marshall has dropped out of contention.*

• bone → a bone of contention

contradiction /ˌkɒntrə'dɪkʃn;
AmE ˌkɑːn-/

a contra,diction in 'terms
a statement or description containing two words
or phrases that contradict each other's meaning:
*They call their project 'a peace offensive', which
seems to me a contradiction in terms.*

contrary /'kɒntrəri; AmE 'kɑːntreri/

contrary to popular be'lief/o'pinion
although it is not what most people consider to be
true: *Contrary to popular belief, many cats dislike
milk.*

on the 'contrary ♦ ,quite the 'contrary
used to emphasize that the opposite of what has
been said is true: *It's not that I don't like him — on

the contrary, he seems very pleasant.* ◇ *I don't find
him funny at all. Quite the contrary.*

to the 'contrary
showing or proving the opposite: *Unless you hear
from me to the contrary, expect me on Friday at
about 6 o'clock.* ◇ *She was convinced that John
was not capable of murder, in spite of all the evidence to the contrary.*

control /kən'trəʊl; AmE -'troʊl/

be in con'trol (of sth)
be able to organize your life well and keep calm:
*In spite of all her family problems, she's really in
control.*

be, get, etc. out of con'trol
be or become impossible to manage or to control:
*The children are completely out of control since their
father left.* ◇ *A truck ran out of control on the hill.*

be under con'trol
be being dealt with successfully: *Don't worry —
everything's under control!* **OPP** get out of hand

bring/get/keep sth under con'trol
succeed in dealing with sth so that it does not
cause any harm: *It took two hours to bring the
fire under control.* ◇ *Please keep your dog under
control!*

• purse → control/hold the purse strings

convenience /kən'viːniəns/

at sb's con'venience (*formal*)
at a time or a place which is suitable for sb: *Can
you telephone me at your convenience to arrange a
meeting?*

• earliest → at your earliest convenience

conventional /kən'venʃənl/

• wisdom → conventional/received wisdom

converted /kɒn'vɜːtɪd; AmE -'vɜːrtɪd/

• preach → preach to the converted

convictions /kən'vɪkʃnz/

• courage → have/lack the courage of your convictions

cooee /'kuːiː/

within 'cooee (of) (*AustralE, New Zealand*)
not far (from): *There's loads of cheap accommodation within cooee of the airport.* ◇ (*figurative*) *The
government is not within cooee of reaching the
growth targets.*

> **NOTE**
> *Cooee* is a noise a person makes as a way of
> attracting sb's attention.

cook /kʊk/

,cook the 'books (*informal*)
change facts or figures in order to make the situation seem better than it is or to hide the fact that
you have stolen money: *The two directors of the*

‚out for the 'count (*BrE*) (*AmE* ‚**down for the 'count**)

unconscious or in a very deep sleep, either because you have been hit very hard or are very tired: *After a whole day of walking around the city, I was out for the count!*

> **NOTE**
> This idiom refers to the rules in boxing. If a boxer is still down when the referee has finished counting to ten, he loses the game.

● last → at the last count

counted /'kaʊntɪd/

stand up and be 'counted
say publicly that you support sb or you agree with sth: *I think that people who disagree with the policy should stand up and be counted.*

counter /'kaʊntə(r)/

over the 'counter
goods, especially medicines, for sale **over the counter** can be bought without written permission from a doctor: *These tablets are available over the counter.*

under the 'counter
(of goods bought or sold in a shop) secretly or illegally: *Before the revolution, such luxuries were only sold under the counter.*

> **NOTE**
> This refers to illegal goods or goods that are only available in small quantities that are hidden, for example under the counter of the store, so that the police or general public cannot see them.

● bargaining → a bargaining counter

counting /'kaʊntɪŋ/

who's 'counting? (*informal*)
used to say that you do not care how many times sth happens: *I've been late for school three times this week — but who's counting?*

country /'kʌntri/

a country 'bumpkin/'cousin (*informal, usually disapproving*)
a person from the countryside who is not used to towns or cities and seems stupid: *He felt a real country bumpkin, sitting in that expensive restaurant, not knowing which cutlery to use.*

go to the 'country (*BrE*)
hold a general election: *The Prime Minister may decide to go to the country in the next few weeks.*

● free → it's a free country
● mother → the mother country

counts /'kaʊnts/

● thought → it's the thought that counts

couple /'kʌpl/

● two → in a couple of shakes **SEE** in two shakes

courage /'kʌrɪdʒ; *AmE* 'kɜːr-/

have/lack the courage of your con'victions
be/not be brave enough to do what you believe to be right: *You say that cruelty to animals is wrong, so why not have the courage of your convictions and join our campaign?*

pluck/screw/summon up (your/the) 'courage (to do sth)
force yourself to be brave enough to do sth: *I had liked her for a long time, and eventually I plucked up the courage to ask her out.* ◇ *I finally screwed up my courage and went to the dentist.*

take your ‚courage in both 'hands
decide to do sth very brave: *I saw him screaming for help far out from the shore, so I took my courage in both hands and swam out to save him.*

● Dutch → Dutch courage

course /kɔːs; *AmE* kɔːrs/

a course of 'action
a way of doing, managing, or achieving sth: *What is the best course of action to take?* ◇ *Two alternative courses of action are open to us: either we deal with him directly or we get the help of a lawyer.*

in/over the course of…
(used with expressions for periods of time) during: *He's seen many changes in the course of his long life.* ◇ *The company faces some major challenges over the course of the next few years.*

in the ordinary, normal, etc. course of e'vents, 'things, etc.
as things usually happen: *In the normal course of events we would not treat her disappearance as suspicious.*

of 'course
1 (also **course** *informal*) used to emphasize that what you are saying is true or correct: *'Don't you like my mother?' 'Of course I do!'* ◇ *'Will you be there?' 'Course I will.'*
2 (also **course** *informal*) used as a polite way of giving sb permission to do sth: *'Can I come, too?' 'Course you can.'* ◇ *'Can I have one of those pens?' 'Of course — help yourself.'*
3 used as a polite way of agreeing with what sb has just said: *'I did all I could to help.' 'Of course,' he murmured gently.*
4 used to show that what you are saying is not surprising or is generally known or accepted: *Ben, of course, was the last to arrive.* ◇ *Of course, there are other ways of doing this.*

of 'course not (also '**course not** *informal*)
used to emphasize the fact that you are saying 'no': *'Are you going?' 'Of course not.'* ◇ *'Do you mind?' 'No, of course not.'*

on 'course for sth/to do sth
likely to achieve or do sth because you have already started to do it: *The American economy is on course for higher inflation than Britain by the end of the year.*

run/take its 'course
(of a series of events, an illness, etc.) develop in the natural or usual way without being changed or stopped: *The doctors agreed to let the illness run*

its course, rather than prescribe drugs which had little chance of success. ◇ *We must allow justice to take its course.*

- collision → be on a collision course (with sb/sth)
- due → in due course
- matter → as a matter of course
- middle → follow/steer/take a middle course
- nature → let nature take its course
- par → be (about) par for the course
- pervert → pervert the course of justice
- stay → stay the course

courses /ˈkɔːsɪz; AmE ˈkɔːrsɪz/

- horses → horses for courses

court /kɔːt; AmE kɔːrt/

hold 'court (*often ironic*)
be the centre of attention in a group of people who find what you say interesting and amusing: *There was Professor Johnson, holding court as usual in the students' coffee bar.*

rule/throw sth out of 'court
make sth not worth considering; completely reject or exclude sth: *The committee ruled any further discussion out of court.* ◇ *My suggestion was ruled out of court because it was too expensive.*

- ball → the ball is in your/sb's court
- laugh → laugh sb/sth out of court

courtesy /ˈkɜːtesi; AmE ˈkɜːrt-/

courtesy of sb/sth
1 (also **by courtesy of sb/sth**) with the official permission of sb/sth and as a favour: *The pictures have been reproduced by courtesy of the British Museum.*
2 given as a prize or provided free by a person or an organization: *Win a weekend in Rome, courtesy of Fiat.*
3 as the result of a particular thing or situation: *Viewers can see the stadium from the air, courtesy of a camera fastened to the plane.*

do sb the courtesy of doing sth
be polite by doing the thing that is mentioned: *Please do me the courtesy of listening to what I'm saying.*

have the courtesy to do sth
know when you should do sth in order to be polite: *You think he'd at least have the courtesy to call to say he'd be late.*

cousin /ˈkʌzn/

- country → a country bumpkin/cousin

Coventry /ˈkʌvəntri; ˈkɒv-; AmE ˈkɑːv-/

- send → send sb to Coventry

cover /ˈkʌvə(r)/

cover all the/your 'bases (*especially AmE*)
consider and deal with all the things that could happen or could be needed when you are arranging sth: *Are you sure we covered all our bases on*

this? ◇ *We cover all the bases from creating a market for your business through closing the sale.*

cover your 'back (*informal*) (*AmE also* **cover your 'ass** ⚠, *slang*)
realize that you may be attacked or criticized for sth later and make sure you avoid this: *Cover your back by getting everything in writing.* **OPP** (lay/leave yourself) wide open (to sth)

cover your 'tracks
be careful not to leave any signs of sth secret or illegal that you have been doing: *He didn't want his wife to know he'd met an old girlfriend so he invented a story to cover his tracks.*

from ,cover to 'cover
from the beginning to the end of a book, magazine, etc: *I've read the newspaper from cover to cover, but I can't find any mention of yesterday's accident.*

under 'cover
1 pretending to be sb else in order to do sth secretly: *a police officer working under cover*
2 under a structure that gives protection from the weather: *We'd better get under cover or we'll get very wet in this rain.*

under cover of sth
hidden or protected by sth: *They hoped to get into the enemy fortress under cover of darkness.*

- blow → blow sb's cover
- judge → don't judge a book by its cover
- multitude → cover/hide a multitude of sins

cow /kaʊ/

have a 'cow (*AmE, slang*)
suddenly become very excited or angry: *My dad spent $500 on a new coat and my mom had a cow.*

- sacred → a sacred cow

cows /kaʊz/

till/until the 'cows come home (*informal*)
for a long time, or for ever: *You can talk till the cows come home, but you'll never persuade me to go with you!*

crack /kræk/

crack a 'joke
tell a joke: *He's always cracking jokes in class.*

the crack of 'dawn (*informal*)
very early in the morning: *We'll have to get up at the crack of dawn to be there by 9 a.m.*

crack the 'whip
use your authority or power to make sb work very hard, usually by treating them in a strict way: *What you need to do is crack the whip and make sure that they do the job properly.*

have a 'crack at (doing) sth ♦ get a 'crack at (doing) sth (*informal*)
make an attempt at doing sth: *Why not let me have a crack at fixing the kettle?* ◇ *When will we get a crack at the championship?*

- fair → a fair crack of the whip
- use → use a sledgehammer to crack a nut

cracked /krækt/

not all, everything, etc. sb/sth is cracked 'up to be (*informal*)
not be as good, interesting, etc. as people claim: *The food in this restaurant is not all it's cracked up to be.* ◇ *She isn't the brilliant skier that she's been cracked up to be.*

cracking /'krækɪŋ/

get 'cracking (*informal*)
start doing sth quickly: *We'll have to get cracking with the painting if we want to be finished by Friday.* ◇ *There's an awful lot to do, so let's get cracking.*

cracks /kræks/

● **paper** → paper over the cracks

cradle /'kreɪdl/

from the ˌcradle to the 'grave
from birth to death; throughout your whole life: *The new ministry was formed to look after citizens' social welfare from the cradle to the grave.*
▶ **ˌcradle-to-'grave** *adj.*: *Their conclusions are based on two cradle-to-grave studies conducted in Germany.*

● **rob** → rob the cradle

cramp /kræmp/

cramp sb's 'style
prevent sb from doing sth freely, or living as they want: *She thinks that being seen with her parents cramps her style.* ◇ *Are you sure you don't mind me coming along? I'd hate to cramp your style!*

cranny /'kræni/

● **nook** → (in) every nook and cranny

crap /kræp/

cut the 'crap (⚠, *slang*)
used to tell sb in an impolite way to stop talking about unimportant things or talking nonsense and get to the main point: *Cut the crap and tell me what you really think, OK?*

● **full** → be full of shit/crap

crash /kræʃ/

ˌcrash and 'burn (*AmE*, *slang*)
1 fail completely: *She shot to fame, then crashed and burned.*
2 fall asleep or collapse because you are very tired

craw /krɔː/

● **stick** → stick in your throat/craw/gullet

crawl /krɔːl/

● **flesh** → make your flesh creep/crawl
● **pub** → a pub crawl

● **skin** → make your skin crawl
● **woodwork** → come/crawl out of the woodwork

crazy /'kreɪzi/

like 'crazy/'mad (*informal*)
very fast, hard, etc: *running/working like crazy*

cream /kriːm/

the ˌcream of the 'crop
the best people or things in a particular group: *Only the cream of the crop of the year's movies are nominated for an award.*

> **NOTE**
> *The cream of something* is the best of a group or people or things.

● **cat** → like the cat that got, stole, etc. the cream

create /kri'eɪt/

● **scene** → create/make a scene
● **stink** → kick up/make/create/raise a stink (about sth)
● **stir** → cause/create a stir

creature /'kriːtʃə(r)/

a creature of 'habit
a person who always does certain things at certain times: *My grandfather is a real creature of habit — he likes his meals at the same time every day.*

credit /'kredɪt/

do sb 'credit ♦ do 'credit to sb ♦ be to sb's 'credit
show sb's good qualities; make sb deserve praise: *The event was arranged with a speed and efficiency that does you credit.* ◇ *Their manager, to her credit, was always strongly opposed to the pay cuts.*

have sth to your 'credit
have achieved sth: *At the age of twenty he already has several major victories to his credit.*

on the 'credit side
used to introduce the good points about sb/sth, especially after the bad points have been mentioned: *If you work for yourself you may not make much money. On the credit side, you will be completely independent.*

creek /kriːk/

up the 'creek (*informal*) (also **up shit 'creek (without a 'paddle)** ⚠, *slang*)
in great difficulty: *Make sure you look after the money and passports — if they get stolen we'll be right up the creek.*

creep /kriːp/

● **flesh** → make your flesh creep/crawl

creeps /kriːps/

● **willies** → give sb the willies/heebie-jeebies/creeps

crème /krem/

the ˌcrème de la ˈcrème (*from French, formal* or *humorous*)
the best people or things of their kind: *This university takes only the crème de la crème of school leavers.* ◇ *Naturally, only the crème de la crème have been invited to the wedding.*

crest /krest/

(on) the crest of a ˈwave
(at) the point of greatest success, wealth, happiness, etc: *He was fortunate to arrive in Hollywood when the film industry was on the crest of a wave.*
OPP (at) a low ebb

● ride → ride the crest of sth

crew /kru:/

● skeleton → a skeleton crew/staff/service

cricket /ˈkrɪkɪt/

it's (just) not ˈcricket (*old-fashioned, BrE, informal*)
it is not a fair or an honourable action or way of behaving

crimp /krɪmp/

put a ˈcrimp in/on sth (*AmE, informal*)
have a bad or negative effect on sth: *I'm sorry to put a crimp in your plans.* ◇ *The extra expense of moving can put a crimp on your budget.*

crisp /krɪsp/

● burn → burn sth to a cinder/crisp

crock /krɒk; AmE krɑːk/

a ˌcrock of ˈshit (△, *slang, especially AmE*)
something that is not true: *'He told me he was working yesterday.' 'What a crock of shit! I saw him shopping in town!'*

crocodile /ˈkrɒkədaɪl; AmE ˈkrɑːk-/

ˈcrocodile tears
an insincere show of sadness: *They never visited her when she was ill, but they came to her funeral and shed (= cried) a few crocodile tears.*

> **❷ ORIGIN**
> In the past, people believed that crocodiles trick people into approaching them by pretending to cry, and then eat them. Another belief was that crocodiles cry after eating somebody as if they are sorry.

Croesus /ˈkriːsəs/

● rich → (as) rich as Croesus

crook /krʊk/

● hook → by hook or by crook

crop /krɒp; AmE krɑːp/

● cream → the cream of the crop

cropper /ˈkrɒpə(r); AmE ˈkrɑːp-/

come a ˈcropper (*BrE, informal*)
1 fall (to the ground): *Pete came a cropper on his motorbike and ended up in hospital.*
2 fail badly, usually when you are expected to do well: *She's so confident she'll pass her exams without doing any work, but I've got a feeling she's going to come a real cropper.*

cross /krɒs; AmE krɔːs/

be/talk at cˌross ˈpurposes
(of two people or groups) misunderstand what the other is referring to or trying to do: *Mary and I spoke about Anne for a minute or two before I realized we were talking at cross purposes: I meant Anne Smith and Mary meant Anne Harris.*

cross a ˌbridge when you ˈcome to it ◆ cross your ˌbridges when you ˈcome to them
deal with a problem only when it happens and not worry about it before then: *'What will you do if you can't afford to run your car next year?' 'I'll cross that bridge when I come to it.'*

cross sb's ˈmind
(often used in negative sentences) (of a thought, etc.) come into sb's mind for a short time: *He intended to marry her and the thought never crossed his mind that she might refuse.* ◇ *It had crossed my mind that I hadn't seen her for a long time so I decided to ring her.*

cross my ˈheart (and hope to ˈdie) (*spoken*)
used for emphasizing that you are sincere when making a promise, or that what you say is true: *'Don't tell anyone else about this, will you?' 'Cross my heart, I won't.'*

cross sb's ˈpath ◆ our/their paths ˈcross
(we/they) meet by chance: *He never crossed my path, thank goodness. He was the last person I wanted to meet.* ◇ *Our paths crossed several times during the war but after that I never saw him again.*

cross the ˈRubicon (*formal*)
reach a point where an important decision is taken which cannot be changed later: *Today we cross the Rubicon. There is no going back.*

> **❷ ORIGIN**
> The *Rubicon*, was a stream which formed the border between Italy and Gaul. When Julius Caesar broke the law by crossing it with his army, it led inevitably to war.

cross ˈswords (with sb)
have an argument (with sb): *At the committee meeting, I crossed swords with Professor Smith over her department's overspending.*

have a (heavy) ˈcross to bear ◆ bear/carry your ˈcross
suffer the trouble(s) that life brings to you: *We all have our crosses to bear.*

This refers to the punishments used in the time of Jesus and described in the Bible.

● **dot** → dot the/your i's and cross the/your t's
● **fingers** → cross your fingers SEE have/keep your fingers crossed

crossed /krɒst; AmE krɔːst/

get your 'lines/'wires crossed ◆ have crossed 'lines/'wires (*informal*)
misunderstand each other: *I think we've got our lines crossed somewhere. I said Venice, not Vienna.* ◇ *We must have got crossed wires. I thought you were going to drive, not me.*

NOTE
This refers to telephone *wires/lines* that are not connected properly.

● **fingers** → have/keep your fingers crossed

crossfire /'krɒsfaɪə(r); AmE 'krɔːs-/

● **caught** → be caught in the crossfire

crossroads /'krɒsrəʊdz; AmE 'krɔːsroʊdz/

at a 'crossroads
at a stage where a decision has to be made: *He's at a crossroads in his career — either he stays in his current job and waits for promotion, or he accepts this new post in Brazil.*

crow /krəʊ; AmE kroʊ/

as the 'crow flies (*informal*)
(of a distance) measured in a straight line: *From here to the village it's five miles as the crow flies, but it's a lot further by road.*

● **eat** → eat crow SEE eat humble pie

crowd /kraʊd/

follow/go with the 'crowd (*often disapproving*)
do as everyone else does because you have no ideas of your own: *Dress in the way you like and try not to follow the crowd.* OPP lead the way

crown /kraʊn/

● **jewel** → the jewel in the crown
● **top** → to top/cap/crown it all

crows /krəʊz; AmE kroʊz/

● **stone** → stone the crows

cruel /kruːəl/

be ,cruel to be 'kind
use unpleasant methods because they are necessary to help sb: *I was worried about Katie getting too involved with Steve so I eventually told her about his drug addiction — you've got to be cruel to be kind sometimes.* OPP kill sb with kindness

crumbles /'krʌmblz/

● **way** → that's the way the cookie crumbles

crunch /krʌntʃ/

if/when it comes to the 'crunch (*informal*)
if/when the moment comes when sth must be decided or done, or a difficulty can no longer be avoided: *She was always threatening to leave him, but when it came to the crunch she didn't have the courage.*

it's 'crunch time (*informal*)
it is the moment when sth must be decided or done, or a difficulty can no longer be avoided: *It's crunch time for him. Either he makes a move now or gives up any hope of winning power.*

crust /krʌst/

● **earn** → earn a/your crust
● **upper** → the upper crust

cry /kraɪ/

cry your 'eyes out
cry a lot and for a long time: *My son cried his eyes out when we told him we couldn't afford a new bike.* OPP laugh your head off

,cry 'foul (*informal*)
complain that sb else has done sth wrong or unfair: *When the Labour party candidate didn't win the election, he cried foul and demanded a recount.*

NOTE
In sport, a *foul* is an action that is against the rules of the game.

cry 'wolf
repeatedly say there is danger, etc. when there is none, or ask for help when there is no need (with the result that people do not think you are telling the truth when there is real danger or when you really need help): *Is the economic future really so bad? Or are the economists just crying wolf?*

❷ ORIGIN
This refers to the traditional story of the shepherd boy who shouted 'Wolf!' just to frighten people, so that when a wolf did come, nobody went to help him.

● **far** → a far cry from sth
● **full** → in full cry
● **hue** → a hue and cry
● **know** → not know whether to laugh or cry
● **moon** → cry/ask for the moon
● **shoulder** → a shoulder to cry on
● **uncle** → cry/say uncle

crying /'kraɪɪŋ/

be a crying 'shame (*spoken*)
used to emphasize that you think sth is extremely bad or shocking: *It's a crying shame to waste all that food.*

a crying 'need (for sth)
a great and urgent need for sth: *There's a crying need for more roads, but at the same time the wildlife needs to be preserved.*

for ,crying out 'loud (*spoken*, *informal*)
used to express anger or frustration: *For crying out loud! How many times have I asked you not to do that?*

it's no good/use crying over spilt 'milk (*saying*)
it is a waste of time worrying, complaining or feeling sad about sth which is done and cannot be changed: *His decision to resign was disappointing, but it's no use crying over spilt milk. We need to concentrate on finding someone to replace him.*

crystal /ˈkrɪstl/

,crystal 'clear
very easy to understand; completely obvious: *After Anne was late for the third time in a week, her boss made it crystal clear that it must not happen again.* **OPP** (as) clear as mud

cucumber /ˈkjuːkʌmbə(r)/

● cool → (as) cool as a cucumber

cudgels /ˈkʌdʒlz/

take up the 'cudgels for sb/sth ◆ take up the cudgels on behalf of sb/sth (*old-fashioned*, *written*)
start to defend or support sb/sth: *The local newspapers have taken up the cudgels on behalf of the woman who was unfairly dismissed from her job because she was pregnant.*

NOTE
A *cudgel* is a short thick stick that is used as a weapon.

cue /kjuː/

(right) on 'cue
just at the appropriate moment: *The bell sounded for the beginning of the lesson, and, right on cue, the teacher walked in.*

take your 'cue from sb
be influenced in your actions by what sb else has done: *In designing the car, we took our cue from other designers who aimed to combine low cost with low petrol consumption.*

cuff /kʌf/

,off the 'cuff
without previous thought or preparation: *I don't know how you can stand up and give an after-dinner speech off the cuff like that.* ◇ *an off-the-cuff remark*

❷ ORIGIN
This expression refers to the fact that in the past, people sometimes used to write notes on their cuffs (= the end of a shirt sleeve at the wrist) to remind them what to say when they were speaking in public, etc.

culpa /ˈkʊlpə/

● mea → mea culpa

cup /kʌp/

not be sb's cup of 'tea (*informal*, *spoken*)
not be the kind of person, thing or activity that you like: *He invited me to the opera but it's not really my cup of tea.* **OPP** be (right) up your street

cupboard /ˈkʌbəd; *AmE* -bərd/

the ,cupboard is 'bare (*BrE*)
used to say that there is no money for sth: *They are seeking more funds but the cupboard is bare.*

❷ ORIGIN
This expression refers to a children's nursery rhyme about Old Mother Hubbard, who had nothing in her cupboard to feed her dog.

'cupboard love (*BrE*)
affection that sb shows towards sb else in order to get sth: *The cat seems especially fond of her, but it's just cupboard love. She's the one who feeds him.*

NOTE
Cupboard here refers to food, which is kept in a cupboard, so this idiom originally meant showing love to somebody in order to get food.

● skeleton → a skeleton in the cupboard/closet

Cupid /ˈkjuːpɪd/

play 'Cupid
try to start a romantic relationship between two people: *Martha was busy playing Cupid as usual, trying to get me to go out with her cousin Terry.*

NOTE
Cupid is the Roman god of love, shown as a baby boy with wings, carrying a bow and arrow.

curate /ˈkjʊərət; *AmE* ˈkjʊrət/

the/a ,curate's 'egg (*BrE*)
sth that has some good things and some bad things about it: *'Is it an interesting book?' 'It's a bit of a curate's egg, good in parts. The dialogue's often quite amusing.'*

❷ ORIGIN
This idiom comes from a story in the magazine *Punch*. A polite *curate* (= an assistant to a priest) is given a bad egg while eating in the house of a very senior priest. When asked if he likes the egg, he replies that 'parts of it are excellent'.

cure /kjʊə(r); *AmE* kjʊr/

● kill → kill or cure
● prevention → an ounce of prevention is better than a pound of cure **SEE** prevention is better than cure

curiosity /ˌkjʊəriˈɒsəti; *AmE* ˌkjʊriˈɑːs-/

curiosity killed the 'cat (*saying*)
used to tell sb not to ask so many questions, especially in reply to a question that you do not want to answer: *'Are you two thinking of getting married by any chance?' 'Now, now. Curiosity killed the cat!'*

curl /kɜːl; *AmE* kɜːrl/

- hair → make sb's hair curl
- toes → make sb's toes curl

curlies /'kɜːliz; *AmE* 'kɜːrliz/

- short → get/have sb by the short and curlies SEE get/have sb by the short hairs

curry /'kʌri; *AmE* 'kɜːri/

curry 'favour (with sb) (*BrE*) (*AmE* **curry 'favor (with sb)**) (*disapproving*)
try to get sb to like or support you by praising or helping them a lot: *They have lowered taxes in an attempt to curry favour with the voters.*

> ❷ ORIGIN
> *Curry* in this phrase means to groom (= clean and comb) a horse. The phrase was originally 'curry *favel*' (= a light brown horse that was thought to be clever and dishonest) and came to mean to try to please somebody who might be useful to you, especially by doing or saying things that you do not mean or believe.

curtain /'kɜːtn; *AmE* 'kɜːrtn/

bring/ring down the 'curtain (on sth) ◆ bring/ring the 'curtain down (on sth)
bring an end to sth: *The BBC has finally decided to bring the curtain down on one of its oldest television programmes.*

the curtain comes down on sth
if **the curtain comes down on sth**, it ends: *On Saturday the curtain came down on another Olympic Games.*

> NOTE
> *Curtain* in these idioms refers to the large curtain at the front of the stage in a theatre, which comes down at the end of a performance.

curtains /'kɜːtnz; *AmE* 'kɜːrtnz/

be 'curtains (for sb/sth) (*informal*)
cause the death of sb or the end of sth: *It'll be curtains for the business if the bank doesn't give us that loan.*

curve /kɜːv; *AmE* kɜːrv/

ahead of/behind the 'curve (*especially AmE, business*)
in advance of or behind a particular trend: *Our expert advice will help you stay ahead of the curve.* ◇ *We've fallen behind the curve when it comes to using the Internet.*

curveball /'kɜːvbɔːl; *AmE* 'kɜːrv-/

throw sb a 'curveball (*AmE*)
surprise sb with a problem, situation, question, etc. that they do not expect and which is difficult to deal with: *Just when you think you have it all under control, life throws you a curve ball.*

> NOTE
> In baseball, a *curveball* is a ball that is difficult to hit because it does not move in a straight line.

cushion /'kʊʃn/

- blow → cushion/soften the blow

cushy /'kʊʃi/

a cushy 'number (*BrE*)
an easy job; a pleasant situation that other people would like: *Sarah's new job sounds like a right cushy number — she only has to go to the office three days a week.*

> ❷ ORIGIN
> *Cushy* means 'easy' or 'pleasant' and comes from Hindi.

customer /'kʌstəmə(r)/

- tough → a tough customer/cookie

cut /kʌt/

> Most idioms containing **cut** are at the entries for the nouns or adjectives in the idioms, for example **cut corners** is at **corners**.

be cut 'out for sb/sth ◆ be cut 'out to be sth
be well suited in character or ability to a person, a job, or an activity: *She wasn't a great journalist. She was more cut out for television reporting.* ◇ *Why did he join the army? He's really not cut out to be a soldier.*

a cut a'bove sb/sth
better than sb/sth: *This is a cut above the average weekly magazine — it publishes very good articles and short stories.*

cut and 'run (*informal*)
make a quick or sudden escape: *She can't rely on Jason — he's the type to cut and run as soon as things get difficult.*

cute /kjuːt/

(as) cute as a 'button (*AmE*)
(usually used about a baby or a child, or sb/sth small) very attractive and charming: *Kate is four, and as cute as a button!*

cutting /'kʌtɪŋ/

(be at) the cutting 'edge (of sth)
(be at) the newest, most advanced stage in the development of sth: *working at the cutting edge of computer technology*

cylinders /'sɪlɪndəz; *AmE* 'sɪlɪndərz/

firing/working on all 'cylinders (*informal*)
using all your energy to do sth; working as well as possible: *The 24-year-old player feels that he is not yet firing on all cylinders.*

D d

dab /dæb/

be a dab 'hand at sth/at doing sth (BrE, informal)
be very good at doing sth: Ask Neil to do it — he's a dab hand at carpentry.

daddy /'dædi/

● sugar → a sugar daddy

daft /dɑːft; AmE dæft/

(as) ,daft as a 'brush (BrE, spoken)
(of a person) very silly

daggers /'dægərz/

be at daggers 'drawn (with sb)
if two people are **at daggers drawn**, they are very angry with each other: They've been at daggers drawn ever since he borrowed her car and smashed it up. **OPP** (as) thick as thieves (with sb)

> **NOTE**
> If you *draw* a weapon (= a gun, a dagger, etc.), you take it out in order to attack somebody.

look 'daggers at sb
look at sb very angrily but not say anything: He looked daggers at her across the room when she mentioned his divorce.

daily /'deɪli/

your daily 'bread
the food or money that you need to live: Each one of us has to earn our daily bread somehow.

daisies /'deɪziz/

● pushing → be pushing up (the) daisies

daisy /'deɪzi/

● fresh → (as) fresh as a daisy

dale /deɪl/

● hill → up hill and down dale

damage /'dæmɪdʒ/

what's the 'damage? (BrE, informal)
how much do I need to pay you?: Thanks for repairing the cooker. What's the damage?

dammit /'dæmɪt/

● near → as near as dammit

damn /dæm/

'damn the consequences, expense, etc. (spoken)
used to say that you are going to do sth even though you know it may be expensive, have bad results, etc: Let's celebrate and damn the expense!

damn it (all) (informal)
used for expressing anger, annoyance, etc: I've broken my pen again, damn it!

damn sb/sth with faint 'praise
praise sb/sth so little that you seem to be criticizing them/it: All he said was that I was 'capable'. Talk about damning someone with faint praise!

Well, the frame's nice!

Pablo couldn't help feeling that she was damning him with faint praise.

not care/give a 'damn (about/for sb/sth) (informal)
not care at all about sb/sth: Steve doesn't give a damn about anybody except himself.

damned /dæmd/

I'll be 'damned (old-fashioned, spoken)
used for expressing surprise: Well, I'll be damned! Isn't that Sarah Parker over there?

I'm/I'll be 'damned if... (BrE also **I'm/I'll be 'blowed if ...**) (spoken)
I certainly will not, do not, etc: I'm damned if I will lend any money to that lazy son of mine. ◇ 'Why is she so late?' 'I'll be blowed if I know.'

damnedest /'dæmdɪst/

do/try your 'damnedest (informal)
try very hard; make a very great effort: He was doing his damnedest to make me feel uncomfortable so that I would leave.

Damocles /'dæməkliːz/

● sword → a/the sword of Damocles

damp /dæmp/

a damp 'squib (BrE, informal)
an event, experience, etc. that is expected to be interesting or exciting, but is in fact boring or

ordinary: *In the end, the party turned out to be rather a damp squib.*

> **NOTE**
> A *squib* is a type of small firework. If it is damp, it will not burn properly.

damper /'dæmpə(r)/

put a 'damper on sth (also **put a 'dampener on sth**) (*informal*)
make an event, etc. less enjoyable or cheerful: *The news of my father's illness put a bit of a damper on the birthday celebrations.*

> **NOTE**
> A *damper* is a device in a piano that is used to reduce the level of the sound produced.

damsel /'dæmzl/

a ,damsel in di'stress (*humorous*)
a woman who needs help from a man, often to solve a practical problem: *When I got a flat tyre I had to wait for my boyfriend to come and help me, like a true damsel in distress!*

> **NOTE**
> *Damsel* is an old word for a young woman who is not married.

dance /dɑːns; *AmE* dæns/

,dance at'tendance on sb (*BrE, formal*)
do a lot of small jobs in order to please sb: *She always has an assistant dancing attendance on her.*

dance to sb's 'tune (*BrE*)
do whatever sb tells you to: *They are richer and more powerful than us so unfortunately we have to dance to their tune.*

- **lead**¹ → lead sb a (merry) dance
- **song** → make a song and dance about sth

dancing /'dɑːnsɪŋ; *AmE* 'dænsɪŋ/

- **singing** → all singing, all dancing

danger /'deɪndʒə(r)/

be on/off the 'danger list (*BrE*)
be so ill that you may die; no longer be very ill: *He's been extremely sick, but thankfully he's off the danger list now.*

dangerous /'deɪndʒərəs/

dangerous 'ground
a situation or subject that is likely to make sb angry, or that involves risk: *We'd be on dangerous ground if we asked about race or religion.*

dare /deə(r); *AmE* der/

Don't you 'dare (do sth)! (*spoken*)
used to tell sb strongly not to do sth: *'I'll tell her about it.' 'Don't you dare!'* ◇ *Don't you dare say anything to anybody.*

how 'dare you, etc. (*spoken*)
used for expressing anger or shock about sth that sb has done: *How dare you speak to me like that!* ◇ *How dare he use my office without permission?*

I dare 'say (*spoken*)
I suppose; it seems probable: *I dare say what you say is true, but it's too late to change our plans now.*

dark /dɑːk; *AmE* dɑːrk/

a dark 'horse (*BrE*)
a person who does not tell other people much about their life, and who surprises other people by having interesting qualities: *You're a dark horse! I had no idea you could play the piano so well.*

> **❷ ORIGIN**
> This phrase comes from horse racing. A *dark horse* was a horse that nobody knew much about and later came to mean somebody who wins a race unexpectedly.

in the 'dark (about sth)
knowing nothing about sth: *Workers were kept in the dark about the plans to sell the company.* ◇ *She arrived at the meeting as much in the dark as everyone else.*

keep it/sth 'dark (from sb) (*BrE, informal*)
keep sth secret: *I've got a new job, but keep it dark, won't you?*

a shot/stab in the 'dark
a guess; sth you do without knowing what the result will be: *The figure he came up with was really just a shot in the dark.*

- **leap** → a leap in the dark
- **whistle** → whistle in the dark

darken /'dɑːkən; *AmE* 'dɑːrk-/

not/never darken sb's ,door a'gain (*old-fashioned* or *humorous*)
not/never come to sb's home again because you are not welcome: *Go! And never darken my door again!*

darn /dɑːn; *AmE* dɑːrn/

'darn it! (*spoken, especially AmE*)
used as a mild swear word to show that you are angry or annoyed about sth, to avoid saying 'damn': *Darn it! I've lost my keys!*

darned /dɑːnd; *AmE* dɑːrnd/

I'll be 'darned! (*spoken, especially AmE*)
used to show that you are surprised about sth: *Well, I'll be darned! Isn't that Lisa over there?*

dash /dæʃ/

cut a 'dash (*BrE*)
impress others by your elegant appearance or behaviour: *She cuts quite a dash with her designer clothes and expensive car.*

- **bolt** → make a bolt/dash for it/sth
- **hopes** → dash/shatter sb's hopes

date /deɪt/

,out of 'date
not modern; not including the latest information: *This atlas is out of date.* ◇ *I'm afraid you must have been using an out-of-date catalogue.*

to 'date
up to and including the present time: *To date, we've received 40 bookings for the trip, so we're doing quite well.*

,up to 'date
1 possessing the most recent information, ideas, etc. about sth/sb: *Are you keeping up to date with the latest developments?* ◇ *I'm not really up to date on John and Mary. Are they still together?*
2 the most recent, modern or fashionable: *His kitchen is **bang up to date**. He's got all the latest technology in it.*
● blind → a blind date
● past → be past its sell-by date

daughter /'dɔːtə(r)/

● father → like father/mother, like son/daughter

daunted /'dɔːntɪd/

nothing 'daunted (*BrE, formal*)
confident about sth difficult that you have to do: *Nothing daunted, the people set about rebuilding their homes after the fire.*

dawn /dɔːn/

● crack → the crack of dawn

dawned /dɔːnd/

● light → (the) light dawned (on sb)

day /deɪ/

,all day and 'every day
without change for a long period of time: *I have to be active. I couldn't just sit around all day and every day now I've retired.*

all in a day's 'work
part of your normal working life and not unusual (especially of events or activities that are considered difficult or unpleasant): *For a nurse, calming the fears of anxious relatives is all in a day's work.*

any day (now) (*spoken*)
very soon: *The letter should arrive any day now.*

'any day (of the week)
used for showing that you prefer one thing or person to another: *I'd rather have him than his brother any day of the week.*

carry/win the 'day (*formal*)
win a contest, an argument, etc.; be successful: *It was a difficult match, but the New Zealand team finally carried the day.*

day after 'day
for many days, one after the other: *Day after day, she came and waited in his office, until finally he agreed to see her.*

day by 'day
all the time; as the days pass: *Day by day she grew more confident about the job.*

day ,in, day 'out
every day for a long period of time: *I drive to work day in, day out, and I'm getting tired of spending so much time travelling.*

the day of 'reckoning (*formal*)
the time when good actions, successes, etc. or bad actions, failures, etc. will be made known and punished or rewarded: *Tomorrow is the day of reckoning; the accountant will tell me what my profits were and how much tax I'll have to pay.*

don't give up the 'day job (*informal, humorous*)
used to tell sb that they should continue doing what they are used to, rather than trying sth new which they are likely to fail at: *So you want to be a writer? Well my advice is, don't give up the day job.*

from day 'one (*spoken*)
from the beginning: *This arrangement has never worked from day one.*

from day to 'day
1 with no thoughts or plans for the future: *They both live from day to day, looking after their sick daughter.*
2 if a situation changes from day to day, it changes often: *A baby's need for food can vary from day to day.*

from ,one day to the 'next
if a situation changes from one day to the next, it is uncertain and not likely to stay the same each day: *In this job, I never know what to expect from one day to the next.*

have had your/its 'day
no longer be as successful, powerful, etc. as you once were/it once was: *He used to be one of the world's top soccer players but now, I'm afraid, he's had his day.*

,if he's, she's, etc. a 'day (*informal*)
(used when talking about sb's age) at least: *She isn't forty! She's fifty-five if she's a day!*

in sb's 'day/time
1 when sb was most successful, famous, etc: *He had, in his day, been one of the greatest opera singers in the world.*
2 at the time when sb was alive; when sb was young: *In my grandmother's time, women were expected to stay at home and look after the children.* ◇ *In my day, nobody would have spoken to the boss like that.*

in 'this day and age
at the present time; nowadays: *It's surprising, in this day and age, to discover that there are still many homes which do not have telephones.*

make sb's 'day (*informal*)
make sb very happy: *Thanks for sending me those flowers. It really made my day!*

make a 'day of it (*spoken*)
make a particular enjoyable activity last for a whole day instead of only part of it: *Instead of going home when we've done our shopping, why*

don't we make a day of it and stay in town for lunch?

not be sb's 'day (*spoken*)
be a day when a lot of things go wrong for sb: *First I tore my jacket, then my car broke down. This is definitely not my day!*

'one day
at some time in the future or in the past: *One day I'd like to go to China.* ◇ *One day we decided to go to the seaside.*

'some day
at a time in the future: *Some day you'll realize what good parents you have.*

take it/things one ,day at a 'time (*spoken*)
not think about what will happen in the future: *I don't know if he'll get better. We're just taking things one day at a time.*

'that'll be the day (*spoken, ironic*)
used for saying that sth is unlikely: *'When I'm rich, I'll buy you a new car.' 'That'll be the day!'*

to the 'day
exactly: *It's ten years to the day since I first came to this town.*

to this 'day
up to now: *To this day I have not been able to find out anything about who my real parents were.*

- black → a black day (for sb)
- call → call it a day
- clear → (as) clear as day
- cold → in the cold light of day
- deed → your good deed for the day
- dog → every dog has his/its day
- dying → till/to/until your dying day
- end → at the end of the day
- evil → the evil hour/day/moment
- field → have a field day
- forth → from that day/time forth
- hair → a bad hair day
- happy → (as) happy as the day is long/as a clam/as Larry
- late → late in the day
- light → (see) the light of day
- live¹ → live to fight another day
- name → name the day
- nice → Have a nice day!
- night → day and night SEE night and day
- night → night and day
- order → the order of the day
- pass → pass the time of day (with sb)
- plain → (as) plain as day
- present → the present day
- rainy → save, keep, etc. it for a rainy day
- red-letter → a red-letter day
- Rome → Rome wasn't built in a day
- save → save the day/situation
- time → not give sb the time of day

daylight /ˈdeɪlaɪt/

,daylight 'robbery (*informal, especially BrE*)
a price or fee that you think is far too high: *£6 000 for an old car like this? That's daylight robbery!*

see 'daylight
begin to understand sth that you didn't understand before: *It was a long time before he finally saw daylight and realized what was going on.*

- broad → in broad daylight

daylights /ˈdeɪlaɪts/

beat/scare the (living) 'daylights out of sb (*informal*)
hit sb/sth very hard and repeatedly; frighten sb very much: *He said if I did it again he'd beat the living daylights out of me!* ◇ *I don't think I'll go to see that new horror film at the cinema. Jane said it scared the daylights out of her.*

days /deɪz/

your, its, etc. days are 'numbered
sb has not long left to live; sth will not last much longer: *Now that we're no longer getting any government support, the theatre's days are numbered.*

'one of these days
at some unspecified time in the future; before a long time has passed: *It's been nice talking to you. We must meet up again one of these days.* ◇ *One of these fine days you'll find that you have no friends left, and who'll help you then?*

(just) one of those 'days
a day on which unpleasant things happen: *It's been one of those days. I lost my keys and then I fell over running for the bus.*

'these days
at the present time, as compared with an earlier time; nowadays: *Divorce is getting more and more common these days.*

'those were the days
used for talking about a better or happier time in the past: *'I got a job as soon as I graduated.' 'Ah, those were the days!'*

- better → have seen/known better days
- born → in all my born days
- early → it's early days (yet)
- end → end your days/life (in sth)
- high → high days and holidays
- nine → a nine days' wonder
- old → the good/bad old days
- salad → your salad days

dead /ded/

cut sb 'dead
pretend not to see sb or not greet sb in order to show your anger, dislike, etc: *Jim has just cut me dead in the street. I'm sure it must be because I criticized his work yesterday.*

dead and 'buried/'gone
dead, especially for a long time; long past and forgotten: *Long after I'm dead and gone, you'll still be*

carrying on the same as you ever were. ◇ *Why bring up old disagreements that have been dead and buried for years?*

(as) dead as a/the 'dodo (*informal*)
no longer in existence; very old-fashioned: *Old business practices are as dead as a dodo in the computer age.*

> **NOTE**
> The dodo was a large bird that could not fly. It is now *extinct* (= it no longer exists).

(as) ˌdead as a 'doornail (*informal*)
completely dead

a dead 'cert (*informal*)
a person or thing that is certain to win, succeed, etc: *'Would you ever bet money on a horse?' 'No, not unless it was a dead cert.'*

> **NOTE**
> *Dead* here means *complete* or *total. Cert* is a short form of *certainty.*

a dead 'duck (*informal*)
a plan, an idea, etc. that has failed or is certain to fail and that is therefore not worth discussing: *The new supermarket is going to be a dead duck; there's no demand for one in this area.*

a dead 'end (*informal*)
a point where no more progress can be made: *Lack of further clues meant that the murder investigation came to a dead end.* ◇ *He was in a dead-end job with no hope of promotion.*

the dead hand of sth
an influence that controls or restricts sth: *We need to free business from the dead hand of bureaucracy.*

ˌdead in the 'water
a person or plan that is **dead in the water** has failed and has little hope of succeeding in the future: *Now the scandal is out, his leadership campaign is dead in the water.*

a dead 'letter
an idea, a proposal, etc. that is no longer valid, useful, etc: *The plans for a new school are a dead letter, now that we know there will be no students for it.*

a dead 'loss
a person or thing that is useless or a complete failure: *This television is a dead loss; the picture fades completely after five minutes.*

dead 'meat (*informal*)
in serious trouble: *If anyone finds out, you're dead meat.*

(in) the ˌdead of (the) 'night ♦ at ˌdead of 'night
in the quietest, darkest hours of the night: *She crept in at dead of night, while they were asleep.* **OPP** in broad daylight

ˌdead on your 'feet
extremely tired: *She'd just got back from a business trip and was dead on her feet.* **OPP** full of beans

a dead 'ringer for sb (*informal*)
a person who looks extremely like sb else: *She's a dead ringer for her mother.*

> **❓ ORIGIN**
> A *ringer* was a person or thing that pretended to be another person or thing. In horse racing for example, a ringer was a horse that was substituted for another in order to cheat in a race.

ˌdead to the 'world (*informal*)
deeply asleep: *Within two minutes of getting into bed, I was dead to the world.*

ˌdead 'wood (*informal*)
people or things that are no longer useful or necessary: *The management wants to cut costs by getting rid of all the dead wood in the factory. Fifty workers are to lose their jobs.*

> **NOTE**
> This refers to the parts of a tree or a branch that are dead and no longer produce fruit, etc.

over ˌmy dead 'body (*spoken*)
used for saying that you will do everything possible to stop sth happening: *'Mum, can I get a tattoo?' 'Over my dead body!'*

sb wouldn't be seen/caught 'dead... (*spoken*)
used to say that you would not do a particular thing because you would feel stupid or embarrassed: *I wouldn't be seen dead in a hat like that.* ◇ *She wouldn't be caught dead in a place like this.*

- **bang** → dead to rights **SEE** bang to rights
- **drop** → drop dead
- **flog** → flog a dead horse
- **kill** → kill sth stone dead
- **knock** → knock sb dead
- **wake** → wake the dead

deaf /def/

(as) deaf as a 'post (*informal*)
unable to hear anything: *You'll have to shout if you want her to hear you. She's as deaf as a post.*

fall on deaf 'ears
(of a question, request, etc.) be ignored or not noticed: *Our request for money fell on deaf ears.*

turn a deaf 'ear (to sth)
refuse to listen (to sth); ignore sth: *She turned a deaf ear to her husband's advice and took the job anyway.*

deal /diːl/

cut a 'deal (with sb) ♦ cut (sb) a 'deal (*business*)
make an arrangement with sb: *She cut a deal with the boss who allowed her to work on the project if she raised half the funds.*

deal sb/sth a 'blow ♦ deal a blow to sb/sth
be a shock for sb; make sth fail, etc: *The death of her father dealt her a terrible blow.* ◇ *Losing his job dealt a blow to his hopes of buying his own house.*

a raw/rough 'deal
unfair treatment: *Many old people feel they are getting a raw deal from the state: they pay money towards a pension all their working life but discover it isn't worth much when they retire.*

- **big** → big deal

- **big** → no big deal
- **done** → a done deal
- **strike** → strike a bargain/deal (with sb)
- **wheel** → wheel and deal

dear /dɪə(r); *AmE* dɪr/

dear me ♦ (dear,) oh dear
used for expressing worry, sympathy, concern, etc: *Dear me! It's started to rain and I've just hung out the washing!*

for dear 'life ♦ for your 'life
because you are in danger: *Run for your life! A tiger has escaped from the circus! ◇ They were clinging for dear life to the edge of the rock.*

hold sb/sth 'dear (*formal*)
feel that sb/sth is of great value: *He laughed at the ideas they held dear.*

- **heart** → be close/dear/near to sb's heart
- **old** → an old dear

dearest /'dɪərɪst; *AmE* 'dɪr-/

- **nearest** → your nearest and dearest

death /deθ/

at death's 'door (*often ironic*)
so ill that you might die: *Come on, get out of bed. You're not at death's door yet!*

be the 'death of sb (*often humorous*)
cause sb a lot of harm or worry: *You children are so badly behaved! You'll be the death of me one day!*

be ,in at the 'death/'kill
be there when sth ends or fails: *I was in at the kill when she finally lost her job.*

,do sth to 'death (*informal*)
talk or write about a subject, or perform a play, etc. so often that it is no longer interesting: *Some people think that the theme of romantic love has been done to death in poetry.*

like death warmed 'up (*BrE*) (*AmE* **like death warmed 'over**) (*informal*)
very ill or tired: *I feel like death warmed up this morning, but I'm going to go to work anyway. ◇ You should really go home to bed. You look like death warmed up.*

put sb to 'death
kill sb as a punishment; execute sb: *The prisoner will be put to death at dawn.*

to 'death
extremely; very much: *to be bored/frightened/scared/worried to death ◇ I'm **sick to death** of your endless criticism.*

to the 'death
until sb dies or is defeated: *There was a fight to the death between two men armed with knives.*

,work yourself/sb to 'death (*informal*)
work, or make sb work, very hard: *That company is working him to death. ◇ She works herself to death and nobody ever thanks her for anything.*

- **catch** → catch your death (of cold)
- **dice** → dice with death

- **die** → die a/the death
- **fate** → a fate worse than death
- **flog** → flog sth to death
- **grim** → hang on/hold on (to sb/sth) like grim death
- **kiss** → the kiss of death
- **life** → (a matter of) life and/or death
- **life** → life after death
- **sign** → sign your own death warrant
- **sound** → sound the death knell of sth
- **sudden** → sudden death
- **tickled** → be tickled to death SEE be tickled pink

debt /det/

be in sb's 'debt (*formal*)
be very grateful to sb because they have helped you: *After my divorce Ann was the only one prepared to listen to my problems, and I am forever in her debt.*

,get/,run into 'debt
begin to owe money: *After she lost her job, she began to run into debt.*

deck /dek/

- **clear** → clear the deck(s)
- **hands** → all hands on deck
- **hit** → hit the deck

deckchairs /'dektʃeərz; *AmE* -tʃerz/

- **rearrange** → rearrange the deckchairs on the Titanic

deed /diːd/

your good deed for the 'day
a helpful, kind thing that you do: *Why don't you do your good deed for the day and cook me dinner?*

deep /diːp/

deep 'down (*informal*)
in your most private thoughts; in reality rather than in appearance: *She's very generous deep down, but this only comes out when you get to know her. ◇ He seems very confident but deep down I think he's quite shy.*

go/run 'deep
(of emotions, beliefs, etc.) be felt in a strong way, especially for a long time: *Dignity and pride run deep in this community.*

go off the 'deep end (*informal*)
suddenly become very angry or emotional: *Don't tell your father that you lost the money — he'll just go off the deep end.*

in deep 'water(s)
in trouble or difficulty: *She was getting into deep water when she tried to argue that murder is sometimes justified for political reasons.*

jump in/be thrown in at the 'deep end (*informal*)
try to do sth difficult without help when you are not prepared or know very little about it: *On the first day of her new teaching job, she was thrown in at the deep end and was told to teach the most badly-behaved class. ◇ I didn't know anything*

about business when I started. I just had to jump in at the deep end.

> **NOTE**
> This phrase refers to the deep end of a swimming pool, where it is too deep to stand.

- **devil** → between the devil and the deep blue sea
- **dig** → dig deep
- **shit** → be in deep shit SEE be in the shit
- **still** → still waters run deep

deer /dɪə(r); *AmE* dɪr/

(be caught/freeze like) a deer in the 'headlights (also **(be caught like) a rabbit in the 'headlights**)
used to describe sb who appears so frightened that they cannot think clearly and do not know what to do or say: *The senator was caught like a deer in the headlights in a TV interview.* ◇ *a deer-in-the-headlights look*

default /dɪ'fɔːlt/

by de'fault
1 a game or competition can be won **by default** if there are no other competitors: *The other team didn't even turn up, so we won by default.*
2 if sth happens **by default**, it happens because you have not made any other decision or choices which would make things happen differently: *It was never my ambition to get into teaching. I became a teacher more by default than by choice.*

in de'fault of sth (*formal*)
because of a lack of sth: *They accepted what he had said in default of any evidence to disprove it.*

defensive /dɪ'fensɪv/

on/onto the de'fensive
acting in a way that shows that you expect to be attacked or criticized; having to defend yourself: *Their questions about the money put her on the defensive.* ◇ *Warnings of an enemy attack forced the troops onto the defensive.* **OPP** on the offensive

degree /dɪ'griː/

- **third** → (give sb) the third degree
- **nth** → to the nth degree

degrees /dɪ'griːz/

by de'grees
little by little; gradually: *The country's economy won't improve straight away, but will only get better by degrees.*

déjà /'deɪʒɑː/

ˌdéjà 'vu (*from French*)
the feeling that you have previously experienced sth which is happening to you now: *I had a strong sense of déjà vu as I walked into the room.*

> **NOTE**
> The meaning of the French phrase is 'already seen'.

deliver /dɪ'lɪvə(r)/

- **goods** → come up with/deliver/produce the goods

delivered /dɪ'lɪvəd; *AmE* dɪ'lɪvərd/

- **signed** → signed, sealed and delivered

delivery /dɪ'lɪvəri/

- **cash** → cash on delivery

delusions /dɪ'luːʒnz/

delusions of 'grandeur (*often humorous*)
a belief that you are more important than you really are: *He's been suffering from delusions of grandeur ever since he became manager.*

demand /dɪ'mɑːnd/

in de'mand
wanted by many people; popular: *Well-qualified young people with experience in marketing are very much in demand at the moment.*

on de'mand
done or happening whenever sb asks: *Feed the baby on demand.*

- **popular** → by popular demand

demon /'diːmən/

the demon 'drink (*BrE, humorous*)
alcoholic drink: *It was the demon drink that made me act in that way.*

demur /dɪ'mɜː(r)/

without de'mur (*formal*)
without objecting or hesitating: *They accepted without demur.*

den /den/

a den of i'niquity/'vice (*disapproving*)
a place where people do bad things: *She thinks that just because we sit around smoking and drinking beer the club must be a real den of iniquity.*

- **lion** → the lion's den

dent /dent/

make a 'dent/'hole in sth (*informal*)
reduce sth: *Having to pay out unexpectedly for car repairs made a big hole in my savings.* ◇ *The embarrassing stories about his past made quite a dent in his reputation.*

department /dɪ'pɑːtmənt; *AmE* -'pɑːrt-/

be sb's department (*spoken*)
be sth that sb is responsible for or knows a lot about: *Don't ask me about it — that's Helen's department, not mine.*

departure /dɪ'pɑːtʃə(r); *AmE* -'pɑːrt-/

- **point** → a point of departure

depends /dɪˈpendz/

it/that (all) deˈpends (*informal*)
perhaps; possibly: *'Would you marry him if he asked you to?' 'I might. It all depends.'* ◇ *'But is it right to send people to prison?' 'It depends what you mean by right!'*

depth /depθ/

ˌin ˈdepth
thoroughly: *The report treats the subject of homelessness in some depth.* ◇ *an in-depth analysis, discussion, etc.*

out of your ˈdepth (*informal*)
in a situation that is too difficult for you to deal with or understand: *When they start talking about economics, I'm out of my depth.*

depths /depθs/

in the depths of sth
at the worst or most unpleasant stage of sth: *in the depths of despair, poverty, depression, etc.* ◇ *in the depths of winter*

• **plumb** → plumb the depths of sth

description /dɪˈskrɪpʃn/

• **beggar** → beggar belief/description

deserting /dɪˈzɜːtɪŋ; AmE dɪˈzɜːrtɪŋ/

• **sinking** → (like rats) deserting/leaving a sinking ship

deserts /dɪˈzɜːts; AmE dɪˈzɜːrts/

get your (just) deˈserts
get what you deserve, especially when it is sth bad: *The family of the victim said that the killer had got his just deserts when he was jailed for life.*

> **NOTE**
> *Deserts* is an old-fashioned word for the rewards or punishments that somebody deserves.

deserve /dɪˈzɜːv; AmE dɪˈzɜːrv/

ˌget what you deˈserve ♦ deˌserve all/everyˈthing you ˈget (*informal*)
used to say that you think sb has earned the bad things that happen to them: *I'm not sorry he's in prison. In my opinion, he got what he deserved.*

deserves /dɪˈzɜːvz; AmE dɪˈzɜːrvz/

he, she, etc. deˌserves a ˈmedal (*spoken*)
used to say that you admire sb because they have done sth difficult or unpleasant: *You deserve a medal for what you've done for him over the years.*

ˌone good ˌturn deserves aˈnother (*saying*)
if sb helps you with sth, you should help them in return

design /dɪˈzaɪn/

• **accident** → (whether) by accident or design

designs /dɪˈzaɪnz/

have deˈsigns on sb/sth
intend to take sb/sth for yourself, for example a job or a person who you find sexually attractive: *Several people have got designs on the office manager's post.* ◇ *I think she's got designs on you, Peter.*

desired /dɪˈzaɪəd; AmE -ˈzaɪərd/

leave a lot, much, etc. to be deˈsired
not be good enough: *Your standard of work has gone down. In fact it leaves a great deal to be desired.* ◇ *The acting in some of those early movies left much to be desired.*

detail /ˈdiːteɪl (AmE also) dɪˈteɪl/

go into ˈdetail(s)
explain sth fully: *I can't go into details now; it would take too long.*

• **devil** → the devil is in the detail(s)

details /ˈdiːteɪlz; AmE also dɪˈteɪlz/

• **devil** → the devil is in the detail(s)

determined /dɪˈtɜːmɪnd; AmE -ˈtɜːrm-/

• **bound** → bound and determined

devices /dɪˈvaɪsɪz/

leave sb to their own deˈvices
leave sb to do sth without your help, or to spend their time as they like: *I've explained everything to him. Now I'm leaving him to his own devices, and we'll see how he manages.* ◇ *The children were usually left to their own devices in the summer holidays.*

devil /ˈdevl/

be a ˈdevil (*BrE*)
said to encourage sb to do sth that they are not sure about doing: *Go on, be a devil, Catherine! Buy yourself some new clothes for once!*

between the ˌdevil and the deep blue ˈsea
in a situation where you have to choose between two things that are equally bad: *In this situation, the government finds itself caught between the devil and the deep blue sea.*

the ˈdevil (*old-fashioned*)
very difficult or unpleasant: *These berries are the devil to pick because they're so small.*

the ˌdevil is in the ˈdetail(s)
used to say that it is the small individual parts of a task, a written document, a design, etc. that may cause most problems and difficulties: *In any negotiation, the devil is in the detail.*

the ˌdevil looks after his ˈown (*saying*)
bad people often seem to have good luck

the devil makes work for idle ˈhands (*saying*)
people who do not have enough to do often start to do wrong: *She blamed the crimes on the local jobless teenagers. 'The devil makes work for idle hands,' she would say.*

a/the 'devil of a job, nuisance, fellow, etc.
(*old-fashioned*)
a difficult or an unpleasant example of sth: *We're
going to have a devil of a job getting the roots of that
tree out of the ground.*

a/the devil's 'advocate
a person who argues against sth, even though
they really agree with it, just to test the arguments
for it: *Helen doesn't really think that women
shouldn't go out to work. She just likes to* **play devil's advocate.**

(the) devil take the 'hindmost (*saying*)
everyone should look after themselves and not
care about others: *I like the way people here always
queue up. Back home we just push and shove, and
the devil take the hindmost!*

go to the 'devil! (*old-fashioned, spoken*)
used, in an unfriendly way, to tell sb to go away

like the 'devil (*old-fashioned, informal*)
very fast, hard, etc: *We had to work like the devil to
be finished on time.* ◇ *I ran like the devil, but I still
missed the bus.*

speak/talk of the 'devil (*informal, saying*)
said when sb who has just been mentioned
appears unexpectedly: *'I haven't seen Leo for a
while.' 'Well, speak of the devil, here he is!'*

who, what, where, etc. the 'devil...
(*old-fashioned, informal*)
used in questions for showing that you are
annoyed or surprised: *Who the devil are you?*
◇ *Where the devil have I put my glasses?*

● **better** → better the devil you know (than the devil you
don't)
● **luck** → the luck of the devil
● **pay** → hell/the devil to pay

devoured /dɪˈvaʊəd; *AmE* dɪˈvaʊərd/

be devoured by sth
be filled with a strong emotion that seems to control you: *She was devoured by envy and hatred.*

diamond /ˈdaɪəmənd/

● **rough** → a diamond in the rough SEE a rough diamond

dibs /dɪbz/

● **bags** → dibs on... SEE bags (I)...

dice /daɪs/

the ˌdice are loaded aˈgainst sb
a person has little chance of succeeding in sth,
perhaps for unfair reasons: *If you apply for a job
when you're over 40, the dice are loaded against
you.*

> ❷ ORIGIN
> This phrase refers to putting a piece of lead
> (= a heavy metal) inside a dice so that it
> always falls in a particular way.

ˌdice with 'death (*informal*)
risk your life by doing sth very dangerous: *Racing
drivers dice with death every time they race.*

> NOTE
> *Dice* means *play dice* or *gamble*.

no 'dice (*spoken, especially AmE*)
used to show that you refuse to do sth or that sth
cannot be done: *'Did you get that job?' 'No dice.'*

> ❷ ORIGIN
> When you throw dice in a game, if they do not
> fall flat or they land on top of each other, the
> throw is invalid and considered *no dice*.

Dick /dɪk/

● **clever** → clever Dick
● **Tom** → every/any Tom, Dick and/or Harry

dicky /ˈdɪki/

not say/hear a 'dicky bird (*BrE, informal*)
say/hear nothing: *Don't look at me! I didn't say a
dicky bird.* ◇ *We haven't heard a dicky bird from her
for weeks.*

> ❷ ORIGIN
> This idiom is from rhyming slang, in which
> *dicky bird* stands for 'word'.

diddly /ˈdɪdli/

'diddly ◆ ˌdiddly-'squat (*AmE, informal*)
(often used in negative sentences) not anything;
nothing: *I don't know what's wrong with him — he
tells me diddly-squat.* ◇ *She doesn't know diddly
about it* (= she doesn't know anything).

die /daɪ/

die a/the 'death (*BrE, informal*)
end suddenly and completely; fail: *Our fund-rais-
ing appeal died a death when the government failed
to support it.* ◇ *He died the death as Othello, and
never got another role after that.*

die in your 'bed
die of old age or illness

die in 'harness
die while you are still working

the die is 'cast (*saying*)
a decision has been made, or a risk has been
taken, and the situation cannot now be changed:
*Once he'd signed the papers, he knew the die had
been cast and there was no turning back.*

> ❷ ORIGIN
> This phrase is associated with Julius Caesar
> who was reported to have said this when he
> took his army across the river Rubicon (see the
> note at *cross the Rubicon*). It's basic meaning is
> 'the dice has been thrown'.

die 'laughing (*informal*)
find sth extremely funny: *I nearly died laughing
when he said that.*

old ˌhabits, traˌditions, etc. die 'hard
used to say that things change very slowly: *'Even
though she's retired, she still gets up at 6 a.m.' 'Well,
I guess old habits die hard.'* ▶ **'diehard** *noun, adj.*:

A few diehards are trying to stop the reforms. ◇ *die-hard supporters of the exiled king*

to 'die for (*informal*)
if you think sth is **to die for**, you really want it, and would do anything to get it: *She was wearing a dress to die for.*

- **flies** → die/drop/fall like flies
- **say** → never say die
- **straight** → (as) straight as a die

differ /'dɪfə(r)/

- **agree** → agree to differ
- **beg** → I beg to differ

difference /'dɪfrəns/

make a, no, some, etc. 'difference (to/in sb/sth)
have an effect/no effect on sb/sth: *The rain didn't make much difference to the game.* ◇ *Your age shouldn't make any difference to whether you get the job or not.* ◇ *Changing schools made a big difference to my life.*

make all the 'difference (to sb/sth)
have an important effect on sb/sth; make sb feel better: *A few kind words at the right time make all the difference if you're upset.*

same 'difference (*spoken*)
used to say that you think the differences between two things are not important: *'She's divorced from her husband.' 'No she's not, she's only separated.' 'Same difference.'*

with a 'difference (*informal*)
(used after nouns) of an unusual kind: *The trad-itional backpack with a difference — it's completely waterproof.*

- **near** → as near as makes no difference **SEE** as near as dammit
- **split** → split the difference
- **world** → a/the world of difference (between A and B)

differences /'dɪfrənsɪz/

- **bury** → bury your differences
- **sink** → sink your differences

different /'dɪfrənt/

be in a different 'league
be much better, bigger, etc. than other similar things, people, etc: *The new designs are in a differ-ent league from those that have been used before.*

a different kettle of 'fish (*informal*)
a person or thing that is completely different from sb/sth else previously mentioned: *You may be able to read French well, but speaking it fluently is a dif-ferent kettle of fish entirely.*

> **NOTE**
> A *kettle* in this idiom is a pan in which you can cook a whole fish.

different 'strokes (for different 'folks) (*AmE*)
used to say that different people like or need dif-ferent things

- **ball** → a (whole) different/new ball game
- **chalk** → as different as chalk and cheese **SEE** (like) chalk and cheese
- **complexion** → put a new/different complexion on sth
- **know** → know different/otherwise
- **language** → speak/talk the same/a different language
- **march** → march to (the beat of) a different drummer/ drum
- **march** → march to a different tune **SEE** march to (the beat of) a different drummer/drum
- **matter** → be another/a different matter
- **sing** → sing a different song/tune
- **story** → a (quite) different story **SEE** (quite) another story
- **wavelength** → be on the same wavelength/on different wavelengths

difficult /'dɪfɪkəlt/

- **life** → make life difficult (for sb)

dig /dɪg/

dig 'deep
1 search thoroughly for information: *You'll need to dig deep into the records to find the figures you want.*
2 try hard to provide the money, equipment, etc. that is needed: *We're asking you to dig deep for the earthquake victims.*

,dig your 'heels in (*informal*)
refuse to do sth or to change your views: *A number of councils have dug their heels in over the govern-ment's request to reduce spending.* **OPP** give way (to sb/sth)

dig your own 'grave ♦ **dig a 'grave for your-self**
do sth that will bring harm to yourself: *If you give up your job now, you'll be digging your own grave, because you won't find it easy to get another one.*

dig yourself (into) a 'hole
get yourself into a bad situation that it will be very difficult to get out of: *When I started lying to him, I realized that I was digging myself into a hole which would be very difficult to get out of.*

dignity /'dɪgnəti/

be,neath sb's 'dignity (*often ironic*)
seeming so unimportant or unpleasant that sb thinks they are too important to do it: *She con-siders it beneath her dignity to help with the house-work now and again.*

,stand on your 'dignity (*formal*)
say firmly that you wish to be treated with the respect that you deserve: *The teacher stood on his dignity and insisted that the students be punished for being rude to him.*

dilemma /dɪ'lemə; daɪ-/

- **horns** → (on) the horns of a dilemma

dim /dɪm/

- **view** → take a dim/poor view of sb/sth

dime /daɪm/

on a 'dime (*AmE*) (*BrE less frequent* **on a 'sixpence**)
1 in a short space or small area: *A 3000 ton train doesn't stop on a dime.* ◊ *These racing boats can turn on a dime.*
2 quickly or suddenly: *Market conditions can turn on a dime* (= change quickly). ◊ *This information enables us to respond to new opportunities on a dime.*

> **NOTE**
> A *dime* is a small coin of the US and Canada which is worth ten cents.

● nickel-and-dime → nickel-and-dime
● penny → a dime a dozen SEE two/ten a penny

dine /daɪn/

● wine → wine and dine (sb)

dinkum /'dɪŋkəm/

● fair → fair dinkum

dinner /'dɪnə(r)/

● dog → a dog's breakfast/dinner

dinners /'dɪnəz; AmE 'dɪnərz/

● hot → more .../more often than sb has had hot dinners

dint /dɪnt/

by dint of sth/doing sth (*formal*)
as a result of (doing) sth; through: *By dint of sheer hard work, she managed to pass all her exams.*

dirt /dɜːt; AmE dɜːrt/

● dish → dish the dirt (on sb)
● pay → hit/strike pay dirt
● treat → treat sb like dirt

dirty /'dɜːti; AmE 'dɜːrti/

dirty great/big (*BrE, informal*)
used to emphasize how large sth is: *When I turned round he was pointing a dirty great gun at me.*

a ˌdirty old 'man (*informal, disapproving*)
an older man who thinks too much about sex: *Lots of dirty old men stood around looking at pornographic magazines.*

a ˌdirty week'end (*BrE, humorous*)
a weekend spent away from home in order to have sex, usually with sb who is not your usual partner: *They went away for a dirty weekend in Brighton.*

a dirty 'word
a thing or an idea that sb finds unpleasant or offensive: *Work is a dirty word to these lazy kids.*

(do sb's) 'dirty work
(do) the unpleasant or dishonest jobs that sb else does not want to do: *Tell him yourself! I don't see why I should have to do your dirty work for you!*

do the 'dirty on sb (*BrE, informal*)
cheat sb or treat them unfairly: *Mike felt that his fellow students had done the dirty on him by telling the lecturer he'd cheated in the exam.*

give sb/get a dirty 'look (*informal*)
look at sb/be looked at in an angry or a disapproving way: *She gave me a dirty look when I suggested that she should go and wash the dishes.*

● hands → get your hands dirty
● talk → talk dirty
● wash → wash your dirty linen in public

disadvantage /ˌdɪsəd'vɑːntɪdʒ; AmE -'væn-/

put sb/be at a disad'vantage
make it/be difficult for sb to succeed: *My lack of experience put me at a disadvantage in comparison with the other candidates for the job.*

disappear /ˌdɪsə'pɪə(r); AmE -'pɪr/

● face → disappear/vanish off the face of the earth

disappearing /ˌdɪsə'pɪərɪŋ; AmE -'pɪrɪŋ/

● act → do/perform/stage a disappearing/vanishing act

disaster /dɪ'zɑːstə(r); AmE -'zæs-/

a di'saster area
1 (*informal*) a place or situation that has a lot of problems, is a failure, or is badly organized: *The room was a disaster area* (= very untidy), *with stuff piled everywhere and nowhere to sit.* ◊ *The current system of taxation is a disaster area.*
2 a place where a disaster has happened and which needs special help: *After the floods, the whole region was declared a disaster area.*

● waiting → an accident/a disaster waiting to happen

discretion /dɪ'skreʃn/

at sb's di'scretion
according to what sb decides or wishes to do: *Bail is granted at the discretion of the court.* ◊ *There is no service charge and tipping is at your discretion.*

di,scretion is the ˌbetter part of 'valour (*BrE*)
(*AmE* **di,scretion is the ˌbetter part of 'valor**)
(*saying*)
you should avoid danger and not take unnecessary risks

> **❓ ORIGIN**
> This comes from Shakespeare's play *Henry IV*.

disguise /dɪs'gaɪz/

● blessing → a blessing in disguise

dish /dɪʃ/

ˌdish the 'dirt (on sb) (*informal*)
tell people unkind or unpleasant things about sb, especially about their private life: *When the newspaper offered her £10 000, she was only too happy to dish the dirt on her friends.*

dishwater /'dɪʃwɔːtə(r)/

● dull → (as) dull as dishwater **SEE** (as) dull as ditchwater

disposal /dɪ'spəʊzl; AmE -'spoʊ-/

at your/sb's dis'posal
available for use as you prefer/sb prefers: *He will have a car at his disposal for the whole month.* ◇ *Well, I'm at your disposal* (= I am ready to help you in any way I can).

disservice /dɪs'sɜːvɪs; dɪ'sɜː-; AmE -'sɜːrv-/

do sb a dis'service
do sth that harms sb and the opinion that other people have of them: *The minister's comments do teachers a great disservice.*

distance /'dɪstəns/

at/from a 'distance
from a place or time that is not near; from far away: *She had loved him at a distance for years.*

go the (full) 'distance
continue playing in a competition or sports contest until the end: *Nobody thought he would last 15 rounds but he went the full distance.*

in/into the 'distance
far away but still able to be seen or heard: *We saw lights in the distance.* ◇ *Alice stood staring into the distance.*

keep your 'distance (from sb/sth) ◆ **keep sb/sth at a 'distance**
not be too friendly or familiar with sb/sth: *She tends to keep her distance from her neighbours, so none of them know her very well.*

● spitting → within shouting distance **SEE** within spitting distance (of sth)

● striking → within striking distance (of sth)

distant /'dɪstənt/

the (ˌdim and) ˌdistant 'past
a long time ago: *stories from the distant past*

in the not too ˌdistant 'future
not a long time in the future; fairly soon: *We're thinking of having a baby in the not too distant future.*

distraction /dɪ'strækʃn/

to di'straction
so that you become upset, excited or angry and not able to think clearly: *The children are **driving me to distraction** today.*

distress /dɪ'stres/

● damsel → a damsel in distress

district /'dɪstrɪkt/

● red-light → the red-light district

ditchwater /'dɪtʃwɔːtə(r)/

● dull → (as) dull as ditchwater

dive /daɪv/

make a 'dive (for sth)
suddenly move or jump forward to do sth or reach sb/sth: *The goalkeeper made a dive for the ball.*

take a 'dive (*informal*)
suddenly get worse: *Profits really took a dive at the end of last year.*

divide /dɪ'vaɪd/

di,vide and 'rule
keep control over people by making them disagree with and fight each other, therefore not giving them the chance to unite and oppose you together: *a policy of divide and rule*

dividend /'dɪvɪdend/

● peace → a/the peace dividend

dividends /'dɪvɪdendz/

● pay → pay dividends

do /duː; də; du/

> Most idioms containing the verb **do** are at the entries for the nouns or adjectives in the idioms, for example **do a runner** is at **runner**.

be/have to do with sb/sth
be connected or concerned with sb/sth: *'What do you want to see me about?' 'It's to do with the letter you sent.'* ◇ *I'm not sure what he does for a living but I know it's something to do with computers.*

could 'do with sth (*spoken*)
want or need sth: *I could really do with a coffee.* ◇ *Her hair could have done with a wash.* ◇ *You look as if you could do with a good night's sleep.*

could/can do with'out sth (*spoken*)
not want sth, for example criticism, advice or complaints: *I could do without him telling me what to say all the time.* ◇ *I could have done without her ringing me up just as I was about to go out.*

do a sb (*informal*)
do or behave as sb did or would do: *Now don't go and do a Mr. Carpenter on us. He told us he was leaving only three weeks before he went, and it took us months to find a replacement.*

do's and 'don'ts (*informal*)
what to do and what not to do; rules: *This book is a useful guide to the do's and don'ts of choosing and buying your first car.*

'do something for sb/sth (*informal*)
make sb/sth look better: *You know, that hat really does something for you!*

it/that (just) won't 'do ◆ **it/that will never 'do** (*especially BrE*)
used to say that a situation is not satisfactory and should be changed or improved: *He's spending every afternoon in the park with his friends instead of going to school, and that just won't do!* ◇ *I feel very upset but it would never do to show it.*

not 'do anything/a lot/much for sb (*informal*)
used to say that sth does not make sb look attractive: *That hairstyle doesn't do anything for her.*

that will 'do (*informal*)
used to order sb to stop doing or saying sth: *That'll do! I've heard enough of your complaints.*

what did you, etc. do with sth?
(usually in perfect and simple past tenses) where did you, etc. put, lose or hide sth?: *What have you done with my scissors? They were on the kitchen table the last time I saw them.*

what do you do for sth?
used to ask how sb manages to obtain the thing mentioned: *It's very quiet, isn't it? What do you do for entertainment out here?*

dock /dɒk; *AmE* dɑːk/

put sb in the 'dock
accuse sb of doing sth wrong: *The government is being put in the dock for failing to warn the public about the flu epidemic.*

> **NOTE**
> The *dock* in a court of law is the place where the person who has been accused of a crime stands or sits during a trial.

doctor /'dɒktə(r); *AmE* 'dɑːk-/

just what the doctor 'ordered (*humorous, saying*)
exactly what sb wants or needs: *Ah, a long, cool, refreshing drink! Just what the doctor ordered!*

doddle /'dɒdl; *AmE* 'dɑːdl/

(it's) a 'doddle (*BrE, informal*)
used to refer to a task or an activity that is very easy: *The first year of the course was an absolute doddle.*

dodo /'dəʊdəʊ; *AmE* 'doʊdoʊ/

● **dead** → (as) dead as a/the dodo

does /dʌz/

that 'does it (*informal*)
used to show that you will not tolerate sth any longer: *That does it! You've called me a liar once too often. I'm leaving!*

dog /dɒg; *AmE* dɔːg/

be like a dog with two 'tails
be extremely happy: *'Is he pleased about his new job?' 'He's like a dog with two tails!'*

a ,dog and 'pony show (*AmE, informal*)
a complicated presentation, event or display that is designed to attract people's attention but which has little real content: *They put on a dog and pony show in the hope of attracting new investors.* ◇ *The protest was just a dog and pony show designed to bring in the media.*

,dog eat 'dog (*informal*)
fierce competition, with no concern for the harm done or other people's feelings: *In the modern business world, it's dog eat dog in the search for success.*

dog sb's 'footsteps
(of a problem or bad luck) seem to follow sb everywhere: *Bad luck seems to have dogged our footsteps from the beginning.*

a ,dog in the 'manger
a person who selfishly stops other people from using or enjoying sth which he/she cannot use or enjoy ▶ **,dog-in-the-'manger** *adj.*: *a dog-in-the-manger attitude*

> **❓ ORIGIN**
> This expression comes from Aesop's fable about a dog which lay in a manger (= a long open box) filled with hay. In this way he stopped the other animals eating the hay, even though he could not eat it himself.

the dog's 'bollocks (*BrE,* ⚠, *slang*)
used to say that sth is excellent or very good: *This song is the dog's bollocks.*

a dog's 'breakfast/'dinner (*BrE, informal*)
a very untidy piece of work; a mess: *Don't ask Julie to help you with the decorating — she made a complete dog's breakfast of painting the kitchen!*

a 'dog's life (*informal*)
a life in which there is not much pleasure or freedom: *It's a dog's life having to do two jobs in order to survive.*

every dog has his/its 'day (*saying*)
(often used to encourage sb) everyone will, at some time in their life, be successful or lucky: *They say every dog has its day, and mine is on Wednesday, when I will be interviewed for a television programme!*

give a dog a bad 'name (and 'hang him) (*saying*)
when a person already has a bad reputation, it is difficult to change it because others will continue to blame or suspect him/her

why keep a ,dog and bark your'self? (*informal, saying*)
if sb can do a task for you, there is no point in doing it yourself: *My mother always cleans the house before the cleaning lady comes, but why keep a dog and bark yourself?*

● **cat** → not have a dog's chance **SEE** not have a cat in hell's chance
● **fight** → fight like cat and dog
● **hair** → the hair of the dog (that bit you)
● **life** → there's life in the old dog yet
● **sick** → (as) sick as a dog
● **tail** → let the tail wag the dog **SEE** the tail (is) wagging the dog
● **tail** → the tail (is) wagging the dog
● **teach** → (you can't) teach an old dog new tricks
● **top** → top dog
● **whipped** → like a whipped dog
● **work** → work like a dog/slave/Trojan

dogbox /'dɒgbɒks; *AmE* 'dɔːgbɑːks/

● **doghouse** → be in the dogbox **SEE** be in the doghouse

doggo /ˈdɒgəʊ; AmE ˈdɔːgoʊ/

● lie → lie doggo

doghouse /ˈdɒghaʊs; AmE ˈdɔːg-/

be in the 'doghouse (*South African* **be in the 'dogbox**) (*informal*)
in a situation where sb is angry with you because you have done sth wrong: *I'm in the doghouse with my wife at the moment: I forgot it was her birthday yesterday!*

Mr Brown was in the doghouse again.

dogs /dɒgz; AmE dɔːgz/

go to the 'dogs (*AmE* also **go to hell in a 'handbasket**) (*informal*)
(often used of a company, an organization, a country, etc.) become less powerful, efficient, etc. than before: *Many people think this country's going to the dogs.*

● rain → rain cats and dogs
● sleeping → let sleeping dogs lie

doing /ˈduːɪŋ/

can't be 'doing with sth (*informal*)
used to say that you do not like sth and are unwilling to accept it: *I can't be doing with people who complain all the time.*

take some 'doing ♦ take a lot of 'doing
be hard work; be difficult: *Getting it finished by tomorrow will take some doing.* ◇ *It's going to take some doing to do the report on time, but we should manage it.*

what is sb/sth doing...?
used to ask why sb/sth is in the place mentioned: *What are these shoes doing on my desk?*

doldrums /ˈdɒldrəmz; AmE ˈdoʊl-/

in the 'doldrums
quiet or depressed: *Property sales have been in the doldrums for some time.* ◇ *He was in the doldrums for the whole winter.*

dollar /ˈdɒlə(r); AmE ˈdɑːl-/

● bet → (you can) bet your bottom dollar/your life (on sth/that...)
● sixty-four → the million dollar question SEE the sixty-four thousand dollar question
● top → pay, earn, charge, etc. top dollar

dollars /ˈdɒləz; AmE ˈdɑːlərz/

● million → look/feel like a million dollars/bucks

done /dʌn/

be 'done for (*informal*)
be in serious trouble: *The supplies are so low that we will be done for in a few days if help doesn't come soon.* ◇ *I think the project is done for — the money's almost gone and we've got no results after three years' hard work.*

be/get 'done for sth/for doing sth (*BrE, informal*)
be caught and punished for doing sth illegal but not too serious: *I got done for speeding on my way back home.*

be/have 'done with sb/sth (*especially BrE*)
no longer be involved with sb/sth or do sth, especially sth unpleasant: *I'm fed up with you lot! I'm done with you for ever!* ◇ *Let's have done with this silly argument.*

be ,over and 'done with
(often used of sth unpleasant, upsetting, etc.) be completely finished: *Well I'm glad that's over and done with. I was so nervous.*

done and 'dusted (*informal*)
if a project, an activity, etc. is **done and dusted**, it is completely finished or ready: *Everybody else seems to think the deal will be done and dusted by lunchtime, but I'm not so sure.*

a done 'deal (*especially AmE*)
used to describe a decision, an arrangement, a project, etc. that is completed and cannot be changed: *The managing director denied that the merger was a done deal, and said they were still in negotiations.*

done 'in (*informal*)
extremely tired: *I feel absolutely done in!* OPP full of beans

the done 'thing (*BrE*)
the socially correct way to behave: *Smoking while somebody else is eating is not the done thing.* ◇ *It's the done thing to dress for dinner in this hotel.*

done to a 'turn (*BrE*)
cooked for exactly the right amount of time: *We had a wonderful dinner, with chicken done to a turn and home-grown vegetables.*

he, she, etc. has gone/been and done sth (*informal*)
used to express surprise, annoyance, etc. at sb's actions: *Someone's gone and locked the door and I haven't got a key!* ◇ *What's he been and done now?*

● been → been there, done that
● easier → easier said than done
● hard → be/feel hard done by

- **harm** → no harm done
- **said** → when all is said and done
- **sooner** → no sooner said than done

donkey /'dɒŋki; AmE 'dɑːŋ-; 'dɔːŋ-/

the 'donkey work (*informal*)
the hard, boring parts of a job: *Why is it always me who has to do the donkey work?*

'donkey's years (*BrE, informal*)
a very long time: *She's lived in that house for donkey's years.*

> ❷ ORIGIN
> This is a play on words between 'years' and 'ears', the joke being that donkeys have long ears.

- **talk** → talk the hind leg(s) off a donkey

donna /'dɒnə; AmE 'dɑːnə/

- **prima** → (a) prima donna

don'ts /dəʊnts; AmE doʊnts/

- **do** → do's and don'ts

doom /duːm/

ˌdoom and 'gloom ♦ ˌgloom and 'doom
a general feeling of having lost all hope and of pessimism (= expecting things to go badly): *Despite the obvious setbacks, it's not all doom and gloom for the England team.*

- **prophet** → a doom merchant **SEE** a prophet of doom

doomsday /'duːmzdeɪ/

till 'doomsday (*informal*)
a very long time; for ever: *This job's going to take me till doomsday.*

> NOTE
> *Doomsday* is the last day of the world when Christians believe that everyone will be judged by God.

door /dɔː(r)/

be on the 'door
work at the entrance to a theatre, club, etc., for example collecting tickets from people as they enter: *We should be able to get in free because I know the guy on the door.*

by/through the back 'door
in an indirect or unofficial way: *She has powerful friends, so she got into the diplomatic service by the back door.*

(from) ˌdoor to 'door
1 from the place of departure to the place you are going to; from building to building: *The whole journey took me four hours from door to door.*
2 from one house, flat/apartment, etc. to the next: *The church distributes leaflets from door to door.* ◇ *a door-to-door salesman*

leave the 'door open (for/on sth)
make sure that there is still the possibility of doing sth: *The management were intelligent enough to leave the door open for further negotiations with the union.*

shut/close the 'door on sth
make it unlikely that sth will happen; refuse to consider an idea, a plan, etc: *I think this company should remain open to ideas and not shut the door on change.* ◇ *She was careful not to close the door on the possibility of further talks.*

- **beat** → beat a path to sb's door
- **darken** → not/never darken sb's door again
- **death** → at death's door
- **foot** → get/have a/your foot in the door
- **lay** → lay sth at sb's door
- **lie** → lie at sb's door
- **open** → open the door to/for sb/sth
- **show** → show sb the door
- **stable** → shut, etc. the barn door after the horse has escaped **SEE** shut/lock/close the stable door after the horse has bolted
- **wolf** → keep the wolf from the door

doornail /'dɔːneɪl; AmE 'dɔːrn-/

- **dead** → (as) dead as a doornail

doors /dɔːz; AmE dɔːrz/

out of 'doors
in the open air; outdoors: *You should spend more time out of doors in the fresh air.*

- **closed** → behind closed doors

doorstep /'dɔːstep; AmE 'dɔːrs-/

on the/your 'doorstep
very near your/sb's home: *It's easy to be concerned with problems across the other side of the world and not see the poverty and unhappiness on your own doorstep.*

dos /duz/

- **fair** → fair dos/do's **SEE** fair's fair

dose /dəʊs; AmE doʊs/

like a dose of 'salts (*old-fashioned, BrE, informal*)
very fast and easily: *We'll go through this house like a dose of salts, cleaning it from top to bottom.*

> NOTE
> *Salts* in this phrase are *laxatives* (= medicine that makes you go to the toilet).

- **medicine** → give sb a taste/dose of their own medicine

dot /dɒt; AmE dɑːt/

dot the/your ˌi's and cross the/your 't's
pay great attention to small details in order to complete sth; be very thorough and careful in what you do or say: *We reached a broad agreement, and decided to dot the i's and cross the t's later.*

on the 'dot (*informal*)
at exactly the right time or at the exact time mentioned: *He always finishes work at 4.30 on the dot.* ◇ *She arrived on the dot of 6.00.*

• year → from, since, etc. the year dot

dotage /'dəʊtɪdʒ; *AmE* 'doʊ-/

be in your 'dotage (*often humorous*)
be old and not always able to think clearly: *Sarah moved back in with her father so that she could look after him in his dotage.* ◇ *Sometimes the kids talk to me as if I'm in my dotage!* **OPP** (in) the first flush of youth, enthusiasm, etc.

dots /dɒts; *AmE* dɑːts/

• connect → connect the dots
• connect → join (up) the dots **SEE** connect the dots

dotted /'dɒtɪd; *AmE* 'dɑːt-/

• sign → sign on the dotted line

double /'dʌbl/

at the 'double (*BrE*) (*AmE* **on the 'double**)
(*informal*)
very quickly; immediately: *Go and get my boots, on the double!* ◇ *The boss wants you to go and see her at the double.*

do a ,double 'take
react to sth surprising or unusual only after a short delay: *I had to do a double take when she walked in — she looked exactly like her mother!*

,double 'Dutch (*BrE, informal*)
language that is impossible to understand: *I wish someone would explain this contract in simple language — it's all double Dutch to me!*

,double or 'quits (*BrE*) (*AmE* **,double or 'nothing**)
(in gambling) a risk in which, if you lose you will have to pay twice the amount of money you owe, or if you win, will not owe anything

> **NOTE**
> *Quits* means that two people are now equal and do not owe each other anything, especially money.

,double 'quick (*BrE, informal*)
very quick(ly): *If the machine starts making a hissing noise, then turn it off double quick.*

a double 'whammy (*informal*)
two unpleasant situations or events that happen at the same time and cause problems for sb/sth: *With this government we've had a double whammy of tax increases and benefit cuts.*

> **❷ ORIGIN**
> This phrase comes from the 1950s American cartoon *L'il Abner*. One of the characters could *shoot a whammy* (= use magic power to make something bad happen to somebody) by pointing a finger with one eye open, or a *double whammy* with both eyes open.

in a ,double 'bind
in a situation in which it is difficult to choose what to do because whatever you choose will have negative results: *Students are caught in a double bind between a lack of jobs if they leave school and a huge bill for higher education if they stay.*

double-edged /,dʌbl 'edʒd/

be a double-edged 'sword/'weapon
be sth that has both advantages and disadvantages: *This new 'miracle diet' is a double-edged sword — it'll make you lose weight fast but you may have some unpleasant side effects.*

doubt /daʊt/

in 'doubt
not certain: *The future of the company is still in doubt.* ◇ *If in doubt, call for an ambulance.*

,no 'doubt
probably, almost certainly: *No doubt you know why I have asked you to come and see me.* ◇ *You will no doubt have already heard that the chairman has resigned.*

without/beyond (a)'doubt
certainly: *This is without doubt the finest wine I have ever drunk.*

• benefit → give sb the benefit of the doubt
• shadow → beyond/without a shadow of (a) doubt
• shadow → there isn't a shadow of a doubt (that...)

doubting /'daʊtɪŋ/

a ,doubting 'Thomas
a person who will not believe sth without proof: *Now, for all you doubting Thomases who thought I couldn't win an important race, here's my medal to prove it!*

> **❷ ORIGIN**
> This expression comes from the Bible. Thomas refused to believe that Jesus had been brought back to life until he saw Jesus for himself and touched his wounds.

doubts /daʊts/

have your 'doubts (about sth)
have reasons why you are not certain about whether sth is good or whether sth good will happen: *I've had my doubts about his work since he joined the company.* ◇ *It may be all right. Personally, I have my doubts.*

down /daʊn/

be down to sb/sth (*informal*)
1 be caused by a particular person or thing: *She claimed her problems were down to the media.* ◇ *Our defeat in last week's game is down to the goalkeeper, who played very badly.*
2 be the responsibility of sb: *It's down to you to check the doors and windows before we leave.*

be down to sth
have nothing except one or a few items of the kind mentioned: *I'm down to my last penny.*

,down and 'out
having no home or job and living on the streets of a city; very poor: *It must be terrible to be down and out in this cold weather.* ▶ **,down-and-'out** *noun* a person who is **down and out** : *Life is hard for the city's down-and-outs.*

down through sth (*written*)
during a long period of time: *Down through the years this town has seen many changes.*

down to sb/sth
even including the last item of a whole list of people or things: *Everybody was affected by the economic crisis, from the president down to the poorest citizen.* ◇ *She's thought of everything down to the tiniest details!*

down 'under (*informal*)
in or to Australia and/or New Zealand: *TV stars from down under*

down with sb/sth!
shouted as a protest against sb/sth: *Down with the dictator!*

downhill /ˌdaʊnˈhɪl/

(all) down'hill ◆ ,downhill all the 'way
(*informal*)
1 very easy compared with the difficulties that came before: *It's all downhill from here. We'll soon be finished.* ◇ *I've done three out of the four parts of the course, so it should be downhill all the way from now on.*
2 getting worse very quickly: *I took on far too much work and after that it was downhill all the way for my health.*

,go down'hill
get worse: *My work has been going downhill ever since my divorce.* ◇ *This restaurant has definitely gone downhill since I last came here.*

down-low /ˈdaʊn ləʊ; AmE loʊ/

keep it on the 'down-low (*AmE, slang*)
keep sth secret; not tell other people about sth: *Her parents wouldn't approve of our relationship so we keep it on the down-low.*

downs /daʊnz/

● **ups** → ups and downs

dozen /ˈdʌzn/

by the 'dozen
many at the same time: *On her birthday, she always receives cards by the dozen.*

● **baker** → a baker's dozen
● **nineteen** → talk, etc. nineteen to the dozen
● **penny** → a dime a dozen **SEE** two/ten a penny
● **six** → it's six of one and half a dozen of the other

drabs /dræbz/

● **dribs** → in dribs and drabs

drag /dræg/

drag your 'feet/'heels
do sth very slowly or delay doing it because you do not want to do it: *How much longer will the government go on dragging its feet about whether to invest more money in the railways?*

● **bootstraps** → drag/pull yourself up by your (own) bootstraps

dragged /drægd/

● **cat** → (look) like sth the cat brought/dragged in

drain /dreɪn/

(go) down the 'drain (*BrE also* **(go) down the 'plughole**) (*informal*)
(be) wasted or lost; (get) much worse: *He watched his business, which had taken so long to build up, go slowly down the drain.*

● **brain** → the brain drain
● **circle** → circle the drain
● **laugh** → laugh like a drain
● **money** → money down the drain

drama /ˈdrɑːmə/

make a 'drama out of sth
make a small problem or event seem more important or serious than it really is: *Oh come on, it's only a tiny scratch — you always make such a drama out of everything!*

draught /drɑːft; AmE dræft/

on 'draught (*BrE*)
(of beer) taken from a barrel (= a large container): *This beer is not available on draught* (= it is available only in bottles or cans).

● **feel** → feel the draught

draw /drɔː/

be fast/quick on the 'draw
1 (*informal*) be quick to understand or react in a new situation: *You can't fool him, he's always quick on the draw.*
2 be quick at pulling out a gun in order to shoot it

draw a 'blank
not find sth that you are looking for: *There was no sign of the murder weapon. The police searched every inch of the forest but drew a blank.*

draw 'breath (*BrE*) (*AmE* **draw a 'breath**)
1 stop doing sth and rest: *She talks all the time and hardly stops to draw breath.*
2 (*literary*) live; be alive: *He was as kind a man as ever drew breath.*

draw a line in the 'sand
set a limit that you refuse to allow sth to go beyond: *The government is trying to draw a line in the sand regarding public sector pay rises.*

draw a 'line under sth (*BrE*)
say that sth is finished and not worth discussing any more: *The company is attempting to draw a line under its recent problems.*

draw the 'line (at sth)
refuse to do or accept sth: *I don't mind cooking dinner for you occasionally, but I draw the line at ironing your shirts!* ◇ *He refused to tolerate her lies any longer. The line had to be drawn somewhere.*

draw the short 'straw (*BrE*) (*AmE* **get the short end of the 'stick**)
be the person in a group who is chosen or forced to do sth unpleasant that nobody wants to do: *You've drawn the short straw, I'm afraid. You're going to have to work on New Year's Day.*

draw 'straws (for sth)
decide on sb to do or have sth, by choosing pieces of paper, etc: *We drew straws for who went first.*

- **full** → draw yourself up/rise to your full height
- **horns** → draw/pull in your horns
- **lots** → cast/draw lots (for sth/to do sth)
- **luck** → the luck of the draw
- **side** → take/draw sb to one side
- **veil** → cast/draw/throw a veil over sth

drawer /drɔː(r)/

- **sharpest** → not the sharpest knife in the drawer

drawing /'drɔːɪŋ/

(it's) back to the 'drawing board
a new plan must be prepared because an earlier one has failed: *She's refused to consider our offer, so it's back to the drawing board, I'm afraid.*

on the 'drawing board
being prepared or considered: *It's just one of several projects on the drawing board.*

drawn /drɔːn/

- **battle** → the battle lines are drawn
- **daggers** → be at daggers drawn (with sb)

dread /dred/

- **think** → I shudder/dread to think (how, what, etc....)

dreaded /'dredɪd/

the dreaded 'lurgy (*BrE, informal, humorous*)
an illness that is easy to catch but not serious, for example a cold: *Ann's not coming out tonight — she's got the dreaded lurgy so she's at home in bed.*

dream /driːm/

dream 'on (*spoken, informal*)
used to tell sb that an idea is not practical or likely to happen: *'Do you think if I ask my boss for a pay rise, I'll get one?' 'Dream on!'*

like a bad 'dream
(of a situation) so unpleasant that you cannot believe it is true: *In broad daylight, the events of the night before seemed like a bad dream.*

not 'dream of sth/of doing sth
(often used with *would*) not even consider sth under any circumstances: *'Don't tell Gary what I've bought him for his birthday.' 'I wouldn't dream*

of it.' ◇ *Only a couple of years ago he would never have dreamt of going abroad on his own, and now he's travelling around India!*

work/go like a 'dream (*informal*)
work/go very well: *The plan worked like a dream, and everybody got what they wanted.* **OPP** go pear-shaped

- **pipe** → a pipe dream

dreams /driːmz/

in your 'dreams (*spoken*)
used to tell sb that sth they are hoping for is not likely to happen: *'I'll be a manager before I'm 30.' 'In your dreams.'*

- **wildest** → beyond your wildest dreams

dress /dres/

- **part** → look/dress the part

dressed /drest/

dressed to 'kill (*informal*)
(especially of a woman) wearing your best clothes, especially clothes that attract attention: *She went to the party dressed to kill.*

dressed (up) to the 'nines (*informal*)
wearing very elegant or formal clothes, especially to attract attention: *She was dressed up to the nines in her furs and jewellery.*

- **mutton** → be mutton dressed (up) as lamb

dribs /drɪbz/

in dribs and 'drabs (*informal*)
in small amounts or numbers: *People started arriving in dribs and drabs from nine o'clock onwards.* ◇ *He paid back the money in dribs and drabs.*

dried /draɪd/

cut and 'dried
(of matters, arrangements or opinions) completely decided and unlikely to be changed: *By the end of the evening their plans for carrying out the robbery were cut and dried, with nothing left to chance.* ◇ *The police thought they had a cut-and-dried case.*

drift /drɪft/

catch/get sb's/the drift (*informal*)
understand the general meaning of what sb says or writes: *Do you catch my drift?* ◇ *My German isn't very good, but I got the drift of what he said.* ◇ *He wasn't the sort of boy you'd introduce to your mother, **if you get my drift*** (= I have not told you all the details, but I am sure you can understand what I mean).

lose the 'drift/'thread of sth
be unable to follow a story, discussion, etc. because you cannot understand the relationship between events, facts, etc: *I had to go out in the middle of the film and when I came back I found I'd lost the thread entirely.* ◇ *When they started talking about artificial intelligence, I completely lost the drift of the argument.*

drink /drɪŋk/

drink sb's 'health
wish sb good health as you lift your glass, and then drink from it

drink like a 'fish (*informal*)
regularly drink too much alcohol: *Her husband drinks like a fish.*

drink sb under the 'table (*informal*)
drink more alcohol than sb without becoming as drunk as they do: *Believe me, she can drink anyone under the table!*

- **demon** → the demon drink
- **drive** → drive sb to drink
- **eat** → eat, drink and be merry
- **horse** → you can take/lead a horse to water, but you can't make it drink
- **meat** → be meat and drink (to sb)
- **spike** → spike sb's drink
- **stiff** → a stiff drink
- **worse** → the worse for drink

drive /draɪv/

drive a coach and 'horses through sth
succeed in avoiding certain rules, conditions, etc. in an obvious and important way, without being punished: *The wage increase we've been given is three times the government's limit. We've driven a coach and horses right through their pay policy.*

drive a hard 'bargain
make sure that you always gain an advantage in business deals, etc: *I wouldn't try to do business with Jack; he's got the reputation of driving a hard bargain.*

drive sb in'sane
make sb more and more angry or irritated, especially over a long period of time: *This job is driving me insane.*

drive sb out of their 'mind/'wits (*informal*)
make sb crazy, or very nervous or worried: *That noise is driving me out of my mind!*

drive sb to 'drink (*often humorous*)
make sb so annoyed, worried, etc. that they begin to drink too much alcohol: *A week with those noisy kids is enough to drive anyone to drink!*

drive a wedge between A and B
make two people become less friendly or loving towards each other: *The disagreements over money finally drove a wedge between them, and they ended up getting divorced.*

> **NOTE**
> A *wedge* is a piece of wood, metal, etc. with one thick end and one thin pointed end that you use to keep two things apart or to split wood or rock.

- **ground** → drive/run/work yourself into the ground
- **home** → drive/hammer sth home (to sb)
- **wall** → drive/send sb up the wall

driven /'drɪvn/

- **pure** → (as) pure as the driven snow

driver /'draɪvə(r)/

- **back-seat** → a back-seat driver
- **driving** → in the driver's seat SEE in the driving seat

driving /'draɪvɪŋ/

the driving 'force (behind sth)
the person or thing that makes sth happen: *She is the driving force behind this new road safety campaign.*

in the 'driving seat (*BrE*) (*AmE* **in the 'driver's seat**)
managing or controlling sth, for example a business: *With a younger person in the driving seat, we can expect some big changes in the company.* **OPP** take a back seat

what sb is 'driving at
the thing sb is trying to say: *What are you driving at? Try to explain what you mean more clearly.* ◇ *I wish I knew what they were really driving at.*

drop /drɒp; AmE drɑːp/

at the ˌdrop of a 'hat (*informal*)
immediately and without hesitating: *He's the sort of person who can sing any song at all at the drop of a hat.*

ˌdrop your 'aitches
not pronounce the 'h' sound, especially at the beginning of a word, where it is pronounced in standard English

> **NOTE**
> This is a feature of some English accents, for example the London one.

drop the 'ball (*AmE, informal*)
make a mistake and spoil sth that you are responsible for: *I could use some help. I don't want to drop the ball on this one.* ◇ *He thinks that you dropped the ball on the Swiss project.*

drop a 'bombshell
announce sth which is unexpected and usually unpleasant: *It was then that he dropped the bombshell — he wasn't planning to come with us.*

drop a 'brick/'clanger (*BrE, informal*)
say or do sth that offends or embarrasses sb, although you did not intend to: *I dropped a real clanger when I mentioned the party. He hadn't been invited.*

drop 'dead
1 (*informal*) die very suddenly
2 (*spoken*) used as a rude way of telling sb to go away: *Drop dead, will you!*

drop a 'hint (to sb) ♦ **drop sb a 'hint**
suggest sth in an indirect way: *He tried to drop a hint about it being time to leave, but they didn't seem to take any notice.* ◇ *She's dropped me a few hints about what she'd like for her birthday.*

drop sb 'in it (*BrE, informal*)
put sb in an embarrassing situation, especially by telling a secret that you should not have told: *Don't mention Paul to my parents or you'll really drop me in it — I haven't told them about him yet.* **OPP** get sb off the hook

a ˌdrop in the ˈocean (*BrE*) (*AmE* a ˌdrop in the ˈbucket)
a very small amount in comparison to the much larger amount that is needed: *$10 million is only a drop in the ocean compared to what is needed to help these people effectively.*

drop sb a ˈline/ˈnote (*informal*)
write a short letter, message, etc. to sb: *I dropped her a line inviting her to my birthday party.*

drop ˈnames
mention famous people you know or have met in order to impress others ▶ **ˈname-dropping** *noun*: *I can't stand all this name-dropping! Does he really know Brad Pitt?*

fit/ready to ˈdrop (*informal*)
very tired; exhausted: *I feel fit to drop.* ◇ *We danced until we were ready to drop.*

let sth ˈdrop
1 do or say nothing more about sb/sth: *I've heard enough about this subject. Can we let it drop now?*
2 mention sb/sth in a conversation, by accident or as if by accident: *He let it drop that the Prime Minister was a close friend of his.*

● **flies** → die/drop/fall like flies
● **heard** → you could have heard a pin drop
● **lap** → drop/dump sth in sb's lap
● **lap** → drop/fall into sb's lap

drops /drɒps; *AmE* drɑːps/

● **bottom** → the bottom drops/falls out of sb's world
● **bottom** → the bottom drops/falls out of the market
● **jaw** → your jaw drops
● **penny** → the penny drops

drown /draʊn/

drown your ˈsorrows (*informal, often humorous*)
try to forget your problems or a disappointment by drinking alcohol: *Whenever his team lost a match he could be found in the pub afterwards drowning his sorrows.*

drowned /draʊnd/

like a drowned ˈrat (*informal*)
very wet: *She came in from the storm looking like a drowned rat.*

drugged /drʌgd/

drugged up to the ˈeyeballs
have taken or been given a lot of drugs: *She was drugged up to the eyeballs, but still in a lot of pain.*

drum /drʌm/

bang/beat the ˈdrum (for sb/sth) (*especially BrE*)
speak with enthusiasm in support of sb/sth: *She's really banging the drum for the new system.*

● **march** → march to (the beat of) a different drummer/drum

drummer /ˈdrʌmə(r)/

● **march** → march to (the beat of) a different drummer/drum

drunk /drʌŋk/

(as) drunk as a ˈlord (*BrE*) (*AmE* **(as) drunk as a ˈskunk**) (*informal*)
very drunk: *I eventually found them in a bar, both as drunk as skunks.* **OPP** (as) sober as a judge

● **blind** → blind drunk
● **roaring** → roaring drunk

dry /draɪ/

(as) dry as a ˈbone
very dry

(as) dry as ˈdust
extremely boring: *Her lectures are very useful, but they're dry as dust.*

milk/suck sb/sth ˈdry
get from sb/sth all the money, help, information, etc. they have, usually giving nothing in return: *It was only later that we found out he'd milked his grandmother dry of all her money before she died.*

not a dry eye in the ˈhouse (*humorous*)
used to say that everyone was very emotional about sth: *There wasn't a dry eye in the house when they announced their engagement.*

run ˈdry
stop supplying water; be all used so that none is left: *The wells in most villages in the region have run dry.* ◇ *Vaccine supplies started to run dry as the flu outbreak reached epidemic proportions.*

● **bleed** → bleed sb dry/white
● **hang** → hang sb out to dry
● **high** → high and dry
● **home** → home and dry
● **powder** → keep your powder dry
● **squeeze** → squeeze sb dry

duck /dʌk/

(take to sth) like a ˌduck to ˈwater
(be able to do sth) naturally and without any difficulty: *'Do the children like living in the country?' 'They've taken to it like ducks to water. They've never been happier!'*

● **dead** → a dead duck
● **lame** → a lame duck
● **sitting** → a sitting duck/target
● **water** → be (like) water off a duck's back

duckling /ˈdʌklɪŋ/

● **ugly** → an ugly duckling

ducks /dʌks/

get/have (all) your ˌducks in a ˈrow (*especially AmE*)
have made all the preparations needed to do sth; be well organized: *We need to get all our ducks in a row before beginning work on the project.*

dudgeon /ˈdʌdʒən/

• **high** → in high dudgeon

due /djuː; duː/

give sb their ˈdue
give sb the praise that they deserve: *Helen may not be bright, but to give her her due, her work is always very accurate.*

in ˌdue ˈcourse
at the right time in the future; eventually: *Thank you for your letter applying for the post of manager. We will be in contact with you again in due course.*

dull /dʌl/

(as) dull as ˈditchwater (*BrE*) (*AmE* **(as) dull as ˈdishwater**)
very boring: *Best-seller or not, the book sounds as dull as ditchwater to me.*

dumb /dʌm/

• **struck** → be struck dumb (with sth)

dump /dʌmp/

• **lap** → drop/dump sth in sb's lap

dumps /dʌmps/

down in the ˈdumps (*informal*)
depressed; miserable: *I've been feeling a bit down in the dumps since I lost my job.* **OPP** on top of the world

dunk /dʌŋk/

• **slam** → be a slam dunk

duration /djuˈreɪʃn; AmE duˈ-/

for the duˈration (*informal*)
until the end of a particular situation: *Kate has the flu so badly that she's confined to her room for the duration.*

dust /dʌst/

after/when the ˈdust settles
when all the exciting events, changes, etc. are over: *When the dust finally began to settle, certain facts about the President's resignation started to emerge.*

leave sb/sth in the ˈdust (*AmE*)
leave sb/sth far behind: *The four-minute mile barrier has been left in the dust by a generation of faster runners.* ◇ *In the local elections, Jackson won easily, leaving all other candidates in the dust.*

let the ˈdust settle (also **wait for the ˈdust to settle**)
wait for a situation to become clear or certain: *Let's not make any decisions now — we'll wait for the dust to settle and then decide what to do.*

not see sb for ˈdust (*informal*)
not see sb because they have left a place very quickly: *If I ever win a lot of money, you won't see me for dust. I'll be on the next plane for New York.*

• **bite** → bite the dust
• **dry** → (as) dry as dust
• **gather** → gather dust
• **gold** → like gold dust

dusted /ˈdʌstɪd/

• **done** → done and dusted

dusty /ˈdʌsti/

a dusty ˈanswer (*old-fashioned*, *BrE*)
an unhelpful or a sharp response to a request or question: *When I asked the company what their policy was on this matter, I received a very dusty answer.*

Dutch /dʌtʃ/

ˌDutch ˈcourage (*BrE*, *informal*)
courage or confidence that you get by drinking alcohol: *I was afraid of having to tell my wife about what had happened, so I went to the pub to get some Dutch courage.*

go ˈDutch (with sb) (*informal*)
share the cost of a meal, etc. equally with sb else: *She always insists on going Dutch when they go out together.*

• **double** → double Dutch

duty /ˈdjuːti; AmE ˈduːti/

duty ˈcalls
used to say that you must do sth that cannot be avoided, especially when you have to stop doing sth pleasant: *Ah, duty calls, I'm afraid — I really must go and finish off those letters.*

on/off ˈduty
(of nurses, police officers, etc.) working/not working at a particular time: *Who's on duty today?* ◇ *What time do you go off duty?*

• **bound** → be/feel duty/honour bound to do sth
• **call** → beyond the call of duty
• **line** → in the line of duty

dying /ˈdaɪɪŋ/

be ˈdying for sth/to do sth (*informal*)
want to have or do sth very much: *I'm dying for a drink.* ◇ *She's heard so much about you. She's dying to meet you.*

be ˈdying of sth (*informal*)
have a very strong feeling of sth, for example hunger or boredom: *We're all dying of curiosity — come on, tell us what happened!* ◇ *I'm dying of thirst.*

till/to/until your ˌdying ˈday
for as long as you live: *I swear I won't forgive her to my dying day!*

E e

eager /'iːɡə(r)/

an eager 'beaver (*informal*)
a person who is enthusiastic about work, etc: *She always starts work early and leaves late. She's a real eager beaver.*

eagle /'iːɡl/

an/sb's ˌeagle 'eye (*informal*)
if sb has an **eagle eye**, they watch things carefully and are good at noticing things: *Nothing the staff did escaped the eagle eye of the manager* (= he saw everything they did). ► ˌeagle-'eyed *adj.*: *An eagle-eyed student spotted the mistake.*

ear /ɪə(r); AmE ɪr/

be out on your 'ear (*informal*)
be forced to leave a job, home, etc. suddenly: *You'll be out on your ear unless your work gets a lot better, my lad.*

beam/grin/smile from ear to 'ear
be smiling, etc. a lot because you are very pleased about sth: *I like your graduation photo, with you grinning from ear to ear and your parents looking so proud.*

go in 'one ear and out the 'other (*informal*)
(of information, advice, an order, etc.) be immediately forgotten or ignored: *He never remembers anything I tell him. It just goes in one ear and out the other.* **OPP** stick in your mind

have sb's 'ear ♦ have the ear of sb (*formal*)
gain the attention of sb important in order to influence them or get their help: *We'll have to gain the ear of the Senator to win support for our cause.*

have an 'ear for sth
be able to recognize and copy sounds well: *The child certainly has an ear for music.*

keep/have an/your ear (close) to the 'ground
(try to) be well-informed about what is or will be happening: *Jane keeps her ear pretty close to the ground and can usually tell you what the mood of the staff is.*

play (sth) by 'ear
1 play (music) which you have heard or remembered but which you have not seen written down: *She can't read music very well, so she plays all the tunes by ear.*
2 (also **play it by 'ear**) (*informal*) decide how to act in a situation as it happens or develops, rather than by planning in advance: *You can't really prepare for the questions the interviewer will ask — you'll just have to play it by ear, I'm afraid.*

- **bend** → bend sb's ear (about sth)
- **cock** → cock an ear/eye at sth/sb
- **deaf** → turn a deaf ear (to sth)

- **flea** → with a flea in your ear
- **lend** → lend an ear (to sb/sth)
- **listen** → listen with half an ear
- **pig** → make a pig's ear (out) of sth
- **silk** → make a silk purse out of a sow's ear
- **talk** → talk sb's ear off
- **thick** → give sb/get a thick ear
- **tin** → have a tin ear (for sth)
- **word** → have a word in sb's ear

earliest /'ɜːliɪst; AmE 'ɜːrl-/

at your earliest con'venience (*written*)
as soon as possible: *Please telephone at your earliest convenience.*

early /'ɜːli; AmE 'ɜːrli/

the ˌearly bird catches the 'worm (*saying*)
you have to get up early or do sth before others in order to be successful ► **an 'early bird** *noun* (*humorous*) a person who gets up, arrives, etc. very early

early 'on
at an early stage of a situation, relationship, period of time, etc: *I knew quite early on that I wanted to marry her.*

it's early 'days (yet) (*BrE*)
it is too soon to be certain about sth: *The new store hasn't had many customers though of course it's early days yet.*

- **bright** → bright and early
- **hours** → the small/early hours
- **night** → have an early/a late night

earn /ɜːn; AmE ɜːrn/

ˌearn a/your 'crust (*BrE, informal*)
earn enough money to live on: *He's a musician now, but he used to earn a crust by cleaning windows.*

> **NOTE**
> The *crust* is the hard, outer surface of bread.

ˌearn your 'keep
be useful, helpful, successful, etc. enough to balance any costs that you cause: *Jill more than earns her keep with the help she gives me around the house.* ◇ *Though it's expensive to buy and maintain, the new computer is earning its keep as we've been able to reduce the number of staff.*

- **spurs** → win/earn your spurs

earnest /'ɜːnɪst; AmE 'ɜːrn-/

in 'earnest
1 more seriously and with more force or effort than before: *The work on the building will begin in earnest on Monday.*
2 very serious and sincere about what you are saying and about your intentions; in a way that shows that you are serious: *You may laugh but I'm **in deadly earnest**.* ◇ *I could tell she was speaking in earnest.*

ears /ɪəz; AmE ɪrz/

be all 'ears (*informal*)
listen very carefully and with great interest: *Go on, tell me what happened — I'm all ears.* **OPP** listen with half an ear

be up to your 'ears in sth
have a lot of sth to deal with: *I'm afraid I'm up to my ears in work at the moment. Can we talk later in the week?*

come to/reach sb's 'ears
hear about sth, especially when other people already know about it: *News of the affair eventually reached her ears.*

his, her, etc. 'ears are burning
a person thinks or knows that other people have been talking about them: *Jenny's ears must have been burning last night: we talked about her for hours.*

his, her, etc. 'ears are flapping (*BrE, informal*)
a person is trying to listen to sb else's conversation: *I think you'd better tell me later when we're alone — ears are flapping here.*

> **NOTE**
> *Flap* here means to move quickly backwards and forwards.

shut/close your 'ears to sb/sth
refuse to listen to sb/sth; ignore sb/sth: *The government has shut its ears to our protests.*

- **believe** → not believe your eyes/ears
- **box** → box sb's ears
- **box** → give sb a box on the ears
- **deaf** → fall on deaf ears
- **music** → be (like) music to your ears
- **prick** → prick up your ears
- **prick** → your ears prick up SEE prick up your ears
- **ring** → ring in your ears/head
- **walls** → walls have ears
- **wet** → (still) wet behind the ears

earshot /ˈɪəʃɒt; AmE ˈɪrʃɑːt/

out of 'earshot (of sb/sth)
too far away to hear sb/sth or to be heard: *We waited until Ted was safely out of earshot before discussing it.*

within 'earshot (of sb/sth)
near enough to hear sb/sth or to be heard: *As she came within earshot of the group, she heard her name mentioned.*

earth /ɜːθ; AmE ɜːrθ/

bring sb/come (back) down to 'earth (with a 'bang, 'bump, etc.)
have to deal, or make sb deal, with sth unpleasant, especially after a time when things seemed to be going well or life was enjoyable: *After such a wonderful trip, losing all her money certainly brought her back down to earth with a bump.* ▸ **,down-to-'earth** *adj.* (*approving*) sensible and practical: *Even though she's a movie star, she's still friendly and down-to-earth.*

cost/pay/charge the 'earth (*BrE, informal*)
cost/pay/charge a lot of money: *It needn't cost the earth to refurbish your offices.*

go to 'earth/'ground (*BrE*)
hide, especially to escape from sb who is chasing you: *His family never saw him again. He went to ground and they heard nothing else of him until he died last year.*

> **NOTE**
> This expression refers to a fox hiding underground when it is hunted.

how, what, why, etc. on 'earth... ♦ **how, why, etc. in the 'world...** (*informal*)
used with questions to express the speaker's surprise, anger, etc: *How on earth did you know I was coming today when I didn't know myself until the last minute?* ◊ *Why on earth would anyone give up such a good job?*

like nothing on 'earth
very ill or unattractive: *After two hours in that tiny boat I felt like nothing on earth.* ◊ *I hadn't slept for 48 hours. I must have looked like nothing on earth.*

nothing on 'earth (*informal*)
absolutely nothing: *Nothing on earth would make me tell anyone our secret.*

run sb/sth to 'earth/'ground (*informal*)
find sb/sth after a long, difficult search: *I spent years looking for the stolen picture but eventually ran it to ground in London.* ◊ *The escaped prisoner was run to ground within a couple of days.*

> **NOTE**
> This comes from hunting and means to chase an animal to its *earth* (= its home or hiding place).

- **ends** → to the ends of the earth
- **face** → disappear/vanish off the face of the earth
- **four** → the four corners of the earth
- **heaven** → a heaven on earth
- **hell** → a hell on earth
- **move** → move heaven and earth (to do sth)
- **promise** → promise (sb) the moon/earth/world
- **salt** → the salt of the earth
- **scum** → the scum of the earth
- **wipe** → wipe sth off the face of the earth

earthly /ˈɜːθli; AmE ˈɜːrθ-/

no earthly 'use, 'reason, etc. (*informal*)
used to emphasize that there is no use, reason, etc. at all: *There's no earthly reason why she shouldn't come with us.*

not (have) an 'earthly (chance) (*BrE, informal*)
(have) no chance at all: *You haven't an earthly chance of beating her at tennis — she is one of the best players in the country.* ◊ *'Any chance of getting a ticket for the concert?' 'Not an earthly, I'm afraid.'*

ease /iːz/

at (your) 'ease
relaxed and confident and not nervous or embarrassed: *I never feel completely at ease with him.*
OPP ill at ease

(stand) at 'ease
(in the military) used as a command to soldiers to tell them to stand with their feet apart and their hands behind their backs

put/set sb at (their) 'ease
make sb feel relaxed, not shy, etc: *Try to put the candidate at ease by being friendly and informal.* ◇ *No matter what situation she was in, somehow she always managed to look completely at her ease.*

● ill → ill at ease
● mind → put/set sb's mind at ease/rest

easier /'iːziə(r)/

,easier ,said than 'done (*saying*)
it is easier to suggest doing sth than actually to do it: *'All you have to do is climb a ladder and mend the roof.' 'Easier said than done — I'm terrified of heights!'*

easily /'iːzəli/

● sit → sit comfortably/easily/well (with sth)

easy /'iːzi/

(as) ,easy as ABC/'pie/falling off a 'log (*informal*)
very easy: *Try using the new photocopier. It's as easy as pie.*

,easy 'come, ,easy 'go (*saying*)
something that has been obtained very easily and quickly may be lost or wasted in the same way: *Her parents have given her all the money she wants, but she's always in debt. With her, it's a case of easy come, easy go.*

,easy/,gently/,slowly 'does it (*informal*)
used for telling sb to be careful, calm, etc: *Easy does it! Just lift it a little bit and I think it'll go through the door.*

,easy 'game
a person or thing that is easy to attack, criticize, or make a victim: *Customers who know nothing about cars are easy game for dishonest dealers.*

,easy 'money
money earned for very little work or effort, often by doing sth dishonest: *There's a lot of easy money to be made in this business.*

,easy on the 'eye, 'ear, etc.
pleasant to look at, listen to, etc: *When decorating your bedroom, it's best to choose colours that are easy on the eye.*

go 'easy on sb (*informal*)
not be too strict with sb, especially when they have done sth wrong: *Go easy on the child, she didn't mean to break the window.*

go 'easy on sth
do not use too much of sth, speak too much about sth, etc: *Go easy on the spices. I don't like very hot curry.* ◇ *When you're talking to Jim, go easy on the subject of marriage — his wife's just left him.*

have an easy 'time of it (*BrE, informal*)
be in a very favourable situation: *She has a very easy time of it in her job — she only works about 30 hours a week.*

I'm 'easy (*BrE, informal*)
used to say that you do not have a strong opinion when sb has offered you a choice: *'Tea or coffee?'* *'Oh, I'm easy — I'll have whatever you're having.'*

on 'easy street (*AmE*)
enjoying a comfortable way of life with plenty of money and no worries: *The box office success of his first movie put him and his family on easy street.* **OPP** (on) skid row

take the easy way 'out
end a difficult situation by choosing the simplest solution, even if it is not the best one: *Rather than trying to save his business, he took the easy way out and declared himself bankrupt.*

take it/things 'easy (*informal*)
relax and avoid working too hard or doing too much; not get angry, excited, etc: *Bob's still running the business on his own. He really ought to be taking things easy at his age.* ◇ *Take it easy, Jenny! There's no need to get so annoyed.* **OPP** be hard at it

● free → free and easy
● option → the soft/easy option
● ride → have/give sb a rough/an easy ride
● touch → a soft/an easy touch

eat /iːt/

eat sb a'live (*informal*)
1 (also **have/eat sb for 'breakfast**) criticize or punish sb severely because you are extremely angry with them
2 (also **have/eat sb for 'breakfast**) defeat sb completely in an argument, a competition, etc: *The defence lawyers are going to eat you alive tomorrow.* ◇ *The union leader eats managers for breakfast!*
3 (usually used in the passive) (of insects, etc.) bite sb many times: *I was being eaten alive by mosquitoes.*

,eat, drink and be 'merry (*saying*)
said to encourage sb to enjoy life now, while they can, and not to think of the future

eat your 'heart out (*spoken*)
used to compare two things and say that one of them is better: *Look at him dance! Eat your heart out, John Travolta* (= he dances even better than John Travolta).

eat your 'heart out (for sb/sth) (*especially BrE*)
be very unhappy because you want sb/sth that you cannot have: *He's eating his heart out for that woman.*

,eat humble 'pie (*BrE*) (*AmE* **eat 'crow**)
say and show that you are sorry for a mistake that you made: *I had to eat humble pie when Harry, who I said would never have any success, won first prize.*

> ❷ ORIGIN
> This comes from a pun on the old word *umbles*, meaning 'offal' (= the inside parts of an animal), which was considered inferior food.

eat like a 'bird
eat very little: *She's so afraid of putting on weight that she eats like a bird.*

eat like a 'horse
eat very large quantities of food: *My brother eats like a horse but never puts on any weight.*

eat sb's 'lunch (*AmE, business*)
take away another company's business or their share of the market: *Unless we're careful, foreign competitors will eat our lunch.*

eat sb out of ,house and 'home (*informal, often humorous*)
eat all the food that sb has: *She eats us out of house and home every time she comes to stay.*

eat your 'words
be forced to admit that what you have said before was wrong: *Nick told everyone that he'd be picked for the team, but when he wasn't chosen he had to eat his words.*

I could eat a 'horse (*spoken*)
I am very hungry: *What's for dinner? I could eat a horse!*

I'll eat my 'hat! (*spoken*)
used to say that you think sth is very unlikely to happen: *They're always late — if they get here before eight o'clock, I'll eat my hat.*

he, she, etc. won't 'eat you (*informal*)
said to encourage sb to speak to or approach sb who seems frightening: *Come on, Emma, Santa Claus won't eat you! If you go closer, he'll give you a present!*

- cake → have your cake and eat it (too)
- dog → dog eat dog

eating /'iːtɪŋ/

have sb eating out of your 'hand
have sb completely in your control so that they will do whatever you want: *Once they knew that they would never be able to escape without his help, he had them eating out of his hand.*

what's 'eating sb? (*spoken*)
used to ask why sb is worried, unhappy, etc: *You seem a bit quiet today. What's eating you?*

ebb /eb/

the ,ebb and 'flow (of sb/sth)
the repeated, often regular, movement from one state to another; the repeated change in level, numbers or amount: *the ebb and flow of money/ seasons* ◇ *She sat quietly, enjoying the ebb and flow of conversation.*

> **NOTE**
> This expression refers to the movement of the sea away from and towards the land.

- low → (at) a low ebb

economical /ˌiːkəˈnɒmɪkl; ˌekə-;
AmE -'nɑːm-/

economical with the 'truth
a way of saying that sb has left out some important facts, when you do not want to say that they are lying: *After the trial he admitted that he had occasionally been economical with the truth.*

edge /edʒ/

have, etc. an/the edge on/over sb/sth
be slightly better, faster, etc. than sb/sth; have an advantage over sb/sth: *Max's design is very good, but I think Paul's has the edge on it.* ◇ *Extra training will give our team an edge over the opposition.*

on 'edge
nervous, worried or anxious: *Most people feel on edge before exams.*

on the ,edge of your 'seat/'chair
very excited and giving your full attention to sth: *The film was so exciting it had me on the edge of my seat right until the last moment.*

take the 'edge off sth
make sth less strong, unpleasant, etc: *He tried to take the edge off the bad news by promising to help them in their difficulties.* ◇ *I had an apple before lunch, which took the edge off my appetite.*

- cutting → (be at) the cutting edge (of sth)
- knife-edge → on a razor's edge **SEE** on a knife-edge
- teeter → teeter on the brink/edge of sth
- teeth → set sb's teeth on edge

edges /'edʒɪz/

- fray → fray at/around the edges/seams
- rough → rough edges

edgeways /'edʒweɪz/

- word → (not) get a word in edgeways

edgewise /'edʒwaɪz/

- word → (not) get a word in edgewise **SEE** (not) get a word in edgeways

educated /'edʒukeɪtɪd/

an ,educated 'guess
a guess made on the basis of facts, good information, etc., and so probably fairly accurate: *I can't tell you exactly how much the building work will cost, but I can make an educated guess.*

eel /iːl/

- slippery → (as) slippery as an eel

effect /ɪ'fekt/

bring/put sth into ef'fect
make sth, for example an idea, a plan, etc. happen: *The government wants to put its new housing policy into immediate effect.*

come/go into ef'fect
(of laws, rules, etc.) begin to be used, applied, etc: *The winter timetable comes into effect in November.*

in ef'fect
in actual practice; in fact: *They may seem different, but in effect, the two systems are almost identical.*

of/to no ef'fect
not having the result hoped for: *Their warnings were of no effect.* ◇ *They tried to persuade him to change his mind, but to no effect.*

take ef'fect
1 have the intended result: *It will be some time before the painkillers take effect.*
2 (*formal*) start to be valid: *Your promotion takes effect from the end of the month.*

to the ef'fect that... ♦ to this/that ef'fect
used when giving the basic meaning of what sb has said or written, without using their exact words: *A letter was sent to the employees to the effect that the store would have to close down.* ◇ *She told me not to interfere, or words to that effect.*

to good, little, etc. ef'fect
with a good, etc. result: *Her talent as a dancer is shown to considerable effect in this new production.*

with effect from... ♦ with immediate ef'fect (*formal*)
starting from...; starting now: *The government has cut the tax on fuel, with effect from 6th April.*

● **ripple** → a ripple effect

effing /'efɪŋ/
effing and 'blinding (*BrE, informal*)
using swear words (= rude and offensive words): *There was a lot of effing and blinding going on.*

effort /'efət; *AmE* 'efərt/
● **last-ditch** → a last-ditch stand/attempt/effort

efforts /'efəts; *AmE* 'efərts/
● **bend** → bend your mind/efforts to sth

egg /eg/
(have) 'egg on your face (*informal*)
be made to look stupid: *Let's think this out carefully. I don't want to end up with egg on my face.*

● **curate** → the/a curate's egg
● **golden** → (kill) the goose that lays the golden egg/eggs **SEE** (kill) the golden goose
● **lay** → lay an egg
● **nest** → a nest egg

eggs /egz/
put all your eggs into one 'basket
risk all your money, effort, etc. on one thing, so that if it is not successful, you have no other chance: *It may be better to invest a small amount of money in several businesses rather than putting all your eggs into one basket.*

● **golden** → (kill) the goose that lays the golden egg/eggs **SEE** (kill) the golden goose
● **omelette** → you can't make an omelette without breaking eggs

● **sure** → (as) sure as eggs is eggs
● **teach** → teach your grandmother to suck eggs

eggshells /'egʃelz/
● **walk** → walk on eggshells

eight /eɪt/
be/have one over the 'eight (*informal*)
be slightly drunk: *From the way he was walking it was obvious he'd had one over the eight.*

> **❷ ORIGIN**
> This may come from a belief that a normal person could only drink eight glasses of beer without becoming drunk.

behind the 'eight ball (*AmE*)
in a difficult situation, with many risks and disadvantages: *Basically, I made mistakes and put us right behind the eight ball.*

> **NOTE**
> In the game of pool, if you hit the eight ball (= the black ball) into one of the holes at the wrong time, you lose the game. If your ball is behind the eight ball, the risks of doing this are greater.

elbow /'elbəʊ; *AmE* -boʊ/
at your 'elbow
very near; within arm's reach: *I always like to have a dictionary at my elbow to check spellings.*

'elbow grease (*informal*)
the effort used in physical work, especially in cleaning: *The bath was so old and stained that we couldn't get it clean no matter how much elbow grease we used.*

'elbow room (*informal*)
1 enough space to move in: *October is a good time to visit as there are fewer tourists and more elbow room in the restaurants.*
2 the freedom to do sth: *Teachers often feel they have little elbow room to try new methods.*

give sb the 'elbow (*BrE, informal*)
tell sb that you no longer want to have a relationship with them: *I hear she's finally given her boyfriend the elbow.*

● **know** → not know your arse/ass from your elbow
● **power** → more power to sb's elbow

elbows /'elbəʊz; *AmE* -boʊz/
● **rub** → rub elbows (with sb) **SEE** rub shoulders (with sb)

elder /'eldə(r)/
an ,elder 'statesman
1 a person who has had an important job in government, business, etc. and who, though he/she may have retired (= stopped work), is still likely to be asked for his/her opinion and advice
2 any experienced and respected person whose advice or work is valued: *He is regarded as TV's elder statesman, having worked for the giant CBS network for nearly twenty years.*

elders /ˈeldəz; AmE ˈeldərz/

your ˌelders and ˈbetters
people who are older and wiser than you and
whom you should respect: *You may not want to
go, but your elders and betters think you should.*

element /ˈelɪmənt/

in your ˈelement
doing sth that you enjoy and do well, especially
with other similar people: *Julie is in her element
with anything mechanical. She just loves fixing
things.*

out of your ˈelement
in a situation that you are not used to and that
makes you feel uncomfortable: *I feel out of my
element talking about politics.*

elephant /ˈelɪfənt/

the ˌelephant in the ˈroom
a serious problem that everyone is aware of but
which they ignore and choose not to mention:
*The growing budget deficit is the elephant in the
room that nobody wants to talk about.*

● white → a white elephant

elephants /ˈelɪfənts/

● pink → see pink·elephants

eleventh /ɪˈlevnθ/

the eˌleventh ˈhour
the moment when it is almost, but not quite, too
late to do sth, avoid sth, etc: *Our pianist had fallen
ill, and then, at the eleventh hour, when we thought
we'd have to cancel the performance, Jill offered to
replace him.* ▶ eˌleventh-ˈhour *adj.*: *an eleventh-
hour decision*

else /els/

if all else ˈfails (*spoken*)
used to introduce an idea or a suggestion that you
could try if nothing else works: *Let's try phoning
her at this number and then emailing her. If all else
fails, we can always contact her parents.*

or else
1 used to introduce the second of two possibilities: *I can't get through to Sally. She's out, or else
she's decided not to answer the telephone.*
2 (*informal*) used to threaten or warn sb: *You'd
better clean up this mess, or else!*

something ˈelse
1 a different thing; another thing: *He said something else that I thought was interesting.*
2 (*informal*) a person, a thing or an event that is
much better than others of a similar type: *I've seen
some fine players, but she's something else.*

embarrassment /ɪmˈbærəsmənt/

an emˌbarrassment of ˈriches
so many good things that it is difficult to choose
just one: *Stratford has an embarrassment of riches,
what with three theatres and lovely countryside too.*

embryo /ˈembriəʊ; AmE -brioʊ/

in ˈembryo
still in a very early stage of development: *We have
just one editor and a reporter, so you could say that
the newspaper exists in embryo.*

> **NOTE**
> An *embryo* is an animal or a plant in the very
> early stages of its development before it is
> born, comes out of its egg, etc.

emperor /ˈempərə(r)/

**the ˌemperor's new ˈclothes ♦ the ˌemperor
has no ˈclothes**
used to describe a situation in which everybody
suddenly realises that they were mistaken in
believing that sb/sth was very good, important,
etc: *Soon, investors will realize that the emperor
has no clothes and there will be a big sell-off in
stocks.*

> **❷ ORIGIN**
> This comes from a story by Hans Christian
> Andersen. Two men offer to make an emperor
> a new suit from a very light material which
> they say stupid people cannot see. When the
> emperor puts on the suit, nobody wants to
> appear stupid so they all praise his new
> clothes. However, when a little boy asks why
> the emperor has no clothes on, everybody
> admits that they can see no clothes and that
> the emperor is naked.

empty /ˈempti/

the ˌempty ˈnest
the situation that parents are in when their children have left home: *the empty nest syndrome*

on an empty ˈstomach
without having eaten anything: *If I travel on an
empty stomach, I always feel sick.*

● glass → (see the) glass half full/half empty

enchilada /ˌentʃɪˈlɑːdə/

the whole enchiˈlada (*AmE, informal*)
the whole situation; everything: *We had a great
time on vacation, and it only cost us $500 for the
whole enchilada.*

> **NOTE**
> An *enchilada* is a Mexican dish with meat and a
> spicy sauce.

● big → the big enchilada

end /end/

at the ˌend of the ˈday (*BrE, spoken*)
when everything has been considered: *At the end
of the day, it's your decision and nobody else's.*

be at an ˈend (*formal*)
be finished: *Our negotiations are at an end, and we
have reached an agreement.*

be at the ˌend of your 'tether (*BrE*) (*AmE* **be at the ˌend of your 'rope**)
having no more patience or strength left: *After two hours of hearing the children shout and argue, I really was at the end of my tether.*

be the 'end (*BrE*, *spoken*)
be very annoying; be impossible to tolerate: *Your children really are the end!* ◇ *I'd seen dirty houses before, but theirs was the absolute end!*

come to a bad/sticky 'end (*informal*)
finish in an unpleasant way; finish by having sth unpleasant happen to you, usually because of your own actions: *The neighbours used to shake their heads at his behaviour and say that he'd come to a bad end.*

days, weeks, etc. on 'end
several days, weeks, etc., one after another: *She stays away from home for days on end.* ◇ *He sits watching TV for hours on end.*

ˌend your 'days/'life (in sth)
spend the last part of your life in a particular state or place: *He ended his days in poverty.*

an ˌend in it'self
a thing that is itself important and not just a part of sth more important: *Speech is not an end in itself, but a means to communicate something.*

ˌend in 'tears (*spoken*)
if you say that sth will **end in tears**, you are warning sb that what they are doing will have an unhappy or unpleasant result: *You'd better keep your promise or it'll end in tears.*

'end it all
kill yourself; commit suicide: *After years of suffering, she had decided to end it all.*

the end justifies the 'means (*saying*)
bad or unfair methods of doing sth are acceptable if the result of that action is good or positive

the ˌend of the 'road/'line
the point where sb/sth cannot continue: *The workers see the closure of the pit as the end of the line for mining in this area.* ◇ *It's the end of the road for our relationship. We just can't agree about anything any more.*

end of 'story (*spoken*)
used when you are stating that there is nothing more that can be said or done about sth: *Look, I told you I can't give you a job here. End of story.*

ˌend to 'end
in a line, with the ends touching: *They arranged the tables end to end.*

get/have your 'end away (*BrE*, *slang*)
have sex

in the 'end
after or in spite of everything that has gone before; finally: *I looked for my keys for hours, and in the end I found them in the car.* ◇ *They tried to get him to confess, and in the end he did.*

keep your 'end up (*BrE*, *informal*)
stay cheerful or perform well in a difficult situation: *She managed to keep her end up even though she was suffering from flu.* ◇ *I had trouble keeping*

my end up in the conversation, because I didn't know anything about the subject.

no 'end (*spoken*)
very much: *Your visit pleased her no end.*

no 'end of (*spoken*)
a lot of: *Making new friends has done him no end of good.* ◇ *We've had no end of offers of help.*

not be the ˌend of the 'world (*spoken*)
not be a disaster: *It wouldn't be the end of the world if you couldn't get into college. I'm sure you'd be able to find a good job anyway.* ◇ *Why are you so upset? It's not the end of the world.*

not know/not be able to tell ˌone end of sth from the 'other (*informal*)
know absolutely nothing about sth, for example a machine: *Don't ask me to fix the car. I don't know one end of an engine from the other.*

not see beyond/past the ˌend of your 'nose
not notice anything apart from what you are doing at present: *I'm so busy running the office that I can't see beyond the end of my nose.*

put an 'end to yourself ♦ put an 'end to it all
kill yourself: *She told me that sometimes she felt so bad that she just felt like putting an end to it all.*

the sth to end all sths
used to emphasize how large, important, exciting, etc. you think sth is: *The movie has a car chase to end all car chases.* ◇ *Many people said that World War I would be the war to end all wars.*

- **beginning** → the beginning of the end
- **bitter** → to the bitter end
- **business** → the business end (of sth)
- **dead** → a dead end
- **deep** → go off the deep end
- **deep** → jump in/be thrown in at the deep end
- **draw** → get the short end of the stick **SEE** draw the short straw
- **hair** → your hair stands on end
- **hear** → hear the end of sth
- **light** → (see the) light at the end of the tunnel
- **loose** → at a loose end
- **means** → (be) a means to an end
- **receiving** → be on/at the receiving end (of sth)
- **rough** → the rough end of the pineapple
- **sharp** → the sharp end (of sth)
- **tail** → (at) the tail end (of sth)
- **thin** → the thin end of the wedge
- **wits** → be at your wits' end
- **wrong** → get (hold of) the wrong end of the stick

end-all /'end ɔːl/

- **be-all** → the be-all and end-all (of sth)

ends /endz/

make (both) ends 'meet
earn enough to pay your living expenses: *Since I lost my job, I'm finding it harder to make ends meet.*

to the ˌends of the 'earth
a very great distance: *He would go to the ends of the earth to be with her.*

- **burn** → burn the candle at both ends
- **loose** → at loose ends **SEE** at a loose end
- **loose** → the loose ends/threads
- **odds** → odds and ends
- **well** → all's well that ends well

enemy /'enəmi/

- **public** → public enemy number one
- **wish** → wouldn't wish sth on my, etc. worst enemy
- **worst** → be your own worst enemy

English /'ɪŋglɪʃ/

the ˌKing's/ˌQueen's 'English (*old-fashioned or humorous*)
(in Britain) correct standard English: *I can't understand a word you're saying. Can't you speak the Queen's English?*

- **plain** → in plain English

Englishman /'ɪŋglɪʃmən/

an ˌEnglishman's ˌhome is his 'castle (*BrE*)
(*AmE* **a ˌman's ˌhome is his 'castle**) (*saying*)
a person's home is a place where they can be private and safe and do as they like

engraved /ɪn'greɪvd/

be engraved on/in your 'heart/'memory/ 'mind
be sth that you will never forget because it affected you so strongly: *Although he was very young at the time, the date of his father's funeral was engraved on his heart.*

> **NOTE**
> *Engrave* means 'cut words or designs on wood, stone, etc.'.

enough /ɪ'nʌf/

ˌcuriously, ˌfunnily, ˌstrangely, etc. e'nough
used to show that sth is surprising: *Funnily enough, I was born on exactly the same day as my wife.*

eˌnough is e'nough (*saying*)
used when you think that sth should not continue any longer: *Enough is enough! I don't mind a joke, but now you've gone too far!*

have had e'nough (of sb/sth)
used when sb/sth is annoying you and you no longer want to do, have or see them/it: *I've had enough of driving the kids around.*

enter /'entə(r)/

enter sb's 'head
be thought of by sb; occur to sb: *It never even entered my head that we might not win.*

enter sb's/your 'name (for sth) ♦ **put sb's/ your 'name down (for sth)**
apply for a place at a school, in a competition, etc. for sb or yourself: *Have you entered your name for the quiz yet?*

- **spirit** → get/enter into the spirit of sth

entering /'entərɪŋ/

- **breaking** → breaking and entering

entirety /ɪn'taɪərəti/

in its/their en'tirety
as a whole, rather than in parts: *The poem is too long to quote in its entirety.*

envelope /'envələʊp; 'ɒn-; *AmE* 'envəloʊp; 'ɑːn-/

- **push** → push the envelope

envy /'envi/

be the envy of sb/sth
be a person or thing that other people admire and that causes feelings of envy: *Our new games console was the envy of all the kids in the street.*

- **green** → green with envy

equal /'iːkwəl/

be without 'equal ♦ **have no 'equal** (*formal*)
be better than anything else or anyone else of the same type: *He was a violinist without equal.*

on equal 'terms (with sb/sth) ♦ **on the same 'terms (as sb/sth)**
with no difference or advantage over another person; as equals: *We're not competing on equal terms; the other team has one more player.* ◇ *A good teacher should treat all her students on the same terms.*

ˌsome (people, members, etc.) are more equal than 'others (*saying*)
although the members of a society, group, etc. appear to be equal, some get better treatment than others

> **❓ ORIGIN**
> This phrase is used by one of the pigs in the book *Animal Farm* by George Orwell: 'All animals are equal but some animals are more equal than others.'

- **things** → other/all things being equal

equals /'iːkwəlz/

- **first** → first among equals

err /ɜː(r); *AmE* er/

err on the side of sth
show slightly too much rather than too little of a quality, especially a good one: *When I am marking exam papers, I always try to err on the side of generosity* (= I give slightly higher marks than the students may deserve).

> **NOTE**
> *Err* is an old-fashioned word meaning 'make a mistake'.

errand /'erənd/

- **fool** → a fool's errand

error /'erə(r)/

the ˌerror of your 'ways (*formal* or *humorous*)
what is wrong and should be changed about the
kind of life you are leading: *While he was in prison,
a social worker visited him in an attempt to make
him see the error of his ways.*

● trial → by trial and error

escape /ɪ'skeɪp/

escape sb's 'notice
not be noticed by sb: *It may have escaped your
notice but I'm very busy right now. Can we talk
later?*

make ˌgood your e'scape (*written*)
manage to escape completely: *In the confusion at
the border, the woman made good her escape.* ◇ *He
made good his escape from a crowd of journalists by
jumping over a fence.*

● narrow → a narrow escape/squeak

escaped /ɪ'skeɪpt/

● stable → shut, etc. the barn door after the horse has
escaped **SEE** shut/lock/close the stable door after the
horse has bolted

essence /'esns/

of the 'essence
absolutely necessary: *Time is of the essence* (= we
must do things as quickly as possible).

etched /etʃt/

be etched on your 'heart/'memory/'mind
be sth that you will never forget because it affected you so strongly: *The image of their son holding
up the championship trophy would be etched on
their memories forever.*

eternal /ɪ'tɜːnl; *AmE* ɪ'tɜːrnl/

● hope → hope springs eternal

even /'iːvn/

be 'even (*informal*)
no longer owe sb money or a favour: *If I pay for the
meals then we're even.*

be/get 'even with sb (*informal*)
cause sb the same amount of trouble or harm as
they have caused you: *I'll get even with him some
day for making those nasty comments about me.*

break 'even
make neither a profit nor a loss: *In the first year of
the business we only just managed to break even.*

even as (*formal*)
just at the same time as sb does sth or as sth else
happens: *Even as he shouted the warning the car
skidded.*

even if/though
in spite of the fact or belief that; no matter
whether: *I'll get there, even if I have to walk.*
◇ *I like her, even though she can be annoying at
times.*

ˌeven 'now/'then
1 in spite of what has/had happened: *I've shown
him the photographs but even now he won't believe
me.* ◇ *Even then she would not admit her mistake.*
2 (*formal*) at this or that exact moment: *The
troops are even now preparing to march into the
city.*

ˌeven the 'score
harm or punish sb who has harmed or cheated
you in the past: *When he discovered how Martha
had tricked him, Jack was determined to even the
score.* **OPP** call it quits

ˌeven 'so
in spite of that: *There are a lot of spelling mistakes;
even so, it's quite a good answer.*

have an even 'chance (of doing sth)
be equally likely to do or not do sth: *She has more
than an even chance of winning tomorrow.*

on an even 'keel
living, working or happening in a calm way, with
no sudden changes, especially after a difficult
time: *After all the troubles of the past weeks, life
seems to be getting back on an even keel again.*

> **NOTE**
> The *keel* is the long piece of wood or steel along
> the bottom of a ship, on which the frame is
> built, and which helps to keep it in a vertical
> position in the water.

● honours → honours are even
● less → even/much/still less

event /ɪ'vent/

in the e'vent
as it actually happened, contrasted with what was
expected: *We all thought he was lazy, but in the
event he worked hard and passed all his exams.*

**in the event of sth ◆ in the event that sth
happens**
if sth happens: *The money will be paid to your family in the event of your death.* ◇ *In the event of an
emergency please call the following number…*

● happy → a/the happy event
● wise → be wise after the event

events /ɪ'vents/

at 'all events ◆ in 'any event
whatever happens; anyway: *James may arrive this
evening or tomorrow morning. In any event, I
would like you to meet him at the airport.* ◇ *At all
events, there will be a change of government.*

a/the ˌturn of e'vents
the way things happen, especially when this is not
expected: *Because of a strange turn of events at
work, she has unexpectedly been offered a very good
job in the sales department.*

ever /'evə(r)/

did you 'ever (…)! (*old-fashioned, informal*)
used to show that you are surprised or shocked:
Did you ever hear anything like it?

ever more... (*formal*)
more and more...: *She grew ever more impatient as time passed.*

ever since (...)
continuously since the time mentioned: *He's had a car ever since he was 18.* ◇ *I was bitten by a dog once and I've been afraid of them ever since.*

'ever so/'ever such (a)... (*spoken, especially BrE*)
very: *Thanks ever so much for all your help.* ◇ *She plays the piano ever so well.* ◇ *He's ever such a nice man.*

if ,ever there 'was (one) (*spoken*)
used to emphasize that sth is certainly true: *That meal was a disaster if ever there was one!*

yours 'ever/ever 'yours
sometimes used at the end of an informal letter, before you write your name

everything /ˈevriθɪŋ/

and everything (*spoken*)
and so on; and other similar things: *Have you got his name and address and everything?* ◇ *She told me about the baby and everything.*

money, winning, etc. isn't 'everything
money, etc. is not the most important thing: *Work isn't everything. You must learn to relax a bit more.*

evidence /ˈevɪdəns/

in 'evidence
present and clearly seen: *There were very few local people in evidence at the meeting.* ◇ *What's the matter with John? His sense of humour hasn't been much in evidence recently.*

turn King's/Queen's 'evidence (*BrE*) (*AmE* **turn State's 'evidence**)
give information against other criminals in order to get a less severe punishment: *One of the gang turned State's evidence and identified at least three others involved in the fraud.*

evil /ˈiːvl; ˈiːvɪl/

the evil 'hour/'day/'moment
the time when you have to do sth difficult or unpleasant: *I'd better go and see the dentist — I can't put off the evil hour any longer.* ◇ *I worried for weeks about how I would tell him the bad news but eventually I couldn't put off the evil day any longer.*

give sb the evil 'eye
look at sb in a very angry, unfriendly or unpleasant way, as if you are trying to harm them by magic power: *I don't know why you're giving me the evil eye — I haven't done anything wrong!*

● lesser → the lesser evil
● necessary → a necessary evil

evils /ˈiːvlz; ˈiːvɪlz/

● lesser → the lesser of two evils

exactly /ɪgˈzæktli/

not exactly (*spoken*)
1 used when you are saying the opposite of what you really mean: *He wasn't exactly pleased to see us — in fact he refused to open the door.* ◇ *It's not exactly beautiful, is it?* (= it's ugly)
2 used when you are correcting sth that sb has said: *'So he told you you'd got the job?' 'Not exactly, but he said they were impressed with me.'*

examined /ɪgˈzæmɪnd/

● head → need, want, etc. your head examined

example /ɪgˈzɑːmpl; AmE -ˈzæmpl/

make an e'xample of sb
punish sb severely for a mistake, crime, etc. so that others will be less likely to do wrong: *The judge decided to make an example of the leaders of the riot in order to prevent other disturbances.*

set (sb) an e'xample ◆ **set (sb) a good, bad, etc. e'xample**
show a standard of work or behaviour for others to follow or copy; show a good, bad, etc. model for others: *She sets us all an example* (= a good example). ◇ *You shouldn't use bad language in front of your children — it sets a bad example.*

● shining → be a shining example (of sb/sth)

excellence /ˈeksələːns; AmE ˌeksəˈlɑːns/

● par → par excellence

excepted /ɪkˈseptɪd/

● present → present company excepted

excepting /ɪkˈseptɪŋ/

● present → excepting present company **SEE** present company excepted

exception /ɪkˈsepʃn/

the ex'ception that proves the 'rule (*saying*)
people say that sth is **the exception that proves the rule** when they are stating sth that seems to be different from the normal situation, but they mean that the normal situation remains true in general: *English people are supposed to be very reserved, but Pete is the exception that proves the rule — he'll chat to anyone!*

make an ex'ception
allow sb not to follow the usual rule on one occasion: *Children are not usually allowed in, but I'm prepared to make an exception in this case.*

take ex'ception to sth
be very offended by a remark, suggestion, etc: *I take great exception to your suggestion that I only did this for the money.*

with the ex'ception of
except; not including: *All his novels are set in Italy with the exception of his last.*

without ex'ception
used to emphasize that the statement you are making is always true and everyone or everything is included: *All students without exception must take the English examination.*

exchange /ɪks'tʃeɪndʒ/

• words → have/exchange words (with sb) (about sth)

excuse /ɪk'skjuːz/

ex'cuse me
1 used before you do or say sth that might annoy sb, or to get sb's attention: *Excuse me, is anybody sitting here?* ◇ *Excuse me, could you tell me the time, please?*
2 used for saying sorry or disagreeing with sb, or for showing that you are annoyed: *Excuse me, but I think you're mistaken.* ◇ *Excuse me, sir, but you can't park there!*
3 used when you are leaving the room for a short time: *Excuse me a minute, I'll be right back.*
4 (*especially AmE*) used for saying sorry for something you have done: *Excuse me, did I step on your toe?*
5 (*especially AmE*) used when you did not hear what sb said and you want them to repeat it

• French → excuse/pardon my French

exhibition /ˌeksɪ'bɪʃn/

make an exhi'bition of yourself (*disapproving*)
behave in a stupid or an embarrassing way that makes people notice you: *She got angry and made a real exhibition of herself at the party.*

existence /ɪg'zɪstəns/

• bane → the bane of sb's life/existence

expect /ɪk'spekt/

what (else) do you ex'pect? (*spoken*)
used to tell sb not to be surprised by sth: *She shouted at you? What do you expect when you treat her like that?*

expected /ɪk'spektɪd/

be (only) to be ex'pected
be likely to happen; be quite normal: *A little tiredness after taking these drugs is to be expected.* ◇ *'I'm afraid I'm very nervous.' 'Don't worry, that's only to be expected.'*

expecting /ɪk'spektɪŋ/

be ex'pecting (*informal*)
be pregnant: *I hear Sue's expecting.*

expense /ɪk'spens/

at sb's ex'pense
1 paid for by sb: *When Joe is travelling at the firm's expense, he goes first class.*
2 (of jokes, etc.) making sb seem foolish: *They all had a good laugh at Pete's expense.*

at the expense of sb/sth
causing damage or loss to sb/sth else: *We could lower the price, but only at the expense of quality.*

go to the expense of sth/of doing sth ◆ go to a lot of, etc. ex'pense
spend money on sth: *They went to all the expense of redecorating the house and then they moved.*

put sb to the expense of sth/of doing sth ◆ put sb to a lot of, etc. ex'pense
make sb spend money on sth: *Their visit put us to a lot of expense.*

• spare → spare no expense/pains/trouble (to do sth/(in) doing sth)

experience /ɪk'spɪəriəns; AmE -'spɪr-/

put sth down to ex'perience (also **chalk it up to ex'perience** *especially AmE*)
accept a failure, loss, etc. as being sth that you can learn from: *When her second novel was rejected by the publisher, she put it down to experience and began another one.*

explain /ɪk'spleɪn/

ex'plain yourself
1 give sb reasons for your behaviour, especially when they are angry or upset because of it: *I really don't see why I should have to explain myself to you.*
2 say what you mean in a clear way: *Could you explain yourself a little more — I didn't understand.*

extent /ɪk'stent/

to...extent
used to show how far sth is true or how great an effect it has: *To a certain extent, we are all responsible for this tragic situation.* ◇ *He had changed to such an extent* (= so much) *that I no longer recognized him.* ◇ *The pollution of the forest has seriously affected plant life and, to a lesser extent, wildlife.* ◇ *To what extent is this true of all schools?*

extra /'ekstrə/

• extra → go the extra mile (for sb/sth)

extreme /ɪk'striːm/

boring, silly, etc. in the ex'treme
extremely boring, silly, etc: *I must admit, it's puzzling in the extreme just how these books found their way here.*

extremes /ɪk'striːmz/

go to ex'tremes ◆ carry/take sth to ex'tremes
behave in a way that is not moderate or normal: *She really goes to extremes, spending such huge sums of money on entertaining her friends.* ◇ *You never go out after dark? That's taking being careful to extremes, isn't it?*

eye /aɪ/

an ‚eye for an 'eye (and a ‚tooth for a 'tooth) (*saying*)
a person who treats sb else badly should be treated in the same way **OPP** two wrongs don't make a right

> **❓ ORIGIN**
> This expression comes from the Bible.

get your 'eye in (*BrE*)
(in ball games) get to the point where you start to judge distances, the speed of the ball, etc., accurately and so start to play well: *The batsman began slowly but once he got his eye in he started to play some very good shots.*

give your eye 'teeth for sth/to do sth (*informal*)
(usually used with *would*) give anything for sth; want sth very much: *I'd give my eye teeth to own a car like that.* ◇ *He'd give his eye teeth for a job in television.*

have an 'eye for sth
be good at judging sth: *He's always had an eye for a bargain.*

have your 'eye on sb/sth
watch sb/sth closely; want to have sth: *A house that I'd had my eye on for some time suddenly came up for sale.*

have an eye to/for the main 'chance (*BrE, usually disapproving*)
be good at using opportunities for your own benefit: *She's certainly got an eye for the main chance. Her business has become highly successful.*

have one eye/half an eye on sth
look at or watch sth while doing sth else, especially in a secret way so that other people do not notice: *During his talk, most of the delegates had one eye on the clock.*

keep an/your 'eye on sb/sth
take responsibility for sb/sth; make sure that sb/sth is safe: *It's my job to keep an eye on how the money is spent.* ◇ *Keep an eye on my bag while I go and make a phone call, will you?*

She found it difficult to relax when she had to keep an eye on young Lucy.

keep your eye on the 'ball
continue to give your attention to what is most important: *We've got to keep our eye on the ball if we want to remain successful.*

keep an 'eye out (for sb/sth) (*informal*)
watch or look carefully (for sb/sth): *Can you keep an eye out for the taxi and let me know when it arrives?*

(be unable to) look sb in the 'eye(s)/'face
(be unable to) look at sb directly (because you feel embarrassed, ashamed, etc.): *I knew he was lying because he wouldn't look me in the eye when he spoke.*

‚my 'eye! (*BrE, spoken*)
used to show that you do not believe sb/sth: *'It's an antique.' 'An antique, my eye!'*

one in the eye for sb/sth (*informal*)
a result, an action, etc. that represents a defeat or disappointment for sb/sth: *The appointment of a woman was one in the eye for male domination.*

(not) see eye to 'eye (with sb) (about/on/over sth)
(not) have the same opinion or attitude as sb else (about a particular issue, problem, etc.): *My boss and I don't see eye to eye over the question of finance.*

under the (watchful) eye of sb
being watched carefully by sb: *The children played under the watchful eye of their father.*

what the eye doesn't 'see (the heart doesn't 'grieve over) (*saying*)
if a person does not know about sth that they would normally disapprove of, then it cannot hurt them: *What does it matter if I do use his desk while he's away? What the eye doesn't see…!*

with an eye to sth/to doing sth
intending to do sth: *She's doing an interpreters' course with an eye to getting a job abroad.*

- apple → the apple of sb's eye
- bat → not bat an eye **SEE** not bat an eyelid
- beady → have your beady eye on sb/sth
- beady → keep a beady eye on sb/sth
- beauty → beauty is in the eye of the beholder
- black → a black eye
- blind → turn a blind eye (to sth)
- blink → in the blink of an eye
- cast → cast/run an eye/your eyes over sth
- catch → catch sb's eye
- close² → keep a close eye/watch on sb/sth
- cock → cock an ear/eye at sth/sb
- corner → out of the corner of your eye
- dry → not a dry eye in the house
- eagle → an/sb's eagle eye
- evil → give sb the evil eye
- far → as far as the eye can/could see
- hit → hit sb in the eye
- meet → meet the/your eye(s)
- meets → there's more to sb/sth than meets the eye
- mind → in your mind's eye
- naked → the naked eye
- pig → in a pig's eye
- please → please the eye
- private → a private eye
- public → in the public eye
- roving → have a roving eye

- twinkling → in the twinkling of an eye
- weather → keep a weather eye on sth/open for sth

eyeball /'aɪbɔːl/

,eyeball to 'eyeball (with sb) (*informal*)
standing very close, facing one another, for example in a fight: *The two men stood eyeball to eyeball, shouting insults at each other.*

- hairy → give sb the hairy eyeball

eyeballs /'aɪbɔːlz/

- drugged → drugged up to the eyeballs
- eyes → be up to your eyes/eyeballs in sth

eyebrows /'aɪbraʊz/

- raise → raise your eyebrows (at sth)

eyeful /'aɪfʊl/

have/get an 'eyeful (of sth) (*BrE, spoken*)
look carefully at sth that is interesting or unusual: *Quick! Come and get an eyeful of this!*

eyelashes /'aɪlæʃɪz/

- bat → bat your eyelashes/eyes

eyelid /'aɪlɪd/

- bat → not bat an eyelid

eyes /aɪz/

all eyes are on sb/sth
if **all eyes are on sb/sth**, everyone is looking at sb/sth in an interested way: *All eyes were on him as he walked onto the stage.*

be all 'eyes
watch with close attention and usually with great interest: *The children were all eyes as, one by one, I took the toys out of the bag.*

be up to your 'eyes/'eyeballs in sth
have a lot of sth to deal with: *He was up to his eyes in debt.*

'Lunch? No way – I'm up to my eyes in here!'

before your (very) 'eyes
right in front of you, where you can see sth very clearly: *There, before my very eyes, he took the plane ticket and ripped it into tiny pieces.*

clap/lay/set 'eyes on sb/sth (*informal*)
see sb/sth: *I've no idea who she is. I've never clapped eyes on her before.* ◇ *The moment I set eyes on the house, I knew I would live there.*

your ,eyes are bigger than your 'stomach
(*informal, humorous*)
used to say that sb has been greedy by taking more food than they can eat: *Can't you finish your food? Your eyes are bigger than your stomach!*

your eyes nearly pop out of your 'head
(*informal*)
sb has an expression of great surprise on their face: *Our eyes nearly popped out of our heads when we saw a giraffe walking down the High Street.*
▸ **'eye-popping** *adj.* (*informal*) very surprising or amazing: *a movie with eye-popping special effects*

for sb's eyes 'only
to be seen only by sb: *This letter is for your eyes only, so keep it locked in your desk.*

have eyes in the back of your 'head (*informal*)
seem to be able to see everything and know what is going on: *You have to have eyes in the back of your head to keep control of six lively children.*

have eyes like a 'hawk
be able to notice or see everything: *Mrs Fielding's bound to notice that chipped glass. The woman has eyes like a hawk!* ▸ **,hawk-'eyed** *adj.*

> **NOTE**
> A *hawk* is a kind of bird of prey (= a bird that kills other creatures for food), and can see small things from very far away.

in the eyes of sb/sth ◆ **in sb's eyes**
according to sb/sth; in sb's opinion: *You may believe that what you are doing is right, but in the eyes of the law it's a crime.*

keep your 'eyes open/peeled/skinned (for sb/sth)
watch carefully (for sb/sth): *Keep your eyes peeled, and if you see anything suspicious, call the police immediately.*

make 'eyes at sb (*informal*)
look at sb in a way that tries to attract them sexually: *He did nothing all evening but make eyes at the girls!*

not take your 'eyes off sb/sth
(often used with *can* or *could*) not stop looking at sb/sth: *She couldn't take her eyes off the beautiful picture.*

only have eyes for sb ◆ **have eyes only for sb**
be interested in, or in love with a particular person and nobody else: *John tried to get Helen to go out with him, but she only had eyes for Chris.*

shut/close your 'eyes to sth
pretend that you have not noticed sth so that you do not have to deal with it: *My son has his faults — and I've never closed my eyes to them — but dishonesty isn't one of them.* ◇ *Politicians seemed to be shutting their eyes to corruption in the police force.*

through the eyes of sb ♦ through sb's eyes
from the point of view of sb: *You must try to see it through the eyes of the parents, not just from the teacher's point of view.* ◇ *Can't you look at the situation through my eyes?*

with your 'eyes open
knowing what you are doing, what to expect, and what the results may be: *If a marriage is to work, both partners must go into it with their eyes open.*

(be able to do sth) with your 'eyes shut/closed
(be able to do sth) very easily, especially because you have done it many times before: *She's driven up to Scotland so often that she can do it with her eyes shut.*

- bat → bat your eyelashes/eyes
- believe → not believe your eyes/ears
- cast → cast/run an eye/your eyes over sth
- cry → cry your eyes out
- eye → (be unable to) look sb in the eye(s)/face
- feast → feast your eyes (on sb/sth)
- meet → meet sb's eyes
- open → open your/sb's eyes (to sth)
- pull → pull the wool over sb's eyes
- scales → the scales fall from sb's eyes
- sight → be a sight for sore eyes
- stars → have stars in your eyes

F f

FA /ˌef 'eɪ/
- sweet → sweet FA

face /feɪs/

be in your 'face (*informal*)
if an attitude, a performance, etc. is **in your face** it is aggressive in style and designed to make people react strongly to it: *This band's famous for their live performances, which are always loud and in your face.* ▶ **in-your-'face** *adj.*: *I don't really like in-your-face action thrillers.*

disappear/vanish off the face of the 'earth
disappear completely: *Keep looking — they can't just have vanished off the face of the earth.*

your/sb's 'face doesn't fit
used to say that sb will not get a particular job or position because they do not have the appearance, personality, etc. that the employer wants, even when this should not be important: *It doesn't matter how qualified you are, if your face doesn't fit, you don't stand a chance.*

your face 'falls
you suddenly look disappointed or upset: *He was quite cheerful until we told him the price. Then his face fell.*

his, her, etc. face is like 'thunder ♦ he, she, etc. has a face like 'thunder
sb looks very angry: *'What's wrong with Julia?' 'I don't know, but she's had a face like thunder all morning.'*

face the 'music (*informal*)
accept the difficulties, criticism and unpleasant results that your words or actions may cause: *He's been cheating us out of our money for years and now it's time for him to face the music.*

ˌface to 'face (with sb/sth)
1 in the presence of sb and close enough to meet, talk, see, etc. them: *The two leaders came face to face for the first time in Moscow this morning.* ◇ *The programme brought Anna face to face with her father for the first time in her life.* ◇ *face-to-face discussions, negotiations, etc.*
2 in a situation where you have to accept that sth is true and deal with it: *The crisis has brought her face to face with a lot of problems she had been trying not to think about.*

Peter and Mary finally came face to face.

ˌface 'up/'down
1 (of a person) with your face and stomach facing upwards/downwards: *She lay face down on the bed.*
2 (of a playing card) with the number or picture facing upwards/downwards: *Place the card face up on the pile.*

get in sb's 'face (*AmE, informal*)
annoy sb by criticizing them or telling them what to do all the time: *She got in my face about staying out of things that don't concern me.* ◇ *I don't care who you are. Don't get in my face.*

in the face of sth
even though sth, usually a danger, problem or unpleasant situation, etc. exists: *In the face of all the evidence against you, how can you say that you're innocent?* ◇ *She married him in the face of opposition from both her parents.* ◇ *In the face of very dangerous conditions, they managed to rescue all the men from the ship.*

let's 'face it (*informal*)
we must accept the unpleasant facts; let's be honest: *Let's face it — we just don't have enough money to buy a new car.* ◇ *Let's face it. He married her for her money, not for love.*

look/stare you in the 'face
(usually used in progressive tenses) (of a fact, an answer, a situation, etc.) be obvious but not noticed: *The answer to the problem had been staring her in the face for years but she hadn't seen it.* ◇ *'Where's that book?' 'There in front of you, looking you in the face.'*

lose 'face
be less respected or look stupid because of sth you have done: *The government can't agree to the changes without losing face.* **OPP** save (sb's) face
▶ **(a) loss of 'face** *noun*: *This gives him an opportunity to change his mind without loss of face.*

on the 'face of it (*informal*)
as sth appears to you when you first look at or consider it, especially when your first impression may be or was wrong: *On the face of it the pay offer looked wonderful, but in fact it wasn't nearly as good as we thought.* ◇ *'Well, what do you think of the new plans?' 'On the face of it, they look good but I think we need to look at them more closely.'*

set your face against sth (*written, especially BrE*)
be strongly opposed to sth and refuse to change your opinion: *Her father had set his face against the marriage.*

take sb/sth at face 'value
accept that sb/sth is exactly as they/it first appears: *You can't take everything she says at face value.* ◇ *A diplomat learns not to take everything at face value.*

to sb's 'face
(say sth) openly, when speaking to sb: *Would you really call her a liar to her face?* ◇ *I think he's guilty but I'd never dare say it to his face.* **OPP** behind sb's back

'what's his/her face (*spoken*)
used to refer to a person whose name you cannot remember: *Are you still working for what's her face?*

- blow → blow up in sb's face
- blue → (do sth) till you're blue in the face
- brave → put a brave face on sth
- brave → put on a brave face
- egg → (have) egg on your face
- eye → (be unable to) look sb in the eye(s)/face
- flat → fall flat on your face
- fly → fly in the face of sth
- laugh → laugh in sb's face
- laugh → laugh on the other side of your face
- long → (pull, wear, etc.) a long face
- nerve → have the face to do sth SEE have the nerve to do sth
- nose → cut off your nose to spite your face
- plain → (as) plain as the nose on your face
- pretty → not just a pretty face
- pull → pull/make faces/a face (at sb/sth)
- red → a red face
- save → save (sb's) face
- show → show your face
- shut → shut your mouth/trap/face/gob!
- slap → a slap in the face
- smash → smash sb's face/head in
- stare → stare sth in the face
- straight → (keep) a straight face
- wipe → wipe sth off the face of the earth
- wipe → wipe the/that smile, grin, etc. off your/sb's face
- written → be written all over sb's face

facelift /'feɪslɪft/

give sth a 'facelift
improve the appearance of sth, for example a building, room, etc: *We've given our offices a facelift — new furniture, new lighting and a new carpet.* ◇ *The whole street needs a facelift.*

NOTE
A *facelift* is an operation to lift and tighten the skin on your face in order to make you look younger.

faces /'feɪsɪz/
- pull → pull/make faces/a face (at sb/sth)

fact /fækt/

,after the 'fact
after sth has happened or been done when it is too late to prevent it or change it: *On some vital decisions employees were only informed after the fact.*

a ,fact of 'life
something difficult or unpleasant that cannot be changed and has to be accepted or dealt with: *Taxes are a fact of life. You just have to pay them.* ◇ *It is a fact of life that some people are born more intelligent than others.*

in (actual) 'fact
1 used to emphasize a statement, especially one that is the opposite of what has just been mentioned: *This £10 note looks genuine but it is, in actual fact, a fake.* ◇ *I thought the talk would be boring but in fact it was very interesting.*
2 used to give extra details about sth that has just been mentioned: *It was cold. In fact, it was freezing.*

is that a 'fact? (*spoken*)
used in reply to a statement that you find interesting or surprising, or that you do not believe: *'She says I'm one of the best students she's ever taught.' 'Is that a fact?'*

- matter → as a matter of fact
- matter → the fact/truth of the matter
- point → in point of fact

facts /fækts/

the ,facts of 'life
the facts about sex, how babies are born, etc., especially when told to children: *When do you think you should tell your children the facts of life?*

the facts speak for them'selves
it is not necessary to give any further explanation about sth because the information that is available already proves that it is true: *The programme producers say they were careful not to present their own opinions, simply letting the facts speak for themselves.*

- hard → hard facts

fade /feɪd/
- woodwork → blend/fade into the woodwork

fail /feɪl/

without 'fail
used for emphasizing that sth always happens or must happen: *She sends me a Christmas card every year without fail.* ◇ *You must be here by 8.30 without fail.*

● **words** → words fail me

fails /feɪlz/

● **else** → if all else fails

faint /feɪnt/

● **damn** → damn sb/sth with faint praise

faintest /'feɪntɪst/

not have the 'faintest/'foggiest (idea) (*BrE, informal*)
have no idea at all about sth; not know anything at all: *I haven't got the faintest idea what to buy Roger for his birthday.* ◇ *'Where are we?' 'I'm afraid I haven't the foggiest.'*

fair /feə(r)/; *AmE* fer/

all's fair in love and 'war (*saying*)
normal rules of behaviour do not apply in situations like war and love: *'I told Sarah that John had another girlfriend.' 'But that's not true; he hasn't.' 'I know, but all's fair in love and war.'*

> **NOTE**
> This is often used with other words to make new expressions, for example *all's fair in friendship and business*.

be 'fair! (*spoken*)
used to tell sb to be reasonable in their judgement of sb/sth: *Be fair! She didn't even know you were coming today.*

be set 'fair (*BrE*)
1 (of weather) be good and with no sign of change: *Apparently the weather is set fair for the rest of the week.*
2 be likely to be successful: *They are set fair to win the championship.*

by ,fair means or 'foul
even if unfair methods are used: *He's determined to buy that company by fair means or foul.*

fair and 'square (also **fairly and 'squarely**)
1 completely and fully: *They were the better team and they beat us fair and square.*
2 directly and with force: *I hit him fair and square on the chin.*

a fair crack of the 'whip (*BrE, informal*)
a fair or reasonable opportunity to do sth or to show that you can do sth: *I don't think he was really given a fair crack of the whip. He only had five minutes to present his suggestions.* ◇ *We all got a fair crack of the whip. We can't complain.*

,fair 'dinkum (*AustralE, New Zealand, informal*)
1 used to emphasize that sth is genuine or true, or to ask whether it is: *It's a fair dinkum Aussie wedding.* ◇ *'Burt's just told me he's packing up in a month.' 'Fair dinkum?'*

2 used to emphasize that behaviour is acceptable: *They were asking a lot for the car, but fair dinkum considering how new it is.*

fair e'nough (*informal*)
1 used for accepting a suggestion, etc: *'I think £200 is a reasonable price.' 'Fair enough. Can I pay you at the end of the week?'*
2 used for showing that you think that sth is reasonable: *Letting the students work the machines on their own is fair enough, but they do need some training first.*

fair 'game
if a person or thing is said to be **fair game**, it is considered acceptable to play jokes on them, criticize them, etc: *The younger teachers were considered fair game by most of the kids.*

> **NOTE**
> In this idiom, *game* refers to birds and animals that people hunt for sport or food.

a fair 'hearing
the opportunity for sb to give their point of view about sth before deciding if they have done sth wrong, often in a court of law: *I'll see that you get a fair hearing.*

fair 'play
not breaking the rules or cheating; honest or correct behaviour: *We want to see fair play in this competition.* ◇ *It may be legal, but it's not fair play.*

a fair 'shake (*AmE, informal*)
a fair chance or fair treatment: *This new pay deal means a fair shake for all the workers.*

(more than) your fair 'share of sth
(more than) the usual, expected or desired amount of sth: *I've had more than my fair share of problems recently, but now things seem to be getting better again.* ◇ *We've all paid our fair share except Delia, who's never got any money.*

fair's 'fair (*BrE* also **fair 'dos/'do's**) (*spoken*)
used, especially as an exclamation, to say that you think that an action, a decision, etc. is acceptable and appropriate because it means that everyone will be treated fairly: *You may not like her, but fair's fair, she's a good teacher.* ◇ *Look, fair's fair. I've helped you lots of times. Now you can help me.*

it's a fair 'cop (*BrE, spoken, humorous*)
used by sb who is caught doing sth wrong, to say that they admit that they are wrong: *He just said, 'it's a fair cop' and handed the bag to one of the policemen.*

make, etc. sth by/with your own fair 'hand (*humorous*)
make, etc. sth yourself: *I made this birthday card for you with my own fair hand.*

play 'fair/'straight (with sb)
act honestly and fairly: *I don't think it's playing fair to blame her for other people's mistakes.*

faire /feə(r)/; *AmE* fer/

● **savoir** → savoir faire

fairer /ˈfeərə(r); AmE ˈferər/
● say → you can't say fairer (than that)

fairly /ˈfeəli; AmE ˈferli/
● fair → fairly and squarely SEE fair and square

fairness /ˈfeənəs; AmE ˈfernəs/
in (all) ˈfairness (to sb)
used to introduce a statement that defends sb who has just been criticized, or that explains another statement that may seem unreasonable: *In all fairness to him, he did try to stop her leaving.*

fair-weather /ˌfeə ˈweðə(r); AmE ˌfer/
a ˌfair-weather ˈfriend (*disapproving*)
somebody who is only a friend when it is pleasant for them, and stops being a friend when you are in trouble: *I really thought she'd be here to help me, but it seems that she's just a fair-weather friend.*

fairy /ˈfeəri; AmE ˈferi/
a/your ˌfairy ˈgodmother
a person who helps you unexpectedly when you most need help: *You'll need a fairy godmother to get you out of your present difficulties.*

❷ ORIGIN
The fairy godmother is the magical character in the story of *Cinderella* who helps Cinderella go to the ball.

fait /feɪt/
a ˌfait accomˈpli (*from French*)
something that has already happened or been done and that you cannot change: *We got married secretly and then presented our parents with a fait accompli.*

faith /feɪθ/
bad ˈfaith
1 lack of trust between two people: *The dispute was the cause of a lot of bad faith and bitterness.*
2 dishonest behaviour: *There were many accusations of bad faith on the part of the government.*

break/keep ˈfaith with sb
break/keep a promise that you have made to sb; stop/continue being loyal to sb: *The government claims they have kept faith with the people by reducing the crime rate.*

good ˈfaith
the intention to do sth right: *They handed over their weapons as a gesture of good faith.*

in bad ˈfaith
knowing that what you are doing is wrong: *She insists that she did not act in bad faith, and that the mistakes were due to a computer error.*

in good ˈfaith
believing that sth is correct; believing that what you are doing is right, especially when it has bad consequences: *When I recommended Simon for the job, I did it in good faith. I didn't realize that he had been in trouble with the police.*

● pin → pin your faith/hopes on sb/sth

faithfully /ˈfeɪθfəli/
Yours faithfully (*BrE, formal, written*)
used at the end of a formal letter before you sign your name, when you have addressed sb as 'Dear Sir/Dear Madam,' etc. and not by their name

fall /fɔːl/

Idioms containing **fall** are at the entries for the nouns or adjectives in the idioms, for example **fall from grace** is at **grace**.

fall about (laughing/with laughter) (*BrE, informal*)
laugh a lot: *When he watches Charlie Chaplin films, he falls about laughing. I don't find them funny at all!*

fall ˈover yourself to do sth (*informal*)
do everything you can for sb because you want to please and impress them: *After he became manager, people were suddenly falling over themselves to help him.*

falling /ˈfɔːlɪŋ/
● easy → (as) easy as ABC/pie/falling off a log

falls /fɔːlz/
● apple → the apple doesn't fall/never falls far from the tree
● bottom → the bottom drops/falls out of sb's world
● bottom → the bottom drops/falls out of the market
● face → your face falls

false /fɔːls/
by/on/under false preˈtences (*BrE*) (*AmE by/on/under false ˈpretenses*)
by lying about your identity, qualifications, financial or social position, etc: *She was sent to prison for six months for obtaining money under false pretences.* ◇ *He got me there under false pretences. He told me he wanted to discuss a business deal, but when I got there, it was a surprise birthday party.*

a false aˈlarm
a warning of sth, especially sth unpleasant or dangerous, which does not in fact happen: *They thought the packet contained a bomb but it was a false alarm.*

(make) a/one false ˈmove (*informal*)
in an already dangerous or risky situation, sth which makes your position even more dangerous: *She's in a difficult financial situation, and if she makes a false move now she could lose everything.* ◇ *'One false move and you're dead,' he shouted at the bank clerk.*

(make) a false ˈstart
an attempt to begin sth that is not successful: *After a few false starts, I finally managed to work the fax machine.* ◇ *He made a few false starts early on in his acting career, but then found success with the Royal Shakespeare Company.*

sound/strike a false 'note
seem wrong, not appropriate, etc. in a certain situation: *I really thought his speech at the conference struck a false note. Instead of saying how serious the housing situation was, he was telling jokes about it.*

• ring → ring true/false/hollow

fame /feɪm/

• claim → claim to fame

familiar /fəˈmɪliə(r)/

have a familiar 'ring (about/to it)
sound familiar: *His complaints have a familiar ring. Others have said exactly the same thing about our designs.* ◇ *The music in the movie had a familiar ring to it. I think it was Schumann.*

familiarity /fəˌmɪliˈærəti/

familiarity breeds con'tempt (*saying*)
you have little respect, liking, etc. for sb/sth that you know too well: *George's father is regarded by everyone as a great artist, but George doesn't think he is. Familiarity breeds contempt!*

family /ˈfæməli/

in the 'family way (*old-fashioned*, *informal*)
pregnant

run in the 'family
(of a physical characteristic or moral quality) be sth that many members of a family have: *He was never going to live long because heart disease runs in both families.* ◇ *Good looks run in the family.*

• big → one big happy family

famous /ˈfeɪməs/

ˌfamous ˌlast 'words (*informal*, *humorous*)
used when you think sb has been too optimistic about sth and is likely to be wrong: *'The journey will only take an hour on the high-speed train.' 'Famous last words! That train is always late!'*

NOTE
Last words in this idiom refers to words spoken by somebody just before they die.

famously /ˈfeɪməsli/

get on/along 'famously (*old-fashioned*, *informal*)
have a very good relationship: *My mother and my mother-in-law are getting on famously.*

fan /fæn/

fan the 'flames (of sth)
make a feeling such as anger, hatred, etc. worse: *His writings fanned the flames of racism.*

• shit → (when) the shit hits the fan

fancy /ˈfænsi/

as, whenever, etc. the fancy 'takes you
as, whenever, etc. you feel like doing sth: *We bought a camper van so we could go away whenever the fancy took us.*

catch/take/tickle sb's 'fancy (*informal*)
please or attract sb: *Mary seems afraid some other girl will catch Alan's fancy.* ◇ *She saw that the picture had taken my fancy and insisted on giving it to me as a present.*

fancy your/sb's 'chances (*informal*)
think, often wrongly, that you will be successful; be confident about what you/sb can do: *He fancies his chances as a racing driver, even though he has hardly ever driven a racing car.* ◇ *'Do you think he'll win?' 'No, I don't fancy his chances at all.'*

(just) fancy 'that (*old-fashioned*, *BrE*, *spoken*)
used as an expression of surprise: *'He passed all his exams with grade A.' 'Well, fancy that.'*

take a 'fancy to sb/sth (*especially BrE*)
begin to like sb/sth; be attracted by sb/sth: *He's taken quite a fancy to Chinese cooking.* ◇ *She's taken a fancy to one of the team.*

• flight → a flight of fancy

fancy-free /ˌfænsi ˈfriː/

• footloose → footloose and fancy-free

Fanny /ˈfæni/

• sweet → sweet Fanny Adams SEE sweet FA

far /fɑː(r)/

as/so 'far as…
as much as; to the extent that: *I will help you as far as I am able.* ◇ *As far as I'm concerned, the whole matter is no longer my responsibility and is now with the police.*

as far as the eye can/could 'see
to the horizon: *There was only sand as far as the eye could see.*

as/so far as it 'goes
to a limited degree, usually less than is satisfactory: *It's a good plan as far as it goes, but there are a lot of things they haven't thought of.*

by 'far
by a very great amount; much: *This is by far the best painting/This is the best painting by far.* ◇ *Our holiday this year was better by far than last year's.*

carry/take sth too, etc. 'far
continue doing sth beyond reasonable limits: *Of course we should show him respect, but I think expecting us to stand up whenever he walks into the room is taking things a bit far.*

(by) far and a'way
(used with superlative adjectives) very much; by a very great amount: *The company has by far and away the biggest share of the car market in this country.* ◇ *Her painting is far and away the best.*

far and 'wide
everywhere and many places; over a large area: *People come from far and wide to visit the monument.* ◇ *The police were searching far and wide for the missing child.*

far be it from me to do sth, but... (*informal*)
used when you are just about to disagree with sb or criticize them and you would like them to think that you do not really want to do this: *Far be it from me to interfere, but don't you think you've been arguing for long enough?*

a far cry from sth
very different from sth: *This house is a far cry from our little flat.* ◇ *Her designs are a far cry from the eccentric clothes she used to make.*

far from sth/doing sth
almost the opposite of sth or of what is expected: *It is far from clear* (= it is not clear) *what he intends to do.* ◇ *Far from being grateful for our help, she said we had ruined the evening.*

far 'from it (*informal*)
not at all; certainly not: *'Isn't he generous with money?' 'Far from it! He spends it all on himself.'* ◇ *'Are you ready, Alex?' 'Far from it, I'm afraid.'*

far 'gone (*informal*)
very drunk, ill, tired, etc: *When we arrived, she was already too far gone to recognize us, and she only lived for a few more hours.* ◇ *She seemed quite far gone, even though she'd only had two glasses of sparkling wine.*

go as/so far as to do sth
be willing to go to extreme or surprising limits in dealing with sth: *She's a brilliant painter, but I wouldn't go so far as to say she is the best in the country.* ◇ *I don't like people smoking but I wouldn't go so far as to forbid it.*

go 'far
(of people) be successful in the future: *Linda is an excellent manager. She should go far.*

go too 'far ◆ go a bit 'far
say or do sth which is considered too extreme or socially unacceptable: *Getting a bit drunk at a party is OK, but arriving completely drunk — that's really going too far.* ◇ *You've gone too far this time, Joanna.*

in so 'far as (also **inso'far as**)
to the extent that: *In so far as I am a judge of these things, the repairs to the car have been done very well.* ◇ *It was a good report in so far as it showed what needs to be done.*

not far 'off/'out/'wrong (*informal*)
almost correct: *She said she thought it would be sold for $200, and she wasn't far wrong: someone paid $235 for it.* ◇ *The original sales' estimate was not far off.*

not go 'far
1 (of money) not be enough to buy a lot of things: *$20 doesn't go very far these days.*
2 (of a supply of sth) not be enough for what is needed: *One loaf won't go far among ten people.*

,so 'far
up to this point; up to now: *There haven't been any accidents in this factory so far, and let's hope that none happen in future.*

,so far, so 'good (*saying*)
used to say that things have been successful until now and you hope they will continue like this, but you know the task, etc. is not finished yet: *'How's the operation going?' 'So far, so good.'*

- **afield →** far/farther/further afield
- **apple →** the apple doesn't fall/never falls far from the tree
- **few →** few and far between
- **near →** so near and yet so far
- **removed →** be far/further/furthest removed from sth

farm /fɑːm; *AmE* fɑːrm/

- **bet →** bet the farm/ranch
- **buy →** buy the farm

farther /'fɑːðə(r); *AmE* 'fɑːrðə-/

- **afield →** far/farther/further afield

fashion /'fæʃn/

after a 'fashion
to some extent but not very well: *'Can you skate?' 'Yes, after a fashion.'* ◇ *'Have you mended the TV?' 'Yes, after a fashion.'*

after the fashion of sb/sth (*formal*)
in the style of sb/sth: *The new library is very much after the fashion of Nash.*

in (a)...'fashion (*formal*)
in a particular way: *How could they behave in such a fashion?* ◇ *She was proved right, in dramatic fashion, when the whole department resigned.*

like it's going out of 'fashion (*spoken*)
used to emphasize that sb is doing sth or using sth a lot: *She's been spending money like it's going out of fashion.*

fast /fɑːst; *AmE* fæst/

as fast as your legs can 'carry you
as quickly as you can: *When he heard the police sirens, he ran off as fast as his legs could carry him.*

fast and 'furious
(of games, amusements, etc.) noisy and very active: *Ten minutes before the race, the betting was fast and furious.*

> **NOTE**
> *Furious* in this idiom means 'with great energy and speed'.

a fast 'talker
a person who can talk very quickly and easily, but who cannot always be trusted: *The salesman was a real fast talker, and somehow managed to convince me to buy the most expensive model!*

a fast 'worker (*informal*)
a person who wastes no time in gaining an advantage, especially a person who can quickly gain sb's affection: *She's a fast worker! She's only been here a*

few days and already the boss has invited her for dinner!

hold 'fast to sth
refuse to stop believing in sth such as a theory, principle, religion, etc: *She knew that whatever happened in her life, she would hold fast to her religious beliefs.*

in the 'fast lane (*informal*)
the exciting and sometimes risky way of life typical of very successful people: *I hear you've just been made chief of the Berlin office, Joan. How's life in the fast lane?* **OPP** in the slow lane

> NOTE
> The *fast lane* is the part of a main road such as a motorway, where vehicles drive fastest.

not so 'fast (*informal*)
often used for telling sb who may have done sth wrong, etc. to stop or wait: *Not so fast, young man! Let me see your ticket!* ◇ *'I'm going out to play now, Dad.' 'Not so fast, David. You've got to tidy your room first.'*

play fast and 'loose (with sb/sth) (*old-fashioned*)
treat sb/sth in a way that shows that you feel no responsibility or respect for them: *If he plays fast and loose with my daughter's feelings, I'll make sure he regrets it.*

stand 'fast/'firm
refuse to move back; refuse to change your opinions or behaviour: *The management have stood firm against demands for a pay increase.* **OPP** shift your ground

> NOTE
> *Fast* here means 'firmly fixed'.

- **buck** → make a fast/quick buck
- **draw** → be fast/quick on the draw
- **hard** → hard and fast
- **pull** → pull a fast one (on sb)
- **stick** → stick fast
- **thick** → thick and fast

fat /fæt/

a 'fat cat (*informal, disapproving*)
a person who earns, or has, a lot of money (especially when compared to people who do not earn much): *The company director is described as a fat cat, who enjoys his luxury lifestyle but doesn't care about his employees.*

(a) 'fat chance (of sth/doing sth) (*spoken*)
used when you think that there is no possibility of sth happening: *He said he'd give me a job if I passed my exam with a grade A. A fat chance I have of that!* ◇ *'Do you think she'll lend me the money?' 'Fat chance.'*

the fat is in the 'fire (*informal*)
something has been said or done that is certain to cause anger, fighting, offended feelings or other trouble: *The fat's in the fire now. Jim has just told his wife that he has taken a job in another town without mentioning it to her first.*

a 'fat lot of good/help/use (*spoken*)
not at all good/helpful/useful: *A fat lot of use that would be! What a stupid idea.* ◇ *He was a fat lot of help, I must say!*

it ain't/it's not ,over till the fat lady 'sings (*saying*)
used near the end of a competition, race, etc. to say that it is not finished yet, especially when you think that the person/team who is losing still have a chance to win: *Some people think he's already lost the election, but it ain't over till the fat lady sings, you know!*

> **❷ ORIGIN**
> This refers to the fact that some operas end with a woman singing before she dies.

run to 'fat
(of people) begin to get fat: *After he stopped playing football he quickly ran to fat.*

- **chew** → chew the fat
- **live¹** → live off/on the fat of the land

fatale /fə'tɑːl; *AmE* fə'tæl/

- **femme** → (be) a femme fatale

fate /feɪt/

a ,fate worse than 'death (*often humorous*)
a terrible experience: *Go on a trip with the Trumans? You're joking. It would be a fate worse than death.*

- **tempt** → tempt fate/providence

father /'fɑːðə(r)/

like ,father/,mother, like 'son/'daughter (*saying*)
a child is similar to its father/mother in a particular way: *Young Jim is turning out to be as hard-working as his dad — like father, like son.*

- **founding** → the founding father(s) of sth
- **wish** → the wish is father to the thought

fatted /'fætɪd/

- **kill** → kill the fatted calf

fault /fɔːlt/

at 'fault
responsible for doing wrong, making a mistake, etc.; to be blamed: *The inquiry will decide who was at fault over the loss of the funds.* ◇ *I don't feel that I am at fault. After all, I didn't know I was breaking a rule.*

to a 'fault (*written*)
used to say that sb has a lot, or even too much of a particular good quality: *He was generous to a fault.*

- **find** → find fault (with sb/sth)

faux /fəʊ; *AmE* foʊ/

(make/commit) a ,faux 'pas (*from French*)
an action or a remark that causes embarrassment because it is not socially correct: *I immediately made a faux pas when I forgot to take my shoes off*

before I went into the house. ◊ *They were kind enough to overlook my faux pas and continued as if nothing had happened.*

> **NOTE**
> The meaning of the French expression is 'wrong step'.

favour (*BrE*) (*AmE* favor) /'feɪvə(r)/

be (all) in favour of sth/of doing sth
support or approve an idea, a course of action, etc: *As far as Joe's suggestion about saving money is concerned, I'm all in favour of it.* ◊ *Some people are in favour of restoring the death penalty for major crimes.* ◊ *All those in favour, raise their hands.*

do me a 'favour
1 (*informal*) used when asking sb to help you: *Do me a favour and answer the door, will you?*
2 (*spoken*) you can't expect me to believe that: *'It's worth £2 000. The man in the antique shop told me.' 'Do me a favour. It's not even worth £200.'*

in sb's/sth's 'favour
to sb's advantage: *The court decided in the employee's favour.* ◊ *The fact that the dollar is falling is in your favour.*

in/out of 'favour (with sb)
supported/not supported or liked/not liked by sb: *I seem to be out of favour with the head of department after my remarks at the meeting.* ◊ *He stays late every afternoon because he wants to stay in favour with the boss.*

● **curry** → curry favour (with sb)
● **fear** → without fear or favour
● **stacked** → the cards/odds are stacked in favour of sb/sth

favourite (*BrE*) (*AmE* favorite) /'feɪvərɪt/

sb's favourite 'son
a performer, politician, sports player, etc., who is popular where they were born: *Everyone in the town was proud and excited to see their favourite son nominated for an Oscar.*

favours (*BrE*) (*AmE* favors) /'feɪvəz; *AmE* 'feɪvərz/

do sb no 'favours ◆ not do sb any 'favours
do sth that is not helpful to sb or that gives a bad impression of them: *You're not doing yourself any favours, working for nothing.* ◊ *The orchestra did Beethoven no favours.*

fear /fɪə(r); *AmE* fɪr/

be/go in fear of your 'life
be afraid all the time that you may be killed, attacked, etc: *After she got involved with the drug dealers, she went in fear of her life.*

for fear of sth/of doing sth ◆ for fear (that)...
because you do not want sth bad to happen: *I'm not going to put it in the washing machine for fear of spoiling it.* ◊ *I had to keep my opinions secret for fear (that) I would lose my job.*

in fear and 'trembling (of sb/sth) (*written*)
feeling very frightened or anxious: *They lived in fear and trembling of being discovered by the police.*

,no 'fear! (*BrE, spoken*)
used to say that you definitely do not want to do sth: *'Who's coming for a midnight swim?' 'No fear! It's much too cold.'*

put the fear of 'God into sb (*informal*)
frighten sb very much, especially in order to force them to do what you want: *The first thing that happens when you go into the army is that they put the fear of God into you.*

there's no fear of sth
there's no possibility or danger of sth happening: *I've got a new alarm clock so there's no fear of me oversleeping again.*

without ,fear or 'favour (*BrE*) (*AmE* **without ,fear or 'favor**) (*formal*)
(judge, decide sth, etc.) in a completely fair way without being influenced by anybody: *The newspaper reprinted the facts, without fear or favour.*

feast /fiːst/

feast your 'eyes (on sb/sth)
look at sb/sth and get great pleasure: *Wow! Come and feast your eyes on this birthday cake!*

feather /'feðə(r)/

a 'feather in your cap
an achievement, a success or an honour which you can be proud of: *It's a real feather in his cap to represent his country in the Olympics.* **OPP** a black mark (against sb)

> **❓ ORIGIN**
> This idiom comes from the American Indian custom of giving a feather to somebody who had been very brave in battle.

feather your (own) 'nest
make yourself richer, especially by spending money on yourself that should be spent on sth else: *He's been feathering his own nest at the expense of the people he was supposed to be helping.*

● **birds** → birds of a feather (flock together)
● **knocked** → you could have knocked me, etc. down with a feather
● **light** → (as) light as air/a feather

feathered /'feðəd; *AmE* 'feðərd/

our feathered 'friends (*informal, humorous*)
birds: *We mustn't forget to put out food for our feathered friends during the cold winter months.*

feathers /'feðəz; *AmE* 'feðərz/

● **fly** → the feathers/fur/sparks will fly
● **ruffle** → ruffle sb's/a few feathers
● **smooth** → smooth (sb's) ruffled feathers
● **spit** → spit blood/venom/feathers

feature /'fiːtʃə(r)/

● **redeeming** → a redeeming feature

fed /fed/

,fed up to the back 'teeth with sb/sth
(also **,sick to the back 'teeth of sb/sth**) (*informal*)
depressed, annoyed or bored by sb/sth: *I'm fed up
to the back teeth with listening to you complaining.*
◇ *She's always playing the same CD, and I'm sick to
the back teeth of it!*

feed /fiːd/

● chicken → chicken feed

feeding /'fiːdɪŋ/

a 'feeding frenzy (*especially AmE*)
a period of time during which sb/sth eats, spends,
etc. a lot in a way that does not seem to be controlled: *The news about their marriage started a
media feeding frenzy, with all the newspapers trying
to get photos and interviews.*

> **NOTE**
> A *feeding frenzy* is an occasion when a group of
> sharks or other fish attack and eat something.

feeds /fiːdz/

● bite → bite the hand that feeds you

feel /fiːl/

be/feel 'out of it/things
not be/feel part of a group, a conversation, an
activity, etc: *I didn't know anybody at the party so
I felt a bit out of it really.*

,feel your 'age
realize from your physical condition, opinion,
views, etc. that you are getting old: *He's not as
energetic as he used to be — beginning to feel his
age, I suppose.* ◇ *Listening to this rap music really
makes me feel my age.*

feel the 'draught (*informal*)
suffer financially as a result of economic, social or
political changes around you: *Because of the world
trade recession, a lot of third world countries are
feeling the draught.*

feel 'free (to do sth) (*informal*)
(used to give sb permission to do sth) you may do
as you want; nobody will object if you do sth: *'May
I borrow your bike?' 'Feel free!'* ◇ *Feel free to come
and go as you like.*

feel (it) in your 'bones (*informal*)
sense or suspect sth without really knowing why:
*That's funny — I felt in my bones that there was
something wrong — and now you tell me there's
been an accident.* ◇ *'How can you be so sure she's
going to win?' 'I can feel it in my bones.'*

feel like sth/like doing sth
want to have or do sth: *Do you know what I feel
like? A nice cup of tea!* ◇ *I'm so tired that I feel like
going straight to bed.*

feel the 'pinch (*informal*)
be under pressure because you do not have as
much money as you had before: *Schools all over
the country are beginning to feel the pinch after
the government cut back its spending on education.*

> **NOTE**
> If you feel a *pinch* from a shoe, it hurts your
> foot because it is too tight.

feel 'strange
not feel comfortable in a situation; have an
unpleasant physical feeling: *She felt strange sitting
at her father's desk.* ◇ *It was terribly hot and I started to feel strange.*

feel your 'way
1 move along carefully, for example when it is
dark, by touching walls, objects, etc.
2 be careful about how you do sth because you
are just learning how to do it or you don't yet have
enough information: *I don't know how they will
react to the proposal, so at the moment I'm still feeling my way.* ◇ *He's only been in the job for three
months, so he's still feeling his way.*

get the 'feel of sth (*informal*)
become familiar with or get used to sth: *When
you're learning to drive a car, you'll probably find
changing gear difficult, but you'll soon get the feel of
it.* ◇ *Once you get the feel of a Ferrari, you'll never
want any other car.*

have a 'feel for sth (*informal*)
have an understanding of sth or be naturally good
at doing it: *A good politician has to have a feel for
what people want.*

not feel your'self
not feel as healthy, happy, etc. as you usually feel:
*I don't feel myself this morning; I think I'll stay at
home.*

● bound → be/feel duty/honour bound to do sth
● hard → be/feel hard done by
● honoured → be/feel honoured (to do sth)
● jelly → be/feel like jelly
● lost → be/feel lost without sb/sth
● million → look/feel like a million dollars/bucks
● sick → be/feel sick at heart
● sorry → be/feel sorry for sb
● sorry → be/feel sorry for yourself
● small → feel that high SEE look/feel small
● small → look/feel small

feelers /'fiːləz; AmE 'fiːlərz/

put out/have 'feelers
try to find out what people think about a particular course of action before you do it: *They're putting out feelers about the possibility of building a
new sports complex in Leeds.*

> **NOTE**
> An insect has *feelers* (= antennae) on its head,
> which it uses to feel or sense things.

feeling /'fiːlɪŋ/

bad/ill 'feeling(s)
anger between people, especially after an argument or a disagreement: *There was a lot of bad
feeling between the two groups of students.*

get/have the 'feeling (that...)
feel that sth is true although you have no direct
knowledge or facts: *I get the feeling that he's got*

another girlfriend somewhere. ◇ *Have you ever had the feeling that you were being watched?*

- **Monday** → that Monday morning feeling
- **sinking** → (get/have) a/that sinking feeling

feelings /ˈfiːlɪŋz/

- **hard** → no hard feelings
- **mixed** → have mixed feelings (about sb/sth)
- **spare** → spare sb's feelings

feet /fiːt/

at sb's 'feet
respecting and admiring sb, and so being influenced by them: *As a young man, he had the whole of Paris at his feet.*

be/get ˌrun/ˌrushed off your 'feet
be very busy: *In the last few days before the holidays, the sales assistants were rushed off their feet.*

fall/land on your 'feet (*informal*)
be lucky in finding a good position, job, place to live, etc., especially when your previous situation was difficult: *Well, you really fell on your feet this time, didn't you? A job in Rome, a large flat, a company car...*

> ❷ ORIGIN
> This expression may refer to the fact that cats are thought to always land safely on their feet, even if they fall or jump from a very high place.

ˌfeet 'first (*informal*)
dead or unconscious: *If you want me to leave this house, you'll have to carry me out feet first* (= you'll have to kill me first).

feet of 'clay
a surprising fault or weakness in the character of sb who is admired and respected: *Why are people always surprised when they discover that their heroes have feet of clay?*

> ❷ ORIGIN
> This idiom comes from a story in the Bible, where the king of Babylon saw an image with a head of gold and feet of clay.

get your 'feet wet (*especially AmE, informal*)
start doing sth that is new for you: *At that time he was a young actor, just getting his feet wet.*

have/keep both/your feet on the 'ground
have a sensible and realistic attitude to life: *He is always talking about his big plans to be a great actor. You should tell him to keep his feet on the ground.* **OPP** have your head in the clouds

on your 'feet
1 standing up: *Working in a restaurant means that you're on your feet all day long.*
2 (of a business, etc.) in a strong position again after a period of difficulty, uncertainty, etc: *Only our party's policies will really get the country on its feet again.* ◇ *The company seems to be back on its feet now.*

put your 'feet up
relax by sitting, or lying down; enjoy a period of rest from work, etc: *After work, I like to have a cup of tea and put my feet up.* ◇ *You've worked for this company for 35 years, Jack. Now it's time for you to put your feet up and relax.*

throw yourself at sb's 'feet
ask for sb to help, protect or forgive you: *He threw himself at her feet and asked for her forgiveness.*

under sb's 'feet
annoying sb because you are getting in their way and/or stopping them from working, etc: *It's difficult to do housework with the children under my feet all the time.*

- **cold** → get/have cold feet
- **dead** → dead on your feet
- **drag** → drag your feet/heels
- **find** → find your feet
- **grass** → not let the grass grow under your feet
- **ground** → cut the ground from under sb/sb's feet
- **itchy** → get/have itchy feet
- **patter** → the patter of tiny feet
- **pull** → pull the carpet/rug out from under sb's feet
- **six** → six feet under
- **stocking** → in your stocking(ed) feet
- **sweep** → sweep sb off their feet
- **think** → think on your feet
- **two** → have two left feet
- **two** → stand on your own two feet
- **vote** → vote with your feet
- **walk** → walk sb off their feet
- **weight** → take the weight off your feet
- **world** → have the world at your feet

fell /fel/

at/in one fell 'swoop
with a single action or movement; all at the same time: *Only a foolish politician would promise to lower the rate of inflation and reduce unemployment at one fell swoop.*

felt /felt/

- **presence** → make your presence felt

femme /fæm; *AmE* fem/

(be) a ˌfemme faˈtale (*from French*)
a beautiful woman that men find sexually attractive but who brings them trouble or unhappiness: *The movie follows the relationship between sexy femme fatale Suzy and young lawyer Jim, which eventually leads to a murderous crime of passion.*

> NOTE
> The meaning of the French expression is 'disastrous woman'.

fence /fens/

- **side** → my, her, the other, the same, etc. side of the fence
- **sit** → sit on the fence

fences /ˈfensɪz/

- **mend** → mend (your) fences (with sb)

fetch /fetʃ/

fetch and 'carry (for sb)
be always doing small jobs for sb; act as if you
were sb's servant: *I hate having to fetch and carry
for my husband all day. Why can't he do more for
himself?*

fettle /'fetl/

in fine/good 'fettle (*old-fashioned, informal*)
healthy and cheerful: *After ten hours' sleep and a
good long run, I was in fine fettle.* **OPP** be, feel, etc.
out of sorts

fever /'fiːvə(r)/

at 'fever pitch
in a state of great excitement or great activity: *The
audience was at fever pitch. I've never seen such
excitement at a concert.* ◇ *We're working at fever
pitch to get the hall ready for the concert at eight.*

few /fjuː/

few and far be'tween
not frequent; not happening often: *Since her illness, the former Senator's public appearances have
been few and far between.* ◇ *Apartments for hire are
few and far between in this part of town.*

have had a few (too many) (*informal*)
have drunk a lot of alcohol: *Look, he's had a few
and he really shouldn't drive home.* ◇ *You've had a
few too many, Paul. You don't know what you're
saying.*

a man/woman of few 'words
a person who does not talk much: *Mr Robins was a
man of few words, but his opinions were always
respected.*

• precious → precious few/little
• quite → a good few **SEE** quite a few
• ruffle → ruffle sb's/a few feathers

fiction /'fɪkʃn/

• truth → truth is stranger than fiction

fiddle /'fɪdl/

fiddle while Rome 'burns (*saying*)
do nothing or waste your time when you should
be dealing with a dangerous or serious situation:
*With the world's population growing fast and mil-
lions getting hungrier every day, the leaders of the
rich nations just seem to be fiddling while Rome
burns.*

> **❷ ORIGIN**
> This phrase refers to the Roman emperor Nero,
> who fiddled (= played the violin) during the
> burning of Rome in AD 64.

on the 'fiddle (*BrE, informal*)
getting money by doing dishonest things, usually
at work, for example stealing from your employer,
making false claims for expenses, etc: *He was on
the fiddle for years and his boss never suspected a
thing.*

• fit → (as) fit as a fiddle
• second → play second fiddle

field /fiːld/

have a 'field day
enjoy a time of great excitement or activity: *Whenever this novelist brings out a new book, the critics
have a field day, and she is attacked from all sides.*
◇ *When the royal family go skiing, press photographers have a field day.*

> **❷ ORIGIN**
> A *field day* was originally a military ceremony
> or exercise.

leave the field 'clear for sb ◆ **leave sb in possession of the 'field**
enable sb to be successful in a particular area of
activity because other people or groups are not
competing with them any longer: *Many of our
more experienced players are injured or resting,
which leaves the field clear for new talent.*

play the 'field (*informal*)
have romantic or sexual relationships with a lot of
different people: *He told me he didn't want to get
married yet because he was having too much fun
playing the field.*

• left → be (way out/over) in left field
• level → a level playing field
• level → level the playing field

fierce /fɪəs; AmE fɪrs/

something 'fierce (*AmE, spoken*)
very much; more than usual: *I sure do miss you
something fierce!*

fifth /fɪfθ/

take/plead the 'fifth (*AmE*)
make use of the right to refuse to answer questions in court about a crime, because you may give
information which will make it seem that you are
guilty

> **❷ ORIGIN**
> From the *Fifth Amendment* of the US Constitu-
> tion, which guarantees this right.

• wheel → a fifth/third wheel

fifty-fifty /ˌfɪfti 'fɪfti/

fifty-'fifty (*informal*)
divided equally between two people, groups or
possibilities: *Let's split the bill fifty-fifty.* ◇ *She has
a fifty-fifty chance of winning.*

fight /faɪt/

fight ˌfire with 'fire
use similar methods in a fight or an argument to
those your opponent is using: *The only way we can
win this match is to fight fire with fire.*

ˌfight for (your) 'life
make a great effort to stay alive, especially when
you are badly injured or seriously ill: *A young cyclist is fighting for his life after the accident.*

,fight it 'out
continue fighting or arguing until one person
wins: *I'm not going to interfere. They can just fight
it out between themselves.*

fight like cat and 'dog (*informal*)
argue fiercely very often: *They fight like cat and
dog, but they are really very fond of each other.*

fight a ,losing 'battle
try without success to achieve or prevent sth: *I'm
fighting a losing battle with my weight. I can't lose
any.* ◇ *The police are fighting a losing battle against
car theft.*

fight your 'own battles
be able to win an argument or get what you want
without anyone's help: *I wouldn't get involved —
he's old enough to fight his own battles.*

fight 'shy of sth/of doing sth
avoid sth or doing sth; not want to do sth: *I tend to
fight shy of getting involved in protests, but in this
case I feel very strongly that we should complain.*

fight ,tooth and 'nail (for sb/sth/to do sth)
fight in a very determined way for what you want:
*We fought the government tooth and nail to prevent
the new road being built.* ◇ *She's prepared to fight
tooth and nail to get the job.*

put up a (good) 'fight
fight or compete bravely against sb/sth stronger
than you: *The team put up a good fight but in the
end they were beaten.* ◇ *She won't accept the decision — she'll put up a fight.*

• **live¹** → live to fight another day
• **pick** → pick a fight/quarrel (with sb)

fighting /'faɪtɪŋ/

a ,fighting 'chance
a slight but real chance of succeeding, avoiding
sth, etc: *With five minutes of the game left, our
team still has a fighting chance of winning.*
◇ *Things don't look very hopeful for John Brown in
the presidential elections, but he's still in with a
fighting chance.*

fighting 'spirit
a feeling that you are ready to fight very hard for
sth or to try sth difficult: *Come on, don't give up
now! Where's your fighting spirit?*

fighting 'talk
comments or remarks that show that you are
ready to fight very hard for sth: *What we want
from the management is fighting talk.*

• **fit** → fighting fit **SEE** (as) fit as a fiddle

figment /'fɪgmənt/

a figment of sb's imagi'nation
something which sb only imagines: *Doctor, are you
suggesting the pain is a figment of my imagination?*

figure /'fɪgə(r); AmE 'fɪgjər/

cut a fine, poor, sorry, etc. 'figure
have a fine, etc. appearance: *In his brand new uni-
form he cut a fine figure.*

a figure of 'fun
somebody who is often laughed at by other
people: *As a young man he was admired, but as an
old man he became a figure of fun.*

go 'figure (*AmE, informal*)
used to say that you do not understand the reason
for sth, or that you do not want to give an explanation for sth because you think it is obvious: *At the
same time that I was criticized for working too fast I
was accused of working too slow. Go figure!*

put a 'figure on sth
give the exact amount or exact value of sth: *It's
difficult to put a figure on a table like this, but it's
probably worth about $5 000.*

• **ballpark** → a ballpark figure

figures /'fɪgəz; AmE 'fɪgjərz/

it/that 'figures (*informal*)
used to say that sth was expected or seems logical: *'We're going to need new offices when the company expands next year.' 'That figures.'* ◇ *'I think he
killed her to get the insurance money.' 'That certainly figures.'*

• **head** → have a (good) head for figures
• **round** → in round figures/numbers

file /faɪl/

(in) single/Indian 'file
in a line, one person after another: *The whole class
walked along behind the teacher in single file.*

> ❷ ORIGIN
> When American Indians walked in a group,
> each person walked in the footsteps of the
> person in front so that they could not be
> counted by the enemy.

• **rank** → (the) rank and file

fill /fɪl/

fill sb's 'boots/'shoes
do sb's job in a satisfactory way when they are not
there: *Mr Carter is retiring and we need a new director to fill his shoes.*

have had your 'fill of sb/sth
have had enough of sb/sth: *I've had my fill of Star
Wars movies. I never want to see another one as long
as I live.*

final /'faɪnl/

• **analysis** → in the last/final analysis
• **straw** → be the last/final straw
• **word** → your/the last/final word (on/about sth)

find /faɪnd/

find 'fault (with sb/sth)
look for faults or mistakes in sb/sth, often so that
you can criticize them/it: *He's always finding fault
with the children, even when they are doing nothing
wrong.* ◇ *I can find no fault with this essay; it's the
best I've ever read.* **OPP** sing sb's/sth's praises

finders

find your 'feet (*informal*)
become used to a new job, place, etc. and start
functioning well: *After moving from teaching to
industry, it took her a long time to find her feet in
a very different job.*

(not) find it in your heart to 'do sth
(also **(not) find it 'in yourself to do sth**) (*literary*)
(not) be able to persuade yourself to do sth: *I wish
you could find it in your heart to forgive her.*
◇ *I can't find it in myself to criticize her work after
she's tried so hard.*

find your 'voice/'tongue (*informal*)
finally be able to speak after being too nervous or
shy to do so: *He sat silent through the first half of
the meeting before he found his tongue.*

find your/its 'way (to/into…)
come to a place or a situation by chance or without intending to: *After several other jobs, he eventually found his way into acting.*

take sb as you 'find them
accept sb as they are without expecting them to
behave in a special way or have special qualities:
*The house is in chaos, so when you come you must
take us as you find us.*

- bearings → find/get your bearings
- match → find/meet your match (in sb)
- needle → like looking for/trying to find a needle in a
  haystack
- scratch → scratch A and you'll find B

finders /'faɪndəz; *AmE* 'faɪndərz/

,finders 'keepers (*saying*)
(often used by children) anyone who finds sth has
a right to keep it: *I just found a pound coin on the
ground. Finders keepers, so it's mine!*

fine /faɪn/

cut it/things 'fine
allow only just enough time to do sth: *Your train
leaves in twenty minutes and you're still here! You're
cutting it a bit fine, aren't you?*

have sth down to a fine 'art (*informal, often
humorous*)
learn through experience how to do sth perfectly:
*I found it difficult to organize the timetables at first,
but now I've got it down to a fine art.* ◇ *She has
complaining in restaurants down to a fine art! Head
waiters are terrified of her.*

not to put too fine a 'point on it
used when you are about to speak very directly or
honestly: *Not to put too fine a point on it, I think
you've been a complete idiot.*

- chance → chance would be a fine thing
- fettle → in fine/good fettle
- line → tread/walk a fine/thin line
- small → the fine print **SEE** the small print
- small → the small print
- talk → you're a fine one to talk **SEE** you can/can't talk
- well → all very well/fine (for sb) (to do sth) but…

fine-tooth /'faɪn tuːθ/

go over/through sth with a ,fine-tooth 'comb
(*informal*)
search or look at sth very closely or carefully:
*I went through the accounts with a fine-tooth comb
checking for mistakes.* ◇ *The police went through
his room with a fine-tooth comb.*

finger /'fɪŋgə(r)/

the ,finger of su'spicion
if **the finger of suspicion** points or is pointed at
sb, they are suspected of having committed a
crime, being responsible for sth, etc: *The woman's
still missing, and the finger of suspicion is now being
pointed at her husband.*

get/pull your 'finger out (*BrE, informal*)
used to tell sb to start doing some work or making
an effort: *I wish the police would get their finger out
and solve the crime!* ◇ *If you pull your finger out,
we might finish on time.*

give sb the 'finger (*AmE, informal*)
raise your middle finger in the air with the back
part of your hand facing sb, done to be rude to sb
or to show them that you are angry: *Did you see
what he just did? He gave me the finger!*

have a finger in every 'pie (*informal*)
be involved in everything that happens: *Jane likes
to have a finger in every pie.*

have/keep your finger on the 'pulse (of sth)
know all that is happening; be aware of new
developments in a particular situation: *Successful
politicians need to keep their finger on the pulse of
the voters.*

> **NOTE**
> A doctor takes your *pulse* by putting his fingers
> on your wrist and counting the number of
> times the blood beats in a minute.

not put your 'finger on sth (*informal*)
not be able to say exactly what is wrong or different about a particular situation: *I knew something
she had said wasn't true, but I couldn't quite put my
finger on it.* ◇ *There's something wrong with these
statistics but I just can't put my finger on what it is.*

- lay → lay a finger on sb
- lift → (not) lift a finger (to do sth)
- little → twist/wind/wrap sb around your little finger
- point → point a/the finger (at sb)

fingernails /'fɪŋgəneɪlz; *AmE* -gərn-/

- bite → bite your nails/fingernails

fingers /'fɪŋgəz; *AmE* 'fɪŋgərz/

get your 'fingers burnt ♦ burn your 'fingers
suffer as a result of doing sth without realizing the
possible bad results, especially in business: *She got
her fingers burnt when she set up a business and
had all her money stolen by her partner.*

**have/keep your 'fingers crossed ♦ cross your
'fingers** (*informal*)
hope that sth will be successful; wish sb good
luck: *I'm going to give my first lecture tomorrow,*

so keep your fingers crossed for me, won't you?
◊ *Good luck, Ingrid.* **Fingers crossed!**

> **NOTE**
> People often cross the first two fingers of one
> hand when they use this expression.

work your ˌfingers to the ˈbone (*informal*)
work very hard: *It's not fair — I work my fingers to
the bone all day and then I have to cook and clean in
the evenings.*

- **green** → green fingers
- **slip** → slip through sb's fingers
- **snap** → snap your fingers
- **sticky** → have sticky fingers
- **thumbs** → be all fingers and thumbs SEE be all thumbs
- **tick** → tick sth off on your fingers
- **till** → have your fingers/hand in the till
- **two** → put/stick two fingers up at sb

fingertips /'fɪŋgətɪps; AmE -gərt-/

have sth at your ˈfingertips
be so familiar with a subject that you can produce
any facts about it easily and quickly: *The director
was well prepared for the interview. She had all the
facts at her fingertips.*

to your ˈfingertips (*BrE*)
(of a particular type of person) completely; in
every way: *He is an artist to his fingertips.* ◊ *She's
a professional to her fingertips.*

finish /'fɪnɪʃ/

be in at the ˈfinish
be present when sth ends: *I was one of the first
people on this project and I certainly want to be in
at the finish.*

finishing /'fɪnɪʃɪŋ/

the finishing ˈtouch(es)
the final details that make sth complete: *We've
been putting the finishing touches to the party
decorations.*

fire /'faɪə(r)/

be/come under ˈfire
1 be shot at: *While defending the town we came
under fire again last night.*
2 be criticized, insulted, etc: *The government is
already under fire over its housing policy.*

fire ˈquestions, ˈinsults, etc. at sb
ask sb a lot of questions one after another or make
a lot of comments very quickly: *The room was full
of journalists, all firing questions at them.*

hold your ˈfire
1 delay or stop shooting for a while: *Hold your
fire! I think they're going to surrender.* **OPP** open fire
(on sb/sth)
2 stop attacking sb: *She told the journalists to hold
their fire. If they didn't listen to her, how would they
know what she thought?*

on ˈfire
giving you a painful burning feeling: *He couldn't
breathe. His chest was on fire.*

play with ˈfire
take unnecessary and dangerous risks: *Be very
careful, Mike. You're playing with fire.* ◊ *If you ask
me she's playing with fire, getting involved with a
married man.*

set sth on ˈfire
1 (also **set ˈfire to sth**) make sth start burning
because you want to destroy or damage it: *Three
youths were accused of setting the house on fire.*
◊ *Demonstrators had set fire to vehicles and equipment.*
2 make sb/sth very interested or excited: *Her new
book has really set the literary critics on fire.*

- **add** → add fuel to the fire/flames
- **baptism** → a baptism of fire
- **fat** → the fat is in the fire
- **fight** → fight fire with fire
- **frying** → out of the frying pan (and) into the fire
- **hang** → hang fire
- **house** → get along/on like a house on fire
- **irons** → have many, etc. irons in the fire
- **open** → open fire (on sb/sth)
- **smoke** → there's no smoke without fire
- **smoke** → where there's smoke, there's fire SEE there's no
smoke without fire
- **world** → not/never set the Thames on fire SEE not/never
set the world on fire
- **world** → not/never set the world on fire

firing /'faɪərɪŋ/

be in the ˈfiring line (*BrE*) (*AmE* **be on the ˈfiring
line**)
be in a position where you are likely to be affected, attacked, criticized, etc: *The newspapers are
criticizing the government's policy again, and the
Prime Minister is in the firing line.* ◊ *In the latest
round of spending cuts, teachers' jobs are again in
the firing line.*

- **cylinders** → firing/working on all cylinders

firm /fɜːm; AmE fɜːrm/

be on firm ˈground
be sure about your beliefs, knowledge, etc.; be
confident: *I don't know a lot about physics, I'm
afraid. I'm on firmer ground with mathematics,
which I studied at university.*

a firm ˈhand
strong discipline and control: *What his son needs,
if you ask me, is a firm hand!*

hold ˈfirm (to sth) (*formal*)
believe sth strongly and not change your mind:
She held firm to her principles.

take a firm ˈline/ˈstand (on/against sth)
make your beliefs known and try to make others
follow them: *We need to take a firm line on tobacco
advertising.* ◊ *They took a firm stand against drugs
in the school.*

- **believer** → be a great/firm believer in sth
- **fast** → stand fast/firm

first /fɜːst; AmE fɜːrst/

at first 'glance/'sight
as things seem at first; judging by first appearances: *At first glance, the exam paper looked fairly difficult, but once I got started I found it quite easy.*

come 'first
be treated as the most important person or thing in sb's life: *His work always came first with Joe, which upset his wife a lot.*

first among 'equals
the person or thing with the highest status in a group: *Our history classes were usually open discussion-groups between us and our teacher, with the teacher as first among equals.*

first and 'foremost
before everything else; most importantly: *First and foremost, we must ensure that the children are safe.* ◇ *Don't forget, he is first and foremost an actor, not a singer.*

first and 'last
mainly; only: *The book is, first and last, an account of a poet's development.* ◇ *I saw him for the first and last time at his father's funeral.*

first 'come, first 'served (*saying*)
people will be dealt with, seen, etc. strictly in the order in which they arrive, apply, etc: *We have 100 tickets for the performance, and they will be distributed on a first come, first served basis.*

(in) the first flush of 'youth, en'thusiasm, etc.
when sb is young or sth is new: *By then, he was no longer in the first flush of youth.* ◇ *In the first flush of enthusiasm, we were able to get everyone interested in helping.*

(at) first 'hand
from your own experience or knowledge, rather than from sb else; directly: *I know at first hand what it is like to be poor; we always had very little money at home.* ◇ *We have a first-hand account of the raid from a witness.*

first of 'all
1 before doing anything else; at the beginning: *First of all, let me ask you something.*
2 as the most important thing: *The content of any article needs, first of all, to be relevant to the reader.*

first 'off/'up (*informal*)
before anything else; to begin with: *First off, we will choose the teams, then we can start the game.*

(give sb, have, etc.) (the) first re'fusal
the opportunity to buy sth before it is offered for sale to others: *She promised to give me first refusal if she ever decides to sell the flat.*

first 'thing (tomorrow, in the morning, etc.)
at the beginning of the period of time mentioned, before doing anything else: *I always like a cup of tea first thing in the morning.* ◇ *Can you lend me some money? I'll pay you back first thing tomorrow.*
OPP last thing (at night)

first things 'first (*often humorous*)
the most important or necessary duties, matters, etc. must be dealt with before others: *First things*

first. We must make sure the electricity is turned off before we start repairing the cooker. ◇ *We have a lot to discuss, but, first things first, let's have a cup of coffee!*

(be) the 'first/'last (person) to do sth
be very willing or likely/unwilling or unlikely to do sth: *I'd be the first person to admit that I'm not perfect.* ◇ *Mary is the last person you'd see in a pub — she hates pubs.*

from the (very) 'first
from the beginning: *They were attracted to each other from the first.*

from first to 'last
from beginning to end; during the whole time: *It's a fine performance that commands attention from first to last.*

get to first 'base (with sb/sth) (also **reach/make first 'base (with sb/sth)**) (*informal, especially AmE*)
successfully complete the first stage of sth: *The project hasn't even reached first base yet. Why all this delay?*

> **NOTE**
> This idiom comes from baseball. *First base* is the first of four positions (= bases) that a player must reach in order to score points.

have first 'call (on sb/sth)
be the most important person or thing competing for sb's time, money, etc. and be dealt with or paid for before other people or things: *The children always have first call on her time.*

in the 'first instance (*formal*)
as the first part of a series of actions: *In the first instance, notify the police and then contact your insurance company.*

make the first 'move
do sth before sb else, for example in order to end an argument or to begin sth: *If he wants to see me he should make the first move.*

put sb/sth 'first
treat sb/sth as the most important person or thing: *A politician should always put the needs of the country first and not his personal ambitions.* ◇ *He never put his family first.*

there's a first time for 'everything (*saying, humorous*)
the fact that something has not happened before does not mean that it will never happen: *'The flood water has never reached the house before.' 'Well, there's a first time for everything.'*

- feet → feet first
- first → in the first place
- flight → in the first/top flight
- head → head first
- hell → see sb in hell first
- know → not know the first thing about sb/sth
- last → last in, first out
- love → love at first sight
- order → of the highest/first order

fish /fɪʃ/

fish for compliments
encourage sb indirectly to say nice things about you: *Stop asking me if you look OK. You're just fishing for compliments.*

fish or cut 'bait (*AmE, informal*)
used to tell sb to make a decision and take the necessary action: *There's been enough discussion. It's time for the government to fish or cut bait.*

> **NOTE**
> *Bait* is the food you put on a hook to catch fish. If you *cut bait*, you stop fishing.

a ˌfish out of 'water (*informal*)
a person who feels uncomfortable or embarrassed in unfamiliar surroundings: *Everybody else knew each other really well, so I felt a bit like a fish out of water.*

have other/bigger fish to 'fry (*informal*)
have more important, interesting or useful things to do: *He's not interested in reviewing small provincial exhibitions like this one; he's got much bigger fish to fry.* ◇ *So you aren't coming out with us tonight? I suppose you've got other fish to fry.*

neither ˌfish nor 'fowl
neither one thing nor another: *Graduate teaching assistants are neither fish nor fowl, neither completely students nor teachers.*

an ˌodd/a ˌqueer 'fish (*old-fashioned, BrE*)
a strange person: *He's an odd fish. He's got a lot of very strange ideas.*

there are plenty/lots more fish in the 'sea
♦ there are (plenty of) other fish in the 'sea (*informal*)
there are many other people or things that are as good as the one sb has failed to get: *'I'll never love anyone as much again.' 'Look, Julie, there are lots more fish in the sea, you know.'*

- **big** → a big fish (in a little pond)
- **candy** → be like shooting fish in a barrel SEE be like taking candy from a baby
- **cold** → a cold fish
- **different** → a different kettle of fish
- **drink** → drink like a fish

fist /fɪst/

make a better, good, poor, etc. 'fist of sth (*BrE, informal*)
make a good, bad, etc. attempt to do sth: *The Irish rugby team are hoping to make a better fist of it than the English did yesterday.*

- **iron** → an iron fist/hand (in a velvet glove)
- **money** → make/lose money hand over fist
- **shake** → shake your fist (at sb)

fit /fɪt/

(as) ˌfit as a 'fiddle (also ˌfighting 'fit)
very healthy and active: *After our walking holiday, I came back feeling fit as a fiddle.*

fit the 'bill (*informal*)
be suitable for a purpose: *We need a new sofa for the living room, and I think this one will fit the bill quite nicely.*

fit (sb) like a 'glove
(of a coat, dress, etc.) be the perfect size or shape for sb: *You look wonderful in that dress. It fits you like a glove.*

have/throw a 'fit (*informal*)
become very excited or angry: *Your father will throw a fit when he sees you've broken yet another window!*

have a pink/blue 'fit (*BrE, informal*)
be very angry: *If your mother catches you smoking, she'll have a pink fit.*

see/think 'fit (to do sth) (*formal, often disapproving*)
think it is right or acceptable to do sth: *You obviously didn't see fit to inform us of what you were going to do.* ◇ *You should warn her about his behaviour if you see fit.*

- **drop** → fit/ready to drop
- **face** → your/sb's face doesn't fit

fits /fɪts/

in ˌfits and 'starts
not steadily; often starting and stopping: *'How's the book?' 'Oh, I'm working on it in fits and starts. I sometimes wonder if I'll ever finish it.'* ◇ *He made progress in fits and starts at first but now he's improving rapidly.*

- **cap** → if the shoe fits (, wear it) SEE if the cap fits (, wear it)

fittest /'fɪtɪst/

- **survival** → (the) survival of the fittest

five /faɪv/

ˌgive sb 'five (*informal*)
hit the inside of sb's hand with the inside of your hand as a greeting or to celebrate a victory: *Give me five!*

- **high** → high five
- **nine** → nine to five

fives /faɪvz/

- **bunch** → a bunch of fives

fix /fɪks/

be/get in a 'fix (*informal*)
be/get in a difficult situation: *I'm in a bit of a fix. Can you help me?*

fix sb with a 'look, 'stare, 'gaze, etc.
look directly at sb for a long time: *He fixed her with an angry stare.*

- **broke** → if it ain't broke, don't fix it

fixed /fɪkst/

how are you, etc. 'fixed (for sth)? (*spoken*)
used to ask how much of sth a person has, or to ask about arrangements: *How are you fixed for cash?* ◇ *How are we fixed for Saturday* (= have we arranged to do anything)*?*

flag /flæg/

fly/show/wave the 'flag
show your support for your country, an organization or an idea in order to encourage or persuade others to do the same: *This exhibition of Scottish painting is our way of flying the flag.* ▸ **'flag-waving** *noun* the expression of strong national feelings, especially in a way that people disapprove of

keep the 'flag flying
continue to support an idea, a principle, an activity, etc. which is in danger of disappearing: *They try to keep the flag flying in the British film industry.* ◇ *There are only two of us left now to keep the flag flying.*

● **red** → like waving a red flag in front of/at a bull **SEE** (like) a red rag to a bull

flagrante /fləˈɡrænti/

in fla'grante (delicto) (*from Latin, literary* or *humorous*)
if sb is found or caught **in flagrante**, they are discovered doing sth that they should not be doing, especially having sex: *One of the gentlemen was caught in flagrante with the wife of the club's President, which of course caused a huge scandal.*

NOTE
The meaning of the Latin phrase is 'in the heat (of the crime)'.

flak /flæk/

get/take (the) 'flak (for sth) (*informal*)
receive severe criticism: *He's taken a lot of flak for his unpopular decisions.* ◇ *Why do I always get the flak when something goes wrong around here?*

NOTE
Flak is bullets from guns on the ground that are shooting at enemy aircraft.

flame /fleɪm/

● **old** → an old flame

flames /fleɪmz/

● **add** → add fuel to the fire/flames
● **fan** → fan the flames (of sth)

flap /flæp/

be in/get into a 'flap (*informal*)
be in/get into a state of worry or excitement: *Julia's getting into a real flap about her exams.*
OPP (as) cool as a cucumber

flapping /ˈflæpɪŋ/

● **ears** → his, her, etc. ears are flapping

flash /flæʃ/

a ,flash in the 'pan (*informal*)
a success which lasts for a short time and is not likely to be repeated: *He scored a lot of goals early in the season, but hasn't scored any since, so it may have been just a flash in the pan.*

❶ ORIGIN
This refers to an old type of gun. Sometimes the gunpowder in the *pan* (= a small container at the top of the gun) exploded but failed to set fire to the gunpowder inside the gun with the result that the gun did not fire a bullet.

flash sb a 'smile, 'look, etc.
smile, look, etc. at sb suddenly and quickly: *She flashed him a quick smile, then was gone before he could say anything.*

in/like a 'flash (*informal*)
very quickly; suddenly: *'Sixty-six!' she answered in a flash.* ◇ *This new liquid will clean your floor in a flash.*

● **quick** → (as) quick as a flash

flat /flæt/

and ,that's 'flat! (*BrE, spoken*)
that is my final decision and I will not change my mind: *I'm not lending you any more money, and that's flat!*

fall 'flat
if a joke, a story, or an event **falls flat**, it completely fails to amuse people or to have the effect that was intended: *I didn't think the comedian was funny at all — most of his jokes fell completely flat.*

fall ,flat on your 'face (*informal*)
fail completely in an attempt to do sth, especially in a noticeable way: *I thought I would pass my driving test easily but I fell flat on my face.*

be flat 'broke (*BrE also* **be stony 'broke**) (*informal*)
have no money at all: *I'm afraid I can't come away with you this weekend — I'm flat broke!*

(as) flat as a 'pancake (*informal*)
completely flat: *There are one or two hills in Norfolk, but otherwise the landscape is as flat as a pancake.*

flat 'out (*informal*)
1 as fast as possible; with all the energy, strength, etc. you have: *If I worked flat out, I could get all the repairs done today.*
2 lying down, especially because you are ill or extremely tired: *He was flat out on the bed.*
3 (*especially AmE*) in a definite and direct way; completely: *I told him flat out 'No'.* ◇ *It's a 30-year mortgage, which we just flat out can't handle.*

in two minutes, ten seconds, etc. 'flat (*informal*)
used to say that sth happened or was done very quickly, in no more than the time stated: *He tidied his room in ten minutes flat.* ◇ *She spent nine*

months writing the first half of the book and then finished it in three months flat.

flattery /ˈflætəri/

flattery will get you 'everywhere/'nowhere (*spoken, humorous*)
praise that is not sincere will/will not get you what you want: *Just remember — flattery will get you nowhere. There's no point in trying to be nice to me so that I'll give you what you want.*

flaunt /flɔːnt/

if you've ˌgot it, 'flaunt it (*humorous, saying*)
used to tell sb that they should not be afraid of allowing other people to see their qualities and abilities: *Don't worry about what other people think! As my grandmother always used to say, 'if you've got it, flaunt it'!*

> **NOTE**
> *Flaunt* means to show something that you are proud of to other people, in order to impress them.

flavour (*BrE*) (*AmE* flavor) /ˈfleɪvə(r)/

flavour of the 'month (*especially BrE*)
a person who is especially popular at the moment: *If I were you, I'd keep quiet at the staff meeting. You're not exactly flavour of the month with the boss at the moment.*

> **❷ ORIGIN**
> In the past, ice cream companies in the US would choose a particular flavour each month to advertise in their stores.

flea /fliː/

with a 'flea in your ear
if sb sends a person away **with a flea in their ear**, they tell them angrily to go away: *When he came to ask for his job back, we sent him away with a flea in his ear.*

flesh /fleʃ/

flesh and 'blood
the human body; a normal person with weaknesses, desires, fears, etc: *'Why did he do it?' 'Look, he'd been away from home for six months and he was lonely. He's only flesh and blood, you know.'*

your (own) ˌflesh and 'blood
a member of your own family: *How can I possibly not help him? He's my own flesh and blood, isn't he?*

in the 'flesh
in sb's actual presence; in person: *It's very strange seeing somebody in the flesh after seeing them on television for years.*

make your 'flesh creep/crawl
make you feel afraid or full of disgust: *This is a movie to make your flesh creep.* ◊ *The way he looked at me made my flesh crawl.*

more than flesh and blood can 'stand, en'dure, etc.
too painful or unpleasant to tolerate: *Sometimes the pain is so bad that it is more than flesh and blood can stand.*

put flesh on (the bones of) sth
develop a basic idea, etc. by giving more details to make it more complete: *The strength of the book is that it puts flesh on the bare bones of his argument.*

- **pound** → (have, demand, claim, etc.) your pound of flesh
- **press** → press (the) flesh
- **spirit** → the spirit is willing but the flesh (it) is weak
- **thorn** → be a thorn in your flesh/side
- **way** → go the way of all flesh

flex /fleks/

flex your 'muscles
show that you are ready and prepared to use your power, abilities, etc: *He's flexing his muscles, waiting for the day he becomes president.*

> **NOTE**
> Athletes *flex* (= stretch and tighten) their muscles before a race, a fight, a game, etc.

flies /flaɪz/

die/drop/fall like 'flies
die, become ill, etc. in large numbers: *During the epidemic people were dropping like flies.*

(there are) no flies on sb (*informal*)
1 sb is not stupid and therefore cannot be tricked or deceived easily: *You can't just tell her that you've lost the money; she'll never believe you. There are no flies on Jane, you know.*
2 sb is skilful or clever at doing sth: *There are no flies on Jim. He can persuade anybody to buy a car from him.*

- **crow** → as the crow flies
- **time** → time flies

flight /flaɪt/

a ˌflight of 'fancy
an idea or a statement that is very imaginative but not practical or sensible: *The idea is not just a flight of fancy. It has been done before.*

in the first/top 'flight
among the best of a particular group: *Everybody hopes that the new manager will be able to keep the team in the top flight next year.*

take 'flight
run away: *The gang took flight when they heard the police car.*

fling /flɪŋ/

have a 'fling (*informal*)
1 enjoy yourself without worrying or thinking seriously about anything, especially when it is the last opportunity you will have: *Before I started training, I had one last fling and went to Paris with a group of friends for the weekend.*

2 have a short sexual relationship with sb: *'Do you know Sally Taylor?' 'Yes, I know her quite well in fact. We had a bit of a fling a few years ago.'*

● mud → fling/sling/throw mud (at sb)

flip /flɪp/

flip your 'lid (*AmE* also **flip your 'wig**) (*informal*)
1 become very angry: *When he saw the damage to his car, he flipped his lid.*
2 go mad; become mentally ill: *After the divorce, she just flipped her lid. She was in hospital for months.*

● bird → flip/give/shoot sb the bird
● toss → flip a coin SEE toss a coin
● toss → flip for sth SEE toss a coin

flit /flɪt/

● moonlight → do a moonlight flit

float /fləʊt; *AmE* floʊt/

float sb's 'boat (*informal*)
be what sb likes: *You can go swimming, hiking or just lie on the beach, whatever floats your boat.*

● air → float/walk on air

flog /flɒg; *AmE* flɑːg; flɔːg/

flog a dead 'horse (*BrE, informal*)
waste your effort by trying to do sth that is no longer possible: *Pam's flogging a dead horse trying to organize the theatre trip. It's quite obvious that nobody's interested.*

> **NOTE**
> If an animal or a person is *flogged*, it/they are hit many times with a whip or a stick, usually as a punishment.

flog sth to 'death (*BrE, informal*)
talk/write about or deal with a subject so often that there is no longer any interest in it: *The word 'new' has really been flogged to death in advertisements, and nobody believes it any more.*

flood /flʌd/

flood the 'market
offer for sale large quantities of a product, often at a low price: *Importers flooded the market with cheap toys just before Christmas.*

floodgates /'flʌdgeɪts/

● open → open the floodgates (to sth)

floods /flʌdz/

be in 'floods (of 'tears) (*informal*)
be crying a lot: *She was in floods of tears after a row with her family.*

floor /flɔː(r)/

hold the 'floor
speak at a public meeting, etc. for a long time, often stopping others from speaking: *The Ameri-*can delegation held the floor for three quarters of an hour, putting forward their proposals.*

take the 'floor
1 stand up to talk in a debate, etc: *Next, the chairman asked the treasurer, Ms Jones, to take the floor.*
2 begin dancing: *A few couples took the floor.*

● ground → be, come, get, etc. in on the ground floor
● wipe → wipe the floor with sb

flotsam /'flɒtsəm; *AmE* 'flɑːt-/

flotsam and 'jetsam
1 parts of boats, pieces of wood or rubbish, etc. that are found floating on the sea or along the shore; any kind of rubbish: *The beaches are wide and filled with interesting flotsam and jetsam.*
2 people who have no home or job and who move from place to place, often rejected by society: *Under the bridge, you see the human flotsam and jetsam of a big city.*

flow /fləʊ; *AmE* floʊ/

go with the 'flow (*informal*)
be relaxed and not worry about what you should do: *He's very stubborn so there's really no point in trying to change his mind. It's best to just go with the flow.*

● ebb → the ebb and flow (of sb/sth)

The situation was out of his control so he decided to relax and just go with the flow.

flower /'flaʊə(r)/

the flower of sth (*literary*)
the finest or best part of sth: *The people of the village will never forget the war and their young men, killed in the flower of youth.*

flown /fləʊn; *AmE* floʊn/

● bird → the bird has flown

flush /flʌʃ/

● first → (in) the first flush of youth, enthusiasm, etc.

fly /flaɪ/

the ,feathers/,fur/,sparks will 'fly (*informal*)
there will be anger, annoyance, etc: *The fur will really fly when she tells him he can't go out tonight.*

fly the 'coop (*informal, especially AmE*)
escape from a place: *He was never happy living at home with his parents, so as soon as possible he flew the coop and got his own place.*

> **NOTE**
> A *coop* is a cage for chickens, hens, etc.

fly 'high
be successful: *The business is flying high at the moment, making large profits and attracting a lot of investors.* ▶ **,high-'flyer** (also **,high-'flier**) *noun*: *academic high-flyers*

fly in the face of 'sth (*written*)
oppose or be the opposite of sth that is usual or expected: *Such a proposal is flying in the face of common sense.*

a/the fly in the 'ointment (*informal*)
a person or thing that stops a situation, an activity, a plan, etc. from being as good or successful as it could be: *We lead a very happy life here. The only fly in the ointment is that there's too much traffic on our road.*

fly into a 'rage, 'temper, etc.
suddenly become very angry: *She flies into a rage every time anybody suggests that she should stop working so hard.*

fly a 'kite (*BrE, informal*)
release a bit of information, etc. in order to test public reaction to sth that you plan to do at a later date: *Let's fly a kite. Tell the papers that the government is thinking of raising the school leaving age to 18, and we'll see what the reaction is.*

> **NOTE**
> A *kite* is a kind of toy that you fly in the air at the end of one or more long strings. It will tell you which way the wind is blowing.

(go) fly a/your 'kite (*AmE, informal*)
used to tell sb to go away and stop annoying you or interfering

,fly the 'nest
1 (of a young bird) become able to fly and leave its nest
2 (*informal*) (of sb's child) leave home and live somewhere else: *Their children have all flown the nest now.*

fly off the 'handle (*informal*)
suddenly become very angry: *There's no need to fly off the handle!*

a fly on the 'wall
a person who watches others without being noticed: *I'd love to be a fly on the wall when the committee is discussing the report I wrote!* ◇ *fly-on-the-wall documentaries* (= in which people are filmed going about their normal lives as if the camera were not there)

let 'fly (at sb/sth) (with sth) (*informal*)
1 throw, shoot, etc. sth with great force: *He aimed his gun and let fly.*

2 attack sb/sth: *When I told him that I couldn't find the letter, he let fly at me.* ◇ *She let fly at her neighbour with a stream of insults.*

on the 'fly (*informal*)
1 if you do sth **on the fly**, you do it quickly while sth else is happening, and without thinking about it very much: *I usually eat my breakfast on the fly.*
2 (in computing) if sth is produced **on the fly**, it is created immediately while the computer program is running: *This is a new program that creates GIF images on the fly.*

he, she, etc. wouldn't harm/hurt a 'fly
he, she, etc. is kind and gentle, and would not hurt anyone: *The dog may look very fierce, but he wouldn't hurt a fly.*

● flag → fly/show/wave the flag
● pigs → pigs might fly
● pigs → when pigs fly **SEE** pigs might fly
● tangent → go/fly off at a tangent

flyer /'flaɪə(r)/

● flying → get off to a flyer **SEE** get off to a flying start

flying /'flaɪɪŋ/

a ,flying 'visit
a very brief visit: *The Prime Minister paid a flying visit to Brussels this afternoon.*

get off to a ,flying 'start ♦ get off to a 'flyer
make a very good, successful start: *She got off to a flying start, gaining several points in the first few minutes.*

go 'flying (*BrE, informal*)
fall, especially as a result of not seeing sth under your feet: *Someone's going to go flying if you don't pick up these toys.*

with ,flying 'colours (*BrE*) (*AmE* **with ,flying 'colors**)
with great success: *We expect your son to pass the exam with flying colours.* ◇ *She came through her French test with flying colours.*

> **❷ ORIGIN**
> In the past, if a ship or an army lost a battle it had to take down its *colours* (= the national flag). The ship or army that won a victory continued to show its flag.

● flag → keep the flag flying

foam /fəʊm; AmE foʊm/

foam at the 'mouth (*informal*)
be extremely angry: *He stood there foaming at the mouth. I've never seen anybody so angry.*

> **NOTE**
> If an animal *foams at the mouth*, it has a mass of small bubbles in and around its mouth, especially because it is very ill or angry.

fodder /'fɒdə(r); AmE 'fɑːd-/

● cannon → cannon fodder

fog /fɒg; *AmE* fɔːg; fɑːg/

in a fog (*informal*)
uncertain and confused: *Thank you for your explanation, but I'm afraid I'm still in a fog over what happened.*

fogey (also **fogy**) /'fəʊgi; *AmE* 'foʊgi/

● **old** → an old fogey/fogy

foggiest /'fɒgiːst; *AmE* 'fɔːgiːst; 'fɑːgiːst/

● **faintest** → not have the faintest/foggiest (idea)

fold /fəʊld; *AmE* foʊld/

fold sb in your 'arms (*literary*)
put your arms around sb and hold them against your body: *When he saw how upset she was, he folded her in his arms.*

● **return** → return to the fold

follow /'fɒləʊ; *AmE* 'fɑːloʊ/

follow in sb's 'footsteps
to do the same job, have the same style of life, etc. as sb else, especially sb in your family: *He followed in his dad's footsteps and became a lawyer.*

follow your 'nose
1 be guided by your sense of smell: *He followed his nose to the kitchen, and found Marina making tomato soup.*
2 go straight forward: *The garage is a mile ahead up the hill — just follow your nose.*
3 act according to what seems right or reasonable, rather than following any particular rules: *In situations like this, I think all we can do is follow our noses.*

follow 'suit
act or behave in the way that sb else has just done: *One of the oil companies put up the price of fuel today, and the others are expected to follow suit.*

> **NOTE**
> If you *follow suit* in card games, you play a card of the same suit (= either hearts, clubs, diamonds or spades) that has just been played.

● **act** → a hard/tough act to follow
● **crowd** → follow/go with the crowd
● **middle** → follow/steer/take a middle course

fonder /'fɒndə(r); *AmE* 'fɑːndə(r)/

● **absence** → absence makes the heart grow fonder

food /fuːd/

be off your 'food
have no appetite, probably because you are ill or depressed: *She's off her food, she's sleeping very badly and she can't concentrate.*

food for 'thought
an event, a remark, a fact, etc. which should be considered very carefully because it is interesting, important, etc: *The lectures were very interesting and gave much food for thought.*

fool /fuːl/

act/play the 'fool
behave in a stupid way to make people laugh, especially in a way that may also annoy them: *It's impossible to have a decent game of tennis with Frank — he acts the fool the whole time.* ◇ *If you played the fool in class a little less and worked a bit harder, you could do quite well.*

> **NOTE**
> In the past, a *fool* was a man employed by a king or queen to entertain people by telling jokes, singing songs, etc.

Unfortunately, Colin tends to act the fool at office parties.

any fool can/could... (*spoken*)
used to say that sth is very easy to do: *Any fool could tell she was lying.*

be ˌno/ˌnobody's 'fool
be a clever person who cannot easily be tricked or cheated by anyone: *You won't be able to cheat her — she's nobody's fool.* ◇ *Don't underestimate him. He's no fool.*

a ˌfool and his ˌmoney are soon 'parted (*saying*)
a foolish person usually spends money too quickly or carelessly, or is cheated by others

a ˌfool's 'errand
a journey, task, etc. that is a waste of time because it was not necessary: *Are you sending me on a fool's errand again? The last time you sent me to get tickets, the play wasn't even on.*

> **NOTE**
> An *errand* is a job that you do for somebody that involves going somewhere to take a message, to buy something, etc.

a fool's 'paradise
a state of happiness which cannot last because sth which you have not thought of is threatening to destroy it: *You've been living in a fool's paradise. How long do you think we can go on spending our money without earning more?*

make a 'fool of sb/yourself
make sb/yourself appear stupid or ridiculous: *Last time you drank champagne, you made a complete fool of yourself.* ◇ *The interviewer made a real fool of me; I just couldn't answer her question.*

,more fool 'you, ,them, etc. (*spoken*)
(used as an exclamation) you, etc., were very foolish to do sth: *'He's not going to accept that job in Vienna.' 'More fool him. He'll never get another chance like that again.'*

(there's) ,no fool like an 'old fool (*saying*)
an older person who behaves foolishly appears more foolish than a younger person who does the same thing, because experience should have taught him not to do it: *Fred is going to marry a woman thirty years younger than him. There's no fool like an old fool.*

fooled /fuːld/

you could have ,fooled 'me! (*informal*)
used for expressing your surprise about a statement, claim, etc: *'He's quite intelligent, you know.' 'You could have fooled me! I've never heard him say anything intelligent at all.'*

foolish /ˈfuːlɪʃ/

● **penny →** penny wise (and) pound foolish

fools /fuːlz/

fools rush 'in (where angels fear to 'tread) (*saying*)
people with little experience attempt to do the difficult or dangerous things which more experienced people would not consider doing

● **suffer →** not suffer fools gladly

foot /fʊt/

foot the 'bill (for sth)
be responsible for paying the cost of sth: *The local council will have to foot the bill for damage done to the roads in last years's floods.*

get/have a/your ,foot in the 'door
start/have started to be accepted in an organization, a group, a profession, etc. that could bring you success: *It's difficult to get your foot in the door as a young actor without any experience.* ▶ **,foot-in-the-'door** *adj.*: *aggressive, foot-in-the-door sales techniques*

get/start off on the right/wrong 'foot (with sb) (*informal*)
start a relationship well/badly: *I seem to have got off on the wrong foot with the new boss.*

have a foot in both 'camps (*informal*)
be involved with two separate groups, etc. that have different ideas: *She works in industry and at a university, so she's got a foot in both camps.*

have ,one foot in the 'grave (*informal, humorous*)
be so old or ill that you probably will not live much longer: *I may be retired, but that doesn't mean I've got one foot in the grave, you know.*

...my 'foot! (*informal, humorous*)
a strong way of saying that you disagree completely with what has just been said: *'Ian can't come because he's tired.' 'Tired my foot! Lazy more like!'*

not/never put/set a foot 'wrong (*informal*)
never make a mistake: *According to her colleagues, she never put a foot wrong.*

on 'foot
walking, in contrast to other ways of travelling: *It'll take you half an hour on foot, or five minutes in the car.*

put your 'foot down (*informal*)
1 drive faster in a car: *If you put your foot down, we might be home by seven o'clock.*
2 use your authority to stop sb doing sth: *When she asked if she could stay out until midnight, I put my foot down and insisted that she come home by eleven at the latest.*

put your 'foot in it (*BrE*) (also **put your foot in your 'mouth** *AmE, BrE*) (*informal*)
say or do sth that upsets, offends or embarrasses sb without intending to: *He really put his foot in it when he mentioned the party to her. She hadn't been invited.*

set 'foot in/on sth
enter or visit a place: *Neil Armstrong was the first man to set foot on the moon, in July 1969.* ◇ *She's been complaining from the moment she set foot in this hotel.*

● **best →** put your best foot forward
● **boot →** the shoe is on the other foot **SEE** the boot is on the other foot
● **hand →** bind/tie sb hand and foot
● **head →** from head to foot/toe
● **shoot →** shoot yourself in the foot
● **wait →** wait on sb hand and foot

football /ˈfʊtbɔːl/

● **political →** a political football

footloose /ˈfʊtluːs/

,footloose and fancy-'free
free to go where you like or do what you want because you have no responsibilities: *Here she was, at forty, footloose and fancy-free in New York.*

footsie /ˈfʊtsi/

play 'footsie (with sb)
touch sb's feet lightly with your own feet, especially under a table, as an expression of affection or sexual interest

footsteps /ˈfʊtsteps/

● **dog →** dog sb's footsteps
● **follow →** follow in sb's footsteps

for /fɔː(r); fə(r)/

A for B
comparing A with B: *The packets of washing powder are all different sizes, but, weight for weight,*

this one is the cheapest. ◇ Man for man, our soldiers are better trained and better equipped than theirs.

for 'all...
1 in spite of...: For all his qualifications, he isn't really very good at the job. ◇ For all her claims to be efficient, she is a very slow worker.
2 used for saying that the thing you mention does not matter or make any difference: He can do what he wants, for all I care (= I don't care what he does). ◇ 'Where's Peter?' 'For all I know, he may be dead.'

for all (the world) to 'see
clearly visible; in a way that is clearly visible: The relief that the audience felt when the performance finished was clear for all to see.

there's/that's...for you
used to say that sth is a typical example of its kind: She calls him at least four times a day, but that's love for you I suppose. ◇ (ironic) He might at least have called to explain. There's gratitude for you!

forbid /fəˈbɪd; AmE fərˈb-/

God/Heaven for'bid (that...) (also humorous or old use, less frequent **Heaven for'fend (that...)**) (spoken)
used to say that you hope that sth will not happen: 'Maybe you'll end up as a lawyer, like me.' 'Heaven forbid!'
(Some people find this use offensive.)

forbidden /fəˈbɪdn; AmE fərˈb-/

for,bidden 'fruit
something that you are not allowed to have, do, etc. and for this reason is more attractive: He felt very attracted to his best friend's wife, but admitted that it was partly because she was forbidden fruit.

> **❷ ORIGIN**
> This expression refers to the story of Adam and Eve in the Bible, in which Eve ate an apple when she wasn't allowed to.

force /fɔːs; AmE fɔːrs/

bring sth into 'force ♦ come into 'force
make a rule, law, etc. start being used; start being used: The government says it will bring the new rules into force on July the first. ◇ After the new housing law comes into force, we will find it easier to buy our own home.

force sb's 'hand
force sb to do sth differently or sooner than planned: By applying pressure to get the law changed, the opposition party wants to force the government's hand.

'force the issue
do sth to make people take action quickly: The management certainly seemed sympathetic to our concerns, but I think it would be best to wait a while and not try to force the issue just yet.

force of 'circumstance
a situation in which you are forced to do sth by factors beyond your control: He claimed he turned

to crime through force of circumstance. He hadn't been able to find a job and his family was starving.

force of 'habit
a tendency always to do things in a certain way because you have always done them in that way: I don't know why I check all the locks every time I leave the house. It's force of habit, I suppose.

force the 'pace (especially BrE)
make sb do sth more quickly or make sth happen more quickly: The government is forcing the pace on economic reforms and the public don't like it.

> **NOTE**
> If you force the pace in a race, you force the other runners to run as fast as you because you want them to get tired.

a force to be 'reckoned with
a person or thing that has a lot of power and influence and should therefore be treated seriously: The increased size of the country's army means that it is now a force to be reckoned with. ◇ Be very careful how you deal with her because she's a force to be reckoned with.

in 'force/'strength
(of people) present in large numbers: The police were out in force to deal with any trouble at the demonstration. ◇ Party members appeared in strength to welcome the Prime Minister.

● driving → the driving force (behind sth)
● show → a show of force
● spent → a spent force
● tour → a tour de force

forces /ˈfɔːsɪz; AmE ˈfɔːrsɪz/

the forces of 'nature
the power of the wind, rain, etc., especially when it causes damage or harm: This is one of the few areas of the country where the forces of nature are in control, which is why people don't live here.

join/combine 'forces (with sb)
work together in order to achieve a shared aim: The two firms joined forces to win the contract.
OPP part company (with/from sb/sth)

fore /fɔː(r)/

be/come to the 'fore (BrE) (AmE **be at the 'fore**)
be or become important and noticed by people; play an important part: She came very much to the fore in the area during the local campaign against the new bypass.

> **NOTE**
> Fore means 'front'.

bring sth to the 'fore
make sth become noticed by people: His political opinions have been brought to the fore recently, particularly after his television appearance last week.

forearmed /ˌfɔːrˈɑːmd; AmE -ˈɑːrmd/

● forewarned → forewarned is forearmed

forefront /'fɔːfrʌnt; AmE 'fɔːrf-/

at/in/to the 'forefront (of sth)
in or into an important or a leading position in a particular group or activity: *The new product took the company to the forefront of the computer software market.* ◇ *The court case was constantly in the forefront of my mind* (= I thought about it all the time).

foregone /'fɔːgɒn; AmE 'fɔːrgɔːn; -gɑːn/

a ,foregone con'clusion
a result that is certain to happen: *It's a foregone conclusion that Spain will win tonight's match.*

forelock /'fɔːlɒk; AmE 'fɔːrlɑːk/

touch/tug your 'forelock (*disapproving*)
show too much respect for a person of a higher rank or status: *This is a democratic country and we don't want people tugging their forelocks.*

> **❷ ORIGIN**
> In the past, people either took off their hats or pulled on their *forelocks* (= the hair above the forehead) to show respect.

foremost /'fɔːməʊst; AmE 'fɔːrmoʊst/

● first → first and foremost

foreseeable /fɔː'siːəbl; AmE fɔːr's-/

for/in the foreseeable 'future
for/in the period of time when you can predict what is going to happen, based on the present circumstances: *The statue will remain in the museum for the foreseeable future.* ◇ *It's unlikely that the hospital will be closed in the foreseeable future* (= soon).

forest /'fɒrɪst; AmE 'fɔːr-; 'fɑːr-/

● wood → not see the forest for the trees **SEE** not see the wood for the trees

forewarned /fɔː'wɔːnd; AmE fɔːr'wɔːrnd/

fore,warned is fore'armed (*saying*)
if you know about problems, dangers, etc. before they happen, you can be better prepared for them: *Jim says that Betty is very angry with me still. Well, forewarned is forearmed, and I'll have to think up an excuse before I see her.*

> **NOTE**
> *Fore-* in these words means 'before something happens' or 'in advance'.

forfend /fɔː'fend; AmE fɔːr-/

● forbid → Heaven forfend (that...) **SEE** God/Heaven forbid (that...)

forget /fə'get; AmE fər'g-/

for'get it (*spoken*)
1 used to tell sb that sth is not important and that they should not worry about it: *'I still owe you for lunch yesterday.' 'Forget it — it was my treat!'*

2 used to tell sb that you are not going to repeat what you said: *'Now, what were you saying about John?' 'Forget it, it doesn't matter.'*
3 used to emphasize that you are saying 'no' to sth: *'Any chance of you helping out here?' 'Forget it, I've got too much to do.'*
4 used to tell sb to stop talking about sth because they are annoying you: *Just forget it, will you?*

● forgive → forgive and forget

forgetting /fə'getɪŋ; AmE fər'getɪŋ/

not forgetting... (*BrE*)
used to include sth in the list of things that you have just mentioned: *I share the house with Jim, Ian and Sam, not forgetting Spike, the dog.*

forgive /fə'gɪv; AmE fər'gɪv/

for,give and for'get
decide to forget an argument, an insult, etc: *Come on, it's time to forgive and forget.* ◇ *Many of his victims find it impossible to forgive and forget.*

forgiven /fə'gɪvn; AmE fər'gɪvn/

he, she, etc. could/might be forgiven for doing sth
used to say that it is easy to understand why sb does or thinks sth, although they may be wrong: *Looking at the crowds out shopping, you could be forgiven for thinking that everyone has plenty of money to spend.*

form /fɔːm; AmE fɔːrm/

good/bad 'form (*old-fashioned, BrE*)
a way of doing things that is socially acceptable/ not socially acceptable: *I think it was very bad form for Joe to arrive late for the funeral.* ◇ *Apparently, good form requires you to wear a hat on these occasions.*

off 'form (*also* **out of 'form**)
in a poor mental or physical state; doing worse than normal: *She had been ill and was off form, so she didn't do so well in the exam.*

on 'form (*also* **in (good) 'form**)
in a good mental or physical state; doing as well as normal: *He's really on form tonight and is answering all the questions correctly and very quickly.* ◇ *The team are in good form this season.*

take 'form (*formal*)
gradually form into a particular shape; gradually develop: *In her body a new life was taking form.*

● matter → (do sth) as a matter of form
● present → on present form
● shape → in any (way,) shape or form
● shape → in the shape/form of sb/sth
● true → true to form

former /'fɔːmə(r); AmE 'fɔːrm-/

be a shadow/ghost of your/its former 'self
not have the strength, influence, etc. that you/sth used to have: *He'd been ill for some time, and he looked a shadow of his former self.* ◇ *The old house, which had once been so full of life, was now just a ghost of its former self.*

fort /fɔːt; AmE fɔːrt/

hold the 'fort (*BrE*) (*AmE* **hold down the 'fort**) (*informal*)
be in charge or taking care of sth while the person usually responsible is not there: *I'm going abroad for a few weeks, and Kathy will hold the fort while I'm away.*

Forth /fɔːθ; AmE fɔːrθ/

● **painting** → be like painting the Forth Bridge

forth /fɔːθ; AmE fɔːrθ/

and 'so forth (also **and 'so on** (**and 'so forth**))
used to show that a story, list, etc. continues in an expected way: *I'm in a bit of a hurry. I've got to pack my bags, find my passport and so on, all before tomorrow morning.*

,back and 'forth (also **,backwards and 'forwards**)
in one direction and then in the opposite one, repeatedly: *The rope swung back and forth from the branch.* ◇ *She travels backwards and forwards between the factory and head office.*

from that day/time 'forth (*literary*)
beginning on that day; from that time: *He never saw his mother again from that day forth.*

hold 'forth (about/on sth) (*disapproving*)
speak for a long time about sth in a way that other people might find boring: *The politician held forth on the importance of living in a society free from social injustice.* ◇ *He's a real bore. He's always holding forth about something or other.*

Fort Knox /ˌfɔːt 'nɒks; AmE ˌfɔːrt 'nɑːks/

be like/as safe as Fort 'Knox
(about a building) be strongly built, with many locks, strong doors, alarms, etc. so that it is very safe and difficult for thieves to enter: *This home of yours is like Fort Knox.* ◇ *Financially, she's as safe as Fort Knox.*

> **❷ ORIGIN**
> *Fort Knox* is a military base in Kentucky where most of the US's store of gold is kept.

fortune /'fɔːtʃuːn; AmE 'fɔːrtʃ-/

fortune 'smiles on sb
a person is lucky and successful: *At first, fortune smiled on him and the business was successful.*

make a 'fortune
make a lot of money: *He made a fortune buying and selling nineteenth-century paintings.*

● **hostage** → a hostage to fortune
● **seek** → seek your fortune
● **small** → a small fortune

forty /'fɔːti; AmE 'fɔːrti/

forty 'winks (*informal*)
a short sleep, especially during the day: *I managed to get forty winks after lunch.*

forward /'fɔːwəd; AmE 'fɔːrwərd/

● **best** → put your best foot forward
● **step** → one step forward, two steps back

forwards /'fɔːwədz; AmE 'fɔːrwərdz/

● **forth** → backwards and forwards SEE back and forth

foul /faʊl/

fall foul of 'sb/'sth
do sth which gets you into trouble with sb/sth: *They fell foul of the law by not paying their taxes.* ◇ *Try not to fall foul of Mr. Jones. He can be very unpleasant.*

● **cry** → cry foul
● **fair** → by fair means or foul

found /faʊnd/

all 'found (*old-fashioned*)
with free food and accommodation in addition to your wages: *My grandmother told me how she used to work as a maid, and was paid £3 a week all found.*

nowhere to be 'found/'seen (also **nowhere in 'sight**)
impossible to find: *They searched the house but the necklace was nowhere to be found.* ◇ *By the time I arrived at the station, the others were nowhere in sight.*

foundations /faʊn'deɪʃnz/

shake/rock the 'foundations of sth ◆ shake/rock sth to its 'foundations
cause people to question their basic beliefs about sth: *This issue has shaken the very foundations of French politics.*

founding /'faʊndɪŋ/

the ,founding 'father(s) of sth (*formal*)
the people who found or start a country, an organization, a branch of science, etc: *Charles Babbage, the founding father of computer science*

four /fɔː(r)/

the four ,corners of the 'earth
the parts of the world furthest away: *People come from the four corners of the earth to attend the annual festival.*

these four 'walls
used when you are talking about keeping sth secret: *Don't let this go further than these four walls* (= don't tell anyone else who is not in the room now).

four-letter /ˌfɔː 'letə(r); AmE ˌfɔːr/

a ,four-letter 'word
a short word that is considered rude or offensive, especially because it refers to sex or other functions of the body: *Four-letter words used to be banned on radio and television.*

fours /fɔːz; AmE fɔːrz/

on all 'fours
with your knees, toes and hands on the floor: *The ceiling of the tunnel was so low that we had to crawl along on all fours.*

fowl /faʊl/

● fish → neither fish nor fowl

frame /freɪm/

be in/out of the 'frame
be taking part/not taking part in sth: *We won our match last week, so we're still in the frame for the championship.*

a frame of 'mind
a particular way of thinking, mood, etc: *You should ask her for permission when she's in a better frame of mind.* ◇ *I wonder what frame of mind he was in when he wrote the letter.*

franca /'fræŋkə/

● lingua → a lingua franca

fray /freɪ/

fray at/around the 'edges/'seams
start to come apart or to fail: *Support for the leader was fraying at the edges.*

> **NOTE**
> If cloth *frays*, the threads in it start to come apart.

frazzle /'fræzl/

be burnt, worn, etc. to a 'frazzle (*informal*)
be completely burnt/extremely tired: *After working all weekend at the hospital, Deborah was worn to a frazzle.*

free /friː/

be in/go into free 'fall
be falling/start to fall rapidly: *Share prices are in free fall in Tokyo this morning.* ◇ *The value of the euro against the dollar went into free fall as soon as the news was announced.*

> **NOTE**
> From the moment you jump out of a plane until the moment your parachute opens, you are in *free fall*.

for 'free
1 without having to pay: *Some children got into the cinema for free by using old tickets.*
2 used for emphasizing how strongly you feel about sth: *The whole plan is a disaster. I can tell you that for free.*

free and 'easy
informal and relaxed: *They had to settle down. Life wasn't free and easy any more.*

(as) free as (the) 'air/as a 'bird
completely free: *You can't imagine what it's like to feel as free as the air. Nobody who hasn't been in prison can imagine it.*

get, have, etc. a free 'hand
be given permission or an opportunity to do what you want in your work, plans, etc: *My boss gives me a free hand in deciding which outside contractor to use.* ◇ *She has a free hand in choosing her staff.*
OPP tie sb's hands

get, take, etc. a free 'ride
have an advantage or a benefit from a situation without doing anything to deserve it: *The free ride is over — either you start working or quit.*

it's a free 'country (*spoken*)
used as a reply when sb suggests that you should not do sth: *It's a free country and I'll say what I like!*

make free with sth (*disapproving*)
use sth a lot, even though it does not belong to you: *I think he'll have something to say about you making free with all his things while he's away.*

of your own free 'will
because you want to do sth rather than because sb has told or forced you to do it: *She left of her own free will.*

● feel → feel free (to do sth)
● home → home free SEE home and dry
● rein → give/allow sb/sth free/full rein
● thing → there's no such thing as a free lunch
● walk → walk free

freedom /'friːdəm/

● manoeuvre → freedom of/room for manoeuvre

freeze /friːz/

● blood → make sb's blood freeze
● tracks → stop/halt/freeze in your tracks

freezes /'friːzɪz/

● hell → when hell freezes over

French /frentʃ/

ex,cuse/,pardon my 'French (*informal, humorous*)
used for saying you are sorry when you have used or are going to use rude or offensive language: *Ouch, bloody hell! Oops, excuse my French!* ◇ *If you'll pardon my French, he's a bloody fool.*

take French 'leave (*BrE, old-fashioned or humorous*)
leave your work, duty, etc. without permission; go away without telling anyone: *I think I might take French leave this afternoon and go to the cinema.*

> **❓ ORIGIN**
> This idiom is said to refer to the eighteenth-century French custom of leaving a dinner or party without saying goodbye to the host or hostess.

frenzy /ˈfrenzi/

● feeding → a feeding frenzy

fresh /freʃ/

(as) fresh as a ˈdaisy
lively or clean and neat: *Even when it's so hot, she looks as fresh as a daisy. How does she do it?*

fresh out of sth (*informal, especially AmE*)
having recently finished a supply of sth: *Sorry, we're fresh out of milk.*

get ˈfresh (with sb) (*informal*)
be rude and too confident in a way that shows a lack of respect for sb or a sexual interest in sb: *Don't get fresh with me!*

● blood → fresh/new/young blood
● breath → a breath of fresh air
● ground → break fresh/new ground

Freudian /ˈfrɔɪdiən/

a ˌFreudian ˈslip
a mistake in speaking or writing which shows what you really think or feel about sb/sth: *'I've never loved, I mean I've never stopped loving, my mother.' 'Was that a Freudian slip?'*

❷ ORIGIN
This is named after Sigmund Freud.

friend /frend/

a ˌfriend in ˈneed (is a ˌfriend inˈdeed) (*saying*)
a friend who helps you when you are in trouble (is a real friend): *I'll always be grateful to Tom for helping me; a friend in need is a friend indeed!*

● fair-weather → a fair-weather friend
● man → man's best friend

friends /frendz/

be (just) good ˈfriends
used to say that two friends are not having a romantic relationship with each other: *People often think Ian and I are a couple, but we're just good friends.*

have ˌfriends in high ˈplaces
know important people with power and influence who can help you: *Ask Geoff to help with the campaign. He's got friends in high places.*

make ˈfriends (with sb)
become sb's friend: *Roger was new to the district but he soon made friends with other boys of his age.* ◇ *She's a very open sort of person and tends to make friends easily.*

what's ... between friends? (*spoken*)
used for refusing an offer by a friend to pay you for sth because the amount is small: *'I owe you €2 for that coffee.' 'Don't be silly, Steve, what's €2 between friends?'*

● feathered → our feathered friends

He never did anything special in his life, but he had friends in high places.

fright /fraɪt/

the ˌfright of your ˈlife
an experience that makes you feel great fear: *I got the fright of my life when I saw the gun pointing at me.* ◇ *He gave me the fright of my life when I saw him hanging out of the window.*

look a ˈfright (*old-fashioned, BrE*)
look ugly or ridiculous: *Oh no, just look at what the hairdresser's done to my hair! I look a fright!*

take ˈfright (at sth) (*written*)
be frightened by sth: *The horse took fright and galloped off as the car passed.*

frighten /ˈfraɪtn/

● life → frighten/scare the life out of sb
● wits → frighten/scare sb out of their wits

frightened /ˈfraɪtnd/

● shadow → be frightened/nervous/scared of your own shadow

frighteners /ˈfraɪtnəz; AmE -nərz/

put the ˈfrighteners on (sb) (*BrE, slang*)
threaten sb so that they will do what you want: *They started putting the frighteners on the witness, sending him threatening letters.*

fringe /frɪndʒ/

● lunatic → the lunatic fringe

fritz /frɪts/

on the ˈfritz (*AmE, informal*)
not working: *The TV is on the fritz again.*

fro /frəʊ; AmE froʊ/

● to → to and fro

full

frog /frɒg; AmE frɔːg; frɑːg/

have a 'frog in your throat (*informal*)
not be able to speak clearly because your throat is sore, you want to cough, etc: *She had a frog in her throat, so she had a drink of water before she went on speaking.*

froing /'frəʊɪŋ; AmE 'froʊɪŋ/

● **toing** → toing and froing

front /frʌnt/

,back to 'front
with the front part where the back should be: *You've got your jumper on back to front.*

,front and 'center (*AmE*)
in or into the most important position: *This is the first TV channel to put kids front and center.*

Oops! Bill had his jumper on back to front.

in the front line (of sth)
doing work that will have an important effect on sth: *a life spent in the front line of research*

on the front 'burner (*informal, especially AmE*)
(of an issue, a plan, etc.) being given a lot of attention because it is considered important: *Anything that keeps education on the front burner is good.*
OPP on the back burner

> **NOTE**
> A *burner* is one of the parts of a cooker/stove, etc. that produces a flame.

up 'front (*informal*)
(of money) as payment in advance: *We finally agreed to pay him half the fee up front and the other half when he'd finished.* ▶ ,up'front *adj.* **1** not trying to hide what you think or do: *If that's what they're doing, they ought to be more upfront about it.* **2** (of money) paid in advance: *There will be an upfront fee of 4%.*

● **cash** → cash up front **SEE** cash down
● **home** → on the home front
● **lead¹** → lead from the front

fruit /fruːt/

the fruit(s) of sth
the good results of an activity or a situation: *Enjoy the fruits of your labours* (= the rewards for your hard work). ◇ *The book is the fruit of years of research.*

● **bear** → bear fruit
● **forbidden** → forbidden fruit

fruitcake /'fruːtkeɪk/

● **nutty** → (as) nutty as a fruitcake

fry /fraɪ/

● **fish** → have other/bigger fish to fry
● **small** → small fry

frying /'fraɪɪŋ/

out of the 'frying pan (and) into the 'fire (*saying*)
out of one situation of danger or difficulty into another (usually worse) one: *It was a case of out of the frying pan into the fire: she divorced her husband, who was an alcoholic, and then married another man with the same problem.*

fuel /'fjuːəl/

● **add** → add fuel to the fire/flames

full /fʊl/

at full 'stretch
to the full extent of your powers, abilities, etc: *We've been working at full stretch for weeks to get the hall ready for the conference.*

be at/below full 'strength
have/not have the necessary number of people to do sth: *We're working below strength at the moment; it's not easy to deliver all the orders on time.* ◇ *When we're working at full strength, we employ 600 people.*

be full of 'shit/'crap (⚠, *slang*)
say, write, etc. stupid or wrong things: *She's so full of shit.* ◇ *You're all full of crap and I'm not listening any more!*

come/go full 'circle
after a long period of changes, return to the position or situation in which sth/you started: *The wheel of fashion has come full circle. I was wearing shoes like that thirty years ago.*

come to a full 'stop (*BrE*)
stop unexpectedly before sth is or seems to be finished: *It's a very strange book — you're in the middle of the story and it suddenly comes to a full stop.* ◇ *She came to a full stop and seemed unable to go on with her speech.*

> **NOTE**
> *Full stop* here refers to the mark (.) used at the end of a sentence.

draw yourself up/rise to your full 'height
stand straight and tall in order to show your determination or high status: *When the sales assistant said he couldn't help her, she drew herself up to her full height and demanded to see the manager.*

(at) full 'blast
with great noise, power, speed, etc: *Tom had his radio on at full blast — it was deafening.* ◇ *The heating was on full blast all day.*

full 'marks (to sb for doing sth) (*BrE*)
used for praising sb for being or doing sth: *Full marks to Hannah for being so helpful this morning.* ◇ *Full marks, Dominic. You sang that very well.*

fullness

the ˌfull 'monty
the full amount that people expect or want: *They'll do the full monty* (= take off all their clothes) *if you pay them enough.*

> **❷ ORIGIN**
> This expression may refer to Field Marshal Montgomery (*'Monty'*), who insisted on a full cooked English breakfast wherever he went; or it might refer to a full three-piece suit from the tailors *Montague Burton.*

full of 'beans
very lively, active and healthy: *Ray is certainly full of beans again after his illness.*

> **❷ ORIGIN**
> This phrase was originally used to talk about horses that were fed on beans.

full of the joys of 'spring
very happy, cheerful and lively: *You look full of the joys of spring this morning.*

'full of yourself (*disapproving*)
feeling successful and very proud of yourself because of it: *He came to see us last week, very full of himself because he had just been promoted.*

(at) full 'pelt/'speed/'tilt
with great speed, force, etc: *The police were chasing him so he ran full pelt down the road.* ◇ *We drove down the road at full tilt.*

full steam/speed a'head
with as much speed or energy as possible: *We were working full steam ahead to finish the project by the end of April.*

> **❷ ORIGIN**
> This expression refers to the order given on a ship by the captain to the engine room.

full 'stop (*BrE*) (also **period** *AmE, BrE*) (*spoken*)
used to emphasize that there is nothing more to say about a subject: *I don't have to give you any reasons. You can't have a motorbike, full stop.* ◇ *I don't like him, period.*

(at) full 'throttle
if you do sth **at full throttle**, you do it with as much speed and energy as you can: *He's determined to live his whole life at full throttle.*

> **NOTE**
> The *throttle* is a device that controls the amount of fuel going into the engine of a vehicle.

in 'full
completely; with nothing missing: *I paid the debt in full.* ◇ *The programme reported on the latest developments in full.* **OPP** in part

in full 'cry
chasing or attacking sth with a lot of noise and enthusiasm: *The newspapers are in full cry over this new banking scandal.* ◇ *The government is having difficulties, and its critics are in full cry again.*

> **NOTE**
> This idiom refers to hounds (= hunting dogs) and the noise they make when they are chasing a fox.

in full 'swing
at the height of sth such as an event, a party, an election, etc.; at the busiest or liveliest time: *When we arrived at 10 o'clock, the party was already in full swing.* ◇ *The tourist season in London is in full swing at the moment.*

in full 'view (of sb/sth)
where you can easily be seen (by sb/sth): *The player committed the foul in full view of the referee, and was sent off the field.*

not the full 'quid (*AustralE, New Zealand, informal*)
not very intelligent: *George always looks to me like he's not the full quid.* **OPP** all there

> **NOTE**
> A *quid* is an informal word for one pound in British money.

to the 'full
as completely or as much as possible: *You'll be able to enjoy life to the full again after your operation.*

- **glass** → (see the) glass half full/half empty
- **hands** → have your hands full
- **know** → know sth full/perfectly/very well
- **measure** → full/short measure
- **pump** → pump sb full of sth
- **rein** → give/allow sb/sth free/full rein
- **seams** → be full to bursting (with sth) **SEE** be bursting/bulging at the seams (with sth)
- **three** → (yes sir, no sir) three bags full (sir)
- **wheel** → the wheel has come/turned full circle

fullness /ˈfʊlnəs/

in the fullness of 'time (*formal*)
when enough time has passed; eventually: *I knew that, in the fullness of time, somebody with your abilities would emerge and become leader.*

fun /fʌn/

for 'fun ◆ for the 'fun of it
for the pleasure or enjoyment of sth, not because it's important or serious: *I entered the competition just for fun — I never thought I'd win.* ◇ *'Why did you say it if you didn't mean it?' 'For the fun of it. I just wanted to see his reaction.'*

fun and 'games (*informal*)
1 activities that are not serious and that other people may disapprove of: *It's not all fun and games at this school — we make our children work hard as well.*
2 (*humorous*) trouble: *We had some fun and games putting up those new shelves yesterday.*

in 'fun
in order to amuse sb, not to upset them: *I didn't mean to upset you. It was only said in fun.*

make 'fun of sb/sth (also **poke 'fun at sb/sth**)
make unkind remarks or jokes about sb: *People enjoy making fun of the clothes I wear, though they seem all right to me.* ◇ *It's a programme that likes to poke fun at the royal family.*

- **figure** → a figure of fun

funeral /ˈfjuːnərəl/

it's 'your funeral (*informal*)
used to tell sb that they, and nobody else, will
have to deal with the unpleasant results of their
own actions: *I think you're making a big mistake,
but if you don't want to listen to me that's fine — it's
your funeral.*

funny /ˈfʌni/

'funny business (*informal*)
something that is suspicious and probably illegal
or dishonest: *Now, behave yourself! I don't want
any of your funny business.* ◇ *If there's any funny
business going on, we'll soon find out.*

fur /fɜː(r)/

● **fly** → the feathers/fur/sparks will fly

furious /ˈfjʊəriəs; AmE ˈfjʊr-/

● **fast** → fast and furious

furniture /ˈfɜːnɪtʃə(r); AmE ˈfɜːrn-/

● **part** → part of the furniture

furrow /ˈfʌrəʊ; AmE ˈfɜːroʊ/

● **plough** → plough a lonely, your own, etc. furrow

further /ˈfɜːðə(r); AmE ˈfɜːrð-/

further along/down the 'road
at some time in the future: *There are certain to be
more job losses further down the road.*

go 'further
1 say more about sth, or make a more extreme
point about it: *I would go even further and suggest
that the entire government is corrupt.*
2 last longer; serve more people: *They watered
down the soup to make it go further.*

go no 'further ♦ not go any 'further
if you tell sb that a secret will **go no further**, you
promise not to tell it to anyone else: *Can I have
your assurance that this will go no further?*

**,nothing could be ,further from my 'mind, the
'truth, etc.**
used to emphasize that what sb has said you are
thinking is definitely not true: *'You must be thinking how terrible I look.' 'Nothing could be further
from my mind. You're as beautiful as always.'*
◇ *People expect the richest people to be the most
generous, but in fact nothing could be further from
the truth.*

take sth 'further
take more serious action about sth or speak to sb
at a higher level about it: *I am not satisfied with
your explanation and I warn you that I intend to
take the matter further.*

● **ado** → without further/more ado
● **afield** → far/farther/further afield
● **removed** → be far/further/furthest removed from sth

furthest /ˈfɜːðɪst; AmE ˈfɜːrð-/

● **removed** → be far/further/furthest removed from sth

fury /ˈfjʊəri; AmE ˈfjʊri/

like 'fury (*informal*)
with great energy, speed, etc: *I worked like fury to
get everything done by five o'clock.*

● **hell** → hell hath no fury (like a woman scorned)

fuse /fjuːz/

● **blow** → blow a fuse
● **short** → be on/have a short fuse

fuss /fʌs/

a ,fuss about 'nothing
a lot of anger or worry about sth that is not
important: *She complained about her food twice in
the restaurant. She was making a lot of fuss about
nothing — I thought everything was fine.*

make a 'fuss of/over sb/sth
pay a lot of attention to sb/sth; show concern,
affection, etc. for sb/sth: *It's sometimes quite pleasant being ill, with people making a fuss of you all the
time.*

fussed /fʌst/

not be 'fussed (about sb/sth) (*BrE, informal*)
not mind about sth; not have feelings about sth:
It'd be good to go there, but I'm not that fussed.

future /ˈfjuːtʃə(r)/

in 'future (*BrE*) (*AmE* **in the 'future**)
from now on: *Please be more careful in future.* ◇ *In
future, make sure the door is never left unlocked.*

● **distant** → in the not too distant future
● **foreseeable** → for/in the foreseeable future

G g

gab /ɡæb/

● **gift** → a gift of/for gab **SEE** the gift of the gab
● **gift** → the gift of the gab

gaff /ɡæf/

● **blow** → blow the gaff (on sb/sth)

gain /ɡeɪn/

gain 'ground
1 (of soldiers) move forward in a battle: *Our men
began to gain ground, forcing the enemy back
towards the river.*
2 (of an idea, development, etc.) become more
popular or successful: *Diesel cars seem to be gaining ground because they are cheaper to run.*

gain 'time
delay sth so that you can have more time to make a decision, deal with a problem, etc: *Instead of answering the question, he asked for a glass of water to gain time.*

gained /geɪnd/

• ventured → nothing ventured, nothing gained

gallery /'gæləri/

play to the 'gallery
behave in an exaggerated way to attract ordinary people's attention: *The most popular and successful politicians in our history have always known how to play to the gallery.*

> **NOTE**
> In a theatre, the *gallery* is the highest level where the cheapest seats are.

• rogues → a rogues' gallery

game /geɪm/

blow/sod △ 'this/'that for a game of soldiers (*BrE, slang*)
used by sb who does not want to do sth because it is annoying or involves too much effort: *After waiting for twenty minutes more, he thought 'sod this for a game of soldiers', and left.*

your/sb's (little) 'game (*informal*)
your/sb's trick, plan or intention: *So that's your little game — getting me moved to a different office and then doing my job for me.*

the ˌgame is not worth the 'candle
(*old-fashioned, saying*)
sth is not worth the effort needed: *After trying to get permission to build the office for a whole year, we gave up, because the game was just not worth the candle.*

> **❷ ORIGIN**
> In the past, candles were used for light at night. If a game or an activity was not worth the cost of the candles required to light the room, it was not worth playing or doing.

the game is 'up (*BrE, informal*)
said to sb who has done sth wrong, when they are caught and the crime or trick has been discovered: *The game's up, Malone. We're arresting you for the murder of Joe Capella. ◊ The game is up for the Democrats. They'll never win the next election after this scandal.*

give the 'game away (*informal*)
(accidentally) reveal your own or another person's secret plan, trick, etc. and so spoil it: *Don't laugh when he comes in or you'll give the game away. The birthday present's got to be a surprise. ◊ He can't keep a secret, so never tell him anything important in case he gives the game away.* **OPP** keep sb guessing

(be/go) on the 'game (*BrE, slang*)
be/become a prostitute

the only game in 'town (*informal*)
the most important thing of a particular type, or the only thing that is available: *When it comes to selling technology, our company is the only game in town. ◊ It may not be great, but right now it's the only game in town.*

play the 'game
behave in a fair and honest way: *That's the third time this week you've left me to finish all your work. You're not playing the game, Luke.*

play sb's 'game ♦ play the same 'game (as sb)
(also **play sb at their own 'game**)
use the same methods as a competitor, an opponent, an enemy, etc: *Safeway started cutting their food prices, so Asda decided to play them at their own game by cutting prices even more.*

what's sb's/your 'game? (*BrE, spoken*)
used to ask why sb is behaving as they are: *Dan's looking very nervous. Why? What's his game?*

• ball → a (whole) different/new ball game
• beat → beat sb at their own game
• easy → easy game
• fair → fair game
• mug → be a mug's game
• name → the name of the game
• numbers → a/the numbers game
• rules → the rules of the game
• skin → have/put skin in the game
• two → two can play at that game
• waiting → a waiting game

gamekeeper /'geɪmkiːpə(r)/

• poacher → poacher turned gamekeeper

games /geɪmz/

play (silly) 'games (with sb)
not treat a situation seriously, especially in order to cheat or deceive sb: *Don't play silly games with me; I know you did it.*

• fun → fun and games

gamut /'gæmət/

run the 'gamut of sth
experience or describe a range of sth: *This poem runs the gamut of emotions from despair to joy.*

> **❷ ORIGIN**
> *Gamut* originally referred to a complete scale of musical notes or the range of a voice or a musical instrument.

gander /'gændə(r)/

have/take a 'gander (at sth) (*informal*)
look at sth: *Come over here and have a gander at what I've got!*

> **❷ ORIGIN**
> This came from a comparison between the way a person walks when they want to look at something, often stretching their neck to get a

better view, and a *gander* (= a male goose), which wanders about, stretching its neck to see things.

● **sauce** → what's sauce for the goose is sauce for the gander

gangbusters /ˈɡæŋbʌstəz; *AmE* -ərz/

like 'gangbusters (*AmE, informal*)
with a lot of energy and enthusiasm: *At the time, we were spending money like gangbusters.*

> ❷ ORIGIN
> A *gangbuster* was a type of police officer in the US who used to find and arrest criminal gangs (= organized groups). The name comes from a radio programme from the 1930s describing FBI (= Federal Bureau of Investigation) cases.

gap /ɡæp/

● **bridge** → bridge the gap (between A and B)

garden /ˈɡɑːdn; *AmE* ˈɡɑːrdn/

everything in the garden is 'lovely/'rosy (*BrE, saying, often ironic*)
everything is satisfactory, is going well, or could not be better: *She pretends that everything in the garden is rosy, but I've heard that she's heavily in debt.*

● **common** → common or garden
● **lead**¹ → lead sb up the garden path

garden-variety /ˈɡɑːdn vəraɪəti; *AmE* ˈɡɑːrdn/

● **common** → garden-variety **SEE** common or garden

garters /ˈɡɑːtəz; *AmE* ˈɡɑːrtərz/

● **guts** → have sb's guts for garters

gas /ɡæs/

● **cooking** → be cooking with gas
● **step** → step on the gas **SEE** step on it

gasp /ɡɑːsp; *AmE* ɡæsp/

● **last** → your/the last gasp

gatepost /ˈɡeɪtpəʊst; *AmE* -poʊst/

between you, me and the 'gatepost (*BrE, informal*)
used to show that what you are going to say next is a secret: *Well, between you, me and the gatepost, I heard that she's pregnant.*

Gates /ɡeɪts/

● **Pearly** → the Pearly Gates

gather /ˈɡæðə(r)/

gather 'dust
(of plans, recommendations, etc.) be forgotten or ignored: *As usual the report was left to gather dust and not dealt with by the authorities for years.*

● **wits** → collect/gather your wits

gauntlet /ˈɡɔːntlət/

run the 'gauntlet
be attacked or criticized by many people at the same time: *The Prime Minister's car had to run the gauntlet of a large group of protesters outside the conference hall.*

> ❷ ORIGIN
> This phrase refers to an old army punishment where a man was forced to run between two lines of soldiers hitting him.

take up the 'gauntlet
accept sb's invitation to fight or compete: *The country needs enormous help to rebuild its economy, and it's time to take up the gauntlet and do what we can.*

throw down the 'gauntlet
invite sb to compete with you; challenge sb: *They have thrown down the gauntlet to the Prime Minister by demanding a referendum.* **OPP** hold out/offer an olive branch (to sb)

> ❷ ORIGIN
> A *gauntlet* is a kind of glove. In medieval times a knight threw his gauntlet at the feet of another knight as a challenge to fight. If he accepted the challenge, the other knight would pick up the glove.

gay /ɡeɪ/

with gay a'bandon (*old-fashioned*)
without thinking about the results or effects of a particular action: *Although she was nervous at first, she was soon singing and dancing with gay abandon.*

> NOTE
> *Gay* here means 'happy and without cares'.

gaze /ɡeɪz/

● **space** → look/stare/gaze into space

gear /ɡɪə(r); *AmE* ɡɪr/

get into 'gear ◆ **get sth into 'gear**
start working, or start sth working, in an efficient way: *Sorry, I can't seem to get my brain into gear this morning.*

(slip/be thrown) out of 'gear
(of emotions or situations) (become) out of control: *She said nothing when he arrived in case her temper slipped out of gear.*

● **ass** → get your ass in gear

general /ˈdʒenrəl/

in 'general
in most cases; usually: *The money is due to come on the first of every month; in general it arrives punctually, but at holiday times it's sometimes late.* **OPP** in particular

● **common** → the common/general run (of sth)

genes /dʒiːnz/

● blood → in the/sb's blood/genes

genie /'dʒiːni/

the ˌgenie is out of the 'bottle
used to say that an action has been taken that will
cause a big and permanent change in people's
lives, especially one which might make a situation
worse: *Now that genetically modified foods are on
our supermarket shelves, the genie is out of the bottle and cannot be put back in.*

let the ˌgenie out of the 'bottle
do sth that causes a big and permanent change in
people's lives, especially one which might make a
situation worse: *Once you make carrying guns
legal, you let the genie out of the bottle.*

> **NOTE**
> In Arabian stories, a *genie* is a spirit with
> magical powers, especially one that lives in a
> bottle or lamp.

gentleman /'dʒentlmən/

a ˌgentleman's a'greement (also **a ˌgentlemen's
a'greement**)
an agreement, a contract, etc. in which nothing is
written down because both people trust each
other not to break it: *'Why don't you tell him you
don't want to sell it now?' 'I can't possibly. It was a
gentleman's agreement and I must keep to it.'*

gently /'dʒentli/

● easy → easy/gently/slowly does it

get /get/

> Most idioms containing the verb **get** are at the
> entries for the nouns or adjectives in the
> idioms, for example **get on sb's nerves** is at
> **nerves**.

can't get 'over sth (*spoken*)
used to say that you are shocked, surprised,
amused, etc. by sth: *I can't get over how rude she
was to me.*

get a'way from it all (*informal*)
go away somewhere on holiday/vacation, etc. in
order to escape from pressures at work, home, city
life, etc: *We went walking to get away from it all for
a while.* ◇ *Why don't you get away from it all and
have a weekend in the mountains?*

get 'hold of sb/sth
obtain sth; reach or contact sb: *Do you know where
I can get hold of a telephone directory for Paris?*
◇ *I spent all morning on the phone trying to get
hold of the manager.*

'get it (in the 'neck) (*informal*)
be criticized, blamed or punished: *You'll get it
when your mother sees all this mess.* ◇ *We'll get it
in the neck if we arrive late.*

get it 'on (with sb) (*slang, especially AmE*)
have sex with sb

get sb 'nowhere/not get sb 'anywhere
not help sb make progress: *His job is getting him
nowhere. He ought to try and find another one.*
◇ *All these questions aren't getting us anywhere.
We need to make a decision.*

'get somewhere/anywhere/nowhere
make some/no progress: *Now at last we're getting
somewhere!* ◇ *You'll get nowhere in life if you don't
work harder.* ◇ *Are you getting anywhere with that
new manager?*

'get there (*informal*)
finally achieve your aim or complete a task: *Peter
is a slow learner, but he gets there in the end.*

**how selfish, stupid, ungrateful, etc. can you
'get?** (*spoken*)
used to express surprise or disapproval that sb has
been so selfish, stupid, etc: *I can't believe he didn't
even say thank you. How ungrateful can you get?*

getting /'getɪŋ/

be getting 'on (*informal*)
1 (of people) be becoming old: *I'm getting on a bit
now and I can't walk as well as I used to.*
2 (of the time) be becoming late: *It's getting on, so
I'd better be off home.*

getting on for... (*especially BrE*)
near to or approaching a particular time, number,
age, etc: *I've lived here getting on for five years now.*
◇ *She's getting on for ninety.*

there's no getting a'way from it (*informal*)
we cannot ignore an important and possibly
unpleasant fact: *There's no getting away from it.
He's simply a better player than me.*

what are you, was he, etc. 'getting at?
(*spoken*)
used to ask, especially in an angry way, what sb
is/was suggesting: *I'm partly to blame? What
exactly are you getting at?*

ghost /gəʊst; AmE goʊst/

give up the 'ghost
1 (*old-fashioned*) die

> **NOTE**
> *Ghost* in this idiom means 'soul' or 'spirit'.

2 (*humorous*) (of a machine, etc.) stop working
because it is so old: *My old computer has finally
given up the ghost, so I'm getting a new one.*
3 (of a person) stop making an effort; stop working: *She persuaded me to carry on when I was
tempted to give up the ghost.*

not have a 'ghost of a chance (of doing sth)
(*informal*)
have no chance at all (of doing sth): *He doesn't
have a ghost of a chance of passing the exam this
year.*

> **NOTE**
> The *ghost* of something is a very small amount
> that is difficult to see, hear, feel, etc.

● former → be a shadow/ghost of your/its former self
● white → (as) white as a sheet/ghost

gift /gɪft/

the gift of the 'gab (*BrE*) (*AmE* **a gift of/for 'gab**) (*informal, sometimes disapproving*)
the ability to speak easily and to persuade other people with your words: *To be a successful sales executive you need the gift of the gab.*

> **❷ ORIGIN**
> *Gab* is possibly from the Irish word for *mouth*. The Irish have a reputation as good talkers.

(not) look a ,gift horse in the 'mouth (*informal*)
(not) find sth wrong with sth given to you free: *He didn't want to accept the offer of a free meal but I told him not to look a gift horse in the mouth.*

> **❷ ORIGIN**
> The usual way to judge the age of a horse is to look at its teeth.

● **God** → God's gift (to sb/sth)

gild /gɪld/

gild the 'lily
try to improve sth which is already perfect, and so spoil it: *The dress is perfect. Don't add anything to it at all. It would just be gilding the lily.*

> **❷ ORIGIN**
> This comes from Shakespeare's play *King John*. *Gild* means 'to cover something with a thin layer of gold'. A *lily* is a very beautiful flower.

gills /gɪlz/

to the 'gills (*informal*)
completely full: *I was stuffed to the gills with chocolate cake.*

> **NOTE**
> *Gills* are the openings on the side of a fish's head that it breathes through.

● **green** → green about the gills

gilt /gɪlt/

take the gilt off the 'gingerbread
spoil sth so that you find it less attractive than before: *He's offered us his villa by the sea for two weeks. Unfortunately, we can only have it in January, which rather takes the gilt off the gingerbread.*

> **❷ ORIGIN**
> In the past, gingerbread was decorated with *gilt* or *gold leaf* (= a very thin sheet of gold).

gingerbread /'dʒɪndʒəbred; *AmE* -dʒərb-/

● **gilt** → take the gilt off the gingerbread

gird /gɜːd; *AmE* gɜːrd/

gird (up) your 'loins (*literary* or *humorous*)
prepare yourself for action, hard work, etc: *There's a lot of hard work to be done before the weekend, so let's gird up our loins and start.*

> **❷ ORIGIN**
> In the Bible, to *gird your loins* meant to pick up your robe and tie it about your waist so that you could run or move much more quickly.

girl /gɜːl; *AmE* gɜːrl/

● **big** → a big girl's blouse
● **old** → old boy/girl
● **poster** → poster child/boy/girl

girls /gɜːlz; *AmE* gɜːrlz/

● **lads** → be one of the lads/boys/girls

give /gɪv/

> Most idioms containing the verb **give** are at the entries for the nouns or adjectives in the idioms, for example **give sb a bell** is at **bell**.

,don't give me 'that (*spoken, informal*)
used to tell sb that you do not accept what they say: *'I didn't have time to do it.' 'Oh, don't give me that!'*

give sb a 'break
give sb a chance; not judge sb too harshly: *Give the lad a break — it's only his second day on the job.*

,give and 'take
be willing to listen to other people's wishes and points of view and to change your demands, if this is necessary: *If we want this marriage to be successful, we both have to learn to give and take.* ► **,give and 'take** noun: *We can't all expect to have exactly what we want. There has to be some give and take.*

give as good as you 'get
defend yourself very well when you fight or argue with sb: *Don't worry about her. She can give as good as she gets.*

give it up (for sb) (*informal*)
show your approval of sb by clapping your hands: *Give it up for Tommy!*

'give me sth/sb (,any day/time) (*spoken*)
used for saying you like sth much more than the thing just mentioned: *I hate going to clubs. Give me a nice meal at a restaurant any day.* ◇ *I don't like cricket very much. Give me football any time.*

give me a 'break! (*spoken*)
used when sb wants sb else to stop doing or saying sth that is annoying, or to stop saying sth that is not true: *I didn't mean it like that, so give me a break!*

give or 'take (sth)
if sth is correct **give or take** a particular amount, it is approximately correct: *It took us three hours, give or take a few minutes.* ◇ *It'll cost about $1 000, give or take.*

give sb what 'for ♦ 'give it to sb (*BrE, spoken*)
punish sb severely: *If you take my car again without asking me, I'll give you what for.* ◇ *The manager will really give it to you when he finds out what you've done.*

I/I'll give you 'that (*spoken*)
used when you are admitting that sth is true: '*I
said an hour ago that I thought we were going the
wrong way, didn't I?*' '*Yes, you did, I'll give you that.*'

given /ˈɡɪvn/

be given to sth/to doing sth (*formal*)
do sth often or regularly: *She's much given to out-
bursts of temper.* ◇ *He's given to going for long
walks on his own.*

gives /ɡɪvz/

what 'gives? (*spoken, informal*)
what is happening?; what is the news?: *I haven't
seen you for a few weeks! What gives?*

glad /ɡlæd/

'glad rags (*old-fashioned, informal*)
smart clothes worn for a party, etc: *We put our
glad rags on and went to the theatre.*

gladly /ˈɡlædli/

● **suffer** → not suffer fools gladly

glance /ɡlɑːns; AmE ɡlæns/

at a (single) 'glance
immediately; with only a quick look: *He could tell
at a glance what was wrong.*

● **first** → at first glance/sight
● **steal** → steal a glance/look (at sb/sth)

glass /ɡlɑːs; AmE ɡlæs/

(see the) ,glass half 'full/half 'empty
used to describe whether sb has a positive or
negative attitude towards sth: *People are prepared
to see the glass half full at the moment rather than
half empty.* ◇ *He's a glass-half-full type of guy (= he
always expects good things to happen).*

● **people** → people (who live) in glass houses shouldn't
throw stones
● **raise** → raise your glass (to sb)

glistens /ˈɡlɪsnz/

● **gold** → all that glitters/glistens/glisters is not gold

glisters /ˈɡlɪstəz; AmE ˈɡlɪstərz/

● **gold** → all that glitters/glistens/glisters is not gold

glitters /ˈɡlɪtəz; AmE ˈɡlɪtərz/

● **gold** → all that glitters/glistens/glisters is not gold

gloom /ɡluːm/

● **doom** → gloom and doom SEE doom and gloom
● **pile** → pile on the agony/gloom

glory /ˈɡlɔːri/

● **reflected** → bathe/bask in reflected glory

glove /ɡlʌv/

● **fit** → fit (sb) like a glove
● **hand** → hand in glove (with sb)
● **iron** → an iron fist/hand (in a velvet glove)

gloves /ɡlʌvz/

the gloves are 'off (*informal*)
in an argument, dispute, etc., stop being gentle
with sb and start fighting them with force and
determination: *Up to now both sides in the dispute
have been cautious, but now the gloves are off and a
serious confrontation is expected.*

> **NOTE**
> This idiom refers to boxers taking off their
> gloves.

'Right, that's it! The gloves are off now!'

● **kid** → handle, treat, etc. sb with kid gloves

glowing /ˈɡləʊɪŋ; AmE ˈɡloʊɪŋ/

in glowing 'terms/'colours (*BrE*) (*AmE* **in glowing 'terms/'colors**)
in a very positive way: *He describes Manchester in
glowing terms. I never realized it was such an interesting place.* ◇ *He spoke of her performance in the
movie in glowing terms.*

glued /ɡluːd/

be 'glued to sth (*informal*)
give all your attention to sth; stay very close to
sth: *He spends every evening glued to the TV.* ◇ *Her
eyes were glued to the screen* (= she did not stop
watching it).

● **spot** → glued/rooted to the spot

glutton /ˈɡlʌtn/

a ,glutton for 'punishment, 'work, etc.
(*informal*)
a person who seems to like doing unpleasant or
difficult things: *You're going to drive all the way to
London and back in a day? You're a glutton for pun-*

ishment, aren't you? ◇ *She's a glutton for work. She stays late every evening.*

> **NOTE**
> A *glutton* is a person who is too fond of food. In this idiom, it refers to a person who seems to be very fond of the thing mentioned.

gnash /næʃ/

gnash your 'teeth
feel very angry and upset about sth, especially because you cannot get what you want: *He'll be gnashing his teeth when he hears that we lost the contract.*

> **NOTE**
> The basic meaning of *gnash your teeth* is to bite or grind them together.

go /gəʊ; AmE goʊ/

> Most idioms containing the verb **go** are at the entries for the nouns or adjectives in the idioms, for example *go for broke* is at **broke**.

as things, people, etc. 'go
compared to the average thing of that type: *As government statements go, this one was fairly honest.* ◇ *As titles for abstract paintings go, 'Field with Figures' is better than most.*

at/in one 'go (*BrE*)
in one single action; all at the same time: *I don't think I'll be able to solve all the problems at one go.* ◇ *He ate the whole cake in one go.*

be a 'go (*AmE, informal*)
be planned and possible or allowed: *We've just heard that the project is a go.*

be on the 'go (*informal*)
be busy and active: *I've been on the go all day and I'm exhausted.* ◇ *She's always on the go. I wish she would just sit down and relax sometimes.*

don't go doing sth (*spoken*)
used to tell or warn sb not to do sth: *Don't go getting yourself into trouble.*

first, second, etc. 'go (*BrE*)
at the first, second, etc. attempt: *I passed my driving test first go.*

go all 'out for sth ♦ go all out to 'do sth (*informal*)
make a very great effort to get or do sth: *We knew that only one of the firms would get the order for computers and so we went all out to get the contract.* ◇ *We must go all out to increase our membership.*

go and do sth (*informal*)
used for expressing anger that sb has done sth: *Why did you have to go and tell him? It was a secret.* ◇ *Look what you've gone and done now! That was my favourite vase.*

go down 'well, 'badly, etc. (with sb) (also **go off 'well**)
used to talk about whether people like sth such as a speech, performance, etc: *Her speech went down well with the audience.*

'go for it (*spoken*)
used for encouraging sb to try and achieve sth that is difficult or considered difficult: *Don't listen to him, Jeannie, go for it! How will you ever know unless you try?*

go 'on (with you) (*old-fashioned*)
used to express the fact that you do not believe sth, or that you disapprove of sth: *Go on with you — you're never forty. You don't look a day over thirty.*

have a 'go (at sb) (*informal*)
attack, criticize (sb): *She had a go at me last night about crashing the car.* ◇ *He's always having a go at me about my spelling.*

have a 'go (at sth/at doing sth) (*informal*)
attempt to do, win or achieve sth: *I'm sure I could do better than that. Let me have a go!* ◇ *I've got the time, so I'll have a go at the decorating myself.*

have sth on the 'go (*informal*)
be dealing with, working on, etc. sth: *She's a very busy architect and always has some project on the go.* ◇ *'Have you got anything interesting on the go at the moment?' 'Yes, I'm working on a programme about the origins of sport.'*

no 'go (*informal*)
impossible; unsuccessful: *I asked him if I could have an extra week's leave, but it was no go.* ◇ *'Could you lend me your car this weekend, Mike?' 'No go, I'm afraid. I need it myself.'*

not (even) 'go there (*informal*)
used to say that you do not want to talk about sth in any more detail because you do not even want to think about it: *We could argue about it all week, so let's not even go there.* ◇ *'Didn't you go on a date with him?' 'Don't even go there!'*

...to 'go
1 still remaining before sth happens, finishes or is completed: *There's only a few seconds to go before the rocket takes off.* ◇ *With only two kilometres to go, Max is still first.*
2 (*informal, especially AmE*) (of food bought in a restaurant, shop, etc.) to be taken away and eaten somewhere else: *Two coffees to go, please.*

goalposts /'gəʊlpəʊsts; AmE 'goʊlpoʊsts/

● **move** → move the goalposts

goat /gəʊt; AmE goʊt/

act/play the 'goat (*informal*)
deliberately behave in a silly or foolish way: *Stop acting the goat or I'll send you out. I'm warning you.*

get sb's 'goat (*informal*)
annoy sb very much: *That woman really gets my goat. She does nothing but complain.* ◇ *It really gets my goat when people smoke in non-smoking areas.*

goats /gəʊts; AmE goʊts/

● **sheep** → sort out/separate the sheep from the goats

gob /gɒb; AmE gɑːb/

● **shut** → shut your mouth/trap/face/gob!

God /gɒd; AmE gɑːd/

(good) 'God ◆ God al'mighty ◆ God in 'heaven ◆ my/oh 'God (spoken)
used for expressing anger, surprise, etc: *Good God! What on earth have you done to my car? ◇ Oh my God! I've broken my watch again! ◇ God almighty! You're not going to wear that terrible old suit to the wedding, are you?*
(Some people find these expressions offensive.)

God 'bless
used when you are leaving sb, to say that you hope they will be safe, etc: *Good night, God bless.*

God ˌrest his/her 'soul ◆ God 'rest him/her (old-fashioned, spoken)
used to show respect when you are talking about sb who is dead: *My grandfather, God rest his soul, would never think of leaving the house without a suit and tie on.*

God's gift (to sb/sth) (ironic)
a person who thinks that they are particularly good at sth or who thinks that sb will find them particularly attractive: *He seems to think he's God's gift to women.*

God 'willing (spoken)
used for expressing your hope that sth will happen: *We've had a lovely holiday and we'll be back again next year, God willing.*

play 'God
behave as if you control events or other people's lives: *It is unfair to ask doctors to play God and end someone's life.*

to 'God/'goodness/'Heaven
used after a verb to emphasize a particular hope, wish, etc: *I wish to God you'd learn to pay attention!*
(Some people find the use of **God** here offensive.)

● act → an act of God
● fear → put the fear of God into sb
● forbid → God/Heaven forbid (that...)
● grace → there but for the grace of God (go I)
● help → God/Heaven help sb
● honest → honest to God/goodness
● hours → work all the hours God sends
● knows → God/goodness/Heaven knows
● love → for the love of God
● man → a man of God/the cloth
● name → in God's/Heaven's name
● name → in the name of God/Heaven
● please → please God
● thank → thank God!

godmother /'gɒdmʌðə(r); AmE 'gɑːd-/

● fairy → a/your fairy godmother

gods /gɒdz; AmE gɑːdz/

● lap → in the lap of the gods

goes /gəʊz; AmE goʊz/

what ˌgoes around 'comes around (saying)
the way sb behaves towards other people will affect the way those people behave towards them in the future: *I feel a little sorry for her but I guess she never helped anyone and what goes around comes round.*

going /'gəʊɪŋ; AmE 'goʊɪŋ/

be going on (for) sth (BrE)
be nearly a particular age, time or number: *It was going on for midnight by the time we left.*

be good 'going ◆ be not bad 'going (informal)
be good progress: *'It only took me two hours to get to Birmingham.' 'That's good going.' ◇ 'I've written 20 pages today.' 'That's not bad going.'*

enough/something to be going 'on with (BrE)
something that is enough for a short time: *£50 should be enough to be going on with.*

have a lot, something, nothing, etc. 'going for you
have many, some, no, etc. achievements, skills, advantages, etc: *As the very intelligent daughter of rich parents, she's got a lot going for her. ◇ No job, no qualifications, nowhere to live. He doesn't have much going for him, does he?*

while the ˌgoing is 'good (BrE) (AmE **while the ˌgetting is 'good**)
before a situation changes and it is no longer possible to do sth: *He thinks the company is going to go bankrupt soon, so he's getting out while the going is good. ◇ Don't you think we should quit while the going is good?*

goings /'gəʊɪŋz; AmE 'goʊɪŋz/

● comings → comings and goings

gold /gəʊld; AmE goʊld/

ˌall that ˌglitters/ˌglistens/ˌglisters is not 'gold (saying)
not everything that seems good, attractive, etc. is actually good, etc: *Don't imagine that because they are rich, they are happy. All that glitters is not gold.*

> **NOTE**
> The verbs in this idiom mean 'shine brightly'.

a 'gold mine
a business or an activity that makes a large profit: *That Internet cafe of his is a real gold mine.*

(as) good as 'gold
(of children) very well-behaved: *The children were good as gold. They sat quietly and read all afternoon.*

like 'gold dust
very difficult to obtain because everyone wants it/ them: *You can't get those new trainers anywhere. They're like gold dust.*

● heart → have a heart of gold
● streets → the streets are paved with gold
● strike → strike gold
● worth → be worth your/its weight in gold

golden /ˈɡəʊldən; AmE ˈɡoʊldən/

the ˈgolden age (of sth)
the period during which sth is very successful, especially in the past: *This book looks back on the golden age of steam engines, and all railway fans will enjoy it immensely.*

a ˈgolden boy
a young man who is very successful and popular: *He had been the golden boy of Welsh rugby.*

(kill) the golden ˈgoose (also **(kill) the goose that lays the golden ˈegg/ˈeggs**)
(destroy) sth that makes you rich, successful, etc: *The government is worried that a new tax might kill the golden goose by scaring away foreign investment.* ◇ *The banks made vast profits from an energy trader that had become the golden goose of Wall Street.*

❷ ORIGIN
This comes from an ancient Greek story about a farmer who had a goose that laid golden eggs. The farmer thought that if he killed the goose he could get all the eggs inside. However, by killing the goose, he lost everything.

a golden ˈhandshake
a large sum of money given to sb when they leave their job, or to persuade them to leave their job: *The directors will each get a large golden handshake and a pension.*

the golden ˈrule
the most important rule, principle, etc. to remember when you are doing sth: *When you're playing a stroke in golf, the golden rule is to keep your eye on the ball.*
- mean → the happy/golden mean
- silence → silence is golden

gone /ɡɒn; AmE ɡɔːn; ɡɑːn/
- dead → dead and buried/gone
- done → he, she, etc. has gone/been and done sth
- far → far gone
- today → here today, gone tomorrow

good /ɡʊd/

Most idioms containing **good** are at the entries for the nouns or verbs in the idioms, for example **a good Samaritan** is at **Samaritan**.

ˌall to the ˈgood
used to say that if sth happens, it will be good, even if it is not exactly what you were expecting: *'I'm afraid we've arrived a bit early.' 'Don't worry. It's all to the good. It means we can start the meeting earlier.'*

as ˈgood as…
so close to sth happening that you consider that it has happened: *I thought the car was as good as sold and then the man suddenly decided not to buy it.* ◇ *She as good as told me she didn't want to come.*

as ˌgood as it ˈgets
used when you are saying that a situation is not going to get any better: *The past year has been very special — as good as it gets as far as I'm concerned.*

be ˈgood for sth
1 be likely to be able to give or provide sth: *I'll ask my aunt if she can help us. She'll be good for a small loan, I'm sure.*
2 be likely to live, last, etc. for a period of time: *This car's probably good for another 20 000 miles.*

be no ˈgood ♦ not be any/much ˈgood
1 not be useful; have no useful effect: *This gadget isn't much good.* ◇ *It's no good trying to talk me out of leaving.*
2 not be interesting or enjoyable: *His latest movie isn't much good.*

do ˈgood
be kind and generous to people who need help, for example by working for a charity: *She tries to do good by visiting prisoners' families when she can.*
▶ ˌdo-ˈgooder *noun* (*informal, disapproving*) a person who tries to help others but does it in a way that is annoying

do sb a good ˈturn
be helpful to sb; do sb a favour: *I did you a good turn, now you do me one.*

do sb ˈgood
help sb; have a good effect on sb: *A trip to the beach would do you a lot of good.*

for ˈgood (*BrE* also **for ˌgood and ˈall**)
permanently; for ever: *I'm going away for good.* ◇ *Today I gave up smoking for good.*

for your (ˌown) ˈgood
(of sth unpleasant) so that you will benefit: *I don't like criticizing you but it's for your own good.* ◇ *I know he doesn't want to do all this extra homework, but it's for his own good.*

good and… (*informal*)
completely: *I won't go until I'm good and ready.*

ˌgood for ˈyou, ˈhim, etc. (especially *AustralE* **good ˈon you, him, etc.**) (*informal*)
used to praise sb for doing sth well: *'I've decided to give up smoking as from tomorrow.' 'Good for you, Philip.'* ◇ *'He's saving up his pocket money to buy a football.' 'Good for him.'*

to the ˈgood
in profit: *She bought the painting for €250 and then sold it for €550, so she's €300 to the good, lucky woman.*

up to no ˈgood (*informal*)
doing or planning sth wrong or dishonest: *He doesn't work but he seems to have lots of money. I'm sure he's up to no good.* ◇ *Where have those children gone? They're probably up to no good.*

goodbye /ˌɡʊdˈbaɪ/

kiss/say goodˈbye to sth ♦ kiss sth goodˈbye (*informal*)
give up hope of getting sth that you want very much: *You'll have to say goodbye to your chances of becoming a doctor if you don't pass the exams.*

◇ *After this letter from the bank, we can kiss good-bye to our trip to Australia.*

goodness /'gʊdnəs/

out of the ˌgoodness of your 'heart
from feelings of kindness, without thinking about what advantage there will be for you: *You're not telling me he offered to lend you the money out of the goodness of his heart?*

● God → to God/goodness/Heaven
● honest → honest to God/goodness
● knows → God/goodness/Heaven knows
● thank → thank goodness/heaven(s)! SEE thank God!

goods /gʊdz/

come up with/deliver/produce the 'goods
(*informal*)
do what you are expected or have promised to do: *You can depend on him to come up with the goods. If he says he'll do something, he always does it.*

goody-goody /'gʊdi gʊdi/

a ˈgoody-goody ◆ a goody ˈtwo-shoes
(*informal, disapproving*)
a person who behaves very well to please people in authority such as parents or teachers: *Don't be such a goody-goody! ◇ He's a real goody two-shoes. He'd never do anything that might get him into trouble.*

goose /guːs/

● cook → cook sb's goose
● golden → (kill) the golden goose
● golden → (kill) the goose that lays the golden egg/eggs SEE (kill) the golden goose
● sauce → what's sauce for the goose is sauce for the gander
● say → he, she, etc. wouldn't say boo to a goose
● wild → a wild goose chase

gooseberry /'gʊzbəri; AmE 'guːsberi/

play 'gooseberry (*BrE*)
be a third person with two people who have a romantic relationship and want to be alone together: *Dave and Michelle invited me to go out with them but I don't want to play gooseberry all evening.*

Gordian /ˌgɔːdiən; AmE ˌgɔːrdiən/

cut/untie the ˌGordian ˈknot
solve a very difficult or complicated problem with forceful action: *Will the negotiators be able to untie the Gordian knot?*

> ❷ ORIGIN
> This expression comes from the legend in which King Gordius tied a very complicated knot and said that whoever untied it would become the ruler of Asia. Alexander the Great cut through the knot with his sword.

gospel /'gɒspl; AmE 'gɑːspl/

take sth as/for 'gospel/ˌgospel 'truth
(*informal*)
believe sth without questioning it or without any real proof: *You can't always take what she says as gospel — she's not the most honest person in the world. ◇ It would be foolish to take everything in the newspapers for gospel.* OPP take sth with a pinch of salt

> NOTE
> *Gospel* is the life and teaching of Jesus as described in the Bible.

grab /græb/

how does...grab you? (*spoken*)
used to ask sb whether they are interested in sth or in doing sth: *How does the idea of a trip to Rome grab you?*

● headlines → grab/hit/make the headlines
● hold → catch/get/grab/take (a) hold of sb/sth

grabs /græbz/

be up for 'grabs (*informal*)
available for anyone who is interested: *The contract for repairing the damaged buildings will soon be up for grabs. ◇ There are thousands of prizes up for grabs in our competition!*

grace /greɪs/

fall from 'grace
lose people's approval, for example through a mistake or immoral behaviour: *The government minister fell from grace as a result of the financial scandal.*

have the (good) grace to do sth
be polite enough to do sth: *Fortunately, she had the grace to apologize as soon as she realized she had offended them. ◇ He didn't even have the grace to say thank you.*

there but for the grace of 'God (go 'I) (*saying*)
used to say that you could easily have been in the same difficult or unpleasant situation that sb else is in: *Whenever I think of poor Fran and her problems, I think there but for the grace of God go I.*

> NOTE
> *Grace* in this expression refers to the kindness that God shows towards the human race.

with (a) good/bad 'grace
in a willing and pleasant/unwilling and rude way: *It is very important in sport to accept defeat with good grace. ◇ I've never seen anybody do anything with such bad grace.*

● saving → a saving grace

graces /'greɪsɪz/

be in sb's good 'graces (*formal*)
have sb's approval and be liked by them: *Having bought them all dinner, he is now firmly in their good graces.*

● airs → airs and graces

grade /greɪd/

make the 'grade (*informal*)
reach a high enough standard in an exam, a job, etc: *You'll never make the grade if you don't work hard before the exams.* ◇ *Do you think she'll ever make the grade as a journalist?*

grain /greɪn/

be/go against the 'grain
be or do sth different from what is normal or natural: *Voting for the Liberal Party goes against the grain with him. He's voted Conservative all his life.* ◇ *It goes against the grain for her to spend a lot of money on clothes.*

> NOTE
> The *grain* is the natural direction of lines in a piece of wood.

grand /grænd/

a/the ,grand old 'age
a great age: *She finally learned to drive at the grand old age of 65.*

a/the ,grand old 'man (of sth)
an old man who is very experienced and respected in a particular profession, etc: *At eighty, he is the grand old man of the British film industry.*

grandeur /'grændʒə(r); -djə(r)/

● delusions → delusions of grandeur

grandmother /'grænmʌðə(r)/

● teach → teach your grandmother to suck eggs

granted /'grɑːntɪd; AmE 'græn-/

take sb/sth for 'granted
not value sb/sth just because they are/it is always there: *Your problem is that you take your wife for granted. When was the last time you told her how much you appreciated her?* ◇ *We take so many things for granted these days: electricity, running water, cars…*

take sth for 'granted (that…)
believe that sth is/will be true, will happen, etc. without checking to make sure: *We took it for granted that there would be some rooms available at the hotel but we were wrong.* ◇ *He took it for granted that he would get the job, and so he was very surprised when he didn't.*

grapes /greɪps/

● sour → sour grapes

grapevine /'greɪpvaɪn/

on/through the 'grapevine
by talking in an informal way to other people: *I heard on the grapevine that you're leaving.*

grasp /grɑːsp; AmE græsp/

grasp the 'nettle (*BrE*)
deal with a difficult matter, firmly and with courage: *The government will have to grasp the nettle. If they don't, the traffic congestion is going to get out of control.*

> ❷ ORIGIN
> This expression refers to the belief that if you touch a nettle (= a plant with leaves that sting) lightly, you will be hurt, but not if you take a firm hold if it.

● straws → clutch/grasp at straws

grass /grɑːs; AmE græs/

the ,grass is (always) 'greener on the other 'side (of the 'fence) (*saying*)
things always seem better in another place, job, etc: *She says she would be able to do business better in France, but the grass is always greener on the other side!*

the ,grass 'roots
the ordinary people in an organization, for example a political party or trade union, and not the officials: *The leaders of this union are losing contact with their members. They need to get back in touch with the grass roots.* ▶ ,grass-'roots *adj.*: *a grass-roots movement*

not let the ,grass grow under your 'feet
be very active and do the things that need to be done very quickly: *The new owner didn't let the grass grow under her feet, and immediately started to change the whole layout of the shop.*

put/turn/send sb out to 'grass (*informal, humorous*)
force sb to stop doing their job, especially because they are old: *Old Harry doesn't seem able to remember anything nowadays. Isn't it time he was put out to grass?*

> NOTE
> This expression refers to old farm horses or other animals, which no longer work and stay in the fields all day.

● kick → kick sth into the long grass
● snake → a snake in the grass

grasshopper /'grɑːshɒpə(r); AmE 'græshɑːp-/

● knee-high → knee-high to a grasshopper

grata /'grɑːtə/

● persona → persona non grata

grateful /'greɪtfl/

● small → be grateful/thankful for small mercies

grave /ɡreɪv/

turn in his, her, etc. 'grave (*BrE*) (*AmE* **roll in his, her, etc. 'grave**)
(of a person who is dead) likely to be very shocked or angry: *Beethoven would turn in his grave if he could hear the way they're playing his music.*

- **cradle** → from the cradle to the grave
- **dig** → dig your own grave
- **foot** → have one foot in the grave
- **silent** → (as) silent as the grave

gravy /'ɡreɪvi/

the 'gravy train (*informal, especially AmE*)
(of a particular job or situation) an easy way of getting a lot of money and other benefits: *Financial services produce very high earnings, and a lot of people are trying to get onto the gravy train.*

gray /ɡreɪ/ (*especially AmE*) = grey

grease /ɡriːs/

grease sb's 'palm (*old-fashioned, informal*)
give sb money in order to persuade them to do sth dishonest: *Luckily, Mick was able to grease a few palms, thus helping his brother to escape.*

> **NOTE**
> This phrase refers to the fact that you put *grease* (= a thick substance like oil) on a machine to make it run smoothly.

- **elbow** → elbow grease
- **oil** → grease the wheels **SEE** oil the wheels
- **squeaky** → the squeaky wheel gets the grease/oil

greased /ɡriːst/

like greased 'lightning (*informal*)
very fast: *After the phone call, he was out of the door like greased lightning.*

great /ɡreɪt/

be a 'great one for sth/for doing sth
do sth a lot; enjoy sth: *I've never been a great one for writing letters.* ◇ *You're a great one for quizzes, aren't you?*

be no great 'shakes (*informal*)
be not very good, efficient, suitable, etc: *He's no great shakes as a teacher.* ◇ *'What did you think of the movie?' 'It was no great shakes.'*

go great 'guns (*informal*)
(usually in the progressive tenses) do sth quickly and successfully: *She's halfway through the race, and is going great guns.* ◇ *He's going great guns on his new book at the moment.*

- **believer** → be a great/firm believer in sth
- **dirty** → dirty great/big
- **many** → a good/great many
- **oaks** → great/tall oaks from little acorns grow

greater /'ɡreɪtə(r)/

- **sum** → be greater/more than the sum of its parts

Greek /ɡriːk/

it's all 'Greek to me (*informal, saying*)
it is too difficult for me to understand: *This contract is written in such complicated language that it's all Greek to me.*

green /ɡriːn/

give sb/get the ˌgreen 'light (*informal*)
allow sb/be allowed to begin sth: *The council has given the green light for work to begin on the new shopping centre.* ◇ *As soon as we get the green light, we'll start advertising for new staff.*

> **NOTE**
> This expression refers to the green light on traffic lights, which means 'go'.

ˌgreen about the 'gills (*informal*)
looking or feeling as if you are going to be sick, especially at sea; seasick: *You look a bit green about the gills. Go up on deck and get some fresh air.*

> **NOTE**
> *Gills* are the openings on the side of a fish's head that it breathes through.

ˌgreen 'fingers (*BrE*) (*AmE* **a ˌgreen 'thumb**)
if you have **green fingers**, you are good at making plants grow: *I do envy you your green fingers. Your garden always looks so beautiful.*

ˌgreen with 'envy
very jealous (= wanting sth that sb else has): *He was green with envy when he saw their expensive new car.*

greener /'ɡriːnə(r)/

- **grass** → the grass is (always) greener on the other side (of the fence)

green-eyed /ˌɡriːn 'aɪd/

the ˌgreen-eyed 'monster (*humorous*)
a feeling of anger or unhappiness because sb you like or love is showing interest in sb else; jealousy: *In next week's programme we'll be looking at the green-eyed monster, jealousy.*

> **❷ ORIGIN**
> This comes from Shakespeare's play *Othello*.

greetings /'ɡriːtɪŋz/

- **season** → (the) season's greetings

grey (*especially BrE*) (*AmE usually* **gray**) /ɡreɪ/

a ˌgrey 'area
an area of a subject or situation that is not clear or does not fit into a particular group or area and is therefore difficult to define or deal with: *The question of police evidence in cases like this is a grey area. We will need to consult our lawyers about it.*

'grey matter (*informal*)
intelligence or mental powers: *Mark hasn't got much grey matter, but he tries hard.*

(men in) grey 'suits
people working in politics, law, etc. who have
power but are not known to the public: *It will be
the men in grey suits who decide whether the Prime
Minister stays or goes.*

grief /griːf/

come to 'grief (*informal*)
be destroyed or ruined; have an accident and hurt
yourself: *His plans came to grief due to poor organization and insufficient financing.* ◇ *A lot of ships
have come to grief along this coast.*

give sb 'grief (about/over sth) (*informal*)
be annoyed with sb and criticize their behaviour:
Stop giving me grief and let me finish this!

good 'grief! (*informal*)
used for expressing surprise or disbelief: *Good
grief! You're not going out dressed like that, are
you?*

grim /grɪm/

hang on/hold on (to sb/sth) like grim 'death
hold sb/sth very tightly, usually because you are
afraid or determined not to let go: *As the horse galloped off, you could see poor Sarah hanging on like
grim death.* ◇ *The robbers tried to steal my bag, but
I held on to it like grim death.*

> **NOTE**
> The word *grim* (= very serious or unpleasant)
> is often used to describe death.

grin /grɪn/

grin and 'bear it (*informal*)
(only used as an infinitive and in orders) accept
sth unpleasant without complaining: *If the trip is
a disaster, you'll just have to grin and bear it.*

Working with Ann wasn't always easy, but Tony
knew he'd just have to grin and bear it.

grin like a Cheshire 'cat
smile widely in a foolish way or as if you are very
pleased with yourself: *She sat there grinning like a
Cheshire cat while we tried to put the tent up.*

> **❶ ORIGIN**
> The Cheshire Cat is a character in Lewis Car-
> roll's story, *Alice in Wonderland*.

● ear → beam/grin/smile from ear to ear

grind /graɪnd/

**grind to a 'halt/'standstill ◆ come to a grind-
ing 'halt**
stop slowly: *All work on the building has ground to
a halt because of a shortage of materials.* ◇ *Every
Friday night traffic comes to a grinding halt in
Hammersmith.*

> **NOTE**
> This idiom refers to the way a very large
> machine slowly stops working, with some of its
> parts *grinding* (= rubbing) together.

● axe → have an axe to grind

grindstone /'graɪndstəʊn; *AmE* -stoʊn/

● nose → keep your nose to the grindstone

grip /grɪp/

get/take a 'grip/'hold on yourself (*informal*)
make an effort to control your feelings, especially
in a difficult situation: *I know you're nervous, but
you must get a grip on yourself. You're due to go on
stage in five minutes.* ◇ *Look, Ben, get a grip, will
you? If we panic now, we'll be finished.*

in the 'grip of sth
experiencing sth unpleasant that cannot be
stopped: *The whole country is in the grip of a serious recession.*

lose your 'grip (on sth) (*informal*)
be unable to control or do sth as well as you did
before: *She's definitely made some bad decisions
recently. I think she's losing her grip.*

grips /grɪps/

come/get to 'grips with sb/sth
begin to understand or to deal properly with a
person, problem, subject, etc: *The government has
yet to get to grips with the problem of crime.* ◇ *I'm
trying to come to grips with Polish grammar.*

grist /grɪst/

grist for/to sb's 'mill
(of an experience, a piece of information, etc.)
useful to sb: *As a novelist, I feel that any experience,
good or bad, is grist to my mill.*

> **NOTE**
> *Grist* is corn that is is ready to be crushed in a
> *mill* in order to make flour.

grit /grɪt/

grit your 'teeth
be determined to continue to do sth in a difficult
or an unpleasant situation: *When I was a boy, I was
forced to have a cold shower every morning. I hated
it but I just had to grit my teeth and do it.* ◇ *She*

shouted at me but I just gritted my teeth and said nothing.

❷ ORIGIN
The basic meaning of *grit your teeth* is to bite your teeth tightly together.

groan /grəʊn; *AmE* groʊn/

groan under the weight of sth (*written*)
used to say that there is a lot or too much of sth: *The dining table was groaning under the weight of all the food.*

NOTE
The phrase suggests that something such as a table is making a low noise because there is too much weight on it.

groove /gruːv/

be (stuck) in a 'groove (*BrE*)
be unable to change sth that you have been doing the same way for a long time and that has become boring: *While other businesses are attracting new customers, this one seems to be stuck in a groove, and has been losing money for the last two years.*

ground /graʊnd/

be, come, get, etc. in on the ground 'floor (*informal*)
become involved at the beginning of a plan, a company, an organization, etc. and possibly profit from this later: *Reg came in on the ground floor and saw the value of his investment double in two years.*

break fresh/new 'ground
make a discovery; use new methods, etc: *We're breaking fresh ground with our new freezing methods.* ▶ **'ground-breaking** *adj.*: *a ground-breaking discovery/report*

cut the ground from under sb/sb's 'feet
suddenly spoil sb's idea or plan by doing sth to stop them from continuing with it: *When he announced that all my figures were out of date, he really cut the ground from under my feet.*

drive/run/work yourself into the 'ground
work so hard that you become extremely tired: *You need to be careful, or you'll run yourself into the ground before long.* ◊ *With only two or three hours' sleep a night, he was driving himself into the ground.*

get (sth) off the 'ground
(of a plan, project, etc.) start happening successfully; make sth start happening successfully: *By this time next year the new company should be just getting off the ground.* ◊ *We're looking for a new manager to help get this project off the ground.*

give/lose 'ground (to sb/sth)
allow sb/sth to obtain more power, influence, etc. than yourself: *The government has lost ground to the opposition, according to the opinion polls.*

hold/stand your 'ground
face a situation and refuse to run away: *In spite of the enemy's fierce attack, we stood our ground and*

eventually they had to retreat. ◊ *After arguing about future policy for three hours, he was still standing his ground.*

on the 'ground
among ordinary people or people closely involved in sth: *On the ground, there are hopes that the fighting will soon stop.* ◊ *There's a lot of support for the policy on the ground.*

run sb/sth into the 'ground
use sth so much that it breaks; make sb work so hard that they are no longer able to work: *In just one year, she managed to run her new car into the ground.* ◊ *These children are running me into the ground.*

thick/thin on the 'ground (*BrE*)
if people or things are **thick/thin on the ground,** there are a lot/not many of them in a place: *Customers are thin on the ground at this time of year.* ◊ *Good science teachers are thin on the ground.*

- **dangerous** → dangerous ground
- **ear** → keep/have an/your ear (close) to the ground
- **earth** → go to earth/ground
- **earth** → run sb/sth to earth/ground
- **feet** → have/keep both/your feet on the ground
- **firm** → be on firm ground
- **gain** → gain ground
- **happy** → a happy hunting ground
- **hit** → hit the ground running
- **moral** → take, claim, seize, etc. the moral high ground
- **neutral** → on neutral ground/territory
- **prepare** → prepare the ground (for sth)
- **riveted** → be riveted to the spot/ground
- **shift** → shift your ground
- **stony** → fall on stony ground
- **suit** → suit sb (right) down to the ground

grow /grəʊ; *AmE* groʊ/

grow like 'Topsy
grow very fast, particularly in an unplanned or uncontrolled way: *After many contributions, our website has grown like Topsy, and is now being completely revised.*

❷ ORIGIN
Topsy was a female character in Harriet Beecher Stowe's novel *Uncle Tom's Cabin*.

- **absence** → absence makes the heart grow fonder
- **grass** → not let the grass grow under your feet
- **money** → money doesn't grow on trees
- **oaks** → great/tall oaks from little acorns grow

growing /'grəʊɪŋ; *AmE* 'groʊɪŋ/

'growing pains
the problems, difficulties, etc. which happen in the early stages of sth: *The troubles that are affecting the company are more than just growing pains.*

❷ ORIGIN
Growing pains are pains that some children feel in their arms and legs when they are growing.

guard /ɡɑːd; AmE ɡɑːrd/

be on/off your 'guard
be prepared/not be prepared for sth, for example
an attack, a danger, a surprise, etc. to happen: *We
must all be on our guard against bomb attacks.*
◇ *He hit me while I was off my guard.*

> **NOTE**
> Your *guard* is a position you take when you
> want to defend yourself, especially in a sport
> such as boxing or fencing.

mount/stand/keep 'guard (over sb/sth)
act as a guard: *Two soldiers stood guard over the
captured weapons.*

● catch → catch sb off (their) guard
● old → the old guard

guernsey /'ɡɜːnzi; AmE 'ɡɜːrnzi/

get a 'guernsey (*AustralE, informal*)
be recognized as being good; be chosen for sth:
*I am afraid that our achievement failed to get a
guernsey in the local press.*

> **❷ ORIGIN**
> A *guernsey* is a kind of shirt worn by a player of
> Australian Rules Football. If you are given or
> get *a guernsey*, you are chosen to play for the
> team.

guess /ɡes/

'anybody's/'anyone's guess (*informal*)
nobody knows: *Who will win the next game is anybody's guess.*

at a 'guess
as a rough estimate: *At a guess, I would say there
were about thirty people in the room.*

‚guess 'what (*informal*)
used to introduce sth surprising or exciting that
you want to tell sb: *Guess what, Angela's getting
married next month!*

your ‚guess is as good as 'mine (*informal*)
neither of us knows the answer: *'If the government
knows how to run the country, why aren't things
getting any better?' 'Your guess is as good as mine!'*

● educated → an educated guess

guessing /'ɡesɪŋ/

keep sb 'guessing (*informal*)
not tell sb about your plans or what is going to
happen next: *It's the kind of book that keeps you
guessing right to the end.* **OPP** give the game away

● prizes → (there are) no prizes for guessing what...,
who..., etc.

guest /ɡest/

be my 'guest (*informal*)
used to give sb permission to do sth that they have
asked to do: *'May I look at this book?' 'Be my guest.'*

guilt /ɡɪlt/

a 'guilt trip (*informal*)
things you say to sb in order to make them feel
guilty about sth: *Don't lay a guilt trip on your child
about schoolwork.*

guinea /'ɡɪni/

a 'guinea pig
a person used in medical or other experiments:
*Students in fifty schools are to act as guinea pigs
for these new teaching methods.*

> **NOTE**
> A *guinea pig* is a small animal with short ears
> and no tail, often kept as a pet or used for
> laboratory research.

gulf /ɡʌlf/

● bridge → bridge the gulf (between A and B) **SEE** bridge
the gap (between A and B)

gullet /'ɡʌlɪt/

● stick → stick in your throat/craw/gullet

gum /ɡʌm/

gum up the 'works (*informal*)
make progress or an activity impossible: *The building was going well, but the delay in delivering more
bricks has really gummed up the works.*

> **NOTE**
> The *works* are the moving parts of an engine.

up a 'gum tree (*BrE, informal*)
in a very difficult or awkward situation: *I've got
bills to pay and the bank is refusing to lend me any
more money. I'm really up a gum tree.*

gun /ɡʌn/

have a 'gun to your head (*informal*)
be forced to do sth that you do not want to do:
*'Why did he go back to his wife?' 'Because he had a
gun to his head. She said she would never let him see
the children again.'*

hold/put a 'gun to sb's head
force sb to do sth that they do not want to do by
making threats: *He had to sack a hundred workers
last week. He didn't want to, but the bank was holding a gun to his head.*

under the 'gun (*AmE, informal*)
experiencing a lot of pressure: *The deadline is in
two days — we're really under the gun.* ◇ *I'm under
the gun to come up with new clients or else.*

● jump → jump the gun
● smoking → a/the smoking gun
● son → a/the son of a gun

guns /ɡʌnz/

● great → go great guns
● spike → spike sb's guns
● stick → stick to your guns

gut /gʌt/

● bust → bust a gut

guts /gʌts/

have the 'guts (to do sth) (*informal*)
have the courage (to do sth): *She didn't have the guts to tell him she was going to move out.* ◇ *He'll never agree to sail across the Atlantic with you. He hasn't got the guts.* ▶ **'gutsy** *adj.*: *a gutsy fighter*

have sb's ,guts for 'garters (*BrE, informal*)
be very angry with sb and punish them severely for sth they have done: *She'd have my guts for garters if she knew I'd lent you her car.*

slog/sweat/work your 'guts out (*informal*)
work very hard: *I've slogged my guts out digging this ditch, and I'm completely exhausted.* ◇ *You sweat your guts out all your life and what do you get when you retire? Next to nothing.* **OPP** not do a stroke (of work)

● blood → blood and guts
● hate → hate sb's guts
● misery → (a) misery guts
● spill → spill your guts (to sb)

gutter /'gʌtə(r)/

the ,gutter 'press (*disapproving*)
popular newspapers which print a lot of shocking stories about people's private lives rather than serious news: *Somebody must control the gutter press in this country.*

> **NOTE**
> The *gutter* is sometimes used to refer to bad social conditions or low moral standards.

Guy /gaɪ/

● Mr → Mr Nice Guy

guy /gaɪ/

● tough → a tough guy
● wise → a wise guy

gyp /dʒɪp/

give sb 'gyp (*BrE, informal*)
cause sb a lot of pain: *My back's been giving me gyp again lately.*

H h

habit /'hæbɪt/

make a 'habit/'practice of sth
do sth regularly: *I don't usually make a practice of staying up so late, but there was a programme on TV I wanted to watch.*

● creature → a creature of habit
● force → force of habit

hackles /'hæklz/

your, his, etc. 'hackles rise
become angry: *Ben felt his hackles rise as the speaker continued.*

make sb's 'hackles rise ♦ raise 'hackles
make sb angry: *He really makes my hackles rise, that man. He's so rude to everybody.* ◇ *Her remarks certainly raised hackles.*

> **NOTE**
> *Hackles* are the hairs on the back of a dog's neck that rise when it is angry or excited.

hair /heə(r); AmE her/

a bad 'hair day (*spoken, humorous*)
a day when everything seems to go wrong: *Today is definitely a bad hair day — you know, one of those days when nothing gets done no matter how hard you try.* ◇ *What's wrong — are you having a bad hair day?*

> **NOTE**
> This expression refers to the fact that if you think your hair looks bad, you feel that you look unattractive and nothing in the day will go right for you.

get in sb's 'hair
annoy sb by preventing them from doing sth: *I can do the housework much more quickly when the children aren't getting in my hair all the time.*

the hair of the 'dog (that 'bit you) (*informal*)
an alcoholic drink taken in the morning in order to help cure the unpleasant effects of drinking too much alcohol the night before: *'Why are you drinking whisky at 8 o'clock in the morning?' 'Hair of the dog. I've got the most terrible hangover.'*

> **❷ ORIGIN**
> In the past, if a person was bitten by a dog, burnt hair from the same dog was used as a protection against infection.

a 'hair's breadth
a very small distance or amount: *He escaped death by a hair's breadth. If the other car had been going any faster, he would certainly have been killed.* ◇ *She was within a hair's breadth of winning.*

> **NOTE**
> *Breadth* means *width*.

your 'hair stands on end (*informal*)
you feel very frightened, nervous or angry: *When I first read the report my hair stood on end.* ◇ *This is a movie which will make your hair stand on end.*

> **NOTE**
> A *hair-raising* adventure, story, etc. is very frightening but often exciting.

keep your 'hair on (also **keep your 'shirt on** *less frequent*) (*BrE, informal*)
used for telling sb who is angry or very excited about sth to keep calm: *Keep your hair on, Mum. You can hardly see the damage.* ◇ *Keep your shirt on! We've got plenty of time to get to the airport.*

let your 'hair down (*informal*)
relax completely and enjoy yourself, especially after a period when you have not been able to do so: *Why don't you let your hair down a bit? Come out with us for the evening.*

> **❷ ORIGIN**
> In the past, women wore their hair tied up when they were in public and only untied their hair in private or in informal situations.

The office party was a good opportunity for everyone to let their hair down.

make sb's 'hair curl (*informal, humorous*)
shock or disturb sb: *The video contains some sex scenes that are enough to make your hair curl.*

not a 'hair out of place
looking very smart, well-dressed, etc: *How does she manage to look so good at the end of a long journey? There's never a hair out of place.*

not harm/touch a hair of sb's 'head
not hurt sb physically in any way at all: *If he harms a hair of my daughter's head, I'll kill him.*

not turn a 'hair
not show strong emotion like fear, surprise or excitement, when others expect you to: *He didn't turn a hair when the judge gave him a 20-year prison sentence.*

- hang → hang by a thread/hair
- hide → not see hide nor hair of sb/sth
- tear → tear your hair (out)

hairs /heəz; *AmE* herz/

put 'hairs on your chest (*informal, humorous*)
(especially of alcoholic drinks) make you feel strong, etc: *This Polish vodka will put hairs on your chest.*

- short → get/have sb by the short hairs
- split → split hairs

hairy /'heəri; *AmE* 'heri/

give sb the hairy 'eyeball (*AmE, informal*)
look at sb in a suspicious or disapproving way: *When I say I'm into hunting, people either laugh or give me the hairy eyeball.*

> **NOTE**
> This refers to looking at somebody with your eyes slightly closed so that your eye is partly covered by your eyelashes.

hale /heɪl/

hale and 'hearty
(especially of old people) strong and healthy: *She was still hale and hearty in her nineties.*

half /hɑːf; *AmE* hæf/

and a 'half (*informal*)
bigger, better, more important, etc. than usual: *That was a meal and a half. I haven't eaten so well for months.*

your better/other 'half (*informal, humorous*)
your wife or husband: *I'll have to ask my better half about that.*

give sb half a 'chance (to do sth) (*informal*)
give sb even a small opportunity (to do sth): *Given half a chance, I'd go and work in the USA, but it's so difficult to get a visa.* ◇ *If you give him half a chance, he'll show how well he can do the job.*

half the 'battle
(complete, achieve, etc.) the most difficult part of sth: *If you manage to keep calm when you're taking your driving test, that's half the battle.*

half the 'fun, 'trouble, etc. of sth (*informal*)
much or a great deal of the enjoyment, etc. of sth: *Half the pleasure of coming home is finding out what's been happening while you were away.* ◇ *'The team should play better with a new manager.' 'That's half the trouble — everybody expects too much of him.'*

half a ˌloaf is better than 'none/no 'bread (*saying*)
you should be grateful for sth, even if it is not as good, much, etc. as you really wanted; something is better than nothing: *They're only going to agree to some of this, but half a loaf is better than none, I suppose.*

half a 'minute, 'tick, 'second, etc. (*informal*)
(wait) a very short time: *I'll be with you in half a moment! I've just got to put my coat on.* ◇ *Just give me half a tick, will you? I've left the keys upstairs.*

the 'half of it
only some of the facts of a particular situation, not all of them: *The public knows that he's had an affair with his secretary, but that's only the half of it.* ◇ *'I hear you've been having trouble with the new managers.' 'You don't know the half of it, Ray. It's been an absolute nightmare.'*

'half the time (*informal*)
most of the time: *Do tell me whether you are coming home for lunch or not. I don't know where you are half the time.*

how the other half 'lives
the life of people in circumstances very different from your own, especially those much richer or poorer: *You should go and see the homeless in our big cities, then you'd know how the other half lives.* ◇ *Look at these photos of houses in Hollywood! How the other half lives, eh?*

in 'half the time
in a much shorter time than expected: *I don't think much of his work. I could have done the same job in half the time, and much better too.*

no half 'measures (*BrE*)
used for emphasizing that you want sth done as well, fully, etc. as possible: *He entertained the visitors very well indeed. There were no half measures: the best food, the best wine, the best silver...*

,not 'half (*BrE, informal*)
used to emphasize a statement or an opinion: *It wasn't half good* (= it was very good). ◇ *'Is it hot outside?' 'Not half. It's much too hot for me.'*

not 'half as good, nice, etc. as sb/sth
not nearly as good, nice, etc. as sb/sth: *She's not half as nice as her sister.* ◇ *His new book isn't half as interesting as his last one.*

not half 'bad (*informal*)
(used to show surprise) not bad at all; good: *The food really isn't half bad, is it?*

too clever, quick, etc. by 'half (*BrE, informal, disapproving*)
much too clever, quick, etc: *That boy is too charming by half — he can get you to do anything he wants.* ◇ *I don't like her at all — she's too clever by half.*

- **eye** → have one eye/half an eye on sth
- **glass** → (see the) glass half full/half empty
- **halves** → go half and half (with sb) SEE go halves (with sb)
- **listen** → listen with half an ear
- **six** → it's six of one and half a dozen of the other

half-cock /ˌhɑːf ˈkɒk; *AmE* ˌhæf ˈkɑːk/

go off at ˌhalf-ˈcock (*informal*)
start without enough preparation, so that the effect or result is not satisfactory: *Let's not go off at half-cock. We must get enough people together before we start the meeting.*

? ORIGIN
This refers to an old type of gun. It it was at *half-cock*, the firing lever (= cock) was not pulled all the way back so that the gun was not completely ready to fire.

half-hour /ˌhɑːf ˈaʊə(r); *AmE* ˌhæf-/

- **hour** → on the hour/half-hour

halfway /ˌhɑːfˈweɪ; *AmE* ˌhæf-/

a ˌhalfway 'house
1 a place where prisoners, mental patients, etc. can stay for a short time after leaving a prison or hospital, before they start to live on their own again: *We're opening several halfway houses for people who've been in this hospital.*
2 something that combines the features of two plans, wishes, etc: *We really wanted to build a completely new hospital, but we didn't have the money, so this extension is a kind of halfway house.*

? ORIGIN
A *halfway house* was originally a place such as an inn (= a pub where you can stay the night) that was halfway between two places, or in the middle of a journey.

- **meet** → meet sb halfway

hallmarks /ˈhɔːlmɑːks; *AmE* -mɑːrks/

have all the 'hallmarks of sb/sth
have all the characteristics or typical features of sb/sth: *The burglary had all the hallmarks of a professional job.*

NOTE
Hallmarks are marks put on gold and silver objects that show the quality of the metal and give information about when and where they were made.

halt /hɔːlt; *BrE* also hɒlt/

- **call** → call a halt (to sth)
- **grind** → come to a grinding halt SEE grind to a halt/ standstill
- **tracks** → stop/halt/freeze in your tracks
- **tracks** → stop/halt sb in their tracks

halved /hɑːvd; *AmE* hævd/

- **trouble** → a trouble shared is a trouble halved

halves /hɑːvz; *AmE* hævz/

do nothing/not do anything by 'halves
do whatever you do completely and thoroughly: *She does nothing by halves. When she decided to write a book, it was 1 000 pages long.*

go 'halves (with sb) ◆ **go ˌhalf and 'half (with sb)** (*informal*)
share the total cost of sth equally with sb else: *If you drive me up to Edinburgh, we'll go halves on the petrol.*

hand

ham /hæm/

ham it 'up (*informal*)
(especially of actors) when people **ham it up**, they deliberately exaggerate their emotions or movements: *When we realized we were being filmed, we all started behaving differently, hamming it up for the cameras.*

NOTE
A *ham* is an informal word for an actor who performs badly, especially by exaggerating emotions.

hammer /'hæmə(r)/

be/go at sb/sth ,hammer and 'tongs (*informal*)
do sth, especially argue or fight, with a lot of energy and noise: *The boss went at me hammer and tongs. I've never seen him so angry.* ◇ *The couple in the flat upstairs are always at it hammer and tongs.*

❷ ORIGIN
This idiom refers to the loud noise made by a blacksmith at work when he is making horseshoes. He uses a pair of *tongs* to hold the hot iron and a *hammer* to beat the iron into the shape of the shoe.

come/go under the 'hammer
be offered for sale at an auction (= a sale at which things are sold to the person who offers the most money): *The house and all its contents are to come under the hammer next Thursday.*

NOTE
The person in charge of an auction hits the table with a *hammer* to show that he/she has accepted the highest offer.

● home → drive/hammer sth home (to sb)

hammering /'hæmərɪŋ/

give sb/get a 'hammering (*BrE, informal*)
beat sb/be beaten severely or easily; punish sb/be punished hard: *Real Madrid gave the other team a hammering.* ◇ *When I was young, I once stole some money from my mother. I got a real hammering when she found out.*

hand /hænd/

ask for/win sb's hand (*old-fashioned*)
ask for/get permission to marry sb: *'Did John ask your father for your hand?' 'No. Nobody does that any more, do they?'*

(close/near) at 'hand
near in distance or time: *Some people think that the end of the world is at hand.* ◇ *It's a very convenient place to live. We've got everything close at hand — shops, schools, and a library.*

bind/tie sb hand and 'foot
remove or restrict sb's freedom of action or movement: *Staying at home to look after a sick parent often means that a person is tied hand and foot.* ◇ *I can do nothing to help you because I'm bound hand and foot by my present contract.*

by 'hand
1 (of a letter, etc.) if a letter is delivered **by hand**, it is delivered by the person who wrote it, or by messenger rather than by post: *There's a postal strike on at the moment, so we'll have to deliver these invitations by hand.*
2 made/done without using machinery: *Several local farmers still milk their cows by hand.* ◇ *These wine glasses were made by hand.*

get out of 'hand
become difficult or impossible to control: *How can we stop price increases getting out of hand?* ◇ *The student teacher saw that the class was getting completely out of hand, so he asked for help.* **OPP** be under control

give sb a 'hand (with sth)
help sb to do sth: *I can't lift this piano on my own. Can you give me a hand, Carlos?* ◇ *Let me give you a hand with these suitcases.*

go hand in 'hand (with sth)
be closely connected (with sth): *Poverty tends to go hand in hand with disease, and raising people's incomes usually helps to improve their health.* ◇ *A bad economic situation and rising crime usually go hand in hand.*

,hand in 'glove (with sb)
very closely associated with sb, usually in sth dishonest: *The terrorists are working hand in glove with the drug traffickers.* ◇ *They are hand in glove with the secret police.*

,hand in 'hand
(of people) holding each other's hand, usually as a sign of affection: *The lovers walked along the river bank, hand in hand.*

hand sth to sb on a 'plate ◆ hand sb sth on a 'plate (*informal*)
give sth to sb without the person concerned having to make any effort to get it: *She was handed the job on a plate. Somebody just telephoned her one afternoon and asked her if she'd like to work for the BBC.* ◇ *A contract's not just going to be handed to you on a plate, you know. You have to earn it.*

have/take a hand in sth/in doing sth
be involved in sth, especially sth bad, wrong, etc: *We think all three of you had a hand in planning the robbery. So, come on, confess.* ◇ *I'm sure he had a hand in creating this problem.*

have to 'hand it to sb (*informal*)
admit, perhaps unwillingly, that you admire sb for their skill, achievements, determination, etc: *You have to hand it to him; he certainly knows how to play tennis.* ◇ *To be honest, I didn't think she could cook, but I have to hand it to her. Tonight's meal was fantastic.*

hold sb's 'hand
give sb help, comfort, support, etc. in a difficult situation: *Industry cannot expect the government to hold its hand every time it has problems.* ◇ *This is Jane's first day in the office, so I've asked Mary to hold her hand a bit.*

in 'hand

1 (of a task, matter, etc.) now being dealt with, thought about, discussed, etc: *Let's stop talking about other subjects and get back to the matter in hand.*

2 still to be used, played, spent, etc.; remaining: *The two teams have an equal number of points, but Liverpool still have a game in hand.* ◇ *The club still has money in hand for the improvements.*

keep your 'hand in

practise a skill occasionally, so that you do not lose it: *The director likes to teach a class occasionally, just to keep her hand in.*

lift/raise a 'hand against sb

to hit or threaten to hit sb: *She never raised a hand against her daughter because she didn't believe in hitting children.*

not do a hand's 'turn (old-fashioned)

do no work: *She hasn't done a hand's turn all week.*

on either/every 'hand (literary)

on both/all sides; in every direction: *We were surrounded on every hand by dancing couples.*

on 'hand

near and available; present: *We have a doctor on hand in case of emergency.*

on (the) 'one hand...on the 'other (hand)...

used to show two different aspects of the same situation: *On the one hand, it's very cheap living here. On the other, it costs a lot to get home!*

out of 'hand

immediately and without thinking about sth fully or listening to other people's arguments: *They rejected my suggestion out of hand.*

put your ˌhand in/into your 'pocket (BrE)

spend or give money: *One of our colleagues is retiring, so I expect they'll want us to put our hands into our pockets for a present.* ◇ *He's one of the meanest men I know. He never puts his hand in his pocket for anything.*

(at) second, third, etc. 'hand

by being told about sth by sb else who has seen it or heard about it, not by experiencing, seeing, etc. it yourself: *I'm fed up of hearing about these decisions third hand!*

show/reveal your 'hand (BrE) (AmE **tip your 'hand**)

do sth which reveals your intentions, plans, etc: *The problem is that we can't say anything to the management without showing our hand, and we wanted to be able to take them by surprise.* ◇ *In court a good lawyer never reveals his hand too soon.*

OPP keep/hold/play your cards close to your chest

> NOTE
> These expressions refer to showing your cards (= your hand) in card playing.

ˌtake sb/sth in 'hand

begin to control or look after sb/sth, especially in order to make improvements in their behaviour, their performance, etc: *That child is very badly behaved; someone should take her in hand.* ◇ *The new manager hopes to take the organization in hand, because in recent months it has been in chaos.*

talk to/tell it to the 'hand (because/'cos the face ain't 'listening) (AmE, informal)

used to say in a rude way that you refuse to listen to what sb is trying to tell you

> NOTE
> This is said while holding your hand up in front of the other person's face.

throw your 'hand in (informal)

stop doing sth or taking part in sth, especially because you are not successful: *If I fail again this time, I shall throw my hand in.*

> NOTE
> When you have no chance of winning in a game of cards, you throw your *hand* (= cards) into the middle of the table.

(ready) to 'hand

(have sth) with or near you; easy to reach or get: *I don't seem to have my diary to hand at the moment — can I ring you back and make an appointment?* ◇ *Surgeons need their instruments ready to hand during an operation.*

turn your 'hand to sth

start doing sth or be able to do sth, especially when you do it well: *Jim can turn his hand to most jobs around the house.*

with your ˌhand on your 'heart ✦ ˌhand on 'heart

speaking very honestly and telling the truth: *I can tell you, hand on my heart, that I never took any money out of your purse.* ◇ *How can you stand there with your hand on your heart and tell me that?*

with one hand tied behind your 'back (informal)

1 unable to use your full powers: *The government has one hand tied behind its back in these negotiations.*

2 very easily; with little effort: *She could run the restaurant with one hand tied behind her back.*

- **big** → give sb a big hand
- **bird** → a bird in the hand is worth two in the bush
- **bite** → bite the hand that feeds you
- **cap** → go cap in hand (to sb)
- **cap** → go hat in hand **SEE** go cap in hand (to sb)
- **cash** → cash in hand
- **count** → be able to count sb/sth on (the fingers of) one hand
- **dab** → be a dab hand at sth/at doing sth
- **dead** → the dead hand of sth
- **eating** → have sb eating out of your hand
- **fair** → make, etc. sth by/with your own fair hand
- **firm** → a firm hand
- **first** → (at) first hand
- **force** → force sb's hand
- **free** → get, have, etc. a free hand
- **heavy** → heavy hand
- **helping** → a helping hand
- **iron** → an iron fist/hand (in a velvet glove)
- **know** → know sth like the back of your hand
- **left** → the left hand doesn't know what the right hand's doing

- **lend** → lend (sb) a hand (with sth)
- **live¹** → live (from) hand to mouth
- **money** → make/lose money hand over fist
- **old** → an old hand (at sth/at doing sth)
- **overplay** → overplay your hand
- **palm** → have sb in the palm of your hand
- **rule** → rule (sb/sth) with a rod of iron/with an iron hand
- **shake** → shake sb by the hand
- **sleight** → sleight of hand
- **stay** → stay your/sb's hand
- **strengthen** → strengthen your hand
- **till** → have your fingers/hand in the till
- **try** → try your hand (at sth/doing sth)
- **upper** → get, have, gain, etc. the upper hand (over sb)
- **wait** → wait on sb hand and foot
- **whip** → get, have, hold, etc. the whip hand (over sb)

handbasket /ˈhændbɑːskɪt; AmE -bæs-/

- **dogs** → go to hell in a handbasket **SEE** go to the dogs

handle /ˈhændl/

get/have a handle on sb/sth (*informal*)
become/be familiar with and so understand sb/sth: *I can't really get a handle on the situation here. What's happening?*

- **fly** → fly off the handle
- **hot** → too hot to handle **SEE** too hot for sb

hands /hændz/

all ˌhands on ˈdeck (also **all ˌhands to the ˈpump**) (*saying, humorous*)
everyone helps or must help, especially in an emergency: *There are 10 staff off sick this week, so it's all hands on deck.* ◇ *When the kitchen staff became ill, it was all hands to the pump and even the manager did some cooking.*

> **NOTE**
> On a ship, a *hand* is a sailor.

at the hands of sb ◆ at sb's ˈhands (*written*)
if you experience sth **at the hands of sb**, they are the cause of it: *So far hundreds of innocent civilians have died at the hands of the terrorists.*

be good with your ˈhands
be skilful at making or doing things with your hands: *I'm not surprised he's become an artist — he always was good with his hands.*

fall into sb's ˈhands/the ˈhands of sb
be taken, captured or obtained by sb: *The city has fallen into enemy hands.* ◇ *These documents must not fall into the hands of the wrong people.*

get your ˈhands dirty
do physical work: *He's not frightened of getting his hands dirty.*

get/lay your ˈhands on sb
(used mostly in threats) catch sb who has done sth wrong: *Just wait until I get my hands on the person who stole my bike!*

get/lay your ˈhands on sth
obtain sth that you want or need very much: *Do you know where I can get my hands on a Russian dictionary? I need to check a translation.* ◇ *I'd buy a new car if only I could lay my hands on the money.*

(get/keep/take your) ˌhands ˈoff (sb/sth) (*spoken*)
used to tell sb not to touch sb/sth: *Those cakes are for tea, so hands off!* ◇ *Keep your hands off my tools, please.*

ˌhands ˈup! (*spoken*)
1 used to tell a group of people to raise one hand in the air if they know the answer to a question, etc: *Hands up all those who want to go swimming.*
2 used by sb who is threatening people with a gun to tell them to raise both hands in the air

have your ˈhands full
be very busy: *I've got my hands full looking after four children.* ◇ *You look as if you've got your hands full today. Would you like me to help you?* **OPP** have time on your hands

in the hands of sb ◆ in sb's ˈhands
in the control of sb or sb's responsibility: *I'll leave the matter in your hands.* ◇ *The future of the industry now lies in the hands of the government.*

in safe/good ˈhands
being taken care of by a responsible person or organization, and unlikely to be harmed or damaged: *When the child is with my mother, I know she's in good hands.* ◇ *It's a good hospital. I'm sure he's in safe hands.*

many hands make light ˈwork (*saying*)
a task is done easily if a lot of people share the work

off sb's ˈhands
no longer the responsibility of sb: *Now that the children are off my hands, I've got more time for other things.*

on sb's ˈhands
1 (of work, etc.) to do: *I've got a lot of work on my hands at the moment.*
2 that sb is responsible for: *I've got the neighbour's children on my hands this afternoon.*

on your ˌhands and ˈknees
with your knees, toes and hands on the ground: *The tunnel was so low in places that we had to crawl along on our hands and knees.* ◇ *She was down on her hands and knees looking for her earring.*

ˌout of sb's ˈhands
no longer in the control of or the responsibility of sb: *I'm afraid the matter is now out of my hands. You'll have to write to the Area Manager.*

ˌplay (right) into sb's ˈhands
do exactly what an enemy, opponent, etc. wants so that they gain the advantage in a particular situation: *The thieves played right into the hands of the law by trying to sell stolen property to a police informer.*

take sth/sb off sb's ˈhands
take sth away from sb who no longer wants it or take a responsibility from sb who needs a rest: *I wish somebody would take this old table off my hands. I haven't got room for it.* ◇ *Look, you and Tony relax at the weekend, and I'll take the children off your hands for a couple of days.*

throw up your hands/arms in de'spair, 'horror, etc. (*often humorous*)
show that you disagree strongly with sth, or are very worried about sth: *When she said she wanted to get a motorbike, her parents threw up their hands in horror.*

win (sth)/beat sb ,hands 'down
win (sth)/beat sb very easily: *Holland won the match hands down. The score was five nil.*

- bare → with your bare hands
- blood → have (sb's) blood on your hands
- change → change hands
- clean → have clean hands
- clean → your hands are clean SEE have clean hands
- courage → take your courage in both hands
- devil → the devil makes work for idle hands
- join → join hands (with sb)
- law → take the law into your own hands
- life → take your life in your hands
- matters → take matters into your own hands
- pair → a pair of hands
- pair → I've only got one pair of hands
- putty → (like) putty in sb's hands
- shake → shake hands (with sb)
- show → a show of hands
- tie → tie sb's hands
- time → have time on your hands
- wash → wash your hands of sb/sth
- wring → wring your hands

handshake /'hændʃeɪk/

- golden → a golden handshake

handwriting /'hændraɪtɪŋ/

- writing → the handwriting (is) on the wall SEE the writing (is) on the wall

handy /'hændi/

,come in 'handy/'useful (*informal*)
be useful when needed: *The money my aunt gave me will come in handy to pay for my music lessons.*

hang /hæŋ/

get the 'hang of sth (*informal*)
learn or begin to understand how to do, use, etc. sth: *I haven't got the hang of how to use the coffee-making machine yet.* ◇ *It took him a long time to get the hang of all the irregular verbs.*

'hang sth (*BrE, spoken*)
used to say that you are not going to worry about sth: *Oh, let's get a taxi and hang the expense!*

hang by a 'thread/'hair
be in a very uncertain situation: *After the operation, his life hung by a thread for several hours.* ◇ *The future of this company hangs by a thread. Unless we get two or three big orders by the end of the month, we're finished.*

hang 'fire
delay or be delayed: *We'll have to hang fire on that decision, I'm afraid.*

❷ ORIGIN
This phrase refers to a gun which does not fire immediately.

hang your 'head (in/for 'shame)
look or feel embarrassed or ashamed: *When I think of how I behaved, I have to hang my head in shame.* ◇ *The thief hung his head as he was led away by the police.* **OPP** hold your head up (high)

hang (on) 'in there (*informal*)
used for encouraging sb to continue trying to achieve sth: *'I'll never find a job.' 'Look, just hang on in there. I'm sure you'll get something soon.'*

hang a 'left/'right (*AmE*)
take a left/right turn

hang on sb's 'words/every 'word
listen to what sb says with great attention: *The professor was talking to a group of students, who hung on her every word.*

hang out/up your 'shingle (*AmE, informal*)
start to do business from your home, especially as a doctor or a lawyer: *After graduating, he decided to hang out a shingle as a consultant.*

hang sb out to 'dry (*AmE, informal*)
leave sb in a difficult situation without your support, especially to avoid receiving any blame yourself: *It was his own party who hung him out to dry for losing the election.*

hang over sb's 'head ♦ hang 'over sb
(of a possible problem, etc.) worry sb: *With the threat of job losses hanging over their heads, the staff are all very worried.* ◇ *She can't enjoy herself with all these financial problems hanging over her.*

hang 'tough (*AmE*)
be determined and refuse to change your attitude or ideas: *Employees are being urged to hang tough and continue negotiations with management.*

hang up your 'boots
stop playing football, etc. because you are too old or ill/sick to continue: *At the age of 38, he decided it was time to hang up his boots.*

let it all hang 'out (*informal*)
express your feelings freely: *Sometimes you just have to let it all hang out and say what you really think.*

- grim → hang on/hold on (to sb/sth) like grim death
- heavy → hang/lie heavy (on sb/sth)
- loose → hang/stay loose
- peg → a peg on which to hang sth
- peg → a peg to hang sth on

hanged /hæŋd/

- well → (you, etc.) may/might as well be hanged/hung for a sheep as (for) a lamb

hangs /hæŋz/

- cloud → a cloud hangs over sb/sth
- question → a question mark hangs over sb/sth
- time → time hangs/lies heavy (on your hands)

ha'porth /'heɪpəθ; AmE -pərθ/

- **spoil** → spoil the ship for a ha'porth/ha'penny-worth of tar

happen /'hæpən/

anything can/might 'happen
used to say that it is not possible to know what the result of sth will be: *'There's no way we're going to win this match!' 'How can you be so sure — anything can happen!'*

- **accidents** → accidents will happen
- **things** → these things happen
- **waiting** → an accident/a disaster waiting to happen

happens /'hæpənz/

as it 'happens
used when you say sth that is surprising, or sth connected with what sb else has just said: *I agree with you, as it happens.* ◇ *As it happened, I had a spare set of keys in my bag.*

it (just) so 'happens that...
by chance: *It just so happened they'd been invited to the party too.*

- **event** → in the event that sth happens
- **shit** → shit happens

happy /'hæpi/

(as) happy as the day is 'long/as a 'clam/as 'Larry (*informal*)
very happy: *Grandpa's as happy as a clam helping the children to fly their kites.*

(not) a ˌhappy 'bunny (*BrE*) (*AmE* (not) a ˌhappy 'camper) (*informal*)
(not) pleased about a situation: *Ailsa has caught a cold and is not a happy bunny.* ◇ *We must make sure that our existing clients are happy campers.*

a/the ˌhappy e'vent (*humorous*)
the birth of a baby: *'When's the happy event, then?' 'At the end of July.'*

a happy 'hunting ground (*humorous*)
a very good place to find what you want: *The Sunday antique market is a happy hunting ground for collectors.*

a/the happy 'medium
a sensible balance between two extremes: *I like to know my colleagues well, but not too well. The sort of friendship I have with them now is a happy medium.* ◇ *In life generally we should try to find the happy medium. Extreme solutions to problems always lead to difficulties.*

many happy re'turns (of the 'day)
used to wish sb a happy and pleasant birthday: *Here's your present. Many happy returns!*

- **big** → one big happy family
- **mean** → the happy/golden mean

hard /hɑːd; AmE hɑːrd/

be hard 'at it
be working hard: *She's been hard at it all day.* ◇ *When I left at six, he was still hard at it.* **OPP** take it/things easy

be/feel hard 'done by (*informal*)
be/feel unfairly treated: *I think you've been hard done by — you worked twice as long as anyone else.*

be 'hard on sb
1 treat, criticize or punish sb too severely: *Don't be too hard on little Emma. She didn't intend to break the cup.*
2 be unfair to sb; be unfortunate for sb: *It's hard on the people who have to work on New Year's Day.*

be hard 'up (*informal*)
have very little money: *In those days we were so hard up that meat was a real luxury.* **OPP** be well off

be hard 'up for sth
have too few or too little of sth: *We're hard up for ideas at the moment.*

do/learn sth the 'hard way
learn sth from experience, especially when this is unpleasant: *I learned the hard way not to trust door-to-door salesmen.* ◇ *Why do you always do everything the hard way?*

fall on hard 'times
become poor: *She has fallen on hard times and hardly has enough money to live on.*

ˌhard and 'fast
(of rules, etc.) that cannot be changed: *These regulations are not hard and fast. They can be changed by general consent.* ◇ *There are no hard-and-fast rules about this.*

> **NOTE**
> *Fast* in this idiom means 'fixed'.

(as) hard as 'nails
(of a person) not sensitive or sympathetic: *She doesn't care what happens to anybody. She's as hard as nails.*

hard 'cash
real money, not shares, cheques, etc: *How much is it worth in hard cash?*

hard 'cheese (*BrE, informal*)
used as a way of saying that you are sorry about sth, usually in an ironic way (= you really mean the opposite): *I've made my decision — I'm going to the sell the car, and if he doesn't agree with that then it's hard cheese.*

(the) ˌhard 'core (*BrE*)
the small central group in an organization, or in a particular group of people, who are the most active or who will not change their beliefs or behaviour: *It's only really the hard core that bother(s) to go to meetings regularly.* ▶ **'hard-core** *adj.* **1** having a belief or a way of behaving that will not change: *a hard-core political activist* **2** relating to pornography (= books, videos, etc. that describe or show naked people and sexual acts) of an extreme kind: *hard-core sex magazines*

hard 'facts
the real or true facts of a situation, etc: *I'm not interested in your opinion. I want hard facts.* ◇ *This is a newspaper which deals in hard facts, not rumours.*

,hard 'going
difficult to understand or needing a lot of effort: *I'm finding his latest novel very hard going.*

,hard 'luck/'lines (*BrE*)
used to tell sb that you feel sorry for them: *'Failed again, I'm afraid.' 'Oh, hard luck.'*

hard of 'hearing
unable to hear well: *He's become rather hard of hearing.* ◇ *The television programme has subtitles for the hard of hearing.*

hard 'put (to it) to do sth ♦ hard 'pressed/'pushed to do sth
able to do sth only with great difficulty: *I'd be hard put to name all the countries in the world.*

the 'hard stuff (*informal*)
strong alcoholic drinks like whisky, brandy, etc: *a drop of the hard stuff*

make hard 'work of sth
make sth more difficult or complicated than it should be: *I don't know why he's making such hard work of his maths homework. It's really quite easy.*

no hard 'feelings
used for saying that you would still like to be friendly with sb you have just beaten in a fight, a competition, an argument, etc: *When he heard that he had won the contract, he turned to his competitor and said, 'No hard feelings, I hope.'*

play hard to 'get (*informal*)
pretend not to be interested in sb/sth in order to increase sb's interest in or desire for you: *She's playing hard to get, but I'm sure she really wants to go out with me.* ◇ *My advice is, play hard to get for a while and they might offer you more money.*

take sth 'hard
be very upset by sth: *He took his wife's death very hard.*

too much like hard 'work
so difficult, tiring, etc. that you do not want to do it: *This job is a bit too much like hard work for me. I'm going to look for something easier.*

- **act** → a hard/tough act to follow
- **die** → old habits, traditions, etc. die hard
- **drive** → drive a hard bargain
- **heels** → hard/hot on sb's heels
- **hit** → hit sb/sth hard
- **nut** → a hard/tough nut (to crack)
- **rock** → (caught/stuck) between a rock and a hard place

hardball /'hɑːdbɔːl; *AmE* 'hɑːrd-/

play 'hardball (*especially AmE*)
used to refer to a way of behaving, especially in politics, that shows that a person is determined to get what they want: *It's time to play hardball with the unions.* ◇ *He's playing hardball with a client of mine.*

harden /'hɑːdn; *AmE* 'hɑːrdn/

,harden your 'heart against sb/sth
no longer be emotionally affected by sb/sth because you feel angry, bitter, etc., towards them/it: *Doctors have to harden their hearts against the suffering they see every day.*

hard-luck /ˌhɑːd 'lʌk; *AmE* ˌhɑːrd/

a hard-'luck story
a story about yourself that you tell sb in order to get their sympathy or help: *He stopped me in the street and told me a long hard-luck story about his wife leaving him. All he really wanted was some money.* ◇ *Don't give me any of your hard-luck stories, John. I don't believe them.*

hardly /'hɑːdli; *AmE* 'hɑːrd-/

- **wait** → I, he, etc. can hardly wait **SEE** I, he, etc. can't wait

hare /heə(r); *AmE* her/

run with the ,hare and hunt with the 'hounds
try to remain friendly with both sides in a quarrel: *I know you want to keep everyone happy, but I'm afraid you can't run with the hare and hunt with the hounds on this issue.*

- **mad** → (as) mad as a March hare

harm /hɑːm; *AmE* hɑːrm/

,no 'harm done (*spoken*)
used to tell sb not to worry because they have caused no serious damage or injury: *Forget it, Dave, no harm done.*

not come to (any) 'harm ♦ come to no 'harm
not be injured, badly treated or damaged, etc: *The child will come to no harm if she stays there.*

out of harm's 'way
in a place where sb/sth cannot cause or suffer injury, accident, loss, etc: *Most people think that dangerous criminals should be locked up out of harm's way.* ◇ *You should put these glasses out of harm's way. They're too valuable to use every day.*

there's no harm in (sb's) doing sth ♦ it does no harm (for sb) to do sth
used to tell sb that sth is a good idea and will not cause any problems: *He may say no, but there's no harm in asking.* ◇ *It does no harm to ask.*

- **fly** → he, she, etc. wouldn't harm/hurt a fly
- **hair** → not harm/touch a hair of sb's head
- **mean** → mean (sb) no harm
- **mean** → not mean (sb) any harm

harness /'hɑːnɪs; *AmE* 'hɑːrnɪs/

in 'harness (*BrE*)
doing your normal work, especially after a rest or a holiday/vacation: *After so many weeks away, it felt good to be back in harness again.*

> **NOTE**
> A *harness* is a set of strips of leather and metal pieces that is used for controlling a horse.

in 'harness (with sb) (*BrE*)
working closely with sb in order to achieve sth: *The manager told us to remember that we're a team, and that we can achieve much greater results if we're working in harness.*

● **die** → die in harness

Harry /'hæri/

● **Tom** → every/any Tom, Dick and/or Harry

harvest /'hɑːvɪst; *AmE* 'hɑːrv-/

● **reap** → reap a/the harvest

hash /hæʃ/

● **mess** → make a mess/hash of sth/of doing sth

haste /heɪst/

more 'haste, less 'speed (*BrE, saying*)
if you try to do sth quickly, you are more likely to make mistakes and so take a longer time than necessary: *I had to send the email twice because I forgot to add the attachment. More haste, less speed!*

● **marry** → marry in haste (, repent at leisure)

hat /hæt/

keep sth under your 'hat (*informal*)
keep sth secret: *I'm going to apply for another job, but keep it under your hat for a while, will you?*
OPP let the cat out of the bag

pick, etc. sth out of a hat (*informal*)
choose sb/sth completely by chance: *We couldn't decide where to go on holiday so we just picked a place out of a hat.*

take your 'hat off to sb ♦ hats 'off to sb (both *especially BrE*) (*AmE* usually **tip your 'hat to sb**) (*informal*)
used for expressing admiration for what sb has done: *I take my hat off to the doctors and nurses of the hospital. They were magnificent.* ◇ *Hats off to you. That's the best fish soup I've ever tasted.*

throw your 'hat into the ring
announce officially that you are going to compete in an election, a competition, etc: *Another candidate has now thrown his hat into the ring for the elections later this year.*

● **cap** → go hat in hand **SEE** go cap in hand (to sb)
● **drop** → at the drop of a hat
● **eat** → I'll eat my hat!
● **knock** → knock sb/sth into a cocked hat
● **old** → old hat
● **pass** → pass round/around the hat **SEE** pass the hat round/around
● **pull** → pull sth/a rabbit out of the hat
● **talk** → talk through your hat

hatch /hætʃ/

down the 'hatch (*informal*)
said before you drink alcohol: *He raised his glass, said 'Down the hatch', and then drank it all at once!*

❼ ORIGIN
This is thought to come from ships, where goods go down through the *hatch* (= an opening in the floor) to be stored for the journey, as if they are being swallowed.

hatches /'hætʃɪz/

● **batten** → batten down the hatches

hatchet /'hætʃɪt/

a 'hatchet job (on sb/sth) (*informal*)
strong criticism that is unfair or intended to harm sb/sth: *The press did a very effective hatchet job on her last movie.*

❼ ORIGIN
In the past in the US, a *hatchet man* was a person who was paid to kill somebody, often using a *hatchet* (= a small axe). A *hatchet job* was originally therefore a murder.

● **bury** → bury the hatchet

hate /heɪt/

hate sb's 'guts (*informal*)
dislike sb very much: *Don't invite that man to the party. I hate his guts.*

● **pet** → your, his, etc. pet hate

hath /hæθ/

● **hell** → hell hath no fury (like a woman scorned)

hats /hæts/

● **hat** → hats off to sb **SEE** take your hat off to sb

hatter /'hætə(r)/

● **mad** → (as) mad as a hatter

haul /hɔːl/

haul 'ass (*AmE*, ⚠, *slang*)
travel or move quickly: *I had just forty-eight hours to haul ass across the country.*

haul sb over the 'coals (*BrE*) (*AmE* **rake sb over the 'coals**) (*informal*)
criticize sb very strongly for sth they have done: *I was hauled over the coals for being late.*

❼ ORIGIN
This was once a form of torture (= an act of causing somebody severe pain as a punishment or to make them say something) in which a person was pulled over hot or burning pieces of coal.

● **long** → be in sth for the long haul
● **long** → a long haul
● **long** → over the long haul

have /hæv; həv; əv/

Most idioms containing the verb **have** are at the entries for the nouns or adjectives in the idioms, for example **have a cow** is at **cow**.

and what 'have you (*spoken*)
other things, people, etc. of the same kind: *He does all sorts of things — building, gardening, fencing and what have you.* ◇ *If you add up the cost of petrol, insurance, repairs and what have you, running a car certainly isn't cheap.*

have 'had it (*informal*)
1 be in a very bad condition; be unable to be repaired: *This television's had it; we'll have to get a new one.* ◇ *The car had had it.*
2 be extremely tired: *I've had it! I'm going to bed.*
3 have lost all chance of surviving sth: *When the truck smashed into me, I thought I'd had it.*
4 be going to experience sth unpleasant: *Dad saw you scratch the car — you've had it now!*
5 (also **have had it up to here (with sb/sth)**) be unable to accept a situation any longer: *I've had it with him — he's let me down once too often.* ◇ *I've had it up to here with these tax forms.*

'have it (that...)
say that...; claim that...: *Rumour has it that you're going to retire. Is that true?* ◇ *She will have it that her brother is a better athlete than you, but I don't believe her.*

have it 'in you (to do sth)
have the unexpected ability, determination, courage, etc. to do sth: *She managed to finish the crossword all on her own! I didn't know she had it in her!*

have it 'in for sb (*informal*)
want to harm or cause trouble for sb because you have had a bad experience with them: *She's had it in for those boys ever since they damaged her roses.* ◇ *The government has had it in for the trade unions for years.*

have it 'off/a'way with sb (*BrE, slang*)
have sex with sb

have it 'out with sb
have a serious discussion with sb in order to end a disagreement, quarrel, etc: *You must stop ignoring Fred because of what he said, and have it out with him once and for all.*

(not) have a lot, anything, etc. 'on
be busy/not busy: *I'm sorry I can't come with you, but I've got a lot on at the moment.* ◇ *I haven't got much on next week, so I might be able to spend some time with the kids.*

have-nots /ˌhæv ˈnɒts; *AmE* ˈnɑːts/

● **haves** → the haves and the have-nots

haves /hævz/

the ,haves and the 'have-nots
the rich people and the poor people: *You can see the haves and the have-nots in this city — the millionaires in their huge houses and the homeless sleeping on the streets.*

having /ˈhævɪŋ/

he, she, etc. isn't 'having any (of it) (*informal*)
he, she, etc. is not willing to listen to or believe sth: *I suggested sharing the cost, but he wasn't having any of it.* ◇ *I tried to persuade her to wait but she wasn't having any.*

havoc /ˈhævək/

play/wreak 'havoc with sth
cause damage, destruction or disorder to sth: *The terrible storms wreaked havoc with electricity supplies, because so many power lines were down.*

haw /hɔː/

● **um** → hum/hem and haw **SEE** um and aah (about sth)

hawk /hɔːk/

● **eyes** → have eyes like a hawk
● **watch** → watch sb/sth like a hawk

hay /heɪ/

make hay while the 'sun shines (*saying*)
make the best use of opportunities and favourable conditions while they last: *Opportunities for starting your own business will never be better, so make hay while the sun shines and go and see your bank manager today.*

● **hit** → hit the sack/hay

haystack /ˈheɪstæk/

● **needle** → like looking for/trying to find a needle in a haystack

haywire /ˈheɪwaɪə(r)/

go 'haywire (*informal*)
go out of control; start functioning or behaving in a very strange way: *My printer's gone haywire. It keeps stopping and starting.*

head /hed/

above/over sb's 'head
too difficult for sb to understand: *It was clear from the expression on his face that the lecture went completely over his head.*

be banging, etc. your head against a brick 'wall (*informal*)
try for a long time to achieve sth, persuade sb to do sth, etc. without success: *I realized they weren't even listening to my protests. I was just banging my head against a brick wall.*

bite/snap sb's 'head off (*informal*)
speak to sb angrily without good reason: *He was only making a suggestion — there's no need to snap his head off!*

The teacher must be having a bad day. I only asked her a question and she bit my head off!

head

bring sth/come to a 'head
if you **bring** a situation **to a head** or it **comes to a head** you are forced to deal with it quickly because it suddenly becomes very bad: *Matters came to a head yesterday when an emergency meeting was called to demand the directors' resignation.* ◇ *Her recent public remarks about company policy have finally brought matters to a head.*

build up/work up, etc. a head of 'steam
develop the energy, enthusiasm or support required to do sth: *The movement for change has been building up a head of steam and the politicians are starting to listen.*

bury/hide your ,head in the 'sand
refuse to deal with unpleasant realities, possible dangers, etc. by pretending they do not exist: *Stop burying your head in the sand, Tim. Don't pretend that everything's all right.*

> **❷ ORIGIN**
> This phrase refers to the common belief that the ostrich buries its head in the sand when it is in danger.

can't make head or/nor 'tail of sth (*informal*)
not be able to understand sth at all: *I can't make head or tail of this picture — is it upside down?*

do sb's 'head in (*BrE, informal*)
make sb feel confused, upset and/or annoyed: *Shut up! You're doing my head in.*

from ,head to 'foot/'toe
all over your body; completely: *She was dressed from head to foot in white.* ◇ *He was covered from head to foot in mud.*

get your 'head down (*informal*)
1 work or study hard: *If you want to pass that French exam, you'll have to get your head down.*
2 go to bed and sleep: *It's time to get our heads down; we have to be up early tomorrow morning.*

get your 'head round sth (*BrE, informal*)
understand sth difficult, often with a lot of effort: *The plan is so complicated — I'm still trying to get my head round it.*

get sth into your/sb's (thick) 'head (*informal*)
succeed in understanding or in making sb understand sth fully: *When are you going to get it into your thick head that you don't need to worry about money? You're rich now.* ◇ *I'm still trying to get it into my head that I'm free to do what I want now.*

get/take it into your 'head that... (*informal*)
think or believe sth, often wrongly: *Somehow she's taken it into her head that her husband is trying to poison her.*

give sb their 'head
give sb the freedom to do what they want: *We must give the new art teacher her head, so that she has the freedom to do things differently.* **OPP** tie sb's hands

> **❷ ORIGIN**
> This idiom refers to allowing a horse to go as fast as it likes when you are riding it.

go to your 'head
1 (of alcohol) make you feel a bit drunk: *I can't drink more than two pints of beer — it goes straight to my head.*
2 (of success, fame, praise, etc.) make you feel too proud of yourself in a way that other people find annoying: *Just because you had a small part in a movie, don't let it go to your head!*

have a good 'head on your shoulders
be a sensible person: *Don't worry about the children — Laura's with them and she's got a good head on her shoulders.*

have a (good) head for 'figures
be good at doing sums, etc: *If you want to be successful in business, you must have a good head for figures.*

have a (good) head for 'heights
be able to stand on a high place without feeling ill or afraid: *I won't go up the church tower with you. I've no head for heights.*

have your head in the 'clouds (*informal*)
not be realistic because you are always thinking of your own hopes, ideas, dreams, etc: *He wants us to start a business together but it would never work. He's got his head in the clouds half the time.* **OPP** have/keep both/your feet on the ground

have your 'head screwed on (the right way) (*informal*)
be sensible: *You can certainly trust Ann with your money. She's got her head screwed on the right way.* **OPP** have a screw loose

a/per 'head
for each person: *The meal shouldn't cost more than $30 a head.*

head and 'shoulders above sb/sth
very much better, greater, etc. than sb/sth: *He's head and shoulders above the other candidates.*

,head 'first
1 moving forwards or downwards with your head in front of the rest of your body: *He fell head first down the stairs.*
2 without thinking carefully about sth before acting: *She got divorced and rushed head first into another marriage.*

(the) head 'honcho (*informal, especially AmE*)
the person who is in charge; the boss: *Claude is the studio's head honcho, so talk to him if you have a problem.*

> **❷ ORIGIN**
> This phrase comes from the Japanese word *hancho*, meaning 'group leader'.

head 'north/'south (*business*)
(about share prices, currencies, etc.) rise/fall in value: *The country's currency headed south for the second day, weakening 1.4%.*

head over 'heels (in 'love)
completely in love: *He's head over heels in love with his new girlfriend.*

head

a ˌhead ˈstart (on/over sb)
an advantage that sb already has before they start doing sth: *Being able to speak French gave her a head start over the other candidates.*

hold your ˈhead up (high)
not feel ashamed, guilty or embarrassed about sth: *After this scandal, he will never be able to hold his head up high again.* **OPP** hang your head (in/for shame)

in over your ˈhead
involved in sth that is too difficult for you to deal with: *After a week in the new job, I soon realized that I was in over my head.*

keep your ˈhead
think clearly and remain calm: *If there is a robbery, you should try to keep your head and do as you are told.*

keep your ˈhead above water
succeed in staying out of debt; manage to deal with tasks, responsibilities, etc: *The company had great difficulty keeping its head above water during the economic crisis.* ◇ *I don't know how she manages to keep her head above water. She has so much to do.*

keep your ˈhead down (*informal*)
1 avoid being noticed or being seen in public: *She's so unpopular with the voters that the Prime Minister has told her to keep her head down until after the election.* ◇ *In the army you soon learn to keep your head down and stay out of trouble.*
2 work very hard: *He kept his head down for weeks before the final exams.*

lose your ˈhead (*informal*)
become unable to act in a calm or sensible way: *It's a very frightening situation, but we mustn't lose our heads.* **OPP** keep a level head

need, want, etc. your ˈhead examined (*informal*)
used for saying that sb is behaving in a crazy or stupid way: *She spent $300 on a pair of shoes? She needs her head examined.*

on sb's (own) head ˈbe it
(often used for warning sb) somebody is alone responsible for the results of their action or decision: *You refuse to go to your own daughter's wedding? On your head be it!* ◇ *On his own head be it if he decides to leave college early.*

out of/off your ˈhead (*BrE, informal*)
1 crazy: *Are you off your head?*
2 not knowing what you are saying or doing because of the effects of alcohol or drugs: *Don't even try to have a proper conversation with him — he's off his head.*

over sb's ˈhead
to a higher position of authority than sb: *He gets angry when you go over his head and talk to his boss.*

put your ˌhead in the lion's ˈmouth
deliberately put yourself in a dangerous or risky situation: *So I put my head in the lion's mouth and asked my boss for a pay rise.*

put sth out of your ˈhead
stop thinking about or wanting sth: *I am not going to let you go to the party, so you can put that idea out of your head.*

rear/raise its (ugly) ˈhead
(used of sth considered unpleasant) appear again after being hidden or forgotten: *Political corruption has reared its ugly head again.* ◇ *Famine has raised its head again in many parts of the world.*

scream, shout, etc. your ˈhead off (*informal*)
scream, shout, etc. a lot and very loudly: *She screamed her head off when I jumped out at her.*

stand/turn sth on its ˈhead
1 turn sth upside down
2 make people think about sth in a completely different way: *He stood the argument on its head, saying that the plan wouldn't save money and would, in fact, cost more.*

take it into your head to do sth
suddenly decide to do sth: *She's taken it into her head to give all her books away.*

turn sb's ˈhead
(of success, praise, etc.) make a person feel too proud in a way that other people find annoying: *You'd better stop giving me all these compliments, or you'll turn my head!*

- bear → like a bear with a sore head
- bill → head/top the bill
- block → put/lay your head/neck on the block
- clear → have/keep a clear head
- enter → enter sb's head
- eyes → have eyes in the back of your head
- eyes → your eyes nearly pop out of your head
- gun → have a gun to your head
- gun → hold/put a gun to sb's head
- hair → not harm/touch a hair of sb's head
- hang → hang over sb's head
- hang → hang your head (in/for shame)
- heart → let your heart rule your head
- hit → hit the nail on the head
- hole → need/want sb/sth like (you need/want) a hole in the head
- ideas → put ideas in/into sb's head SEE give sb ideas
- knock → I'll knock your block/head off!
- knock → knock sth on the head
- laugh → laugh your head off
- level → keep a level head
- old → (have) an old head on young shoulders
- price → a price on sb's head
- ring → ring in your ears/head
- roof → a roof over your head
- rush → have a rush of blood to the head
- scratch → scratch your head (over sth)
- shake → shake your head
- short → win, lose, etc. by a short head
- smash → smash sb's face/head in
- soft → be/go soft in the head
- standing → do sth standing on your head
- talk → talk through the back of your head
- talk → talk your head off
- thick → a thick head

- **top** → off the top of your head
- **use** → use your head
- **wet** → wet the baby's head

headless /'hedləs/

run around like a ˌheadless 'chicken
be very busy and active trying to do sth, but not
very organized, with the result that you do not
succeed: *What a day! I've been running around like
a headless chicken all day!*

> **NOTE**
> After a chicken's head is cut off its body may
> continue to move for a few moments.

headlights /'hedlaɪts/

- **deer** → (be caught/freeze like) a deer in the headlghts
- **deer** → (be caught like) a rabbit in the headlights **SEE** (be caught/freeze like) a deer in the headlights

headlines /'hedlaɪnz/

grab/hit/make the 'headlines (*informal*)
be an important item of news in newspapers or on
the radio or television: *His reputation has suffered
a lot since the scandal over his love affair hit the
headlines.*

heads /hedz/

bang/knock your/their 'heads together
(*informal*)
force people to stop arguing and behave in a sensible way: *I'd like to bang those stupid politicians'
heads together.*

heads or 'tails? (*spoken*)
used to ask sb which side of a coin they think will
be facing upwards after it has been thrown in the
air in order to decide sth by chance: *'Let's toss for
it. Heads or tails?' 'Heads.' 'Heads it is. You win.'*

ˌheads will 'roll (for sth) (*spoken, usually
humorous*)
used to say that some people will be punished
because of sth that has happened: *Have you seen
this article about police corruption? Heads will roll,
I'm sure.* ◇ *When the spy scandal was exposed,
many said that heads should roll in the government.*

> **❷ ORIGIN**
> This comes from the idea that when people
> were punished by having their heads cut off,
> the heads rolled along the ground.

put your, their, etc. 'heads together (*informal*)
think about or discuss sth as a group: *If we all put
our heads together, we might find a way to solve the
problem.*

- **two** → two heads are better than one

head-to-head /ˌhed tə 'hed/

(go) head-to-'head (with sb)
(deal with sb) in a very direct and determined
way, especially in a competition between two
people, organizations, etc: *They are set to meet
head-to-head in next week's final.*

headway /'hedweɪ/

make 'headway
make progress, especially when this is slow or difficult: *We are making little headway with the negotiations.* ◇ *The boat was unable to make much
headway against the tide.*

health /helθ/

- **clean** → a clean bill of health
- **drink** → drink sb's health

heap /hiːp/

collapse, fall, etc. in/into a 'heap
fall down heavily and not move: *He collapsed in a
heap on the floor.*

- **bottom** → at the bottom/top of the pile/heap
- **scorn** → heap/pour scorn on sb/sth
- **scrap** → on the scrap heap

heaps /hiːps/

heaps 'better, 'more, 'older, etc.
(*BrE, informal*)
a lot better, etc: *Help yourself — there's heaps more.*
◇ *He looks heaps better than when I last saw him.*

hear /hɪə(r); AmE hɪr/

can't hear yourself 'think (*informal*)
there is so much noise around you that you cannot
think clearly: *Can you turn the volume down? I
can't hear myself think in here.*

hear/see the 'end/the last of sb/sth
(often used with not, never, etc.) keep being
reminded of sth because sb is always talking
about it: *We'll never hear the end of her visit to
Buckingham Palace.* ◇ *If we don't get her a dog,
we'll never hear the end of it.*

ˌhear, 'hear!
called out, usually at a public meeting, etc. to
express agreement and approval: *'It is the wish of
this government that both unemployment and inflation be reduced to acceptable levels.' 'Hear, hear!'*

not 'hear of sth
not allow sth to happen: *'May I pay for the phone
call?' 'Don't be silly! I wouldn't hear of it!'* ◇ *He
won't hear of his daughter becoming a police officer.
He thinks it's much too dangerous.*

(do) you 'hear me? (*spoken*)
used to tell sb in an angry way to pay attention
and obey you: *You can't go — do you hear me?*

- **dicky** → not say/hear a dicky bird
- **last** → hear/see the last of sb/sth
- **things** → see/hear things

heard /hɜːd; AmE hɜːrd/

you could have heard a 'pin drop
it was extremely quiet: *When the play finished you
could have heard a pin drop.*

- **last** → the last I heard
- **voice** → make your voice heard

hearing /'hɪərɪŋ; AmE 'hɪrɪŋ/

in/within (sb's) 'hearing
near enough to sb so that they can hear what is
said: *She shouldn't have said such things in your
hearing.*

● **fair** → a fair hearing
● **hard** → hard of hearing

heart /hɑːt; AmE hɑːrt/

at 'heart
used to say what sb is really like even though they
may seem to be different: *He seems strict but he's a
very kind man at heart.* **OPP** on the surface

be close/dear/near to sb's 'heart
be a person or thing that sb is very fond of, concerned about, interested in, etc: *The campaign to
keep our local hospital open is something that is
very close to my heart.*

by 'heart (*BrE* also **off by 'heart**)
using only your memory: *There was a time when I
knew the whole poem by heart.*

break sb's 'heart
make sb feel extremely unhappy: *That boy is
breaking his mother's heart with his wild ways.*
◇ *It's a job I would like, but it won't break my heart
if I don't get it.* ▶ **'heartbreak** *noun: He causes his
mother nothing but heartbreak.* **'heartbreaking,
'heartbroken** *adj.: a heartbreaking story ◇ We
were heartbroken by the news.*

He broke her heart and then just walked away.

do sb's heart 'good (to do sth)
make sb feel happy, more cheerful, hopeful, etc: *It
did my heart good to see him looking so well.*

(come) (straight) from the 'heart
(be) genuine and sincere: *The letter comes straight
from the heart. He means every word of it.*

have a 'heart (*spoken*)
used for asking sb to be sympathetic or kind: *'We'll
work until midnight.' 'Have a heart, Joe. Can't we
stop earlier than that?'*

have a heart of 'gold
have a very kind and helpful nature, even though
it is not always obvious: *I know he's often bad-tempered but really, you know, he's got a heart of gold.*

have a heart of 'stone
be a person who does not show others sympathy
or pity: *Don't ask her to give any money to the fund
— she's got a heart of stone.* ▶ **,stony-'hearted** *adj.*

(your) heart and 'soul
with a lot of energy and enthusiasm: *She puts her
heart and soul into the job.* ◇ *A dancer must throw
herself heart and soul into every performance.*

your heart 'bleeds for sb (*ironic*)
used to say that you do not feel sympathy or pity
for sb: *'I have to get up at 6 o'clock tomorrow!'
'Oh, my heart bleeds for you — I have to do
that every single day!'* ▶ **,bleeding 'heart** *noun*
(*disapproving*) a person who is too kind and sympathetic towards people that other people think
do not deserve kindness: *a bleeding-heart liberal*

your heart goes 'out to sb
you feel great pity or sympathy for sb: *My heart
goes out to all those who lost friends and relatives
in the disaster.*

your heart is in your 'mouth (*informal*)
you feel very anxious or afraid: *My heart was in my
mouth as I waited to hear whether the jury would
find me guilty or not guilty.*

your, his, etc. heart is in the right 'place
used to say that sb's intentions are kind and sincere even though they sometimes do the wrong
thing: *I know she gets angry sometimes, but basically her heart is in the right place.*

your/sb's 'heart is not in it
sb does not give all their enthusiasm, interest and
energy to sth: *He agreed to write the book for a
large sum of money, but his heart wasn't in it, and
it was never finished.*

your heart 'leaps
used to say that you have a sudden feeling of happiness or excitement: *Her heart leapt when she
heard a knock on the door, thinking it might be
him.* **OPP** your heart sinks

your ,heart misses a 'beat
used to say that you have a sudden feeling of fear,
excitement, etc: *For a moment she thought she saw
the dead man's face looking in through the window
and her heart missed a beat.*

the 'heart of the matter
the most central and important part of a situation,
problem, etc: *And now we come to the heart of the
matter. Who is going to pay for all this?*

your heart 'sinks
used to say that you suddenly feel sad or
depressed about sth: *My heart sank when I realized
I would have to walk home in the rain.* **OPP** your
heart leaps

in good 'heart (*BrE*)
happy and cheerful: *Despite their bad living conditions and lack of money, the families were still in
good heart.*

in your ,heart of 'hearts
in your deepest feelings or thoughts: *I know in my
heart of hearts that you're right, but I still find it
difficult to accept.*

heat

let your ˌheart rule your ˈhead
act according to what you feel rather than what you think is sensible: *Don't let your heart rule your head. I know you like him but are you sure you can really trust him?*

lose ˈheart
become discouraged: *The revolutionaries lost heart after their leader was killed.*

lose your ˈheart (to sb/sth) (*formal*)
fall in love (with sb/sth): *I've quite lost my heart to those little kittens of yours. Can we take one home?*

a man, woman, etc. after your own ˈheart
a person you particularly like because they have the same interests, opinions, etc. as you: *You love football too? Then you're a man after my own heart!*

not have the ˈheart (to do sth)
not be able or willing to do sth which could hurt sb else: *I didn't have the heart to take the money from him — it was all he had.*

ˌrip/ˌtear the ˈheart out of sth
destroy the most important part or aspect of sth: *Protestors say that closing the factory will tear the heart out of the local economy.*

set your ˈheart/ˈmind on sth/on doing sth ♦ have your heart/mind ˈset on sth/on doing sth
want sth very much; want to do or achieve sth very much: *When she was a small girl, her heart was set on a horse of her own. ◊ He set his mind on becoming a doctor. ◊ I have my heart set on a new guitar.*

take ˈheart (from sth)
feel more positive about sth, especially when you thought that you had no chance of achieving sth: *The government can take heart from the results of the latest opinion polls.*

take sth to ˈheart
1 be very upset or offended by sb's criticism: *Her review of your book is stupid. Don't take it so much to heart.*
2 pay great attention (to sb's suggestions, etc.): *I'm pleased to see that they have taken my suggestions to heart and followed my advice.*

to your heart's conˈtent
as much or as long as you want: *This weekend I'll be able to read to my heart's content.*

> **NOTE**
> *Content* in this idiom means *contentment* (= a feeling of happiness or satisfaction).

with all your ˈheart/your whole ˈheart
used for emphasizing how strongly you feel about sth: *She hoped with all her heart that she would never have to see him again. ◊ I love you with all my heart.*

with a ˌheavy/ˌsinking ˈheart
with a feeling of sadness or fear: *It was with a heavy heart that he left the school for the last time.*
OPP with a light heart

● **absence** → absence makes the heart grow fonder
● **bless** → bless your, his, etc. heart SEE bless you, him, etc.

● **bottom** → from the bottom of your heart
● **change** → a change of heart
● **cross** → cross my heart (and hope to die)
● **eat** → eat your heart out (for sb/sth)
● **engraved** → be engraved on/in your heart/memory/mind
● **etched** → be etched on your heart/memory/mind
● **find** → (not) find it in your heart to do sth
● **goodness** → out of the goodness of your heart
● **hand** → hand on heart
● **hand** → with your hand on your heart
● **harden** → harden your heart against sb/sth
● **home** → home is where the heart is
● **interests** → have sb's (best) interests at heart
● **light** → with a light heart
● **open** → open your heart (to sb)
● **pour** → pour your heart out (to sb)
● **search** → search your heart/soul/conscience
● **sick** → be/feel sick at heart
● **sob** → sob your heart out
● **steal** → steal sb's heart
● **strike** → strike fear, terror, etc. into sb/sb's heart
● **way** → the way to sb's heart
● **wear** → wear your heart on your sleeve
● **win** → win sb's heart
● **young** → be, stay, etc. young at heart

heartbeat /ˈhɑːtbiːt; *AmE* ˈhɑːrt-/

a ˈheartbeat away (from sth)
very close to sth: *The offices are a heartbeat away from Singapore's business centre. ◊ With all her musical talent, it seems that success is just a heartbeat away.*

in a ˈheartbeat
very quickly, without thinking about it: *If I was offered another job, I'd leave in a heartbeat.*

hearts /hɑːts; *AmE* hɑːrts/

● **heart** → in your heart of hearts

heartstrings /ˈhɑːtstrɪŋz; *AmE* ˈhɑːrt-/

● **tug** → tug at sb's heartstrings

hearty /ˈhɑːti; *AmE* ˈhɑːrti/

● **hale** → hale and hearty

heat /hiːt/

if you can't stand the ˈheat (get out of the ˈkitchen) (*informal*)
used to tell sb to stop trying to do sth if they find it too difficult, especially in order to suggest that they are less able than other people: *'It seems a bit risky to me. Are you sure we should do this?' 'Well, if you can't stand the heat…'*

in the ˌheat of the ˈmoment
while in a state of strong emotion or excitement: *I must apologize for the rude things I said yesterday in the heat of the moment.*

take the 'heat out of sth
make a situation less tense, emotional, dangerous, etc: *The police tried to take the heat out of the situation by withdrawing for a while.* **OPP** add fuel to the fire/flames

turn on the 'heat (*informal*)
put increased pressure on sb in order to make them do sth: *If he doesn't pay us we'll have to turn on the heat.*

heave-ho /ˌhiːv ˈhəʊ; *AmE* ˈhoʊ/

give sb the (old) heave-'ho (*informal*)
dismiss sb from their job; end a relationship with sb: *'Are Julie and Mike still together?' 'Oh no, she gave him the old heave-ho a couple of months ago.'*

❷ ORIGIN
Heave-ho was originally the cry of sailors when pulling up the anchor.

heaven /ˈhevn/

a heaven on 'earth
a place or situation where everything is perfect: *The island is a real heaven on earth.* **OPP** a hell on earth

a ˌmarriage/ˌmatch made in 'heaven
a combination of two people or things which seems perfect: *When she married Dave, everyone thought that theirs was a match made in heaven.* ◇ *A merger between the two leading mobile phone networks would appear to be a marriage made in heaven, but will consumers lose out?*

- forbid → God/Heaven forbid (that...)
- forbid → Heaven forfend (that...) **SEE** God/Heaven forbid (that...)
- God → God in heaven
- God → to God/goodness/Heaven
- help → God/Heaven help sb
- high → smell/stink to high heaven
- knows → God/goodness/Heaven knows
- manna → manna from heaven
- move → move heaven and earth (to do sth)
- name → in God's/Heaven's name
- name → in the name of God/Heaven
- seventh → be in (your) seventh heaven

heavens /ˈhevnz/

(Good) 'Heavens! ✦ **Heavens a'bove!** (*spoken*)
used to show that you are surprised or annoyed: *Good Heavens! What have you done to your hair?*

the heavens 'open
it suddenly begins to rain very heavily: *We were walking back from the bus stop when suddenly the heavens opened.*

heavy /ˈhevi/

get 'heavy (*informal*)
become very serious, because strong feelings are involved: *They started shouting at me and it soon got very heavy.*

hang/lie 'heavy (on sb/sth)
1 (of a feeling or sth in the air) be very noticeable in a particular place in a way that is unpleasant: *Smoke lay heavy on the far side of the water.* ◇ *Despair hangs heavy on the air.*
2 make sb/sth feel uncomfortable or anxious: *The crime lay heavy on her conscience.*

ˌheavy 'going
boring, tiring, difficult, etc: *I do find her novels very heavy going.* ◇ *The last part of the journey was rather heavy going because of the muddy paths.*

NOTE
The *going* is the condition of the ground, especially in horse racing.

heavy 'hand
a way of doing sth or of treating people that is much stronger and less sensitive than it needs to be: *the heavy hand of management* **OPP** a light touch ▸ ˌheavy-'handed *adj.*: *a heavy-handed approach/manner*

the 'heavy mob/brigade (*BrE, informal*)
a group of strong, often violent people employed to do sth such as protect sb: *I had to laugh when he turned up at the meeting with his heavy mob, as if he was a mafia boss or something.*

a heavy 'silence/'atmosphere
a situation when people do not say anything, but feel embarrassed or uncomfortable: *There was a heavy silence for a few minutes before anybody spoke.*

make heavy 'weather of sth/of doing sth
make sth seem more difficult than it really is: *You're making very heavy weather of repairing that bike. What's the problem?* **OPP** make light work of sth

- heart → with a heavy/sinking heart
- time → time hangs/lies heavy (on your hands)

heck /hek/

for the 'heck of it (*informal*)
just for pleasure rather than for a reason: *'Why are you doing that?' 'Just for the heck of it.'*

what the 'heck! (*informal*)
used to say that you are going to do sth that you know you should not do: *It means I'll be late for work but what the heck!*

hedge /hedʒ/

ˌhedge your 'bets (*informal*)
try to reduce the risk of losing your money, being wrong about sth, etc. by choosing two or more courses of action at the same time: *She's invested her money in two quite different businesses, so she's hedging her bets.*

NOTE
This idiom refers to putting money on more than one horse in a race to increase your chances of winning money.

heebie-jeebies /ˌhiːbi ˈdʒiːbiz/

- willies → give sb the willies/heebie-jeebies/creeps

heed /hiːd/

give/pay 'heed (to sb/sth) ✦ **take 'heed (of sb/sth)** (*formal*)
pay careful attention to sb/sth: *They gave little heed to the rumours.* ◇ *I paid no heed at the time but later I had cause to remember what he'd said.*

heel /hiːl/

come to 'heel ✦ **bring sb to 'heel**
obey the rules; make sb obey the rules: *He'll soon come to heel if I start to get nasty with him.* ◇ *Tell him you'll leave him if he does it again. That'll bring him to heel, I'm sure.*

> **NOTE**
> If you tell a dog to *come to heel*, you make it come close to you.

down at 'heel
(of sb's appearance) looking poor: *Since he lost his job, he has begun to look rather down at heel.*

> **NOTE**
> This idiom refers to the worn heels of old shoes.

turn/spin on your 'heel
suddenly turn around and leave, often because you are angry or annoyed: *Quite unexpectedly he turned on his heel and walked out of the door.*

under the 'heel of sb (*literary*)
completely in sb's control; dominated by sb: *For years, the country was under the heel of a dictator.*

● Achilles → an/sb's Achilles' heel

heels /hiːlz/

at/on sb's 'heels
following closely behind sb: *Every day she walks past my house, with her little black dog at her heels.*

hard/hot on sb's 'heels
following sb closely because you want to catch them: *Jane has the most points at the moment, but the other competitors are hot on her heels.* ◇ *The police are hard on his heels.*

take to your 'heels
run away very quickly: *The burglars took to their heels when they heard the police arrive.*

● cool → cool your heels
● dig → dig your heels in
● drag → drag your feet/heels
● head → head over heels (in love)
● kick → kick up your heels
● kick → kick your heels
● show → show (sb) a clean pair of heels
● tread → tread on sb's heels

height /haɪt/

● full → draw yourself up/rise to your full height

heights /haɪts/

● head → have a (good) head for heights

hell /hel/

all 'hell breaks/is let loose (*informal*)
there is suddenly an angry, noisy reaction to sth; suddenly everything becomes confused, noisy, etc: *When soldiers fired shots into the crowd, all hell broke loose.* ◇ *All hell broke loose when they heard that their pay had been cut.*

beat/knock/kick the 'hell out of sb/sth (*informal*) (also **beat/knock/kick the 'shit out of sb/sth** △, *slang*)
beat, etc. sb/sth very hard: *If the crowd had managed to get hold of the robber, they would have beaten the hell out of him.* ◇ *The gang knocked the hell out of him for no reason at all.*

(just) for the 'hell of it (*informal*)
just for fun, with no particular reason: *The youths had nothing to do so they went round breaking windows just for the hell of it.*

from 'hell (*informal*)
used to describe a very unpleasant person or thing; the worst that you can imagine: *They are the neighbours from hell.*

get the hell 'out (of…) (*spoken*)
get out of or leave a place very quickly: *Here come the police. Let's get the hell out of here.* ◇ *Get the hell out of my house and don't come back!*
(Some people find the use of this idiom offensive.)

give sb 'hell (*informal*)
1 make life unpleasant for sb: *Her back is giving her hell at the moment; she's in constant pain.*
2 shout at or speak angrily to sb because they have done sth wrong: *His mother gave him hell for coming home so late.*

go to 'hell (*spoken, offensive*)
used to tell sb to go away or to stop saying/doing sth because it is annoying: *He wanted to come back but she told him to go to hell.* ◇ *'Why don't you answer my question, Jim?' 'Oh, go to hell, will you? I'm tired of your stupid questions.'*

hell for 'leather (*old-fashioned, BrE, informal*)
with the greatest possible speed, energy, etc: *I saw a man going hell for leather down the street, with two policemen running after him.*

> **❷ ORIGIN**
> This is from horse riding. A rider can hit a horse with a strip of leather to make it run faster.

hell hath no 'fury (like a woman 'scorned) (*BrE, saying*)
used to refer to sb, usually a woman, who has reacted very angrily to sth, especially the fact that her husband or lover has been unfaithful (= has had a sexual relationship with another woman): *He should have known better than to leave her for that young girl. Hell hath no fury like a woman scorned.*

> **NOTE**
> *Hath* is an old form of *has*.

a/one hell of a... (*spoken*, *slang*)
sb/sth that is very bad, good, unusual, impressive,
etc: *We had a hell of a good time at the night club.*
◇ *I had one hell of a hangover the next morning.*

> **NOTE**
> This is sometimes written as 'a/one helluva'.

a ,hell on 'earth
a place or situation that is extremely bad or
unpleasant: *Life for the ordinary soldiers was hell
on earth.* **OPP** a heaven on earth

(come) ,hell or high 'water
whatever the difficulties or opposition may be:
*Come hell or high water, we've got to reach the
injured men tonight.*

Hell's 'teeth (*old-fashioned*, *BrE*, *spoken*)
used to express anger or surprise: *Hell's teeth, look
at the time! I'm going to be late for work!*

like 'hell
1 (*informal*) very hard, very much, very fast, etc.
in an effort to do sth: *I had to run like hell to catch
the bus.*
2 (*spoken*) used to give emphasis when saying no
to a suggestion, idea, etc: *'He thinks you're going to
lend him your car this weekend.' 'Like hell I am.'*
(Some people find this use offensive.)

play (merry) 'hell with sb/sth (*BrE*, *informal*)
disturb, upset or trouble sb/sth very much: *These
storms play merry hell with our TV reception.*

scare, annoy, etc. the 'hell out of sb (*informal*)
scare, annoy, etc. sb very much: *The sight of a man
with a gun scared the hell out of her.* ◇ *Louise suddenly surprised the hell out of us by announcing
that she was pregnant!*

see sb in 'hell first (*informal*)
used to emphasize that you have no intention of
agreeing to or doing what sb has suggested: *You
want me to invite that woman to this house? I'll see
her in hell first.*

to 'hell and back (*informal*)
used to say that sb has been through a difficult
situation: *We'd been to hell and back together and
we were still good friends.*

to 'hell with sb/sth (*spoken*)
used to express anger or dislike and to say that
you no longer care about sb/sth and will take no
notice of it/them: *To hell with this stupid car. I'm
going to buy a new one.*
(Some people find this use offensive.)

what the 'hell! (*spoken*)
it doesn't matter; I don't care: *'Do you want a cig-
arette?' 'No, thanks, I've given up. Oh, what the
hell! Yes, I will have one, after all.'*
(Some people find this use offensive.)

when 'hell freezes over (*informal*)
if you say something will happen **when hell
freezes over**, you mean that you think it will
never happen: *'They might give you a pay rise
soon.' 'Yeah, right. When hell freezes over!'*

- **bat** → like a bat out of hell
- **cat** → not have a cat in hell's chance

- **catch** → catch hell **SEE** catch it
- **dogs** → go to hell in a handbasket **SEE** go to the dogs
- **hope** → not have a hope in hell
- **pay** → hell/the devil to pay
- **raise** → raise Cain/hell
- **road** → the road to hell is paved with good intentions
- **snowball** → not have a snowball's chance in hell (of
  doing sth)
- **sure** → (as) sure as hell

hell-bent /ˌhel ˈbent/

be ,hell-'bent on sth/on doing sth
be absolutely determined to do sth stupid, dangerous, etc: *Have you seen how fast he drives that
car? I'd say he was hell-bent on killing himself.*

helm /helm/

at the 'helm/'tiller
in control of an organization, etc: *The company
began to make profits again with the new managing
director at the helm.*

> **NOTE**
> A *helm* or a *tiller* is used for controlling the dir-
> ection of a ship or a boat.

take (over) the 'helm
take control of an organization, etc. from another
person: *When Mr Davies retired, his daughter took
the helm.*

help /help/

can't help (doing) sth ♦ can't help but do sth
not be able to avoid or resist doing sth: *A klepto-
maniac is a person who can't help stealing things.*
◇ *'I'm sorry, I can't help it,' she said, bursting into
tears.* ◇ *He's a bit of a fool, but you can't help but
like him.*

God/Heaven 'help sb (*spoken*)
used to say that you are afraid sb will be in danger
or that sth bad will happen to them: *God help us if
this doesn't work.*
(Some people find this use offensive.)

not if 'I can help it
used for saying you do not want sth to happen:
*'Your daughter told me that she wants to leave
school when she's 16.' 'Not if I can help it.'*

so 'help me ('God)
used when making a serious promise, threat, etc:
*I'll catch the man who did this to my son, so help me
God.* ◇ *I'll kill him, so help me.*

> **NOTE**
> In a court of law a witness swears to 'tell the
> truth, the whole truth and nothing but the
> truth, so help me God'.

there's no 'help for it (*especially BrE*)
it is not possible to avoid doing sth that may harm
sb in some way: *There's no help for it. We shall have
to call the police.*

- **fat** → a fat lot of good/help/use

helping /'helpɪŋ/

a ,helping 'hand
help: *The new charity tries to offer a helping hand to young people who have become addicted to drugs.* ◇ *A helping hand would be very welcome at the moment.*

hem /hem/

● um → hum/hem and haw **SEE** um and aah (about sth)

hen /hen/

(as) rare/scarce as hen's 'teeth (*old-fashioned*)
extremely rare: *Critics always complain that good movies that the whole family can see together are as scarce as hen's teeth.*

> NOTE
> This refers to the fact that hens do not have teeth.

hence /hens/

...days, weeks, etc. 'hence (*formal*)
a number of days, etc. from now: *The true consequences will only be known several years hence.*

herd /hɜːd; AmE hɜːrd/

● ride → ride herd on sb/sth

here /hɪə(r); AmE hɪr/

,here and 'now
1 at this moment; immediately: *I'm afraid I can't tell you the answer here and now. I'll try and find out for you later.*
2 the present situation: *Don't worry so much about the future. You need to concentrate more on the here and now.*

,here and 'there
to or in various places: *Here and there in the crowd I saw people I recognized.*

,here 'goes ◆ ,here we 'go
said before you begin to do sth dangerous, exciting, difficult, etc: *Is everybody ready? OK, here goes. Turn on the electricity and let's see what happens.*

,here goes 'nothing (*AmE*)
said before you begin to do something that you do not think will be successful: *'Well, here goes nothing!' she said, getting ready to jump.*

,here, there, and 'everywhere
in, to, or from many different places: *The letters came from here, there, and everywhere.* ◇ *We searched here, there, and everywhere, but couldn't find the document they wanted.*

,here we go a'gain
often used for showing you are angry or annoyed that sth is starting to happen again: *Here we go again! They're digging up the road — it's the third time this year.* ◇ *Here we go again — another train cancelled. This is getting ridiculous.*

,here you 'are ◆ ,here you 'go (*spoken*)
used when you are giving sth to sb: *Here you are. This is what you were asking for.* ◇ *Here you go. Four copies, is that right?*

here's to sb/sth!
used for wishing sb/sth health, success, happiness, etc., especially when lifting your glass and drinking a toast to sb/sth: *Here's to the happy couple! May they have a long and happy marriage!* ◇ *What a wonderful meal. Here's to the cook!* ◇ *Here's to success!*

neither ,here nor 'there
not important because it is not connected with the subject being discussed; irrelevant: *The fact that she's the director's daughter is neither here nor there. She's the most suitable person for the job.* ◇ *What might have happened is neither here nor there.*

herring /'herɪŋ/

● red → a red herring

hesitates /'hezɪteɪts/

he who 'hesitates (is 'lost) (*saying*)
if you delay in doing sth you may lose a good opportunity: *You should have applied for that job. I'm sure you would have got it. Remember, he who hesitates...*

hey /heɪ/

hey 'presto (*BrE*) (*AmE* '*presto*)
people sometimes say **hey presto** when they have just done sth so quickly and easily that it seems to have been done by magic: *You just press the button and, hey presto, a perfect cup of coffee!*

> ❷ ORIGIN
> *Presto* is an Italian word meaning 'quick' or 'quickly'.

what the 'hey! (*AmE, spoken*)
it doesn't matter; I don't care: *This is probably a bad idea, but what the hey!*

hide /haɪd/

hide your ,light under a 'bushel (*BrE*)
not let people know that you are good at sth: *We didn't know you could play the guitar! You've been hiding your light under a bushel all this time!*

> ❷ ORIGIN
> This phrase comes from the Bible.

not see ,hide nor 'hair of sb/sth (*spoken*)
not see sb/sth for some time: *I haven't seen hide nor hair of her for a month.*

> NOTE
> *Hide* here means 'skin'.

● head → bury/hide your head in the sand
● multitude → cover/hide a multitude of sins
● rhinoceros → have a hide/skin like a rhinoceros
● save → save sb's/your (own) neck/skin/hide

hiding /ˈhaɪdɪŋ/

be on a ˌhiding to ˈnothing (*BrE, informal*)
have no hope of succeeding, whatever happens:
The Government is on a hiding to nothing in these elections.

high /haɪ/

be for the ˈhigh jump (*BrE, informal*)
be about to be punished, criticized, dismissed, etc:
When your father sees your school report, you'll be for the high jump.

> **❷ ORIGIN**
> This was first used as a military term and refers to the punishment of hanging somebody.

be/get on your ˌhigh ˈhorse
be annoyed because you think that sb has not treated you with enough respect: *When they suggested that she might have made a mistake, she got on her high horse and asked them how they dared question her ability.*

have a ˈhigh old time (*old-fashioned, informal*)
enjoy yourself very much: *When I left them they were having a high old time singing and dancing on the tables!*

ˌhigh and ˈdry
in a difficult situation without help or money:
When the travel company went bankrupt, many holidaymakers were left high and dry abroad or waiting at the airport.

> **NOTE**
> This expression refers to boats left on the beach after the level of the sea has fallen.

ˌhigh and ˈlow
(search, etc. for sth) in every possible place; everywhere: *I've been hunting high and low for that pen, where did you find it?*

ˌhigh and ˈmighty (*informal*)
behaving as though you think you are more important than other people: *He's too high and mighty to mix with ordinary people like us!*

(as) high as a ˈkite (*informal*)
in an excited state, especially because of drugs, alcohol, etc: *He was as high as a kite when they came to arrest him.*

ˌhigh days and ˈholidays
festivals and special occasions: *This 19th-century dish was traditionally made on high days and holidays, and is still often eaten at Christmas.*

ˌhigh ˈfive (*especially AmE*)
an action to celebrate victory or to express happiness in which two people raise one arm each and hit their open hands together: *Way to go! High five!* ◇ *Her teammates cheered and gave her a high five.*

ˌhigh ˈjinks (*old-fashioned, informal*)
a lot of fun and amusement: *They got up to all sorts of high jinks on the trip.*

> **❷ ORIGIN**
> This refers to a particular game that was played at drinking parties.

the ˈhigh point/spot of sth
the best, most interesting, entertaining, etc. part of sth: *The high spot of our trip was the visit to Rome.* ◇ *It was the high point of the evening.*

in ˌhigh ˈdudgeon (*old-fashioned, written*)
in an angry or offended mood, and showing other people that you are angry: *After being refused entry to the club, he went off in high dudgeon.*

on ˈhigh
1 (*formal*) in a high place: *We gazed down into the valley from on high.*
2 (*humorous*) the people in senior positions in an organization: *An order came down from on high that from now on lunchbreaks were to be half an hour and no longer.*
3 in heaven: *The disaster was seen as a judgement from on high.*

on the ˌhigh ˈseas
in international waters; on a part of the sea which does not belong to any country: *What happens if a crime is committed on the high seas?*

run ˈhigh
(especially of feelings) be strong and angry or excited: *As usual, emotions ran high at the awards ceremony last night.*

smell/stink to high ˈheaven (*informal*)
1 have a very strong and unpleasant smell: *When was the last time you cleaned the dog kennel? It stinks to high heaven.*
2 seem to be very dishonest or morally unacceptable: *This whole deal stinks to high heaven. I'm sure somebody was bribed.*

take the ˈhigh road (in sth) (*AmE*)
take the most positive course of action: *He took the high road in his campaign.*

- **fly** → fly high
- **friends** → have friends in high places
- **hell** → (come) hell or high water
- **moral** → take, claim, seize, etc. the moral high ground
- **order** → of a high order **SEE** of the highest/first order
- **profile** → adopt, keep, etc. a high/low profile
- **riding** → riding high
- **sights** → set your sights high/low
- **small** → feel that high **SEE** look/feel small
- **spirits** → be in high/low spirits
- **time** → it's high/about time (that)...

highest /ˈhaɪɪst/

- **order** → of the highest/first order

highly /ˈhaɪli/

- **speak** → speak highly of sb
- **think** → think highly of sb/sth

hightail /ˈhaɪteɪl/

ˈhightail it (*informal, especially AmE*)
leave somewhere very quickly: *As soon as the bell went for the end of lessons, Jack ran out of the school gates and hightailed it for home.*

high-water /ˌhaɪ ˈwɔːtə(r)/ (AmE also) ˈwɑːt-/

high-'water mark
the highest stage of achievement: *This was the high-water mark of the ancient Greek civilization.*

highway /ˈhaɪweɪ/

● **way** → my way or the highway

highways /ˈhaɪweɪz/

ˌhighways and 'byways
(on/along) all the roads, large and small, of a country, an area, etc: *She travelled the highways and byways of Scotland collecting folk songs and local traditions.*

hike /haɪk/

take a 'hike (AmE, informal)
a rude way of telling sb to go away: *Take a hike, will you?*

hill /hɪl/

a ˌhill of 'beans (old-fashioned, AmE, informal)
something that is not worth much: *He's so rich that as far as he's concerned, the money he lost doesn't amount to a hill of beans.*

over the 'hill (informal)
no longer young; past your best: *Some people think if you're 30, you're over the hill!*

up ˌhill and down 'dale
to or from many places; everywhere: *They cycled up hill and down dale, glad to be away from the city.*

hills /hɪlz/

● **old** → (as) old as the hills

hilt /hɪlt/

(up) to the 'hilt
(support, etc. sb) completely: *I will support you to the hilt on this.*

hind /haɪnd/

● **talk** → talk the hind leg(s) off a donkey

hindmost /ˈhaɪndməʊst; AmE -moʊst/

● **devil** → (the) devil take the hindmost

hint /hɪnt/

take a/the 'hint
understand what sb wants you to do, even though they tell you in an indirect way: *She yawned and said, 'Goodness, it's late.' 'OK,' said Pete, 'I can take a hint. I'll go now.'* ◇ *Sarah hoped he'd take the hint and leave her alone.*

● **drop** → drop a hint (to sb)

hip /hɪp/

● **joined** → joined at the hip
● **shoot** → shoot from the hip

hire /ˈhaɪə(r)/

● **ply** → ply for hire/trade/business

history /ˈhɪstri/

go down in/make 'history
be or do sth so important that it will be recorded in history: *Roger Bannister made history as the first man to run a mile in less than four minutes.* ◇ *This battle will go down in history as one of our most important victories.*

the 'history books
the record of great achievements in history: *She has earned her place in the history books.*

● **rest** → the rest is history

hit /hɪt/

be/make a (big, etc.) 'hit with sb
be liked very much by sb when they first meet you: *You've made quite a hit with my mother. She really likes you.* ◇ *The new teacher is a big hit with all the students as well as the other members of staff.*

hit (it) 'big (informal)
be very successful: *The band has hit big in the US.*

hit the 'books (AmE)
study hard and read a lot about sth: *You're going to hit the books and make something of yourself.* ◇ *My exams are soon so I'd better start hitting the books.*

hit the 'bottle (informal)
regularly drink too much: *She managed to resist alcohol for a year, then hit the bottle again when her husband died.* ◇ *He's really hitting the bottle at the moment.*

hit the 'buffers (informal)
if a plan, sb's career, etc. **hits the buffers**, it suddenly stops being successful: *His big ideas for expanding the business hit the buffers yesterday when the board of directors rejected his proposals.*

hit the 'deck (*informal*)
1 fall to the ground suddenly: *When we heard the shooting we hit the deck.* ◇ *The champion landed another heavy punch and the challenger hit the deck for the third time.*
2 (*AmE*) get out of bed: *Come on! It's time to hit the deck.*

hit the ground 'running (*informal*)
start doing sth and continue very quickly and successfully: *What we need for this project is someone who will hit the ground running.*

> ❷ ORIGIN
> This idiom possibly refers to soldiers who are expected to land from parachutes or from helicopters and get straight into action.

hit sb/sth 'hard
affect sb/sth very badly: *The death of her daughter hit her very hard.*

> NOTE
> In the passive, we usually say 'hard hit by' instead of 'hit hard by': *Pensioners have been particularly hard hit by the rise in heating costs.*

hit sb in the 'eye (*informal*)
be very obvious or striking: *The strange combination of colours hits you in the eye as soon as you enter the room.*

'hit it (*spoken*)
used to tell sb to start doing sth, such as playing music: *Hit it, Louis!*

hit it 'off (with sb) (*informal*)
quickly form or have a good relationship with sb: *I met a girl at the party, and we hit it off straight away.*

hit the 'jackpot
suddenly win, earn, etc. a lot of money; suddenly be very successful: *She's hit the jackpot with her latest book — it's sold millions.*

a 'hit list (*informal*)
a list of people, organizations, etc. against whom some unpleasant action is being planned: *The gang have drawn up a hit list of about 50 politicians.* ◇ *Be careful how you speak to her because I think you're on her hit list.*

hit the nail on the 'head (*informal*)
say sth that is exactly right: *'So you want to move to another department.' 'You've hit the nail on the head. That's exactly what I want.'* OPP be/fall wide of the mark

hit the 'road (also **hit the 'trail** *especially AmE*) (*informal*)
begin a journey: *Well, we'd better hit the road, we've a long way to go.*

hit the 'roof/'ceiling (*informal*)
suddenly become very angry: *Every time I mention Patricia, Sam hits the roof.*

When Dad found out I'd crashed the car, he hit the roof.

hit the 'sack/'hay (*informal*)
go to bed: *I think it's time to hit the sack.*

> ❷ ORIGIN
> *Sack* and *hay* both refer to simple beds. In the past a bed was often just a sack or piece of rough cloth with hay inside. Sailors in the navy also slept in hammocks (= a type of bed hung between two posts, etc.) similar to sacks.

hit the 'skids (*especially AmE*)
begin to decline or get worse very quickly: *In February shares hit the skids, and in one day $1 bn was wiped off the value of the company.*

hit the 'spot (*informal*)
if sth **hits the spot** it does exactly what it should do: *I decided I wasn't really hungry, but the coffee really hit the spot and I drank a whole pot.*

hit the 'streets ♦ hit the 'shops/'stores (*informal*)
become widely available for sale: *The new games console hits the streets tomorrow.*

hit sb when they're 'down
continue to hurt sb when they are already defeated: *You wouldn't hit a man when he's down, would you?*

hit sb where it 'hurts
affect sb where they will feel it most: *After four years of marriage, she really knows how to hit him where it hurts, and isn't afraid to do it either.*

take a 'hit
be damaged or badly affected by sth: *The airline industry took a hit last year.*

- brick → hit a brick wall **SEE** be/come up against a brick wall
- headlines → grab/hit/make the headlines

- **home** → hit/strike home
- **know** → not know what hit you
- **mark** → hit/miss the mark
- **nerve** → hit/touch a (raw) nerve
- **note** → hit/strike the right/wrong note
- **pay** → hit/strike pay dirt
- **rock** → hit/reach rock bottom
- **six** → hit/knock sb/sth for six
- **smash** → a smash hit
- **stride** → hit (your) stride SEE get into your stride

hit-and-miss /ˌhɪt ən ˈmɪs/

‚hit-and-'miss (also ‚hit-or-'miss *less frequent*)
not done in a careful or planned way and therefore not likely to be successful: *The advertisements were rather hit-and-miss and not based on proper market research.* ◇ *They use rather hit-and-miss techniques for selecting new staff.*

hit-and-run /ˌhɪt ən ˈrʌn/

‚hit-and-'run
a road accident in which a driver leaves the place where the accident happened without stopping to give help, leave his name, etc: *a hit-and-run accident/driver*

hitch /hɪtʃ/

hitch your ‚wagon to a 'star ✦ hitch your wagon to sb/sth
try to succeed by forming a relationship with sb/sth that is already successful: *She quit the group and hitched her wagon to the dance band 'Beats'.* ◇ *We must be careful. We don't want to hitch our wagon to the wrong star.*

> NOTE
> *Hitch* means to tie or attach something to something else.

- **lift** → thumb/hitch a lift

hitched /hɪtʃt/

get 'hitched (*informal*)
get married: *They got hitched last year without telling anybody about it.*

hither /ˈhɪðə(r)/

‚hither and 'thither (*especially literary*)
in many different directions: *When you look down at the square, you see all the people hurrying hither and thither.*

> NOTE
> *Hither* and *thither* are old words for 'here' and 'there'.

hits /hɪts/

- **shit** → (when) the shit hits the fan

hobby /ˈhɒbi; AmE ˈhɑːbi/

a 'hobby horse
a subject that sb feels strongly about and likes to talk about: *Sorry, I'm starting to get on my hobby horse!* (= talk about my favourite subject).

Hobson /ˈhɒbsn; AmE ˈhɑːbsn/

‚Hobson's 'choice
the choice of taking what is offered or nothing at all, in reality no choice at all: *It's Hobson's choice really, as this is the only room they have empty at the moment.*

> ❷ ORIGIN
> This expression refers to a 17th-century Cambridge man, Tobias Hobson, who hired out horses; he would give his customers the 'choice' of the horse nearest the stable door or none at all.

hoc /hɒk; AmE hɑːk/

- **ad** → ad hoc

hock /hɒk; AmE hɑːk/

be in 'hock (to sb) (*informal*)
owe money: *I'm in hock for about €5 000.*

> ❷ ORIGIN
> *Hock* comes from the Dutch word for prison.

hog /hɒɡ; AmE hɔːɡ; hɑːɡ/

go the ‚whole 'hog (*informal*)
do sth thoroughly or completely: *They painted the kitchen and then decided to go the whole hog and do the other rooms as well.*

- **road** → a road hog

hog-wild /ˌhɒɡ ˈwaɪld; AmE ˌhɔːɡ; ˌhɑːɡ/

go 'hog-wild (*AmE, informal*)
behave in an uncontrolled or excited manner: *Just because your Mom and Dad aren't here it's no reason to go hog-wild.*

hoist /hɔɪst/

- **petard** → be hoist/hoisted by/with your own petard

hold /həʊld; AmE hoʊld/

> Most idioms containing **hold** are at the entries for the nouns and adjectives in the idioms, for example **hold your fire** is at **fire**.

catch/get/grab/take (a) 'hold of sb/sth
have or take sb/sth in your hands: *He caught hold of her wrists so she couldn't get away.* ◇ *Lee got hold of the dog by its collar.* ◇ *Quick, grab a hold of that rope.*

hold 'good/'true
be or remain true, valid, correct, etc: *This principle holds true in every case.* ◇ *Will your promise hold good even if you don't get the money?*

'hold it (*informal*)
wait a moment: *Hold it a second! I just have to make sure the doors are locked.*

hold your 'own
remain in a strong position when sb is attacking you, competing with you, etc: *There was a lot of competition but she managed to hold her own.* ◊ *'How's your father?' 'He's holding his own, but only just. We'll just have to hope that he'll start getting better soon.'*

on 'hold
delayed until a later time or date: *We can't find the money, so all our plans are on hold at the moment.* ◊ *We'll have to put the decision on hold until we get more details.*

take (a) 'hold
begin to have complete control over sb/sth; become very strong: *Panic took hold of him and he couldn't move.* ◊ *They managed to get out of the house just before the flames took hold.* ◊ *It is best to treat the disease early before it takes a hold.*

holding /ˈhəʊldɪŋ; AmE ˈhoʊ-/

leave sb holding the 'baby (*AmE also* **leave sb holding the 'bag**) (*informal*)
leave sb to take the responsibility or blame for sth: *It's always the same. We all agree to do something, then you all say you're too busy to arrange it, and I'm left holding the baby.* ◊ *You two were going to fly off and leave me holding the bag.*

there's no 'holding/'stopping sb
a person cannot be prevented from doing sth because of their enthusiasm, energy, determination, etc: *There was no holding him once he started talking about his life in India.* ◊ *You know Hannah — once she's decided to do something there's no stopping her.*

holds /həʊldz; AmE hoʊldz/

(with) ˌno ˌholds 'barred
(of fighting, competition, etc.) with no or very few rules or restrictions: *This started off as a very clean election campaign, but now it's no holds barred.* ◊ *a no-holds-barred row over the latest political scandal*

> **NOTE**
> In wrestling, *no holds barred* means that there are no rules about which ways of holding your opponent are allowed and which are not.

hole /həʊl; AmE hoʊl/

in a 'hole (*informal*)
in a difficult situation: *He had got himself into a hole and it was going to be difficult to get out of it.*

in the 'hole (*AmE, informal*)
in debt; owing money: *We started the current fiscal year $3 million in the hole.*

need/want sb/sth like (you need/want) a ˌhole in the 'head (*informal*)
definitely not need/want sb/sth at all: *I had to get home before midnight, and just then I needed a flat tyre like a hole in the head.*

- **dent** → make a dent/hole in sth
- **dig** → dig yourself (into) a hole
- **money** → money burns a hole in your pocket
- **sleeve** → have an ace in the hole **SEE** have an ace/a trick up your sleeve

holes /həʊlz; AmE hoʊlz/

- **pick** → pick holes (in sth)

holiday /ˈhɒlədeɪ; AmE ˈhɑːl-; BrE also -di/

- **busman** → a busman's holiday

holidays /ˈhɒlədeɪz; AmE ˈhɑːl-; BrE also -diz/

- **high** → high days and holidays

holies /ˈhəʊliz; AmE ˈhoʊliz/

- **holy** → holy of holies

hollow /ˈhɒləʊ; AmE ˈhɑːloʊ/

- **beat** → beat sb/sth hollow
- **ring** → ring true/false/hollow

holy /ˈhəʊli; AmE ˈhoʊli/

ˌholy of 'holies (*humorous*)
a special place which only particular people can enter: *This room is the holy of holies. It contains the most valuable books in the world.* ◊ *The boss invited me into his holy of holies this morning. What a fantastic office he's got!*

> **NOTE**
> In a Jewish temple, the *holy of holies* is the inner part, which only the chief priest can enter.

home /həʊm; AmE hoʊm/

at 'home
1 (feeling) comfortable or relaxed, as if you are in your own home: *I like the city. I feel at home here.* ◊ *Come in and make yourself at home while I finish cooking the dinner.*
2 (of a sports event) at your own ground, club, etc: *We're at home to Oxford United on Saturday, and the week after we're away to Luton.*
3 (of a subject, topic of conversation, etc.) know about and feel confident discussing sth: *I'm not really at home with French literature. My speciality is the language.*

bring home the 'bacon (*informal*)
be successful in sth; be the person who earns money for a family, an organization, etc: *The firm wants very much to get this contract, and we're expecting you to bring home the bacon.* ◊ *He's the one who brings home the bacon, not his wife.*

bring sth 'home to sb
make sb realize how important, difficult or serious sth is: *This documentary brought home the tragedy of the poor to many people.* ◊ *Visiting that hospital for the mentally ill really brought home to me how sad some people's lives are.*

come 'home (to sb)
become fully clear or understood: *The danger of the situation we were in suddenly came home to me.*

drive/hammer sth 'home (to sb)
make sure that sb understands sth completely, for example by repeating it often: *The instructor tried to drive home to us the need for safety precautions before diving.* ◊ *Police used statistics to hammer home their warning about car theft.*

hit/strike 'home
1 (of an insult, a remark, criticism, etc.) affect or hurt sb in the intended way; make sb really understand sth: *His criticism of my work struck home. I knew he was right.* ◊ *My remarks last week obviously hit home because he has not been late for work since.*
2 (of a punch, a blow, an arrow, a bullet, etc.) hit sb/sth where you intended; hit the target: *The punch hit home and Ferguson fell to the floor.*

home and 'dry (*BrE*) (*AmE* home 'free)
in a safe or good position because you have successfully completed or won sth: *When we've won four out of six games, we'll know that we're home and dry.* ◊ *All they have to do is sign the contract and then we'll be home free.*

a 'home bird
a person who spends most of the time at home because they are happiest there: *Sheila's a home bird really. She likes to spend her free time around the house or in the garden.*

a ,home from 'home (*BrE*) (*AmE* a ,home away from 'home)
a place where you feel as comfortable, happy, etc. as in your own home: *They used to stay in their aunt's apartment in Brighton every summer. It was a real home from home.*

,home is where the 'heart is (*saying*)
a home is where the people you love are: *When I ask him if he's happy travelling around the world all the time, he just says, 'Home is where the heart is. If my wife and children are with me, then I'm happy.'*

home sweet 'home (*often ironic*)
used to say how pleasant your home is (especially when you really mean that it is not pleasant at all)

a ,home 'truth
an honest criticism of a person said directly to them: *It's time someone told you a few home truths, my boy!*

on the 'home front
happening at home, or in your own country, rather than in a foreign country: *There will be heavy snow across most of France, while on the home front we can expect to see similar conditions at least until the weekend.*

on the ,home 'straight/'stretch
approaching the end of a task, project, course, etc: *Ten exams done and two more to do — you're on the home straight now.* ◊ *I never thought the prison sentence would end, but I feel I'm on the home straight now.*

> **NOTE**
> This refers to the last part of a horse race when the horses are approaching the finishing line.

when he's, it's, etc. at home? (*BrE, informal, humorous*)
used to emphasize a question about sb/sth: *'Shirley Hills wants to meet you.' 'Who's she when she's at home?'*

- charity → charity begins at home
- chickens → (your/the) chickens come home to roost
- close² → close to home
- cows → till/until the cows come home
- eat → eat sb out of house and home
- Englishman → an Englishman's home is his castle
- Englishman → a man's home is his castle SEE an Englishman's home is his castle
- house → set up house/home (with sb/together)
- lights → the lights are on but nobody's home
- press → press sth home
- press → press home your advantage
- ram → ram sth home
- romp → romp home/to victory
- spiritual → be sb's spiritual home
- write → be nothing, not much, etc. to write home about

homework /'həʊmwɜːk; *AmE* 'hoʊmwɜːrk/
do your 'homework (on sth)
find out the facts, details, etc. of a subject in preparation for a meeting, a speech, an article, etc: *He had just not done his homework for the interview. He couldn't answer our questions.*

honcho /'hɒntʃəʊ; *AmE* 'hɑːntʃoʊ/
- head → (the) head honcho

honest /'ɒnɪst; *AmE* 'ɑːn-/
honest! (*spoken*)
used to emphasize that you are not lying: *I didn't mean it, honest!*

honest to 'God/'goodness
used for emphasizing the truth of what you are saying: *I didn't tell anybody — honest to God!*
▶ ,honest-to-'goodness *adj.* (*approving*) simple and good: *This book is an honest-to-goodness attempt to describe life as a political leader.*

make an honest 'woman of sb (*old-fashioned* or *humorous*)
marry a woman who you have been having a sexual relationship with: *When are you going to make an honest woman of her, Peter?*

honesty /'ɒnəsti; *AmE* 'ɑːn-/
in all 'honesty
speaking honestly: *I can't in all honesty say that I've had much experience of this kind of work, but I'm willing to try it.*

honey /'hʌni/
- land → a/the land of milk and honey

honeymoon /'hʌnimuːn/
a/the 'honeymoon period
a period of time at the beginning of sth, for example a relationship, a job, a period in govern-

ment, etc., when everybody is pleased with you and there appear to be no problems: *The honeymoon period is over now for the new President.*

honour (*BrE*) (*AmE* honor) /'ɒnə(r); *AmE* 'ɑːnər/

do sb an 'honour ♦ do sb the 'honour (of doing sth) (*formal*)
do sth to make sb feel very proud and pleased: *Would you do me the honour of dining with me?*

have the 'honour of sth/of doing sth (*formal*)
be given the opportunity to do sth that makes you feel proud and happy: *May I have the honour of the next dance?*

(there is) honour among 'thieves (*saying*)
used to say that even criminals have standards of behaviour that they respect

in 'honour of sb/sth ♦ in sb's/sth's 'honour
in order to show respect and admiration for sb/sth: *a ceremony in honour of those killed in the explosion* ◇ *A banquet was held in her honour.*

on your 'honour (*old-fashioned*)
1 used to promise very seriously that you will do sth or that sth is true: *I swear on my honour that I knew nothing about this.*
2 be trusted to do sth: *You're on your honour not to go into my room.*

● **bound →** be/feel duty/honour bound to do sth
● **point →** a point of honour
● **word →** your, his, etc. word of honour

honoured (*BrE*) (*AmE* honored) /'ɒnəd; *AmE* 'ɑːnərd/

be/feel honoured (to do sth)
feel proud and happy: *I was honoured to have been mentioned in his speech.*

honours (*BrE*) (*AmE* honors) /'ɒnəz; *AmE* 'ɑːnərz/

do the 'honours (*often humorous*)
perform a social duty or ceremony, such as pouring drinks, making a speech, etc: *Harry, could you do the honours? Tom and Angela both want gin and tonic.* ◇ *His father was ill, so Charles did the honours with the welcome speech.*

honours are 'even (*BrE*)
no particular person, team, etc. is doing better than the others in a competition, an argument, etc: *After a competitive first day of the series, I'd say honours are even.*

hoof /huːf/

'hoof it (*informal*)
go somewhere on foot; walk somewhere: *We hoofed it all the way to 42nd Street.*

> **NOTE**
> This comes from the noun *hoof*, which is the hard part of the foot of some animals, for example horses.

on the 'hoof (*BrE, informal*)
if you do sth **on the hoof**, you do it quickly and without giving it your full attention because you are doing sth else at the same time: *We made the decision on the hoof, late at night and without really thinking about the consequences.*

> **NOTE**
> Meat that is sold, transported, etc. *on the hoof* is sold, etc. while the cow or sheep is still alive.

hook /hʊk/

by ˌhook or by 'crook
(of sth difficult) by any method, whether it is honest or not: *Don't worry — we'll have the money ready by 4 o'clock, by hook or by crook.*

> ❷ **ORIGIN**
> This may come from the practice in the past of allowing workers to use the tools of their trade (*billhooks* for farm workers, *crooks* for shepherds) to pull down loose wood from their employer's trees to use as firewood.

get sb off the 'hook (*informal*)
help sb to avoid punishment, etc: *You're going to need a very clever lawyer to get you off the hook.*

hook, line and 'sinker
if you accept sth **hook, line and sinker**, you accept it completely, either because you have been deceived or because you believe things too easily: *Are you telling me that you swallowed his absurd lies hook, line and sinker?*

> **NOTE**
> All three words in this expression are items used for catching a fish.

let sb off the 'hook (*informal*)
allow sb to escape from a difficult situation or punishment: *We'll let you off the hook this time, but if you make any more mistakes like that, you'll lose your job.* ◇ *There won't be time for me to read my report to the committee, so that's let me off the hook.*

> **NOTE**
> This expression refers to a fish escaping after it has been caught.

off the 'hook
if you leave or take the telephone **off the hook**, you take the receiver (= the part that you pick up) off the place where it usually rests, so that nobody can call you: *So many people were calling me that in the end I got tired of it and left the phone off the hook.*

● **ring →** ring off the hook
● **sling →** sling your hook

hookey (also **hooky**) /'hʊki/

● **truant →** play hookey/hooky **SEE** play truant

hooks /hʊks/

get your 'hooks into sb
gain influence or control over sb: *He was perfectly happy living alone until that woman got her hooks into him.*

hoops /huːps/

• jump → jump through hoops
• shoot → shoot hoops

hoot /huːt/

not care/give a 'hoot (about sb/sth) (also **not care/give two 'hoots (about sb/sth)**) (*informal*)
not care at all: *I don't care two hoots about having money, as long as I'm happy.*

hop /hɒp; AmE hɑːp/

• catch → catch sb on the hop
• jump → hop to it SEE jump to it

hope /həʊp; AmE hoʊp/

be beyond 'hope (of sth)
be in a situation where no improvement is possible: *After so many months, the captives were beyond hope of escape and of ever seeing their families again.*

hold out little, etc. 'hope (of sth/that…) ♦ **not hold out any, much, etc. 'hope**
offer little, etc. reason for believing that sth will happen: *The doctors did not hold out much hope for her recovery.*

hope against 'hope (that…)
continue to hope for sth, even if this seems useless or foolish: *It was a couple of days since the earthquake, but the family were still hoping against hope that their son was safe.*

hope for the 'best
hope that everything will go well, even if there are doubts that it will: *There is nothing more the doctors can do. All we can do now is hope for the best.*

hope springs e'ternal (*saying*)
human beings never stop hoping: *She's sure that he'll come back to her one day. I'm not so sure, but hope springs eternal.*

> **❷ ORIGIN**
> This comes from *An Essay on Man* by Alexander Pope: 'Hope springs eternal in the human breast'.

I should 'hope so/not ♦ **so I should 'hope** (*spoken*)
used to say that you feel very strongly that sth should/should not happen: *'Nobody blames you.' 'I should hope not!'* ◇ *'She did apologize.' 'So I should hope!'*

in the hope of sth ♦ **in the hope that…**
because you want sth to happen: *I called early in the hope of catching her before she went to work.* ◇ *He asked her again **in the vain hope** that he could persuade her to come* (= it was impossible).

not have a ,hope in 'hell (*informal*)
not have any chance at all: *You haven't got a hope in hell of winning the race — you're far too slow!*

not a 'hope ♦ **some 'hope(s)!** (*BrE, spoken*)
there is no or little chance of sth happening: *Some hope of your becoming manager — you're far too lazy!* ◇ *'Your dad will lend you the money, won't he?' 'Not a hope.'*

• live¹ → live in hope
• ray → the one/a ray of hope

hopes /həʊps; AmE hoʊps/

build up/raise sb's 'hopes
make sb feel hopeful about sth or persuade them that sth good is going to happen: *Don't raise her hopes too much. She may not win.*

dash/shatter sb's 'hopes
destroy sb's hopes of doing or getting sth: *Any hopes that the museum would be built this year were dashed yesterday when the council announced its plans to spend less money on the arts.* ◇ *His poor performance in the exam shattered his hopes of becoming a lawyer.*

• pin → pin your faith/hopes on sb/sth

hopping /'hɒpɪŋ; AmE 'hɑːp-/

,hopping 'mad (about/over sth) (*informal*)
extremely angry about sth: *Anne was hopping mad about the sales figures.*

horizon /hə'raɪzn/

on the ho'rizon
soon to happen: *The change of government means that there are new developments on the horizon.*

• cloud → a (small) cloud on the horizon

horn /hɔːn; AmE hɔːrn/

• blow → blow/toot your own horn SEE blow your own trumpet

hornet /'hɔːnɪt; AmE 'hɔːrnɪt/

a 'hornet's nest
a lot of trouble: *When Charles got the manager's job, it stirred up a real hornet's nest, because everyone was angry about his fast promotion.*

> **NOTE**
> A *hornet* is a large wasp that has a very powerful sting.

horns /hɔːnz; AmE hɔːrnz/

draw/pull in your 'horns
start being more careful in your behaviour, especially by spending less money than before: *After making huge losses, the company had to draw in its horns by cancelling some major projects.*

(on) the horns of a di'lemma
(in) a situation in which you must make a choice between things which are equally unpleasant: *I'm really on the horns of a dilemma. I need the car but I can't afford it.*

- **bull** → take the bull by the horns
- **lock** → lock horns (with sb) (over sth)

horror /'hɒrə(r); AmE 'hɔːr-; 'hɑːr-/

,horror of 'horrors (*BrE, humorous* or *ironic*)
used to emphasize how bad a situation is: *I stood up to speak and — horror of horrors — realized I had left my notes behind.*

- **shock** → shock horror

horse /hɔːs; AmE hɔːrs/

(straight) from the horse's 'mouth (*informal*)
(of information, etc.) directly from the person who really knows because they are closely connected with its source: *'How do you know he's leaving?' 'I got it straight from the horse's mouth. He told me himself.'*

> **❷ ORIGIN**
> This may come from horse racing and the humorous suggestion that you had heard from the horse itself whether it would win the race.

you can ,take/,lead a horse to ,water, but you ,can't make it 'drink (*saying*)
you can give sb the opportunity to do sth, but you cannot force them to do it if they do not want to

- **cart** → put the cart before the horse
- **dark** → a dark horse
- **eat** → eat like a horse
- **eat** → I could eat a horse
- **flog** → flog a dead horse
- **gift** → (not) look a gift horse in the mouth
- **high** → be/get on your high horse
- **hobby** → a hobby horse
- **stable** → shut, etc. the barn door after the horse has escaped **SEE** shut/lock/close the stable door after the horse has bolted
- **wrong** → back the wrong horse

horses /'hɔːsɪz; AmE 'hɔːrsɪz/

change/swap horses in mid'stream
change to a different or new activity while you are in the middle of sth else; change from supporting one person or thing to another: *'I don't believe in changing horses in midstream,' he said. 'Give this policy a chance before you think of changing it.'*

hold your 'horses (*informal*)
used for asking sb to stop for a moment, speak more slowly, etc: *Hold your horses! We haven't finished the last question yet.*

,horses for 'courses (*BrE*)
people or things should only be used for the purpose which they are most suitable for: *I think Johnson would be much better for this job. It's a question of horses for courses.*

> **NOTE**
> This expression refers to the fact that horses race better on a track that suits them.

- **drive** → drive a coach and horses through sth
- **wild** → wild horses couldn't/wouldn't drag sb there, prevent sb doing sth, etc.

- **wishes** → if wishes were horses, beggars would/might ride

hostage /'hɒstɪdʒ; AmE 'hɑːs-/

a ,hostage to 'fortune
an action which may cause you great trouble in the future: *Are you really sure you want to know who your real mother is? It may be taking a hostage to fortune, you know.*

hot /hɒt; AmE hɑːt/

be ,hot to 'trot (*informal*)
1 be very enthusiastic about starting an activity: *She's hot to trot and ready to start work next week if we want her to.*
2 be excited in a sexual way

go ,hot and 'cold (all 'over) (*informal*)
suddenly feel very worried, upset or frightened when you remember sth very unpleasant: *I go hot and cold all over when I think of that train accident. It was so terrible.*

hot 'air (*informal*)
impressive but worthless or empty promises: *Don't believe anything she says. It's all hot air.*

(all) hot and 'bothered (*informal*)
worried and upset: *Ministers are getting all hot and bothered about official secrets getting out.* ◇ *You're looking a bit hot and bothered. Is everything OK?*

a 'hot line (to sb)
a special telephone line to an important person, such as a president, etc. which is used in emergencies: *The President of the United States spoke on the hot line with the Prime Minister about the crisis.*

,hot off the 'press
news that is **hot off the press** has just appeared in the newspapers and is fresh and usually exciting: *Listen to this story — it's hot off the press!*

> **NOTE**
> Paper that has just been printed on a *press* (= printing machine) is still warm.

hot on sb's/sth's 'tracks/'trail (*informal*)
close to catching or finding the person or thing that you have been chasing or searching for: *The burglar ran away, with the police hot on his trail.*

a hot po'tato (*informal*)
a very sensitive matter that is difficult or embarrassing to deal with: *His resignation is a political hot potato.*

a 'hot spot (*informal*)
1 a place where fighting is common, especially for political reasons: *As a journalist, I get sent to one hot spot after another.*
2 a place where there is a lot of activity or entertainment: *We went clubbing in some of Ibiza's most famous hot spots.*

hot 'stuff (*informal, especially BrE*)
1 sb/sth of very high quality: *He's really hot stuff as a tennis player.*

2 a sexually attractive person; a film/movie, book, etc. that is exciting in a sexual way: *She seems to think he's really hot stuff.* ◇ *His new book is really hot stuff.*

hot under the 'collar (*informal*)
annoyed, embarrassed or excited: *He gets very hot under the collar if people disagree with him.*

When he saw the phone bill, Dad got a bit hot under the collar.

in hot pur'suit (of sb/sth)
chasing sb; trying to catch sb: *He grabbed the jewels and ran, with several customers in hot pursuit.*

in the 'hot seat (*informal*)
a position of responsibility in which you must deal with difficult questions, criticism or attacks: *Our radio phone-in today is on transport, and the Minister of Transport will be in the hot seat, ready to answer your questions.*

in hot 'water (*informal*)
in trouble: *She got into hot water for being late.* ◇ *The new clerk was in hot water because she forgot to ask for a receipt for the money.* ◇ *This sort of behaviour will land him in hot water.*

make it 'hot for sb (*informal*)
make a situation very difficult or uncomfortable for sb: *If you insist on staying here, I can make it very hot for you.*

more …/more often than sb has had hot 'dinners (*informal, often humorous*)
used for emphasizing how much/many or how often sb has done sth: *He's won more medals than you've had hot dinners.* ◇ *She's been to France more often than you've had hot dinners.*

not so/too 'hot (*informal*)
not very well, healthy, etc.; not very good: '*How do you feel today?*' '*Not so hot.*' ◇ *Her work's not too hot, is it? I thought she'd be better than this!*

sell/go like 'hot cakes (*informal*)
be sold quickly in great quantities: *The band's latest record is selling like hot cakes.*

too 'hot for sb (also **too hot to 'handle**) (*informal*)
(too) difficult, dangerous, etc. for sb: *When the scandal became public, things got too hot for the Minister and she resigned.* ◇ *The newspapers won't print the story — it's just too hot to handle.*

- blow → blow hot and cold
- cat → like a cat on a hot tin roof **SEE** like a cat on hot bricks
- cat → like a cat on hot bricks
- heels → hard/hot on sb's heels
- strike → strike while the iron is hot

hotfoot /'hɒtfʊt; *AmE* 'hɑːt-/

'hotfoot it (*informal*)
walk or run somewhere quickly: *Once the police arrived, we hotfooted it out of there.*

hots /hɒts; *AmE* hɑːts/

get/have the 'hots for sb (*informal*)
be sexually attracted to sb: *I reckon Jim's really got the hots for you!*

hounds /haʊndz/

- hare → run with the hare and hunt with the hounds

hour /'aʊə(r)/

at an un,earthly/un,godly 'hour (*informal*)
very early or very late, especially when this is annoying: *The job involved getting up at some unearthly hour to catch the first train.* ◇ *I heard him come home at some ungodly hour again last night.*

in your ,hour of 'need (*often humorous*)
when you really need help: *Where were you in my hour of need? Sitting in a cafe with your friends!*

on the 'hour/half-'hour
at exactly 5 o'clock, 6 o'clock, etc./ 5.30, 6.30, etc: *Buses leave here for Oxford on the hour.*

- eleventh → the eleventh hour
- evil → the evil hour/day/moment
- bottom → the bottom of the hour
- top → the top of the hour

hours /'aʊəz; *AmE* 'aʊərz/

,after 'hours
after the period during which a shop, pub, etc. is open: *Pubs are not allowed to sell drinks after hours.*

at 'all hours
at any time during the night or day; all the time: *He comes here at all hours, sometimes in the middle of the night.*

keep… 'hours
if you **keep** regular, strange, etc. **hours**, the times at which you do things, especially getting up or going to bed, are regular, strange, etc: *Keeping irregular hours is hard on children, so try to set a regular bedtime and a regular time to get up.*

the 'small/'early hours (also the wee (small) 'hours)
the period of time very early in the morning, soon after midnight: *He died in the early hours of Saturday morning.* ◊ *We stayed up talking into the small hours.*

till/until 'all hours
until very late at night or early next morning: *She sat up till all hours trying to finish her essay.*

work all the ,hours God 'sends (*informal*)
work all the time: *'You look tired, Jane.' 'I'm working all the hours God sends at the moment trying to finish my thesis.'* **OPP** not do a stroke (of work)

house /haʊs/

bring the 'house down (*informal*)
make everyone laugh a lot or clap their hands loudly, especially at a performance in the theatre: *Their act brought the house down when they played in London.* ◊ *'Did he sing well?' 'He brought the house down!'*

get on like a 'house on fire (*BrE*) (*AmE* get along like a 'house on fire) (*informal*)
quickly develop a very friendly relationship with sb: *I was worried about introducing my boyfriend to my parents, but they got on like a house on fire.*

a ,house of 'cards
a plan, an organization, etc., that is so badly arranged that it could easily fail: *His plans collapsed like a house of cards when he was told he hadn't won the scholarship.*

keep 'house
cook, clean and do all the other jobs around the house: *She had given up her career to devote herself to the task of keeping house and raising a family.*

on the 'house
(especially of alcoholic drinks) given to a customer free by the hotel, restaurant, bar, etc: *Drinks are on the house tonight!*

put/set your (own) 'house in order
organize your own business or improve your own behaviour before you try to criticize sb else: *A government official warned the newspaper industry to put its own house in order before it started to tell other industries how they should be run.*

set up 'house/'home (with sb/together)
to make a place your home: *They got married and set up home together in Hull.*

- clean → clean house
- doghouse → in the doghouse
- dry → not a dry eye in the house
- eat → eat sb out of house and home
- halfway → a halfway house
- open → (keep) open house
- pack → pack the house

household /'haʊshəʊld; *AmE* -hoʊld/

a ,household 'name/'word
a name/word that is extremely well known: *The business she founded made her into a household name.* ◊ *Microsoft is a household name.*

houseroom /'haʊsruːm; -rʊm/

not give sb/sth 'houseroom (*BrE*)
not want sb/sth in your house because you dislike or do not approve of it/them; completely reject sb/sth: *I wouldn't give that ugly old furniture houseroom.* ◊ *She won't give any of these theories houseroom.*

houses /'haʊsɪz/

go all round the 'houses (*BrE, informal*)
do sth or ask a question in a very complicated way instead of in a simple, direct way: *If you want to ask her something, just ask her directly — there's no need to go all round the houses!*

- people → people (who live) in glass houses shouldn't throw stones
- safe → (as) safe as houses

housetops /'haʊstɒps; *AmE* -tɑːps/

shout, etc. sth from the 'housetops/'rooftops (*informal*)
tell sth to everyone: *Don't shout it from the housetops, will you? I want to keep it a secret just between us for a while.* ◊ *He was in love and wanted to shout it from the rooftops.* **OPP** keep quiet about sth

how /haʊ/

how 'can/'could you! (*spoken*)
used to show that you strongly disapprove of sb's behaviour or are very surprised by it: *Ben! How could you? After all they've done for us!* ◊ *Ugh! How can you eat that stuff?*

how 'come (...)? (*spoken*)
used to say you do not understand how sth can happen and would like an explanation: *'They've decided not to buy the house.' 'How come? I thought they definitely wanted it.'* ◊ *If she spent five years in Paris, how come her French is so bad?*

,how do you 'do (*becoming old-fashioned*)
used as a formal greeting when you meet sb for the first time. The usual reply is also *How do you do?*

how's 'this/'that for a...? (*informal*)
used for asking for sb's reaction to sth: *'How's that for a surprise present?' 'It looks wonderful. Thank you!'* ◊ *'Well, how's that for bad hotel service?' 'Unbelievable.'*

huddle /'hʌdl/

get/go into a 'huddle (with sb)
move close to sb so that you can talk about sth without other people hearing: *Every time she asked a question, the group went into a huddle before giving her an answer.*

hue /hjuː/

a ,hue and 'cry
loud opposition, protest, etc: *There was a great hue and cry among the parents when it was announced that the school was to close.* ◊ *If the government raises taxes too much, there'll be a real hue and cry.*

This phrase refers to the medieval law 'hu e cri', which stated that the public had to chase and try to catch a criminal.

huff /hʌf/

,huff and 'puff
1 breathe heavily while making a great physical effort: *They huffed and puffed as they carried the sofa upstairs.*
2 make it obvious that you are annoyed about sth without doing anything to change the situation: *After much huffing and puffing, he agreed to help.*

in a 'huff (*informal*)
in a bad mood, especially because sb has annoyed or upset you: *She went off in a huff.*

hum /hʌm/

● um → hum/hem and haw **SEE** um and aah (about sth)

human /'hju:mən/

● milk → the milk of human kindness

humble /'hʌmbl/

● eat → eat humble pie

hump /hʌmp/

give sb/get the 'hump (*BrE, informal*)
annoy sb/become annoyed, angry, etc: *She gets the hump when people don't listen to her.* ◇ *'What's wrong with Jake?' 'Oh, I don't know. He's got the hump about something.'*

over the 'hump (*informal*)
past the largest, worst or most difficult part of a job, illness, etc: *I'll be over the hump when I've done this exam — then there'll be just two left.*

● bust → bust sb's ass/balls/butt/hump
● bust → bust your ass/balls/butt/hump

hundred /'hʌndrəd/

a hundred/thousand/million and one things/ things to do, etc. (*informal*)
very many or too many (things to do, people to see, etc.): *I'm so busy — I've got lectures to prepare and a hundred and one letters to write — I just don't know where to start.* ◇ *She's always got a thousand and one excuses for everything.*

a/one hundred per 'cent
completely: *I agree with you one hundred per cent.*

● miles → not a hundred/thousand/million miles away/ from here
● nine → ninety-nine times out of a hundred **SEE** nine times out of ten

hung /hʌŋ/

● well → (you, etc.) may/might as well be hanged/hung for a sheep as (for) a lamb

hunkers /'hʌŋkəz; AmE -kərz/

on your 'hunkers
sitting on your heels with your knees bent up in front of you: *The little boy took out his favourite red sports car, and was delighted when Tom went down on his hunkers and admired the toy.*

hunt /hʌnt/

● hare → run with the hare and hunt with the hounds

hunting /'hʌntɪŋ/

● happy → a happy hunting ground

hurry /'hʌri; AmE 'hɜ:ri/

in a 'hurry
1 very quickly or more quickly than usual: *He had to leave in a hurry.*
2 not having enough time to do sth: *Sorry, I haven't got time to do it now — I'm in a hurry.*

in a 'hurry to do sth
impatient to do sth: *My daughter is in such a hurry to grow up.*

in no 'hurry (to do sth) ◆ **not in a/any 'hurry (to do sth)**
1 having plenty of time: *I don't mind waiting — I'm not in any particular hurry.* ◇ *Serve this lady first — I'm in no hurry.*
2 not wanting or not willing to do sth: *We were in no hurry to get back to work after the holidays.*

I, he, etc. won't do sth again in a 'hurry (*spoken*)
used to say that sb does not want to do sth again because it was not enjoyable: *I won't be going there again in a hurry — the food was terrible.*

● tearing → (be in) a tearing hurry/rush

hurt /hɜ:t; AmE hɜ:rt/

it won't/wouldn't 'hurt sb to do sth
it will/would be better for sb to do sth; it would be a good idea for sb to do sth: *It wouldn't hurt her to walk instead of going in the car all the time.*

● fly → he, she, etc. wouldn't harm/hurt a fly

hurts /hɜ:ts; AmE hɜ:rts/

● hit → hit sb where it hurts

hustle /'hʌsl/

,hustle and 'bustle
busy and excited activity: *I can't concentrate on my work with all this hustle and bustle going on around me.* ◇ *I've always loved the hustle and bustle of big cities.*

Hyde /haɪd/

● Jekyll → a Jekyll and Hyde

hymn /hɪm/

● sing → sing from the same song/hymn sheet

hysterics /hɪˈsterɪks/

have hyˈsterics (*spoken*)
be extremely upset and angry: *My mum'll have hysterics when she sees the colour of my hair.*

I i

i /aɪ/

● **dot** → dot the/your i's and cross the/your t's

ice /aɪs/

ˌbreak the ˈice
make a social situation more informal and relaxed, especially at the beginning of a meeting, party, etc: *If you serve drinks as soon as they arrive it will help to break the ice.* ➤ **an ˈice-breaker** *noun*: *James told a very funny joke, which was a good ice-breaker.*

cut no ˈice (with sb)
not impress or influence sb: *Her aggressive manner may be very useful at work, but it cuts no ice with me.* ◇ *Public protests don't cut much ice with this government.*

put sth on ˈice
decide to take no action on sth for a period of time; postpone sth: *They have put the plans for the new hospital on ice because of the economic situation.* ◇ *My plans for going to the USA are on ice for the moment.*

● **thin** → be skating/walking on thin ice

iceberg /ˈaɪsbɜːɡ; AmE -bɜːrɡ/

● **tip** → be the tip of the iceberg

icing /ˈaɪsɪŋ/

the icing on the ˈcake
something attractive, but not necessary, which is added to sth already very good: *The meal was perfect, the wonderful view from the restaurant the icing on the cake.*

idea /aɪˈdɪə; AmE -ˈdiːə/

get the iˈdea (*informal*)
understand sth when it has been explained to you: *'Do you understand how it works now?' 'Yes, I think I've got the idea. Thanks for showing me.'*

have no iˈdea ♦ not have the first, slightest, etc. iˈdea
not know sth at all; not know how to do sth at all: *I've no idea what time it is.* ◇ *Don't ask him to mend it; he hasn't got the first idea about cars.*

you have no iˈdea... (*spoken*)
used to show that sth is hard for sb else to imagine: *You've no idea how much traffic there was tonight.*

the (very) iˈdea! (*old-fashioned, spoken*)
used to express surprise or disapproval at the way sb behaves: *She expected me to pay for everything. The idea!*

run aˈway with the idea/notion (*spoken*)
believe sth that is not true: *Don't run away with the idea that you're going to be famous just because you've appeared on television once.*

ˈthat's an idea! (*spoken*)
used to reply in a positive way to a suggestion that sb has made: *Hey, that's an idea! And we could get a band, as well.*

ˈthat's the idea! (*spoken*)
used to encourage people and to tell them that they are doing sth right: *That's the idea! You're doing just fine.*

● **right** → have the right idea

ideal /aɪˈdiːəl/

● **world** → in an ideal/a perfect world

ideas /aɪˈdɪəz; AmE -ˈdiːəz/

give sb iˈdeas (also **put iˈdeas in/into sb's head**)
give sb hopes about sth that may not be possible or likely; make sb act or think in an unreasonable way: *Don't keep telling him about your adventures in Africa. You're giving him ideas.* ◇ *Who's been putting ideas into his head?*

● **buck** → buck up your ideas; buck your ideas up

idle /ˈaɪdl/

● **bone** → bone idle
● **devil** → the devil makes work for idle hands

if /ɪf/

ˌif and ˈwhen
used to say sth about an event that may or may not happen: *If and when we ever meet again I hope he remembers what I did for him.*

if ˈanything
used to express an opinion about sth, or after a negative statement to suggest that the opposite is true: *I'd say he was more like his father, if anything.* ◇ *She's not thin — if anything she's a little plump.*

if ˌI were ˈyou
used to introduce a suggestion or a piece of advice: *If I were you, I wouldn't buy that car. You can see it's been in an accident.*

if it wasn't/weren't for...
used to say that sb/sth stopped sb/sth from happening: *If it weren't for you, I wouldn't even be here today.*

if ˈnot
1 used to introduce a different suggestion, after a sentence with *if* : *I'll go if you're going. If not* (= if you are not) *I'd rather stay at home.*
2 used after a *yes/no* question to say what will or should happen if the answer is 'no': *Are you ready? If not, I'm going without you.* ◇ *Do you want that cake? If not, I'll have it.*

3 used to suggest that sth may be even larger, more important, etc. than was first stated: *They cost thousands if not millions of pounds to build.*

if 'only
used to express a wish that something had happened or would happen: *If only she'd done what I told her, she wouldn't be in this trouble.* ◇ *If only you'd let me explain.*

ifs /ɪfs/

,ifs and/or 'buts
(often used in negative sentences) used to stop sb arguing, protesting or making excuses when you tell them to do sth: *I want this work finished by Friday and no ifs and buts.*

ignorance /'ɪɡnərəns/

,ignorance is 'bliss (*saying*)
if you do not know about sth, you cannot worry about it: *Some doctors believe ignorance is bliss and don't give their patients all the facts.*

ill /ɪl/

for ,good or 'ill (*formal*)
whether the effect of an action, fact, etc. is good or bad: *Look, for good or ill, you chose this profession. You can't just leave it now.*

,ill at 'ease
nervous, especially in a social situation: *He always feels ill at ease at parties.* ◇ *She looked very ill at ease during her speech.* **OPP** at (your) ease

it's an ,ill 'wind (that blows ,nobody any 'good) (*saying*)
no problem is so bad that it does not bring some advantage to sb: *The fire destroyed half the village. For the builders business has never been better. It's an ill wind...*

speak/think 'ill of sb (*formal*)
say or think bad things about sb: *You shouldn't speak ill of the dead.*

● **bode** → bode well/ill (for sb/sth)
● **feeling** → bad/ill feeling(s)
● **wish** → wish sb/sth ill

image /'ɪmɪdʒ/

be the image of sb/sth ◆ **be the living/spitting/very image of sb/sth**
be very similar to, or look exactly like sb/sth else: *She's the spitting image of her mother.*

imagination /ɪˌmædʒɪ'neɪʃn/

● **figment** → a figment of sb's imagination
● **stretch** → by no stretch of the imagination
● **stretch** → not by any stretch of the imagination

immediate /ɪ'miːdiət/

● **effect** → with immediate effect **SEE** with effect from...

immemorial /ˌɪmə'mɔːriəl/

● **time** → from/since time immemorial

impression /ɪm'preʃn/

be under the im'pression that...
believe, usually wrongly, that...: *I was under the impression you were coming tomorrow, not today.*

in /ɪn/

anything/nothing/something 'in it
any/no/some truth in what is being said: *'Is there anything in the story that he is leaving the company?' 'No, I'm sure there's nothing in it.'/'Yes, I think there's something in it.'*

anything/nothing/something in it for sb (*informal*)
any/no/some advantage, especially financial, to sb: *He wanted to know more about the business but I told him there was nothing in it for him.*

be in at sth
present when sth happens: *They were in at the start of the economic boom.*

be 'in for sth
1 be about to get or experience sth unpleasant, for example a shock, a surprise, trouble, bad weather, etc: *He'll be in for a big surprise when he opens that letter.* ◇ *I think we're in for trouble with the new boss.*
2 be taking part in sth, for example a competition; be trying to get sth, for example a job: *I'm in for both the 100 metres race and the long jump.* ◇ *I hope Jan gets that professorship she's in for.*

be 'in for it (*BrE* also **be 'for it**) (*informal*)
be going to get into trouble or be punished: *We'd better hurry or we'll be in for it.*

be/get 'in on sth (*informal*)
knowing about sth; included in sth: *I'd like to be in on this project if you'll have me.* ◇ *She wants to get in on what the others are doing.* ◇ *Shall we let him in on the secret?*

be/keep (well) 'in with sb (*informal*)
be friendly with sb, not because you like them, but because they may be useful to you: *If you want to do well in this company, keep well in with the boss.*

,in and 'out (of sth)
going regularly to a place: *I've been in and out of the travel agency all this week, trying to arrange my holiday.* ◇ *After the accident, he was in and out of hospital for a couple of years.*

in that (*written*)
for the reason that; because: *She was fortunate in that she had friends to help her.*

inch /ɪntʃ/

every ,inch a/the 'leader, 'star, 'hero, etc.
a leader, star, hero, etc. in every way; completely a leader, star, hero, etc: *She is every inch a movie star.* ◇ *That horse looks every inch a winner.* ◇ *He looked every inch the romantic hero.*

give sb an 'inch (and they'll ,take a 'yard/'mile) (*saying*)
if you say yes to sb for a small request, they will want much more: *Joe could borrow my car occasionally, and then he started to borrow it every night! Give him an inch...!*

,inch by 'inch
very slowly and with great care or difficulty: *She crawled forward inch by inch.*

not budge/give/move an 'inch
refuse to change your position, decision, etc. even a little: *We tried to negotiate a lower price but they wouldn't budge an inch.*

within an 'inch of sth/of doing sth
very near/close to sth/to doing sth: *I came within an inch of death in that car accident.* ◇ *They came within an inch of winning the match.* ◇ *They beat him within an inch of his life* (= very severely).

• trust → not trust sb an inch

inconsiderable /,ɪnkən'sɪdrəbl/

not incon'siderable (*formal*)
large; large enough to be considered important: *We have spent a not inconsiderable amount of money on the project already.*

Indian /'ɪndiən/

an ,Indian 'summer
1 a period of unusually dry, warm weather in the autumn: *We had a splendid Indian summer last October.*
2 a period of success or happiness near the end of sb's life: *He made his best movies in his seventies; it was for him a real Indian summer.*

• file → (in) single/Indian file

Indians /'ɪndiənz/

• chiefs → there are too many chiefs and not enough Indians

industry /'ɪndəstri/

• captain → a captain of industry

infinitum /,ɪnfɪ'naɪtəm/

• ad → ad infinitum

influence /'ɪnfluəns/

under the 'influence
(used of sb driving a car) having had too much alcohol to drink: *She was fined £500 for driving under the influence.*

information /,ɪnfə'meɪʃn; AmE ,ɪnfər'm-/

for your infor'mation
1 (*abbr.* **FYI**) written on documents that are sent to sb who needs to know the information in them but does not need to deal with them
2 (*informal*) used to tell sb that they are wrong about sth: *For your information, I don't even have a car.*

• mine → a mine of information (about/on sb/sth)

iniquity /ɪ'nɪkwəti/

• den → a den of iniquity/vice

initiative /ɪ'nɪʃətɪv/

(do sth) on your own i'nitiative
do sth which is your own idea, not a suggestion or an order from another person: *Did you ask him to organize a meeting, or was it on his own initiative?*

take the i'nitiative
lead people by being the first to act in a situation: *France took the initiative in the peace talks.* ◇ *California took the initiative in banning smoking in public places.*

injury /'ɪndʒəri/

do sb/yourself an 'injury (*often humorous*)
hurt sb/yourself physically: *I nearly did myself an injury carrying those heavy suitcases.*

• add → add insult to injury

injustice /ɪn'dʒʌstɪs/

do yourself/sb an in'justice
judge yourself/sb unfairly: *We may have been doing him an injustice. This work is good.*

ink /ɪŋk/

much ,ink has been 'spilled (on/over sth)
a lot has been written about sth: *Much ink has been spilled on the life of Shakespeare.*

• red → red ink

inner /'ɪnə(r)/

the ,inner 'man/'woman
1 your mind or soul: *Prayer and meditation are good for the inner man.*
2 (*humorous*) your appetite: *It's time to do something for the inner man; let's look for a restaurant.*

innings /'ɪnɪŋz/

a good 'innings (*BrE, informal*)
used about sb who has died or who is at the end of their life or career to say that they have had a long life or career: *He's had a good innings but now it's time for him to retire and let someone younger take over as director.*

> NOTE
> In cricket, an *innings* is the period of time that a team or a person spends batting (= hitting the ball). A *good innings* is one that lasts a long time and in which a lot of 'runs' (= points) are scored.

inroads /'ɪnrəʊdz; AmE -roʊdz/

make inroads in/into sth
1 reduce the amount of sth: *Repairs to the house had made deep inroads into their savings.*
2 advance successfully into a new area: *Doctors are making great inroads in the fight against cancer.* ◇ *Their products are already making inroads in these new markets.*

jackpot /'dʒækpɒt; AmE -pɑːt/

● hit → hit the jackpot

jam /dʒæm/

be in a 'jam (*informal*)
be in a difficult situation: *I'm in a bit of a jam. Could you give me a lift to the train station?*

jam on the 'brake(s) ◆ **jam the 'brake(s) on**
make a vehicle stop very suddenly by operating the brakes with force: *The car skidded as he jammed on the brakes.*

jam to'morrow (*BrE, informal*)
good things that are promised for the future but never happen: *They refused to settle for a promise of jam tomorrow.*

> ❷ ORIGIN
> This comes from Lewis Carroll's *Through the Looking-Glass* (1871) in which the Queen says to Alice 'The rule is, jam tomorrow and jam yesterday but never jam today.'

● money → money for jam **SEE** money for old rope

Jane /ˌdʒeɪn/

● plain → a plain Jane

jaw /dʒɔː/

your 'jaw drops
your mouth opens because you are very surprised: *When they told her that she had won a million dollars, her jaw dropped in amazement.*
▶ **'jaw-dropping** *adj.*: *Taking the desert road was a jaw-dropping experience.*

jaws /dʒɔːz/

the jaws of 'death, de'feat, etc. (*literary*)
used to describe an unpleasant situation that almost happens: *The team snatched victory from the jaws of defeat.*

jazz /dʒæz/

and all that 'jazz (*spoken, informal*)
and things like that: *I was no good at history at school — dates and battles and all that jazz.*

Jekyll /'dʒekl/

a Jekyll and 'Hyde
a person with two separate personalities or ways of behaving, one good, pleasant, etc. and one evil, unpleasant, etc: *He's a real Jekyll and Hyde. At home he shouts at his wife and children all the time; at work he's always charming and friendly.*

> ❷ ORIGIN
> This comes from a story by Robert Louis Stevenson, *Dr Jekyll and Mr Hyde*, in which Dr Jekyll takes a drug which separates the good and bad sides of his personality into two characters. All the negative aspects go into the character of Mr Hyde.

jelly /'dʒeli/

be/feel like 'jelly (also **turn to 'jelly**)
(of legs or knees) feel weak because you are nervous or frightened.: *She couldn't move — her head was swimming, her mouth was dry and her legs felt like jelly.*

● shake → shake like a jelly/leaf

jest /dʒest/

in 'jest
as a joke: *The remark was made half in jest.*
◇ *'Many a true word is spoken in jest,'* thought Rosie (= people often say things as a joke that are actually true).

jet /dʒet/

the 'jet set
the group of very rich and fashionable people who travel a lot, either on business or for pleasure: *She's really joined the jet set now, skiing in St. Moritz, winter holidays in Barbados, shopping in Paris...* ▶ **'jet-setter** *noun* a person who belongs to the jet set: *His job takes him to New York, Tokyo, Rome and Madrid. He's a real jet-setter.*

jetsam /'dʒetsəm/

● flotsam → flotsam and jetsam

jewel /'dʒuːəl/

the jewel in the 'crown
the most attractive or valuable part of sth: *The research facility is considered the jewel in the crown of the nation's technology industry.*

jinks /dʒɪŋks/

● high → high jinks

jitters /'dʒɪtəz; AmE -tərz/

get/have the 'jitters (*informal*)
feel anxious and nervous, especially before an important event or before having to do sth difficult: *I always get the jitters before exams.* ◇ *Louise had the pre-wedding jitters so badly she nearly didn't make it to the church.*

Job /dʒəʊb; AmE dʒoʊb/

a Job's 'comforter (*old-fashioned*)
a person who is sympathetic but says things which make you feel even more unhappy than you are already: *Ann came to see me when I was in hospital. She was a real Job's comforter! She told me about somebody who had the same operation as me, and then died a month later.*

> ❷ ORIGIN
> Job is a character in the Bible. His friends pretended to comfort him but were actually criticizing him.

● patience → the patience of a saint/of Job

job /dʒɒb; AmE dʒɑːb/

do a good, bad, etc. 'job (on sth) ♦ **make a good, bad, etc. job of sth**
do sth well, badly, etc: *They did a very professional job.* ◇ *You've certainly made an excellent job of the kitchen* (= for example, painting it).

do the 'job/'trick (*informal*)
do what is needed or wanted: *These pills should do the job. You'll feel better in no time.* ◇ *I tried many different ways to stop smoking. Acupuncture finally did the trick.*

give sb/sth up as a bad 'job (*informal*)
decide that it is impossible to do sth or to change sb and then stop trying to do it: *'Are you still studying Japanese?' 'No, I gave it up as a bad job. It was far too difficult for me!'*

Good 'job! (*AmE, spoken*)
used to tell sb that they have done well at sth: *You finished already? Good job!*

(it's) a good job/thing (that)… (*spoken*)
(it's) lucky: *It's a good job he was here. We couldn't have moved the piano without him.* ◇ *It's a good job my luggage was insured.*

(and) a ˌgood job/thing 'too (*spoken*)
used to show that you are pleased to hear some news, especially if you have been waiting for it for a long time: *'They've cut the price of petrol.' 'And a good thing too.'* ◇ *He's given up smoking, and a good job too in my opinion.*

have a (hard/difficult) job doing/to do sth
find it difficult to do sth: *I had a job getting to work on time this morning. The traffic was terrible.* ◇ *He had a hard job to make himself heard.*

a job of 'work (*BrE, old-fashioned or formal*)
work that you are paid to do or that must be done: *There was a job of work waiting for him that he was not looking forward to.*

just the 'job/'ticket (*informal*)
exactly what is wanted or needed: *That cup of tea was just the job.*

more than your 'job's worth (to do sth) (*BrE, spoken*)
not worth doing because it is against the rules or because it might cause you to lose your job: *I'm afraid I can't do that. It would be more than my job's worth.*

on the 'job
1 while actually working, and not drinking coffee, talking, wasting time, etc: *I've been on the job all day, and I feel exhausted.* ◇ *At work we can smoke in the canteen, but not on the job.*
2 (*BrE, slang*) having sex

- **best** → make the best of sth/things/a bad job
- **day** → don't give up the day job
- **hatchet** → a hatchet job (on sb/sth)
- **lie** → lie down on the job
- **put-up** → a put-up job
- **snow** → a snow job
- **walk** → walk off the job

jobs /dʒɒbz; AmE dʒɑːbz/

jobs for the 'boys (*BrE, informal, disapproving*)
good jobs, positions or contracts that are given to people only or mainly because they are friends, relatives or supporters: *The city officials here are completely corrupt. It's jobs for the boys.*

- **odd** → odd jobs

Joe /dʒəʊ; AmE dʒoʊ/

Joe 'Bloggs (*BrE*) (*AmE* **Joe 'Blow**) (*informal*)
a way of referring to a typical ordinary person: *What will this promised cut in taxes really mean to Joe Bloggs and his family?* ◇ *As the son of a senator, of course he has advantages that the average Joe Blow doesn't have.*

Joe 'Public (*BrE*) (*AmE* **John ˌQ. 'Public**) (*informal*)
people in general; the public: *Once again, it seems that Joe Public is paying the price for inefficient management.*

jog /dʒɒg; AmE dʒɑːg/

jog sb's 'memory
help sb to remember sth: *So you don't remember Mary Woodson? Well, here's a photograph of you with her which might jog your memory.*

John /dʒɒn; AmE dʒɑːn/

- **Joe** → John Q. Public **SEE** Joe Public

joie /ʒwʌ/

ˌjoie de 'vivre (*from French, written*)
a feeling of great happiness and enjoyment of life: *After the depressing events of the last few months, Mina felt that it was time to put a little joie de vivre back into their lives.*

> **NOTE**
> This French phrase means 'joy of living'.

join /dʒɔɪn/

join the 'club
said as a reply to sb who tells you their bad news when you are or have been in the same situation yourself; an expression of sympathy: *'I failed the exam again!' 'Join the club! Pete, Sarah and I have as well, so don't worry!'*

join 'hands (with sb)
1 if two people **join hands**, they hold each other's hands
2 work together in doing sth: *Education has been reluctant to join hands with business.*

- **battle** → do/join battle (with sb)
- **beat** → if you can't beat them, join them
- **connect** → join (up) the dots **SEE** connect the dots
- **forces** → join/combine forces (with sb)

joined /dʒɔɪnd/

joined at the 'hip
1 (*humorous*) used to say that two people are never apart and spend a great deal of time together: *She and Scott didn't separate all night. It's like they're joined at the hip or something.*
2 used to say that two things are closely connected to each other: *Astronomy isn't physics, but they're joined at the hip.* ◊ *The two companies are joined at the hip through their joint ownership of the TV station.*

joint /dʒɔɪnt/

out of 'joint
1 (of a bone) pushed out of its correct position
2 not working or behaving in the normal way: *Time is thrown completely out of joint in the opening chapters of the book.*

● **case** → case the joint
● **nose** → put sb's nose out of joint

joke /dʒəʊk; AmE dʒoʊk/

be/get/go beyond a 'joke
be no longer funny; be serious: *This has got beyond a joke! Open this door and let me out at once!* ◊ *The state of the roads in this country is beyond a joke.*

be no ''joke
be serious or difficult: *Trying to find a job nowadays is no joke.* ◊ *It's no joke living on such a small income.*

the joke's on 'sb (*informal*)
used to say that sb who tried to make another person look ridiculous now looks ridiculous instead

make a 'joke of sth
laugh about sth that is serious or should be taken seriously: *Don't make a joke of it! I could lose my job because of this!*

take a 'joke
find a joke or trick which is played on you amusing and accept it: *He didn't think it was funny at all when we put that pin on his chair. He really can't take a joke, can he?*

● **crack** → crack a joke
● **practical** → (play) a practical joke (on sb)

joker /dʒəʊkə(r); AmE dʒoʊk-/

the joker in the 'pack
a person or thing who could change the way that things will happen in a way that cannot be predicted: *Everyone knew each other well, except for the new guy Jason, who was the joker in the pack.*

> **NOTE**
> The *pack* here is a set of playing cards. In every pack there are two extra cards, which are called *jokers*.

joking /dʒəʊkɪŋ; AmE dʒoʊkɪŋ/

joking a'part/a'side (*BrE*)
used to show that you are now being serious after you have said sth funny: *No, but joking apart, do you think we should go and see if she's OK?*

you must be 'joking! ✦ **you're 'joking!** (*informal*)
used to show that you do not believe sth, or that you find sth ridiculous: *'It's the best movie I've ever seen.' 'You must be joking!'* ◊ *'The boss wants us to work late again.' 'What? You're joking!'*

jolly /dʒɒli; AmE dʒɑːli/

jolly 'good! (*old-fashioned, BrE, spoken*)
used to show that you approve of sth that sb has just said: *So you and Alan are going away for the weekend, are you? Jolly good.*

'jolly well (*old-fashioned, BrE*)
used to emphasize a statement when you are annoyed about sth: *If you don't come now, you can jolly well walk home!*

Joneses /dʒəʊnzɪz; AmE dʒoʊn-/

keep up with the 'Joneses (*informal, disapproving*)
try to have all the possessions and social achievements that your neighbours or other people around you have, especially by buying what they buy: *First the Smiths got a swimming pool, and now their neighbours, the Sinclairs, are building one. It's silly the way people always have to keep up with the Joneses.*

> **NOTE**
> *Jones* is a very common surname, and is used to refer to neighbours in general.

jot /dʒɒt; AmE dʒɑːt/

not one/a 'jot (or 'tittle) (*informal*)
not even the smallest amount: *There's not a jot of truth in the story.* ◊ *It seems that his divorce has not affected him one jot.* ◊ *She doesn't seem to care a jot what I do.*

jowl /dʒaʊl/

● **cheek** → cheek by jowl (with sb/sth)

joy /dʒɔɪ/

(get/have) no 'joy (from sb) (*informal*)
(get/have) no success or luck in getting sth you want: *I tried to find that record but no joy.* ◊ *'I've just been fishing.' 'Any joy?' 'Yes, I caught a big one.'* ◊ *You won't get any joy from her. She doesn't give money to any kind of charity.*

● **bundle** → a bundle of joy
● **pride** → your pride and joy

joys /dʒɔɪz/

● **full** → full of the joys of spring

judge /dʒʌdʒ/

don't judge a ,book by its 'cover (*saying*)
used to say that you should not form an opinion about sb/sth from their appearance only: *When we arrived we found that the hotel we'd booked looked awful, but as they say, you should never judge a book by its cover.*

● **sober** → (as) sober as a judge

judgement (*especially BrE*) (*AmE* usually judgment) /'dʒʌdʒmənt/

- **better** → against your better judgement
- **pass** → pass judgement (on/about sb/sth)
- **sit** → sit in judgement (on/over sb)
- **value** → a value judgement

juggling /'dʒʌɡlɪŋ/

- **act** → a balancing/juggling act

jugular /'dʒʌɡjələ(r)/

go for the 'jugular (*informal*)
attack sb's weakest point during a discussion in an aggressive way: *Harry decided that there was no point trying to be nice to these people — he would have to go straight for the jugular.*

> **NOTE**
> The *jugular vein* is a large vein in the neck that carries blood from the head to the heart.

jump /dʒʌmp/

be/stay one jump a'head (of sb/sth)
have/keep your advantage over sb by taking action before they do or by making sure you know more than they do: *For years he has managed to stay one jump ahead of the police.* ◇ *People who are successful in business are always one jump ahead of the competition.*

go (and) jump in a/the 'lake (*spoken*)
used to tell sb in a rude way to go away or to stop doing something: *I'm sick of you and your stupid questions. Go and jump in the lake!* ◇ *She made me so angry that I told her to go jump in a lake.*

jump down sb's 'throat (*informal*)
react to sth that sb has said or done by suddenly speaking to them angrily: *He asked her a very simple question and she jumped down his throat. He couldn't believe it.* ◇ *It's not my fault. Don't jump down my throat.*

jump the 'gun (*informal*)
do sth before the right time: *They jumped the gun by building the garage before they got permission from the town council.*

> **NOTE**
> This idiom refers to an athlete in a race who starts running before the starter has fired the gun.

jump the 'lights (*informal*)
drive on when the traffic lights are red: *A policeman stopped us for jumping the lights.*

jump out of your 'skin (*informal*)
make a quick, sudden movement because sth has suddenly frightened you: *When I heard the explosion, I nearly jumped out of my skin.* ◇ *She nearly jumped out of her skin when somebody banged on the door in the middle of the night.*

The sight of a spider made her jump out of her skin.

jump the 'queue (*BrE*) (*AmE* **jump the 'line, cut in 'line**)
go to the front of a line of people without waiting for your turn: *I get very angry with people who jump the queue.* ▸ **'queue-jumping** (*BrE*) (*AmE* **'line-jumping** *less frequent*) *noun*: *This practice encourages queue-jumping for medical services.*

'jump the shark (*AmE*)
if a television programme **jumps the shark**, it starts to decline in quality and introduces ridiculous ideas in order to maintain the interest of the public

> **? ORIGIN**
> This comes from the TV series *Happy Days*, in which on one show a character jumped over a shark while waterskiing.

jump 'ship
1 (of a sailor) leave the ship on which you are serving, without permission: *Two of the sailors jumped ship in New York.*
2 leave an organization that you belong to, suddenly and unexpectedly: *When they realized that the company was in serious financial trouble, quite a few of the staff jumped ship.*

jump through 'hoops
do sth difficult or complicated in order to achieve sth: *How did you manage to get permission for this? Did you have to jump through hoops?*

> **NOTE**
> This refers to the circus, where animals are made to jump through a *hoop* (= a large ring of plastic, iron, etc.).

jump 'to it (*AmE* also **hop 'to it**) (*informal*)
used to tell sb to hurry and do sth quickly: *You have got ten minutes to clean this room. Now jump to it.* ◇ *Hop to it, will you? We don't have much time.*

- **bandwagon** → climb/jump on the bandwagon
- **conclusions** → jump/leap to conclusions
- **deep** → jump in/be thrown in at the deep end
- **high** → be for the high jump
- **quantum** → a quantum jump SEE a quantum leap
- **running** → take a running jump

jungle /'dʒʌŋgl/

- **law** → the law of the jungle

jury /'dʒʊəri; AmE 'dʒʊri/

the jury is/are (still) 'out (on sth)
people have not yet decided if sth is good or bad:
*No one knows whether the government's housing
policy is popular or not. The jury is still out on that
until the next election.* ◇ *Was he a good leader? The
jury is still out on that question.*

NOTE

The *jury* is a group of members of the public
who listen to the facts of a case in a court of law
and decide whether or not a person is guilty of
a crime. They leave the courtroom to discuss
the case and make their decision in secret.

just /dʒʌst/

could/might just as well...
used to say that you/sb would have been in the
same position if you had done sth else, because
you got little benefit or enjoyment from what you
did do: *The weather was so bad we might just as
well have stayed at home.*

just about (*informal*)
1 almost; nearly: *I've just about finished my essay.*
◇ *'Do you feel all right?' 'I suppose so, just about.'*
2 approximately; about: *The company has lost just
about a million pounds this year.* ◇ *It was just about
midnight when they arrived.*

just like 'that
suddenly and unexpectedly: *She announced that
she was leaving her job at the end of this week, just
like that.*

just a 'minute/'moment/'second (*informal*)
used to ask sb to wait for a short time: *'Is Mr Burns
available?' 'Just a second, please, I'll check.'*

just 'now
1 at this moment: *Come and see me later — I'm
busy just now.*
2 during this present period: *Business is good just
now.*
3 only a short time ago: *I saw her just now.*

just 'so
1 as it should be; with everything in its proper
place or with everything done properly: *He likes
his office to be just so, with everything in its place.*
2 (*old-fashioned, formal*) yes, I agree: *'This must
never happen again.' 'Just so.'*

just 'then
at that moment: *Just then, someone knocked at the
front door.*

not just 'yet
not now but probably quite soon: *I can't give you
the money just yet.*

that's just 'it (also **that's just the 'trouble**)
(*informal*)
that is exactly the problem: *'You only need to spend
£5 more and you can get a really good dictionary.'
'That's just it, I'm afraid — I haven't got another £5.'*

justice /'dʒʌstɪs/

bring sb to 'justice
arrest sb for a crime and put them on trial in a
court of law: *It is his job to bring the murderer to
justice.*

do justice to 'sb/'sth ◆ ˌdo sb/sth 'justice
say or do sth which shows that you know or recognize the true value of sb/sth; show the true
value of sth: *They were not hungry and couldn't do
justice to her excellent cooking.* ◇ *This picture
doesn't do him justice; he's much better-looking in
real life.*

ˌdo yourself 'justice
do sth as well as you can in order to show other
people how good you are: *She's a very good painter, but in her recent work she hasn't done herself
justice.* ◇ *He didn't do himself justice in the match.
He hadn't trained hard enough.*

- **pervert** → pervert the course of justice
- **poetic** → poetic justice
- **rough** → rough justice

justifies /'dʒʌstɪfaɪz/

- **end** → the end justifies the means

K k

keel /kiːl/

- **even** → on an even keel

keen /kiːn/

(as) ˌkeen as 'mustard (*BrE, informal*)
wanting very much to do well at sth; enthusiastic:
*She's as keen as mustard. She always gets here first
in the morning and she's the last to leave work in the
evening.*

- **mad** → be mad keen (on sb/sth)

keep /kiːp/

Most idioms containing the verb **keep** are at
the entries for the nouns or adjectives in the
idioms, for example **keep your nose clean** is at
nose.

ˌkeep 'going
1 make an effort to live normally when you are in
a difficult situation or when you have experienced
great suffering: *You just have to keep yourself busy
and keep going.*

2 (*spoken*) used to encourage sb to continue doing sth: *Keep going, Sarah, you're nearly there.*

,keep sb 'going (*informal*)
be enough for sb until they get what they are waiting for: *Why don't you have an apple to keep you going till dinner time?*

,keep it 'up
used to tell sb to continue doing sth as well as they are already doing it: *They've done well so far. I just wonder how long they can keep it up.*

,keep sth to your'self
not tell other people about sth: *I don't want John to know about this, so keep it to yourself.*
OPP spread the word

keep your,self to your'self
avoid meeting people socially or becoming involved in their affairs: *My neighbour keeps himself to himself. We smile and say 'good morning,' but that's all.*

keepers /'ki:pəz; *AmE* 'ki:pərz/

• finders → finders keepers

keeping /'ki:pɪŋ/

in sb's 'keeping
being taken care of by sb: *The documents were all in the safe keeping of the family solicitor, and would remain so until her death.*

in 'keeping (with sth)
appropriate or expected in a particular situation; in agreement with sth: *The furniture should be in keeping with the style of the house.*

out of 'keeping (with sth)
not appropriate or expected in a particular situation; not in agreement with sth: *Her remarks were quite out of keeping with the formality of the occasion.*

keeps /ki:ps/

for 'keeps (*informal*)
permanently; for ever: *'Are you really giving me this beautiful ring?' 'Yes, it's yours. For keeps.'*

ken /ken/

beyond/outside your 'ken (*old-fashioned*)
not within your knowledge or understanding: *Such things are beyond my ken.*

> **NOTE**
> Ken is an old word for 'knowledge'.

kettle /'ketl/

• different → a different kettle of fish
• pot → the pot calling the kettle black

key /ki:/

• lock → under lock and key

kibosh /'kaɪbɒʃ; *AmE* -bɑːʃ/

put the 'kibosh on sth (*old-fashioned*, *informal*)
stop sth from happening: *Melissa's parents put the kibosh on her plans for a big party at her house on her birthday.*

kick /kɪk/

get a 'kick from/out of sth (*informal*)
get a feeling of excitement, enjoyment, etc. out of sth: *She got a real kick from seeing her photo in the newspaper.*

,kick against the 'pricks
harm yourself by protesting when it is useless to do so: *People in prison learn very quickly not to kick against the pricks. If they complain, the prison officers make their lives very difficult.*

> **❷ ORIGIN**
> This idiom comes from the Bible and refers to the fact that an animal such as an ox may kick when it is *pricked* (= pushed with a stick) to make it move, but will still have to move.

kick (some/sb's) 'ass/'butt (⚠ *slang*, *AmE*)
act in a very firm, controlling or aggressive manner: *Now let's kick some butt!*▶ 'kick-ass *adj.* (⚠ *slang*, *AmE*) very good: *a kick-ass rock band*

,kick the 'bucket (*BrE*, *informal* or *humorous*)
die: *He got married for the first time when he was 75 and a week later he kicked the bucket.*

> **❷ ORIGIN**
> This idiom refers to the killing of animals for food. They were hung from a wooden frame (the *bucket*), which they would kick as they were dying.

kick the 'habit, 'drug, 'booze, etc.
stop doing sth harmful that you have done for a long time: *According to research, only one smoker in a hundred is able to kick the habit without some kind of help.*

kick your 'heels (*BrE*, *informal*)
have nothing to do while you are waiting for sth: *I've been kicking my heels here for an hour, waiting for the passport office to open.*

kick sb in the 'teeth (*informal*)
treat sb badly or fail to give them help when they need it: *The workers feel they've been kicked in the teeth by their employers. They have met all their orders this year but are still being made redundant.*
▶ a kick in the 'teeth *noun*: *I expected to get that job. It was a real kick in the teeth when I didn't.*

kick sth into the long 'grass ♦ kick sth into 'touch (both *BrE*)
reject, remove or stop dealing with a problem: *He tends to deal with disputes by kicking them into the long grass.*

> **NOTE**
> In rugby and football, if a ball is kicked into *touch* (= the area outside the lines that mark the sides of the playing field), play stops.

,**kick over the 'traces** (*old-fashioned, BrE*)
start to behave badly and refuse to accept any discipline or control: *She smokes and she drinks. She's
really kicking over the traces, and her parents don't
know what to do with her.*

> ❷ ORIGIN
> This phrase refers to a horse that has managed
> to lift its leg(s) over the long thin strips of lea-
> ther (the *traces*) that attach it to a carriage or
> wagon so that it can kick more easily. The
> driver then cannot control it.

kick the 'tyres (*BrE*) (*AmE* **kick the 'tires**)
(*especially AmE*)
test the quality of sth; see if sth is suitable for you:
*We now spend longer kicking the tyres before invest-
ing in new companies.* ▶ **'tyrekicker** (*BrE*) (*AmE*
'tirekicker) *noun* a possible customer who asks a
lot of questions about a product but never buys
anything: *Your sales team can waste a huge amount
of time on tyrekickers.*

a kick up the 'backside (also **a kick in the 'pants**)
(*informal*)
a shock, strong criticism, etc. which encourages sb
to do sth or to behave better: *What he needs is a
good kick up the backside. Then he'd do some work.*

> NOTE
> Your *backside* is the part of the body that you
> sit on.

kick up a 'fuss, 'row, etc. (*informal*)
complain very noisily and loudly about sth: *He
kicked up a real fuss about the slow service in the
restaurant.* ◇ *Every time her newspaper arrives
late, she kicks up a fuss.*

kick up your 'heels (*informal, especially AmE*)
be relaxed and enjoy yourself: *Now that he's more
confident in his job, perhaps he can kick up his heels
and stop looking so worried all the time.*

,**kick sb up'stairs** (*informal*)
move sb to a job that seems to be more important
but which actually has less power or influence:
*They couldn't sack him, so they kicked him upstairs
onto the board of directors, where he could do less
damage.*

kick sb when they're 'down
continue to hurt sb when they are already defeated, etc: *George generally believed that you should
never kick a man when he's down, but thought that
this time he might make an exception.*

'**kick yourself** (*informal*)
be angry with yourself for sth you have done or
not done: *Buy it. It's a real bargain. You'll kick yourself if you don't.* ◇ *I told John that Susan was really
lazy. Then somebody told me that she was a good
friend of his. I could have kicked myself for being so
stupid.*

- **hell** → beat/knock/kick the hell out of sb/sth
- **hell** → beat/knock/kick the shit out of sb/sth **SEE** beat/
  knock/kick the hell out of sb/sth
- **stink** → kick up/make/create/raise a stink (about sth)

kicking /'kɪkɪŋ/

- **alive** → alive and kicking

kicks /kɪks/

for 'kicks (*informal*)
(especially of crime or violence) done for excitement and pleasure: *They destroyed the telephone
boxes just for kicks.* ◇ '*Why did he steal the car?*'
'*Just for kicks. He was bored.*'

kid /kɪd/

handle, treat, etc. sb with kid 'gloves
treat sb very carefully and gently because you do
not want to upset them or make them angry: *She
is so easily upset that I feel I have to treat her with
kid gloves all the time.*

> NOTE
> *Kid gloves* are made of very soft leather from
> the skin of a *kid* (= a young goat).

like a kid in a 'candy store/shop (*AmE*)
used to say that sb is very happy and excited about
sth: *It was my first time in a championship game, so
I felt like a kid in a candy store.* ◇ *I'm like a kid in a
candy store when it comes to technology. It all looks
so good!*

- **kids** → kid stuff **SEE** kids' stuff
- **new** → a/the new kid on the block

kidding /'kɪdɪŋ/

,**no 'kidding** (*spoken*)
1 (*sometimes ironic*) used to emphasize that sth is
true or that you agree with sth that sb has just
said: '*It's cold!*' '*No kidding!*'
2 used to show that you mean what you are saying: *I want the money back tomorrow. No kidding.*

you're 'kidding ♦ you must be 'kidding
(*spoken*)
used to show that you are very surprised at sth
that sb has just said: '*Did you hear about Christine?
She won some money on the lottery.*' '*You're kidding! How much?*' ◇ *You've called the police? You're
kidding me!*

kids /kɪdz/

'**kids' stuff** (*BrE*) (*AmE* '**kid stuff**)
something that is very easy to do or understand:
'*What did you think of the maths exam?*' '*Kids'
stuff. I'm sure I've passed.*'

kill /kɪl/

,**kill the fatted 'calf**
welcome home sb who has been away for a long
time by having a big celebration: *My brother's
coming home tomorrow, so I expect my parents will
be killing the fatted calf for him.*

> ❷ ORIGIN
> This is from a story in the Bible, in which a
> father arranges a special meal when his son
> returns to the family after a long time away. A
> *fatted calf* is a young cow that has been given
> extra food to make it fat.

,kill or 'cure (*BrE*)
extreme action which will either be a complete
success or a complete failure: *This new chemical
will either clean the painting perfectly or it will
damage it badly. It's kill or cure.*

kill sth stone 'dead (*informal*)
completely destroy sth; end sth: *This has killed my
chances of promotion in this company stone dead.*

kill 'time, a couple of 'hours, etc. ♦ have
'time, a couple of 'hours, etc. to kill
do sth to help pass the time while you are waiting
for sth: *'What did you do at the airport when your
plane was late?' 'We killed time by playing cards
and doing crosswords.'* ◇ *I had two hours to kill
before the train left, so I went to see a movie.*

kill two birds with one 'stone
manage to achieve two aims by doing one thing: *If
we have to go to Manchester for the meeting, then
let's visit Auntie Joan on the way there. We can kill
two birds with one stone.*

,kill sb with 'kindness
harm sb by being too kind to them, usually without realizing what you are doing: *The patient
needs lots of exercise. Don't let him stay in bed —
you'll kill him with kindness.* **OPP** be cruel to be kind

'kill yourself ('laughing) (*BrE, informal*)
laugh a lot: *It was a very funny video. We killed ourselves laughing from beginning to end.* ◇ *He just
stood there killing himself laughing.*

'kill yourself doing sth (*informal*)
make a very great effort to do sth: *It would be good
to leave at 7 o'clock, but don't kill yourself getting
here by then. We can leave a bit later if we need to.*
◇ *I nearly killed myself finishing the report in time
for this meeting.*

• death → be in at the death/kill
• dressed → dressed to kill
• looks → if looks could kill...

killed /kɪld/

• curiosity → curiosity killed the cat

killing /'kɪlɪŋ/

,make a 'killing (*informal*)
make a lot of money quickly: *He was clever. He
invested a lot of money in property. When prices
went up, he made a killing.* **OPP** lose your shirt

kilter /'kɪltə(r)/

out of 'kilter
out of harmony or balance; not working properly:
*Long-haul flights tend to throw your body clock out
of kilter for a couple of days.*

kin /kɪn/

• kith → kith and kin
• next → your next of kin

kind /kaɪnd/

in 'kind
1 (of payment) in the form of goods or services,
not money: *People in the country used to pay the
doctor in kind with meat, vegetables, eggs and
things like that.*
2 do the same thing to sb as they have done to
you, usually something unpleasant: *If they attack
our troops, we will retaliate in kind.*

'kind of/'sort of (*informal*)
used with adjectives, adverbs and verbs when
something is difficult to describe or when the
word you use is not exactly what you mean: *She
kind of smiled at me.* ◇ *My new dress is sort of
green.* ◇ *He said it sort of nervously.*

NOTE
These phrases are sometimes written or
spoken as *kinda* or *sorta*.

nothing of the 'kind/'sort (*informal*)
not at all as sb said or as you expected: *The brochure said it would be a beginners' course but it's
nothing of the sort.* ◇ *I said nothing of the kind.
She completely misunderstood me.*

of a 'kind
people or things with similar characteristics: *Uncle
Fred and your father are two of a kind; football and
work, that's all they seem to be interested in.* ◇ *He
always uses the same style of photography and similar music so all his films are very much of a kind.*

of a 'kind/'sort (*disapproving*)
(used after a noun) of poor quality; not what sb/
sth should be: *He is a poet of a kind.* ◇ *They gave us
meat of a sort; we could hardly eat it.*

one of a 'kind
the only one like this: *My father was one of a kind
— I'll never be like him.*

something of the/that 'kind/'sort
something like what has been said: *'He's resign-
ing.' 'I'd suspected something of the kind.'*

• cruel → be cruel to be kind

kindly /'kaɪndli/

look 'kindly on/upon sb/sth (*formal*)
approve of sb/sth: *He hoped they would look kindly
on his request.*

not take 'kindly to sb/sth
find it difficult to accept sb/sth: *I don't take kindly
to criticism from him.* ◇ *She didn't take kindly to
my suggestion.*

kindness /'kaɪndnəs/

• kill → kill sb with kindness
• milk → the milk of human kindness

King /kɪŋ/

• English → the King's/Queen's English
• evidence → turn King's/Queen's evidence

knee

king /kɪŋ/

a ˌking's 'ransom (*literary*)
a very large amount of money: *We don't exactly get paid a king's ransom in this job.*

> **❷ ORIGIN**
> In the past, if a king was captured in a war, his country would pay a ransom for his release.

● **live¹** → live like a king
● **uncrowned** → (be) the uncrowned king/queen (of sth)

kingdom /'kɪŋdəm/

blow, send, etc. sb to kingdom 'come (*informal*)
kill sb, especially with a gun, a bomb or other very violent methods: *'If you try to call the police, I'll blow you to kingdom come.'*

till/until kingdom 'come (*old-fashioned*)
for a long time, for ever: *You can dig here until kingdom come, but you will never find water.*

> **NOTE**
> The expression *kingdom come* in these two idioms means heaven or the next world.

kiss /kɪs/

ˌkiss and 'tell
a way of referring to sb talking publicly, usually for money, about a past sexual relationship with sb famous: *Despite all the money the tabloids were offering for her story, she was determined not to kiss and tell.*

kiss (sb's) 'arse (*BrE*) (*AmE* **kiss (sb's) 'ass**) (⚠, *slang*)
be very nice to sb in order to persuade them to help you or to give you sth

> **NOTE**
> A more polite way to express this is 'lick sb's boots'.

ˌkiss sth 'better (*spoken*)
take away the pain of an injury by kissing it: *Come here and let me kiss it better.*

the kiss of 'death (*informal, often humorous*)
an action or event that seems good, but is certain to make sth else fail: *When the chairman said he had every confidence in me, I knew it was the kiss of death. A week later I was looking for another job.*

the kiss of 'life (*BrE*)
1 a method of helping sb who has stopped breathing to breathe again by placing your mouth on theirs and forcing air into their lungs: *He gave the child the kiss of life, but unfortunately it was too late to save her.*
2 any thing or action that saves an organization, business, etc: *This loan is the kiss of life that our company needs.*

● **goodbye** → kiss sth goodbye **SEE** kiss/say goodbye to sth
● **steal** → steal a kiss (from sb)

kit /kɪt/

get your 'kit off (*BrE*, *slang*)
take your clothes off

● **caboodle** → the whole kit and caboodle **SEE** the whole caboodle

kitchen /'kɪtʃɪn/

everything but/bar the kitchen 'sink (*informal, humorous*)
many more things than are necessary: *She was only staying for a few days, but she brought everything with her bar the kitchen sink!*

They always take everything but the kitchen sink when they go on holiday.

kite /kaɪt/

● **fly** → fly a kite
● **fly** → (go) fly a/your kite
● **high** → (as) high as a kite

kith /kɪθ/

kith and 'kin (*old-fashioned*)
friends and relatives: *He has returned to live in Italy, where he'll be surrounded by his kith and kin.*

kittens /'kɪtnz/

have 'kittens (*BrE*, *informal*)
be nervous and anxious, especially when you are waiting for news of sth: *Your poor mother's having kittens. She hasn't heard anything from Simon for three weeks.*

knee /niː/

● **bended** → on bended knee(s)
● **mother** → at your mother's knee

knee-high /ˌniː ˈhaɪ/

knee-high to a 'grasshopper (*informal*, *humorous*)
(of a child) very small; very young: *I haven't seen you since you were knee-high to a grasshopper!*

knees /niːz/

bring sb to their 'knees
show sb that they are weak; defeat sb, especially in a war

bring sth to its 'knees
badly affect an organization, etc. so that it can no longer function: *The strikes brought the industry to its knees.*

your/sb's 'knees are knocking (*informal*)
if your/sb's **knees are knocking**, they are shaking because you are nervous or afraid: *It was the first time I'd ever spoken in public, and my knees were knocking!*

on your 'knees
1 kneeling down: *He was on his knees praying.* ◇ *She was on her knees looking for the coin.*
2 in a very weak state: *The country's economy is on its knees.*

- bee → the bee's knees
- hands → on your hands and knees
- weak → be/go weak at the knees

knell /nel/

- sound → sound the death knell of sth

knickers /ˈnɪkəz; AmE -kərz/

get/have your 'knickers in a twist (*BrE*) (*AmE* **get/have your 'panties in a knot**) (*informal*)
react too strongly to a difficult situation by getting angry, upset, confused, etc: *The boss is getting his knickers in a twist about these sales figures.* ◇ *Don't get your panties in a knot about it! It's no big deal.*

- wet → wet your pants/knickers

knife /naɪf/

get your 'knife into sb ✦ **have your 'knife in sb** (*informal*)
harm and continue to harm sb (usually not physically) whom you consider your enemy: *He's had his knife into me for months, and every time I make a mistake, he tells my boss.*

go under the 'knife (*informal*)
have a medical operation: *Peter hates his nose so much that he's seriously considering going under the knife to have it made smaller.*

like a knife through 'butter
(cut/go) through sth hard easily: *It went through the metal door like a knife through butter.*

put/stick the 'knife in ✦ **put/stick the 'knife into sb** (*informal*)
criticize sb or deliberately try to harm them: *The senator has quite a few enemies that would love to stick the knife in if they got the chance.*

turn/twist the 'knife (in the wound)
deliberately remind sb of sth they are already upset about, and so upset them even more: *After the divorce, her friend turned the knife in the wound by saying she had always thought that the marriage wouldn't last.* ◇ *All right. I know I was stupid. You don't have to twist the knife.*

- atmosphere → you could cut the atmosphere with a knife
- sharpest → not the sharpest knife in the drawer

knife-edge /ˈnaɪf edʒ/

on a 'knife-edge (also **on a 'razor's edge**)
in a very dangerous or difficult situation where there is a risk of sth terrible happening: *He was balanced on a knife-edge between life and death.* ◇ *The future of this company is on a razor's edge.*

knifepoint /ˈnaɪfpɔɪnt/

at 'knifepoint
while being threatened, or threatening sb, with a knife: *She was attacked at knifepoint.*

knight /naɪt/

a knight in shining 'armour (*BrE*) (*AmE* **a knight in shining 'armor**) (*usually humorous*)
a man who arrives to help you when you are in trouble or danger: *My car broke down at the roundabout. Luckily, a knight in shining armour stopped to help me.*

knit /nɪt/

knit your 'brows
frown (= move your eyebrows together), to show that you are thinking hard, feeling angry, etc: *She knitted her brows, trying to think how she could have spent so much money in one week.*

knives /naɪvz/

the knives are 'out (for sb)
the situation has become so bad that people are preparing to make one person take the blame, for example by taking away their job: *The knives are out for the minister. People are calling for his resignation.*

knobs /nɒbz; AmE nɑːbz/

with 'knobs on (*BrE, slang*)
used to say that sth is a more complicated version of what you mention: *It isn't art — it's just a horror movie with knobs on!*

knock /nɒk; AmE nɑːk/

I'll knock your 'block/'head off! (*BrE, spoken*)
used to threaten sb that you will hit them

knock sb 'dead (*spoken*)
impress sb very much: *You look fabulous — you'll knock 'em dead tonight.*

know

knock sb/sth into a cocked 'hat (*BrE*)
be very much better than sb/sth: *This new software is going to knock everything else on the market into a cocked hat.*

> **NOTE**
> A *cocked hat* is an old-fashioned kind of hat with three corners often worn in the army and navy.

knock it 'off! (*spoken*)
used to tell sb to stop making a noise, annoying you, etc: *Knock it off, will you? I'm trying to work.*

knock sb off their 'perch/'pedestal
show that sb does not deserve to be admired so much: *These revelations will really knock him off his pedestal.*

knock sth on the 'head (*BrE, informal*)
stop doing sth; stop sth from happening: *By lunchtime we were all exhausted so we knocked it on the head.* ◇ *The increase in airfares has knocked our plan to travel this year on the head.*

knock sb 'sideways (*informal*)
surprise or shock sb so much that they are unable to react immediately: *Losing his job has really knocked him sideways.*

knock 'spots off sb/sth (*BrE, informal*)
be very much better than sb/sth else: *This book knocks spots of all the other books on Napoleon.* ◇ *You'll knock spots off her. You're a much better player.*

knock the 'stuffing out of sb (*informal*)
make sb feel weak, mentally and/or physically: *When his wife left him, it seemed to knock the stuffing out of him.* ◇ *This flu has really knocked the stuffing out of me.*

> **NOTE**
> *Stuffing* in this idiom refers to the soft material used to fill cushions, toys, etc.

take a (hard, nasty, etc.) 'knock
have an experience that makes sb/sth less confident or successful; be damaged: *His reputation has taken a bit of a knock since the newspapers printed stories about his private life.*

- **heads** → bang/knock your/their heads together
- **hell** → beat/knock/kick the hell out of sb/sth
- **hell** → beat/knock/kick the shit out of sb/sth **SEE** beat/knock/kick the hell out of sb/sth
- **loop** → knock/throw sb for a loop
- **sense** → knock/talk some sense into sb
- **shape** → get/knock/lick sb/sth into shape
- **six** → hit/knock sb/sth for six
- **socks** → blow/knock sb's socks off
- **touch** → knock on wood **SEE** touch wood

knocked /nɒkt; *AmE* nɑːkt/

you could have knocked me, etc. down with a 'feather (*informal*)
used to tell sb about a very surprising experience: *When they said how much the painting was worth, you could have knocked me down with a feather!*

knocking /'nɒkɪŋ; *AmE* 'nɑːkɪŋ/

- **knees** → your/sb's knees are knocking

knot /nɒt; *AmE* nɑːt/

- **Gordian** → cut/untie the Gordian knot
- **knickers** → get/have your panties in a knot **SEE** get/have your knickers in a twist
- **tie** → tie the knot

knots /nɒts; *AmE* nɑːts/

- **rate** → at a rate of knots
- **tie** → tie sb/yourself (up) in knots

knotted /'nɒtɪd; *AmE* 'nɑːtɪd/

- **stuffed** → get knotted **SEE** get stuffed

know /nəʊ; *AmE* noʊ/

before you know where you 'are
before you have time to realize that sth has happened: *We were whisked off in a cab before we knew where we were.* ◇ *Before she knew where she was, her bag had been snatched and the thief was running away with it.*

be not to 'know
have no way of realizing or being aware that you have done sth wrong: *'I'm sorry I called when you were asleep.' 'Don't worry — you weren't to know.'*

for all 'I, 'you, etc. know (*spoken*)
used to emphasize that you sb does not know sth: *She could be dead for all I know.*

in the 'know (*informal*)
having information or knowledge that most other people do not have: *Only a few of us were in the know about the date of the wedding. We didn't want the press to find out.* ◇ *People in the know say that this is the best Spanish wine you can buy.*

it ˌtakes one to 'know one (*informal, disapproving*)
you are the same kind of person as the person you are criticizing: *'Your brother is a real idiot.' 'Well, it takes one to know one.'*

know sb/sth 'backwards (*informal, especially BrE*)
know sb/sth extremely well: *He must know the play backwards by now — he's seen it six times!*

know 'best
know what should be done in a situation because you have knowledge and/or experience: *'I want to get up.' 'But the doctor said you were to stay in bed, and he knows best.'* ◇ *Everyone said that I shouldn't go there alone but I thought I knew best.*

know 'better (than that/than to do sth)
be sensible enough not to do sth: *You left the car unlocked? I thought you'd know better.* ◇ *He knows better than to judge by appearances.*

know sb by 'sight
recognize sb and know who they are, without having spoken to them: *I haven't actually met Dr. Galston, but I know him by sight of course.*

know

know 'different/'otherwise (*informal*)
have more information about sth: *She thought he was upset about the divorce, but I knew different.*

know sth ,full/,perfectly/,very 'well
used when you wish to indicate that the person you are speaking to already knows sth you have just said or are about to say: *You know full well that smoking is forbidden in this room.* ◇ *You know perfectly well what I am referring to.*

know sb/sth inside 'out (*informal*)
know sb/sth very well: *You've read that book so often that you must know it inside out by now.* ◇ *She knows me inside out. I can't hide anything from her.*

know sth like the back of your 'hand (*informal*)
know a place very well: *As a taxi driver, you have to know the city like the back of your hand.*

know no 'bounds
(usually with abstract nouns) be without limits; be very great: *His generosity knows no bounds.*

know your own 'mind
know what you want or like: *At 25 you're old enough to know your own mind and make these decisions for yourself.*

know your 'place
behave in a way that shows that you know what your social position is and which people are more important than you: *My grandfather believed that life was simpler when he was young, when everybody knew their place.*

know the 'score (*informal*)
know the true situation, especially if this is bad: *Look, you know the score, we can't afford a car right now.*

know your 'stuff (*informal*)
know everything that you should know about a job, a subject, etc: *I was very impressed by your lawyer. He really knows his stuff.*

know a thing or two (about sb/sth) (*informal*)
know a lot about sb/sth from your own experience: *After ten years as a teacher, I know a thing or two about how children learn.* ◇ *'How much do you know about computers?' 'Oh, I know a thing or two.'*

know your way a'bout/a'round (sth)
be familiar with a place, with how things are done etc.; be experienced: *I'd used the library before, so I knew my way around and found the book quite quickly.*

know what it is to be/do sth
have personal experience of being/doing sth: *I know what it is to be a mother, so believe me when I say it is very hard work.*

know what you're 'doing/a'bout (*informal*)
have experience of doing sth and therefore understand it fully: *'I'm worried about David using that machine.' 'Don't worry. He knows what he's doing.'*

know what you're 'talking about (*informal*)
have good knowledge of sth; be an expert on sth: *I really enjoyed that lecture. She certainly knows what she's talking about.* ◇ *That history teacher*

doesn't know what he's talking about. He makes a lot of mistakes.

know what's 'good for you
know what is necessary for you to do to be successful, etc.; know how to avoid trouble: *If you know what's good for you, young man, you'll talk to nobody about what you've seen here tonight.*

know what's 'what (*informal*)
know all that needs to be known in a particular situation or in general: *Ask Ann. She knows what's what. She's been here for years.*

know where you 'are/'stand
know what your position is; know what sb expects of you: *I don't know where I stand with him. I don't know what he feels about me.* ◇ *Has she talked to you about your chances of promotion? Do you know where you stand?*

know where you're 'going
know clearly what you want to achieve (in life, in your job, etc.): *He knows exactly where he's going. He wants to be an actor.*

know which side your 'bread is buttered (*informal*)
know what to do in order to gain advantages, stay in a favourable situation, etc: *I'm sure Ray will make a special effort to please the new supervisor — after all, he knows which side his bread is buttered!*

let sb 'know
tell sb about sth: *I don't know if I can come, but I'll let you know soon.* ◇ *Let me know how I can help.*

not know any 'better
not behave well, politely, etc. because you have never learned how to: *You can't blame him for his bad table manners; he doesn't know any better.*

not know you're 'born (*BrE, spoken*)
not realize how easy your life or situation is compared to other people's: *Young people today don't know they're born. Life was much harder when I was a child.*

not know your ,arse from your 'elbow (*BrE*) (*AmE* **not know your ,ass from your 'elbow**) (△, *slang*)
be very stupid or completely lacking in skill: *Don't ask him to organize things! He doesn't know his arse from his elbow!*

not know 'beans about sth (*AmE, informal*)
know nothing about a subject: *I really don't know beans about economics.*

not know the first thing a'bout sb/sth
know nothing at all about sb/sth: *I don't know the first thing about Chinese history.*

not know sb from 'Adam (*informal*)
not know who sb is: *This man came into the office and he said that he knew me. I didn't know him from Adam, which was a bit embarrassing.*

not know the 'meaning of the word (*disapproving*)
not have enough experience of sth to understand what it really is; not be capable of really understanding sth: *Love? He doesn't know the meaning*

of the word. ◇ *They talk about justice, but they don't know the meaning of the word.*

not know what 'hit you (*informal*)
be so surprised by sth that you do not know how to react: *You should have seen his reaction! He didn't know what had hit him!* `OPP` see sth coming

not know what you're 'missing
not realize how good, amusing, interesting, etc. sth is because you have never tried it: *'I'm not really interested in snowboarding.' 'Oh, you should give it a try. You don't know what you're missing.'*

not know what to 'do with yourself
not know how to spend your time: *I hardly know what to do with myself when the children go back to school. I have so much free time.*

not know whether you're 'coming or 'going (*informal*)
be confused about what you are doing, because you are doing too many things at the same time: *I've got so much work to do that I don't know whether I'm coming or going.*

not know whether to 'laugh or 'cry (*informal*)
be unable to decide how to react to a bad or unfortunate situation: *Can you believe she said that to me? I didn't know whether to laugh or cry!*

not know which way/where to 'look (*informal*)
not know how to react or behave in an embarrassing situation: *When a half-naked woman walked into the room, nobody knew where to look.*

not know which way/where to 'turn
not know what to do, where to get help, etc. in a difficult situation: *She didn't know where to turn for help when her daughter started taking drugs.*

(well) what do you 'know (about 'that)? (*informal*)
used to express surprise: *Well, what do you know? Look who's here!*

you 'know (*informal*)
1 used when you are thinking of what to say next: *He's, you know, strange. It's hard to explain.*
2 used to show that what you are referring to is known or understood by the person you are speaking to: *You know I bought a new bag? Well, someone stole it last night.*
3 used to emphasize sth that you are saying: *I'm not stupid, you know.*

,you know as well as 'I do
used when you are trying to convince sb that sth is true: *You know as well as I do that if she finds out, she'll stop us going.*

you know 'who/'what (*spoken*)
used to refer to sb/sth without mentioning a name: *I saw you know who this morning. She didn't even say hello to me.*

you never 'know (with sb/sth)
you cannot be sure (about the behaviour of sb/sth or the quality of sth): *Don't throw away those old stamps. You never know, they might be valuable one day.* ◇ *You never know with him; one day he's smiling and laughing, the next day he won't speak to anybody.*

● **answers** → have/know all the answers
● **better** → better the devil you know (than the devil you don't)
● **end** → not know/not be able to tell one end of sth from the other
● **left** → the left hand doesn't know what the right hand's doing
● **pat** → have/know sth down pat **SEE** have/know/get sth off pat
● **pat** → have/know/get sth off pat
● **ropes** → show sb/learn/know the ropes
● **tell** → I know what **SEE** I/I'll tell you what
● **want** → not want to know (about sth)
● **world** → I don't know what the world's coming to **SEE** what is the world coming to?

knowing /'nəʊɪŋ; *AmE* 'noʊ-/

there's no 'knowing/'saying/'telling...
it is impossible to know/say/tell: *There is no telling what he may do when he gets angry.* ◇ *There's no saying what will happen.*

knowledge /'nɒlɪdʒ; *AmE* 'nɑːl-/

be common/public 'knowledge
be sth that everyone knows, especially in a particular community or group: *What do you mean you're surprised he's leaving? I thought it was common knowledge that he was looking for another job!*

come to sb's 'knowledge (*formal*)
become known by sb: *It has come to our knowledge that you have been taking time off without permission.*

to your 'knowledge
from the information you have, although you may not know everything: *'Are they divorced?' 'Not to my knowledge.'*

● **best** → to the best of your belief/knowledge
● **safe** → safe in the knowledge that...
● **working** → have a working knowledge of sth

known /nəʊn; *AmE* noʊn/

let it be 'known/make it 'known that... (*formal*)
make sure that people are informed about sth, especially by getting sb else to tell them: *The President has let it be known that he does not intend to run for election again.*

make yourself 'known to sb
introduce yourself to sb: *I made myself known to the hotel manager.*

● **best** → for a/some reason/reasons best known to himself, herself, etc.
● **better** → have seen/known better days
● **truth** → if (the) truth be known/told

knows /nəʊz; *AmE* noʊz/

God/goodness/Heaven knows (*spoken*)
1 I do not know; no one knows: *'What's going to happen next?' 'God knows.'*

2 used for adding emphasis to a statement, opinion, etc: *God knows how he manages to survive on such a small salary.* ◇ *I'm no gardening expert, goodness knows!*
(Some people may find the use of **God knows** offensive.)

● Lord → Lord (only) knows (what, where, why, etc.)...

knuckle /'nʌkl/

● near → near the knuckle

knuckles /'nʌklz/

● rap → give sb, get, etc. a rap over the knuckles
● rap → rap sb over the knuckles

Ll

labour (*BrE*) (*AmE* labor) /'leɪbə(r)/

a ˌlabour of ˈlove
a hard task that you do because you want to, not because it is necessary: *This tablecloth is a real labour of love. It took her years to make it.*

labour the ˈpoint
continue to repeat or explain sth that is already clear: *I think you've said enough — there's no need to labour the point.*

lack /læk/

● courage → have/lack the courage of your convictions
● trying → not for lack/want of trying

Lad /læd/

● Jack → a Jack the Lad

ladder /'lædə(r)/

● top → (at) the top of the tree/ladder

ladies /'leɪdiːz/

a ˈladies' man
a man who likes the company of women and is successful with them: *Jim had always been a bit of a ladies' man, and he didn't marry until he was 45.*

lads /lædz/

be one of the ˈlads/ˈboys/ˈgirls (*informal*)
be a member of a group of friends of the same sex and a similar age, who meet regularly to enjoy themselves: *His wife doesn't understand that he likes being one of the lads from time to time.* ◇ *She's never really been one of the girls. She much prefers the company of men.*

lady /'leɪdi/

● bag → a bag lady
● fat → it ain't/it's not over till the fat lady sings

lager /'lɑːgə(r)/

a ˈlager lout (*BrE*)
a young man who drinks too much alcohol and then behaves in a noisy and unpleasant way: *The police are planning to crack down on lager louts this summer.*

lake /leɪk/

● jump → go (and) jump in a/the lake

lam /læm/

on the ˈlam (*AmE, informal*)
escaping from sb, especially from the police: *The man disappeared just before he was due to go to jail and has been on the lam ever since.*

lamb /læm/

● mutton → be mutton dressed (up) as lamb
● slaughter → (like) a lamb/lambs to the slaughter
● two → in two shakes of a lamb's tail **SEE** in two shakes
● well → (you, etc.) may/might as well be hanged/hung for a sheep as (for) a lamb

lame /leɪm/

a ˌlame ˈduck (*informal*)
a person or an organization that is not very successful and needs help: *My uncle is a bit of a lame duck. The family has to help him all the time.* ◇ *The shipping industry had become a lame duck.*

land /lænd/

in the ˌland of the ˈliving (*humorous*)
alive: *Nice to see you. I'm glad to see that you're still in the land of the living.*

in the ˌland of ˈNod (*old-fashioned, humorous*)
asleep: *Pete and Joe were still in the land of Nod, so I went out for a walk in the morning sunshine.*

> **❷ ORIGIN**
> This expression developed from the similarity between the verb 'nod off', meaning to fall asleep, and a place in the Bible called 'the land of Nod'.

land a ˈblow, ˈpunch, etc.
succeed in hitting sb/sth: *She landed a punch on his chin.*

a/the land of ˌmilk and ˈhoney
a place where life is pleasant and easy and people are very happy: *She had always longed to travel to the United States and to see what she imagined as the land of milk and honey.*

> **❷ ORIGIN**
> This phrase comes from the Bible, referring to the Promised Land.

see, etc. how the ˈland lies (*BrE*)
find out about a situation: *Let's wait and see how the land lies before we do anything.*

● feet → fall/land on your feet
● lie → the lay of the land **SEE** the lie of the land
● live¹ → live off/on the fat of the land

- **live¹** → live off the land
- **promised** → the promised land
- **soup** → land yourself/sb in the soup **SEE** be in the soup
- **spy** → spy out the land

landscape /ˈlændskeɪp/

- **blot** → a blot on the landscape

lane /leɪn/

- **fast** → in the fast lane
- **memory** → take a trip down memory lane **SEE** go down/take sb down memory lane
- **slow** → in the slow lane

language /ˈlæŋgwɪdʒ/

mind/watch your 'language
be careful about what you say in order not to upset or offend sb: *Watch your language, young man!*

speak/talk the same/a different 'language
share/not share ideas, experiences, opinions, etc., that make real communication or understanding possible: *Unions and managers are at last beginning to speak the same language.* ◇ *Artists and scientists simply talk a different language.*

lap /læp/

drop/dump sth in sb's 'lap (*informal*)
make sth the responsibility of another person: *They dropped the problem firmly back in my lap.*

drop/fall into sb's 'lap (*informal*)
be obtained without any effort: *A job's not going to just fall in your lap, you know. You'll have to go out and find one!*

in the lap of the 'gods
used to say that the success of something is uncertain because it depends on luck or on things beyond your control: *I don't know what's going to happen — it's in the lap of the gods now. All we can do is wait.*

in the lap of 'luxury
in easy, comfortable conditions, and enjoying the advantages of being rich: *It was a wonderful hotel. I really enjoyed living in the lap of luxury for a couple of weeks.*

- **last** → the last lap

large /lɑːdʒ; AmE lɑːrdʒ/

at 'large
1 (after a noun) as a whole, in general: *The public at large does not know enough about this problem.*
2 (of a dangerous person or animal) free; not captured: *Her killer is still at large.* **OPP** under lock and key

by and 'large (*informal*)
used when you are saying something that is generally, but not completely, true: *By and large, I enjoyed my time at school.*

in 'large part ◆ in ˌno small 'part (*formal*)
to a large extent: *The speech was in large part an attack on the Prime Minister.* ◇ *She was in no small*

part responsible for the success of this company and we mustn't forget that.

(as) large as 'life (*humorous*)
used of sb who is seen in person, often unexpectedly: *I thought she'd left the country, but there she was, large as life, in the supermarket!*

- **loom** → loom large
- **writ** → writ large

larger /ˈlɑːdʒə(r) AmE ˈlɑːrdʒə(r)/

larger than 'life
looking or behaving in a way that is more interesting or exciting than other people, and so is likely to attract attention: *He's one of those larger than life characters.*

lark /lɑːk; AmE lɑːrk/

be ˌup/ˌrise with the 'lark
get up early in the morning: *She was up with the lark this morning.*

> **NOTE**
> A *lark* in this idiom refers to a kind of bird that sings early in the day.

blow/sod △ 'that for a lark (*BrE, slang*)
used by sb who does not want to do sth because it involves too much effort: *Sod that for a lark! I'm not doing any more tonight.*

> **NOTE**
> A *lark* is a thing that you do for fun or as a joke.

Larry /ˈlæri/

- **happy** → (as) happy as the day is long/as a clam/as Larry

last /lɑːst; AmE læst/

at (long) 'last
at the end of a period of waiting, trying etc.; finally: *At long last she's got a job in a theatre in Stratford.*

at the last 'count
according to the latest information about the numbers of sth: *She'd applied for 30 jobs at the last count.*

at the last 'minute/'moment
as late as possible; almost too late: *Why do you always have to arrive at the last moment?*
▶ ˌlast-'minute *adj.*: *last-minute changes of plan, decisions, preparations, etc.*

the day, week, month, etc. before 'last
the day, week, etc. just before the most recent one; two days, weeks, etc. ago: *I haven't seen him since the summer before last.*

every last...
every person or thing in a group: *We spent every last penny we had on the house.*

have the last 'laugh (*informal*)
be successful at sth in the end, even though other people thought that this was not possible: *When he invented this machine, everybody laughed at it, but he's sold 10 000 of them. He certainly had the last laugh.*

have the last 'word
make the final point in a discussion or an argument: *She always likes to have the last word in any argument.*

hear/see the 'last of sb/sth
hear/see sb/sth for the last time: *That was the last I ever saw of her.* ◇ *Unfortunately, I don't think we've heard the last of this matter.*

,last but not 'least ◆ **,last but by no means 'least**
used to say that the last person or thing on a list, etc. is as important as the others: *He thanked everyone for their help: Mr Watkins, Ms Smith, Ms Jackson, and, last, but by no means least, Mr Jones.*

your/the last 'gasp
the point at which you/sth can no longer continue living, fighting, existing, etc: *People are saying that the group's latest actions are simply the last gasp of a dying campaign.*

> NOTE
> A *gasp* is a quick deep breath.

the last I 'heard (*spoken*)
used to give the most recent news you have about sb/sth: *The last I heard he was still working at the garage.*

,last 'in, ,first 'out
used, for example in a situation when people are losing their jobs, to say that the last people to be employed will be the first to go

the last 'lap
the final part of sth which has taken a long time: *Her medical studies finish next year, so she's on the last lap now.* ◇ *They are on the last lap of their journey round the world.*

> NOTE
> A *lap* is a single circuit of a running or race track.

(as) a last re'sort
a thing you decide to do when everything else has failed: *Nobody wanted to lend me the money. As a last resort I asked my brother-in-law, and luckily he was able to help me.*

last 'thing (at night)
immediately before going to bed or to sleep: *They always had a cup of cocoa last thing at night.* **OPP** first thing (tomorrow, in the morning, etc.)

the ,last 'word (in sth)
the most recent, most fashionable, etc. of its type: *They say that this new car is the last word in luxury.* ◇ *This is the last word in computer technology.*

on your/its ,last 'legs
about to die or stop functioning very soon; be very weak or in bad condition: *This photocopier is on its last legs.*

to/till the 'last
until the last possible moment, especially until death: *He died protesting his innocence to the last.* ◇ *They loved each other till the last.*

- **analysis** → in the last/final analysis
- **breathe** → breathe your last

- **famous** → famous last words
- **first** → (be) the first/last (person) to do sth
- **first** → first and last
- **first** → from first to last
- **hear** → hear/see the end/the last of sb/sth
- **laughs** → he who laughs last laughs longest
- **straw** → be the last/final straw
- **week** → a week yesterday, last Monday, etc.
- **word** → your/the last/final word (on/about sth)

last-ditch /ˌlɑːst ˈdɪtʃ; *AmE* ˌlæst/

a ,last-ditch 'stand/at'tempt/'effort
a final attempt to avoid defeat: *They are making a last-ditch stand to save the company.* ◇ *This is a last-ditch attempt to stop the strike.*

> ❓ ORIGIN
> *Ditch* in this idiom refers to a long channel built to defend an area against attack.

latch /lætʃ/

on the 'latch (*BrE*)
closed but not locked: *Can you leave the door on the latch so I can get in?*

late /leɪt/

,late in the 'day (*disapproving*)
(do sth) later than you should: *It's a bit late in the day to tell me you can't come. I've already bought the tickets.*

late of... (*formal*)
until recently working or living in the place mentioned: *Professor Jones, late of York University*

of 'late (*formal*)
recently: *He has been feeling rather unwell of late. He ought to see the doctor.*

- **better** → better late than never
- **night** → have an early/a late night

later /ˈleɪtə(r)/

later 'on (*informal*)
at a time in the future; after the time you are talking about: *I'm going out later on.* ◇ *Much later on, she realized what he had meant.*

- **see** → see you later
- **sooner** → sooner or later
- **sooner** → sooner rather than later

lather /ˈlɑːðə(r); *AmE* ˈlæð-/

get into a 'lather ◆ **work yourself into a 'lather** (*BrE, informal*)
get anxious or angry about sth, especially when it is not necessary: *Look, don't worry! There's no point getting yourself into a lather over this!*

> ❓ ORIGIN
> The idiom originally described the heavy sweat that you can see on the coat of a horse that has run very hard as a mass of white bubbles, like *lather*, the bubbles produced by mixing soap with water.

in a 'lather (*BrE, informal*)
in a nervous, angry or excited state: *What's going on? Chris has just come rushing into my office all in a lather, saying something about a lost report.*

laugh /lɑːf; *AmE* læf/

don't make me 'laugh (*spoken*)
used to show that you think what sb has just said is impossible or stupid: *'Will your dad lend you the money?' 'Don't make me laugh!'*

for a 'laugh ♦ **for 'laughs**
for fun and amusement: *'Why did you hide her glasses?' 'Oh, just for a laugh.'* ◇ *We all went swimming at 2 a.m. for a laugh.*

have a (good) 'laugh (about sth)
find sth amusing: *I was angry at the time but we had a good laugh about it afterwards.*

laugh all the way to the 'bank (*informal*)
make a lot of money easily and feel very pleased about it: *With profits continuing to rise, both investors and company bosses are laughing all the way to the bank.*

laugh your 'head off
laugh very loudly and for a long time: *If old Mr Bradley could see you now he'd laugh his head off.*
OPP cry your eyes out

laugh in sb's 'face (*informal*)
show in a very obvious way that you have no respect for sb: *When I made my suggestion at the meeting, everybody just laughed in my face.*

laugh like a 'drain (*BrE*)
laugh very loudly: *When I told him what had happened he laughed like a drain, as if it was the funniest thing he'd ever heard.*

laugh on the other side of your 'face (*BrE, informal*)
be forced to change from feeling pleased or satisfied to feeling disappointed or annoyed: *If you think you've tricked me, then you're wrong! You'll soon be laughing on the other side of your face!*

laugh sb/sth out of 'court (*BrE, informal*)
refuse, in an unpleasant way, to consider sb's suggestion, opinion, etc. seriously because you think it's stupid: *When she suggested trying the new treatment, they laughed her out of court.*

laugh up your 'sleeve (at sb/sth) (*informal*)
be secretly amused by sth: *Only he knew the whole story about the money. He must have been laughing up his sleeve all along.*

you have to 'laugh (*spoken*)
used to say that you think there is a funny side to a situation: *Well, I'm sorry you've lost your shoes, but you've got to laugh, haven't you?*

● know → not know whether to laugh or cry
● last → have the last laugh
● raise → raise a laugh/smile

laughing /'lɑːfɪŋ; *AmE* 'læfɪŋ/

be 'laughing (*spoken, informal*)
be in a fortunate position; have no worries: *If you can play like that in tomorrow's game you'll be laughing!*

a 'laughing stock
a person that everyone laughs at because they have done sth stupid: *I can't wear this to the party! I'll be a laughing stock!*

no laughing 'matter
something which is too serious to joke about: *Trying to find a place to live at the moment is no laughing matter.*

● die → die laughing

laughs /lɑːfs; *AmE* læfs/

a barrel/bundle of 'laughs (*informal, often ironic*)
very amusing; a lot of fun: *Life hasn't exactly been a barrel of laughs lately.*

he who laughs ˌlast laughs 'longest (*saying*)
do not be too proud of your present success; in the end another person may be more successful than you: *You think just because you've won this game, that means you're the best player. Well, wait until the championship. Remember, he who laughs last laughs longest.*

● laugh → for laughs **SEE** for a laugh

laurels /'lɒrəlz; *AmE* 'lɔːr-; 'lɑːr-/

look to your 'laurels
do sth to protect your good position or reputation from competition by others: *He thinks he's the best in the class but there's a new girl who is very good. He's going to have to look to his laurels.*

● rest → rest on your laurels

Law /lɔː/

● Murphy → Murphy's Law
● Sod → Sod's Law

law /lɔː/

go to 'law (*BrE*)
ask a court of law to settle a problem or disagreement: *They went to law to get their property back.*

have the 'law on sb (*BrE, informal*)
(often used as a threat) report sb to the police: *If you have just one more noisy party, I'll have the law on you.*

law and 'order
a situation in which most people in a country respect and obey the law; public order: *There has been a breakdown in law and order in some parts of the country.* ◇ *The President praised the forces of law and order* (= the police and the army).

the ˌlaw of 'averages
the principle that one thing will happen as often as another if you try enough times: *Keep applying for jobs and by the law of averages you'll get one sooner or later.*

the ‚law of the 'jungle
a situation in which people are prepared to harm other people in order to succeed: *The police daren't go into certain parts of the city. It's the law of the jungle in there.* ◇ *In this business it's the law of the jungle.*

a law unto him'self, her'self, etc.
a person who does what they want, even when this is against the rules and customs of a group or society in general: *That man is a law unto himself. He comes to work when he likes, and when he's here he doesn't do what he's supposed to do.*

take the law into your own 'hands
take action personally against sb who has broken the law or done sth wrong, instead of calling the police: *I knew who had stolen my car, so I took the law into my own hands. I went to his house and beat him up. The police arrested both of us!*

there's no 'law against sth (*spoken*)
used to tell sb who is criticizing you that you are not doing anything wrong: *I'll sing if I want to — there's no law against it.*

- **lay** → lay down the law
- **letter** → the letter of the law
- **long** → the long arm of the law
- **Parkinson** → Parkinson's law
- **possession** → possession is nine points/tenths/parts of the law
- **word** → your, his, etc. word is law
- **wrong** → on the wrong side of the law

lay /leɪ/

lay sth at sb's door (*formal*)
blame sb for sth: *The failure of the talks cannot be laid at the government's door.*

lay sth 'bare
reveal sth which has never been seen before: *She laid bare her feelings for him.* ◇ *The report lays bare the shocking housing conditions in this city.*

lay 'claim to sth
state that you have a right to sth: *'The Lamb and Flag' lays claim to being the oldest pub in London.*

lay down your 'arms
stop fighting in a war etc: *Tell your men to lay down their arms — the war's over.*

lay down the 'law (*informal, disapproving*)
give sb orders and express your opinions in an unpleasant, aggressive way, often when you have no right to do so: *He came in here this morning and started laying down the law about all kinds of things. Who does he think he is?*

lay down your 'life (for sb/sth) (*literary*)
die for your country, a cause etc: *Thousands of young men laid down their lives in the war so that we could live in freedom.*

lay an 'egg (*informal, especially AmE*)
fail or make a mistake: *He laid an egg with these proposals with the very people he wanted most to convince.* ◇ *Columnists sometimes lay an egg, but Martin has laid an ostrich omelette.*

lay a 'finger on sb (*informal*)
(often in negative sentences) touch sb with the intention of hurting them physically: *If you lay a finger on her, I'll call the police.*

lay it on 'thick/with a 'trowel (also **pile it on 'thick, pile it 'on**)
say that sth is much better or much worse than it really is because you want to impress or annoy sb: *He said that she was his favourite author and that she deserved the Nobel Prize for literature. He really laid it on with a trowel.* ◇ *My father really piled it on, shouting at me for ages about my exam results.*

lay it on the 'line (*informal*)
tell sb sth in an honest, direct and forceful way: *She laid it on the line, telling us that we would fail the exam unless we worked harder.*

lay sb 'low (*informal*)
(of an illness) cause sb to go to bed or be unable to work normally: *That flu laid her low for a couple of weeks.*

lay 'siege to sth
surround a building, especially in order to speak to or question the person or people living or working there: *The press and paparazzi laid siege to the star's London flat in the hope of getting a photograph of her.*

> **NOTE**
> A *siege* is a military operation in which an army tries to capture a town by surrounding it and stopping the supply of food, etc. to the people inside.

lay sb to 'rest (*formal*)
bury sb: *He was laid to rest beside his parents.*

lay sth to 'rest
stop sth by showing that it is not true: *The media speculation about their relationship has finally been laid to rest.*

lay sth 'waste ♦ lay 'waste to sth (*formal*)
destroy everything, especially in a war: *As the army retreated, it laid waste to thousands of acres of farmland.*

- **block** → put/lay your head/neck on the block
- **cards** → put/lay your cards on the table
- **eyes** → clap/lay/set eyes on sb/sth
- **hands** → get/lay your hands on sb
- **hands** → get/lay your hands on sth
- **lie** → the lay of the land **SEE** the lie of the land

lays /leɪz/

- **golden** → (kill) the goose that lays the golden egg/eggs **SEE** (kill) the golden goose

lead¹ /liːd/

give a 'lead (on sth)
give people encouragement to do sth by doing it yourself first: *The government should give a lead on protection of the environment.*

lead sb a'stray
encourage sb to behave in a silly or criminal way: *Small children are easily led astray by older chil-*

dren. ◇ *He's a weak character, who's easily led astray.*

lead sb by the 'nose
make sb do everything you want; control sb completely: *Unfortunately, she's allowed herself to be led by the nose for years, so it doesn't surprise me that she isn't happy.*

lead sb a (merry) 'dance
cause sb a lot of trouble or worry: *Where have you been? You've led us a merry dance — we've been looking all over for you!*

lead from the 'front
take an active part in what you are telling or persuading others to do: *If you want to succeed in this business, you need to lead from the front. We need people who can motivate their team to get the best possible results.*

lead (sb) 'nowhere
have no successful result for sb: *This discussion is leading nowhere.*

lead sb to be'lieve (that...)
make sb think sth is true, usually wrongly: *I was led to believe that I didn't need a visa to enter the country, and now it appears that I do.* ◇ *She led me to believe that she was a student, but she wasn't.*
OPP put/set sb straight (about/on sth)

lead sb up the garden 'path (*informal*)
cause sb to believe sth that is not true; deceive sb: *I think you're just leading us up the garden path — now, come on, tell us the truth!* ◇ *He had led her up the garden path, telling her he wasn't married.*

lead the 'way
1 go in front of sb in order to show them the way: *She led the way to the conference hall.*
2 be the first to do or develop sth: *The United States was leading the way in space research.*
OPP follow/go with the crowd

- **charmed →** lead/have a charmed life
- **horse →** you can take/lead a horse to water, but you can't make it drink
- **life →** lead/live the life of Reilly/Riley

lead² /led/

go ,down like a lead bal'loon (*informal*)
be very unsuccessful; not be accepted by people: *As you can imagine, the new proposals went down like a lead balloon, so we'll have to think again.*
OPP go down a bomb

> **NOTE**
> *Lead* is a heavy soft grey metal (symbol = Pb).

- **swing →** swing the lead

leading /'liːdɪŋ/

a ,leading 'light (in/of sth)
an important and respected member of a group, an organization, a profession, etc: *Mr Harris is a leading light in the local business community.*

a ,leading 'question
a question that you ask in a particular way in order to get the answer you want: *That's a leading question.* ◇ *Lawyers are experts on leading questions. You have to be very careful when you answer them.*

- **blind →** the blind leading the blind

leads /liːdz/

- **thing →** one thing leads to another

leaf /liːf/

take a leaf out of sb's 'book
follow sb's example because you admire them and their way of doing sth: *If you're having difficulty with the children, take a leaf out of Sandra's book. She knows how to control them.*

> **NOTE**
> *Leaf* is an old word for a page.

- **new →** turn over a new leaf
- **shake →** shake like a jelly/leaf

league /liːg/

be out of sb's 'league (*informal*)
be too difficult, expensive, etc. for sb: *You can't afford a lawyer like that. She's way out of your league.*

in 'league (with sb)
making secret plans with sb: *They accused him of being in league with the terrorists, which of course he denied.*

not be in the same 'league/'class/'street (*informal*)
be of a much lower standard than sb/sth: *He was a good painter, but not in the same league as Picasso.* ◇ *We're not in the same class as the Swiss ski team. They're the best in the world.*

- **different →** be in a different league

leak /liːk/

take a 'leak (*slang*)
pass urine (= waste liquid) from the body: *I'm just going to take a leak before we leave.*

- **spring →** spring a leak

lean /liːn/

- **backwards →** bend/lean over backwards to do sth

leap /liːp/

a leap in the 'dark
an action or a risk that you take without knowing anything about the activity or what the result will be: *The government is being accused of taking a leap in the dark as it prepares to radically change the education system.*

,look before you 'leap (*saying*)
think carefully about the possible risks and effects before you decide to do sth: *I know you don't like this job but don't just accept the first job offered to you. Remember to look before you leap.*

- **conclusions →** jump/leap to conclusions
- **quantum →** a quantum leap

leaps

leaps /liːps/

by/in ,leaps and 'bounds
in large amounts or very quickly: *My knowledge of German increased by leaps and bounds when I lived in Germany for a year.* ◇ *Production is going up in leaps and bounds.* **OPP** step by step

● heart → your heart leaps

learn /lɜːn; *AmE* lɜːrn/

learn your 'lesson
learn what to do or what not to do in the future because you have had a bad experience in the past: *I used to carry a lot of money on me, until one day my bag was stolen. Since then, I've learned my lesson.*

● hard → do/learn sth the hard way
● live[1] → live and learn
● ropes → show sb/learn/know the ropes

lease /liːs/

a (,new) lease of 'life (*BrE*) (*AmE* **a (,new) lease on 'life**)
a chance for sb/sth to live/last longer; a chance to get more enjoyment and satisfaction out of life: *The successful heart operation gave him a new lease of life.* ◇ *The outside of the city hall has just been thoroughly cleaned and it's given the old place a new lease on life.*

leash /liːʃ/

● strain → strain at the leash
● tight → keep sb/sth on a tight leash **SEE** keep a tight rein on sb/sth

least /liːst/

at 'least
1 (of a number) not less than: *There were at least 70 000 people at the concert.* **OPP** at (the) most
2 the minimum sb should do: *I know it's difficult for him to telephone me, but he could at least write.*
3 used for talking about the only advantage or good point of sb/sth: *This car is slow, it uses a lot of petrol, but at least it doesn't break down.*
4 used to show you are not completely sure of sth: *It's true. At least, I think so.*

at the (very) 'least
used after amounts to show that the amount is the lowest possible: *It'll take a year, at the very least.*

(,not) in the 'least
(used in negative sentences, questions and *if* clauses) (not) at all: *She wasn't in the least afraid.* ◇ *If you are in the least worried about it, then ask somebody for help.*

the (very) 'least you can/could do
the minimum you should do: *The least you can do is apologize.* ◇ *'Thank you so much for helping me.' 'Well, it was the least I could do.'*

,least 'said ,soonest 'mended (*BrE, saying*)
a bad situation will pass or be forgotten most quickly if nothing more is said about it: *She's still very angry, of course, but if you ask me it's a case of least said soonest mended.*

not 'least (*written*)
especially: *There are a lot of complaints about the new road, not least because of the noise.*

● last → last but by no means least
● last → last but not least
● line → (choose, follow, take, etc.) the line of least resistance
● said → the less/least said, the better
● say → to say the (very) least

leather /'leðə(r)/

● hell → hell for leather

leave /liːv/

> Most idioms containing **leave** are at the entries for the nouns or adjectives in the idioms, for example **leave sb cold** is at **cold**.

,leave 'go (of sth) (*BrE, informal*)
stop holding on to sth: *Leave go of my arm — you're hurting me!*

leave it at 'that (*informal*)
say or do no more about sth: *We talked about it for a few minutes, I made a few suggestions, and we left it at that.* ◇ *We've done enough for today. Let's leave it at that, shall we?*

,leave it 'out (*BrE, spoken*)
used to tell sb to stop doing sth: *Leave it out, will you? I'm trying to study!*

leave sb 'to it (*informal*)
allow sb to continue doing sth on their own, without your help: *Oh well, we'll leave you to it, Derek — you seem to be managing very well by yourself.*

take it or 'leave it
1 used to say that you do not care if sb accepts or rejects your offer: *$200 is my final offer, take it or leave it.*
2 (*informal*) (with *can*, not used in the negative) not feel strongly about sth, not mind sth: *'Do you like Indian food?' 'I can take it or leave it.'*

take (your) 'leave (of sb) (*formal*)
say goodbye: *With a nod and a smile, she took leave of her colleagues.*

without (so much as) a ,by your 'leave (*old-fashioned*)
without asking permission; rudely: *What do you think you're doing, coming in here without so much as a by your leave?*

> **NOTE**
> *Leave* in this phrase means 'permission'.

leaving /'liːvɪŋ/

● sinking → (like rats) deserting/leaving a sinking ship

leeway /'liːweɪ/

make up 'leeway (*BrE*)
get out of a bad position that you are in, especially because you have lost a lot of time: *By now, James*

was so far behind in the race that he knew he had little chance of making up the leeway.

left /left/

be (way out/over) in left 'field (*AmE, informal*)
completely wrong; strange or unusual: *He's way out in left field if he thinks we're going to support him on this.*

> **NOTE**
> This idiom refers to the left part of the field in baseball.

the ˌleft hand doesn't know what the ˌright hand's 'doing (*saying, informal*)
one part of an organization, a group, etc. does not know what another part is doing: *First I got a letter from them saying they couldn't return my money, and then the next day they sent me a cheque. Obviously the left hand doesn't know what the right hand's doing.*

left ˌout in the 'cold
excluded from a group or an activity; ignored: *Everyone had something to do or somewhere to go. I felt left out in the cold.*

ˌleft, right and 'centre ♦ ˌright, left and 'centre (*BrE*) (*AmE* ˌleft, right and 'center, ˌright, left and 'center**) (*informal*)
in or from all directions: *He was shouting orders left, right and centre.* ◇ *She was criticized right, left and centre for her views on education.*

- **hang** → hang a left/right
- **right** → left and right **SEE** right and left
- **two** → have two left feet

left-handed /ˌleft 'hændɪd/

- **backhanded** → a left-handed compliment **SEE** a backhanded compliment

leg /leg/

break a 'leg! (*spoken*)
used to wish sb good luck: *You'd better leave now if you want to arrive early for the exam. Break a leg!*

> **NOTE**
> It is thought that wishing for something bad to happen will prevent it from happening. This expression is used especially in the theatre.

get your 'leg over (*BrE, informal*)
have sex

'leg it (*informal, especially BrE*)
run, especially in order to escape from sb: *We saw the police coming and legged it down the road.*

not have a ˌleg to 'stand on (*informal*)
not be able to prove what you say: *He claims he wasn't there, but four people saw him, so he doesn't have a leg to stand on.*

- **arm** → cost/pay an arm and a leg
- **pull** → pull sb's leg
- **shake** → shake a leg
- **talk** → talk the hind leg(s) off a donkey

legend /'ledʒənd/

- **living** → a legend in your own lifetime **SEE** a living legend

legs /legz/

have 'legs (*informal*)
if a news story, film/movie, etc. **has legs**, people will continue to be interested in it, or it will be successful, popular, etc. for a long time: *We'll soon see if the movie has legs.* ◇ *Some economists believe that the recovery still has legs.*

- **fast** → as fast as your legs can carry you
- **last** → on your/its last legs
- **stretch** → stretch your legs
- **tail** → with your tail between your legs

leg-up /'leg ʌp/

give sb a 'leg-up
1 (*BrE, informal*) help sb climb up or onto sth, for example, a horse or a wall: *I gave him a leg-up.*
2 (*informal*) help sb, usually by giving them money: *His father gave him a leg-up when he was starting his business.*

leisure /'leʒə(r)/; *AmE* 'liːʒər/

at (your) 'leisure
without needing to hurry, at a convenient time for you: *I'm not going to read this report now; I'll read it later at my leisure.*

lend /lend/

lend 'colour to sth (*BrE*) (*AmE* **lend 'color to sth**)
make sth seem probable: *The tracks outside the house lend colour to her claim that somebody tried to break in last night.*

lend an 'ear (to sb/sth)
listen to what sb is telling you: *He's a good friend. He's always ready to lend a sympathetic ear.*

lend (sb) a 'hand (with sth)
help sb (to do sth): *I saw two men pushing a broken-down car along the road so I stopped to lend them a hand.* ◇ *She stayed with us for three weeks and didn't once lend a hand with the housework!*

lend your 'name to sth (*formal*)
let it be known in public that you support or agree with sth: *Famous actors sometimes lend their names to political causes.*

lend sup'port, 'weight, 'credence, etc. to sth
make sth seem more likely to be true or genuine: *This latest evidence lends support to her theory.*

length /leŋθ/

at 'length
1 (*literary*) after a long time: *'I'm not sure,' he said at length.*
2 in great detail and taking a long time: *She talked at length about her work in hospitals.*

the length and 'breadth of sth
everywhere in an area: *I've travelled the length and breadth of Europe, but I've never seen such beautiful scenery as here.*

● arm → keep sb at arm's length

lengths /leŋθs/

go to any, great, etc. 'lengths (to do sth)
try very hard (to do sth); do whatever is necessary: *She went to great lengths to find this book.* ◊ *They were prepared to go to any lengths to help their son.*

leopard /'lepəd; AmE -ərd/

a leopard cannot change its 'spots (*saying*)
a person's character does not change: *A dictator is unlikely to become a good leader in a democracy. A leopard cannot change its spots.*

less /les/

even/much/still 'less
and certainly not: *I don't want even to see her, much less speak to her.* ◊ *I don't like beer, even less do I like warm, weak English beer.*

less is 'more
used to say that it is more effective to give a small amount of detail, information, etc. than a large amount: *When it comes to Web design, less is more.*

no 'less (*often ironic*)
used to suggest that sth is surprising or impressive: *She's having lunch with the Director, no less.*

no less than...
used to emphasize a large amount: *The guide contains details of no less than 115 hiking routes.*

lesser /'lesə(r)/

the ˌlesser of two 'evils ♦ the ˌlesser 'evil
the less unpleasant of two unpleasant choices: *Neither candidate seemed capable of governing the country. People voted for him as the lesser of two evils.*

lesson /'lesn/

● learn → learn your lesson
● object → an object lesson
● teach → teach sb a lesson

let /let/

> Most idioms containing **let** are at the entries for the nouns or adjectives in the idioms, for example **let off steam** is at **steam.**

ˌlet 'fall sth
mention sth in a conversation, by accident or as if by accident: *She let fall a further heavy hint.*

ˌlet sb 'go
1 allow sb to be free: *Will they let the hostages go?*
2 make sb have to leave their job: *They're having to let 100 employees go because of falling profits.*

ˌlet sb/sth 'go ♦ ˌlet 'go (of sb/sth)
1 stop holding sb/sth: *Let go of me! You're hurting!* ◊ *Don't let go of my hand, or you'll get lost.*
2 give up an idea or an attitude, or control of sth: *It's time to let the past go.* ◊ *Some people find it hard to let go of their inhibitions.*

ˌlet yourself 'go
1 behave in a relaxed way without worrying about what people think of your behaviour: *Come on, enjoy yourself, let yourself go!*
2 stop being careful about how you look and dress, etc: *He has let himself go since he lost his job.*

let sb 'have it (*spoken, informal*)
punish sb or speak to them very angrily: *She annoyed me so much that I let her have it.* ◊ *Dad will let you have it when he sees that mess.*

let it 'go (at 'that)
say or do nothing more about sth: *I could have disagreed with him, but I let it go. I don't like arguments.* ◊ *The police spoke firmly to the boy about the damage and then let it go at that.*

ˌlet me 'see/'think
used when you are thinking or trying to remember sth: *Now let me see — where did he say he lived?*

letter /'letə(r)/

the ˌletter of the 'law (*often disapproving*)
the exact words of a law or rule rather than its general meaning: *They insist on sticking to the letter of the law.*

to the 'letter
with attention to every detail; exactly: *I followed your instructions to the letter.*

● dead → a dead letter
● open → an open letter
● poison → a poison pen letter

level /'levl/

do/try your level 'best (to do sth)
try as hard as you can: *I'll do my level best to be there by ten o'clock, but I can't promise anything.*

keep a level 'head
remain calm and sensible, even in difficult situations: *She managed to keep a level head when all the others panicked.* **OPP** lose your head ► **level-'headed** *adj.*: *Nurses need to be level-headed.*

ˌlevel 'pegging (*BrE*)
making progress at the same rate as another person or group: *There's ten minutes left, and the teams are still level pegging.*

> **❷ ORIGIN**
> In some games, a player puts a *peg* (= a short piece of wood, plastic, etc.) in one of a series of numbered holes to mark their score. If both players' pegs are *level*, their scores are equal.

a ˌlevel 'playing field
a situation in which everyone has the same opportunities: *Many small businesses complain that they are not competing on a level playing field and that they are the ones who lose out.*

,level the 'playing field
create a situation where everyone has the same opportunities: *There is a high demand for new laws and restrictions to be introduced in order to level the playing field.*

on the 'level (*AmE* also **on the ,up and 'up**) (*informal*)
honest; legal: *I promise you that he's on the level. He's never been involved in anything criminal.*

● sink → sink to sb's level

liberties /'lɪbəti:z; *AmE* -bərti:z/

take 'liberties (with sb/sth)
be more free with sb/sth than you should be: *The translator has taken too many liberties with this. The original meaning is lost.* ◇ *He uses our phone without asking, which I think is taking liberties.*

liberty /'lɪbəti; *AmE* -bərti/

at 'liberty (to do sth) (*formal*)
having permission to do sth: *You are at liberty to leave, if you wish.*

take the liberty of doing sth (*formal*)
do sth without permission: *I have taken the liberty of giving your address to a friend who is visiting London. I hope you don't mind.*

licence (*BrE*) (*AmE* **license**) /'laɪsns/

artistic/poetic 'licence (*often ironic*)
the freedom of artists or writers to change facts in order to make a story, painting, etc. more interesting or beautiful: *In the book, a fair amount of artistic licence has been taken with the timing of historical events so that they fit with the story.* ◇ *I allowed myself a little poetic licence in describing the table as an antique.*

> **NOTE**
> *Licence* in this idiom means 'freedom to do or say whatever you want'.

a licence to print 'money (*disapproving*)
used to describe a business which makes a lot of money with little effort: *Many people think that the national lottery is nothing more than a licence to print money.*

lick /lɪk/

at a (fair) 'lick (*informal*)
fast; at a high speed: *You must have been driving at a fair lick to get here so quickly!*

lick sb's 'boots (*informal*) (*BrE* also **lick sb's 'arse** ⚠, *slang*) (*AmE* also **lick sb's 'ass** ⚠, *slang*)
show too much respect for sb in authority because you want to please them: *It makes me very angry when I see Andrew licking Mr Smith's boots all the time.*

a lick of 'paint (*informal*)
a coat of fresh paint: *All this house needs is a good clean and a lick of paint.*

lick your 'wounds
spend time trying to get your strength and confidence back after a defeat or disappointment: *'He heard this morning that he hasn't got the job.' 'Where is he?' 'Licking his wounds somewhere, probably.'*

● lips → lick/smack your lips
● shape → get/knock/lick sb/sth into shape

licking /'lɪkɪŋ/

● beating → take a licking SEE take a beating

lid /lɪd/

keep/put a/the 'lid on sth
try to make sure that people do not do sth or find out about sth: *The government wants to keep the lid on discussion of tax reforms at the moment.*

lift, blow, etc. the 'lid off sth (*informal*)
tell people unpleasant or shocking facts about sth: *The story in today's paper really lifts the lid off the use of drugs in horse racing.*

put the (tin) 'lid on sth (*BrE, informal*)
bring to an end an activity, your hopes or plans: *I've got a place at an American university but I can't afford to go, so that's put the lid on that.* ◇ *It rained and rained, which put the tin lid on our plans for a picnic in the park.*

● flip → flip your lid

lie /laɪ/

give the 'lie to sth (*formal*)
show that sth is not true: *These statistics give the lie to the government's claim that inflation is under control.*

lie at sb's 'door (*formal*)
(of the responsibility for a mistake, etc.) belong to sb: *The main problem is the design of the building and the responsibility for that lies clearly at the architect's door.*

lie 'doggo (*old-fashioned, informal*)
be very still or hide somewhere so that you will not be found: *I lay doggo in the yard while the police searched the house for me.*

lie down on the 'job (*informal*)
not do a job properly: *I'm not going to employ anybody here who lies down on the job. I only want people who work hard.*

lie in 'state
(of the body of an important person) be placed for people to see before it is buried

lie in 'store (for sb)
(of events, etc.) be waiting to happen (to sb): *I wonder what lies in store for us in our new life in California.*

lie in 'wait
hide and wait for sb so that you can attack them: *The police think the murderer must have been lying in wait for his victim.*

lie 'low (*informal*)
hide or keep quiet for a short time: *The thieves lay low for a few days in a farmhouse, then tried to leave the country with the money.*

the ˌlie of the ˈland (*BrE*) (*AmE* **the ˌlay of the ˈland**)
1 the way the land in an area is formed and what physical characteristics it has
2 the way a situation is now and how it is likely to develop: *Check out the lie of the land before you make a decision.*

lie through your ˈteeth (*informal*)
tell very obvious lies without being embarrassed: *The witness was clearly lying through his teeth.*

lie your way into/out of sth
get yourself into/out of a situation by telling lies: *I lied my way into the concert by claiming to be a journalist.* ◇ *You can't lie your way out of it this time, I'm afraid.*

● **bed** → have made your bed and have to lie on it
● **bottom** → be/lie at the bottom of sth
● **heavy** → hang/lie heavy (on sb/sth)
● **live¹** → live a lie
● **sleeping** → let sleeping dogs lie
● **tell** → I tell a lie
● **white** → a white lie

lies /laɪz/

● **land** → see, etc. how the land lies
● **pack** → a pack of lies
● **rub** → there is/lies the rub
● **therein** → therein lies...
● **time** → time hangs/lies heavy (on your hands)
● **tissue** → a tissue of lies

lieu /luː; *BrE also* ljuː/

in lieu (of sth) (*formal*)
instead of: *They took cash in lieu of the prize they had won.* ◇ *We work on Saturdays and have a day off in lieu during the week.*

life /laɪf/

be sb's ˈlife
be the most important person or thing to sb: *My children are my life.* ◇ *Writing is his life.*

bring sb/sth to ˈlife
make sb/sth more lively, interesting or attractive: *It was only her performance that brought the movie to life.* ◇ *If you put a couple of pictures on the wall it might bring the room to life a bit.*

come to ˈlife
1 become more interesting, exciting or full of activity: *The match finally came to life in the final minutes of the second half.*
2 start to act or move as if alive: *In my dream all my toys came to life.*

frighten/scare the ˈlife out of sb
frighten sb very much: *Don't do that! You scared the life out of me creeping up on me like that!*

get a ˈlife (*spoken*)
used to tell sb to stop being boring and to do sth more interesting: *Simon, all you do is sit at home all day playing video games. Get a life!*

lead/live the life of Reilly/ˈRiley (*informal*)
have a comfortable and enjoyable life without any worries: *He inherited a lot of money and since then he's been living the life of Riley.*

life after ˈdeath
the possibility or belief that people continue to exist in some form after they die: *Do you believe in life after death?*

(a matter of) ˌlife and/or ˈdeath (*informal*)
used to describe a situation that is very important or serious: *We need that business deal, it's a matter of life or death to the company.* ◇ *It's hardly a life-and-death decision whether we drive or take the train, is it?*

the life and ˌsoul of the ˈparty (*BrE*)
very cheerful or enthusiastic: *People always expect Jane to be the life and soul of the party.*

life is ˈcheap (*disapproving*)
used to say that there is a situation in which it is not thought to be important if people somewhere die or are treated badly: *In areas like this, drugs are hard currency and life is cheap.*

(have) a life of its ˈown
(of an object) seeming to move or function by itself without a person touching or working it: *When he was painting, he said, the brush used to take on a life of its own and take him in directions he never intended to go.*

lose your ˈlife
be killed: *Sixty people lost their lives in the air crash.* ▸ **loss of ˈlife** *noun*: *Fortunately there was no loss of life in the fire.*

make life ˈdifficult (for sb)
cause problems for sb: *She does everything she can to make life difficult for him.*

make sb's life a ˈmisery
make sb's life very unpleasant or difficult: *Ever since he joined the company he's made my life a misery.* ◇ *Her arthritis makes her life a misery; she's in constant pain.*

the ˈman/ˈwoman in your life (*informal*)
the man or woman that you are having a sexual or romantic relationship with

not for the ˈlife of me, etc.
used for saying that you cannot do sth, however hard you try: *I can't for the life of me remember his first name.* ◇ *He couldn't for the life of him understand why she was so annoyed with him.*

not on your ˈlife (*spoken*)
used to refuse very firmly to do sth: *Go out and miss the football match on TV? Not on your life!* ◇ *Lend him $50? Not on your life.*

see ˈlife
see and experience different ways of living, for example by travelling, working with many different kinds of people, etc: *She's done many different jobs all over the world. She's seen life, that's for sure.* ◇ *He's certainly seen a bit of life.*

such is ˈlife (*informal*)
used when you are disappointed about sth but know that you must accept it: *He didn't get the prize he was hoping for. But such is life, I suppose.*

take sb's 'life (*formal*)
kill sb: *In my opinion, the state does not have the right to take a person's life.*

take your ,life in your 'hands
risk being killed, injured, attacked, etc: *You take your life in your hands if you let him drive.* ◇ *The reason that his photos are so good is because he takes his life in his hands to get them.*

take your own 'life (*formal*)
kill yourself; commit suicide: *His children died in a house fire and shortly afterwards he took his own life.*

,that's 'life (also ,**c'est la 'vie** *from French*) (*spoken*)
used when you are disappointed about sth but know that you must accept it: *Some people are born intelligent and some people are not. That's life.* ◇ *I didn't get that job I wanted. They said I didn't have enough experience. Oh well, c'est la vie.*

there's ,life in the old dog 'yet (*humorous*)
a person is old but is still active and enjoys life: *At 70 he's decided to go round the world. There's life in the old dog yet!* ◇ *I'm not too old to enjoy myself! There's life in the old dog yet, you know.*

this is the 'life!
used to show that you are very happy with the situation you are in: *Sunshine, a swimming pool and champagne. This is the life!*

to the 'life
(of a painting, sculpture, description, etc.) exactly like the person/thing painted, etc: *This new portrait really is Prince Charles to the life.* ◇ *When I read her description of him, I could see him again so clearly. It was him to the life.*

what a 'life!
used to show that you think your life is very difficult or unpleasant: *Three hours travelling to work in a crowded train every day. What a life!* ◇ *Cooking, cleaning and ironing seven days a week. What a life!*

where there's 'life (, there's 'hope) (*saying*)
in a terrible situation you must not give up hope because there is always a chance that it will improve: *The game isn't over yet — we could still win. Where there's life there's hope.*

- **bane** → the bane of sb's life/existence
- **bet** → (you can) bet your bottom dollar/your life (on sth/that...)
- **breathe** → breathe (new) life into sth
- **charmed** → lead/have a charmed life
- **dear** → for your life SEE for dear life
- **dog** → a dog's life
- **end** → end your days/life (in sth)
- **fact** → a fact of life
- **facts** → the facts of life
- **fear** → be/go in fear of your life
- **fight** → fight for (your) life
- **fright** → the fright of your life
- **kiss** → the kiss of life
- **large** → (as) large as life
- **larger** → larger than life
- **lay** → lay down your life (for sb/sth)

- **lease** → a (new) lease of life
- **lease** → a (new) lease on life SEE a (new) lease of life
- **light** → the light of sb's life
- **prime** → in the prime of (your) life
- **real** → in real life
- **risk** → risk life and limb
- **save** → can't do sth to save your life
- **slice** → a slice of life
- **spring** → spring to/into life/action
- **staff** → the staff of life
- **story** → that's the story of my life
- **time** → at my, your, etc. time of life
- **time** → have the time of your life
- **true** → true to life
- **variety** → variety is the spice of life
- **walk** → a walk of life
- **way** → a/the/sb's way of life

lifetime /'laɪftaɪm/

the chance, etc. of a 'lifetime
a wonderful opportunity, etc. that you are not likely to get again: *This is your chance to win the trip of a lifetime!*

- **living** → a legend in your own lifetime SEE a living legend

lift /lɪft/

(not) lift a 'finger (to do sth) (*informal*)
(not) make any effort at all to do sth, especially to help sb: *He didn't lift a finger to help me when I was in trouble.* ◇ *She does all the work in the house. Nobody else lifts a finger.*

thumb/hitch a 'lift
stand by the side of the road with your thumb out because you want a driver to stop and take you somewhere: *We tried to hitch a lift, but nobody stopped to pick us up.*

- **hand** → lift/raise a hand against sb
- **roof** → lift/raise the roof

lifts /lɪfts/

- **rising** → a rising tide lifts all boats

light /laɪt/

be in sb's 'light
be between sb and a source of light: *Could you move, please? You're in my light.*

be light on sth
not have enough of sth: *We seem to be light on fuel.*

be/go out like a 'light (*informal*)
fall asleep very quickly or suddenly lose consciousness: *She went out like a light after an exhausting day at work.* ◇ *One minute she was talking and laughing and the next minute she was out like a light. It was very frightening.*

bring sth to 'light
show information, evidence, etc: *The police investigation brought to light evidence of more than one crime.* ◇ *These documents have brought new information to light about Shakespeare's early life.*

cast/shed/throw (new) 'light on sth
make a problem, etc. easier to understand: *This book sheds new light on the role of the CIA.* ◇ *'Can you throw any light on the matter?'*

come to 'light
become known; be revealed: *It recently came to light that he'd been in trouble with the police before.*

in a ˌgood, ˌbad, ˌfavourable, etc. 'light
if you see sth or put sth **in a good, bad, etc. light**, it seems good, bad, etc: *You must not view what happened in a negative light.* ◇ *They want to present their policies in the best possible light.*

in the 'light of sth (*BrE*) (*AmE* **in 'light of sth**)
after considering sth: *In the light of what you have just told me, I am prepared to increase your loan to £5 000.*

(as) light as 'air/a 'feather
weighing very little; very light: *I love this jacket — it's really warm but it's as light as a feather.* ◇ *Her sponge cakes are as light as air.* **OPP** weigh (half) a ton

(see the) ˌlight at the end of the 'tunnel
(see) the possibility of success, happiness, etc. in the future, especially after a long period of difficulty: *Business has been bad recently, but I think we're beginning to see some light at the end of the tunnel.*

(the) light 'dawned (on sb)
somebody suddenly understood or began to understand sth: *I puzzled over the problem for ages before the light suddenly dawned on me.*

(see) the light of 'day
be thought of or discovered by sb, or become known to a lot of people at a particular time: *It was then that the idea of a European parliament first saw the light of day.*

the light of sb's 'life
the person sb loves more than any other: *Elizabeth was his only child, the light of his life.*

a light 'touch
the ability to deal with sth in a delicate and relaxed way: *She handles this difficult subject with a light touch.* **OPP** heavy hand

make 'light of sth
treat sth or behave as if sth is less serious, important etc. than it really is: *She was in great pain but she always made light of it.* ◇ *They made light of their difficulties but it was obvious that things were going badly.*

make light 'work of sth (*informal*)
do sth very easily; defeat sb very easily: *She made light work of that translation.* ◇ *They made light work of their match against Lazio and won the championship.* **OPP** make heavy weather of (doing) sth

see the 'light
1 understand or accept sth after you have spent a lot of time thinking about it: *I think he's finally seen the light and is going to retire while he's still able to enjoy himself.*
2 change what you believe as a result of a religious experience: *She was an atheist but now she says she's seen the light.*

set 'light to sth (*especially BrE*)
make sth start burning: *A spark from the fire had set light to a rug.*

with a light 'heart
with a feeling of happiness or relief: *She left the doctor's with a light heart. There was nothing wrong with her after all.* **OPP** with a heavy/sinking heart ▸ **light-'hearted** *adj.* **1** (of a person) cheerful and happy **2** (of a situation, etc.) amusing, not serious: *The programme takes a light-hearted look at the tourist industry.*

● **cold** → in the cold light of day
● **green** → give sb/get the green light
● **hands** → many hands make light work
● **hide** → hide your light under a bushel
● **leading** → a leading light (in/of sth)
● **shining** → be a shining light **SEE** be a shining example (of sb/sth)
● **sweetness** → be all sweetness and light
● **travel** → travel light

lightly /ˈlaɪtli/

get off/be let off 'lightly (*informal*)
be lucky and escape serious injury, punishment or trouble: *Only two years in prison for stealing all that money? I think he got off very lightly.*

lightning /ˈlaɪtnɪŋ/

at/with ˌlightning 'speed
very fast: *The lecturer talked at lightning speed.* ◇ *They're a very efficient company. They reply to your letters with lightning speed.*

ˌlightning never strikes (in the same place) 'twice (*saying*)
an unusual or unpleasant event is not likely to happen in the same place or to the same person twice

● **catch** → catch lightning in a bottle
● **greased** → like greased lightning

lights /laɪts/

the lights are 'on but nobody's 'home (*saying, humorous*)
used to describe sb who is stupid, not thinking clearly or not paying attention: *Don't try discussing anything intelligent with Alice. The lights are on but nobody's home, I'm afraid.*

● **bright** → the bright lights
● **jump** → jump the lights
● **shoot** → shoot the lights

like /laɪk/

> Most idioms containing **like** are at the entries for the nouns or adjectives in the idioms, for example **like gold dust** is at **gold**.

and the 'like (*informal*)
and similar people or things: *Professional people include lawyers, doctors, architects and the like.*

anything/nothing/something like that
anything, etc. of that kind: *Do you do aerobics or play tennis, or anything like that?* ◇ *She's an expert in the preservation of paper or something like that.* ◇ *No, there's nothing like that available yet.*

how would 'you like it?
used to emphasize that sth bad has happened to you and you want some sympathy: *How would you like it if someone called you a liar?*

I like your 'nerve, 'cheek, etc. ◆ I like 'that! (*informal, ironic*)
used for saying that you think sb's behaviour is very unreasonable or unfair: *She crashed into my car and now she wants me to pay for hers to be repaired. Well I like her nerve!* ◇ *He wants me to do his work for him while he goes to a football game! Well, I like that!*

if you 'like (*spoken*)
1 used to politely agree to sth or to suggest sth: *'Shall we stop now?' 'If you like.'* ◇ *If you like, we could go out this evening.*
2 used when you express sth in a new way or when you are not confident about sth: *It was, if you like, the dawn of a new era.*

(as) like as 'not ◆ like e'nough ◆ most/very 'like (*informal*)
quite/very probably: *As like as not, he'll be late. He usually is.*

(just) like 'that
without hesitating: *I asked him for some money and he gave it to me just like that.*

likely /ˈlaɪkli/

as ˌlikely as 'not ◆ most/very 'likely
very probably: *As likely as not she's forgotten all about it.*

a 'likely story (*spoken, ironic*)
used for showing that you do not believe what sb has said: *They said they'd found the wallet on the ground outside the pub — a likely story!*

not (bloody△, etc.) 'likely! (*spoken, especially BrE*)
used to disagree strongly with a statement or a suggestion: *Sign a blank cheque for you? Not bloody likely!*

likes /laɪks/

the likes of sb (*informal*)
people like sb: *She didn't want to associate with the likes of me.*

liking /ˈlaɪkɪŋ/

for 'your liking
if you say, for example, that sth is too hot **for your liking**, you mean that you would prefer it to be less hot: *The town was too crowded for my liking.*

to sb's 'liking (*formal*)
suitable, and how sb likes sth: *The coffee was just to his liking.*

lily /ˈlɪli/

● **gild** → gild the lily

limb /lɪm/

out on a 'limb (*informal*)
in a risky or difficult position because you are saying or doing sth which does not have the support of other people: *When he started that company, he really went out on a limb. It might have been a disaster.* ◇ *I seem to be out on a limb here. Does nobody agree with my idea?*

> **NOTE**
> A *limb* in this phrase is a large branch of a tree.

● **risk** → risk life and limb
● **tear** → tear sb limb from limb

limbo /ˈlɪmbəʊ; *AmE* -boʊ/

in 'limbo
in a state of uncertainty or between two states: *We're in limbo at the moment because we've finished our work in this country and now we're waiting for our next contract.* ◇ *Our plans for renting an apartment in Spain are in limbo at the moment.*

> **❷ ORIGIN**
> In some Christian beliefs, *limbo* is a state that is neither heaven nor hell, where some souls live.

limelight /ˈlaɪmlaɪt/

out of/in the 'limelight
receiving no/a lot of public attention: *If you are married to a Prime Minister, you are always in the limelight.*

> **❷ ORIGIN**
> In theatres, *lime* used to be burnt in front of the stage to give a bright light.

limit /ˈlɪmɪt/

be the (absolute) 'limit (*old-fashioned, spoken*)
be a very annoying person or thing: *You're the limit, Michael. I've been waiting for you for over two hours. Where on earth have you been?* ◇ *The trains on this line are the absolute limit. They are never on time.*

● **sky** → the sky's the limit

limits /ˈlɪmɪts/

within 'limits
1 to a certain extent; not completely: *'Do you support what he says?' 'Yes, within limits!'*
2 as long as it is reasonable; to a reasonable degree: *I will do anything I can to help you, within limits, of course.*

● **bounds** → off limits SEE out of bounds

line /laɪn/

all along/down the 'line ◆ right down the 'line (*informal*)
completely; at every stage: *We've had problems with this software all along the line. It was a complete waste of money.* ◇ *He supported their campaign right down the line.*

linen

bring sb/sth into 'line (with sb/sth)
make sb/sth behave, function, etc. in the same way as other people, organizations, etc: *We're trying to bring our production methods more into line with our Japanese competitors.* ◇ *He's a very clever child but he's naughty. I feel that he needs bringing into line a bit.*

in line for sth
likely to get sth: *She's in line for promotion.*

in the ˌline of 'duty
while doing a job: *A police officer was injured in the line of duty yesterday.*

(be) in/out of 'line with sb/sth
be in agreement/disagreement with sth: *Her views on education are quite out of line with the official view.* ◇ *The changes being made are in line with the new policy.*

(choose, follow, take, etc.) the line of least re'sistance
(to choose, etc.) the easiest way of doing sth: *You'll never get anywhere in life if you always take the line of least resistance.*

line your (own)/sb's 'pocket(s) (*informal*)
make a lot of money dishonestly, especially by stealing it from your employer: *He'd been lining his pockets for years before it was discovered.*

on the 'line
(of a job, your career, reputation, etc.) at risk: *If I don't get enough contracts this month, my job will be on the line.* ◇ *By making such a controversial movie, he has really put his reputation on the line.*

somewhere, etc. along/down the 'line
at some particular moment or stage during sth: *'How did it happen?' 'I don't know. I just know that somewhere along the line we stopped loving each other.'* ◇ *The report looks at where the market is heading and what we can expect further down the line.*

tread/walk a fine/thin 'line
be in a difficult or dangerous situation where you could easily make a mistake: *He was walking a fine line between being funny and being rude.*

- bottom → the bottom line
- draw → draw a line in the sand
- draw → draw a line under sth
- draw → draw the line (at sth)
- drop → drop sb a line/note
- end → the end of the road/line
- firing → be in/on the firing line
- firm → take a firm line/stand (on/against sth)
- front → in the front line (of sth)
- hook → hook, line and sinker
- hot → a hot line (to sb)
- jump → cut in line **SEE** jump the queue
- jump → jump the line **SEE** jump the queue
- lay → lay it on the line
- order → out of line **SEE** out of order
- overstep → overstep the mark/line
- party → the party line

- pitch → pitch a line/story/yarn (to sb)
- sign → sign on the dotted line
- step → be/get out of line **SEE** step out of line
- step → step out of line
- toe → toe the line

linen /ˈlɪnɪn/

- wash → wash your dirty linen in public

lines /laɪnz/

on/along the lines of … ♦ on/along (the) … lines (*spoken*)
1 in the way that is mentioned: *The new system will operate **along the same lines as** the old one.*
2 similar to sth; in a similar way, style, etc. to sth: *I'm looking for a silver teapot, something along the lines of this one here.*
3 used for giving a summary of sth you have read or heard: *'What did he say in his defence?' 'Something along the lines of his being so drunk that he didn't realize what he was doing.'*

- battle → the battle lines are drawn
- crossed → get your lines/wires crossed
- crossed → have crossed lines/wires
- hard → hard luck/lines
- read¹ → read between the lines

lingua /ˈlɪŋgwə/

a ˌlingua 'franca (*from Italian*)
a shared language that is used for communication by people whose main languages are different: *In the middle of the 20th century, English became the lingua franca of the world.* ◇ *The majority of our group being South American, we used Spanish as a lingua franca.*

lining /ˈlaɪnɪŋ/

- cloud → every cloud has a silver lining

link /lɪŋk/

a link in the 'chain
one of the stages in a process or a line of argument: *Many people believe that coming from a broken home may be one of the first links in the chain that eventually leads to a life of crime.*

- weak → the weak link (in the chain)

lion /ˈlaɪən/

the ˌlion's 'den
a difficult situation in which you have to face a person or people who are unfriendly or aggressive towards you: *Before each one of her press conferences, she felt as if she were going into the lion's den.*

> ❷ ORIGIN
> This idiom comes from the story of Daniel in the Bible, who went into a lion's *den* (= home) as a punishment but was not hurt by the lion.

the 'lion's share (of sth) (*BrE*)
the largest part of sth that is being shared: *The lion's share of the awards have gone to American stars again.*

> ❓ ORIGIN
> This idiom comes from one of Aesop's fables. The lion is helped by other animals to kill a stag, but then refuses to share it with them.

● head → put your head in the lion's mouth

lions /'laɪənz/

● wolves → throw sb to the wolves/lions

lip /lɪp/

● bite → bite your lip
● stiff → (keep) a stiff upper lip

lips /lɪps/

lick/smack your 'lips
1 move your tongue over your lips, especially before eating sth good
2 (*informal*) show that you are excited about sth and want it to happen soon: *They were licking their lips at the thought of clinching the deal.*

my lips are 'sealed (*informal, humorous*)
I promise not to tell your secret: *Don't worry, I won't tell anybody. My lips are sealed.*

on everyone's 'lips
if sth is **on everyone's lips**, they are all talking about it: *The question on everyone's lips at the moment is: will they get married or not?*

● pass → not pass your lips
● read¹ → read my lips

lip-service /'lɪp ˌsɜːvɪs; *AmE* ˌsɜːrvɪs/

● pay → pay lip-service to sth

list /lɪst/

● danger → be on/off the danger list
● hit → a hit list

listen /'lɪsn/

listen with half an 'ear
not listen with your full attention: *I was watching television and listening with half an ear to what he was telling me.* **OPP** be all ears

litmus /'lɪtməs/

● the litmus test SEE acid → the acid test (of sth)

little /'lɪtl/

a little 'bird told me (that…) (*spoken*)
I have heard about sth but I do not want to say who told me: *A little bird told me you might be applying for another job. Is that true?* ◇ *'How did you know I was getting married?' 'Oh, a little bird told me.'*

little by 'little
slowly; gradually: *Her English is improving little by little.* ◇ *Little by little she began to feel better.*

make 'little of sth
1 treat sth as unimportant or less important than expected: *She made little of all the problems in the department and said everything was all right.*
2 hardly understand sth: *I read the article on the relationship between physics and art, but I'm afraid I could make little of it.*

more than a little ex'cited, 'shocked, etc.
quite or very excited, shocked, etc: *Peter was more than a little disappointed not to be chosen for the team.* ◇ *I was more than a little surprised to see it still there two days later.*

twist/wind/wrap sb around/round your little 'finger (*informal*)
be able to persuade or influence sb very easily, usually because they like you: *I can twist my parents round my little finger.*

● account → of little/no account
● avail → to little/no avail
● better → little/no better than
● bit → little by little SEE bit by bit
● oaks → great/tall oaks from little acorns grow
● precious → precious few/little
● purpose → to little/good/some/no purpose
● short → little/nothing short of sth
● wonder → it's no/small/little wonder (that)…

live¹ /lɪv/

ˌlive and 'breathe sth
be very enthusiastic about sth: *He just lives and breathes football.*

live and 'learn
1 learn through your mistakes or experience: *I left my bike unlocked for five minutes and it was stolen. You live and learn I suppose.*
2 used for expressing surprise at sth new which you have just heard, read, etc: *It says in this book that the Romans were the first to have a state postal service. Well, you live and learn, don't you?*

live and 'let live (*saying*)
used to say that you should accept other people's opinions and behaviour even though they are different from your own: *If we could all learn to live and let live a little more, the world would be a much happier place.*

live beyond/within your 'means
live on more/less money than you have or earn: *They seemed wealthy but they were living well beyond their means.* ◇ *I find it very hard to live within my means.*

live by/on your 'wits
earn money by clever or sometimes dishonest means: *Patrick did not go to college, as expected, but learned to live very successfully on his wits.*

live (from) ˌhand to 'mouth
spend all the money you earn on basic needs such as food, without being able to save any money: *There's no way we can even think about travelling to Europe this year, as we are literally living from hand to mouth.* ▶ ˌhand-to-'mouth *adj.*: *a hand-to-mouth existence*

live in 'hope
believe there is a chance that what you want to happen will happen one day: *The situation doesn't look too good, but we live in hope.* ◇ *The Johnsons live in hope that one day their son will come home.*

live in 'sin (*old-fashioned* or *humorous*)
live together and have a sexual relationship with sb, without being married: *Are you two married yet or are you still living in sin?*

live it 'up (*informal*)
have a very enjoyable time, often spending a lot of money: *Since his retirement he has been living it up in the south of Spain.* ◇ *We are very careful with our money, but for two weeks a year while we're on holiday, we really live it up.*

live a 'lie
keep sth important about yourself a secret from other people, so that they do not know what you really think, what you are really like, etc: *In the end she found that she couldn't go on living a lie, and told him the truth.*

live like a 'king
live in very comfortable surroundings, enjoying all the advantages of being rich: *In this luxury resort, you can live like a king.* ◇ *One day we'll be rich, and you and I will live like kings.*

live off/on the ˌfat of the 'land (*informal*)
have plenty of money to spend on the best food, drink, entertainment, etc: *Money was no problem then. We were living off the fat of the land in those days.* ◇ *It's always the same: the rich live off the fat of the land and complain that the poor are lazy.*

live off the 'land
eat whatever food you can grow, kill or find yourself: *Having grown up on a farm, Jack was more used to living off the land than the rest of the group.*

ˌlive to fight another 'day (*saying*)
used to say that although you have failed or had a bad experience, you will continue: *She only just lost the election, so she lives to fight another day.*

live to tell the 'tale (*informal, often humorous*)
survive a terrible experience: *Only one man out of fifteen lived to tell the tale.* ◇ *It will be a difficult experience, but I expect you'll live to tell the tale!*

live up to your/its repu'tation
be as good, bad, etc. as people say: *The restaurant lived up to its reputation. We had a wonderful meal.*

- borrowed → be/live on borrowed time
- life → lead/live the life of Reilly/Riley
- pockets → be/live in each other's pockets
- rough → live/sleep rough

live² /laɪv/

go 'live
(of a computer system) become operational (= ready to be used): *Good news! Our website is going live tomorrow!*

a live 'wire (*informal*)
a lively and enthusiastic person: *You must invite her to your party — she's a real live wire.* ◇ *We need a live wire like him in this department. Let's give him the job.* **OPP** a wet blanket

NOTE
A wire that is *live* is connected to a source of electrical power, so has a great deal of energy.

lived /lɪvd/

you haven't 'lived
used to tell sb that if they have not had a particular experience their life is not complete: *You've never been to New York? You haven't lived!*

lively /'laɪvli/

look 'lively/'sharp (*BrE, informal*)
do sth quickly; hurry up: *Come on, look lively or we won't get to the station in time.*

lives¹ /lɪvz/

- half → how the other half lives

lives² /laɪvz/

- nine → have nine lives

living /'lɪvɪŋ/

be ˌliving 'proof of sth
show sth is true simply by being alive or existing: *He plays tennis and golf. He's living proof that a heart attack doesn't mean the end of an active life.*

in/within ˌliving 'memory
that can be remembered by people who are alive now: *These are the worst floods in Britain within living memory.*

a living 'legend (also **a ˌlegend in your own 'lifetime**)
a person who has become famous while still alive: *Her 30-year study of chimpanzees made her a living legend.*

- image → be the living/spitting/very image of sb/sth
- land → in the land of the living
- world → (think) the world owes you a living

lo /ləʊ; AmE loʊ/

ˌlo and be'hold (*humorous*)
used when telling a story to introduce sb's unexpected appearance: *I walked into the restaurant and, lo and behold, there was my boss with his wife.*

❷ ORIGIN
The phrase uses old words that tell you to look at something. It means 'look and see'.

load /ləʊd; AmE loʊd/

get a load of 'this (*spoken*)
used to tell sb to look at or listen to sb/sth: *Get a load of this. They want to build a new road right across here.*

a load of (old) 'rubbish, 'nonsense, etc. (*informal*)
nonsense; worthless: *Don't bother to watch that film. It's a load of old rubbish.*

- bricks → a few, two, etc. bricks short of a load
- mind → (take) a load/weight off sb's mind

be lost for 'words
be so surprised, confused, etc. that you do not know what to say: *When he told me what she'd done to him I was lost for words.*

be 'lost in sth
be giving all your attention to sth so that you do not notice what is happening around you: *to be lost in thought/admiration*

be 'lost on sb
not be understood or noticed by sb: *I'm afraid that joke was lost on me.* ◇ *Good writing is lost on him. He's just not interested in literature.*

be lost to the 'world
be giving all your attention to sth so that you do not notice what is happening around you: *When I went into his office he was staring out of the window, apparently lost to the world.*

be/feel 'lost without sb/sth
feel unable to work or live without sb/sth: *I left my watch at home and I feel lost without it.* ◇ *I'm completely lost without my diary.*

get 'lost! (*informal*)
an impolite way of telling sb to go away, or of refusing sth: *I told him to get lost, but it makes no difference, he just keeps following me around.*

give sb/sth up for 'lost (*formal*)
stop looking for sb/sth because you no longer expect to find them/it: *The fishermen had been given up for lost in the storm but they have now arrived safely back.*

a lost 'cause
an ambition, project or aim which seems certain to end in failure: *For many years he supported the development of the electric car, but he now thinks it's a lost cause.* ◇ *Trying to help him to improve his pronunciation is a lost cause.*

make up for lost 'time
do sth quickly or very often because you wish you had started doing it sooner: *The building work is now behind schedule, but contractors are confident that they can make up for lost time.*

- love → there's no love lost between A and B
- time → there's no time to be lost

lot /lɒt; AmE lɑ:t/

a bad 'lot (*old-fashioned, BrE*)
a person who is dishonest: *I'm not surprised. I always said he was a bad lot, didn't I?*

by 'lot
using a method of choosing sb to do sth in which each person takes a piece of paper, etc. from a container and the one whose paper has a special mark is chosen: *The committee is chosen by lot and its members change annually.*

throw in your 'lot with sb
decide to join a person or an organization, so that you share their luck, both good and bad: *He left his job in the National Theatre to throw in his lot with a small travelling theatre company.*

lots /lɒts; AmE lɑ:ts/

cast/draw 'lots (for sth/to do sth)
decide who is going to do sth by using a method in which each person takes a piece of paper or a stick and the person who has the paper with a special mark on or the shortest stick is chosen: *They drew lots to see who should speak to the parents.*

loud /laʊd/

,loud and 'clear (*informal*)
said in a very clear voice or expressed very clearly: *The message of the book is loud and clear: smoking kills.* ◇ *He let us know loud and clear that he would not accept students arriving late for his lectures.*

,out 'loud
in a voice that can be heard by other people: *I almost laughed out loud.* ◇ *Please read the letter out loud.* **OPP** under your breath

- crying → for crying out loud
- think → think out loud

louder /ˈlaʊdə(r)/

- actions → actions speak louder than words

lout /laʊt/

- lager → a lager lout

love /lʌv/

(just) for 'love/for the 'love of sth
if you do sth **for love**, you do it without payment or other reward, because you like the work or the person you are working for: *She works in the museum during the summer but she doesn't get paid. She helps for the love of it.*

for the love of 'God (*old-fashioned, spoken*)
used when you are expressing anger and the fact that you are impatient: *For the love of God, be quiet! I'm trying to concentrate.*

give/send my love to sb (*informal*)
used to send friendly greetings to sb: *Give my love to Mary when you see her.* ◇ *Bob sends his love.*

love at first 'sight
falling in love with sb the first time you meet them: *I never really believed in love at first sight until I met my husband.*

'love from ♦ lots of 'love (from) (*written, informal*)
used at the end of a letter to a friend or to sb you love, followed by your name: *Lots of love, Jenny*

love is 'blind (*saying*)
when you are in love with sb, you cannot see their faults: *I don't like him at all, but she's crazy about him. Well, they say love is blind, don't they?*

,love you and 'leave you (*spoken, humorous*)
used to say that you must go, although you would like to stay longer: *Well, time to love you and leave you I'm afraid.*

make 'love (to sb)
have sex (with sb): *They made love all night long.*

not for love or/nor 'money (*informal*)
used to say that it is impossible to do sth or get
sth: *The show is sold out. You can't get a ticket for
love nor money.*

there's no 'love lost between A and B
(*informal*)
two people dislike each other: *They may have been
the best of friends when they were younger but
there's no love lost between them now.*

● cupboard → cupboard love
● fair → all's fair in love and war
● labour → a labour of love
● tough → tough love

lovely /'lʌvli/

lovely and 'warm, 'cold, 'quiet, etc. (*BrE,
spoken*)
used when you are emphasizing that sth is good
because of the quality mentioned: *It's lovely and
warm in here.*

● garden → everything in the garden is lovely/rosy

low /ləʊ; AmE loʊ/

be/run 'low (on sth)
not have much of sth left: *We're running low on
fuel. Do you think we'll have enough to get home?*

(at) a low 'ebb
not as good, strong, successful, etc. as usual: *Business confidence is at a low ebb at the moment.
◇ Our family fortunes are at a bit of a low ebb.*
OPP (on) the crest of a wave

> NOTE
> This idiom refers to a very low tide, when the
> sea is a long way from the land.

● high → high and low
● lay → lay sb low
● lie → lie low
● profile → adopt, keep, etc. a high/low profile
● sights → set your sights high/low
● sink → sink so low
● spirits → be in high/low spirits
● stoop → stoop so low (as to do sth)

low-down /'ləʊ daʊn; AmE loʊ-/

give sb/get the 'low-down (on sb/sth)
(*informal*)
give sb/get the important and true facts about sb/
sth: *Can you give me the low-down on this deal with
the Bank of China?*

lower /'ləʊə(r); AmE loʊ-/

lower the 'tone (of sth)
make the general character and attitude of sth,
such as a place, a piece of writing or the atmosphere of an event, less polite or respectable: *Residents were afraid that a fast-food restaurant would
lower the tone of the street.*

'lower yourself (by doing sth)
(usually used in negative sentences) behave in a
way that makes other people respect you less:
I wouldn't lower myself by working for him.

● sights → raise/lower your sights
● temperature → raise/lower the temperature

luck /lʌk/

any 'luck? (*spoken*)
used to ask sb if they have been successful with
sth: *'Any luck?' 'No, they're all too busy to help.'*

be down on your 'luck (*informal*)
have no money because of a period of bad luck: *He
employed a retired soldier who was down on his
luck to tidy up the garden.*

do sth for 'luck
1 do sth because you believe it will bring you
good luck, or because this is a traditional belief:
Take something blue. It's for luck.
2 do sth for no particular reason: *I hit him once
more for luck.*

good 'luck (with sth) (*spoken*)
used to wish sb success with sth: *Good luck with
your exams. ◇ Good luck! I hope it goes well.*

good 'luck to sb (*spoken*)
used to say that you do not mind what sb does as
it does not affect you, but you hope they will be
successful: *It's not something I would care to try
myself but if she wants to, good luck to her.*

you're in 'luck ♦ your 'luck is in
you are lucky at the moment: *I knew my luck was
in today when all the traffic lights were green on my
way to work. And now I've found that money I lost.*

just my, his, etc. 'luck (*informal*)
my, his, etc. typical bad luck: *I wanted the steak
but there wasn't any left. Just my luck! ◇ They sold
the last tickets to the people in front of us. Just our
luck.*

the luck of the 'devil ♦ the luck of the 'Irish
very good luck: *You need the luck of the devil to get
a seat on the train in the rush hour. ◇ It was the
luck of the Irish that saved him.*

the ˌluck of the 'draw
the result of chance only: *Some teachers get a job
near home, others are sent hundreds of miles away.
It's the luck of the draw.*

no such 'luck (*informal*)
unfortunately not: *I thought I might finish early
today, but no such luck.*

tough/bad 'luck (*informal*)
1 (*BrE*) used to show sympathy for sth unfortunate that has happened to sb: *'I failed by one
point.' 'That's tough luck.'*
2 (also **tough**) (also **tough 'shit, tough 'titty** ⚠,
slang) (*ironic*) used to show that you do not feel
sorry for sb who has a problem: *'If you take the
car, I won't be able to go out.' 'Tough luck!' ◇ If you
don't like the idea, tough. You should have said
something earlier.*

- **beginner** → beginner's luck
- **best** → the best of luck (to sb)
- **better** → better luck next time
- **chance** → as chance/luck would have it
- **hard** → hard luck/lines
- **hard-luck** → a hard-luck story
- **pot** → take pot luck
- **push** → push your luck
- **try** → try your luck (at sth)
- **worse** → worse luck

lucky /'lʌki/

lucky 'you, 'me, etc. (*spoken*)
used to show that you think sb is lucky to have sth, be able to do sth, etc: *'I'm off to Paris.' 'Lucky you!'*

'you'll, 'he'll, etc. be lucky (also **'you, 'he, etc. should be so lucky**) (*spoken*)
what you expect or hope for is unlikely to happen: *You were hoping I'd come and collect you from the airport after midnight? You'll be lucky! Try a taxi!* ◇ *'Come and see us if you are ever in Australia.' 'I should be so lucky.'*

- **strike** → strike (it) lucky
- **thank** → thank your lucky stars (that...)
- **third** → third time lucky

lull /lʌl/

- **storm** → the calm/lull before the storm

lump /lʌmp/

have a 'lump in your throat
feel a tight feeling in your throat caused by a strong emotion: *I didn't cry but I did have a lump in my throat.*

(like it or) 'lump it (*informal*)
accept sth unpleasant because there is no other choice: *I'm sorry you're not happy about it but you'll just have to lump it.* ◇ *That's the situation — like it or lump it!*

lumps /lʌmps/

take your 'lumps (*AmE, informal*)
accept bad things that happen to you without complaining: *If we make mistakes, we'll take our lumps.*

lunatic /'lu:nətɪk/

the ˌlunatic 'fringe (*disapproving*)
members of an organization or group who are more extreme than the others; extreme groups: *It's the lunatic fringe of the Animal Liberation Front which smashes the windows of butchers' shops, not ordinary members like us.*

❷ ORIGIN
The word *lunatic* means crazy. It comes from the Latin word *luna*, meaning 'moon', because people believed that the changes in the moon caused temporary madness.

lunch /lʌntʃ/

ˌout to 'lunch (*informal, especially AmE*)
crazy, stupid or confused: *She has talent physically but mentally she's out to lunch.* ◇ *I respect his scholarship, but he's out to lunch on this matter.*

- **eat** → eat sb's lunch
- **thing** → there's no such thing as a free lunch

lurch /lɜ:tʃ; AmE lɜ:rtʃ/

leave sb in the 'lurch (*informal*)
leave sb who is in a difficult situation and needs your help: *You can't resign now and leave us all in the lurch. It wouldn't be fair.*

lurgy /'lɜ:gi AmE 'lɜ:rgi/

- **dreaded** → the dreaded lurgy

luxury /'lʌkʃəri/

- **lap** → in the lap of luxury

lying /'laɪɪŋ/

(not) take sth lying 'down (*informal*)
accept an insult or offensive act without protesting or reacting: *I'm not going to take this stupid decision lying down. If necessary, I'll take the company to court.* ◇ *She's the kind of person who won't take defeat lying down.* **OPP** put up a (good) fight

lyrical /'lɪrɪkl/

- **wax** → wax lyrical (about sth)

M m

machine /mə'ʃi:n/

- **cog** → a cog in the machine/wheel

mackerel /'mækrəl/

- **sprat** → (be) a sprat to catch a mackerel

mad /mæd/

be mad 'keen (on sb/sth) (*informal*)
be very interested in or enthusiastic about sb/sth: *She's been mad keen on African music ever since she came back from Zimbabwe last year.* ◇ *He's mad keen on getting into the army.*

(as) mad as a 'hatter (*informal*)
(of a person) crazy

❷ ORIGIN
The Mad Hatter was a character in Lewis Carroll's *Alice's Adventures in Wonderland*. Because of the chemicals used in hat-making, workers often suffered from mercury poisoning, which can cause loss of memory and damage to the nervous system.

(as) mad as a March 'hare (*informal*)
(of a person) crazy

> ❷ ORIGIN
> A *March hare* refers to a hare (= an animal like
> a large rabbit) that behaves very strangely in
> the breeding season.

- barking → be barking mad
- crazy → like crazy/mad
- hopping → hopping mad (about/over sth)
- raving → (stark) raving mad/bonkers

made /meɪd/

be made 'up (about/with sth) (*BrE, informal*)
be very pleased or satisfied (about/with sth): *I'm
really made up with the new job. It's the type of
work I've always wanted.*

have it 'made (*informal*)
be sure of success; have everything that you want:
With his brains and energy, he's got it made. ◇ *A
good job, a beautiful house, lovely children: she's
really got it made.*

(be) 'made for sb/each other
be completely suited to sb/each other: *Jen and
Alan seem made for each other, don't they?*

what sb is 'made of (*informal*)
how sb reacts in a difficult situation: *Let's see what
he's made of.* ◇ *Go out and show them what you're
made of* (= show them that you are strong, intelligent, etc.)!

madness /'mædnəs/

- method → there's method in sb's madness

magic /'mædʒɪk/

(have) a/the magic 'touch
(have) a special ability that means you do sth very
well: *She seems to have a magic touch with the children and they do everything she asks.*

- weave → weave your magic

maid /meɪd/

- old → an old maid

mail /meɪl/

- snail → snail mail

main /meɪn/

in the 'main
mostly; on the whole: *In the main, the students did
well in the exam.*

- eye → have an eye to/for the main chance

majority /mə'dʒɒrəti; AmE -'dʒɔːr-; -'dʒɑːr-/

- silent → the silent majority

make /meɪk/

> Most idioms containing the verb **make** are at
> the entries for the nouns or adjectives in the
> idioms, for example **make no bones about
> (doing) sth** is at **bones**.

make as if to do sth (*written*)
make a movement that makes it seem as if you are
just going to do sth: *He made as if to speak.*

make a 'break for it (*informal*)
try to escape from prison, etc: *Six prisoners shot a
guard and made a break for it in a stolen car.*

make 'do (with sth) ◆ **make sth 'do**
manage with sth that is not really satisfactory:
*I really need a large frying pan but if you haven't
got one I'll have to make do with that small one.*
◇ *I didn't have time to go shopping today so we'll
just have to make do.*

make a 'go of sth (*informal*)
be successful in sth: *We've had quite a few problems
in our marriage, but we're both determined to make
a go of it.*

make 'good (*informal*)
become rich and successful, especially when you
have started your life poor and unknown: *He's a
local boy* **made good**.

make good sth
1 pay for, replace or repair sth that has been damaged or lost: *The suitcase went missing at the airport so the airline have agreed to make good the
loss.* ◇ *The mechanic explained that they would
have to make good the damage to the body of the
car before they resprayed it.*
2 do what you promised, threatened, intended,
etc. to do: *When she became President she made
good her promise to ensure equal pay for both men
and women.*

'make it
1 be successful in your job: *She's a very good dancer but I'm not sure she'll make it as a professional.*
◇ *He wants to be a professor by the time he's 30. Do
you think he'll make it?*
2 succeed in reaching a place: *The train leaves in
ten minutes. Hurry up or we won't make it.*
◇ *I don't think we'll make it before dark.*
3 survive after an illness, accident, etc: 'Do you
think she's going to make it, doctor?' 'It's really too
soon to say.'

'make it with sb (*AmE, slang*)
have sex with sb

make like… (*AmE, informal*)
pretend to be, know or have sth in order to
impress people: *He makes like he's the greatest
actor of all time.*

make the 'most of sth
get as much good as you can out of sth: *The meeting finished early so I decided to make the most of
being in London and do some shopping.* ◇ *The
opportunity won't come again so make the most of
it now.*

make the 'most of yourself, himself, etc.
look as attractive as possible: *She's a pretty girl but she doesn't make the most of herself.*

make 'much of sb/sth (*written*)
treat sb/sth as important: *The media made much of the fact that she was the first woman pilot to fly a jumbo jet.*

make nothing 'of sth
1 treat sth as easy or unimportant: *What a hill! But even with her heavy bag, Amy made nothing of it and was moving at top speed.* **OPP** make heavy weather of sth/of doing sth
2 not be able to understand or make sense of sth: *He went to bed again and thought it over but could make nothing of it. The more he thought about it, the less he understood.*

,make or 'break (*informal*)
the thing which decides whether sth succeeds or fails: *This movie is make or break for the production company.* ◇ *This is a make-or-break year for us.*

'make something of yourself
be successful in your life: *She has the education, the talent and the brains to really make something of herself.*

on the 'make (*informal, disapproving*)
1 trying openly to become successful, rich, etc: *Jack was a young man on the make. Not so much for fame, but for money.*
2 trying to find a sexual partner: *He thought I was on the make so came over and asked me to dance.*

Maker /'meɪkə(r)/
● meet → meet your Maker

making /'meɪkɪŋ/
be the 'making of sb/sth
be the reason that sb/sth succeeds or develops well: *It was only a small part in a TV show, but it was the making of her.* ◇ *Those two years of hard work were the making of him.*

in the 'making
developing into sth or being made: *He's very good at public speaking — I think he's a politician in the making.*

of your own 'making
(used about a problem or difficulty) caused by you rather than by sb/sth else: *The problem is of your own making, so don't try to blame anyone else.*

makings /'meɪkɪŋz/
have the 'makings of sth
(of a person) have the necessary qualities or character to become sth: *She's got the makings of a good tennis player, but she needs to practise much harder.*

malice /'mælɪs/
with ,malice a'forethought (*law*)
with the deliberate intention of committing a crime or harming sb: *Suddenly Guy, more by way of a nervous twitch than with malice aforethought, pulled the trigger.*

mama /'mæmə/
● boy → a mama's boy **SEE** a mummy's/mother's boy

man /mæn/
be sb's 'man/'woman
be the best person to do a particular job, etc: *If you need a driver, then I'm your man.* ◇ *If you need a good music teacher, she's your woman.*

be 'man enough (to do sth/for sth)
be brave enough (to do sth): *He won't fight — he's not man enough!*

be no good/use to 'man or 'beast (*informal*)
be completely useless: *Since the Chernobyl disaster the land round here has been no use to man or beast.*

be your own 'man/'woman
act or think independently, not following others or being ordered to do things: *Working for himself meant that he could be his own man.*

every man has his 'price ◆ everyone has their 'price (*saying*)
everyone can be persuaded to do sth against their moral principles if you offer them enough money

it's every ,man for him'self (*saying*)
you must think about your own interests, safety, etc. first, before the interests, etc. of other people: *In business, it's every man for himself.*

make a 'man of/out of sb
make a young man develop and become more adult: *My father was very old-fashioned. He was always trying to 'make a man of me' by taking me fishing or camping with him.*

a/the ,man about 'town
a man who frequently goes to fashionable parties, clubs, theatres, etc.

,man and 'boy
from when sb was young to when they were old or older: *He's been doing the same job for 50 years — man and boy.*

the ,man (and/or ,woman) in the 'street (*BrE* also **the man (and/or woman) on the ,Clapham 'omnibus** *old-fashioned*)
an average or ordinary person, either male or female: *You have to explain it in terms that the man in the street would understand.*

a ,man of 'God/the 'cloth (*old-fashioned, formal*)
a religious man, especially a priest or a clergyman

the ,man of the 'match (*BrE, sport*)
the man who plays the best in a game of football, cricket, etc.

a ,man of the 'people
(especially of a politician) a man who understands and is sympathetic to ordinary people: *The main reason he was so popular was that despite being one of the most powerful men in the country, he was also a man of the people.*

a ,man of 'straw
a weak or cowardly person: *You don't need to be frightened of him — he's a man of straw.*

maneuver

This idiom compares a person to a model of a man filled with *straw* (= stems of grain plants such as wheat, etc. that have been cut and dried).

,man to 'man
between two men who are treating each other honestly and equally: *I'm telling you all this man to man.* ◇ *a man-to-man talk*

man's best 'friend
a way of describing a dog

a 'man's man
a man who is more popular with men than with women

one man's ,meat is another man's 'poison (*saying*)
used to say that different people like different things; what one person likes very much, another person does not like at all: *I'm amazed that Tim enjoys cricket so much. Still, one man's meat is another man's poison, as they say.*

to a 'man (*written*)
used to emphasize that sth is true of all the people being described: *To a man, they all agreed.*

you can't keep a good man 'down (*saying*)
a person who is determined or wants sth very much will succeed: *He failed his driving test twice, but passed on the third try — you can't keep a good man down!*

- dirty → a dirty old man
- Englishman → a man's home is his castle SEE an Englishman's home is his castle
- few → a man/woman of few words
- grand → a/the grand old man (of sth)
- inner → the inner man/woman
- ladies → a ladies' man
- life → the man/woman in your life
- marked → a marked man
- new → a new man
- odd → the odd man/one out
- old → old man
- one → as one man SEE as one
- parts → a man/woman of (many) parts
- poor → be a/the poor man's sth/sb
- possessed → like a man/woman possessed
- right-hand → your right-hand man
- twice → be twice the man/woman (that sb is)
- white-van → white-van man
- word → be a man/woman of his/her word
- world → a man/woman of the world

maneuver /mə'nuːvə(r)/ (*AmE*) = manoeuvre

manger /'meɪndʒə(r)/

- dog → a dog in the manger

manna /'mænə/

manna from 'heaven
something unexpected, for example a gift of money, which comes to help you when you are in difficulties: *That cheque for £1000 from my aunt came like manna from heaven as I had three or four big bills to pay.*

❷ ORIGIN
This phrase comes from the Bible. *Manna* was the food the Israelites found in the desert.

manner /'mænə(r)/

all 'manner of sb/sth
many different types of people or things: *The problem can be solved in all manner of ways.*

in the manner of sb/sth (*formal*)
in a style that is typical of sb/sth: *a painting in the manner of Raphael*

in a ,manner of 'speaking
if you think about it in a certain way: *'Are they married?' 'In a manner of speaking — they've lived together for 15 years.'*

(as if) to the ,manner 'born (*formal*)
as if a job, a social position, etc. were completely natural to you: *He rides round in a Rolls Royce as if to the manner born.*

manoeuvre (*BrE*) (*AmE* **maneuver**) /mə'nuːvə(r)/

freedom of/room for ma'noeuvre
the chance to change the way that sth happens and influence decisions that are made: *Small businesses have limited room for manoeuvre.*

many /'meni/

as many as…
used to show surprise that the number of people or things involved is so large: *There were as many as 200 people at the lecture.*

a good/great many
very many; a lot: *A good many people think she's right.* ◇ *There are a great many places in the world I'd like to visit.*

map /mæp/

(be) off the 'map
(be) far away from other places; (be) remote: *It's a little house in the country, a bit off the map.*

put sb/sth on the 'map
make sb/sth famous or important: *Her performance in her first film really put her on the map.* ◇ *The newspaper story put the village on the map.*

- wipe → wipe sth off the map SEE wipe sth off the face of the earth

marbles /'mɑːblz; *AmE* 'mɑːrblz/

lose your 'marbles (*informal*)
become crazy or mentally confused: *They say the old man has lost his marbles because of the strange things he's been saying, but I'm not so sure.*

STUDY PAGES

HOW IDIOMS ARE FORMED

An idiom usually begins as a phrase with a literal meaning which then starts to be used in a figurative or an idiomatic way. For example, in the past it was a sign of respect to *take your hat off to someone* when meeting them or entering their house. From this literal meaning, the phrase came to be used more generally to mean 'show respect or express admiration for what someone has done':

I take my hat off to her for all the hard work she's done.

In many ways idioms reflect the history and way of life of the people who have spoken English over the ages. Here are some more examples:

FARMING

A large number of idioms come from a time when far more people worked on the land than they do now. Many idioms relate to farm work such as **ploughing** (e.g. *plough a lonely furrow*), **sowing seeds** (e.g. *plant/ sow the seeds of sth*), **harvesting crops** (e.g. *you reap what you sow*), **threshing** (e.g. *separate the wheat from the chaff*), and **hay making** (e.g *make hay while the sun shines*).

In the same way there are many idioms which refer to **farm animals**:

the black sheep of the family	*take the bull by the horns*
like lambs to the slaughter	*pigs might fly*
till the cows come home	*don't count your chickens*

Blacksmiths and Millers

Two important figures in rural life were the **blacksmith**, who worked with metal, and the **miller**, who ground people's grain into flour.

Blacksmith	**Milling**
strike while the iron is hot	*grist to the mill*
have many irons in the fire	*put somebody through the mill*

TRANSPORT

Horses

Before the invention of the motor car the main means of transport was the horse. As a result many idioms relate to **horses** and **carts**:

put the cart before the horse	*eat like a horse*
flog a dead horse	*ride a coach and horses through sth*

Several refer to the **equipment** that is placed on a horse so you can ride on it and control it:

get the bit between your teeth	*keep a tight rein on sth*
kick over the traces	*give free rein to sth*
in harness	*be in the saddle*

Ships and Sailing

In the past, travelling by ship was often the fastest means of transport and there are many idioms connected with the **sea** and **sailing**:

Everything should be plain sailing from now on.
His criticisms really took the wind out of my sails.
With a new manager at the helm, the team's fortunes should improve.
In my first week in the job, Ellen offered to show me the ropes.

Trains

The arrival of the **railways** led to many new idioms based on the steam engine and the idea of tracks and rails.

Steam is associated with ideas of power and energy:

The economy should pick up steam next year.
It does you good to let off steam once in a while.
The process has run out of steam.

Tracks and **rails** suggest the path that someone should follow:

Tom went off the rails after his divorce.
We're on track to make a profit this year.
Their grand plan hit the buffers before it even got started.

Cars and planes

The dramatic effect of the **car** and the **plane** on society and people's lives can be seen in the large number of idioms they have generated:

Cars	**Planes**
be in the driving seat	*get (sth) off the ground*
get into gear/move up a gear	*be flying high*
get the green light	*fly by the seat of your pants*
live life in the fast lane	*have a soft/bumpy landing*

SCIENCE AND TECHNOLOGY

As our ancestors' lives were dominated by the land and the seasons, these days our lives are shaped by science and technology. **Chemistry** gave us the *acid test* and *litmus test*, from **physics** we had a *quantum leap*, while **psychology** has left us with *Freudian slips*.

Many idioms relate to **machines**. We say that someone is *firing on all cylinders*, knows *the nuts and bolts* of a subject and if they have an unimportant position in a large organization then they're just a *cog in the machine*.

Electronic machinery has also generated many idioms:

He's a live wire.	*She has a short fuse.*
We're on the same wavelength.	*He really pushes my buttons.*
You're getting your wires crossed.	*I need to recharge my batteries.*

ORIGINS: Sport and Entertainment

Leisure activities have always been a rich source of idioms, from sports and games to entertainments such as the theatre and cinema.

SPORTS

Over the years, many idioms have entered the English language from the world of sport. From **golf** we have the expression *below par* (= not as good as usual) while **cricket** gave us *have a good innings* (= have a long and successful life or career).

Sport continues to produce many new expressions. Here are a few examples with the sports they come from:

baseball	*play hardball; a ballpark figure; be way out in left field*
boxing	*pull your punches; out for the count; on the ropes*
football/rugby	*move the goalposts; a level playing field; kick sth into touch*
basketball	*a slam dunk* (= a great success)
pool	*behind the eight ball* (= at a disadvantage)

GAMES

There are a large number of idioms related to playing **cards** and **dice**. These frequently refer to common themes:

hiding or revealing your plans and intentions: *keep your cards close to your chest; lay your cards on the table; play your ace; show your hand; have an ace up your sleeve*

probability and chance: *on the cards; the cards/odds are stacked against you; the dice are loaded; I wouldn't bet on it*

the way you deal with a situation: *play your cards right; overplay your hand; pass the buck; cash in your chips; have had your chips*

taking risks: *a safe bet; dice with death; at stake; hedge your bets*

ENTERTAINMENT

Here are some of the idioms that have come from different forms of entertainment over the ages:

theatre	*behind the scenes; take centre stage; play to the gallery; pleased as Punch* (from Punch and Judy puppet shows)
music and opera	*play second fiddle; dance to sb's tune; sing a different song/tune; sing from the same hymn sheet; it's not over till the fat lady sings; a prima donna*
magic	*pull a rabbit out of a hat; hey presto; try every trick in the book*
radio	*be on the same wavelength; the sixty-four thousand dollar question*
journalism	*hot off the press; hit the headlines*
cinema	*cut to the chase; it's in the can; it's a wrap*

ORIGINS: Literature and Quotations

Many idioms have entered English from literature and history.

FABLES AND FAIRY TALES

The stories we are told as children often remain with us for the rest of our lives and some have even entered the language as idioms.

Idioms from **Aesop's fables** include: *sour grapes, the goose that laid the golden eggs, the lion's share* and *the boy who cried wolf*.

Two of **Hans Christian Andersen**'s most famous stories are *the ugly duckling* and *the emperor's new clothes*.

English fairy tales gave us *a peeping Tom* and *the streets are paved with gold*.

Several idioms come from the **1001 Arabian Nights**: *an Aladdin's cave, let the genie out of the bottle* and *open sesame*.

THE CLASSICAL WORLD

Many English phrases come from ancient **Greek** and **Roman** history:

From **ancient myths**: *an Achilles' heel, Pandora's box* and *play Cupid*.

From **ancient history**: *as rich as Croesus, rest on your laurels* and *hold out an olive branch*.

The life of **Julius Caesar** and **Alexander the Great** gave us: *cross the Rubicon, the die is cast* and *cut the Gordian knot*.

SHAKESPEARE AND THE BIBLE

The **King James Bible** and the complete works of **Shakespeare** have had a profound influence on the English language. Here are a few examples:

Shakespeare	The Bible
gild the lily	*the salt of the earth*
hoist by your own petard	*fall by the wayside*
pomp and circumstance	*the writing is on the wall*
your pound of flesh	*hide your light under a bushel*

FAMOUS QUOTATIONS

Many well-known phrases from **books** and **poems** have become part of the language, these include:

hope springs eternal (from a poem by **Alexander Pope**, 1688-1744)
ships that pass in the night (**Henry Wadsworth Longfellow**, 1807-1882)
Big Brother (from the novel *1984* by **George Orwell**, 1903- 1950)

HISTORICAL FIGURES

Famous figures from history have also left their mark on the language. The American president **Richard Nixon** talked about *the silent majority*, while **Napoleon** *met his Waterloo* in 1815. The English political leader **Oliver Cromwell** famously gave rise to the expression *warts and all* when he asked a painter to portray him as he was, not as he would like to be.

S6 The Language and Structure of Idioms

The words and structures used within idioms are often quite unusual:

OLD-FASHIONED WORDS AND MEANINGS

Many idioms are old and contain words that are no longer used apart from within these phrases. Some examples of **archaic words** include:

> *a **damsel*** (= a lady) *in distress*
> *your next of **kin*** (= family)
> *whys and **wherefores*** (= for what (purpose))
> ***hither** and **thither*** (= to here and to there)

Other words are only ever used in idiomatic expressions and are never found in other contexts, for example: *put the **kibosh** on sth, be in **cahoots**,* or *in high **dudgeon***.

Some words used in idioms seem familiar but actually have a **different meaning** from the one that is current today. Examples include:

- *get their just deserts* – the word ***deserts*** here means 'what sb deserves'
- *curry favour* – ***curry*** is an old verb meaning 'groom a horse'
- *money is no **object*** – meaning 'money is no objection'
- *hold fast; stick fast; hard and fast* – ***fast*** usually means 'quick'. However in these phrases it means 'fixed' or 'firm'.

FOREIGN WORDS AND FOREIGN PHRASES

In several cases, a word that is used in an idiom derives from a **foreign language**, for example:

> *the head **honcho*** (= the person in charge) from Japanese
> *the whole **caboodle*** (= everything) from Dutch
> *run **amok*** (= be out of control) from Malay
> *a big **cheese*** (= an important person) from Hindi

Sometimes whole expressions from other languages have entered English. Phrases from French are the most common, although Latin terms are frequently used in legal and academic contexts:

French	Latin
the crème de la crème	*ad infinitum*
raison d'être	*in loco parentis*
faux pas	*quid pro quo*
vis-à-vis	*non sequitur*
tour de force	*status quo*

Looking at something suggests giving it your **attention**:

You need to keep your eye on him (= pay attention to what he does).
The police turned a blind eye to it (= ignored it).

2 **you hear with your ears:**
The news finally reached her ears (= she heard about it).
Walls have ears (= other people may be listening).
The authorities turned a deaf ear to my request (= ignored it).

3 **you speak with your mouth, tongue and lips:**

mouth	tongue	lip
watch your mouth	*have a loose tongue*	*my lips are sealed*
keep your mouth shut	*have a sharp tongue*	*on everyone's lips*
take the words out of my mouth	*a slip of the tongue*	*bite my lip/tongue*

YOUR NOSE IS FOR INVESTIGATING

The nose is often associated with **finding** or **investigating** things,
probably from a comparison with the way a dog investigates by
following a smell or sniffing things. Examples include:

Just follow your nose.
He was having a nose around.
Keep your nose out of my business and it's opposite *stick your nose in.*

MANY HANDS MAKE LIGHT WORK

For most **work** you need to use your hands and many idioms reflect this:

a helping hand	*have your hands full*
lend sb a hand	*get your hands dirty*

If you hold something in your hands you can control it, so 'hand'
sometimes refers to **control**:

in/out of hand (= in/out of control)
out of my hands (= not my responsibility)
take sb in hand (= begin to control or look after him/her)
have a free hand (= be free to take your own decisions)

If you kill someone with a knife you will get blood on your hands.
Responsibility for a crime or bad action is sometimes shown in terms
of having clean or unclean hands:

You'll have blood on your hands.
He's anxious to prove that his hands are clean.
I wash my hands of the whole matter (= I will not be responsible
  for what happens in future).

There are hundreds of idioms that people use to describe feelings and emotions. Here you will find some of these idioms grouped by the following themes:

- angry/annoyed
- confused
- energy/health
- happy
- love/attraction
- proud/confident/ ashamed
- sad/upset
- scared/frightened
- surprised/unprepared
- worried/nervous

For more information on the individual idioms look at the appropriate place in the dictionary where each idiom can be found.

ANGRY/ANNOYED
There are many idioms related to being angry. Here are a few:

become angry: *fly off the handle* *hit the roof/ go through the roof* *have a fit/hysterics* *go ballistic/mental*	**become a little angry or excited:** *get hot under the collar* *get the hump* *lose your cool* *get bent out of shape*
bored or irritated *I'm sick and tired of it.* *I'm fed up to the back teeth with it.* *be climbing the walls* *browned off*	**offend or annoy someone:** *put his nose out of joint* *tread on her toes* *rub him up the wrong way* *put her back up*
show your anger: *give him a black look* *look daggers at her* *shake your fist at them*	**attack or punish someone:** *jump down my throat* *bite her head off* *nail him to the wall*

CONFUSED

being confused: *lose your bearings* *in a fog, in a spin, in a whirl* *completely at sea* *tie yourself in knots* *not know if you're coming or going*	**can't understand something:** *can't make head or tail of it* **start to understand something** *get to grips with it* *get the hang of it* *get your head round it*

ENERGY/HEALTH

full of energy: *full of beans* *as fresh as a daisy* *bright-eyed and bushy-tailed*	**very tired:** *dead on your feet* *on your hands and knees* *fit/ready to drop*
feeling very well and healthy: *feel like a million dollars* *working/firing on all cylinders* *(as) fit as a fiddle*	**feel unwell:** *under the weather* *feel like death warmed up* *not so/too hot*

C Look at the following and check the main part of the dictionary for more information on each expression.

Idioms you can use when…

1 …you don't know the answer to something

> I haven't a clue.
> Search me.
> Your guess is as good as mine.
> Goodness knows.
> I haven't got the foggiest.
> I have no idea.

2 …you want to tell somebody to keep calm

> Keep you hair on!
> Keep your shirt on!
> It's not the end of the world.
> Don't get your knickers in a twist.
> Don't make a mountain out of a molehill.
> Take it easy.

3 …you understand what somebody is telling you

> I get the message.
> I get the picture.
> I take your point.
> Enough said.
> Tell me about it.
> Say no more.

4 …you do not believe what somebody has told you

> Pull the other one!
> As if!
> Come off it!
> Tell me another!
> You're joking!
> A likely story!

D Choose an idiom that could be used in reply to the following. There are two sentences for each of bubbles above.

1 Where's Mark?
2 Harry is going to star in a Hollywood movie.
3 I don't think you should mention this to Jane – it would only upset her.
4 John's broken my stereo – I'm going to kill him!
5 When I was a teenager, I used to date Madonna.
6 I'd better not go out tonight – I need to save money.
7 How far is Denver from Chicago?
8 My computer's crashed and I've lost all my work – I could scream!

It's as Easy as ABC

There are a lot of expressions in English that use *as x as y* to mean 'very x'.

A Choose which adjective is the correct one to complete the idiom.

1 as _____ as falling off a log
   painful   funny   easy

2 as _____ as a mule
   stubborn   mad   lazy

3 as _____ as a fiddle
   fit   fine   free

4 as _____ as a cucumber
   crisp   cool   green

5 as _____ as a bee
   annoying   noisy   busy

6 as _____ as a pancake
   flat   sweet   pale

B The nouns in the idioms have been mixed up. Find the right combination.

1 Their little girl is as bright as *a bird*.   a button

2 He answered the question as quick as *a bat*.   _____

3 In her new dress, Rachel looked as pretty as *gold*.   _____

4 Without his glasses, he's as blind as ~~a button~~.   _____

5 You're out of prison now and as free as *a flash*.   _____

6 The children behaved well; they were as good as *a picture*. _____

C In these phrases, two of the nouns are commonly used in idioms. Can you identify the one that is not?

a hatter   a March hare   potatoes   day   air   a feather

as mad as…   as plain as…   as light as…

monkeys   the nose on your face   a bubble

D Comparisons with 'like'
We can say that a good swimmer 'swims like a fish'. Choose the correct noun from the box to complete these sentences.

wildfire   a leaf   a headless chicken   hot cakes   a light

1 Before I sang my solo, I was shaking like _____ .

2 We need to order some more of those umbrellas. They're selling like _____ .

3 I was so tired, I went out like _____ .

4 The rumour spread like _____ .

5 She was running around like _____ trying to get everything done.

All Eyes

A Choose the idiom which would be appropriate in the following situations:

1 You're so proud of your child.
  a He's the apple of my eye.
  b He's for my eyes only.
  c He looks a sight.

2 You're pleased to see someone.
  a She's robbed me blind.
  b I take a dim view of her.
  c She's a sight for sore eyes.

3 She's good at noticing things around her.
  a She can see things in her mind's eye.
  b She has eyes in the back of her head.
  c She can see her way clear to doing that.

4 There's too much information for you to see clearly.
  a I can't see the wood for the trees.
  b I just watch the world go by.
  c I need to keep my eyes open.

5 He looks terrible.
  a I take a dim view of him.
  b He looks a sight.
  c I know him by sight.

6 You don't want anyone else to see something.
  a This is for your eyes only.
  b Keep your eyes peeled.
  c Feast your eyes on this.

B Julie's talking about her friend Clare. Use the idioms in the box to replace the phrases 1–9, changing the form as necessary.

turn a blind eye	love is blind	not take your eyes off sb
cry your eyes out	have (got) a roving eye	see the light
with your eyes open	set eyes on sb	swear blind

couldn't take her eyes off

It all started on holiday. She just **1** *couldn't stop looking at* this guy. I didn't like him and could tell he **2** *was always looking for the chance to start a new sexual relationship* but she just wouldn't listen – **3** *when people are in love they just don't see things clearly*, as they say.

They started spending a lot of time together but then, one night, she caught him kissing someone else. Well, you know Clare. She would never **4** *pretend not to notice something*, so she marched over, threw her drink over him and told him she never wanted to **5** *see him* again.

That night she **6** *cried a lot* but I'm glad she **7** *understood what the real situation was*. She **8** *says definitely* that she'll never trust another man again and that next time she'll go into a relationship **9** *knowing what to expect,* but she'll change her mind when she meets the right person.

Naming Names

A Places

Complete the sentences with the name of a place or a nationality. The words are in the box below, but be careful – there are a few extra words that you will not need!

The other children said they'd send him to _Coventry_ if he told the teacher.

I wouldn't do her job for all the tea in _____ .

You're taking wine with you to France? Isn't that a bit like taking coals to ___ _____ ?

4 Don't try to rush things. _____ wasn't built in a day, you know.

5 I can't believe he won the game! He has the luck of the _____ , that boy.

6 I don't want you to pay for my meal as well as your own. Let's go _____ .

China	Greek	Irish	Rome	American	~~Coventry~~
French	Newcastle	Indian	Dutch	Cheshire	

B People

All the answers in this crossword are people's names. If you need help, one word in each clue will lead you to the correct part of the dictionary.

Across(→)

2 He likes to have a good time, this *lad*. (4)

4 We would all like to live this man's *life*. (5)

5 He's the American *uncle*. (3)

7 This is the *prince* that every girl would like to meet. (8)

9 It's easy when he's your *uncle*. (3)

11 He's *Mr Hyde*'s other side. (6)

Down (↓)

1 His *choice* is no choice at all. (6)

2 Mr *Blow* or Mr *Public*, just ordinary guys. (3)

3 He has the golden *touch*. (5)

6 He's the *real* thing, the best example. (5)

8 By his *law*, everything that can go wrong, will go wrong. (6)

10 This *old* man is in the police force. (4)

on the 'market
available for sale: *This computer isn't on the market yet. You should be able to buy one early next year.* ◇ *This house only came on the market yesterday.* ◇ *We're putting a new range of cosmetics on the market next month.*

play the 'market
buy and sell stocks and shares in order to make a profit: *He's been playing the market for 30 years, but is quick to warn people of the risks involved.*

- **black** → the black market
- **bottom** → the bottom drops/falls out of the market
- **buyer** → a buyer's market
- **corner** → corner the market (in sth)
- **flood** → flood the market
- **open** → on the open market
- **price** → price yourself/sth out of the market
- **seller** → a seller's market

marks /mɑːks; AmE mɑːrks/

on your ,marks, get ,set, 'go!
used to tell runners in a race to get ready and then to start: *He raised the starting gun. 'On your marks, get set, go!' he shouted, and fired into the air.*

- **full** → full marks (to sb for doing sth)

marriage /'mærɪdʒ/

- **heaven** → a marriage/match made in heaven
- **shotgun** → a shotgun wedding/marriage

marrow /'mærəʊ; AmE -roʊ/

- **chill** → chill sb to the bone/marrow

marry /'mæri/

marry in 'haste (, repent at 'leisure) (*saying*)
people who marry quickly, without really getting to know each other, will discover later that they have made a mistake

marry 'money
marry a rich person: *His sister married money — she lives in Bermuda now.*

mass /mæs/

be a 'mass of sth
be full of or covered with sth: *The garden was a mass of flowers.*

mast /mɑːst; AmE mæst/

- **nail** → nail your colours to the mast

master /'mɑːstə(r); AmE 'mæs-/

be your own 'master/'mistress
be free to make your own decisions rather than being told what to do by sb else: *There's no point trying to tell him what to do. He's his own master, as you know.*

- **past** → a past master (in/of/at sth)

masters /'mɑːstəz; AmE 'mæstərz/

- **serve** → serve two masters

mat /mæt/

go to the 'mat (with sb) (for sb/sth) (*AmE, informal*)
support or defend sb/sth in an argument with sb: *We went to the mat for him because he'd helped us in the past.*

take sb/sth to the 'mat (*AmE, informal*)
to get involved in an argument with sb/sth: *He took them to the mat on that issue.*

> **NOTE**
> Both of these idioms come from the sport of wrestling, in which two people fight by holding each other and trying to force the other person to the ground or mat.

- **welcome** → lay, put, roll, etc. out the welcome mat (for sb)

match /mætʃ/

be no 'match for sb/sth
not as good, etc. as sb/sth; not be able to compete successfully against sb/sth: *He's no match for Woods. Woods is much the better player.* ◇ *We are no match for the Japanese when it comes to making cameras.*

find/meet your 'match (in sb)
meet sb who is as good at doing sth as you are, and perhaps better: *He thought he could beat anyone, but he's finally found his match.* ◇ *As a saleswoman, she's met her match in Lorna.*

- **heaven** → a marriage/match made in heaven
- **man** → the man of the match
- **mix** → mix and match
- **shooting** → the whole shooting match
- **slanging** → a slanging match

matter /'mætə(r)/

as a matter of 'course
as a regular habit, or as a normal way of behaving: *Before making any important decision, I discuss it with my wife as a matter of course.* ◇ *As a matter of course, you should go to the dentist at least once a year.*

as a matter of 'fact (*spoken*)
used when you are telling sb sth interesting, new or important: *I'm going home early today. As a matter of fact, it's my birthday.* ◇ *I don't agree, as a matter of fact.*

(do sth) as a matter of 'form
(do sth) because it is polite, or because it is the usual way of doing sth: *We knew everyone agreed, but we had a vote as a matter of form.* ◇ *I need your signature, just as a matter of form.*

be another/a different 'matter
be very different: *I know which area they live in, but whether I can find their house is a different matter altogether.*

be the 'matter (with sb/sth)
be the reason for unhappiness, pain, problems, etc: *What's the matter, Gail? You look ill.* ◇ *John's been very quiet recently. I wonder if there's anything the matter with him.* ◇ *Don't worry, there's nothing*

March /mɑːtʃ; AmE mɑːrtʃ/

● mad → (as) mad as a March hare

march /mɑːtʃ; AmE mɑːrtʃ/

march to (the beat of) a different 'drummer/ 'drum (also **march to a different 'tune** *less frequent*)
behave in a different way from other people; have different attitudes or ideas: *She was a gifted and original artist who marched to a different drummer.*

● quick → quick march
● steal → steal a march on sb

marching /'mɑːtʃɪŋ; AmE 'mɑːrtʃɪŋ/

get your 'marching orders (*BrE, informal*)
be ordered to leave a place, a job, etc: *When he kept arriving late he got his marching orders.*

> ❷ ORIGIN
> These were originally the orders given for soldiers to depart.

give sb their 'marching orders (*BrE, informal*)
tell sb to leave a job, a relationship, etc: *When she found out he was seeing another woman, she gave him his marching orders.*

mare /meə(r); AmE mer/

a 'mare's nest
1 an idea or a discovery that seems interesting and exciting but is found to be false or have no value: *I fancy this will prove to be a mare's nest! We have had these mysteries before.*

> NOTE
> A *mare* is a female horse or donkey. They do not make nests and so a mare's nest does not exist.

2 a difficult or complicated situation; a mess: *This area of the law is a veritable mare's nest.* ◇ *My hair is a mare's nest!*

marines /mə'riːnz/

● tell → (go) tell it/that to the marines

mark /mɑːk; AmE mɑːrk/

be close to/near the 'mark
almost correct or accurate: *The estimate of the total cost had been pretty close to the mark, in fact.* ◇ *She thinks it will take six months to complete the job, but I think eight would be nearer the mark.*

be ,quick/,slow off the 'mark
be quick/slow to do sth or understand sth: *You have to be quick off the mark when you answer a newspaper advertisement for an apartment.* ◇ *Jenny was rather slow off the mark, and they had to explain the joke to her.*

> NOTE
> In athletics, your *mark* is your starting point in a race.

get off the 'mark
start scoring, especially in cricket: *Stewart got off the mark with a four.*

,hit/,miss the 'mark
succeed/fail in achieving or guessing sth: *He blushed furiously and Robyn knew she had hit the mark.*

,leave/,make your/its 'mark (on sth/sb)
do sth important, that has a lasting effect or makes a lasting impression (on sth/sb): *As Minister for Education, he left his mark on British politics.* ◇ *Her two unhappy marriages have left their mark* (= have made her an unhappy person).

,make your 'mark
become famous because you are very good at sth: *He's an actor who has made his mark in comedy shows.*

,mark my 'words (*old-fashioned, spoken*)
(often used for introducing a warning) listen carefully to what I am saying: *He'll be back, mark my words! He never stays away for long.*

mark 'time
stay in one situation, job, etc., not making any progress, but waiting for an opportunity to do so: *'What are you doing at the moment?' 'I'm just marking time until somebody offers me a better job.'*

> NOTE
> If soldiers *mark time*, they march on one spot without moving forward.

,mark 'you (*old-fashioned spoken, especially BrE*)
used to remind sb of sth they should consider in a particular case: *She hasn't had much success yet. Mark you, she tries hard.*

,up to the 'mark
as good as it/they should be: *His English and history are very good, but his maths is not really up to the mark.* ◇ *I don't think we should promote her. She's just not up to the mark.*

● black → a black mark (against sb)
● high-water → high-water mark
● overshoot → overshoot the mark
● overstep → overstep the mark/line
● question → a question mark hangs over sb/sth
● question → there's a question mark (hanging) over sb/ sth
● toe → toe the mark **SEE** toe the line
● wide → be (a long) way off the mark **SEE** be/fall wide of the mark

marked /mɑːkt; AmE mɑːrkt/

a marked 'man
a man who is in danger of being killed by his enemies: *When they discovered he was a spy, he became a marked man.*

market /'mɑːkɪt; AmE 'mɑːrk-/

in the 'market for sth (*informal*)
interested in buying sth: *I'm not in the market for a car as expensive as that.* ◇ *Do you know anyone in the market for some stereo equipment?*

13 If you understand what somebody means, even if they do not say it directly, *you get the _____.*

  a picture   **b** painting   **c** scene

14 If something is a very small amount compared to what is needed, it is *a drop in the _____.*

  a sea   **b** river   **c** ocean

15 If you wouldn't like to do something at all, you wouldn't do it *for all the tea in _____.*

  a England   **b** China   **c** India

16 If something sells very quickly in large quantities, it *sells like hot _____.*

  a toast   **b** bread   **c** cakes

17 If you are completely wrong, you are *way out in left _____.*

  a field   **b** pitch   **c** court

18 If an emotion can clearly be seen in somebody's expression, it is *written all over his/her _____.*

  a face   **b** look   **c** eyes

19 If something is very easy to see or understand, it's *as plain as _____.*

  a Jane   **b** day   **c** pie

20 If you give an important visitor a very special welcome, you *put out the red _____.*

  a carpet   **b** mat   **c** flag

21 If you have a nervous feeling in your stomach, you *have _____ in your stomach.*

  a birds   **b** snakes   **c** butterflies

22 If something is back to normal after a difficult period, it is *back on an even _____.*

  a board   **b** keel   **c** deck

23 If you say '*It's no use crying over spilt _____*', you think that it is a waste of time to worry or complain about something that is done and cannot be changed.

  a water   **b** soup   **c** milk

24 Somebody you are very pleased or relieved to see is *a sight for _____ eyes.*

  a sore   **b** tired   **c** red

25 If you deal with a difficult or dangerous situation in a direct and brave way, you *take the bull by the _____.*

  a leg   **b** tail   **c** horns

Put Yourself to the Test

The following two pages give you an opportunity to test yourself on the idioms that have been focused on in the study pages.
The questions do not follow the same order as the study pages.

1 Someone who is unfriendly and never shows emotion is *a cold* _____ .
  a frog   **b** stone   **c** fish

2 If you make a lot of money very quickly, you *make money hand over*
_____ .
  a hand   **b** fist   **c** foot

3 If something is normal or what you would expect, it is *par for the*
_____ .
  a pitch   **b** course   **c** field

4 If you lie to someone as a joke, you *pull their* _____ .
  a leg   **b** nose   **c** hair

5 If something is very easy, it is *a piece of* _____ .
  a pie   **b** cake   **c** chocolate

6 If something is the original and best version of something, it is *the real*
_____ .
  a McCoy   **b** McDonald   **c** McCartney

7 If you speak in an unkind and unpleasant way, you *have a sharp* _____ .
  a heart   **b** mouth   **c** tongue

8 If you recognize a name or word, it *has a familiar* _____ *to it.*
  a ring   **b** sound   **c** noise

9 If you have a lot of things to do and a lot of responsibilities, you *have a lot on your* _____ .
  a dish   **b** plate   **c** table

10 If you are not as well or cheerful as usual, you are *under the* _____ .
  a rain   **b** clouds   **c** weather

11 If you know a place very well, you know it *like the back of your* _____ .
  a head   **b** hand   **c** eyes

12 If something happens suddenly or unexpectedly, it happens *out of the*
_____ .
  a black   **b** white   **c** blue

the matter. ◇ *There's something the matter with this radio. It's stopped working.*

be (all) a matter of sth/doing sth
depend on sth/doing sth: *Success in business is all a matter of experience.* ◇ *Doing anything well is a matter of practice.*

be a matter of o'pinion
be sth which people disagree about: *'She's a great singer.' 'That's a matter of opinion'* (= I do not agree).

the 'fact/'truth of the matter
used when you want to show you are being honest, or when you are telling sb sth unusual or surprising: *I didn't take anything, and that's the truth of the matter.* ◇ *The fact of the matter is that they only got married so she could stay in the country.*

for 'that matter (*spoken*)
used to say that the second thing mentioned is just as important or true as the first thing: *Don't shout at your mother like that — or at anyone else, for that matter.* ◇ *She thought that TV — and staying indoors, for that matter — was bad for children.*

a matter of 'days, 'miles, 'pounds, etc.
a particular number of days, miles, etc., especially when this number is small: *Don't worry, it'll only be a matter of hours before he gets back.* ◇ *It will only cost us a matter of a few pounds.* ◇ *Travelling by boat could take us a matter of weeks.*

no matter who, what, where, when, etc.
used to say that sth is always true, whatever the situation is, or that sb should certainly do sth: *Don't open the door, no matter who comes.* ◇ *No matter what he says, don't trust him.* ◇ *I'll find her, no matter where she's hiding.*

• grey → grey matter
• heart → the heart of the matter
• laughing → no laughing matter
• mind → mind over matter
• time → it's only, just, etc. a matter/a question of time (before...)

matters /ˈmætəz; *AmE* ˈmætərz/

take matters into your own 'hands
do sth yourself, because you are tired of waiting for sb else to do it: *The police were doing nothing about finding my car, so I decided to take matters into my own hands and look for it myself.*

• mince → not mince matters **SEE** not mince your words

mature /məˈtʃʊə(r); -ˈtjʊə(r); *AmE* -ˈtʃʊr; -ˈtʊr/

on mature re'flection/conside'ration (*formal*)
after thinking about sth carefully and for a long time: *He wanted to ban his staff from using the Internet at work, but on mature reflection he decided that this would not be good for morale.*

max /mæks/

to the 'max
to the highest level or greatest amount possible: *She believes in living life to the max.*

may /meɪ/

be that as it 'may ♦ that's as 'may be (*formal*)
in spite of that: *I know he's tried hard; be that as it may, his work is just not good enough.* ◇ *'That dress cost $800.' 'That's as may be, I still don't like it.'*

McCoy /məˈkɔɪ/

• real → the real McCoy

mea /meɪə/

mea 'culpa (*from Latin, often humorous*)
used when you are admitting that sth is your fault: *'Who broke this glass?' 'Mea culpa,' Frank said.*

meal /miːl/

make a 'meal of/out of sth (*informal*)
do sth with more effort and care than it really needs; treat sth as more serious than it really is: *Just write her a short note — don't make a meal of it.* ◇ *It's only a small mistake. There's no need to make such a meal out of it, is there?* **OPP** make nothing of sth (1)

a 'meal ticket (*informal*)
a person or thing that you see only as a source of money and food: *He suspected that he was just a meal ticket for her.* ◇ *I hoped the guitar would become my meal ticket.*

• square → a square meal

mean /miːn/

be no mean... (*approving*)
be a thing of a very high quality; be a very good example of sth: *His mother was a painter and he's no mean artist himself.* ◇ *Cycling around France at the age of 75 is no mean feat.*

be/mean 'nothing to sb (*informal*)
not be important for sb; not be a person that sb loves: *Why should he go to the funeral? The dead man was nothing to him.* ◇ *The danger meant nothing to them.*

the happy/golden 'mean (*approving*)
a course of action that is not extreme: *To be honest, I don't like either of the proposals. What we really need is a golden mean between the two.*

I mean (*spoken*)
used to explain or correct what you have just said: *I blame the parents. I mean, would you allow a 13-year-old to stay out until 2 o'clock in the morning?*

mean 'business (*informal*)
be serious about what you plan to do; be determined: *He means business. If we try to escape, he'll shoot us.* ◇ *I'm not joking. This time I really mean business.*

mean (sb) no 'harm ✦ not mean (sb) any 'harm
not have any intention of hurting sb: *Try not to worry about what he said. I know you thought he was rude, but he didn't mean any harm by it.*

mean to 'say
used to emphasize what you are saying or to ask sb if they really mean what they say: *I mean to say, you should have known how he would react!* ◊ *Do you mean to say you've lost it?*

'mean well (*usually disapproving*)
have good intentions, although their effect may not be good: *Your father means well, I know, but I wish he'd stop telling us what to do.* ◊ *She's always suggesting ways I could improve my cooking. I know she means well but it really annoys me.* ▶ ,**well-'meaning** *adj.*: *She's very well-meaning, but she only makes the situation worse.*

● **supposed →** what's that supposed to mean?
● **world →** be/mean (all) the world to sb

meaning /'miːnɪŋ/

get sb's 'meaning (*informal*)
understand what sb is really saying: *I get your meaning. You don't need to say any more.*

● **know →** not know the meaning of the word

means /miːnz/

by 'all means (*spoken*)
used to say that you are very willing for sb to have sth or do sth: *'Can I smoke?' 'By all means.'* ◊ *'Do you think I could borrow this dictionary?' 'Yes, by all means.'*

by means of sth (*formal*)
with the help of sth: *The load was lifted by means of a crane.*

by 'no (manner of) means ✦ not by 'any (manner of) means
in no way at all; definitely not: *She is by no means poor, believe me. She only pretends to be.* ◊ *He hasn't won yet, not by any manner of means.*

(be) a ,means to an 'end
a thing you do in order to achieve or obtain sth else: *He saw his college education simply as a means to an end — a well-paid job.*

● **end →** the end justifies the means
● **fair →** by fair means or foul
● **last →** last but by no means least
● **live¹ →** live beyond/within your means
● **ways →** ways and means

meant /ment/

be meant to be sth
be generally considered to be sth: *This restaurant is meant to be excellent.*

meantime /'miːntaɪm/

in the 'meantime/'meanwhile
in the time between two things happening: *In five minutes, there's the news. In the meantime, here's some music.* ◊ *The bus doesn't leave until six*

o'clock. *In the meantime we can go and have a coffee.* ◊ *I hope to go to medical school eventually. In the meanwhile, I'm going to study chemistry.*

measure /'meʒə(r)/

beyond 'measure (*formal*)
very much: *His relief was beyond measure.* ◊ *It has improved beyond measure.*

(do sth) for good 'measure
(do sth) extra in order to make certain that e̶̶ ̶ thing is all right, safe, etc: *Put a couple̶̶   ̶̶e̶ spoonfuls of tea in the pot for good measure. There's nothing worse than weak tea.* ◊ *I've put new locks on all the doors, and just for good measure, I've put locks on all the downstairs windows too.*

full/short 'measure
the whole of sth or less of sth than you expect or should have: *We experienced the full measure of their hospitality.* ◊ *The concert only lasted an hour, so we felt we were getting short measure.*

get/have/take the 'measure of sb ✦ get/have/take sb's 'measure (*formal*)
form an opinion about sb's character or abilities so that you can deal with them: *The champion soon had the measure of his young opponent.*

in great, large, etc. 'measure (*formal*)
to a great extent or degree: *His success is in great measure the result of good luck.* ◊ *You are in large measure responsible for all our problems.* ◊ *My expectations had been met in full measure.*

in some, equal, etc. 'measure (*formal*)
to some, etc. extent or degree: *The introduction of a new tax accounted in some measure for the downfall of the government.* ◊ *Our thanks are due in equal measure to every member of the team.*

make sth to 'measure (*BrE*)
make a piece of clothing especially for sb, by taking personal measurements: *All his shirts are made to measure.* ▶ ,**made-to-'measure** *adj.*: *a made-to-measure suit*

measures /'meʒəz; AmE 'meʒərz/

● **half →** no half measures

meat /miːt/

be meat and 'drink (to sb)
be sth that a person enjoys very much or is very interested in: *Stories about the royal family are meat and drink to journalists.*

● **dead →** dead meat
● **man →** one man's meat is another man's poison

meat-and-potatoes /,miːt ən pə-'teɪtəʊz AmE -toʊz /

,**meat-and-po'tatoes** (*AmE*)
dealing with or interested in the most basic and important aspects of sth: *a meat-and-potatoes argument* ◊ *My father always was a meat-and-potatoes man* (= a person who likes simple things).

,mind over 'matter
the influence of the mind on the body; the power to change things by thinking: *'How does he manage to work when he's so ill?' 'Mind over matter.'*

,mind your own 'business (*spoken, informal*)
think about your own affairs and not ask questions about or try to get involved in other people's lives: *'Who was the girl I saw you with last night?' 'Mind your own business!'* ◇ *I was sitting in a cafe minding my own business when a man came up to me and hit me in the face.*

mind your ,P's and 'Q's (*informal*)
be careful how you behave; remember to be polite: *Sally's got very strict ideas about how her children should behave, so mind your P's and Q's.*

❓ ORIGIN
This expression probably refers to the *P* in 'please' and the pronunciation of 'thank you' which sounds like *Q*.

mind the 'shop (*BrE*) (*AmE* **mind the 'store**)
be in charge of sth for a short time while sb is away: *Who's minding the shop while the boss is abroad?*

mind 'you (*spoken*)
1 used to add to what you have just said, especially sth that makes it less strong: *It's a fantastic restaurant. Expensive, mind you.* ◇ *I've heard they're getting divorced. Mind you, I'm not surprised — they were always arguing.*
2 used after a word you want to emphasize: *When we were children, we used to walk, walk mind you, five miles to and from school every day.*

,mind your 'backs! (*informal*)
used to tell people to move out of your way, for example when you are carrying something: *Mind your backs! I'm coming through!*

never 'mind
1 (*especially BrE*) used to tell sb not to worry or be upset: *You failed your driving test? Never mind, the best drivers always fail the first time.*
2 used to suggest that sth is not important: *This isn't the place I wanted to take you to — but never mind, it's just as good.*
3 used to emphasize that what is true about the first thing you have said is even more true about the second: *I never thought she'd win once, never mind twice!*

never mind (about) (doing) sth
used to tell sb that they should not think about sth or do sth because it is not as important as sth else, or because you will do it: *Never mind the washing-up — we haven't got time.* ◇ *Never mind saying how sorry you are, who's going to pay for the damage you've done?*

,never you 'mind (*informal*)
used to tell sb not to ask about sth because you are not going to tell them: *'How much did you pay for it?' 'Never you mind.'* ◇ *Never you mind why I want it, just give it to me.*

put you in mind of sb/sth (*old-fashioned*)
remind you of sb/sth: *Her way of speaking puts me in mind of my mother.* ◇ *That music always puts me in mind of holidays in Turkey.*

put/set sb's 'mind at ease/rest
do or say sth to sb which stops them worrying about sth: *If you'd phoned me it would have put my mind at ease.* ◇ *He was nervous about meeting my parents, so I tried to set his mind at rest.*

put/set/turn your 'mind to sth
give all your effort and attention to sth or to achieving sth: *You could be a very good writer if you put your mind to it.* ◇ *He can turn his mind to the detail if he has to.*

put/get sth out of your 'mind
stop thinking about sth; try to forget sth: *Let's put the problems with the bank out of our minds and try to enjoy ourselves a bit. There's no point worrying all the time.*

take sb's 'mind off sth
make sb forget about sth unpleasant for a short time: *I went out to see a movie to try to take my mind off my problems.* ◇ *We're trying to take his mind off things a bit.*

to 'my mind (*spoken*)
in my opinion: *To my mind, his earlier works are better.*

a practical, scientific, etc. turn of 'mind
a practical, scientific, etc. way of thinking about things: *He's got a very practical turn of mind. He can fix anything.*

turn sth over in your 'mind
think about sth, for example an offer, a plan, etc., very carefully before you make a decision: *I've been turning over the job offer in my mind all weekend. I really don't know what to do.*

with sth in mind
for a particular reason: *He wrote the book with his son in mind* (= for his son). ◇ *I went out for a drive, with no particular destination in mind.*

- **bend** → bend your mind/efforts to sth
- **blow** → blow your/sb's mind
- **bore** → bore sb out of their mind
- **cast** → cast your mind back to sth
- **change** → change your mind
- **close**[1] → close your mind (to sth)
- **concentrate** → concentrate the mind
- **cross** → cross sb's mind
- **drive** → drive sb out of their mind/wits
- **engraved** → be engraved on/in your heart/memory/mind
- **etched** → be etched on your heart/memory/mind
- **frame** → a frame of mind
- **heart** → have your heart/mind set on sth/on doing sth **SEE** set your heart/mind on sth/on doing sth
- **heart** → set your heart/mind on sth/doing sth
- **know** → know your own mind
- **language** → mind/watch your language
- **one-track** → have a one-track mind
- **open** → have/keep an open mind (on/about sth)
- **peace** → peace of mind
- **piece** → give sb a piece of your mind
- **presence** → presence of mind
- **prey** → play on sb's mind **SEE** prey on sb's mind
- **prey** → prey on sb's mind

- push → push sth to the back of your mind
- read¹ → read sb's mind/thoughts
- right → (not) in your right mind
- sieve → have a mind/memory like a sieve
- sight → out of sight, out of mind
- slip → slip sb's memory/mind
- speak → speak your mind
- step → mind/watch your step
- stick → stick in your mind
- stoned → stoned out of your mind
- unsound → of unsound mind
- weigh → weigh on your mind

minds /maɪndz/

- meeting → a meeting of minds
- two → be in/of two minds about sth/about doing sth

mine /maɪn/

a mine of infor'mation (about/on sb/sth)
a person, book, etc. that can give you a lot of information on a particular subject: *My grandmother was a mine of information on the family's history.* ◇ *People criticize television, but for children it's a mine of information.*

- gold → a gold mine
- guess → your guess is as good as mine

minority /maɪˈnɒrəti; AmE -ˈnɔːr-; -ˈnɑːr-/

be in a/the mi'nority
form much less than half of a large group: *Men are in the minority in this profession.*

be in a minority of 'one (*often humorous*)
be the only person to have a particular opinion or to vote a particular way: *Hannah didn't like the music, but she realized that she'd be in a minority of one if she said anything negative about it.*

mint /mɪnt/

in mint con'dition
new or as good as new; in perfect condition: *The books were 30 years old but they were in mint condition.* ◇ *My bicycle isn't exactly in mint condition so I really can't ask much for it.*

make, etc. a 'mint (of money) (*informal*)
make a lot of money: *They've made a mint of money with their new range of travel books.* ◇ *You can earn a mint selling ice cream on the beach in July and August.* **OPP** take a bath

> **NOTE**
> A *mint* is a place where money is made.

minus /ˈmaɪnəs/

- plus¹ → plus or minus

minute /ˈmɪnɪt/

(at) any 'minute/'moment ('now)
very soon: *Hurry up! He'll be back any minute now.*

the minute/moment (that)…
as soon as…: *I want to see him the minute he arrives.*

not for a/one 'minute/'moment/'second/ 'instant (*informal*)
not at all; definitely not: *I didn't think for a minute that he was married.* ◇ *Not for one instant would I ever consider going there on holiday again.*

this 'minute
immediately; now: *Come down from there this minute!* ◇ *I don't know what I'm going to do yet — I've only just this minute found out.*

to the 'minute
exactly: *The train arrived at 9.05 to the minute.*

up to the 'minute (*informal*)
1 fashionable and modern: *She's a tremendous follower of fashion. Everything she wears is up to the minute.*
2 having the most recent information: *Our reporters will keep you up to the minute with the latest developments in Florida.* **OPP** out of date

- born → there's one born every minute
- just → just a minute/moment/second
- last → at the last minute/moment
- New York → a New York minute
- wait → wait a minute/moment/second

miracles /ˈmɪrəklz/

- wonders → work/do wonders/miracles (for/on/with sb/ sth)

mirrors /ˈmɪrəz; AmE ˈmɪrərz/

- smoke → smoke and mirrors

mischief /ˈmɪstʃɪf/

do sb/yourself a 'mischief (*BrE, informal or humorous*)
hurt sb/yourself: *You could do yourself a mischief wearing such tight trousers!*

make 'mischief
deliberately do or say sth that annoys or upsets sb; make trouble for sb: *She told those lies because she was jealous and wanted to make mischief.*

miserable /ˈmɪzrəbl/

- sin → (as) miserable/ugly as sin

misery /ˈmɪzəri/

(a) 'misery guts (*informal*)
a way to describe sb who is never happy or who complains a lot: *What's the matter with you, misery guts?* ◇ *He used to be good fun, but he seems to be turning into an old misery guts.*

put sb/sth out of their/its 'misery
1 (*informal*) stop sb worrying by telling them sth that they are anxious to know: *You can't keep telling him to wait for your answer. Put him out of his misery and tell him now.* **OPP** prolong the agony
2 kill an animal which is badly injured or very ill in order to end its suffering: *I can't let a horse go on suffering such terrible pain. Can you put it out of its misery, please.*

- life → make sb's life a misery

miss /mɪs/

he, she, etc. doesn't miss a 'trick (also **he, she, etc. doesn't 'miss much**) (*spoken*)
used to say that sb notices every opportunity to gain an advantage: *I'm sure Julie knows your secret — she never misses a trick!* ◇ *How did he know it was the right time to sell all his shares in the company? He doesn't miss much, does he?*

give sth a 'miss (*informal, especially BrE*)
decide not to do sth: *I usually go to a yoga class on Mondays, but I think I'll give it a miss this week.*

,miss the 'boat (*informal*)
lose the opportunity to do or get sth because you do not act quickly enough: *I'm afraid we've missed the boat — all the tickets for Saturday's performance have been sold.*

a ,miss is as ,good as a 'mile (*saying*)
there is no real difference between only just failing in sth and failing in it badly because the result is still the same: *What's the difference between failing an exam with 35% or 10%? Absolutely nothing; a miss is as good as a mile.*

- **mark** → hit/miss the mark
- **near** → a near miss

misses /'mɪsɪz/

- **heart** → your heart misses a beat

missing /'mɪsɪŋ/

- **know** → not know what you're missing

mission /'mɪʃn/

,mission ac'complished
used when you have successfully completed what you have had to do: *Mission accomplished. Let's go and have a drink.*

mistake /mɪ'steɪk/

and 'no mistake! (*old-fashioned, especially BrE*)
used to show that you are sure about the truth of what you have just said: *The dinner party was a disaster, and no mistake!*

by mi'stake
accidentally; without intending to: *I took your bag instead of mine by mistake.*

in mi'stake for sth
thinking that sth is sth else: *Children may eat pills in mistake for sweets.*

,make no mi'stake (about sth) (*spoken*)
used to emphasize what you are saying, especially when you want to warn sb about sth: *Make no mistake (about it), this is one crisis that won't just go away.*

mistaking /mɪ'steɪkɪŋ/

there's no mi'staking sb/sth
sb/sth is easy to recognize; sth is obvious: *There's no mistaking her voice — she's got a very strong Scottish accent.* ◇ *There's no mistaking the new mood of optimism in the country.*

mistress /'mɪstrəs/

- **master** → be your own master/mistress

mix /mɪks/

,mix and 'match
combine things in different ways for different purposes: *You can mix and match courses to suit your requirements.*

'mix it (with sb) (*BrE*) (*AmE* ,**mix it 'up (with sb)**) (*informal*)
argue with sb or cause trouble: *Don't take any notice of what he says. You know what he's like — always trying to mix it.*

mixed /mɪkst/

be/get mixed 'up in sth
be/become involved in sth, especially sth illegal or dishonest: *What have you got yourself mixed up in now?*

be/get mixed 'up with sb
be/become friendly with or involved with sb that other people do not approve of: *I told her I didn't think she should get mixed up with that group, but as usual she ignored my advice.*

have ,mixed 'feelings (about sb/sth)
have both positive and negative feelings (about sb/sth): *I've got mixed feelings about leaving college — it's great to finish my studies, but I'm rather worried about finding a job.* ◇ *They had mixed feelings about their new boss. She seemed very pleasant but not very organized.*

a ,mixed 'bag/'bunch (*informal*)
a group of people or things of different types or of different abilities: *The entries to the competition were a real mixed bag — some excellent, some awful.* ◇ *This year's students are rather a mixed bunch.*

a ,mixed 'blessing
sth good, pleasant, fortunate, etc. which also has disadvantages: *Living in such a beautiful old castle is something of a mixed blessing. Just think of the heating bills, for example.*

mixer /'mɪksə(r)/

a good/bad 'mixer
a person who finds it easy/difficult to talk to people they do not know, for example at a party: *Whoever we appoint for this position will be dealing directly with our clients. We are looking for someone who is friendly, a good mixer, reliable and practical.*

mob /mɒb; AmE mɑːb/

- **heavy** → the heavy mob/brigade

mockers /'mɒkəz; AmE 'mɑːkərz/

put the 'mockers on sth (*BrE, informal*)
stop sth from happening or spoil its chances for success: *According to the weather forecast, it's going to rain, which will really put the mockers on our plans for a barbecue.*

mockery /'mɒkəri; AmE 'mɑːk-/

make a 'mockery of sth
make sth seem worthless or foolish: *This decision makes a mockery of the party's economic policy.*

> **NOTE**
> If you *mock* a person or thing, you laugh at them/it in an unkind way.

mod /mɒd; AmE mɑːd/

(with) all mod 'cons (*BrE, informal*)
used to describe a house or flat/apartment that has all the things that make living there easier and more comfortable, for example a washing machine, a shower, etc: *From the outside it looks rather old, but inside it's got all mod cons — even a microwave oven.* ◇ *We want a campsite with all mod cons.*

> **NOTE**
> This phrase is a short form of 'modern conveniences'.

Mohammed /mə'hæmɪd/

- **mountain** → if the mountain will not come to Muhammad, Muhammad must go to the mountain

mold /məʊld; AmE moʊld/ (*AmE*) = mould

molehill /'məʊlhɪl; AmE 'moʊl-/

- **mountain** → make a mountain out of a molehill

moment /'məʊmənt; AmE 'moʊ-/

at the 'moment
now; at the present time: *'The number is engaged at the moment.' 'OK, I'll phone again later.'* ◇ *I'm unemployed at the moment.*

the man, woman, etc. of the 'moment
the person most admired and talked about at a particular time: *This is the woman of the moment: the first Olympic gold medalist in gymnastics in this country.*

the ,moment of 'truth
a time when sb/sth is tested, or when important decisions are made: *He asked her if she still loved him. It was a moment of truth.* ◇ *Right, now for the moment of truth. Switch it on and see if it works!*

of 'moment
(*after nouns*) very important: *matters of great moment*

pick/choose your 'moment
carefully choose the right time to do sth: *I wanted to make sure she agreed, so I picked my moment, when she was in a good mood.* ◇ (*ironic*) *You told her you wanted a divorce two days after her operation! You really picked your moment, didn't you?*

- **evil** → the evil hour/day/moment
- **heat** → in the heat of the moment
- **just** → just a minute/moment/second
- **last** → at the last minute/moment
- **minute** → (at) any minute/moment/(now)
- **minute** → not for a/one minute/moment/second/instant
- **minute** → the minute/moment (that)...
- **psychological** → the psychological moment
- **short** → at a moment's notice **SEE** at (very) short notice
- **spur** → (do sth) on the spur of the moment
- **time** → for the moment/present **SEE** for the time being
- **wait** → wait a minute/moment/second
- **weak** → a moment of weakness **SEE** a weak moment
- **weak** → a weak moment

moments /'məʊmənts; AmE 'moʊ-/

have your/its 'moments
have short times that are better, more interesting, etc. than others: *My job's rather boring most of the time but it does have its moments.* ◇ *'What did you think of the play?' 'Well, it had its moments, but on the whole it wasn't very good.'*

Monday /'mʌndeɪ; -di/

,Monday morning 'quarterback (*AmE, informal, disapproving*)
a person who criticizes or comments on an event after it has happened: *It's easy to play Monday morning quarterback and say that he made a poor decision.* ▶ **,Monday morning 'quarterback** *verb* criticize or comment on an event after it has happened: *I don't like to Monday morning quarterback any work that is done by another investigator.* **,Monday morning 'quarterbacking** *noun*: *This is the worst kind of Monday-morning quarterbacking.*

> **❷ ORIGIN**
> The *quarterback* directs the play in an American football game. Most games are played on a Sunday so Monday morning is the day after the game finished.

that Monday 'morning feeling
a feeling of being depressed because you have to start a new week back at work: *In my new job, I never have that awful Monday morning feeling.*

money /'mʌni/

be in the 'money (*informal*)
have a lot of money to spend: *I'll be in the money if I get this job.*

be 'made of money (*informal*)
be rich; have a lot of money: *I can't afford that! I'm not made of money, you know!* ◇ *Why do people always think that lawyers are made of money?*

for 'my money (*informal*)
in my opinion: *For my money, he's one of the greatest pianists of all time.*

get/have your 'money's worth
get good value for the money you have spent: *What an exciting final it was! The crowd certainly had its money's worth.* ◇ *The movie was only an hour long, so we felt that that we didn't really get our money's worth.*

good 'money
a lot of money; money that you earn with hard work: *Thousands of people paid good money to watch the band perform.* ◇ *Don't waste good money on that!*

have ˌmoney to 'burn
have so much money that you can spend as much as you like: *I was staying at the Ritz — I had money to burn in those days!* ◊ *He's got money to burn. He's just spent $4 000 on a picture of Mickey Mouse.*

have more ˌmoney than 'sense
have a lot of money, and waste it by spending it in a foolish way: *Collectors with more money than sense pay thousands of pounds for these spoons.*

make/lose money ˌhand over 'fist (*informal*)
make/lose money very fast and in large quantities: *Some of these tennis players are making money hand over fist.*

money burns a 'hole in your pocket (*informal*)
sb spends or wants to spend money very quickly and carelessly: *She can't wait to spend her prize money — it's burning a hole in her pocket.* ◊ *He gets paid on Friday and by Monday he's spent it all. Money just burns a hole in his pocket.*

money doesn't grow on 'trees (*saying*)
used to say that you should be careful about how much money you spend because the amount you have is limited: *I can't give you any more pocket money, Alice. Money doesn't grow on trees, you know.*

ˌmoney down the 'drain (*informal*)
a waste of money: *Her father feels that all her expensive education will just be money down the drain if she gets a job in a cafe.*

money for old 'rope (also **money for 'jam**)
(both *BrE, informal*)
money that is earned very easily and with very little effort: *All I have to do in my job is answer the phone occasionally — it's money for old rope.*

money 'talks (*saying*)
if you have a lot of money you can get special treatment, have more power, persuade people to do things, etc: *Of course he'll get what he wants. Money talks, doesn't it?*

on the 'money (*AmE*)
correct; accurate: *His prediction was right on the money.* **OPP** off beam

put 'money into sth
invest money in sth: *She put the money into stocks and shares.* ◊ *The Government should put more money into the film industry.*

put (your) 'money on sb/sth
1 bet that a horse, dog, etc. will win a race: *He put his money on Second Wind for the 3.30.*
2 (*informal*) be certain that sb will do sth, or that sth will happen: *I'd put money on him passing that exam.* ◊ *I wouldn't put any money on that car lasting much longer.*

put your money where your 'mouth is
(*informal*)
show that you really mean what you say, by actually doing sth, giving money, etc. rather than just talking about it: *The government talks about helping disabled people, but doesn't put its money where its mouth is.* ◊ *You think she'll win? Come on, then, put your money where your mouth is* (= have a bet with me).

a (good) run for your 'money (*informal*)
1 a lot of satisfaction or pleasure from sth; good value for sth: *I've had a good run for my money as director of this company, but now I think it's time someone younger took over.*
2 strong and satisfying competition, opposition, etc: *They may not beat your team but they'll certainly give you a good run for your money.*

throw ˌgood money after 'bad (*disapproving*)
spend more money in an attempt to get back the money which has been lost, although this is unlikely to be successful: *The Government was throwing good money after bad by investing money in industries that would never make a profit.*

throw your 'money about/around (*informal*)
spend money in a careless and obvious way: *He's always throwing his money around to try to impress people.* **OPP** tighten your belt

throw 'money at sth (*disapproving*)
spend a lot of money trying to do sth which will probably not succeed: *They threw money at the business, but it failed in its first year.* ◊ *The government throws money at social problems but it doesn't do much good.*

- coin → coin money
- colour → see the colour of sb's money
- easy → easy money
- fool → a fool and his money are soon parted
- licence → a licence to print money
- love → not for love or/nor money
- marry → marry money
- pays → you pays your money and you takes your choice
- pin → pin money
- rolling → (be) rolling in it/money
- smart → the smart money is on sb/sth
- time → time is money

monkey /'mʌŋki/

I don't/couldn't give a 'monkey's (*BrE, slang*)
used to say, in a way that is not very polite, that you do not care about sth, or are not at all interested in it: *To be honest, I couldn't give a monkey's whether you go or not.*

make a 'monkey out of sb
make sb seem stupid or foolish: *No one makes a monkey out of me.*

'monkey business (*informal*)
dishonest or silly behaviour: *There's money missing from the office and it's not the first time it's happened. I think there's some monkey business going on.* ◊ *That's enough monkey business. Let's get down to more serious matters. This is a meeting, not a party.*

a/the ˌmonkey on sb's 'back
1 a difficult problem that sb cannot solve or get rid of: *The accusations of fraud remain a monkey on her back.*
2 (*slang*) the state of being unable to stop using drugs

,monkey's 'wedding (*South African*)
used to describe a period of time when it is raining
while the sun is shining: *Look! It's a monkey's wedding!*

● brass → brass monkey weather **SEE** brass monkeys

monkeys /'mʌŋkiz/

● brass → brass monkeys

monster /'mɒnstə(r); *AmE* 'mɑːn-/

● green-eyed → the green-eyed monster

month /mʌnθ/

month after 'month
over a period of several months: *Prices continue to
rise month after month.*

,month by 'month
as the months pass; each month: *Her pain
increased month by month.*

(not for/in) a ,month of 'Sundays (*spoken*)
used to emphasize that sth will never happen: *'Do
you think she'll be able to sell the house at that
price?' 'Not in a month of Sundays. It's far too
much.'*

● flavour → flavour of the month

monty /'mɒnti; *AmE* 'mɑːnti/

● full → the full monty

mood /muːd/

**be in the mood for sth/for doing sth ✦ be in
the mood to do sth**
have a strong desire to do sth; feel like doing sth:
*I'm in the mood for going out and having a good
time. ◇ She said she wasn't in the mood to dance.*

**be in no mood for sth/for doing sth ✦ be in
no mood to do sth**
not want to do sth; not feel like doing sth: *I'm in
no mood for jokes — just tell me the truth.*

moon /muːn/

be over the 'moon (*informal, especially BrE*)
be very happy and excited: *'How does it feel to have
won the championship?' 'I'm over the moon.'*

❷ ORIGIN
This comes from a line in an old children's
poem: *Hey diddle, diddle, the cat and the fiddle,
the cow jumped over the moon....*

cry/ask for the 'moon (also **want the 'moon**)
(*BrE, informal*)
want or ask for sth you cannot get, or sth that will
not be given to you: *Is it asking for the moon to
hope for peace in this country? ◇ I don't want the
moon; I just want him to listen to me for once.*

● once → once in a blue moon
● promise → promise (sb) the moon/earth/world

moonlight /'muːnlaɪt/

do a moonlight 'flit (*BrE, informal*)
leave the place where you have been living in
quickly and secretly, usually to avoid paying your
debts, rent, etc: *When I called to get the money she
owed me, I found she'd done a moonlight flit.*

moons /muːnz/

many 'moons ago (*literary*)
a very long time ago: *Many moons ago, when I was
young...*

moot /muːt/

be a moot 'point/'question
be a subject that people disagree on or are uncertain about: *It's a moot point whether women or
men make better drivers.*

❷ ORIGIN
A *moot* was a group of people who met to discuss questions of local or national law during
the Anglo-Saxon period. A *moot point* was a
question of law discussed at this meeting.

moral /'mɒrəl; *AmE* 'mɔːr-; 'mɑːr-/

(give sb) ,moral sup'port
(give sb) your friendship, encouragement,
approval, etc. rather than financial or practical
help: *Will you stay and give me some moral support
while I explain to him why I'm late? ◇ Your moral
support alone isn't enough. We need money to fund
this cause.*

**take, claim, seize, etc. the moral 'high
ground**
claim that your side of an argument is morally better than your opponents' side; argue in a way that
makes your side seem morally better: *Don't you
try to take the moral high ground with me! You're
just as bad as I am!*

more /mɔː(r)/

be 'more than glad, ready, etc. (to do sth)
be very glad, etc. (to do sth): *If you ever want to
borrow the car, I'll be more than happy to lend it to
you. ◇ The project's made very good progress — I'm
more than satisfied.*

more 'like (it) (*informal*)
1 better; more satisfactory: *This is more like it!
Fresh vegetables — not that canned rubbish. ◇ Turn
the music up louder! That's more like it!*
2 used to give what you think is a better description of sth: *'How many people were there — about
40?' 'No, more like 20.' ◇ Just talking? Arguing
more like it.*

,more or 'less
1 almost: *I've more or less finished reading the
book. ◇ She's finished, more or less.*
2 approximately: *It cost €200, more or less.*

● less → less is more

morning /'mɔːnɪŋ; AmE 'mɔːrnɪŋ/

the morning 'after (the night be'fore)
(*informal*)
the morning after an occasion when sb has drunk too much alcohol and is feeling tired, ill/sick, etc: *She was suffering from the effects of the morning after.* ◇ *a morning-after headache*

morning, noon and 'night
at all times of the day and night (used to emphasize that sth happens very often or that it happens continuously): *When Sally was a baby she used to cry morning, noon and night.*

● Monday → Monday morning quarterback
● Monday → that Monday morning feeling

mortal /'mɔːtl; AmE 'mɔːrtl/

● shuffle → shuffle off this mortal coil

mortar /'mɔːtə(r); AmE 'mɔːrt-/

● bricks → bricks and mortar

most /məʊst; AmE moʊst/

at (the) 'most
not more than this amount; as a maximum: *I'll be away for a week, or perhaps ten days at the most.* ◇ *There were 50 people there at the very most.*
OPP at least

mother /'mʌðə(r)/

at your ,mother's 'knee
when you were very young: *I learnt these songs at my mother's knee.*

be 'mother (*old-fashioned, informal* or *humorous*)
pour the tea: *The tea's ready. Shall I be mother?*

the 'mother country
the country where you or your family were born and which you feel a strong emotional connection with: *The cafe was a meeting place for the immigrants, a welcome reminder of the tastes of the mother country.*

the 'mother (and 'father) of (all) sth (*informal*)
used to emphasize that sth is very large, important, etc: *There was the mother of all storms that night. It lasted for hours.* ◇ *Sorry we're so late. We got stuck in the mother of all traffic jams on the way.*

your ,mother 'tongue
the language you first learned to speak as a child; your native language: *She was born in Singapore, but her mother tongue is French.*

● boy → a mummy's/mother's boy
● father → like father/mother, like son/daughter
● necessity → necessity is the mother of invention

motion /'məʊʃn; AmE 'moʊʃn/

put/set sth in 'motion (also **set the wheels in 'motion**)
do what is necessary to make a start on a project, plan, meeting, etc: *The Government wants to put the new reforms in motion before the election.* ◇ *It*

will be many years before we see any results, but at least we know that the wheels are in motion.

> **NOTE**
> This expression refers to starting a large and complicated piece of machinery.

motions /'məʊʃnz; AmE 'moʊʃnz/

go through the 'motions (of doing sth)
do sth or say sth because you have to, not because you really want to: *He went through the motions of welcoming her friends, but then quickly left the room.* ◇ *She's not really interested in the subject — she's just going through the motions.*

mould (*BrE*) (*AmE* **mold**) /məʊld; AmE moʊld/

break the 'mould (of sth) (*BrE*) (*AmE* **break the 'mold (of sth)**)
change what people expect from a situation, especially by acting in a dramatic and original way: *After a string of defeats, he finally broke the mould by getting through to the semi-finals of a major competition.*

> **NOTE**
> A *mould/mold* is a container that you pour a liquid or soft substance into, which then becomes solid in the same shape as the container.

mount /maʊnt/

● guard → mount/stand/keep guard (over sb/sth)

mountain /'maʊntən; AmE 'maʊntn/

if the ,mountain will not come to Mu'hammad, Mu,hammad must go to the 'mountain (also **Mohammed**) (*saying*)
if a person cannot or refuses to come and see you, you must go and see them: *He's refused to fly to the USA to see the Defence Secretary, so it's a case of if the mountain won't come to Muhammad...*

> **❷ ORIGIN**
> This phrase comes from a story about the prophet Muhammad.

make a ,mountain out of a 'molehill
(*disapproving*)
make a small or unimportant problem seem much more serious than it really is: *It's not such a big problem! You're making a mountain out of a molehill!*

mountains /'maʊntənz; AmE 'maʊntnz/

● move → move mountains (to do sth) **SEE** move heaven and earth (to do sth)

mouse /maʊs/

● cat → (play) cat and mouse (with sb)
● poor → (as) poor as a church mouse
● quiet → (as) quiet as a mouse

mouth /maʊθ/

be all 'mouth (*BrE* also **be all mouth and (no) 'trousers**) (*informal*)
if you say sb is **all mouth**, you mean that they talk a lot about doing sth, but are, in fact, not brave enough to do it: *Don't be scared of her. She won't hurt you — she's all mouth.*

down in the 'mouth (*informal*)
unhappy and depressed: *Why is she looking so down in the mouth?*

make sb's 'mouth water
make sb feel hungry; make sb want to do or have sth very much: *The smell of your cooking is making my mouth water.* ◇ *The sight of all that money made his mouth water.* ► **'mouth-watering** *adj.*: *a mouth-watering smell*

run off at the 'mouth (*AmE, informal*)
talk too much, in a way that is not sensible: *I'm sorry. I didn't mean to run off at the mouth like that.*

- **big** → me and my big mouth
- **born** → be born with a silver spoon in your mouth
- **foam** → foam at the mouth
- **foot** → put your foot in your mouth **SEE** put your foot in it
- **gift** → (not) look a gift horse in the mouth
- **head** → put your head in the lion's mouth
- **heart** → your heart is in your mouth
- **horse** → (straight) from the horse's mouth
- **live¹** → live (from) hand to mouth
- **melt** → melt in your mouth
- **money** → put your money where your mouth is
- **open** → open your (big) mouth
- **shoot** → shoot your mouth off (about sth)
- **shut** → keep your mouth/trap shut **SEE** shut your mouth/trap/face/gob!
- **shut** → shut sb's mouth
- **shut** → shut your mouth/trap/face/gob!
- **taste** → leave a bad/nasty taste in the/your mouth
- **watch** → watch your mouth/tongue
- **word** → by word of mouth
- **words** → put words in/into sb's mouth
- **words** → take the words (right) out of sb's mouth

mouths /maʊðz/

out of the ,mouths of 'babes (and 'sucklings) (*saying*)
used when a small child has just said sth that seems very wise or clever: *It was my daughter who told me I should enjoy life more. She's only four years old, but out of the mouths of babes...*

move /muːv/

get a 'move on (*spoken*)
hurry; do sth faster: *You'd better get a move on or you'll be late.* **OPP** take your time (doing sth/to do sth/over sth) (1)

make a 'move
1 (*BrE, informal*) leave one place in order to go to another: *It's getting late. I think it's time we made a move.* ◇ *I've been in this job far too long already, it's time I made a move.*
2 (also **make your 'move**) do the action that you intend to do or need to do in order to achieve sth: *We're waiting to see what our competitors will do before we make a move.* ◇ *The rebels waited until nightfall before making their move.*

> **NOTE**
> This phrase refers to moving your pieces in a game such as chess.

make a 'move on sb (*informal*)
1 try to start a sexual relationship with sb: *He made a move on me at the party.*
2 (*sport*) try to pass sb who is front of you in a race: *Singleton made a move on Bell to promote himself into second position.*

move the 'goalposts (*informal, disapproving, especially BrE*)
change the rules for sth, or the conditions under which it is done, so that the situation becomes more difficult for sb: *Our union is angry at the management for moving the goalposts during the pay talks. Every time agreement is reached they put up another obstacle.*

Bob began to suspect that they were not being honest and were moving the goalposts.

move heaven and 'earth (to do sth) (also **move 'mountains (to do sth)**)
do everything you can in order to help sb, achieve sth, etc: *His friends moved heaven and earth to free him from prison.* ◇ *Faith can move mountains* (= achieve the impossible).

not move a 'muscle
(of a person) stay very still, without moving: *The patient didn't move a muscle for weeks.*

on the 'move
1 moving or travelling from one place to another: *The army is on the move at last.*
2 very active or busy: *It is important for patients to keep on the move while they are recovering.* ◇ *I can't wait to sit down and relax — I've been on the move all day.*

- ass → move your ass **SEE** get your ass in gear
- false → (make) a/one false move
- first → make the first move
- inch → not budge/give/move an inch
- spirit → (do sth) as/if/when the spirit moves you

mover /'muːvə(r)/
- prime → a prime mover

movers /'muːvəz; *AmE* 'muːvərz/
,movers and 'shakers
people with power in important organizations: *He is one of the principle movers and shakers in the political arena.*

moves /muːvz/
- spirit → (do sth) as/if/when the spirit moves you

moving /'muːvɪŋ/
get 'moving (*informal*)
begin, leave, etc. quickly: *It's late: we ought to get moving.* ◇ *The tourist trade doesn't really get moving until June.*

get sth 'moving (*informal*)
cause sth to make progress: *The new management really got the business moving.*

the moving 'spirit
the person who begins and leads a group, for example a political party, a group of artists, etc: *He was one of the moving spirits in the establishment of the United Nations.*

Mr /'mɪstə(r)/
Mr 'Big (*informal, disapproving*)
the most important person in a group, an area, etc: *Harry Turner, considered the local Mr Big of the criminal underworld, was found dead today at his home.*

,Mr 'Nice Guy (*informal*)
a way of describing a man who is very honest and thinks about the wishes and feelings of other people: *He is famous for being football's Mr Nice Guy.* ◇ *I've given them plenty of chances, but now I've had enough. It's no more Mr Nice Guy!*

Mr 'Right (*informal*)
the man who would be the ideal husband for a particular woman: *I'm not going to get married in a hurry — I'm waiting for Mr Right to come along.*

much /mʌtʃ/
as 'much (as)
the same (as): *Please help me — you know I'd do as much for you.* ◇ *I thought as much* (= that's what I expected).

as much as sb can/could 'do (not) to do sth
used to say that sth is/was difficult to do: *No dessert for me, thanks. It was as much as I could do to finish the main course.*

be not so much sth as sth
be one thing but also something else which is more important: *He's not so much unintelligent as uninterested in schoolwork.*

be too 'much (for sb)
1 be stronger or better than sb; beat sb: *Cambridge were too much for Oxford in the boat race this year.*
2 be more than sb is able to do: *A cycling holiday would be too much for an unfit person like me.*
3 used for showing that sb/sth annoys you: *His rudeness towards her is just too much.*

'much as/though
although: *Much as I'd like to stay, I really must leave now.* ◇ *He agreed, much though he disliked the idea of selling the business.*

not be much of a sth
not be a good sth: *You're not much of a help, standing there with your hands in your pockets.* ◇ *I'm not much of a cook.* ◇ *It wasn't much of a speech really.*

not much 'in it
used to say that there is little difference between two things: *I won, but there wasn't much in it* (= our scores were nearly the same).

not 'up to much (*BrE*)
not very good: *His French isn't up to much but his German is excellent.* ◇ *The weather wasn't up to much, unfortunately.*

,so much for 'sb/'sth
1 used to show that you have finished talking about sth: *So much for the situation in the Far East. Now let's turn our attention to South America.*
2 used to suggest that sth has not been useful or successful: *She gave the job to the other manager. So much for all her promises to me.*

,so much 'so that
to such an extent that: *His nose wouldn't stop bleeding — so much so that we had to take him to hospital.*

'this much
used to introduce sth positive or definite: *I'll say this much for him — he never leaves a piece of work unfinished.*

very 'much so
used for emphasizing 'yes': *'I understand you are interested in German politics.' 'Yes, very much so.'*

without so much as sth/as doing sth ◆ not so much as sth/as doing sth
used for emphasizing that sb does not do sth that you expected them to do: *She took the money without so much as a thank you.* ◇ *He didn't so much as look at her when she came in.*

muchness /'mʌtʃnəs/
be ,much of a 'muchness
be very similar (especially of people or things which are not very good): *It's hard to choose between them — they're all much of a muchness.*

◇ *All the restaurants round here are much of a muchness.*

muck /mʌk/

where there's ˌmuck there's 'brass (*BrE, saying*)
used to say that sb has made a lot of money from an unpleasant or a dirty business activity: *When they saw his enormous house and flash car they looked at each other, both thinking 'Where there's muck there's brass.'*

> **NOTE**
> *Muck* is dirt or mud. *Brass* is an old-fashioned word for 'money'.

mud /mʌd/

fling/sling/throw 'mud (at sb) (*informal*)
try to damage sb's reputation by telling other people bad things about them: *Just before an election, politicians really start to sling mud at each other.* ► **'mud-slinging** *noun*: *There's too much mud-slinging by irresponsible journalists.*

ˌmud 'sticks (also **if you ˌthrow enough 'mud, ˌsome of it will 'stick**) (*saying*)
people remember and believe the bad things they hear about other people, even if they are shown to be false: *Although he was proved innocent, mud sticks, and he found it very difficult to get a job afterwards.*

• clear → (as) clear as mud
• name → your, his, etc. name is mud

muddy /'mʌdi/

muddy the 'waters (*disapproving*)
make sth which seemed clear and easy to understand before seem much less clear now: *Recent research findings have muddied the waters considerably — nuclear scientists are having to re-examine all their existing theories.* ◇ *They're just muddying the waters with all this new information.*

mug /mʌg/

be a 'mug's game (*disapproving, especially BrE*)
an activity which brings little or no benefit to you: *Don't start smoking — it's a mug's game.* ◇ *The money's terrible in this job — it's a real mug's game.*

> **NOTE**
> *Mug* here means 'fool'.

Muhammad /məˈhæmɪd/

• mountain → if the mountain will not come to Muhammad, Muhammad must go to the mountain

mule /mjuːl/

• stubborn → (as) stubborn as a mule

multitude /'mʌltɪtjuːd; *AmE* -tuːd/

cover/hide a ˌmultitude of 'sins (*often humorous*)
used to say that sth is not as good as it looks, sounds, etc: *The term 'abstract art' covers a multitude of sins.* ◇ *A coat of paint can hide a multitude of sins.*

> **❷ ORIGIN**
> This expression comes from the Bible. A *multitude* is a very large number of things.

mum /mʌm/

keep 'mum (*informal*)
say nothing about a secret; stay silent: *I just kept mum when she asked me where Ben was. She'd be furious if she knew.* ◇ *Please will everyone keep mum about Saturday. We want to give them a real surprise.* **OPP** blow the gaff (on sb/sth)

ˌmum's the 'word! (*informal*)
used for telling sb to keep a secret or for telling sb that you will keep a secret: *'Nobody must mention this project outside the office. I hope that's clear.' 'We understand, John. Mum's the word!'*

> **NOTE**
> These two idioms refer to the sound you make when your mouth is closed.

mummy /'mʌmi/

• boy → a mummy's/mother's boy

munchies /'mʌntʃɪz/

have the 'munchies (*informal*)
suddenly feel hungry: *Can I borrow some money? I've got the munchies and I haven't got any money to buy anything.*

> **NOTE**
> *Munchies* is connected with the word *munch*, which means 'eat something steadily and often noisily'.

murder /'mɜːdə(r); *AmE* 'mɜːrd-/

get away with 'murder (*informal, often humorous*)
do sth wrong without being punished, criticized, etc: *His latest book is rubbish! He seems to think that because he's a famous author he can get away with murder!* ◇ *She lets the students get away with murder.*

I could 'murder a... (*spoken*)
used to say that you very much want to eat or drink sth: *I could murder a coffee.*

he, she, etc. will 'murder you (*spoken*)
used to warn sb that another person will be very angry with them: *Your brother will murder you when he finds out what you've done to his car!*

• scream → scream bloody murder **SEE** scream blue murder
• scream → scream blue murder

murky /'mɜːki; AmE 'mɜːrki/
● waters → (be in/get into) murky/uncharted waters

murmur /'mɜːmə(r); AmE 'mɜːrm-/

(do sth) with‚out a 'murmur
(do sth) without complaining: *She paid the extra money for the trip without a murmur.*

Murphy /mɜːfiː; AmE mɜːrfiː/

‚Murphy's 'Law (*humorous*)
a statement of the fact that, if anything can possibly go wrong, it will go wrong: *Of course it had to be the day of my job interview that the car broke down — it's Murphy's Law.*

> **❷ ORIGIN**
> This expression was named after Edward A. Murphy, Jr., an engineer in the US Air Force.

muscle /'mʌsl/
● move → not move a muscle

muscles /'mʌslz/
● flex → flex your muscles

music /'mjuːzɪk/

be (like) ‚music to your 'ears
(of information, etc.) be sth that is pleasant to hear: *The news that she'd finally left was like music to my ears.* ◇ *The bell at the end of the lesson is always music to my ears.*

● face → face the music

must /mʌst; məst/

if you 'must (do sth)
used to say that sb may do sth but you do not really want them to: *'Can I smoke?' 'If you must.'* ◇ *It's from my boyfriend, if you must know.*

mustard /'mʌstəd; AmE -tərd/

(not) cut the 'mustard
(not) be as good as expected or required: *I didn't cut the mustard as a hockey player.*

> **❷ ORIGIN**
> *Mustard* in this expression may possibly refer to an old-fashioned slang word used in American English, meaning 'the best of anything'.

● keen → (as) keen as mustard

muster /'mʌstə(r)/
● pass → pass muster

mutton /'mʌtn/

be mutton dressed (up) as 'lamb (*BrE, informal, disapproving*)
used to describe a woman who is trying to look younger than she really is, especially by wearing clothes that are designed for young people: *Have you seen her? Mutton dressed as lamb. Somebody should remind her that she's 55, not 25.*

> **NOTE**
> *Mutton* is the meat from an adult sheep, while *lamb* is the meat from a young sheep.

N n

nail /neɪl/

nail your colours to the 'mast (*especially BrE*)
show clearly which side you support: *It's time to nail our colours to the mast and condemn this dreadful policy.* **OPP** sit on the fence

> **❷ ORIGIN**
> In this expression, *colours* are flags. In a battle at sea, a ship would *nail its colours to the mast* to show its intention to continue fighting and not surrender.

a nail in sb's/sth's 'coffin
something, especially one of a series of things, which makes the failure or destruction of sth more likely: *If we don't succeed with this campaign, it'll be the final nail in our coffin.* ◇ *The new tax has driven another nail into the coffin of the British film industry.*

nail sb to the 'wall (*informal*)
punish sb and/or make them suffer because you are very angry with them: *I'm going to nail him to the wall for what he's done!*

on the 'nail (*informal*)
(of payment) without delay: *They're good customers who always pay on the nail.*

● fight → fight tooth and nail (for sb/sth/to do sth)
● hit → hit the nail on the head

nails /neɪlz/
● bite → bite your nails/fingernails
● hard → (as) hard as nails
● tough → (as) tough as nails

naked /'neɪkɪd/

the naked 'eye
the normal power of your eyes without the help of an instrument: *Bacteria are invisible to the naked eye.*

the naked 'truth
the truth, which may be unpleasant: *If you want the naked truth about it, he'll certainly give it to you!*

● stark → buck naked **SEE** stark naked

name /neɪm/

by 'name
using the name of sb/sth: *She asked for you by name.* ◇ *The principal knows all the students by name.* ◇ *I only know her by name* (= I have heard about her but I have not met her).

by the name of... (*written*)
who is called: *The play stars a young actor by the name of Tom Rees.*

go by the name of...
use a name that may not be your real one: *Although she was born Mary Jones, she now goes by the name of Natasha, which she feels is more appropriate to her glamorous image.*

have (sb's 'name on it ♦ with your 'name on it (*informal*)
if sth **has your name on it**, or there is sth **with your 'name on it**, it is intended for you: *He took my place and got killed. It should have been me — that bullet had my name on it.* ◊ *Don't worry — there's a job somewhere with your name on it!*

(not) have sth to your 'name (*informal*)
(not) possess sth: *I've only got two dresses to my name.* ◊ *She didn't have a penny to her name when she arrived here.*

in ˌall but 'name
used to describe a situation which exists in reality but that is not officially recognized: *He runs the company in all but name.*

in 'God's/'Heaven's name ♦ in the name of 'God/'Heaven
used especially in questions to show that you are angry, surprised or shocked: *What in God's name was that noise?* ◊ *Where in the name of Heaven have you been?*

in the name of 'sb/'sth ♦ in sb's/sth's 'name
1 using the authority of sb/sth; as a representative of sb/sth: *I arrest you in the name of the law.*
2 used to give a reason or an excuse for doing sth, often when what you are doing is wrong: *new laws introduced in the name of national security*
3 for sb; showing that sth officially belongs to sb: *The reservation was made in the name of Brown.* ◊ *The car is registered in my name.*

in ˌname 'only
officially recognized but not existing in reality: *He's party leader in name only.*

make a 'name for yourself ♦ make your 'name
become successful and well known because of your skill in doing sth very well: *She quickly made a name for herself as one of the best brain surgeons in the country.* ◊ *He made his name in the theatre and then moved into movies.*

name the 'day
choose the date for a wedding: *They are engaged but they haven't named the day yet.*

your, his, etc. name is 'mud (*informal, usually humorous*)
used to say that sb is not liked or popular because of sth they have done: *Your name will be mud at home if you don't write to your family soon.* ◊ *My name is mud at the moment. It's all because I forgot to pay the phone bill.*

name 'names
give the names of people who are involved in sth, especially sth wrong or illegal: *If the newspapers really know the people responsible for these terrible*

crimes, then they should name names. ◊ *I won't name names, but there are some people in this room who have broken several of the club's rules.*

the name of the 'game (*informal*)
the thing that is considered central or really important in a particular situation: *Survival is the name of the game when you're in the jungle.* ◊ *In the art world good publicity is the name of the game, not talent.*

a name to 'conjure with
1 the name of a well-known, very respected and admired person, group or thing in a particular field: *My father went to school with Bill Gates — now there's a name to conjure with!*
2 (*humorous*) used when you mention a name that is difficult to remember or pronounce: *The soup was called chlodnik — now there's a name to conjure with!*

put a 'name to sb/sth
know or remember what sb/sth is called: *I recognize his face but I can't put a name to it.*

take sb's name in 'vain
show a lack of respect when using sb's name: *I get very upset when people take God's name in vain.* ◊ (*humorous*) *Have you been taking my name in vain again?*

❷ ORIGIN
This expression comes from the Bible.

you ˌname it, sb's 'got it (*informal*)
sb has everything you can think of: *He's got an amazing collection of jazz records — you name it, he's got it.*

- **big** → a big name/noise/shot
- **clear** → clear sb's name
- **dog** → give a dog a bad name (and hang him)
- **enter** → enter sb's/your name (for sth)
- **enter** → put sb's/your name down (for sth) SEE enter sb's/your name (for sth)
- **household** → a household name/word
- **lend** → lend your name to sth
- **middle** → be sb's middle name
- **rose** → a rose by any other name (would smell as sweet)
- **what** → what's-his 2;-her/-its/-their-name
- **worthy** → worth the name SEE worthy of the name

nameless /'neɪmləs/

somebody, who will/shall remain/be 'nameless (*humorous*)
used to say that you will not mention sb's name, either because the people listening to you already know who you are talking about, or because you do not want to embarrass sb: *Somebody, who will remain nameless, actually managed to drink two bottles of champagne!*

names /neɪmz/

- **call** → call sb names
- **drop** → drop names
- **name** → name names

nanny /'næni/

the 'nanny state (*BrE*)
a disapproving way of talking about the fact that
government seems to get too involved in people's
lives and to protect them too much, in a way that
limits their freedom: *We're living in a nanny state;
the government watches over you for everything
and nobody takes responsibility for their own
actions anymore.*

> **NOTE**
> In this phrase, the state or government is being
> compared to a *nanny*, a woman whose job is to
> take care of young children, telling them what
> to do, how to behave, etc.

napping /'næpɪŋ/

● catch → catch sb napping

narrow /'nærəʊ; *AmE* -roʊ/

a narrow e'scape/'squeak
a situation where sb only just avoids injury, danger or failure: *We had a narrow escape on the way
here. The wind blew a tree down just in front of us.
We could have been killed.*

● straight → keep to, stay on, etc. the straight and narrow

nasty /'nɑːsti; *AmE* 'næsti/

get/turn 'nasty
1 become threatening and violent: *You'd better do
what he says or he'll turn nasty.*
2 become bad or unpleasant: *It looks as though
the weather is going to turn nasty again.*

a nasty piece of 'work (*BrE, informal*)
a very unpleasant and dangerous person: *Keep
away from Bill Smith — he's a very nasty piece of
work.* ◇ *The factory manager was a nasty piece of
work. We were all terrified of him.*

● cheap → cheap and nasty
● rough → cut up rough/nasty
● taste → leave a bad/nasty taste in the/your mouth

native /'neɪtɪv/

go 'native (*often humorous*)
(of a person staying in another country) try to live
and behave like the local people: *She was one of a
number of artists who had emigrated in the 1990s
and gone native.*

naturally /'nætʃrəli/

come 'naturally (to sb/sth)
if sth **comes naturally** to you, you are able to do it
very easily and very well: *Making money came naturally to him.*

nature /'neɪtʃə(r)/

against 'nature
not natural; not moral: *Murder is a crime against
nature.*

(get, go, etc.) back to 'nature
return to a simple kind of life in the country, away
from cities and technology: *'Did you enjoy your
camping trip?' 'Well, not really. Getting back to
nature isn't really my thing. I'd have preferred to
stay in a luxury hotel!'*

in the nature of 'sth
similar to sth; a type of sth; in the style of sth: *His
speech was in the nature of an apology.*

in the 'nature of things
used for saying that sth that happens is normal in
a particular situation and not at all surprising:
*Don't worry about it. It's in the nature of things for
children to argue with their parents when they're
teenagers.* ◇ *In the nature of things, people who
have power don't like losing it.*

let ,nature take its 'course
not try to change or influence a situation: *As a
parent, sometimes you need to sit back and let
nature take its course; if you try to stop your child
from making any mistakes it can be more damaging
in the end.*

● call → a call of nature
● forces → the forces of nature
● second → be second nature (to sb)

nauseam /'nɔːziæm/

● ad → ad nauseam

near /nɪə(r); *AmE* nɪr/

as ,near as 'dammit (also **as ,near as makes no
'difference**) (*BrE, spoken*)
very nearly; so nearly sth or so like sth that you
can consider it the same: *The bill for the meal was
£100, as near as dammit. It's some paint to
cover that scratch on the car. It's not an exact match
but it's as near as makes no difference.*

> **NOTE**
> *Dammit* is a way of writing *damn it* (an expres-
> sion showing you are annoyed or impatient)

near e'nough (*BrE, spoken*)
used to say that sth is so nearly true that the difference does not matter: *We've been here twenty
years, near enough.*

a near 'miss
a situation in which an accident, usually involving
two moving objects, is only just avoided: *There
was another near miss this afternoon just over
Heathrow Airport when a jet nearly hit a small private plane.* ◇ *He drove like a maniac. We had one
near miss after another.*

near the 'knuckle (*BrE, informal*)
(about a remark, joke, etc.) likely to offend people
or make them feel embarrassed: *His act is too near
the knuckle for me.*

nowhere/not anywhere 'near
not nearly: *The bus was nowhere near full.* ◇ *The
test wasn't anywhere near as difficult as I expected.*

so ,near and ,yet so 'far
used to describe a situation in which sb is very
near to success, but finally fails: *He came second

in the piano competition, only one point behind the winner. So near and yet so far.

- bone → close to/near the bone
- heart → be close/dear/near to sb's heart
- mark → be close to/near the mark
- pretty → pretty near SEE pretty much/well
- thing → a close/near thing

nearest /ˈnɪərɪst; AmE nɪr-/

your ˌnearest and ˈdearest (*informal, often humorous*)
your close family and friends: *It must be difficult for him here, living so far away from his nearest and dearest.*

nearly /ˈnɪəli; AmE ˈnɪrli/

not ˈnearly
much less than; not at all: *It's not nearly as hot as last year.* ◇ *There isn't nearly enough time to get there now.*

- eyes → your eyes nearly pop out of your head
- pretty → pretty nearly SEE pretty much/well

necessarily /ˌnesəˈserəli; BrE also ˈnesəsərəli/

ˌnot necesˈsarily
used to say that sth is possibly true but not definitely or always true: *The more expensive articles are not necessarily better.* ◇ *Biggest doesn't necessarily mean best.* ◇ (*spoken*) *'We're going to lose.' 'Not necessarily.'*

necessary /ˈnesəsəri; AmE -seri/

a ˌnecessary ˈevil
a thing that is unpleasant or even harmful, but which must be accepted because it brings some benefit: *Injections against tropical illnesses are a necessary evil when you are planning to travel to that part of the world.* ◇ *I suppose all these security measures are a necessary evil.*

necessity /nəˈsesəti/

neˌcessity is the ˌmother of inˈvention (*saying*)
a very difficult new problem forces people to think of, design, produce, etc. a solution to it: *'So how did you manage to open the bottle?' 'I used a bit of wire and a stick. Necessity is the mother of invention, as the saying goes.'*

- virtue → make a virtue of necessity

neck /nek/

be up to your ˈneck in sth ♦ be in sth up to your ˈneck
1 have a lot of sth to deal with: *I've been up to my neck in job applications for weeks.*
2 be deeply involved in sth, especially sth dangerous or criminal: *He says he knows nothing about the drug smuggling, but the police are sure he's in it* (= trouble) *up to his neck.*

break your ˈneck (doing sth/to do sth) (*informal*)
make a great effort: *There's no need to break your neck trying to get here by five. We can always wait for you.*

by a ˈneck
if a person or an animal wins a race **by a neck**, they win it by a short distance: *The final was very close, with Molina finally winning by a neck.*

ˌget it in the ˈneck (*BrE, informal*)
be shouted at or punished because of sth that you have done: *Look at the time! I really should get back to work, or I'll get it in the neck.*

> **❷ ORIGIN**
> This refers to the punishment of being killed by hanging or having your head cut off.

in your, this, etc. ˌneck of the ˈwoods (*informal*)
in a particular area or part of the country: *Hi, Jim! What are you doing in this neck of the woods?* ◇ *Not much happens in our neck of the woods. It's very quiet.*

ˌneck and ˈneck (with sb/sth) (also **ˌnip and ˈtuck (with sb)** *especially AmE*)
(in a race, competition, etc.) level with each other: *With another 100 metres to go, Jones and Saville are neck and neck.*

- block → put/lay your head/neck on the block
- brass → brass neck/nerve
- breathe → breathe down sb's neck
- millstone → be a millstone around/round sb's neck
- pain → a pain in the neck
- risk → risk your neck
- save → save sb's/your (own) neck/skin/hide
- scruff → by the scruff of sb's/the neck
- stick → stick your neck out
- wring → wring sb's neck

need /niːd/

if need(s) ˈbe
if it is necessary: *We should have enough money, but if need be, we can cash one of our traveller's cheques.* ◇ *Give him a tablet now to relieve the pain; you can give him another one later if needs be.*

that's ˈall I need (*informal*)
used when sth bad happens in a situation which is already bad: *The car's broken down? That's all I need!*

- crying → a crying need (for sth)
- friend → a friend in need (is a friend indeed)
- hole → need/want sb/sth like (you need/want) a hole in the head
- hour → in your hour of need

needle /ˈniːdl/

like looking for/trying to find a ˌneedle in a ˈhaystack
very difficult to find: *How can we ever find the quotation if you don't even know what part of the book it comes from? It'll be like looking for a needle in a haystack.*

needles /ˈniːdlz/

- pins → have pins and needles
- tenterhooks → be on pins and needles SEE (be) on tenterhooks

needless /ˈniːdləs/

,needless to 'say
as you would expect: *Needless to say, the students who had studied maths before did better in the statistics exam.* ◇ *He got home from the party at 5 a.m. Needless to say, his parents were furious.*

> **NOTE**
> If something is *needless*, it is not necessary.

needs /niːdz/

needs 'must (when the devil drives) (*saying*)
in particular situations it is necessary for you to do sth you do not like or enjoy: *Of course I'd rather go to the beach than sit here studying for my exams, but needs must I suppose.*

neighbourhood (*BrE*) (*AmE* neighborhood) /ˈneɪbəhʊd; *AmE* ˈneɪbər-/

in the neighbourhood of
(of a number or an amount) approximately; not exactly: *It cost in the neighbourhood of £500.*

nelly /ˈneli/

not on your 'nelly (*old-fashioned, BrE, informal*)
definitely not: *You want to borrow my new car? Not on your nelly!*

> **❷ ORIGIN**
> *Nelly* was short for *Nelly Duff*, which was rhyming slang for *puff*, an informal word for your life.

nerve /nɜːv; *AmE* nɜːrv/

have a 'nerve (*informal*)
behave in a way that other people think is rude or not appropriate: *She had a nerve, arriving half an hour late for the meeting.* ◇ *She borrowed my new bicycle without asking.* **What a nerve!**

have the nerve to do sth (*BrE* also have the face to do sth) (*informal*)
do sth that other people think is rude or not appropriate without feeling embarrassed or ashamed: *He had the nerve to ask me for a pay rise after only three weeks in the job.* ◇ *I don't know how she's got the face to criticize my designs. She doesn't know anything at all about architecture.*

hit/touch a (raw) 'nerve
say sth which upsets sb because they are very sensitive about that subject: *You touched a raw nerve when you talked to the manager about the need for better communications within the company.*

- brass → brass neck/nerve
- strain → strain every nerve/sinew (to do sth)

nerves /nɜːvz; *AmE* nɜːrvz/

a bag/bundle of 'nerves (*informal*)
a person who is very frightened, worried or nervous about sth: *She was a bundle of nerves at the start of the interview but she became more confident later.* ◇ *He's a bag of nerves. He needs a break.*

get on sb's 'nerves (*informal*)
annoy sb a lot: *It really gets on my nerves the way he only ever talks about his job and his car.* ◇ *By the end of the week, they were all getting on each other's nerves.*

have nerves of 'steel
not be easily frightened in a difficult or dangerous situation: *She won't be nervous about doing it. She's got nerves of steel.*

- war → a war of nerves

nervous /ˈnɜːvəs; *AmE* ˈnɜːrvəs/

- shadow → be frightened/nervous/scared of your own shadow

nest /nest/

a 'nest egg (*informal*)
a sum of money saved for the future: *She has a nice little nest egg which she intends to use for travelling round the world one day.*

> **❷ ORIGIN**
> A *nest egg* was an egg left in a nest to encourage a chicken to continue to produce more eggs.

- empty → the empty nest
- feather → feather your (own) nest
- fly → fly the nest
- hornet → a hornet's nest
- mare → a mare's nest

net /net/

cast/spread your net 'wide
consider a wide range of possibilities or cover a large area, especially to try to find sb/sth: *Unless we spread our net a bit wider, this company will never get enough business.*

- slip → slip through the net

nettle /ˈnetl/

- grasp → grasp the nettle

network /ˈnetwɜːk; *AmE* -wɜːrk/

- old → the old boy network

neutral /ˈnjuːtrəl; *AmE* ˈnuː-/

on neutral 'ground/'territory
in a place that has no connection with either of the people or sides who are meeting and so does not give an advantage to either of them: *We decided to meet on neutral ground.*

never-never /ˌnevə ˈnevə(r); AmE ˌnevər ˈnevər/

on the ˌnever-ˈnever (BrE, informal)
on hire purchase (= by making payments over a long period of time): *He bought a new car on the never-never.*

new /njuː; AmE nuː/

(as) ˌgood as ˈnew ♦ like ˈnew
in very good condition, as it was when it was new: *I've had your coat cleaned — it's as good as new now.*

a new ˈbroom (sweeps clean) (BrE, saying)
a person who has just started to work for an organization, a department, etc., especially in a senior job, and who is likely to make a lot of changes: *The new managing director is clearly a new broom. He's already got rid of ten members of staff and now he's looking at our working methods.*

a/the ˌnew kid on the ˈblock (informal)
sb who is new to a place, an organization, etc: *Despite his six years in politics, he was still regarded by many as the new kid on the block.*

a ˌnew ˈman (BrE)
a man who shares the work in the home that is traditionally done by women, such as cleaning, cooking and taking care of children. New men are considered sensitive and not aggressive: *He is comfortable with his 'new man' image, and has been known to leave the office early to go home and cook dinner for his family.*

a ˌnew one on ˈme
a story, joke or piece of information that you have not heard before and which you may find difficult to believe: *Butter that always stays soft — that's a new one on me.* ◇ *No, I've never heard that story before. It's a new one on me.*

turn over a new ˈleaf
change your way of behaving and start a better life: *This is a new project to help ex-prisoners turn over a new leaf.*

what's ˈnew? (spoken, informal)
used as a friendly greeting: *Hi! What's new?*

- **ball** → a (whole) different/new ball game
- **blood** → fresh/new/young blood
- **brave** → a brave new world
- **clean** → (as) clean as a new pin
- **complexion** → put a new/different complexion on sth
- **emperor** → the emperor's new clothes
- **ground** → break fresh/new ground
- **pastures** → pastures new
- **ring** → ring out the old (year) and ring in the new
- **teach** → (you can't) teach an old dog new tricks

Newcastle /ˈnjuːkɑːsl; AmE ˈnuːkæsl/

- **coals** → (carry/take) coals to Newcastle

news /njuːz; AmE nuːz/

be bad ˈnews (for sb/sth)
be likely to cause problems for sb/sth: *Central heating is bad news for indoor plants.*

be good ˈnews (for sb/sth)
be likely to be helpful or give an advantage for sb/sth: *The cut in interest rates is good news for homeowners.*

break the ˈnews (to sb)
be the first to tell sb some bad news: *I'm sorry to be the one to break the news.*

it's/that's ˌnews to ˈme
used to express surprise at some information that you have just heard: *'Max is thinking of leaving his job.' 'Really? That's news to me. I thought he was happy there.'*

ˌno news is ˈgood news (saying)
if there were bad news you would hear it, so if you have not heard anything that means everything must be all right: *He's been in the mountains for a week without contacting us. I just hope no news is good news.*

newt /njuːt; AmE nuːt/

- **pissed** → (as) pissed as a newt

New York /ˌnjuː ˈjɔːk; AmE ˌnuː ˈjɔːrk/

a New York ˈminute (AmE)
a very short period of time; very quickly: *Everything can change in a New York minute.* ◇ *I loved the hotel and would stay there again in a New York minute!*

> **NOTE**
> This may refer to the idea that everything and everybody moves quickly in New York.

next /nekst/

as good, well, etc. as the ˈnext person
as good/well etc. as most other people: *I can swim as well as the next person, but I can't compete with her — she's an Olympic champion.*

the next best ˈthing
the best alternative for a thing that you cannot have: *I couldn't find any more of that Italian ice cream but this is the next best thing in my opinion.*

your ˌnext of ˈkin (formal)
your closest living relative or relatives: *The hospital need to contact her next of kin — she is very ill indeed.* ◇ *This form must be signed by your next of kin.*

> **NOTE**
> Kin is an old word for your family or your relatives.

the ˈnext thing (I knew)... (informal)
used when sb tells a story and wants to say that sth happened suddenly or unexpectedly: *I was just walking down the road and the next thing I knew someone was pointing a gun at my face.*

next to ˈnothing
a very small amount; almost nothing: *He knows a great deal about flowers but next to nothing about trees and shrubs.* ◇ *He was able to buy the neighbouring farm for next to nothing.*

notes /nəʊts; AmE noʊts/

● compare → compare notes (with sb)

nothing /'nʌθɪŋ/

be/have nothing to 'do with sb/sth
1 have no connection with sb/sth: *Wynne-Williams plc is nothing to do with Owen Wynne-Williams. It's a completely different company.* ◇ *Go away! It's got nothing to do with you* (= you have no right to know about it).
2 avoid or refuse contact with sb/sth: *I want nothing to do with your schemes.* ◇ *She will have absolutely nothing to do with that organization. She doesn't approve of it.*

for 'nothing
1 without paying; free: *We got into the concert for nothing because my uncle works there.* ◇ *They were giving packets of sweets away for nothing at the supermarket this morning.*
2 (do sth and) not achieve what you wanted; (do sth) for no reason or purpose: *All that hard work for nothing!* ◇ *When I got to Berlin, he'd already left. I'd made the journey for nothing.*

have nothing on sb (*informal*)
1 have much less of a particular quality than sth/sb: *I'm quite a fast worker, but I've got nothing on her!* ◇ *Although all four children could play the piano well, the three boys had nothing on Joan, who played like an angel.*
2 (of the police, etc.) have no information that could show sb to be guilty of sth: *Look, they've got nothing on you, so stop worrying!* **OPP** have something on sb

not for 'nothing do I, will they, etc. ...
used to emphasize that there is a good reason for sth: *Not for nothing did people call him the king of rock and roll.*

'nothing but
only: *Nothing but the freshest vegetables are used in our restaurant.*

,nothing 'doing (*informal*)
used to refuse a request: *'Can you lend me ten dollars?' 'Nothing doing!'*

'nothing if not sth (*informal*)
(used for emphasis) very; very much a particular type of person: *She's nothing if not fair.* ◇ *Her work is nothing if not original.*

(there's) nothing 'in it
1 (*informal*) used to talk about a contest where the competitors are level and it is hard to say who will win: *Right up to the end of the game, there was nothing in it. Either team could have won.*
2 (of a rumour, report, story, etc.) there's no truth in it: *There was a rumour that he was about to resign, but apparently there's nothing in it.*

'nothing less than
(used for emphasis) very; completely: *Their defeat was nothing less than amazing.* ◇ *Her survival was nothing less than a miracle.*

nothing 'like (*informal*)
not; not at all like sth: *It's nothing like as bad as he said.* ◇ *We've sold nothing like enough books to make a profit.* **OPP** something like sb/sth

nothing 'more than
(used for emphasis) only: *The injury isn't serious — it's nothing more than a sprained ankle.*

,nothing 'much
not a great amount of sth; nothing of great value or importance: *There's nothing much in the fridge.* ◇ *I got up late and did nothing much all day.*

there's nothing (else) 'for it (but to do sth)
there is only one possible action in a particular situation: *When the river flooded, there was nothing for it but to move everything upstairs.* ◇ *There was nothing for it but to try to swim to the shore.*

there's nothing like sth
used to say that you enjoy sth very much: *There's nothing like a brisk walk on a cold day!*

there's nothing 'to it (*informal*)
it is easy to do: *It's not difficult to use. All you have to do is pull these two switches and it starts. You see, there's nothing to it!* ◇ *I finished the work very quickly. There was nothing to it really.*

nothings /'nʌθɪŋz/

● sweet → sweet nothings

notice /'nəʊtɪs; AmE 'noʊ-/

● escape → escape sb's notice
● short → at a moment's notice **SEE** at (very) short notice

notion /'nəʊʃn; AmE 'noʊʃn/

● idea → run away with the idea/notion

nouveau /'nuːvəʊ; AmE 'nuːvoʊ/

the ,nouveau 'riche (*from French, disapproving*)
people who have recently become rich and like to show how rich they are in a very obvious way: *As a member of the nouveau riche, Tom can often be seen at New York's most fashionable venues.*

> **NOTE**
> The meaning of the French phrase is 'new rich'.

now /naʊ/

,any minute, day, time, etc. 'now
in the next few minutes, days, etc: *The cab will be here any minute now.*

as of 'now
from now on; from this moment on: *As of now, smoking is forbidden in this house.*

it's ,now or 'never
you must do sth now because you will not get another opportunity to do it: *If we don't climb it now, we never will. It's now or never.*

(every) now and a'gain/'then
occasionally: *We see each other every now and again.* ◇ *She sat by the window, looking out now and then to see if they were coming.* ◇ *'How often do you go to the theatre?' 'Now and then. Not often.'* **OPP** all the time (2)

now for 'sb/'sth
used when turning to a fresh activity or subject: *And now for some travel news.*

,now, 'now (*informal*)
1 used for comforting sb who is upset: *Now, now, darling. What's the matter? Stop crying and tell me what's happened.*
2 used for introducing a friendly warning or criticism: *Now, now, that's no way to speak to your father!*

now... now...
at one time... at another time...: *Her moods kept changing — now happy, now sad.*

'now then
1 used for getting sb's attention before you start to tell them or ask sth: *Now then, let's begin the next exercise.* ◇ *Now then, lads, what's going on here?*
2 used when you are trying to remember sth: *The capital of Cuba? Now then, let me think...*

'now what? (*spoken*)
1 (also **what is it 'now?**) used when you are annoyed because sb is always asking questions or interrupting you: *'Yes, but Dad...' 'Now what?'*
2 used to say that you do not know what to do next in a particular situation: *Well, that idea didn't work. Now what?*

nth /enθ/

for the nth 'time (*informal*)
used when you are stating that sth is the last in a long series and emphasizing how often sth has happened, especially when you are annoyed: *I told him, for the nth time, to tidy his room but he's done nothing to it at all.*

to the nth de'gree (*informal*)
to the greatest possible amount, level, etc.; very much: *This book is boring to the nth degree.*

> **NOTE**
> In mathematics, *n* is used to represent a number whose value is not mentioned.

nude /nju:d; *AmE* nu:d/

in the 'nude
wearing no clothes; naked: *It's a painting of the Duchess of Alba in the nude.* ◇ *People sunbathe in the nude on the rocks above the creek.*

nudge /nʌdʒ/

,nudge 'nudge, ,wink 'wink ♦ a ,nudge and a 'wink
used to suggest sth to do with sex without actually saying it: *They've been spending a lot of time together, nudge nudge, wink wink.*

null /nʌl/

,null and 'void (*formal*)
(of a legal agreement) no longer effective or valid: *The contract was declared null and void.*

number /'nʌmbə(r)/

do a 'number on sb/sth (*informal, especially AmE*)
hurt, damage or criticize sb/sth seriously: *Sun and pollution can really do a number on your skin.* ◇ *To*

the delight of Republicans, the press did a number on your senator (= criticized him severely).

have sb's 'number (*informal*)
really understand what type of person sb is and what they plan to do: *Don't worry, I've got his number. I shall be very careful in any business I do with him.* ◇ *You can't fool me, you know. I've got your number.*

your/sb's (lucky) 'number comes up (*informal*)
sb is very lucky in a competition, etc: *If my lucky number comes up, we'll spend a weekend in Venice.*

your/sb's number is 'up (*informal*)
sb is about to die or experience sth very unpleasant: *There's no point worrying about getting killed in a plane crash. When your number's up, your number's up.* ◇ *The police have the evidence they need to arrest him, so it looks as if his number's up.*

,number 'one (*informal*)
1 the most important or best person or thing: *We're number one in the used car business.* ◇ *He's the world's number one athlete.*
2 (*often disapproving*) yourself: *She doesn't care about other people and their problems. She just looks after number one.* ◇ *Take care of number one and forget everybody else. That's his philosophy.*

your/sb's number 'two (*informal*)
the second most important person in a company, an organization, etc: *Brian Jones is the new number two at the ministry.*

● **amount** → any amount/number of sth
● **cushy** → a cushy number
● **opposite** → your opposite number
● **public** → public enemy number one

numbered /'nʌmbəd; *AmE* 'nʌmbərd/

● **days** → your, its, etc. days are numbered

numbers /'nʌmbəz; *AmE* -bərz/

by 'numbers
sth done easily but without imagination; following instructions: *I'm not a very good cook, I just do it by numbers.* ◇ *The last thing we want is teaching by numbers, reducing learning to a mechanical process.*

by the 'numbers (*AmE*)
following closely the accepted rules for doing sth: *I want this to go smooth and by the numbers.*

a/the 'numbers game
a way of considering an activity, etc. that is concerned only with the number of people doing sth, things achieved, etc., not with who or what they are: *Candidates were playing the numbers game as the crucial vote drew closer.*

● **round** → in round figures/numbers
● **safety** → there's safety in numbers
● **weight** → weight of numbers

nut /nʌt/

do your 'nut (*BrE, informal, spoken*)
be very angry or worried: *He'll do his nut when he sees all that mess.* ◇ *She's doing her nut because she*

hasn't heard from her son for weeks. She's sure that something terrible must have happened.

> **NOTE**
> *Nut* is an informal word for your head.

a hard/tough 'nut (to 'crack) (*informal*)
a very difficult problem to solve; a very difficult person to deal with: *Persuading drivers to leave their cars at home and use public transport will be a very tough nut to crack.* ◇ *You'll find it difficult to make him change his mind. He's a tough nut.*

,off your 'nut (*BrE, informal, spoken*)
crazy: *Is he completely off his nut?*

> **NOTE**
> *Nut* is an informal word for your head.

● **use** → use a sledgehammer to crack a nut

nuts /nʌts/

the nuts and 'bolts (of sth) (*informal*)
the most important and practical details of sth: *Jim put together the nuts and bolts of the deal; I added the details.* ◇ *He worked there long enough to learn the nuts and bolts of the business.*

> **NOTE**
> *Nuts* and *bolts* are small pieces of metal that are screwed together to fasten things together.

● **soup** → from soup to nuts

nutshell /'nʌtʃel/

(put sth) in a 'nutshell (*informal*)
(say or express sth) in a very clear way, using few words: *Unemployment is rising, prices are increasing; in a nutshell, the economy is in trouble.* ◇ *'Do you like his idea?' 'To put it in a nutshell, no.'*

nutty /'nʌti/

(as) nutty as a 'fruitcake (*informal, humorous*)
(of a person) completely crazy: *He's as nutty as a fruitcake. Do you know what he did yesterday? He had lunch outside in the pouring rain.*

O o

oaks /əʊks; AmE oʊks/

great/tall ,oaks from little acorns 'grow (*saying*)
large and successful organizations, businesses, etc. sometimes begin in a very small or modest way: *Welcome to my new website! It may not look much at the moment, but great oaks from little acorns grow!*

> **NOTE**
> An *oak* is a large tree and the *acorn* is its fruit.

oar /ɔː(r)/

put/stick your 'oar in (*BrE, informal*)
interfere in the affairs of other people: *This project is nothing to do with Dave. Why does he keep trying to stick his oar in all the time?*

oath /əʊθ; AmE oʊθ/

on/under 'oath (*law*)
having made a formal promise to tell the truth in a court of law: *Is she prepared to give evidence on oath?* ◇ *The judge reminded the witness that he was still under oath.*

oats /əʊts; AmE oʊts/

get your 'oats (*BrE, informal*)
have sex regularly

● **sow**[1] → sow your wild oats

object /'ɒbdʒɪkt; AmE 'ɑːbdʒekt; -dʒɪkt/

money, expense, etc. is no 'object
there is no need to worry about the amount of money, etc., because there is enough or because it has no importance: *Choose whatever you like from the menu. It's your birthday so money is no object.* ◇ *He was ready to travel anywhere. Distance was no object.*

an 'object lesson
a practical example of what you should or should not do in a particular situation: *It was an object lesson in how not to make a speech. He did absolutely everything wrong.*

> **❷ ORIGIN**
> An *object lesson* was a school lesson that used real objects as a way of teaching in a very direct and practical way.

occasion /ə'keɪʒn/

have occasion to do sth (*formal*)
have a reason or need to do sth: *If you ever have occasion to visit Zurich, you will always be welcome to stay with us.*

on oc'casion(s)
sometimes; not very often: *I don't smoke cigarettes but I like to smoke a cigar on occasion.*

● rise → rise to the occasion/challenge
● sense → a sense of occasion

ocean /'əʊʃn; AmE 'oʊʃn/

an ocean of sth (BrE also **oceans of sth**) (*informal*)
a large amount of sth: *oceans of food*

● drop → a drop in the ocean

odd /ɒd; AmE ɑːd/

,odd 'jobs
various small, practical tasks, repairs, etc. in the home, often done for other people: *I've got some odd jobs to do around the apartment; the bedroom door needs to be painted and the light fixed.* ► **odd-'job man** *noun* (*especially BrE*) a person who is employed to do odd jobs

the odd man/one 'out
a person or thing that is different from others or does not fit easily into a group or set: *That's the problem with 13 people in a group. If you need to work in pairs, there's always an odd one out.* ◇ *Tom is nearly always the odd man out. He never wants to do what we want to do, or go where we want to go.*

● fish → an odd/a queer fish

odds /ɒdz; AmE ɑːdz/

against all (the) 'odds
in spite of great difficulties or problems; although it seemed impossible: *Against all the odds this little-known man succeeded in becoming President.* ◇ *It's a romantic story of love surviving against all odds.*

be at 'odds (with sb/sth) (about/over sth)
1 not be in agreement with sb about sth: *I'm at odds with her on the question of nuclear energy.*
2 (of two things) not match or correspond to each other: *His colourful way of dressing is strangely at odds with his shy personality.*

it makes no 'odds (to sb/sth) (*spoken, especially BrE*)
used to say that sth is not important: *It makes no odds to me what you decide to do.*

odds and 'ends (BrE also **odds and 'sods**) (*informal*)
small items that are not valuable or are not part of a larger set: *She's got all kinds of interesting odds and ends on her desk.* ◇ *I've got a few odds and ends* (= small jobs) *to do before leaving.*

the odds 'are (that...) (also (**it's**) **odds-'on (that...)**)
it is very likely that: *I don't think we can come. The odds are that we won't be able to get a babysitter — not on Christmas Eve.* ◇ *It was odds-on that they would decide to get married, so no one was surprised.*

the odds are a'gainst sth/sb doing sth
sth is very unlikely: *The odds are against them winning, I'm afraid.* ◇ *The odds are against her because she's less experienced than the other applicants.*

over the 'odds (*informal*)
more than the usual price: *He paid over the odds for that bike and now he's regretting it.*

what's the 'odds? (BrE, *informal*)
what difference does it make?; what does it matter?: *Work this weekend or next weekend? What's the odds? You get the same money.*

● stacked → the cards/odds are stacked against sb/sth
● stacked → the cards/odds are stacked in favour of sb/sth

odds-on /,ɒdz 'ɒn; AmE ,ɑːdz 'ɑːn; 'ɔːn/

● odds → (it's) odds-on (that...) **SEE** the odds are (that...)

odour (BrE) (AmE odor) /'əʊdə(r); AmE 'oʊ-/

be in good/bad 'odour (with sb) (*formal*)
have/not have sb's approval and support: *He's in rather bad odour with his boss at the moment.*

off /ɒf; AmE ɔːf; ɑːf/

be ,off for 'sth (*informal*)
have a particular amount of sth: *How are we off for coffee* (= how much have we got)*?*

,off and 'on ◆ ,on and 'off
not regularly; not continuously: *It rained on and off all week.*

offence (BrE) (AmE offense) /ə'fens/

no of'fence (*spoken*)
used to say that you do not mean to upset or insult sb by sth you say or do: *No offence, but I'd really like to be on my own.*

offensive /ə'fensɪv/

be on the of'fensive
be attacking sb/sth rather than waiting for them to attack you: *The Scots were on the offensive for most of the game.* ◇ *The government is very much on the offensive in the fight against drugs.* **OPP** on/onto the defensive

go on(to) the of'fensive ◆ take the of'fensive
start attacking sb/sth before they start attacking you: *The president decided to take the offensive by developing a new strategy to discourage competition.*

offer /'ɒfə(r); AmE 'ɔːf-; 'ɑːf-/

have sth to 'offer
have sth available that sb wants: *Barcelona has a lot to offer its visitors in the way of entertainment.* ◇ *He's a young man with a great deal to offer* (= who is intelligent, has many skills, etc.).

on 'offer
1 that can be bought, used, etc: *The following is a list of courses currently on offer.* ◇ *Prizes worth more than $20 000 are on offer to the winner.*

2 (*especially BrE*) on sale at a lower price than normal for a short period of time: *Italian coffee is on (special) offer this week.*

under 'offer (*BrE*)
if a house or building is **under offer**, sb has agreed to buy it at a particular price: *They've already sold two of their properties, and the third is currently under offer.*

● olive → hold out/offer an olive branch (to sb)

offering /'ɒfərɪŋ; *AmE* 'ɔːf-; 'ɑːf-/
● peace → a peace offering

offices /'ɒfɪsɪz; *AmE* 'ɔːf-; 'ɑːf-/
through sb's good 'offices (*formal*)
with sb's help: *He eventually managed to find employment, through the good offices of a former colleague.*

offing /'ɒfɪŋ; *AmE* 'ɔːf-; 'ɑːf-/
in the 'offing (*informal*)
likely or about to happen soon: *There's a pay rise in the offing, I hear.*

❷ ORIGIN
The *offing* is the furthest part of the sea that you can see from land. Ships that are *in the offing* will soon arrive at the land.

often /'ɒfn; 'ɒftən; *AmE* 'ɔːfn; 'ɔːftən; 'ɑːf-/
every so 'often
occasionally: *I usually drink tea, but every so often I have coffee after dinner.*

(as) often as 'not ♦ more often than 'not
frequently; usually: *As often as not I watch TV after dinner.*

oil /ɔɪl/
be no 'oil painting (*BrE, humorous*)
used to say that a person is not attractive to look at: *He's no oil painting but he's a marvellous actor.*

oil the 'wheels (*BrE*) (*AmE* **grease the 'wheels**)
help sth to happen easily and without problems, especially in business or politics: *He doesn't worry about bureaucratic procedures because he knows just where to oil the wheels.*

● burn → burn the midnight oil
● pour → pour oil on troubled water(s)
● squeaky → the squeaky wheel gets the grease/oil

ointment /'ɔɪntmənt/
● fly → a/the fly in the ointment

OK (also **okay**) /əʊ'keɪ; *AmE* oʊ-/
be doing O'K/o'kay (*informal*)
be successful; be making a lot of money: *'How's business?' 'We're doing OK, thanks.'* ◇ *They're doing more than okay with those new restaurants. They're making a fortune.*

give sb/get the O'K/o'kay (*informal*)
give sb/receive approval or permission: *I'm waiting to get the OK before I start on the project.* ◇ *He can't start until his boss gives him the OK.*

Old /əʊld; *AmE* oʊld/
the Old 'Bill (*BrE, informal*)
the police: *Put it down or I'll call the Old Bill!*

old /əʊld; *AmE* oʊld/
any old how (*spoken*)
in a careless or untidy way: *You can't just dress any old how for such an important occasion.*

any old thing, time, place, etc. (*spoken*)
it does not matter which thing, when, where, etc: *Come on, let's go out now — you can do the housework any old time.* ◇ *We can't have any old person looking after the kids — it has to be someone reliable.*

for 'old times' sake
because of pleasant memories of things you did together in the past: *I saw John Smith today. I hadn't seen him for years. We had a drink together for old times' sake.* ◇ *I lent him the money for old times' sake.*

the 'good/'bad old days
an earlier period of time in your life or in history that is seen as better/worse than the present: *That was in the bad old days of very high inflation.*

it's the (same) old 'story
something unpleasant or bad which happens again and again: *He says we haven't got enough money for a trip overseas. It's the same old story every year.*

of 'old (*formal or literary*)
in or since past times: *in days of old* ◇ *We know him of old* (= we have known him for a long time).

of the 'old school
following old methods, standards, etc: *He's one of the old school, a teacher who believes in discipline and politeness.*

(as) old as the 'hills
very old; ancient: *That joke's as old as the hills!*

an old 'bag (*disapproving, offensive*)
an annoying and unpleasant woman: *Some old bag came in here complaining that we'd charged her too much.*

an old 'bat (*BrE, informal, disapproving*)
a silly or annoying old person: *She never hears what I'm saying to her — the silly old bat.*

old 'boy/'girl (*informal*)
1 an older man/woman: *There's a nice old boy living next door.*
2 a former pupil of a school: *He's one of our most famous old boys.* ◇ *We have an old girls' reunion every five years.*

the old 'boy network (*BrE, informal*)
the practice of men who went to the same school using their influence to help each other at work or socially

an/that old 'chestnut (*informal*)
a joke or story that has often been repeated and as a result is no longer amusing: *'He told us all about the police arresting him for climbing into his own house.' 'Oh, no, not that old chestnut again.'*

an old 'dear (*informal*)
an old woman: *And then this old dear came in looking very ill, so I asked the doctor to see her before the other patients.*

an old 'flame (*informal*)
a person you were once in love with; a former boyfriend or girlfriend: *My mother has an old flame who sends her a bottle of perfume once a year.*

an old 'fogey/'fogy (*usually disapproving*)
(usually of an older person) a person with very old-fashioned or traditional views, opinions, etc: *I'm not such an old fogey that I can't remember what it was like to be a student.*

> NOTE
> A young person with old-fashioned views, style of dress, etc. is sometimes called a 'young fogey': *He's one of the young fogies who write for the 'Spectator'.*

the ,old 'guard
the original or older members of a group or an organization, who are often against change but whose ideas and ways of working are being replaced: *The old guard in European politics is being challenged by fresh new ideas.*

an old 'hand (at sth/at doing sth)
a person who is very experienced at sth: *Pete's an old hand at negotiating our contracts — he's been at the firm nearly twenty years, so he knows all the procedures.* **OPP** (still) wet behind the ears

,old 'hat
something that is old-fashioned and no longer interesting: *This is supposed to be a new method of learning English, but frankly, it's a bit old hat.* **OPP** all the rage

(have) an old head on young 'shoulders
used to describe a young person who acts in a more sensible way than you would expect for a person of their age: *He's only seventeen, but he has an old head on young shoulders and remains calm under pressure.*

an old 'maid (*old-fashioned, disapproving*)
a woman who has never married and is now no longer young

old 'man (*informal*)
a person's husband or father: *I go to see my old man every month. He's 77 now, you know.* ◇ *Ask your old man if he can mend it.*

the ,old school 'tie (*BrE*)
an informal system in which upper class men educated at the same private school help each other with jobs, contracts, etc. in their adult lives: *People say that the bank is run on the old school tie system.*

an old 'wives' tale (*disapproving*)
an old idea or belief that has proved not to be scientific: *When you're expecting a baby, people tell you all sorts of old wives' tales.* ◇ *The belief that make-up ruins your skin is just an old wives' tale.*

old 'woman (*informal, especially BrE*)
1 a person's wife or mother: *Give your old woman a surprise and take her out for a nice meal.*
2 (*disapproving*) a man who worries about things that are not important: *My boss is a real old woman. He gets so annoyed if I make even the smallest mistake.*

● chip → a chip off the old block
● dirty → a dirty old man
● fool → (there's) no fool like an old fool
● grand → a/the grand old age
● grand → a/the grand old man (of sth)
● high → have a high old time
● life → there's life in the old dog yet
● money → money for old rope
● poor → poor old sb/sth
● reopen → reopen old wounds
● ring → ring out the old (year) and ring in the new
● ripe → at/to a ripe old age
● settle → settle an old score
● teach → (you can't) teach an old dog new tricks
● tough → (as) tough as old boots

olive /'ɒlɪv; AmE 'ɑːlɪv/

hold out/offer an 'olive branch (to sb)
show that you want to make peace with sb: *After their argument, he was the first one to hold out an olive branch.* **OPP** throw down the gauntlet

> **❷ ORIGIN**
> The olive branch is an ancient symbol of peace.

omelette (*AmE also* omelet) /'ɒmlət; AmE 'ɑːm-/

you can't make an ,omelette without breaking 'eggs (*saying*)
you cannot make an important change in sth without causing problems for sb: *I know that all these changes in the industry are painful to many people, but you can't make an omelette without breaking eggs.*

omnibus /'ɒmnɪbəs; AmE 'ɑːm-/

● man → the man (and/or woman) on the Clapham omnibus **SEE** the man (and/or woman) in the street

on /ɒn; AmE ɑːn; ɔːn/

be 'on about sth (*informal*)
talk about sth; mean sth: *I didn't know what he was on about. It didn't make sense.*

be/go/keep 'on about sth (*informal, disapproving*)
keep talking about the same thing so that people become bored or annoyed: *What's she on about now?* ◇ *Don't keep on about your terrible journey. It's so boring.*

be/go/keep 'on at sb (to do sth) (*informal, disapproving*)
keep criticizing sb or telling them what to do, etc: *He keeps on at her all the time about her smoking.*

onside /ˌɒnˈsaɪd; AmE ˌɑːn-; ˌɔːn-/

get/keep sb on'side
get/keep sb's support: *The government needs to keep the major national newspapers onside to help win votes in the election.*

onto /ˈɒntə; ˈɒntu; AmE ˈɑːn-; ˈɔːn-/

be 'onto sb
1 (*informal*) know about what sb has done wrong: *She knew the police would be onto them.*
2 (also **get 'onto sb**) be talking to sb, usually in order to ask or tell them sth: *They've been onto me for ages to get a job.* ◇ *I must get onto the local council about all the rubbish in the street.*

be 'onto sth
know about sth or be in a situation that could lead to a good result for you: *Researchers believe that they are onto something big.* ◇ *She's onto a good thing with that new job.*

open /ˈəʊpən; AmE ˈoʊ-/

be 'open to sth
be willing to consider sth: *We are open to any suggestions you care to make.*

have/keep an ˌopen 'mind (on/about sth)
be willing to change your opinion (on/about sth): *I've still got an open mind on the question of nuclear defence.* ▸ **ˌopen-'minded** *adj.*: *You can talk to her about anything — she's very open-minded.*

(out) in(to) the 'open
no longer/not hidden or secret: *The whole banking scandal came into the open after somebody found some confidential documents on a train.*

in the open 'air
outside; not indoors: *In summer I think it's nice to eat in the open air.* ▸ **ˌopen-'air** *adj.*: *an open-air swimming pool*

on the ˌopen 'market
available to buy without any restrictions: *Firearms are not freely available on the open market.* **OPP** the black market

an ˌopen 'book
a person whose behaviour, attitudes, thoughts, etc. are very easy to understand, either because you know them very well or because they are very open and honest: *After living with her for 20 years, she's an open book to me.* ◇ *His life is an open book. He has no secrets.* **OPP** a closed book (to sb)

open the 'door to/for sb/sth
provide sb with the chance or opportunity to do sth new, interesting, etc: *Going to university opened the door to a whole new world for her.*

open your/sb's 'eyes (to sth)
realize or make sb realize the truth about sth: *The trip to China really opened our eyes.* ◇ *He opened my eyes to the beauty of poetry.* ▸ **an 'eye-opener** *noun*: *The programme on police methods was a real eye-opener for me.*

open 'fire (on sb/sth)
start shooting (at sb/sth): *The officer gave the order to open fire on the enemy.* **OPP** hold your fire

open the 'floodgates (to sth)
1 remove the restrictions or controls which for a long time have prevented a lot of people from doing sth they want to do: *If the case is successful, it may open the floodgates to more damages claims against the industry.*
2 do sth which allows sb to express feelings which have been kept under control for a long time: *The discussion sessions allow people to open the floodgates to their deepest fears.*

open your 'heart (to sb)
tell sb about your feelings, problems or worries: *She longed to be able to open her heart to someone who would understand.*

(keep) open 'house
be willing to receive guests in your home at any time, and give them food, drink, etc: *It was always open house at their place.*

an ˌopen invi'tation (to sb)
1 an invitation to sb to visit you at any time
2 if sth is **an open invitation** to criminals, etc., it encourages them to commit a crime by making it easier: *Leaving your camera on the seat in the car is an open invitation to thieves.*

an ˌopen 'letter
a letter containing a protest, piece of advice, etc. to a well-known person, which is published in a newspaper: *In an open letter to the Prime Minister, six well-known authors attacked the government's policy on the arts.*

open your (big) 'mouth (*informal*)
say sth when you should not: *Why do you always have to open your big mouth? Can't you just keep quiet sometimes?*

an open 'question (also **open to 'question**)
a matter that cannot be decided easily or that people hold several different views on: *Whether private schools give children a better education is open to question.* ◇ *It's an open question whether meat is bad for you.*

an ˌopen 'secret
a fact that is supposed to be a secret but that everyone knows: *It's an open secret that they're getting married.*

open 'sesame (*humorous*)
an easy way to gain or achieve sth that is usually very difficult to get: *Academic success is not always an open sesame to a well-paid job.* ◇ *The bank had just closed but I banged on the door and — open sesame — they let me in!*

> ❷ ORIGIN
> This expression comes from the story *Ali Baba and the Forty Thieves*. The words *open sesame* opened the door of the thieves' cave where they kept their treasure.

open the way for sb/sth (to do sth)
make it possible for sb to do sth or for sth to happen: *A group of diplomats went first, in order to open the way for a personal visit by the President.*

with ˌopen 'arms
if you welcome sb **with open arms**, you are extremely happy and pleased to see them: *Don't*

expect her to welcome you with open arms. She's still very angry with you. OPP *give sb/get the cold shoulder*

- burst → burst (sth) open
- door → leave the door open (for/on sth)
- eyes → keep your eyes open/peeled/skinned (for sb/sth)
- eyes → with your eyes open
- heavens → the heavens open
- options → keep/leave (all) your options open
- weather → keep a weather eye on sth/open for sth
- wide → be wide open
- wide → (lay/leave yourself) wide open (to sth)

open-and-shut /ˌəʊpən ən ˈʃʌt; AmE ˌoʊ-/

an ˌopen-and-shut ˈcase
(of a legal case, crime, etc.) so clear or simple that it can be dealt with or solved very easily and quickly: *It's an open-and-shut case. His fingerprints were on the gun and he can't prove where he was that night.*

openers /ˈəʊpnəz; AmE ˈoʊ-; ˈəʊpnərz/

for ˈopeners (*informal, especially AmE*)
to begin with; for a start: *For openers, I don't think his work is very original.*

operation /ˌɒpəˈreɪʃn; AmE ˌɑ:p-/

come into opeˈration
start working; start having an effect: *The new rules come into operation from next week.*

in opeˈration
working, being used or having an effect: *The system needs to be in operation for six months before it can be assessed.* ◇ *Temporary traffic controls are in operation on New Road.*

put sth into opeˈration
make sth start working; start using sth: *It's time to put our plan into operation.*

operative /ˈɒpərətɪv; AmE ˈɑ:pərətɪv; -reɪt-/

the ˌoperative ˈword
used to emphasize that a particular word or phrase is the most important one in a sentence: *I was in love with her — 'was' being the operative word.*

opinion /əˈpɪnjən/

be of the opinion that… (*formal*)
think or believe that…: *I'm firmly of the opinion that smoking should be banned in all public places.*

have a good, bad, high, low, etc. oˈpinion of sb/sth
think that sb/sth is good, bad, etc: *The boss has a very high opinion of her.*

- considered → your considered opinion
- contrary → contrary to popular belief/opinion
- matter → be a matter of opinion

opportunity /ˌɒpəˈtjuːnəti; AmE ˌɑːpərˈtuː-/

- window → a window of opportunity

opposed /əˈpəʊzd; AmE əˈpoʊzd/

as opˈposed to (*written*)
used to make a contrast between two things: *200 people attended, as opposed to 300 the previous year.* ◇ *This exercise develops suppleness as opposed to* (= rather than) *strength.*

opposite /ˈɒpəzɪt; -sɪt; AmE ˈɑːpəzət/

your ˌopposite ˈnumber
a person who holds the same position as you in another country, organization, company, etc: *The American Secretary of State will meet his Russian opposite number tomorrow.* ◇ *She's my opposite number in IBM.*

the ˌopposite ˈsex
the other sex: *He found it difficult to talk to members of the opposite sex.*

opposites /ˈɒpəzɪts; -sɪts; AmE ˈɑːpəzəts/

ˌopposites atˈtract
used to say that people who are very different are often attracted to each other: *'Aren't you surprised that Peter and Sally are together?' 'A little. But they say opposites attract, don't they?'*

opposition /ˌɒpəˈzɪʃn; AmE ˌɑːpə-/

in oppoˈsition to sb/sth
1 disagreeing strongly with sb/sth, especially with the aim of preventing sth from happening: *Protest marches were held in opposition to the proposed law.*
2 contrasting two people or things that are very different: *Leisure is usually defined in opposition to work.*

option /ˈɒpʃn; AmE ˈɑːp-/

the ˌsoft/ˌeasy ˈoption (*often disapproving*)
an easier way of doing sth; an easier course of action because it involves less effort, difficulty, etc: *If you want to go for the soft option, you can get the qualification in three years rather than two.* ◇ *He decided to take the easy option and give them what they wanted.*

options /ˈɒpʃnz; AmE ˈɑːp-/

keep/leave (all) your ˈoptions open
avoid making a decision now so that you still have a choice in the future: *Doing business with him is sometimes quite stressful. He likes to keep all his options open until the very last minute.*

oranges /ˈɒrɪndʒɪz; AmE ˈɔːr-; ˈɑːr-/

- apples → apples and oranges

order /'ɔ:də(r); AmE 'ɔ:rd-/

in 'order
1 (of an official document) that can be used because it is all correct and legal: *If the documents are not in order, the apartment cannot be sold.*
2 (*formal*) as it should be: *Is everything in order for you, sir?*
3 if sth is **in order**, it is a suitable thing to do or say on a particular occasion: *I think a drink would be in order.*

in/of the 'order of (*BrE*) (*AmE* **on the 'order of**) (*formal*)
(of an amount) about; approximately: *They own a business worth in the order of fifteen million euros.* ◇ *We employ in the order of 4 000 people in this factory.*

in order that (*formal*)
so that sth can happen: *All those concerned must work together in order that agreement can be reached on this issue.*

in order to do sth
with the purpose or intention of doing or achieving sth: *She arrived early in order to get a good seat.* ◇ *In order to get a complete picture, further information is needed.*

of the highest/first 'order ◆ of a high 'order
of the best, worst, most extreme, etc. type: *It was a scandal of the first order.*

on 'order
requested from a shop/store, factory, etc. but not yet received: *We've got 500 copies of the book on order. They should be here later this week.*

the ˌorder of the 'day
what is normally done, etc. or should be done in a particular situation; the usual attitudes, beliefs, etc. of a particular group of people: *Dinner jackets and evening dresses are the order of the day at these parties.*

ˌout of 'order
1 (of a machine, etc.) broken or not working properly: *The phone is out of order again.* ◇ *There was a notice on the toilet door saying 'out of order'.*
2 (*BrE*) (*AmE* **out of 'line**) (*informal*) (of behaviour, remarks, etc.) not acceptable in a particular situation: *Your remarks were completely out of order at a meeting like that.*

● apple-pie → in apple-pie order
● house → put/set your (own) house in order
● law → law and order
● pecking → a/the pecking order
● short → in short order
● tall → a tall order
● working → in running order SEE in (full/good) working order

ordered /'ɔ:dəd; AmE 'ɔ:rdərd/

● doctor → just what the doctor ordered

orders /'ɔ:dəz; AmE 'ɔ:dərz/

be in/take (holy) 'orders
be/become a priest: *He wanted to take holy orders, but his father had other plans for him.*

be under 'orders (to do sth)
have been ordered or commanded (to do sth): *Prisoners of war were under orders to reveal only their name, rank and number.*

● marching → get your marching orders
● marching → give sb their marching orders
● starters → under starters orders

ordinary /'ɔ:dnri; AmE 'ɔ:rdneri/

in the ordinary 'way (*BrE*)
used to say what normally happens in a particular situation: *In the ordinary way, she's not a nervous person.*

out of the 'ordinary
unusual; strange: *His new book is certainly out of the ordinary. I've never read anything like it before.*

other /'ʌðə(r)/

> Most idioms containing **other** are at the entries for the nouns and verbs in the idioms, for example **in other words** is at **words**.

every other (person/thing)
every second (person/thing): *We go abroad for two weeks every other year.* ◇ *I buy milk every other day.*

the ˌother 'day, 'morning, etc.
only a few days ago: *The other evening we went for a drive in the country.* ◇ *I saw Jake the other day while I was shopping.*

other than
1 except: *I don't know any French people other than you.* ◇ *We're going away in June but other than that I'll be here all summer.*
2 (*written*) different or differently from; not: *I have never known him to behave other than selfishly.*

'somebody/'something/'somewhere or other
used when you do not think it is necessary to be more exact about sb/sth, or to show that the person/thing/place mentioned does not have much importance or value in your opinion: *'What did you have for pudding?' 'Oh, something or other covered with cream.'* ◇ *'Where's your pen?' 'Oh, I lent it to someone or other at work and they forgot to give it back.'*

otherwise /'ʌðəwaɪz; AmE 'ʌðərwaɪz/

or 'otherwise
used to refer to sth that is different from or the opposite of what has just been mentioned: *It was necessary to discover the truth or otherwise of these statements.* ◇ *We insure against all damage, accidental or otherwise.*

● know → know different/otherwise

ounce /aʊns/

● prevention → an ounce of prevention is better than a pound of cure SEE prevention is better than cure

out /aʊt/

be (all) out to do sth ♦ be (all) out for sth
want or plan to do or get sth: *I think he's out to kill me.* ◇ *I'm not interested in a few thousand dollars. I'm out for a million!*

‚out and a'bout (*BrE*)
able to go outside again after an illness: *I saw Mrs Neve in town this morning. I was pleased to see her out and about again.*

'out of it (*informal*)
not aware of what is happening, usually because of drinking too much alcohol, or taking drugs: *He looks completely out of it.*

'out there (*informal*)
strange; far from what most people consider normal: *Her art's kind of out there; maybe that's why it doesn't sell very well.*

'out with it!
used to make sb tell you sth they are hiding, or hesitating to tell you: *Come on, out with it! I want to know the truth!*

outs /aʊts/

• ins → the ins and outs (of sth)

outset /'aʊtset/

at/from the 'outset (of sth)
at/from the beginning of sth: *I made it clear right from the outset that I disapproved.*

outside /,aʊt'saɪd/

at the out'side
(of an amount, a number, etc.) at the most; as a maximum: *I doubt if this factory makes more than 500 cars a year at the very outside.*

on the out'side
1 used to describe how sb appears or seems: *On the outside she seems calm, but I know she's quite worried.*
2 not in prison: *Life on the outside took some getting used to again.*

the outside 'world ♦ the world out'side
the rest of the world; somewhere where you are in contact with or have the normal way of life of most people: *After 15 years in a monastery, he got a job in the outside world. It was quite a shock for him.*

• ken → beyond/outside your ken

outstay /,aʊt'steɪ/

• welcome → outstay/overstay your welcome

oven /'ʌvn/

• bun → have a bun in the oven

over /'əʊvə(r); AmE 'oʊ-/

(all) over a'gain
once more; for a second time: *I'm not sure if I could stand seeing that DVD all over again.* ◇ *He told me*

the work was so bad that I would have to do it over again.

‚over and a'bove
in addition to sth: *Higher safety standards are needed over and above the ones already in place.* ◇ *He gets a big annual bonus, over and above his basic salary.*

‚over and 'over (a'gain)
many times; repeatedly: *Her doctor warned her over and over about the dangers of smoking.*

‚over 'easy/'medium/'hard (*AmE*)
(used about eggs) fried on both sides for a short time/for a moderate length of time/for a longer time: *I'll have two eggs over easy and a cup of coffee, please.*

overboard /'əʊvəbɔːd; AmE 'oʊvərbɔːrd/

go 'overboard (about/for sb/sth) (*informal*)
be too excited or enthusiastic about sth or about doing sth: *I told her just to cook a simple meal but she went completely overboard.* ◇ *He doesn't just like her. He's gone completely overboard about her.*

throw sth 'overboard
reject or get rid of sth: *All ideas of reform were thrown overboard when the new government came to power.*

overdo /,əʊvə'duː; AmE ,oʊvər'duː/

over'do it/things
do too much: *He rather overdid it last Saturday playing football, and now he's aching all over.* ◇ *I've been overdoing things a bit recently. I really need a rest.*

overdrive /'əʊvədraɪv; AmE 'oʊvərd-/

go, etc. into 'overdrive
begin to work much harder, increase production, etc: *Production at the factory has shifted into overdrive in an attempt to meet the new orders on time.*

> **NOTE**
> *Overdrive* is an extra high gear in a vehicle, that you use when you are driving at high speeds.

over-egg /,əʊvər 'eg; AmE 'oʊ-/

‚over-egg the 'pudding
used to say that you think sb has done more than is necessary, or has added unnecessary details to make sth seem better or worse than it really is: *If you're telling lies, keep it simple — never over-egg the pudding.*

overplay /,əʊvə'pleɪ; AmE ,oʊvər'p-/

overplay your 'hand
spoil your chance of success by judging your position to be stronger than it really is: *Some say that the actors overplayed their hand, asking for too much money for each appearance.*

> **NOTE**
> This comes from card games. If you *overplay your hand*, you play in a way that is too confident because you think your cards are better than they really are.

overshoot /,əʊvə'ʃuːt; AmE ,oʊvər'ʃ-/

overshoot the 'mark
make a mistake when you are judging the amount, etc. of sth: *He overshot the mark by about $3 million.*

> **❷ ORIGIN**
> If you *overshoot the mark*, you shoot an arrow further than you intended and miss the target.

overstay /,əʊvə'steɪ; AmE ,oʊvər's-/

● welcome → outstay/overstay your welcome

overstep /,əʊvə'step; AmE ,oʊvər's-/

overstep the 'mark/'line
go beyond the limit of what is polite or acceptable: *He has really overstepped the mark this time, shouting at the referee like that.*

overtime /'əʊvətaɪm; AmE 'oʊvərt-/

● working → be working overtime

overtures /'əʊvətʃʊəz; -tjʊəz; AmE 'oʊvərtʃərz; -tʃʊrz/

make 'overtures (to sb)
try to make friends, start a business relationship, have discussions, etc. with sb: *On my first day at work everyone made friendly overtures.* ◇ *If we want to stay in business I think we ought to start making overtures to the bank manager!*

owes /əʊz; AmE oʊz/

● world → (think) the world owes you a living

owl /aʊl/

● night → a night owl

own /əʊn; AmE oʊn/

> Most idioms containing **own** are at the entries for the nouns and verbs in the idioms, for example **off your own bat** is at **bat**.

come ,into your/its 'own
have the opportunity to show how good or useful you are or sth is: *When the traffic's as bad as this, a bicycle really comes into its own.* ◇ *It was only when she became Health Secretary that she came into her own.*

get your 'own back (on sb) (*informal*)
do sth to sb in return for harm they have done to you; get revenge: *I got my own back by writing a very rude article about him in the newspaper.*

(all) on your 'own
1 alone; without anyone else: *Why are you sitting here on your own?*
2 without help: *She made it all on her own.*

oyster /'ɔɪstə(r)/

● world → the world is your oyster

Pp

P /piː/

● mind → mind your P's and Q's

pace /peɪs/

do sth at your own 'pace
do sth at the speed you prefer: *When you are learning a language at home, you can work at your own pace.*

keep 'pace (with sb/sth)
1 move, progress or develop at the same speed or rate as sb/sth: *In this business we have to keep pace with our foreign competitors.* ◇ *He isn't really keeping pace with the other children in his class.*
2 keep informed about sth which is changing very fast: *I find it difficult to keep pace with all the political changes that are taking place.*

set the 'pace
do sth at a speed which other people must follow if they want to be successful; lead by being better, cleverer, more original, etc. than other people: *Jones set the pace in the 5 000 metres.* ◇ *This new style of bicycle has really set the pace for the rest of the industry.* ▶ **'pacesetter** *noun: Richard Rogers is a pacesetter in modern architecture.*

> **NOTE**
> In athletics, one person in a race *sets the pace* for the other competitors by running faster than them.

(not) stand the 'pace
not be able to work, live or compete under pressure: *You want to be a journalist? Are you sure you could stand the pace?*

● force → force the pace
● snail → at a snail's pace

paces /'peɪsɪz/

go through your 'paces ◆ show your 'paces
perform a particular activity in order to show other people what you are capable of doing: *The team went through their paces in front of an adoring public.*

put sb/sth through their/its 'paces
test sb's/sth's ability to do sth by making them/it show how well they/it can actually perform certain actions, tasks, etc: *We watched the trainer putting the police dog through its paces.* ◇ *They're putting the new machinery through its paces.*

> **NOTE**
> These expressions refer to judging the performance of a horse before deciding to buy it.

pack /pæk/

ahead of the 'pack
if a person, company, etc. is **ahead of the pack**, they start to do sth before other people, especially their rivals: *The company was ahead of the pack in recognizing the huge potential of the Internet.*

,pack your 'bags (*informal*)
prepare to leave a place permanently, especially after a disagreement: *He hadn't paid any rent for three months so she told him to pack his bags.*

,pack it 'in (*informal, especially BrE*)
stop doing sth: *Your guitar playing is getting on my nerves. Pack it in, will you?* ◇ *I didn't like my last job so I packed it in.*

a ,pack of 'lies (*informal*)
a lot of lies told at the same time: *The police discovered that her story was a pack of lies.* ◇ *He told me a pack of lies when I asked him about previous jobs.*

,pack a (hard, etc.) 'punch (*informal*)
1 be able to hit very hard: *He's a boxer who packs a nasty punch!*
2 have a powerful effect on sb: *Their latest advertising campaign packs a hard punch.* ◇ *Don't drink too much of his home-made beer — it packs quite a punch!*

,pack them 'in ◆ ,pack the 'house
attract a large audience; fill a theatre, hall, etc: *This group's been playing for twenty years but they're still packing them in.* ◇ *The city orchestra always plays to a packed house.*

● joker → the joker in the pack

packed /pækt/

packed (together) like sar'dines (*informal*)
(of people) pressed tightly together in a way that is uncomfortable or unpleasant: *On the tube in the rush hour the passengers are packed like sardines.*

> **NOTE**
> *Sardines* are a type of fish that are usually sold packed tightly together in small tins.

packet /'pækɪt/

make, lose, spend, etc. a 'packet (*informal*)
make, etc. a large amount of money: *He went to the USA and made a packet in office property.* ◇ *We spent a packet on our weekend away — everything was so expensive.*

packing /'pækɪŋ/

● send → send sb packing

page /peɪdʒ/

be on the same 'page (*especially AmE*)
think the same way or have the same opinion about sth: *I just want to make sure we're all on the same page about this.*

● printed → the printed word/page

paid /peɪd/

put 'paid to sth (*informal*)
make it impossible for sth to happen or continue: *Her poor exam results have put paid to any chance she had of getting into medical school.*

paid-up /ˌpeɪd 'ʌp/

a (fully) ,paid-up 'member, etc.
1 a person who has paid the money necessary to become a member of a group, etc: *The society has got over 10 000 paid-up members.*
2 (*informal*) a strong and enthusiastic supporter of a group, etc: *He is a fully paid-up supporter of the Green Party.*

pain /peɪn/

on/under pain of sth (*formal*)
with the threat of having sth done to you as a punishment if you do not obey a command: *They were forbidden on pain of death to talk to any of the other prisoners.* ◇ *We were told to pay within three days, on pain of a €1 000 fine if we didn't.*

a pain in the 'neck (*BrE also* **a pain in the 'arse** ⚠/**'bum**/**'backside**) (*AmE also* **a pain in the 'ass** ⚠/**'butt**) (*informal*)
a person or thing that you find annoying: *Her new boyfriend is a real pain in the neck — he never stops talking.*

pains /peɪnz/

be at (great) pains to do sth
put a lot of effort into doing sth correctly: *The manager was at great pains to point out that no one would lose their job after reorganization.* ◇ *She was at pains to make us feel welcome in her home.*

for your 'pains (*especially BrE, often ironic*)
as payment, reward or thanks for sth you have done: *I helped them in the shop for a week, and all I got for my pains was a box of chocolates.*

take (great) 'pains with sth/to do sth ◆ go to great 'pains to do sth
make a great effort to do sth well, carefully, properly, etc: *It looks easy but in fact he went to great pains to achieve that particular effect in his paintings.* ◇ *She takes great pains with the flower arrangements.*

● growing → growing pains
● spare → spare no expense/pains/trouble (to do sth/(in) doing sth)

paint /peɪnt/

paint a terrible, depressing, rosy, etc. 'picture (of sb/sth)
describe sth in a particular way; give a particular impression of sb/sth, often a negative one: *You paint a depressing picture of your childhood!* ◇ *People who don't like students paint the worst possible picture of their behaviour.* ◇ *The book paints a vivid picture of life in the city.*

paint the town 'red (*informal*)
go to a lot of different bars, clubs, etc. and enjoy
yourself: *It was the end of term and students
decided to go out and paint the town red.*

paint sth with a ,broad 'brush
describe sth in a general way, ignoring the
details: *His description of national politics is
painted with a very broad brush, although some
areas are described in a little more detail than
others.* ▶ **,broad-'brush** *adj.* [only before noun]
dealing with sth in a general way rather than considering details: *a broad-brush approach*

● corner → back/paint sb/yourself into a corner
● lick → a lick of paint

painted /'peɪntɪd/

● black → he, it, etc. is not as black as he, it, etc. is painted

painting /'peɪntɪŋ/

be like painting the Forth 'Bridge (*BrE*)
if a job is **like painting the Forth Bridge**, it is so
big that by the time you get to the end you have to
start at the beginning again: *Cleaning a house this
size is a bit like painting the Forth Bridge. As soon as
I've finished it's time to start again!*

NOTE
The *Forth Bridge* is a very big bridge over the
river Forth in Edinburgh.

● oil → be no oil painting

pair /peə(r); *AmE* per/

I've only got one pair of 'hands (*spoken*)
used to say that you are too busy to do anything
else: *Give me a chance! I've only got one pair of
hands you know!*

a pair of 'hands (*informal*)
a person who can do, or is doing, a job: *We need an
extra pair of hands if we're going to finish on time.*
◇ *Colleagues regarded him as a **safe pair of hands**
(= sb who can be relied on to do a job well).*

● show → show (sb) a clean pair of heels

pairs /peəz; *AmE* perz; peərz/

in 'pairs
in groups of two objects or people: *Students
worked in pairs on the project.*

pajamas /pə'dʒɑːməz; *AmE* -'dʒæm-/ (*AmE*) = pyjamas

pale /peɪl/

be,yond the 'pale
considered socially unacceptable: *Her behaviour
towards her employees is completely beyond the
pale. She treats them like servants.*

❷ ORIGIN
A *pale* was a boundary made of wooden posts
or the safe area inside this. In the fourteenth
and fifteenth centuries, the part of Ireland that

was under English rule was called *the Pale*. The
area outside this was *beyond the Pale* and considered wild and dangerous by the English.

**'pale beside/next to sth ♦ 'pale in/by com-
parison (with/to sth) ♦ 'pale into insignifi-
cance**
seem less important when compared with sth
else: *Last year's riots pale in comparison with this
latest outburst of violence.*

palm /pɑːm/

have sb in the ,palm of your 'hand
have sb completely under your control or influence: *Her boyfriend will do anything for her; she's
got him in the palm of her hand.*

● grease → grease sb's palm

pan /pæn/

go down the 'pan (*BrE, slang*)
be wasted or spoiled: *That's another brilliant idea
down the pan.*

NOTE
Pan is an informal word for the bowl of a toilet.

● flash → a flash in the pan
● frying → out of the frying pan (and) into the fire

pancake /'pænkeɪk/

● flat → (as) flat as a pancake

Pandora /pæn,dɔːrə/

Pandora's 'box
a source of great trouble and suffering, although
this may not be obvious at the beginning: *The publication of her diaries opened up a real Pandora's
box.*

❷ ORIGIN
In Greek mythology, Pandora was the first
woman on earth. The gods sent her to earth
with a box that she was forbidden to open, but
she opened it and all the evils flew out of it into
the world.

panic /'pænɪk/

'panic stations (*BrE, informal*)
a situation in which people feel anxious and there
is a lot of confused activity, especially because
there is a lot to do in a short period of time: *At
the moment it's panic stations in the office because
we're preparing for the president's visit next week.*

❷ ORIGIN
In the navy, a call to *action stations* means that
each sailor takes the position that they should
have when in battle. *Panic stations* is a humorous comparison with this.

press/push the 'panic button (*BrE*)
react in a sudden or an extreme way to sth unexpected that has frightened you: *Although the team
lost yet another match on Saturday, their manager
is refusing to press the panic button.*

pant /pænt/

• puff → puff and pant/blow

panties /'pæntiz/

• knickers → get/have your panties in a knot SEE get/have your knickers in a twist

pants /pænts/

scare, bore, etc. the 'pants off sb (*informal*)
scare, bore, etc. sb very much: *He would creep up behind people and scare the pants off them.* ◇ *He was clearly boring the pants off his audience.*

• ants → have ants in your pants
• catch → catch sb with their pants down
• kick → a kick in the pants SEE a kick up the backside
• seat → (fly) by the seat of your pants
• wear → wear the pants SEE wear the trousers
• wet → wet your pants/knickers

paper /'peɪpə(r)/

on 'paper
considering sth from what is written down about it, rather than what is actually true in practice; in theory: *This idea looks very good on paper, but I'm not sure that it's very practical.*

,paper over the 'cracks
try to hide a problem or disagreement in a way that is temporary and not likely to be successful: *These new prison reforms are just papering over the cracks. What we need is a fundamental change in the prison system.*

NOTE
This expression refers to putting wallpaper on a wall in order to hide the cracks in the plaster.

a ,paper 'tiger
a person or thing that is less strong, powerful, dangerous, etc. than they/it appears: *He claimed that the enemies of his party were paper tigers and not to be feared.*

❷ ORIGIN
This is a translation of a Chinese expression that became well known when it was used by Mao Zedong.

• pen → put pen to paper
• punch → he, she, etc. couldn't punch his, her, etc. way out of a paper bag
• worth → not worth the paper it's printed/written on

papers /'peɪpəz; AmE 'peɪpərz/

• walking → get your walking papers
• walking → give sb their walking papers

par /pɑː(r)/

be below/under 'par
less well, good, etc. than is usual or expected: *I've been feeling rather below par recently — I think it's time I took a break.* ◇ *His performance at the concert was well under par.*

be on a 'par with sb/sth
be equal to sb/sth; be at the same level as sb/sth in importance, rank, value, etc: *He doesn't think his salary is on a par with his position in the company.* ◇ *As actors, I would say they were on a par.*

be (about) ,par for the 'course (*disapproving*)
be normal; be what you would expect to happen: *'The food on this plane is terrible.' 'Well, that's about par for the course.'*

NOTE
This idiom refers to the game of golf. *Par* is the number of times a good player should hit the ball to complete a particular hole or course.

be up to/above 'par
of an acceptable standard, quality, etc.; better than the usual standard, quality, etc: *You don't need to worry. Your work is well above par.* ◇ *His driving wasn't quite up to par and he lost the race.*

,par 'excellence (*from French*)
(only used after the noun it describes) better than all the others of the same kind; a very good example of sth: *She turned out to be an organizer par excellence.*

parade /pə'reɪd/

• rain → rain on sb's parade

paradise /'pærədaɪs/

• fool → a fool's paradise

paragon /'pærəgən; AmE -gɑːn/

a paragon of 'virtue
a person who is without faults; a completely perfect person: *We don't expect all election candidates to be paragons of virtue.*

parallel /'pærəlel/

in 'parallel (with sb/sth)
with and at the same time as sb/sth else: *The new degree and the existing certificate courses would run in parallel.* ◇ *Ann wanted to pursue her own career in parallel with her husband's.*

parcel /'pɑːsl; AmE 'pɑːrsl/

• part → be part and parcel of sth

pardon /'pɑːdn; AmE 'pɑːrdn/

,pardon 'me (*spoken*)
1 (*especially AmE*) used to ask sb to repeat sth because you did not hear it or do not understand it: *'You look miles away.' 'Pardon me?'*
2 used by some people to say 'sorry' when they have accidentally made a rude noise or done sth wrong

,pardon me for 'doing sth (*informal*)
used to show that you are upset or offended by the way that sb has spoken to you: *'This is a meeting for women only, so get out and mind your own business.' 'Oh, pardon me for existing!'* ◇ *'Oh, just shut up.' 'Well, pardon me for breathing!'*

• beg → I beg your pardon
• French → excuse/pardon my French

parentis /pəˈrentɪs/

• loco → in loco parentis

park /pɑːk; AmE pɑːrk/

• walk → a walk in the park

parker /ˈpɑːkə(r); AmE ˈpɑːrk-/

• nosy → a nosy parker

Parkinson /ˈpɑːkɪnsn; AmE ˈpɑːrk-/

'Parkinson's law (*humorous*)
the idea that work will always take as long as the time you have to do it: *I don't know why this report is taking me so long. Parkinson's law, I suppose.*

> ❼ ORIGIN
> This is the title of a book by C. Northcote Parkinson about inefficient administration.

parrot-fashion /ˈpærət fæʃn/

(learn, repeat, etc. sth) 'parrot-fashion (*BrE, disapproving*)
(learn, repeat, etc. sth) without understanding the meaning: *When we were at school we used to learn history parrot-fashion; all I can remember now is the dates.*

> NOTE
> This idiom refer to the fact that parrots can learn phrases and repeat them after you without understanding what they mean.

• sick → (as) sick as a parrot

part /pɑːt; AmE pɑːrt/

be part and parcel of sth
be an essential part of sth: *Long hours spent planning lessons are part and parcel of a teacher's job.*

the better/best part of sth
most of sth: *I worked at the camp for the better part of the summer. ◇ He had lived there for the best part of fifty years.*

for the 'most part
mainly; on the whole; generally: *I agree with you for the most part but there are a few details I'd like to discuss further.*

for 'my, 'his, etc. (own) part
as far as I am, he is, etc. concerned: *For my part I don't care whether they win or not.*

have/play/take/want no 'part in/of sth
not be involved or refuse to be involved in sth, especially because you disapprove of it: *He had no part in the decision. ◇ I want no part of this sordid business.*

have a part to 'play (in sth)
be able to help sth: *We all have a part to play in the fight against crime.*

in 'part
partly; to some extent: *Her success was due in part to luck.* ❴OPP❵ in full

look/dress the 'part
have an appearance or wear clothes that are suitable for a particular job, position, etc: *I think Tim Evans should play Robin Hood. He really looks the part. ◇ He's a funny kind of bank manager; he doesn't dress the part at all.*

on sb's part ♦ on the part of sb
(of an action) done, made or performed by sb: *The argument started because of an angry remark on his part. ◇ If you want to go camping, son, there'd be no objection on our part.*

part 'company (with/from sb/sth)
1 leave sb; separate and go in different directions: *We walked down into town together and then parted company at the station. ◇ They've finally parted company after a long, unhappy marriage.*
2 disagree with sb: *I'm afraid I have to part company with you on the question of nuclear energy.*
3 (*humorous*) come apart; separate: *In the high winds the sail and the boat parted company.*

part of the 'furniture (*informal*)
sb who has worked or been in a particular place for such a long time that people hardly notice them: *The librarian had been there so long he seemed like part of the furniture.*

play a/your 'part (in sth)
be involved in sth; be a reason for sth happening: *You too can play a part in helping your community. ◇ Arguments within the party played a part in the downfall of the government.*

take sth in good 'part (*BrE*)
accept sth slightly unpleasant without complaining or being offended: *They played a trick on her by putting a plastic spider in her bed, but she took it in good part. ◇ He took my criticism in good part.* ❴OPP❵ take sth amiss

take 'part (in sth)
be one of a group of people doing sth together; participate in sth: *He's taking part in a golf competition this weekend. ◇ She never takes part in any community activities.*

take sb's 'part (*BrE*)
defend or support what sb has said or done, especially in an argument: *Personally I take Emma's part on this matter. ◇ He never takes my part in an argument.*

• discretion → discretion is the better part of valour
• large → in no small part SEE in large part

parted /ˈpɑːtɪd; AmE ˈpɑːrt-/

• fool → a fool and his money are soon parted

Parthian /ˈpɑːθiən; AmE ˈpɑːrθiən/

• parting → a Parthian shot SEE a parting shot

particular /pəˈtɪkjələ(r); AmE pərˈt-/

in par'ticular
1 especially or particularly: *He loves reading, science fiction in particular.*

parting

2 special or specific: *Peter was lying on the sofa doing nothing in particular.* ◇ *Is there anything in particular you'd like for dinner?* ◇ *She directed the question at no one in particular.* **OPP** in general

parting /ˈpɑːtɪŋ; AmE ˈpɑːrt-/

a/the ˌparting of the ˈways
1 the place where two or more people who have been travelling together separate and take different routes: *We travelled to India together, and in Delhi it was the parting of the ways. Ray went on to China and I went on to Australia.*
2 the time when two or more people who have been working, living, etc. together separate and begin a new period in their lives: *After college it was the parting of the ways. We all went to live in different parts of the country and gradually we lost touch.*

a ˌparting ˈshot (also **a ˌParthian ˈshot**)
a remark or action, often an unkind one, that somebody makes just as they are leaving: *As Jim walked out of the door, his parting shot was, 'I never want to see any of you again.'*

❷ ORIGIN
Parthia was a kingdom in ancient times. The Parthians used to fire arrows at the enemy as they were retreating from battle.

parts /pɑːts; AmE pɑːrts/

a man/woman of (many) ˈparts
a person who can do many different things well: *My grandfather was a man of many parts: a talented musician, a good cook and not a bad painter.*

round/in ˌthese ˈparts (*old-fashioned*)
in this area: *We don't see many tourists round these parts.* ◇ *What are the food specialities in these parts?*

● possession → possession is nine points/tenths/parts of the law
● private → private parts
● sum → be greater/more than the sum of its parts

party /ˈpɑːti; AmE ˈpɑːrti/

be (a) ˈparty to sth (*formal*)
take part in a (secret) plan, agreement, etc., and therefore be partly responsible for it: *'Were you a party to this, Anna?' 'No, Mrs Jones, I was away on holiday at the time.'* ◇ *How many people were party to the plan?*

the ˌparty ˈline
the beliefs or policies of a political party: *Ministers in the government are expected to follow the party line.* ◇ *She has gone against the party line again.* ◇ *No one seems to know exactly what the party line is on this issue.*

your ˈparty piece (*BrE, informal*)
the same song, poem, trick, etc. that you often do in order to entertain people at parties: *His party piece is to stand on his head and drink a glass of water.*

the party's ˈover
a period of freedom, enjoyment, very good luck, etc. has now come to an end and life is about to return to normal: *We've had a good time while the manager's been away, but now the party's over.*

● life → the life and soul of the party

pas /pɑː/

● faux → (make/commit) a faux pas

pass /pɑːs; AmE pæs/

come to such a ˈpass ◆ come to a pretty ˈpass (*old-fashioned* or *humorous*)
reach a sad or difficult state: *Things have come to a pretty pass when children are begging in the streets.*

let sth ˈpass
pay no attention to sth that sb says or does because you think it is better not to argue about it or criticize it: *He started saying terrible things about my mother again but I let it pass. It only makes things worse if I say something.*

make a ˈpass at sb (*informal*)
make a direct approach to sb you are interested in sexually: *He can't resist making a pass at every woman he meets.*

not pass your ˈlips
1 if words do **not pass your lips**, you say nothing
2 if food or drink does **not pass your lips**, you eat or drink nothing: *He promised her that nothing would pass his lips before dinner.*

ˌpass the ˈbuck (*informal*)
refuse to accept responsibility for a mistake, an accident, an important decision, etc. and try to get another person, organization, etc. to accept responsibility for it instead: *The same thing happens after every disaster. All the officials involved just try to pass the buck.* **OPP** the buck stops here ▶ **ˈbuck-passing** noun: *The public is tired of all this political buck-passing. They just want to know who was responsible for the decision.*

❷ ORIGIN
The *buck* is a small object in a poker game that is placed in front of the player whose turn it is to deal.

pass the ˈhat round/around ◆ pass round/around the ˈhat (*informal*)
collect money from a number of people, for example to buy a present for sb: *Anthony had his car radio stolen, so his friends passed the hat round and bought him a new one.*

pass ˈjudgement (on/about sb/sth) (*especially BrE*) (*AmE usually* **pass ˈjudgment (on/about sb/sth)**)
give your opinion about sb/sth, especially if this is critical: *Don't be too quick to pass judgement, you're not perfect yourself, you know.*

pass ˈmuster
be good enough; be acceptable: *I didn't think Charlie's parents would like me, but evidently I pass muster.*

❷ ORIGIN
Muster is the calling together of soldiers, sailors, etc. for inspection. If you *pass muster*, you pass the inspection without criticism.

pass the/your 'time (doing sth)
spend your time (doing sth), often while you are waiting for sth else: *They told each other jokes to pass the time while waiting for the next train.* ◇ *We passed our time making plans for the weekend.*

pass the time of 'day (with sb)
greet sb and have a short conversation with them about things that are not very important: *I don't know any of the neighbours very well, only just enough to pass the time of day.*

pass 'water (*formal*)
pass urine (= waste liquid) out of your body; urinate

● ships → be (like) ships that pass in the night

passage /ˈpæsɪdʒ/

● bird → a bird of passage

passing /ˈpɑːsɪŋ; *AmE* ˈpæs-/

in 'passing
done or said while you are giving your attention to sth else: *'What did the minister say about educational reform?' 'Not very much. He just mentioned it in passing.'* ◇ *Could I just say in passing that…?*

past /pɑːst; *AmE* pæst/

be/look 'past it (*BrE, informal*)
1 (of a person) be too old to do sth as well as you used to in the past: *He might look past it, but I bet he can run faster than you.*
2 (of a thing) be no longer in good condition or functioning well because of its age: *Those shoes are a bit past it, aren't they? You need a new pair.*

be past your/its 'best
be no longer as strong, fresh, young, beautiful, etc. as before: *What do you mean, somebody over 35 is past their best? That's nonsense.* **OPP** in the prime of (your) life

be past its 'sell-by date (*informal*)
be no longer useful or valued: *His ideas on economics are well past their sell-by date.*

NOTE
The *sell-by date* is the date written on food packaging after which the food must not be sold.

I wouldn't put it 'past sb (to do sth)
used to say that you think sb is quite capable of doing sth surprising, unusual, etc: *'Do you think he'd ever steal from his friends?' 'I wouldn't put it past him.'*

a ˌpast 'master (in/of/at sth)
a person who is very good at doing sth: *He's a past master at making other people feel guilty.*

● blast → a blast from the past
● caring → be beyond/past caring (about sth)
● distant → the (dim and) distant past

● end → not see beyond/past the end of your nose
● rake → rake over the ashes/the past
● thing → a thing of the past

pasting /ˈpeɪstɪŋ/

give sb/get a 'pasting (*informal, especially BrE*)
1 beat sb/be beaten very easily: *Our team was given a real pasting on Saturday. We lost 6-0.* ◇ *The Democrats got a real pasting at the local elections.*
2 criticize sb/be criticized very severely: *His new film got a pasting in the newspaper yesterday.* ◇ *She gave me a real pasting for handing in my essay a week late.*

pasture /ˈpɑːstʃə(r); *AmE* ˈpæs-/

put sb out to 'pasture (*informal, humorous*)
ask sb to leave a job because they are getting old; make sb retire: *Isn't it time some of these politicians were put out to pasture?*

❷ ORIGIN
This expression refers to old farm horses or other animals, which no longer work and stay in the fields (= *pastures*) all day.

pastures /ˈpɑːstʃəz; *AmE* ˈpæs-/

ˌpastures 'new
a new job, place to live, way of life, etc: *After 10 years as a teacher, Jen felt it was time to move on to pastures new.* ◇ *Without warning, she left him for pastures new.*

pat /pæt/

give sb/yourself a ˌpat on the 'back ♦ pat sb/yourself on the 'back (for doing sth)
praise sb/yourself for sth they/you have done well: *I think we should pat James on the back for working so hard.* ◇ *I feel I can give myself a pat on the back for finishing everything on time.*

have/know/get sth off 'pat (*BrE*) (*AmE* **have/know sth down 'pat**)
know or have learned sth so well that you can repeat it at any time: *I'm afraid I haven't got the answer off pat.* ◇ *She has all our names and cellphone numbers down pat.*

stand 'pat (*especially AmE*)
refuse to change your mind about a decision you have made or an opinion you have: *There has been a lot of controversy over the new proposals, but the government is standing pat.* **OPP** shift your ground

patch /pætʃ/

go through, hit, etc. a 'bad/'sticky patch
come to a difficult time in your business, marriage, etc: *We've struck a bad patch in our marriage.* ◇ *High inflation meant that her business went through a sticky patch.*

not be a 'patch on sb/sth (*informal, especially BrE*)
not be nearly as good as sb/sth: *The film isn't a patch on the book.*

path /pɑːθ; AmE pæθ/

- beat → beat a path to sb's door
- lead¹ → lead sb up the garden path
- primrose → the primrose path (to ruin, destruction, etc.)
- smooth → smooth the path/way
- tread → tread a difficult, solitary, etc. path

paths /pɑːθs; AmE pæθs/

- cross → our/their paths cross SEE cross sb's path

patience /'peɪʃns/

the patience of a 'saint/of 'Job
very great patience: *I don't know how she does it — she's got the patience of a saint, that woman!* ◊ *You need the patience of Job to deal with customers like that.*

> ❷ ORIGIN
> Job was a character in the Bible who lost his family, his home and his possessions, but still did not reject God.

- try → try sb's patience

patter /'pætə(r)/

the patter of tiny 'feet (*informal or humorous*)
a way of referring to children when sb wants, or is going to have, a baby: *We can't wait to hear the patter of tiny feet.*

Paul /pɔːl/

- rob → rob Peter to pay Paul

pause /pɔːz/

give (sb) pause for 'thought ♦ give (sb) 'pause (*formal*)
make sb think seriously about sth or hesitate before doing sth: *His remarks on the conditions in our prisons gave me pause for thought. Until that moment I'd never realized things were so bad.*

- pregnant → a pregnant pause/silence

pave /peɪv/

,pave the 'way (for sb/sth)
make the arrival of sb/sth easier; prepare for sb/sth: *Babbage's early work on calculating machines in the nineteenth century paved the way for the development of computers.*

paved /peɪvd/

- road → the road to hell is paved with good intentions
- streets → the streets are paved with gold

pay /peɪ/

be in the pay of sb/sth ♦ be in sb's/sth's pay (*usually disapproving*)
be working for sb or for an organization, often secretly: *He's been in the pay of our rivals for the last ten years.*

'hell/the 'devil to pay (*informal*)
a lot of trouble: *There'll be hell to pay when your father sees that broken window.*

hit/strike 'pay dirt (*informal, especially AmE*)
suddenly be in a successful situation, especially one that makes you rich: *The band hit pay dirt two years ago with their first album, but have since been less successful.*

> ❷ ORIGIN
> This comes from mining. *Pay dirt* is earth that contains valuable minerals or metal such as gold.

pay 'dividends
produce great advantages or profits: *Learning a foreign language will always pay dividends.* ◊ *Hard work while you're young pays dividends later.*

> NOTE
> If you invest in a company, the money you receive as your share of the profit is called a *dividend*.

pay for it'self
(of a new system, sth you have bought, etc.) save as much money as it cost: *The rail pass will pay for itself after only about two trips.*

pay 'lip-service to sth
if a person **pays lip-service to sth**, they pretend to support or agree with sth, without proving their support by what they actually do: *He doesn't really believe in equal opportunities. He just pays lip-service to it because he doesn't want to appear old-fashioned.*

pay the 'price/'penalty (for sth/for doing sth)
suffer as a result of bad luck, a mistake or sth you have done: *They've made a lot of mistakes in the past and now they're paying the price.* ◊ *I'm really paying the penalty for all those late nights. I feel terrible today.*

pay your re'spects (to sb) (*formal*)
show respect for sb by visiting them, attending their funeral, etc: *At the funeral the whole neighbourhood came out to pay their respects (to him).*

pay through the 'nose (for sth) (*informal*)
pay a very high price for sth: *Why pay through the nose for a used car? Come to Smith's for prices you can afford!*

pay 'tribute to sb/sth
show that you respect or admire sb/sth: *Members of the musical profession paid tribute to the late Leonard Bernstein.*

> ❷ ORIGIN
> In the past, people often had to *pay tribute* to a ruler, which meant paying money in return for protection or for not being attacked.

pay sb/sth a visit ♦ pay a visit to sb/sth
visit sb/sth: *I think it's time we paid Jo a visit, don't you?*

pay your/its (own) 'way
(of a person, group, etc.) have or make enough money to support yourself/itself: *I had to work in*

pennies /'peni:z/

• pinch → pinch pennies

penn'orth /'penəθ; *AmE* -nərθ/

• two → put in your two pennyworth/penn'orth

penny /'peni/

,in for a 'penny, ,in for a 'pound (*saying*)
once you have decided to start doing sth, you may
as well do it as well as you can, even if this means
spending a lot of time, energy, money, etc: *The
new carpet made everything else look old, so we
thought 'in for a penny, in for a pound', and we
painted the room and bought a new sofa too!*

the ,penny 'drops (*informal, especially BrE*)
suddenly understand the meaning or significance
of sth: *She never understands jokes. It usually takes
about half an hour for the penny to drop.* ◇ *There
was a long silence on the stage, and then the penny
finally dropped — it was my turn to speak.*

> **NOTE**
> This is a comparison with the way a machine
> starts after a coin is inserted.

a ,penny for your 'thoughts (also **a 'penny for
them**) (*saying*)
used to ask sb what they are thinking about: *A
penny for your thoughts, Hugh! You haven't said
anything all evening!*

penny ,wise (and) pound 'foolish
used to say that sb is very careful about small matters but much less sensible about larger, more
important things: *When it comes to a used car,
don't be penny wise and pound foolish. Spend the
money to have the vehicle checked out.*

turn up like a bad 'penny (*informal*)
appear when you are not welcome or not wanted,
especially when this happens regularly: *He turns
up like a bad penny every time there's a chance of a
free meal or a drink.*

two/ten a 'penny (*BrE*) (*AmE* **a ,dime a 'dozen**)
very cheap or very common, and therefore not
valuable: *In the small towns on the coast, lobsters
are two a penny.* ◇ *Finding a job will be difficult.
History teachers are ten a penny at the moment.*

• pretty → a pretty penny
• spend → spend a penny

pennyworth /'peniwɜːθ; *AmE* -wɜːrθ/

• two → put in your two pennyworth/penn'orth

people /'piːpl/

of 'all people/places/things
used to emphasize that the person/place/thing is
the most or least likely in the circumstances: *You
of all people should be sympathetic, having just had
a similar accident yourself.* ◇ *If it's a rest they need,
then why go to New York of all places?*

**people (who live) in glass ,houses shouldn't
throw 'stones** (*saying*)
you should not criticize other people for faults
that you have yourself: *'He said you weren't entirely honest in business.' 'Oh, did he? Well tell him from
me that people who live in glass houses shouldn't
throw stones. He'll know what I mean.'*

• man → a man of the people
• things → be all things to all men/people

pep /pep/

a 'pep talk (*informal*)
a talk by sb to give people confidence or encouragement: *Just before the exams, our teacher gave us
all a pep talk.*

per /pɜː(r); pə(r)/

as per sth
following sth that has been decided: *The work was
carried out as per instructions.*

as per 'usual/'normal (*spoken*)
in the usual or normal manner: *'What time is the
lesson?' 'Thursday at 3 o'clock, as per usual.'* ◇ *'Is
he in a bad mood this morning?' 'Yes, as per normal.'*

• head → a/per head
• hundred → a/one hundred per cent

perch /pɜːtʃ; *AmE* pɜːrtʃ/

• knock → knock sb off their perch/pedestal

perfect /'pɜːfɪkt; *AmE* 'pɜːrf-/

• practice → practice makes perfect
• world → in an ideal/a perfect world

perfectly /'pɜːfɪktli; *AmE* 'pɜːrf-/

• know → know sth full/perfectly/very well

perform /pə'fɔːm; *AmE* pər'fɔːrm/

• act → do/perform/stage a disappearing/vanishing act

peril /'perəl/

(do sth) at your (own) 'peril
(often used as a warning) at the risk of serious
danger: *People who go climbing in winter do so at
their own peril.* ◇ *You go in Mike's car at your peril.
He's a terrible driver.*

period /'pɪəriəd; *AmE* 'pɪr-/

• full → period SEE full stop
• honeymoon → a/the honeymoon period

perish /'perɪʃ/

,perish the 'thought! (*spoken, often humorous*)
I hope it will not happen; may it never happen: *'A
picnic is a good idea but what if it rains?' 'Perish the
thought!'*

perpetuity /,pɜːpə'tjuːəti; *AmE* ,pɜːrpə'tuː-/

in perpe'tuity (*formal*)
for all time in the future; forever: *They do not own
the land in perpetuity.*

person /ˈpɜːsn; AmE ˈpɜːrsn/

about/on your ˈperson (*formal* or *humorous*)
carried with you, for example in a pocket or bag:
*You don't happen to have a pen about your person,
do you?*

in ˈperson
personally; physically present: *I'm sorry, I won't be
able to come in person, but I'll send my assistant.*

in the person of sb (*formal*)
in the form or shape of sb: *Help arrived in the person of his mother.*

• next → as good, well, etc. as the next person

persona /pɜːˈsəʊnə; AmE pɜːrˈsoʊnə/

perˌsona non ˈgrata (*from Latin*)
a person who is not welcome in a particular place
because of sth they have said or done: *Persona non
grata in Hollywood, Jake moved to New York to try
and make a living on the stage.*

NOTE
The meaning of *non grata* is 'not pleasing'.

personally /ˈpɜːsənəli; AmE ˈpɜːrs-/

take sth ˈpersonally
feel personally offended by sb's general remark,
etc: *I was talking about people having smelly socks,
and I'm afraid Mike took it personally.* ◇ *Look, don't
take this personally, Sue, but there are several
people in this office who are not working hard
enough.*

persons /ˈpɜːsnz; AmE ˈpɜːrsnz/

• respecter → be no respecter of persons

perspective /pəˈspektɪv; AmE pərˈs-/

get, put, etc. sth in/out of perˈspective
be able/not be able to see or understand the relative importance of particular events, facts, etc:
*When you're depressed, it's very easy to get things
out of perspective. Everything worries you.* ◇ *Let's
try and put your present problems in perspective,
then you'll see that things aren't as bad as you think.*

persuasion /pəˈsweɪʒn; AmE pərˈs-/

of a/the… persuasion (*formal* or *humorous*)
of the type mentioned: *As a young man, Max had
always been of an artistic persuasion.* ◇ *peers of the
Liberal persuasion*

pervert /pəˈvɜːt; AmE pərˈvɜːrt/

perˌvert the course of ˈjustice (*law*)
tell a lie or do sth in order to prevent the police,
etc. from finding out the truth about a crime: *He
was arrested and charged with attempting to pervert the course of justice.*

pet /pet/

your, his, etc. pet ˈhate (*BrE*) (*AmE* **your, his,
etc. pet ˈpeeve**)
something that you particularly dislike: *She didn't
mind people smoking, but her pet hate was people
blowing smoke in her face.*

petard /pəˈtɑːd; AmE pəˈtɑːrd/

be hoist/hoisted by/with your own peˈtard
(*BrE*)
be caught in the trap that you were preparing for
another person

❷ ORIGIN
This is from Shakespeare's play *Hamlet*. A
petard was a small bomb.

Pete /piːt/

for ˌPete's ˈsake (*BrE*)
used to emphasize that it is important to do sth, or
when you are annoyed or impatient about sth: *For
Pete's sake, what are you doing in that bathroom?
You've been in there for nearly an hour.*

Peter /ˈpiːtə(r)/

• rob → rob Peter to pay Paul

pew /pjuː/

ˌtake a ˈpew (*BrE, spoken, humorous*)
used to tell sb to sit down: *Good to see you! Take a
pew and I'll get us a drink.*

NOTE
A *pew* is a long wooden seat in a church.

phase /feɪz/

in ˈphase/out of ˈphase (with sth) (*BrE*)
working/not working together in the right way:
The traffic lights were out of phase.

phone /fəʊn; AmE foʊn/

• telephone → be on the telephone/phone

phrase /freɪz/

a ˌturn of ˈphrase
a particular way of saying sth or describing sth:
She has a very amusing turn of phrase.

• coin → to coin a phrase

pick /pɪk/

ˌpick and ˈchoose
take time and care to choose sth you really want:
*There are so few jobs in banking at the moment that
you're not really in a position to pick and choose.*

pick sb's ˈbrains (*informal*)
ask sb who knows a lot about a particular subject
for information or ideas: *I need some help with this
project. Can I pick your brains?*

pick a 'fight/'quarrel (with sb)
deliberately start a fight or an argument (with sb): *Why do you always pick fights with other boys?* ◊ *At work he's always picking quarrels.*

pick 'holes (in sth) (*informal*)
criticize sth or find fault with sth, for example a plan, a reason, an argument, etc: *It's easy for you to pick holes in my explanation, but have you got a better one?*

pick a 'lock
open a lock without a key, using sth such as a piece of wire: *I can't find my front door key. I don't suppose you know how to pick a lock, do you?*

the pick of the 'bunch (*informal*)
the best example of a group of people or things: *This Australian wine is the pick of the bunch.*

pick sb's 'pocket
steal money or other things from sb's pocket without them realizing: *I can't find my wallet. I think somebody's picked my pocket!* ► *If she's not careful she'll get her pocket picked.* ► **'pickpocket** *noun* a person who picks pockets: *Be careful of pickpockets when you're on the underground in London.*

pick up the 'pieces
do what you can to get your life, a situation, etc. back to normal after a disaster, shock, etc: *After his son was killed in a car accident, it took him a long time to pick up the pieces.* ◊ *It's always the same with her husband. He upsets everyone and then leaves her to pick up the pieces.*

pick up 'speed
go faster: *The train began to pick up speed.*

pick up the 'tab (for sth) (*informal*)
pay the bill, especially for a group of people in a restaurant, etc: *Her father picked up the tab for all the champagne at the wedding.*

pick up the 'threads
start sth, for example an activity, a relationship, a career, again after a break: *It's not easy for women returning to work to pick up the threads of their earlier careers.*

pick your 'way (across, over, etc. sth)
walk carefully, choosing the safest, driest, etc. place to put your feet: *She picked her way delicately over the rough ground.*

pick a 'winner
1 choose a horse, etc. that you think is most likely to win a race
2 (*informal*) make a very good choice: *Good choice, George. I think you've picked a winner there!*

take/have your 'pick (of sth)
choose whatever you like: *With that much money you can have your pick of any car in the showroom.* ◊ *There's ham, cheese or egg sandwiches. Take your pick!*

● **bone** → have a bone to pick with sb
● **moment** → pick/choose your moment
● **steam** → get up/pick up steam

pickle /ˈpɪkl/

in a (real, right, etc.) 'pickle (*informal*)
in a difficult situation; in a mess: *Things are in a real pickle at the moment, I'm afraid. My assistant's left and I'm completely lost without him!* ◊ *Can you help me? I'm in a bit of a pickle.*

picnic /ˈpɪknɪk/

be no 'picnic (*informal*)
be difficult or unpleasant: *Living with someone like her is no picnic, believe me.*

● **bricks** → a few, two, etc. sandwiches short of a picnic **SEE** a few, two, etc. bricks short of a load

picture /ˈpɪktʃə(r)/

be/look a 'picture
look very beautiful or special: *The park looks a picture in the summer.*

be the ˌpicture of 'health, 'happiness, etc.
be completely or extremely healthy, etc: *She's the picture of happiness in this photo.* ◊ *He's the picture of misery, isn't he? Look at him standing there in the rain.*

get the 'picture (*spoken*)
understand sth: *I get the picture — you want me to keep it a secret.*

in/out of the 'picture (*informal*)
involved/not involved in a situation: *Morris is likely to win, with Jones out of the picture now.*

put/keep sb in the 'picture (*informal*)
give sb the information they need in order to understand a particular situation, etc: *Before you start work, let me put you in the picture about the way the office is run.*

● **big** → the big picture
● **paint** → paint a terrible, depressing, rosy, etc. picture (of sb/sth)
● **pretty** → (as) pretty as a picture
● **side** → a/one side of the story/picture

pie /paɪ/

ˌpie in the 'sky (*informal*)
ideas that are not practical; false hopes or promises: *Most voters know that the big promises which politicians make before an election are just pie in the sky.* ◊ *He says he's going to make a movie in Hollywood, but I think it's all pie in the sky.*

> **❷ ORIGIN**
> This comes from a song written in 1911 by Joe Hill, who worked to improve the rights of workers in America. The song criticizes religion for creating false hopes in the poor: 'Work and pray, Live on hay, You'll get pie in the sky when you die.'

● **American** → as American as apple pie
● **cake** → a piece/share/slice of the pie **SEE** a share/slice of the cake
● **easy** → (as) easy as ABC/pie/falling off a log

- **eat** → eat humble pie
- **finger** → have a finger in every pie
- **nice** → (as) nice as pie

piece /piːs/

give sb a piece of your 'mind (*informal*)
angrily tell sb your true opinion of them; criticize sb angrily: *If he doesn't turn that music down soon, I'm going to give him a piece of my mind.* **OPP** bite your tongue

(all) in one 'piece (*informal*)
not hurt or harmed, especially after being in danger or in an accident: *'Are you all right, Richard?' 'Yes, thanks. I'm still in one piece, I think. I've torn my jacket, that's all.'*

(all) of a 'piece (with sth) (*formal*)
possessing the same character or qualities; consistent (with sth): *When you see a lot of his paintings together, you feel that his work is all of a piece.* ◇ *This latest programme is all of a piece with current popular science programmes on TV.*

,piece by 'piece
one part at a time: *He took his motorcycle apart piece by piece, cleaned it, and put it back together.*

a piece of 'cake (*informal*) (*BrE* also **a piece of 'piss** △, *slang*)
(of a task, etc.) very easy to do: *After climbing mountains in the Swiss Alps, going up English hills is a piece of cake.* ◇ *Taking photos should be a piece of cake with the new camera I've got.* **OPP** a tall order

- **action** → a piece/slice of the action
- **cake** → a piece/share/slice of the pie **SEE** a share/slice of the cake
- **long** → how long is a piece of string?
- **nasty** → a nasty piece of work
- **party** → your party piece
- **say** → say your piece
- **villain** → the villain of the piece

pièce /pjes/

your/the ,pièce de ré'sistance (*from French*)
the most important or impressive part of a group or series of things: *I hope you all enjoyed your main course. And now for my pièce de résistance: chocolate gateau!*

pieces /'piːsɪz/

fall to 'pieces
1 (usually used in the progressive tenses) (of things) become very old and in bad condition because of long use: *Our car is falling to pieces, we've had it so long.*
2 (of a person, an organization, a plan, etc.) stop working; be destroyed: *He's worried that the business will fall to pieces without him.*

go (all) to 'pieces (*informal*)
(after a terrible shock, etc.) become so upset or nervous that you can no longer lead your life normally: *After he lost his job he just seemed to go to pieces.* **OPP** pull yourself together

- **bits** → bits and pieces
- **bits** → pick, pull, etc. sb/sth to bits/pieces
- **pick** → pick up the pieces
- **tear** → tear sb/sth to pieces/shreds

pig /pɪg/

in a pig's 'eye (*AmE, informal*)
used to say that you think that sth is not at all true or that sth will definitely not happen: *He told you his father owns the company? In a pig's eye!* ◇ *'Apparently this is the best hotel in town.' 'In a pig's eye it is!'*

make a 'pig of yourself (*informal*)
eat and drink too much; be greedy: *She always makes such a pig of herself.*

make a pig's 'ear (out) of sth (*BrE, informal*)
do sth very badly: *He made a real pig's ear of his geography exam.*

(buy) a pig in a 'poke
if you buy **a pig in a poke**, you buy or pay for sth without seeing it or examining it carefully first: *Make sure you take the car for a proper test drive — you don't want to buy a pig in a poke, do you?*

> **NOTE**
> *Poke* is an old word for a small sack or bag.

a pig of a sth (*BrE, informal*)
a difficult or unpleasant thing or task: *I've had a pig of a day.*

- **guinea** → a guinea pig
- **middle** → (be) pig/piggy in the middle
- **sweat** → sweat like a pig

pigeon /'pɪdʒɪn/

be sb's pigeon (*old-fashioned, BrE*)
be sb's responsibility or business: *Somebody needs to write a report on training for the manager, but it's not my pigeon.* ◇ *Gustav will have to tell them first, it's his pigeon.*

pigeons /'pɪdʒɪnz/

- **cat** → put/set the cat among the pigeons

piggy /'pɪgi/

- **middle** → (be) pig/piggy in the middle

pigs /pɪgz/

,pigs might 'fly (*BrE*) (*AmE* when **,pigs 'fly**) (*ironic, saying*)
used when you do not believe sth will ever happen: *'You might get into the football team if you practise hard.' 'Yes, and pigs might fly!'*

pike /paɪk/

come down the 'pike (*AmE, informal*)
happen; become noticeable: *We're hearing a lot about new inventions coming down the pike.*

> **NOTE**
> *Pike* here is short for 'turnpike', which is a type of large road in the US.

pikestaff /ˈpaɪkstɑːf; *AmE* -stæf/

● plain → (as) plain as a pikestaff

pile /paɪl/

make a/your 'pile (*informal*)
make a lot of money: *If you want to make a pile, don't go into the restaurant business.*

pile on the 'agony/'gloom (*informal, especially BrE*)
1 make sth unpleasant sound much worse than it really is in order to gain sympathy from other people: *He always piles on the agony when he has a cold; you'd think he was dying.*
2 make sb feel even worse about an unpleasant situation: *The latest fare increase just piles on the gloom for rail passengers, who already feel they are paying too much.*

● bottom → at the bottom/top of the pile/heap
● lay → pile it on thick; pile it on **SEE** lay it on thick/with a trowel

pill /pɪl/

be on the 'pill
(of women) be regularly taking a medicine that will stop you getting pregnant (= the contraceptive pill)

sugar/sweeten the 'pill
make sth unpleasant seem less unpleasant: *He tried to sweeten the pill by telling her she'd only be in hospital a few days.*

● bitter → a bitter pill (for sb) (to swallow)

pillar /ˈpɪlə(r)/

be driven, pushed, etc. from ˌpillar to 'post
be forced to go from one person or situation to another without achieving anything: *Vast numbers of refugees have been pushed from pillar to post in that area.*

a pillar of so'ciety, etc.
a person who is respected in society, etc.; a person of importance: *I couldn't believe that a pillar of the community like him had been caught stealing from his employer.*

● strength → a pillar/tower of strength

pillow /ˈpɪləʊ; *AmE* -loʊ/

'pillow talk (*informal*)
a conversation in bed between lovers when promises are made which should not be taken too seriously, or secrets are revealed: *'He said he'd never been so deeply in love in the whole of his life.' 'That was just pillow talk.' ◇ 'How did he find out about that?' 'Pillow talk, probably.'*

pilot /ˈpaɪlət/

● automatic → be on automatic pilot

pin /pɪn/

ˌpin your 'faith/'hopes on sb/sth
put your trust in sb/sth; hope for sb/sth: *He's pinning his faith on the revival of the economy. ◇ The idea that he'll be out of prison in five years is all she's got to pin her hopes on.*

'pin money (*informal*)
a small amount of money that you earn, especially when this is used to buy things that you want rather than things that you need: *She teaches a little French now and then, just for pin money.*

> ❷ ORIGIN
> This was originally the money given to a woman by her husband to pay for her clothes and other personal items.

● clean → (as) clean as a new pin
● heard → you could have heard a pin drop

pinch /pɪntʃ/

at a 'pinch/'push (*BrE*) (*AmE* **in a 'pinch**) (*informal*)
possible if you try very hard or if it is absolutely necessary: *We usually only accept 55 guests but at a pinch, we could take 60.*

pinch 'pennies (*informal*)
try to spend as little money as possible: *We've been pinching pennies all year so that we can visit my relatives in Australia in December.* ▸ **'penny-pinching** *adj.*: *penny-pinching governments* **'penny-pinching** *noun* **'penny-pincher** *noun*

take sth with a pinch of 'salt (*informal*)
not believe everything sb says: *She told me she knew people in the movie industry, but I took that with a pinch of salt. ◇ I take everything he says with a large pinch of salt.* **OPP** take sth as/for gospel/gospel truth

● feel → feel the pinch

pineapple /ˈpaɪnæpl/

● rough → the rough end of the pineapple

pink /pɪŋk/

in the 'pink (*old-fashioned, informal*)
in very good health or excellent physical condition: *Here are some tips to keep you in the pink.*

see pink 'elephants (*informal*)
see things that are not really there, because you are drunk

● fit → have a pink/blue fit
● tickled → be tickled pink

pins /pɪnz/

have ˌpins and 'needles
have an uncomfortable feeling in your arm or leg when it has been in the same position for a long time: *The best thing to do when you have pins and needles in your leg is to stamp your foot on the floor several times.*

on your 'pins (*old-fashioned, informal*)
on your legs; when standing up or walking: *He's not as steady on his pins as he used to be. I worry about him going out.*

• tenterhooks → be on pins and needles **SEE** (be) on tenterhooks
• two → for two pins

pint /paɪnt/

• quart → get/pour/put a quart into a pint pot

pip /pɪp/

pip sb at/to the 'post (*BrE, informal*)
beat sb in a race, competition, etc. by only a small amount or at the last moment: *We thought we'd won the contract, but we were pipped at the post by a rival company.* ◇ *I was winning the race until Tina came up behind me and pipped me to the post.*

pipe /paɪp/

a 'pipe dream
a hope, belief, plan, etc. that will probably never come true: *She's got this pipe dream about being a pop star.*

❷ ORIGIN
This expression refers to smoking the drug opium, which makes you sleep and gives you powerful dreams.

put 'that in your pipe and smoke it (*informal*)
used after telling sb an unpleasant fact or truth, to say that they should accept it: *I'm not giving you any more money to spend on that car. So put that in your pipe and smoke it!*

pipeline /'paɪplaɪn/

in the 'pipeline
already being considered, planned, prepared or developed, but not yet ready: *We have an interesting new database program in the pipeline. It should be on sale early next year.*

piper /'paɪpə(r)/

• pays → he who pays the piper calls the tune

pique /piːk/

,pique sb's 'interest, curi'osity, etc. (*especially AmE*)
make sb very interested in sth: *The programme has certainly piqued public interest in this rare bird.*

piss /pɪs/

be on the 'piss (*BrE, ⚠, slang*)
be out at a pub, club, etc. and drinking a large amount of alcohol: *I'm not sure if Jerry will be at work today — he was out on the piss with his mates last night.*

'piss yourself (laughing) (*BrE, ⚠, slang*)
laugh very hard: *Poor Kath — she was lying on the floor and we were all pissing ourselves laughing!*

take the 'piss (out of sb/sth) (*BrE, ⚠, slang*)
make fun of sb/sth: *He told me he thought I had a fantastic singing voice, but I think he was taking the piss* (= he was only joking). ◇ *Are you taking the piss out of me?*

• piece → a piece of piss **SEE** a piece of cake

pissed /pɪst/

(as) pissed as a 'newt (*BrE, ⚠, slang*)
very drunk **OPP** (as) sober as a judge

pit /pɪt/

make a 'pit stop (*informal, especially AmE*)
stop for a short time during a long journey by road for a rest, meal, etc: *I'm getting a bit hungry. Shall we make a pit stop at the next service station?*

NOTE
In motor racing, a *pit stop* is an occasion when a car stops during a race for more fuel, etc.

the pit of your/the 'stomach
the bottom of the stomach where people say they feel strong feelings, especially fear: *He had a sudden sinking feeling in the pit of his stomach.*

,pit your 'wits (against sb/sth)
compete with sb/sth in a test of intelligence or knowledge: *He's pitting his wits against the computer chess game.*

• bottomless → a bottomless pit (of sth)

pitch /pɪtʃ/

make a 'pitch for sb/sth ♦ make a 'pitch to sb (*especially AmE*)
make a determined effort to get sth or to persuade sb of sth: *Both presidential candidates have promised to make a pitch for better roads and schools.*

,pitch a 'line/'story/'yarn (to sb) (*informal*)
tell sb a story or make an excuse that is not true: *He assured me that it really happened, but I reckon he was just pitching me a line.*

• fever → at fever pitch
• queer → queer sb's pitch

pitched /pɪtʃt/

a ,pitched 'battle
1 a fight that involves a large number of people: *There was a pitched battle earlier today between police and demonstrators. Two hundred people were injured, ten seriously.*
2 a military battle fought with soldiers arranged in prepared positions

pits /pɪts/

be the 'pits (*informal*)
be very bad; be the worst kind of sth: *The teaching at this school is the pits.* ◇ *This newspaper really is the pits.* **OPP** be the bomb

pity /'pɪti/

,more's the 'pity (*BrE, informal*)
unfortunately: *He can't read and he doesn't want to learn, more's the pity.*

place /pleɪs/

all 'over the place (*informal*)
1 everywhere: *In my job I have to travel all over the place.*
2 not neat or tidy; not well organized: *There were books and papers all over the place. ◇ Your calculations are all over the place* (= completely wrong).

(not) be sb's 'place to do sth
not have the right to do sth, for example to criticize sb, suggest sth, etc: *'Why didn't you tell him?' 'It wasn't my place to.' ◇ He told his secretary that it wasn't her place to question what he said.*

fall, drop, etc. into 'place
1 because of a new piece of information, the relationship between several events, facts, etc. suddenly becomes clear: *When I found out that he was Lucy's uncle, everything fell into place. ◇ When we got the final result of our experiment, everything slotted into place.*
2 (of a complex situation) finally reach a satisfactory conclusion: *Last year everything was so difficult; then John changed his job, I started work, the children moved school and everything finally fell into place.*

give 'place to sb/sth (*formal*)
be replaced by sb/sth: *Houses and factories gave place to open fields as the train gathered speed.*

if ,I was/were in 'your place
used to introduce a piece of advice you are giving to sb: *If I were in your place, I'd resign immediately.*

in the 'first place
1 used at the beginning of a sentence to introduce the different points you are making in an argument: *In the first place it's not your car, and in the second you're not old enough to drive it. Is that clear?*
2 used at the end of a sentence to talk about why sth was done or whether it should have been done or not: *I should never have taken that job in the first place.*

in 'my, 'your, etc. place
in my, your, etc. situation: *I wouldn't like to be in your place.*

in 'place
prepared and ready: *Everything seems to be in place for a successful peace conference.*

in place of sb/sth ♦ in sb's/sth's 'place
instead of sb/sth: *You can use milk in place of cream in this recipe. ◇ He was unable to go to the ceremony, but he sent his son in his place.*

out of 'place
1 not in the correct place: *Some of these files seem to be out of place.*
2 not suitable for a particular situation: *Your silly remarks were completely out of place at such an important meeting. ◇ I feel quite out of place at a smart party like this.*

a place in the 'sun
(of a person) a very favourable position, especially in your professional life: *When he was offered a professorship at Caltech, he felt that he had finally found his place in the sun.*

> **❷ ORIGIN**
> This is a translation of a phrase used in Pascal's *Pensées* in the seventeenth century.

put sb in their 'place
remind sb forcefully of their real position in society or at work: *That young man needs putting in his place. He behaves as if he were the manager here.*

take 'place
happen: *The meeting will take place at eight o'clock. ◇ Some strange things had taken place in that old castle.*

take sb's 'place ♦ take the place of sb
do sth which another person was doing before; replace sb: *Miss Jones has left the school and this term her place has been taken by Mr Carter. ◇ I was sick, so Bill took my place at the meeting.*

take your 'place
1 go to the physical position that is necessary for an activity: *We all took our places round the table.*
2 take or accept the status in society that is correct or that you deserve: *He is ready now to take his place as one of the fastest swimmers in history.*

- hair → not a hair out of place
- heart → your, his, etc. heart is in the right place
- know → know your place
- pedestal → put/set/place sb on a pedestal
- premium → put/place a premium on sth
- pride → (give sth) pride of place
- rock → (caught/stuck) between a rock and a hard place
- shoes → put yourself in sb's shoes/place
- think → behave/act as if you own the place **SEE** think you own the place
- think → think you own the place

placed /pleɪst/

be well, ideally, better, etc. placed for sth/to do sth
1 be in a good, ideal, etc. position or have a good, ideal, etc. opportunity to do sth: *Engineering graduates are well placed for a wide range of jobs. ◇ The company is now better placed to take advantage of the new legislation.*
2 be situated in a pleasant or convenient place: *The hotel is ideally placed for restaurants, bars and clubs.*

places /'pleɪsɪz/

change/swap 'places (with sb)
(of two people, groups, etc.) exchange seats, positions, situations, etc: *The Smiths can afford to go away a lot because they haven't got a family to bring up. But I wouldn't want to change places with them. ◇ Can you see the whiteboard where you are, or would you like to swap places?*

'go places (*informal*)
be successful or likely to be successful in your life or job: *If you're young, energetic and want to go*

places, write to this address and we'll send you a job application form. ◇ *He's a young architect who's really going places.*

• **friends** → have friends in high places
• **people** → of all people/places/things

plague /pleɪɡ/

• **avoid** → avoid sb/sth like the plague

plain /pleɪn/

be (all) plain 'sailing (*AmE* also **be clear 'sailing**)
be simple and free from trouble: *Life with him isn't all plain sailing, you know.* ◇ *She answered the first question well and from then on it was all plain sailing.*

in plain 'English
simply and clearly expressed, without using technical language: *I don't understand these documents at all. Why can't they write them in plain English?*

(as) plain as a 'pikestaff ♦ (as) plain as 'day ♦ (as) plain as the nose on your 'face (*informal*)
easy to see or understand; obvious: *It's as plain as a pikestaff; this government is ruining the economy.* ◇ *You can't miss the sign, it's right there, as plain as the nose on your face.*

a plain 'Jane (*disapproving*)
a girl or woman who is not very pretty or attractive: *She was a shy girl, who always thought of herself as a plain Jane.*

planet /'plænɪt/

be on another 'planet ♦ what 'planet is sb on? (*spoken, humorous*)
used to suggest that sb's ideas are not realistic or practical: *He can't really think we're going to finish the job today, can he? What planet is he on?*

'That thing? What planet are you on?'

plank /plæŋk/

• **walk** → walk the plank

planks /plæŋks/

• **thick** → (as) thick as two short planks

plant /plɑːnt; *AmE* plænt/

• **seeds** → plant/sow the seeds of sth

plate /pleɪt/

have enough, a lot, etc. on your 'plate (*informal*)
have enough, a lot of things, etc. to do or be responsible for: *I can't help you next week, I've got too much on my plate.* ◇ *She has a lot on her plate at the moment; that's why she looks so worried all the time.*

• **hand** → hand sth to sb on a plate

platter /'plætə(r)/

• **silver** → (hand sth to sb) on a silver platter

play /pleɪ/

> Most idioms containing **play** are at the entries for the nouns or adjectives in the idioms, for example **play ball (with sb)** is at **ball**.

bring/call/put sth into 'play
make sth begin to work or operate; involve sth in sth: *The exercise brings many skills into play.* ◇ *This latest decision calls many new factors into play.*

come into 'play
begin to operate or be active; have an effect or influence: *It's time for the first part of our plan to come into play.* ◇ *A lot of different factors came into play in making this decision.*

have money, time, etc. to 'play with (*informal*)
have plenty of money, time, etc. for doing sth: *We need to make a decision now, as we haven't got much time to play with.*

in/out of 'play
(of the ball) in/out of a position where it can be played according to the rules of the game: *The defender kicked the ball out of play.* ◇ *The ball's in play, so play on.*

make great, much, etc. 'play of/with sth
put a lot of emphasis on sth; behave as if sth is very important: *The English love of gardening is something he makes great play of in his latest book.* ◇ *He always makes great play of the fact that he went to a famous school.*

make a 'play for sb/sth (*especially AmE*)
make a well-planned attempt to get sth you want: *He was making a play for a top government position.* ◇ *If you want to make a play for her, send her flowers.*

playing /'pleɪɪŋ/

what's sb 'playing at?
used to ask in an angry way about what sb is doing: *What do you think you're playing at?*

• **level** → a level playing field
• **level** → level the playing field

plea /pli:/

● cop → cop a plea

plead /pli:d/

● fifth → take/plead the fifth

please /pli:z/

if you 'please
1 (old-fashioned, formal) used when politely asking sb to do sth: Take a seat, if you please.
2 (old-fashioned, especially BrE) used to say that you are annoyed or surprised at sb's actions: And now, if you please, he wants me to rewrite the whole thing!

,please the 'eye
be very attractive to look at: We are proud to present our new lunchtime buffet, where we're sure you will find dishes to please the eye as well as the palate (= they look and taste good).

,please 'God
used to say that you very much hope or wish that sth will happen: Please God, don't let him be dead.

,please your'self (spoken)
used to tell sb that you are annoyed with them and do not care what they do: 'I don't think I'll bother finishing this.' 'Please yourself.'

,please your'self ♦ ,do as you 'please
be able to do whatever you like: There were no children to cook for, so we could just please ourselves.

pleased /pli:zd/

I'm (very) pleased to 'meet you (formal)
said when you are meeting sb for the first time, often as you shake hands: 'John, this is Dr Savary.' 'I'm pleased to meet you.'

none too 'pleased
not pleased; angry: She was none too pleased at having to do it all again.

only too 'pleased (to do sth)
very happy or willing to do sth: We're only too pleased to help.

(as) ,pleased as 'Punch (BrE)
very pleased; delighted: My brother was as pleased as Punch when he passed his driving test.

> **❷ ORIGIN**
> This idiom refers to the character Mr Punch in the traditional puppet play Punch and Judy.

'pleased with yourself (often disapproving)
too proud of sth you have done: He was looking very pleased with himself.

pleasure /'pleʒə(r)/

at your/sb's 'pleasure (formal)
as you want; as sb else wants: The land can be sold at the owner's pleasure.

have had the 'pleasure (formal)
have been introduced to sb before: 'Tony, have you met Angela Evans?' 'No, I don't think I've had the pleasure.'

it's a 'pleasure
used after sb thanks you for doing sth to help them: 'Thanks for the meal.' 'It's a pleasure.'

with 'pleasure (formal)
used for accepting an offer, invitation, etc. or for saying that you are willing to do what sb has requested: 'Would you like to come and have lunch on Sunday?' 'With pleasure. I'd love to come.'

pledge /pledʒ/

sign/take the 'pledge (old-fashioned)
promise never to drink alcohol: He hasn't been much fun since he took the pledge.

> **❷ ORIGIN**
> In the nineteenth century there were anti-drinking campaigns, when people were encouraged to sign a promise (= a pledge) never to drink alcohol.

plot /plɒt; AmE plɑ:t/

lose the 'plot (BrE, informal)
lose your ability to understand or deal with what is happening: You should have seen Jimmy yesterday. I really thought he'd lost the plot! **OPP** get your act together

the plot 'thickens (often humorous)
used to say that a situation is becoming more complicated and difficult to understand: Aha, so both Karen and Steve had the day off work yesterday? The plot thickens!

plough (BrE) (AmE plow) /plaʊ/

,plough a lonely, your own, etc. 'furrow (literary)
do things that other people do not do, or be interested in things that other people are not interested in: There are several English teachers at the school, but Jeanne continues to plough a lonely furrow, teaching French and German.

> **NOTE**
> A furrow is a long narrow cut in the ground made by a plough (= a large piece of farming equipment used for cutting the soil).

ploughshares (BrE) (AmE plowshares) /'plaʊʃeəz; AmE -ʃeərz; -ʃerz/

● swords → beat/turn swords into ploughshares

pluck /plʌk/

pluck sth out of the 'air
say a name, number, etc. without thinking about it, especially in answer to a question: I just plucked a figure out of the air and said: 'Would £1 000 seem reasonable to you?'

● courage → pluck/screw/summon up (your/the) courage (to do sth)

plug /plʌg/

● pull → pull the plug on sth

plughole /ˈplʌɡhəʊl; AmE -hoʊl/

• drain → (go) down the plughole SEE (go) down the drain

plumb /plʌm/

plumb the 'depths of sth
reach the lowest or most extreme point of sth:
When his friend was killed, he plumbed the depths of despair.

❓ ORIGIN
Originally, this referred to finding out the depth of the sea, etc. by dropping a weight tied to a rope into the water.

plunge /plʌndʒ/

take the 'plunge (*informal*)
decide to do sth new, difficult or risky, especially after thinking about it for some time: *After working for twenty years he's decided to take the plunge and go back to college.* OPP get/have cold feet

NOTE
A *plunge* is an act of jumping or diving into water.

plus¹ /plʌs/

plus or 'minus
used when the number mentioned may actually be more or less by a particular amount: *The margin of error was plus or minus three percentage points.*

plus² /pluː/

plus ça 'change (, plus c'est la même 'chose) /ˌpluː sæ ˈʃɒnʒ; AmE ˈʃɔːʒ/ (*from French, saying*)
some things never really change, even though details such as time and people involved may be different: *Despite assurances that this year's competition would welcome new talent and new ideas, none of the newcomers have reached the final round. Plus ça change…*

NOTE
The meaning of the full expression in French is 'the more it changes, the more it stays the same'.

ply /plaɪ/

ply for 'hire/'trade/'business (*BrE*)
look for customers, passengers, etc. in order to do business: *There are plenty of taxis plying for hire outside the theatre.*

ply your 'trade (*written*)
do your work or business: *This is the restaurant where he plied his trade as a cook.*

pneumonia /njuːˈməʊniə; AmE nuːˈmoʊ-/

• sneezes → if A catches a cold, B gets pneumonia SEE when A sneezes, B catches a cold

poacher /ˈpəʊtʃə(r); AmE ˈpoʊtʃ-/

poacher turned 'gamekeeper (*BrE*)
a person who has changed from one situation or attitude to the opposite one, especially sb who used to oppose people in authority but is now in a position of authority: *He used to represent an oil company but now works for an environmental organization; a real case of the poacher turned gamekeeper.*

pocket /ˈpɒkɪt; AmE ˈpɑːk-/

be ˌin/ˌout of 'pocket (*especially BrE*)
have gained/lost money as a result of sth: *That one mistake left him thousands of pounds out of pocket.* ◇ *Even after paying the extra fee, we were still £100 in pocket.*

in sb's 'pocket (*informal*)
in sb's control, under sb's influence, etc: *She makes all the decisions, not him. He's completely in her pocket.* ◇ *The gang had hundreds of police officers in their pockets.* OPP be your own man/woman

out of your own 'pocket
with your own money: *He paid for the trip out of his own pocket.*

• hand → put your hand in/into your pocket
• line → line your (own)/sb's pocket(s)
• money → money burns a hole in your pocket
• pick → pick sb's pocket

pockets /ˈpɒkɪts; AmE ˈpɑːk-/

be/live in each other's 'pockets (*BrE*)
if two people are **in each other's pockets**, they are too close to each other or spend too much time with each other: *They live together, work together and socialize together. If you ask me, it can't be healthy to live in each other's pockets like that.*

pod /pɒd; AmE pɑːd/

• peas → as alike/like as (two) peas in a pod

poetic /pəʊˈetɪk; AmE poʊ-/

poetic 'justice
a punishment or reward that is deserved: *If you ask me it's poetic justice. He tried to get you fired, and now he's lost his job himself.*

• licence → artistic/poetic licence

point /pɔɪnt/

ask, tell, etc. sb point 'blank
ask, tell, etc. sb very directly, and perhaps rudely: *I told him point blank that we no longer wanted him to work for us.* ◇ *She asked me point blank why I didn't like her.*

❓ ORIGIN
Point blank originally referred to firing a gun or shooting an arrow directly at the centre of a target from very close to it.

be on the 'point of doing sth
be about to do sth: *I was on the point of posting the letter when I saw it didn't have a stamp on it.*

beside the 'point
of no importance to the matter being discussed; irrelevant: *His political interests are beside the point. All I want to know about him is whether he can do the job properly.*

come/get (straight) to the 'point
talk about the most important problem, matter, etc. immediately rather than have a general conversation first: *Stop avoiding the issue and come to the point!* ◇ *Let me get straight to the point. I don't think you'll pass this exam unless you work harder.*

get the 'point (of sth)
understand sb's explanation: *You haven't got the point of what I'm trying to say.* ◇ *Oh, I see. I get the point.*

have a 'point (there)
have made a good suggestion; have a good idea: *He's got a point there; if you sell the house now you'll lose money, so why not wait till next year?* ◇ *Animal rights campaigners have a point when they say that a lot of animal testing is unnecessary.*

if/when it ,comes to the 'point
if/when the time comes when you have to do or decide sth: *I'm not frightened of flying, but when it comes to the point I'd rather travel by train.*

in point of 'fact
used to say what is true in a situation: *'Picasso painted this picture in 1935.' 'In point of fact, Joanna, he painted it in 1934.'* ◇ *I'll visit you next time I'm in Berlin. In point of fact, I'm supposed to be going there next month, so why don't I come and see you then?*

make your 'point
explain your opinion fully; tell sb exactly what you mean: *They were all talking so loudly I didn't get a chance to make my point.* ◇ *Look, I think you've made your point, Mr Davies. Perhaps we should hear somebody else's opinion.*

make a 'point of doing sth
make sure you do sth; make an effort to do sth because you think it is the correct way to do things: *I always make a point of locking up at night.* ◇ *She made a point of thanking all the staff before she left the office.*

,more to the 'point
more important to the subject being discussed than what has already been mentioned: *Drinking and driving is against the law and, more to the point, extremely dangerous.*

point a/the 'finger (at sb)
say you think sb is responsible for sth; accuse sb of doing sth: *It was his wife who pointed the finger at him in the end.*

,point of 'contact
a place where you go or a person that you speak to when you are dealing with an organization: *The receptionist is the first point of contact most people have with the clinic.*

a ,point of de'parture
1 a place where a journey starts
2 (*formal*) an idea, a theory or an event that is used to start a discussion, an activity, etc: *Professor Brown's recent article will certainly be the point of departure for future research on the subject.*

a ,point of 'honour (*BrE*) (*AmE* **a ,point of 'honor**)
a thing that sb considers to be very important for their honour or reputation: *His refusal to talk to the press about his private life had always been a point of honour for him.*

(get to, reach, etc.) the ,point of ,no re'turn
the time when you must continue with what you have decided to do, because it is not possible to get back to an earlier situation: *We've invested so much in the project that we simply must finish it. We've reached the point of no return.*

a ,point of 'view
1 sb's opinion about sb/sth: *I don't agree with her, but she has a right to her point of view.*
2 one way of looking at or judging sth: *From the businessman's point of view these new hourly flights to Paris are just what is needed.*

point the 'way (to/towards sth)
show how things will develop in future: *New high-speed trains are pointing the way to a new age of European travel.*

take sb's 'point
understand and accept the truth of what sb has said, especially during an argument, discussion, etc: *I take your point, Simon, but I don't think it's as simple as you think.* ◇ *'Look, Jane. I know a lot more about physics than you, so why do you keep disagreeing with what I say?' 'OK, point taken.'*

to the 'point
expressed in a simple, clear way without any extra information or feelings: *The speech was short and to the point.*

to the 'point of sth/of doing sth
to such an extent that a stronger description could be used: *The restaurant staff were unhelpful to the point of rudeness.* ◇ *His remarks were unkind to the point of being cruel.*

up to a (certain) 'point
to some extent; not completely: *I'm willing to help you up to a point, but after that you'll have to look after yourself.* ◇ *I agree with you up to a point, but not completely.*

- **case** → a case in point
- **fine** → not to put too fine a point on it
- **high** → the high point/spot of sth
- **labour** → labour the point
- **moot** → be a moot point/question
- **saturation** → saturation point
- **score** → score a point/points (off/over/against sb)
- **sore** → a sore point (with sb)
- **stretch** → stretch a point
- **strong** → be your strong point/suit
- **tipping** → a/the tipping point

points

points /pɔɪnts/

have your 'good, 'plus, etc. points
have some good qualities or aspects: *Europe has its good points, but I prefer the American way of life.* ◇ *She often seems rather unfriendly, but I suppose she's got her plus points.*

• brownie → brownie points
• possession → possession is nine points/tenths/parts of the law
• score → score a point/points (off/over/against sb)

poison /'pɔɪzn/

a ,poison 'pen letter
an unpleasant letter which is not signed and is intended to upset the person who receives it: *Most politicians get poison pen letters, sometimes threatening their lives.*

what's your 'poison? (*spoken, humorous*)
used to ask sb what alcoholic drink they would like: *Right, would anyone like a drink? Bill, what's your poison?*

• man → one man's meat is another man's poison

poisoned /'pɔɪznd/

a poisoned 'chalice (*especially BrE*)
a thing which seems attractive when it is given to sb but which soon becomes unpleasant: *He inherited a poisoned chalice when he took over the job as union leader.*

> **NOTE**
> A *chalice* is a large cup for holding wine.

poke /pəʊk; AmE poʊk/

have a ,poke a'round (*informal*)
look carefully around a place to see what you can find; try to find out information about sb/sth: *I thought I'd go and have a poke around the new shopping mall later. Do you want to come with me?*

take a 'poke at sb/sth (*old-fashioned, AmE, informal*)
make an unkind remark about sb/sth; laugh at sb/sth: *Then he took a poke at my hair, telling me I looked like a scarecrow!*

• fun → poke fun at sb/sth SEE make fun of sb/sth
• nose → poke/stick your nose in/into sth
• pig → (buy) a pig in a poke

poker /'pəʊkə(r); AmE 'poʊ-/

• stiff → (as) stiff as a poker

pole /pəʊl; AmE poʊl/

be up the 'pole (*old-fashioned, BrE, informal*)
1 be mad, crazy, etc: *My neighbour's really up the pole. I can hear him singing and shouting night after night.*
2 be in trouble or difficulties: *The whole industry is up the pole at the moment. Nobody knows what its future will be.*

• touch → not touch sb/sth with a ten-foot pole SEE not touch sb/sth with a bargepole

poles /pəʊlz; AmE poʊlz/

• apart → be poles/worlds apart

polish /'pɒlɪʃ; AmE 'pɑːl-/

• spit → spit and polish

political /pə'lɪtɪkl/

a po,litical 'football
an issue or a problem that causes argument and disagreement and that different political groups use to gain votes: *It is sad that education is still being used as a political football, instead of action being taken to improve it.*

politically /pə'lɪtɪkli/

po,litically cor'rect (*abbr.* **PC**)
used to describe language or behaviour that deliberately tries to avoid offending particular groups of people: *These days everybody has to be politically correct. I even heard someone the other day calling a short person 'vertically challenged'!*

pomp /pɒmp; AmE pɑːmp/

pomp and 'circumstance
formal and impressive ceremony: *The Prince was welcomed with warmth, but not with all the pomp and circumstance he was used to.*

> **❼ ORIGIN**
> This comes from Shakespeare's play *Othello* and refers to the impressive clothes, decorations, music, etc. that are part of an official ceremony.

pond /pɒnd; AmE pɑːnd/

across the 'pond (*informal, especially BrE*)
on the other side of the Atlantic Ocean from Britain/the US: *And now let's hear some news and gossip from across the pond, with our reporter in New York.*

pony /'pəʊni; AmE 'poʊni/

• dog → a dog and pony show
• Shanks → (on) Shanks's pony

poor /pɔː(r); pʊə(r); AmE pɔːr; pʊr/

be a/the ,poor man's 'sb/'sth
be a person or thing that is similar to but of a lower quality than a particular famous person or thing: *Try some of this sparkling white wine — the poor man's champagne.*

be/come a poor second, third, etc. (*especially BrE*)
finish a long way behind the winner in a race, competition, etc: *The Socialists won the election easily with 40% of the vote, with the Democrats coming a poor second with only 26%.*

(as) poor as a church 'mouse
very poor: *She was as poor as a church mouse, living on a tiny pension.* **OPP** (as) rich as Croesus

,**poor old 'sb/'sth** (*informal*)
used to express sympathy: *Poor old Mrs Kirk's just gone into hospital again.* ◊ *She sat down to rest her poor old legs.*

a poor re'lation
sb/sth with less importance, respect or power than others: *At the peace conference, our country was treated very much as the poor relation.*

• spirits → in good/poor spirits SEE be in high/low spirits
• view → take a dim/poor view of sb/sth

pop /pɒp; *AmE* pɑːp/

pop your 'clogs (*BrE, humorous*)
die: *I haven't seen you for so long I thought you'd popped your clogs!*

pop the 'question (*informal*)
ask sb to marry you: *Where were you when he popped the question?*

• eyes → your eyes nearly pop out of your head

popular /'pɒpjələ(r); *AmE* 'pɑːp-/

by popular de'mand
because a lot of people have asked for sth: *By popular demand, the play will run for another week.*

• contrary → contrary to popular belief/opinion

porkies /'pɔːkiz; *AmE* 'pɔːrkiz/

• tell → tell porkies

porridge /'pɒrɪdʒ; *AmE* 'pɔːr-; 'pɑːr-/

do 'porridge (*BrE, old-fashioned, informal*)
be in prison serving a sentence: *He's doing porridge again, this time for armed robbery.*

> **❓ ORIGIN**
> This comes from the fact that as porridge is a cheap food that makes the stomach feel full, it was often served in prisons.

port /pɔːt; *AmE* pɔːrt/

any port in a 'storm (*saying*)
when you are in trouble you will accept help, etc. that would be unacceptable otherwise: *When he went to work there he had been unemployed for a year. It was a case of any port in a storm.*

a ,port of 'call (*informal*)
a place where you go or stop for a short time, especially when you are going to several places: *Our first port of call this morning is the bank.*

> **NOTE**
> These two idioms refer to ports where ships stop for a short time during a voyage.

pose /pəʊz; *AmE* poʊz/

• strike → strike a pose/an attitude

positive /'pɒzətɪv; *AmE* 'pɑːz-/

• proof → proof positive
• think → think positive

possessed /pə'zest/

like a man/woman pos'sessed ♦ **like one pos'sessed**
with a lot of force or energy: *He flew out of the room like a man possessed.*

what(ever) pos'sessed sb to do sth?
used to ask why sb did sth bad, stupid, unexpected, etc: *'She drove straight to the airport and got on the first plane.' 'What possessed her to do that?'*

> **❓ ORIGIN**
> This phrase refers to the belief that people can be controlled ('possessed') by an evil spirit.

possession /pə'zeʃn/

possession is nine points/tenths/parts of the 'law (*saying*)
if you already have or control sth, it is difficult for sb else to take it away from you, even if they have the legal right to it

take pos'session (of sth) (*formal*)
become the owner of sth: *He couldn't pay his taxes, so the government took possession of his property.*

• field → leave sb in possession of the field SEE leave the field clear for sb

possibility /,pɒsə'bɪləti; *AmE* ,pɑːs-/

• realms → beyond/within the realms of possibility

possible /'pɒsəbl; *AmE* 'pɑːs-/

as quickly, much, soon, etc. as 'possible
as quickly, much, soon, etc. as you can: *We will get your order to you as soon as possible.*

possum /'pɒsəm; *AmE* 'pɑːsəm/

play 'possum (*informal*)
pretend to be asleep or not aware of sth, in order to deceive sb: *Jake decided that his best course of action would be to play possum and wait for her to give up.*

> **NOTE**
> A *possum* is a small Australian and American animal that pretends to be dead when it is in danger.

post /pəʊst; *AmE* poʊst/

• deaf → (as) deaf as a post
• pillar → be driven, pushed, etc. from pillar to post
• pip → pip sb at/to the post

postal /'pəʊstl; *AmE* 'poʊstl/

go 'postal (*AmE, informal*)
become extremely angry or start behaving in a violent and angry way: *According to one eye witness, the man 'went postal, and started hitting his computer'.*

> **❓ ORIGIN**
> This expression originated in the USA in the 1990s, where there were several incidents of postal workers losing control and shooting members of the public in post offices.

posted /'pəʊstɪd; AmE 'poʊst-/

keep sb 'posted (on/of/about sth) (*informal*)
keep sb informed: *There's no news at the moment,
but I'll keep you posted.* ◇ *He said he'd keep me posted of his movements.*

poster /'pəʊstə(r); AmE 'poʊ-/

'poster child/boy/girl (*AmE*)
a person or thing that is seen as representing a
particular quality or activity: *My aunt sees me as
the poster child for failed relationships.* ◇ *He's the
IT industry's poster boy for success.*

post-haste /ˌpəʊst 'heɪst; AmE ˌpoʊst/

ˌpost-'haste (*literary*)
with great speed: *I shall send the invitations off
post-haste.*

> **❷ ORIGIN**
> This comes from the old phrase *haste, post,
> haste,* which was written on letters to tell the
> *post* (= the person taking the letters) to ride
> quickly to deliver them.

pot /pɒt; AmE pɑːt/

go (all) to 'pot (*informal*)
be spoiled because people are not working hard or
taking care of things: *This whole country's going to
pot.* ◇ *She used to write very nicely, but her handwriting's really gone to pot now she uses a computer
all the time.*

the ˌpot calling the kettle 'black (*saying,
informal*)
used to say that you should not criticize sb for a
fault that you have yourself: *'You haven't done any
work all morning.' 'Neither have you! Talk about the
pot calling the kettle black!'*

> **❷ ORIGIN**
> When cooking was done over a fire, the smoke
> made cooking pots turn black.

take ˌpot 'luck (*informal*)
choose sth or go somewhere without knowing
very much about it, but hope that it will be good,
pleasant, etc: *'Did somebody recommend the hotel
to you?' 'No, we just took pot luck. It was the first
hotel in the brochure.'* ◇ *You're welcome to stay for
supper, but you'll have to take pot luck* (= eat whatever is available).

- melting → in the melting pot
- quart → get/pour/put a quart into a pint pot
- watched → a watched pot never boils

potato /pə'teɪtəʊ; AmE -toʊ/

- couch → a couch potato
- hot → a hot potato

potatoes /pə'teɪtəʊz; AmE -toʊz/

- small → small potatoes **SEE** small beer

potshot /'pɒtʃɒt; AmE 'pɑːtʃɑːt/

take a 'potshot/'potshots (at sb/sth) (*informal*)
1 fire at sb without aiming carefully: *Somebody
took a potshot at him as he drove past.*
2 criticize sb suddenly and without thinking: *The
newspapers took potshots at his attempts to get into
the movie business.*

> **❷ ORIGIN**
> This was originally a shot fired from a close
> distance to kill an animal for food (for the pot).
> As the shot required no skill it broke the rules
> of sport.

pound /paʊnd/

**(have, demand, claim, etc.) your pound of
'flesh**
(take, demand, etc.) the full amount that sb owes
you, even if this will cause them trouble or suffering: *They want their pound of flesh; they want
every penny we owe them by next Monday.*
◇ *I didn't realize working here was going to be such
hard work. They really demand their pound of flesh,
don't they?*

> **❷ ORIGIN**
> This phrase comes from Shakespeare's *Mer-
> chant of Venice,* in which the moneylender
> Shylock demanded a pound of flesh from An-
> tonio's body if he could not pay back the
> money he borrowed.

- penny → in for a penny, in for a pound
- penny → penny wise (and) pound foolish
- prevention → an ounce of prevention is better than a
  pound of cure **SEE** prevention is better than cure

pour /pɔː(r)/

pour your 'heart out (to sb)
tell sb all about your troubles, feelings, etc: *When I
asked her what was the matter, she burst into tears
and poured out her heart to me.*

pour oil on troubled 'water(s)
try to settle a disagreement or dispute; take action
which will calm a tense or dangerous situation: *He
was always having rows with his son and his wife's
attempts to pour oil on troubled water usually made
things worse.* ◇ *There's going to be big trouble
unless somebody pours oil on troubled waters fast.*
OPP add fuel to the fire/flames

> **❷ ORIGIN**
> Sailors used to pour oil on a rough sea to calm
> the water in order to make a sea rescue easier.

- cold → pour/throw cold water on sth
- quart → get/pour/put a quart into a pint pot
- scorn → heap/pour scorn on sb/sth

pours /pɔːz; AmE pɔːrz/

- rains → it never rains but it pours
- rains → when it rains, it pours **SEE** it never rains but it
  pours

powder /'paʊdə(r)/

keep your 'powder dry (old-fashioned)
remain ready for a possible emergency: *The bank is not cutting interest rates at the moment, preferring to keep its powder dry in case it's forced to cut them in the future.*

> **❷ ORIGIN**
> This comes from advice given by Oliver Cromwell to his troops when they were crossing a river before battle. *Powder* here refers to the gunpowder used to fire bullets.

(go to) powder your 'nose (old-fashioned or humorous)
a polite way of referring to the fact that a woman is going to the toilet: *I'm just going to powder my nose and I'll be with you in a minute.*

take a 'powder (AmE, informal)
leave suddenly; run away: *She hung about all morning getting in my way, so in the end I told her to take a powder.*

power /'paʊə(r)/

be the (real) power behind the 'throne
be the person who really controls a family, business, country, etc., even though people think sb else controls it: *It's not the president who makes the important decisions; his wife is the real power behind the throne.*

do sb/sth a 'power/'world of good
(old-fashioned)
do sb/sth a lot of good; benefit sb/sth: *She's under a lot of stress at work, and a few days at the coast would do her a power of good.*

more power to sb's 'elbow (old-fashioned, BrE, informal)
used to express support or encouragement for sb to do sth: *'He's so angry at his train being late every morning that he's made an official complaint.' 'Good for him. More power to his elbow.'*

● corridors → the corridors of power

powers /'paʊəz; AmE 'paʊərz/

the ˌpowers that 'be (often ironic)
the people who control a country, an organization, etc: *It's the powers that be who decide things. We just have to live with their decisions.*

practical /'præktɪkl/

for (all) 'practical purposes
in actual fact; in reality: *Your daughter does so little work at school, Mrs Brown, that for all practical purposes she might as well not be here at all.*

(play) a ˌpractical 'joke (on sb)
play a trick on sb which involves physical action, using an object, etc: *They put a frog in his bed as a practical joke.* ► **a ˌpractical 'joker** *noun* a person who plays practical jokes

practice /'præktɪs/

in 'practice
in reality; in fact; in a real or normal situation: *The pilot is there to fly the plane, but in practice it flies itself most of the time.* ◇ *In theory it should work very well, but in practice it doesn't.*

ˌin/ˌout of 'practice
having practised/having not practised a skill regularly for a period of time: *I've got to keep in practice if I'm going to win this race.* ◇ *I haven't played the piano for a while so I'm a bit out of practice.*

ˌpractice makes 'perfect (saying)
a way of encouraging people by telling them that if you do an activity regularly you will become very good at it: *If you want to learn a language, speak it as much as you can. Practice makes perfect!*

put sth into 'practice
actually do or carry out sth which was only planned or talked about before: *It's not always easy to put your ideas into practice.*

● habit → make a habit/practice of sth
● sharp → sharp practice

practise (BrE) (AmE practice) /'præktɪs/

ˌpractise what you 'preach (saying)
live or act the way you advise others to live or act: *He's always telling me to go on a diet, but he doesn't practise what he preaches. He needs to lose weight too!*

praise /preɪz/

praise sb/sth to the 'skies
praise sb/sth very much; say sb/sth is very good, beautiful, etc: *She's always praising you to the skies: she says she's never had such a good assistant before.* **OPP** not have a good word to say for/about sb/sth

● damn → damn sb/sth with faint praise

praises /'preɪzɪz/

● sing → sing sb's/sth's praises

prayer /preə(r); AmE prer/

not have a 'prayer (of doing sth)
have no chance of succeeding: *She's done no work at all this term, so she doesn't have a prayer of passing her exams.*

● wing → on a wing and a prayer

prayers /preəz; AmE preərz; prerz/

● answer → the answer to sb's prayers

preach /priːtʃ/

preach to the con'verted (AmE also **preach to the 'choir**)
tell people to support a view or an idea when they already support it: *Why do they keep telling us about the importance of women in industry? They're preaching to the converted here.*

● practise → practise what you preach

precious /'preʃəs/

precious 'few/'little (*informal*)
very few/little: *There are precious few places round here where you can get good Indian food.*

precise /prɪ'saɪs/

to be (more) pre'cise (also **more pre'cisely**)
used to show that you are giving more detailed and accurate information about sth you have just mentioned: *The shelf is about a metre long — well, 98 cm, to be precise.* ◇ *The problem is due to discipline, or, more precisely, the lack of discipline, in schools.*

preference /'prefrəns/

give (a) preference to sb/sth
treat sb/sth in a way that gives them an advantage over other people or things: *Preference will be given to graduates of this university.*

in preference to sb/sth
rather than sb/sth: *She was chosen in preference to her sister.*

pregnant /'pregnənt/

a pregnant 'pause/'silence
a pause/silence in which everyone is waiting or listening for sth, or a moment of silence which is full of meaning: *There was a pregnant pause while everyone waited to hear what she had to say.*

prejudice /'predʒudɪs/

without 'prejudice (to sth) (*law*)
without affecting any other legal matter: *They agreed to pay compensation without prejudice* (= without admitting guilt).

premium /'priːmiəm/

at a 'premium
having great value or importance; difficult or expensive to buy, find, obtain, etc: *During a war, ordinary foods like bread or meat are often at a premium.* ◇ *Good mathematics teachers are always at a premium in this country.*

put/place a 'premium on sth
consider sth very important or valuable: *This company puts a high premium on the loyalty of its employees.*

prepare /prɪ'peə(r); AmE -'per/

prepare the 'ground (for sth)
do something which makes it possible or easier for sth to happen: *By making her his deputy, the chairman was preparing the ground for her to replace him after he retired.* ◇ *The meeting was to prepare the ground for next week's peace talks.*

presence /'prezns/

in sb's 'presence ✦ in the presence of sb
with sb in the same place: *The document was signed in the presence of two witnesses.* ◇ *She asked them not to discuss the matter in her presence.*

make your 'presence felt
do sth which makes people notice your importance, strength, abilities, etc: *In the first half of the game the Turkish team really made their presence felt.* ◇ *The demonstrators made their presence felt by shouting and waving banners.*

presence of 'mind
the ability to react quickly and stay calm in a difficult or dangerous situation: *A little girl from Leeds showed remarkable presence of mind yesterday when she saved her brothers from a fire in their home.* ◇ *The boy **had the presence of mind to** switch off the gas.*

present /'preznt/

all present and cor'rect (*BrE*) (*AmE* all present and ac'counted for) (*spoken*)
used to say that all the things or people who should be there are now there: *'Now, is everybody here?' 'All present and correct, Sir!'*

> **NOTE**
> This is used in the army to inform an officer that none of the soldiers in his or her unit are missing, injured, etc.

at 'present
now; at the moment: *How many people are living in this house at present?*

make a 'present of sth (to sb)
make it easy for sb to take or steal sth from you, or to gain an advantage over you, because you have been careless: *Before you go out, lock all the doors and windows. Don't make a present of your property (to thieves).*

on 'present form
judging by sb/sth's present performance or behaviour; as things are at the moment: *On present form I'd say he should win easily.* ◇ *A painting by Durant could sell for over a million on present form.*

present company ex'cepted (also **excepting present 'company**)
used as a polite remark to show that the criticisms you are making are not directed at the people you are talking to: *My feeling is that the people around here, present company excepted of course, are rather unfriendly.*

the present 'day
modern times; now: *These customs have continued right up to the present day.* ◇ *Present-day attitudes to women are very different.*

- time → for the moment/present SEE for the time being
- time → (there's) no time like the present

press /pres/

get/have a good, bad, etc. 'press
get/have good, bad, etc. things said about you in the newspapers, on television, etc: *The royal family's been getting a good press recently, for a change.* ◇ *Zoos have been getting a bad press over the last few years.*

,press (the) 'flesh
(of a famous person or a politician) shake hands with members of the public, especially in order to persuade them to vote for you: *The presidential candidates were out on the streets again today, smiling for the cameras and pressing the flesh.*

,press sth 'home
make a point in an argument or discussion with force: *She kept pressing home the point that more money should be spent on education.*

press ,home your ad'vantage
make good use of the fact that you are in a stronger position than your opponent, enemy, etc: *Once they realized that the management was so weak, the union leaders pressed home their advantage and asked for another three days' holiday.*

,press sb/sth into 'service
use sb/sth for a purpose that they were not trained or intended for because there is nobody or nothing else available: *Every type of boat was pressed into service to rescue passengers from the sinking ferry.*

> **❷ ORIGIN**
> This expression originally referred to forcing someone to join the army or navy.

- gutter → the gutter press
- hot → hot off the press
- panic → press/push the panic button
- push → press sb's buttons **SEE** push sb's buttons

pressed /prest/

be pressed/pushed for 'money, 'space, 'time, etc.
have very little money, time, etc: *I'll have to do those letters tomorrow — I'm a bit pressed for time this afternoon.* ◇ *I'm afraid we're a bit pushed for space in this office.*

- hard → hard pressed/pushed to do sth

pressure /'preʃə(r)/

put 'pressure on sb (to do sth) ♦ **bring pressure to 'bear (on sb) (to do sth)**
force or try to persuade sb to do sth: *The landlord is putting pressure on us to move out.* ◇ *If the management won't listen, we'll have to bring some more pressure to bear.*

under 'pressure
1 if a liquid or a gas is kept **under pressure**, it is forced into a container so that when the container is opened, the liquid or gas escapes quickly
2 being forced to do sth: *The director is under increasing pressure to resign.*
3 made to feel anxious about sth you have to do: *The team performs well under pressure.*

presto /'prestəʊ; AmE 'prestoʊ/

- hey → hey presto

pretences (BrE) (AmE pretenses) /prɪ'tensɪz/

- false → by/on/under false pretences

They put pressure on him to sign the contract.

pretty /'prɪti/

not just a pretty 'face (*humorous*)
used to emphasize that you have particular skills or qualities: *'I hear you passed all your exams.' 'Yes, I'm not just a pretty face, you know!'*

,not a pretty 'sight (*humorous*)
a very unpleasant or shocking sight: *When he stepped out of that boxing ring, he wasn't a pretty sight, I can tell you.*

(as) ,pretty as a 'picture
very pretty: *This charming cottage dates back to the 15th century and is as pretty as a picture, with its thatched roof and secluded garden.*

pretty 'much/'well (*BrE also* **pretty 'nearly**) (*AmE also* **pretty 'near**) (*spoken*)
almost; just about: *This nightclub is pretty much the best this town can offer.* ◇ *I'm pretty well disgusted by your behaviour.* ◇ *It's worth pretty near a thousand dollars.*

a pretty 'penny (*old-fashioned*)
a lot of money: *Have you seen the neighbour's new car? That must have cost a pretty penny.*

- pass → come to a pretty pass **SEE** come to such a pass
- sitting → be sitting pretty

prevention /prɪ'venʃn/

pre,vention is better than 'cure (*BrE*) (*AmE* **an ounce of pre,vention is better than a pound of 'cure**) (*saying*)
it is better to stop sth bad from happening rather than try to deal with the problems after it has happened: *Remember that prevention is better than cure, so brush your teeth at least twice a day and visit your dentist for regular check-ups.*

preview /'priːvjuː/

- sneak → a sneak preview

prey /preɪ/

be/fall 'prey to sth (*formal*)
be harmed or affected by sth bad: *He was often prey to doubt and despair.* ◇ *Thousands of small businesses are falling prey to high interest rates.*

> NOTE
> *Prey* is an animal, a bird, etc. that is hunted,
> killed and eaten by another animal.

,prey on sb's 'mind (also **,play on sb's 'mind**)
worry or trouble sb very much: *The death of his
father is really preying on his mind at the moment.
He thinks it was his fault.* ◇ *The question of whether
to accept the new job and move to Scotland had been
playing on his mind for days.*

price /praɪs/

at 'any price
without considering how much it might cost or
how many unpleasant things you might have to
do (to achieve sth): *They wanted victory at any
price.* ◇ *Be elected president at any price; that's his
aim.*

at a 'price
(get sth) only by paying a high price, by spending
a lot of time, effort, etc: *Accommodation is only
available in the city centre at a price.* ◇ *He knew he
could be a successful businessman, but at a price —
he'd hardly ever see his family.*

beyond/without 'price (*formal* or *literary*)
so valuable that it cannot be bought; priceless:
These paintings are almost beyond price.

not at 'any price
used to say that no amount of money would persuade you to do or sell sth: *'What about joining the
army?' 'Not at any price. That's the last thing I want
to do.'*

a 'price on sb's head
a reward for finding or killing a criminal: *In the
Wild West there were cowboys who used to hunt
down any man with a price on his head.*

price yourself/sth out of the 'market
demand such a high price for sth that no one
wants to buy it: *If you charge too much, you'll price
yourself out of the market.*

put a 'price on sth
give the value of sth in money: *Any businessman
will tell you it's hard to put a price on public confidence.* ◇ *I've never seen a vase like this before, so I'm
afraid I can't put a price on it.*

what price...? (*BrE, spoken*)
1 used to say that you think that sth you have
achieved may not be worth all the problems and
difficulties it causes: *What price fame and fortune?*
2 used to say that sth seems unlikely: *What price
England winning the World Cup?*

● **cheap** → cheap at twice the price **SEE** cheap at the price
● **man** → everyone has their price **SEE** every man has his
  price
● **pay** → pay the price/penalty (for sth/for doing sth)

prick /prɪk/

**prick your 'conscience ◆ your 'conscience
pricks you**
make you feel guilty about sth; feel guilty about
sth: *Her conscience pricked her as she lied to her
sister.*

,prick up your 'ears ◆ your 'ears prick up
start to listen carefully: *'And the winner is ...' He
pricked up his ears. '... Michael Poole.'*

> NOTE
> This expression refers to the way dogs, horses
> and other animals raise their ears when they
> listen with attention.

pricks /prɪks/

● **kick** → kick against the pricks
● **prick** → your conscience pricks you **SEE** prick your conscience

pride /praɪd/

your ,pride and 'joy
sb/sth that you are very proud and pleased to
have: *That car's his pride and joy.* ◇ *His granddaughter is his real pride and joy.*

pride comes before a 'fall (*saying*)
if you are too proud or confident, sth may happen
which will make you look foolish: *Remember,
John, pride comes before a fall. Don't go round talking about your success in business all the time.*

(give sth) pride of 'place
the best or most important position: *All the entries
in the flower show are good, but pride of place must
go to Cynthia Jones's roses.* ◇ *Sally gave her award
pride of place on the mantelpiece.*

take 'pride in sb/sth
be proud of sb/sth; consider sth to be worth doing
well: *She takes a lot of pride in running such a successful business.*

● **swallow** → swallow your pride

prim /prɪm/

prim and 'proper
(of a person) very correctly behaved and easily
shocked by anything that is rude: *Don't invite her
to the party. She's so prim and proper.*

prima /'priːmə/

(a) ,prima 'donna (*from Italian, disapproving*)
a person who thinks they are very important
because they are good at sth, and who behaves
badly when they do not get what they want: *Stop
behaving like a prima donna — you're not the only
person around here.* ◇ *In her new film, Victoria
plays a prima donna television presenter.*

> NOTE
> The *prima donna* is the main woman singer in
> an opera performance or an opera company.
> The phrase means 'first lady'.

prime /praɪm/

in the prime of (your) 'life
at the time in your life when you are strongest or
most successful: *He was struck down in the prime
of his life by a heart attack.* ◇ *What do you mean,
I'm old? I'm still in the prime of life!* **OPP** be past
your/its best

a prime 'mover
a person or a thing that starts sth and has an important influence on its development: *The prime mover in setting up the group was ex-lawyer James Stanley.* ◇ *Economic factors are the prime mover of change.*

prime the 'pump
give sb, an organization, etc. financial help in order to support a project, business, etc. when it is beginning: *The government should really prime the pump in new high technology projects. That's the only way they'll be able to survive in the current economic climate.* ▸ **'pump-priming** *noun: The nation is relying on pump-priming to get the economy started.*

❷ ORIGIN
Originally, this was a way of making a pump work properly by adding water to it.

primrose /'prɪmrəʊz; AmE -roʊz/

the primrose 'path (to ruin, destruction, etc.) (*literary*)
an easy life that is full of pleasure but that causes you harm in the end: *If we followed your advice we'd all be walking down the primrose path to ruin.*

❷ ORIGIN
This phrase comes from Shakespeare's play *Hamlet*.

Prince /prɪns/

Prince 'Charming (*usually humorous*)
a man who seems to be a perfect boyfriend or husband because he is attractive, kind, etc: *I'm still waiting for my Prince Charming!*

NOTE
This expression refers to a character in fairy tales such as *Cinderella*.

principle /'prɪnsəpl/

in 'principle
1 according to the general principles or theory: *In principle the machine should work in any climate, but we haven't actually tried it out abroad yet.*
2 in general but not necessarily in detail: *In principle I agree with you, but I'm not sure that it's the most effective solution to the problem.*

on 'principle
because of your beliefs or ideas about what is right or how people should behave: *I quite like meat, but I don't eat it on principle.*

print /prɪnt/

get into 'print
have your work printed and published, especially for the first time: *If you want to get into print, you have to know the right people.*

in 'print
1 (of a book) still available from the company that publishes it: *Is this edition still in print?*

2 (of a person's work) printed in a book, newspaper, etc: *It was the first time he had seen his name in print.*

out of 'print
(of a book) no longer available from the company that publishes it: *Her first novel is now out of print.*

- licence → a licence to print money
- small → the fine print **SEE** the small print

printed /'prɪntɪd/

the printed 'word/'page
stories, articles, etc. printed in a book, magazine, newspaper, etc.

- worth → not worth the paper it's printed/written on

priorities /praɪ'ɒrətiz; AmE -'ɔːr-; -'ɑːr-/

get your pri'orities right/straight
do or get things in the right order of importance: *If you think enjoying yourself is more important, then you need to get your priorities straight.* ◇ *The country has got its priorities right — it has invested in industry to achieve economic success.*

prisoners /'prɪznəz; AmE 'prɪznərz/

take no 'prisoners
be extremely aggressive and show no sympathy for other people in trying to achieve your aims: *She took no prisoners in her dealings with the unions.* ◇ *Her take-no-prisoners approach has been remarkably successful.*

private /'praɪvət/

a ,private 'eye (*informal*)
a detective who is not in the police, but who can be employed to find out information, find a missing person, follow sb, etc: *They hired a private eye to look for more evidence.*

private 'parts
a polite way of referring to the sexual organs without saying their names

prizes /'praɪzɪz/

(there are) no prizes for guessing what…, who…, etc. (*informal*)
(it is) not difficult to guess or find the answer to sth: *No prizes for guessing who does all the work around here.*

pro /prəʊ; AmE proʊ/

- quid → quid pro quo

probability /ˌprɒbə'bɪləti; AmE ˌprɑːb-/

in ,all proba'bility (*written*)
very probably: *The changes were, in all probability, made before 1600.*

problem /'prɒbləm; AmE 'prɑːb-/

do you have a 'problem with that? (*spoken*)
used to show that you are impatient with sb who disagrees with you

,it's/,that's not 'my problem (*spoken*, *informal*)
used to show that you do not care about sb else's
difficulties: *Well, I'm sorry you feel that way, but
I'm afraid it's not my problem.*

no 'problem (*spoken*, *informal*)
1 (also **not a 'problem**) used for saying that you
can do sth or are happy to do sth for sb: *'Can you
be here at 7.30 tomorrow morning?' 'No problem.'*
2 used after sb has thanked you or said they are
sorry for sth: *'Thanks for the ride.' 'No problem.'*

that's 'your, 'his, etc. problem (*spoken*, *informal*)
used to show that you think sb should deal with
their own difficulties: *If she doesn't like it, that's
her problem, not mine!*

what's your 'problem? (*spoken*, *informal*)
used to show that you think sb is being unreasonable: *What's your problem? I only asked if you could
help me for ten minutes.*

problems /'prɒbləmz; *AmE* 'prɑːb-/

● teething → have, etc. teething problems/troubles

probs /prɒbz; *AmE* prɑːbz/

no 'probs (*spoken*)
used to mean 'there is no problem': *I can let you
have it by next week, no probs.*

process /'prəʊses; *AmE* 'prɑːses; 'proʊ-/

in the 'process (of doing sth)
1 while doing sth: *In the process of cleaning the
furniture, I found six coins.* ◇ *He was supposed to
be cutting my hair, but he nearly cut off my ear in
the process.*
2 in the middle of doing sth: *We're still in the process of trying to find somewhere to live.*

prodigal /'prɒdɪgl; *AmE* 'prɑːd-/

a/the prodigal 'son (*formal*, *disapproving* or
humorous)
a person who leaves home as a young man and
wastes his money and time on a life of pleasure,
but who is later sorry about this and returns to his
family: *All the family went to the airport to welcome
home the prodigal son.*

> **❷ ORIGIN**
> This expression comes from a story in the
> Bible.

produce /prə'djuːs; *AmE* -'duːs/

● goods → come up with/deliver/produce the goods

production /prə'dʌkʃn/

on production of sth (*formal*)
when you show sth: *Discounts will only be given on
production of your student ID card.*

profile /'prəʊfaɪl; *AmE* 'proʊ-/

adopt, keep, etc. a ,high/,low 'profile
try/try not to attract other people's interest,
attention, etc: *If I were you, I'd try and keep a low
profile until she's forgotten about the whole thing.*
◇ *In the run-up to the elections all three candidates
maintained a high profile.*

in 'profile
(of a face) seen from the side: *In profile he's got a
nose like an eagle!*

programme (*BrE*) (*AmE* program)
/'prəʊgræm; *AmE* 'proʊ-/

get with the 'programme (*informal*)
(usually in orders) used to tell sb that they should
change their attitude and do what they are supposed to be doing: *Frank, we have work to do,
remember? Get with the programme.* ◇ *You're
through if you don't get with the program.*

prolong /prə'lɒŋ; *AmE* -'lɔːŋ; -'lɑːŋ/

pro,long the 'agony
make an unpleasant situation last longer than is
necessary: *Don't prolong the agony. Just say yes or
no, and then I'll know where I stand.* **OPP** put sb/sth
out of their/its misery

promise /'prɒmɪs; *AmE* 'prɑːm-/

I (can) 'promise you (*informal*)
used as a way of encouraging or warning sb about
sth: *I can promise you, you'll have a wonderful time.*
◇ *If you don't take my advice, you'll regret it, I
promise you.*

promise (sb) the 'moon/'earth/'world
(*informal*)
make very big or impossible promises that you are
unlikely to keep: *He promised her the moon, but
after ten years of marriage they hardly had enough
to live on.*

promised /'prɒmɪst; *AmE* 'prɑːm-/

the promised 'land
a place or situation in which people expect to find
happiness, wealth, freedom etc: *For millions of
people in Europe, the USA was seen as the promised
land.* ◇ *The Prime Minister's speech seemed to suggest that we had already reached the promised land.*

> **❷ ORIGIN**
> This expression comes from the Bible and
> refers to the land that God promised the
> Israelites.

promises /'prɒmɪsɪz; *AmE* 'prɑːm-/

he, it, etc. promises 'well
sb/sth seems likely to do well in future: *The new
trainee promises well.* ◇ *The harvest promises well
this year.*

proof /pruːf/

the proof of the 'pudding (is in the 'eating)
(*saying*)
you can only say sth is a success after it has actually been tried out or used: *I know you didn't think
it was a very good product, but just look at the fantastic sales figures. That's the proof of the pudding.*

NOTE
Proof in this idiom refers to a way of testing something.

proof 'positive
definite or convincing proof: *It's proof positive of her belief in the company that she's investing her own money in it.*

• living → be living proof of sth

prop /prɒp; AmE prɑːp/

,prop up the 'bar (*informal, disapproving*)
spend a lot of time drinking in a pub or a bar: *'Where's Paul?' 'Propping up the bar in the King's Head, as usual.'*

proper /'prɒpə(r); AmE 'prɑːp-/

,good and 'proper (*BrE, spoken*)
completely; thoroughly: *That's messed things up good and proper.*

• prim → prim and proper

property /'prɒpəti; AmE 'prɑːpərti/

• public → be public property

prophet /'prɒfɪt; AmE 'prɑːf-/

a ,prophet of 'doom ♦ a 'doom merchant
a person who always expects that things will go very badly: *Various prophets of doom have suggested that standards in education are worse than ever.*

proportion /prə'pɔːʃn; AmE -'pɔːrʃn/

,keep sth in pro'portion
react to sth in a sensible way and not think it is worse or more serious than it really is: *Listen, I know you're all upset but let's try to keep things in proportion, shall we?*

out of (all) pro'portion (to sth)
greater or more important, serious, etc. than it really is or should be: *When you're depressed, it's very easy to get things out of proportion.* ◊ *The punishment is out of all proportion to the crime.*

propose /prə'pəʊz; AmE -'poʊz/

propose a 'toast (to sb)
ask people to wish sb health, happiness and success by raising their glasses and drinking: *I'd like to propose a toast to the bride and groom.*

❷ ORIGIN
In the past, the name of a lady who was being wished health and happiness was supposed to improve the flavour of the wine like the pieces of spiced toast that people put in their wine.

pros /prəʊz; AmE proʊz/

the pros and 'cons (of sth)
the arguments for and against sth; the advantages and disadvantages (of sth): *Your idea is interesting, but let's look carefully at its pros and cons before we take any decisions.*

❷ ORIGIN
This expression comes from the Latin words *pro*, meaning 'for', and *contra*, meaning 'against'.

protest /'prəʊtest; AmE 'proʊ-/

under 'protest
unwillingly and after expressing disagreement: *The new contract was finally accepted, but only under protest.*

proud /praʊd/

do sb 'proud (*old-fashioned, BrE*)
look after a guest very well, especially by giving them good food, entertainment, etc: *We spent the holidays with them and they really did us proud.*

do yourself/sb 'proud
do sth that makes you proud of yourself or that makes other people proud of you: *The team did us proud by winning 3-0 on Saturday.*

proves /pruːvz/

• exception → the exception that proves the rule

providence /'prɒvɪdəns; AmE 'prɑːv-/

• tempt → tempt fate/providence

prowl /praʊl/

be/go on the 'prowl
1 (of animals) move around quietly while hunting for food: *Our cats go on the prowl at night, and then they sleep here all day.*
2 (of people) be moving around quietly because you are trying to catch sb or intending to commit a crime: *Look out for burglars on the prowl. If you see anything suspicious, call the police immediately.*

psychological /ˌsaɪkə'lɒdʒɪkl; AmE -'lɑːdʒ-/

the ,psychological 'moment
the best time to do sth in order for it to be successful: *The publication of her first novel came at the psychological moment, and she became well known very quickly.*

pub /pʌb/

a 'pub crawl (*BrE, informal*)
a visit to several pubs, going straight from one to the next and drinking in each one: *We went on a pub crawl last night.*

Public /'pʌblɪk/

• Joe → John Q. Public **SEE** Joe Public

public /'pʌblɪk/

be ,public 'property
be known or talked about by everyone: *When you're famous, you and your life suddenly become public property.*

go 'public

1 (of a company) sell shares to the public: *We're hoping to go public early next year.*

2 make a public statement about a private matter because you think this is the right thing to do: *He decided to go public about his drug problem in order to warn other athletes of the dangers.*

in the public 'eye

well known because you are often seen on television or in newspapers: *The royal family are always in the public eye.*

public ,enemy number 'one

a person or a thing that is thought to be the greatest threat to a group or community: *Genetically modified foods have replaced nuclear power as public enemy number one.* ◇ *The gangster Kline became America's public enemy number one during the Depression.*

- **knowledge** → be common/public knowledge
- **wash** → wash your dirty linen in public

pudding /ˈpʊdɪŋ/

- **over-egg** → over-egg the pudding
- **proof** → the proof of the pudding (is in the eating)

puff /pʌf/

,puff and 'pant/'blow (*informal*)

breathe quickly and loudly through your mouth after physical effort: *Eventually, puffing and panting, he arrived at the gate.*

- **huff** → huff and puff

puffed /pʌft/

be puffed up with 'pride, etc.

be too full of pride, etc: *He felt grown-up, puffed with self-importance.*

pull /pʊl/

on the 'pull (*BrE, slang*)

(of a person) trying to find a sexual partner: *What are you all dressed up for? Are you going out on the pull again tonight?*

pull the ,carpet/,rug out from under sb's 'feet (*informal*)

take the help, support or confidence away from sb suddenly: *I was just about to ask her out when she pulled the rug out from under my feet by telling me she's getting married next month.* ◇ *The bank's pulled the carpet out from under his feet, unfortunately. It looks as if he'll have to sell the business.*

pull/make 'faces/a 'face (at sb/sth)

produce an expression on your face to show that you do not like sb/sth or in order to make sb laugh: *What are you pulling a face at now?* ◇ *The little girl stood outside the window of the cafe making faces at everybody.* ▶ **'face-pulling** *noun*: *He amazed the audience with his silent mime and face-pulling performance.*

pull a 'fast one (on sb) (*slang*)

tell lies or cheat sb, for example in order to get their money, possessions, etc.; deceive sb: *Don't*

try to pull a fast one on me. I'm not stupid, you know.

pull sb's 'leg (*informal*)

tell sb sth which is not true, as a joke: *'You came first! You've won the prize!' 'Really? Or are you just pulling my leg?'* ▶ **'leg-pulling** *noun*: *The news of his engagement was greeted with much leg-pulling by his friends.*

pull the 'other one (— it's got 'bells on!) (*BrE, spoken*)

used to show that you do not believe what sb has just said: *'I've been offered a job in New York.' 'Pull the other one!' 'No, really!'*

pull out all the 'stops (*informal*)

do everything you can to make sth successful: *We'll have to pull out all the stops to get this order ready by the end of the week.*

> **❷ ORIGIN**
> You pull out the *stops* on an organ when you want to make the music very loud.

pull the 'plug on sth (*informal*)

destroy or bring an end to sth, for example sb's plans, a project, etc: *The banks are threatening to pull the plug on the project.* ◇ *They've pulled the plug on that new comedy show on Channel Four.*

pull your 'punches (*informal*)

(usually used in negative sentences) express sth less strongly than you are able to, for example to avoid upsetting or shocking sb: *Her articles certainly don't pull any punches.* ◇ *I don't believe in pulling punches. If they're wrong, let's say so.*
OPP not mince your words

pull sth/a ,rabbit out of the 'hat (*informal*)

suddenly produce sth as a solution to a problem: *We had almost given up hope when Mick pulled a rabbit out of the hat by coming up with a great new idea.*

> **NOTE**
> This is a trick that is often done by magicians.

pull 'rank (on sb)

make unfair use of your senior position, authority, etc. in an organization, etc: *I was really looking forward to going to Rome on business, but then my manager pulled rank on me and said she was going instead.*

> **NOTE**
> The position, especially a high one, that somebody has in the army, etc. is called a *rank*.

pull your 'socks up (*BrE, informal*)

work harder, be more determined, etc: *You really must pull your socks up if you want to beat Jackie in the competition.*

pull 'strings (for sb) (*AmE also* **pull 'wires**) (*informal*)

use your influence in order to get an advantage for sb: *She doesn't want me to pull any strings for her; she says she prefers to be offered a place on her own merit.* ◇ *I'm sure his uncle in the BBC must have pulled strings for him.*

pull the 'strings
(secretly) control the actions of other people: *I don't understand this situation at all. I want to know exactly who is pulling the strings.*

> **NOTE**
> These two expressions refer to the strings that are attached to a puppet (= a model of a person or an animal) that you pull to make different parts of its body move.

pull up 'stakes (*AmE*)
leave your home and go to live in a different place: *When the factories and businesses closed, most of the community were forced to pull up stakes and move south.* **OPP** put down (new) roots

> **NOTE**
> *Stakes* in this phrase are the sticks or posts that are put up in order to support a tent, mark a particular place, etc.

pull your 'weight
do your fair share of the work: *If everyone pulls their weight we're going to win this prize with no trouble at all.* ◊ *She's annoyed because she feels that certain people are not pulling their weight.*

pull the 'wool over sb's eyes (*informal*)
deceive sb; hide the truth from sb: *It's no use you trying to pull the wool over my eyes; you didn't go to school again today, did you?* **OPP** open your/sb's eyes (to sth)

> **❷ ORIGIN**
> This idiom may refer to a time in the past when judges and other important people wore wigs made of wool. If somebody pulled the wig over their eyes, they were not be able to see what was happening.

pull yourself to'gether
bring your feelings under control and start acting normally; stop feeling sorry for yourself: *I know she's upset but it's time for her to pull herself together and stop crying.* **OPP** go (all) to pieces

- **bootstraps** → drag/pull yourself up by your (own) bootstraps
- **finger** → get/pull your finger out
- **horns** → draw/pull in your horns
- **short** → bring/pull sb up short

pulling /ˈpʊlɪŋ/

like pulling 'teeth
very difficult: *It was like pulling teeth to get the kids to work together.*

pulse /pʌls/

- **finger** → have/keep your finger on the pulse (of sth)

pump /pʌmp/

pump sb full of sth
fill sb with sth, especially drugs: *They pumped her full of painkillers.*

pump 'iron (*informal*)
do exercises in which you lift heavy weights in order to strengthen your muscles: *I should take more exercise, but I'm not interested in pumping iron at the local gym three evenings a week.*

pump sb's 'stomach
remove the contents of sb's stomach using a pump, because they have swallowed sth harmful: *She had to go to the hospital and have her stomach pumped.* ▸ **'stomach pump** *noun*

- **hands** → all hands to the pump **SEE** all hands on deck
- **prime** → prime the pump

Punch /pʌntʃ/

- **pleased** → (as) pleased as Punch

punch /pʌntʃ/

he, she, etc. couldn't ˌpunch his, her, etc. way out of a paper 'bag (*informal, humorous*)
a person is so weak, shy, etc. that they would never dare react forcefully to sth: *You don't need to worry about what Jim would do; he couldn't punch his way out of a paper bag.*

punch above/below your 'weight
do an activity that might be considered above/below your abilities: *Scotland is punching above its weight in research output.*

- **pack** → pack a (hard, etc.) punch

punches /ˈpʌntʃɪz/

- **pull** → pull your punches
- **roll** → roll with the punches

pup /pʌp/

sell sb/buy a 'pup (*old-fashioned, BrE, informal*)
sell sb or be sold sth that has no value or is worth much less than the price paid for it: *I'm wondering whether this really is a genuine Rolex. Do you think I've been sold a pup?*

> **❷ ORIGIN**
> The idea behind this idiom seems to be that someone dishonestly sells a young dog with no experience to someone who is expecting a more valuable older trained dog.

pure /pjʊə(r); *AmE* pjʊr/

ˌpure and 'simple
and nothing else: *This man is a bully, pure and simple.* ▸ **ˌpurely and 'simply** *adv.*: *I am basing my opinion purely and simply on the facts of the case.*

(as) pure as the driven 'snow (*often humorous*)
innocent or morally good: *I don't think you're really in a position to criticize her. You're hardly as pure as the driven snow yourself!*

purpose /ˈpɜːpəs; *AmE* ˈpɜːrpəs/

on 'purpose
deliberately: *He took the worst jobs he could find on purpose, and then wrote a book about his experiences.* ◊ *Don't shout at me like that. I didn't break it on purpose.*

purposes

to little/good/some/no 'purpose (*formal*)
with little, good, etc. result or effect: *Another meeting was held, to little purpose.* ◇ *She had used the profits to good purpose and upgraded their software.*

● **accidentally** → accidentally on purpose

● **serve** → serve the purpose (of doing sth) **SEE** serve a, his, its, etc. purpose

purposes /'pɜːpəsɪz; AmE 'pɜːr-/

● **cross** → be/talk at cross purposes

● **intents** → for/to all intents and purposes

● **practical** → for (all) practical purposes

purse /pɜːs; AmE pɜːrs/

control/hold the 'purse strings (*informal*)
be the person who controls the amount of money spent and the way in which it is spent: *I'm the one who controls the purse strings in this office, and you must come to me if you want any more money.*

● **silk** → make a silk purse out of a sow's ear

pursuit /pə'sjuːt; AmE pər'suːt/

● **hot** → in hot pursuit (of sb/sth)

push /pʊʃ/

give sb/get the 'push (*BrE, informal*)
1 tell sb/be told to leave your job: *He was stealing from the firm so the manager gave him the push.* ◇ *The company is in trouble. Who will be the next to get the push?*
2 end a relationship with sb/be rejected by sb you have had a relationship with: *His girlfriend gave him the push and he's a bit upset.* ◇ *Why is it always me that gets the push? What's wrong with me?*

if/when ,push comes to 'shove (*informal*)
if/when there is no other choice; if/when everything else has failed: *I don't want to sell the house, but if push comes to shove, I might have to.*

> **NOTE**
> *Shove* means to push somebody in a rough way.

push the 'boat out (*BrE, informal*)
spend a lot of money on food, drinks, etc. when celebrating a special occasion: *They really pushed the boat out for their daughter's wedding.* **OPP** pinch pennies

,push sb's 'buttons (also **,press sb's 'buttons** especially in *BrE*) (*informal*)
make sb react, especially in an angry or excited way: *I almost never lose my temper, but this guy can really push my buttons.* ◇ *I've known him for years, but I still don't really know what pushes his buttons.*

push the 'envelope
do sth in an extreme way in order to find out to what degree sth is possible: *Advertisements seem to be pushing the envelope of taste every day.* ◇ *People these days like to push the envelope with extreme sports.* ▶ **'envelope-pushing** noun, adj.: *envelope-pushing technology*

> **❷ ORIGIN**
> This expression comes from the aeroplane industry. A plane's *envelope* was the limit of its performance. Test pilots would need to *push (the edge of) the envelope* to see what the plane could and could not do.

push your 'luck ♦ 'push it/things (*informal*)
(often used as a warning) take a risk because you have successfully avoided problems in the past: *You've already got a good pay rise. Now don't push your luck by asking for more leave.* ◇ *Look, boys, I told you ten minutes ago to leave, so don't push it. Get out of here now or I'll call the police.*

push sth to the ,back of your 'mind
try to forget about sth unpleasant: *I tried to push the thought to the back of my mind.*

● **panic** → press/push the panic button

● **pinch** → at a pinch/push

pushed /pʊʃt/

● **hard** → hard pressed/pushed to do sth

● **pressed** → be pressed/pushed for money, space, time, etc.

pushing /'pʊʃɪŋ/

be ,pushing '40, '50, etc. (*informal*)
be nearly 40, 50, etc. years old: *My grandmother's pushing eighty but she's as fit as ever.*

be ,pushing up (the) 'daisies (*old-fashioned, humorous*)
be dead and in a grave: *I'll be pushing up daisies by the time that happens.*

> **NOTE**
> A *daisy* is a small white flower that often grows in grass.

put /pʊt/

> Most idioms containing the verb **put** are at the entries for the nouns or adjectives in the idioms, for example **put your foot in it** is at **foot**.

put it a'bout (*BrE, informal*)
have many sexual partners: *He was a man who had always put it about.*

put it 'on (*informal*)
pretend that you are hurt, angry, etc: *She's not really scared. She's only putting it on.*

put it 'there!
used when you are offering to shake hands with sb because you agree with them or want to praise them

'put it to sb that… (*formal*)
suggest sth to sb to see if they can argue against it: *I put it to you that you are the only person who had a motive for the crime.*

put sb 'through it (*especially BrE, informal*)
force sb to do sth difficult or unpleasant: *During the training they really put you through it; I was exhausted!*

put to'gether
used when comparing or contrasting sb/sth with a group of other people or things to mean 'combined' or 'in total': *Your department spent more last year than all the others put together.*

putty /'pʌti/

(like) putty in sb's 'hands (*informal*)
willing to do anything sb wants or tells you to do: *As soon as she starts crying, I'm putty in her hands.*
OPP (as) stubborn as a mule

> **NOTE**
> *Putty* is a soft flexible substance used for fixing glass in windows.

put-up /'pʊt ʌp/

a ,put-up 'job (*BrE, informal*)
something that is planned to trick or deceive sb: *The whole thing was a put-up job. He set fire to the shop himself so that he could claim the insurance money.*

pyjamas (*BrE*) (*AmE* pajamas) /pə'dʒɑːməz; *AmE* -'dʒæm-/

● cat → the cat's whiskers/pyjamas

Pyrrhic /'pɪrɪk/

a ,Pyrrhic 'victory
a victory which is achieved at too high a price and therefore not worth having: *It was a Pyrrhic victory. They won the strike but then most of them lost their jobs.*

> **❷ ORIGIN**
> This idiom refers to Pyrrhus, King of Epirus, who in 279BC defeated the Romans but lost all his best officers and men.

Q q

Q /kjuː/

,QE'D
that is what I wanted to prove and I have proved it: *He can't have done it. The bank was robbed at 6.30 and he was with me at the time. QED.*

> **❷ ORIGIN**
> This is an abbreviation of a Latin phrase, *quod erat demonstrandum*, meaning *which was to be demonstrated*.

● Joe → John Q. Public **SEE** Joe Public
● mind → mind your P's and Q's

q /kjuː/

● quiet → on the q.t. **SEE** on the quiet

qua /kweɪ; kwɑː/

● sine → a sine qua non (of/for sth)

quaking /'kweɪkɪŋ/

(be) ,quaking/,shaking in your 'boots/'shoes
be very worried or frightened: *The prospect of facing the team again in the semi-final had everyone quaking in their boots.*

quandary /'kwɒndəri; *AmE* 'kwɑːn-/

in a 'quandary
uncertain about what to do in a particular situation: *She's in a bit of a quandary about which of the jobs to accept.*

quantity /'kwɒntəti; *AmE* 'kwɑːn-/

● unknown → an unknown quantity

quantum /'kwɒntəm; *AmE* 'kwɑːn-/

a quantum 'leap (also **a quantum 'jump** *less frequent*)
a sudden very large increase, advance or improvement in sth: *This latest research represents a quantum leap in our understanding of the universe.*
◇ *The quantum leap in writing technology came with the introduction of personal computers.*

> **NOTE**
> In physics, a *quantum jump* is a sudden change in a physical quality such as energy from one fixed level to another.

quarrel /'kwɒrəl; *AmE* 'kwɔːr-; 'kwɑːr-/

● pick → pick a fight/quarrel (with sb)

quart /kwɔːt; *AmE* kwɔːrt/

get/pour/put a ,quart into a pint 'pot (*BrE*)
try to do sth impossible, especially to try to put sth into a space which is too small for it: *30 people in this small room! You can't put a quart into a pint pot, you know.*

> **NOTE**
> A *pint* is 0.568 litres and a *quart* is 1.136 litres.

quarterback /'kwɔːtəbæk; *AmE* 'kwɔːrtərbæk/

● Monday → Monday morning quarterback

quarters /'kwɔːtəz; *AmE* 'kwɔːtərz; 'kwɔːrt-/

● close² → at close quarters

Queen /kwiːn/

● English → the King's/Queen's English
● evidence → turn King's/Queen's evidence

queen /kwiːn/

'queen it over sb
(of women) behave in an unpleasant way to sb because you think you are better or more important than they are: *She sits in her office queening it over all the junior staff.*

● uncrowned → (be) the uncrowned king/queen (of sth)

queer /kwɪə(r); AmE kwɪr/

queer sb's 'pitch ♦ queer the 'pitch (for sb)
(BrE, informal)
spoil sb's plans or their chances of getting sth:
Somebody must have told her boss about her plans
to leave. Who was trying to queer her pitch?

● fish → an odd/a queer fish

question /'kwestʃən/

beyond/without 'question
without any doubt: She is without question the best
student in the class. ◇ The view is, beyond question,
the most spectacular in the whole area.

bring/call/throw sth into 'question
cause sth to become a matter for doubt and discussion: Scandals like this call into question the
honesty of the police. ◇ The high number of accidents has brought government policy on industrial
safety into question.

,good 'question! (spoken)
used to show that you do not know the answer to
an important question: 'How much is all this going
to cost?' 'Good question!'

in 'question (formal)
1 that is being discussed: On the day in question
we were in Cardiff. ◇ The money in question doesn't
belong to you; it belongs to your sister.
2 in doubt; uncertain: The future of public transport is not in question.

it's (just, etc.) a 'question of sth
it concerns sth; it is really about sth: It's not a question of money; it's much more a question of principle. ◇ If it's a question of paying you a bit more,
then I think we can consider that.

out of the 'question
impossible and so not worth considering: An
expensive holiday is out of the question this year.

There was a question mark hanging over the new
building project.

**a 'question mark hangs over sb/sth ♦ there's
a 'question mark (hanging) over sb/sth**
there is some doubt about sb/sth: A question mark
hangs over the future of this club. ◇ There's a question mark over his loyalty to the company.

there's some/no question of sth/of doing sth
there is some/no possibility of sth/doing sth: I'm
afraid there is no question of you leaving work early
this afternoon. ◇ Apparently there is some question
of our getting three days' extra leave this year. I hope
we do.

without 'question
if you do sth **without question**, you do it without
arguing or complaining: I expect officers to obey
my orders without question. ◇ Her version of events
was accepted without question.

● beg → beg the question
● leading → a leading question
● moot → be a moot point/question
● open → open to question **SEE** an open question
● pop → pop the question
● sixty-four → the million dollar question **SEE** the sixty-
four thousand dollar question
● sixty-four → the sixty-four thousand dollar question
● time → it's only, just, etc. a matter/a question of time
(before...)
● vexed → a vexed question

queue /kju:/

● jump → jump the queue

quick /kwɪk/

cut sb to the 'quick
hurt sb's feelings; offend sb deeply: It cut her to the
quick to hear him criticizing her family like that.

> **NOTE**
> The quick is the soft, sensitive flesh that is
> under your nails.

have a quick 'temper
become angry easily: Just be careful how you tell
him — he's got a very quick temper and he's quite
scary when he's angry! ▶ **,quick-'tempered** adj.:
She's quite a quick-tempered woman.

,quick and 'dirty (informal)
used to describe sth that is usually complicated,
but is being done quickly and simply in this case:
Read our quick-and-dirty guide to web page design.

(as) quick as a 'flash
very fast or suddenly: Quick as a flash he replied
that he had never seen it before. ◇ When the cat
appeared, the bird flew away, as quick as a flash.

,quick 'march
used for telling sb to walk faster: Come on! Quick
march or we'll miss the bus.

> **NOTE**
> 'Quick march' is also a command given to sol-
> diers.

a **'quick one** (*BrE, informal*)
a drink, usually alcoholic, which you have a short time for before doing sth else: *Have you got time for a quick one before your train goes?*

- **buck** → make a fast/quick buck
- **double** → double quick
- **draw** → be fast/quick on the draw
- **mark** → be quick/slow off the mark
- **uptake** → be quick/slow on the uptake

quid /kwɪd/

,**quid pro 'quo** (*from Latin*)
a thing that is given in return for sth else: *The management have agreed to begin pay talks as a quid pro quo for suspension of strike action.*

> NOTE
> The meaning of the Latin phrase is 'something for something'.

- **full** → not the full quid

quids /kwɪdz/

quids 'in (*BrE, informal*)
in a position of having made a profit, especially a good profit: *I've just received three cheques so we're quids in at the moment.*

> NOTE
> A *quid* is an informal word for one pound in money.

quiet /'kwaɪət/

keep quiet about sth ♦ keep sth quiet
say nothing about sth; keep sth secret: *I've decided to resign but I'd rather you kept quiet about it.*

on the 'quiet (also **on the q.t.** *old-fashioned*) (*informal*)
without telling anyone; secretly: *Well, just on the quiet, she's actually leaving her job next month. Don't tell anyone, will you?* ◇ *Just remember that whatever I tell you is on the q.t.*

> NOTE
> *Q.t.* is an abbreviation of 'quiet'.

(as) quiet as a 'mouse
(of a person) saying very little or making very little noise: *He's quiet as a mouse in class.* ◇ *Be as quiet as a mouse when you go upstairs — the baby's asleep in our bedroom.*

- **peace** → peace and quiet

quite /kwaɪt/

not ,quite the 'thing
1 not considered socially acceptable: *It wouldn't be quite the thing to turn up in jeans and trainers.*
2 (*old-fashioned*) not healthy or normal

'**quite a/some sb/sth** (*informal*)
used to show that you think sb/sth is impressive, unusual, remarkable, etc: *That's quite some swimming pool you've got there. It's huge!* ◇ *We found it quite a change when we moved abroad.*

quite the 'best, the 'worst, etc. sth (*informal*)
absolutely the best, worst, etc: *It was quite the worst film I've ever seen.*

quite a 'few (*BrE* also **a good 'few**)
a fairly large number: *I've been there quite a few times.* ◇ *They've been here a good few years now.*

quite 'so (*BrE, formal*)
used to agree with sb or to show that you understand them: *'It's a very interesting book.' 'Quite so. That's why I wanted you to read it.'*

quite some 'time
quite a long time: *Quite some time has passed since I last saw my brother.*

- **contrary** → quite the contrary SEE on the contrary
- **there** → be not all/quite there

quits /kwɪts/

be 'quits (with sb) (*informal*)
1 be in a position in which neither of two people owe each other money any more: *If I give you $10, then we're quits, aren't we?*
2 have done sth unpleasant to sb who did sth unpleasant to you: *He crashed my motorbike last year and now I've crashed his car, so we're quits.*

- **call** → call it quits
- **double** → double or quits

qui vive /,kiː 'viːv/

on the qui 'vive
paying close attention to a situation, in case sth happens: *He's always on the qui vive for a business opportunity.*

quo /kwəʊ; *AmE* kwoʊ/

- **quid** → quid pro quo
- **status** → the status quo

quoi /kwɑː/

- **sais** → je ne sais quoi

quote /kwəʊt; *AmE* kwoʊt/

'**quote (…'unquote)** (*spoken*)
used by a speaker to show the beginning (and end) of a word, phrase, etc. that has been said or written by sb else: *This, quote, 'novel of the century', unquote, is probably the most boring book I've ever read.*

R r

R /ɑː(r)/
• three → the three R's

rabbit /'ræbɪt/
• deer → (be caught like) a rabbit in the headlights **SEE** (be caught/freeze like) a deer in the headlights
• pull → pull sth/a rabbit out of the hat

race /reɪs/

a ,race against 'time/the 'clock
a situation in which you have to do sth or finish sth very fast before it is too late: *It was a race against time to reach the shore before the boat sank.*

a/the ,race to the 'bottom (*business*)
the idea that economic competition will lead to lower standards, worse conditions for workers, and workers in some countries losing their jobs to lower-paid workers in other countries: *They fear that globalization only creates a race to the bottom.*

• one-horse → a one-horse race
• rat → the rat race

rack /ræk/

go to ,rack and 'ruin
get into bad condition because of lack of care: *The house has gone to rack and ruin over the last few years.* ◇ *The country is going to rack and ruin under this government.*

> **NOTE**
> *Rack* in this idiom means 'destruction'.

on the 'rack
in a state of anxiety, stress, pain, etc: *After three weeks had passed and she had still not heard from her daughter, Joan was on the rack.*

> **❷ ORIGIN**
> The *rack* was an instrument of torture, used in the past for punishing and hurting people. Their arms and legs were tied to a wooden frame and then pulled in opposite directions, stretching the body.

rack your 'brains (also **wrack your 'brains** *less frequent*) (*informal*)
try very hard to think of sth or remember sth: *I've been racking my brains all day trying to remember his name.*

• peg → off the rack **SEE** off the peg

radar /'reɪdɑː(r)/

below/under the 'radar (screen)
if something is **below/under the radar**, people are not aware of it: *The conflict has slipped below the radar screens of the mass media.* ◇ *Experts say a lot of corporate crime stays under the radar.*

on/off the 'radar (screen)
used to say that people are aware or not aware of sth, or are thinking or not thinking about it: *Foreign policy is just not on most people's radar screens.* ◇ *Eastern Europe has remained off the radar of most UK investors.*

rag /ræg/

lose your 'rag (*BrE, informal*)
become very angry and behave in an uncontrolled way: *He really lost his rag when the children broke another window with their ball.*

the 'rag trade (*old-fashioned, informal*)
the business of designing, making and selling clothes: *He's worked in the rag trade all his life.*

• chew → chew the rag **SEE** chew the fat
• red → (like) a red rag to a bull

rage /reɪdʒ/

all the 'rage (*informal*)
very popular or fashionable: *Short hair is all the rage at the moment.* **OPP** old hat

ragged /'rægɪd/

,run sb 'ragged (*informal*)
make sb do a lot of work or make a big effort so that they become tired: *You look really exhausted. Have the children been running you ragged?*

rags /rægz/

from ,rags to 'riches (*informal*)
from being very poor to being very rich, especially in a short period of time: *She went from rags to riches in less than five years.* ► **,rags-to-'riches** *adj.*: *It was a real rags-to-riches story.*

• glad → glad rags

> **NOTE**
> If a person is in *rags*, they are wearing very old torn clothes.

rails /reɪlz/

get back on the 'rails (*informal*)
become successful again after a period of failure, or begin functioning normally again: *Even after losing all three of their last matches, the club assures fans that they will get back on the rails in time for their next game.*

go off the 'rails (*BrE, informal*)
start behaving in a way which shocks or upsets other people: *Away from the routine of army life some ex-soldiers go completely off the rails.*

> **NOTE**
> These idioms refer to a train leaving the track that it runs on.

rain /reɪn/

come ,rain, come 'shine ♦ (come) ,rain or 'shine (*informal*)
whatever the weather is like; whatever happens: *They met in the park, come rain or shine, every Saturday morning for twenty years.*

rain cats and 'dogs (also **rain 'buckets**) (*informal*)
(usually used in progressive tenses) rain very heavily: *We can't possibly play golf today. It's raining cats and dogs out there.* ◇ *It's been raining buckets all morning.*

❷ ORIGIN
The expression 'raining cats and dogs' may come from Norse mythology. Cats were supposed to have an influence over the weather, while dogs were the signal of storms.

,rain on sb's 'parade (*AmE*)
spoil sth for sb: *Drugs again rained on the Olympics' parade as another athlete tested positive for an illegal substance.*

take a 'rain check (on sth) (*informal, especially AmE*)
used to refuse an offer or invitation but to say that you will accept it later: *'Would you like to try that new restaurant tonight?' 'I'm afraid I'm busy tonight, but can I take a rain check?'*

❷ ORIGIN
A *rain check* was originally a ticket that was given to spectators at an outdoor event if it was cancelled or interrupted by rain. They could then use this ticket at a future event.

● right → (as) right as rain

rains /reɪnz/

it never ,rains but it 'pours (*BrE*) (*AmE* **when it ,rains, it 'pours**) (*saying*)
when one thing goes wrong, so do others: *It never rains but it pours! First I found that the car had been stolen and then I lost the keys to my office.*

rainy /'reɪni/

save, keep, etc. it for a ,rainy 'day (*informal*)
save money or things for a time in the future when you might need them: *'Don't spend it all at once,' his aunt said . 'Save some of it for a rainy day.'*

raise /reɪz/

raise 'Cain/'hell (*informal*)
complain or protest noisily and angrily, often as a way of getting sth you want: *He'll raise hell if we don't finish on time.* ► **'hell-raiser** *noun* a violent and destructive person

❷ ORIGIN
Cain was the first murderer in the Bible.

raise your 'eyebrows (at sth)
show, by the expression on your face, that you disapprove of or are surprised by sth: *Eyebrows were raised when he arrived at the wedding in jeans.* ◇ *When he said he was leaving, there were a lot of raised eyebrows.*

raise your 'glass (to sb)
hold up your glass and wish sb happiness, good luck, etc. before you drink: *Now, would everybody please raise their glasses and drink a toast to the bride and groom.*

raise a 'laugh/'smile
do or say sth that makes other people laugh/smile: *If the speeches are not going well, ask Paula to speak; she can always raise a laugh.* ◇ *His jokes didn't even raise a smile, which was embarrassing.*

raise the 'spectre of sth (*BrE*) (*AmE* **raise the 'specter of sth**)
make people afraid that sth unpleasant might happen: *The news of more cuts has raised the spectre of redundancies once again.*

NOTE
A *spectre* is an old word for a ghost.

raise sb's 'spirits
make sb happier: *Good weather always raises her spirits.*

raise your 'voice
speak in a louder voice, often because you are angry: *Don't raise your voice at me. It wasn't my fault.* ◇ *They heard **raised voices** and saw two men engaged in an argument.*

raise a/your voice a'gainst sb/sth
say publicly that you do not agree with sb's actions, plans, etc: *He was the only person to raise his voice against the plan.*

● ante → raise/up the ante
● hackles → raise hackles **SEE** make sb's hackles rise
● hand → lift/raise a hand against sb
● head → rear/raise its (ugly) head
● hopes → build up/raise sb's hopes
● roof → lift/raise the roof
● sights → raise/lower your sights
● stink → kick up/make/create/raise a stink (about sth)
● temperature → raise/lower the temperature

raison /'reɪzō ; AmE 'reɪzoʊn/

his, your, etc. ,raison 'd'être /,reɪzō 'detrə; AmE ,reɪzoʊn/ (*from French*)
the most important reason for sb's/sth's existence: *Work seems to be her sole raison d'être.*

NOTE
The meaning of the French phrase is 'reason for being'.

rake /reɪk/

rake over the 'ashes/the 'past (*informal, disapproving*)
discuss with sb unpleasant things that happened between you in the past: *When they met each other again, ten years after the divorce, they both tried hard not to rake over the past.*

● haul → rake sb over the coals **SEE** haul sb over the coals
● thin → (as) thin as a rake

ram /ræm/

ram sth 'home (*especially BrE*)
force sb to understand sth important: *The terrible injuries I saw in that accident really rammed home for me the importance of wearing seat belts.*

rampage /ˈræmpeɪdʒ/

be/go on the 'rampage
run round the streets causing damage to shops/ stores, cars, etc: *After their team lost, some of the crowd went on the rampage through the town.*

ramrod /ˈræmrɒd; AmE -rɑːd/

,ramrod 'straight ◆ (as) ,straight as a 'ramrod
(of a person) with a very straight back and looking serious and formal: *As she walked in she could feel the tension in the room, with her mother sitting ramrod straight in her chair.*

> NOTE
> A *ramrod* is a long straight piece of iron used in the past to push explosive into a gun.

ranch /rɑːntʃ; AmE ræntʃ/

● **bet** → bet the farm/ranch

range /reɪndʒ/

in/within 'range (of sth)
near enough to be reached, seen or heard: *He shouted angrily at anyone within range.*

out of 'range (of sth)
too far away to be reached, seen or heard: *The cat stayed well out of range of the children.*

rank /ræŋk/

(the) ,rank and 'file
(the) ordinary members of a group or an organization: *I can see that you are happy with the plan but what will the rank and file think?* ◇ *The rank-and-file members don't elect the leader.* **OPP** (the) top brass

> NOTE
> In the military, the *rank and file* are ordinary soldiers who are not officers.

● **pull** → pull rank (on sb)

ranks /ræŋks/

break 'ranks
(of the members of a group) refuse to support a group or an organization of which they are members: *Large numbers of MPs felt compelled to break ranks over the issue.*

> NOTE
> This idiom refers to soldiers, police etc. failing to remain in line.

come up/rise through the 'ranks
after starting your career at the bottom or low down in an organization, finally reach a high position in it: *The new managing director has come up through the ranks, which is quite unusual these days.*

> NOTE
> In the military, the *ranks* refers to the position of ordinary soldiers rather than officers. Some may become officers if they have the right qualities.

● **close¹** → close ranks

ransom /ˈrænsəm/

hold sb to 'ransom
1 hold sb as a prisoner until money has been paid for their release: *The kidnappers held the little girl to ransom for more than eight hours.*
2 try to force sb to do what you want by using threats: *The government said that the workers were holding the country to ransom by demanding a ten per cent pay rise.*

● **king** → a king's ransom

rant /rænt/

,rant and 'rave (*disapproving*)
show that you are angry by shouting or complaining loudly for a long time: *He stood there for about twenty minutes ranting and raving about the colour of the new paint.*

rap /ræp/

,rap sb over the 'knuckles ◆ give sb, get, etc. a ,rap over the 'knuckles (*informal*)
criticize sb/be criticized for doing sth wrong: *He got a rap over the knuckles for spending too much money on his business lunches.*

take the 'rap (for sb/sth) (*informal*)
be blamed or punished, especially for sth you did not do: *She was prepared to take the rap for the broken window, even though it was her brother who had kicked the ball.*

● **beat** → beat the rap

raptures /ˈræptʃəz; AmE ˈræptʃərz/

be in/go into 'raptures (about/over sb/sth)
be extremely enthusiastic about sb/sth you like: *Each time I mention your name, he goes into raptures about you.*

rare /reə(r); AmE rer/

a rare 'bird
a person or thing that is unusual, often because they have/it has two very different interests or qualities: *Jill is a very rare bird, a good politician and an excellent listener.*

> ❷ ORIGIN
> This expression is a translation of the Latin idiom 'rara avis'.

● **hen** → (as) rare/scarce as hen's teeth

raring /ˈreərɪŋ; AmE ˈrer-/

,raring to 'go (*informal*)
very enthusiastic about starting sth: *We've finished our training and now we're all raring to go.*

rat /ræt/

the 'rat race (*disapproving*)
intense competition for success in jobs, business, etc., typical of a big city: *Paul got caught up in the rat race and was never at home.* ◇ *They longed to escape from the rat race and move out of the city.*

● **drowned** → like a drowned rat
● **smell** → smell a rat

rate /reɪt/

at 'any rate (*spoken*)

1 used to say that a particular fact is true in spite of what has happened in the past or what may happen in the future: *Well, that's one good piece of news at any rate.*

2 used to show that you are being more accurate about sth that you have just said: *He said he'd be here on the 5th. At any rate, I think that's what he said.*

3 used to show that what you have just said is not as important as what you are going to say: *There were maybe 80 or 90 people there. At any rate, the room was packed.*

at a rate of 'knots (*BrE, informal*)

very fast: *You must have been going at a rate of knots to have finished so soon.* **OPP** at a snail's pace

> **NOTE**
> The speed of a boat or ship is measured in *knots*.

at 'this/'that rate (*spoken*)

if the situation continues as it is: *This traffic's terrible. At this rate we'll never get to the airport on time.*

the ˌgoing 'rate (for sth)

the usual amount of money paid for goods or services at a particular time: *They pay slightly more than the going rate for freelance work.*

rather /ˈrɑːðə(r); AmE ˈræðər/

rather than

instead of sb/sth: *I think I'll have a cold drink rather than coffee.* ◇ *Why didn't you ask for help, rather than trying to do it on your own?*

rather you, etc. than 'me (also **sooner you, etc. than 'me**) (*especially BrE*)

used for saying that you are pleased that you do not have to do a difficult or unpleasant thing: *'She works every weekend.' 'Rather her than me.'*

would rather… (than)

would prefer to: *She'd rather die than give a speech.* ◇ *'Do you want to come with us?' 'No, I'd rather not.'* ◇ *Would you rather walk or go by car?* ◇ *'Do you mind if I smoke?' 'I'd rather you didn't.'*

● steep → be a bit/rather steep

rattle /ˈrætl/

ˌrattle sb's 'cage (*informal*)

annoy sb: *Who's rattled his cage?* **OPP** smooth (sb's) ruffled feathers

rave /reɪv/

● rant → rant and rave

raving /ˈreɪvɪŋ/

(stark) raving 'mad/'bonkers (*informal*)

completely crazy; suddenly very angry with sb: *Are you stark raving mad, jumping off a moving train?* ◇ *When I told her I'd crashed her car, she went stark raving bonkers.*

raw /rɔː/

catch/touch sb on the 'raw (*BrE*)

upset sb by reminding them of sth they are particularly sensitive about: *She touched him on the raw by criticizing his driving.*

in the 'raw

in a way that does not hide the unpleasant aspects of sth: *If you want to see life in the raw, get a job as a police officer.*

● deal → a raw/rough deal

ray /reɪ/

the one/a ray of 'hope

the one small sign of improvement in a difficult situation: *They've actually stopped fighting, so perhaps there's a ray of hope after all.* ◇ *Our one ray of hope is the bank. They might agree to lend us the money we need.*

a ray of 'sunshine (*informal*)

a person or thing that makes sb's life happier: *She calls her granddaughter her 'little ray of sunshine'.*

rays /reɪz/

● catch → catch some rays

razor /ˈreɪzə(r)/

● knife-edge → on a razor's edge **SEE** on a knife-edge

razzle /ˈræzl/

be/go out on the 'razzle (*BrE, informal*)

go out drinking, dancing and enjoying yourself: *It's a long time since I went out on the razzle, but your birthday will be a wonderful excuse.*

reach /riːtʃ/

reach for the 'stars

try to be successful at sth that is difficult: *She decided very early that she was going to reach for the stars and get to the top of her profession.*

within (easy) 'reach (of sth)

close to sth: *The house is within easy reach of schools and sports facilities.*

● ears → come to/reach sb's ears

● first → reach/make first base (with sb/sth) **SEE** get to first base (with sb/sth)

● rock → hit/reach rock bottom

read[1] /riːd/

ˌread between the 'lines

find or look for a hidden or extra meaning in sth a person says or writes, usually their real feelings about sth: *Reading between the lines, it was obvious that he was feeling lonely.*

ˌread sb like a 'book (*informal*)

understand sb so well that you can guess what they will say or do before they say or do it: *She found that after living with him for a year or more, she could read him like a book.*

,read sb's 'mind/'thoughts (*informal*)
understand what sb is thinking, feeling, planning,
etc: *I can't read your mind! If you don't tell me
what's worrying you, I can't help you.*

,read my 'lips (*spoken*)
used to tell sb to listen carefully to what you are
saying: *Read my lips: no new taxes* (= I promise
there will be no new taxes).

read (sb) the 'Riot Act (*BrE*)
tell sb forcefully and angrily that you will punish
them if they do not stop behaving badly; be angry
with sb who has behaved badly: *The headmaster
came in and read the Riot Act. He said he would
keep us in after school if there was one more complaint about us.*

> **❷ ORIGIN**
> In 1715 the Riot Act was passed in Parliament.
> Groups of more than twelve people were not
> allowed to meet in public. If they did, an offi-
> cial came to read them the Riot Act, which
> ordered them to stop the meeting.

read² /red/

,take sth/it as 'read (*BrE*)
consider that sth does not need discussing
because everyone already knows, understands,
or agrees about it: *Can I take it as read that we all
agree on this matter?*

ready /'redi/

at the 'ready
prepared for immediate action or use: *Cameras
and microphones at the ready, they waited for the
new President to appear.*

make 'ready (for sth) (*formal*)
prepare (for sth): *Everyone is very busy here making ready for the royal visit.*

ready, steady, 'go! (*BrE*) (also (get) ready, (get)
set, 'go! *AmE, BrE*)
what you say to tell people to start a race

,ready to 'roll (*informal*)
ready to start: *The show is just about ready to roll.*

ready when 'you are
used for telling sb that you are ready and are waiting for them to do sth: *'When would you like me to
begin?' 'Ready when you are.'*

● drop → fit/ready to drop
● rough → rough and ready

real /'riːəl; *BrE* usually rɪəl/

for 'real
1 if you do sth **for real**, you do sth which is genuine or serious, rather than imagined, practised or
talked about, etc: *You might think that jumping out
of a plane is easy, but when you do it for real, it's
terrifying. ◇ He's joked about emigrating to Canada
in the past, but this time I think it's for real.*
2 genuine: *Do you think this offer of a free flight is
for real?*

get 'real (*informal*)
used to tell sb that they are behaving in a stupid or
unreasonable way: *You really think people are
going to listen to your crazy ideas? Get real!*

in real 'life
not the life people have in books, films/movies,
plays, etc: *She plays the role of a pianist in the
movie, but in real life she can't play a note.*

the ,real Mc'Coy (*informal*)
the original and therefore the best type of sth; the
best example of sth: *It's an American flying jacket,
the real McCoy. ◇ This apple pie is the real McCoy. I
haven't eaten one like this for years.*

> **❷ ORIGIN**
> This idiom possibly refers to the American
> boxing champion Kid McCoy. So many people
> pretended to be him that he started calling
> himself Kid 'The Real' McCoy.

the real 'thing (*informal*)
the genuine thing: *Are you sure it's the real thing
(= love), not just infatuation? ◇ Synthetic dia-
monds don't have the quality of the real thing.*

reality /ri'æləti/

in re'ality
used to say that a situation is different from what
has just been said or from what people believe:
*Outwardly she looked confident but in reality she
felt extremely nervous.*

realms /relmz/

beyond/within the realms of possi'bility
impossible/possible: *A successful outcome is not
beyond the realms of possibility.*

reap /riːp/

reap a/the 'harvest (*BrE*)
benefit or suffer as a direct result of sth that you
have done: *His attacking policies have reaped a particularly good harvest overseas, where he is well
known as a shrewd businessman.*

you ,reap what you 'sow (*saying*)
you have to deal with the bad effects or results of
sth that you originally started: *He's so mean! When
I went to him for some sympathy and understanding, all he said was 'you reap what you sow'!*

> **NOTE**
> These two phrases refer to farmers cutting and
> collecting crops from a field.

(sow the wind,) reap the 'whirlwind (*especially
AmE*)
suffer as a result of your actions: *We will reap the
whirlwind of those actions for years, if not decades,
to come.*

> **❷ ORIGIN**
> This expression comes from the Bible. A *whirl-
> wind* is a strong wind that spins very fast and
> causes a lot of damage.

rear /rɪə(r); AmE rɪr/

bring up the 'rear
1 be the last person or group to appear in a line or procession: *The President led the way out of the courtyard, followed by senior officials. Junior officials brought up the rear.*
2 finish last in a race or competition: *Smith finished in 2nd place, Warren in 3rd, with poor Davis bringing up the rear in 12th place.*

● head → rear/raise its (ugly) head

rearrange /ˌriːəˈreɪndʒ/

rearrange the ˌdeckchairs on the Tiˈtanic
if sth is like **rearranging the deckchairs on the Titanic**, it is an activity that is not worth doing because it cannot improve the situation: *None of the staff believe that the new system will improve anything. It's simply a case of rearranging the deckchairs on the Titanic.*

> ❷ ORIGIN
> This expression refers to the famous ship that sank after hitting an iceberg on its first voyage.

reason /ˈriːzn/

within 'reason
on the condition that it is sensible or reasonable: *She wanted it repaired immediately and said she would pay whatever we asked, within reason.*

● best → for a/some reason/reasons best known to himself, herself, etc.
● rhyme → there's no rhyme or reason to/for sth
● rhyme → without rhyme or reason SEE there's no rhyme or reason to/for sth
● sense → (make sb) see sense/reason
● stands → it stands to reason (that...)

rebound /ˈrɪbaʊnd/

on the 'rebound
while you are sad and confused, especially after a relationship has ended: *She married John on the rebound from Geoff. I knew it wouldn't last.*

> NOTE
> If a ball *rebounds*, it bounces back after it has hit a hard surface.

recall /rɪˈkɔːl/

beyond reˈcall
impossible to bring back to the original state; impossible to remember: *When the plans to build the new highway were announced, we knew that the beautiful landscape around our house would soon be damaged beyond recall.*

received /rɪˈsiːvd/

● wisdom → conventional/received wisdom

receiving /rɪˈsiːvɪŋ/

be on/at the reˈceiving end (of sth) (*informal*)
be the person that an action, etc. is directed at, especially an unpleasant one: *He's been on the receiving end of a lot of criticism recently.*

recharge /ˌriːˈtʃɑːdʒ; AmE -ˈtʃɑːrdʒ/

recharge your 'batteries (*informal*)
rest for a while to get more energy for the next period of activity: *You've been working too much. What you need is a few days away to recharge your batteries.*

A couple of weeks on the beach helped Tim and Tina to recharge their batteries.

recipe /ˈresəpi/

a recipe for diˈsaster, sucˈcess, etc.
a method or an idea that seems likely to have a particular result: *That idea sounds like a recipe for disaster.* ◇ *What's her recipe for success?*

reckoned /ˈrekənd/

● force → a force to be reckoned with

reckoning /ˈrekənɪŋ/

in/into/out of the 'reckoning (*especially BrE*)
(especially in sport) among/not among those who are likely to win or be successful: *Phelan is fit again and could come into the reckoning.*

● day → the day of reckoning

recognition /ˌrekəgˈnɪʃn/

change, alter, etc. beyond/out of (all) recogˈnition
change, etc. such a lot that people do not recognize you, it, etc: *I went back to Birmingham after 20 years and it had changed beyond all recognition.* ◇ *She had changed beyond all recognition since I last saw her.*

record

record /'rekɔːd; AmE 'rekərd/

be/go on 'record ♦ **put sth on 'record**
say sth publicly, for example in a newspaper, so that what you say is written down: *He is on record as saying that he never wanted to become President, but now he's fighting for the job.*

(just) for the 'record
so that the facts should be recorded or remembered correctly: *I'd like to state, just for the record, that I disagree with the committee's decision.*

,off the 'record
if you tell sb sth **off the record**, it is not yet official and you do not want them to repeat it publicly: *If you speak to me off the record, I won't quote you by name.* ◇ *It was an off-the-record remark and you shouldn't have attached my name to it.*

on 'record
officially noted or written down: *It was the warmest day on record.*

put/set the 'record straight (*informal*)
give a correct version, explanation of events, facts, etc. because you think sb has made a mistake: *I think there has been some misunderstanding so I'd like to set the record straight.*

● track → a track record

red /red/

in the 'red (*informal*)
in debt: *At this time of year we are usually in the red.* **OPP** in the black

> **❷ ORIGIN**
> In bank accounts, an amount that was owed used to be written in red figures, not black.

not have a red 'cent (*AmE, informal*)
have no money at all: *I wish I could come with you, but I don't have a red cent at the moment.* **OPP** (be) rolling in it/money

on ,red a'lert
prepared for an emergency or for sth dangerous to happen: *Following the bomb blast, local hospitals have been put on red alert.*

(as) red as a 'beetroot (*BrE*) (*AmE* **(as) red as a 'beet**) (*informal*)
with red cheeks, because you feel angry, embarrassed or hot: *I could feel myself going red as a beetroot when she said that my work had been chosen for the prize.* ◇ *My face is always as red as a beet when I come out of the sauna.*

the red 'carpet
a very special welcome given to an important visitor: *When I went to my girlfriend's house for the first time, her family really put out the red carpet for me.* ◇ *It was an unofficial visit so the guests didn't get the usual red carpet treatment.*

> **NOTE**
> A strip of red carpet is usually laid on the ground for an important visitor to walk on when he or she arrives.

a red 'face (*informal*)
embarrassment: *There are going to be a lot of red faces at the bank when they discover their mistake.*

a red 'herring
a fact, etc. which sb introduces into a discussion because they want to take people's attention away from the main point: *Look, the situation in French agriculture is just a red herring. We're here to discuss the situation in this country.*

> **❷ ORIGIN**
> This idiom comes from the custom of using the scent of a smoked, dried herring (which was red) to train dogs to hunt.

red 'ink (*business*)
debts, losses or money that is owed: *The company opened the fiscal year with $315.9 million in red ink.* ◇ *The health care industry is bleeding red ink* (= losing a lot of money).

red in ,tooth and 'claw
involving opposition or competition that is violent and without pity: *nature, red in tooth and claw*

(like) a red rag to a 'bull (*BrE*) (*AmE* **like waving a red flag in front of/at a 'bull**)
certain to make a particular person very angry or even violent: *Don't mention anything about religion to your uncle. It's like a red rag to a bull.*

> **NOTE**
> This expression refers to the belief that bulls do not like the colour red.

red 'tape (*disapproving*)
official rules that seem more complicated than necessary and prevent things from being done quickly: *Do you know how much red tape you have to go through if you want to import a car?*

> **❷ ORIGIN**
> This phrase comes from the custom of tying up official documents with red ribbon or tape.

see 'red (*informal*)
suddenly become very angry: *Cruelty to animals makes him see red.*

● paint → paint the town red

redeeming /rɪ'diːmɪŋ/

a redeeming 'feature
sth good or positive about sb/sth that is otherwise bad: *Her one redeeming feature is her generosity.* ◇ *The only redeeming feature of the hotel was the swimming pool. Apart from that, it was the worst hotel I've ever stayed in.*

red-handed /,red 'hændɪd/

● catch → catch sb red-handed

red-letter /,red 'letə(r)/

a red-'letter day
a very special day which is remembered because sth important or good happened: *Today was a red-letter day. We heard we had won a free trip to Japan.*

❷ ORIGIN
Religious holidays and other important dates used to be printed in red on calendars.

red-light /ˌred ˈlaɪt/

the red-ˈlight district
the part of a city where prostitutes work and sex shops are found: *I got lost and found myself in the red-light district all alone!*

redress /rɪˈdres/

redress the ˈbalance
make a situation equal or fair again: *They have won the last two games, so today we'll be trying to redress the balance.*

reduced /rɪˈdjuːst; AmE -ˈduːst/

reˌduced ˈcircumstances
the state of being poorer than you were before. People say 'living in reduced circumstances' to avoid saying 'poor': *As time passed, his reduced circumstances became more and more obvious to his friends and colleagues.*

reference /ˈrefrəns/

in/with ˈreference to (*formal* or *written*)
used to say what you are talking or writing about: *With reference to your letter of July 22…*

reflect /rɪˈflekt/

reflect well, badly, etc. on sb/sth
make sb/sth appear to be good, bad, etc. to other people: *This incident reflects badly on everyone involved.*

reflected /rɪˈflektɪd/

bathe/bask in reflected ˈglory
get attention and fame not because of sth you have done but through the success of sb else connected to you: *She wasn't happy to bathe in the reflected glory of her daughter's success, as she wanted to succeed on her own.*

reflection /rɪˈflekʃn/

a sad, poor, etc. reflection on sth
a thing which damages sb's/sth's reputation: *The increase in crime is a sad reflection on our society today.*

● mature → on mature reflection/consideration

refresh /rɪˈfreʃ/

reˌfresh sb's/your ˈmemory
remind sb/yourself of sth that you have forgotten: *Refresh my memory, will you? How many children has he got?* ◊ *Before I interviewed Ms Waters, I read her book again just to refresh my memory.*

refusal /rɪˈfjuːzl/

● first → (give sb, have, etc.) (the) first refusal

regard /rɪˈɡɑːd; AmE rɪˈɡɑːrd/

have reˈgard to sth (*law*)
remember and think carefully about sth: *It is always necessary to have regard to the terms of the contract.*

in/with reˈgard to sb/sth (*formal*)
concerning sb/sth: *a country's laws in regard to human rights* ◊ *The company's position with regard to overtime is made clear in the contracts.*

in this/that reˈgard (*formal*)
concerning what has just been mentioned: *I have nothing further to say in this regard.*

regards /rɪˈɡɑːdz; AmE rɪˈɡɑːrdz/

as regards sb/sth (*formal*)
about or concerning sb/sth: *As regards the method of payment, a decision will be made after the contract has been signed.*

region /ˈriːdʒən/

in the region of
approximately: *He earns somewhere in the region of €50 000.*

regular /ˈreɡjələ(r)/

(as) regular as ˈclockwork
very regularly; happening at the same time in the same way; reliable: *She arrives at work on her bicycle at 8.45 every day, as regular as clockwork.*

rein /reɪn/

give/allow sb/sth free/full ˈrein ✦ give/allow free/full ˈrein to sth
not restrict, limit or control sth: *In a novel the author need not keep to the facts, but a textbook is not the place to give free rein to your imagination.*
OPP keep a tight rein on sb/sth

NOTE
A *rein* is a long leather band that is fastened around a horse's neck and used by the rider to control the speed of the horse.

● tight → keep a tight rein on sb/sth

reinvent /ˌriːɪnˈvent/

reinvent the ˈwheel
waste time creating sth that already exists and works well: *There's no point in us reinventing the wheel. Why can't we just leave things as they are?*

relation /rɪˈleɪʃn/

● poor → a poor relation

relatively /ˈrelətɪvli/

ˈrelatively speaking
used when you are comparing sth with all similar things: *Relatively speaking, these jobs provide good salaries.*

religion /rɪˈlɪdʒən/

get reˈligion (*informal*, *often disapproving*)
suddenly become interested in religion: *He got religion while he was touring in Australia.*

remain /rɪˈmeɪn/

- **nameless** → somebody, who will/shall remain/be nameless

remember /rɪˈmembə(r)/

something to reˈmember sb by (*informal*)
a punishment, especially a physical one: *If I ever catch you stealing my apples again, I'll give you something to remember me by.*

remembered /rɪˈmembəd; rɪˈmembərd/

be reˈmembered as/for sth
be famous or known for a particular thing that you have done in the past: *He is best remembered as the man who brought jazz to Britain.* ◇ *A natural journalist, he will be remembered for his words rather than his actions.*

removed /rɪˈmuːvd/

be far/further/furthest reˈmoved from sth
be very different from sth; not be connected with sth: *Many of these books are far removed from the reality of the children's lives.*

reopen /ˌriːˈəʊpən; AmE -ˈoʊ-/

reopen old ˈwounds
remind sb of sth unpleasant that happened or existed in the past: *Look, let's try not to reopen any old wounds this time, OK?*

repair /rɪˈpeə(r); AmE -ˈper/

beyond reˈpair
impossible to repair: *The engine was damaged beyond repair.*

in good, bad, etc. reˈpair (also **in a good, bad, etc. state of reˈpair**) (*formal*)
in good, bad, etc. condition: *The house is in a terrible state of repair.* ◇ *If it were in a better state of repair, this old table would be worth a lot of money.*

reputation /ˌrepjuˈteɪʃn/

- **live¹** → live up to your/its reputation

reserve /rɪˈzɜːv; AmE rɪˈzɜːrv/

in reˈserve
available to be used in the future or when needed: *The money was being kept in reserve for their retirement.* ◇ *200 police officers were held in reserve.*

residence /ˈrezɪdəns/

in ˈresidence
having an official position in a particular place such as a college or university: *a writer/an artist/a musician in residence*

resistance /rɪˈzɪstəns/

- **line** → (choose, follow, take, etc.) the line of least resistance

résistance /reˈzɪstõs; AmE -stɑːns/

- **pièce** → your/the pièce de résistance

resort /rɪˈzɔːt; AmE rɪˈzɔːrt/

- **last** → (as) a last resort

respect /rɪˈspekt/

in reˈspect of (*formal*)
1 concerning: *Large increases can now be expected in respect of fuel prices.*
2 in payment for sth: *Please state the money you have received in respect of overtime worked.*

with (all due) reˈspect (*formal*)
used before disagreeing with sb in order to seem polite: *With all due respect, Mr Jones, I cannot agree with you.*

with respect to sth (*formal*)
(often used in business) concerning sth; with reference to sth: *With respect to your enquiry about the new pension scheme, I have pleasure in enclosing our leaflet.*

respecter /rɪˈspektə(r)/

be no respecter of ˈpersons
treat everyone in the same way, without being influenced by their importance, wealth, etc: *Though still young, she was a very confident girl. She was no respecter of persons and never thought before she spoke.*

respects /rɪˈspekts/

- **pay** → pay your respects (to sb)

rest /rest/

and the ˈrest (*spoken*)
used to say that the actual amount or number of sth is much higher than sb has stated: *'We've run up a cost of £250 …' 'And the rest, and the rest!'*

and (all) the ˈrest (of it) (*spoken*)
used at the end of a list to mean everything else that you might expect to be on the list: *After I've paid the rent, I'm left with only €40 a week to pay for food, clothes, travelling and all the rest of it.*

at ˈrest
1 (*technical*) not moving: *At rest the insect looks like a dead leaf.*
2 dead and therefore free from trouble or anxiety. People say 'at rest' to avoid saying 'dead': *She now lies at rest in the family grave.*

come to ˈrest
stop moving: *The car crashed through the barrier and came to rest in a field.* ◇ *His eyes came to rest on Clara's face.*

for the ˈrest (*BrE*, *formal*)
as far as other less important matters are concerned: *The most important thing in life is to do your duty. For the rest I care nothing.*

rhinoceros

(why don't you) give it a 'rest! (*BrE, spoken*)
used to tell sb to stop doing sth or talking about
sth because they are annoying you: *Give it a rest
will you! That's the third time you've criticized my
driving this morning.*

give sth a 'rest (*informal*)
stop doing sth for a while: *He first started his university degree some ten years ago, but gave it a rest
for a few years before starting again last year.*

I ,rest my 'case (*spoken, law*) or (*humorous*)
have no more to say about sth, especially because
you think you have proved your point: *You see
what I mean about him always arriving late? It's
nearly ten o'clock and he's not here yet. I rest my
case!*

rest as'sured (that...) (*formal*)
be completely certain or confident that...: *You can
rest assured that we will do everything we can to get
your money back.*

the rest is 'history
used when you are telling a story to say that you
do not need to tell the end of it, because everyone
knows it already: *She moved here two years ago,
met Steve last summer, and the rest is history.*

,rest on your 'laurels (*usually disapproving*)
be satisfied with the success you have already
gained and so no longer try to improve your position, etc: *I know you got a very good degree from
Oxford but what are you going to do with your life
now? You can't rest on your laurels for ever, you
know.*

> **❷ ORIGIN**
> Laurel leaves were used in Roman times to
> make a crown for the winner of a race or com-
> petition.

- **God** → God rest him/her
- **God** → God rest his/her soul
- **lay** → lay sb to rest
- **lay** → lay sth to rest
- **mind** → put/set sb's mind at ease/rest
- **wicked** → there's no peace/rest for the wicked

retreat /rɪˈtriːt/

- **beat** → beat a (hasty) retreat

retrospect /ˈretrəspekt/

in 'retrospect
thinking about a past event or situation, often
with a different opinion of it from the one you
had at the time: *In retrospect, I think that I was
wrong.* ◇ *The decision seems extremely odd, in
retrospect.*

return /rɪˈtɜːn; AmE rɪˈtɜːrn/

by re'turn (of 'post) (*BrE*)
using the next available post; as soon as possible:
Please reply by return of post.

in re'turn (for sth)
1 as a way of thanking sb or paying them for sth
they have done: *What will you give me in return for
this information?*

2 as a response or reaction to sth: *I asked her opinion, but she just asked me a question in return.*

re,turn the 'compliment
do or say the same pleasant thing that sb else has
done or said to you: *Thanks for a lovely meal. We'll
try and return the compliment very soon.*

re,turn to the 'fold (*literary*)
come back to a group or community (especially a
religious or political society): *She left the party 10
years ago but has recently returned to the fold.*

> **NOTE**
> A *fold* is a place where sheep are kept and so
> can mean a group of people who share the
> same ideas and beliefs.

- **interest** → pay sth back/return sth with interest
- **point** → (get to, reach, etc.) the point of no return

returns /rɪˈtɜːnz; AmE rɪˈtɜːrnz/

- **happy** → many happy returns (of the day)

reveal /rɪˈviːl/

- **hand** → show/reveal your hand

revelation /ˌrevəˈleɪʃn/

come as/be a reve'lation (to sb)
be a completely new or surprising experience; be
different from what was expected: *His performance in the race today was a revelation to everyone.*
◇ *My trip to Texas was a revelation.*

reverse /rɪˈvɜːs; AmE rɪˈvɜːrs/

go/put sth into re'verse
start to happen or make sth happen in the opposite way: *In the 1980s economic growth went into
reverse.*

in re'verse
in the opposite order or way; backwards: *The
secret number is my phone number in reverse.*
◇ *We did a similar trip to you, but in reverse.*

revert /rɪˈvɜːt; AmE rɪˈvɜːrt/

revert to 'type (*formal*)
return to the way you would expect sb to behave
when you remember their family, sex, work, history, etc: *The team had two very unexpected wins,
but have now reverted to type and lost the last two
games.*

reward /rɪˈwɔːd; AmE rɪˈwɔːrd/

- **virtue** → virtue is its own reward

rhinoceros /raɪˈnɒsərəs; AmE -ˈnɑːs-/

have a hide/skin like a rhi'noceros (*informal*)
be tough and not easily offended; have no fear of
criticism from others: *Say what you like about him,
he won't care; he's got a skin like a rhinoceros.*

rhyme /raɪm/

there's no ˌrhyme or 'reason to/for sth
• without ˌrhyme or 'reason
no sense or logical explanation: *There has been no rhyme or reason to market movements in recent weeks.* ◇ *Changes were being made without rhyme or reason.*

> **❷ ORIGIN**
> This phrase comes from Shakespeare's play *As You Like It*: 'But are you so much in love as your rhymes speak?' 'Neither rhyme nor reason can express how much'.

ribbons /'rɪbənz/

cut, tear, etc. sth to 'ribbons
cut, tear, etc. sth very badly: *She was so furious when she discovered her husband with another woman that she cut all his clothes to ribbons.*

rich /rɪtʃ/

(as) rich as 'Croesus (*informal*)
extremely rich **OPP** (as) poor as a church mouse

> **❷ ORIGIN**
> Croesus was a very rich king in Lydia, Asia Minor, in the sixth century BC.

that's 'rich (*spoken, especially BrE*)
used to say that a criticism sb makes is surprising and not reasonable, because they have the same fault: *Me? Lazy? That's rich, coming from you!*

• stinking → be stinking rich
• strike → strike it rich

riche /riːʃ/

• nouveau → the nouveau riche

riches /'rɪtʃɪz/

• embarrassment → an embarrassment of riches
• rags → from rags to riches

rid /rɪd/

be 'rid of sb/sth (*formal*)
be free of sb/sth that has been annoying you or that you do not want: *I was glad to be rid of the car when I finally sold it.* ◇ (*BrE*) *He was a nuisance and we're all **well rid of** him* (= we'll be much better without him).

get 'rid of sb/sth
make yourself free of sb/sth that is annoying you or that you do not want; throw sth away: *Try and get rid of your visitors before I get there.* ◇ *I can't get rid of this headache.* ◇ *We got rid of all the old furniture.*

• want → want rid of sb/sth

riddance /'rɪdns/

good 'riddance (to sb/sth)
an unkind way of saying that you are pleased that sb/sth has gone: *'Goodbye and good riddance!' she said to him angrily as he left.*

riddled /'rɪdld/

be 'riddled with sth
be full of sth, especially sth bad or unpleasant: *His body was riddled with cancer.* ◇ *Her typing was slow and riddled with mistakes.*

ride /raɪd/

be/go along for the 'ride (*informal*)
join a group of people because you are interested in what they are doing, although you do not want to take an active part in it: *Some of the group are not really interested in politics — they're just along for the ride.*

have/give sb a rough/an easy 'ride (*informal*)
to experience/not experience difficulties when you are doing sth; to make things difficult/easy for sb: *She hasn't always had an easy ride in her business life.* ◇ *The government has been given a rough ride by the popular press recently.*

let sth 'ride (*informal*)
decide to do nothing about a problem that you know you may have to deal with later: *The manager knows who is leaving work early, but he's decided to let it ride for the moment.* **OPP** nip sth in the bud

ride the 'crest of sth
enjoy great success or support because of a particular situation or event: *The band is riding the crest of its last tour.*

ride 'herd on sb/sth (*AmE, informal*)
keep watch or control over sb/sth: *Police are riding herd on crowds of youths on the streets.*

ride 'roughshod over sb/sth (*especially BrE*)
(*AmE usually* **run 'roughshod over sb/sth**)
treat sb/sb's feelings, ideas, protests, etc. with no respect at all because you do not consider them important: *The local authority rode roughshod over the protests of parents and closed down the school.*

> **NOTE**
> *Roughshod* is an old word to describe a horse that was wearing shoes with nails that stick out.

ride 'shotgun (*AmE, informal*)
ride in the front passenger seat of a car or truck: *My turn to ride shotgun today!*

> **❷ ORIGIN**
> Originally, this referred to an armed guard who travelled in the seat next to the driver.

ride a/the 'wave of sth
enjoy or be supported by the particular situation or quality mentioned: *Schools are riding a wave of renewed public interest.*

take sb for a 'ride (*informal*)
cheat or deceive sb: *If you've paid $8 000 for that car you've been taken for a ride!*

• bumpy → give sb/have a bumpy ride
• free → get, take, etc. a free ride
• storm → ride out/weather the storm (of sth)
• wishes → if wishes were horses, beggars would/might ride

ridiculous /rɪˈdɪkjələs/

● **sublime** → from the sublime to the ridiculous

riding /ˈraɪdɪŋ/

be riding for a ˈfall
behave in a way which will cause problems for you later: *He's riding for a fall if he keeps talking to the boss so rudely.*

riding ˈhigh
very successful or confident: *The company has been riding high for the last two years, but will their success continue?*

Right /raɪt/

● **Mr** → Mr Right

right /raɪt/

as of ˈright (also **by ˈright**) (*formal*)
according to the law: *The house is hers as of right but it is not clear who owns the furniture and paintings.*

be all right (by/with sb)
be convenient (for sb); be allowed: *'Yes, thank you, I will stay the night if it's all right with you.' ◇ Is it all right to park here?*

do ˈright by sb (*old-fashioned*)
treat sb fairly: *The factory will close but the company have promised to do right by the workforce and find jobs for those who want them.*

get sth ˈright/ˈstraight
understand sth clearly and correctly: *Have I got this right? You want me to jump off the bridge and onto a moving train? Never! ◇ Let's get one thing straight. I'm the boss and I tell you what to do.*

have the right iˈdea
have found a very good or successful way of living, doing sth, etc: *He's certainly got the right idea, retiring at 55.*

I'm all ˈright, Jack (*BrE, informal*)
used by or about sb who is happy with their own life and does not care about other people's problems: *He has a typical 'I'm all right, Jack' attitude — as long as he's doing well he doesn't care about anyone else.*

in your own ˈright
because of your own skills, qualifications, work, etc. and not because of other people: *She is the daughter of a world-famous actor but this prize will make her famous in her own right.*

in the ˈright
in a legally or morally correct position in a particular situation: *The problem with Kate is that she always thinks she's in the right. She will never accept that sometimes she gets things wrong.*
OPP in the wrong

(not) in your right ˈmind
(not) mentally normal: *Nobody in their right mind would buy a used car without driving it first.*

it'll be all ˌright on the ˈnight (*saying*)
used to say that a performance, an event, etc. will be successful even if the preparations for it have not gone well

it's/that's all ˈright
used as a response to sb thanking you or saying sorry for sth: *'Thank you so much for the flowers.' 'Oh, that's all right.' ◇ 'Sorry I didn't call you yesterday.' 'Oh, it's all right — I'd forgotten all about it.'*

it's ˌall right for ˈsome
used to show that you are jealous of another person's good luck: *Jane's going to Paris next week — it's all right for some, isn't it?*

make (all) the right ˈnoises (*informal*)
behave as if you support or agree with sth, usually because it is fashionable or to your advantage to do so: *The doctors are making the right noises about the reforms to the health service, but I'm not sure that they actually agree with them.*

put sth ˈright
correct sth; repair sth: *There seems to be a mistake in my hotel bill. I wonder if you could put it right, please? ◇ There's nothing seriously wrong with your television. I can put it right in ten minutes.*

put/set sb ˈright
1 tell sb the truth about sth because they have not understood or they have the wrong information: *She was telling everybody that I'd written the report so I soon put her right.*
2 make sb feel better: *These tablets should put you right.*

right you ˈare! (*BrE, informal*)
used to show that you accept a statement or an order: *'Two teas, please.' 'Right you are!'*

ˌright and ˈleft ♦ ˌleft and ˈright
everywhere: *She owes money right and left.*

(as) right as ˈrain (*informal*)
in good health or condition: *Get lots of fresh air and rest and you'll soon be feeling as right as rain again.*

right aˈway/ˈoff
immediately; without any delay: *They asked him to start right away. ◇ I told him right off what I thought of him.*

right eˈnough (*spoken*)
certainly; in a way that cannot be denied: *You heard me right enough (= so don't pretend that you did not).*

right ˈnow
1 at this moment: *He's not in the office right now.*
2 immediately: *Do it right now!*

right ˈon (*spoken*)
used to express strong approval or encouragement ► **ˌright-ˈon** *adj.* (*informal, sometimes disapproving*) having political opinions or being aware of social issues that are fashionable and left-wing: *They pretend to be so right-on, but are they really?*

,right side 'up (*AmE*)
with the top part turned to the top; in the correct, normal position: *I dropped my toast, but luckily it fell right side up.*

right a 'wrong
do sth to correct an unfair situation or sth bad that you have done: *The families have now been given back their land, in an attempt to right a wrong that was committed generations ago.*

see sb (all) 'right (*AmE* also **do sb 'right**) (*informal*)
make sure that sb is treated correctly, paid properly for sth they have done, etc: *If I die, then the company will see my wife right.*

'she'll be right (*AustralE, informal*)
used to say that everything will be all right, even if there is a problem now: *Don't worry, she'll be right, mate.* ◇ *a 'she'll be right' attitude*

too 'right/'true (*informal*)
used for showing that you completely agree with sb/sth: *Too right! This is the worst team we've had for years.*

would ,give your right 'arm for sth/to do sth (*informal*)
want sth very much: *I'd give my right arm to own a horse like that.*

- ballpark → be in the same/right ballpark
- bit → a bit of all right
- cards → play your cards right
- foot → get/start off on the right/wrong foot (with sb)
- hang → hang a left/right
- heart → your, his, etc. heart is in the right place
- left → left, right and centre
- left → right, left and centre SEE left, right and centre
- left → the left hand doesn't know what the right hand's doing
- line → right down the line SEE all along/down the line
- might → might is right
- note → hit/strike the right/wrong note
- priorities → get your priorities right/straight
- serve → serve sb right (for doing sth)
- side → be on the right/wrong side of 40, 50, etc.
- side → get/keep on the right/wrong side of sb
- things → put things right
- track → be on the right/wrong track
- two → two wrongs don't make a right

right-hand /'raɪt hænd/

your ,right-hand 'man (*informal*)
an assistant who you trust with everything: *'I'd like to introduce you to Peter Davies, my right-hand man. He'll help you when I am away.'*

rights /raɪts/

by 'rights
according to what should happen or what you would expect: *By rights I should feel sorry for shouting at her, but I don't.*

put/set sth to 'rights
correct a situation, especially one which is unfair; put things in their right places or right order: *As a young politician, she wanted to set the world to rights.* ◇ *It took me ages to put things to rights after the workmen had left.*

within your 'rights
having the moral or legal right to do sth: *They were acting perfectly within their rights when they refused to let you into their house.*

- bang → dead to rights SEE bang to rights

riled /raɪld/

be/get (all) ,riled 'up (*informal, especially AmE*)
be/get very annoyed about sth: *Instead of getting all riled up about this, we should try to figure out what to do.*

Riley /'raɪli/

- life → lead/live the life of Riley

ring /rɪŋ/

give sb a 'ring (*BrE, informal*)
make a telephone call to sb: *I'll give you a ring tomorrow.*

ring a 'bell (*informal*)
sound familiar; help you remember sth, but not completely: *That name rings a bell but I can't remember exactly where I've heard it before.*

ring the 'changes (on sth) (*BrE*)
make changes to sth in order to have greater variety: *I'm pleased to see that they're ringing the changes in the staff canteen. The new menus are much more interesting.*

> **❷ ORIGIN**
> This expression refers to bell-ringing, where the bells can be rung in different orders.

ring in your 'ears/'head
make you feel you can still hear sth: *Months later, the applause at the Berlin concert was still ringing in her ears.*

,ring off the 'hook (*AmE*)
(of a telephone) ring many times: *The phone has been ringing off the hook with offers of help.*

,ring out the ,old (year) and ,ring in the 'new
celebrate the end of one year and the start of the next one

ring 'true/'false/'hollow
seem true/false/insincere: *What you've said about Jim just doesn't ring true. Are we talking about the same person?* ◇ *His apology rings a little hollow.*

- brass → the brass ring
- curtain → bring/ring down the curtain (on sth)
- familiar → have a familiar ring (about/to it)
- hat → throw your hat into the ring

ringer /'rɪŋə(r)/

- dead → a dead ringer for sb

rings /rɪŋz/

run 'rings around/round sb/sth (*informal*)
do sth very well and so make your opponent look foolish: *I don't want to compete against her in the debate, she'll run rings around me.*

ringside /'rɪŋsaɪd/

have a ringside 'seat/'view (*informal*)
be in a very good position to see sth happen: *My flat overlooks the central square, so I had a ringside view of the demonstration.*

> **NOTE**
> At a boxing match or a circus, a *ringside seat* is one which is closest to the ring.

Riot /'raɪət/

• read[1] → read (sb) the Riot Act

riot /'raɪət/

run 'riot
get out of control: *They allow their children to run riot — it's not surprising that the house is always in such a mess.* ◇ *His imagination ran riot as he thought what he would do if he won the money.*

rip /rɪp/

let sth 'rip (*informal*)
allow a car, boat, etc. to go as fast as possible: *There's a straight road ahead. Let it rip!*

let 'rip (at sb) (with sth) (*informal*)
speak or do sth with great force, enthusiasm, etc. and without control: *He was furious. He let rip at me with a stream of abuse.* ◇ *In the last song, the singer really let rip.*

rip sb/sth a'part/to 'shreds, 'bits, etc.
destroy sth; criticize sb/sth very strongly: *Can you believe it? I spent all that time preparing my report, only to have it ripped to shreds!* **OPP** praise sb/sth to the skies

• heart → rip/tear the heart out of sth

ripe /raɪp/

at/to a 'ripe old age ♦ at/to the ripe old age of…
at/to a very old age: *My grandmother lived to a ripe old age.* ◇ *My uncle was still driving a car at the ripe old age of 89.*

• time → the time is ripe (for sb) (to do sth)

ripple /'rɪpl/

a 'ripple effect
a situation in which an event or action has an effect on sth, which then has an effect on sth else: *His resignation will have a ripple effect on the whole department.*

> **NOTE**
> A *ripple* is a small wave on the surface of a liquid, especially water in a lake, etc.

rise /raɪz/

get a 'rise out of sb
make sb react in an angry way by saying sth that you know will annoy them, especially as a joke: *Don't take any notice of him — he's just trying to get a rise out of you.* ◇ *She always got a rise out of him by copying his accent.*

give 'rise to sth (*formal*)
cause sth to happen or exist: *The novel's success gave rise to a number of sequels.*

,rise and 'shine (*old-fashioned*)
used for telling sb to get out of bed in the morning: *Rise and shine, everyone, we've got a lot to do today.*

,rise from the 'ashes
become successful or powerful again after defeat or destruction: *Can a new party rise from the ashes of the old one?*

> ❷ **ORIGIN**
> This idiom refers to the story of the phoenix, a mythological bird which burns to death and then *rises from the ashes* to be born again.

rise to the 'bait
act or react to sth in exactly the way another person wants you to: *I knew he was trying to get me angry, but I didn't rise to the bait.*

> **NOTE**
> A fisherman uses *bait* to attract fish to his hook.

rise to the oc'casion/'challenge
do sth successfully in a difficult situation, emergency, etc: *When the lead singer became ill, Cathy had to take her place. Everyone thought she rose to the occasion magnificently.* ◇ *This company must be prepared to rise to the challenge of a rapidly changing market.*

• full → draw yourself up/rise to your full height
• hackles → make sb's hackles rise
• hackles → your, his, etc. hackles rise
• lark → be up/rise with the lark
• ranks → come up/rise through the ranks

rising /'raɪzɪŋ/

a rising ,tide lifts all 'boats (*saying, especially AmE*) (*politics*)
used to say that everybody benefits when a country's economy grows and improves: *Anger over inequality is absent during periods of expansion, because a rising tide lifts all boats.*

> ❷ **ORIGIN**
> This expression is often associated with US President John F. Kennedy.

risk /rɪsk/

at 'risk (from/of sth)
in danger of sth unpleasant or harmful happening: *As with all diseases, certain groups will be more at risk than others.* ◇ *If we go to war, innocent lives will be put at risk.*

risks

at the 'risk of doing sth
used to introduce sth that may sound stupid or may offend sb: *At the risk of showing my ignorance, how exactly does the Internet work?*

at risk to yourself/sb/sth
with the possibility of harming yourself/sb/sth: *He dived in to save the child at considerable risk to his own life.*

do sth at your ,own 'risk
do sth even though you have been warned about the possible dangers and will have to take responsibility for anything bad that happens: *Persons swimming beyond this point do so at their own risk* (= on a notice). ◇ *Valuables are left at their owner's risk* (= on a notice).

risk ,life and 'limb
risk being killed or injured in order to do sth: *She risked life and limb to save her son from the fire.*

risk your 'neck (*informal*)
take a big risk by doing sth dangerous, stupid, etc: *I'm not going to risk my neck complaining about the boss.* **OPP** save sb's/your (own) neck/skin/hide

run the 'risk (of doing sth) ◆ **run 'risks**
be or put yourself in a situation in which sth bad could happen to you: *We'd better give them what they want. We don't want to run the risk of losing their business.* ◇ *Investment is all about running risks.*

take a 'risk ◆ **take 'risks**
do sth even though you know that sth bad could happen as a result: *That's a risk I'm not prepared to take.* ◇ *You have no right to take risks with other people's money.* **OPP** play (it) safe

risks /rɪsks/

- risk → run risks **SEE** run the risk (of doing sth)
- risk → take risks **SEE** take a risk

river /'rɪvə(r)/

- sell → sell sb down the river

riveted /'rɪvɪtɪd/

be ,riveted to the 'spot/'ground
be so shocked or frightened that you cannot move: *As he walked away, she wanted to run after him but she felt frozen, riveted to the spot.*

road /rəʊd; AmE roʊd/

off the 'road
(of a car) needing to be repaired and therefore impossible to use: *We'll have to go by bus. My car's off the road at the moment.*

on the 'road
1 travelling, especially for long distances or periods of time: *The band has been on the road for six months.*
2 (of a car) in good condition so that it can be legally driven: *It will cost about €700 to get the car back on the road.*
3 moving from place to place, and having no permanent home: *Life on the road can be very hard.*

on the ,road to re'covery, 'stardom, etc.
on the way to achieving sth desirable: *The operation was a success and the patient is now well on the road to recovery.* ◇ *After many years struggling to get their company started, they are now firmly on the road to success.*

on the ,road to 'ruin, di'saster, etc.
following a course of action that will lead to ruin, disaster, etc: *I don't know whether it was losing his job or the divorce that set him on the road to ruin.*

one for the 'road (*spoken*)
a last alcoholic drink before you leave a party, etc: *How about one for the road, Jim?*

a 'road hog (*informal, disapproving*)
a person who drives in a dangerous way without thinking about the safety of other road users

> **NOTE**
> If you *hog the road*, you drive so that other vehicles cannot pass.

the road to ,hell is paved with good in'tentions (*saying*)
it is not enough to intend to do good things, behave better, etc.; you must actually do them, be better, etc.

- end → the end of the road/line
- further → further along/down the road
- high → take the high road (in sth)
- hit → hit the road
- show → get the show on the road

roaring /'rɔːrɪŋ/

do a roaring 'trade (in sth) (*informal*)
sell sth very quickly or do a lot of business: *Toy stores do a roaring trade at this time of year.*

,roaring 'drunk
extremely drunk and noisy: *They came home roaring drunk again last night.* **OPP** stone-cold sober

a ,roaring suc'cess (*informal*)
a very great success: *The band was such a roaring success that they have been asked to stay for an extra week.* ◇ *His movies haven't exactly been a roaring success, have they?*

roasting /'rəʊstɪŋ; AmE 'roʊ-/

give sb/get a 'roasting (*informal*)
criticize sb or be criticized in an angry way: *I'd better go. I'll get a roasting if I'm late again!*

rob /rɒb; AmE rɑːb/

,rob sb 'blind (*informal*)
get a lot of money from sb by deceiving them or charging them too much for sth: *He robbed his clients blind, taking about 25% of their profits.*

,rob the 'cradle (*AmE, informal*)
have a sexual relationship with a much younger person: *She robbed the cradle when she married me.* ▸ **'cradle-rob** (*AmE*) (*BrE* **'cradle-snatch**) *verb*, **'cradle-robber** (*AmE*) (*BrE* **'cradle-snatcher**) *noun*: *Tim, you're such a cradle snatcher. She's like ten years younger than you!*

329 | **rolled**

rob ,Peter to pay 'Paul (*saying*)
take money from one area and spend it in
another: *Government spending on education has
not increased. Some areas have improved, but only
as a result of robbing Peter to pay Paul.*

robbery /'rɒbəri; AmE 'rɑːb-/
● daylight → daylight robbery

robin /'rɒbɪn; AmE 'rɑːb-/
● round → a round robin

Robinson /'rɒbɪnsn; AmE 'rɑːb-/
● say → before you can say Jack Robinson

rock /rɒk; AmE rɑːk/

**(caught/stuck) between a ,rock and a 'hard
place**
in a situation where you have to choose between
two things, both of which are unpleasant: *The
workers now feel that they are caught between a
rock and a hard place. They don't agree with the
new terms and conditions, but if they go on strike
they may lose their jobs altogether.*

hit/reach ,rock 'bottom ♦ be at ,rock 'bottom
reach or be at the lowest point or level that is possible: *Demand for new cars is at rock bottom. This
month's sales figures are the lowest in ten years.
◇ I really hit rock bottom after my marriage broke
up.* ► **,rock-'bottom** *adj.*: *For rock-bottom prices,
come to McArthur's Furniture Store.*

rock the 'boat (*informal*)
do sth that might upset sb/sth, cause problems or
change the balance of a situation in some way:
*Politicians who are prepared to rock the boat are
popular with newspapers but not with their parties.*

● foundations → shake/rock sth to its foundations
● foundations → shake/rock the foundations of sth
● solid → (as) solid as a rock
● steady → (as) steady as a rock

rocker /'rɒkə(r); AmE 'rɑːk-/

,off your 'rocker (*informal spoken, especially BrE*)
(of a person) crazy: *Spend a thousand pounds on a
dress! Are you off your rocker?*

rocket /'rɒkɪt; AmE 'rɑːkɪt/

give sb a 'rocket (*BrE, informal*)
criticize sb very strongly for doing sth wrong: *His
boss gave him a rocket for losing the contract.*

it's not 'rocket science
used in order to emphasize that sth is not complicated or difficult to do or understand: *Oh, I'm sure
I'll manage. It's not exactly rocket science, is it?*

**you don't have to be a 'rocket scientist (to do
sth) ♦ it doesn't take a 'rocket scientist (to do
sth)**
used to emphasize that sth is easy to understand:
*Of course this model sells more than the others — it's
the cheapest! It doesn't take a rocket scientist to
work that one out.*

rocks /rɒks; AmE rɑːks/

on the 'rocks
1 in danger of failing or being destroyed: *Their
marriage is on the rocks. ◇ The economy of this
country is on the rocks. Something must be done
before it's too late.*
2 (of drinks) served with ice but no water: *'How
would you like your whisky?' 'On the rocks, please.'*

rod /rɒd; AmE rɑːd/

make a rod for your own 'back
do sth which is likely to cause problems for yourself, especially in the future: *I think she's making a
rod for her own back by not telling him she's leaving. When he finds out, there'll be trouble.*

● beat → a rod/stick to beat sb with
● rule → rule (sb/sth) with a rod of iron/with an iron hand
● spare → spare the rod and spoil the child

rogues /rəʊgz; AmE roʊgz/

a ,rogues' 'gallery (*informal, humorous*)
a collection of photographs of criminals: *Have you
seen these photos of the new teachers? What a
rogues' gallery!*

roll /rəʊl; AmE roʊl/

be on a 'roll (*informal*)
be experiencing a period of success at what you
are doing: *Don't stop me now — I'm on a roll!*

'roll on...! (*BrE, spoken*)
used to say that you want sth to happen or arrive
soon: *Roll on the spring! I hate winter. ◇ Roll on
Friday!*

roll up your 'sleeves (*informal*)
get ready for hard work: *We've just moved into a
bigger house and there's a lot to do. I guess we'll just
have to roll up our sleeves and get on with it.*
OPP put your feet up

roll with the 'punches
adapt yourself to a difficult situation: *Well, there's
nothing we can do to change things. We'll just have
to learn to roll with the punches.*

NOTE
This idiom comes from a technique used in
boxing, where the boxer moves away from the
punch to avoid a direct hit.

● grave → roll in his, her, etc. grave SEE turn in his, her, etc. grave
● heads → heads will roll (for sth)
● ready → ready to roll
● tongue → roll/slip/trip off the tongue

rolled /rəʊld; AmE roʊld/

(all) rolled into 'one
several qualities/things combined in one place,
person, object, etc: *It's a penknife, scissors, cork-
screw all rolled into one. ◇ He's a writer, scientist
and journalist rolled into one.*

rolling /'rəʊlɪŋ; AmE 'roʊlɪŋ/

,rolling in the 'aisles (*informal*)
laughing a lot: *The comedian was very good indeed. He had the audience rolling in the aisles.*

(be) 'rolling in it/money (*informal*)
(be) very rich: *She's been the managing director of the company for 10 years, so she must be rolling in it by now.*

a rolling 'stone (gathers no 'moss) (*saying*)
a person who moves from place to place, job to job, etc. and so does not have a lot of money, possessions or friends but is free from responsibilities

● ball → get/keep/set/start the ball rolling

Rome /rəʊm; AmE roʊm/

Rome wasn't built in a 'day (*saying*)
it takes time, patience, and hard work to do a difficult or important job: *She asked me why the report wasn't finished yet so I reminded her that Rome wasn't built in a day.*

when in 'Rome (do as the 'Romans do) (*saying*)
follow the example of other people and act as they do, especially if you are a stranger or new to a place or situation: *I don't take cabs usually but it seemed to be what everyone did in the city; so I thought 'when in Rome…'*

● fiddle → fiddle while Rome burns

romp /rɒmp; AmE rɑːmp/

'romp home/to victory (*informal*)
win easily, especially in a race, an election, etc: *The Queen's horse romped home in the first race. ◇ The Democratic Party romped to victory in the recent elections.*

roof /ruːf/

go through the 'roof (*informal*)
1 become very angry: *He went through the roof when I told him I'd lost the money.*
2 (of prices, numbers) rise or increase very high very quickly: *Prices have gone through the roof since the oil crisis began.*

lift/raise the 'roof (also **bring the 'roof down**) (*informal*)
(of a large group of people) make a very loud noise, for example by shouting or singing: *The audience raised the roof when the band played their favourite song. ◇ The crowd brought the roof down when the home team scored. I had never ever heard such cheering.*

a 'roof over your head (*informal*)
a place to live; a house: *Everyone needs a roof over their heads but thousands remain homeless.*

under one/the same 'roof (*informal*)
in the same house, etc: *There were three generations of the family living under one roof.*

under your 'roof
in your home: *I don't want that woman under my roof ever again!*

● cat → like a cat on a hot tin roof SEE like a cat on hot bricks
● hit → hit the roof/ceiling

rooftops /'ruːftɒps; AmE -tɑːps/

● housetops → shout, etc. sth from the housetops/rooftops

room /ruːm; rʊm/

no room to swing a 'cat (*informal*)
(of a room) very small; not big enough: *In most modern student accommodation there's not enough room to swing a cat. ◇ I'd love a bigger kitchen. There isn't room to swing a cat in this one.*

> **❷ ORIGIN**
> *Cat* in this phrase does not mean the animal, but probably a special kind of whip (= a piece of rope or leather attached to a handle), called a 'cat-o'-nine-tails', that was used to punish sailors.

● elbow → elbow room
● elephant → the elephant in the room
● manoeuvre → freedom of/room for manoeuvre

roost /ruːst/

● chickens → (your/the) chickens come home to roost
● rule → rule the roost

root /ruːt/

get to the 'root of sth
be able to see or do sth about the main cause (of a problem, etc.): *We must get to the root of the drugs problem.* **OPP** scratch the surface (of sth)

,root and 'branch
completely; thoroughly: *The independence movement has been destroyed root and branch.*

the ,root 'cause (of sth)
the main cause of sth, such as a problem or difficult situation: *Poverty is the root cause of most of the crime in the city.*

take 'root
become firmly established: *His ideas on education never really took root; they were just too extreme.*

> **NOTE**
> If a plant *takes root* it develops roots and attaches itself to the ground.

rooted /'ruːtɪd/

● spot → glued/rooted to the spot

roots /ruːts/

put down (new) 'roots
go to live in a place and gradually become part of a local community: *We've moved around a lot because of my job and it seems to get more difficult to put down new roots each time.* **OPP** pull up stakes

● grass → the grass roots

rope /rəʊp; *AmE* roʊp/

give sb enough 'rope (and he'll/she'll 'hang himself/herself) (*saying*)
deliberately give sb enough freedom for them to make a mistake and get into trouble: *The question was vague, giving the candidate enough rope to hang herself.*

● end → be at the end of your rope SEE be at the end of your tether
● money → money for old rope

ropes /rəʊps; *AmE* roʊps/

on the 'ropes (*informal*)
very near to failure or defeat: *The company is on the ropes; unless the bank extends their loan, they're finished.*

> NOTE
> This idiom refers to a boxer that is against the ropes of a boxing ring.

show sb/learn/know the 'ropes (*informal*)
explain to sb/learn/know how to do a particular job, task, etc. correctly: *It will take me a couple of weeks to learn the ropes but after that I should be fine.* ◊ *Mrs Brian will show you the ropes.*

> ❷ ORIGIN
> This expression refers to a sailor learning the different ropes for the sails of a ship.

rose /rəʊz; *AmE* roʊz/

a 'rose by any other name (would smell as 'sweet) (*saying*)
what is important is what people or things are, not what they are called

> ❷ ORIGIN
> This phrase comes from Shakespeare's play *Romeo and Juliet.*

rose-coloured (*BrE*) (*AmE* **rose-colored**) /'rəʊz kʌləd; *AmE* 'roʊz kʌlərd/

● spectacles → look at, see, etc. sth through rose-tinted/rose-coloured spectacles

roses /'rəʊzɪz; *AmE* 'roʊz-/

be all 'roses ◆ be a bed of 'roses (also **be ˌroses, ˌroses all the 'way**) (*informal*)
be easy, comfortable or pleasant: *Being a rock star isn't all roses, you know.* ◊ *Don't expect married life to be a bed of roses, because it's not.*

everything's coming up 'roses (*informal*)
everything is happening as well as or better than you hoped: *She's had an unhappy time recently but everything seems to be coming up roses for her now.*

put the 'roses back in your cheeks (*BrE, informal*)
make you look healthier because you are not so pale: *A week in the countryside will put the roses back in your cheeks.*

● smelling → come up/out of sth smelling of roses

rose-tinted /'rəʊz tɪntɪd; *AmE* 'roʊz/

● spectacles → look at, see, etc. sth through rose-tinted/rose-coloured spectacles

rosy /'rəʊzi; *AmE* 'roʊzi/

● garden → everything in the garden is lovely/rosy

rot /rɒt; *AmE* rɑːt/

the rot sets 'in
a situation starts to get worse: *The rot really set in when the team's best player left the club last year.*

● stop → stop the rot

rotten /'rɒtn; *AmE* 'rɑːtn/

● apple → a bad/rotten apple
● spoil → spoil sb rotten

rough /rʌf/

cut up 'rough/'nasty (*informal*)
behave or react in an angry, bad-tempered or violent way: *I didn't want to ask Joe for money, but Billy had cut up rough when I couldn't pay him back.*

in 'rough (*especially BrE*)
if you write or draw sth **in rough**, you make a first version of it, not worrying too much about mistakes or details: *I've already written the essay in rough, but I need to write it out again this evening.*

live/sleep 'rough
live or sleep outside in the streets because you have no home or money: *Hundreds of people are sleeping rough on the streets of the city.*

ˌrough and 'ready
1 simple and prepared quickly but good enough for a particular situation: *I can give you a rough-and-ready estimate of the cost of the work now and a more detailed estimate later.*
2 (of a person) not very polite, educated or fashionable: *His approach was rather rough and ready, but he was very popular with his customers.*

rough and 'tumble
1 a situation in which people compete with each other and are aggressive in order to get what they want: *In the rough and tumble of politics you can't trust anyone.*
2 a noisy but not serious fight: *The toddlers often join in the rough and tumble of the older children's games.*

a ˌrough 'diamond (*BrE*) (*AmE* **a ˌdiamond in the 'rough**)
a person who has many good qualities even though they do not seem to be very polite, educated, etc: *Don't be put off by your first impressions — he's something of a rough diamond.*

> NOTE
> A *rough diamond* is a diamond that has not yet been cut or polished.

rough 'edges
small parts of sth or of a person's character that are not yet as good as they should be: *The ballet*

still had some rough edges. ◇ *He had the rough edges knocked off him at school.*

the ˌrough end of the ˈpineapple (*AustralE, informal*)
a situation in which sb is treated badly or unfairly: *The team got the rough end of the pineapple when it came to decisions by the referee.*

ˈrough it (*informal*)
live in a way that is not very comfortable for a short time: *We can sleep on the beach. I don't mind roughing it for a night or two.*

rough ˈjustice
punishment or rewards given without enough care so that people feel they have been unfairly treated: *The pensioners complained that they had received rough justice when their claim for an increase in benefits was rejected without discussion.*

take the ˌrough with the ˈsmooth
accept the unpleasant part of sth as well as the pleasant: *It certainly isn't all fun and games when you're a student, but you have to learn to take the rough with the smooth.*

● **bit** → a bit of rough
● **deal** → a raw/rough deal
● **ride** → have/give sb a rough/an easy ride

roughshod /ˈrʌfʃɒd; *AmE* -ʃɑːd/

● **ride** → run roughshod over sb/sth SEE ride roughshod over sb/sth

roulette /ruːˈlet/

● **Russian** → play Russian roulette

round /raʊnd/

in round ˈfigures/ˈnumbers
approximately, to the nearest 10, 100 or 1 000: *In round figures, how much will the work cost?*

ˌround aˈbout (*especially BrE*) (*AmE usually* **aˌround aˈbout**)
1 in the area near a place: *in Oxford and the villages round about*
2 approximately: *We're leaving around about ten.* ◇ *A new roof will cost round about £3 000.*

ˌround ˈhere (*especially BrE*) (*AmE usually* **aˌround ˈhere**)
near where you are now or where you live: *There are no decent schools round here.*

a ˌround ˈrobin
a letter of protest, etc. that has been signed by many people in such a way that no single person can be blamed or punished for sending it: *Did you sign that round robin that was sent to the manager this week?*

> **❷ ORIGIN**
> This comes from the navy. Originally it was a letter of protest in which the signatures were written in a circle so that nobody could see who had signed it first.

stand a ˈround (of drinks)
buy a drink at the same time for each of your friends in a pub, bar, etc: *It's my turn to stand a round, so what are you all having?*

roundabouts /ˈraʊndəbaʊts/

● **swings** → swings and roundabouts

rounds /raʊndz/

do the ˈrounds (of sth) (*BrE*) (*also* **make the ˈrounds** *AmE, BrE*)
1 go from place to place or from person to person: *We did the rounds of the local cafes but he wasn't in any of them.*
2 be passed from person to person: *News of her resignation soon made the rounds and it wasn't long before another company offered her work.* ◇ *This virus seems to be doing the rounds at the moment.*

route /ruːt; *AmE also* raʊt/

en ˈroute (*from French*)
on the way; while travelling from/to a particular place: *We stopped for a picnic en route.* ◇ *The bus broke down en route from Boston to New York.*

roving /ˈrəʊvɪŋ; *AmE* ˈroʊ-/

have a roving ˈeye (*old-fashioned*)
be always looking for a chance to start a new love affair or get sth that you want: *Be careful of Brian — he's got a roving eye.*

row /rəʊ; *AmE* roʊ/

in a ˈrow
(of a number of events, etc.) happening one after another; consecutively: *We've won five games in a row.*

● **ducks** → get/have (all) your ducks in a row
● **skid** → (on) skid row

rub /rʌb/

rub sb's ˈnose in it (*also* **rub it ˈin**) (*informal*)
continue reminding sb about a mistake they have made or an unpleasant truth: *She's always rubbing my nose in it. She's never forgiven me for not taking that job.* ◇ *I know I made the wrong decision, but there's no need to rub it in, is there?*

rub ˈsalt into the wound/into sb's wounds
make sb who is already feeling upset, angry, etc. about sth feel even worse: *She was already upset about not getting the job, but when they gave it to one of her own trainees it really rubbed salt into the wound.*

rub ˈshoulders (with sb) (*AmE also* **rub ˈelbows (with sb)**) (*informal*)
meet and spend time with rich or famous people, socially or as part of your job: *I used to rub shoulders with some very wealthy people when I worked in banking.*

rub sb up the wrong 'way (*BrE*) (*AmE* **rub sb the wrong 'way**) (*informal*)
make sb annoyed or angry, often without intending to, by doing or saying sth that offends them: *She's a very good lawyer but she does sometimes rub clients up the wrong way.*

there is/lies the 'rub (*formal* or *humorous*)
that is the main difficulty: *To get a job you need somewhere to live, and there's the rub — I have nowhere to live and so I can't get a job.*

> ❷ ORIGIN
> This expression comes from Shakespeare's play *Hamlet*.

● **two** → not have two brain cells, pennies, etc. to rub together

Rubicon /'ru:bɪkən; *AmE* -kɑ:n/

● **cross** → cross the Rubicon

rude /ru:d/

a rude a'wakening (*written*)
a sudden, unexpected discovery of an unpleasant fact, truth, etc: *If he thinks that the exam's going to be easy, he's going to get a rude awakening.*

ruffle /'rʌfl/

ruffle sb's/a few 'feathers (*informal*)
annoy sb by doing sth that upsets and disturbs them: *All this talk of a strike has clearly ruffled the management's feathers.* **OPP** smooth (sb's) ruffled feathers

> NOTE
> This refers to the way the wind disturbs the smooth surface of a bird's feathers so that they stick out.

ruffled /'rʌfld/

● **smooth** → smooth (sb's) ruffled feathers

rug /rʌg/

● **carpet** → sweep sth under the rug **SEE** sweep/brush sth under the carpet
● **pull** → pull the carpet/rug out from under sb's feet

ruin /'ru:ɪn/

● **rack** → go to rack and ruin

ruins /'ru:ɪnz/

in 'ruins
badly damaged or destroyed: *The city was in ruins at the end of the war.* ◇ *Their life was in ruins after the death of their only child.*

rule /ru:l/

as a (general) 'rule
usually: *It's lucky for you that I'm still awake. As a rule I'm in bed by eleven.*

make it a 'rule to do sth
always do sth because you think it is a good idea or the right thing to do: *I make it a rule to invite all my students to a party at my house once a year.*

a rule of 'thumb
a quick, practical, but not exact, way of measuring or calculating sth: *As a rule of thumb you need a litre of paint to every 12 square metres of wall.*

> ❷ ORIGIN
> This phrase may come from the fact that people often used their thumbs to estimate measurements.

rule the 'roost (*informal*)
be the person who controls a group, family, community, etc: *It is a family firm, where the owner's mother rules the roost.*

> NOTE
> A *roost* is a place where birds sleep.

rule (sb/sth) with a rod of 'iron/with an iron 'hand (*informal*)
control sb/sth in a very strong or strict way: *They ruled the country with an iron hand and anybody who protested was arrested.*

● **court** → rule/throw sth out of court
● **divide** → divide and rule
● **exception** → the exception that proves the rule
● **golden** → the golden rule
● **heart** → let your heart rule your head

rules /ru:lz/

bend/stretch the 'rules
allow sb to break the rules to some extent because you think there is a good reason: *We don't normally employ people over 50, but in your case we're prepared to bend the rules a little.*

play by sb's 'rules ◆ play by your own 'rules
if sb **plays by their own rules** or makes other people **play by their rules**, they set the conditions for doing business or having a relationship: *If we want to win this contract, we're going to have to play by their rules for a while.*

play by the 'rules
deal fairly and honestly with people: *You know how we conduct business here, and I expect you all to play by the rules in future.*

the rules of the 'game
the standards of behaviour that most people accept or that actually operate in a particular area of life or business: *It was a very competitive and aggressive business, so I had to learn the rules of the game very quickly.*

run /rʌn/

> Most idioms containing **run** are at the entries for the nouns or adjectives in the idioms, for example **run dry** is at **dry**.

give sb/get/have the 'run of sth (*informal*)
allow sb/be allowed to use freely a house, etc. that belongs to another person: *He was very kind*

and let us have the run of his house while he was at work.

on the 'run
1 (of an escaped prisoner, criminal, etc.) be running away or hiding from the police: *Four prisoners escaped this morning. Three of them were caught but one of them is still on the run.*
2 be very busy or active: *She's been on the run all day. It's not surprising she's tired.*
3 (of an enemy, opponent, etc.) in the process of being defeated: *Liverpool have got Manchester United on the run.* ◇ *The rebels are on the run now. Victory is ours.*

'run for it (*informal*)
run away from danger very quickly: *Run for it. There's a bomb in here!*

runaround /'rʌnəraʊnd/

give sb the 'runaround (*informal*)
treat sb badly by not telling them the truth, or by not giving them the help or the information they need, and sending them somewhere else: *Residents claim they were given the runaround by the local council, from whom they had no help at all.*

run-in /'rʌn ɪn/

have a 'run-in with sb (*informal*)
have an argument or disagreement with sb: *She had a run-in with her son's teacher this morning. She doesn't think he gives the children enough homework.*

runner /'rʌnə(r)/

do a 'runner (*BrE, informal*)
leave or escape from sb/a place, often after doing sth wrong: *He stole all the money in the office and did a runner.* ◇ *'What happened to his wife?' 'She did a runner. Nobody's seen her for months.'*

running /'rʌnɪŋ/

come 'running
be pleased to do what sb wants: *He expects his wife to come running every time he wants something.*

in/out of the 'running (for sth) (*informal*)
having some/no chance of succeeding or achieving sth: *She's definitely in the running for a prize.* ◇ *He's out of the running for the Paris job now.*

make the 'running (*BrE, informal*)
lead or be very active in sth, which other people must then follow or join: *In the field of electronics, it's the Japanese who are making the running.*

> NOTE
> This idiom refers to the person in a race who determines the speed of the race by running faster than the others.

a running 'battle
an argument, a dispute, etc. which continues over a long period of time: *There's been a running battle between John and his neighbour for years about their garden wall.*

> NOTE
> *Running* here means 'continuing'.

take a running 'jump (*old-fashioned, spoken*)
used to tell sb in an angry or impolite way to go away: *He asked me if I'd sell him the painting for $30, so I told him to take a running jump.*

,up and 'running
working fully and correctly: *It will be a lot easier when we have the database up and running.*

• hit → hit the ground running
• working → in running order **SEE** in (full/good) working order

run-of-the-mill /,rʌn əv ðə 'mɪl/

,run-of-the-'mill (*often disapproving*)
ordinary, with no special or interesting features: *a run-of-the-mill job*

runs /rʌnz/

• chill → a chill runs/goes down sb's spine
• shiver → a shiver runs/goes down sb's spine

rush /rʌʃ/

have a rush of blood to the 'head (*humorous*)
because of a strong emotion, suddenly (decide to) do sth foolish or dangerous: *I don't really know why I bought that vase. I just had a rush of blood to the head and wrote a cheque.*

• bum → give sb/get the bum's rush
• fools → fools rush in (where angels fear to tread)
• tearing → (be in) a tearing hurry/rush

rushed /rʌʃt/

• feet → be/get run/rushed off your feet

Russian /'rʌʃn/

play ,Russian rou'lette
take dangerous risks: *The airline was accused of playing Russian roulette with the lives of their passengers.*

> NOTE
> *Russian roulette* is a dangerous game in which a person shoots a gun at their own head. The gun only contains one bullet so the person does not know if it will fire or not.

rut /rʌt/

in a 'rut
in a fixed, rather boring way of doing things: *I suddenly realized one day that I'd been in a rut for years: same job, same flat, same friends, ...*

> NOTE
> A *rut* is a deep track that a wheel makes in soft ground and which causes wheels to get stuck.

Ss

sack /sæk/

give sb/get the 'sack (*informal*)
tell sb/be told to leave a job, usually because of sth that you have done wrong: *If you don't work harder you'll get the sack.* ◇ *She gave him the sack because he was always late.*

❷ ORIGIN
This may refer to a servant losing their job. They were given their *sack* (= bag) of belongings and told to leave the house.

● hit → hit the sack/hay

sackcloth /'sækklɒθ; AmE -klɔ:θ/

put on, wear, etc. ˌsackcloth and 'ashes
behave in a way that shows that you are sorry for sth that you have done: *Look, I've said I'm sorry! What do you want me to do — put on sackcloth and ashes?*

❷ ORIGIN
This comes from the Bible. People wore *sackcloth* (= a rough material) and put *ash* (= the grey powder left after something burns) on their face and hair to show that a person who they loved had died or that they were sorry for something they had done.

sacred /'seɪkrɪd/

nothing is 'sacred
often used by sb to complain that people do not respect traditions, ideas, values, etc. as much as they should: *For journalists these days nothing is sacred* (= they will write about anything).

a sacred 'cow (*disapproving*)
a person, belief or institution that a group of people greatly respect and never criticize: *The National Health Service is a political sacred cow. No one likes to criticize it.*

❷ ORIGIN
In the Hindu religion, cows are respected and never harmed.

saddle /'sædl/

be in the 'saddle
be in a position of responsibility and control in an organization: *It's too early to say if she is a good manager. She hasn't been in the saddle for very long.*

NOTE
In horse riding the *saddle* is the leather seat for the rider.

safe /seɪf/

play (it) 'safe
avoid danger; act safely, even if another course of action would be quicker, more successful, etc: *I know all these locks seem unnecessary but I believe it's always better to play safe.* **OPP** take a risk

ˌsafe and 'sound
safe; not hurt or harmed: *Fortunately, the police found the missing children safe and sound.*

(as) safe as 'houses (*BrE*)
very safe; not dangerous: *Investing your money with us is as safe as houses.*

a safe 'bet (*informal*)
something that is likely to be right or successful: *If you want a cheap holiday with lots of sunshine, then Spain is a safe bet.*

safe in the knowledge that...
confident because you know that sth is true or will happen: *She went out safe in the knowledge that she looked fabulous.*

to be on the 'safe side
to be careful or prepared; just in case sth unpleasant or unexpected happens: *I'll go and check that the gas is off, just to be on the safe side.* ◇ *You'd better take an umbrella, to be on the safe side.*

● better → better (to be) safe than sorry
● Fort Knox → be like/as safe as Fort Knox
● hands → in safe/good hands

safety /'seɪfti/

there's ˌsafety in 'numbers (*saying*)
it is safer for a group of people to do something which could be dangerous for one person alone: *We decided there was safety in numbers, so we asked everyone in the office to sign our letter of complaint.*

said /sed/

eˌnough 'said
used to say that you understand a situation and there is no need to say any more: *'He's a politician, remember.' 'Enough said.'*

the less/least said, the 'better (*saying*)
it is better in a difficult situation to say nothing or very little, because otherwise you might make it worse: *He's very angry and she's very upset, so don't say anything about cars or accidents. Remember, the less said, the better.*

there's something, not much, etc. to be 'said for sth/for doing sth ◆ sth has something, not much, etc. to be 'said for it
sth has a lot of advantages or good qualities: *There's a lot to be said for eating sensibly.* ◇ *There's not much to be said for this book; in fact, it's the worst book I've ever read.*

when ˌall is said and 'done
when all the facts are considered: *She doesn't have a lot of experience but, when all is said and done, she's the best person for the job.*

you 'said it! (*informal*)
I agree completely; that is very true: *'That was the most boring lecture I've ever heard.' 'You said it!'*

- **easier** → easier said than done
- **least** → least said soonest mended
- **sooner** → no sooner said than done
- **well** → well said!

sail /seɪl/

sail close to the 'wind
behave in a way that is almost illegal or socially unacceptable: *She's been late for work three times this week, which is sailing close to the wind, I think.*

sailing /'seɪlɪŋ/

- **plain** → be clear sailing SEE be (all) plain sailing

sails /seɪlz/

- **trim** → trim your sails
- **wind¹** → take the wind out of sb's sails

saint /seɪnt/

- **patience** → the patience of a saint/of Job

sais /seɪ/

,je ne sais 'quoi /ˌʒə nə seɪ 'kwɑː/ (*from French, often humorous*)
a good quality that is difficult to describe: *He has that je ne sais quoi that distinguishes a professional from an amateur.* ◇ *It has a certain je ne sais quoi that really appeals to me.*

> **NOTE**
> The meaning of the French phrase is 'I do not know what'.

sake /seɪk/

for God's, heaven's, pity's, etc. 'sake
used to emphasize that it is important to do sth; used to show that you are annoyed about sth: *For God's sake try and control yourself!* ◇ *Do be careful, for goodness' sake.* ◇ *Oh, for heaven's sake!*
(Some people find the use of **God** here offensive.)

for its 'own sake
because you are interested in it, and not because you could gain an advantage from doing it: *I'm not learning Arabic for any special reason; I'm doing it for its own sake, because I enjoy it.*

for the sake of sb/sth ♦ for sb's/sth's sake
in order to help sb/sth or because you like sb/sth: *They stayed together for the sake of the children.* ◇ *You can do it. Please, for my sake.* ◇ *I hope you're right, for all our sakes* (= because this is important for all of us).

for the sake of 'argument
as a starting point for a discussion; to discuss things in theory only: *For the sake of argument, let's say that prices continue to rise by 20 per cent a year.*

- **old** → for old times' sake
- **Pete** → for Pete's sake

salad /'sæləd/

your 'salad days (*old-fashioned*)
the time when you are young and do not have much experience of life: *Back in my salad days my friends and I used to go dancing every Saturday night.*

> **❷ ORIGIN**
> This comes from Shakespeare's play *Antony and Cleopatra*.

sale /seɪl/

for 'sale
available to be bought, especially from the owner: *I'm sorry, it's not for sale.* ◇ *They've put their house up for sale.*

on 'sale
1 available to be bought, especially in a shop/store: *Tickets are on sale from the booking office.* ◇ *The new model goes on sale next month.*
2 (*especially AmE*) being offered at a reduced price: *All video equipment is on sale today and tomorrow.*

salt /sɔːlt; BrE also sɒlt/

the salt of the 'earth
a very good and honest person that you can always depend on: *Tim's the salt of the earth — he'd do anything he can for you.* **OPP** the scum of the earth

> **❷ ORIGIN**
> This expression comes from the Bible.

- **pinch** → take sth with a pinch of salt
- **rub** → rub salt into the wound/into sb's wounds
- **worth** → worth your/its salt

salts /sɔːlts; BrE also sɒlts/

- **dose** → like a dose of salts

Sam /sæm/

- **Uncle** → Uncle Sam

Samaritan /səˈmærɪtən/

a ,good Sa'maritan
a person who gives help and sympathy to people who need it: *He stole money from an old woman while pretending to be a good Samaritan and help carry her shopping.*

> **❷ ORIGIN**
> This comes from a story told by Jesus in the Bible.

same /seɪm/

> Idioms containing **same** are at the entries for the nouns and verbs in the idioms, for example **be in the same boat** is at **boat**.

,all/just the 'same
in spite of this; nevertheless: *I don't want a lift, but thanks all the same.* ◇ *'You don't need a raincoat!*

The weather's fine!' 'All the same, I think I'll take one; you never know.'

(the) ˌsame aˈgain (*spoken*)
used to ask sb to serve you the same drink as before: *Same again, please!*

ˌsame ˈhere (*spoken*)
used to say that the same is also true of you: *'I thought it was a terrible movie.' 'Same here.'*

(the) ˌsame to ˈyou
used to reply to a greeting, an insult, etc: *'Have a good weekend.' 'And the same to you.'* ◇ *'Get lost!' 'Same to you!'*

sand /sænd/

● draw → draw a line in the sand
● head → bury/hide your head in the sand

sands /sændz/

● shifting → (the) shifting sands (of sth)

sandwiches /ˈsænwɪtʃɪz; -wɪdʒ-/

● bricks → a few, two, etc. sandwiches short of a picnic **SEE** a few, two, etc. bricks short of a load

sardines /ˌsɑːˈdiːnz; AmE ˌsɑːrˈd-/

● packed → packed (together) like sardines

satisfaction /ˌsætɪsˈfækʃn/

to sb's satisˈfaction
1 if you do sth **to sb's satisfaction**, they are pleased with it: *The affair was settled to the complete satisfaction of the client.*
2 if you prove sth **to sb's satisfaction**, they believe or accept it: *Can you demonstrate to our satisfaction that your story is true?*

saturation /ˌsætʃəˈreɪʃn/

satuˈration point
so full that you cannot add any more: *The refugee camps have reached saturation point.*

sauce /sɔːs/

what's ˌsauce for the ˌgoose is ˌsauce for the ˈgander (*old-fashioned, saying*)
if one partner in a marriage or relationship can behave in a particular way, then the other partner should also be allowed to behave in this way: *If she can go out with her friends, why can't I? What's sauce for the goose is sauce for the gander.*

> **NOTE**
> A *gander* is a male goose.

sausage /ˈsɒsɪdʒ; AmE ˈsɔːs-/

not a ˈsausage (*old-fashioned, informal*)
nothing at all: *There's nothing in here at all. Not a sausage!*

save /seɪv/

can't do sth to ˌsave your ˈlife (*informal*)
cannot do sth at all or can only do sth very badly: *He can't cook to save his life.*

save sb's ˈbacon (*informal*)
rescue sb from a difficult or dangerous situation: *Thank you for helping me with my exam preparation. You really saved my bacon.* **OPP** throw sb to the wolves/lions

save your ˈbreath (*spoken*)
do not waste your time speaking to sb because they will not listen to your comments, advice, suggestions, etc: *Save your breath. He never listens to anybody.*

> **❓ ORIGIN**
> This phrase comes from a longer saying: 'save your breath to cool your porridge'.

save the ˈday/situˈation
do sth that changes probable failure into success: *Jones saved the day for England with a last-minute goal.*

save (sb's) ˈface
do sth in order to keep the respect of other people: *The announcement was an attempt by the government to save face.* **OPP** lose face
▶ **ˈface-saving** *adj.*: *face-saving measures*

save sb's/your (own) ˈneck/ˈskin/ˈhide (*informal*)
save sb or yourself from a dangerous or unpleasant situation: *Don't rely on him for help, he's only interested in saving his own skin.* **OPP** risk your neck

● blushes → save/spare sb's blushes

saved /seɪvd/

ˌsaved by the ˈbell
saved from a difficult, embarrassing, etc. situation at the last moment: *Saved by the bell! He was just asking me why my report was two weeks late when you came in.*

> **NOTE**
> This expression refers to the bell that marks the end of a round in a boxing match.

saving /ˈseɪvɪŋ/

a ˌsaving ˈgrace
a quality which prevents sb/sth from being completely bad: *She can be difficult at times. Her saving grace is her sense of humour.*

savoir /ˈsævwɑː(r)/

savoir ˈfaire (*from French, approving*)
the ability to behave in the appropriate way in certain situations: *He was renowned throughout the diplomatic world for his savoir faire.*

> **NOTE**
> The meaning of the French phrase is 'know how to do'.

say /seɪ/

as they 'say (also **as the saying 'goes**)
often used before or after a saying or an idiom: *We can kill two birds with one stone, as they say.* ◇ *He was, as the saying goes, as mad as a hatter.*

before you can say Jack 'Robinson
(*old-fashioned*)
very quickly or suddenly: *I'll do that for you. I'll have it finished before you can say Jack Robinson.*

have your 'say (*informal*)
give your opinion about sth: *You've had your say, now let me have mine.*

have something, nothing, etc. to 'say for yourself
1 be able/unable to explain your actions: *I've asked him what he was doing here in the middle of the night, but he's got nothing to say for himself.*
2 be able/unable to hold a conversation or express your opinions: *She seems very nice but she doesn't have much to say for herself.*

I 'must say (*spoken*)
used to emphasize an opinion: *Well, I must say, that's the funniest thing I've heard all week.*

I ˌwouldn't say 'no (to sth) (*spoken*)
used to say that you would like sth or to accept sth that is offered: *I wouldn't say no to a pizza.* ◇ *'Tea, Brian?' 'I wouldn't say no.'*

let us say…
used when making a suggestion or giving an example: *I can let you have it for, well let's say £100.*

ˌnever say 'die (*saying*)
do not stop trying or hoping for sth: *Never say die, buddy. I've been in worse situations than this.* ◇ *Billy was an enthusiastic player with the never-say-die attitude that supporters love to see.*

'not to say
used to suggest that you could, with good reason, use a stronger word to describe sb/sth: *He is very difficult, not to say impossible, to understand.*

say 'cheese!
used to ask sb to smile before you take their photograph: *Is everybody ready? Right, say cheese!*

ˌsay no 'more (*spoken*)
it is not necessary for sb to continue speaking because you already understand the situation: *'He's only 21, and he's marrying a rich old lady of 65.' 'Say no more!'*

say your 'piece (*informal*)
say exactly what you feel or think: *I went to see the boss this morning and I said my piece about our working conditions. He wasn't very happy about it.*

say 'what? (*AmE, spoken*)
used to express surprise at what sb has just said: *'He's getting married.' 'Say what?'*

say 'when
used to ask sb to tell you when you should stop pouring a drink or serving food for them because they have enough

(just) say the 'word
used to show that you are willing and ready to do something as soon as sb asks: *If you need any help, just say the word.*

that is to 'say
in other words: *We'll meet again three days from now, that is to say on Friday.*

to ˌsay the (very) 'least
used to say that you are using the least strong way of saying sth: *I'm not very happy with his work, to say the least.*

to say 'nothing of sth
and also; not forgetting: *She is an expert in Chinese, to say nothing of speaking several European languages.*

ˌwhat would/do you 'say (to sth/doing sth)?
(*spoken*)
would you like sth/to do sth?: *What would you say to a weekend in Paris?* ◇ *Let's eat out tonight. What do you say?*

whatever you 'say (*spoken*)
used to agree to sb's suggestion because you do not want to argue: *'Just do it now!' 'Whatever you say.'*

who can 'say (…)? (*spoken*)
used to say that nobody knows the answer to a question: *Who can say what will happen next year?*

who's to 'say (…)? (*spoken*)
used to say that sth might happen or might have happened in a particular way, because nobody really knows: *Who's to say we wouldn't have succeeded if we'd had more time?*

he, she, etc. wouldn't say ˌboo to a 'goose
(*informal*)
sb is very shy and afraid of upsetting or annoying people: *How could he ever succeed in politics? He wouldn't say boo to a goose.*

> **NOTE**
> People shout *Boo!* when they want to surprise or frighten somebody.

you can say 'that again! (*spoken*)
I agree completely; I know that already: *'She's the most boring person I've ever met.' 'You can say that again!'*

you can't say 'fairer (than 'that) (*BrE, spoken*)
used to say that you think the offer you are making is reasonable or generous: *Look, I'll give you £100 for it. You can't say fairer than that.*

you don't 'say! (*spoken, often ironic*)
used to express surprise: *'My brother's an astronaut, you know.' 'You don't say!'* ◇ *'I was in the Scouts for six years.' 'You don't say.'* (= I'm not interested/surprised).

- **dare** → I dare say
- **dicky** → not say/hear a dicky bird
- **goodbye** → kiss/say goodbye to sth
- **mean** → mean to say
- **needless** → needless to say

- **sorry** → I'm sorry to say
- **suffice** → suffice (it) to say (that)…
- **uncle** → cry/say uncle
- **word** → not/never have a good word to say for/about sb/ sth

saying /'seɪɪŋ/

it ˌgoes without 'saying (that…) ♦ **that ˌgoes without 'saying**
it is obvious, already known or natural (that…): *Of course I'll visit you in hospital. It goes without saying!* ◊ *'You realize that this is a very responsible job, don't you?' 'Yes, that goes without saying.'*

it's/that's not 'saying much, etc.
used to show that what you have just said is not particularly remarkable or impressive: *She's a better player than me, but that's not saying much* (= because I'm a very bad player).

- **knowing** → there's no knowing/saying/telling…
- **mind** → if you don't mind me/my saying so…
- **say** → as the saying goes **SEE** as they say

says /sez/

(it) does (eˌxactly) what it says on the 'tin (*informal, saying*)
used to say that sth is as good or effective as it claims to be, or that it really does what it claims to do. This expression is especially used when you are comparing publicity and advertisements with actual products: *I paid £150 for this camera and am more than happy with it. It does exactly what it says on the tin!*

it, etc. says a 'lot, 'much, etc. about/for sb/sth (that…)
something reveals a lot, etc. about sb's/sth's qualities, personality, etc: *It says much about the high quality of these instruments that many of them are still in use today.* ◊ *The kind of car you drive says a great deal about you.*

what/whatever sb says, 'goes (*informal, often humorous*)
when a particular person in authority gives an order, this order must be obeyed: *Sarah wanted the kitchen painted green, and whatever she says, goes.* ◊ *Don't argue with me. I'm the boss here and what I say goes.*

who 'says (…)? (*spoken*)
used to disagree with a statement or an opinion: *Who says I can't do it?*

say-so /'seɪ səʊ; AmE soʊ/

on sb's 'say-so
based on a statement that sb makes without giving any proof: *He hired and fired people on his partner's say-so.*

scales /skeɪlz/

the ˌscales fall from sb's 'eyes (*literary*)
sb finally understands the truth about sth: *It wasn't until much later that the scales fell from his eyes and he realized that she'd been lying to him.*

---

❷ ORIGIN
In the Bible, this expression describes the moment when St Paul suddenly began to believe in Jesus and was able to see again.

- **tip** → tip the balance/scales
- **tip** → tip the scales at sth

scarce /skeəs; AmE skers/

ˌmake yourself 'scarce (*informal*)
leave the place you are in in order to avoid an embarrassing or difficult situation: *I could see they wanted to be alone, so I made myself scarce.*

- **hen** → (as) rare/scarce as hen's teeth

scare /skeə(r); AmE sker/

scare the 'shit out of sb ♦ **scare sb 'shitless** (⚠, *slang*)
frighten sb very much: *You scared the shit out of me, creeping around in the dark like that!*

- **daylights** → beat/scare the (living) daylights out of sb
- **life** → frighten/scare the life out of sb
- **wits** → frighten/scare sb out of their wits

scared /skeəd; AmE skerd/

- **shadow** → be frightened/nervous/scared of your own shadow
- **witless** → be scared/bored witless

scene /siːn/

arrive/come on the 'scene
arrive in/at a place, probably to change the existing situation: *John and I were really happy together until she came on the scene.* ◊ *By the time the police arrived on the scene, it was too late.*

create/make a 'scene
complain noisily, behave badly, etc. especially in a public place: *Please don't create a scene in public.*

(not) sb's 'scene (*informal*)
(not) the kind of place, activity, etc. that sb likes or feels comfortable with: *The resort wasn't really our scene. Most of the people were much older than us and there wasn't any nightlife.* ◊ *I don't like going to clubs. A quiet evening with friends is much more my scene.*

set the 'scene/'stage (for sth)
1 give sb the information they need in order to understand what comes next: *The first few chapters of the book just set the scene.*
2 create the conditions in which sth can easily happen: *His arrival set the scene for another argument.* ◊ *With so many economic and political problems, the stage was set for another war.*

scenes /siːnz/

behind the 'scenes
(of discussions, arrangements, etc.) not seen by the public: *The general public knows very little about what happens behind the scenes in politics.* ◊ *There was a lot of behind-the-scenes activity at the peace conference.*

NOTE
This expression refers to the parts of the stage
in a theatre which the audience cannot see.

scent /sent/

be on the 'scent (of sb/sth)
have information that will lead you to sb/sth: *The
police are on the scent of the criminals.*

put/throw sb off the 'scent
give sb false information to prevent them from
finding out or knowing sth: *I threw the police off
the scent by pretending I was in Mexico City on the
day of the crime.*

NOTE
Animals such as dogs follow the *scent* (= smell)
of other animals, especially when hunting.

scheme /skiːm/

the/sb's 'scheme of things
the way the world and other things are or seem to
be organized: *Low-paid workers like us don't have a
very important place in the scheme of things.*
◇ *Don't worry too much about your exam results;
they're not really important in the great scheme of
things.*

school /skuːl/

a school of 'thought
theories or opinions held by particular groups of
people: *There are two schools of thought on this
matter.*

* old → of the old school
* old → the old school tie
* tell → tell tales out of school

schtum (also shtum) /ʃtʊm/

keep 'schtum/'shtum (*BrE, informal*)
say nothing: *I think we'd better keep schtum about
this money, don't you?* OPP open your (big) mouth

❓ ORIGIN
Shtum is a Yiddish word from the German
stumm, meaning 'silent'.

science /ˈsaɪəns/

have/get sth down to a 'science (*especially
AmE, often humorous*)
have a very precise and efficient way of doing sth,
especially sth that is normally done in a casual or
informal way: *When Tom says he has shopping
down to a science, he isn't kidding.*

* blind → blind sb with science
* rocket → it's not rocket science

scientist /ˈsaɪəntɪst/

* rocket → it doesn't take a rocket scientist (to do sth)
* rocket → you don't have to be a rocket scientist (to
  do sth)

Fred has cake making down to a science.

score /skɔː(r)/

on 'that/'this score
as far as that/this is concerned: *The accommodation is excellent so I don't think we need to worry on
that score.*

‚score a 'point/'points (off/over/against sb)
(*especially BrE*)
defeat sb in an argument; deliberately say sth that
makes sb appear stupid: *Why don't you try to solve
the problem instead of scoring points over each
other?* ◇ *I don't like David. He's always trying to
score points off everybody.* ▶ **'point-scoring** *noun*:
political point-scoring

* even → even the score
* know → know the score
* settle → settle a score/an account (with sb)
* settle → settle an old score

scorn /skɔːn; AmE skɔːrn/

heap/pour 'scorn on sb/sth
speak about sb/sth in a way that shows that you
do not respect them or have a good opinion of
them: *She poured scorn on his plans to get rich
quickly.*

scot-free /ˌskɒt ˈfriː; AmE ˌskɑːt/

get off/go ‚scot-'free (*informal*)
escape from a situation without receiving the punishment you deserve: *It seemed so unfair that she
was punished while the others got off scot-free!*

❓ ORIGIN
This idiom comes from the old English word
sceot, meaning a 'tax'. People were *scot-free* if
they didn't have to pay the tax.

scrap /skræp/

on the 'scrap heap (*informal*)
no longer wanted or considered useful: *With the
closure of the factory, thousands of workers have
been thrown on the scrap heap.*

scrape /skreɪp/

scrape (up) an ac'quaintance with sb
(*informal*)
try to become friends with sb because they might
be useful to you

scrape (the bottom of) the 'barrel
(*disapproving*)
use things or people of a low quality because all
the good ones have already been used: *TV is terrible at the moment, it's nothing but old movies.
They're really scraping the barrel, aren't they?*

• bow¹ → bow and scrape

scratch /skrætʃ/

do sth from 'scratch
do sth from the beginning, not using any work
done earlier: *The fire destroyed all the plans. Now
we'll have to start again from scratch.*

scratch ,A and you'll find 'B
(used to speak about particular types of people in
general) carefully consider or examine sb/sth and
you will find that they are different from their outside appearance: *Scratch a senator from Texas and
you'll find a cowboy.*

scratch your 'head (over sth)
think hard in order to find an answer to sth: *We're
all scratching our heads for a solution to this
problem.*

scratch the 'surface (of sth)
deal with, understand, or find out about only a
small part of a subject or problem: *This report only
scratches the surface of the problem.* **OPP** get to the
bottom of sth

up to 'scratch
at the good standard that is expected or needed:
*The level of safety in our power stations must be
brought up to scratch. ◇ If he doesn't come up to
scratch, get rid of him.*

> **❷ ORIGIN**
> This expression comes from boxing: the line in
> the ring which the boxers have to come to
> when they start to fight is called the *scratch*.

,you scratch 'my back and ,I'll scratch 'yours
(*saying*)
used to say that if sb helps you, you will help
them, even if this is unfair to others ▶ **'back-
scratching** *noun*: *There is too much back-scratch-
ing in local politics in this town.*

scream /skriːm/

scream blue 'murder (*BrE*) (*AmE* **scream
bloody 'murder**) (*informal*)
shout, scream, etc. very loudly and for a long
time; make a lot of noise or fuss because you disagree very strongly with sth: *Jill will scream blue
murder if Ann gets promoted and she doesn't.*

screen /skriːn/

• silver → the silver screen
• small → the small screen

screw /skruː/

have a 'screw loose
be slightly crazy: *He dresses his cats up in little
coats for the winter. Sometimes I think he must have
a screw loose.* **OPP** have your head screwed on (the right
way)

screw 'him, 'you, 'that, etc. (△, *slang*)
an offensive way of showing that you are annoyed
or do not care about sb/sth

a ,turn of the 'screw
another problem or difficulty added to a situation
which is already very bad: *In this recession a rise in
interest rates is just another turn of the screw for
businesses.*

> **❷ ORIGIN**
> This idiom refers to a method of torturing
> people. *Thumbscrews* were used to crush
> people's thumbs, and turning them tightened
> them.

• courage → pluck/screw/summon up (your/the) courage
(to do sth)

screwed /skruːd/

• head → have your head screwed on (the right way)

screws /skruːz/

put the 'screws on (sb) (*informal*)
force sb to do sth, especially by frightening and
threatening them: *The electricity company is really
putting the screws on. We've got a week to pay
before our supply is cut off!*

> **NOTE**
> This idiom refers to *thumbscrews* (see note
> above at *a turn of the screw*).

scrounge /skraʊndʒ/

be/go on the 'scrounge (for sth) (*BrE*, *informal*,
disapproving)
ask sb for money, food, etc. without doing any
work for it or paying for it: *She's always on the
scrounge for cigarettes. Why doesn't she buy her
own?*

scruff /skrʌf/

by the scruff of sb's/the 'neck
(hold sb or an animal) by the back of the neck:
*The barman took her by the scruff of the neck and
threw her out.*

scum /skʌm/

the ,scum of the 'earth (*informal*)
a person or a group of people thought to be
worthless, evil or completely without good qualities: *Drug dealers are the scum of the earth.*
OPP the salt of the earth

> **NOTE**
> *Scum* is a layer of dirt on the surface of water.

sea /siː/

all, completely, etc. at 'sea
confused; not organized: *We're still completely at sea trying to understand the new regulations.*

● devil → between the devil and the deep blue sea
● fish → there are plenty/lots more fish in the sea

seal /siːl/

a ˌseal of apˈproval
the formal support or approval of a person or an organization: *Our project has the director's seal of approval.*

set the 'seal on sth (*formal*)
be the highest or best thing to happen in a successful career, project, etc: *His Nobel prize set the seal on a brilliant career in physics.*

sealed /siːld/

● lips → my lips are sealed
● signed → signed, sealed and delivered

seams /siːmz/

be bursting/bulging at the 'seams (with sth)
(also **be full to 'bursting (with sth)**) (*informal*)
be very or too full (of sth): *All of our schools are bursting at the seams; we have to build new ones urgently.*

● apart → come/fall apart at the seams
● fray → fray at/around the edges/seams

seamy /ˈsiːmi/

the 'seamy side (of life, etc.)
the unpleasant, dishonest or immoral aspects (of life, etc.): *It's well known that the world of entertainment has its seamy side: drug abuse, corruption, alcoholism…*

search /sɜːtʃ; AmE sɜːrtʃ/

search your 'heart/'soul/'conscience (*formal*)
think carefully about your feelings or your reasons for doing sth: *If I searched my heart I'd probably find that I don't always tell the truth.*
▶ **'heart-searching, 'soul-searching** *nouns*: *His divorce forced him to do a lot of soul-searching.*

ˌsearch 'me (*spoken*)
I don't know; I've no idea: *'What's the capital of Queensland?' 'Search me!'*

seas /siːz/

● high → on the high seas

season /ˈsiːzn/

ˌin/ˌout of 'season
1 (of fruit, vegetables, fish, etc.) available/not available in shops/stores because it is the right/wrong time of year for them: *Peaches are in season at the moment.*
2 at the time of year when many/few people go on holiday/vacation: *Hotels are much cheaper out of season.*

3 during the time of year when you can/cannot hunt animals: *You can't shoot ducks out of season.*

(the) season's 'greetings (*written*)
used as a greeting at Christmas, especially on Christmas cards

● silly → the silly season

seat /siːt/

(fly) by the seat of your 'pants
act without careful thought and without making a plan in advance, hoping that you will be lucky and successful: *He made careful plans and then found that everything had changed at the last minute, so in the end he had to fly by the seat of his pants.*

> **❓ ORIGIN**
> This idiom was first used by pilots to describe flying by using the way the plane felt as a guide to its condition. The *seat of your pants* is the part of your trousers/pants that you sit on.

take a back 'seat
change to a less important role or function: *After forty years in the business, it's time for me to take a back seat and let someone younger take over.* **OPP** in the driving seat

● box → in the box seat
● catbird → in the catbird seat
● driving → in the driver's seat **SEE** in the driving seat
● edge → on the edge of your seat/chair
● hot → in the hot seat
● ringside → have a ringside seat/view

seats /siːts/

● bums → bums on seats

second /ˈsekənd/

be second 'nature (to sb)
be sth that you do automatically, without thinking about it, because you have done it for so long or so often: *It took a while to learn to drive, but now it's second nature (to me).*

be second only to sb/sth
be in a position where only one person or thing is better, more important, etc: *As a pianist, he was second only to Rubinstein.*

get your second 'wind (*informal*)
find energy, strength or enthusiasm after feeling tired or after a period when you produce little: *After midnight the dancers seemed to get their second wind and went on till dawn.*

> **NOTE**
> This expression comes from running; after feeling out of breath at the beginning of a race, you later find it easier to breathe.

have second 'thoughts
change your opinion about sth; have doubts about sth: *We were going to go to Italy, but we had second thoughts and came here instead.*

seeing

on 'second thoughts (BrE) (AmE on 'second thought)
used when you want to change what you have said or decided: *On second thoughts, I won't have water, I'll have a cup of tea.*

play second 'fiddle
have a lower or less important position than another person: *She wants to be the boss, not play second fiddle to somebody else.* **OPP** call the shots/the tune

> **NOTE**
> *Fiddle* is an informal word for 'violin'.

,second 'best
not as good as the best; not exactly what you want: *The two teams seemed evenly matched, but Arsenal came off second best* (= did not win). ◇ *Sometimes you have to settle for* (= be content with) *second best.*

a/your second 'childhood
a period in life, especially in old age, when you sometimes act like a child, forget things, etc: *I have to feed her and dress her. She's really in her second childhood.*

,second 'sight
the special ability to know what will happen in the future or what is happening somewhere else: *Sometimes I think I've got second sight because my dreams seem to come true.*

second to 'none
very good; as good as the best: *This airline's safety record is second to none.*

without a second 'thought
immediately; without stopping to think about sth further: *He dived in after her without a second thought.*

- **bite** → a second/another bite at/of the cherry
- **just** → just a minute/moment/second
- **minute** → not for a/one minute/moment/second/instant
- **split** → a split second
- **wait** → wait a minute/moment/second

secrecy /'si:krəsi/
- **swear** → swear sb to secrecy

secret /'si:krət/
- **open** → an open secret
- **top** → top secret
- **trade** → a trade secret

see /si:/

> Most idioms containing **see** are at the entries for the nouns or adjectives in the idioms, for example **see stars** is at **stars**.

be glad, etc. to see the 'back of sb/sth
(*informal, especially BrE*)
be happy that you will not have to deal with or see sb/sth again because you do not like them/it: *Was I pleased to see the back of her!* ◇ *This year's been awful, I'll be glad to see the back of it.*

see a lot, nothing, etc. of sb
often, never, etc. see sb socially: *'Do you see much of Jennifer these days?' 'No, but I see a great deal of her sister.'*

see sb/sth for what they 'are/it 'is
realize that sb/sth is not as good, pleasant, etc. as they seem/it seems: *I used to really like him, but now I can see him for what he really is — selfish and arrogant!*

,see for your'self
see or experience sth yourself so that you will believe it is true: *Don't you believe she's here? Well, come in and see for yourself.*

'see to it (that...)
make certain (that): *I want you to see to it that she never comes in here again.* ◇ *This report must be sent to Head Office immediately. Would you see to it for me?*

'see you (a'round) ♦ ,see you 'later (also (I'll) be 'seeing you) (*spoken*)
used to say goodbye to sb who you expect to see again soon

so I 'see!
used to say that sb does not need to tell you about the present situation because it is obvious, especially when you are not happy about it: *'I'm afraid I'm a bit late this morning.' 'So I see.'*

you 'see (*spoken*)
used when you are explaining sth: *You see, the thing is, we won't be finished before Friday.*

seed /si:d/

go/run to 'seed (*informal*)
(of a person) become untidy or dirty because you no longer care about your appearance, etc: *I was very surprised when I saw her. She has really run to seed in the last few months.*

> **❷ ORIGIN**
> This idiom refers to the fact that when the flower in a plant dies, seeds are produced.

seeds /si:dz/

plant/sow the 'seeds of sth
start a process which will develop into sth large, important, etc: *What first planted the seeds of doubt in your mind?* ◇ *The seeds of conflict were sown when oil was discovered on the border between the two countries.*

seeing /'si:ɪŋ/

seeing as/that...
because; considering that; since: *Seeing as we're both going the same way, can I give you a lift?*

,seeing is be'lieving (*saying*)
if you see sth, you can be sure that it is true or that it really exists: *He might be telling the truth, but seeing is believing, I always say.*

- **see** → (I'll) be seeing you **SEE** see you (around)

seek /siːk/

seek your 'fortune (*literary*)
try to find a way to become rich, especially by going to another place: *At the age of twenty, he decided to emigrate and seek his fortune in Canada.*
▶ **'fortune seeker** *noun*

seen /siːn/

● **better** → have seen/known better days
● **dead** → sb wouldn't be seen/caught dead...
● **found** → nowhere to be found/seen

self /self/

● **former** → be a shadow/ghost of your/its former self

sell /sel/

sell sb down the 'river (*informal*)
act very unfairly to sb who trusts you; betray sb you have promised to help: *The workers thought that their own leaders had sold them down the river.*

> ❷ ORIGIN
> This idiom comes from the days of slavery in the US. A slave who was sold to an owner further down the Mississippi river would experience worse conditions than in the states further north.

sell sb 'short
cheat sb by giving them less than they have paid for: *He sold us short! We paid for five kilos of mushrooms and only got four!*

sell your 'soul (*informal, often humorous*)
do something morally or legally wrong in order to get sth that you want very much: *He'd sell his soul to get that job.*

> NOTE
> This expression refers to selling your soul to the devil in exchange for power, money, etc.

sell yourself/sb/sth 'short
describe yourself/sb/sth as being less good, valuable, etc. than you, etc. really are: *Don't sell yourself short when you go for an interview.* ◇ *It was a great idea, but you sold it short.*

● **hot** → sell/go like hot cakes
● **pup** → sell sb/buy a pup

sell-by /'sel baɪ/

● **past** → be past its sell-by date

seller /'selə(r)/

a ˌseller's 'market
a situation in which people selling sth have an advantage, because there is not a lot of a particular item for sale, and prices can be kept high: *We just can't afford to buy a house at the moment. It's a seller's market, and there's nothing we can do about it.* **OPP** a buyer's market

send /send/

send sb 'packing (*informal*)
tell sb firmly or rudely to go away because they are annoying or disturbing you; dismiss sb from a job: *He wanted to borrow money off me, but I sent him packing.* ◇ *They caught him stealing company property and he was sent packing.*

send sb to 'Coventry (*BrE*)
refuse to speak to sb, as a way of punishing them for sth they have done: *Joe worked all through the strike, so when it was over, the other workers sent him to Coventry.*

> ❷ ORIGIN
> This may come from the English Civil War when the city of Coventry was a strong supporter of Parliament. Supporters of the King who were taken prisoner were sometimes sent there.

● **chill** → send a chill up/down sb's spine **SEE** a chill runs/goes down sb's spine
● **grass** → put/turn/send sb out to grass
● **love** → give/send my love to sb
● **shiver** → send a shiver up/down sb's spine **SEE** a shiver runs/goes down sb's spine
● **wall** → drive/send sb up the wall

sends /sendz/

● **hours** → work all the hours God sends

sense /sens/

in 'no sense
not in any way: *In no sense do I agree with this suggestion.*

in a 'sense ♦ in 'one sense
considered in one way, rather than in other ways: *In a sense we are all responsible for the problem of starvation in the world.*

knock/talk some 'sense into sb (*informal*)
try to persuade sb to stop behaving in a stupid way, sometimes using rough or violent methods: *I wish somebody would knock some sense into our politicians.* ◇ *Try and talk some sense into her before she makes the wrong decision.*

make 'sense
1 have a meaning that you can easily understand: *This sentence doesn't make sense — there's no verb in it.*
2 be a sensible or practical thing to do: *It makes sense to buy a house now because prices will certainly go up soon.*
3 be easy to understand or explain: *John wasn't making much sense on the phone.*

make 'sense of sth
understand sth that is difficult or not very clear: *I don't understand these instructions. Can you make any sense of them?*

(make sb) see 'sense/'reason
(make sb) begin to act and think more reasonably than before: *Ah, you've given up smoking! I'm glad you've seen sense at last.* ◇ *It's time somebody made him see reason.*

a sense of oc'casion
a feeling or an understanding that an event is important or special: *Candles on the table gave the evening a sense of occasion.*

● money → have more money than sense
● sixth → a sixth sense

senses /'sensɪz/

come to your 'senses
1 (also **bring sb to their 'senses**) stop behaving in an unreasonable or stupid way; do sth to stop sb behaving in this way: *At last he has come to his senses. He now understands that a restaurant in this part of town will never succeed.*
2 wake up from being unconscious: *When I came to my senses I found myself in a hospital bed.*

take ˌleave of your 'senses (*informal, humorous*)
behave as if you are mad: *You want €25 000 for it? Have you taken leave of your senses?* ◇ *I think my aunt has taken leave of her senses. She wants to make a will leaving all her money to a dogs' home.*

sent /sent/

● things → these things are sent to try us

separate /'seprət/

go your separate 'ways
(of two or more people) stop seeing each other socially, because you are living in different places, doing different jobs, etc: *After school we went our separate ways.*

● men → sort out/separate the men from the boys
● sheep → sort out/separate the sheep from the goats
● wheat → sort out/separate the wheat from the chaff

sequitur /'sekwɪtə(r)/

a ˌnon 'sequitur (*from Latin, formal*)
a statement that does not seem to follow what has just been said in any natural or logical way: *In the middle of a discussion about the weather, Liz started talking about fish. Everyone ignored the non sequitur completely.*

> **NOTE**
> The Latin phrase means 'it does not follow'.

seriously /'sɪəriəsli; AmE 'sɪr-/

take sb/sth 'seriously
consider or treat sth as important or serious: *We told him he was in danger but he didn't take us seriously.*

seriousness /'sɪəriəsnəs; AmE 'sɪr-/

in all 'seriousness
seriously; not jokingly: *Surely you're not telling me, in all seriousness, that you want to work in a factory for the rest of your life!* **OPP** (with) tongue in cheek

serve /sɜːv; AmE sɜːrv/

serve a, his, its, etc. 'purpose ◆ serve the 'purpose (of doing sth) (*BrE* also **serve his, its, etc. 'turn**)
be useful for a particular purpose or period of time; be good or useful enough for sb: *It's not a very good radio, but it serves its purpose.* ◇ *He used his friends and then abandoned them when they had served their turn.*

serve sb 'right (for doing sth) (*informal*)
used to say that sth that has happened to sb is their own fault and they deserve it: *After the way you've treated her, it will serve you right if she never speaks to you again!* ◇ *I told you the dog would bite if you teased it. It serves you right.*

serve two 'masters
(usually used in negative sentences) support two opposing parties, principles, etc. at the same time: *Government ministers are not allowed to work for private companies as nobody can serve two masters at once.*

> **❓ ORIGIN**
> This expression comes from the Bible.

● time → do/serve time

served /sɜːvd; AmE sɜːrvd/

● first → first come, first served

serves /sɜːvz; AmE sɜːrvz/

● memory → if memory serves
● memory → if my memory serves me well, correctly, etc.

service /'sɜːvɪs; AmE 'sɜːrv-/

be at sb's 'service (*formal*)
be ready to help sb: *If you need to know anything else, I'm at your service.*

be of 'service (to sb) (*formal*)
be helpful (to sb): *If I can be of service, please let me know.*

do sb a/no 'service (*formal*)
do sth that is helpful/not helpful to sb: *She was doing herself no service by remaining silent.*

see 'service
1 be in the army, navy or air force: *He saw service in Korea and later in Vietnam.*
2 be used: *This new type of engine won't see service until next year.*

● press → press sb/sth into service
● skeleton → a skeleton crew/staff/service

sesame /'sesəmi/

● open → open sesame

set /set/

> Most idioms containing **set** are at the entries for the nouns or adjectives in the idioms, for example **set the pace** is at **pace**.

be, look, etc. (all) 'set (for sth/to do sth)
be ready or prepared to do sth: *They were all set to go out when the phone rang.* ◇ *The team looks set for another easy win.*

be (,dead) 'set against sth/against doing sth
be strongly opposed to sth: *I've tried to persuade him to move house, but he's dead set against it.* ◇ *She's not very well, but she's set against going to the doctor.*

be (,dead) 'set on sth/on doing sth
want to do or have sth very much; be determined to do or have sth: *She's dead set on leaving her job and emigrating to Canada.*

sets /sets/

● rot → the rot sets in

settle /'setl/

settle a 'score/an ac'count (with sb) ◆ **settle an old 'score**
hurt or punish sb who has harmed or cheated you in the past; get revenge: *I've got a score to settle with him after the terrible things he said about my girlfriend.* ◇ *Before he left the school, he wanted to settle an old score with one of his classmates.*
OPP call it quits

● dust → let the dust settle
● dust → wait for the dust to settle **SEE** let the dust settle

settles /'setlz/

● dust → after/when the dust settles

seven /'sevn/

the seven year 'itch (*informal*)
the wish for a new sexual partner because you are bored with your husband or wife: *He's started looking at all the women in the office. It must be the seven year itch.*

sevens /'sevnz/

● sixes → be at sixes and sevens

seventh /'sevnθ/

be in (your) seventh 'heaven
be extremely happy: *When she has all her grandchildren around her, she's in seventh heaven.*

> ℗ ORIGIN
> This comes from the belief that there are seven heavens and that God and the most important angels live in the highest or seventh heaven.

sex /seks/

● opposite → the opposite sex

shade /ʃeɪd/

put sb/sth in the 'shade (*informal*)
be much better or more successful than sb/sth: *The new player really puts the rest of the team in the shade.* **OPP** cannot hold a candle to sb/sth

shadow /'ʃædəʊ; AmE -doʊ/

be frightened/nervous/scared of your own 'shadow
be very easily frightened; be very nervous: *Since the attack he's been a changed man. He's nervous of his own shadow and doesn't like to go out alone at night.*

beyond/without a ,shadow of (a) 'doubt
◆ **there isn't a ,shadow of a 'doubt (that…)**
there is no doubt at all (that…); absolutely certainly: *He's innocent beyond a shadow of a doubt.* ◇ *There isn't a shadow of doubt in my mind about the safety of the system.*

in/under the 'shadow of
1 very close to: *The new market is in the shadow of the City Hall.*
2 when you say that sb is **in/under the shadow of** another person, you mean that they do not receive as much attention as that person: *Most of her childhood had been spent in the shadow of her elder sister.*

● former → be a shadow/ghost of your/its former self

shaft /ʃɑːft; AmE ʃæft/

give sb the 'shaft (*AmE, informal*)
treat sb unfairly: *It seems to me that the big corporations are keeping all the money for themselves and giving the shaft to ordinary consumers, as usual.*

shaggy-dog /,ʃægi 'dɒg; AmE -'dɔːg/

a ,shaggy-'dog story (*informal*)
a long, complicated story or joke, which has no proper ending and is not very funny: *He told us this joke, which turned out to be a shaggy-dog story, and I hate those!*

> ℗ ORIGIN
> This expression comes from the subject of one particular story of this kind, a dog with long, untidy (*shaggy*) hair.

shake /ʃeɪk/

more … than you can shake a 'stick at
(*informal*)
used to emphasize the large number of sth: *This music magazine has more reviews than you can shake a stick at.*

shake your 'fist (at sb)
hold up your fist (= your closed hand) at sb because you are angry or because you want to threaten them: *He got out of the car, shaking his fist in anger at the driver in the car behind.*

shake 'hands (with sb) ◆ **shake sb's 'hand**
◆ **shake sb by the 'hand**
take hold of sb's hand and move it up and down as a greeting or to show that you agree about sth: *The television pictures of the two presidents shaking hands were shown all over the world.*

shake your 'head
move your head from side to side as a way of saying 'no', or to show sadness, disagreement, disap-

proval, etc: *She didn't say anything — she just shook her head and sighed.*

shake a 'leg (*old-fashioned, informal*)
used to tell sb to start to do sth or to hurry: *Come on, shake a leg or we'll be late!*

shake like a 'jelly/'leaf (*informal*)
shake with fear; be very afraid or nervous: *Before I went into the exam room I was shaking like a leaf.*

shake (hands) on it/on sth
shake hands with sb to show that you have made an agreement, a deal, etc: *'OK, I'll let the car go for $5 000.' 'Do you want to shake on it?' ◇ Let's shake on it.*

• **fair** → a fair shake
• **foundations** → shake/rock sth to its foundations
• **foundations** → shake/rock the foundations of sth

shakers /'ʃeɪkəz; AmE 'ʃeɪkərz/

• **movers** → movers and shakers

shakes /ʃeɪks/

• **great** → be no great shakes
• **two** → in a couple of shakes SEE in two shakes
• **two** → in two shakes of a lamb's tail SEE in two shakes

shaking /'ʃeɪkɪŋ/

• **quaking** → (be) quaking/shaking in your boots/shoes

shame /ʃeɪm/

put sb/sth to 'shame
be much better than sb/sth: *This new stereo puts our old one to shame.*

'shame on you, him, etc. (*spoken*)
an exclamation said to sb who has behaved badly or done sth they should be ashamed of: *You forgot your mother's birthday? Shame on you!*

• **crying** → be a crying shame

Shanks /ʃæŋks/

(on) Shanks's 'pony (*BrE, informal*)
walking, rather than travelling by car, bus, etc.; on foot: *'How are we going to get there?' 'I suppose it'll have to be Shanks's pony.' ◇ You young people go everywhere by car these days. When I was young all we had was Shanks's pony.*

> **NOTE**
> *Shanks* is an informal word for your legs.

shape /ʃeɪp/

be in (good, bad, etc.) 'shape
1 (of a person) be in good, bad, etc. health or physical condition: *He's in good shape for a man of his age. ◇ She goes to the gym three times a week to stay in shape.*
2 (of a thing) be well, badly, etc. organized or in good, bad, etc. condition: *The economy's in very bad shape and is likely to get worse.*

be out of 'shape
1 not having the normal shape: *The wheel had been twisted out of shape.*
2 (of a person) not be in good physical condition: *I hadn't been training for months and was really out of shape.*

be the ,shape of ,things to 'come (also **be a ,taste of ,things to 'come**)
be a sign or an example of how things are likely to be in the future: *These new computers are the shape of things to come. ◇ Telephones with television screens: could this be a taste of things to come?*

get (yourself) (back) into 'shape
take exercise, etc. to become fit and healthy (again): *After she had the baby, she started swimming every day, to get back into shape.*

get/knock/lick sb/sth into 'shape
make sb/sth more acceptable or organized; improve sb/sth: *Do you think you can lick this company into shape?*

give 'shape to sth (*formal*)
express or explain a particular idea, plan, etc.

in any (way,) shape or 'form (*informal*)
of any kind: *I don't approve of violence in any shape or form.*

in the shape/form of sb/sth
follows a general word and introduces a particular example of it: *There was entertainment on the ship, in the form of a disco and a cinema. ◇ Help arrived in the shape of a policeman.*

'shape up or ship 'out (*AmE, informal*)
used to tell sb that if they do not improve, work harder, etc. they will have to leave their job, position, etc: *Two players have been told by the manager to shape up or ship out.*

take 'shape
develop to a point where you can see what sth will finally be like: *After months of discussion, a peace agreement is gradually taking shape. ◇ An idea for a new book started to take shape in his mind.*

• **bent** → get bent out of shape (about/over sth)

shapes /ʃeɪps/

come in all ,shapes and 'sizes
be of many different forms or types: *Pasta comes in all shapes and sizes. ◇ The containers come in all shapes and sizes.*

share /ʃeə(r); AmE ʃer/

share and share a'like (*saying*)
share things equally: *Children must learn to share and share alike.*

• **cake** → a piece/share/slice of the pie SEE a share/slice of the cake
• **fair** → (more than) your fair share of sth
• **lion** → the lion's share (of sth)

shared /ʃeəd; AmE ʃerd/

• **trouble** → a trouble shared is a trouble halved

shark /ʃɑːk; AmE ʃɑːrk/

• jump → jump the shark

sharp /ʃɑːp; AmE ʃɑːrp/

have a sharp 'tongue (*informal*)
(of a person) often speak in an unkind or unpleasant way: *You've got to be careful of her, she's got a sharp tongue.* ▸ **sharp-'tongued** *adj.*: *a sharp-tongued old man*

(as) sharp as a 'tack (*AmE*)
intelligent with a quick and lively mind: *My grandmother's 85 but she's still sharp as tack.*

> **NOTE**
> A tack is a kind of small nail or pin.

the 'sharp end (of sth) (*BrE, informal*)
the job or activity of greatest difficulty or responsibility: *He started work **at the sharp end** of business, as a salesman.* ◇ *As head of the school, I'm at the sharp end if there are complaints.*

sharp 'practice
clever but dishonest methods of business, etc: *There's a lot of sharp practice in the second-hand car business.*

• lively → look lively/sharp

sharpest /'ʃɑːpɪst; AmE 'ʃɑːrpɪst/

not the sharpest knife in the 'drawer (also **not the sharpest tool in the 'box**) (*humorous*)
not intelligent: *I know he's good-looking, but he's not exactly the sharpest knife in the drawer, is he?*
OPP a/one smart cookie

shatter /'ʃætə(r)/

• hopes → dash/shatter sb's hopes

shave /ʃeɪv/

• close² → a close shave/call

shebang /ʃɪ'bæŋ/

the ˌwhole she'bang (*informal*)
the whole thing; everything: *It's not just a computer we need. We're going to have to get a printer, a scanner, a CD-writer, the whole shebang.*

shed /ʃed/

• light → cast/shed/throw (new) light on sth

sheep /ʃiːp/

like 'sheep (*disapproving*)
if people behave **like sheep**, they all do what the others are doing, without thinking or deciding for themselves: *If John says that something must be done, they do it. They just follow his orders like sheep.*

sort out/separate the ˌsheep from the 'goats
separate the good people from the bad people: *The exams at the end of the first year usually separate the sheep from the goats.*

> **ⓘ ORIGIN**
> This comes from the belief that on Judgement Day (= the day the world ends) God will judge everybody who ever lived and decide who was good (= the sheep) and who was bad (= the goats).

• black → a/the black sheep (of the family)
• count → count sheep
• well → (you, etc.) may/might as well be hanged/hung for a sheep as (for) a lamb
• wolf → a wolf in sheep's clothing

sheet /ʃiːt/

• clean → a clean sheet/slate
• sing → sing from the same song/hymn sheet
• white → (as) white as a sheet/ghost

sheets /ʃiːts/

• three → (be) three sheets to the wind

shelf /ʃelf/

buy, get, etc. sth off the 'shelf
buy, etc. sth which is not made especially for sb, and is found in an ordinary shop/store: *Did they buy the computer system off the shelf or was it designed specially for them?*

on the 'shelf (*informal*)
1 (especially of women) not married and unlikely to marry because you are no longer young: *Some women used to think they were on the shelf if they weren't married at 30.*
2 not wanted by anyone; not used: *Unemployed people often feel they've been left on the shelf.*

Angie's biggest fear was ending up on the shelf.

shell /ʃel/

come out of your 'shell ◆ **bring sb out of their 'shell** (*informal*)
become less shy and more confident when talking to other people: *When Anna first joined the club, it took her a long time to come out of her shell.*

go, retreat, withdraw, etc. into your 'shell
become more shy and avoid talking to other people: *If you ask him about his family, he goes into his shell.*

Sherlock /ˈʃɜːlɒk; *AmE* ˈʃɜːrlɑːk/

• shit → No shit, Sherlock! **SEE** No shit!

shift /ʃɪft/

shift your 'ground (*usually disapproving*)
change your opinion or position, especially during an argument or a discussion: *He's shifted his ground on many major policy issues.* **OPP** stand fast/firm

shifting /ˈʃɪftɪŋ/

(the) ,shifting 'sands (of sth)
used to describe a situation that changes so often that it is difficult to understand or deal with it: *the shifting sands of the digital age*

shine /ʃaɪn/

take the 'shine off sth (*informal*)
make sth seem much less good than it did at first: *Allegations of cheating have taken the shine off the successful exam results.*

take a 'shine to sb/sth (*informal*)
begin to like sb/sth as soon as you see/meet them/it: *I think you'll get the job — they seemed to take quite a shine to you.*

• rain → come rain, come shine
• rain → (come) rain or shine
• rise → rise and shine

shines /ʃaɪnz/

• hay → make hay while the sun shines
• think → think the sun shines out of sb's arse/backside
• think → think the sun shines out of sb's ass **SEE** think the sun shines out of sb's arse/backside

shingle /ˈʃɪŋɡl/

• hang → hang out/up your shingle

shining /ˈʃaɪnɪŋ/

be a shining e'xample (of sb/sth) (also **be a shining 'light**)
be a very good example of sb/sth, which other people can follow or copy: *Their friends think Phillip and Joan are a shining example of a happily married couple.* ◇ *His books on grammar are a shining light in a very difficult and confused field.*

• knight → a knight in shining armour

ship /ʃɪp/

when your 'ship/'boat comes in (*informal*)
when you are suddenly successful or have a lot of money: *Perhaps, when our ship comes in, we'll both be able to leave our jobs.*

• jump → jump ship
• shape → shape up or ship out

• sinking → (like rats) deserting/leaving a sinking ship
• spoil → spoil the ship for a ha'porth/ha'penny-worth of tar
• tight → run a tight ship

ships /ʃɪps/

be (like) ,ships that ,pass in the 'night (*informal*)
(of people) meet for a short time, by chance, and perhaps for the only time in your lives: *We met on a course in Spain and had a wonderful time together. But we both knew that we were just ships that pass in the night.*

> **❷ ORIGIN**
> This is from a poem by Longfellow: 'Ships that pass in the night, and speak each other in passing,...'.

shirt /ʃɜːt; *AmE* ʃɜːrt/

lose your 'shirt (*informal*)
lose all or a lot of your money and possessions: *'How did you two get on at the races?' 'I won $300 and Paul lost his shirt.'* **OPP** make a killing

put your 'shirt on sth (*BrE, informal*)
bet a lot or all of your money in a horse race, etc.; invest all your money in sth: *I've put my shirt on Diamond Lady in the 10.15.* ◇ *He put his shirt on the future of the company.*

the ,shirt off sb's 'back
anything that sb has, including the things they really need themselves, that sb else takes from them or they are willing to give: *He's the type of person who would give the shirt off his back if he thought it would help.*

• hair → keep your shirt on **SEE** keep your hair on
• stuffed → a stuffed shirt

shirtsleeves /ˈʃɜːtsliːvz; *AmE* ˈʃɜːrt-/

in (your) 'shirtsleeves
wearing a shirt without a jacket, etc. on top of it: *Even though it was the middle of winter, it was so hot in the office that we were all in our shirtsleeves.*

shit /ʃɪt/

be in the 'shit ✦ be in ,deep 'shit (△, *slang*)
be in a lot of trouble: *I'll be in the shit if I don't get this work finished today.* ◇ *You're in deep shit now.*

like 'shit (△, *slang*)
very bad, ill/sick etc.; really badly: *I woke up feeling like shit.* ◇ *We get treated like shit in this job.*

No 'shit! (△, *slang*)
1 used to show that you are surprised, impressed, etc. or to show that what you are saying is true: *'That guy's my brother.' 'No shit! Really?'*
2 (also **No shit, Sherlock!**) used when you think sb has said sth that is obvious or that you already know: *'If it rains we'll all get wet.' 'No shit, Sherlock!'*

> **NOTE**
> *Sherlock* in this expression refers to Sherlock Holmes, the fictional detective.

not give a 'shit (about sb/sth) (△, slang)
not care at all about sb/sth: *I don't give a shit what Marie thinks. I'll do what I want!*

shit all over sb/sth (△ slang, especially AmE)
treat sb/sth very badly: *We're supposed to be helping them and they shit all over us every chance they get.*

shit 'happens (△, slang)
used to express the idea that we must accept that bad things often happen without reason: *'We were all really sorry to hear about you and Rachel.' 'Yeah, well, shit happens.'*

(when) the ,shit hits the 'fan (△, slang)
(when) sb in authority finds out about sth bad or wrong that sb has done: *When the committee finds out what actually happened, the shit will really hit the fan.*

- act → get/have your act together **SEE** get your act together
- creek → up shit creek (without a paddle) **SEE** up the creek
- crock → a crock of shit
- full → be full of shit/crap
- hell → beat/knock/kick the shit out of sb/sth **SEE** beat/knock/kick the hell out of sb/sth
- luck → tough shit **SEE** tough/bad luck (2)
- scare → scare the shit out of sb
- shoot → shoot the bull/shit **SEE** shoot the breeze
- thick → (as) thick as shit **SEE** (as) thick as two short planks

shithouse /ˈʃɪthaʊs/
- built → be built like a brick shithouse **SEE** be built like a tank

shitless /ˈʃɪtləs/
- scare → scare sb shitless

shiver /ˈʃɪvə(r)/
a 'shiver runs/goes down sb's spine ◆ send a 'shiver up/down sb's spine
feel, or make sb feel, excitement or anxiety: *This piece of music sends shivers down my spine.* ◇ *When I heard all those people shouting and screaming, a shiver ran down my spine.*

shivers /ˈʃɪvəz; AmE ˈʃɪvərz/
give sb/get the 'shivers (*informal*)
make sb feel fear and horror: *That old portrait gives me the shivers.* ◇ *I get the shivers every time I hear his name.*

shock /ʃɒk; AmE ʃɑːk/
,shock 'horror (*BrE, informal, often humorous*)
used when you pretend to be shocked by sth that is not really very serious or surprising: *Shock horror! You're actually on time for once!*

shoe /ʃuː/
- boot → the shoe is on the other foot **SEE** the boot is on the other foot
- cap → if the shoe fits (wear it) **SEE** if the cap fits (wear it)

shoes /ʃuːz/
be in sb's shoes (*informal*)
be in sb's position: *I'd leave that job immediately if I were in his shoes.*

put yourself in sb's shoes/place
consider what you would do or feel if you were in the position of sb else: *Put yourself in his shoes! If your mother had just died, how would you feel?*

- fill → fill sb's boots/shoes
- quaking → (be) quaking/shaking in your boots/shoes
- step → step into sb's shoes

shoestring /ˈʃuːstrɪŋ/
(do sth) on a 'shoestring (*informal*)
(do sth) with very little money: *In the early years, the business was run on a shoestring.*

shoo-in /ˈʃuː ɪn/
be a 'shoo-in (*AmE, informal*)
be a person or team that will win easily or will definitely be chosen for sth: *He's a shoo-in for governor.* ◇ *She was a shoo-in to win the award.*

shoot /ʃuːt/
shoot your 'bolt (*informal*)
make a final attempt to do something, especially if this attempt comes too early to be successful: *In an argument it's important not to shoot your bolt too soon. Keep one or two good points for the end.*

> ❷ ORIGIN
> In this idiom, *bolt* refers to an arrow that was shot from a crossbow.

shoot the 'breeze (also shoot the 'bull/'shit △)
(both *AmE, informal*)
talk in a friendly, informal way; chat: *We sat around in the bar, shooting the breeze.*

shoot sb/sth 'down (in 'flames) (*informal*)
be very critical of sb's ideas, opinions, suggestions, etc: *I thought it was a brilliant idea, but she shot it down in flames.*

,shoot from the 'hip
react quickly without thinking carefully first: *As a manager, he was sometimes accused of shooting from the hip, but he was always popular with his colleagues.*

> NOTE
> This refers to firing a shot from a handgun immediately after taking it from your belt, without taking proper aim.

shoot 'hoops (*AmE, informal*)
play basketball: *Hey Joe! Do you want to shoot some hoops?*

,shoot it 'out (with sb) (*informal*)
fight against sb with guns, especially until one side is killed or defeated: *The gang decided to shoot it out with the police.* ▸ 'shoot-out *noun*: *The movie ended with a shoot-out, which of course the hero won.*

shoot the 'lights (*informal*)
go through red traffic lights: *In this city people shoot the lights all the time.*

shoot the 'messenger
blame the person who gives the news that sth bad has happened, instead of the person who is really responsible: *'You look awesome! But..."But what?' 'Well, don't shoot the messenger here but those pants make you look a little... large.'*

shoot your 'mouth off (about sth)
1 talk publicly or carelessly about things which should be secret: *This is a secret. Please don't shoot your mouth off to everyone about it.*
2 talk loudly and with too much pride about sth: *Mark is always shooting his mouth off about all the money he earns.* **OPP** watch your mouth/tongue

shoot yourself in the 'foot (*informal*)
do or say sth stupid which is against your own interests: *You'd better prepare your argument carefully — you don't want to shoot yourself in the foot.*

● bird → flip/give/shoot sb the bird

shooting /ˈʃuːtɪŋ/

the ,whole 'shooting match (*BrE, informal*)
everything, or a situation which includes everything: *The whole shooting match is being computerized, which should significantly reduce delays.*

● candy → be like shooting fish in a barrel **SEE** be like taking candy from a baby

shop /ʃɒp; AmE ʃɑːp/

all 'over the shop (*AmE also* **all 'over the lot**)
(*informal*)
everywhere: *I've been looking for you all over the shop. Where have you been?* ◇ *Since you explained idioms to me, I keep seeing them all over the shop.*

,set up 'shop (*especially BrE*)
start a business (in a particular place): *He worked as a writer for several years, then set up shop as a small publisher.* ◇ *The young lawyer set up shop in a new office in the centre of town.* **OPP** shut up shop

● bull → like a bull in a china shop
● closed → a closed shop
● kid → like a kid in a candy store/shop
● mind → mind the shop
● shut → shut up shop
● talk → talk shop

shops /ʃɒps; AmE ʃɑːps/

● hit → hit the shops/stores

short /ʃɔːt; AmE ʃɔːrt/

at (very) short 'notice (*also* **at a moment's 'notice**)
with very little warning; without much time to prepare: *In this job you have to be able to work weekends at short notice.*

be caught/taken 'short (*BrE, informal*)
suddenly need to go to the toilet in a place where it is difficult to find one

be in ,short sup'ply
not be enough of sth; be scarce: *During the war, many things were in short supply.*

be on/have a short 'fuse (*informal*)
be likely to get angry easily, because you are tired, stressed, etc: *Your father's having trouble at work, so his temper's on a short fuse today.* ◇ *Be careful what you say to the director. She has a very short fuse.*

> **NOTE**
> A *fuse* is a piece of string or paper which is lit to make a bomb explode.

be ,short and 'sweet (*informal*)
last for a short time, but still be good or pleasant; be good because it is short: *The patient is very tired, so make your visit short and sweet.* ◇ *The chairman promised to make the introduction short and sweet.*

be/run short of sth
not have enough of sth; only have a small amount of sth left: *We're running short of butter. Can you get some more today?* ◇ *I'm a bit short of money at the moment.* **OPP** be well off for sth

bring/pull sb up 'short
make sb stop what they are doing because sth attracts their attention or because they suddenly realize sth: *His criticism of my work pulled me up short, because I thought he was pleased with it.*

come 'short (*South African, informal*)
have an accident; get into trouble: *Kim broke her collarbone and Lisa and a couple others also came short.* ◇ *We've seen a lot of IT companies come short through aggressive expansion.*

cut sb 'short
stop sb speaking: *She was just about to say who had got the job, but I cut her short and asked her to keep it secret.*

cut sth 'short
make sth end before the natural time; interrupt sth: *We'll have to cut our stay short, I'm afraid. My husband's father is seriously ill.* ◇ *Our conversation was cut short by the arrival of the teacher.*

fall 'short of sth
fail to reach the standard that you expected or need: *Your performance at work has fallen short of what is required in this company.*

for 'short
as a shorter way of saying sth: *Her name's Joanna, but her friends call her 'Jo' for short.*

get/have sb by the short 'hairs (*also* **get/have sb by the short and 'curlies**) (*informal*)
get/have sb in a position where they must agree to what you want: *We can't go on strike because the boss will simply hire new staff. He's got us by the short and curlies.*

> **NOTE**
> *Short and curlies* refers to the hairs on a person's body.

give sb/sth short 'shrift ◆ get short 'shrift
give sb/sth/get little attention or sympathy: *Mrs Jones gave my suggestion very short shrift. I was*

quite surprised. ◇ *When Ann complained about the toilets, she got very short shrift.*

> **❷ ORIGIN**
> *Shrift* was the act of confessing your crimes, etc. to a priest and being forgiven. If a person was *given short shrift* they were only allowed a short time to do this between being found guilty and being executed or punished.

go 'short (of sth)
not have as much of sth as you need: *Give the boy some money. I don't want him to go short.*

in 'short
in a few words; briefly: *This picture has been badly damaged, and besides, it's not signed: in short, it's worthless.*

in ˌshort 'order
quickly and without trouble: *A decision will have to be made in short order if the new system is to be in place by September.*

in the 'short run
concerning the immediate future: *In the short run, unemployment may fall.* **OPP** in the long run

little/nothing short of 'sth
used when you are saying that sth is almost true, or is equal to sth: *Last year's figures were little short of disastrous.* ◇ *The transformation has been nothing short of a miracle.*

make short 'work of sth/sb
do or finish sth very quickly; defeat sb very easily: *The children certainly made short work of the chocolate biscuits!* ◇ *The champion made very short work of the challenger in the title fight.*

a short back and 'sides (*BrE*)
a conventional haircut for men where the hair is cut very short around the ears and above the neck

a ˌshort 'cut (to sth)
1 a shorter way to go to a place: *I usually take a short cut behind the post office to get to college.*
2 a way of doing sth more quickly or easily: *Producing good cheese takes time — there are really no short cuts.*

short of sth/of doing sth
without sth or without doing sth; unless sth happens: *Short of a miracle, we're certain to lose.* ◇ *Short of asking her to leave* (= and we don't want to do that), *there's not a lot we can do about the situation.*

win, lose, etc. by a short 'head
win, lose, etc. but by only a little: *The competition was tough but the winner by a short head was John Smith.*

> **❷ ORIGIN**
> This expression refers to a close finish in horse racing.

- **bricks** → a few bricks short of a load
- **bricks** → a few, two, etc. sandwiches short of a picnic **SEE** a few, two, etc. bricks short of a load
- **draw** → draw the short straw
- **draw** → get the short end of the stick **SEE** draw the short straw

- **long** → the long and (the) short of it
- **long** → to make a long story short **SEE** to cut a long story short
- **measure** → full/short measure
- **sell** → sell sb short
- **sell** → sell yourself/sb/sth short
- **stop** → stop short
- **term** → in the long/medium/short term
- **thick** → (as) thick as two short planks

shot /ʃɒt; *AmE* ʃɑːt/

be (all) 'shot (to 'pieces) (*informal*)
be destroyed or in very bad condition: *All my dreams were shot to pieces when I heard the news.* ◇ *This engine's totally shot. I'll have to get a new one.*

be/get 'shot of sb/sth (*BrE, informal*)
get rid of sb/sth that you do not want/like or which has given you trouble: *It's time we got shot of this car — it's falling apart.*

have/take a 'shot (at sth/at doing sth) (also **give sth a 'shot**) (*informal*)
try to do sth: *We all had a shot at solving the riddle.* ◇ *I don't know if I'll be any good at editing the newsletter, but I'll give it a shot.*

(do sth) like a 'shot (*informal*)
(do sth) immediately or quickly, without hesitating: *I'd be off like a shot if he offered me a job abroad.* ◇ *If she wanted him, he'd go back to her like a shot.*

(fire) a (warning) shot across sb's 'bows
do sth to warn an enemy, a competitor, etc. that you will take further action against them if necessary: *The President's speech on Friday was a shot across the bows of the banks. If they don't change their policies, he will change the law.*

> **❷ ORIGIN**
> This expression refers to encounters between ships of hostile nations. One ship might fire a shot at another, not in order to hit it, but to warn it to move.

a shot in the 'arm (*informal*)
a thing or an action that gives sb/sth new energy, help or encouragement or provides a quick solution to a problem: *The discovery of gas reserves was a much-needed shot in the arm for the economy.*

> **❷ ORIGIN**
> This phrase refers to an injection of a drug.

shot through with sth
containing a lot of a particular colour, quality or feature: *He spoke in a voice shot through with emotion.*

- **best** → give it your best shot
- **big** → a big name/noise/shot
- **dark** → a shot/stab in the dark
- **long** → a long shot
- **long** → not by a long shot **SEE** not by a long chalk
- **parting** → a Parthian shot **SEE** a parting shot

shotgun /'ʃɒtgʌn; AmE 'ʃɑːt-/

a ˌshotgun 'wedding/'marriage (old-fashioned, informal)
a marriage which takes place because the woman is pregnant

> **NOTE**
> This expression probably refers to the father of a woman, who threatens to shoot the man unless he marries her.

● ride → ride shotgun

shots /ʃɒts; AmE ʃɑːts/

● call → call the shots/the tune

shoulder /'ʃəʊldə(r); AmE 'ʃoʊ-/

be, stand, act, etc. ˌshoulder to 'shoulder (with sb)
be supporting sb or in agreement with sb: We fought shoulder to shoulder to defend our country. ◇ I stand shoulder to shoulder with Julia on this important issue.

put your shoulder to the 'wheel
start working very hard at a particular task: We're really going to have to put our shoulders to the wheel if we want to get this ready on time. **OPP** take it/things easy

a shoulder to 'cry on
a person who listens to your troubles and offers sympathy and kindness: When you're depressed, you need a shoulder to cry on.

● chip → have a chip on your shoulder
● cold → give sb/get the cold shoulder
● looking → be looking over your shoulder
● straight → straight from the shoulder

shoulders /'ʃəʊldəz; AmE 'ʃoʊldərz/

on sb's 'shoulders
if blame, guilt, etc. is **on sb's shoulders**, they must take responsibility for it: I feel like all the responsibility is on my shoulders, which is quite stressful.

● head → have a good head on your shoulders
● head → head and shoulders above sb/sth
● old → (have) an old head on young shoulders
● rub → rub shoulders (with sb)
● weight → be a weight off your shoulders

shout /ʃaʊt/

be ˌin with a 'shout (of sth/of doing sth) (informal)
have a good chance of winning sth or of achieving sth: The interview seemed to go well, so I think I'm in with a shout of getting the job.

give sb a 'shout (spoken)
tell sb sth: Give me a shout when you're ready.

● write → be nothing, not much, etc. to shout about **SEE** be nothing, not much, etc. to write home about

shouting /'ʃaʊtɪŋ/

● bar → be all over bar the shouting
● spitting → within shouting distance **SEE** within spitting distance (of sth)

shove /ʃʌv/

'shove it (informal, especially AmE)
used to say rudely that you will not accept or do sth: 'The boss wants that report now.' 'Yeah? Tell him he can shove it.'

● push → if/when push comes to shove

show /ʃəʊ; AmE ʃoʊ/

be on 'show
be shown or displayed, often for sale: A couple of the new models are on show at the BMW garage. ◇ At weddings the gifts given by the guests are often on show.

do sth/be for 'show
do sth/be done to attract attention or admiration, and for no other purpose: That expensive computer is just for show; he doesn't really know how to use it.

get the ˌshow on the 'road (spoken)
start an activity or a journey, especially one that needs a lot of organization: Right, everyone! Let's get this show on the road!

(jolly) good 'show! (old-fashioned, BrE, informal)
used to show that you like sth or to say that sb has done sth well

have something, nothing, little, etc. to 'show for sth
have or produce sth, etc. as a result of your efforts, work, etc: Students who fail the final exam have nothing to show for years of hard work.

it (just/only) goes to 'show (that...)
used to say that sth is an example of a general truth or principle: He had all his money stolen? It just goes to show you should always lock your desk.

put on a good, poor, wonderful, etc. show
make a good, poor, etc. attempt at doing sth, especially in spite of difficulties: Considering that the children had no help, they put on a marvellous show.

run the show (sometimes disapproving)
be in control of a plan, a project, an organization, etc: Why does Sheila always have to run the show? There are plenty of other people who could organize the event just as well as her.

show (sb) a clean pair of 'heels (informal)
1 run away: They ran after her, but she showed them a clean pair of heels.
2 get ahead of sb in a competition: As makers of quality software, they've shown the rest of the industry a clean pair of heels.

show sb the 'door (informal)
tell sb to leave because of an argument or bad behaviour: If she spoke to me like that, I'd show her the door!

show your 'face
be in or go to a place, especially when you are not welcome: After what happened yesterday, I don't

know how you dare show your face here. ◇ *If he ever shows his face in here again, there'll be trouble.*

show good 'cause (for sth/for doing sth) (*law*)
give a good reason for sth: *Can you show good cause for your accusation?* ◇ *She could show no good cause for being in the office at midnight.*

a show of 'force
an act which clearly shows your power or gives a warning to people not to act against you: *The government sent in tanks as a show of force, and the rebels left the town.*

a show of 'hands
a method of voting in which each person shows their opinion by raising their hand: *If you like, we can settle this debate with a show of hands.*

show your 'teeth (*BrE*)
do sth that shows that you are able to act aggressively and use your power in a situation if it is necessary: *Up until now the police have been very patient with the strikers, but today they really showed their teeth.*

show the 'way
do sth first so that other people can follow: *The future lies in changing the way we do business, and this Internet company is showing the way.*

show sb who's 'boss
make it clear to sb that you have more power and authority than they have: *I think it's time we showed these people who's boss, don't you?*

show 'willing (*BrE*)
show that you are ready to help, work hard, etc. if necessary: *The meeting wasn't due to start for another half an hour, but she thought she'd better go early to show willing.*

- **dog** → a dog and pony show
- **flag** → fly/show/wave the flag
- **hand** → show/reveal your hand
- **paces** → show your paces **SEE** go through your paces
- **ropes** → show sb/learn/know the ropes
- **steal** → steal the show

shreds /ʃredz/

in 'shreds
1 very badly damaged: *After a stressful week, her nerves were in shreds.* ◇ *The country's economy is in shreds.*
2 torn in many places: *The document was in shreds on the floor.*

- **tear** → tear sb/sth to pieces/shreds

shrift /ʃrɪft/

- **short** → get short shrift **SEE** give sb/sth short shrift
- **short** → give sb/sth short shrift

shrinking /ˈʃrɪŋkɪŋ/

a ˌshrinking 'violet (*humorous*)
a very shy person who is easily frightened: *I can't imagine why a dynamic young woman like her is marrying a shrinking violet like him.*

shtum /ʃtʊm/

- **schtum** → keep schtum/shtum

shudder /ˈʃʌdə(r)/

- **think** → I shudder/dread to think (how, what, etc....)

shuffle /ˈʃʌfl/

lose sb/sth in the 'shuffle (*AmE*)
(usually used in the passive) not notice sb/sth or pay attention to sb/sth because of a confusing situation: *She was so busy at work, her marriage was getting lost in the shuffle.* ◇ *We feel that if schools are too big, it's easy for a student to be lost in the shuffle.*

shuffle off this mortal 'coil (*old-fashioned* or *humorous*)
die: *They believe that when they shuffle off this mortal coil their souls will become stars.*

> ❷ ORIGIN
> This expression comes from Shakespeare's play *Hamlet*.

shufti /ˈʃʊfti/

have/take a 'shufti (at sb/sth) (*BrE*, *informal*)
have a (quick) look (at sb/sth): *I don't mind having a shufti at the bike, but I can't afford to buy it.*

> ❷ ORIGIN
> This comes from military slang, from an Arabic word meaning *try to see*.

shut /ʃʌt/

ˌput up or 'shut up (*especially BrE*)
used to tell sb to stop just talking about sth and actually do it, show it, etc: *Come on, Scott. Put up or shut up. Let's see how fearless you really are.*

shut sb's 'mouth
stop sb from saying sth, especially from revealing a secret: *His employers tried to shut his mouth by offering him money, but he told the story to the newspapers anyway.*

shut your 'mouth/'trap/'face/'gob! (also **keep your 'mouth/'trap shut**) (*slang*)
a rude way of telling sb to be quiet or stop talking: *'Shut your face', Roger said, 'or I'll kick you out.'* ◇ *Why can't you learn to keep your big mouth shut?*

> NOTE
> *Trap* and *gob* are slang words for 'mouth'.

shut up 'shop (*BrE*, *informal*)
close a business permanently or stop working for the day: *The family ran a small grocer's for years, but when the old man died they shut up shop.* ◇ *It's 6 o'clock — time to shut up shop and go home.*

- **door** → shut/close the door on sth
- **ears** → shut/close your ears to sb/sth
- **eyes** → shut/close your eyes to sth
- **eyes** → (be able to do sth) with your eyes shut/closed
- **stable** → shut/lock/close the stable door after the horse has bolted

shutters /'ʃʌtəz; AmE 'ʃʌtərz/

,bring/,put down the 'shutters
stop letting sb know what your thoughts or feelings are; stop letting yourself think about sth: *He brought down the shutters on the terrible image of the car accident.*

shy /ʃaɪ/

● fight → fight shy of sth/of doing sth
● once → once bitten, twice shy

sick /sɪk/

be off 'sick
not be at work or school because you are not well: *He broke his arm and was off sick for a fortnight.*

be 'sick (*BrE*)
bring food from your stomach back out through your mouth; vomit: *I was sick three times in the night.* ◇ *The dog had been violently sick on the floor.*

be/feel sick at 'heart (*formal*)
be very unhappy or disappointed: *When I realized the accident was my fault, I felt sick at heart.*

make sb 'sick (*informal*)
make sb angry or disgusted: *You make me sick, lying around in front of the TV all day!* ◇ *Look how much these people are earning! It makes you sick.*

(as) sick as a 'dog (*informal*)
feeling very ill; vomiting a lot: *I was sick as a dog last night.*

(as) sick as a 'parrot (*BrE, humorous*)
very disappointed: *She was as sick as a parrot when she found out that her sister had been nominated for a prize and she hadn't.*

'sick of sb/sth ♦ ,sick and 'tired of sb/sth (*informal*)
bored with or annoyed by sb, or by sth that has been happening for a long time which you want to stop: *I'm sick and tired of hearing you complaining all day long.*

sick to your 'stomach
disgusted or angry: *I feel sick to my stomach every time I think about the way that child was punished.*

● fed → sick to the back teeth of sb/sth **SEE** fed up to the back teeth with sb/sth
● worried → be sick with worry **SEE** be worried sick

side /saɪd/

be (a bit, a little, etc.) on the 'cold, 'small, etc. side (*informal*)
be slightly too cold, small, etc: *These boots are a bit on the big side, but they're quite comfortable.* ◇ *It's a little on the cold side this morning.*

be on the ,right/,wrong side of '40, '50, etc. (*informal, often humorous*)
be younger/older than 40, 50, etc: '*How old is she?*' '*On the wrong side of forty, I'd say.*'

be on sb's 'side
support and agree with sb: *I'm definitely on your side in this.* ◇ *Whose side are you on anyway?*

be on the side of the 'angels
having correct moral principles and behaving correctly: *The policemen in Scobie's crime novels are not always on the side of the angels.*

come down/out on the side of sb/sth
decide, especially after considering sth carefully, to choose or support sth/sb: *After much discussion, they finally came down on the side of nuclear energy.* ◇ *In the argument that followed, my father came down firmly on my side.*

from ,side to 'side
moving to the left and then to the right: *He shook his head slowly from side to side.* ◇ *The ship rolled from side to side.*

get/keep on the right/wrong 'side of sb
try to please sb and not annoy them/annoy sb and make them dislike you: *She got on the wrong side of her boss after criticizing him in a meeting.*

have sth on your 'side
have sth as an advantage that will make it more likely that you will achieve sth: *She may not win this year, but she does have youth on her side.*

leave/put sth on/to one 'side
put sth in a separate place so that you can deal with it later: *After you've taken the bread out of the oven, leave it on one side to cool.* ◇ *Leaving that to one side for now, are there any other questions?*

let the 'side down (*especially BrE*)
fail to give your friends, family, etc. the help and support they expect, or behave in a way that makes them disappointed: *Everyone in the sales team has increased their sales except you. You're letting the side down badly.*

not leave sb's 'side
stay with sb, especially in order to take care of them: *While he was in hospital she didn't leave his side for more than a couple of hours at a time.*

on the 'side
1 in addition to your main job: *He's a teacher but he does some journalism on the side.*
2 (*informal*) secretly: *Even after he was married he still had a girlfriend on the side.*

the other side of the 'coin
the other aspect of the situation; a different or opposite way of looking at a situation: *Third World countries receive a lot of money from developed countries, but the other side of the coin is that they have to spend this money on expensive imports.*

,side by 'side (with sb/sth)
1 close together and facing in the same direction: *The two dogs lay side by side on the floor.* ◇ *There were two children ahead, walking side by side.*
2 together, without any difficulties: *Party members fought side by side with trade unionists for a change in the law.* ◇ *We have been using both systems, side by side, for two years.*

my, her, the other, the same, etc. side of the 'fence
my, the opposite, the same, etc. point of view or position in an argument: *The former allies are now on opposite sides of the fence.* ◇ *Make up your mind — which side of the fence are you on?*

a/one side of the 'story/'picture
only one way of looking at a situation: *There are two sides to this story, and you've only heard Jim's.* ◇ *This programme on the dispute only shows one side of the picture.*

take/draw sb to one 'side
take sb away from a group of people in order to speak to them in private: *She took me to one side to explain why she hadn't given me the job.*

this side of…
before a particular time, event, age, etc: *They aren't likely to arrive this side of midnight.*

- **bed** → get up on the wrong side of the bed **SEE** get out of bed on the wrong side
- **bit** → a bit on the side
- **bright** → look on the bright side
- **credit** → on the credit side
- **err** → err on the side of sth
- **grass** → the grass is (always) greener on the other side (of the fence)
- **know** → know which side your bread is buttered
- **laugh** → laugh on the other side of your face
- **right** → right side up
- **safe** → to be on the safe side
- **seamy** → the seamy side (of life, etc.)
- **sides** → from/on every side **SEE** from/on all sides
- **sides** → take sb's side **SEE** take sides
- **thorn** → be a thorn in your flesh/side
- **time** → have time on your side **SEE** time is on sb's side
- **time** → time is on sb's side
- **wrong** → from/on the wrong side of the tracks
- **wrong** → on the wrong side of the law

sidelines /'saɪdlaɪnz/

on the 'sidelines
watching sth but not taking an active part in it; waiting to take an active part in sth: *The Prime Minister's husband talked about what it was like on the sidelines of political life.* ◇ *He's waiting on the sidelines for a chance to re-enter politics.*

> **NOTE**
> The *sidelines* are the lines along the sides of a sports field that mark the outer edges.

sides /saɪdz/

from/on all 'sides ♦ from/on every 'side
from every direction: *People are criticizing him from all sides.*

see both 'sides (of the question, problem, etc.)
understand why one person or group has an opinion, and why a different person or group disagrees with it: *When people are in politics, it's difficult for them to see both sides of a question.*

take 'sides ♦ take sb's 'side
support one person or group in an argument or disagreement: *I refuse to take sides in this argument. It's nothing to do with me.* ◇ *Whenever we quarrel, you always take Carole's side.* **OPP** sit on the fence

- **short** → a short back and sides

- **split** → split your sides (laughing/with laughter)
- **two** → two sides of the same coin

sideways /'saɪdweɪz/

- **knock** → knock sb sideways

siege /siːdʒ/

under 'siege
1 surrounded by an army or the police: *The city has now been under siege for more than three weeks.*
2 being criticized all the time or put under pressure by problems, questions, etc: *The dollar came under siege on Monday, falling to its lowest for three years.*

- **lay** → lay siege to sth

sieve /sɪv/

have a mind/memory like a 'sieve (*informal*)
forget things easily or quickly: *I'm terribly sorry I didn't remember your birthday — I've got a memory like a sieve.*

> **NOTE**
> A *sieve* is a kitchen tool with small holes in it, used for separating solids from liquids or very small pieces of food from larger pieces.

sight /saɪt/

be in/within 'sight
1 be close enough to be seen: *In fine weather the mountains are just within sight.*
2 likely to happen, almost a reality: *Prison reform is now within sight.* ◇ *The end of our problems is in sight at last.*

be a ˌsight for sore 'eyes (*spoken*)
be a person or thing that you are happy to see; be welcome or much needed: *Ah! You're a sight for sore eyes!*

do sth on 'sight
do or feel sth as soon as you see sb/sth: *She complained constantly about the hotel, which she hated on sight.* ◇ *The soldiers were ordered to shoot on sight.*

hate, be sick of, etc. the 'sight of sb/sth (*informal*)
hate, etc. sb/sth very much: *I'm sick of the sight of him!*

keep sight of sb/sth ♦ keep sb/sth in sight
1 stay in a position where you can see sb/sth: *If you keep the tower in sight, you won't get lost.*
2 remain aware of sth; not forget sth: *It's important to keep sight of the fact that you have a small chance of winning.*

look a 'sight (*old-fashioned, BrE*)
be ugly or untidy: *She looked a real sight. A yellow hat, pink dress, black stockings, blue shoes.* ◇ *Your bedroom looks a sight. Go and tidy it.*

lose 'sight of sth
(of a purpose, aim, etc.) stop considering sth; forget sth: *The government seem to have lost sight of their aims and are now just trying to survive.*

,out of 'sight, ,out of 'mind (*saying*)
used to say that sb will quickly be forgotten when they are no longer with you **OPP** absence makes the heart grow fonder

a (damn, etc.) sight 'better, 'worse, etc. (than sb/sth) (*informal*)
a lot better, etc. (than sb/sth): *Life would be a sight easier if we had a little more money!* ◇ *A car that big would use a darn sight more petrol than ours.*

a (damn, etc.) sight too 'good, too 'much, etc. (*informal*)
much too good, etc: *There's a damn sight too much rubbish on TV.*

sight un'seen
if you buy sth **sight unseen**, you do not have an opportunity to see it before you buy it: *We bought the table sight unseen and were pleased to find it was perfect for our kitchen.*

- **first** → at first glance/sight
- **found** → nowhere in sight **SEE** nowhere to be found/seen
- **know** → know sb by sight
- **love** → love at first sight
- **pretty** → not a pretty sight
- **second** → second sight
- **stand** → you, he, etc. can't stand the sight/sound of sb/sth

sights /saɪts/

raise/lower your 'sights
increase/reduce your hopes and ambitions: *You should raise your sights and apply for the director's job.* ◇ *Some women feel that staying at home and having a family means lowering their sights.*

see the 'sights
visit the famous places in a city, country, etc: *We spent our first day in Rome seeing the sights.*
▶ **'sightseeing, 'sightseer** *nouns*: *We spent the afternoon sightseeing.* ◇ *There are always sightseers outside Buckingham Palace.*

Even as a child, Joe set his sights high.

set your sights 'high/'low
be ambitious/not ambitious; expect a lot/little from your life: *If you set your sights high, you could do anything.*

set your 'sights on sth/on doing sth ◆ **have your sights 'set on sth/on doing sth**
try to achieve or get sth: *She's set her sights on an Olympic gold.* ◇ *He has his sights on owning the biggest property company in the USA.*

> **NOTE**
> You look through the *sights* of a gun to aim at the target.

sign /saɪn/

(be) a ,sign of the 'times
something that shows the way the world is changing: *Seventy per cent of last year's graduates are still unemployed — a sign of the times, I'm afraid.*

sign on the dotted 'line (*informal*)
sign your name at the bottom of a contract and so agree to a deal, etc: *The job isn't mine until I've signed on the dotted line.*

sign your own 'death warrant
do sth that results in your own death, defeat or failure: *By refusing to play pop music this new radio station is signing its own death warrant.*

- **pledge** → sign/take the pledge

signed /saɪnd/

,signed, ,sealed and de'livered ◆ **,signed and 'sealed**
definite, because all the legal documents have been signed: *At the conference they hope to have a treaty signed, sealed and delivered by Tuesday.*

silence /'saɪləns/

,silence is 'golden (*saying*)
it is sometimes best not to say anything in a difficult or dangerous situation

> **NOTE**
> The complete saying is 'speech is silver, silence is golden'.

- **conspiracy** → a conspiracy of silence
- **heavy** → a heavy silence/atmosphere
- **pregnant** → a pregnant pause/silence

silent /'saɪlənt/

give sb/get the 'silent treatment
refuse to talk to sb, usually because you are angry with them; be treated in this way: *Are you going to talk to me now, or are you still giving me the silent treatment?*

(as) ,silent as the 'grave
without any noise at all: *The playground, which had been filled with the noises of children at play, suddenly became silent as the grave.*

the ,silent ma'jority
the large number of people in a country who think the same as each other, but do not express their

views publicly: *The government is appealing to the silent majority to support its foreign policy.*

❷ ORIGIN
The US President, Richard Nixon, used this phrase during the Vietnam War.

silk /sɪlk/

make a silk ˌpurse out of a sow's 'ear
succeed in making sth good out of material that does not seem very good at all: *If you're serious about taking up painting, invest in good quality brushes and canvas. After all, it's no good trying to make a silk purse out of a sow's ear.*

● smooth → (as) smooth as silk

silly /'sɪli/

ˌdrink, ˌlaugh, ˌshout, etc. yourself 'silly (*informal*)
drink, laugh, shout, etc. so much that you cannot behave in a sensible way: *Everyone was too busy laughing themselves silly to notice her quietly leave the room.*

play 'silly buggers (with sth) (*BrE, informal*)
behave in a stupid and annoying way: *Stop playing silly buggers and answer the question.*

the 'silly season (*BrE*)
the time, usually in the summer, when newspapers are full of unimportant stories because there is little serious news

silver /'sɪlvə(r)/

(hand sth to sb) on a silver 'platter
give sth to sb without expecting them to do or give anything in return: *I don't like her at all — she expects to be handed everything on a silver platter as if she's better than other people.*

NOTE
A *platter* is a large plate that is used for serving food.

the silver 'screen (*old-fashioned*)
the film industry: *the heroes and heroines of the silver screen*

● born → be born with a silver spoon in your mouth
● cloud → every cloud has a silver lining
● tongue → a silver/smooth tongue

simple /'sɪmpl/

● pure → pure and simple

sin /sɪn/

(as) miserable/ugly as 'sin (*spoken*)
used to emphasize that sb is very unhappy or ugly: *He arrived at the party looking as miserable as sin.* ◇ *Some babies are as ugly as sin at that age.*

● live¹ → live in sin

sincerely /sɪn'sɪəli; AmE -'sɪrli/

Yours sincerely (*BrE*) (*AmE* **Sincerely (yours)**) (*formal, written*)
used at the end of a formal letter before you sign your name, when you have addressed sb by their name

sine /'saɪn/

a sine qua 'non (of/for sth) /ˌsaɪneɪ kwɑː 'nəʊn; AmE 'noʊn/ (*from Latin, formal*)
something that is essential before you can achieve sth else: *Many people believe that grammar is the sine qua non of language learning.*

NOTE
In Latin, this means 'without which not'.

sinew /'sɪnjuː/

● strain → strain every nerve/sinew (to do sth)

sing /sɪŋ/

sing a different 'song/'tune
(be forced to) change your opinion: *Anne says she wants a large family but I'm sure she'll be singing a different tune when she's had one or two children.*

sing for your 'supper (*old-fashioned*)
do sth for sb in order to get what you want or need: *Susan has to clean her room before she's allowed to go out with her friends — she really has to sing for her supper!*

sing from the same 'song/'hymn sheet (*informal*)
say the same things and agree about a subject, especially in public: *We really need to make sure we are all singing from the same hymn sheet before the press conference.*

sing sb's/sth's 'praises (*informal*)
praise sb/sth very much or with great enthusiasm; say that sb/sth is very good: *Both her grandsons are doctors, and she never stops singing their praises.* ◇ *One day he's singing your praises; the next day he's telling you you're stupid.* **OPP** find fault (with sb/sth)

singing /'sɪŋɪŋ/

ˌall 'singing, ˌall 'dancing (*BrE, informal*)
(of a machine or system) having a lot of advanced technical features and therefore able to perform many different functions: *With these extras your PC will become the all singing, all dancing box the salesman claimed it would be.*

single /'sɪŋgl/

● file → (in) single/Indian file

sings /sɪŋz/

● fat → it ain't/it's not over till the fat lady sings

sink /sɪŋk/

sink your 'differences
agree to forget or ignore your past arguments or disagreements: *The two groups sank their political differences and joined together to beat the ruling party.*

,sink or 'swim (*saying*)
be in a situation where you will either succeed without help from other people, or fail completely: *The government refused to give the company any help, and just left it to sink or swim.*

,sink so 'low ◆ **sink to sth**
have such low moral standards that you do sth very bad: *Stealing from your friends? How could you sink so low?* ◇ *I can't believe that anyone would sink to such depths.*

sink to sb's 'level
stop behaving well and begin to behave badly, especially in an argument or a fight, because other people are behaving in this way: *Use words, not violence, or you'll just be sinking to their level.*

● kitchen → everything but/bar the kitchen sink
● teeth → get/sink your teeth into sth
● trace → sink, vanish, etc. without (a) trace

sinker /'sɪŋkə(r)/

● hook → hook, line and sinker

sinking /'sɪŋkɪŋ/

(like rats) deserting/leaving a sinking 'ship (*humorous, disapproving*)
used to talk about people who leave an organization, a company, etc. that is having difficulties, without caring about the people who are left: *One by one, employees began looking for other jobs, like rats deserting a sinking ship.* ◇ *I might have known he'd be the first rat to desert this sinking ship!*

(get/have) a/that 'sinking feeling (*informal*)
a feeling that sth bad has happened/is going to happen: *Most people know that sinking feeling you get when a bill arrives in the post.*

● heart → with a heavy/sinking heart

sinks /sɪŋks/

● heart → your heart sinks

sins /sɪnz/

(do/be sth) for your sins (*spoken humorous, especially BrE*)
be/do sth as a punishment: *'I hear you're going to be the new manager.' 'Yes, for my sins.'*

● multitude → cover/hide a multitude of sins

sir /sɜː(r); sə(r)/

,no 'sir! ◆ **,no sir'ree!** (*spoken, especially AmE*)
certainly not: *We will never allow that to happen! No sir!*

,yes 'sir! ◆ **,yes sir'ree!** (*spoken, especially AmE*)
used to emphasize that sth is true: *That's a fine car you have. Yes sirree!*

sirree /sɜːˈriː; səˈriː/

● sir → no sirree! SEE no sir!
● sir → yes sirree! SEE yes sir!

sisters /'sɪstəz; AmE 'sɪstərz/

● skin → be (all) brothers/sisters under the skin

sit /sɪt/

sit comfortably/easily/well (with sth) (*written*)
seem right, natural, suitable, etc. in a particular place or situation: *His views did not sit comfortably with the management line.*

sit in 'judgement (on/over sb) (*especially BrE*) (*AmE usually* **sit in 'judgment (on/over sb)**)
judge or decide if sb is wrong or right, even if you have no right to do so: *What gives you the right to sit in judgement over us?*

sit on the 'fence
avoid deciding between two sides of an argument, discussion, quarrel, etc: *Either you support me or you don't. You can't sit on the fence all your life.* ◇ *Politicians cannot sit on the fence. People expect them to have clear views.* **OPP** take sides ▸ **'fence-sitter** *noun* a person who cannot or does not want to decide which side of an argument, etc. to support

sit 'tight
not move; not change your position, in the hope that your present difficulties will be solved or go away: *If your car breaks down on the motorway, sit tight and wait for the police.* ◇ *In a period of recession businessmen have to sit tight and hope for better times in the future.*

sitting /'sɪtɪŋ/

be ,sitting 'pretty (*informal*)
be rich, successful or in a pleasant situation: *If you make win our competition, then you'll be sitting pretty.*

do sth in/at one 'sitting
do sth in one continuous period of activity, without getting up from your chair: *I read the book in one sitting.*

a ,sitting 'duck/'target
a person or thing that is very easy to attack or criticize: *It's always easy to criticize teachers; they're just sitting ducks.*

situ /'sɪtjuː; 'saɪt-; AmE 'saɪtuː/

in 'situ (*from Latin*)
in the original or correct place: *Much of the original furniture has been left in situ so that we can view the room almost as it looked a hundred years ago.*

> **NOTE**
> *Situ* literally means 'position'.

situation /ˌsɪtʃuˈeɪʃn/

situations vacant (*written*)
used in newspapers to show that details of jobs on offer are below: *the 'situations vacant' column*

* catch-22 → a catch-22 situation
* chicken-and-egg → a chicken-and-egg situation
* save → save the day/situation

six /sɪks/

hit/knock sb/sth for 'six (*BrE*)
1 (often of sth unpleasant) surprise sb a lot: *It really hit me for six to find that my father had written about me in his book.*
2 completely destroy a plan, an idea, a suggestion, etc.; knock sb/sth over/down: *The stock market crash has hit the economy for six.* ◇ *Toby took a step backwards and knocked the vase for six.*

> NOTE
> In cricket, if you hit the ball a long distance you score six runs.

it's six of ˌone and half a dozen of the 'other (*saying*)
used to say that there is no real difference between two possible choices: *Patrick said John started the fight, but I think it was probably six of one and half a dozen of the other.* ◇ *I've tried both ways of getting to Oxford and as far as I can see it's six of one and half a dozen of the other* (= they both take the same time).

six feet 'under (*informal, humorous*)
dead and buried in the ground: *By then, all the witnesses were six feet under.*

sixes /'sɪksɪz/

be at ˌsixes and 'sevens (*informal*)
be in a state of confusion; not be well organized: *I'm completely at sixes and sevens this week. My secretary's ill, I've got a report to write, and we're moving offices.*

sixpence /'sɪkspəns/

* dime → on a sixpence SEE on a dime

sixth /sɪksθ/

a sixth 'sense
a special ability to know sth without using any of the five senses that include sight, touch, etc: *A kind of sixth sense told her that there was someone else in the room, and she turned round quickly.*

sixty-four /ˌsɪksti 'fɔː(r)/

the sixty-four thousand dollar 'question (also **the million dollar 'question**)
a very important question which is difficult or impossible to answer: *The sixty-four thousand dollar question for modern astronomy is 'Is there life elsewhere in the universe?'*

> ❓ ORIGIN
> This phrase originated in the 1940s as 'the sixty-four dollar question'. It came from a popular US radio quiz programme at the time on which the top prize was $64.

size /saɪz/

cut sb down to 'size
show that sb is less important than they seem or think: *Failing his exams has certainly cut him down to size.*

that's about the 'size of it (*spoken*)
that is a good or fair description of the situation: *'So you're leaving college just to go travelling?' 'Yes, that's about the size of it.'*

sizes /'saɪzɪz/

* shapes → come in all shapes and sizes

skates /skeɪts/

get/put your 'skates on (*BrE, informal*)
hurry up: *If you don't put your skates on, you'll be late for work.*

skating /'skeɪtɪŋ/

* thin → be skating/walking on thin ice

skeleton /'skelɪtn/

a skeleton 'crew/'staff/'service
the minimum number of staff necessary to run an organization or service: *At weekends we have a skeleton staff to deal with emergencies.*

a skeleton in the 'cupboard/'closet
something shocking, embarrassing, etc. that has happened to you or your family in the past that you want to keep secret: *The new presidential candidate is certainly popular, but does he have any skeletons in the closet?*

skid /skɪd/

(on) skid 'row (*informal, especially AmE*)
people who are **on skid row** live in a very poor part of town where there are many social problems: *When he went bankrupt he lost everything, and ended up living on skid row for a few years.*
OPP on easy street

> ❓ ORIGIN
> This expression came from the phrase *skid road*, referring to the poor part of towns where loggers (= people who cut down trees or cut and transported wood) lived. Originally a *skid road* was a road made of large pieces of wood, used for moving logs to the mill.

skids /skɪdz/

on the 'skids (*informal*)
moving towards disaster; declining: *It was clear months ago that the firm was on the skids.* **OPP** fly high

put the 'skids under sb/sth (*informal*)
make sb/sth fail; stop sb/sth doing sth: *Unfortunately the government has put the skids under the hospital building programme.*

* hit → hit the skids

skies /skaɪz/

* praise → praise sb/sth to the skies

skin /skɪn/

be (all) brothers/sisters under the 'skin
be men/women with similar feelings, in spite of outside appearances, position, etc: *Actors and politicians are brothers under the skin. They both need public approval.*

be (all/just/nothing but) skin and 'bone(s) (*informal*)
be very or too thin: *After two years in prison, he was nothing but skin and bone.*

do sth by the ˌskin of your 'teeth (*informal*)
only just do sth; nearly fail to do sth: *We thought we'd miss the plane, but in the end we caught it by the skin of our teeth.*

get under sb's 'skin (*informal*)
attract or disturb sb: *I've tried to forget her, but I know that I've got her under my skin.* ◇ *He gets under his opponents' skins and they make stupid mistakes.*

have/put skin in the 'game (*AmE, especially business*)
take an active interest in the success or failure of a particular project, activity, etc. because you are involved in a personal or financial way: *If you want someone to make efficient choices, they have to have a little skin in the game.*

> **❷ ORIGIN**
> This expression was first used by the US investor Warren Buffett to describe a situation in which senior managers own or buy shares in the company that they manage and so to have a personal interest in the company's success or failure.

it's no skin off 'my, 'your, 'his, etc. nose (*informal*)
used to say that sb is not upset or annoyed about sth because it does not affect them in a bad way: *It's no skin off my nose if the price of cigarettes goes up. I don't smoke.*

make your 'skin crawl
make you feel afraid or full of disgust: *His smile made my skin crawl.*

skin sb a'live
(used as a threat or warning) punish sb very severely: *Your mother would skin you alive if she knew you'd started smoking!*

(have) a thick/thin 'skin (*informal*)
(be) not affected/affected by criticism or unkind remarks: *A traffic warden needs a thick skin to take so much abuse from motorists.* ◇ *He's got rather a thin skin for a politician. He'll have to learn to take the odd unkind remark.* ► **ˌthick-'skinned, ˌthin-'skinned** *adj.*

- **jump** → jump out of your skin
- **rhinoceros** → have a hide/skin like a rhinoceros
- **save** → save sb's/your (own) neck/skin/hide
- **slip** → slip on a banana skin
- **soaked** → be/get soaked to the skin
- **way** → there's more than one way to skin a cat

skin-deep /ˌskɪn 'diːp /

- **beauty** → beauty is only skin-deep

skinned /skɪnd/

- **eyes** → keep your eyes open/peeled/skinned (for sb/sth)

skip /skɪp/

'skip it (*spoken, informal*)
used to tell sb impolitely that you do not want to talk about sth or repeat what you have said: *'What were you saying?' 'Oh, skip it!'*

skunk /skʌŋk/

- **drunk** → (as) drunk as a skunk

sky /skaɪ/

the sky's the 'limit (*spoken, informal*)
there is no limit or end to sth, especially sb's success or progress: *For an ambitious young woman in this business, the sky's the limit.*

- **pie** → pie in the sky

sky-high /ˌskaɪ 'haɪ/

- **blow** → blow sb/sth sky-high

slack /slæk/

cut sb some 'slack (*informal, especially AmE*)
make things easier than usual for sb; allow sb more freedom to do things than they would normally have: *I know I made a mistake, but it's my first week on the job, so cut me some slack, OK?*

take up the 'slack
improve the way money or people are used in an organization: *The export market has failed to take up the slack in recent years, which has led to financial losses.*

> **NOTE**
> The *slack* is the part of a rope that is hanging loosely. If there is no slack, the rope is tight.

slam /slæm/

be a 'slam dunk (*AmE*)
be something that is certain to be successful: *The case looked like a slam dunk for the prosecution.*

> **NOTE**
> In basketball, a *slam dunk* is the act of jumping up and putting the ball through the net with a lot of force.

slanging /'slæŋɪŋ/

a 'slanging match (*BrE, informal*)
a noisy, angry argument: *It started as a peaceful discussion, but it ended in a real slanging match.*

> **NOTE**
> *Slanging* in this idiom comes from the old verb *slang*, meaning 'to attack somebody with rude and offensive language'.

slap

slap /slæp/

(a bit of) slap and 'tickle (*old-fashioned, BrE, informal*)
kissing and cuddling between lovers: *We used to do anything to get a bit of slap and tickle when we were young lads.*

a slap in the 'face
an action that seems to be intended as a deliberate insult to sb: *The bank refused to lend her any more money, which was a real slap in the face for her.* **OPP** give sb/yourself a pat on the back

a slap on the 'wrist (*informal*)
a small punishment or warning: *I got a slap on the wrist from my secretary today for leaving the office so untidy.*

slate /sleɪt/

(put sth) on the 'slate (*informal*)
(put sth) on your account in a shop, a bar, etc. to be paid for later: *Can I put this on the slate?*

> **NOTE**
> A *slate* is a thin sheet of a type of dark grey stone that was used in the past to write on.

- clean → a clean sheet/slate
- wipe → wipe the slate clean

slaughter /'slɔːtə(r)/

(like) a lamb/lambs to the 'slaughter
(do sth or go somewhere) without protesting, probably because you do not realize that you are in danger: *When the war started, thousands of young men went off to fight, like lambs to the slaughter.*

> **NOTE**
> *Slaughter* is the killing of animals for their meat.

slave /sleɪv/

be a slave to/of sth
be a person whose life is completely controlled by sth, for example a habit, a job, an interest, etc: *She's a slave to fashion; she's always buying new clothes.*

- work → work like a dog/slave/Trojan

sledgehammer /'sledʒhæmə(r)/

- use → use a sledgehammer to crack a nut

sleep /sliːp/

be able to do sth in your 'sleep (*informal*)
be able to do sth very easily because you have done it many times before: *He'd done the journey so many times before that he almost felt as if he could do it in his sleep.*

,go to 'sleep (*informal*)
(of your leg, arm, hand, etc.) be unable to feel anything in your leg, etc. because it has been in a particular position for a long time

not lose any sleep over sb/sth ♦ lose no sleep over sb/sth (*informal*)
not worry a lot about sb/sth: *The business does have problems at present but it's nothing I'm going to lose any sleep over.*

not sleep a 'wink ♦ not get a 'wink of sleep
not sleep at all: *I didn't sleep a wink last night because I was worrying about my driving test.*

put sb/sth to 'sleep
1 give sb drugs (= an anaesthetic) before an operation to make them unconscious: *Before the operation we'll put you to sleep, so don't worry, you won't feel a thing.*
2 kill a sick or injured animal by giving it drugs so that it dies without pain: *She took her old dog to the vet and he put it to sleep.*

sleep like a 'log/'top (also **sleep like a 'baby**) (*informal*)
sleep very well; sleep without waking: *After our long walk yesterday, I slept like a log.*

'sleep on it
not make a decision until the following day so that you can have more time to think about it: *If you aren't sure what to do, sleep on it and give us your decision tomorrow.*

sleep 'tight! (*informal, spoken*)
used especially to children before they go to bed to say that you hope they sleep well: *Good night, Pat, sleep tight!*

- beauty → get your beauty sleep
- rough → live/sleep rough

sleeping /'sliːpɪŋ/

let ,sleeping dogs 'lie (*saying*)
do not disturb a situation which could cause trouble: *I was very careful about what I said. It's best to let sleeping dogs lie, I think.*

sleeve /sliːv/

have an ,ace/a ,trick up your 'sleeve (*BrE*)
(*AmE* **have an ,ace in the 'hole**) (*informal*)
have an idea or plan which you keep secret and can use if you need to (especially in order to gain an advantage over sb): *They think they've won the contract but we've still got a couple of aces up our sleeve.*

have/keep sth up your 'sleeve (*informal*)
have a good idea, plan or piece of information which you are not telling anyone about now, but which you intend to use later: *John was smiling to himself all through the meeting; I'm sure he's got something up his sleeve.*

- laugh → laugh up your sleeve (at sb/sth)
- wear → wear your heart on your sleeve

sleeves /sliːvz/

- roll → roll up your sleeves

slog

sleight /slaɪt/

ˌsleight of ˈhand
1 something done with very quick and skilful movements of the hand(s) so that other people cannot see what really happened: *The trick is done simply by sleight of hand.*
2 skilful use of facts or figures to give people the wrong impression of sth or to make them believe sth which is not true: *We now realize that much of Burt's research was presented with a statistical sleight of hand.*

slice /slaɪs/

a ˌslice of ˈlife
a story, play or film/movie that shows aspects of ordinary life: *In this book Dickens shows us a slice of nineteenth-century London life.*

- action → a piece/slice of the action
- cake → a piece/share/slice of the pie **SEE** a share/slice of the cake
- way → any way you slice it

sliced /slaɪst/

- best → the best thing since sliced bread

slightest /ˈslaɪtəst/

not in the ˈslightest
not at all; not in the least: *Flying doesn't worry me in the slightest.*

sling /slɪŋ/

sling your ˈhook (*BrE, informal*)
(often used in orders) go away: *That boy's a real nuisance. I tried telling him to sling his hook but he simply ignored me.*

- mud → fling/sling/throw mud (at sb)

slings /slɪŋz/

the ˌslings and ˈarrows (of sth)
the problems and difficulties (of sth): *As a politician you have to deal with the slings and arrows of criticism from the newspapers.*

> **❓ ORIGIN**
> This comes from Shakespeare's play *Hamlet*: 'the slings and arrows of outrageous fortune'.

slip /slɪp/

give sb the ˈslip (*informal*)
get away from sb who is following you: *The police were chasing us but we managed to give them the slip.*

let ˈslip sth
give sb information that is supposed to be secret: *She tried not to let slip what she knew.* ◇ *I happened to let it slip that he had given me $2 000 for the car.*

slip sb's ˈmemory/ˈmind
forget about sth or forget to do sth: *I was supposed to go to the dentist today, but it completely slipped my mind.*

a ˈslip of a boy, girl, etc. (*old-fashioned*)
a small or thin, usually young, person: *They were amazed that such a slip of a girl could cause so much trouble.*

a slip of the ˈtongue/ˈpen
a small mistake when speaking or writing: *Did I say North Street? Sorry, that was a slip of the tongue — I meant South Street.*

slip on a baˈnana skin (*informal*)
(usually of a public figure) make a stupid mistake: *The new minister slipped on a banana skin before he had been in the job a week.*

slip through sb's ˈfingers
(of an opportunity, money, etc.) escape or be missed: *I wouldn't let a wonderful opportunity like this slip through your fingers if I were you.*

slip through the ˈnet
when sb/sth **slips through the net**, an organization or a system fails to find them/it and deal with them/it: *We tried to contact all former students, but one or two slipped through the net.*

there's ˌmany a ˈslip ('twixt ˌcup and ˈlip) (*saying*)
(of plans, hopes, etc.) nothing is completely certain until it happens because things can easily go wrong: *We should get to London before 7 o'clock, but there's many a slip 'twixt cup and lip.* ◇ *She aims to get to the top in the company, but there's many a slip…*

> **NOTE**
> The word *'twixt* is a short form of the old word *betwixt*, meaning 'between'.

- Freudian → a Freudian slip
- tongue → roll/slip/trip off the tongue

slippery /ˈslɪpəri/

(as) slippery as an ˈeel (*informal*)
dishonest and good at not answering questions, etc: *The man the police want to talk to is slippery as an eel, and has so far escaped arrest.* **OPP** (as) straight as a die (2)

the slippery ˈslope
a situation or way of behaving that could quickly lead to danger, disaster, failure, etc: *Starting with shoplifting, he was soon on the slippery slope towards a life of crime.*

slipping /ˈslɪpɪŋ/

be ˈslipping (*informal*)
(of sb's behaviour or performance) not be as good, tidy, efficient, etc. as usual; not be up to sb's usual high standard: *You're slipping, Edwina: this letter is full of typing errors.* ◇ *That's three times he's beaten me — I must be slipping!*

slog /slɒg; AmE slɑːg/

ˌslog/ˌslug it ˈout (*BrE, informal*)
(of people, organizations, competitors, etc.) fight very hard until one person or group finally wins: *The boxers slugged it out to the finish.* ◇ *The two teams will slog it out for second place.*

NOTE
In this idiom, *slug* and *slog* are both informal
words meaning 'to hit very hard'.

• guts → slog/sweat/work your guts out

slope /sləʊp; AmE sloʊp/

• slippery → the slippery slope

slouch /slaʊtʃ/

be no 'slouch (at sth/at doing sth) (*informal*)
be good at sth/at doing sth: *He's no slouch in the
kitchen — you should try his spaghetti bolognese.*

slow /sləʊ; AmE sloʊ/

do a slow 'burn (*AmE, informal*)
slowly get angry: *It makes me do a slow burn when
it takes longer to check out at the grocery store than
it took to shop.* **OPP** fly into a rage, temper, etc.

go 'slow (on sth)
show less enthusiasm for achieving sth: *The government is going slow on tax reforms.*

in the 'slow lane
not making progress as fast as other people, countries, companies, etc: *According to the latest survey,
the country is expected to remain in the slow lane of
economic recovery.* **OPP** in the fast lane

NOTE
The *slow lane* is the part of a motorway/free-
way in which the traffic moves slowly.

• mark → be quick/slow off the mark
• uptake → be quick/slow on the uptake

slowly /'sləʊli; AmE 'sloʊli/

slowly but 'surely
used for describing definite but slow progress in
sth: *Attitudes to women at work are changing slowly but surely.*

• easy → easy/gently/slowly does it

slug /slʌg/

• slog → slog/slug it out

slum /slʌm/

'slum it (*informal, often humorous*)
live in worse conditions than you do usually: *What
are you doing coming on the bus today? Are you
slumming it?*

sly /slaɪ/

do sth on the 'sly
do sth secretly: *She didn't seem to have much appetite for dinner. I wonder if she's been eating chocolates on the sly?* **OPP** (out) in(to) the open

smack /smæk/

• lips → lick/smack your lips

small /smɔːl/

be grateful/thankful for small 'mercies
be happy that a bad situation is not even worse:
*The thieves took the TV and stereo but didn't take
any jewellery, so let's be thankful for small mercies.*

it's a ˌsmall 'world (*saying*)
used when you meet or hear about sb you know,
in an unexpected place: *It turns out that he's a
friend of my brother's! It's a small world, isn't it?*

look/feel 'small (also **feel 'that high**)
feel stupid, embarrassed or ridiculous in front of
other people: *Why did you tell everyone that I'd
failed all my school exams? I felt so small.* ◇ *Mrs
Jones made him feel that high when she criticized
his work in front of everybody.*

NOTE
When using the expression *feel that high*, you
often use your thumb and finger to indicate
something small.

small 'beer (*BrE*) (*AmE* **small po'tatoes**)
something that has little importance or value:
*Jacob earns about $40 000, but that's small beer
compared with his brother's salary.*

a ˌsmall 'fortune (*informal*)
a lot of money: *This house cost hardly anything
when we bought it, but now it's worth a small fortune.*

'small fry (*informal*)
people, groups or businesses that are not considered to be important or powerful: *These local
companies are only small fry compared to the huge
multinationals.* **OPP** a big name/noise/shot

the 'small print (*BrE*) (*AmE* **the 'fine print**)
the parts of a written agreement or legal contract
that are printed in very small letters, but which
may contain important information: *Make sure
you read the small print before signing the contract.*

the small 'screen
(the) television (when contrasted with cinema):
*Cinema films reach the small screen very quickly
these days.*

(make) 'small talk
(take part in) polite conversation about unimportant things: *Maria introduced me to her parents,
and we sat there making small talk for a while.*

• hours → the small/early hours
• large → in no small part **SEE** in large part
• still → the still small voice
• sweat → don't sweat the small stuff
• way → do sth in a big/small way
• wonder → it's no/small/little wonder (that)…

smart /smɑːt; AmE smɑːrt/

a ˌsmart 'alec/aleck (*informal, disapproving*)
a person who tries to show that they are cleverer
than everyone else: *Some smart alec wrote in to
say that the last edition of the newspaper contained
37 printing errors.*

a/one smart 'cookie (*AmE, informal*)
a clever person with good ideas: *Jed is one smart cookie. I'm sure he'll do the right thing.*

the 'smart money is on sb/sth
if **the smart money is on** sb or sth, people with intelligence or knowledge think sb will succeed or sth will happen: *This year, the smart money is on Roe to win the tournament.*

smash /smæʃ/

smash sb's 'face/'head in (*BrE, informal*)
hit sb very hard in the face/head: *Give me the money or I'll smash your head in.*

a ˌsmash 'hit (*informal*)
(of a record, play or film/movie) very popular and a great success: *Still at number one, it's The Rubber Band, with their smash hit, 'Love me'.* ◊ *The, actress Donna May has been in 15 Broadway smash hits.*

smell /smel/

ˌsmell a 'rat (*informal*)
think or suspect that sth is wrong or that sb is trying to deceive you: *She says that the business is making a lot of money, but I smell a rat somewhere. The figures are too good to be true.*

● **high** → smell/stink to high heaven
● **sweet** → the sweet smell of success
● **wake** → wake up and smell the coffee

smelling /'smelɪŋ/

come up/out of sth smelling of 'roses (*informal*)
still have a good reputation, even though you have been involved in sth that might have given people a bad opinion of you: *Nobody ever knew the details and he came out of the deal smelling of roses.*

smile /smaɪl/

● **ear** → beam/grin/smile from ear to ear
● **raise** → raise a laugh/smile

smiles /smaɪlz/

be all 'smiles
be very happy and smiling, especially after feeling sad or worried about sth: *He was really depressed about the business last week, but he's all smiles now. A very big order has just come in.*

● **fortune** → fortune smiles on sb

smithereens /ˌsmɪðə'riːnz/

blow, smash, etc. sth to smithe'reens (*informal*)
destroy sth completely by breaking it into small pieces: *The bomb blew the car to smithereens.*

smoke /sməʊk; AmE smoʊk/

go up in 'smoke
1 be destroyed by fire: *Their home went up in smoke before their eyes.*

2 (of plans, etc.) be destroyed or ruined: *Her plans to become a member of parliament went up in smoke when the newspapers printed a story about her drink problem.*

smoke and 'mirrors
used to describe ways of tricking people or of hiding the truth: *He said the government had used smoke and mirrors to raise taxes.* ◊ *The commission has declared war on the smoke and mirrors of sales promotions.*

ˌsmoke like a 'chimney (*informal*)
smoke a lot of cigarettes: *You think I smoke a lot? You should meet Joe — he smokes like a chimney.*

there's no ˌsmoke without 'fire (*BrE*)
(*AmE* **where there's smoke, there's 'fire**) (*saying*)
if a lot of people are saying that sth bad is happening, it must be partly true: *Although he had been found not guilty in court, people are saying that there's no smoke without fire.*

● **blow** → blow smoke (up sb's ass)
● **pipe** → put that in your pipe and smoke it

smokescreen /'sməʊkskriːn; AmE 'smoʊk-/

a 'smokescreen
sth that hides your real intentions, feelings, or activities: *She couldn't answer the question, so she tried to put up a smokescreen by talking angrily about the interviewer's rudeness.*

> **NOTE**
> A *smokescreen* is a cloud of smoke used to hide soldiers, ships, etc. during a battle.

smoking /'sməʊkɪŋ; AmE 'smoʊk-/

a/the ˌsmoking 'gun
something that seems to prove that sb has done sth wrong or illegal: *This memo could be the smoking gun that investigators have been looking for.*

smooth /smuːð/

(as) smooth as 'silk (also **(as) smooth as a baby's 'bottom** *humorous*)
very smooth: *He had just shaved and his face was as smooth as a baby's bottom.*

smooth the 'path/'way
make it easier for sth to happen: *The President's speech smoothed the way for talks with the rebel leaders.*

smooth (sb's) ruffled 'feathers
make sb feel less angry or offended: *Her note of apology was meant to smooth ruffled feathers, but it only seemed to make things worse.* **OPP** ruffle sb's/ a few feathers

● **rough** → take the rough with the smooth
● **tongue** → a silver/smooth tongue

snail /sneɪl/

at a 'snail's pace (*informal*)
very slowly: *My grandmother drove the car at a snail's pace.*

Traffic was moving at a snail's pace through the centre of the city.

'snail mail (*informal, humorous*)
used especially by people who use email on computers to describe the system of sending letters by ordinary mail: *I'd love to hear from you, either by email or snail mail.*

snake /sneɪk/

a ˌsnake in the 'grass (*disapproving*)
a person who pretends to be your friend but who cannot be trusted: *We used to be friends, but who knew he'd turn out to be such a snake in the grass?*

snap /snæp/

be a 'snap (*AmE, informal*)
be very easy to do: *This job's a snap.*

snap your 'fingers
1 attract sb's attention by making a sound with your thumb and middle finger: *Waiters don't like customers in restaurants who snap their fingers and shout 'waiter!'*
2 show you do not care about sb/sth: *He snapped his fingers at the committee and walked angrily out of the room.*

ˌsnap 'out of it ♦ ˌsnap sb 'out of it (*informal*)
try to stop feeling unhappy or depressed; help sb stop feeling this way: *For heaven's sake, Ann, snap out of it! Things aren't that bad! ◇ She wouldn't talk to anyone for days, but her friends helped snap her out of it.*

ˌsnap 'to it (*informal*)
used, especially in orders, to tell sb to start working harder or more quickly: *Come on! Snap to it!*

● head → bite/snap sb's head off

snappy /'snæpi/

ˌmake it 'snappy (*informal*)
used to tell sb to do sth quickly or to hurry: *If you don't make it snappy, we'll miss the train. ◇ Come on, make it snappy! There's not much time left!*

snatches /'snætʃɪz/

in 'snatches
for short periods rather than continuously: *Sleep came to him in brief snatches.* **OPP** at a stretch

sneak /sniːk/

a ˌsneak 'preview
an opportunity to look at or watch sth, for example a book or a film/movie, before it is shown to the public: *She gave me a sneak preview of her latest painting.*

sneezed /sniːzd/

not to be 'sneezed/'sniffed at (*informal*)
important or worth having: *If I were you, I'd take the job. A salary like that's not to be sneezed at.*

sneezes /'sniːzɪz/

when A 'sneezes, B catches a 'cold (also **if A catches a 'cold, B gets pneu'monia** *less frequent*)
if one person, organization, country, etc. has a problem, the effects of this on another person, organization or country are much more serious: *When Wall Street sneezes, the world catches a cold.*

sniff /snɪf/

have a (good) ˌsniff a'round
examine a place carefully: *Come and visit our website and have a sniff around!*

> **NOTE**
> This refers to the way that a dog *sniffs* (= smells) something in order to find out more about it.

not get a 'sniff of sth (*informal*)
not succeed in obtaining sth: *I worked in Hollywood for years, but I never got a sniff of the big money.*

sniffed /snɪft/

● sneezed → not to be sneezed/sniffed at

sniffles /'snɪflz/

get, have, etc. the 'sniffles (*informal*)
get, have, etc. a slight cold: *'Are you ill?' 'No, I've just got the sniffles.'*

snit /snɪt/

be in a 'snit (*AmE*)
be bad-tempered and refuse to speak to anybody for a time because you are angry about sth: *She was in quite a snit. Hope it wasn't something I said. ◇ What are you in such a snit about?*

snook /snuːk/

● cock → cock a snook at sb/sth

snow /snəʊ; AmE snoʊ/

a 'snow job (*AmE, informal*)
an attempt to deceive sb or to persuade them to support sth by telling them things that are not

true, or by praising them too much: *That guy gave me a real snow job. If I'd known the truth I never would have given him the money.*

● **pure** → (as) pure as the driven snow

snowball /'snəʊbɔːl; AmE 'snoʊ-/

not have a ˌsnowball's chance in 'hell (of doing sth) (*informal*)
have no chance at all of doing sth: *Look at this traffic! I'm afraid we haven't got a snowball's chance in hell of getting to the airport in time.* **OPP** a sporting chance

> **NOTE**
> This idiom refers to the belief that hell is a place of fire.

snowed /snəʊd; AmE snoʊd/

be snowed 'under (with sth)
have more things, especially work, than you feel able to deal with: *I'd love to come but I'm completely snowed under at the moment.*

snuff /snʌf/

'snuff it (*BrE, slang, humorous*)
die: *Old Jack was over 90 when he snuffed it.*

up to 'snuff (*informal*)
of the required standard or quality; in good health: *Many people believe that the new senator is not up to snuff politically.* ◇ *I haven't felt up to snuff for several weeks.*

snuffles /'snʌflz/

get, have, etc. the 'snuffles (*informal*)
get, have, etc. a cold: *According to research, non-drinkers are more likely to develop the winter snuffles than moderate drinkers.*

snug /snʌg/

(as) snug as a bug (in a rug) (*informal, humorous*)
very warm and comfortable: *In his sleeping bag he'll be as snug as a bug in a rug.*

SO /səʊ; AmE soʊ/

be so much/many sth
be completely sth; be just or only sth: *All his fine speeches are so much rubbish if he doesn't keep his promises.* ◇ *All these politicians are just so many names to me. I don't know any of them.*

...or so
used after a number, an amount, etc. to show that it is not exact: *He stayed for a week or so.* ◇ *Take a kilo or so of sugar...*

so as to do sth
with the intention of doing sth: *We went early so as to get good seats.*

'so much/many (sth)
a certain amount/number (of sth): *At the end of every working week I have to write in my notebook that I drove so many miles at so much per litre.*

soaked /səʊkt; AmE soʊkt/

be/get ˌsoaked to the 'skin
(of a person) be/get very wet: *Don't go out in this rain — you'll get soaked to the skin.*

soapbox /'səʊpbɒks; AmE 'soʊpbɑːks/

be/get on your 'soapbox (*informal*)
express the strong opinions that you have about a particular subject: *Don't mention the Internet in front of him, or he'll get on his soapbox and we'll be here all night listening to his opinions about the evils of modern technology.*

> **NOTE**
> A *soapbox* is a small box that somebody speaking in public, especially outdoors, might stand on so that they could be seen and heard more easily.

SOB /ˌes əʊ 'biː; AmE oʊ/

● **son** → SOB **SEE** a/the son of a bitch

sob /sɒb; AmE sɑːb/

sob your 'heart out
cry noisily for a long time because you are very sad: *After the argument she spent an hour sobbing her heart out in the bedroom.* **OPP** laugh your head off

a 'sob story (*informal, disapproving*)
a story that sb tells you so that you will feel sorry for them, especially one that does not have that effect or is not true: *Then she gave me another of her sob stories, this time about an argument with her boyfriend.*

sober /'səʊbə(r); AmE 'soʊ-/

(as) sober as a 'judge
not at all affected by alcohol: *I was driving, so of course I was sober as a judge.* **OPP** (as) drunk as a lord

● **stone-cold** → stone-cold sober

sock /sɒk; AmE sɑːk/

put a 'sock in it (*old-fashioned, BrE, informal*)
be quiet; stop talking or making a noise: *Put a sock in it, will you? I'm on the phone.*

> **❓ ORIGIN**
> This expression may refer to early gramophones, which had no volume controls. To play records more quietly, people used to put a sock into the trumpet.

'sock it to sb (*informal or humorous*)
do sth or tell sb sth in a strong and effective way: *Go in there and sock it to 'em!*

socks /sɒks; AmE sɑːks/

blow/knock sb's 'socks off (*informal*)
surprise or impress sb very much: *With that dress and your new haircut you'll knock their socks off!*

● **bless** → bless his, her, etc. (little) cotton socks
● **pull** → pull your socks up

Sod /sɒd; AmE sɑːd/

,Sod's 'Law (BrE, humorous)
the tendency for things to happen in just the way
that you do not want, and in a way that is not useful: *The band always plays better when they're not
being recorded — but that's Sod's Law, isn't it?*

sod /sɒd; AmE sɑːd/

● game → blow/sod this/that for a game of soldiers
● lark → blow/sod that for a lark

sods /sɒdz; AmE sɑːdz/

● odds → odds and sods SEE odds and ends

soft /sɒft; AmE sɔːft/

be/go soft in the 'head (informal, disapproving)
be/become crazy or stupid: *Sometimes I talk to
myself in the street; people must think I'm soft in
the head.*

have a soft 'spot for sb/sth (informal)
particularly like sb/sth: *I've always had a soft spot
for my little cousin Clare.*

● option → the soft/easy option
● touch → a soft/an easy touch

soften /'sɒfn; AmE 'sɔːfn/

● blow → cushion/soften the blow

softly-softly /,sɒftli 'sɒftli; AmE ,sɔːftli
'sɔːftli/

a/the softly-'softly approach (BrE, informal)
a/the gentle, patient and careful way of doing sth,
especially when dealing with people: *The police
are now trying a more softly-softly approach with
football hooligans.* **OPP** like a bull in a china shop

sold /səʊld; AmE soʊld/

be 'sold on sth (informal)
be very enthusiastic about sth: *We were really sold
on the idea.*

soldiers /'səʊldʒəz; AmE 'soʊldʒərz/

● game → blow/sod this/that for a game of soldiers

solid /'sɒlɪd; AmE 'sɑːl-/

(as) solid as a 'rock
extremely solid and reliable: *The Irish team were
solid as a rock in defence.* ▸ ,rock-'solid adj.: *The
company has a rock-solid reputation.*

some /sʌm; səm/

'some such
used to say that sth is similar to another thing or
things: *I think this music's by Bartok or some such
composer.*

something /'sʌmθɪŋ/

have something 'on sb (informal)
have information about sb which is proof of their
criminal activities or which would make them

embarrassed if you told other people: *The press
have got something on him, but for the moment
they're keeping quiet.* **OPP** have nothing on sb (2)

or something (informal)
or another similar thing: *Would you like some coffee or something?* ◊ *Why won't you tell her? Are you
frightened of her or something?* ◊ *Let's go for a walk
or something.*

something 'else
1 a different thing; another thing: *He said something else that I thought was interesting.*
2 (informal) a person, a thing or an event that is
much better than others of a similar type: *I've seen
some fine players, but she's something else!*

'something like that ♦ ,something like 'sb/'sth
similar or partly the same as sb/sth; approximately (a number): *'Is he a travel agent?' 'Yes, something like that.'* ◊ *Something like twenty people
came to the meeting.* **OPP** nothing like

something of a sth
quite or rather a sth; sth to an extent: *He has something of a reputation as a sportsman.* ◊ *Our walk
home turned out to be something of an adventure.*

there's 'something about sb/sth
sb/sth has a strange, attractive or unusual quality
that influences you, but which is difficult to
explain: *There's something about her I don't like,
but I can't put it into words.*

son /sʌn/

a/the ,son of a 'bitch (also **SOB** especially in AmE)
(△, slang)
an offensive way to refer to a person that you
think is bad or very unpleasant: *That's the son of
a bitch who stole my car!*

a/the son of a 'gun (AmE, informal, spoken)
a person or thing that you are annoyed with: *My
car's at the shop — the son of a gun broke down
again.*

● father → like father/mother, like son/daughter
● favourite → sb's favourite son
● prodigal → a/the prodigal son

song /sɒŋ; AmE sɔːŋ/

(buy sth, go, etc.) for a 'song (informal)
(buy sth, be sold, etc.) for much less money than
its real value: *I bought this car for a song.*

make a song and 'dance about sth (informal,
disapproving)
worry or be excited about sth which is not very
important: *My aunt makes a real song and dance
about people arriving late, so hurry up.*

on 'song (informal)
working or performing well: *The whole team was
on song.*

● sing → sing a different song/tune
● sing → sing from the same song/hymn sheet

soon /suːn/

,anytime 'soon (*especially AmE*)
used in negative sentences and questions to refer to the near future: *Do you think she'll be back anytime soon?*

none too 'soon
1 almost too late: *They were rescued none too soon; they'd already finished all the food and only had water for another day.*
2 used for saying that sb should have done sth a long time ago: *'I've mended the lamp in the children's room.' 'None too soon. It's been broken for weeks.'*

he, she, etc. would just as soon do A (as B)
sb wants to do one thing as much as another thing; it does not matter to sb what they do: *Susan can have my ticket for the show. I'd just as soon stay at home (as go out) anyway.* ◇ *He'd just as soon have pizza as a hamburger.*

● **fool →** a fool and his money are soon parted
● **speak →** speak too soon

sooner /'suːnə(r)/

no ,sooner ,said than 'done
(of a request) done immediately: *When he said he wanted to go to the zoo on his birthday it was no sooner said than done.*

no sooner...than... (*written*)
used to show that one thing, which is unexpected, happens immediately after another thing: *No sooner had she got in the bath than the front door bell rang.*

the ,sooner the 'better
very soon; as soon as possible: *'When shall I tell him?' 'The sooner the better.'*

,sooner or 'later
at some time in the future, even if you are not sure exactly when: *The police will find him sooner or later.*

,sooner rather than 'later
after a short time rather than after a long time: *We urged them to sort out the problem sooner rather than later.*

I, etc. would sooner do sth (than sth else)
I, etc. would prefer to do sth (than do sth else): *She'd sooner share a house with other students than live at home with her parents.*

● **rather →** sooner you, etc. than me SEE rather you, etc. than me

soonest /'suːnəst/

● **least →** least said soonest mended

sore /sɔː(r)/

a ,sore 'point (with sb)
a subject or matter that makes sb feel angry or hurt: *The tax increases are a sore point with Jake, as he's going to lose a lot of money.*

stand/stick out like a sore 'thumb (*informal*)
be very obvious or noticeable in an unpleasant way: *He's going to stick out like a sore thumb if he*

doesn't wear a suit to the wedding. **OPP** merge into the background

● **bear →** like a bear with a sore head
● **sight →** be a sight for sore eyes

sorrow /'sɒrəʊ; *AmE* 'sɑːroʊ; 'sɔː-/

do sth more in ,sorrow than in 'anger
do sth because you feel sad or sorry rather than angry: *They said they were threatening legal action more in sorrow than in anger.*

sorrows /'sɒrəʊz; *AmE* 'sɑːroʊz; 'sɔː-/

● **drown →** drown your sorrows

sorry /'sɒri; *AmE* 'sɑːri; 'sɔːri/

be/feel 'sorry for sb
feel sympathy or pity for sb: *I feel sorry for all the people who are alone at Christmas.*

be/feel 'sorry for yourself (*informal, disapproving*)
be/feel unhappy because you think other people have treated you badly, etc: *You can't sit there feeling sorry for yourself all day.*

I'm 'sorry to say
used for saying that sth is disappointing: *He didn't accept the job, I'm sorry to say.*

● **better →** better (to be) safe than sorry

sort /sɔːt; *AmE* sɔːrt/

● **kind →** kind of/sort of
● **kind →** nothing of the kind/sort
● **kind →** of a kind/sort
● **kind →** something of the/that kind/sort
● **men →** sort out/separate the men from the boys
● **sheep →** sort out/separate the sheep from the goats
● **wheat →** sort out/separate the wheat from the chaff

sorts /sɔːts; *AmE* sɔːrts/

be, feel, etc. out of 'sorts (*especially BrE*)
be, feel, etc. ill or bad-tempered: *I was out of sorts for a couple of weeks after I came out of hospital.* ◇ *What's the matter with Jane? She looks rather out of sorts today.* **OPP** in fine/good fettle

it takes all 'sorts (to make a 'world) (*saying*)
different people like different things; different people have different characters and abilities: *'I don't understand Bill. He spends nearly all weekend cleaning and polishing his car.' 'Well, it takes all sorts.'*

of 'sorts (*informal*)
used when you are saying that sth is not a good example of a particular type of thing: *He offered us an apology of sorts and we accepted it.*

soul /səʊl; *AmE* soʊl/

be the soul of sth
be a perfect example of a good quality: *She's the soul of discretion.*

sound

good for the 'soul (*humorous*)
good for you, even if it seems unpleasant: *'Want a ride?' 'No thanks. Walking is good for the soul.'*

* bare → bare your soul
* body → body and soul
* body → keep body and soul together
* God → God rest his/her soul
* heart → (your) heart and soul
* life → the life and soul of the party
* search → search your heart/soul/conscience
* sell → sell your soul

sound /saʊnd/

like, love, etc. the ˌsound of your own 'voice (*disapproving*)
talk too much, usually without listening to others: *That man does like the sound of his own voice. We couldn't stop him talking.*

(as) sound as a 'bell (*informal*)
in perfect condition: *There's nothing wrong with her. She's been examined and she's sound as a bell.*

sound a'sleep
deeply and peacefully asleep: *He had fallen sound asleep in the chair by the fire.* ◊ *The children are sound asleep upstairs.*

sound the 'death knell of sth
be the reason why sth ends, goes out of fashion, or is replaced: *The arrival of large supermarkets sounded the death knell of many small local shops.*

> NOTE
> The *death knell* is the ringing of a bell to announce a person's death.

* false → sound/strike a false note
* note → sound/strike a note (of sth)
* safe → safe and sound
* stand → you, he, etc. can't stand the sight/sound of sb/sth
* suspiciously → look/sound suspiciously like sth

soup /suːp/

be in the 'soup ✦ land yourself/sb in the 'soup (*informal*)
be in, or get yourself or sb into, trouble or difficulties: *If we don't get paid soon, we'll be in the soup.* ◊ *I've really landed myself in the soup this time; I've crashed my father's car.*

from ˌsoup to 'nuts (*AmE, informal*)
from beginning to end: *She told me the whole story from soup to nuts.*

> NOTE
> This refers to a long meal that often begins with soup and ends with nuts.

sour /'saʊə(r)/

go/turn 'sour
become less enjoyable, pleasant or good: *Relations between the two nations have recently gone sour.*

sour 'grapes (*saying*)
used to describe the behaviour of sb who pretends that sth they cannot have is of little value or interest: *When she failed the entrance exam, she started saying that she never wanted to go to college anyway, but I think that's just sour grapes.*

> ❷ ORIGIN
> This idiom comes from one of Aesop's fables. A fox cannot reach some grapes so he decides that they are not ready to eat.

south /saʊθ/

* head → head north/south

sow¹ /səʊ; *AmE* soʊ/

sow your wild 'oats (*informal*)
(usually used of young men) enjoy yourself before you get married and settle down: *The problem is that he never sowed his wild oats before he got married, and he wants to sow them now.*

> ❷ ORIGIN
> *Wild oats* are weeds that grow in fields and look like real oats. Sowing them would be a silly or useless activity.

* reap → you reap what you sow
* seeds → plant/sow the seeds of sth

sow² /saʊ/

* silk → make a silk purse out of a sow's ear

space /speɪs/

in the space of a 'minute, an 'hour, a 'morning, etc.
during the period of a minute, an hour, etc: *I went from Glasgow to Edinburgh twelve times in the space of a few days.*

look/stare/gaze into 'space
look straight in front of you without looking at a particular thing, usually because you are thinking about sth: *I asked her twice if she was ready to leave but she just sat there staring into space.*

* breathing → a breathing space
* waste → a waste of space
* watch → watch this space

spade /speɪd/

* call → call a spade a spade

spades /speɪdz/

in 'spades (*informal*)
in large amounts or to a great degree: *He'd got his revenge now, and in spades.*

> NOTE
> *Spades* are one of the four kinds of playing cards. They are the highest cards in the game of bridge.

span /spæn/

● spick → spic and span SEE spick and span

spanner /'spænə(r)/

put/throw a 'spanner in the works (*BrE*) (*AmE* **throw a ('monkey) 'wrench in the works**) (*informal*)
spoil or prevent the success of sb's plan, idea, etc: *Let's get this finished before the boss comes along and throws a spanner in the works.*

> **NOTE**
> A *spanner* or *wrench* is a metal tool used for fastening things tightly. The *works* are the moving parts of a machine.

spare /speə(r); AmE sper/

go 'spare (*BrE, informal*)
be very angry: *When she found the children drawing on the walls, she went spare.*

spare sb's 'feelings
be careful to avoid offending or upsetting sb: *Eric got no votes at all, but we didn't tell him because we wanted to spare his feelings.* ◊ *She didn't spare my feelings at all — she told me exactly why she didn't like me.*

spare no expense/pains/trouble (to do sth/ (in) doing sth)
spend as much time, money or effort as is necessary: *His twenty-first birthday party was amazing — his parents had spared no expense.* ◊ *The ship's crew will spare no pains to make your Mediterranean cruise unforgettable.* ◊ *It will be a wonderful trip, no expense spared.*

spare the 'rod and spoil the 'child (*saying*)
if you do not punish a child for behaving badly, he/she will behave badly in future

a spare 'tyre (*BrE*) (*AmE* **a spare 'tire**)
a roll of flesh around the waist: *He went on a diet to try and lose his spare tyre.*

to 'spare
if you have time, money, etc. **to spare**, you have more than you need: *I've got absolutely no money to spare this month.* ◊ *We arrived at the airport with five minutes to spare.*

● blushes → save/spare sb's blushes

spark /spɑːk; AmE spɑːrk/

● bright → (a) bright spark

sparks /spɑːks; AmE spɑːrks/

● fly → the feathers/fur/sparks will fly

spate /speɪt/

in (full) 'spate (*especially BrE*)
1 (of a river) containing more water and flowing more strongly than usual: *After heavy rain, the river was in spate.*

2 (of a person) completely involved in talking and not likely to stop or not able to be interrupted: *Celia was in full spate as usual, so I just sat there waiting for her to finish.*

speak /spiːk/

no sth/nothing/not anything to 'speak of
nothing very important or worth mentioning: *We looked through his private papers, but we didn't find anything to speak of.* ◊ *He's got no money to speak of.*

so to 'speak (also **as it 'were**)
used to emphasize that you are expressing sth in an unusual or amusing way: *They were all very similar. All cut from the same cloth, so to speak.* ◊ *Night fell and the city became, as it were, a different place entirely.*

speak for it'self/them'selves
be so clear or obvious that no explanation or comment is needed: *The expressions on their faces spoke for themselves — they hated the song.*

speak for my'self, him'self, etc.
express what you think or want yourself, rather than sb else doing it for you: *I'm quite capable of speaking for myself, thank you!*

speak for your'self (*spoken, informal*)
used to tell sb that a general statement they have just made is not true of you: *'We didn't play very well.' 'Speak for yourself!'* (= I think that I played well).

speak 'highly of sb
praise sb because you admire or respect their personal qualities or abilities: *His teacher speaks very highly of him.* ◊ *Professor Heynman was very highly spoken of by his students.* **OPP** not/never have a good word to say for/about sb/sth

speak your 'mind
say exactly what you think, in a very direct way: *I like a man who speaks his mind.* **OPP** bite your tongue

speak too 'soon
say sth, and find afterwards that what you said is not true: *'I'm glad Simon didn't come.' 'You spoke too soon. Here he comes now.'*

speak 'volumes (about/for sb/sth)
show or express a lot about the nature or quality of sb/sth: *Her face spoke volumes. You could see how much she had suffered.* ◊ *The progress he's made since the operation speaks volumes for his courage.*

● actions → actions speak louder than words
● devil → speak/talk of the devil
● facts → the facts speak for themselves
● ill → speak/think ill of sb
● language → speak/talk the same/a different language

speaking /'spiːkɪŋ/

be on 'speaking terms (with sb)
1 know sb well enough to speak to them, perhaps sb famous or important: *He's on speaking terms with a number of senior politicians.*

2 (also **be 'speaking (to sb)**) be talking to each other again after an argument: *Tony and Craig had a big row and are not on speaking terms.* ◇ *You're lucky I'm still speaking to you after what you did!*

- manner → in a manner of speaking
- relatively → relatively speaking
- strictly → strictly speaking

spec /spek/

do sth on 'spec (*BrE, informal*)
go somewhere without a ticket, an appointment, etc. in the hope that you will be able to get sth you want: *That restaurant's very popular. You'll never get a table if you just turn up on spec.*

> **NOTE**
> *Spec* is short for *speculation* (= doing something without knowing all the facts).

spectacle /'spektəkl/

make a 'spectacle of yourself
draw attention to yourself by behaving or dressing in a ridiculous way in public: *He made a spectacle of himself by shouting at the barman.*

spectacles /'spektəklz/

look at, see, etc. sth through ,rose-tinted/ ,rose-coloured 'spectacles
notice only the pleasant things in life and think things are better than they really are; be too optimistic: *She is convinced the company will make a big profit, but then she does tend to see things through rose-tinted spectacles.*

spectre (*BrE*) (*AmE* **specter**) /'spektə(r)/

- raise → raise the spectre of sth

speed /spiːd/

a ,turn of 'speed
a sudden increase in speed: *She put on a turn of speed at the end of the race and won easily.*

up to 'speed (on sth)
1 (of a person, company, etc.) performing at an expected rate or level: *the cost of bringing the chosen schools up to speed*
2 (of a person) having the most recent and accurate information or knowledge: *I'll bring you up to speed on the latest developments.*

- full → (at) full pelt/speed/tilt
- full → full steam/speed ahead
- haste → more haste, less speed
- lightning → at/with lightning speed
- pick → pick up speed

spell /spel/

(be) under sb's 'spell
(be) so attracted to or interested in sb that you are in their power and will do what they say: *When he tells a story, the children are completely under his spell.*

> **NOTE**
> If somebody puts a *spell* on you, they say a phrase with magic power that gives them control over you.

- weave → weave a spell (over sb)

spend /spend/

spend the 'night with sb/together
stay with sb for a night and have sex with them: *James told me Kim and Robin spent the night together.*

spend a 'penny (*old-fashioned, BrE, informal*)
go to the toilet; urinate: *Do you want to spend a penny before we leave?*

> **❷ ORIGIN**
> In the past, public toilets in England had coin operated locks, which cost one penny to open.

spent /spent/

a ,spent 'force
a person or group that no longer has any power or influence: *The new album is proof that this band is not a spent force just yet.*

spice /spaɪs/

- variety → variety is the spice of life

spick /spɪk/ (also **spic**)

,spick and 'span (also **,spic and 'span**)
clean, tidy and fresh: *The boss likes everything spick and span in the office.*

spike /spaɪk/

spike sb's 'drink
add (more) alcohol or drugs to sb's drink, without their knowledge: *…I discovered later that they'd spiked my drink. That's why I was so ill!*

spike sb's 'guns (*BrE*)
spoil sb's plans because you do not want them to succeed: *She was jealous of David's progress in the company, so she spiked his guns by telling the boss that David had a drinking problem.*

> **❷ ORIGIN**
> This refers to pushing a metal *spike* (= a thin object with a sharp point) into the enemy's gun or cannon so that it cannot be fired.

spill /spɪl/

spill the 'beans (*informal*)
tell sb sth that should be kept secret or private: *We were trying to keep it a secret from Pete, but Marcia spilled the beans.* ◇ *Come on, spill the beans! What did your father say?* **OPP** keep sth under your hat

spill (sb's) 'blood (*formal* or *literary*)
kill or wound people: *Nothing can justify spilling innocent blood.*

spill your 'guts (to sb) (*AmE, informal*)
tell sb everything you know or feel about sth, because you are upset: *I know you're upset about*

what I did, but did you have to spill your guts to my
parents?

spilled /spɪlt/

● ink → much ink has been spilled (on/over sth)

spills /spɪlz/

● thrills → (the) thrills and spills (of sth)

spilt /spɪlt/

● crying → it's no good/use crying over spilt milk

spin /spɪn/

in a (flat) 'spin
very confused, worried or excited: *Her resignation
put her colleagues in a spin.*

spin your 'wheels
use your time, energy, etc. without achieving anything: *I had the feeling that the company was spinning its wheels and getting nowhere.* ▶ **'wheel-
spinning** *noun*: *Save yourself some wheel-spinning
and head to the library.*

spin (sb) a 'yarn/'tale
tell sb a story, usually a long one, which is often
not true: *She came an hour late and spun him a
yarn about her car breaking down.*

> **❷ ORIGIN**
> Sailors used to spin yarns (= long threads) to
> make ropes. They were also famous for telling
> unlikely stories of their adventures, which is
> perhaps the origin of the idiom.

● heel → turn/spin on your heel

spine /spaɪn/

● chill → send a chill up/down sb's spine **SEE** a chill runs/
goes down sb's spine
● shiver → send a shiver up/down sb's spine **SEE** a shiver
runs/goes down sb's spine

spirit /'spɪrɪt/

(do sth) as/if/when the spirit 'moves you
(do sth) when you want to, rather than when you
have to or are forced to: *She works in the garden
occasionally, when the spirit moves her.*

be with sb in 'spirit
be thinking of sb who is in another place because
you would like to be with them but cannot be: *I'm
afraid I can't come to the wedding, but I'll be with
you in spirit.*

get/enter into the 'spirit of sth
take part in an activity or event with enthusiasm:
*Every year he gets into the spirit of Christmas by
decorating his whole house with coloured lights.
◇ The party went well because everyone entered into
the spirit of things.*

the ˌspirit is 'willing but the ˌflesh (it) is 'weak
(*saying, humorous*)
you intend to do good things but are too tired,
lazy, etc. to actually do them

ˌthat's the 'spirit!
used to encourage sb or to tell them that they are
doing sth well: *'I'm rather tired, but I think I can
run another mile.' 'That's the spirit!'*

● fighting → fighting spirit
● moving → the moving spirit

spirits /'spɪrɪts/

be in high/low 'spirits (also **in good/poor
'spirits**)
be happy and cheerful/sad and miserable: *John
was in rather low spirits all evening.* ▶ **ˌhigh-
'spirited, ˌlow-'spirited** *adj.*: *high-spirited children*

● raise → raise sb's spirits

spiritual /'spɪrɪtʃuəl/

be sb's ˌspiritual 'home
be a place where sb could be happy, because they
like the people, customs, culture, etc. there: *I've
always thought that Australia was his spiritual
home.*

spit /spɪt/

spit and 'polish (*informal*)
cleaning and polishing: *This table will look as good
as new with a bit of spit and polish.*

spit 'blood/'venom/'feathers
show that you are very angry; speak in an angry
way: *That man made me so angry that by the end of
the meeting I was spitting blood!*

ˌspit it 'out! (*spoken*)
usually used in orders to tell sb to say sth when
they seem frightened or unwilling to speak: *What
did you tell her about me? Come on, spit it out!*

spite /spaɪt/

in 'spite of sth
if you say that sb does/did sth **in spite of** a fact,
you mean it is surprising that that fact does/did
not prevent them from doing it; despite: *In spite of
his age, he still leads an active life. ◇ They went
swimming in spite of all the danger signs. ◇ English
became the official language for business **in spite of
the fact that** the population was largely Chinese.*

(do sth) in 'spite of yourself
(do sth) even though you do not want or expect
to: *He was a bit depressed so I tried to cheer him up
with a joke. He smiled in spite of himself.*

● nose → cut off your nose to spite your face

spitting /'spɪtɪŋ/

within 'spitting distance (of sth) (*BrE*) (also
within 'shouting distance *AmE, BrE*) (*informal*)
very near a place: *We live within spitting distance of
the sea.*

● image → be the living/spitting/very image of sb/sth

splash /splæʃ/

make, cause, etc. a 'splash (*informal*)
attract a lot of attention, for example in the newspapers, because you are famous: *Their wedding created quite a splash in the newspapers.*

spleen /spliːn/

• vent → vent your spleen

spliced /splaɪst/

get 'spliced (*old-fashioned, BrE, informal*)
get married

> **NOTE**
> The basic meaning of *splice* is to join the ends of two pieces of rope together.

split /splɪt/

split the 'difference
agree on an amount of sth, such as money, which is halfway between two others: *John offered €60, but Peter wanted €100. Finally they split the difference and agreed on €80.*

split sth down the 'middle
divide people into two groups, who disagree: *The local Conservative party is split down the middle on the matter of taxation.*

split 'hairs (*disapproving*)
pay too much attention in an argument to differences that are very small and not important: *You might think I'm just splitting hairs, but what exactly do you mean by 'a significant improvement'?* ▶ **'hair-splitting** *noun*

a ˌsplit 'second
a very short time: *I heard a loud explosion and a split second later I was on the floor.* ▶ **ˌsplit-'second** *adj.*: *split-second timing/reactions*

split your 'sides (laughing/with laughter)
laugh a lot; laugh loudly: *When she started singing in that funny voice, we nearly split our sides.*

split the 'ticket (*AmE, politics*)
vote for candidates from more than one party: *Election officials are reminding voters that they may 'split their ticket' in the November election, unlike a state primary election.*

spoil /spɔɪl/

spoil sb 'rotten (*informal*)
give sb everything they want or ask for: *She spoils the kids rotten.*

spoil the ˌship for a ha'porth/ha'penny-worth of 'tar (*saying*)
spoil sth good because you did not spend any or enough money on a small but essential part of it: *Always buy good quality floppy disks. Don't spoil the ship for a ha'porth of tar.*

> **❷ ORIGIN**
> *Ship* in this idiom was originally *sheep* and *ha'porth* or *ha'penny-worth* referred to a very small amount of money. The basic meaning of the idiom was originally 'allow a sheep to die

because you won't buy a very small amount of tar', tar being used to treat cuts on a sheep's body.

• cooks → too many cooks spoil the broth
• spare → spare the rod and spoil the child

spoiled /spɔɪld/

• choice → be spoilt/spoiled for choice

spoiling /'spɔɪlɪŋ/

be ˌspoiling for a 'fight, argument, etc.
want to fight, argue, etc. with sb very much: *Are you spoiling for a fight?* ◇ *The teachers' union is spoiling for a fight with the Government.*

spoilt /spɔɪlt/

• choice → be spoilt/spoiled for choice

spoke /spəʊk; AmE spoʊk/

put a 'spoke in sb's wheel (*BrE*)
make it difficult for sb to do sth or to carry out their plans: *If the management try to cut our pay, we can put a spoke in their wheel by going on strike.*

> **❷ ORIGIN**
> *Spoke* may be an incorrect translation from Dutch of *spaak* meaning 'bar' or 'stick'.

spoken /'spəʊkən; AmE 'spoʊ-/

• word → the spoken/written word

sponge /spʌndʒ/

• towel → throw in the towel/sponge

spoon /spuːn/

• born → be born with a silver spoon in your mouth
• wooden → get, win, take, etc. the wooden spoon

sport /spɔːt; AmE spɔːrt/

be a (good) 'sport (*informal*)
be generous, cheerful and pleasant, especially in a difficult situation: *She's a good sport.* ◇ *Go on, be a sport* (= used when asking sb to do sth for you).

sporting /'spɔːtɪŋ; AmE 'spɔːrtɪŋ/

a ˌsporting 'chance
a reasonable chance of success: *I know it's going to be tough, but I think I'm in with a sporting chance of winning.* **OPP** not have a cat in hell's chance

spot /spɒt; AmE spaːt/

ˌglued/ˌrooted to the 'spot
not able to move, for example because you are frightened or surprised: *He shouted at her to run, but she just stood there, glued to the spot.* ◇ *She stood there rooted to the spot when she saw the body.*

on the 'spot
1 at the place where sth is happening: *Our man on the spot is Geoff Davies. He's going to tell us exactly what's happening in Cairo.*
2 immediately; without any delay: *The police officer asked me for my driving licence and I gave it to him on the spot.* ◇ *on-the-spot fines*

put sb on the 'spot
put sb in a difficult position, perhaps by asking them a difficult or embarrassing question: *Her question about my future plans really put me on the spot.*

● **bang** → bang/spot on
● **black** → a black spot
● **blind** → a/sb's blind spot
● **bright** → a/the bright spot
● **high** → the high point/spot of sth
● **hit** → hit the spot
● **hot** → a hot spot
● **riveted** → be riveted to the spot/ground
● **soft** → have a soft spot for sb/sth
● **tight** → in a tight corner/spot

spotlight /'spɒtlaɪt; AmE 'spɑːt-/

in/under the 'spotlight
getting attention from newspapers, television and the public: *Unemployment has once again come under the spotlight.* ◇ *He's a shy man, who really doesn't enjoy being in the spotlight.*

spots /spɒts; AmE spɑːts/

● **knock** → knock spots off sb/sth
● **leopard** → a leopard cannot change its spots

spout /spaʊt/

be/go up the 'spout (*BrE, slang*)
be/go wrong; be spoilt or not working: *It looks like our holiday plans are up the spout.* ◇ *This information the bank sent me is totally up the spout.*

> **❷ ORIGIN**
> *Spout* was the name given to a lift in a pawnbroker's shop which took goods up to an area where they were stored. If somebody had items *up the spout,* they were in financial trouble. The expression gradually came to mean difficulties in general.

sprat /spræt/

(be) a ˌsprat to catch a 'mackerel (*informal*)
(be) a fairly small or unimportant thing which is offered or risked in the hope of getting sth bigger or better: *The competition and prize of a free car is a sprat to catch a mackerel. The publicity will mean good business for months to come.*

> **NOTE**
> *Sprat* and *mackerel* are both types of fish. *Sprats* are very small.

spread /spred/

spread like 'wildfire
(especially of news or disease) travel or spread very quickly: *Rumours about a fall in the price of oil spread like wildfire in the city.* ◇ *Cholera spread like wildfire through the camps.*

spread your 'wings
become more independent and confident enough to try new activities, etc: *Studying at university should help you to spread your wings and become independent.*

spread the 'word
tell people about sth: *Because of her contacts in the business world, he asked Kate to spread the word about his latest venture.* **OPP** keep sth to yourself

spread yourself too 'thin
try to do so many different things at the same time that you do not do any of them properly: *Are you sure you can manage an evening job as well? Don't you think you're spreading yourself a bit too thin?*

● **net** → cast/spread your net wide

spring /sprɪŋ/

be ˌno spring 'chicken (*humorous*)
be no longer young: *I'm no spring chicken, but I still like going on long walks.* ◇ *Are you sure he should be playing squash at his age? He's no spring chicken, you know!*

spring a 'leak
(of a boat, roof, container, etc.) start to let water in: *The boat sprang a leak halfway across the lake.*

spring to/into 'life/'action
(of a person or thing) suddenly become active or start to work: *As soon as he heard the alarm bell, he sprang into action.* ◇ *This machine will spring into life at the touch of a button.*

spring a 'trap
1 make a trap for catching animals close suddenly
2 try to trick sb into doing or saying sth; succeed in this: *The burglars were arrested after the police sprung a trap on them last night.*

● **full** → full of the joys of spring
● **mind** → come/spring to mind

springs /sprɪŋz/

● **hope** → hope springs eternal

spur /spɜː(r)/

(do sth) on the ˌspur of the 'moment
if you do sth **on the spur of the moment**, you do it as soon as you think of it, without planning or preparation: *When they telephoned me with the offer of a job abroad, I decided on the spur of the moment to accept.* ◇ *It was a spur-of-the-moment decision.*

spurs /spɜːz; AmE spɜːrz/

win/earn your 'spurs (*formal*)
become successful or famous: *You'll win your spurs as a teacher if you can control class 5.*

spy /spaɪ/

ˌspy out the ˈland
find out about a situation, a place, an organization, etc. before you make a decision: *The manager is sending Mark to Iceland to spy out the land. He wants to know whether we can do business there.*

square /skweə(r); AmE skwer/

be/go back to square ˈone (also **start again from square ˈone**) (*informal*)
start sth again from the beginning because your first idea, plan, action, etc. has failed or has been stopped: *The experiment didn't work, so it's back to square one, I'm afraid.*

> **❷ ORIGIN**
> This may refer to going back to the beginning or first square of a board game such as 'snakes and ladders'.

be (all) ˈsquare (with sb) (*informal*)
1 have the same score in a competition: *Liverpool were all square with Chelsea at half-time.*
2 (of two people) not owe money (or anything else) to each other: *Here's a pound — now we're square.*

be a square ˈpeg (in a round ˈhole) (*BrE, informal*)
not fit well or easily into an organization, a job, etc. because you are different: *I don't have the right personality for the job. I feel like a square peg in a round hole.* **OPP** in your element

square your/an acˈcount (with sb) ♦ **square acˈcounts (with sb)**
1 pay sb the money you owe them: *You can square your account at the end of the week.*
2 hurt sb, usually because they have done sth bad to you: *I'm here to square accounts with Murphy for what he did to my sister.*

square the ˈcircle
(try to) do sth that is or seems impossible: *The Government is trying to square the circle when it says it will spend more on the health service without raising taxes.*

> **❷ ORIGIN**
> This is a mathematical task that was considered impossible, involving making a square exactly equal in area to a particular circle.

a square ˈmeal
a large and satisfying meal: *The children get three square meals a day.*

● **fair** → fair and square

squarely /ˈskweəli; AmE ˈskwerli/

● **fair** → fairly and squarely SEE fair and square

squeak /skwiːk/

● **narrow** → a narrow escape/squeak

squeaky /ˈskwiːki/

the squeaky wheel gets the ˈgrease/ˈoil (*AmE*)
used to say that a person who complains or talks a lot gets most attention: *In politics, the squeaky wheel gets the grease so it is vital for consumers to speak up and be heard. ◇ It's the squeaky wheel that gets the oil, but what about the shy student?*

squeeze /skwiːz/

put the ˈsqueeze on sb (to do sth) (*informal*)
put pressure on sb to act in a particular way; make a situation difficult for sb: *Rising fuel prices are putting the squeeze on farmers and transport businesses.*

ˌsqueeze sb ˈdry
get as much money, information, etc. out of sb as you can: *The war, as well as the economic sanctions imposed by foreign powers, have squeezed the economy dry.*

● **tight** → a tight squeeze

squib /skwɪb/

● **damp** → a damp squib

stab /stæb/

have a stab at sth/at doing sth (*informal*)
try sth/doing sth, especially if you have never done it before: *I had a stab at fishing once but I found it boring.*

stab sb in the ˈback ♦ **get, etc. a stab in the ˈback** (*informal*)
do or say sth that harms sb who trusts you; be treated this way: *Jane promised to support me at the meeting, but then she stabbed me in the back by supporting David instead.* ▶ **a ˈback-stabber, ˈback-stabbing** *nouns*: *This party is full of back-stabbers. ◇ There is always a lot of back-stabbing in academic life.*

● **dark** → a shot/stab in the dark

stable /ˈsteɪbl/

shut/lock/close the stable door after the horse has ˈbolted (*BrE*) (*AmE* **shut, etc. the barn door after the horse has eˈscaped**)
take action to prevent sth bad from happening after it has already happened: *Last week all their silver was stolen; this week they're putting in a burglar alarm! That's really shutting the stable door after the horse has bolted.*

stack /stæk/

● **blow** → blow your stack SEE blow your top

stacked /stækt/

the cards/odds are stacked aˈgainst sb/sth
it is not likely that sb/sth will succeed, because they/it will have many problems or difficulties: *The cards are stacked against this plan. The public are against it.*

the cards/odds are stacked in 'favour of sb/
sth (*BrE*) (*AmE* **the cards/odds are stacked in
'favor of sb/sth**)
it is likely that sb/sth will succeed because the
conditions are good or because sb/sth has an
advantage: *The odds are heavily stacked in favour
of Manchester United, who are having a very successful season and who will be playing in front of
the home crowd.*

Emily had the impression that the odds were
stacked in favour of her opponent.

staff /stɑːf; *AmE* stæf/

the ˌstaff of 'life (*literary*)
a basic food, especially bread

● **skeleton** → a skeleton crew/staff/service

stag /stæg/

go 'stag (*AmE, old-fashioned, informal*)
(of a man) go to a party without a partner: *Our
dates were sick and we went stag.*

stage /steɪdʒ/

be/go on the 'stage
be/become an actor: *Maria has always wanted to
go on the stage.*

● **act** → do/perform/stage a disappearing/vanishing act
● **scene** → set the scene/stage (for sth)

stake /steɪk/

(be/have a lot, etc.) at 'stake
that can be won or lost, depending on the success
of a particular action: *The team must win the game
on Saturday to stay in the competition. With so
much at stake, everyone has to play their best.*
◇ *This decision has put our lives at stake.*

> **NOTE**
> *Stake* in this idiom refers to the amount of
> money that somebody bets when they are
> gambling and which they could lose.

stake (out) a/your 'claim to sb/sth
say that you have a special interest in sb/sth, or
have a right to own sth, especially to warn other
people not to take it: *Both countries have staked
out a claim to the land.*

> **❷ ORIGIN**
> If you staked out your claim to some land, you
> put *stakes* (= wooden posts) in the ground to
> mark the limits of land that you claimed was
> yours.

stakes /steɪks/

in the... stakes
used to say how much of a particular quality a
person has, as if they were in a competition in
which some people are more successful than
others: *John doesn't do too well in the personality
stakes.*

● **pull** → pull up stakes

stand /stænd/

> Most idioms containing **stand** are at the entries
> for the nouns and adjectives in the idioms, for
> example **stand on ceremony** is at **ceremony**.

you, he, etc. can't 'stand sb/sth ◆ you, he,
etc. can't 'stand the sight/sound of sb/sth
(*informal*)
you, he, etc. dislikes or hates sb/sth or seeing/
hearing sb/sth: *If you can't stand the sight of blood,
you won't make a very good nurse!* ◇ *I can't stand
the sight of her.* **OPP** think the world of sb/sth

make a 'stand (against/for/over/about/on
sth) ◆ take a 'stand (on/over sth)
argue, protest or fight because of sth you believe
in: *This must never happen again; it's time to make
a stand.* **OPP** sit on the fence

stand or 'fall by sth
succeed or fail, or be judged good or bad, because
of one thing: *A salesman stands or falls by the number of sales he makes — if he doesn't make enough,
he loses his job.*

standard /'stændəd; *AmE* -dərd/

● **bog** → bog standard

standby /'stændbaɪ/

on 'standby
1 ready to do sth immediately if needed or asked:
*The emergency services were put on standby after a
bomb warning.*
2 ready to travel or go somewhere if a ticket or
sth that is needed suddenly becomes available:
He was on standby for the flight to New York.

standing /'stændɪŋ/

do sth standing on your 'head (*informal*)
do sth very easily, without any effort: *This exam's
no problem. I could do it standing on my head.*

leave sb/sth 'standing (*informal*)
be much better than sb/sth: *In maths and science
she leaves the others standing.*

stands /stændz/

it ˌstands to 'reason (that…) (*informal*)
it is quite clear, obvious or easy to understand: *It stands to reason that the less you eat, the thinner you get.*

- hair → your hair stands on end

standstill /'stændstɪl/

- grind → grind to a halt/standstill

star /stɑː(r)/

- hitch → hitch your wagon to a star

stare /steə(r); AmE ster/

stare sth in the 'face
be unable to avoid sth: *They were staring defeat in the face.*

- face → look/stare you in the face
- space → look/stare/gaze into space

stark /stɑːk; AmE stɑːrk/

stark 'naked (*BrE*) (*AmE* buck 'naked)
completely naked: *He always walks around his apartment buck naked.*

stars /stɑːz; AmE stɑːrz/

have 'stars in your eyes
if you have stars in your eyes, you are happy and excited about the future, because you believe that you will be successful and famous: *Hundreds of young actors, all with stars in their eyes, are here for the auditions.* ▶ ˌstarry-'eyed *adj.*: *I was just a starry-eyed teenager, dreaming of singing on Broadway.*

see 'stars (*informal*)
see small bright lights for a few moments, for example after being hit on the head: *There was a bang. I saw stars, and the next thing I knew, I was lying on the kitchen floor.*

- reach → reach for the stars
- thank → thank your lucky stars (that…)

start /stɑːt; AmE stɑːrt/

ˌdon't 'start (also ˌdon't 'you start) (*spoken, informal*)
used to tell sb not to complain or be critical: *Don't start! I told you I'd be late.*

for a 'start ♦ to 'start with (also for 'starters *informal*)
used for giving the first of several things or reasons: *You're not going to marry him. For a start, you're too young. For another thing, you hardly know him.* ◇ *She wasn't keen on the idea to start with.*

'start something/anything (*informal*)
begin a fight or an argument: *Don't try to start anything with him, he has a knife.* ◇ *Are you trying to start something?*

- ball → get/keep/set/start the ball rolling
- false → (make) a false start
- flying → get off to a flying start
- foot → get/start off on the right/wrong foot (with sb)
- head → a head start (on/over sb)
- square → start again from square one SEE be/go back to square one

started /'stɑːtɪd; AmE 'stɑːrtɪd/

you, he, she, etc. 'started it (*spoken, informal*)
you, he, she, etc. began a fight or an argument: *'Stop fighting, you two!' 'He started it!'*

starters /'stɑːtəz; AmE 'stɑːrtərz/

under ˌstarters 'orders
(of a runner, rider, etc.) waiting for a signal to start the race

- start → for starters SEE for a start

starts /stɑːts; AmE stɑːrts/

- fits → in fits and starts

starving /'stɑːvɪŋ; AmE 'stɑːrvɪŋ/

be 'starving (for sth) (also be 'starved *especially AmE*) (*informal*)
feel very hungry: *When's dinner? I'm starving!*

State /steɪt/

- evidence → turn State's evidence SEE turn King's/Queen's evidence

state /steɪt/

be in a 'state ♦ get into a 'state (*informal*)
1 be/get worried, nervous or upset: *Her husband was injured in a car crash yesterday, so she's in a terrible state.* ◇ *He got into a state over his driving test.*
2 be/get dirty or untidy: *This house is in a real state!* OPP be/look a picture

a state of af'fairs
general situation or circumstances: *We know little about the present state of affairs in China.*

ˌstate of the 'art
using the most modern or advanced techniques or methods; as good as it can be at the present time: *The security system we're using is state of the art.* ◇ *This computer uses state-of-the-art technology.*

the state of 'play
what is happening now in a situation which is developing or changing: *We go to our correspondent for the latest state of play in the peace talks.*

- lie → lie in state
- nanny → the nanny state
- repair → in a good, bad, etc. state of repair SEE in good, bad, etc. repair

statesman /'steɪtsmən/

- elder → an elder statesman

stations /'steɪʃnz/

• action → action stations
• panic → panic stations

status /'steɪtəs; AmE also 'stætəs/

the status 'quo (from Latin)
the situation as it is now, or as it was before a recent change: *The conservatives are keen to maintain the status quo.*

a 'status symbol
an expensive possession which shows people that you are rich: *These cars are regarded as status symbols in Britain.*

stay /steɪ/

be here to 'stay ♦ have come to 'stay
be accepted or used by most people and therefore a permanent part of our lives: *It looks as if televised trials are here to stay.* **OPP** here today, gone tomorrow

stay! (spoken)
used to tell a dog not to move

stay the 'course
continue doing sth until it has finished or been completed, even though it is difficult: *Very few of the trainees have stayed the course.*

stay your/sb's 'hand (old-fashioned or literary)
stop yourself/sb from doing sth; prevent sb from doing sth: *He reached for his keys, but Rosa stayed his hand.*

stay the 'night (especially BrE)
sleep at sb's house for one night: *You can always stay the night at our house.*

stay 'put (informal)
stay where you are; not travel, escape, look for another job, etc: *I'd like to move house, but my wife wants to stay put.*

• clear → steer/stay/keep clear (of sb/sth)
• jump → be/stay one jump ahead (of sb/sth)
• loose → hang/stay loose
• way → keep/stay out of sb's way

stead /sted/

in sb's/sth's 'stead (formal)
instead of sb/sth: *Foxton was dismissed and John Smith was appointed in his stead.*

stand sb in good 'stead
be useful to sb: *Learning German will stand her in good stead when she goes to work in the export department.*

steady /'stedi/

go 'steady (with sb) (old-fashioned, informal)
have sb as a regular boyfriend or girlfriend: *Martin and Ingrid have been going steady for nearly a year.*

(as) steady as a 'rock
extremely steady and calm; that you can rely on: *Even though she must have been frightened, her voice was as steady as a rock and she looked him straight in the eyes when she spoke.*

steady 'on! (informal)
be more careful about what you do or say; slow down: *Steady on, you two, let's not get angry!* ◊ *Steady on, you'll break it!*

• ready → ready, steady, go!

steal /stiːl/

be a 'steal (especially AmE)
be for sale at an unexpectedly low price: *This suit is a steal at $80.* **OPP** cost/pay an arm and a leg

steal a 'glance/'look (at sb/sth) (written)
look quickly at sb/sth, so that nobody notices you looking: *He stole a glance at her out of the corner of his eye.*

steal sb's 'heart (literary)
make sb fall in love with you: *As he became more well known, his good looks and charm stole young girls' hearts all across the country.*

steal a 'kiss (from sb) (literary)
kiss sb suddenly or secretly: *This is the place where he first stole a kiss from me, when I was only twelve.*

steal a 'march on sb (written)
do sth before sb else, and so gain an advantage: *The 'Daily News' stole a march on our paper by printing the story first.*

> **❷ ORIGIN**
> This expression probably comes from the military, referring to armies secretly marching to higher ground in order to be in a better position than the enemy.

steal the 'show
attract more attention and praise than other people in a particular situation: *Actors don't like working with animals because they often steal the show.*

steal sb's 'thunder
spoil sb's attempt to surprise or impress, by doing sth first: *He had planned to tell everyone about his discovery at the September meeting, but his assistant stole his thunder by talking about it beforehand.*

> **❷ ORIGIN**
> In the eighteenth century, the writer John Dennis invented a machine that made the sound of thunder for use in his new play. The play was not a success, and was taken off and replaced by another play. When Dennis went to see the other play, he was angry to hear his thunder machine being used and complained that '...they will not let my play run, but they steal my thunder'.

• beg → beg, borrow or steal

steam /stiːm/

> **NOTE**
> All these idioms refer in different ways to engines that are powered by steam, particularly the kind that were used on trains.

get up/pick up 'steam
1 gradually increase speed: *As the train came out of the tunnel, it picked up steam.*

2 (*informal*) gradually get bigger, more active or popular: *The election campaign is getting up steam now; it is only two weeks to election day.* ◇ *I'm trying to get up enough steam to finish writing this book, but it's not easy.*

,let off 'steam (*informal*)
release energy, strong feelings, nervous tension, etc. by intense physical activity or noisy behaviour: *He lets off steam by going to the gym after work.* ◇ *All children need to let off steam from time to time.*

run out of 'steam (*informal*)
lose the energy, enthusiasm, etc. that you had before: *His presidential campaign began well but ran out of steam after a couple of months.*

(get/go somewhere) under your own 'steam (*BrE, informal*)
(get/go somewhere) without help from others: *Don't worry about arranging transport for us. We can get there under our own steam.*

● full → full steam/speed ahead
● head → build up/work up, etc. a head of steam

steamed /stiːmd/

be/get (all) steamed 'up (about/over sth) (*BrE*) (*AmE* be 'steamed (about sth)) (*informal*)
be/become very angry or excited (about sth): *There's no need to get so steamed up over such a small problem.*

steel /stiːl/

of 'steel
having a quality like steel, especially a strong, cold or hard quality: *She felt a hand of steel* (= a strong, firm hand) *on her arm.* ◇ *There was a hint of steel in his voice* (= he sounded cold and firm).

● nerves → have nerves of steel

steep /stiːp/

be a bit/rather 'steep (*informal*)
(of a price or a request) be too much; be unreasonable: *€6? That seems a bit steep for a small piece of cheese.* ◇ *It's a bit steep to expect us to work longer hours for no extra money.*

steeped /stiːpt/

be 'steeped in sth (*written*)
have a lot of a particular quality: *This is a city steeped in history.*

steer /stɪə(r); AmE stɪr/

● bum → a bum steer
● clear → steer/stay/keep clear (of sb/sth)
● middle → follow/steer/take a middle course

stem /stem/

from ,stem to 'stern
all the way from the front of a ship to the back: *It was a small boat, less than thirty feet from stem to stern.*

,stem the 'tide (of sth)
stop the large increase of sth bad: *The police are unable to stem the rising tide of crime.*

step /step/

be in/out of 'step (with sb/sth)
1 putting your feet on the ground in the right/wrong way, according to the rhythm of the music or the people you are moving with: *I found myself marching in step with the music.*
2 having ideas that are the same as or different from other people's: *He's completely out of step with other cancer specialists; his ideas about treatment are quite different.* ◇ *The government no longer seems to be in step with the attitudes of the people.*

fall into 'step (beside/with sb) (*written*)
change the way you are walking so that you start walking in the same rhythm as the person you are walking with: *He caught her up and fell into step beside her.*

mind/watch your 'step
1 walk carefully: *Mind your step, it's wet there.*
2 behave or act carefully: *You've got to watch your step with Simon. He gets angry very quickly.*

one step ,forward, two steps 'back (*saying*)
used to say that every time you make progress, something bad happens that means that the situation is worse than before: *Trying to get the law changed has been a frustrating business. It's a case of one step forward, two steps back.*

a/one step a'head (of sb/sth)
when you are **one step ahead** of sb/sth, you manage to avoid them or to achieve sth more quickly than they do: *One of the reasons why they're so successful as a business is because they always seem to be one step ahead of the competition.*

,step by 'step
slowly, one thing after another; gradually: *If you take it step by step, learning a language is easy.* ◇ *There are step-by-step instructions on how to build your bookcase.*

step into the 'breach
do sb's job or work when they are suddenly or unexpectedly unable to do it: *The cook at the hotel fell ill, so the manager's wife stepped into the breach.*

NOTE
This comes from the military. A *breach* was a hole that had been made in the walls that defended you from your enemies. If you *stepped into the breach* you stood in front of the hole and tried to stop people from entering.

step into sb's 'shoes
take over a job from another person: *Mike stepped into his father's shoes when his father retired as director.*

'step on it (also **step on the 'gas** especially in *AmE*) (*informal*)
drive a car faster; accelerate: *You'll be late if you don't step on it.*

step out of 'line ◆ be/get out of 'line
behave badly or break the rules: *The teacher warned them that she'd punish anyone who stepped out of line.*

● **tread** → step on sb's toes **SEE** tread on sb's toes

steps /steps/

take steps to do sth
take the necessary action to achieve or get sth: *The government is taking steps to control the rising crime rate.*

● **step** → one step forward, two steps back

stern /stɜːn; AmE stɜːrn/

● **stem** → from stem to stern

sterner /stɜːnə(r); AmE stɜːrnə(r)/

be made of sterner 'stuff
(of a person) have a stronger character and be more able to deal with difficulties and problems than other people: *Did she cry? I thought she was made of sterner stuff.*

stew /stjuː; AmE stuː/

be in a 'stew (about/over sth) ◆ get (yourself) into a 'stew (about/over sth) (*informal*)
be/become very worried or nervous (about sth): *She's in a stew over what she's going to wear to the party tonight.*

let sb 'stew (in their own 'juice) (*informal*)
leave sb to worry and suffer the unpleasant effects of their own actions: *We told her not to trust him but she wouldn't listen — so let her stew in her own juice!*

stick /stɪk/

get/take 'stick from sb (*BrE, informal*)
be angrily told you are wrong or at fault; be blamed or criticized: *The new member of the team took a lot of stick from the crowd. He played terribly.* ◇ *The government has been getting a lot of stick from the press recently.*

give sb 'stick (*BrE, informal*)
criticize sb: *The crowd gave the players a lot of stick for their terrible performance.*

‚stick 'em 'up! (*spoken*)
used to tell sb to put their hands above their head when you are pointing a gun at them: *This is a robbery! Stick 'em up!*

stick 'fast
be firmly fixed in a place and unable to move or be moved: *The boat was stuck fast in the mud.*

stick in your 'mind
(of a memory, an idea, a picture, etc.) be remembered for a long time because it made a strong impression on you: *The image of the dead child's face stuck in my mind for years.* ◇ *That poem has always stuck in my mind.*

stick in your 'throat/'craw/'gullet (*informal*)
if sth **sticks in your throat**, it is difficult or impossible to agree with or accept: *It really sticks in my throat that I get paid less than the others for doing the same job.*

stick your 'neck out (*informal*)
do or say sth which other people are afraid to do, and as a result attract attention or trouble: *Joe stuck his neck out at the meeting; he told the boss that the new sales policy wasn't working.*

stick to your 'guns (*informal*)
refuse to change your actions, opinions, etc. in spite of criticism: *If the government sticks to its guns we'll get through this economic crisis.*

● **beat** → a rod/stick to beat sb with
● **boot** → put/stick the boot in
● **carrot** → the carrot and/or (the) stick
● **cleft** → be (caught) in a cleft stick
● **draw** → get the short end of the stick **SEE** draw the short straw
● **knife** → put/stick the knife in/into sb
● **mile** → stand/stick out a mile
● **mud** → if you throw enough mud, some of it will stick **SEE** mud sticks
● **nose** → poke/stick your nose in/into sth
● **oar** → put/stick your oar in
● **shake** → more … than you can shake a stick at
● **sore** → stand/stick out like a sore thumb
● **tell** → tell sb where to put/stick sth
● **two** → put/stick two fingers up at sb
● **wrong** → get (hold of) the wrong end of the stick

sticks /stɪks/

(out) in the 'sticks (*informal*)
in the country, far from towns and cities: *I like living out in the sticks, but it can be a bit boring.*

‚up 'sticks (and go, etc.) (*BrE, informal*)
leave your home in order to move to another one: *Things weren't working out for them here, so they upped sticks and went to Chicago.*

● **mud** → mud sticks

sticky /'stɪki/

have sticky 'fingers (*informal*)
be likely to steal sth: *Be careful about leaving your things lying around. Some people here have got very sticky fingers!*

(be on) a ‚sticky 'wicket (*BrE, informal*)
a situation in which it is difficult to defend yourself against criticism or attack: *Don't be too confident about getting the contract. After our problems with the last one we're on a sticky wicket there.*

> **NOTE**
> In the game of cricket, a *sticky wicket* is a playing area that is drying out after rain and so is more difficult for the person hitting the ball to play on.

● **end** → come to a bad/sticky end
● **patch** → go through, hit, etc. a bad/sticky patch

stiff /stɪf/

(as) stiff as a 'board
(of things) very firm and difficult to bend or move: *He left his gloves outside in the snow, and when he found them again they were as stiff as a board.*

(as) stiff as a 'poker (*informal*)
(usually of people) very straight or upright in the way you sit or stand: *The old lady was sitting upright in her chair, stiff as a poker.*

a ,stiff 'drink
a strong alcoholic drink: *That was a shock — I need a stiff drink!*

(keep) a stiff upper 'lip
keep calm and hide your feelings when you are in pain or in a difficult situation: *The English gentleman is famous for his stiff upper lip.*

● **bore** → bore sb stiff

still /stɪl/

be still going 'strong (*informal*)
1 be still active, successful or working: *After nine hours of chess, both players are still going strong.* ◇ *My car was made in the nineties, but it's still going strong.*
2 be still strong and healthy, in spite of being old: *She's 91 years old and still going strong.*

the still of the 'night (*literary*)
the time during the night when it is silent and calm

the still small 'voice
the voice of your conscience, especially when you are thinking of doing sth wrong or bad

still waters run 'deep (*saying*)
a person who seems to be quiet or shy may surprise you by knowing a lot or having deep feelings: *I know he seems very quiet and content with his life, but still waters run deep, you know.*

● **less** → even/much/still less

sting /stɪŋ/

a ,sting in the 'tail (*informal*)
an unpleasant feature that comes at the end of a story, an event, etc: *Roald Dahl's stories often have a sting in the tail; that's why I like them.*

take the 'sting out of sth
(of a situation) take away the part that is unpleasant or dangerous: *We can pay the electricity bill in monthly instalments if we want, which takes the sting out of it.*

stink /stɪŋk/

kick up/make/create/raise a 'stink (about sth) (*informal*)
show that you are angry about a situation, often by protesting in public: *He kicked up a stink about the noise from the new nightclub, writing to all the papers and complaining to the council.*

● **high** → smell/stink to high heaven

stinking /'stɪŋkɪŋ/

be stinking 'rich (*informal, usually disapproving*)
be extremely rich: *He doesn't need to work for a living — he's stinking rich.*

stint /stɪnt/

do sth without 'stint (*written*)
do sth generously and in large amounts: *She praises her pupils without stint.*

stir /stɜː(r)/

cause/create a 'stir
make a number of people feel interest, excitement or shock: *His sudden resignation caused quite a stir.*

stir sb's/the 'blood
make sb excited or enthusiastic: *His political speeches are designed to stir the blood.*

stir your 'stumps (*old-fashioned, BrE, informal*)
begin to move; hurry: *You stir your stumps and get ready for school, my girl!*

> **NOTE**
> *Stump* is an informal word for 'leg'.

stitch /stɪtʃ/

not have a stitch 'on ◆ **without a stitch 'on** (*informal*)
have no clothes on; be naked: *When he came into my room, I didn't have a stitch on. I was so embarrassed!* ◇ *We left our clothes along the river bank and went swimming without a stitch on.*

a ,stitch in 'time (saves 'nine) (*saying*)
if you act immediately when sth goes wrong, it will save you a lot more work later, because the problem will get worse if you leave it: *We'd better fix that leak before it does any permanent damage. A stitch in time…*

stitches /'stɪtʃɪz/

in 'stitches (*informal*)
laughing a lot: *The film had the audience in stitches.*

stock /stɒk; AmE stɑːk/

(be) in/out of stock
(be) available/not available for sale in a shop/store: *Have you got any mozzarella cheese in stock?* ◇ *The book you want is out of stock at the moment.*

take 'stock (of sb/sth)
think again carefully (about sb/sth); think about what sth really means: *After a year in the job, she decided it was time to take stock* (= think again whether it was the job she wanted). ◇ *He stopped to take stock of what he had read.*

● **laughing** → a laughing stock
● **lock** → lock, stock and barrel

stocking /'stɒkɪŋ; AmE 'stɑːkɪŋ/

in your ˌstocking(ed) 'feet (old-fashioned)
wearing socks or stockings but not shoes: *Our feet were too sore to put into shoes, so we walked home in our stockinged feet.*

stocks /stɒks; AmE stɑːks/

on the 'stocks
in the process of being made, built or prepared: *Our new model is already on the stocks and will be available in the spring.*

> **NOTE**
> *Stocks* refers to the frame that supports a ship or boat when it is being built.

stock-still /ˌstɒk 'stɪl; AmE ˌstɑːk-/

be, stay, stand, etc. ˌstock-'still
be, stay, etc. still, without moving at all: *When I heard footsteps on the stairs, I stood stock-still and held my breath.*

> **NOTE**
> *Stock-still* means as still as a *stock* (= an old word for a piece of wood).

stomach /'stʌmək/

have no 'stomach for sth
have no desire or appetite for sth because you find it unpleasant: *He has no stomach for this kind of job. He should never have become a salesman.*

turn sb's 'stomach ♦ make sb's 'stomach turn
make sb feel sick or disgusted: *The thought of eating a raw egg turns my stomach.*

- **empty** → on an empty stomach
- **eyes** → your eyes are bigger than your stomach
- **pit** → the pit of your/the stomach
- **pump** → pump sb's stomach
- **sick** → sick to your stomach
- **strong** → have a strong stomach

stone /stəʊn; AmE stoʊn/

be carved/set in 'stone
(of a decision, plan, etc.) unable to be changed: *People should remember that our proposals aren't carved in stone.*

leave no stone un'turned
try everything possible to find or obtain sth: *The police left no stone unturned in their efforts to find the little girl.*

ˌstone the 'crows ♦ ˌstone 'me (old-fashioned, BrE)
used to express surprise, shock, anger, etc: *Stone the crows! You're not going out dressed like that, are you?*

a 'stone's throw
a very short distance: *We're just a stone's throw from the shops.*

- **blood** → like getting blood out of/from a stone
- **heart** → have a heart of stone
- **kill** → kill sth stone dead

- **kill** → kill two birds with one stone
- **rolling** → a rolling stone (gathers no moss)

When the brochure said the hotel was just a stone's throw from the beach...

stone-cold /ˌstəʊn 'kəʊld; AmE ˌstoʊn 'koʊld/

ˌstone-cold 'sober
having drunk no alcohol at all: *By the time I arrived at the party, everyone else had had quite a few drinks, whereas I was stone-cold sober.* **OPP** blind drunk

stoned /stəʊnd; AmE stoʊnd/

ˌstoned out of your 'mind (slang)
not behaving or thinking normally because of the effects of an illegal drug such as marijuana

stones /stəʊnz; AmE stoʊnz/

- **people** → people (who live) in glass houses shouldn't throw stones

stony /'stəʊni; AmE 'stoʊni/

fall on stony 'ground
fail to produce the result or the effect that you hope for; have little success: *She tried to warn him, but her words fell on stony ground.*

- **flat** → be stony broke **SEE** be flat broke

stools /stuːlz/

- **two** → fall between two stools

stoop /stuːp/

stoop so 'low (as to do sth) (written)
lower your moral standards far enough to do sth bad or unpleasant: *I hope none of my friends would stoop so low as to steal.* ◇ *She suggested placing an ad in a magazine for a boyfriend, but I'd never stoop so low.*

stop

stop /stɒp; AmE staːp/

stop at 'nothing
do anything, even sth immoral or criminal in order to get sth: *He'd stop at nothing to make a success out of his business.*

stop the 'rot
stop sth getting worse, especially in politics or business: *Our company's profits were falling, so a new director was appointed to stop the rot.*

stop 'short
1 (also **stop sb short**) suddenly stop doing sth or make sb stop sb doing sth: *When I read how many people had died, I stopped short and stared in disbelief at the newspaper.*
2 (**stop short of sth/of doing sth**) nearly but not actually do sth, for example because you are afraid or you think it is a bad idea: *The manager told her that he was unhappy with her work, but he stopped short of dismissing her from her job.*

- full → come to a full stop
- full → full stop
- pit → make a pit stop
- tracks → stop/halt sb in their tracks
- tracks → stop/halt/freeze in your tracks

stopping /'stɒpɪŋ; AmE 'staːpɪŋ/

- holding → there's no holding/stopping sb

stops /stɒps; AmE staːps/

- buck → the buck stops here
- pull → pull out all the stops

store /stɔː(r)/

be in 'store (for sb)
be coming in the future; be about to happen: *I can see trouble in store. ◇ There's a surprise in store for you.*

put/set (no, great, little, etc.) 'store by sth
think that sth has (no, great, little, etc.) importance or value: *She sets little store by what her husband says. ◇ Why do some people put such great store by their horoscopes?*

store up 'trouble, etc. for yourself
have problems in the future because of things that you are doing or not doing now: *If you don't deal with the problem now, you'll be storing up trouble for yourself later.*

- kid → like a kid in a candy store/shop
- lie → lie in store (for sb)
- mind → mind the store SEE mind the shop

stores /stɔːz; AmE stɔːrz/

- hit → hit the shops/stores

storm /stɔːm; AmE stɔːrm/

the ˌcalm/ˌlull before the 'storm (*saying*)
a period of unnatural calm before an attack, violent activity, etc: *What the country was experiencing was not peace, but just the calm before another storm.*

dance, talk, etc. up a 'storm (*informal, especially AmE*)
dance, talk, etc. with enthusiasm and energy: *They spent the evening celebrating the end of the exams, dancing up a storm at the college party. ◇ Campbell won an award for his first novel, and has been writing up a storm ever since.*

ride out/weather the 'storm (of sth)
manage to survive a difficult period or situation: *The government has managed to ride out the recent storm. ◇ Many companies are having difficulty weathering the present economic storm.*

a storm in a 'teacup (*BrE*) (*AmE* **a tempest in a 'teapot**) (*informal*)
a small or unimportant problem which is treated as much more serious than it really is: *Don't worry. It's a storm in a teacup. Everyone will have forgotten about it by tomorrow.*

take sb/sth by 'storm
1 take or seize a town, castle, building, etc. with a sudden and fierce attack: *The police took the building by storm; two people were injured during the operation.*
2 be extremely successful very quickly in a particular place or among particular people: *Lord of the Rings took the whole world by storm; it was one of the most successful movies ever made.*

- port → any port in a storm

story /'stɔːri/

(quite) another 'story ♦ a (quite) different 'story
1 very different from what has just been said: *Her English is excellent, but her French is another story.*
2 used when you are talking about one thing and then mention another thing, which you are not going to talk about on that occasion: *I once met Paul McCartney, but that's another story. I'll tell you about that one day.*

so the story 'goes... ♦ the story 'goes (that)...
used to describe sth that people are saying, although it may not be correct: *He used to be a doctor, or so the story goes.*

that's the ˌstory of my 'life (*informal*)
used for saying that sth that happens to you or to another person is typical of the bad luck you always have: *'I meet somebody I really like and she tells me she's married. That's the story of my life!'*

- cock → a cock and bull story
- end → end of story
- hard-luck → a hard-luck story
- likely → a likely story
- long → it's a long story
- long → to make a long story short SEE to cut a long story short
- old → it's the (same) old story
- pitch → pitch a line/story/yarn (to sb)
- shaggy-dog → a shaggy-dog story
- side → a/one side of the story/picture
- sob → a sob story
- tall → a tall story
- tell → tell a different, another, etc. tale/story

● tell → tell its own tale/story
● tell → tell the same tale/story (of sth)

straight /streɪt/

give it to me 'straight (*spoken, informal*)
used when you want sb to tell you sth in an honest and direct way, especially if you think it will be unpleasant: *So, now you've met him, give it to me straight — what do you think of him?*

go 'straight (*informal*)
(of a former criminal) live according to the law: *After his years in prison, he was determined to go straight this time.*

keep to, stay on, etc. the ˌstraight and 'narrow (*informal*)
live your life according to strict moral principles: *She's stopped drinking and now she's trying to stay on the straight and narrow.*

> ❷ ORIGIN
> This phrase comes from the Bible, describing the path to Heaven.

play it 'straight (also **play a straight 'bat**)
be honest and not try to deceive sb: *'Do you think we should try and hide this from the newspapers?' 'No, play it straight; I'm sure the public will see our point of view.'*

> ❷ ORIGIN
> These idioms refer to one way of holding the bat in the game of cricket.

put/set sb 'straight (about/on sth)
make sure that sb is not mistaken about the real facts in a situation: *He thought I was a doctor of medicine, so I put him straight and told him I was a doctor of philosophy.* **OPP** lead sb to believe (that...)

put sth 'straight
make sth neat and tidy; organize or settle sth properly: *Please put all your papers straight before you leave the office.* ◇ *When he discovered that he was dying, he started to put all his affairs straight.*

(earn/get) straight 'A's (*especially AmE*)
(get) the best marks/grades in all your classes: *She got straight A's in all her exams.* ◇ *He's always been **a straight A student**.*

(as) straight as an 'arrow
in a straight line or direction: *You can't get lost if you follow this track. It runs as straight as an arrow through the middle of the forest.*

(as) straight as a 'die
1 in a straight line or direction: *The road runs northwards, as straight as a die.*
2 honest: *Carol would never steal anything — she's as straight as a die.* **OPP** (as) slippery as an eel

ˌstraight a'way
immediately; without delay: *I'll do it straight away.*

(keep) a straight 'face
manage not to laugh: *When she told me about her accident with the pig, I couldn't keep a straight face.*

ˌstraight from the 'shoulder
honestly and directly: *He's an outspoken politician who speaks straight from the shoulder.*

ˌstraight 'off/'out (*informal*)
without hesitating: *She asked him straight off what he thought about it all.* ◇ *I told her straight out that she was wrong.*

ˌstraight 'up (*BrE, spoken, informal*)
used for telling sb that what you are saying is completely true: *'I got the best marks in the class.' 'Straight up?' 'Straight up.'*

● fair → play fair/straight (with sb)
● home → on the home straight/stretch
● priorities → get your priorities right/straight
● ramrod → (as) straight as a ramrod **SEE** ramrod straight
● record → put/set the record straight
● right → get sth right/straight
● think → think straight

strain /streɪn/

strain at the 'leash (*informal*)
want to be free from control; want to do sth very much: *Why don't you let her leave home? Can't you see she's straining at the leash?* ◇ *He's straining at the leash to leave Britain for somewhere sunnier.*

> NOTE
> A *leash* is a long piece of leather, chain or rope used for holding and controlling a dog.

strain every 'nerve/'sinew (to do sth) (*written*)
try as hard as you can (to do sth): *He strained every sinew to help us, but didn't succeed.*

strange /streɪndʒ/

be/make strange 'bedfellows
be two very different people or things that you would not expect to find together: *Art and rugby may seem strange bedfellows, but the local rugby club donated £5 000 to help fund an art exhibition.*

> NOTE
> A *bedfellow* is a person who shares a bed with somebody else.

● feel → feel strange

stranger /'streɪndʒə(r)/

be no/a 'stranger to sth (*formal*)
be familiar/not familiar with sth because you have/have not experienced it many times before: *He is no stranger to controversy.*

● truth → truth is stranger than fiction

strapped /stræpt/

be ˌstrapped for 'cash (*informal*)
have very little money: *I can't come to the club tonight — I'm a bit strapped for cash.*

straw /strɔː/

be the last/final 'straw (also **be the ˌstraw that breaks the camel's 'back**)
be the last in a series of bad events, etc. that makes it impossible for you to accept a situation any longer: *I've had a terrible day, and this traffic is the last straw, I can't take any more.*

a straw in the 'wind (*BrE*)
an unimportant incident or piece of information which shows you what might happen in the future: *Journalists are always looking for straws in the wind.*

- **bricks** → make bricks without straw
- **draw** → draw the short straw
- **man** → a man of straw

straws /strɔːz/

clutch/grasp at 'straws
try all possible means to find a solution or some hope in a difficult or unpleasant situation, even though this seems very unlikely: *The doctors have told him that he has only 6 months to live, but he won't accept it. He's going to a new clinic in Switzerland next week, but he's just clutching at straws.*

- **draw** → draw straws (for sth)

strays /streɪz/

- **waifs** → waifs and strays

streak /striːk/

- **yellow** → a yellow streak

stream /striːm/

be/come on 'stream
(of a factory, machine etc.) be/start working or operating: *The new printing machines come on stream in March.* ◇ *We're waiting for the new software to come on stream; it will make our jobs much easier.*

go, swim, etc. with/against the 'stream/'tide
behave/not behave in the same way as most other people: *He's a fashion designer who's always swum against the stream; his work is very original.* ◇ *Why do you always have to go against the tide?*

street /striːt/

be (right) up your 'street (*especially BrE*)
(*AmE* usually **be (right) up your 'alley**) (*informal*)
be suitable for you: *Why don't you apply for this job? It looks right up your street.* **OPP** not be sb's cup of tea

- **easy** → on easy street
- **league** → not be in the same league/class/street
- **man** → the man (and/or woman) in the street

streets /striːts/

be 'streets ahead (of sb/sth) (*BrE, informal*)
be very much better (than sb/sth): *Japan is streets ahead of us in computer technology.*

on the 'streets (*informal*)
1 without a home: *He was weak and ill and he knew he wouldn't survive on the streets.*
2 working as a prostitute: *She's been on the streets since she was fifteen.*

the streets are ˌpaved with 'gold (*saying*)
used to say that it seems easy to make money in a place: *More and more people are moving to the big cities, where they believe the streets are paved with gold.*

> **❷ ORIGIN**
> In the traditional story of Dick Whittington, Dick goes to London because he is told that it is so rich that even the streets are paved with gold, but later finds out that this is not true.

- **hit** → hit the streets
- **walk** → walk the streets

strength /streŋθ/

go from ˌstrength to 'strength
have more and more success: *Since she became the boss, the company's gone from strength to strength.*

on the strength of sth
mainly because of sth: *I got the job on the strength of my experience in sales.* ◇ *They were sent to prison on the strength of a tiny piece of evidence.*

a ˌpillar/ˌtower of 'strength
a person who gives you the courage and determination to continue when you are in a bad situation: *My wife has been a tower of strength during my illness.* ◇ *During your five years in prison, Terry was a pillar of strength.*

- **force** → in force/strength
- **full** → be at/below full strength

strengthen /'streŋθn/

ˌstrengthen your 'hand
give you more power to do sth or act against sb/sth: *The new anti-drug laws will strengthen the hand of the police.*

strengths /streŋθs/

play to your 'strengths
give your attention and effort to things that you do well; give sb the opportunity to do this: *Each member of the team should have a task that plays to their strengths.*

stretch /stretʃ/

at a 'stretch
(of periods of time) without stopping; continuously: *She practises the piano for hours at a stretch.* **OPP** in snatches

by 'no stretch of the imagination ♦ not by 'any stretch of the imagination
it is completely impossible to say; by no means: *By no stretch of the imagination could you call him clever.* ◇ *You couldn't say that factory was beautiful, not by any stretch of the imagination!*

stretch your 'legs
walk about after sitting or lying for a long time: *I'd been working at my desk all morning, so I went outside to stretch my legs for ten minutes.*

stretch a 'point
allow sb to break the rules for a good reason: *You are usually only allowed one hour for lunch, but I'm prepared to stretch a point if there's an emergency.*

- full → at full stretch
- home → on the home straight/stretch
- rules → bend/stretch the rules

strictly /'strɪktli/

strictly 'speaking
if you are using words or rules in their exact or correct sense: *Strictly speaking, nobody under 18 can join this club, but as you are nearly 18…* ◇ *Strictly speaking, a tomato is a fruit, not a vegetable.*

stride /straɪd/

get into your 'stride (*BrE*) (*AmE* **hit (your) 'stride**)
begin to do sth with confidence and at a good speed after a slow, uncertain start: *She found the job difficult at first, but now she's got into her stride and she loves it.*

put sb off their 'stride/'stroke
make sb take their attention off what they are doing and stop doing it so well: *All sorts of things can put a player off his stroke.*

(match sb) ,stride for 'stride
keep doing sth as well as sb else, even though they keep making it harder for you: *We've managed to match our closest competitors stride for stride as regards prices.*

take sth in your 'stride (*BrE*) (*AmE* **take sth in 'stride**)
accept and deal with sth difficult without worrying about it too much: *Joey was upset when we moved house, but Ben seems to have taken it all in his stride.*

- breaking → without breaking stride

strides /straɪdz/

make great, rapid, etc. 'strides (in sth/in doing sth)
improve quickly or make fast progress (in sth/in doing sth): *Ann's made huge strides in her piano-playing.* ◇ *Tom has made enormous strides at school this year.*

strike /straɪk/

strike a 'balance (between A and B)
find a sensible middle point between two demands, extremes, courses of action, etc: *We need to strike a balance between protecting him and letting him become more independent.* ◇ *Children need to strike a balance between work and play at school.*

strike a 'bargain/'deal (with sb)
come to an agreement (with sb), especially after a lot of discussion or argument: *They struck a bargain with the landlord to pay less rent in return for painting the house.*

strike a blow for/against/at sth
act forcefully in support of/against sth (for example a belief, principle or group of people): *The protest was a chance to strike a blow for freedom.* ◇ *The new law would strike a blow against racism.*

strike ,fear, ,terror, etc. into sb/sb's 'heart (*formal*)
make sb feel fear, terror, etc: *His crimes struck horror into the nation's heart.*

strike 'gold
find happiness, wealth, etc.; find exactly what you need: *She hasn't always been lucky with her boyfriends, but I think she's struck gold this time.* ◇ *We've struck gold here. This book has everything we need.*

strike it 'rich (*informal*)
become rich suddenly: *He struck it rich when a relative died and left him two million.*

strike (it) 'lucky (*informal*)
have good luck: *We certainly struck it lucky with the weather — it's beautiful today.* ◇ *He bets on the horses, and sometimes he strikes lucky.*

strike a 'pose/an 'attitude
sit, stand or lie in a position in order to attract attention: *He was striking a pose, leaning against the ship's rail.*

,strike while the ,iron is 'hot (*saying*)
do sth immediately because now is a particularly good time to do it: *He seems in a good mood. Why don't you strike while the iron is hot and ask him now?*

> **❷ ORIGIN**
> A blacksmith (= a person who makes things out of iron) must *strike* (= hit) the iron while it is hot enough to be bent into the shape required.

- chord → strike/touch a chord (with sb)
- false → sound/strike a false note
- home → hit/strike home
- note → hit/strike the right/wrong note
- note → sound/strike a note (of sth)
- pay → hit/strike pay dirt

strikes /straɪks/

- lightning → lightning never strikes (in the same place) twice

striking /'straɪkɪŋ/

within 'striking distance (of sth)
near enough to be reached or attacked; near: *In one minute the aircraft can be within striking distance of the target.* ◇ *There are lakes, mountains and forests all within striking distance.* **OPP** out of range (of sth)

string /strɪŋ/

have/keep sb on a 'string
make sb do what you want because you have control over them: *Of course, he's rich and powerful enough to keep several people on a string.*

> **NOTE**
> This idiom refers to a puppet (= a model of a person or an animal) that is controlled with strings attached to parts of its body.

- bow² → have another string/more strings to your bow
- long → how long is a piece of string?

strings /strɪŋz/

(with) no 'strings attached (also **without 'strings**)
with no special rules, conditions or limits: *I got a loan of $5 000 with no strings attached.* ◇ *It was a relationship without strings* (= without responsibility or commitment) *which suited them both.*

- apron → (tied to) your mother's, wife's, etc. apron strings
- bow² → have another string/more strings to your bow
- pull → pull strings (for sb)
- pull → pull the strings
- purse → control/hold the purse strings

strip /strɪp/

- tear → tear a strip off sb SEE tear sb off a strip

stroke /strəʊk; AmE strəʊk/

at a/one (single) 'stroke
(something happens) as a result of one sudden action or event: *All my problems were solved at a stroke when an aunt left me some money.*

not do a 'stroke (of 'work)
not do any work at all: *He's useless — he hasn't done a stroke of work today.* ◇ *'Does your husband help in the house?' 'No, he doesn't do a stroke.'*
OPP work like a dog/slave/Trojan

on/at the ˌstroke of 'eight, 'midnight, etc.
at exactly eight o'clock, midnight, etc: *She gets to work at the stroke of nine every day.*

- stride → put sb off their stride/stroke

strokes /strəʊks; AmE strəʊks/

- different → different strokes (for different folks)

strong /strɒŋ; AmE strɔːŋ/

be 'strong on sth
1 be good at sth: *I'm not very strong on dates* (= I can't remember the dates of important events).
2 have a lot of sth: *The report was strong on criticism, but short on practical suggestions.*

be your 'strong point/suit
be a thing that you do well: *Writing letters has never been my strong point.* ◇ *Logic is definitely not his strong suit.*

come on 'strong (with sb) (*informal*)
make your feelings clear in an aggressive way: *Do you think I came on too strong at that meeting?*

have a strong 'stomach
not feel sick or upset when you see or do unpleasant things: *You've got to have a strong stomach to watch animals being killed.*

- bit → a bit thick/strong
- still → be still going strong

struck /strʌk/

be 'struck by/on/with sb/sth (*informal*)
be impressed or interested by sb/sth; like sb/sth very much: *I was struck by her youth and enthusiasm.* ◇ *We're not very struck on that new bar.*

be struck 'dumb (with sth)
be suddenly unable to speak (because of shock, fear, etc.): *We were struck dumb at the sight of three armed soldiers in the kitchen.* ◇ *The witnesses were struck dumb with terror.* ▶ **'dumbstruck** *adj.*: *When I found out that I had won first prize, I was dumbstruck.*

struggle /'strʌɡl/

- uphill → an uphill struggle/battle/task

strut /strʌt/

ˌstrut your 'stuff (*informal*)
proudly show your ability, especially at dancing or performing: *I saw you at the club last night, strutting your stuff on the dance floor!*

stubborn /'stʌbən; AmE -bərn/

(as) ˌstubborn as a 'mule (*often disapproving*)
very determined not to change your opinion or attitude; obstinate: *If you tell her what to do, she won't do it because she's as stubborn as a mule. Why not just suggest it to her?*

stuck /stʌk/

ˌget stuck 'in ♦ ˌget stuck 'into sth (*BrE, informal*)
start doing sth in an enthusiastic way: *Here's your food. Now get stuck in* (= start eating). ◇ *We got stuck into the job immediately.*

stuff /stʌf/

do your 'stuff (*informal*)
do sth you are good or skilled at (often while other people watch): *Joy got her guitar and went on stage to do her stuff.*

not give a 'stuff (*BrE, slang*)
not care at all about sth: *I don't give a stuff what you think!*

stuff and 'nonsense (*spoken, old-fashioned*)
used to say that you think sth is not true or stupid: *A hotel for the night? Stuff and nonsense! You're staying here with us.*

stuff him, that, etc. (*spoken, informal*)
used to show strong dislike of sb or a refusal to do what they want: *'Switch that radio off, I'm trying to work!' 'Stuff you, I'll do what I like!'* ◇ *He wants me to do extra work this week. Well, he can stuff it!*

that's the 'stuff (*informal*)
used for telling sb that they are doing sth correctly or well, or doing sth good: *'I'd like my hair cut shorter at the front.' 'Like this?' 'Yeah, that's the stuff.'*

● hard → the hard stuff
● hot → hot stuff
● kids → kid stuff SEE kids' stuff
● know → know your stuff
● sterner → be made of sterner stuff
● strut → strut your stuff
● sweat → don't sweat the small stuff

stuffed /stʌft/

get 'stuffed (also **get 'knotted** *less frequent*) (*BrE, spoken*)
used to tell sb in a rude and angry way to go away, or that you do not want sth: *If they don't offer you more money, tell them to get stuffed.* ◇ *Get stuffed, you idiot!*

a stuffed 'shirt (*informal, disapproving*)
a person who is very serious, formal or old-fashioned: *This office is full of stuffed shirts; there's no one fun that I can have a laugh with.*

stuffing /'stʌfɪŋ/

● knock → knock the stuffing out of sb

stumps /stʌmps/

● stir → stir your stumps

style /staɪl/

be (not) sb's 'style
be (not) the type of thing that sb enjoys; be (not) the way sb usually behaves: *Classical music's not my style; I prefer rock.* ◇ *I don't like living in town much. The country is more my style.* ◇ *I'm sure he didn't say that; it's not his style at all. He's always so polite.*

in (great, grand, etc.) style
in an impressive way: *She always celebrates her birthday in style.* ◇ *He won the championship in fine style.*

● cramp → cramp sb's style

subject /'sʌbdʒɪkt; -dʒekt/

● change → change the subject

sublime /sə'blaɪm/

from the sub,lime to the ri'diculous
used to describe a situation in which sth serious, important or of high quality is followed by sth silly, unimportant or of poor quality: *His works as an artist range from the sublime to the ridiculous, with very little in between.*

❷ ORIGIN
From the sublime to the ridiculous is only one step is a translation of a phrase that was first said by Napoleon Bonaparte.

substance /'sʌbstəns/

a woman, man, person, etc. of 'substance (*formal*)
a person who is important, powerful or rich: *In those days, a station master was a man of substance in the community.*

succeeds /sək'siːdz/

nothing suc,ceeds like suc'cess (*saying*)
success encourages you and often leads to more success: *The first task the students do should be one they are likely to do well. This is because nothing succeeds like success.*

success /sək'ses/

● roaring → a roaring success
● succeeds → nothing succeeds like success
● sweet → the sweet smell of success

such /sʌtʃ/

... and such
and similar things or people: *The centre offers activities like canoeing and sailing and such.*

as 'such
1 in the usual sense or meaning of the word: *There is no theatre as such in the town, but plays are sometimes performed in the town hall.*
2 considering sth only in theory, not in practice or in relation to a particular person or thing: *I am not interested in money as such, but I do like the freedom it can buy.*
3 because sb/sth is what it is: *The government is the main contributor and, as such, controls the project.*

such as
1 for example: *Wild flowers such as orchids and primroses are becoming rare.* ◇ *'I met a lot of important people in Canada.' 'Such as?'* (= give me an example).
2 of a kind that; like: *Opportunities such as this don't come along every day.*

,such as it 'is
used to say that there is not much of sth or that it is of poor quality: *You're welcome to join us for lunch, such as it is — we're only having soup and bread.*

suck /sʌk/

,suck it and 'see (*BrE, informal*)
used to say that the only way to know if sth is suitable is to try it: *With so many different models of mobile phone available, the best way to find out if one is right for you is to suck it and see.*

,suck it 'up (*AmE, informal*)
accept sth bad and deal with it well, controlling your emotions: *I admired the way he never stopped trying. Even when the audience started shouting abuse at him, he sucked it up and continued singing.*

● dry → milk/suck sb/sth dry
● teach → teach your grandmother to suck eggs

sudden /'sʌdn/

,all of a 'sudden
suddenly and unexpectedly: *I was sitting reading my book when all of a sudden the lights went out.*

,sudden 'death
a way of deciding the winner of a game when scores are equal at the end. The players or teams continue playing and the game ends as soon as one of them gains the lead: *If no one scores in the next five minutes the game will go to sudden death.* ◇ *They won the match after an exciting sudden-death play-off.*

suffer /'sʌfə(r)/

not suffer fools 'gladly
not be patient or polite with people who are less intelligent than you: *He says what he thinks and doesn't suffer fools gladly. Some people consider him a bit arrogant.*

> **NOTE**
> *Suffer* here means 'accept somebody annoying or unpleasant without complaining'.

sufferance /'sʌfərəns/

on 'sufferance
if you do sth **on sufferance**, sb allows you to do it although they do not really want you to: *He's only staying here on sufferance.*

suffice /sə'faɪs/

suffice (it) to say (that)... (*formal*)
used for saying that you could say much more about sb/sth but you do not want or need to: *I won't tell you all that was said at the meeting. Suffice it to say that they approved our plan.*

> **NOTE**
> *Suffice it* here means 'it is enough'.

sugar /'ʃʊɡə(r)/

a 'sugar daddy (*informal*)
an older man who has a much younger woman as a girlfriend and gives her presents, money, etc: *When you tell him that he's a sugar daddy, he gets very angry. He says she isn't interested in his money, only in him.*

● **pill** → sugar/sweeten the pill

suggestion /sə'dʒestʃən; *AmE* also səg'dʒ-/

at/on sb's sug'gestion
because sb suggested it: *At his suggestion, I bought the more expensive printer.*

suit /suːt; *BrE* also sjuːt/

,suit your/sb's 'book (*BrE, informal*)
be convenient or useful for you/sb: *Well, if you're honest and hard-working, that suits our book.*

suit sb (right) ,down to the 'ground (*BrE, informal*)
suit sb completely: *I've found a job that suits me down to the ground: the pay's great and I can work from home.*

,suit your'self (*informal*)
1 do exactly what you like: *I choose my assignments to suit myself.*
2 usually used in orders to tell sb to do what they want, even though it might annoy you: *'I don't want anything to eat, I'm on a diet.' 'All right, suit yourself!'*

● **birthday** → in/wearing your birthday suit
● **follow** → follow suit
● **strong** → be your strong point/suit

suits /suːts; *BrE* also sjuːts/

● **grey** → (men in) grey suits

sum /sʌm/

be greater/more than the ,sum of its 'parts
be better or more effective as a group than you would think just by looking at the individual members of the group: *After their victory, the captain was full of praise for his team, saying that it was a classic case of the whole being greater than the sum of its parts.*

in 'sum (*formal*)
used to introduce a short statement of the main points of a discussion, speech, etc: *In sum, there are significant gaps in technological development across countries.*

summer /'sʌmə(r)/

● **Indian** → an Indian summer
● **swallow** → one swallow doesn't make a summer

summon /'sʌmən/

● **courage** → pluck/screw/summon up (your/the) courage (to do sth)

sun /sʌn/

under the 'sun
of any kind; in the world: *He's tried every medicine under the sun, but nothing works.* ◇ *I've got stamps from every country under the sun.*

● **catch** → catch the sun
● **hay** → make hay while the sun shines
● **place** → a place in the sun
● **think** → think the sun shines out of sb's arse/backside
● **think** → think the sun shines out of sb's ass **SEE** think the sun shines out of sb's arse/backside

Sunday /'sʌndeɪ; -di/

your Sunday 'best (*informal, humorous*)
your best clothes: *She got all dressed up in her Sunday best to meet her boyfriend's parents.*

Sundays /'sʌndeɪz; -diz/

● **month** → (not for/in) a month of Sundays

sundry /ˈsʌndri/

,all and ˈsundry (*informal*)
everyone; people of all kinds: *I don't like you talking about my personal problems to all and sundry.*

sunk /sʌŋk/

be ˈsunk in sth
be in a state of unhappiness or deep thought: *She just sat there, sunk in thought.*

sunny-side /ˈsʌni saɪd/

,sunny-side ˈup (*AmE*)
(of an egg) fried on one side only: *How'd you like your eggs - scrambled or sunny-side up?*

sunshine /ˈsʌnʃaɪn/

● **ray** → a ray of sunshine

supper /ˈsʌpə(r)/

● **sing** → sing for your supper

supply /səˈplaɪ/

● **short** → be in short supply

support /səˈpɔːt; *AmE* səˈpɔːrt/

● **moral** → (give sb) moral support

suppose /səˈpəʊz; *AmE* səˈpoʊz/

I don't suppose you could...
used as a very polite way of asking sb to do sth for you: *I don't suppose you could carry this bag for me, could you?*

I supˈpose so
used for showing that you agree but you are not happy about it: *'Can I borrow the car?' 'Yes, I suppose so, but be careful.'* ◇ *'Can I invite him to the party?' 'I suppose so.'*

supposed /səˈpəʊzd; *AmE* səˈpoʊzd/

(not) be supˈposed to (do sth)
1 (not) be expected or required to do sth by rules, the law, an agreement, etc: *She's supposed to do an hour's homework every evening.* ◇ *We're not supposed to be at the party for an hour yet.*
2 (used only in negative sentences) be not allowed to do sth: *You're not supposed to walk on the grass.*

what's ˈthat supposed to mean? (*informal*)
used when you are angry at what sb has said, or do not fully understand it: *'You aren't the most popular person at school, you know.' 'What's that supposed to mean?'*

sure /ʃʊə(r); ʃɔː(r); *AmE* ʃʊr/

be sure to do sth (also **be sure and do sth**) (*spoken*)
used to tell sb to do sth: *Be sure to give your family my regards.* ◇ *Be sure and call me tomorrow.*

for ˈsure (*informal*)
definitely: *'What time will you be here?' 'I don't know for sure yet.'* ◇ *I'll be there for sure; don't worry.*

make ˈsure (of sth/that...)
1 check that sth is true or has been done: *I think the door's locked, but I'd better go and make sure.* ◇ *Have you made sure that we've got enough money?*
2 do sth in order to be certain that sth else happens: *I want to make sure that the party is a success.* ◇ *Make sure there's enough to eat tonight.*

(as) sure as eggs is ˈeggs (*old-fashioned, BrE, informal*)
absolutely certain; without any doubt: *If he goes on driving at that speed, he'll end up in hospital, as sure as eggs is eggs.*

(as) sure as ˈhell (*AmE, informal*)
certainly; without doubt: *Joe sure as hell won't want to dress up in a suit and tie.*

sure eˈnough
exactly as expected or as sb said: *She said she was going to give up her job and, sure enough, she did.* ◇ *They said it would rain, and, sure enough, it did.*

ˈsure of yourself (*sometimes disapproving*)
very confident: *She seems very sure of herself.*

,sure ˈthing (*spoken, especially AmE*)
yes; of course: *'Will you come tonight?' 'Sure thing!'* ◇ *'Can you help me with this table?' 'Sure thing.'*

to be ˈsure (*formal*)
used to admit that sth is true: *He is intelligent, to be sure, but he's also very lazy.*

surely /ˈʃʊəli; ˈʃɔːli; *AmE* ˈʃʊrli/

● **slowly** → slowly but surely

surface /ˈsɜːfɪs; *AmE* ˈsɜːrfɪs/

below/beneath the ˈsurface
what you cannot see but can only guess at or feel: *She seems very calm but beneath the surface I'm sure that she's very upset.* ◇ *Beneath the surface of this beautiful city there is terrible poverty and suffering, which tourists never see.*

on the ˈsurface
when you consider the obvious things, and not the deeper, hidden things: *On the surface she can be very pleasant and helpful, but underneath she's got problems.* ◇ *The plan seems all right on the surface.*

● **scratch** → scratch the surface (of sth)

surprise /səˈpraɪz; *AmE* sərˈp-/

surˌprise, surˈprise (*spoken, ironic*)
used when you are not surprised about sth: *'There's nothing worth watching on TV tonight.' 'Surprise, surprise'* (= there is usually nothing worth watching).

take sb by surˈprise
happen to sb unexpectedly; surprise sb: *His decision to retire took us all by surprise.*

survival /sə'vaɪvl; AmE sər'v-/

(the) sur,vival of the 'fittest
the principle that only the people or things that are best adapted to their surroundings will continue to exist: *In this climate of economic recession, many businesses are at risk, and it really is a case of survival of the fittest.*

NOTE
Fittest means 'most suitable'.

suspicion /sə'spɪʃn/

be a,bove/be,yond su'spicion
be so good or honest that nobody thinks you would do sth bad: *He is absolutely beyond suspicion.*

be under su'spicion (of sth)
be the person that the police think has committed a crime (although they cannot prove it yet): *He was still under suspicion and he knew the police were watching him.*

• finger → the finger of suspicion

suspiciously /sə'spɪʃəsli/

look/sound suspiciously like sth (*often humorous*)
be very similar to sth: *Their latest single sounds suspiciously like the last one.*

swallow /'swɒləʊ; AmE 'swɑːloʊ/

one ,swallow doesn't make a 'summer (*saying*)
you must not take too seriously a small sign that sth is happening or will happen in the future: *'We got a big order from Sweden this morning. Things are getting better.' 'One swallow doesn't make a summer, you know. Don't be too optimistic.'*

NOTE
This expression refers to the fact that swallows (= small birds with a tail with two points) spend the winter in Africa but fly to northern countries for the summer.

swallow the 'bait (*informal*)
accept an offer, etc. which has been made or prepared specially by sb in order to get you to do sth: *When people read the words 'Free Gift' on a magazine they usually swallow the bait and buy it.*

NOTE
A fisherman uses *bait* to attract fish to his hook.

swallow your 'pride
decide to act in a way you are ashamed of or embarrassed by because you want or need sth very much: *She is very independent and it was hard for her to swallow her pride and ask for help.*

swap /swɒp; AmE swɑːp/

• horses → change/swap horses in midstream
• places → change/swap places (with sb)

swathe /sweɪð/

cut a 'swathe through sth
(of a person, fire, etc.) pass through a particular area destroying a large part of it: *The new road cut a swathe through the countryside.*

NOTE
A *swathe* was the area of grass, etc. cut by one movement of a *scythe* (= a curved tool used for cutting grass).

sway /sweɪ/

hold 'sway (over sb/sth) (*literary*)
(of a person, a movement, an idea, etc.) have power, control or great influence over sb/sth: *Rebel forces hold sway over much of the island.* ◇ *These ideas held sway for most of the century.*

swear /sweə(r); AmE swer/

swear 'blind (that)… (*informal*)
say that sth is definitely true: *She swore blind that she had not taken the money, and I believe her.*

swear like a 'trooper (*old-fashioned, BrE*)
use many swear words; use bad language: *She's only fourteen, but she swears like a trooper.*

NOTE
A *trooper* is a soldier.

swear sb to 'secrecy
make sb promise not to tell a secret: *Before telling her what happened, I had sworn her to secrecy.* ◇ *Everyone was sworn to secrecy about what had happened.*

sweat /swet/

be in a 'sweat
1 (also **be all of a 'sweat**) (*informal*) be wet with sweat because it is hot or you have been running, etc: *I had to run to work this morning because I got up late. I was in a real sweat when I arrived.*
2 (also **be in a cold 'sweat**) be very frightened or worried about sth: *I woke up during the night in a cold sweat worrying about the exam.*

break 'sweat (*BrE*) (*AmE* **break a 'sweat**) (*informal*)
use a lot of physical effort: *He hardly needed to break sweat to reach the final.*

by the sweat of your 'brow (*literary*)
by your own hard work or physical effort: *They had to live by the sweat of their brow.*

don't 'sweat it (*AmE, spoken*)
used to tell sb to stop worrying about sth: *If we're a few minutes late he'll wait for us, so don't sweat it.*

don't sweat the 'small stuff (*AmE, spoken*)
used to tell sb not to worry about small details or unimportant things

no 'sweat (*spoken*)
used as a way of saying that sth is not difficult or any trouble: *'Thanks for driving me to the station.' 'No sweat* (= it is no trouble).*' ◇ 'How was the exam?' 'I passed that one, no sweat.'*

sweat 'blood (*informal*)
1 work very hard; make a very great effort: *I sweated blood to get that essay finished on time.*
2 be very worried or afraid: *He sweats blood every time the telephone rings, in case it's the police.*

sweat it 'out (*informal*)
suffer an unpleasant situation; wait for sth unpleasant to end: *I hate this job, but I'm going to sweat it out and hope something better comes along.* ◇ *After the competition we just had to sit there and sweat it out until the result was announced.*

sweat like a 'pig (*informal*)
sweat very much: *It's 35 degrees inside the factory, and the workers are sweating like pigs.*

● **blood** → blood, sweat and tears
● **guts** → slog/sweat/work your guts out

sweep /swiːp/

sweep the 'board
win all or most of the prizes, games, money, etc: *At the awards ceremony last night France swept the board, with six major prizes.*

sweep sb off their 'feet
attract sb very strongly because you are exciting, charming, etc: *She's waiting for a nice young man to come and sweep her off her feet.* ◇ *I was swept off my feet by his wit and charm.*

● **carpet** → sweep sth under the rug **SEE** sweep/brush sth under the carpet
● **clean** → make a clean sweep (of sth)

sweet /swiːt/

do sth in your ˌown sweet 'time/'way
(*informal*)
do sth how and when you want to, even though this might annoy other people: *I tried to give her some advice but she just went on in her own sweet way.* ◇ *It's no use trying to hurry him. He'll do it in his own sweet time.*

have a sweet 'tooth
like to eat sweet things: *I've got a sweet tooth, so I'd find it difficult to give up sugar in my tea.*

keep sb 'sweet (*informal*)
be pleasant and nice to sb, so that they will treat you well: *I have to keep my mother sweet because I want to borrow the car.*

she's 'sweet (*AustralE, New Zealand, informal*)
everything is all right: *'Sorry mate.' 'Nah, she's sweet mate, no need to apologize.'*

sweet F'A (also *less frequent* sweet Fanny 'Adams)
(*BrE, informal*)
nothing; nothing important: *'What happened while I was away?' 'Sweet FA.'*

sweet 'nothings (*informal, usually humorous*)
pleasant but unimportant words said by lovers: *He was whispering sweet nothings in her ear.*

the sweet smell of suc'cess (*informal*)
the pleasant feeling of being successful

● **home** → home sweet home
● **short** → be short and sweet

sweeten /ˈswiːtn/

● **pill** → sugar/sweeten the pill

sweetness /ˈswiːtnəs/

be all ˌsweetness and 'light
1 (of a person) be pleasant, friendly and polite: *She's all sweetness and light as long as you're doing what she wants.*
2 (of a situation) be enjoyable and easy to deal with: *Their quarrel seems to be over. Everything's all sweetness and light at the moment.*

swim /swɪm/

in(to) the 'swim (of things) (*informal*)
involved in things that are happening in society or in a particular situation: *After being away for two years, it took her a while to get back into the swim of things.*

● **sink** → sink or swim

swine /swaɪn/

● **cast** → cast pearls before swine

swing /swɪŋ/

get in/into the 'swing (of sth) (*informal*)
become involved in sth and start to do it well and enjoy it: *I've only been at college a week, so I haven't got into the swing of things yet.* ◇ *He was just getting in the swing of his performance when all the lights went out.*

go with a 'swing (*BrE*)
(of a party or entertainment) be lively, enjoyable and successful: *Their house-warming party really went with a swing.*

swing both 'ways (*informal*)
be bisexual (= sexually attracted to both men and women)

ˌswing into 'action
start to act efficiently and quickly: *When the police heard about the the bomb, they swung into action, searching the area with dogs and moving the public to safety.*

ˌswing the 'lead (*old-fashioned, BrE, informal*)
(usually used in the progressive tenses) pretend to be ill/sick when you are not, especially to avoid work: *I don't think there's anything wrong with her — she's just swinging the lead.*

> **❷ ORIGIN**
> The *lead* (pronounced /led/) may refer to a weight at the bottom of a line that sailors used to measure how deep the water was. *Swinging the lead* was possibly considered an easy job, and so came to mean avoiding hard work.

● **full** → in full swing
● **room** → no room to swing a cat
● **tip** → swing the balance **SEE** tip the balance/scales

swings

swings /swɪŋz/

,swings and 'roundabouts (*BrE, informal*)
used when you want to say that gaining one thing usually means losing another thing: *Higher earnings mean more tax, so it's all swings and roundabouts.* ◇ *What you gain on the swings you'll probably lose on the roundabouts.*

> NOTE
> *Swings* and *roundabouts* are both types of equipment found at a fairground.

switch /swɪtʃ/

● asleep → asleep at the switch **SEE** asleep at the wheel

swoop /swuːp/

● fell → at/in one fell swoop

sword /sɔːd; *AmE* sɔːrd/

a/the sword of 'Damocles (*literary*)
a bad or unpleasant thing that might happen to you at any time and that makes you feel worried or frightened: *Now the news of my divorce is public, I'm relieved in a way. It had been hanging over my head like the sword of Damocles.*

> ❷ ORIGIN
> This expression comes from the Greek legend in which *Damocles* had to sit at a meal with a sword hanging by a single hair above his head. He had praised King Dionysius' happiness, and Dionysius wanted him to understand how quickly happiness can be lost.

● double-edged → be a double-edged sword/weapon
● pen → the pen is mightier than the sword

swords /sɔːdz; *AmE* sɔːrdz/

beat/turn swords into 'ploughshares (*literary*)
stop fighting and return to peaceful activities

> ❷ ORIGIN
> This comes from the Bible. A *ploughshare* is a blade that forms part of a *plough* (= a large piece of farming equipment used for cutting the soil).

● cross → cross swords (with sb)

syllable /'sɪləbl/

● words → in words of one syllable

symbol /'sɪmbl/

● status → a status symbol

sympathy /'sɪmpəθi/

in 'sympathy with sth (*written*)
happening because sth else has happened: *Share prices slipped again today, in sympathy with the German market.*

out of 'sympathy with sb/sth (*written*)
not agreeing with or not wanting to support sb/sth: *It is generally believed that he is out of sympathy with government policies.*

sync /sɪŋk/

in/out of 'sync (*informal*)
moving or working/not moving or working at exactly the same time and speed as sb/sth else: *The soundtrack is not in sync with the picture.* ◇ *Can we try that part of the dance again? I think we were out of sync.*

> NOTE
> *Sync* is a short form of *synchronization*.

system /'sɪstəm/

get sth out of your 'system (*informal*)
do sth so that you no longer feel a very strong emotion or have a strong desire: *Tell him how angry you really feel. That'll get it out of your system.* ◇ *When I was young I was obsessed with ballet, but by the time I left school I had got it out of my system.*

systems /'sɪstəmz/

all systems 'go (for sth) (*informal*)
used to say that everything is ready to begin sth: *The wind had dropped, the sun was shining and it was all systems go for the airshow.* ◇ *The campaign team are in place, so it's all systems go!*

Tt

T /tiː/

to a 'T/'tee (*BrE, informal*)
exactly; perfectly: *This new job suits me to a T* (= it is perfect for me). ◇ *This portrait is excellent — it's Rosemary to a T.*

> ❷ ORIGIN
> This may be a short form of the old phrase *to a tittle* which meant 'to the smallest detail'. A *tittle* was a small mark or point on a letter.

t /tiː/

● dot → dot the/your i's and cross the/your t's
● quiet → on the q.t. **SEE** on the quiet

tab /tæb/

● pick → pick up the tab (for sth)

table /'teɪbl/

on the 'table (*BrE*)
used in business, to talk about a suggestion, plan or amount of money which is being discussed or offered: *In today's meeting there were several new proposals on the table.* ◇ *The company can put an extra one per cent on the table, in return for an agreement on overtime.*

● cards → put/lay your cards on the table
● drink → drink sb under the table

take

tables /ˈteɪblz/

turn the 'tables (on sb)
do sth which means that you now have an advantage over sb who previously had an advantage over you: *They beat us 3-0 last year, but we turned the tables on them this year — we won 5-0.*

> **NOTE**
>
> If two people are playing a board game on a table and then one of them turns the table around, the two players will exchange positions in the game so that the person who was losing will now be winning.

● wait → wait (on) tables

tabs /tæbz/

keep (close) 'tabs on sb/sth (*informal*)
watch sb/sth very carefully; keep informed about sb/sth: *I'm not sure about Johnson — we'd better keep tabs on him until we know we can trust him.* ◇ *I'm keeping tabs on the number of private phone calls you all make from the office.*

tacks /tæks/

● brass → get down to brass tacks

tail /teɪl/

on sb's 'tail (*informal*)
(of the police, a spy, etc.) following behind sb very closely: *I had the feeling there was someone on my tail.*

(at) the tail 'end (of sth)
(at) the final or last part (of sth): *I didn't hear most of the conversation — I only came in at the tail end.*

the tail (is) wagging the 'dog (also **let the tail wag the 'dog**)
used to describe a situation where a small, unimportant thing controls a larger, more important thing: *In this company the workers tell the manager what he can and cannot do. It's a real case of the tail wagging the dog.*

turn 'tail (and run, flee, etc.)
run away from a fight or a dangerous situation: *As soon as he saw the police he turned tail and fled.*

with your tail between your 'legs (*informal*)
feeling ashamed, embarrassed or unhappy because you have been defeated or punished: *They thought they would win easily, but they've gone home with their tails between their legs.*

> **NOTE**
> This idiom refers to the way a dog behaves when it is punished.

● chase → chase your (own) tail
● head → can't make head or/nor tail of sth
● nose → nose to tail
● sting → a sting in the tail
● top → top and tail sth
● two → in two shakes of a lamb's tail **SEE** in two shakes

tails /teɪlz/

● dog → be like a dog with two tails
● heads → heads or tails?

take /teɪk/

> Most idioms containing the verb **take** are at the entries for the nouns or adjectives in the idioms, for example **take sth with a pinch of salt** is at **pinch**.

be on the 'take (*informal*)
accept money from sb for helping them in a dishonest or illegal way: *It now seems that some of the officials were on the take, accepting bribes and then issuing fake passports.*

I, you, etc. can't take sb 'anywhere (*informal, often humorous*)
used to say that you cannot trust sb to behave well in public: *You've got soup all over your shirt — I can't take you anywhere, can I?*

take sth as it 'comes
deal with difficulties as they happen, without worrying too much: *I don't plan for the future. I like to take life as it comes.*

'take it (*informal*)
(often used with can/could) be able to bear or tolerate sth difficult or unpleasant such as stress, criticism or pain: *They argued so much that finally he couldn't take it any more and he left her.* ◇ *People are rude to her in her job, and she feels she's taken it for long enough.*

'take it (that…)
think or suppose (that sth is true, will happen, etc.): *'I take it that you won't be back for lunch,' she said as they left.* ◇ *You speak French, I take it?*

take it from 'here/'there
1 continue doing sth that sb else has started: *I explained how to start the machine, and let him take it from there.* ◇ *You work out who you want in your team and I'll take it from there.*
2 if sb says that they/we will **take it from here/there**, they mean that they/we will do sth and then decide what to do next: *We'll work out a business plan, see what the bank says, and then take it from there.*

take it from 'me (that…) (*informal*)
you should believe me, because I have personal experience of…: *Take it from me that it's not easy to become a professional writer.*

take it on/upon yourself to do sth
decide to do sth without asking anyone for permission: *He took it upon himself to dismiss my secretary, which he had no right to do.*

take it 'out of sb ♦ take a lot 'out of sb
make sb very tired or weak: *Driving all day really takes it out of you.* ◇ *That flu bug has really taken it out of her.*

take it 'out on sb (*informal*)
behave in an unpleasant way towards sb because you feel angry, disappointed, etc., although it is not their fault: *I know you've had a bad day at work, but don't take it out on me.*

take sb 'out of himself, herself, etc.
amuse or entertain sb and so make them feel less
worried about their problems or less unhappy:
*She was very depressed when they split up. We took
her away for a few days to try to take her out of
herself.*

takes /teɪks/

have what it 'takes (to do sth) (*informal*)
have the qualities, ability, etc. needed to be successful: *He's certainly ambitious, but if you ask me
he hasn't really got what it takes to be the best.*

taking /'teɪkɪŋ/

**be sb's for the 'taking ◆ be there for the
'taking**
if sth is **yours for the taking** or **there for the taking**, it is easy to get: *She was surprised to find the
money on the kitchen table, just there for the taking.*
◇ *With the team's closest rivals out of the championship, the title was theirs for the taking.*

tale /teɪl/

- live[1] → live to tell the tale
- old → an old wives' tale
- spin → spin (sb) a yarn/tale
- tall → a tall tale SEE a tall story
- tell → tell a different, another, etc. tale/story
- tell → tell its own tale/story
- tell → tell the same tale/story (of sth)

tales /teɪlz/

- tell → tell tales (about sb/sth)
- tell → tell tales out of school

talk /tɔːk/

be all 'talk (and no action) (*disapproving*)
be a person who talks a lot about what they are
going to do or have done without actually doing
much: *Don't listen to her promises — she's all talk
and no action.*

be the talk of sth (*informal*)
be sth that everyone is interested in and talking
about: *His collection is the talk of the Milan fashion
shows.* ◇ *Overnight, she became the talk of the
town* (= famous).

'you can/can't talk (also **look who's 'talking,
you're a 'fine one to talk**) (*spoken*)
you should not criticize sb because you are also
guilty of the same fault: *'He's always late for
appointments.' 'You can talk! You're hardly ever on
time yourself.'* ◇ *'George is so careless with money.'
'Look who's talking!'*

'talk about... (*spoken*)
used to emphasize sth: *Did you watch the programme on the Labour Party last night? Talk about
biased!*

talk 'big (*disapproving*)
tell people how good you are or promise many
things: *The President talks big but he doesn't do
anything.*

talk 'dirty (*informal*)
talk to sb about sex in order to make them sexually excited: *I love it when you talk dirty.*

talk sb's 'ear off (*especially AmE, informal,
especially disapproving*)
if sb **talks your ear off** they talk to you a lot: *That
guy on the plane talked my ear off — I couldn't wait
to land!*

talk your 'head off (*informal*)
talk a lot: *He talked his head off all evening.*

talk the hind leg(s) off a 'donkey (*informal,
humorous*)
(usually used with *can* or *could*) talk for a long
time: *He would make a good politician — he could
talk the hind legs off a donkey!*

talk 'shop
talk about your work or business in a social situation with sb who works with you: *Are you two
talking shop again? Why don't you forget business
for a while and come and meet my friends?* ▸ **'shop
talk** *noun*: *We've discussed more intimate things
than just shop talk.*

talk through the back of your 'head (*informal*)
talk nonsense: *If he says that he's going to win the
prize, he's talking through the back of his head.*

talk through your 'hat (*old-fashioned, informal*)
(usually used in progressive tenses) say silly
things while you are talking about a subject you
do not understand: *Don't take any notice of him.
He's talking through his hat, as usual.*

talk to a brick 'wall (*informal*)
used when sb refuses to listen to your advice,
ideas, explanations, etc: *Talking to him is like talking to a brick wall. He just won't listen.*

talk 'tough (on sth) (*informal, especially AmE*)
tell people very strongly what you want: *Before
the elections, the party talked tough on crime, but
little has been done since they've been in power.*

talk 'turkey (*informal, especially AmE*)
discuss the practical details of sth seriously and
honestly: *Look, Mark, it's time we talked turkey.
How much money can you invest in the company?*

talk your way out of sth/out of doing sth
make excuses and give reasons for not doing sth;
manage to get yourself out of a difficult situation:
*He tried to talk his way out of it by saying someone
else was responsible.* ◇ *I'd like to see her talk her
way out of this one* (= the present trouble).

- cross → be/talk at cross purposes
- devil → speak/talk of the devil
- fighting → fighting talk
- hand → talk to/tell it to the hand (because the face ain't
  listening)
- language → speak/talk the same/a different language
- pep → a pep talk
- pillow → pillow talk
- sense → knock/talk some sense into sb
- small → (make) small talk

talker /'tɔːkə(r)/

- fast → a fast talker

talking /'tɔːkɪŋ/

'now you're talking (*spoken*)
used for showing interest and enthusiasm about sth just said, for example a good suggestion: *'Why don't we go to Paris for the weekend?' 'Now you're talking!'*

talking of sb/sth (*spoken, especially BrE*)
used for saying that you intend to say more about sb/sth just mentioned: *'I was out last night with Dave, Mark and Angela...' 'Talking of Mark, did he tell you about his latest business idea?'*

● know → know what you're talking about
● talk → look who's talking **SEE** you can/can't talk

talks /tɔːks/

● money → money talks

tall /tɔːl/

stand 'tall (*especially AmE*)
show that you are proud and able to deal with anything: *Speaking on television, she said that her former manager's advice to stand tall and be proud of herself was what helped her to succeed.*

a ˌtall 'order
a very difficult task or request: *Finishing this work by the end of the week is a tall order, but I'll try.* **OPP** child's play

a ˌtall 'story (*especially BrE*) (*AmE usually* **a ˌtall 'tale**)
a story which is very difficult to believe: *What she says about her grandfather being a foreign prince sounds like a tall story to me.* ◇ *There were many tall tales told later about the events of that day.*

● oaks → great/tall oaks from little acorns grow
● walk → walk tall

tandem /'tændəm/

in 'tandem (with sb/sth)
together (with sb/sth); at the same time (as sb/sth): *These two computers are designed to work in tandem.* ◇ *She runs the business in tandem with her husband.*

tangent /'tændʒənt/

go/fly off at a 'tangent (*BrE*) (*AmE* **go off on a 'tangent**)
change suddenly from talking or thinking about one thing to talking or thinking about another: *One moment the professor is working hard on a problem in physics, the next he's gone off at a tangent and he's talking about bees.*

NOTE
A *tangent* is a straight line that touches the outside of a curve but does not cross it.

tango /'tæŋgəʊ; AmE -goʊ/

● two → it takes two to tango **SEE** it takes two (to do sth)

tank /tæŋk/

in the 'tank (*AmE, informal, business*)
(about the price of shares, bonds, etc.) falling quickly: *Technology stocks are doing well, but everything else is in the tank.*

● built → be built like a tank

tantrum /'tæntrəm/

throw a 'tantrum (*BrE also* **throw a 'wobbly**) (*informal*)
suddenly become very angry and behave in an unreasonable way: *When you were a child, you were always throwing tantrums.* ◇ *My mum would throw a wobbly if she knew what we'd been doing.*

tap /tæp/

(be) on 'tap
(be) ready and available for immediate use: *I've got plenty of people on tap to help us if we need them.*

tape /teɪp/

● red → red tape

taped /teɪpt/

have sb/sth 'taped (*BrE, informal*)
understand sb/sth completely and have learned how to deal with them/it successfully: *He can't fool me — I've got him taped.*

tar /tɑː(r)/

tar sb/sth with the same 'brush
judge a whole group of people or things unfairly because of your bad experience with one or a few of them: *Because his older brother had been a troublemaker at the school, Paul was automatically tarred with the same brush. It wasn't fair!*

● spoil → spoil the ship for a ha'porth/ha'penny-worth of tar

target /'tɑːgɪt; AmE 'tɑːrgɪt/

● sitting → a sitting duck/target

task /tɑːsk; AmE tæsk/

take sb to 'task (about/for/over sth)
criticize sb forcefully (for doing sth wrong): *I was taken to task for arriving late.* ◇ *She took the Government to task over its economic record.* **OPP** give sb/yourself a pat on the back

● uphill → an uphill struggle/battle/task

taste /teɪst/

be in bad, the worst possible, etc. 'taste
be offensive and not at all appropriate: *Most of his jokes were in very poor taste.*

be in good, the best possible, etc. 'taste
be appropriate and not at all offensive: *They made a few jokes about the management, but it was all done in good taste.*

leave a bad/nasty 'taste in the/your mouth
(of an experience) make you feel angry, bitter, or disgusted: *The idea that the money had been stolen from her sick mother left a nasty taste in the mouth.* ◇ *When you see someone being treated so unkindly, it leaves a bad taste in your mouth.*

to 'taste
in the quantity that is needed to make sth taste the way you prefer: *Add salt and pepper to taste.*

• **accounting** → there's no accounting for taste(s)
• **acquired** → an acquired taste
• **medicine** → give sb a taste/dose of their own medicine
• **shape** → be a taste of things to come **SEE** be the shape of things to come

tat /tæt/

• **tit** → tit for tat

tatters /'tætəz; AmE -tərz/

be in 'tatters
1 (of clothes) be torn in many places: *He got into a fight and came home with his clothes in tatters.*
2 (of a plan, an idea, a person's feelings, etc.) be ruined or badly damaged: *She's failed her exams, and now all her hopes of becoming a doctor are in tatters.* ◇ *His career and his reputation are both in tatters after the scandal.*

tea /ti:/

wouldn't do sth for all the tea in 'China (*informal*)
never; not for any reason at all: *'If you marry him you'll be a rich woman.' 'I wouldn't marry him for all the tea in China.'*

• **cup** → not be sb's cup of tea

teach /ti:tʃ/

teach your grandmother to suck 'eggs (*BrE, informal*)
tell or show sb how to do sth that they can already do well, and probably better than you can: *I don't know why he's telling Rob how to use the computer. It seems to me like teaching your grandmother to suck eggs.*

teach sb a 'lesson (also **'teach sb (to do sth)**)
learn from a punishment or because of an unpleasant experience, that you have done sth wrong or made a mistake: *He needs to be taught a lesson* (= he should be punished). ◇ *Losing all his money in a card game has taught him a lesson he'll never forget.* ◇ *That'll teach you! Perhaps you'll be more careful in future!*

(you can't) teach an old dog new 'tricks (*saying*)
(you can't) make old people change their ideas or ways of working, etc: *My grandmother doesn't want a computer. She says you can't teach an old dog new tricks.*

• **thing** → can/could teach/tell sb a thing or two (about sb/sth)

teacup /'ti:kʌp/

• **storm** → a storm in a teacup

teapot /'ti:pɒt; AmE -pɑ:t/

• **storm** → a tempest in a teapot **SEE** a storm in a teacup

tear /teə(r); AmE ter/

tear your 'hair (out) (*informal*)
be very worried or angry: *Why are you so late home? Your mother and I have been tearing our hair out wondering where you were!*

Sid was tearing his hair out trying to get the report finished on time.

tear sb ,limb from 'limb (*often humorous*)
attack sb very violently: *Julian looked so angry that I thought he was going to tear his brother limb from limb.*

tear yourself/sth 'loose (from sb/sth) ✦ **tear 'loose**
escape from sb/sth by using great force; become separated from sb/sth in this way: *He put his arms round my neck but I tore myself loose and ran for help.* ◇ *As he held onto the bushes, he felt them tear loose from the rock.*

tear sb 'off a strip ✦ **tear a 'strip off sb** (*BrE, informal*)
criticize sb because you are angry about sth they have said or done: *The boss tore all the staff off a strip for using the Internet for personal matters during office hours.*

tear sb/sth to 'pieces/'shreds
criticize sb/sth; completely destroy sth: *The press tore the Government's economic plans to shreds.* ◇ *The Prime Minister tore his opponents' arguments to pieces.* **OPP** praise sb/sth to the skies

• **heart** → rip/tear the heart out of sth
• **loose** → break/cut/tear (sth) loose from sb/sth
• **wear** → wear and tear

tell

tearing /'teərɪŋ; *AmE* 'terɪŋ/

(be in) a tearing 'hurry/'rush (*especially BrE*)
(be) in a very great hurry: *I was late for a meeting and in a tearing hurry.*

tears /tɪəz; *AmE* tɪrz/

- **blood** → blood, sweat and tears
- **bore** → bore sb to tears
- **crocodile** → crocodile tears
- **end** → end in tears

tee /tiː/

- **T** → to a T/tee

teeter /'tiːtə(r)/

teeter on the 'brink/'edge of sth
be very close to a very unpleasant or dangerous situation: *The country is teetering on the brink of civil war.*

NOTE
If something *teeters*, it stands or moves in an unsteady way as if it is going to fall.

teeth /tiːθ/

cut your 'teeth on sth
learn or gain experience from sth: *It was a small experimental theatre company and many of today's most successful actors cut their teeth there.*

get/sink your 'teeth into sth (*informal*)
put effort and enthusiasm into sth that is difficult enough to keep you interested: *This job is too easy. Why can't they give me something I can really get my teeth into?*

have 'teeth (*BrE, informal*)
(of an organization, a law, etc.) be powerful and effective: *It appears that the new legislation doesn't have any teeth, since there has been no improvement in working conditions.*

(do sth) in the teeth of danger, opposition, etc.
(do sth) when or even though it is dangerous or people oppose it, etc: *The new law was passed in the teeth of strong opposition.* ◇ *They crossed the Atlantic in the teeth of a force 10 wind.*

set sb's 'teeth on edge
1 (of a sound) make sb feel physically uncomfortable: *That noise is really setting my teeth on edge! Can you stop?*
2 annoy sb; make sb feel tense: *It sets my teeth on edge when I hear him talk to his mother so rudely.*

- **armed** → armed to the teeth (with sth)
- **bare** → bare your teeth
- **bit** → get/take the bit between your teeth
- **eye** → give your eye teeth for sth/to do sth
- **fed** → fed up to the back teeth with sb/sth
- **fed** → sick to the back teeth of sb/sth **SEE** fed up to the back teeth with sb/sth
- **gnash** → gnash your teeth
- **grit** → grit your teeth
- **hell** → Hell's teeth
- **hen** → (as) rare/scarce as hen's teeth

- **kick** → kick sb in the teeth
- **lie** → lie through your teeth
- **pulling** → like pulling teeth
- **show** → show your teeth
- **skin** → do sth by the skin of your teeth

teething /'tiːðɪŋ/

have, etc. 'teething problems/troubles
experience small problems or difficulties in the development of a product, business, etc., or when sth new first becomes available to the public: *If your new car is having teething troubles, take it back to the garage where you bought it.*

NOTE
When a baby is *teething*, its first teeth are starting to grow, which is painful for the baby.

telegraph /'telɪɡrɑːf; *AmE* -ɡræf/

- **bush** → bush telegraph

telephone /'telɪfəʊn; *AmE* -foʊn/

be on the 'telephone/'phone
1 be using the telephone: *Mr Perkins is on the telephone but he'll be with you in a moment.* ◇ *You're wanted* (= sb wants to speak to you) *on the telephone.*
2 (*BrE*) have a telephone in your home or place of work: *They live on a small island and are not on the phone.*

tell /tel/

don't 'tell me (*spoken, informal*)
used to say that you know or can guess what sb is going to say, especially because it is typical of them: *Don't tell me, you were late again!*

I tell a 'lie (*spoken*)
used to say that sth you have just said is not true or correct: *We first met in 1982, no, I tell a lie, it was 1983.*

I 'tell you ♦ I can 'tell you ♦ I'm 'telling you ♦ I can't 'tell you how, etc. ... (*spoken*)
used to emphasize what you are saying, especially when it is surprising or difficult to believe: *It's not as easy as it looks, I'm telling you.* ◇ *I can't tell you how happy I felt* (= it is difficult to describe my happiness, because it was so great).

I/I'll tell you 'what ♦ I know 'what (*spoken*)
said before making a suggestion: *I tell you what — let's ask Fred to lend us his car.* ◇ *I know what! Why don't you buy her a CD?*

tell it how/like it 'is (*informal*)
tell sb sth honestly and directly: *All right, I'll tell it like it is. I don't love you Rachel, and I never have.*

(go) tell it/that to the ma'rines (*saying, informal*)
used to say that you do not believe what sb is saying, promising, etc: *'I'll never smoke again!' 'Yeah? Go tell that to the marines.'*

❓ ORIGIN
This comes from the saying 'that will do for the marines but the sailors won't believe it'.

tell its 'own tale/story
explain or show sth, without the need of any more explanations or comment: *The burned buildings and broken glass in the streets tell their own story.*

'tell me (*spoken*)
used to introduce a question: *Tell me, have you had lunch yet?*

'tell me about it (*spoken*)
used to say that you understand what sb is talking about and have had the same experience: *'I get so annoyed with Steve!' 'Tell me about it. He drives me crazy.'*

tell me a'nother (*spoken*)
used for saying that you do not believe sb because they are joking or exaggerating: *'I caught a fish that weighed 5 kilos.' 'Tell me another! I bet it didn't even weigh one kilo.'*

tell 'porkies (*BrE, informal, humorous*)
(usually used in progressive tenses) say sth that is not true: *Can this be true, or is somebody telling porkies?*

> **❷ ORIGIN**
> In rhyming slang, *porky-pies* means 'lies'.

tell the same tale/story (of sth)
show the same thing: *The faces of these children tell the same tale of hunger and misery.*

tell a 'different, a'nother, etc. tale/story
give some information that is different from what you expect or have been told: *She sounded very calm, but her face told a different story.*

tell 'tales (about sb/sth) (*BrE*)
tell sb, especially sb in authority, that another person has done something wrong: *How did the boss know that I was late for work this morning? I think somebody's been telling tales about me.*

tell ,tales out of 'school
talk about the private affairs of a group or an organization to people who do not belong to it: *I shouldn't tell tales out of school, but my company is in serious trouble.*

tell the 'time (*BrE*) (*AmE* **tell 'time**)
read the time from a clock, etc: *She's only five — she hasn't learnt to tell the time yet.*

tell sb ,where to get 'off ✦ tell sb ,where they get 'off (*BrE, informal*)
tell sb angrily that you do not like the way they are behaving and you no longer accept it: *He gets drunk every time we go to a party, so I've told him where to get off.*

tell sb where to 'put/'stick sth ✦ tell sb what they can 'do with sth (*informal*)
make it clear to sb that you are angry and are rejecting what they are offering you: *I was so furious I nearly told him where to stick his rotten job!*

tell the (whole) 'world
tell sth to everyone; tell sth publicly: *Keep your voice down! We don't want to tell the whole world about it!*

to tell (you) the 'truth
used when admitting sth: *To tell the truth, I fell asleep in the middle of her talk.*

what did I 'tell you? (also **I 'told you so**)
used for telling sb who did not listen to your warnings or take your advice that they were wrong and you were right: *'I've got terrible stomach-ache.' 'What did I tell you? You should never have drunk the tap water.' ◇ 'She didn't like the present.' 'I told you so. I knew she didn't like perfume.'*

you ,never can 'tell ✦ you can ,never 'tell (*saying*)
you can never be sure; you can never know exactly what will happen: *'Is he happy?' 'I don't know. You can never tell with him.' ◇ 'Who's going to win?' 'In weather conditions like these you never can tell.'*

- **end** → not know/not be able to tell one end of sth from the other
- **hand** → talk to/tell it to the hand (because the face ain't listening)
- **kiss** → kiss and tell
- **live¹** → live to tell the tale
- **thing** → can/could teach/tell sb a thing or two (about sb/sth)
- **time** → only time will tell
- **time** → time (alone) will tell

telling /'telɪŋ/

you're telling 'me! (*spoken, informal*)
used for saying that you already know and completely agree with what sb has just said: *'Cooking for ten people is hard work.' 'You're telling me.'*

- **knowing** → there's no knowing/saying/telling...
- **tell** → I'm telling you SEE I tell you

temper /'tempə(r)/

keep/lose your 'temper (with sb)
manage/fail to control your anger: *You must learn to keep your temper. ◇ He loses his temper very quickly if you argue with him.*

- **quick** → have a quick temper

temperature /'temprətʃə(r); AmE also -tʃʊr/

have/run a 'temperature
have a higher body temperature than normal: *She's got a headache and she's running a temperature.*

raise/lower the 'temperature (*informal*)
increase/decrease the amount of excitement, emotion, etc. in a situation: *His angry refusal raised the temperature of the meeting. ◇ The government tried to lower the political temperature by agreeing to some of the demands.*

take sb's 'temperature
measure the heat of sb's body, using a thermometer: *The nurse took my temperature; it was 38°.*

tempest /'tempɪst/

• storm → a tempest in a teapot SEE a storm in a teacup

tempt /tempt/

tempt 'fate/'providence
take a risk or do something dangerous: *'I don't think I'll insure my boat.' 'Don't tempt fate. It's best to insure it.'*

ten /ten/

ˌten out of 'ten (for sth) (*BrE, often ironic*)
used to say that sb has guessed sth correctly or done sth very well: *Not brilliant, Robyn, but I'll give you ten out of ten for effort.*

ˌten to 'one
it is very likely that...; very probably: *Ten to one they'll never find out who did it anyway.*

• nine → nine times out of ten
• penny → two/ten a penny

tender /'tendə(r)/

at a ˌtender 'age ♦ at the tender ˌage of '8, '12, etc.
used in connection with sb who is still young and does not have much experience: *We were sent to boarding school at a tender age.* ◇ *At the tender age of seventeen I left home.*

ten-foot /'ten fʊt/

• touch → not touch sb/sth with a ten-foot pole SEE not touch sb/sth with a bargepole

tenterhooks /'tentəhʊks; AmE -tərh-/

(be) on 'tenterhooks (*AmE also* **be on ˌpins and 'needles**)
(be) very tense, excited or anxious about what might happen: *We were kept on tenterhooks for hours while the judges chose the winner.*

> **❷ ORIGIN**
> In the past, a *tenterhook* was used to keep material stretched on a drying frame during manufacture.

tenths /tenθs/

• possession → possession is nine points/tenths/parts of the law

term /tɜːm; AmE tɜːrm/

in the 'long-/'medium-/'short term
used to describe what will happen a long/medium/short time into the future: *In the short term, we can send the refugees food and clothing, but in the long term we must do something about the underlying problems.* ► **ˌlong-'term, ˌshort-'term** *adj.*: *a long-term approach* ◇ *short-term problems*

terms /tɜːmz; AmE tɜːrmz/

be on good, bad, friendly, etc. 'terms (with sb)
have a good, bad, friendly, etc. relationship with sb: *He's not on very good terms with his wife's family.* ◇ *I'm on **first-name terms** with my boss now* (= we call each other by our first names).

come to 'terms with sth
learn to accept sth that is difficult or unpleasant: *He finally came to terms with his father's death.*

do sth on sb's/your (own) 'terms
do sth in a way that sb chooses/you choose because they/you are in a position of power: *They agreed to stop fighting, but on their own terms: all prisoners to be released, and talks to be held immediately.*

in terms of... ♦ in ... terms
used to show how sth is explained, described or judged: *In terms of money, it's a great job.* ◇ *In energy terms, this new power station can produce ten times as much as the old type.*

• contradiction → a contradiction in terms
• equal → on the same terms (as sb/sth) SEE on equal terms (with sb/sth)
• glowing → in glowing terms/colours
• nodding → be on nodding terms with sb
• speaking → be on speaking terms (with sb)
• uncertain → in no uncertain terms

territory /'terətri; AmE -tɔːri/

ˌcome/ˌgo with the 'territory
be a normal and accepted part of a particular job, situation, etc: *As a doctor, he has to work long hours and some weekends, but that goes with the territory I suppose.*

• neutral → on neutral ground/territory

test /test/

put sb/sth to the 'test
test sb/sth; find out whether sb/sth is good, bad, true, real, etc: *The second part of the contest will put your general knowledge to the test.*

stand the test of 'time
be considered valuable or useful by people for many years: *Dickens' books have stood the test of time — they are as popular now as they were a century ago.*

test the 'water/'waters
try to find out whether sth is likely to succeed, by asking people for their opinions before you do sth: *Your idea might not be popular with people, so before you start marketing it you should test the waters.*

• acid → the acid test (of sth)
• acid → the litmus test SEE the acid test (of sth)

tested /'testɪd/

• tried → tried and tested/trusted

tête-à-tête /ˌteɪt ɑːˈteɪt/

a ˌtête-à-ˈtête (*from French*)
a private conversation between two people: *When I last saw her, she was having a tête-à-tête with Maria.* ◇ *I hate to interrupt your tête-à-tête, but could somebody answer the phone?*

NOTE
The meaning of the French phrase is 'head-to-head'.

tether /ˈteðə(r)/

• end → be at the end of your tether

Thames /temz/

• world → not/never set the Thames on fire SEE not/never set the world on fire

thank /θæŋk/

have sb to thank (for sth)
used when you are saying who is responsible for sth: *I have my parents to thank for my success.*

I'll thank you (not) to do sth ◆ I'll thank you for sth/for doing sth (*formal, spoken*)
used when you are angry or annoyed, to ask sb in a formal way (not) to do sth: *I'll thank you not to interfere in my personal affairs.*

thank 'God! ◆ thank 'goodness/'heaven(s)!
used as an expression of relief: *Thank God you've arrived. I was so worried.*
(Some people find the phrase thank God offensive.)

thank your lucky 'stars (that...)
be very grateful (that...): *You should thank your lucky stars that you're young and healthy.*

he, she, etc. won't 'thank you for sth
used to say that sb will not be pleased or will be annoyed about sth: *John won't thank you for interfering.*

thankful /ˈθæŋkfl/

• small → be grateful/thankful for small mercies

thanks /θæŋks/

(be) no thanks to sb/sth
(be) in spite of sb/sth: *It's no thanks to you that we arrived on time — you kept wanting to stop!*

thanks to sb/sth (*sometimes ironic*)
because of sb/sth: *We won the game thanks to a lot of hard work from everyone in the team.* ◇ *We lost the match, thanks to a few silly mistakes.*

• vote → a vote of thanks

that /ðæt/

and (all) 'that (*BrE, informal*)
and that sort of thing; and all the other things: *My brother's got a farm, with chickens, cows, pigs and all that.* ◇ *Her paintings are well done and all that, but I find them rather boring.*

at 'that
1 when that happened: *He said she was a fool. At that, she walked out of the room.*
2 (*informal*) as well; either: *She suggested that we should write to our Member of Parliament, and it's not such a bad idea at that.*

is that 'so? (*informal*)
1 used for telling sb that you are not frightened by their actions or threats: *'If you don't shut your mouth I'll kick you out of the house.' 'Is that so? You just try it!'*
2 used to express surprise or interest at what sb has said: *'He owns twenty cars.' 'Is that so?'*

'not that
used to state that you are not suggesting sth: *She hasn't written — not that she said she would.*

that is (to say)
1 in other words: *I'm between jobs at the moment; that's to say unemployed.* ◇ *It cost him a week's wages, that is, €300.*
2 used to give more information or to correct what has already been said: *She's a housewife — when she's not teaching English, that is.* ◇ *Let him explain it — if he can, that is.* ◇ *Nobody wants to do it. Nobody except me, that is.*

'that's a good one (*informal*)
1 said in reply to a joke or clever remark
2 (*ironic*) said in reply to a stupid remark or action: *'Can you make dinner? I'm tired.' 'Tired? That's a good one. You've done nothing all day!'*

that's (about) 'it (*informal*)
1 used for saying that an activity, a job, etc. is finished: *That's it for today. We can go home now.* ◇ *That's about it. I've said all I wanted to say.*
2 used to agree with what sb has just said: *'You mean you won't get more than $500 for the job?' 'That's about it.'*

(and/so) ˌthat's 'that
used to show that sth is finished or decided, and there should be no more discussion or argument: *So that's that. At last we're all agreed.* ◇ *You're going to bed now, and that's that! I don't want any argument!*

them /ðem/

ˌthem and 'us
used to describe a situation in which two groups are opposed to each other, often with one group more powerful than the other: *We should try to get away from a 'them and us' attitude between employers and workers.*

theme /θiːm/

• variations → variations on the theme of sth

then /ðen/

and 'then some (*spoken*)
and even more (than has already been mentioned): *It rained for two hours and then some.*

theory /ˈθɪəri; *AmE* ˈθɪri; ˈθiːəri/

in ˈtheory
used to say that a particular statement is supposed to be true but may in fact be wrong: *In theory, these machines should last for ten years or more.* ◇ *That sounds fine in theory, but have you really thought it through?*

there /ðeə(r); *AmE* ðer/

be not all/quite ˈthere (*informal*)
think slowly because of low intelligence, illness, drugs, etc: *Are you sure he's all there?* **OPP** all there

be ˈthere for sb
be available if sb wants to talk to you or if they need help: *You know I'll always be there for you.*

ˌso ˈthere! (*informal*)
(often said by children) used for emphasizing your satisfaction with sth or for emphasizing a refusal, etc: *I got a better mark than you. So there!* ◇ *Well, you can't have it, so there!*

(do sth) ˌthere and ˈthen ♦ (do sth) ˌthen and ˈthere
(do sth) at that time and place; immediately: *I took one look at the car and offered to buy it then and there.*

ˌthere you ˈare (also ˌthere you ˈgo) (*spoken*)
1 used when you give sth to sb: *I've got your newspaper. There you are.* ◇ *There you go. That's €3 change.*
2 used when explaining or showing sth to sb: *You cook it on both sides for three minutes and there you are. The perfect steak.*
3 used when sth happens which shows that you were right: *There you are. I told you we'd miss the train.*

there you ˈgo (aˈgain)
used to criticize sb because they are behaving badly again or saying the same things again and again: *There you go again — as soon as we disagree you start shouting at me!* ◇ *There he goes again — always complaining about something.*

there ˌis ˈthat
said when agreeing with sth: *'Flying is quick, but it's very expensive.' 'Yes, there is that.'*

(and/but/so) there it ˈis ♦ (and/but/so) there you ˈgo ♦ (and/but/so) there we/you ˈare
that is the situation; those are the facts: *I don't like my job, but I need the money, so there it is.* ◇ *Soup and bread isn't the best of meals, but there you go.*

ˌthere's ˈsth for you (*spoken*)
used to say that sth is a very good example of sth: *She visited him every day he was in the hospital. There's devotion for you.* ◇ (*ironic*) *He didn't even say thank you. There's gratitude for you!*

ˈthere's a good boy, girl, dog, etc. (*informal*)
used to praise or encourage small children or animals: *Finish your dinner, there's a good lad.* ◇ *Sit! There's a good dog.*

ˌthere, ˈthere! (*old-fashioned*)
used to comfort a small child: *There, there! Never mind, you'll soon feel better.*

therein /ˌðeərˈɪn; *AmE* ˌðer-/

therein lies… (*formal*)
used to emphasize the result of a particular situation: *He works extremely hard and therein lies the key to his success.*

thick /θɪk/

give sb/get a thick ˈear (*BrE, informal*)
hit sb/be hit on the side of the head, as a punishment: *If you don't behave yourself you'll get a thick ear.*

in the ˈthick of sth/of doing sth
1 in the busiest or most active part of sth/doing sth: *He was in the thick of preparing the food for the party, so I didn't interrupt.*
2 in the most crowded part of sth: *If there's trouble, you usually find him in the thick of it.*

ˌthick and ˈfast
quickly and in great numbers or quantities: *Replies to our advertisement are coming in thick and fast.* ◇ *By midnight, the snow was falling thick and fast.*

(as) thick as ˈthieves (with sb) (*informal*)
(of two or more people) very friendly with each other, especially in a way that makes other people suspicious: *Those two are as thick as thieves — they go everywhere together.* **OPP** be at daggers drawn

(as) thick as two short ˈplanks (*informal*)
(also **(as) thick as ˈshit** ⚠, *slang*) (*BrE*)
(of a person) very stupid: *Because she's a model, people assume she's as thick as two short planks, but she isn't.* **OPP** (as) bright as a button

> **NOTE**
> *Thick* is the opposite of thin and can also mean 'stupid' in informal language.

a thick ˈhead (*informal*)
a physical condition in which your head is painful or you cannot think clearly as a result of an illness or of drinking too much alcohol: *I've got a really thick head this morning.* **OPP** have/keep a clear head

(be) thick with sth/sb
(be) full of sth/sb: *The air was thick with the scent of roses.* ◇ *The street was thick with reporters and photographers.*

through ˌthick and ˈthin
in spite of all the difficulties and problems; in good and bad times: *He's been a good friend to her through thick and thin.*

● **bit** → a bit thick/strong
● **ground** → thick/thin on the ground
● **lay** → lay it on thick/with a trowel
● **lay** → pile it on thick SEE lay it on thick/with a trowel
● **skin** → (have) a thick/thin skin

thickens /ˈθɪkənz/

● **plot** → the plot thickens

thicker /ˈθɪkə(r)/

● **blood** → blood is thicker than water

thief /θiːf/

like a ˌthief in the ˈnight
secretly or unexpectedly: *In the end I left like a thief in the night, without telling anybody or saying goodbye.*

thieves /θiːvz/

- honour → (there is) honour among thieves
- thick → (as) thick as thieves (with sb)

thin /θɪn/

appear, etc. out of thin ˈair
appear, etc. suddenly from nowhere or nothing: *The car seemed to appear out of thin air. I didn't have time to brake.* ◇ *She seems to conjure wonderful costumes out of thin air.*

be skating/walking on ˌthin ˈice
be in a risky or dangerous situation: *They were skating on very thin ice, publishing the election result before it had been confirmed.*

be/get thin on ˈtop (*informal*)
without much hair on the head; be/go bald: *Max is only 30 but he's already getting a bit thin on top.*

disappear, etc. into thin ˈair
disappear, etc. suddenly and in a mysterious way: *The money vanished into thin air. Nobody knows what happened to it.*

have a thin ˈtime (of it) (*BrE, informal*)
be in an unsuccessful period in your business: *Small businesses are having a thin time of it at the moment, and many are closing down.*

(as) thin as a ˈrake
(of a person) very thin: *You're as thin as a rake. You certainly don't need to diet.*

the thin ˌend of the ˈwedge (*especially BrE*)
used for saying that you fear that one small request, order, action, etc. is only the beginning of sth larger and more serious or harmful: *The government says it only wants to privatize one or two railway lines, but I think it's the thin end of the wedge. They'll all be privatized soon.*

> **NOTE**
> A *wedge* is a piece of wood, metal, etc. with one thick end and one thin pointed end that you use to keep two things apart or to split wood or rock.

- ground → thick/thin on the ground
- line → tread/walk a fine/thin line
- skin → (have) a thick/thin skin
- spread → spread yourself too thin
- thick → through thick and thin
- wear → wear thin

thing /θɪŋ/

aˌmount/ˌcome to the same ˈthing
it does not matter how something happens or is done, the result in the end is the same: *Whether it was your fault or his fault, it still amounts to the same thing. My car's wrecked.*

be just the ˈthing (also **be the very ˈthing** *less frequent*)
be exactly what you need or want: *Hot lemon juice and honey is just the thing for a cold.* ◇ *A week by the sea, with plenty of swimming and walking, would be the very thing.*

be no bad ˈthing (that)...
used to say that although sth seems to be bad, it could have good results: *We didn't want the press to get hold of the story, but it might be no bad thing.*

be onto a good ˈthing
be in a position or situation which brings you a lot of benefits: *They've offered her a company car and a huge salary. She's onto a good thing there.*

can/could teach/tell sb a ˈthing or two (about sb/sth) (*informal*)
be able to help sb, or teach sb how to do sth, because you have more experience: *He thinks he knows a lot about farming, but old Bert could teach him a thing or two.*

a close/near ˈthing ✦ a close-run ˈthing (*informal*)
1 a competition, an election, a race, etc. which you only just succeed in winning: *I know we won, but believe me, it was a near thing. They could easily have beaten us.*
2 a punishment, an accident, etc. which you only just avoided: *The police searched the house but they didn't find him. It was a close-run thing.*

do your own ˈthing (*informal*)
live, act or behave as you want, not as others tell you to do; be independent: *Mark's father wanted him to be a doctor, but Mark wanted to do his own thing and run an art gallery.*

for ˈone thing, ...(, and for aˈnother, ...)
one reason is..., and another reason is...: *You ought to stop smoking, you know. For one thing, you're damaging your health, and for another, you can't afford it!* ◇ *'Why don't you get a car?' 'Well for one thing, I can't drive!'*

have a ˈthing about sb/sth (*informal*)
have very strong feelings, either positive or negative, about sb/sth: *I think she's got a thing about David. She keeps looking at him.* ◇ *I've got a thing about smoking, and I don't allow anybody to smoke in my house.*

it isn't my, his, etc. ˈthing
it is not sth that you really enjoy or are interested in: *I'm afraid pubs and clubs aren't really my thing. I'd prefer to go to a restaurant with a few friends.*

it's ˌone thing to do ˈA, it's (quite) aˌnother (thing) to do ˈB ✦ A is ˈone thing, B is (quite) aˈnother
used for saying that you find the first thing acceptable or possible but the second thing definitely unacceptable or impossible: *It's one thing to write a short article; it's quite another to write a whole book on the subject.* ◇ *Romance is one thing, marriage is quite another.*

it's a... thing (*informal*)
it is sth that only a particular group understands: *You wouldn't understand the attraction of fast cars — it's a man thing.*

make a (big) 'thing of/out of sth (*informal*)
make sth seem much more serious or important
than it really is: *It was only a small mistake, but
he made a really big thing out of it.*

,one (damned/damn) thing after a'nother
(*spoken*)
used to complain that a lot of unpleasant things
keep happening to you: *It's just one thing after
another, isn't it? First the car wouldn't start, and
then the bus was late.*

(what with) ,one thing and a'nother
(because of) several different events, tasks,
duties, etc: *What with one thing and another I
haven't had time to sit down all day.*

,one thing leads to a'nother (*informal*)
used to suggest that the way one event or action
leads to others is so obvious that it does not need
to be stated: *He offered me a ride home one night,
and, well, one thing led to another and now we're
engaged!*

there's no such ,thing as a free 'lunch (*spoken*)
used to say that it is not possible to get sth for
nothing: *I think you should be very careful about
accepting his help. Remember, there's no such thing
as a free lunch.*

> ❷ **ORIGIN**
> In the past, some pubs/bars offered their cus-
> tomers a 'free' lunch, but they had to buy
> drinks first.

there's only ,one thing 'for it
there is only one possible course of action: *Well,
there's only one thing for it, I'm afraid. You're going
to have to tell him what you've done and hope he
forgives you.*

the (whole)... thing (*informal*)
a situation or an activity of the type mentioned:
*She really didn't want to be involved in the whole
family thing.*

the (only) thing 'is... (*spoken*)
used before mentioning a worry or problem you
have with sth: *I'd love to come — the only thing is I
might be late.*

the ,thing (about/with sth) 'is (*spoken*)
used to introduce an important fact, reason or
explanation: *I know you want to expand the business. The thing is, we haven't got the money to do
that.* ◇ *I'm sorry I didn't call you. The thing is, I've
been really busy lately.*

a thing of the 'past
sth that no longer happens or exists: *Everybody
sends emails these days. Letter-writing has become
a thing of the past.*

- **best** → the best thing since sliced bread
- **chance** → chance would be a fine thing
- **done** → the done thing
- **first** → first thing (tomorrow, in the morning, etc.)
- **job** → (it's) a good job/thing (that)...
- **job** → (and) a good job/thing too
- **know** → know a thing or two (about sb/sth)
- **know** → not know the first thing about sb/sth
- **last** → last thing (at night)

- **next** → the next best thing
- **next** → the next thing (I knew)...
- **quite** → not quite the thing
- **real** → the real thing
- **sure** → sure thing
- **think** → have another thing coming **SEE** have another
  think coming

things /θɪŋz/

all things con'sidered
considering all the facts, especially the problems
or difficulties, of a situation: *She's had a lot of
problems since her husband died but she seems quite
cheerful, all things considered.*

and 'things (like 'that) (*spoken, informal*)
used when you do not want to complete a list: *She
likes nice clothes and things like that.* ◇ *I've been
busy shopping and things.*

as things 'stand
the present situation is that: *As things stand, we
won't finish the job on time, but we might if we get
some extra help.*

be all ,things to all 'men/'people (*saying*)
change the way you behave or what you say to try
to please the people you are with: *The President's
attempts to be all things to all men had disastrous
consequences.*

'do things to sb (*informal*)
have a powerful emotional effect on sb: *That song
just does things to me.*

in 'all things (*formal*)
in every situation; always: *I believe in honesty in all
things.* ◇ *Moderation in all things is my motto.*

(just) ,one of those 'things
used to say that unfortunate things do happen
sometimes and we must accept this fact: *He
doesn't love me any more and there's absolutely
nothing I can do about it. It's just one of those
things.*

other/all things being 'equal
if nothing else changes; if other conditions remain
the same: *Other things being equal, prices will rise
if people's incomes rise.*

,put things 'right
do sth to improve a difficult situation or correct a
mistake: *The company is inefficient. A good director
could put things right very quickly.*

'see/'hear things (*informal*)
see/hear things that are not really there: *So it was
you that was playing the piano! I thought I was
hearing things.* ◇ (*humorous*) *Tom's washing the
dishes — I must be seeing things!*

these ,things are sent to 'try us (*saying*)
used to say that you should accept an unpleasant
situation or event because you cannot change it:
*'My car broke down again.' 'Oh well, these things are
sent to try us.'*

,these things 'happen
used to tell sb not to worry about sth they have
done: *'Sorry — I've spilt some wine.' 'Never mind,
these things happen.'*

think

,things that go ,bump in the 'night (informal, humorous)
strange or frightening noises, or things that cannot be explained by science: I don't believe in ghosts or spirits, or things that go bump in the night.

● best → make the best of sth/things/a bad job
● day → take it/things one day at a time
● easy → take it/things easy
● feel → be/feel out of it/things
● fine → cut it/things fine
● first → first things first
● look → by/from the look(s) of it/things
● mind → have your mind on other things
● mind → your mind is on other things
● nature → in the nature of things
● overdo → overdo it/things
● people → of all people/places/things
● push → push it/things
● scheme → the/sb's scheme of things
● shape → be a taste of things to come SEE be the shape of things to come
● turned → as it/things turned out
● way → have it/things/everything (all) your (own) way SEE get/have your (own) way
● work → work it/things (so that...)

think /θɪŋk/

anyone would 'think (that)... (also you would have 'thought (that)...)
(of sb's strange or surprising behaviour) if you did not know the truth, it would seem that...: Don't be so nervous! Anyone would think you'd never been to a party before!

come to 'think of it (also 'thinking about it) (informal)
said when you suddenly remember or realize sth: I first met her in 1997. No, come to think of it, it was 1996.

give sb something to 'think about (informal)
do or say sth to sb which shows how angry or determined you are: This letter will give him something to think about.

have another think 'coming (also have another thing 'coming) (informal)
used to tell sb that they are wrong about sth and must change their plans or opinions: If she thinks that married life is going to be easy, she's got another think coming.

if/when you 'think about it
used to draw attention to a fact that is not obvious or has not previously been mentioned: They do have a big house, when you think about it.

I should think 'so/'not (also I should think she, etc. 'is/'does/'did, etc.)
used for emphasis when agreeing that sth is right or correct: 'He didn't give the waiter a tip.' 'I should think not, after such bad service.' ◇ 'He finally apologized for what he said.' 'I should think so.' ◇ 'I'm very angry with my son.' 'I should think you are. He's behaved very badly indeed.'

I shudder/dread to 'think (how, what, etc....) (informal, often humorous)
I am afraid to think or ask myself about sth, because the answer might be terrible or unpleasant: I shudder to think when he last had a bath. ◇ 'How much more work is there?' 'I dread to think!'

just 'think
used when you feel interest, shock or excitement at sth: Just think of the money we spend renting this place. ◇ I'll be on television in front of millions of viewers! Just think!

not 'think of sth/of doing sth
(used with wouldn't, couldn't, won't or can't) definitely not do sth; never do sth: I wouldn't think of buying one of those ugly modern houses.

that's what sb thinks (informal)
what sb thinks will happen will not happen, especially because the speaker is going to do sth to prevent it: 'Your team doesn't have a chance of winning.' 'That's what you think!'

,think a'gain
consider a decision again and perhaps change your idea or intention: I'd advise you to think again before leaving your wife.

,think a'loud ♦ ,think out 'loud
speak your thoughts about sth, for example a problem, to yourself or to others, probably without organizing them as in normal speech: 'What?' 'Oh, don't worry. I was just thinking out loud.'

think (the) 'better of sb
have a higher opinion of sb: She has behaved appallingly — I must say I thought better of her.

think 'better of it/of doing sth
decide not to do sth that you were intending to do: He was about to say something, but then he thought better of it and kept quiet.

think 'big (informal)
have big plans for the future; be ambitious: If you want to be successful in life, you've got to think big.

think 'highly of sb/sth
have a very high opinion of sb/sth: Her teachers think highly of her. ◇ His paintings are highly thought of by the critics.

think 'nothing of sth/of doing sth ♦ not think 'anything of sth/of doing sth
1 consider sth as normal or easy, when other people consider it as difficult, dangerous, etc: He thinks nothing of working 14 hours a day.
2 think that sth is not important: I saw a man outside the door, but I didn't think anything of it at the time. I realized later that he must have been the thief.

think nothing 'of it (spoken, formal)
said as a polite reply when sb has thanked you or said sorry for sth: 'I'm terribly sorry for all the trouble I've caused you.' 'Think nothing of it.'

think on your 'feet
think very quickly: When he asked me why I wasn't at work, I had to think on my feet and I invented an excuse about going to see the doctor. ◇ Lawyers in court need to be able to think on their feet.

think out of the 'box (also **think outside the 'box**)

think about sth, or how to do sth, in a new, different or creative way (especially in business): *The company is looking for adventurous, creative people who can think out of the box and are not afraid of experimenting.* ◇ *Thinking out of the box would improve public education.*

think you 'own the place (also **behave/act as if you 'own the place**) (*disapproving*)

behave in a very confident way that annoys other people, for example by telling them what to do: *What does she think she's doing, coming in here acting as if she owns the place!*

think 'positive

think in a confident way about what you can do: *If you don't think positive, you won't win.* ► **,positive 'thinking** noun: *He believes in the power of positive thinking.*

'think straight

think in a clear or logical way: *You're not thinking straight. If you leave your job, how will you support your family?*

think the sun shines out of sb's 'arse △/'back'-side (*BrE*) (*AmE* **think the sun shines out of sb's 'ass △**) (*slang*)

have a very high opinion of sb and think that everything they do is good: *We need more money for this job. I think you should be the one to ask the boss — he thinks the sun shines out of your backside!*

(not) think 'twice about sth/about doing sth

(not) think carefully before deciding to do sth; (not) hesitate: *You should think twice about employing someone you've never met.* ◇ *If they offered me a job abroad, I wouldn't think twice about taking it!*

think the 'world of sb/sth

like, admire or respect sb/sth very much: *The children think the world of their new teacher.* **OPP** you, he, etc. can't stand sb/sth

to 'think (that)…

used to show that you are surprised or shocked by sth: *I can still hardly believe it! To think that the President stayed at my hotel!* ◇ *To think that he was killed on the last day of the war. It's so sad.*

who does sb think they 'are? (*disapproving, informal*)

sb has no right to behave in a certain way: *Who do you think you are, taking my books without asking?* ◇ *She just walked into my office without knocking! Who does she think she is?*

- fit → see/think fit (to do sth)
- hear → can't hear yourself think
- ill → speak/think ill of sb
- let → let me see/think

thinking /'θɪŋkɪŋ/

put your 'thinking cap on (*informal*)

try to solve a problem by thinking hard about it: *Now, how are we going to find this money? Let's put our thinking caps on.*

- think → thinking about it **SEE** come to think of it
- way → to my, your, etc. way of thinking
- wishful → wishful thinking

third /θɜːd; *AmE* θɜːrd/

(give sb) the ,third de'gree (*informal*)

question sb for a long time and in a thorough way; use threats or violence to get information from sb: *The soldiers were given the third degree in order to make them reveal the information.* ◇ *Why are you giving me the third degree?*

> **❷ ORIGIN**
> This expression comes from Freemasonry (= a secret society). In order to reach the highest level of the organization and become a *Third Degree Mason*, members are interrogated.

third time 'lucky (*AmE* also **third time is the 'charm**)

used when you have failed to do sth twice and hope that you will succeed the third time: *I missed again! Oh well, third time lucky!*

- wheel → a fifth/third wheel

this /ðɪs/

,this and 'that (also **,this, that and the 'other**) (*informal*)

a number of different things: *We talked about this and that for a while and then had dinner.*

this is 'it (*informal*)

1 said when you are agreeing that a point made by sb is important: *'People prefer their cars to public transport, you see.' 'Well, this is it.'*
2 said when you have come to an important moment: *Well this is it, Mike. Good luck in Australia. Don't forget to write…*

thither /'ðɪðə(r)/

- hither → hither and thither

Thomas /'tɒməs; *AmE* 'tɑːməs/

- doubting → a doubting Thomas

thorn /θɔːn; *AmE* θɔːrn/

be a thorn in your 'flesh/'side

be a person or thing that repeatedly annoys you or stops you doing sth: *This patient is a real thorn in my side. He's always complaining of feeling sick and I can never find anything wrong with him.*

thought /θɔːt/

I 'thought as much

that is what I thought or expected: *'She's been lying to you; she hasn't really got any money at all.' 'I thought as much.'*

it's the 'thought that counts (*saying*)

the fact that sb remembered about sth is more important than the size or value of a present: *She didn't send him a present for his birthday, only a card, but it's the thought that counts.*

- food → food for thought

- pause → give (sb) pause for thought
- perish → perish the thought!
- school → a school of thought
- second → on second thought SEE on second thoughts
- second → without a second thought
- think → you would have thought (that)… SEE anyone would think (that)…
- train → a train of thought
- wish → the wish is father to the thought

thoughts /θɔ:ts/

- collect → collect yourself/your thoughts
- penny → a penny for your thoughts
- read¹ → read sb's mind/thoughts
- second → have second thoughts
- second → on second thoughts

thousand /'θaʊznd/

- bat → bat a thousand
- hundred → a hundred/thousand/million and one things/things to do, etc.
- miles → not a hundred/thousand/million miles away/from here
- sixty-four → the sixty-four thousand dollar question

thrall /θrɔ:l/

in (sb's/sth's) 'thrall ♦ in 'thrall to sb/sth (*literary*)
controlled or strongly influenced by sb/sth: *The country's economy is still largely in thrall to the big companies.*

thread /θred/

thread your way through (sth)
move through a place by moving round and between people or things: *I threaded my way through the busy streets.*

- drift → lose the drift/thread of sth
- hang → hang by a thread/hair

threads /θredz/

- loose → the loose ends/threads
- pick → pick up the threads

three /θri:/

(yes sir, no sir) three bags 'full (sir) (*old-fashioned, humorous*)
said when you agree to do sth that sb asks you but think that they are rather rude or unreasonable: *Our new manager doesn't want to hear our opinions, all he wants is, 'Yes sir, no sir, three bags full sir.'*

> **❷ ORIGIN**
> This phrase is from the nursery rhyme, 'Baa, baa, black sheep'.

(give) three 'cheers (for sb/sth)
shout 'hurray' three times to show admiration or support for sb/sth: *You all deserve three cheers for working so hard.* ◇ *Three cheers for the winner — hip, hip, hurray!*

the three 'R's (*old-fashioned*)
reading, writing and arithmetic as the basic school subjects

> **NOTE**
> When you say these three subjects, they all have the sound /r/ at or near the beginning of the word.

(be) three sheets to the 'wind (*old-fashioned*)
(be) drunk: *By 11 o'clock he was three sheets to the wind and we had to take him home in a cab.*
OPP stone-cold sober

> **❷ ORIGIN**
> This idiom comes from sailing: if three *sheets* (= the ropes attached to the sails) are loose, the wind blows the sails about and the boat moves in a very unsteady way.

threshold /'θreʃhəʊld; AmE -hoʊld/

be on the 'threshold of sth (*formal*)
be at an important moment when sth begins, changes or develops: *The country seemed to be on the threshold of war.* ◇ *Now, on the threshold of a new career, he seems confident and happy.*

> **NOTE**
> The *threshold* is the floor or ground at the bottom of a doorway, considered as the entrance to a building or room.

thrills /θrɪlz/

(the) thrills and 'spills (of sth) (*informal*)
the exciting mixture of sudden successes and difficulties: *He loves the thrills and spills of Grand Prix motor racing.*

throat /θrəʊt; AmE θroʊt/

cut your own 'throat
do sth that is likely to harm you, especially when you are angry and trying to harm sb else: *You cut your own throat when you told him to leave. How are you going to manage alone?*

ram, force, thrust, etc. sth down sb's 'throat (*informal*)
try to make sb accept or believe an idea or belief by talking about it all the time: *I'm tired of having her opinions rammed down my throat all the time!* ◇ *He was always forcing Marxist theories down our throats.*

- clear → clear your throat
- frog → have a frog in your throat
- jump → jump down sb's throat
- lump → have, etc. a lump in your throat
- stick → stick in your throat/craw/gullet

throats /θrəʊts; AmE θroʊts/

(be) at each other's 'throats ♦ (be) at one another's 'throats
(be) angrily fighting or arguing with each other: *Within six months of their marriage, Sue and Rodney were at each other's throats.*

throes /θrəʊz; AmE θroʊz/

in the throes of sth/doing sth
doing a difficult task; experiencing a difficult
period or event: *The movie's about a country in
the throes of change.* ◇ *He's in the throes of divorce
at the moment.*

throne /θrəʊn; AmE θroʊn/

● **power** → be the (real) power behind the throne

throttle /'θrɒtl; AmE 'θrɑːtl/

● **full** → (at) full throttle

through /θruː/

,through and 'through
completely; in every way: *He's a gentleman
through and through.* ◇ *This letter is my bank manager through and through.*

throw /θrəʊ; AmE θroʊ/

Most idioms containing **throw** are at the
entries for the nouns or adjectives in the
idioms, for example **throw the book at sb** is at
book.

$100, £50, etc. a 'throw (*informal*)
used to say how much items cost each: *The tickets
for the dinner were £50 a throw.*

thrown /θrəʊn; AmE θroʊn/

● **deep** → jump in/be thrown in at the deep end

thrust /θrʌst/

the cut and 'thrust (of sth) (*BrE*)
the lively exchange of opinions or ideas; competi-
tiveness: *He enjoys the cut and thrust of business.*

thumb /θʌm/

thumb your 'nose at sb/sth
show that you have no respect for sb/sth, sometimes by making a rude sign with your thumb on
the end of your nose: *A photograph shows one of
the crowd thumbing his nose at the speaker.*

under sb's 'thumb (*informal*)
completely controlled or influenced by another
person: *Now that they're married, she's completely
under his thumb and never sees her old friends.*

● **green** → a green thumb SEE green fingers
● **lift** → thumb/hitch a lift
● **rule** → a rule of thumb
● **sore** → stand/stick out like a sore thumb

thumbs /θʌmz/

be all 'thumbs (also **be all ,fingers and 'thumbs**)
be unable to hold sth without dropping or damaging it; be clumsy: *He's all thumbs when it comes
to fixing machines.*

hold 'thumbs (*South African*)
hope that your plans will be successful or that sth
will take place in the way that you want it to: *Let's
hold thumbs that you get the job.*

(give sb/sth/get) the thumbs 'up/'down
used to show that sth has been accepted/rejected
or that it is/is not a success: *I asked him whether I
could borrow the car, and he gave me the thumbs
up.* ◇ *I'm afraid it's thumbs down for your new proposal — the boss doesn't like it.* ◇ *We've got the
thumbs up for the new swimming pool.*

> ❷ ORIGIN
> In contests in ancient Rome the public put
> their thumbs up if they wanted a gladiator to
> live, and down if they wanted him to be killed.

● **twiddle** → twiddle your thumbs

thunder /'θʌndə(r)/

● **blood** → blood and thunder
● **face** → he, she, etc. has a face like thunder
● **face** → his, her, etc. face is like thunder
● **steal** → steal sb's thunder

tick /tɪk/

get, buy, etc. sth on 'tick (*old-fashioned, BrE,
informal*)
get food or other goods and pay for them later:
*You can only buy things on tick in small shops where
they know you well.*

> ❷ ORIGIN
> *Tick* is probably a short form of *ticket* and
> referred to the written note (an IOU) given by a
> person borrowing something to the lender as
> proof that they would pay them back or return
> the goods.

,tick sth off on your 'fingers
check a list of things by saying them aloud, and
touching your fingers one after another at the
same time

what makes sb 'tick (*informal*)
what makes sb behave or think in the way they
do: *I've never really understood what makes her
tick.* ◇ *Money is what makes him tick.*

> NOTE
> *Tick* here is the sound a watch or clock makes
> as the hands move forward every second.

ticket /'tɪkɪt/

'that's the ticket (*old-fashioned, BrE, informal*)
used to say that sth is just what is needed or that
everything is just right

● **job** → just the job/ticket
● **meal** → a meal ticket
● **split** → split the ticket

tickets /'tɪkɪts/

be 'tickets (*South African, informal*)
be the end: *It's tickets for the team that loses.* ◇ *If
he doesn't get this contract, it'll be tickets for Kurt.*

tickle

tickle /'tɪkl/

- fancy → catch/take/tickle sb's fancy
- slap → (a bit of) slap and tickle

tickled /'tɪkld/

be tickled 'pink (also **be tickled to 'death**)
(*old-fashioned, informal*)
be very pleased or amused: *My grandmother will
be tickled pink to get an invitation to the wedding.*
OPP (as) sick as a parrot

tide /taɪd/

the tide 'turns
things change, especially for the better: *For a long
time there has been little political freedom, but slowly the tide is turning.*

- rising → a rising tide lifts all boats
- stem → stem the tide (of sth)
- stream → go, swim, etc. with/against the stream/tide

tie /taɪ/

tie sb's 'hands
(often used in the passive) stop sb doing sth, by
taking away their power or freedom: *Employers
now have the right to dismiss workers who go on
strike and this has tied the unions' hands considerably.* ◇ *I'm afraid my hands are tied. I can't allow
anyone to bring visitors into the club. It's against the
rules.* **OPP** get, have, etc. a free hand

tie sb/yourself (up) in 'knots
become or make sb very confused: *The interviewer
tied the Prime Minister up in knots. He looked a
complete fool.* ◇ *He tied himself up in knots when
he tried to explain why he had lipstick on his face.*

tie the 'knot (*informal*)
get married: *When did you two decide to tie the
knot?*

tie one 'on (*old-fashioned, AmE, slang*)
get very drunk

- hand → bind/tie sb hand and foot
- old → the old school tie

tied /taɪd/

- hand → with one hand tied behind your back

tiger /'taɪgə(r)/

- paper → a paper tiger

tight /taɪt/

in a tight 'corner/'spot (*informal*)
in a very difficult situation: *He's in a bit of a tight
spot at the moment. The bank has given him one
week to find $2 000.*

keep a tight 'rein on sb/sth (also **keep sb/sth
on a tight 'leash**)
control sb/sth very carefully; give sb/sth very little freedom: *The company must keep a tight rein on
spending.* ◇ *She keeps her children on a tight leash
to make sure they don't get into trouble.* **OPP** give/
allow sb/sth free/full rein

> **NOTE**
> A *leash* is used to hold and control a dog, and a
> *rein* is used to control a horse.

run a ,tight 'ship
run an organization in a strict and efficient way:
*The boss runs a very tight ship and everybody is
expected to work very hard.*

a ,tight 'squeeze
a situation where you do not have much space to
put things in: *We managed to get all the luggage in
the car but it was a tight squeeze.*

They were all packed up and ready to go but it
was a tight squeeze.

- sit → sit tight
- sleep → sleep tight!

tighten /'taɪtn/

tighten your 'belt
spend less money, eat less food, etc. because there
is little available: *In wartime everyone has to tight-
en their belts.* ◇ *We'll have to tighten our belts if we
want to save any money for a summer break this
year.* **OPP** throw your money about/around ▶ **'belt-
tightening** *noun*: *Continued government belt-
tightening has helped to reduce public debt.*

tightrope /'taɪtrəʊp; AmE -roʊp/

tread/walk a 'tightrope ♦ **be on a 'tightrope**
be in a situation where you must act very carefully: *I'm walking a tightrope at the moment; one more
mistake and I might lose my job.*

> **NOTE**
> A *tightrope* is a rope high up in the air that an
> acrobat walks along at a circus.

tiles /taɪlz/

- town → a night (out) on the town/on the tiles **SEE** (out)
  on the town

till /tɪl/

have your ˌfingers/ˌhand in the 'till
(*BrE, informal*)
steal, especially small amounts of money from a
shop/store, business, etc. where you work: *He lost
his job after they found he'd had his hand in the till.*

tiller /'tɪlə(r)/

● **helm** → at the helm/tiller

tilt /tɪlt/

tilt at 'windmills
waste your energy attacking imaginary enemies:
*For some reason he thinks everyone is out to get
him, but he's really just tilting at windmills.*

> ❷ **ORIGIN**
> This expression comes from Cervantes' novel
> *Don Quixote*, in which the hero thought that
> the windmills he saw were giants and tried to
> fight them.

● **full** → (at) full pelt/speed/tilt

time /taɪm/

(and) about 'time ('too) ◆ **(and) not before
'time** (*spoken*)
said when the speaker is pleased that sth has happened but thinks that it should have happened
sooner: *Here comes the bus — and about time too.*
◇ *Julia's been promoted, and not before time, considering the amount of work she does.*

against 'time (*also* **against the 'clock**)
if you do sth **against time**, you do it as fast as you
can because you do not have much time: *We've
only got two days to find a replacement, so we're
racing against time.* ◇ *They're working against the
clock to try and get people out of the rubble alive.*

ahead of/behind 'time
early/late: *He arrived ahead of time, and had to
wait.* ◇ *The trains are running behind time again
today.*

all the 'time ◆ **the whole 'time**
1 during the whole of a particular period of time:
The letter was in my pocket the whole time (= while
I was looking for it).
2 very often; repeatedly: *She leaves the lights on
all the time.* **OPP** (every) now and again/then

'any time (*spoken*)
used after sb has thanked you for helping them,
etc: *'Thanks for the lift.' 'Any time.'*

at a 'time
separately or in groups of two, three, etc. on each
occasion: *We had to go and see the principal one at
a time.* ◇ *She ran up the stairs two at a time.*

at the 'time
at a particular moment in the past; then:
*I remember watching the first men on the moon on
television; I was only six at the time.*

at 'my, 'your, etc. time of life
at my, your, etc. age (especially used about older
people): *Learn to drive at my time of life? Don't be
silly!*

be ahead of/before/in advance of your 'time
have ideas or invent things before people are
ready to accept them: *He was sure that it was possible to fly to the moon, but he was ahead of his time
and people laughed at him.* ◇ *She was a feminist
before her time.* **OPP** be behind the times

be before sb's 'time
be before the period that a person can remember
or was involved in: *The Beatles were a bit before my
time.* ◇ *There used to be fields behind this house,
but that was before your time* (= before you started living here).

be (stuck) in a 'time warp
not having changed at all from a time in the past
although everything else has: *Her whole house
seems to be stuck in a time warp. It's like something
out of the 1950s.* **OPP** keep up, move, etc. with the
times

do/serve 'time (*informal*)
be in prison: *He had done time for robbing a bank.*
◇ *Two of the gang are serving time for murder.*

every 'time
whenever there is a choice: *I don't really like
cities — give me the countryside every time.*

for the time 'being (*also* **for the 'moment/'present**)
now, and for a short time in the future: *He can stay
with us for the time being until he finds a place of
his own.* ◇ *I'm happy here for the moment, but I
might want to move soon.*

from/since ˌtime imme'morial
from ancient times; from a very long time ago: *The
Barton family have lived in this village since time
immemorial.*

from ˌtime to 'time
occasionally; sometimes: *We go to the theatre from
time to time.* **OPP** all the time (2)

give sb a rough, hard, bad, etc. 'time (of it)
(*informal*)
make sb's life very difficult because you do not
like them: *Ever since I started work here, she's been
shouting at me and giving me a hard time.*

have a lot of 'time for sb/sth (*informal,
especially BrE*)
like, admire or respect sb/sth very much: *I've got a
lot of time for the police. I think they've got a very
difficult job.*

have no 'time for sb/sth ◆ **not have much
'time for sb/sth** (*informal*)
dislike and have no respect for sb/sth: *I have no
time for lazy people like him.* ◇ *I haven't got any
time for people who tell lies.*

have a (hard, rough, bad, etc.) 'time of it
(*informal*)
experience difficulties, problems, etc: *We're having a time of it at the moment with the builders in
the house.* ◇ *Businesses are having a hard time of it
right now.*

have the ˌtime of your 'life (*informal*)
enjoy yourself; be very happy or excited: *The children had the time of their lives at the circus.*

have 'time on your hands (*informal*)
have more free time than you want or need: *Now the children have left home, she's got a lot more time on her hands.* **OPP** have your hands full

(all) in good 'time (*spoken*)
used to say that sth will be done or will happen at the appropriate time and not before: *Be patient, Emily! All in good time.*

in good 'time
well before the time sth starts or happens: *Make sure you get there in good time to buy your ticket.*

in (less than/next to) 'no time
so soon or so quickly that it is surprising: *The kids will be leaving home in no time.* ◇ *She started learning Chinese last year and in less than no time she could hold a conversation in it.* ◇ *The meal was ready in next to no time.*

in your own good 'time (*informal*)
when you want to, and not when other people tell you to: *There's no point in getting impatient. She'll finish the job in her own good time.*

in your own 'time
in your free time, and not at work: *Please make private phone calls in your own time, Mr Davies, not when you are at work.*

in 'time
1 not late: *Make sure that you get here in time for the concert.*
2 after quite a long time; eventually: *You will feel better in time.*
3 (play, sing, or dance to music) at the right speed: *The violins didn't seem to be in time with the rest of the orchestra.*

it's ˌhigh/aˌbout 'time (that)... (*spoken*)
used for saying that sth should be done or happen immediately or very soon: *It's high time that this room was properly cleaned!* ◇ *So you've started work! It's about time!* (= you should have started a long time ago).

it's only, just, etc. a matter/a question of 'time (before...)
used to say that a thing will definitely happen in the future, although it may not happen immediately: *Don't worry, you'll get a job if you keep looking. It's just a matter of time.* ◇ *It's only a question of time before the fighting spreads to the city.*

keep 'time
1 (of a clock or watch) always show the correct time: *It's an old watch, but it keeps very good time.*
2 sing, play, or dance to music at the right speed: *Keep time with the music, Fiona. You're singing too fast.*

lose/waste no 'time (in doing sth)
do sth quickly and without delay: *As soon as she arrived back home, she lost no time in visiting all her old friends.*

make good, etc. 'time
go as fast as, or faster than you expected or hoped: *On the first part of the trip we made good time.*

make 'time (to do sth)
make sure you have enough time to do sth: *I'm very busy, but I'll try to make time to do it.*

make up the 'time
do sth at a different time, because you cannot do it at the usual or correct time: *He had a long lunch break on Tuesday and so he made up the time by working late on Wednesday.*

'many a time ♦ **'many's the time (that)...** (*old-fashioned*)
many times; frequently: *Many's the time we've thought about emigrating to Australia, but then we wouldn't see our grandchildren growing up.*

(the) next, first, second, etc. time a'round/ 'round
on the next, first, second, etc. occasion that the same thing happens: *He repeated none of the errors he'd made first time round.* ◇ *This time around it was not so easy.*

not give sb the ˌtime of 'day
refuse to speak to sb because you do not like or respect them: *Since the success of her novel, people shake her hand who once wouldn't have given her the time of day.*

(there's) no time like the 'present (*saying*)
the best time to do sth is now: *'When do you want me to start the decorating?' 'Well, no time like the present, is there?'*

of all 'time
that has ever been made, lived, etc: *Which do you think is the best movie of all time?* ▶ **'all-time** *adj.*: *My all-time favourite movie is 'Gone with the Wind'.*

(right) on 'time (*also* **bang on 'time**) (*informal*)
at the correct time, neither early nor late; punctual: *I always have to wait for you — you're never on time.* ◇ *The train came in bang on time for once.*

play for 'time
try to delay sth or prevent sth from happening now because you think there will be an advantage to you if you act later: *If I can play for time a bit longer, they might lower their price.*

take your 'time (doing sth/to do sth/over sth)
1 do sth as slowly as you like; do not hurry: *There's no rush — take your time.* **OPP** get a move on
2 be late; do sth too slowly: *You certainly took your time to get here. I've been waiting an hour!* ◇ *The shop assistant took her time serving me.*

there's no time to 'lose ♦ **there's no time to be 'lost** (*saying*)
you must act quickly: *Come on, there's no time to lose! The plane leaves in half an hour!*

ˌtime after 'time ♦ **ˌtime and (ˌtime) a'gain**
very often; many times, repeatedly: *He makes the same mistake time after time.* ◇ *Time and again she's tried to give up smoking, but she never succeeds.*

time 'flies (*saying*)
time seems to pass very quickly: *How time flies! I've got to go now.* ◇ *Time has flown since I started working here.*

❓ ORIGIN
This is a translation of the Latin phrase 'tempus fugit'.

time hangs/lies 'heavy (on your 'hands)
time seems to pass very slowly because you are bored or have nothing to do: *In prison, time hangs heavy.*

time is getting 'on
it is getting late; there is not much time left: *We'd better hurry up and finish; time's getting on.*

time is 'money (*saying*)
time is valuable, and should not be wasted

❓ ORIGIN
This saying was first used by the American politician Benjamin Franklin in 1748.

time is on sb's 'side (also **have time on your side**)
sb has enough time to do sth; the more that time passes, the more sb will be helped: *Although she failed the exam, time is on her side; she is young enough to take it again next year.* ◇ *The longer we wait to sell the house, the more it will be worth, so we've got time on our side.*

the time is 'ripe (for sb) (to do sth) ♦ **the time is 'ripe for sth/for doing sth** (*literary*)
it is the right time to do sth: *I think the time's ripe for him to leave home if he wants to.* ◇ *The time is ripe for a change in this country.*

time 'was (when)… (*old-fashioned*)
used to say that sth used to happen in the past: *Time was when you could go for a walk in the country and not see another person for miles.*

time (alone) will 'tell ♦ **only time will 'tell** (*saying*)
used to say that you will have to wait for some time to find out the result of a situation: *Only time will tell if the treatment has been successful.*

- **beat** → beat time
- **better** → better luck next time
- **bide** → bide your time
- **big** → big time
- **borrowed** → be/live on borrowed time
- **buy** → buy time
- **crunch** → it's crunch time
- **day** → in sb's day/time
- **day** → take it/things one day at a time
- **easy** → have an easy time of it
- **first** → there's a first time for everything
- **forth** → from that day/time forth
- **fullness** → in the fullness of time
- **gain** → gain time
- **half** → half the time
- **half** → in half the time
- **high** → have a high old time
- **long** → long time no see
- **lost** → make up for lost time
- **mark** → mark time
- **nick** → in the nick of time
- **nth** → for the nth time
- **once** → once upon a time

- **pass** → pass the time of day (with sb)
- **pass** → pass the/your time (doing sth)
- **payback** → it's payback time
- **quite** → quite some time
- **race** → a race against time/the clock
- **stitch** → a stitch in time (saves nine)
- **sweet** → do sth in your own sweet time/way
- **tell** → tell (the) time
- **test** → stand the test of time
- **thin** → have a thin time (of it)
- **third** → third time is the charm **SEE** third time lucky
- **third** → third time lucky
- **whale** → have a whale of a time

times /taɪmz/

at all 'times
always: *Our representatives are ready to help you at all times.*

at 'times
sometimes: *At times I wonder whether he'll ever get a job.*

be behind the 'times
be old-fashioned in the way you live, work, think, etc: *You're behind the times if you think a visit to the dentist has to be painful.* **OPP** be ahead of/before/in advance of your time

keep up, move, etc. with the 'times
change in the same way as the rest of society changes: *In business it's important to keep up with the times.* ◇ *People's tastes change with the times.* **OPP** be (stuck) in a time warp

- **best** → at the best of times
- **hard** → fall on hard times
- **nine** → ninety-nine times out of a hundred **SEE** nine times out of ten
- **old** → for old times' sake
- **sign** → (be) a sign of the times

tin /tɪn/

have a tin 'ear (for sth) (*informal*)
be unable to hear the difference between musical notes or to enjoy music: *Even those of us with a tin ear can recognize a waltz.*

- **cat** → like a cat on a hot tin roof **SEE** like a cat on hot bricks
- **says** → (it) does (exactly) what it says on the tin

tiny /'taɪni/

- **patter** → the patter of tiny feet

tip /tɪp/

be on the tip of your 'tongue
used when you are speaking and cannot remember a word, name, etc. but feel that you will remember it very soon: *What's her name? You know, that tall Italian girl…it's on the tip of my tongue…Claudia, that's it!*

be the tip of the 'iceberg
what you can see of a problem or difficult situation is only one small part of a much larger hid-

den problem: *The 1 000 homeless people in London sleeping in night shelters are only the tip of the iceberg. There are many thousands of homeless people in the capital.*

NOTE
Only ¹/₇ or ¹/₈ of an iceberg can be seen above the water.

tip the 'balance/'scales (also **swing the 'balance**)
be the reason that finally causes sb to do sth or sth to happen in one way rather than another: *They were both very good candidates for the job but she had more experience and that tipped the balance.*

tip the scales at sth
weigh a particular amount: *He tipped the scales at just over 80 kilos.*

tip sb the 'wink ♦ tip the 'wink to sb
(*BrE, informal*)
give sb secret information that they can use to gain an advantage for themselves: *'How did you know the job was available?' 'A friend tipped me the wink and so I telephoned immediately.'*

● hand → tip your hand **SEE** show/reveal your hand
● hat → tip your hat to sb **SEE** take your hat off to sb

tipping /ˈtɪpɪŋ/

it's 'tipping (it) down (*BrE, informal*)
it is raining heavily: *There's no way I'm playing football in this weather — it's tipping it down.*

a/the 'tipping point
the point at which, after a series of small changes, sth reaches a level where it begins to change dramatically or starts to have an important effect on sth/sb : *We're at a tipping point; if we spend just a bit more, we will get a large increase in productivity.*

tiptoe /ˈtɪptəʊ; AmE -toʊ/

on 'tiptoe/'tiptoes
standing or walking on the front part of your foot, with your heels off the ground, in order to make yourself taller or to move very quietly or lightly: *She had to stand on tiptoe to reach the top shelf. ◇ We crept around on tiptoes so as not to disturb him.*

tire /ˈtaɪə(r)/

never tire of doing sth
do sth a lot, especially in a way that annoys people: *He went to Harvard — as he never tires of reminding us.*

● spare → a spare tire **SEE** a spare tyre

tired /ˈtaɪəd; AmE ˈtaɪərd/

be/get tired of sth/doing sth
be/get bored or annoyed with sth/doing sth: *We got tired of the country and we moved into town. ◇ I'm tired of listening to his complaints.*

● sick → sick and tired of sb/sth **SEE** sick of sb/sth

tires /ˈtaɪərz/

● kick → kick the tires **SEE** kick the tyres

tissue /ˈtɪʃuː; BrE also ˈtɪsjuː/

a ,tissue of 'lies (*literary*)
a story, an excuse, etc. that is full of lies: *This official report on the nuclear energy industry is a tissue of lies.*

tit /tɪt/

,tit for 'tat
a situation in which you do sth unpleasant to sb because they have done sth unpleasant to you: *He hit me, so I hit him back — it was tit for tat. ◇ the routine tit for tat when countries expel each other's envoys*

Titanic /taɪˈtænɪk/

● rearrange → rearrange the deckchairs on the Titanic

titty /ˈtɪti/

● luck → tough titty **SEE** tough/bad luck (2)

tizzy /ˈtɪzi/ (also **tizz**)

be/get in/into a 'tizzy/'tizz (about sth)
(*informal*)
be/become excited, nervous or confused, especially about sth that is not important: *He was in such a tizz about his homework.*

to /tuː; tu; tə/

,to and 'fro
from one place to another and back, repeatedly; from side to side repeatedly: *They travel to and fro between London and Paris. ◇ She held the baby in her arms and rocked her to and fro.*

(all) to your'self, him'self, etc.
for only you, him, etc. to have, use, etc: *The boss was away last week so we had the office to ourselves.*

toast /təʊst; AmE toʊst/

be 'toast (*slang*)
be in very serious trouble: *If Dad finds out about this, we're toast!*

> **❷ ORIGIN**
> This probably comes from the US film *Ghostbusters*.

be the toast of...
be sb who is praised by a lot of people in a particular place because of sth that they have done well: *Eddie was the toast of Hollywood yesterday after winning three awards for his latest film.*

● propose → propose a toast (to sb)
● warm → (as) warm as toast

-to-be /tə ˈbi/

-to-be
(in compounds) future: *his bride-to-be ◇ mothers-to-be* (= pregnant women)

tod /tɒd; AmE taːd/

on your 'tod (*old-fashioned*, *BrE*, *informal*)
on your own; alone: *Are you going to be alright here all on your tod?*

> ❷ ORIGIN
> This comes from rhyming slang: after Tod Sloan, an American jockey, whose name rhymes with 'alone'.

today /təˈdeɪ/

here to,day, gone to'morrow
if sth is **here today, gone tomorrow**, it only exists or stays for a short time: *The restaurant staff don't tend to stay for very long — they're here today, gone tomorrow.* **OPP** be here to stay

toe /təʊ; AmE toʊ/

go toe to 'toe (*AmE*)
fight or compete with sb directly: *I am not sure we could go toe to toe with them and win.*

toe the 'line (*AmE* also **toe the 'mark**)
obey the orders and accept the ideas, aims and principles of a particular group or person: *The Prime Minister is angry because some members of the government are not toeing the line.* **OPP** overstep the mark/line

- head → from head to foot/toe
- top → from top to toe

toes /təʊz; AmE toʊz/

keep sb on their 'toes (*informal*)
make sure that sb is ready to deal with anything that might happen by doing things that they are not expecting: *Regular surprise visits help to keep the staff on their toes.* ◇ *This job really keeps me on my toes.*

make sb's 'toes curl
make sb feel embarrassed or uncomfortable about sth: *After yesterday's embarrassing incident, she really didn't want to go to work. Just thinking about it was enough to make her toes curl.* ▸ **'toe-curling** *adj.*: *a toe-curling performance*

on your 'toes
ready to deal with anything that might happen: *We were all on our toes, waiting for the game to begin.*

- tread → step on sb's toes SEE tread on sb's toes
- tread → tread on sb's toes

toffee /ˈtɒfi; AmE ˈtɔːfi; ˈtɑːfi/

can't do sth for 'toffee (*old-fashioned*, *BrE*, *informal*)
if sb **can't do sth for toffee**, they are very bad at doing it: *He can't dance for toffee!*

together /təˈɡeðə(r)/

to'gether with
1 including: *Together with the Johnsons, there were 12 of us in the villa.*
2 in addition to; as well as: *I sent them my order, together with a cheque for £40.*

togged /tɒɡd; AmE taːɡd; tɔːɡd/

be ,togged 'out/'up (in sth) (*informal*)
be wearing clothes for a particular activity or occasion: *They were all togged up in their skiing gear.*

toing /ˈtuːɪŋ/

,toing and 'froing
1 movement or travel backwards and forwards between two or more places: *All this toing and froing between London and Paris is making him tired.*
2 a lot of unnecessary or repeated activity or discussion: *There's been a lot of toing and froing next door today. I wonder what's happening.* ◇ *After a great deal of toing and froing, I decided not to change jobs after all.*

token /ˈtəʊkən; AmE ˈtoʊ-/

by the ,same 'token
for the same reasons: *The penalty for failure will be high. But, by the same token, the rewards for success will be great.*

told /təʊld; AmE toʊld/

all 'told
(used with numbers) with everything/everyone included: *So far there have been fourteen arrests all told.*

- little → a little bird told me (that…)
- tell → I told you so SEE what did I tell you?
- truth → if (the) truth be known/told

toll /təʊl; AmE toʊl/

take its 'toll (on sb/sth) (also **take a (heavy) 'toll (of sth)**)
have a bad effect on sb/sth; cause a lot of damage, deaths, suffering, etc: *The present economic crisis is taking a heavy toll. Thousands of firms have gone bankrupt.* ◇ *His job is taking its toll on him. He needs a rest.*

Tom /tɒm; AmE taːm/

every/any ,Tom, ,Dick and/or 'Harry (*usually disapproving*)
any ordinary person; people of no special value to you: *We don't want just any Tom, Dick or Harry marrying our daughter.*

- Peeping → a Peeping Tom

tomorrow /təˈmɒrəʊ; AmE təˈmaːroʊ; -ˈmɔːr-/

do sth as if/like there's no to'morrow (*informal*)
do sth with a lot of energy, as if this is the last time you will be able to do it: *She's spending money like there's no tomorrow.*

- jam → jam tomorrow
- today → here today, gone tomorrow

ton /tʌn/

be/come down on sb like a ton of 'bricks (*informal*)
criticize sb angrily because they have done sth wrong: *The first time I made a mistake, he came down on me like a ton of bricks.* ◇ *If I find anyone drunk in this factory I'll be down on them like a ton of bricks.*

● **weigh** → weigh (half) a ton

tone /təʊn; *AmE* toʊn/

set the 'tone (of/for sth)
create or establish a general feeling or atmosphere among a group of people (about a particular subject): *His very clever and very funny speech set the tone for the rest of the evening.*

● **lower** → lower the tone (of sth)

tongs /tɒŋz; *AmE* taːŋz; tɔːŋz/

● **hammer** → be/go at sb/sth hammer and tongs

tongue /tʌŋ/

get your 'tongue round/around sth
manage to say a difficult word correctly: *I sometimes find it difficult to get my tongue around the word 'sixth'.*

roll/slip/trip off the 'tongue
be easy to say or pronounce: *It's not a name that exactly trips off the tongue, is it?*

a ˌsilver/ˌsmooth 'tongue
the ability to talk in a very pleasing and polite way, to make people do what you want: *It was his silver tongue that got him the job.* ► ˌsilver-'tongued, ˌsmooth-'tongued *adj.*: *smooth-tongued salesmen*

(with) tongue in 'cheek (*also* **with your tongue in your 'cheek**)
if you say sth **with your tongue in your cheek,** you are not being serious and mean it as a joke: *I never know if Charlie's serious or if he's speaking with tongue in cheek.* ◇ *a tongue-in-cheek remark* **OPP** in all seriousness

● **bite** → bite your tongue
● **cat** → (has the) cat got your tongue?
● **find** → find your voice/tongue
● **loose** → have a loose tongue
● **loosen** → loosen sb's tongue
● **mother** → your mother tongue
● **peace** → hold your peace/tongue
● **sharp** → have a sharp tongue
● **slip** → a slip of the tongue/pen
● **tip** → be on the tip of your tongue
● **watch** → watch your mouth/tongue

tongues /tʌŋz/

set 'tongues wagging (*informal*)
cause people to start talking about sb's private affairs: *A careless remark about his family really set tongues wagging.*

tongues 'wag (*informal*)
there is a lot of talk about sb's private life, etc: *Don't tell anyone your secret — you know how tongues wag around here.*

tool /tuːl/

● **sharpest** → not the sharpest tool in the box **SEE** not the sharpest knife in the drawer

tools /tuːlz/

ˌdown 'tools (*BrE*)
stop work, either at the end of the day or to go on strike: *The workers have threatened to down tools as a protest against the dismissals.*

the tools of the/your 'trade
the things you need to do your job: *We are proud to make David's boots, because they are the tools of his trade as a professional footballer.* ◇ *Ambulancemen now believe that helicopters are vital tools of the trade.*

toot /tuːt/

● **blow** → blow/toot your own horn **SEE** blow your own trumpet

tooth /tuːθ/

● **fight** → fight tooth and nail (for sb/sth/to do sth)
● **long** → (be) long in the tooth
● **red** → red in tooth and claw
● **sweet** → have a sweet tooth

top /tɒp; *AmE* taːp/

at the top of your 'voice
very loudly: *He was shouting at the top of his voice.* **OPP** in an undertone

be/get on 'top of sth
be able to manage and control problems and difficulties successfully: *I've finally got on top of my new job but it took a long time.*

be/go ˌover the 'top (*abbr.* **OTT**) (*informal, especially BrE*)
(of a person) do sth in a wild, excited or extreme way; (of sth) be unnecessarily extreme: *They went completely over the top at their wedding. I've never seen anything like it!* ◇ *His remarks were a bit over the top.*

come out on 'top (of sth)
become, etc. more successful than others: *It was a hard match but Sampras came out on top in the end.* ◇ *Our new model has come out on top in export markets this year.*

from ˌtop to 'bottom
completely and thoroughly: *We searched the house from top to bottom.*

from ˌtop to 'toe
from the head to the feet; completely: *We were covered in mud from top to toe.*

get on 'top of sb
(of a problem, too much work, etc.) make sb feel very worried or depressed: *She's letting things get on top of her at work.*

off the ‚top of your 'head (*informal*)
as a guess; without having time to think carefully:
*Off the top of my head I'd say it would cost $2 000 to
do the repairs.* ◇ *'What's the population of Liverpool?' 'I'm afraid I couldn't tell you off the top of
my head.'*

on top of sb/sth
1 in addition to sth; also: *On top of his salary, he
gets about €150 in commission every week.*
2 too close to sth/sb: *These houses are all built on
top of one another.* ◇ *He was right on top of* (= driving very close behind) *the car in front.*

on ‚top of the 'world
very happy or proud: *I'm on top of the world; I've
just had a baby son.* ◇ *You'll feel on top of the world
after a good rest.* **OPP** down in the dumps

pay, earn, charge, etc. top 'dollar
pay, earn, charge, etc. a lot of money: *If you want
the best, you have to pay top dollar.* ◇ *We can help
you get top dollar when you sell your house.*

‚take it from the 'top (*informal*)
go back to the beginning of a song, piece of music,
speech, etc. and repeat it: *OK, take it from the top,
and no mistakes this time!*

‚top and 'tail sth (*BrE*)
cut the top and bottom parts off fruit and vegetables to prepare them to be cooked or eaten:
*There's no need to top and tail the gooseberries, just
steam or bake them with sugar.*

(the) ‚top 'brass (*BrE, informal*)
people with power and authority: *The top brass
got a huge pay rise.* **OPP** (the) rank and file

> **NOTE**
> Officers in the military wear *brass* (= a bright
> yellow metal) or gold badges to show their
> position.

‚top 'dog (*informal*)
a person, group or country that is better or more
powerful than all the others: *He's top dog in television drama now.*

the top of the 'hour (*especially AmE*)
(on a TV/radio programme, etc.) the beginning of
an hour on a clock: *We have more news coming up
at the top of the hour.* **OPP** the bottom of the hour

(at) the top of the 'tree/'ladder
(at) the highest position in a career: *Anyone can
get to the top of the ladder if they try hard enough.*

‚top 'secret
used to describe very secret government information: *These defence plans are top secret, known only
to a very few people.* ◇ *The file was marked TOP
SECRET.*

the ‚top 'ten, 'twenty, etc.
the ten, twenty, etc. best-selling pop records each
week: *The song didn't even make* (= get into) *the
top twenty.*

to ‚top/‚cap/‚crown it 'all (*spoken*)
used to introduce the final piece of information
that is worse than the other bad things you have
already mentioned: *We went to a horrible restaur-*
*ant. The food was awful, the music was far too loud,
and to top it all, the waiter was rude to us.*

up 'top (*BrE, informal*)
used to talk about sb's intelligence: *He doesn't have
much up top, I'm afraid.*

● **bill** → head/top the bill
● **blow** → blow your top
● **bottom** → at the bottom/top of the pile/heap
● **flight** → in the first/top flight
● **sleep** → sleep like a log/top
● **thin** → be/get thin on top

Topsy /ˌtɒpsi; *AmE* ˈtɑːpsi/
● **grow** → grow like Topsy

torch /tɔːtʃ; *AmE* tɔːrtʃ/
put sth to the 'torch (*literary*)
set fire to sth deliberately: *The original castle was
put to the torch in the 18th century, although it was
rebuilt later.*

● **carry** → carry a torch for sb

torn /tɔːn; *AmE* tɔːrn/
that's 'torn it (*BrE, informal*)
used to say that sth has happened to spoil your
plans: *'Oops, that's torn it,' she thought, as she realized she'd ruined the surprise.*

toss /tɒs; *AmE* tɔːs/
not give a 'toss (about sb/sth) (*BrE, slang*)
not care at all about sb/sth: *I don't give a toss what
he thinks!*

toss a 'coin ✦ 'toss for sth (*especially BrE*)
(also **flip a 'coin, 'flip for sth** usually both *AmE*)
throw a coin in the air in order to decide sth:
*Right, who's going to wash the dishes tonight? Shall
we toss a coin?*

> **NOTE**
> Before the coin is thrown, one person chooses
> either 'heads' (= the side of the coin marked
> with a head) or 'tails' (= the other side). If the
> side chosen lands upwards this person wins the
> toss and the other person loses.

● **argue** → argue the toss

toss-up /ˈtɒs ʌp; *AmE* ˈtɔːs/
be a 'toss-up (between A and B) (*informal,
especially BrE*)
be a situation in which either of two choices,
results, etc. is equally possible: *'Have you decided
on the colour yet?' 'It's a toss-up between the blue
and the green.'*

> **NOTE**
> This expression refers to tossing a coin in order
> to make a decision about something.

touch /tʌtʃ/

be, etc. in/out of 'touch (with sth)
have/not have recent knowledge or news of sth,
and so fully/not fully understand it: *I try to keep in
touch with what's happening by reading the newspapers.* ◇ *Our politicians are old and out of touch*
(= unaware of people's real feelings).

be, keep, etc. in 'touch (with sb)
communicate with sb regularly: *We are in touch
with our central office every day.* ◇ *I've stayed in
touch with some of my university friends.*

be out of 'touch (with sb)
no longer communicate with sb, so that you no
longer know what is happening to them: *Now my
husband and I are divorced, people assume we're
out of touch, but we're not. We see each other quite
regularly.*

get in 'touch with sb/sth
make contact with sb/sth (by phone, letter, visit,
etc.): *Here's my phone number in case you need to
get in touch with me.*

have, etc. a ˌtouch of 'class
have, etc. quality, in design, character, etc: *His
clothes are old and unfashionable, but nevertheless
he has a real touch of class.*

lose 'touch/'contact (with sb/sth)
not write/speak to sb or not hear/read about sb/
sth as you did in the past: *She lost touch with most
of her old friends when she moved to London.*

lose your 'touch
lose the skill or ability to do sth which you used to
do very well: *I don't know what's happened to her
playing. She seems to have lost her touch.* ◇ *He's not
as good a salesman as he used to be. He's losing his
touch.*

not touch sb/sth with a 'bargepole (*BrE*) (*AmE*
not touch sb/sth with a ten-foot 'pole) (*informal*)
refuse to get involved with sb/sth or in a particular situation: *I don't know why she's marrying that
man. I wouldn't touch him with a bargepole.*
◇ *I wouldn't touch the job with a ten-foot pole.*

> **NOTE**
> A *barge* is a large boat with a flat bottom which
> is sometimes moved using a very long pole.

put sb in 'touch with sb/sth
arrange for sb to contact, meet, etc. a person or an
organization that you already know: *He put me in
touch with the British Council in Paris.*

a soft/an easy 'touch (*informal*)
a kind and perhaps easily deceived person whom
people ask for money, help, etc: *Ask Tony to lend
you some money. He's a soft touch.* **OPP** a tough cus-
tomer/cookie

> **❷ ORIGIN**
> *Touch* was a slang term used by criminals to
> refer to the act of stealing something from
> someone, particularly from a pocket. A *soft* or
> *easy touch* was someone that it was easy to
> steal from.

touch 'base (with sb) (*informal*)
make contact with sb again: *She travels to Boston
every week to touch base with her office.* ◇ *I spent
an hour or two sending emails and touching base
with my friends.*

touch 'bottom
1 reach the ground at the bottom of an area of
water
2 (*BrE*) reach the worst possible state or condition: *Her career really touched bottom with that
movie.*

touch 'wood (*BrE*) (*AmE* **knock on 'wood**)
(*saying*)
used for expressing the hope that your good luck
will continue: *We haven't had a serious accident
yet, touch wood.*

> **NOTE**
> This refers to the custom of touching some-
> thing made of wood to prevent bad luck.
> People still often try to touch something made
> of wood when they say this.

- chord → strike/touch a chord (with sb)
- common → the common touch
- finishing → the finishing touch(es)
- forelock → touch/tug your forelock
- hair → not harm/touch a hair of sb's head
- kick → kick sth into touch **SEE** kick sth into the long grass
- light → a light touch
- magic → (have) a/the magic touch
- Midas → the Midas touch
- nerve → hit/touch a (raw) nerve
- raw → catch/touch sb on the raw

touch-and-go /ˌtʌtʃ ən 'ɡəʊ; *AmE* 'ɡoʊ/

be ˌtouch-and-'go (whether...) (*informal*)
be very uncertain whether sth will happen or not;
be risky: *It was touch-and-go whether the work
would be finished in time.*

> **❷ ORIGIN**
> This idiom possibly refers to a ship sailing in
> shallow water. The bottom of the ship might
> touch the sea bed for a moment but the ship
> still remains undamaged and able to continue
> moving.

touched /tʌtʃt/

be touched with sth
have a small amount of a particular quality: *His
hair was touched with grey.* ◇ *Some of her poems
are touched with real genius.*

tough /tʌf/

be/get 'tough (on/with sb)
be strict with sb whose behaviour you do not like;
be ready to punish sb: *It's time to get tough with
football hooligans.* ◇ *be tough on crime*

(as) tough as 'nails (*informal*)
1 very strong and able to deal successfully with
difficult conditions or situations: *She's almost 90
but she's still as tough as nails.*
2 not feeling or showing any emotion

(as) tough as old 'boots (*informal*)
1 (of food) be very tough and difficult to chew: *This steak's as tough as old boots.*
2 very strong and able to bear pain, criticism, etc. without complaining or giving up: *Don't worry, she'll soon recover. She's tough as old boots.*

a tough 'customer/'cookie (*informal*)
a person who knows what they want and is not easily influenced by other people: *Self-confident, ambitious and positive, Paula is a tough cookie who is bound to do well.*

a 'tough guy (*informal*)
a strong, independent-minded person who seems to be afraid of nothing: *The most famous 'tough guy' in American movies was John Wayne.*

tough 'love
treating sb in a harsh way in order to help them improve their situation or change the way they behave: *She believes in 'tough love' for dealing with disruptive youngsters.*

when the ˌgoing gets 'tough (the ˌtough get 'going) (*saying*)
when conditions or progress become difficult, then strong and determined people work even harder to succeed: *I know it's going to be hard work, but you can always call me when the going gets tough.*

- act → a hard/tough act to follow
- hang → hang tough
- luck → tough/bad luck
- luck → tough **SEE** tough/bad luck (2)
- luck → tough shit **SEE** tough/bad luck (2)
- luck → tough titty **SEE** tough/bad luck (2)
- nut → a hard/tough nut (to crack)
- talk → talk tough (on sth)

tour /tʊə(r); tɔː(r); *AmE* tʊr/

a tour de 'force (*from French*)
an extremely skilful performance or achievement: *a literary/cinematic tour de force*

> **NOTE**
> This is a French phrase that means 'an act of strength'.

- whistle-stop → a whistle-stop tour

tow /təʊ; *AmE* toʊ/

in 'tow (*informal*)
following closely behind; with you: *Mrs Bridge arrived with her four children in tow.*

towel /'taʊəl/

throw in the 'towel/'sponge (*informal*)
stop doing sth because you know that you cannot succeed; admit defeat: *It's a bit early to throw in the towel — you've only just started the job.*

> **NOTE**
> This idiom comes from boxing: throwing in the towel or sponge is a sign that a fighter accepts defeat.

tower /'taʊə(r)/

- ivory → an ivory tower
- strength → a pillar/tower of strength

town /taʊn/

go to 'town (on/over sth) (*informal*)
put a lot of money, energy, etc. into sth: *When they give parties they really go to town* (= spend a lot of money, invite a lot of people, etc.). ◇ *She decided to go to town and redecorate all the rooms in the house.*

(out) on the 'town (also **a night (out) on the 'town/on the 'tiles**) (*informal*)
visiting restaurants, clubs, theatres, etc. for entertainment, especially at night: *For a birthday treat they took him out on the town.* ◇ *The students went for a night on the tiles after the last exam.*

- game → the only game in town
- man → a/the man about town
- one-horse → a one-horse town
- paint → paint the town red

trace /treɪs/

sink, vanish, etc. without (a) 'trace
disappear completely: *The boat sank without trace.* ◇ *Many pop stars sink without a trace. After five years no one can even remember their names.*

traces /'treɪsɪz/

- kick → kick over the traces

track /træk/

ˌback on 'track
going in the right direction again after a mistake, failure, etc: *I tried to get my life back on track after my divorce.*

be on the right/wrong 'track
be thinking or acting in the right/wrong way to find the answer to a problem: *We haven't found a solution to the problem yet, but I think we're on the right track.* ◇ *You're on the wrong track, I'm afraid. The information you want isn't here.*

be ˌon 'track
be doing the right thing in order to achieve a particular result: *Curtis is on track for the gold medal.*

keep/lose 'track (of sb/sth)
stay/not stay informed about sb/sth; remember/forget about the number of sth, the time, etc: *It's hard to keep track of how much money we spend every month.* ◇ *I've lost track of the number of times I've lost my keys.*

a ˌtrack 'record
all a person's or an organization's successes or failures in the past: *In business your track record is more important than your qualifications.*

- beaten → off the beaten track

tracks /træks/

make 'tracks (for sth) (*spoken*)
leave one place to go to another: *It's getting late; I think we'd better make tracks.*

stop/halt sb in their 'tracks ♦ stop/halt/ freeze in your 'tracks
suddenly make sb stop by frightening or surprising them; suddenly stop because sth has frightened or surprised you: *The question stopped Alice in her tracks.* ◊ *The horse **stopped dead** in its tracks and refused to move.*

● **cover** → cover your tracks
● **hot** → hot on sb's/sth's tracks/trail
● **wrong** → from/on the wrong side of the tracks

trade /treɪd/

a ,trade 'secret
1 a secret about a particular company's method of production: *The ingredients of Coca-Cola are a trade secret.*
2 (*humorous*) a secret about how you make or do sth: *'Can I have a recipe for this cake?' 'No, you can't. It's a trade secret.'*

● **ply** → ply for hire/trade/business
● **ply** → ply your trade
● **rag** → the rag trade
● **roaring** → do a roaring trade (in sth)
● **tools** → the tools of the/your trade
● **tricks** → the tricks of the trade

trades /treɪdz/

● **jack** → a jack of all trades

trail /treɪl/

● **blaze** → blaze a/the trail
● **hit** → hit the trail SEE hit the road
● **hot** → hot on sb's/sth's tracks/trail

train /treɪn/

bring sth in its 'train (*written*)
have sth as a result: *Unemployment brings great difficulties in its train.*

in sb's 'train (*written*)
following behind sb: *In the train of the rich and famous came the journalists.*

in 'train (*formal*)
being prepared; happening: *The plans for the Queen's birthday celebrations are all in train.* ◊ *Changes to the law have been set in train.*

a train of 'thought
the connected series of thoughts that are in your head at a particular time: *The phone ringing interrupted my train of thought.*

● **gravy** → the gravy train

trap /træp/

fall into/avoid the trap of doing sth
do/avoid doing sth that is a mistake but which seems at first to be a good idea: *Parents sometimes*

fall into the trap of trying to do everything for their children.

● **shut** → keep your mouth/trap shut SEE shut your mouth/trap/face/gob!
● **spring** → spring a trap

travel /'trævl/

travel 'light
travel with very little luggage: *We're travelling light with one small bag each.*

tread /tred/

,tread the 'boards (*humorous*)
be an actor: *He has recently been treading the boards in a new play at the National.*

> **NOTE**
> The *boards* refers to the stage of a theatre.

tread 'carefully, 'warily, etc.
be very careful about what you do or say: *The government will have to tread very carefully in handling this issue.* **OPP** throw caution to the wind(s)

tread a difficult, solitary, etc. 'path
choose and follow a particular way of life, way of doing sth, etc: *A restaurant has to tread the tricky path between maintaining quality and keeping prices down.*

,tread on sb's 'heels
follow sb closely: *In the end she left the meeting room, with her assistant treading hard on her heels.*

,tread on sb's 'toes (*especially BrE*) (*AmE usually* **,step on sb's 'toes**) (*informal*)
offend or annoy sb, especially by getting involved in sth that is their responsibility: *Now that we have proper job descriptions we are less likely to tread on each other's toes.*

,tread 'water
1 keep yourself upright in deep water by moving your arms and legs
2 make no progress while you are waiting for sth to happen: *For the past year I've been treading water, in a boring job with no hope of promotion.*

● **line** → tread/walk a fine/thin line
● **tightrope** → tread/walk a tightrope

treat /triːt/

go down a 'treat (*BrE, informal*)
be very successful or enjoyable: *'Did the children like the story?' 'Yes, it went down a treat.'* ◊ *Mm! ice cream. That'll go down a treat.*

treat sb like 'dirt (*informal*)
treat sb very badly and without respect: *He treated his wife like dirt. She finally left him after ten terrible years.*

work a 'treat (*BrE, informal*)
be very effective or successful: *His idea worked a treat.*

● **trick** → trick or treat

treatment /'tri:tmənt/

● silent → give sb/get the silent treatment

tree /tri:/

be out of your 'tree (*BrE* also **be out of your 'box**) (*informal*)
crazy or strange; behaving in a crazy or stupid way, perhaps because of drugs or alcohol: *She must be out of her tree, going swimming in this weather.*

● apple → the apple doesn't fall/never falls far from the tree
● barking → be barking up the wrong tree
● gum → up a gum tree
● top → (at) the top of the tree/ladder

trees /tri:z/

● money → money doesn't grow on trees
● wood → not see the forest for the trees **SEE** not see the wood for the trees
● wood → not see the wood for the trees

trembling /'tremblɪŋ/

● fear → in fear and trembling (of sb/sth)

trial /'traɪəl/

by ˌtrial and 'error
trying different ways of doing sth until you find the right one: *I didn't know how to use the camera at first, so I had to learn by trial and error.*

a ˌtrial 'run
a first try at doing sth, to test it or for practice: *Take the car for a trial run before you buy it.*

trials /'traɪəlz/

ˌtrials and tribu'lations
difficulties and troubles: *The novel is about the trials and tribulations of adolescence.*

tribulations /ˌtrɪbju'leɪʃnz/

● trials → trials and tribulations

tribute /'trɪbju:t/

● pay → pay tribute to sb/sth

trice /traɪs/

in a 'trice
very quickly or suddenly: *He was gone in a trice.*

trick /trɪk/

ˌtrick or 'treat
said by children who visit people's houses at Halloween (= October 31) and threaten to play tricks on people who do not give them sweets/candy

try, use, etc. every trick in the 'book
try any method you know to get sth or get sb to do sth you want: *He'll use every trick in the book to try and stop you.*

Walter tried every trick in the book to impress Kate but nothing seemed to work.

ˌturn a 'trick/'tricks (*AmE, slang*)
have sex with sb for money: *Things got so bad for her financially that she even considered turning tricks to pay the rent.*

● job → do the job/trick
● miss → he, she, etc. doesn't miss a trick
● sleeve → have an ace/a trick up your sleeve

tricks /trɪks/

a bag/box of 'tricks (*informal*)
a set of methods or equipment that sb can use: *Hotel managers are using a whole new bag of tricks to attract their guests.*

be up to your (old) 'tricks (*informal, disapproving*)
be acting in your usual way, which the speaker does not like: *Tom's just been released from prison — he'll soon be up to his old tricks again, I expect.*

how's 'tricks? (*old-fashioned, informal*)
used as a friendly greeting

the ˌtricks of the 'trade
the clever or expert ways of doing things, especially used by people in their jobs: *She's only been here a couple of months, so she's still learning the tricks of the trade.*

● teach → (you can't) teach an old dog new tricks
● trick → turn a trick/tricks

tried /traɪd/

ˌtried and 'tested/'trusted (*BrE*) (*AmE* ˌtried and 'true*)
that you have used or relied on in the past successfully: *We'll be using a tried and tested technique to solve the problem.*

trim /trɪm/

be, keep, etc. in 'trim (*BrE, informal*)
be, remain, etc. fit and healthy: *For a man of his age he keeps in good trim.* **OPP** be out of shape (2)

trip

,trim your 'sails
1 arrange the sails of a boat to suit the wind so that the boat moves faster
2 reduce your costs: *Increasingly, businesses are having to trim their sails in order to survive.*

trip /trɪp/

- guilt → a guilt trip
- memory → take a trip down memory lane **SEE** go down/take sb down memory lane
- tongue → roll/slip/trip off the tongue

Trojan /ˈtrəʊdʒən; AmE ˈtroʊ-/

- work → work like a dog/slave/Trojan

trolley /ˈtrɒli; AmE ˈtrɑːli/

off your 'trolley (*BrE, informal*)
crazy; stupid: *He's completely off his trolley!*

> **NOTE**
> This idiom is similar to 'go off the rails' but refers to a tram (= a vehicle driven by electricity than runs on rails in the street) that has become disconnected from the power in the overhead track.

trooper /ˈtruːpə(r)/

- swear → swear like a trooper

trot /trɒt; AmE trɑːt/

on the 'trot (*BrE, informal*)
one after the other: *The bus has been late for five days on the trot.*

- hot → be hot to trot

trouble /ˈtrʌbl/

get sb into 'trouble (*old-fashioned*)
make a woman who is not married pregnant

give (sb) (some, no, any, etc.) 'trouble
cause problems or difficulties: *My back's been giving me a lot of trouble lately.* ◊ *The children didn't give me any trouble at all when we were out.*

look for 'trouble
behave in a way that is likely to cause an argument, violence, etc: *Bored youths hang around outside looking for trouble.*

take trouble over/with sth ✦ take trouble doing/to do sth (also **go to the trouble/a lot of trouble to do sth**)
use a lot of time, care and effort in doing sth: *She takes a lot of trouble with her writing, which is why it's so good.* ◊ *I don't want you to go to too much trouble.*

there's 'trouble brewing (*informal*)
a difficult situation is starting to develop: *There's trouble brewing in the car industry.*

a trouble ,shared is a trouble 'halved (*saying*)
if you talk to sb about your problems and worries, instead of keeping them to yourself, they seem less serious: *You really should tell someone how*

you feel. *After all, a trouble shared is a trouble halved.*

- ask → ask for trouble/it
- just → that's just the trouble **SEE** that's just it
- spare → spare no expense/pains/trouble (to do sth/(in) doing sth)

troubled /ˈtrʌbld/

- pour → pour oil on troubled water(s)

troubles /ˈtrʌblz/

- teething → have, etc. teething problems/troubles

trousers /ˈtraʊzəz; AmE -zərz/

- catch → catch sb with their trousers down **SEE** catch sb with their pants down
- mouth → be all mouth and (no) trousers **SEE** be all mouth
- wear → wear the trousers

trowel /ˈtraʊəl/

- lay → lay it on thick/with a trowel

truant /ˈtruːənt/

play 'truant (*BrE*) (*AmE* **play 'hookey/'hooky** *informal*) (*old-fashioned*)
stay away from school without permission: *Is she off school because she's ill, or is she playing truant?*

truck /trʌk/

have/want no 'truck with sb/sth (*BrE*)
not want to deal with or be involved with sb/sth: *He'll have no truck with anyone on the political left.*

true /truː/

come 'true
(of a hope, wish, etc.) really happen: *What the fortune teller said about your future really came true.* ◊ *Winning the medal was like a **dream come true**.*

,out of 'true
if an object is **out of true**, it is not straight or in the correct position: *That picture's out of true. Can you straighten it up?*

so ,bad, ,stupid, etc. it isn't 'true (*informal*)
used to emphasize that sb/sth is very bad, stupid, etc: *His brother is so lazy it isn't true!*

too ,good to be 'true
used to say that you cannot believe that sth is as good as it seems: *'I'm afraid you were quoted the wrong price.' 'I thought it was too good to be true.'*

your, his, etc. true 'colours (*BrE*) (*AmE* **your, his, etc. true 'colors**) (*often disapproving*)
what a person is really like: *Once he got into power he showed his true colours.*

true to 'form
in the usual or typical way or as you expect: *True to form, he arrived early.* ◊ *The meeting went true to form, with a lot of boring speeches.*

true to 'life
(of a book, film/movie, etc.) seeming real rather
than invented: *I don't think the characters are very
true to life.*

- **hold** → hold good/true
- **right** → too right/true
- **ring** → ring true/false/hollow
- **tried** → tried and true SEE tried and tested/trusted

truly /ˈtruːli/

yours 'truly
1 (*informal, often humorous*) I/me: *Steve came
first, Robin second, and yours truly came last.*
◇ *And of course, all the sandwiches will be made by
yours truly.*
2 (**Yours Truly**) (*AmE, formal, written*) used at the
end of a formal letter before you sign your name

- **well** → well and truly

trump /trʌmp/

a/your 'trump card
sth that gives you an advantage over other people,
especially when they do not know what it is and
you are able to use it to surprise them: *Many
schools use small classes as their trump card in marketing campaigns.* ◇ *He waited until the last minute
to play his trump card and tell them about his plans
to cut costs.*

> **NOTE**
> In some card games, one of the four suits is
> chosen to have a higher value than the others.
> The cards in that suit are *trump cards*.

trumpet /ˈtrʌmpɪt/

- **blow** → blow your own trumpet

trumps /trʌmps/

ˌcome/ˌturn up 'trumps (*informal*)
1 be very helpful or generous to sb who has a
problem: *I asked a lot of people if they could lend
me the money, but finally it was my sister who came
up trumps.*
2 do better than expected: *On the day of the
match the team turned up trumps* (= won the
game).

trust /trʌst/

in sb's 'trust ✦ **in the trust of sb**
being looked after by sb: *The family pet was left in
the trust of a neighbour.*

not trust sb an 'inch
not trust sb at all: *He says he just wants to help you
but I wouldn't trust him an inch if I were you.*

take sth on 'trust
believe what sb says even though you do not have
any proof or evidence to show that it is true: *I took
it on trust that the painting was genuine. I had no
reason to believe he would try to deceive me.*

trust 'you, 'him, 'her, etc. (to do sth) (*spoken,
informal*)
used when sb does or says sth that you think is
typical of them: *Trust you to forget my birthday!*
◇ *Trust it to rain at the weekend!*

trusted /ˈtrʌstɪd/

- **tried** → tried and tested/trusted

truth /truːθ/

if (the) ˌtruth be 'known/'told
used to tell sb the true facts about a situation,
especially when these are not known by other
people: *None of the students really liked the new
teacher. In fact, if the truth be told, everyone was
rather afraid of him.*

in 'truth (*written*)
used to emphasize the true facts about a situation:
*She laughed and chatted but was, in truth, not hav-
ing much fun.*

ˌtruth is stranger than 'fiction (*saying*)
used to say that things that actually happen are
often more surprising than stories that are
invented

(the) ˌtruth will 'out (*saying*)
the truth about sth cannot be hidden for ever

- **bend** → bend the truth
- **economical** → economical with the truth
- **gospel** → take sth as/for gospel/gospel truth
- **home** → a home truth
- **matter** → the fact/truth of the matter
- **moment** → the moment of truth
- **naked** → the naked truth
- **tell** → to tell (you) the truth

try /traɪ/

try your 'hand (at sth/doing sth)
try sth for the first time, for example a skill or a
sport: *I've always wanted to try my hand at golf.*

ˌtry it 'on (with sb) (*BrE, informal*)
do sth that you know is wrong, in order to see if sb
will accept this behaviour or not: *The price he
asked was far too much. I think he was just trying
it on.* ◇ *Don't try it on with me, pal, or you'll be
sorry.*

try your 'luck (at sth)
try to do or get sth, hoping you will succeed: *A
friend told me the job was available, so I thought
I'd try my luck.*

try sb's 'patience
make sb feel impatient: *Jim's constant complaining
was really beginning to try her patience.*

- **damnedest** → do/try your damnedest
- **level** → do/try your level best (to do sth)
- **things** → these things are sent to try us
- **utmost** → do/try your utmost (to do sth)

trying /ˈtraɪɪŋ/

not for lack/want of 'trying
used to say that although sb has not succeeded in sth, they have tried very hard: *He's had no success in finding a job, though not for lack of trying.*

● **needle** → like looking for/trying to find a needle in a haystack

tube /tjuːb; *AmE* tuːb/

go down the 'tube/'tubes (*informal*)
(of a plan, company, situation, etc.) fail: *The education system is going down the tubes.*

tuck /tʌk/

● **neck** → nip and tuck (with sb) **SEE** neck and neck (with sb/sth)

tucker /ˈtʌkə(r)/

● **best** → your best bib and tucker

tug /tʌg/

tug at sb's 'heartstrings
make sb feel strong emotions of sadness and pity: *Advertisers often use babies and children to tug at your heartstrings.*

● **forelock** → touch/tug your forelock

tumble /ˈtʌmbl/

● **rough** → rough and tumble

tune /tjuːn; *AmE* tuːn/

be ˌin/ˌout of 'tune (with sb/sth)
1 be on/not on the right musical note: *They were both singing out of tune.*
2 be in/not in agreement with sb/sth; be/not be happy or comfortable with sb/sth: *He's out of tune with modern ideas about education.* ◇ *I don't like London — I just don't feel in tune with city life.*

to the tune of $500, etc. (*informal*)
used to emphasize how much money sth has cost: *We're paying rent to the tune of £200 a week.*

● **call** → call the shots/the tune
● **change** → change your tune
● **dance** → dance to sb's tune
● **march** → march to a different tune **SEE** march to (the beat of) a different drummer/drum
● **pays** → he who pays the piper calls the tune
● **sing** → sing a different song/tune

tunnel /ˈtʌnl/

(have) ˌtunnel 'vision (*disapproving*)
(have) an interest in only one small part of sth instead of the whole of it: *He's got tunnel vision about music. He thinks only the classics are worth listening to.*

● **light** → (see the) light at the end of the tunnel

tuppence /ˈtʌpəns/

not care/give 'tuppence for/about sb/sth
(*old-fashioned, BrE, informal*)
think sb/sth is not important; not care about sb/sth: *She loves him, but he doesn't care tuppence for her.* ◇ *The police don't give tuppence for our rights.*

> **NOTE**
> *Tuppence* is an old word meaning 'two pence'.

turf /tɜːf; *AmE* tɜːrf/

a 'turf war (*informal*)
an argument or a dispute about who owns or controls an area: *Street violence has escalated as a result of a turf war between rival neighbourhood gangs.* ◇ *Turf wars are inevitable when two departments are merged.*

> **NOTE**
> In informal language, your *turf* is the place where you live and/or work, especially when you think of it as your own.

turkey /ˈtɜːki; *AmE* ˈtɜːrki/

● **cold** → cold turkey
● **talk** → talk turkey

turn /tɜːn; *AmE* tɜːrn/

> Most idioms containing **turn** are at the entries for the nouns or adjectives in the idioms, for example **turn the corner** is at **corner**.

at every 'turn
everywhere or every time you try to do sth: *I keep meeting her at every turn.* ◇ *My plans always seem to go wrong at every turn.*

by 'turn(s)
used when talking of contrasting feelings or actions which follow each other: *He looked surprised, worried and angry by turn.* ◇ *When they told me I had got the job in New York, I felt by turns excited and anxious.*

do sth out of 'turn
1 do sth when you have no right to do it because another person should have done it before you; not in the correct order: *There was an argument in the doctor's waiting room because somebody had gone in to see him out of turn.*
2 say or do sth that you should not say because you have no right to or because it's not the right time or place to say it: *It is not the first time that Julia has said something out of turn.* ◇ *I apologize if I've spoken out of turn.*

give sb a 'turn (*old-fashioned*)
frighten or shock sb: *You gave me quite a turn, creeping up on me like that!*

in 'turn
1 one after another: *The teacher spoke to all of us in turn.*
2 as a result of sth in a series of events: *Increased production will, in turn, lead to higher profits.* ◇ *She was very angry with me and I in turn was very upset.*

on the 'turn (*especially BrE*)
going to change soon: *That's the third time they've won this season. I think their luck is on the turn.*

turn sth ,inside 'out/,upside 'down
1 make a place very untidy when you are searching for sth: *I've turned this drawer inside out but I can't find my passport.* ◇ *The thieves turned the office upside down but they didn't find anything valuable.*
2 cause large changes: *The new manager turned the old systems inside out.*

turn round/around and do sth (*informal*)
say or do sth unexpected and unfair: *He just turned round and told her that he was leaving. She couldn't believe it.*

turned /tɜːnd; *AmE* tɜːrnd/

as it/things turned 'out
as later events showed: *I didn't need my umbrella as it turned out* (= because it didn't rain later).

be well, badly, etc. turned 'out
be well, badly, etc. dressed: *Her children are always smartly turned out.*

● **poacher** → poacher turned gamekeeper
● **wheel** → the wheel has come/turned full circle

turns /tɜːnz; *AmE* tɜːrnz/

take 'turns doing sth/to do sth (*BrE* also **take it in 'turns to do sth**)
do sth one person after another: *My wife and I take it in turns to write to our daughter in Canada.* ◇ *There weren't enough computers for everybody, so we had to take turns using them.*

● **tide** → the tide turns
● **worm** → the worm turns

turn-up /'tɜːn ʌp; *AmE* 'tɜːrn-/

a ,turn-up for the 'book(s) (*BrE, informal*)
an unusual or unexpected event: *Everyone thought John would win, so when Richard won it was a real turn-up for the books.*

❷ ORIGIN
This expression comes from gambling. A *turn-up* was a horse, etc. that won unexpectedly, to the benefit of bookmakers, and *books* are the records of bets.

turtle /'tɜːtl; *AmE* 'tɜːrtl/

turn 'turtle
(of a boat) turn upside down: *We turned turtle right in front of everybody at the yacht club. It was so embarrassing.*

NOTE
This expression refers to the fact that if a turtle is turned on its back, it is helpless and unable to move.

twain /tweɪn/

never the ,twain shall 'meet (*saying*)
used to say that two things are so different that they cannot exist together: *People in the area where I grew up were either landowners or farmers, and never the twain shall meet.*

NOTE
Twain is an old word meaning 'two'.

twice /twaɪs/

be 'twice the man/woman (that sb is)
be much better, stronger, healthier, etc. than sb or than before: *How dare you criticize him? He's twice the man that you are!*

twice 'over
not just once but twice: *There was enough of the drug in her stomach to kill her twice over.*

● **cheap** → cheap at twice the price **SEE** cheap at the price
● **lightning** → lightning never strikes (in the same place) twice
● **once** → once bitten, twice shy
● **once** → once or twice
● **think** → (not) think twice about sth/about doing sth

twiddle /'twɪdl/

,twiddle your 'thumbs (*informal*)
do nothing while you are waiting for sth to happen: *I had to sit at home twiddling my thumbs, waiting for the phone to ring.*

NOTE
If you *twiddle your thumbs*, you move them around each other while your fingers are joined together.

twinkling /'twɪŋklɪŋ/

in the ,twinkling of an 'eye
very quickly: *Her mood can change in the twinkling of an eye.*

twist /twɪst/

,twist sb's 'arm (*informal, often humorous*)
force or persuade sb to do sth, but not by using physical force: *'Do you think Jane will lend us her car?' 'I think we could probably twist her arm.'*

'twist in the wind (*especially AmE*)
be in a bad, difficult or uncertain situation particularly one in which you receive the blame for sth: *When the scandal broke, his business partners left him to twist in the wind.* ◇ *The government left people twisting in the wind* (= not sure what would happen to them).

● **bend** → (drive sb/be/go) round the bend/twist
● **knickers** → get/have your knickers in a twist
● **knife** → turn/twist the knife (in the wound)
● **little** → twist/wind/wrap sb around your little finger

'twixt /twɪkst/

● **slip** → there's many a slip ('twixt cup and lip)

two /tuː/

be in two 'minds about sth/about doing sth
(*BrE*) (*AmE* **be of two 'minds about sth/about doing sth**)
be unable to decide about sth: *I was in two minds about leaving London; my friends were there, but at the same time I really wanted to work abroad.*

a 'day, 'moment, etc. or two
one or a few days, moments, etc: *May I borrow it for a day or two?*

fall between two 'stools (*BrE*)
not be successful, acceptable, etc. because it is neither one thing nor another: *The book falls between two stools. It's neither a love story nor a crime story.*

for two 'pins (*old-fashioned, BrE*)
used to say that you would like to do sth, even though you know that it would not be sensible: *I spend so much money on this car. For two pins I'd sell it.*

have two left 'feet (*informal*)
be very awkward in your movements, especially when you are dancing or playing a sport: *I'm a hopeless dancer. I've got two left feet.*

in two 'shakes ♦ in a couple of 'shakes
(also **in two ,shakes of a 'lamb's tail** *old-fashioned*) (*informal*)
very soon: *I've just got to make a phone call. I'll be with you in two shakes.*

it takes 'two (to do sth) (also **it takes two to 'tango**) (*saying*)
used to say that sth cannot be the fault or responsibility of one person alone: *You've only heard his side of the story. It takes two to have an argument, you know.* ◊ *The company is ready to sign the agreement now, but it takes two to tango and the negotiations may continue for several days yet.*

(there are) no two ways a'bout it (*informal*)
used for saying that there is only one possible way to consider a particular situation or fact: *There are no two ways about it — these sales figures are terrible!*

not have two brain cells, pennies, etc. to rub to'gether (*BrE, informal*)
be very stupid, have no money, etc: *How can they afford a new car? They haven't got two pennies to rub together.*

,one or 'two
a few: *We've had one or two problems — nothing serious, though.*

put in your two 'pennyworth/'penn'orth (*BrE*) (*AmE* **put in your two 'cents' worth**) (*informal*)
give your opinion about sth, even if other people do not want to hear it: *I expect you've already made up your mind, but I'll put in my two pennyworth anyway.* ◊ *The public will get a chance to put in their two cents' worth at a public hearing.*

put ,two and ,two to'gether
guess the truth from what you see, hear, etc: *He's inclined to* **put two and two together and make five** (= make an incorrect guess from what he sees, hears, etc.).

put/stick two 'fingers up at sb (*BrE, informal*)
form the shape of a V with the two fingers nearest your thumb and raise your hand in the air with the back part of it facing sb, done to be rude to them or to show them that you are angry: *He must have been furious — he stuck two fingers up at them and walked out of the room.*

stand on your own two 'feet
not need the help of other people; be independent: *I left home to show my parents that I can stand on my own two feet.* ◊ *Isn't it about time you learned to stand on your own two feet?*

that makes 'two of us (*informal*)
I agree with your opinion; I am in the same situation: *'I think he's behaving very badly.' 'That makes two of us.'* ◊ *'I'm bored with this job.' 'That makes two of us.'*

,two can play at 'that game (*saying*)
used when you threaten to behave as badly, etc. as sb has just behaved towards you: *'He told the boss that you were going home early every day.' 'Oh did he? Well, two can play at that game. I think I'll tell the boss about him coming in late every morning.'*

two heads are better than 'one (*saying*)
two people who are trying to solve a problem together achieve more than one person who works alone

two ,sides of the same 'coin
used to talk about two ways of looking at the same situation: *According to some people, great opportunity and great danger are two sides of the same coin.*

two ,wrongs don't make a 'right (*saying*)
used for saying that it is wrong or useless to harm sb because they have harmed you: *Don't be stupid! You want to hurt him just because he hurt you! Two wrongs don't make a right, you know.* **OPP** an eye for an eye (and a tooth for a tooth)

two's 'company (, three's a 'crowd) (*saying*)
two people, especially two lovers, are happier alone than within a group of three: *'Do you want to come with us?' 'I don't think so. Two's company...'*

- **bird** → a bird in the hand is worth two in the bush
- **dog** → be like a dog with two tails
- **hoot** → not care/give two hoots (about sb/sth) **SEE** not care/give a hoot (about sb/sth)
- **kill** → kill two birds with one stone
- **know** → know a thing or two (about sb/sth)
- **lesser** → the lesser of two evils
- **number** → your/sb's number two
- **penny** → two/ten a penny
- **serve** → serve two masters
- **step** → one step forward, two steps back
- **thick** → (as) thick as two short planks
- **thing** → can/could teach/tell sb a thing or two (about sb/sth)
- **ways** → cut both/two ways

two-shoes /'tuː ʃuːz/

- **goody-goody** → a goody two-shoes **SEE** a goody-goody

type /taɪp/

(not) be sb's 'type (*informal*)
(not) be the kind of person that sb likes: *Mark isn't really her type — she prefers quiet, sensitive men.* ◇ *Gerry is more my type.*

● revert → revert to type

tyre (*BrE*) (*AmE* tire) /'taɪə(r)/

● spare → a spare tyre

tyres /'taɪəz; *AmE* 'taɪərz/

● kick → kick the tyres

U u

ugly /'ʌgli/

an ˌugly 'duckling (*informal*)
a person or thing that at first does not seem attractive or likely to succeed but that later becomes successful or much admired: *He's got the looks of a film star now, but he was a real ugly duckling as a child.*

> **❷ ORIGIN**
> This comes from a children's story by Hans Christian Andersen, in which a young swan is raised with ducklings. They have to stop teasing him about his ugliness when he grows into a beautiful swan.

● sin → (as) miserable/ugly as sin

um /ʌm/

ˌum and 'aah (about sth) (also **ˌhum/ˌhem and 'haw** *less frequent*) (*informal*)
speak but say nothing important because you need more time to think about a problem, matter, etc: *He ummed and aahed for about half an hour and then finally said he would lend me the money.* ◇ *After a lot of **umming and aahing**, he finally said yes to the plan.*

> **NOTE**
> *Um, aah,* etc. are sounds that people make when they hesitate or do not know what to say next.

umbrage /'ʌmbrɪdʒ/

take 'umbrage (at sth) (*formal or humorous*)
be offended or angry because of sth, often without a good reason: *She took umbrage at my remarks about her hair.*

unawares /ˌʌnə'weəz; *AmE* -'werz/

catch/take sb una'wares
surprise sb; do sth when sb does not expect it: *Her sudden refusal took me unawares.* ◇ *You caught us unawares by coming so early.*

uncertain /ʌn'sɜːtn; *AmE* ʌn'sɜːrtn/

in ˌno unˌcertain 'terms
clearly and forcefully: *I told him in no uncertain terms what I thought of his behaviour.*

uncharted /ˌʌn'tʃɑːtɪd; *AmE* -'tʃɑːrt-/

● waters → (be in/get into) murky/uncharted waters

Uncle /'ʌŋkl/

Uncle 'Sam (*informal*)
a way of referring to the United States of America or the US government: *He owed $20 000 in tax to Uncle Sam.*

> **❷ ORIGIN**
> The name probably comes from expanding the initials US.

uncle /'ʌŋkl/

cry/say 'uncle (*AmE*)
admit that you have been beaten or defeated: *They're determined to make the President cry uncle in the budget debate.*

> **❷ ORIGIN**
> Originally, this comes from children's games in which the child has to say the word 'uncle' to admit defeat.

● Bob → (and) Bob's your uncle

uncrowned /ˌʌn'kraʊnd/

(be) the ˌuncrowned 'king/'queen (of sth)
the person considered to be the best, most famous or successful in a particular place or area of activity: *Because of her expertise, she is regarded as the uncrowned queen of music in Pakistan.*

> **NOTE**
> A king or queen who is *uncrowned*, has not yet had a crown placed on their head.

understand /ˌʌndə'stænd; *AmE* -dər's-/

● believe → give sb to believe/understand (that)...

understanding /ˌʌndə'stændɪŋ; *AmE* -dər's-/

on the underˈstanding that... (*formal*)
used to introduce a condition that must be agreed before sth else can happen: *They agreed to the changes on the understanding that they would be introduced gradually.*

understood /ˌʌndə'stʊd/

ˌmake yourself underˈstood
make your meaning clear, especially in another language: *He doesn't speak much Japanese but he can make himself understood.*

undertone /'ʌndətəʊn; *AmE* 'ʌndərtoʊn/

in an 'undertone ✦ in 'undertones
in a quiet voice: *'I must leave now,' he said in an undertone.* **OPP** at the top of your voice

undivided /ˌʌndɪˈvaɪdɪd/

get/have sb's undivided at'tention (*often humorous*)
receive sb's full attention: *I'll just finish writing this sentence, and then you can have my undivided attention.*

unearthly /ʌnˈɜːθli; AmE -ˈɜːrθ-/

● hour → at an unearthly/ungodly hour

unglued /ʌnˈɡluːd/

come un'glued (*AmE, informal*)
1 become very upset: *I don't know why, but whenever I take my child to the doctor's she comes unglued.*
2 if a plan, etc. **comes unglued**, it does not work successfully: *Personally, I'm not sorry the building plans have come unglued. It means they'll leave the public park alone.*

Sally started to think that her plans to fly across the Atlantic were coming unglued.

ungodly /ʌnˈɡɒdli; AmE -ˈɡɑːd-/

● hour → at an unearthly/ungodly hour

unison /ˈjuːnɪsn/

in unison (with sb/sth)
1 if people do or say sth **in unison**, they all do it at the same time: *'Good morning, Mrs Crawford' the children shouted in unison.*
2 if people or organizations are working **in unison**, they are working together, because they agree with each other: *I am pleased to report that the various committees are now working in unison to thoroughly investigate this matter.*

unknown /ʌnˈnəʊn; AmE -ˈnoʊn/

an ,unknown 'quantity
a person or thing that you do not know anything or enough about: *His ability to make decisions in a crisis is an unknown quantity. ◇ Our new director is still an unknown quantity.*

unknown to sb
without the person mentioned being aware of it: *Unknown to me, he had already signed the agreement.*

unseen /ʌnˈsiːn/

● sight → sight unseen

unsound /ʌnˈsaʊnd/

of ,unsound 'mind (*law*)
not responsible for your actions because of a mental illness or condition: *He escaped a prison sentence by reason of unsound mind at the time the crime was committed.*

unstuck /ʌnˈstʌk/

come un'stuck (*BrE, informal*)
be unsuccessful; fail: *His plan to escape came badly unstuck. ◇ She came unstuck in the last part of the exam.*

untie /ʌnˈtaɪ/

● Gordian → cut/untie the Gordian knot

unturned /ʌnˈtɜːnd; AmE ʌnˈtɜːrnd/

● stone → leave no stone unturned

up /ʌp/

be up to sb
1 be sb's right to decide: *Shall we have an Indian or a Chinese meal? It's up to you. ◇ The decision's not up to me.*
2 be sb's responsibility or duty: *It's up to us to help people in need.*

be 'up (with sb/sth) (*spoken*)
be wrong with sb/sth: *I could tell something was up from the looks on their faces. ◇ What's up with the car? It won't start.*

on the ,up and 'up (*informal*)
1 (*BrE*) getting better, becoming more successful, etc: *Her health is on the up and up. Soon she'll be out of hospital. ◇ Business is on the up and up.*
2 (*AmE*) honest: *Before we give him the job, are you sure he's on the up and up?*

up a'gainst it (*informal*)
in a difficult situation: *Two of the staff are sick and the order has to be ready for delivery by this evening, so we're really up against it.*

up and a'bout (*BrE*)
out of bed after being ill/sick or sleeping: *She was off work for a week, but she's up and about again now. ◇ On a Saturday he's not up and about till about eleven o'clock.*

up and 'down
sometimes good and sometimes bad: *One moment he seems well, the next he's sick again — he's up and down all the time. ◇ My relationship with him was very up and down.*

up and down sth
all over sth; everywhere in a place: *People up and down the country are giving money to the earthquake appeal.*

,up and 'leave, 'go, etc. (*informal*)
leave, go, etc. quickly and unexpectedly: *Without saying anything, she just upped and went.*

up before sb/sth
appearing in front of sb in authority for a judgement to be made about sth that you have done: *He came up before the local magistrate for speeding.*

up for sth
1 on offer for sth: *The house is up for sale.*
2 being considered for sth, especially as a candidate: *Two candidates are up for election.*
3 willing to take part in a particular activity: *We're going clubbing tonight. Are you **up for it**?*

up to sth
1 (also **up to doing sth**) physically or mentally capable of sth: *She didn't feel up to going to work today.* ◇ *At my age, I just don't think I'm up to climbing 200 steps.* ◇ *He's just not up to the job, I'm afraid.*
2 (*spoken*) doing sth, especially sth bad: *What's she up to?* ◇ *We used to get up to all sorts of things when we were that age.*

,up 'yours! (△, *slang*)
an offensive way of being rude to sb, for example because they have said sth that makes you angry: *'Go and cook me my dinner.' 'Oh, up yours! Do it yourself!'*

uphill /ˌʌpˈhɪl/

an uphill 'struggle/'battle/'task
something that is difficult and takes a lot of effort over a long period of time: *After the recent scandal, he faces an uphill struggle to win back public support before the next election.*

upon /əˈpɒn; *AmE* əˈpɑːn/

(almost) u'pon you (*formal*)
if sth in the future is **almost upon you**, it is going to arrive or happen very soon: *The busy summer season was almost upon us again.*

upper /ˈʌpə(r)/

get, have, gain, etc. the ,upper 'hand (over sb)
get, etc. power or control over sb, especially in a fight, competition, etc: *Our team gained the upper hand in the second half of the match.* ◇ *The police claim they have the upper hand in their fight against the drug dealers.*

the ,upper 'crust (*informal*)
people who are in the highest social class

> ❷ ORIGIN
> In the past, the top or *upper crust* of a loaf of bread was the best part, which the more important members of the household ate.

● stiff → (keep) a stiff upper lip

uppers /ˈʌpəz; *AmE* ˈʌpərz/

on your 'uppers (*BrE, informal*)
having very little money: *Joe paid for lunch, which was great because we were both on our uppers, as usual.* **OPP** (be) rolling in it/money

> ❷ ORIGIN
> *Uppers* refers to the top part of a boot or shoe. If you are walking *on your uppers*, your shoes are old and worn down.

upright /ˈʌpraɪt/

● bolt → bolt upright

ups /ʌps/

,ups and 'downs
times of success, happiness, etc. and times of failure, unhappiness, etc: *I suppose every marriage has its ups and downs.* ◇ *I've watched the ups and downs of his business with great interest.*

upset /ʌpˈset/

upset the/sb's 'apple cart (*informal*)
do sth that spoils a plan or stops the progress of sth: *Another, much cheaper hairdresser has opened next door, which has upset the apple cart.*

upside /ˈʌpsaɪd/

● turn → turn sth inside out/upside down

upstairs /ˌʌpˈsteəz; *AmE* -ˈsterz/

● kick → kick sb upstairs

uptake /ˈʌpteɪk/

be ,quick/,slow on the 'uptake (*informal*)
understand things quickly/understand even simple things with difficulty: *He's a very good worker but he's a bit slow on the uptake sometimes. You have to explain everything twice.*

use /juːz/

be in/out of 'use
be/not be being used: *We'll have to find a classroom that's not in use.* ◇ *The road's out of use while it's being repaired.*

be no 'use (to sb) (also **be of no 'use** *formal*)
be useless: *You can throw those away — they're no use to anyone.*

be of 'use (to sb) (*formal*)
be useful: *These maps might be of use to you on your trip.* ◇ *Can I be of any use* (= can I help)?

,come into/,go out of 'use
start/stop being used: *When did this word come into common use?* ◇ *The present system will go out of use next year.*

I, you, etc. could use a 'drink, etc. (*spoken*)
I, you, etc. need a drink, etc: *We could use some extra help just at the moment.*

have no 'use for sb/sth
strongly dislike sb/sth: *I have no use for people like John. You can never trust them.*

it's no 'use (doing sth)
used to say that there is no point in doing sth because it will not be successful or have a good result: *The bus has already gone, so it's no use running.* ◇ *It's no use. I just can't remember the word.*

make 'use of sb/sth
use sb/sth for your own advantage: *Make full use of every chance you get to speak English.*

put sth to good 'use
benefit from using sth: *She'll be able to put her experience to good use in the new job.*

use your 'head (*BrE* also **use your 'loaf**)
(*informal*)
think carefully; use your intelligence: *Use your loaf! Meena can't read English, so there's no point in writing her a letter!*

> ❷ **ORIGIN**
> In rhyming slang, *loaf of bread* stands for 'head'.

use a ˌsledgehammer to crack a 'nut
use more force than is necessary: *It was a small and peaceful demonstration so I don't know why there was such a big police presence. It was like using a sledgehammer to crack a nut.*

what's the 'use (of doing sth)? (also **what 'use is there (in doing sth)?**)
used for emphasizing that you think an action, etc. will not achieve anything: *What's the use of worrying about the weather? You can't do anything about it.* ◇ *'Why don't you try talking to her?' 'What's the use? She's already made up her mind.'*

● fat → a fat lot of good/help/use
● man → be no good/use to man or beast

useful /ˈjuːzfl/

make yourself 'useful
help other people: *Come on, Hannah. Make yourself useful and peel those potatoes for me.*

● handy → come in handy/useful

uses /ˈjuːsɪz/

have your, his, its, etc. 'uses (*informal, often humorous*)
be useful sometimes: *I know you don't like him, but he has his uses — he's a great cook!*

usual /ˈjuːʒuəl; -ʒəl/

as 'usual
in the same way as what happens most of the time or in most cases: *Steve, as usual, was the last to arrive.* ◇ *As usual at that hour, the place was deserted.* ◇ *Despite her problems, she carried on working as usual.*

● business → it's business as usual
● per → as per usual/normal

utmost /ˈʌtməʊst; *AmE* -moʊst/

do/try your 'utmost (to do sth)
try as hard as you can (to do sth): *I tried my utmost to stop them.* ◇ *Don't blame her — she did her utmost to finish it on time.*

vacuum /ˈvækjuəm/

do sth in a 'vacuum
do sth alone or separately from other people, events, etc., especially when there should be a connection: *No novel is written in a vacuum. There are always influences from past writers.*

vain /veɪn/

in 'vain
without success: *They tried in vain to persuade her to go.* ◇ *All our efforts were in vain.*

● name → take sb's name in vain

valour (*BrE*) (*AmE* **valor**) /ˈvælə(r)/

● discretion → discretion is the better part of valour

value /ˈvæljuː/

a 'value judgement (*especially BrE*) (*AmE* usually **a 'value judgment**) (*disapproving*)
a judgement about sth that is based on sb's personal opinion and not on facts: *'She's quite a good driver for a woman.' 'That's a real value judgement. Women drive just as well as men.'* ◇ *He's always making value judgements.*

● face → take sb/sth at face value

van /væn/

in the 'van (*BrE, formal*)
at the front or in the leading position: *The eight warships in the van opened fire on the advancing fleet.*

● white-van → white-van man

vanish /ˈvænɪʃ/

● face → disappear/vanish off the face of the earth

vanishing /ˈvænɪʃɪŋ/

● act → do/perform/stage a disappearing/vanishing act

variance /ˈveəriəns; *AmE* ˈver-; ˈvær-/

at 'variance (with sb/sth) (*formal*)
disagreeing with or opposing sb/sth: *These conclusions are totally at variance with the evidence.*

variations /ˌveəriˈeɪʃnz; AmE ˌver-/

variations on the theme of sth
different ways of doing or saying the same thing:
*Her new book of short stories offers variations on
the theme of man's desire to succeed.*

variety /vəˈraɪəti/

variety is the spice of 'life (*saying*)
a variety of different activities, interests, places or
people in your life makes it more enjoyable: *We
never go on holiday to the same place twice. It's
good to see different things, and you know what
they say — variety is the spice of life.*

veil /veɪl/

cast/draw/throw a 'veil over sth (*written*)
say nothing or no more about something unpleasant: *It is kinder to draw a veil over some of his later
movies.*

velvet /ˈvelvɪt/

● iron → an iron fist/hand (in a velvet glove)

vengeance /ˈvendʒəns/

do sth with a 'vengeance (*informal*)
do sth with great energy or force: *After the holidays I need to start working with a vengeance.*
◇ *The rain came down with a vengeance.*

venom /ˈvenəm/

● spit → spit blood/venom/feathers

vent /vent/

give (full) 'vent to sth (*informal*)
express a strong negative feeling freely and forcefully: *I tried to stop myself giving full vent to my
anger.*

vent your 'spleen (*literary*)
express your anger in speech or writing: *He vented
his spleen on the assembled crowd.*

> **❷ ORIGIN**
> In the past, people believed that the *spleen*
> (= a small organ near the stomach that con-
> trols the quality of the blood cells) was
> responsible for making someone feel sad or
> bad-tempered. From this, it came to mean a
> person's *anger*.

ventured /ˈventʃəd; AmE ˈventʃərd/

nothing ˌventured, nothing 'gained (*saying*)
used to say that you have to take risks if you want
to achieve things and be successful: *Go on, apply
for the job. You know what they say — nothing ventured, nothing gained.*

verge /vɜːdʒ; AmE vɜːrdʒ/

on/to the verge of sth/of doing sth
at or close to the point or time when sb does sth or
sth happens: *She was on the verge of tears.* ◇ *We're
on the verge of signing a new contract.*

verse /vɜːs; AmE vɜːrs/

● chapter → chapter and verse

vessel /ˈvesl/

● burst → burst a blood vessel

vested /ˈvestɪd/

have a vested 'interest (in sth)
have a personal reason for wanting sth to happen,
especially because you get some advantage from
it: *He has a vested interest in Mona leaving the firm*
(= perhaps because he may get her job).

vexed /vekst/

a vexed 'question
a difficult problem that people often talk and
argue about: *They're discussing the vexed question
of private health insurance.*

vice /vaɪs/

● den → a den of iniquity/vice

vicious /ˈvɪʃəs/

a vicious 'circle
a difficult situation or problem where one thing
makes another thing happen, which then makes
the first thing happen again: *He spends too much
on drink because he's worried about his financial
problems, and so the situation gets worse and
worse. It's a vicious circle.*

victim /ˈvɪktɪm/

fall 'victim (to sth) (*written*)
be injured, damaged or killed by sth: *Many plants
have fallen victim to the sudden frost.*

victory /ˈvɪktəri/

● Pyrrhic → a Pyrrhic victory
● romp → romp home/to victory

vie /viː/

● life → c'est la vie SEE that's life

view /vjuː/

(have, etc. sth) in 'view (*formal*)
(have, etc.) sth as an idea, plan, etc. in your mind:
*What the protesters have in view is a world without
nuclear weapons.* ◇ *He wanted to get rich, and he
went abroad with this end in view.*

in view of sth
because of sth; considering sth: *In view of all this
rain, the game may have to be cancelled.*

on 'view
shown or displayed to the public: *A lot of exciting
new designs are on view at the Boat Show this year.*

take a dim/poor 'view of sb/sth
disagree with or dislike sb/sth: *Farmers tend to
take a dim view of the public walking over their
land.* ◇ *The judge said he took a very poor view of
their behaviour.*

villain

take the view (that) (*formal*)
be sb's opinion that…: *I take the view that medical care should be provided by the State.*

with a view to sth/to doing sth (*formal*)
with the plan or hope of doing sth: *He's painting and decorating the house with a view to selling it for a good price.*

- bird's-eye → a bird's-eye view (of sth)
- full → in full view (of sb/sth)
- long → take the long view (of sth)
- point → a point of view
- ringside → have a ringside seat/view
- worm's-eye → a worm's-eye view

villain /ˈvɪlən/

the 'villain of the piece (*especially humorous*)
a person or thing that is responsible for a particular problem, difficulty, etc: *Nicolette's the villain of the piece, since she's the person who started all this trouble.*

> NOTE
> The *villain* is the principal evil character in a book, a play, etc.

vine /vaɪn/

- wither → wither on the vine

violet /ˈvaɪələt/

- shrinking → a shrinking violet

virtue /ˈvɜːtʃuː; AmE ˈvɜːrtʃuː/

by/in 'virtue of sth (*formal*)
because of sth: *I was invited to a party at the embassy simply by virtue of being British.*

make a ˌvirtue of neˈcessity
act in a good or moral way, and perhaps expect praise for this, not because you chose to but because in that particular situation you had no choice

ˌvirtue is its own reˈward (*saying*)
the reward for acting in a moral or correct way is the knowledge that you have done so, and you should not expect more than this, for example praise from other people or payment

- paragon → a paragon of virtue

vis-à-vis /ˌviːz ɑ: ˈviː/

vis-à-'vis (*from French, written*)
1 in relation to: *Britain's role vis-à-vis the United States*
2 in comparison with: *It was felt that the company had an unfair advantage vis-à-vis smaller companies elsewhere.*

> ❷ ORIGIN
> This phrase originally meant *face-to-face* in French.

vision /ˈvɪʒn/

- tunnel → (have) tunnel vision

visit /ˈvɪzɪt/

- flying → a flying visit
- pay → pay a visit to sb/sth
- pay → pay sb/sth a visit

vivre /viːvrə/

- joie → joie de vivre

voice /vɔɪs/

be in good, poor, etc. 'voice
be singing well, badly, etc: *The soprano was in excellent voice.*

give 'voice to sth
express your feelings, worries, etc: *The speaker stopped, allowing the crowd time to give voice to their frustration and feelings.*

keep your 'voice down
used to tell sb to speak more quietly: *Keep your voices down, won't you? The children are asleep.*

make your 'voice heard
express your opinions, feelings, etc. so that other people hear or notice: *This programme gives ordinary people a rare chance to make their voices heard.*

a voice (crying) in the 'wilderness
a warning of a danger given by a person or small group which most people do not pay any attention to: *A few scientists in the early 1980s were warning of the dangers of AIDS but nobody took them seriously. They were just a voice in the wilderness.*

> ❷ ORIGIN
> This comes from a description of John the Baptist in the Bible.

with ˌone 'voice
(of a group of people) in complete agreement: *It's very rare to find the unions and management speaking with one voice, but on the question of safety at work there is total agreement.*

- find → find your voice/tongue
- raise → raise a/your voice against sb/sth
- raise → raise your voice
- sound → like, love, etc. the sound of your own voice
- still → the still small voice
- top → at the top of your voice

void /vɔɪd/

- null → null and void

volte-face /ˌvɒlt ˈfɑːs; AmE ˌvɔːlt-/

a volte-'face (*from French, formal*)
a complete change of opinion or plan: *This represents a volte-face in government policy.*

> ❷ ORIGIN
> This is a French adaptation of an Italian phrase and refers to turning to face the opposite direction.

volumes /ˈvɒljuːmz; AmE ˈvɑːl-; -jəmz/

- speak → speak volumes (about/for sb/sth)

vote /vəʊt; *AmE* voʊt/

put sth to the 'vote
decide sth by asking people for their votes: *The issue was put to the vote.*

a ,vote of 'thanks
a short formal speech in which you thank sb for sth and ask other people to join you in thanking them: *I'd like to propose a vote of thanks to Ms Waters for her interesting talk.*

,vote with your 'feet
show that you dislike or disagree with sth by leaving a place or an organization: *If shoppers don't like the new market, they'll vote with their feet and go elsewhere.*

vu /vuː/
● déjà → déjà vu

W w

wag /wæg/
● tail → let the tail wag the dog SEE the tail (is) wagging the dog
● tongues → tongues wag

wagging /'wægɪŋ/
● tail → the tail (is) wagging the dog
● tongues → set tongues wagging

wagon /'wægən/

be/go on the 'wagon (*informal*)
no longer drink/decide to stop drinking alcohol, either for a short period of time or permanently, especially if you drink a lot: *'Would you like a gin and tonic?' 'No thanks. I'm on the wagon.'*

> **❷ ORIGIN**
> This idiom refers to the *water wagon*, which in America sprayed roads with water to prevent clouds of dust. If somebody starts drinking alcohol again, they are said to *fall off the wagon*.

● hitch → hitch your wagon to sb/sth/a star

waifs /weɪfs/

,waifs and 'strays
1 people with no home, especially children in a big city: *There are lots of waifs and strays living on the streets here.*
2 (*humorous*) lonely people with nowhere else to go: *My wife is always inviting various waifs and strays from work to our house. She seems to attract them.*

wait /weɪt/

I, he, etc. can't 'wait ◆ I, he, etc. can hardly 'wait
used when you are emphasizing that sb is very excited about sth or keen to do it: *The children **can't wait for** Christmas to come.* ◇ *I can hardly wait to see him again.*

,wait and 'see
be patient and wait to find out about sth later: *'Where are you taking me?' 'Wait and see.'* ◇ *There's nothing we can do at the moment. We'll just have to wait and see.*

'wait for it (*spoken, especially BrE*)
1 wait until you receive the order or signal to do sth: *Are you all ready? Wait for it! Now!*
2 used for telling sb that you are about to say sth amusing or surprising: *'What did you have?' 'We had roast duck and — wait for it — caviar!'*

wait a 'minute/'moment/'second
1 wait for a short time: *Can you wait a second while I make a call?*
2 used when you have just noticed or remembered sth, or had a sudden idea: *Wait a minute — this isn't the right key.*

wait on sb ,hand and 'foot (*disapproving*)
do almost everything for sb, for example cook meals, bring everything they ask for, etc: *My father expects my mother to wait on him hand and foot.*

wait (on) 'tables (*AmE*)
work serving food to people in a restaurant: *I wait on tables at a restaurant near my apartment.* ◇ *She worked her way through college waiting tables.*

'wait till/until... (*spoken*)
used to show that you are very excited about telling or showing sth to sb: *Wait till you see what I've found!*

(just) you 'wait
used to emphasize a threat, warning or promise: *Just you wait till your father gets home!* ◇ *I'll be famous one day, just you wait!*

● dust → wait for the dust to settle SEE let the dust settle
● lie → lie in wait

waiting /'weɪtɪŋ/

an ,accident/a di,saster waiting to 'happen
a thing or person that is very likely to cause danger or a problem in the future because of the condition it is in or the way they behave: *For many months local residents had been complaining that the building was unsafe, and that it was an accident waiting to happen.*

keep sb 'waiting
make sb wait or be delayed, especially because you arrive late: *I'm sorry to have kept you waiting.*

a 'waiting game
a policy of delaying making a decision or doing sth because this puts you in a stronger position: *They're **playing** a waiting game, delaying their offer until they know what the others are offering.*

what are we 'waiting for? (*spoken*)
used to suggest that you should all start doing what you have been discussing: *Well, what are we waiting for? Let's get started!*

what are you 'waiting for? (*spoken*)
used to tell sb to do sth now rather than later: *If the car needs cleaning, what are you waiting for?*

wake /weɪk/

in the wake of sb/sth
coming after and resulting from sb/sth; behind sb/sth: *Disease began spreading in the wake of the floods.* ◇ *The tourists left all sorts of rubbish in their wake.* **OPP** in advance (of sth)

> **NOTE**
> As a ship moves through the water, it leaves a *wake* (= disturbed water) behind it.

wake the 'dead
(of a noise) be very loud: *He must have heard it — that doorbell's loud enough to wake the dead.*

wake up and smell the 'coffee (*AmE, informal*)
used to tell sb that they are wrong about a particular situation or have not been aware of sth and it is time that they realized and accepted the truth: *It's time to wake up and smell the coffee: you're not going to pass this course unless you start working harder.*

wake-up /'weɪk ʌp/

a 'wake-up call
an event that makes people realize that they must take action in a dangerous situation: *The recent storms and floods have been a wake-up call for many people about the reality of climate change.*

walk /wɔːk/

(try to) run before you can 'walk (*informal*)
try to do sth that is difficult before you have succeeded in doing sth easy: *The important thing about cooking is not to try and run before you can walk. Get the basics right and the rest will follow.*

take a 'walk (*informal, especially AmE*)
used to tell sb to go away when you are angry with them: *She told him to take a walk.*

walk all 'over sb (*informal*)
1 treat sb badly, without considering them or their needs: *Tell him what you think of him — don't let him walk all over you like that.*
2 defeat sb easily: *The only time I played chess with my wife, she walked all over me.* ▶ **'walkover** *noun* an easy victory: *We beat them 12-0: it was a walkover.*

walk 'free
be allowed to leave a court of law, etc., without receiving any punishment: *Family and friends of the victim were stunned as the man who they believed was guilty walked free.*

a walk in the 'park (*especially AmE*)
used to say that sth is easy to do: *We succeeded, but it was not a walk in the park for any of us.*

'walk it (*spoken*)
win easily in a competition: *If you play like that on the day of the match, you'll walk it.*

a walk of 'life
a person's job or position in society: *The people at the meeting came from all walks of life — students, writers, business people, and so on.*

walk off the 'job (*AmE*)
stop working in order to go on strike: *Engineers and other employees walked off the job Tuesday to demand higher pay and shorter hours.*

walk sb off their 'feet (*informal*)
make sb walk so far or so fast that they are very tired: *She may be over seventy, but I'm sure she could walk some of you younger ones off your feet.*

walk on 'eggshells
be very careful not to upset sb: *I always felt as if I had to walk on eggshells around him so that I wouldn't hurt his feelings.*

walk the 'plank
1 (in the past) walk along a board placed over the side of a ship and fall into the sea, as a punishment
2 (*informal*) be forced to leave your job or position: *The food and the service is terrible in this restaurant. If you ask me, whoever is in charge should be made to walk the plank!*

walk the 'streets
walk around the streets of a town or city: *Is it safe to walk the streets alone at night?*

walk 'tall
feel proud and confident: *When I finally got a job after years of unemployment, I felt I could walk tall again.*

- **air** → float/walk on air
- **aisle** → go/walk down the aisle
- **line** → tread/walk a fine/thin line
- **tightrope** → tread/walk a tightrope

walking /'wɔːkɪŋ/

give sb their 'walking papers ◆ get your 'walking papers (*AmE, informal*)
dismiss sb from their job; be dismissed: *The coach has been given his walking papers after the team lost again on Saturday.*

a walking 'dictionary, encyclo'pedia, etc. (*informal*)
used to describe a human or living example of the thing mentioned: *Geoff is a walking encyclopedia. He knows about everything.* ◇ *She's a walking dictionary* (= she knows a lot of words).

- **thin** → be skating/walking on thin ice

wall /wɔːl/

drive/send sb up the 'wall (*informal*)
make sb very annoyed; drive sb crazy: *That noise is driving me up the wall.*

go to the 'wall (*informal*)
fail because of lack of money: *Smaller companies are always the first to go to the wall in an economic recession.*

have your 'back to the wall
be in a difficult situation with no easy solution: *Inflation and unemployment have risen this year and the Government has lost a lot of support. The Prime Minister really has his back to the wall now.*

off the 'wall (*informal*)
unusual and amusing; slightly crazy: *Some of his ideas are really off the wall.* ◇ *They've both got a rather off-the-wall sense of humour.*

- **brick** → be/come up against a brick wall
- **brick** → hit a brick wall **SEE** be/come up against a brick wall
- **fly** → a fly on the wall
- **head** → be banging, etc. your head against a brick wall
- **nail** → nail sb to the wall
- **talk** → talk to a brick wall
- **writing** → the handwriting (is) on the wall **SEE** the writing (is) on the wall
- **writing** → the writing (is) on the wall

walls /wɔːlz/

,**walls have 'ears** (*saying*)
somebody may be listening, so be careful what you say: *You'd better keep your voice down. Walls have ears, you know.*

- **bouncing** → be bouncing off the walls
- **climbing** → be climbing the walls
- **four** → these four walls

wand /wɒnd; *AmE* wɑːnd/

- **wave** → wave a (magic) wand (and do sth)

wane /weɪn/

be on the 'wane (*written*)
be becoming smaller or less strong: *Their political power is on the wane.*

> **NOTE**
> When the moon is *on the wane* it appears smaller in the sky.

- **wax** → wax and wane

want /wɒnt; *AmE* wɑːnt; wɔːnt/

for (the) want of sth
because of a lack of sth; because sth is not available: *For the want of a better name, I'm calling this book 'My Early Years'.* ◇ *We went for a walk for want of anything better to do.*

in want of sth (*formal*)
needing sth: *The present system is in want of a total review.*

not want to 'know (about sth) (*informal*)
not care about sth; not want to become involved with sth: *She was in desperate need of help but nobody seemed to want to know.* ◇ *If she wants money, I don't want to know about it.*

want for 'nothing
have everything you need or want: *They both earn good salaries so their children want for nothing.*

want 'rid of sb/sth (*BrE, spoken, informal*)
want to be free of sb/sth that has been annoying you or that you do not want: *Are you trying to say you want rid of me?*

- **hole** → need/want sb/sth like (you need/want) a hole in the head
- **moon** → want the moon **SEE** cry/ask for the moon
- **none** → have/want none of it/that
- **part** → have/play/take/want no part in/of sth
- **truck** → have/want no truck with sb/sth
- **trying** → not for lack/want of trying
- **waste** → waste not, want not

war /wɔː(r)/

a ,war of 'nerves
an attempt to defeat your opponents by putting pressure on them so that they lose courage or confidence: *A big American company is trying to take over our company; it's a real war of nerves.*

a ,war of 'words
a fierce argument or disagreement over a period of time between two or more people or groups: *the political war of words over tax*

- **fair** → all's fair in love and war
- **turf** → a turf war

warm /wɔːm; *AmE* wɔːrm/

keep sb's 'seat, etc. warm (for them)
(*informal*)
remain in a job, an official position, etc. until sb is ready to take it, especially so that a third person cannot do so: *She's not the regular driver — she's just keeping his place warm for him until he gets back.*

(as) warm as 'toast
pleasantly warm compared to the cold air outside etc: *I'll light the fire and we'll soon be as warm as toast in here.*

warm the 'cockles (of sb's 'heart) (*BrE*)
make sb feel happy or sympathetic: *Ah! It warms the cockles of my heart to see the children so happy.*

warmed /wɔːmd; *AmE* wɔːrmd/

- **death** → like death warmed over/up

warp /wɔːp; *AmE* wɔːrp/

- **time** → be (stuck) in a time warp

warpath /'wɔːpɑːθ; *AmE* 'wɔːrpæθ/

be/go on the 'warpath (*informal*)
be angry and ready for an argument or a fight about sth: *Look out — the boss is on the warpath again!*

> **?** ORIGIN
> In the past, if Native Americans were *on the warpath*, they were going to war or preparing to attack somebody.

warrant /'wɒrənt; *AmE* 'wɔːr-; 'wɑːr-/

- **sign** → sign your own death warrant

wars /wɔːz; AmE wɔːrz/

in the 'wars (*spoken*)
slightly injured because you have been in a fight
or have hurt yourself in an accident: *My nephew is
always in the wars. Whenever I see him, he's covered
in plasters.*

warts /wɔːts; AmE wɔːrts/

,warts and 'all (*informal*)
including all the faults as well as the good points:
She still loves him, warts and all.

> ❷ ORIGIN
> The story is that Oliver Cromwell asked the
> painter Sir Peter Lely to paint him exactly as he
> appeared, including all his bad features such
> as his *warts* (= a small hard lump that grows
> on the skin).

wash /wɒʃ; AmE wɑːʃ; wɔːʃ/

it will (all) come out in the 'wash (*spoken*)
1 used to say that the truth about a situation will
be made known at some time in the future: *You
can't hide what you've done for ever. It'll come out
in the wash, you know.*
2 used to make sb less anxious by telling them
that any problems or difficulties will be solved in
the future: *'Some of the documents still haven't
arrived!' 'Don't worry, there's probably been a slight
mix-up — it'll all come out in the wash.'*

wash your dirty linen in 'public (*BrE,
disapproving*)
talk or write about unpleasant or embarrassing
private difficulties in public: *Nobody must mention
these problems at the meeting. I don't want our dirty
linen washed in public.*

> NOTE
> In this idiom, *linen* refers to clothes, especially
> underwear.

wash your 'hands of sb/sth
refuse to deal with or be responsible for sb/sth
any longer: *After the way she's behaved, I'm never
going to help her again! I wash my hands of her!*
◇ *I can't just wash my hands of the whole business.
I've got responsibilities.*

> ❷ ORIGIN
> This idiom refers to Pontius Pilate in the Bible,
> who refused to take a decision about what
> should happen to Jesus.

sth won't/doesn't 'wash (with sb)
used to say that sb's explanation, excuse, etc. is
not valid or that you/sb else will not accept it:
That excuse simply won't wash with me.

waste /weɪst/

go/run to 'waste
not be used and therefore wasted: *What a pity to
see all that food go to waste!*

waste your 'breath (on sb/sth)
speak to sb or about sb/sth but not have any
effect: *Don't waste your breath on her. She doesn't
take advice from anybody.* ◇ *I feel like I'm just wasting my breath trying to explain things to him.*

,waste not, 'want not (*saying*)
if you never waste anything, for example food or
money, you will have it when you need it: *Come
on, finish your food, children. Waste not, want not!*

a waste of 'space (*spoken*)
a person who is useless or no good at anything:
*What did you have to ask him along for? He's a com-
plete waste of space!*

● lay → lay sth waste
● lay → lay waste to sth
● time → lose/waste no time (in doing sth)

watch /wɒtʃ; AmE wɑːtʃ; wɔːtʃ/

be on the 'watch (for sb/sth)
being looking carefully for sb/sth that you expect to
see, especially in order to avoid possible danger:
*The police warned tourists to be on the watch for car
thieves.*

keep 'watch (for sb/sth)
stay awake or watch sb/sth carefully in case of
possible danger or problems: *I'll keep watch while
you sleep.* ◇ *The doctors are keeping watch for any
change in her condition.*

watch the 'clock (*disapproving*)
often check what time it is, because you are impatient for sth to finish or to happen: *Someone who
spends all their time watching the clock is usually
not a good worker.* ▶ **'clock-watching** *noun*: *Don't
spend the afternoon clock-watching.* **'clock-
watcher** *noun*

'watch it (*informal*)
1 used to warn sb to be careful: *Watch it! There's a
car coming.*
2 used to tell sb that they are behaving badly and
will be punished if they continue: *If you do that
again, there'll be trouble, so watch it.*

watch sb/sth like a 'hawk
watch sb/sth very carefully: *Unless you watch him
like a hawk, he'll go off without finishing the work.*
OPP turn a blind eye (to sth)

> NOTE
> A *hawk* is a bird that kills other creatures for
> food, and can see small things from very far
> away.

watch your 'mouth/'tongue
be careful what you say in order not to offend sb
or make them angry: *Now, you just watch your
mouth around your grandparents, Billy!* **OPP** shoot
your mouth off (about sth)

watch this 'space (*informal*)
used in orders, to tell sb to wait for more news
about sth to be announced: *I can't tell you any
more right now, but watch this space.*

watch the 'world go by
watch what is happening around you, but do little
yourself: *It was one of those cafes with a terrace
where you can sit and watch the world go by.*

● close² → keep a close eye/watch on sb/sth
● language → mind/watch your language
● step → mind/watch your step

watched /wɒtʃt; AmE wɑːtʃt; wɔːtʃt/

a watched pot never 'boils (*saying*)
used to say that when you are impatient for sth to happen, it seems to take longer: *Looking out of the window won't make him arrive any quicker! Don't you know that a watched pot never boils?*

water /'wɔːtə(r); AmE also 'wɑːt-/

be (like) water off a ,duck's 'back (*informal*)
used to say that sth, especially criticism, has no effect on sb: *His book got bad reviews, but it was all water off a duck's back — he doesn't care at all what they say.*

be (all) water under the 'bridge (*spoken*)
be an event, a mistake, etc. that has already happened and is now forgotten or no longer important: *We had a terrible quarrel five years ago but that's all water under the bridge.*

hold 'water (*informal*)
(of a theory, etc.) remain true even when examined closely: *Your argument just doesn't hold water.*

> **NOTE**
> If a container *holds water*, no water escapes.

like 'water (*informal*)
in large amounts; in great quantity: *They're still spending money like water.*

- **blood** → blood is thicker than water
- **blow** → blow sb/sth out of the water
- **cold** → pour/throw cold water on sth
- **dead** → dead in the water
- **deep** → in deep water(s)
- **duck** → (take to sth) like a duck to water
- **fish** → a fish out of water
- **head** → keep your head above water
- **hell** → (come) hell or high water
- **horse** → you can take/lead a horse to water, but you can't make it drink
- **hot** → in hot water
- **mouth** → make sb's mouth water
- **pass** → pass water
- **pour** → pour oil on troubled water(s)
- **test** → test the water/waters
- **tread** → tread water

Waterloo /ˌwɔːtə'luː; AmE ˌwɔːtər'luː; 'wɑːt-/

- **meet** → meet your Waterloo

waters /'wɔːtəz; AmE 'wɔːtərz; AmE also 'wɑːt-/

(be in/get into) murky/uncharted 'waters
(be in/get into) a difficult or dangerous situation that you do not know anything about: *As I opened up the computer to try and fix the problem, I realized that I was getting into completely uncharted waters and decided to leave it to the experts.*

> **NOTE**
> *Murky* water is dark or dirty. If somebody is in *uncharted waters*, they are in an area of sea or ocean that is not known or recorded on a map.

- **muddy** → muddy the waters
- **still** → still waters run deep
- **test** → test the water/waters

waterworks /'wɔːtəwɜːks; AmE 'wɔːtərwɜːrks; 'wɑːt-/

turn on the 'waterworks (*informal, disapproving*)
start crying, especially in order to get sympathy or attention: *You can turn off the waterworks for a start, as that won't make me change my mind.*

wave /weɪv/

wave a (magic) 'wand (and do sth)
find a quick and easy way of doing sth that is very difficult or impossible; do sth as if by magic: *I'm sorry, but I can't just wave a magic wand and solve your problems.* ◇ *If you could wave a wand, what sort of apartment would you really like?*

> **NOTE**
> A *wand* is a straight thin stick that is held by a person who is performing magic.

- **crest** → (on) the crest of a wave
- **flag** → fly/show/wave the flag
- **ride** → ride a/the wave of sth

wavelength /'weɪvleŋθ/

be on the same 'wavelength/on different 'wavelengths (*informal*)
have the same/different opinion or feelings about sth: *I find him difficult to talk to — we're on completely different wavelengths.* ◇ *On the subject of marriage, Judith and I are on the same wavelength.*

waves /weɪvz/

make 'waves (*informal*)
be active in a way that makes people notice you, and that may sometimes cause problems: *It's taken us a long time to find an answer to this problem, so please don't make waves now.*

waving /'weɪvɪŋ/

- **red** → like waving a red flag in front of/at a bull **SEE** (like) a red rag to a bull

wax /wæks/

,wax and 'wane (*literary*)
increase then decrease in strength, importance, etc. over a period of time: *The government's popularity has waxed and waned over the past year.*

> **NOTE**
> These two verbs describe the changing shape of the moon in the sky. When the moon *waxes*, more of it is visible, and when it *wanes* we see less of it.

wax 'lyrical (about sth) (*written*)
talk or write about sth with enthusiasm: *He began to wax lyrical about the new car he would buy with his earnings.*

- **ball** → the whole ball of wax

way /weɪ/

across the 'way (BrE also **over the 'way**)
on the other side of the street, etc: *Music blared from the open window of the house across the way.*

,all the 'way
1 (also **the ,whole 'way**) during the whole journey/period of time: *She didn't speak a word to me all the way back home.*
2 completely; as much as it takes to achieve what you want: *I'm fighting him all the way.* ◇ *You can count on my support — I'm with you all the way.*

(that's/it's) always the 'way (*spoken*)
used to say that things often happen in a particular way, especially when it is not convenient: *'I was already late, and then I got stuck in a traffic jam.' 'Yes, that's always the way, isn't it?'*

any way you 'slice it (*AmE, informal*)
however you choose to look at a situation: *Any way you slice it, consumers pay more for certain products in some countries than others.*

be in a bad 'way
be very ill or in serious trouble: *He was attacked in the street last night and he's in quite a bad way, I understand.* ◇ *'I hear the company's in a bad way.' 'Yes, it's lost a lot of money.'*

be on the way 'out/'in
be going out of/coming into fashion: *Short skirts are on the way out.*

be (well) on the/your way to/towards sth
be about to achieve sth in the near future (usually sth good): *We're on the way towards an election victory.* ◇ *He's well on the way to establishing himself among the top ten players in the world.*

'be/be 'born/be 'made that way
(of a person) behave or do things in a particular manner because it is part of your character: *It's not his fault he's so shy — he was born that way.*

be under 'way
have started and be now progressing or taking place: *A major search is under way to find the escaped prisoners.* ◇ *Negotiations are under way to resolve the dispute.*

by the 'way (also **by the 'by/'bye** *less frequent*) (*spoken*)
1 used for introducing sth you have just thought of, which may or may not be connected to what has just been said: *I had a meeting with Graham at work today... by the way, I've invited him and his wife to lunch on Sunday.*
2 used for saying that sth is not important in the present situation or discussion: *Her academic qualifications are by the by. What we need is someone dynamic and creative.*

by way of sth
1 (of a journey) passing through a place: *They're going to Poland by way of France and Germany.*
2 as a kind of sth; as sth: *What are you thinking of doing by way of a vacation this year?* ◇ *The flowers are by way of a 'thank-you' for all her help.*

come your 'way
happen to you or come into your possession, temporarily or permanently: *Some good luck came his*

way. ◇ *When my grandmother dies, quite a lot of money will be coming my way.*

do sth in a big/small 'way
do sth to a great/small extent; do sth on a large/small scale: *He's got himself into debt in a big way.* ◇ *She collects antiques in a small way.*

do sth on/along the 'way
1 do sth as you go somewhere: *Buy a burger and eat it on the way.*
2 do sth while you do sth else; do sth during the process of doing sth else: *I've succeeded in this business, and met a lot of nice people along the way.*

'either way ♦ **,one way or the 'other**
used to say that it does not matter which one of two possibilities happens, is chosen or is true: *Was it his fault or not? Either way, an explanation is due.* ◇ *We could meet today or tomorrow — I don't mind one way or the other.*

every 'which way (*informal*)
in all directions: *Her hair tumbled every which way.*

get in the 'way (of sth)
prevent sb from doing sth; prevent sth from happening: *He wouldn't allow emotions to get in the way of him doing his job.*

get into/out of the way of sth/of doing sth
become used to doing sth/lose the habit of doing sth: *The women had got into the way of going out for a walk every evening.*

get sth out of the 'way
deal with a task or difficulty so that it is no longer a problem or worry: *I'm glad I've got that visit to the dentist out of the way.*

get/have your (own) 'way (also **have it/things/everything (all) your (own) 'way**)
get, believe or do what you want, usually in spite of the wishes or feelings of others: *She always gets her own way in the end.* ◇ *All right, have it your own way — I'm tired of arguing.*

give 'way
break or fall down: *The bridge gave way under the weight of the lorry.* ◇ *Her legs suddenly gave way and she fell to the floor.*

give 'way (to sb/sth)
1 allow sb/sth to go first: *Give way to traffic coming from the left.*
2 feel and express a strong emotion, without trying to hide it or stop it: *She refused to give way to despair.*
3 allow sb to have what they want: *In arguments, I'm always the first to give way.* ◇ *We must not give way to their demands.* **OPP** dig your heels in
4 be replaced by sth: *The storm gave way to bright sunshine.*

go all the 'way (with sb) (*informal*)
have full sexual intercourse with sb

go a long/some way towards doing sth
help very much/a little in achieving sth: *The new law goes a long way towards solving the problem.*

go out of your 'way (to do sth)
make a special effort to do sth, usually to help or please sb: *She went out of her way to cook a really nice meal.*

go your own 'way
do what you want, especially against the advice of others: *Teenagers always go their own way, and it's no use trying to stop them.*

go sb's 'way
1 travel in the same direction as sb: *I'm going your way. Do you want a lift?*
2 (of events) be favourable to sb: *Did you hear Alan got the job? It seems that things are going his way at last.*

go the way of all 'flesh
die or come to an end: *Poor old Johnson has gone the way of all flesh, and the world is certainly a poorer place for it.*

❷ ORIGIN
This expression is associated with the Bible. It was made famous by the book 'The Way of All Flesh' (1903) by Samuel Butler.

have a way of doing sth
used to say that sb often does sth, or that sth often happens in a particular way, especially when it is out of your control: *He has a way of arriving when you're least expecting him.* ◇ *Long-distance relationships have a way of not working out.*

have a way with sb/sth
have a special ability to deal with sb/sth: *She's a very good teacher. She has a way with children.* ◇ *She's got a way with words* (= she is very good at expressing herself).

have your (wicked) 'way with sb (*old-fashioned*, *humorous*)
persuade sb to have sex with you

in a 'way ♦ in 'one way (also **in 'some ways**)
to a certain extent (but not completely): *In a way, living in the town is better than the country, because there's much more to do.* ◇ *In one way, I'm sorry we didn't stay longer.* ◇ *I agree with you in some ways.*

in his, her, its, etc. (own) 'way
in a manner that is appropriate to or typical of a person or thing but that may seem unusual to other people: *I think she does love you in her own way.*

in the/sb's 'way
stopping sb from moving or doing sth: *You'll have to move — you're in my way.* ◇ *I left them alone, as I felt I was in the way.*

keep/stay out of sb's 'way
avoid sb: *He's got a lot of work to do at the moment, so if I were you I'd stay out of his way until he's got it finished.*

look the other 'way
ignore sb/sth deliberately: *We only had three tickets but the woman at the door looked the other way and let all four of us in.*

lose your 'way
1 become lost: *We lost our way in the dark.*
2 forget or move away from the purpose or reason for sth: *I feel that the project has lost its way.*

a lot, not much, etc. in the way of sth
a lot, etc. of sth: *We don't do a lot in the way of exercise.* ◇ *Is there much in the way of nightlife around here?*

make 'way (for sb/sth)
make enough space for sb/sth; allow sb/sth to pass: *Could you move your books to make way for the food?* ◇ *People made way for my wheelchair.*

make your 'way (to/towards sth)
go (to/towards sth): *Would passengers please make their way to gate 15 for the flight to Paris.* ◇ *Don't worry, we can **make our own way** to the airport* (= get there without help, a ride, etc.).

make your 'way in sth
succeed in sth, especially a job: *She's trying to make her way in the fashion business.* ◇ *The time had come to leave home and start to make his way in the world.*

,my way or the 'highway (*AmE*, *informal*)
used to say that sb else has either to agree with your opinion or to leave: *Right now there is only one rule here. It's my way or the highway.*

,no 'way (*informal*)
definitely not; never: *'Are you going to stay at school after you're 16?' 'No way. I want to get a job.'* ◇ *No way am I going to speak to him again!*

not stand in sb's 'way
not try to stop sb from doing sth: *If you want to become a singer, we won't stand in your way.*

(in) ,one way and/or a'nother/the 'other
in various different ways now considered together: *One way and another we had a very good time when we were students.*

on your/the/its 'way
1 coming; going: *If she phones again, tell her I'm on my way* (= coming to see her). ◇ *I'd better be on my way soon* (= leave soon).
2 during the journey: *I bought some bread on the way home.*
3 (of a baby) not yet born: *She's got two children and another one on the way.*

the ,other way a'round/'round
1 in the opposite position, direction or order: *I think it should go on the other way round.*
2 the opposite situation: *I didn't leave you. It was the other way around* (= you left me).

,out of the 'way
1 no longer stopping sb from moving or doing sth: *I moved my legs out of the way so that she could get past.* ◇ *I didn't say anything until Dad was out of the way.*
2 finished; dealt with: *Our region is poised for growth once the election is out of the way.*
3 far from a town or city: *It's a lovely place, but it's a bit out of the way.* ◇ *a little out-of-the-way place on the coast*
4 used in negative sentences to mean 'unusual': *She had obviously noticed nothing out of the way.*

,out of your 'way
not on the route that you planned to take: *I'd love a ride home — if it's not out of your way.*

see your 'way ('clear) to doing sth
find that it is possible or convenient to do sth: *Could you see your way clear to lending me some money until next week?*

see which way the 'wind blows
see what most people think, or what is likely to happen before you decide how to act yourself: *Most politicians are careful to see which way the wind's blowing before they make up their minds.*

,that's the 'way (*informal*)
used for showing pleasure or approval of what sb is doing or has done: *That's the way. Just keep playing like that and you'll win.*

that's the way the cookie 'crumbles
(also **that's the way it 'goes**) (*informal*)
that is the situation and we cannot change it, so we must accept it: *She met somebody else and left me. That's the way the cookie crumbles, I suppose.*

there's more than 'one way to skin a 'cat
(*saying, humorous*)
there are many different ways to achieve sth: *Have you thought about a different approach? There's more than one way to skin a cat.*

to 'my, 'your, etc. way of thinking
in my, etc. opinion: *To his way of thinking, mobile phones should be banned on public transport.*

'way back (*informal*)
a long time ago: *We've known each other since way back.* ◇ *I first met her way back in the fifties.*

a/the/sb's way of 'life
the typical pattern of behaviour of a person or group: *the British/rural/traditional way of life*

the ,way of the 'world
what often happens; what is common: *Marriages don't always last for ever. That's the way of the world, I'm afraid.*

way to 'go! (*AmE, informal, spoken*)
used to tell sb that you are pleased about sth they have done: *Good work, guys! Way to go!*

the way to sb's 'heart
the way to make sb like or love you: *The way to a man's heart is through his stomach* (= by giving him good food).

work, etc. your way through sth
read or do sth from the beginning to the end of sth: *He worked his way through the dictionary learning ten new words every day.* ◇ *He's eating his way through all the restaurants that are recommended in the Good Food Guide.*

,work your way through 'college, etc.
have a paid job while you are a student: *She had to work her way through law school.*

,work your way 'up
start with a badly paid, unimportant job and work hard until you get a well paid, important job: *He's worked his way up from an office junior to managing director.*

- **clear** → clear the way (for sth/for sth to happen)
- **downhill** → downhill all the way
- **easy** → take the easy way out
- **family** → in the family way
- **feel** → feel your way
- **find** → find your/its way (to/into...)
- **hard** → do/learn sth the hard way
- **harm** → out of harm's way

- **know** → know your way about/around (sth)
- **know** → not know which way/where to look
- **know** → not know which way/where to turn
- **laugh** → laugh all the way to the bank
- **lead¹** → lead the way
- **lie** → lie your way into/out of sth
- **long** → go back a long way
- **long** → have come a long way
- **long** → have a long way to go
- **middle** → find, etc. a/the middle way **SEE** follow/steer/ take a middle course
- **open** → open the way for sb/sth (to do sth)
- **ordinary** → in the ordinary way
- **pave** → pave the way (for sb/sth)
- **pay** → pay your/its (own) way
- **pick** → pick your way (across, over, etc. sth)
- **point** → point the way (to/towards sth)
- **punch** → he, she, etc. couldn't punch his, her, etc. way out of a paper bag
- **roses** → be roses, roses all the way **SEE** be all roses
- **rub** → rub sb up the wrong way
- **show** → show the way
- **smooth** → smooth the path/way
- **sweet** → do sth in your own sweet time/way
- **talk** → talk your way out of sth/out of doing sth
- **thread** → thread your way through (sth)
- **wide** → be (a long) way off the mark **SEE** be/fall wide of the mark
- **will** → where there's a will there's a way
- **wing** → wing your/its way (to...)
- **wrong** → take sth the wrong way

ways /weɪz/

be ,set in your 'ways
be unable or unwilling to change your behaviour, habits or ideas, usually because you are old: *He's too set in his ways now to think about a career change.*

you, etc. can't have it 'both ways
you must choose between two things even though you would like both of them: *You want an interesting job that pays well, and yet one where you don't have many responsibilities. Well, you can't have it both ways.*

cut both/two 'ways
have an effect both for and against sb/sth: *Banning imports of cars could cut both ways: other countries may ban the import of cars produced here.*

in ,more ways than 'one
used to show that sth that has been said has more than one meaning: *She's a big woman, in more ways than one* (= she is big in size, and also important or powerful).

,ways and 'means
the methods and materials available for doing sth: *'How will you get the money?' 'Don't worry, there are ways and means.'*

- **change** → change your ways
- **error** → the error of your ways
- **mend** → mend your ways
- **parting** → a/the parting of the ways

- separate → go your separate ways
- swing → swing both ways
- two → (there are) no two ways about it
- way → in some ways SEE in a way

wayside /'weɪsaɪd/

fall by the 'wayside
not be able to continue sth that needs effort, discipline, etc.; begin to be dishonest, immoral, etc: *25 students began the course but a number have fallen by the wayside and only 12 will be taking the exam.*

❷ ORIGIN
This is from a story in the Bible in which the seeds that fell *by the wayside* (= by the side of a path) did not grow.

wazoo /wæ'zuː/

,out/,up the wa'zoo (*AmE*, △, *slang*)
in large numbers or amounts: *She's got awards up the wazoo.*

weak /wiːk/

be/go ,weak at the 'knees (*informal*)
be/become weak because of illness, strong emotion, etc: *He felt dizzy and a bit weak at the knees.* ◇ *Her smile made me go weak at the knees* (= with nervousness, love, etc.). ▸ ,weak-'kneed *adj.* not brave or determined

the weak 'link (in the 'chain)
the point at which a system or an organization is most likely to fail: *She went straight for the one weak link in the chain of his argument.*

a weak 'moment ♦ a moment of 'weakness
a time when you do or agree to sth you would not normally do: *In a weak moment I agreed to let them stay at our house, but later I wished I hadn't.* ◇ *I was on a very strict diet but in a moment of weakness I ate a cream cake.*

- spirit → the spirit is willing but the flesh (it) is weak

weakness /'wiːknəs/

- weak → a moment of weakness SEE a weak moment

weapon /'wepən/

- double-edged → be a double-edged sword/weapon

wear /weə(r); *AmE* wer/

,wear and 'tear
damage or loss of quality because of normal use: *After having the car for five years you expect some wear and tear.* ◇ *The guarantee does not cover normal wear and tear.*

wear your ,heart on your 'sleeve
show other people your emotions, especially love: *He wears his heart on his sleeve and often gets hurt.*

❷ ORIGIN
This phrase is from Shakespeare's play *Othello*.

wear 'thin
begin to become less; become less interesting or amusing: *My patience is beginning to wear very thin.* ◇ *Don't you think that joke's wearing a bit thin?* (= we have heard it many times before)

wear the 'trousers (*BrE*) (*AmE* wear the 'pants) (*often disapproving*)
(especially of a woman) be the partner in a marriage who makes the decisions and tells the other person what to do: *It's not difficult to see who wears the trousers in their house!*

- worse → the worse for wear

wearing /'weərɪŋ; *AmE* 'wer-/

- birthday → in/wearing your birthday suit

weather /'weðə(r)/

keep a 'weather eye on sth/open for sth
watch sth very carefully for signs of change so that you will be prepared for a problem, difficulty, etc: *It's an ambassador's job to keep a weather eye open for any important political changes.*

under the 'weather (*informal*)
slightly ill, sick or depressed; not as well/cheerful as usual: *She was off work for two weeks and she still seems a bit under the weather.*

- brass → brass monkey weather SEE brass monkeys
- heavy → make heavy weather of sth/of doing sth
- storm → ride out/weather the storm (of sth)

weathers /'weðəz; *AmE* 'weðərz/

in 'all weathers (*BrE*)
in all kinds of weather, good and bad: *She goes out jogging in all weathers.*

weave /wiːv/

weave your 'magic ♦ weave a 'spell (over sb) (*especially BrE*)
perform or behave in a way that attracts and interests sb very much or makes them react in a particular way: *Will Owen be able to weave his magic against Spain on Wednesday?*

wedding /'wedɪŋ/

- monkey → monkey's wedding
- shotgun → a shotgun wedding/marriage

wedge /wedʒ/

- drive → drive a wedge between A and B
- thin → the thin end of the wedge

wee /wiː/

- hours → the wee (small) hours SEE the small/early hours

week /wiːk/

,week after 'week (*informal*)
continuously for many weeks: *Week after week the drought continued.*

,week by 'week
as the weeks pass: *Week by week he grew a little stronger.*

week ,in, week 'out
happening every week: *I'm tired of the same old routine week in, week out.*

a ,week to'morrow, on 'Monday, etc. (*BrE*)
(also a ,week from to'morrow, 'Monday, etc. *AmE, BrE*)
seven days after the day that you mention: *It's my birthday a week on Tuesday.*

a ,week 'yesterday, last 'Monday, etc.
(*especially BrE*)
seven days before the day that you mention: *It was a week yesterday that we heard the news.*

weekend /,wi:k'end; *AmE* 'wi:kend/

• dirty → a dirty weekend

weigh /weɪ/

weigh 'anchor
(of a ship and its passengers) leave a place: *We weighed anchor in the afternoon and started for the Philippines.*

> NOTE
> This means 'to lift the anchor out of the water' before sailing away.

weigh on your 'mind
(of a problem or difficulty) make you feel worried and anxious: *The safety of the missing children was weighing on their minds.*

weigh (half) a 'ton (*informal*)
be very heavy: *These suitcases weigh a ton! What have you got in them?* **OPP** (as) light as air/a feather

weigh your 'words
carefully choose the words you use when you speak or write: *He spoke very slowly, weighing his words.*

weight /weɪt/

be a ,weight off your 'shoulders
used to say that you are glad that you do not have to worry about sth any longer: *Finally paying off my debts was a great weight off my shoulders.*

put/throw your 'weight behind sth
use all your influence and power to support sth: *Several of the country's leading politicians have thrown their weight behind the campaign.*

take the 'weight off your feet (*informal*)
used to tell sb who is tired to sit down: *Here, take the weight off your feet and I'll bring you a cup of tea and a biscuit.*

throw your 'weight about/around (*informal*)
use your position of authority or power in an aggressive way in order to get what you want: *He started throwing his weight around, shouting at everyone and telling them what to do.*

weight of 'numbers
the combined power, strength or influence of a group: *They got what they wanted by sheer weight of numbers.*

• carry → carry weight
• groan → groan under the weight of sth
• mind → (take) a load/weight off sb's mind
• pull → pull your weight
• punch → punch above/below your weight
• worth → be worth your/its weight in gold

weird /wɪəd; *AmE* wɪrd/

weird and wonderful
clever and attractive, but unusual or strange: *People were wearing all sorts of weird and wonderful clothes.*

welcome /'welkəm/

lay, put, roll, etc. out the 'welcome mat (for sb) (*especially AmE*)
make sb feel welcome; try to attract visitors, etc: *The country has put out the welcome mat for international investors.*

outstay/overstay your 'welcome
(of a guest) stay too long so that you are no longer welcome: *We visited some friends in France, but we didn't want to overstay our welcome and left after a couple of days.*

you're 'welcome (*especially AmE*)
used as a polite reply when a person thanks you: *'Thanks for your help.' 'You're welcome.'*

well /wel/

,all being 'well
if everything happens as you expect and hope: *We'll see you in July then, all being well.*

,all very 'well/'fine (for sb) (to do sth) but...
(*informal*)
used to criticize or reject a remark that sb has made, especially when they were trying to make you feel happier about sth: *'Why don't you try to relax more?' 'Look, it is all very well to say that, but how can I possibly relax with four small children in the house?'*

,all well and 'good (*informal*)
good but not completely satisfactory: *That's all well and good, but why didn't he call her to say so?*

all's well that 'ends well (*saying*)
if the final result is good, earlier difficulties and problems are not important

> **ℹ ORIGIN**
> This is the title of a play by Shakespeare.

as well (as sb/sth)
in addition to sb/sth; too: *Are they coming as well?* ◇ *They sell books as well as newspapers.* ◇ *She's a talented musician as well as being a photographer.*

be (just) as 'well (to do sth)
be sensible or wise (to do sth): *It's just as well to lock the door, even if you only go out for a short while.*

be doing 'well
be getting healthier after an illness; be in good health after a birth: *Mother and baby are both doing well.*

what's it to 'you, 'him, 'her, etc.? (*informal*)
(said when you are annoyed) you, etc. have no
right to know sth; what does it matter to you,
etc: *What's it to her how I spend my money?*

(and) what's 'more ♦ **what is 'more**
(and) more importantly; (and) in addition: *I don't
like pubs. They're noisy, smelly, and what's more,
expensive.*

what's 'up? (*informal*)
1 what's the matter?: *What's up with him? He
looks furious.*
2 (*especially AmE*) what's new?; what's happening?: *Hey Jo, what's up?*

what's 'what (*spoken*)
what things are useful, important, etc: *She certainly knows what's what.*

what's with sb? (*AmE, spoken*)
used to ask why sb is behaving in a strange way:
*What's with you? You haven't said a single word all
morning.*

what's with sth? (*AmE, spoken*)
used to ask the reason for sth: *What's with all this
walking? Can't we take a cab?*

what's 'yours? (*informal*)
(said in a pub or bar) what would you like to
drink?

whatever /wɒt'evə(r); AmE wət-; wɑːt-/

or what'ever (*spoken*)
or something of a similar type: *It's the same in any
situation: in a prison, hospital or whatever.*

what'ever you do
used to warn sb not to do sth under any circumstances: *Don't tell Paul, whatever you do!*

wheat /wiːt/

sort out/separate the ˌwheat from the 'chaff
separate people or things of a better quality from
those of a lower quality: *When all the applications
came in, our first task was to separate the wheat
from the chaff.*

NOTE
Chaff is the outer covering of the seeds of grain
such as *wheat*, which is separated from the
grain before it is used.

wheel /wiːl/

at/behind the 'wheel (of sth)
driving a car: *Who was at the wheel when the car
crashed?*

NOTE
Wheel in this phrase refers to the steering
wheel of a car.

a fifth/third 'wheel (*AmE*)
an unwanted, extra or unnecessary person: *No, I
don't think I'll join you. Whenever I go out with you
guys I just feel like a fifth wheel.*

NOTE
This refers to adding an extra unnecessary
wheel to a vehicle.

take the 'wheel
start to drive a car, replacing sb else: *When we got
halfway, Sarah took the wheel and I had a rest.*

ˌwheel and 'deal (*disapproving*)
do a lot of complicated deals in business or politics, often in a dishonest way: *He's spent the last
three years wheeling and dealing in the City.*
◇ *I don't want to go into politics — there's too much
wheeling and dealing.* ▶ ˌwheeler-'dealer *noun*

the ˌwheel has come/turned full 'circle
(*saying*)
sth that changed greatly has now returned to its
original state or position: *How long does it take for
the wheel of fashion to come full circle?*

- asleep → asleep at the wheel/switch
- big → a big cheese/wheel
- cog → a cog in the machine/wheel
- reinvent → reinvent the wheel
- shoulder → put your shoulder to the wheel
- spoke → put a spoke in sb's wheel
- squeaky → the squeaky wheel gets the grease/oil

wheels /wiːlz/

(there are) ˌwheels within 'wheels
used to describe a situation which is difficult to
understand because it involves complicated or
secret processes and decisions: *In making political
agreements there are always wheels within wheels.*
◇ *There are wheels within wheels in this organization — you never really know what's going on.*

- motion → set the wheels in motion SEE put/set sth in
  motion
- oil → grease the wheels SEE oil the wheels
- spin → spin your wheels

where /weə(r); AmE wer/

where it's 'at (*informal*)
where the most exciting things are happening (in
music, art, etc.): *For dance music, New York's where
it's at right now.*

wherefores /'weəfɔːrz; AmE 'werf-/

- whys → the whys and (the) wherefores (of sth)

whet /wet/

ˌwhet sb's 'appetite
make sb feel hungry; make sb interested in sth:
*Don't eat too much of this dish. It's only to whet
your appetite for the main course.* ◇ *One of my
teachers lent me a book about climbing, and it really
whetted my appetite.*

NOTE
If you *whet* a knife, sword, etc., you make it
sharper.

which /wɪtʃ/

ˌwhich is 'which
used to talk about distinguishing one person or
thing from another: *The twins are so alike I can't
tell which is which.*

while /waɪl/

while away the time, etc. (doing sth)
pass the time (doing sth), usually because you are
waiting for sth or have nothing better to do: *I had
ten hours to wait in Rome, so I whiled away the time
wandering around the museums.*

● **worth** → (well) worth your while (to do sth)

whip /wɪp/

get, have, hold, etc. the 'whip hand (over sb)
have power or control (over sb): *The government
knows that the army have the whip hand.* ◇ *Our
opponents had the whip hand over us right from
the beginning.*

● **crack** → crack the whip
● **fair** → a fair crack of the whip

whipped /wɪpt/

like a whipped 'dog
ashamed, embarrassed or unhappy because you
have been defeated or punished: *I hate it but when
I get angry with him, he just looks at you like a
whipped dog.*

whipping /'wɪpɪŋ/

a 'whipping boy
a person who is blamed or punished for the mistakes of another person: *The directors are clearly
responsible for what happened, but they're sure to
find a whipping boy lower down the company.* ◇ *It
was your fault, and I am not going to be your whipping boy.*

> **❷ ORIGIN**
> In the past when a royal prince made a mistake
> in his lessons, another boy was whipped
> (= punished) for his mistakes.

whirl /wɜːl; AmE wɜːrl/

give sth a 'whirl (*informal*)
try sth, to see if it is enjoyable, interesting, etc: *I've
never had Indonesian food but I'll give it a whirl.*

in a 'whirl
confused and excited: *My mind was in a whirl as I
realized that this decision would change our lives.*

whirlwind /'wɜːlwɪnd; AmE 'wɜːrl-/

● **reap** → (sow the wind,) reap the whirlwind

whisker /'wɪskə(r)/

**be, come, etc. within a whisker of sth/of
doing sth** (*BrE*)
almost do sth: *They came within a whisker of being
killed.*

do sth by a 'whisker (*informal*)
do sth, but nearly fail; do sth, but only just: *He
missed the first prize by a whisker.* ◇ *You escaped
serious injury by a whisker, so consider yourselves
very lucky.*

whiskers /'wɪskəz; AmE 'wɪskərz/

● **cat** → the cat's whiskers/pyjamas

whistle /'wɪsl/

you, etc. can 'whistle for it (*BrE, spoken*)
used to say that you are not going to give sb sth
that they have asked for: *'The boss wants that sales
report this afternoon.' 'Well, he can whistle for it.'*

whistle in the 'dark
try not to show that you are afraid, are in danger,
etc: *He seems confident we'll get the money we need,
but I think he's just whistling in the dark.*

● **blow** → blow the whistle (on sb/sth)
● **clean** → (as) clean as a whistle
● **wet** → wet your whistle

whistles /'wɪslz/

● **bells** → bells and whistles

whistle-stop /'wɪsl stɒp; AmE staːp/

a ˌwhistle-stop 'tour
short visits to different places made, for example,
by a politician during an election campaign: *The
Prime Minister left on a whistle-stop tour of the
north of England today.* ◇ *The new manager's gone
on a whistle-stop tour of all the offices.*

> **❷ ORIGIN**
> In the US, a *whistle stop* is a small town or sta-
> tion that trains only stop at if somebody gives a
> signal.

whit /wɪt/

not a/one 'whit (*old-fashioned*)
not at all; not the smallest amount: *The party
leaders care not a whit about the principles of
democracy and freedom.*

white /waɪt/

(as) ˌwhite as a 'sheet/'ghost (*informal*)
very pale in the face, because of illness, fear or
shock: *She went as white as a sheet when she heard
the news.*

a white 'Christmas
a Christmas when it snows

a white 'elephant
a thing that is useless and no longer needed,
although it may have cost a lot of money: *That
theatre is a real white elephant. It cost millions to
build and nobody ever goes there.*

> **❷ ORIGIN**
> This comes from the story that in Siam (now
> Thailand), the king would give a white ele-
> phant as a present to somebody that he did not
> like. That person would have to spend all their
> money on looking after the rare animal.

a white 'lie
a small or harmless lie that you tell to avoid hurting sb: *When she asked me if I liked her new dress I had to tell a white lie. I thought it looked awful, but I couldn't say so!*

- black → (in) black and white
- black → in black and white
- bleed → bleed sb dry/white
- whiter → whiter than white

whiter /'waɪtə(r)/

,whiter than 'white
(of a person) completely honest and morally good: *The government must be seen to be whiter than white.*

white-van /,waɪt 'væn/

,white-'van man (*BrE, informal*)
used to refer to a man driving a white van in an aggressive way. Many companies use white delivery vans and their drivers are often considered stupid and rude: *Who enjoys driving to work with the constant traffic jams, roadworks and the impatient hooting of white-van man?*

whizz-kid /'wɪz kɪd/

a 'whizz-kid (also 'whiz-kid) (*informal*)
a person who is very good and successful at sth, especially at a young age: *'Who's the new manager?' 'A financial whizz-kid from Harvard Business School.'*

who /huː/

who am 'I, are 'you, etc. to do sth?
used when you think sb has no right or authority to do sth: *Who are you to tell me I can't leave my bicycle here? It's not your house.* ◇ *I don't agree, but then who am I to say what she should do?*

who's 'who
people's names, jobs, status, etc: *You'll soon find out who's who in the office.*

whole /həʊl; AmE hoʊl/

Most idioms containing **whole** are at the entries for the nouns and verbs in the idioms, for example **go the whole hog** is at **hog**.

as a 'whole
considered as one general group: *The population as a whole were not very interested in the issue.*

on the 'whole
considering everything; in general: *On the whole her school work is improving, though her spelling is still poor.*

a 'whole lot (*informal*)
very much; a lot: *I'm feeling a whole lot better.*

a 'whole lot (of sth) (*informal*)
a large number or amount: *There were a whole lot of people I didn't know.*

the ,whole 'lot
everything; all of sth: *I've sold the whole lot.*

whoop /wuːp; huːp/

,whoop it 'up (*informal*)
1 enjoy yourself very much with a noisy group of people: *Of course I'm in a bad mood! I've been stuck here working while you've been whooping it up in the bar with your friends!*
2 (*AmE*) make people excited or enthusiastic about sth: *The emcee came on stage and really whooped it up for the next act.*

whoopee /wʊ'piː/

make 'whoopee (*old-fashioned, informal*)
celebrate in a noisy way: *Here's a photo of us making whoopee at Dave's wedding.*

why /waɪ/

why 'ever...?
used in questions to mean 'why?', expressing surprise: *Why ever didn't you tell us?*

,why 'not? (*informal*)
used to make a suggestion, or agree to a suggestion: *'Why not go and see a movie?' 'OK.'* ◇ *'Let's go and see a movie.' 'OK, why not?'*

whys /waɪz/

the ,whys and (the) 'wherefores (of sth)
the reasons (for sth): *I don't really want to know all the whys and the wherefores. Just tell me what happened.*

wick /wɪk/

get on sb's 'wick (*BrE, informal*)
annoy sb: *She's always talking about herself — she gets on my wick.*

wicked /'wɪkɪd/

there's no peace/rest for the 'wicked (*usually humorous*)
used when sb is complaining that they have a lot of work to do: *Well, it's been nice talking to you, but I really must go. No rest for the wicked!*

wicket /'wɪkɪt/

- sticky → (be on) a sticky wicket

wide /waɪd/

be/fall wide of the 'mark (also be (a long) way off the 'mark)
be not at all correct or accurate: *No one knew where Bangalore was, and their guesses were all wide of the mark.* OPP on the nose

be wide 'open
(of a competition, an election, etc.) with no obvious winner: *The presidential election is wide open.*
OPP a one-horse race

give sb/sth a wide 'berth
avoid meeting sb; avoid going near or using sth: *He's so boring I always try to give him a wide berth at parties.* ◇ *The roads are very dangerous there — I'd give them a wide berth and go by train.*

a 'wide boy (BrE, informal, disapproving)
a man who makes money in dishonest ways: *If he offers you a business deal, say no. He's a bit of a wide boy.*

(lay/leave yourself) wide 'open (to sth)
(put yourself) in a situation where you can easily be criticized, blamed, attacked, etc: *By not saying anything in your defence, you're leaving yourself wide open to their accusations.* ◇ *The soldiers were wide open to attack.* **OPP** cover your back

● far → far and wide
● net → cast/spread your net wide

wife /waɪf/

● world → (all) the world and his wife

wig /wɪg/

● flip → flip your wig SEE flip your lid

wild /waɪld/

run 'wild (informal)
grow or behave in an uncontrolled way: *Their parents believed in letting the children run wild when they were young and it doesn't seem to have done them any harm.* ◇ *I just let the roses run wild in this part of the garden.*

a ,wild 'goose chase
a (long) search for sth that you cannot find because you have been given the wrong information: *He gave us the wrong directions to the station and that led us off on a wild goose chase.* ◇ *Peter's story sent the police on a wild goose chase. They soon realized he'd been lying.*

> ❷ ORIGIN
> In the past, this was a sport in which horse riders had to follow the exact course taken by the first rider, like the way that geese fly by following a leader. Later it referred to any unplanned or irregular course taken by one person and followed by another, and then came to mean something that was like trying to find a wild goose: that is, a difficult or hopeless task.

wild 'horses couldn't/wouldn't drag sb there, prevent sb doing sth, etc. (informal, humorous)
nothing would make or persuade sb to go somewhere, do sth, etc: *Wild horses wouldn't keep me at home on a Saturday night.*

● hog-wild → go hog-wild
● sow[1] → sow your wild oats

wilderness /'wɪldənəs; AmE -dərn-/

in the 'wilderness
(of politicians) no longer having power, influence or importance because they no longer hold high office: *After a few years in the wilderness she was allowed to return to a job in the government.*

● voice → a voice (crying) in the wilderness

wildest /'waɪldəst/

beyond your wildest 'dreams
much greater or better than you ever expected, imagined, etc: *The success of our first album was beyond our wildest dreams.*

wildfire /'waɪldfaɪə(r)/

● spread → spread like wildfire

will /wɪl/

against your 'will
without wanting to: *I was forced to sign the document against my will.*

at 'will
when, where, how, etc. you want to: *The animals are allowed to wander at will in the park.* ◇ *The younger soldiers started shooting at will* (= they fired their guns without waiting for the order).

where there's a ,will there's a 'way (saying)
a person who really wants something very much and is determined to get it will find a way of getting it or doing it: *'Have you had any luck in contacting Sue?' 'Not yet, but where there's a will there's a way!'*

with a 'will (written)
with energy and enthusiasm: *She started digging the garden with a will.* ◇ *With a will they set to work.*

● best → with the best will in the world
● free → of your own free will

willies /'wɪliz/

give sb the 'willies/heebie-'jeebies/'creeps
(informal)
make sb feel nervous or afraid: *Being alone in this old house gives me the willies.* ◇ *He gives me the creeps. He's got such strange eyes.*

willing /'wɪlɪŋ/

● God → God willing
● show → show willing
● spirit → the spirit is willing but the flesh (it) is weak

wills /wɪlz/

● battle → a battle of wills

willy-nilly /,wɪli 'nɪli/

do sth ,willy-'nilly (informal)
1 do sth whether you want to or not: *She was forced willy-nilly to accept the company's proposals.*
2 do sth in a careless way without planning: *Don't just use your credit card willy-nilly.*

> NOTE
> This expression is a shortened form of 'willing or not willing'.

win /wɪn/

I, you, etc. ˌcan't 'win (*spoken*)
whatever you do, you cannot succeed completely or please everyone: *If I spend time with Phil, Jane's unhappy. If I spend time with her, he's jealous. I just can't win.* ▸ **ˌno-'win** *adj.* (of a situation, policy, etc.) that will end badly whatever you decide to do: *They're in a no-win situation at the moment. Whatever they do, someone criticizes them.*

win sb's 'heart
make sb love you: *The children have won the old man's heart.* ◇ *The actress who played Natasha won the hearts of the audience.*

ˌwin or 'lose
whether you succeed or fail: *Win or lose, we'll know we've done our best.*

you can't win them 'all ♦ **you 'win some, you 'lose some** (*spoken*)
used to express sympathy for sb who has been disappointed about sth: *'I made a terrible speech this evening.' 'Well, you can't win them all. Don't worry about it.'*

'you win (*spoken*)
used to agree to what sb wants after you have failed to persuade them to do or let you do sth else: *OK, you win, I'll admit I was wrong.*

- **day** → carry/win the day
- **hand** → ask for/win sb's hand
- **hands** → win (sth)/beat sb hands down
- **spurs** → win/earn your spurs

wind¹ /wɪnd/

break 'wind
let gas out from the intestine (= the tube along which food passes after it has been through the stomach) through the anus

get 'wind of sth (*informal*)
hear about sth secret or private: *A journalist got wind of a story about the nuclear research centre.*

get/have the 'wind up (about sth) (*BrE, informal*)
become/be frightened about sth: *I heard that he's selling his business and moving away. I think he's got the wind up about something or other.*

go, run, etc. like the 'wind
go, run, etc. very fast: *We had to drive like the wind to get there in time.* ◇ *She ran like the wind.*
OPP at a snail's pace

in the 'wind
about to happen soon, although you do not know exactly when: *I can see some changes in the wind.* ◇ *The soldiers sensed that something was in the wind.*

put the 'wind up sb (*BrE, informal*)
make sb frightened about sth: *He really put the wind up her with his stories of rats in the kitchen.*

take the 'wind out of sb's sails (*informal*)
make sb suddenly less confident or angry, especially when you do or say sth that they do not expect: *When he just smiled and agreed with her, it rather took the wind out of her sails.*

- **caution** → throw caution to the wind(s)
- **change** → a wind/the winds of change
- **ill** → it's an ill wind (that blows nobody any good)
- **sail** → sail close to the wind
- **second** → get your second wind
- **straw** → a straw in the wind
- **three** → (be) three sheets to the wind
- **twist** → twist in the wind
- **way** → see which way the wind blows

wind² /waɪnd/

- **little** → twist/wind/wrap sb around/round your little finger

windmills /'wɪndmɪlz/

- **tilt** → tilt at windmills

window /'wɪndəʊ; AmE 'wɪndoʊ/

be, go, etc. out/out of the 'window (*informal*)
(of a chance, an opportunity, a job, etc.) disappear; be lost: *All my hopes of finding a good job in television have gone out of the window.* ◇ *Don't throw this opportunity out of the window.*

a ˌwindow of oppor'tunity
a limited period of time when you can do something that you want to do or need to do: *The government's difficulties provided the opposition with a window of opportunity to present an alternative policy to the voters.*

a ˌwindow on the 'world
a way of learning about other people and other countries: *News programmes try to provide a window on the world.*

winds /wɪndz/

- **change** → a wind/the winds of change

wine /waɪn/

ˌwine and 'dine (sb)
go to restaurants, etc. and enjoy good food and drink; entertain sb by buying them good food and drink: *Too much wining and dining is making him fat.* ◇ *Our hosts wined and dined us very well.*

wing /wɪŋ/

on a ˌwing and a 'prayer
with only a very slight chance of success: *He started the business in his own home, on a wing and a prayer, but it looks like he's really going to make a success of it.*

> ❷ **ORIGIN**
> This expression was first used in the military to describe how pilots flying very badly damaged planes succeeded in returning to base.

on the 'wing (*literary*)
(of a bird) flying

take/have sb under your 'wing
give sb help and protection: *When new children arrive at the school, she takes them under her wing.*

wings

take 'wing (*literary*)
(of a bird or an aircraft) start flying away

'wing it (*informal*)
do sth without planning or preparing it first;
improvise: *I didn't know I'd have to make a
speech — I just had to wing it.*

'wing your/its way (to…)
go or be sent somewhere very quickly: *An invitation to the wedding will be winging its way to you
very soon.*

wings /wɪŋz/

(wait, stand, etc.) in the 'wings
(wait, etc.) ready to do sth, especially to take the
place of another person: *If the party leader should
resign, there are plenty of other politicians waiting
in the wings.* ◇ *There are many younger tennis players in the wings, waiting for the chance to show
their abilities.*

> NOTE
> The *wings* are the areas at either side of the
> stage that cannot be seen by the audience,
> where actors wait to come onto the stage.

- **clip** → clip sb's wings
- **spread** → spread your wings

wink /wɪŋk/

- **nod** → a nod is as good as a wink (to a blind man)
- **nudge** → a nudge and a wink
- **nudge** → nudge nudge, wink wink
- **sleep** → not get a wink of sleep **SEE** not sleep a wink
- **tip** → tip sb the wink

winks /wɪŋks/

- **forty** → forty winks

winner /'wɪnə(r)/

be onto a 'winner (*informal*)
be doing sth, especially selling sth, that is likely to
be successful: *He is the sole importer of this product, and he certainly thinks he's onto a winner.*

- **pick** → pick a winner

wipe /waɪp/

wipe the 'floor with sb (*informal*)
defeat sb completely and easily in an argument,
competition, etc: *They started arguing about the
education reforms, and she wiped the floor with
him.* ◇ *Italy wiped the floor with Austria, beating
them 5-0.*

wipe sth off the ,face of the 'earth (also **wipe
sth off the 'map**)
completely destroy sth: *If a meteor hit us, whole
cities would be wiped off the face of the earth.* ◇ *The
fall in prices wiped a lot of small businesses off the
map.*

wipe the slate 'clean
agree to forget about past mistakes or arguments
and start again with a relationship: *We're both to
blame. Let's wipe the slate clean and start again.*

> ❷ ORIGIN
> In the past, people wrote on a slate with *chalk*
> (= a soft white stone). If you wiped it, you
> rubbed off the marks written on it.

**wipe the/that 'smile, 'grin, etc. off your/sb's
face**
1 used to tell sb to stop smiling, etc. because it is
annoying or not appropriate: *Wipe that smile off
your face or I'll send you out of the classroom.*
2 make sb feel less happy or satisfied with sth:
*The news from the stock market soon wiped the
smile off his face.*

wire /'waɪə(r)/

go, come, etc. (right) down to the 'wire
(*informal*)
if you say that a situation goes **down to the wire**,
you mean that the result will not be decided or
known until the very end: *Most people are predicting a very close game, quite possibly going right
down to the wire.*

> NOTE
> In this idiom, the *wire* refers to the finishing
> line in races.

- **live²** → a live wire

wires /'waɪəz; *AmE* 'waɪərz/

- **crossed** → get your lines/wires crossed
- **pull** → pull wires **SEE** pull strings (for sb)

wisdom /'wɪzdəm/

conventional/received 'wisdom
the view or belief that most people have: *Conventional wisdom has it that riots only ever happen in
big cities.*

> ❷ ORIGIN
> The term *conventional wisdom* was first used
> by the economist John Kenneth Galbraith in his
> book *The Affluent Society.*

in your, his, etc. (infinite) 'wisdom
used when you are saying that you do not understand why sb has done sth: *The government in its
wisdom has decided to support the ban.*

- **pearls** → pearls of wisdom

wise /waɪz/

be ,wise after the e'vent (*often disapproving*)
know what should have been done in a particular
situation, but only after it has happened: *'If we'd
been more careful, the fire would never have happened.' 'It's no good being wise after the event — we
can't do anything now.'*

be/get 'wise to sb/sth (*informal*)
be/become aware of sth or aware of sb's (usually
bad) behaviour: *When did you first get wise to what
was happening?* ◇ *He thought he could fool me but
I'm wise to him.*

put sb 'wise (to sth) (*informal*)
inform sb about sth: *If Raquel hadn't have put me
wise, I would have believed him.*

a 'wise guy (*informal disapproving, especially AmE*)
a man who speaks or behaves as if he knows much
more than other people: *OK, wise guy, what do you
think we should do then?*

● penny → penny wise (and) pound foolish
● word → a word to the wise

wiser /ˈwaɪzə(r)/

be none the 'wiser/'no wiser ◆ not be any the
'wiser
1 not understand sth, even after it has been
explained to you: *I've read the instructions, but
I'm still none the wiser.*
2 not know or find out about sth bad that sb has
done: *If you put the money back, no one will be any
the wiser.*

wish /wɪʃ/

(just) as you 'wish (*formal, especially BrE*)
I will do what you want; I will agree with your
decision: *We can meet at my house or yours, as
you wish.*

I 'wish! (*spoken*)
used to say that sth is impossible or very unlikely,
although you wish it were possible; if only: *'You'll
have finished by tomorrow.' 'I wish!'*

the wish is father to the 'thought (*saying*)
we believe a thing because we want it to be true

> ❷ ORIGIN
> This phrase was used in Shakespeare's play
> *Henry IV*.

wish sb/sth 'well ◆ wish sb/sth 'ill (*formal*)
hope that sb/sth succeeds or has good luck; hope
that sb/sth fails or has bad luck: *I wish you well in
your new job.* ◇ *She said she wished nobody ill.*

wouldn't wish sth on my, etc. worst 'enemy
(*informal*)
used for saying that sth is so unpleasant, painful,
etc. that you would not like anyone to experience
it: *It's a terrible job — it's dirty, noisy and boring. I
wouldn't wish a job like that on my worst enemy.*

your wish is my com'mand (*humorous*)
I am ready to do anything you ask me to do: *'Put
the kettle on, will you?' 'Your wish is my command.'*

> ❷ ORIGIN
> These are the words of the genie (= a spirit
> with magical powers) in the story about Alad-
> din in *The Thousand and One Nights*.

wishes /ˈwɪʃɪz/

if wishes were ˌhorses, beggars would/might
'ride (*saying*)
wishing for sth does not make it happen

wishful /ˈwɪʃfl/

ˌwishful 'thinking
the belief that sth you want to happen is happening or will happen, although this is actually not
true or is very unlikely: *Prices seem to have stopped*

rising in the shops, or is that just wishful thinking
on my part?

wit /wɪt/

to 'wit (*old-fashioned, formal*)
used when you are about to be more exact about
sth you have just referred to: *I told him I only spoke
one foreign language, to wit French.*

with /wɪð; wɪθ/

be 'with sb (*informal*)
1 understand what sb is saying or explaining: *I'm
sorry, but I'm not with you. What exactly did you
mean by 'cut and paste'?* ◇ *'Are you with me?' 'No,
you've lost me. Can you explain it again?'*
2 be in support of or agreement with sb: *'What do
you think, Jonathan?' 'I'm with Sarah on this.'*
3 used to ask a customer, etc. to wait for a short
time: *I'm just serving this lady. I'll be with you in a
minute.*

get 'with it (*informal*)
become aware of the most recent ideas, developments, events, etc: *You never seem to know what's
happening in the world around you. Time you got
with it, Paul.*

'with it (*informal*)
1 (*old-fashioned*) (of sb/sth) fashionable and up
to date: *Her clothes are very with it, aren't they?*
◇ *He was wearing very with-it sunglasses.*
2 thinking quickly and clearly: *I'm a bit tired this
morning. I'm not really with it.*

with 'that (*written*)
straight after that; then: *He muttered a few words
of apology and with that he left.*

wither /ˈwɪðə(r)/

ˌwither on the 'vine (*formal*)
gradually come to an end or stop being effective:
*He used to be so ambitious, but his ambition seems
to have withered on the vine.*

> NOTE
> If a grape *withers on the vine*, it dries up and
> dies before it can be picked.

witless /ˈwɪtləs/

be scared/bored 'witless (*informal*)
be extremely frightened or bored: *Despite his reputation as a tough guy, he admits that he was 'scared
witless' when he first arrived in New York.*

witness /ˈwɪtnəs/

be (a) 'witness to sth
1 (*formal*) see sth take place: *He has been witness
to a terrible murder.*
2 (*written*) show that sth is true; provide evidence
for sth: *His good health is a witness to the success of
the treatment.*

bear/give 'witness (to sth)
provide evidence of the truth of sth: *The huge
crowd bore witness to the popularity of this man.*

wits /wɪts/

be at your wits' 'end
be so confused or worried that you do not know
what you should do: *I can't pay the bills, the bank
won't lend me any money, and I don't know what to
do — I'm at my wits' end.*

collect/gather your 'wits
try to become calm and think clearly: *After such a
shock I found it difficult to gather my wits.*

frighten/scare sb out of their 'wits
frighten sb very much: *I was scared out of my wits
when I looked out of the window and saw the aircraft's engine on fire.*

have/keep your 'wits about you
be/remain quick to think and act in a demanding,
difficult or dangerous situation: *Mountaineering is
dangerous, so you need to keep your wits about you.*

● **battle** → a battle of wits
● **drive** → drive sb out of their mind/wits
● **live¹** → live by/on your wits
● **pit** → pit your wits (against sb/sth)

wives /waɪvz/

● **old** → an old wives' tale

wobbly /'wɒbli; AmE 'wɑːbli/

● **tantrum** → throw a wobbly **SEE** throw a tantrum

woe /wəʊ; AmE woʊ/

woe be'tide sb (*formal* or *humorous*)
there will be trouble for sb: *Woe betide anyone who
arrives late!*

wolf /wʊlf/

keep the 'wolf from the door (*informal*)
make sure that you have enough money to pay for
the basic things like food, rent, heating, etc: *Their
wages are just enough to keep the wolf from the
door.*

a wolf in sheep's 'clothing
a person who appears friendly and nice but is really dangerous

● **cry** → cry wolf
● **lone** → a lone wolf

wolves /wʊlvz/

throw sb to the 'wolves/'lions
allow sb to be attacked or remain in a difficult
situation, perhaps because they are no longer useful or important to you: *When he became politically
unpopular the rest of his party just threw him to the
wolves.* **OPP** save sb's bacon

woman /'wʊmən/

● **few** → a man/woman of few words
● **honest** → make an honest woman of sb
● **inner** → the inner man/woman
● **life** → the man/woman in your life
● **man** → be sb's man/woman
● **man** → be your own man/woman

● **old** → old woman
● **parts** → a man/woman of (many) parts
● **possessed** → like a man/woman possessed
● **twice** → be twice the man/woman (that sb is)
● **word** → be a man/woman of his/her word
● **world** → a man/woman of the world

wonder /'wʌndə(r)/

I ˌshouldn't 'wonder (if …) (*informal*)
I would not be surprised to find out (that …): *It's
paid for with stolen money, I shouldn't wonder.*

it's no/small/little 'wonder (that)…
it's not surprising: *If you walked all the way, it's
little wonder you're late.* ◇ *'The heating's gone off.'
'I thought it was cold. No wonder!'*

it's a 'wonder (that)… (*especially spoken*)
it is surprising or strange (that)…: *Did you see the
car after the crash? It's a wonder that they survived!*

● **nine** → a nine days' wonder

wonderful /'wʌndəfl; AmE -dərfl/

● **weird** → weird and wonderful

wonders /'wʌndəz; AmE 'wʌndərz/

ˌwonders will ˌnever 'cease (*spoken, usually
ironic*)
used to express surprise and pleasure at sth: *'The
train was on time today.' 'Wonders will never cease
(= I am surprised, because usually it is late).'*

**work/do 'wonders/'miracles (for/on/with sb/
sth)** (*informal*)
have a very good effect (on sb/sth); quickly succeed: *Getting the job did wonders for her self-confidence.* ◇ *This washing powder will work miracles
on those difficult stains.* ▶ **'miracle-worker** *noun*:
*I just don't have enough time to finish it. I'm sorry,
but I'm not a miracle-worker.*

wood /'wʊd/

not out of the 'wood(s) (*informal*)
not yet free from dangers or difficulties: *Our sales
figures look much better this month, but we're not
out of the woods yet.*

not see the ˌwood for the 'trees (*BrE*) (*AmE* **not
see the ˌforest for the 'trees**) (*informal*)
not have a clear understanding of a situation
because you are only looking at small aspects of
it and not considering the situation as a whole:
*The situation is so complex that many people are
unable to see the wood for the trees.*

● **dead** → dead wood
● **touch** → knock on wood **SEE** touch wood
● **touch** → touch wood

wooden /'wʊdn/

don't take any wooden 'nickels (*AmE*)
used when saying goodbye to sb to mean 'be careful', 'take care of yourself': *Well, see you around
Tom. Don't take any wooden nickels.*

get, win, take, etc. the ˌwooden ˈspoon (*BrE*, *informal*)
come last in a race or competition: *England must win this match if they are to avoid taking the wooden spoon.*

> **❓ ORIGIN**
> It was a custom at the University of Cambridge to give a wooden spoon to the student of mathematics who had the lowest mark/grade for their year.

woods /wʊdz/

- **babe** → a babe in the woods
- **neck** → in your, this, etc. neck of the woods

woodwork /ˈwʊdwɜːk; *AmE* -wɜːrk/

blend/fade into the ˈwoodwork
behave in a way that does not attract any attention; disappear or hide: *I decided the best thing to do would be to try and fade into the woodwork and hope that no one noticed me.*

come/crawl out of the ˈwoodwork (*informal*, *disapproving*)
if you say that sb **comes/crawls out of the woodwork**, you mean that they have suddenly appeared in order to express an opinion or to take advantage of a situation: *When he won the lottery, all sorts of distant relatives came out of the woodwork.*

> **NOTE**
> These idioms refer to the fact that insects or small animals, especially unpleasant ones, often hide in holes in wooden parts of a room or building.

wool /wʊl/

- **pull** → pull the wool over sb's eyes
- **wrap** → wrap sb up in cotton wool

word /wɜːd; *AmE* wɜːrd/

be as ˌgood as your ˈword
do what you have promised to do: *You'll find that she's as good as her word — she always comes if she says she will.*

be a man/woman of his/her ˈword
be a person who always does what he/she has promised to do: *If he said he'd help you, he will — he's a man of his word.*

by ˌword of ˈmouth
in spoken, not written, words: *The news spread by word of mouth.*

> **NOTE**
> 'By word of mouse' (= a computer mouse) is a humorous version of this that refers to communication by email, etc.

(right) from the word ˈgo (*informal*)
from the very beginning: *I knew from the word go that it would be difficult.*

(not) get a word in ˈedgeways (*BrE*) (*AmE* **(not) get a word in ˈedgewise**) (*informal*)
(usually used with *can* or *could*) (not) be able to say sth, because sb else is talking too much: *I tried to tell him what I thought, but I couldn't get a word in edgeways.*

give sb your ˈword (that…) ◆ **have sb's ˈword (that…)**
promise sb/be promised (that…): *I give you my word that I'll pay you tomorrow.* ◇ *I've got his word that he'll fix the car by the weekend.*

go ˌback on your ˈword
not do what you have promised; break a promise: *He said he wouldn't charge more than €150, but he went back on his word and gave me an invoice for €200.*

have a ˈword (with sb) (about sth)
have a short conversation about sth, especially in private: *Can I have a word, Marie? It's about Jane.*

have a word in sb's ˈear (*BrE*)
speak to sb in private about sth: *Can I have a word in your ear, John?*

in a ˈword (*spoken*)
used for giving a very short, usually negative, answer or comment: *In a word, 'stupid' is how I'd describe him.*

keep/break your ˈword
do/fail to do what you have promised: *Do you think she'll break her word and tell everyone?*

your/the last/final ˈword (on/about sth)
your, etc. final decision or statement about sth: *'Will you take £900?' 'No, £1 000 and that's my last word.'* ◇ *Is that your final word on the matter?*

leave ˈword (with sb)
leave a message with sb: *He left word with his secretary about where to contact him if necessary.*

(upon) my ˈword! (*old-fashioned*)
used to express surprise: *My word! That was quick!*

not be the ˈword for it
used to say that a word or an expression does not describe sth fully or strongly enough: *Unkind isn't the word for it! I've never seen anyone treat an animal so cruelly!*

not/never have a good word to ˈsay for/about sb/sth (*informal*)
not/never have anything positive to say about sb/sth: *She rarely has a good word to say about her neighbours.* ◇ *Nobody has a good word to say for the new computer system.* **OPP** praise sb/sth to the skies

not a ˈword (to sb) (about sth)
do not say anything to sb/anybody about sth: *Not a word to Jean about the party — it's a surprise!* ◇ *Remember, not a word about how much it cost.*

put in a (good) ˈword (for sb)
say sth good about sb to sb else in order to help them: *If you put in a good word for me, I might get the job.*

the spoken/written ˈword
the language, in speaking/writing: *The spoken word is often very different from the written word.*

take sb at their 'word
believe exactly what sb says or promises: *She said I could go and stay with her in Paris whenever I wanted, so I took her at her word.*

take sb's 'word for it
believe sth that sb has said: *You know more about cars than I do, so if you think it needs a new gearbox, I'll take your word for it.* ◇ *Can I take your word for it that the text has all been checked?*

,word for 'word
in exactly the same words; translated directly from another language: *I repeated what you said, word for word.* ◇ *It probably won't sound very natural if you translate it word for word.* ◇ *a word-for-word account, translation, etc.*

your, his, etc. ,word is (as ,good as) your, his, etc. 'bond
used to say that sb always does what they promise to do: *Don't worry, you can trust my brother. His word's as good as his bond.*

your, his, etc. ,word is 'law
used to say that sb has complete power and control: *Their father is very old-fashioned. His word is law in their house.*

your, his, etc. ,word of 'honour (*BrE*)
(*AmE* **your, his, etc. ,word of 'honor**)
used to refer to sb's sincere promise: *He gave me his word of honour that he'd never drink again.*

a ,word to the 'wise
used to introduce some advice, especially when only a few words are necessary: *The band are now touring the UK. A word to the wise though — make sure you book tickets early.*

- **breathe →** (not) breathe a word (about/of sth) (to sb)
- **dirty →** a dirty word
- **four-letter →** a four-letter word
- **hang →** hang on sb's words/every word
- **household →** a household name/word
- **know →** not know the meaning of the word
- **last →** have the last word
- **last →** the last word (in sth)
- **mum →** mum's the word!
- **operative →** the operative word
- **printed →** the printed word/page
- **say →** (just) say the word
- **spread →** spread the word

words /wɜːdz; *AmE* wɜːrdz/

have/exchange 'words (with sb) (about sth)
(*especially BrE*)
argue or quarrel with sb because you do not like the way they have behaved: *I had to have words with him about his behaviour.* ◇ *They both got angry and had words.*

in 'other words
expressed in a different way; that is to say: *'I don't think this is the right job for you, Pete.' 'In other words, you want me to leave. Is that it?'*

(not) in so/as many 'words
(not) in exactly the same words that sb says were used: *Did he actually say in so many words that there was no hope of a cure?*

in words of one 'syllable
using very simple language so that sb will understand: *They didn't seem to understand my explanation, so I explained it all again in words of one syllable.*

a play on 'words
a clever or amusing use of a word that has more than one meaning, or of words that have different meanings but sound similar/the same; a pun: *When Elvis Presley had his hair cut off in the army he said, 'Hair today and gone tomorrow'. It was a play on words — the usual expression is 'here today and gone tomorrow.'* ▸ **'wordplay** *noun*: *Many of the jokes are based on puns and wordplay.*

put 'words in/into sb's mouth
say or suggest that sb has said sth, when they have not: *You're putting words in my mouth. I didn't say the whole house was dirty, I just said the living room needed a clean.*

take the words (right) out of sb's 'mouth
say exactly what another person was going to say: *'The speed limit on motorways should be raised.' 'I agree completely! You've taken the words right out of my mouth!'*

too funny, sad, etc. for 'words
extremely funny, sad, etc: *The man in the post office was too stupid for words.*

words 'fail me
I cannot express how I feel (because I am too surprised, angry, etc.): *Words fail me! How could you have been so stupid?*

- **actions →** actions speak louder than words
- **eat →** eat your words
- **famous →** famous last words
- **few →** a man/woman of few words
- **hang →** hang on sb's words/every word
- **loss →** at a loss for words
- **lost →** be lost for words
- **mark →** mark my words
- **mince →** not mince your words
- **war →** a war of words
- **weigh →** weigh your words

work /wɜːk; *AmE* wɜːrk/

Most idioms containing **work** are at the entries for the nouns or adjectives in the idioms, for example **work like a charm** is at **charm**.

all ,work and no 'play (makes ,Jack a dull 'boy)
(*saying*)
it is not healthy to spend all your time working, you need to relax too

be at 'work
be having an influence or effect: *Why did they lose the election? Several factors were at work...* ◇ *Evil forces are at work in this organization.*

go/set about your 'work
start to do your work: *She went cheerfully about her work.*

go/set to 'work (on sth) (also **get (down) to 'work (on sth)**)
start working on a particular task: *I set to work on the car, giving it a good clean.* ◇ *I ought to get to work on that report.*

have your 'work cut out (to do sth/doing sth) (*informal*)
be likely to have difficulty doing sth: *You'll have your work cut out to get there before nine. It's 8.30 already.* ◇ *I won't be able to come with you today. I've got my work cut out for me at the moment.*

in/out of 'work
having/not having a paid job: *I've been out of work for a year.* ◇ *Is your husband in work at the moment?* ◇ *an out-of-work actor*

put/set sb to 'work (on sth)
make sb start work (doing sth): *On his first day in the office they put him to work on some typing.*

'work it/things (so that...) (*informal*)
plan sth carefully to get the result you want; organize or arrange sth: *Can you work it so that we get free tickets?* ◇ *I worked things so that I could take all my leave in July and August.*

,work like a 'dog/'slave/'Trojan (*informal*)
work very hard: *She worked like a slave to pass her exams.* **OPP** not do a stroke (of work)

worker /'wɜːkə(r); AmE 'wɜːrk-/

● fast → a fast worker

working /'wɜːkɪŋ; AmE 'wɜːrkɪŋ/

be working 'overtime (*informal*)
be very active or too active: *There was nothing to worry about. It was just her imagination working overtime.*

have a ,working 'knowledge of sth
know sth well enough to be able to use it: *I speak good French and I have a working knowledge of Italian and Spanish.* ◇ *I've used this software a bit so I do have a working knowledge of it.*

in (full/good) working 'order (also **in running 'order**)
(of a machine) in good condition; working well: *For Sale: Fridge in good working order, £60.*

● cylinders → firing/working on all cylinders

works /wɜːks; AmE wɜːrks/

,good 'works
kind acts to help others: *The company produced a report giving details of its good works for the community and the environment.*

in the 'works
something that is **in the works** is being discussed, planned or prepared and will happen or exist soon: *The rumour is that there is a sequel to the movie in the works, although this has not been confirmed.*

the (whole) 'works (*informal*)
everything that you could want, need or expect: *We went to the chip shop and had the works: fish, chips and mushy peas.*

● gum → gum up the works
● spanner → throw a (monkey) wrench in the works **SEE** put/throw a spanner in the works

world /wɜːld; AmE wɜːrld/

be, live, etc. in a world of your 'own
seem not to be aware of things happening around you; be a person who has ideas that other people think are strange: *I'm not surprised he didn't know about it — he lives in a world of his own, that boy.*

be/mean (,all) the 'world to sb
be very important to sb; be loved very much by sb: *Her job means the world to her.* ◇ *They've only got one child and he's all the world to them.*

come/go 'down/'up in the world
become less/more successful; become poorer/richer: *Since she left Harvard she's gone down in the world.*

come into the 'world (*literary*)
be born: *Our lives changed completely when little Oliver came into the world.* **OPP** breathe your last

for all the 'world as if/though... ◆ for all the 'world like sb/sth (*written*)
exactly as if...; exactly like sb/sth: *She stood up and shouted at him, then sat down and went on with her work for all the world as if nothing had happened.*

have the ,world at your 'feet
have many advantages, and so have many opportunities to choose from; be very successful and admired: *When you're young you've got the world at your feet.* ◇ *She's got money; she's well-educated; the world is at her feet.*

in an ,ideal/a ,perfect 'world
used to say that sth is what you would like to happen or what should happen, but you know it cannot: *In an ideal world we would be recycling and reusing everything.*

in the 'world
used to emphasize what you are saying: *There's nothing in the world I'd like more than to visit New York.* ◇ *Don't rush — we've got **all the time in the world**.*

a man/woman of the 'world
a person with a lot of experience of life, who is not easily surprised or shocked

not (do sth) for (all) the 'world
used to say that you would never do sth: *I wouldn't sell that picture for all the world.*

not/never set the 'world on fire (*BrE* also **not/never set the 'Thames on fire**) (*informal*)
never do anything exciting, unusual or wonderful: *He's good, but he'll never set the world on fire. He's not dynamic enough.*

> **NOTE**
> The Thames is the large river that runs through London.

worlds

the... of this world (*informal*)
used to refer to people of a particular type: *We all envy the Bill Gateses of this world* (= the people who are as rich and successful as Bill Gates).

out of this 'world (*informal*)
unusually good: *She cooked a meal which was out of this world.*

see the 'world
travel, live or work in many different parts of the world: *A lot of students take a year off after university to travel and see the world.*

what is the world 'coming to? (*also* **I don't know ˌwhat the world's 'coming to**) (*saying*)
used as an expression of anger, shock, complaint, etc., at changes in people's behaviour, the political situation, etc: *When I read the news these days I sometimes wonder what the world's coming to.* ◇ *Instant tea? What is the world coming to?*

(all) the ˌworld and his 'wife (*informal*)
everyone; a large number of people: *The world and his wife was in Brighton that day.*

the ˌworld is your 'oyster
you have the freedom to do what you want, go where you want, etc. in the future because you are young, successful, rich, etc: *What do you mean, you don't know what to do with your life? The world is your oyster!*

a/the 'world of difference (between A and B) (*informal*)
a lot of difference (between A and B): *There's a world of difference between 'speed' and 'haste'.*

the (whole) world 'over
everywhere in the world: *People are the same the whole world over.* ◇ *Writers the world over joined in protest against her imprisonment.*

(think) the world ˌowes you a 'living (*disapproving*)
(think that) society is responsible for doing everything for you and you should not have to make any effort yourself: *Why don't you go out and get a job? The world doesn't owe you a living, you know.*

- **best** → with the best will in the world
- **bottom** → the bottom drops/falls out of sb's world
- **brave** → a brave new world
- **care** → not have a care in the world
- **care** → without a care in the world
- **dead** → dead to the world
- **earth** → how, why, etc. in the world... **SEE** how, what, why, etc. on earth...
- **end** → not be the end of the world
- **long** → not long for this world
- **lost** → be lost to the world
- **next** → the next world
- **outside** → the outside world
- **outside** → the world outside **SEE** the outside world
- **power** → do sb/sth a power/world of good
- **promise** → promise (sb) the moon/earth/world
- **small** → it's a small world
- **tell** → tell the (whole) world
- **think** → think the world of sb/sth

- **top** → on top of the world
- **watch** → watch the world go by
- **way** → the way of the world
- **window** → a window on the world
- **worlds** → be worlds/a world away (from sth)

worlds /wɜːldz; *AmE* wɜːrldz/

be 'worlds/a world away (from sth)
be very different (from sth): *Life in the country today is worlds away from how it was a hundred years ago.*

- **apart** → be poles/worlds apart
- **best** → the best of both/all (possible) worlds
- **worst** → the worst of both/all (possible) worlds

worm /wɜːm; *AmE* wɜːrm/

the ˌworm 'turns (*informal*)
even a patient, calm person will get angry if they are repeatedly badly treated: *He's often rude to his secretary and she doesn't say anything — but one day the worm will turn.*

- **early** → the early bird catches the worm

worms /wɜːmz; *AmE* wɜːrmz/

- **can** → a can of worms

worm's-eye /'wɜːmz aɪ; *AmE* 'wɜːrmz/

a worm's-eye 'view
the opinion of sb who is closely involved in sth: *I'm afraid I can't give you a general overview of the situation. I can only offer you a worm's-eye view that is based on my own experience.*

worried /'wʌrid; *AmE* 'wɜːr-/

be worried 'sick ◆ **be sick with 'worry**
be extremely worried: *Where have you been? I've been worried sick about you.*

you had me 'worried (*spoken*)
used to tell sb that you were worried because you did not understand what they said correctly: *You had me worried for a moment — I thought you were going to resign!*

worries /'wʌriz; *AmE* 'wɜːriz/

'no worries! (*especially AustralE, informal*)
it's not a problem; it's all right (often used as a reply when sb thanks you for sth): *'Could you help me with this?' 'Sure, no worries.'*

worry /'wʌri; *AmE* 'wɜːri/

ˌnot to 'worry (*informal, especially BrE*)
it is not important; it does not matter: *'Oh, damn! We've missed the train!' 'Not to worry. There'll be another one in five minutes.'*

'you should worry! (*informal*)
used for telling sb that they have no need to worry: *You think you're going to fail the exam! You should worry! You're the best in the class.*

- **worried** → be sick with worry **SEE** be worried sick

worth

worse /wɜːs; *AmE* wɜːrs/

be ˌworse ˈoff
be poorer, unhappier, etc. than before or than sb else: *The increase in taxes means that we'll be £40 a month worse off than before.* **OPP** be better off

we, you, he, etc. can/could/might do ˈworse (than…)
it is a good idea to do sth; sth is a good decision: *If you're looking for a good career, you could do worse than a job in banking.*

come off ˈworse
lose a fight, competition, etc. or suffer more compared with others: *Don't worry about him. People who try to hurt him usually find they come off a lot worse than he does.*

go from ˌbad to ˈworse
(of an already bad situation) become even worse: *Under the new management things have gone from bad to worse.*

none the ˈworse for sth
1 not less valuable, attractive, enjoyable, useful, etc. because of sth: *It's rather old-fashioned but none the worse for that.* ◇ *She's a very strict teacher, but none the worse for that.*
2 not injured or damaged by sth: *One of the drivers had been in a crash but, luckily, was none the worse for the experience.*

the ˌworse for ˈdrink
drunk: *He was the worse for drink when the time came for his speech.* **OPP** stone-cold sober

the ˌworse for ˈwear (*informal*)
1 in a poor condition because of being used a lot: *Your dictionary is looking a bit the worse for wear. Isn't it time you bought a new one?*
2 drunk: *Ellen came back from the pub rather the worse for wear.*

ˌworse ˈluck (*BrE, spoken*)
used to show that you are disappointed about sth: *I'm working tonight, so I can't come to the party, worse luck.*

- **bark** → his, her, etc. bark is worse than his, her, etc. bite
- **better** → for better or (for) worse
- **better** → so much the better/worse (for sb/sth)
- **better** → take a turn for the better/worse
- **fate** → a fate worse than death

worst /wɜːst; *AmE* wɜːrst/

be your ˌown worst ˈenemy
be a person who often creates problems or difficulties for himself/herself: *He spends all his money on clothes, and then finds that he's got nothing left to live on — if you ask me, he's his own worst enemy.*

bring out the ˈworst in sb
make sb show their worst qualities: *Pressure can bring out the worst in people.* **OPP** bring out the best in sb

do your ˈworst
be as harmful, unpleasant, violent, etc. as you can: *I refuse to pay this bill. Let them do their worst.* ◇ *The electricity company did their worst and cut off the supply.*

get the ˈworst of it ✦ come off ˈworst
be defeated in a fight, etc.; be affected more seriously than other people, etc: *The dog had been fighting and had obviously got the worst of it.* ◇ *Small businesses have come off worst in the economic crisis.*

if the ˌworst comes to the ˈworst (*AmE* also **if ˌworst comes to ˈworst**)
if the most unpleasant or unfortunate thing happens: *If the worst comes to the worst, we'll just have to sell the car.*

the worst of ˈboth/ˈall (possible) worlds
all the disadvantages of every situation: *Rail passengers feel that they are getting the worst of both worlds — expensive fares and an unreliable service.* **OPP** the best of both/all (possible) worlds

- **best** → at best/worst
- **wish** → wouldn't wish sth on my, etc. worst enemy

worth /wɜːθ; *AmE* wɜːrθ/

be ˈworth it
be worth the time, money, effort, risk, etc. you have spent/taken doing sth: *A dishwasher costs a lot of money, but it's worth it.* ◇ *Don't drink and drive. It's not worth it.*

be ˌworth your/its ˌweight in ˈgold
be very useful or valuable: *My assistant is worth her weight in gold.*

do sth for ˌall you are ˈworth
do sth with as much energy and effort as possible: *I shouted for all I was worth but no one heard me.*

for ˌwhat it's ˈworth (*spoken*)
used to emphasize that what you are saying is only your opinion or suggestion and may not be very helpful: *That's my opinion, for what it's worth.* ◇ *This is the first drawing I made, for what it's worth.*

make sth ˌworth sb's ˈwhile (*informal*)
pay sb well for doing sth for you: *If you can work on Saturdays and Sundays, we'll make it worth your while.*

not worth the paper it's ˈprinted/ˈwritten on
(of a written agreement, document, report, etc.) not having any value, especially legally, or because the person involved does not intend to do what they say they will: *The promises in this letter aren't worth the paper they're written on.*

ˌworth your/its ˈsalt
deserving respect, especially because you do your job well: *Any teacher worth his salt knows that students who enjoy a lesson learn the most.*

> **❓ ORIGIN**
> This may refer to the fact that in Roman times soldiers were given an allowance of salt as part of their pay. The Latin word *salarium* (= the money given to Roman soldiers to buy salt) is the origin of the word 'salary'.

(well) worth your 'while (to do sth)
interesting or useful to do: *It would be well worth your while to come to the meeting.*

- **bird** → a bird in the hand is worth two in the bush
- **game** → the game is not worth the candle
- **job** → more than your job's worth (to do sth)
- **money** → get/have your money's worth
- **two** → put in your two cents' worth SEE put in your two pennyworth/penn'orth
- **worthy** → worth the name SEE worthy of the name

worthy /'wɜːði; *AmE* 'wɜːrði/

worthy of the 'name (also **worth the 'name**) (*formal*)
deserving to be called good: *Any doctor worthy of the name would help an injured man in the street.*

wound /wuːnd/

- **rub** → rub salt into the wound/into sb's wounds

wounds /wuːndz/

- **lick** → lick your wounds
- **reopen** → reopen old wounds

wrack /ræk/

- **rack** → wrack your brains SEE rack your brains

wrap /ræp/

wrap sb up in cotton 'wool (*informal*)
protect sb too much from dangers or risks: *If you keep your children wrapped up in cotton wool, they'll never learn to be independent.*

- **little** → twist/wind/wrap sb around/round your little finger

wrapped /ræpt/

be ˌwrapped 'up in sb/sth
be so involved with sb/sth that you do not pay enough attention to other people or things: *She's so wrapped up in her own problems that she hasn't got time to listen to anyone else at the moment.*

wraps /ræps/

keep sth, stay, etc. under 'wraps (*informal*)
keep sth, stay, etc. secret or hidden: *These letters have lain under wraps since the 1960s.* ◇ *Next year's event is still being kept under wraps.*

wreak /riːk/

- **havoc** → play/wreak havoc with sth

wrench /rentʃ/

- **spanner** → throw a (monkey) wrench in the works SEE put/throw a spanner in the works

wring /rɪŋ/

ˌwring your 'hands
twist and rub your hands together because you are very worried, upset or anxious: *He stood there,*
wringing his hands in despair. ◇ *It's no use just wringing our hands — we must do something.*
▶ **'hand-wringing** *noun*: *No amount of hand-wringing can change the situation.*

ˌwring sb's 'neck (*spoken, informal*)
used as an expression of anger or as a threat: *If I find the person who did this, I'll wring his neck!*

> **NOTE**
> If you *wring* a bird's neck, you twist it in order to kill the bird.

wringer /'rɪŋə(r)/

go/put sb through the 'wringer (*informal*)
have, or make sb have, a difficult or unpleasant experience, or a series of them: *He's been through the wringer lately, what with his divorce, and then losing his job.* ◇ *Those interviewers really put me through the wringer!*

> **NOTE**
> In the past, a *wringer* was a device that squeezed the water out of clothes that had been washed.

wrist /rɪst/

- **slap** → a slap on the wrist

writ /rɪt/

ˌwrit 'large (*literary*)
1 easy to see or understand: *Mistrust was writ large on her face.*
2 (used after a noun) being a larger or more obvious example of the thing mentioned: *The party's new philosophies are little more than their old beliefs writ large.*

> **NOTE**
> *Writ* in this idiom means *written.*

write /raɪt/

be nothing, not much, etc. to write 'home about (also **be nothing, not much, etc. to 'shout about**) (*informal*)
not be very good or special; be ordinary: *The play was OK, but it wasn't anything to write home about.* ◇ *The food was nothing much to shout about.*

writing /'raɪtɪŋ/

in 'writing
in the form of a letter, document, etc. (that gives proof of sth): *All telephone reservations must be confirmed in writing.* ◇ *You should get his promises in writing.*

the ˌwriting (is) on the 'wall (*AmE* **the ˌhand-writing (is) on the 'wall**) (*saying*)
used when you are describing a situation in which there are signs that sb/sth is going to have problems or is going to fail: *The writing is on the wall for the club unless they can find £20 000.* ◇ *The President refuses to see the handwriting on the wall* (= that he will soon be defeated).

❷ ORIGIN
This phrase comes from the Bible story in which strange writing appeared on a wall during a feast given by King Belshazzar, predicting his death and the end of his kingdom.

written /ˈrɪtn/

be written all over sb's 'face
(of an emotion) be clearly seen on sb's face: *You could see he was guilty; it was written all over his face.*

have sb/sth written all 'over it (*informal*)
show clearly the influence or characteristics of sb/sth: *It's been badly organized, as usual — it's got the council written all over it.*

- word → the spoken/written word
- worth → not worth the paper it's printed/written on

wrong /rɒŋ; AmE rɔːŋ/

ˌback the wrong 'horse (*BrE*)
support the person, group etc. that later loses a contest or fails to do what was expected: *I certainly backed the wrong horse when I said United would win the Cup Final.* ◇ *Many people who had voted for the party in the election were now feeling that they had backed the wrong horse.*

> **NOTE**
> In horse racing, if you *back the wrong horse* you bet money on a horse that does not win the race.

from/on the ˌwrong side of the 'tracks (*informal*)
from or living in a poor area or part of town: *She married a man from the wrong side of the tracks.*

get sb 'wrong (*spoken*)
not understand correctly what sb means: *Please don't get me wrong, I'm not criticizing you.*

get (hold of) the ˌwrong end of the 'stick (*BrE, informal*)
understand sb/sth in the wrong way: *You've got the wrong end of the stick. He doesn't owe me money, I owe him!* **OPP** get sth right/straight

go 'wrong
1 make a mistake with sth: *It doesn't work. We must have gone wrong somewhere. Pass me the instruction manual.* ◇ *Where did we go wrong* (= what mistakes did we make for things to be so bad)?
2 (of a machine) stop working correctly: *This television keeps going wrong. I'm fed up with it.*
3 not progress or develop as well as you expected or intended: *Their marriage started to go wrong when he lost his job.* ◇ *What else can go wrong* (= what other problems are we going to have)?

in the 'wrong
responsible for a mistake, an accident, a quarrel, etc: *She is clearly in the wrong. She had no right to take the book.* ◇ *The accident wasn't my fault. The other driver was totally in the wrong.* **OPP** in the right

on the ˌwrong side of the 'law
in trouble with the police: *The TV presenter found himself on the wrong side of the law after hitting a cyclist while driving.*

take sth the wrong 'way
be offended by a remark that was not intended to be offensive: *Don't take this the wrong way, but don't you think you should get your hair cut?*

you can't go 'wrong (with sth) (*spoken*)
used to say that sth will always be acceptable in a particular situation: *For a quick meal you can't go wrong with pasta.*

- barking → be barking up the wrong tree
- bed → get up on the wrong side of the bed **SEE** get out of bed on the wrong side
- far → not far off/out/wrong
- foot → get/start off on the right/wrong foot (with sb)
- foot → not/never put/set a foot wrong
- note → hit/strike the right/wrong note
- right → right a wrong
- rub → rub sb up the wrong way
- side → be on the right/wrong side of 40, 50, etc.
- side → get/keep on the right/wrong side of sb
- track → be on the right/wrong track

wrongs /rɒŋz; AmE rɔːŋz/

- two → two wrongs don't make a right

wrote /rəʊt; AmE roʊt/

that's all she 'wrote (*AmE, informal*)
used when you are stating that there is nothing more that can be said about sth or that sth is completely finished: *And that's all she wrote for today, folks, because it's time for me to go.* ◇ *All you have to do is point and shoot and that's all she wrote.*

Y y

yank /jæŋk/

yank sb's 'chain (*AmE*, *informal*)
tell sb sth which is not true, as a joke: *Did you mean what you said, or were you just yanking my chain?*

> **NOTE**
> *Yank* means pull something hard, quickly and suddenly.

yards /jɑːdz; *AmE* jɑːrdz/

● **nine** → the whole nine yards

yarn /jɑːn; *AmE* jɑːrn/

● **pitch** → pitch a line/story/yarn (to sb)
● **spin** → spin (sb) a yarn/tale

yeah /jeə/

oh 'yeah? (*spoken*)
used when you are commenting on what sb has just said: *'We're off to France soon.' 'Oh yeah? When's that?'* ◇ (*ironic*) *'I'm going to be rich one day.' 'Oh yeah?'* (= I don't believe you.)

year /jɪə(r); jɜː(r); *AmE* jɪr/

all (the) year 'round
all year; all the time: *The zoo is open to visitors all year round.*

from, since, etc. the year 'dot
(*AmE* **from, since, etc. the year 'one**) (*informal*)
from, etc. a very long time ago: *The case contained old papers going back to the year dot.*

year after 'year
every year for many years: *The hotel has won the top prize year after year.*

year by 'year
as the years pass; each year: *Year by year their affection for each other grew stronger.*

year in, year 'out
(all year and) every year: *He had travelled on the 7.40 train to London year in, year out for thirty years.*

year on 'year (*business*)
(used especially when talking about figures, prices, etc.) each year, compared with the last year: *Spending has increased year on year.* ◇ *a year-on-year increase in unemployment*

● **century** → the turn of the century/year
● **seven** → the seven year itch

years /jɪəz; jɜːz; *AmE* jɪrz/

not/never in a hundred, etc. 'years (*spoken*)
used to emphasize that you will/would never do sth: *I'd never have thought of that in a million years.*

put 'years on sb
make sb feel or look much older: *The shock of losing his job put years on him.*

take 'years off sb
make sb feel or look much younger: *The new hairstyle takes years off her.*

● **donkey** → donkey's years

yellow /'jeləʊ; *AmE* 'jeloʊ/

a 'yellow streak (*disapproving*)
the quality of being easily frightened; cowardice: *He won't fight? I always thought he had a yellow streak in him.*

> **NOTE**
> *Yellow* is often used to describe somebody who is a coward.

yes /jes/

yes and 'no
said when you cannot answer either 'yes' or 'no' because the situation is not simple: *'Have you got a car?' 'Well, yes and no. We have, but it's not working at the moment.'*

yesterday /'jestədeɪ; 'jestədi; *AmE* -tərd-/

● **born** → I wasn't born yesterday

yet /jet/

as 'yet
until now or until a particular time in the past: *an as yet unpublished report* ◇ *As yet little is known about the disease.*

yore /jɔː(r)/

of 'yore (*old use* or *literary*)
long ago: *in days of yore*

young /jʌŋ/

be, stay, etc. young at 'heart
(of an old person) still feel and behave like a young person: *He says that the secret of living to 100 is to remain young at heart.*

you're only young 'once (*saying*)
young people should enjoy themselves as much as possible, because they will have to work and worry later in their lives: *'Don't you think Tony should get a job over the summer?' 'Well, you're only young once — there's plenty of time for that later.'*

● **blood** → fresh/new/young blood
● **old** → (have) an old head on young shoulders

younger /'jʌŋgə(r)/

be getting 'younger (*spoken*)
used to say that people seem to be doing sth at a younger age than they used to, or that they seem younger because you are now older: *The band's fans are getting younger.* ◇ *Why do police officers seem to be getting younger?*

not be getting any 'younger (*spoken*)
be getting older: *I can't possibly walk all the way to the beach — I'm not getting any younger, you know.*

yours /jɔːz; AmE jʊrz/

,you and 'yours (*informal*)
you and your family: *You must provide a safe future for you and yours.*

Zz

Z /zed; AmE ziː/

catch/get some 'Z's (*informal, especially AmE*)
sleep: *I headed home to catch some Z's before our night out.*

> **NOTE**
> In this expression, *Z's* is pronounced /ziːz/ (or sometimes /zedz/ in British English), and is used in cartoons to represent the sound people sometimes make when they sleep.

Time to catch some Z's!

● A → from A to Z

Key to Study Pages

S14–S15 That is to Say…

B 1 if you ask me
   2 you're kidding
   3 for one thing
   4 on top of that
   5 funnily enough
   6 I take your point
   7 that's that
   8 you said it
   9 believe me
  10 at the end of the day

D 1 Any phrase from group 1
   2 Any phrase from group 4
   3 Any phrase from group 3
   4 Any phrase from group 2
   5 Any phrase from group 4
   6 Any phrase from group 3
   7 Any phrase from group 1
   8 Any phrase from group 2

S16 It's as Easy as ABC

A 1 easy
   2 stubborn
   3 fit
   4 cool
   5 busy
   6 flat

B 1 a button
   2 a flash
   3 a picture
   4 a bat
   5 a bird
   6 gold

C The expressions that are NOT used are:
- as mad as monkeys
- as plain as potatoes
- as light as a bubble

D 1 a leaf
   2 hot cakes
   3 a light
   4 wildfire
   5 a headless chicken

S17 As the Saying Goes…

A 1 Better late than never.
   2 It's the thought that counts.
   3 It's no good/use crying over spilt milk.
   4 More haste, less speed.

B

A	B	C
1	c	v
2	a	iii
3	d	i
4	e	iv
5	b	ii

S18 Look Here!

A **Well/Happy**
    She looks the picture of health.
    He was all smiles.

   Angry/Unhappy
    She had a face like thunder.
    He gave her a dirty look.

   Unwell/Ill
    You look rather off colour.
    He doesn't look so hot.

   Old
    She's starting to look her age.
    He looks a bit past it.

   Well-dressed
    We were all in our Sunday best.
    He cut quite a dash in his suit.

   Unattractive
    He's no oil painting.
    She's not much to look at.

B 1 It's written all over your face.
   2 She's the spitting image of her sister/of Joan.
   3 It's difficult to keep a straight face.
   4 She's a sight for sore eyes.
   5 She's (a bit) down in the mouth.

S19 It Takes all Sorts…

A 1 live wire
2 wet blanket
3 rough diamond
4 dark horse
5 nosy parker
6 law unto herself

B

S20 We're in Business

A 1 do a roaring trade
2 shut up shop
3 in the red
4 set up shop
5 cut your losses
6 make ends meet
7 the rat race
8 make good on your debts
9 make money hand over fist

B making money/being rich
hit the jackpot
make a fortune
be rolling in it
be in the money
make a killing

losing money/being poor
take a beating
be hard up
be out of pocket
lose your shirt
strapped for cash

S21 Just What the Doctor Ordered

A Good Health
you are in the pink
you feel like a million dollars
you are on form
you are in shape
you are in good nick

Bad Health 😞
you are green about the gills
you are under the weather
you have been in the wars
you feel the worse for wear
you are off your food

B 1 clean bill of health
2 recharge my batteries
3 turn for the worse
4 fighting fit
5 went downhill
6 on the mend

C 1 flies   **4** rain
2 fiddle   **5** picture
3 needles

S22 It's the Bee's Knees!

A 1 snail   **4** lion
2 donkey   **5** grasshopper
3 duck   **6** beaver

B 1 I felt like a fish out of **water** when I started in this company.
2 I decided to take the bull by the **horns** and tell the boss what I thought.
3 The tourist office sent us on a wild goose **chase** to a hotel which had closed down.
4 I always get butterflies in my **stomach** before I have to give a speech.
5 The boss has always got a bee in his **bonnet** about reducing costs.

C Hold your *horses*.
She had *kittens*.
Hair of the *dog*.
He's no spring *chicken*.
Don't count your *chickens*.
He's a dark *horse*.

D 1 She had kittens.
2 Hold your horses.
3 He's no spring chicken.
4 He's a dark horse.
5 Hair of the dog.
6 Don't count your chickens.

S23 All Hands on Deck!

A

B 1 on an even keel
2 time and tide
3 all hands on deck
4 stuck his oar in
5 port of call
6 plain sailing
7 a drop in the ocean
8 on the crest of a wave

S24-25 Be a Good Sport

A 1 hit/knock sb for six = **cricket**
2 below par = **golf**
3 cover all bases = **baseball**
4 be way out in left field = **baseball**
5 move the goalposts = **football**
6 neck and neck = **horse-racing**
7 out of your depth = **swimming**
8 have a good innings = **cricket**
9 be thrown in at the deep end = **swimming**
10 on the ropes = **boxing**
11 win/lose by a short head = **horse-racing**
12 out for the count = **boxing**

B 1 a ballpark figure
2 on the ropes
3 a level playing field
4 on a par with
5 hitting below the belt
6 way off base

C 1 b
2 d
3 c
4 f
5 a
6 e

D 1 set the ball rollling
2 on his guard
3 on the ball
4 out of his depth
5 throw in the towel
6 catch the Prime Minister off guard
7 pulled any punches
8 wide of the mark
9 won by a short head
10 gave him a run for his money
11 par for the course
12 no-holds-barred

S26 Body and Soul

A

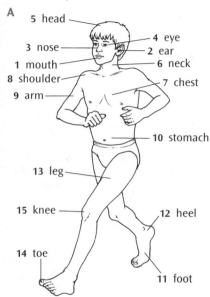

5 head
4 eye
3 nose
2 ear
1 mouth
6 neck
8 shoulder
7 chest
9 arm
10 stomach
13 leg
15 knee
12 heel
14 toe
11 foot

B 1 made my mouth water
2 all ears
3 no skin off my nose
4 more to it than meets the eye
5 put our heads together
6 in this neck of the woods
7 get it off your chest
8 cold shoulder
9 right arm
10 eyes were bigger than your stomach
11 stand on his own two feet
12 hot on his heels
13 pulling your leg
14 to keep the class on their toes
15 weak at the knees

S27 Eat, Drink and Be Merry

1 B Wine and *dine*
2 C have enough on your *plate*
3 C recipe for *disaster*
4 B food for *thought*
5 B have your *cake* and eat it
6 D let's talk *turkey*
7 A as easy as *pie*
8 B saved my *bacon*
9 C one man's *meat* is another man's poison
10 C meat and *potatoes*
11 B a piece of *cake*
12 B go *bananas*
13 B can't bake for *toffee*
14 D go *pear*-shaped
15 D in a *stew*
16 A the *icing* on the cake
17 C Eat, drink and be *merry*

S28 True Colours

A 1 black
2 red
3 grey
4 white

B 1 c
2 f
3 d
4 a
5 b
6 e

C 1 red
2 blue
3 pink
4 white
5 silver
6 red
7 black

S29 Naming Names

A 1 Coventry
   2 China
   3 Newcastle
   4 Rome
   5 Irish
   6 Dutch

B

S30 All Eyes

A 1 a
   2 c
   3 b
   4 a
   5 b
   6 a

B 1 couldn't take her eyes off
   2 had a roving eye
   3 love is blind
   4 turn a blind eye
   5 set eyes on him
   6 cried her eyes out
   7 saw the light
   8 swears blind
   9 with her eyes open

S31 All Ears

A 1 ear
   2 music
   3 ear
   4 noise
   5 ear
   6 noise
   7 sound
   8 ear
   9 ring
  10 music

B 1 It has a familiar ring to it.
   2 He loves the sound of his own voice.
   3 It's/That's like music to my ears.
   4 I'll play it by ear.
   5 I'll have to face the music.
   6 It goes in one ear and out the other.

C 1 ... I couldn't *believe* my ears.
   2 ... the advice fell on *deaf* ears.
   3 ... you could have heard a *pin* drop.
   4 Keep you ear to the *ground* ...
   5 ... but made a *pig's* ear of it,
     I'm afraid.
   6 Jack has been *bending* my ear about
     his financial problems...

S32–33 Flavour of the Month

A   Taste   Smell
      mouth   odour
      sweet   nose
      bitter   sniff
      flavour   stink
      sour   scent
      lips
      tongue

B 1 tongue
   2 sour
   3 mouth
   4 sweet
   5 lips

C   1 – 16 – 3 – 11 – 9 – 5 – 19 – 12 –
     4 – 13 – 7 – 10 – 14 – 18 – 8 – 2 –
     15 – 6 – 17 – 20

D 1 Derby was *born with a silver spoon
     in his mouth* and admits...
   2 Judy will offend a lot of people if she
     keeps *shooting her mouth off.*
   3 ... you need to *keep your nose to the
     grindstone.*
   4 When I get out of prison I plan to
     keep my nose clean.
   5 She *has a sharp tongue* when she's
     angry.
   6 ... in the hope that it would *loosen
     his tongue.*

E 1 b
   2 a
   3 a
   4 c
   5 a

C 1 He left the children in safe hands.
   2 The situation is getting out of hand.
   3 I know this place like the back of my
     hand.
   4 The police let the criminal slip
     through their fingers.
   5 He felt nervous and was all fingers
     and thumbs.

S35–36 Put Yourself to
           the Test

1 c	10 c	19 b
2 b	11 b	20 a
3 b	12 c	21 c
4 a	13 a	22 b
5 b	14 c	23 c
6 a	15 b	24 a
7 c	16 c	25 c
8 a	17 a	
9 b	18 a	

S34 Hands Up!

A

B 1 touch
   2 finger
   3 clutching
   4 glove
   5 thumb
   6 knuckles

Pronunciation and phonetic symbols

Phonetic symbols are used to show the pronunciation of keywords such as **action** /ˈækʃn/. All the main words of an idiom are also keywords so their pronunciation can be found within the dictionary. For the idiom itself, the typical stress pattern is marked (see below for **stress in idioms**).

Consonants

p	pen	/pen/
b	bad	/bæd/
t	tea	/tiː/
d	did	/dɪd/
k	cat	/kæt/
g	get	/get/
tʃ	chain	/tʃeɪn/
dʒ	jam	/dʒæm/
f	fall	/fɔːl/
v	van	/væn/
θ	thin	/θɪn/
ð	this	/ðɪs/
s	see	/siː/
z	zoo	/zuː/
ʃ	shoe	/ʃuː/
ʒ	vision	/ˈvɪʒn/
h	hat	/hæt/
m	man	/mæn/
n	now	/naʊ/
ŋ	sing	/sɪŋ/
l	leg	/leg/
r	red	/red/
j	yes	/jes/
w	wet	/wet/

The symbol (r) indicates that British pronunciation will have /r/ only if a vowel sound follows directly at the beginning of the next word, for example the word **after** /ˈɑːftə(r)/ when used in the idiom **after all**; in all other situations, the /r/ is omitted. For American English, the /r/ sounds should always be pronounced.

Vowels and dipthongs

iː	see	/siː/	
i	happy	/ˈhæpi/	
ɪ	sit	/sɪt/	
e	ten	/ten/	
æ	cat	/kæt/	
ɑː	father	/ˈfɑːðə(r)/	
ɒ	got	/gɒt/	(British English)
ɔː	saw	/sɔː/	
ʊ	put	/pʊt/	
u	actual	/ˈæktʃuəl/	
uː	too	/tuː/	
ʌ	cup	/kʌp/	
ɜː	fur	/fɜː(r)/	
ə	about	/əˈbaʊt/	
eɪ	say	/seɪ/	
əʊ	go	/gəʊ/	(British English)
oʊ	go	/goʊ/	(American English)
aɪ	my	/maɪ/	
ɔɪ	boy	/bɔɪ/	
aʊ	now	/naʊ/	
ɪə	near	/nɪə(r)/	(British English)
eə	hair	/heə(r)/	(British English)
ʊə	pure	/pjʊə(r)/	(British English)

Nasalized vowels marked with /˜/ may be found in certain words taken from French, as in **raison** /ˌreɪzɔ̃/ which appears in the idiom *raison d'être*.

British English and American English

If there is a difference between British English and American English in the pronunciation of a word, then the British English form is given first with *AmE* written before the American pronunciation, for example:

dot /dɒt; *AmE* dɑːt/

If only part of a word is pronounced differently, then only the part that is different is shown. Hyphens (-) represent the rest of the word. For example:

crocodile /ˈkrɒkədaɪl; *AmE* ˈkrɑːk-/

Stress in idioms

Idioms are shown with stress marks. For example, the idiom **a ˌleading ˈquestion** has two stress marks; a *primary*, or strong, stress mark on the word **ˈquestion** and a *secondary*, or weaker, stress mark on **ˌleading**. Idioms are usually shown with at least one primary stress mark. You should not change the position of this stress when speaking or the special meaning of the idiom may be lost.

If more than one stress pattern is possible, or if the stress depends on the context, then no stress mark is given. For example **be light on sth** has no stress mark as the stress falls on the part of the idiom labelled **sth**; in this situation, the stress is usually omitted as its position will depend upon which words take the place of **sth**.

Sometimes you may see an idiom with two primary stress marks. For example, in **he who ˈhesitates (is ˈlost)** both the words *hesitate* and *lost* are given a primary stress mark. The second primary stress mark appears in a part of the idiom that is sometimes omitted and is therefore given in brackets. If the words in brackets are not spoken, then the other word with a primary stress mark, e.g. *hesitates*, takes the primary stress. If the words in brackets are spoken, then the primary stress falls on the word marked within the bracketed phrase.